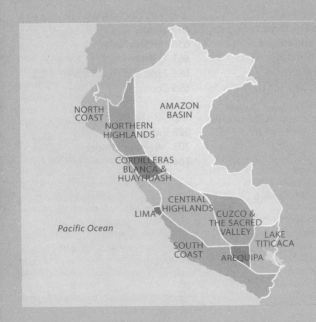

NORTH
COAST

NORTHERN
HIGHLANDS

AMAZON
BASIN

CORDILLERAS
BLANCA &
HUAYHUASH

CENTRAL
HIGHLANDS

LIMA

CUZCO &
THE SACRED
VALLEY

LAKE
TITICACA

Pacific Ocean

SOUTH
COAST

AREQUIPA

Contents

Essentials

Planning your trip

Where to go

The variety that Peru offers the visitor is enormous. The problem, if you're on a tight schedule, is how to fit it all in. Above all, don't attempt too much. Take it easy and give yourself time to appreciate one of the most beautiful and fascinating countries on earth. There are four main areas: the **southern circuit**, the **northern circuit**, the **central highlands** and the **jungle**. From them you can select the elements that suit you best and, providing the transport links are okay, you can tailor your own itinerary. If short of time, flying gives you the greatest flexibility and, since almost all flights depart from Lima, you will have the opportunity to sample some of the capital's museums, nightlife and gastronomy.

At the end of the Inca Trail is the Intipunku, the Gate of the Sun. Through it you not only see Machu Picchu for the first time, but you are transported back through history to the cultures from which the Inca civilization developed. Caral, between the Andes and the Pacific Ocean, predates any other city-state in South America (3200-3000 BC).

The 2500-year-old fortress temple of Chavín de Huantar, in the lee of the snow-covered peaks of the Cordillera Blanca, represents one of the most influential societies of pre-Columbian times. The Nazca Lines, huge outlines of animals and geometric patterns etched into the southern coastal desert between 200 BC and AD 600, continue to puzzle scientists. Near the elegant colonial city of Trujillo, on Peru's northern coast, are Chan Chán, the largest adobe city in the world, and the massive adobe pyramids of Huaca del Sol, Huaca de la Luna and El Brujo.

Further north still, the pyramid complex of Sipán has revealed some of the finest examples of pre-Columbian jewellery, pottery and textiles to be found on the continent. Also here are the mysterious and evocative ruins of Tucumé, a huge city of 26 pyramids, and Sicán, whose pyramids rise out of a forest of carob trees. In the northeast, where the Andean mountains drop to meet the vast Amazonian lowlands, the cities and cliffside tombs of the cloud people lie hidden in the forest. The most visited of these, Kuélap, is the greatest pre-Columbian fortress in the Americas.

Machu Picchu's near neighbour, Cuzco, is the gateway to natural history. Its festivals are a microcosm of 3000 others across the country. It gives access to the jungle reserves of Manu and Tambopata, where the tally of birds, mammals, reptiles, butterflies and plants has yet to be fully catalogued. Without doubt, Peru is the best place on earth for seeing jungle wildlife, but Cuzco is not the sole point of entry. From the Amazon city of Iquitos you can access Pacaya-Samiria on whose tracks and waterways you can view Peru's wild heart to your own heart's content. In northern Peru, just as in Cuzco, the sporting possibilities are endless: hiking to ruined cities, whitewater rafting or biking down the mountains. Huaraz in the Cordillera Blanca is a mecca for climbers and there are fabulous treks in the Chachapoyas area.

Look south beyond Cuzco to the islands in the sparkling waters of Lake Titicaca, where communities preserve traditions untouched by modernity. In the magnificent city of Arequipa, watched over by volcanoes, the high walls of the Santa Catalina Convent conceal a perfectly preserved miniature colonial town which was, until recently, closed to the outside world. Nearby are the Colca and Cotahuasi canyons, remarkable chasms twice as deep as the Grand Canyon, where you can trek along pre-Hispanic agricultural terraces that are still in use, and look for mighty condors rising on the thermals.

Packing for Peru

Everybody has their own preferences, but a good principle is to take half the clothes and twice the money that you think you will need. Always take out a good travel insurance policy.

Listed here are those items most often mentioned. These include an inflatable travel pillow and strong shoes. You should also take waterproof clothing and waterproof treatment for leather footwear. Wax earplugs are vital for long bus trips or in noisy hotels. Also important are flip-flops, which can be worn in showers to avoid athlete's foot, and a sheet sleeping bag to avoid sleeping on dirty sheets in cheap hotels.

Other useful things include: a clothes line, a nailbrush, a vacuum flask, a water bottle, a universal sink plug of the flanged type that will fit any waste-pipe, string, a Swiss Army knife (don't carry it in your hand luggage when flying), an alarm clock, candles (for power cuts), a torch/flashlight, pocket mirror, an adaptor for recharging all your electronic kit, a padlock for the doors of the cheapest hotels (or for the tent zip if camping), a small first-aid kit, sun hat, lip salve with sun protection, contraceptives, waterless soap, wipes and a small sewing kit. Always carry toilet paper, especially on long bus trips. The most security conscious may also wish to include a length of chain and padlock for securing luggage to a bed or bus seat, and a lockable canvas cover for your rucksack. Contact lens wearers note that lens solution can be difficult to find in Peru. Ask for it in a pharmacy, rather than an opticians.

Itineraries

One to two weeks

While a one-week visit to Peru would be very restrictive, there are certain places that fit neatly into seven days of travelling. If you find yourself with any time to spare, a few extra days in Lima visiting its fascinating museums will give you an overview of what you'll be seeing later. And in the meantime, you can experience the capital's great nightlife.

Cuzco and Machu Picchu You could spend one or two weeks in southern Peru, which offers a very rewarding short circuit covering the most important and popular sites in this part of the country. Trips to Cuzco and Machu Picchu, the crown jewels of the Inca Empire, frequently comprise a week (or less), but if you plan to hike the Inca Trail or any of the challenging alternatives, you need to consider two weeks in the region. Beautiful Titicaca, the highest navigable lake in the world, and the white city of Arequipa can be combined with Cuzco into a fortnight, using air, rail and road travel.

Nazca and the Paracas Peninsula As an alternative to the highlands, try a week or two on the southern coast, taking in the Paracas Peninsula, with its marine birdlife, and the incredible Nazca and Palpa lines.

The Cordillera Blanca Huaraz, in the Cordillera Blanca, is only seven hours by road from Lima and one of the world's premier high-altitude recreation areas, with unparalleled ease of access. A week's hiking or climbing in the Cordillera and neighbouring areas is a practical option. Over the course of two weeks it can also easily be linked with the coastal archaeological sites near the colonial city of Trujillo (eg Chan Chán, the Huacas del Sol and de la Luna) and further north, around Chiclayo (eg Lambayeque with the Brüning and Sipán museums, Túcume and Sicán). Alternatively, the Cajamarca area includes the pleasant city itself, plus thermal baths, archaeological and more recent historical sites and beautiful countryside. To get there quickly from Huaraz, you have to return to the coast for flights from Lima or bus services from Lima, Trujillo or Chiclayo.

The jungle Peru's eastern jungle includes zones with some of the highest levels of biodiversity in the world. There are two distinct areas where tourism infrastructure has been developed, north and southeast, and a central zone that is growing in popularity. One itinerary could include the southeastern jungle, which contains the Manu National Park and the Tambopata National Reserve. These provide wonderful opportunities for those interested in plants, or for watchers of birds, butterflies and animals.

A trip to the southeastern jungle is usually combined with a visit to Cuzco, but it need not be. Flying both ways to Puerto Maldonado is the only viable option if short of time. Travelling overland to the Amazon Basin is another option. The adventurous way is from Cuzco to Puerto Maldonado (tours often involve going one way by road, the other by air), but from Lima to the central jungle, via Tarma, is easy enough for people to do on a holiday weekend (and is therefore crowded at such times). The Amazonian city of Iquitos is the jumping-off point for the northern jungle, where there is a good network of jungle lodges on the river or its tributaries. Flying to Iquitos is an option, either from Lima, or from Tarapoto, which can be reached by a beautiful road that descends from the mountains just north of Chachapoyas. Alternatively, you can travel overland to Pucallpa and then take a river boat downstream to Iquitos.

The Andes A trip to the central Andes from Lima can be done fairly quickly, calling at Huancayo, Huancavelica and Ayacucho in a week to 10 days. Alternatively, the route from Cuzco to the Central Highlands is rewarding. By bus it is a demanding route, but with paving in progress and a new flight service between the two cities, this journey is becoming much easier. Obviously the more time you allow, the more variety you'll see, especially in the Mantaro Valley near Huancayo, and the places of historical interest around Ayacucho. These are also two of the best places to buy handicrafts.

Three to four weeks
Adding an extra week or two to the basic southern itinerary would allow you to see much more of Cuzco, especially the Sacred Valley of the Incas. You can also head out and explore the Colca or Cotahuasi canyons from Arequipa, or, from Puno, the shores and islands of Lake Titicaca.

Chachapoyas and the far north Cajamarca gives access to the more remote Chachapoyas region, which contains a bewildering number of pre-Hispanic archaeological sites. Aim to spend a minimum of one week here. Access by road is from the southwest through Celendín. There is also a more northerly road route to Chachapoyas from Chiclayo, where you should stop to see the nearby archaeological sites.

You can break up a tour of archaeological sites and mountains with some action by surfing at Puerto Chicama (north of Trujillo) and there are many more beaches in the far north near Piura and Tumbes. Tumbes also has wildlife parks, such as coastal mangroves, unlike those in other parts of the country.

The Central Highlands If you're planning on spending more time in the Central Highlands, one variation would be to travel overland from Cerro de Pasco via Oyón and Churín to Huacho, on the coast north of Lima. You would then be close to the intriguing city of Caral. Another good option is to combine the Central Highlands with the Cordillera Blanca, taking a series of buses between Huaraz and Huánuco, via La Unión and Huallanca. Finally, the Cordillera Huayhuash offers some rewarding long-distance, high-altitude trekking. It is most easily reached from Huaraz, via Chiquián, but should not be attempted unless you have a week or so to spare.

When to go

Peru's high season in the highlands is from May to September, when the weather is most stable for hiking and climbing. At this time the days are generally clear and sunny, though nights can be very cold at high altitude. During the wettest months in the highlands, November to April, some roads become impassable and hiking trails can be very muddy. April and May, at the end of the highland rainy season, is a beautiful time to see the Peruvian Andes, but the rain may linger, so be prepared. For a more detailed description of conditions in the Cordillera Blanca, see page 348.

On the coast, high season is September, and Christmas to February. The summer months are from December to April, but from approximately May to October much of this area is covered with *la garúa*, a blanket of cloud and mist. At this time only the northern beaches near Tumbes are warm and pleasant enough for swimming.

The best time to visit the jungle is during the dry season, from April to October. During the wet season (November to April), it is oppressively hot (40°C and above) and while it only rains for a few hours at a time, which is not enough to spoil your trip, it is enough to make some roads virtually impassable, making travel more difficult.

The high season for foreign tourism is from June to September while national tourism peaks on certain holidays, Christmas, Semana Santa and Fiestas Patrias. Prices rise and accommodation and bus tickets are harder to come by. If you know when you will be travelling buy your tickets in advance.

Every bit as important as knowing where to go and what the weather will be like, is Peru's festival calendar. At any given time of the year there'll be a festival somewhere in the country, drawing people from miles around. Check the websites of **PromPerú**, www.peru.info, and **South American Explorers**, www.saexplorers.org, and see the Festivals and events listings under each relevant town.

What to do

Birdwatching

Peru is the number one country in the world for birdwatching. Its varied geography and topography, and its wildernesses of so many different life zones, have endowed it with the greatest biodiversity and variety of birds on Earth. Some 18.5% of all the world's bird species and 45% of all neotropical birds occur in Peru. For this reason, Peru is is often dubbed 'the bird continent' by professional birders.

Birds breed all year round, but there's a definite peak in breeding activity – and consequently birdsong – just before the rains come in Oct, and this makes it rather easier to locate many birds between Sep and Christmas.

Details of the following key sites are given in the main travelling text: Paracas National Reserve (page 307); Loma de Lachay (page 406); Huascarán Biosphere Reserve (page 349); Chiclayo (page 442) and the route via Abra Patricia to Moyobamba (page 529); Iquitos (page 600); Manu Biosphere Reserve (page 620); and Tambopata National Reserve (page 627). A great 3- to 4-week combination trip would be to spend 16 days in Manu, then 2-3 days in the highlands at Abra Málaga and 2-3 days in the Huascarán Biosphere Reserve. A trip into the Marañón Valley and Abra Patricia (Chiclayo-Moyobamba) can be substituted for Manu; this allows access to some of the most sought-after endemics, but would produce far fewer species. More information on the birds of Peru is given in the Flora and fauna section on page 689.

Contact
PromPerú, www.peru.info, for details on bird-watching, or www.perubirdingroutes.com.

Climbing
The Cordillera Blanca is an ice climber's paradise. It takes just 1 or 2 days to reach the snowline on most mountains in the most intensive grouping of glaciated peaks in South America. The statistics are impressive: more than 50 summits between 5000 m and 6000 m (with over 20 surpassing 6000 m); and 663 glaciers. It is not unusual for climbers to reach 3 or more 6000-m summits, climbed Alpine-style, during a 3-week trip. The degree of difficulty ranges from Pisco (5752 m), an excellent acclimatizer or novice's mountain (still demanding), to Copa (6173 m), of moderate difficulty, and the tremendous challenges of Alpamayo (5957 m), Artesonraju (6025 m), Quitaraju (6036 m) and Ranrapalca (6162 m). Huaraz is the main climbing centre of the Cordillera Blanca, and has a growing infrastructure. It is also home to the Peruvian Mountain Guide Association.

The Huayhuash is a little more remote and Chiquián, northwest of the range, and Cajatambo to the south, have few facilities for climbers. It is possible to contact guides, arrieros, porters and cooks in Chiquián, although it is best to enquire in Huaraz first. The Huayhuash has some of the most

spectacular ice walls in Peru. The Jirishancas and Yerupajas (Grande and Chico) are the most popular and demanding.

The cordilleras Vilcabamba and Vilcanota have the enticing peaks of Salkantay (6271 m) and Ausangate (6398 m), but Cuzco is not developed for climbing. This is one of the genuine attractions of Peruvian andinismo – there is always another mountain more remote to feed the appetite. Huagurunchu (5730 m), for instance, in the central Andes, is barely known and Coropuna, Peru's 3rd highest at 6425 m, is hardly ever climbed.

Rock climbing is great in the quebradas, where the rock is most solid (frost-shattered higher up) this is becoming more popular, particularly in the Quebrada de Llaca, near Huaraz, and for beginners at Monterrey. Other rock climbs in the Huaraz area are the boulders of Huanchac, the 'Sphinx', or Torre de Parón and routes in the Rurec Valley.

Contact
Asociación de Guías de Montaña del Perú (AGMP), Casa de Guías, Plaza Ginebra 28-g, Huaraz, T043-421811, www.casadeguias.com.pe.

Cultural tourism
This covers more esoteric pursuits, such as archaeology and mystical tourism. Several of the tour operators listed on page 60 offer customized packages for special-interest groups. Cultural tourism is a rapidly growing niche market. Under the umbrella heading turismo vivencial, PromPerú has a variety of interesting community-based tourism projects in archaeology, agro-tourism, education, llama trekking, nature tourism and traditional medicine; for details see Tourist information, page 65. Private operators and some language schools offer the opportunity to get involved in community projects.

The Instituto Nacional de Cultura, in the Museo de la Nación, see page 86, should be contacted by archaeologists for permits and information. The Museo Nacional de Antropología y Arqueología in Pueblo Libre, see page 87, is the centre for archaeological investigation and the **Museo de la Nación** holds interesting exhibitions.

Contact

Until Oct 2010, **Insituto Nacional de Cultura** (INC), was the governing body, www.inc.gob.pe, and in the text below the INC is still referred to. **Ministerio de Cultura**, ww.mcultura.gob.pe. PromPerú, www.peru.info.

Diving

Diving off the Paracas Peninsula is rewarding, as is the warmer tropical ocean, with larger fish, off Tumbes. It is also practised in the Bahía de Pucusana. The best season for visibility is Mar-Nov because the rivers from the mountains don't deposit silt into the sea. See also Lima, page 114.

Contact

Peru Divers, Lima, www.perudivers.com. Operators are listed in the Activities and tours sections throughout the book.

Kayaking

Peru offers outstanding whitewater kayaking for all standards of paddlers from novice to expert. Some first descents remain unattempted owing to logistical difficulties, though they are slowly being ticked off by a dedicated crew of local and internationally renowned kayakers. For the holiday paddler, it's probably best to join up with a raft company who will gladly carry all your gear (plus any non-paddling companions) and provide you with superb food while you enjoy the river from an unladen kayak. There is a small selection of kayaks available in Peru for hire from about US$20-30 a day. For complete novices, some companies offer 2- to 3-day kayak courses on the Urubamba and Apurímac that can be booked locally. Kayaking is also offered on Lake Titicaca. For expedition paddlers, bringing your own kayak is the best option though it is becoming increasingly expensive to fly with your boats around Peru. A knowledge of Spanish is indispensable.

Contact

Kayaking operators are listed in the Activities and tours sections throughout the book; many also offer whitewater rafting.

Mountain biking

With its amazing diversity of trails, tracks and rough roads, Peru is surely one of the last great mountain-bike destinations yet to be fully discovered. Whether you are interested in a 2-day downhill blast from the Andes to the Amazon jungle or an extended off-road journey, then Peru has some of the world's best biking opportunities. The problem is finding the routes as trail maps are virtually non-existent and the few main roads are often congested with traffic and far from fun to travel along. A few specialist agencies run by dedicated mountain bikers are now exploring the intricate web of paths, single tracks and dirt roads that criss-crosses the Andes, putting together exciting routes to suit every type of cyclist. When signing up for a mountain-bike trip, remember that you are in the Andes so if you are worried about your fitness and the altitude, make sure you do a predominantly downhill trip.

There a now a couple of companies offering imported high-quality, full-suspension mountain bikes with superb hydraulic disc brakes. Valued at over US$2500 each, these bikes are a dream to ride, for the novice and the expert alike. The guides at these companies are experts in making sure you get the very best out of these state-of-the-art machines. Whatever the quality of the bike, check that it is regularly maintained and that the guide gives you a full explanation on its use. In the wrong hands, or poorly maintained, bikes can cause problems and you may have very little come back, especially if booking and paying from overseas. Other things to check: the company must be operating in Peru legally. Trips should have a support vehicle for the duration, not just dropping you off and meeting you at the end. Guides should carry a first aid kit, at the very least a puncture repair kit (preferably a comprehensive tool kit) and be knowledgeable about bike mechanics. Bikes do go wrong, punctures are frequent and people do fall off, so it is essential that your guide provides this minimum cover.

Contact

Amazonas Explorer, Cuzco, www.amazonas-explorer.com. **Mountain Bike Adventures**, Huaraz, www.chakinaniperu.com. **Perú Bike**, Lima, www.perubike.com.

Parapenting and hang-gliding

Vuelo libre is its name in Peru. Flying from the coastal cliffs is easy and the thermals are good. The Callejón de Huaylas is more risky owing to variable thermals, crosswinds and a lack of good landing sites, but there is a strong allure to flying at 6000 m in front of the glaciers of Huascarán. The area with the greatest potential is the Sacred Valley of Cuzco, which has excellent launch sites, thermals and reasonable landing sites. The season in the sierra is May-Oct, with the best months being Aug and Sep. Some flights in Peru have exceeded 6500 m.

While the attraction of parapenting or hang-gliding in the sierras is very great, with mountains on all sides and steep valleys below, most pilots are to be found in Lima. Arranging a tandem jump or a course is easy: just go to Parque del Amor in Miraflores in the afternoon and see who is hanging around waiting for the thermals and the breeze. Jumping off the cliff gives a completely different perspective on the city as you fly above the Pacific breakers and the traffic on the coastal boulevard, with a pelican's view of the blocks of flats and offices. There are other launch sites on the coast south of Lima, in the Callejón de Huaylas, Arequipa, the Central Highlands and in the Cuzco region.

Contact

Aeroxtreme, Lima, www.aeroxtreme.com. **Andean Trail Perú**, Lima, www.andean trailperu.com. **Fly Adventure**, Lima, www.flyadventure.net. **Infinity**, www.infinity cross.com and **Peru Fly**, Lima, www.perufly. com. Make sure the operator has the backing of the **Asociación Peruana de Vuelo Libre** (APVL), http://apvl.pe/. Also see Activities and tours on pages 115 and 165.

Rafting

Peru is rapidly becoming one of the world's premier destinations for whitewater rafting. Several of its rivers are rated in the world's top 10 and a rafting trip, be it for 1 or 10 days, is now high on any adventurer's 'must-do' list of activities while travelling in Peru. It is not just the adrenalin rush of big rapids that attract, it is the whole experience of accessing areas beyond the reach of motor vehicles that few if any have ever visited. This may be tackling sheer-sided, mile-deep canyons, travelling silently through pristine rainforest, or canoeing across the stark altiplano, high in the Andes.

If you are looking to join a rafting expedition of some length, then it is definitely worth signing up before you set foot in Peru. Some long expeditions have fewer than 2 or 3 scheduled departures a year and the companies that offer them only accept bookings well in advance as they are logistically extremely difficult to organize. For the popular day trips and expeditions on the Apurímac there are regular departures (the latter in the dry season only). If you can spare a couple of days to wait for a departure then it is fine to book in Cuzco. It also gives you the chance to talk to the company that will be operating your tour. There are day-trip departures all year and frequent multi-day departures in the high season. Note that the difficulty of the sections changes between the dry and rainy season; some become extremely difficult or un-runnable in the rainy season (Dec-Mar). The dry season is Apr/May to Sep (but can be as late as Nov).

In 2010 a new regulatory body for rafting operators was set up to ensure that companies are able to run professional trips, that they employ international-standard safety techniques, that guides are adequately qualified and legally allowed to work in Peru and that equipment is regularly checked. It is hoped that, once fully in place in 2011, this body will weed out the poor practices, equipment and guides that have undermined this fun and exciting sport.

Contact

Operators are listed in the Activities and tours sections throughout the book. The majority are in Cuzco. For more information on staying safe when rafting, turn to page 277.

Surfing

Peru is a top, internationally renowned surfing destination. Its main draws are the variety of waves and the year-round action. Point break, left and right reef break and waves of up to 6 m can all be found during the following seasons: Sep-Feb in the north and Mar-Dec in the south, though May is often ideal south of Lima.

Ocean swells are affected by 2 currents; the warm El Niño in the north and the cold Humboldt current in the south arriving from Antarctica. Pimentel, near Chiclayo, is the dividing point between these 2 effects but a wet suit is normally required anywhere south of Piura.

The biggest wave is at Pico Alto (sometimes 6 m in May), south of Lima, and the largest break is 800 m at Chicama, near Trujillo. There are more than 30 top surfing beaches. North of Lima these include: Chicama, Pacasmayo, Punta Tur, Punta Nonura, El Golf, Cabo Blanco, Los Organos and Máncora (all left break). South of Lima the best beaches are: Punta Hermosa, Punta Rocas (right break) and Pico Alto (right break, best in May), the pick of the bunch; Huaico/Santa Rosa (left break), Cabo Negro (left break), Sangallán (right break); El Olón and Piedras Negras (left breaks) and Caleta La Cruz (right break), are all near Ilo.

International competitions are held at Pico Alto (Balin Open in May) and Punta Rocas (during the summer months). A surfing magazine, *Tablista*, is published bimonthly. Also look out for the free *X3Mag* and, of course, Footprint's *Surfing the World*.

Contact

Eco-Innovation Tours, www.eco-innovation tours.com. **Federación Deportiva Nacional de Tabla (Fenta)**, Lima, www.surfingperu. com.pe. **Olas Peru Surf Travel**, Lima, www.olasperusurftravel.com. See also www.olasperu.com for surf news. **Peru Surf Guides**, Lima, www.perusurfguides.com.

Trekking

Peru has some outstanding circuits around the Nevados. The best known are the Llanganuco to Santa Cruz loop, see page 374; the Ausangate circuit, see page 215; and a strenuous trek around the Huayhuash, see page 400. For treks from Caraz, see page 373, for treks from Carhuaz, see page 369, and for information on trekking in the Cordillera Blanca and Huayhuash, see page 349. Other good areas are the Colca Canyon, the Chincheros area and the upper Cañete Valley.

The other type of trekking for which Peru is justifiably renowned is walking among ruins, and, above all, for the Inca Trail (see page 196). However, there are many other walks of this type in a country rich in archaeological heritage. Some of the best are: the valley of the Río Atuen near Leymebamba and the entire Chachapoyas region (see page 503); the Tantamayo ruins above the Marañón (see page 587); the Cotahuasi Canyon (see page 293); and beyond Machu Picchu to Vilcabamba (see page 206) and Choquequirao. People tend to think of the Inca Trail to Machu Picchu as the only stretch of Inca roadway that can be walked. It is, however, just a fraction of the Inca road network. See the colour section for details of trekking the Capaq Ñan (the Royal Road).

Most walking is on clear trails, well trodden by *campesinos* who populate most parts of the Peruvian Andes. If you camp on their land, ask permission first and, of course, do not leave any litter. Tents, sleeping bags, mats and stoves can easily be hired in Huaraz and Cuzco but check carefully for quality.

Trekking and climbing companies show very little concern for their clients about acute mountain sickness, AMS (an exception is **Monttrek** in Huaraz). Almost every climb or trek in Peru is scheduled faster than the recommended 300 m per day, even the very popular Santa Cruz trek near Huaraz. Unlike Nepal, where guides go out of their way to prevent AMS in travellers, few ask whether you are acclimatized. You should be wary of agencies wanting to sell you trips with fast ascents.

Contact
See above under Climbing for the **Asociación de Guías de Montaña del Perú**. Trekking companies are listed in the Activities and tours sections throughout the book. See the colour section for more detailed descriptions of some of the treks listed above.

Getting there

Air

From Europe and the Middle East
There are direct flights to Lima only from Amsterdam (**KLM** via Bonaire) and Madrid (**Iberia**, **Air Europa** and **LAN**). Air France is due to start Paris-Lima flights in 2011. From London, Frankfurt, Rome, Milan, Lisbon or other European cities, the best connections are made in Madrid, or via Brazilian or US gateways. From Tel Aviv, make connections in either Madrid or Miami.

From North America
Miami is the main gateway to Peru, together with Atlanta, Dallas, Houston, Los Angeles and New York. Airlines, not all direct, include **American**, **Continental**, **Delta**, **LAN**, **TACA**, **Copa** and **AeroMéxico**. Daily connections can be made from almost all major North American cities. From Toronto, **Air Canada** flies to Lima, but not daily. From Vancouver, there are no direct flights or connections; fly via one of the above gateways.

From Australia and New Zealand
There are no obvious connecting flights. One option would be to go to Buenos Aires from Sydney or Auckland (four flights a week with **Aerolíneas Argentinas**) and fly on from there (several daily flights). Alternatively, fly to Los Angeles and travel down.

From South Africa
From Johannesburg, make connections in Buenos Aires or São Paulo.

From Latin America
There are regular flights, in many cases daily, to Peru from most South American countries. The **LAN** group has the most routes to Lima within the continent. The **TACA** group also has quite extensive coverage, including to Central America and Mexico.

From Asia

From Hong Kong, Seoul and Singapore, connections have to be made in Los Angeles. Make connections in Los Angeles or Miami if flying from Tokyo.

Prices and discounts

Most airlines offer discounted fares on scheduled flights through agencies who specialize in this type of fare. The very busy seasons are 7 December-15 January and 10 July-10 September. If you intend travelling during those times, book as far ahead as possible. During February-May and September-November special offers may be available. Examples of fares on scheduled airlines are: from the UK a return with flexible dates will cost about £620, low season 2010 prices. A low season return from Miami to Lima cost from US$590 in 2010. From Sydney, Australia, return fares start at US$1600. Note that taxes and fuel surcharges may apply to these fares.

If you buy discounted air tickets always check the reservation with the airline concerned to make sure the flight still exists. Also remember the IATA airlines' schedules change in March and October each year, so if you're going to be away a long time it's best to leave return flight coupons open. In addition, check whether you are entitled to any refund or re-issued ticket if you lose, or have stolen, a discounted air ticket. Some airlines require the repurchase of a ticket before you can apply for a refund, which will not be given until after the validity of the original ticket has expired. Travel insurance in some cases covers lost tickets.

Discount flight agents

Using the web to book flights, hotels and other services directly is an increasingly popular way of making holiday reservations. You can get some good deals this way. Be aware, though, that cutting out the travel agents is denying yourself the experience that they can give, not just in terms of the best flights to suit your itinerary, but also advice on documents, insurance and other matters before you set out, safety, routes, lodging and times of year to travel. A reputable agent will also be bonded to give you some protection if arrangements collapse while you are travelling.

In the UK and Ireland

Journey Latin America, 12-13 Heathfield Terr, London W4 4JE, T020-8747 8315, www.journeylatinamerica.co.uk.
STA Travel, T0871-230 0040, www.statravel.co.uk. 45 branches in the UK, including many university campuses. Specialists in low-cost flights and tours, good for student IDs and insurance.

Trailfinders, 194 Kensington High St, London W8 7RG, T020-7938 3939, www.trailfinders.com. 22 branches in London and throughout the UK. Also 2 branches in Ireland (Dublin, Cork) and 2 travel centres in Australia (Brisbane, Sydney, www.trailfinders.com.au).
Trips Worldwide, 14 Frederick Pl, Clifton, Bristol BS8 1AS, T0800-840 0850, www.tripsworldwide.co.uk.

North America

Discount Airfares Worldwide On-Line, www.etn.nl/discount.htm. A hub of consolidator and discount agent links.
eXito, 108 Rutgers Av, Fort Collins, CO 80525, USA, T1-800-655-4053 (USA), T1-800-670 2605 (Canada), www.exitotravel.com.
STA Travel, T1-800-781-4040, www.statravel.com. 18 branches in the USA, including university campuses.
Travel CUTS, in all major Canadian cities and on university and college campuses, T1-866-246-9762, www.travelcuts.com. Specialist in student discount fares, IDs and other travel services.

Australia and New Zealand
Flight Centre, with offices throughout Australia and other countries. In Australia call T133 133 or www.flightcentre.com.au. **STA Travel**, see above. In NZ: 130 Cuba St, Wellington, T04-385 0561, T0800-474400, www.statravel.co.nz. Also in major towns and university campuses.
Travel.com.au, Level 10, 17 York St, Sydney, NSW 2000, T1300 130 481, www.travel.com.au.

Airport information

All international flights arrive at **Jorge Chávez Airport** in Callao, 16 km from the centre of the city of Lima, T01-511 6055, www.lap.com.pe. The *aduana* (customs) process is relatively painless and efficient (a push-button, red light/green light system operates for customs baggage checks – see also Customs, page 49). Taxi services to town have their booths before the gate separating arriving passengers from the general public. If you do not opt for one of these companies, taxi drivers await passengers in the entrance hall. Their fares vary little from the transport companies. Do not try to get a cab outside the airport perimeter unless you know exactly what you are doing. This is not a safe choice. For full details, see Lima Ins and outs, page 72.

Jorge Chávez airport has all the facilities one would expect at an international airport: money exchange, mobile phone rental, car hire, tourist information and shops. See page 118 for more detail on the services available.

Baggage allowance

There is always a weight limit for your baggage, but airlines do not use a standard baggage allowance system. You should therefore find out from the carrier exactly how much weight you are permitted. Some airlines allow only one piece of luggage, others two, usually with an additional charge for the second. In general the maximum weight of checked-in baggage will be 20 kg or 23 kg per case. You may find that allowances are different in each direction of your journey. Carry-on luggage is normally restricted by both size and weight. At busy times of the year it can be very difficult and expensive to bring items such as bikes and surfboards along. Airlines may let you pay a penalty for overweight baggage, but you should verify this in advance. Do not assume that you can bring extra luggage. The weight limit for internal flights is often 20 kg per person, but can be considerably less if the plane is very small.

Airlines recommend that you arrive at the airport three hours before international flights and two hours before domestic flights. Check-in for international flights closes one hour before departure, 30 minutes for domestic flights, after which you may not be permitted to board. Drivers of cars entering the car park are subject to a document check.

Tax

There is a US$31 departure tax for international flights. It may be paid in dollars or soles. It is sometimes included in the international flight ticket, but do not assume this. For national flights the airport tax is US$7, payable only in soles or dollars. Some airlines allow you to pay the tax when you check in. If you don't pay it then, you must pay at the airport tax offices before security. When making a domestic connection in Lima, you are not required to pay airport tax. Contact airline personnel at baggage claim and they will escort you to your departure gate. Tickets purchased in Peru also have the 19% state tax, but this will be included in the price of the ticket.

Border crossings

The main entry points into Peru on land are as follows:

From Bolivia Desaguadero (town has the same name either side of the border) and Yunguyo–Kasani on the southeastern side of Lake Titicaca, see page 255. There is also an unpaved crossing on the north shore Puerto Acosta–Tilali, see page 249.

From Chile Arica–Tacna, see page 339.

From Ecuador At Aguas Verdes–Huaquillas, see page 472; Macará–La Tina see page 463; and at La Balsa Zumba– Namballe, see page 527.

From Brazil The Assis Brasil–Iñapari crossing, see page 628, is being upgraded as part of the Interoceánica highway and will soon be a straightforward crossing. There is another border crossing between Brazil and Colombia and Peru from Leticia (Colombia) and Tabatinga (Brazil) to Santa Rosa in Peru, see page 605; this is a river crossing only.

Reconfirming flights

It is very important to reconfirm your flights when flying internally in Peru or leaving the country. This can be done in the case of e-tickets by checking-in online, 24-48 hours in advance. Otherwise, phone or visit the airline office directly 48-72 hours in advance. Some travel agents may reconfirm a flight, but you may have to pay a service charge. If you do not reconfirm your internal or international flight, you may not get on the plane. See also Customs, page 49.

Road and river

Peru has land and river borders with neighbouring countries and they are heavily used, see Border crossings box, above.

Getting around

Although Peru's geography is dominated by the Andes, one of the world's major mountain ranges, great steps have been taken to improve major roads and enlarge the paved network linking the Pacific coast with the Highlands. This also means that there are various options, albeit on rougher roads, for the traveller wishing to go to northern Peru from the centre of the country (or vice versa), avoiding Lima. But it is worth taking some time to plan an overland journey in advance, checking which roads are finished, which have roadworks and which will be affected by the weather. The highland and jungle wet season, from mid-October to late March, can seriously hamper travel, so allow extra time if planning to go overland at this time. Peru also, unfortunately, suffers more than its fair share of natural disasters, such as earthquakes and the El Niño weather phenomenon, see page 688. This can have dramatic effects on overland travel.

Air

If you only have a couple of weeks, travelling by air is the sensible option. It allows access to most major regions and means you can spend more time at your destination and less getting there. On the downside, though, you will see less of the country and will meet fewer people than if you travel overland. A further complication is that national companies offering internal flights rarely seem to operate for more than a couple of years. Services therefore change frequently so you should check on the internet, or immediately on arrival in Peru, what flights are available. Always give yourself at least an extra day between national and international flights to allow for schedule changes or cancellations.

Carriers serving the major cities are **Star Perú**, www.starperu.com, **LAN**, www.lan.com and **Peruvian Airlines**, www.peruvianairlines.pe. For destinations such as Andahuaylas, Ayacucho, Cajamarca, Huancayo, Huánuco and Huaraz flights are offered by **LC Busre**, www.lcbusre.com.pe. **Grupo TACA**, www.grupotaca.com, offers a service on the Lima–Cuzco route. Flights start at about US$100 one-way anywhere in the country from Lima, but prices vary greatly between airlines, with **LAN** being the most expensive for non-Peruvians. Prices often increase at holiday times (Semana Santa, May Day, Inti Raymi, 28-29 July, Christmas and New Year), and for elections. During these times and the northern hemisphere summer, seats can be hard to come by, especially on the Lima–Cuzco–Lima route, so book early. There are no deals for round-trip tickets.
▸▸ *For contact details of national airlines, see Lima Transport, page 118.*

It is common for flight times to change, earlier or later, or be cancelled because of weather delays especially in the wet season. Do not be surprised or perturbed by this, often there is nothing the airline can do. Flights are often overbooked so it is very important to reconfirm your tickets, as mentioned above, and be at the airport well in advance. By law, the clerk can start to sell reserved seats to stand-by travellers 30 minutes before the flight.

Internal flight prices are given in US dollars but can be paid in soles and the price should include the 19% general sales tax. Tickets are not interchangeable between companies but sometimes exceptions will be made in the case of cancellations. Do check with companies for special offers. If the price sounds too good to be true, double check your ticket to make sure you are not being sold a ticket for Peruvian nationals; these tickets are often half price but you need to show Peruvian ID to get on the plane.

To save time and hassle, travel with carry-on luggage only (48 cm x 24 cm x 37 cm). This will guarantee that your luggage arrives at the airport when you do.

Rail

Peru's national rail service was privatized in 1999. The lines of major interest to the traveller are Cuzco–Machu Picchu, on which three companies operate services (see page 194) and Puno–Juliaca–Cuzco, run by **PerúRail**, www.perurail.com. The other railway that carries passengers is the line from Lima–Huancayo, with a continuation to Huancavelica in the Central Highlands. The service from the capital to Huancayo runs on several weekends through the year; check www.fcca.com.pe for the latest schedule. Huancayo–Huancavelica has daily passenger services. Train schedules may be cut in the rainy season.

On almost any trip to the Amazon Basin, a boat journey will be required at some point, either to get you to a jungle lodge, or to go between river ports. Motorized canoes with canopies usually take passengers to jungle lodges. They normally provide life jackets and have seats that aren't very comfortable on long journeys, so a cushion may come in handy. Being open to the elements, the breeze can be a welcome relief from the heat and humidity in the daytime, but they can also be cold in the early morning and if there is any rain about it will blow into your face. Take a waterproof to keep you dry and warm. You sit very close to the water and you soon learn to respect the driver's knowledge of the river.

Public river transport: there are various types of vessel, a *lancha* is a large riverboat; a *rápido* or *deslizador* is a speedboat (some are faster than others); a *yate* is a small to medium wooden colectivo, usually slow, and a *chalupa* is a small motor launch used to ferry passengers from the *lanchas* to shore. Standards are variable and generally not as high as in Brazil, but improving. There are some good boats; the best *lanchas* are on the Iquitos–Pucallpa and Iquitos–Yurimaguas routes. Not all *rápidos* are safe or reliable. Always look at several vessels and talk to the staff before choosing.

Accommodation is either in a cabin for two or four passengers (on the best boats some cabins have a private bath), which will be more expensive than slinging your hammock in the general hammock area. Some boats have two classes of hammock space. If you choose to sleep in a hammock, hang it away from lightbulbs (they aren't switched off at night and attract all sorts of strange insects) and away from the engines, which usually emit noxious fumes and, of course, noise. Another useful tip is not to sling your hammock near the bottom of the stairwell on double-decked river boats, as this is where the cook slaughters the livestock every morning. Do try to find somewhere sheltered from the cold, damp night breeze. Take rope for hanging your hammock, plus string and sarongs for privacy. Use a double hammock of material (not string) for warmth; you may need a blanket as well. It may be possible to sleep on board ahead of departure and on arrival if in the middle of the night.

Food is also of variable quality, often monotonous, and sometimes meagre; you need to take your own plate, cutlery and cup, plenty of drinking water (the silt in the rivers will clog filters; purifying tablets may not kill giardia), extra snacks and seasonings. Local produce can sometimes be purchased on route. There is usually (not always) a bar on board (often expensive) serving beer, soft drinks and a few snacks. Departures are after sunset and the first night's meal is not included.

Departure times are marked on a chalk-board on each vessel. All say '*sin falta*' ('without fail') but that does not necessarily mean the boat leaves at that time, nor even on that day. Flexibility is indispensable, always allow extra time. How long the trip takes depends on whether going upstream or downstream, the water level, the size and state of the engine, the amount of cargo (boats go very loaded from Pucallpa to Iquitos), how long they wait at intermediate ports, the weather, etc. The quality of your experience depends on the level of crowding, especially if travelling hammock class. Boats travel near shore upstream and in the middle of the river downstream. To flag down a boat at intermediate points along the river, use a white sheet during the day or strong light at night; sometimes they don't bother stopping even when they see you are calling. Pay the captain or *mestre* (manager) on the boat; avoid touts. On some boats staff collect the fares in the middle of the first night, once passengers are all in their hammocks. You need to take a bag to put your rubbish in (rather than doing as the other passengers do, ie chucking it all overboard), toilet paper, mosquito repellent and long-sleeved shirts/long trousers for after dusk. DEET is the best mosquito repellent but it will be washed directly into the river and it is lethal to most fish. Being able to speak Spanish is essential. Thieves are a problem; do not leave anything out of sight, not even your shoes under your hammock at night. Also take great care of your belongings when embarking and disembarking. Women travellers can expect the usual unwanted attention, but it becomes more uncomfortable when confined to the small boat.

Road

Peru's road network is being upgraded and better roads mean better bus services and improved conditions for drivers. Peru, however, is no different from other Latin American countries in that travelling by road at night or in bad weather should be treated with great care. It is also true that there are many more unpaved than paved roads, so extended overland travel is not really an option if you only have a few weeks' holiday. Detailed accounts of major and minor road conditions are given in the travelling text.

The Pan-American Highway runs north–south through the coastal desert and is mostly in good condition. Also paved and well-maintained is the direct road that branches off the Pan-American at Pativilca and runs up to Huaraz and on to Caraz. The northern route from Chiclayo through to Tarapoto is fully paved, as is the spur to Jaén. Cajamarca has a paved connection to the coast to serve the Yanacocha mining operation. The Central Highway from Lima to Huancayo is mostly paved. It continues (mostly paved) to Pucallpa in the Amazon Basin. There is also a paved road from La Oroya to Tarma and Satipo. South of Lima, there's the paved 'Liberatores' highway from Pisco to Ayacucho. From Nazca to Abancay and on to Cuzco is paved. This is now the main route from Lima to Cuzco. The main roads in and to the Sacred Valley from Cuzco are also paved. The Cuzco–Puno highway is fully paved and is a fast, comfortable journey to rival the train. The paved road continues along the south shore of Lake Titicaca to Desaguadero on the Bolivian border. From there the paving runs down the western slope of the Andes to Moquegua and the coast, one of the nicest highways in the country. Also in the south, the road that runs into the sierra to Arequipa is in good condition. From Arequipa the road to Puno is paved. Roads from Arequipa to Mollendo and Matarani are also excellent.

All other roads in the mountains are dirt, some good, some very bad. Each year they are affected by heavy rain and mud slides, especially those on the eastern slopes of the mountains. Repairs can be delayed because of a shortage of funds. This makes for slow travel and frequent breakdowns. Note that some of these roads can be dangerous or impassable in the rainy season. Check beforehand with locals (not with bus companies, who only want to sell tickets) as accidents are common at these times.

Bus

Services along the coast to the north and south as well as inland to Huancayo, Ayacucho and Huaraz are generally good, but since 2008 the number of accidents and hold-ups on buses has increased. You should also be prepared for blockades of highways by strikes and protests, which may cause delays. On long-distance journeys it is advisable to pay a bit extra and take a reliable company. All major bus companies operate modern buses with two decks on interdepartmental routes. The first deck is called *bus-cama*, the second *semi-cama*. Both have seats that recline, *bus-cama* further than *semi-cama*. These buses usually run late at night and are more expensive than ordinary buses, which tend to run earlier in the day. Many buses have toilets and show movies. Each company has a different name for its regular and *cama* or *ejecutivo* services. In the text below prices give only a general idea of bus fares; there is great variation between companies and between days of the week. Look out for promotional offers.

Cruz del Sur and Ormeño are bus lines covering most of the country. Cruz del Sur, generally regarded as a class above the others, accepts Visa cards and gives 10% discount to ISIC and Under26 cardholders (you may have to insist). There are many smaller but still excellent bus lines that run only to specific areas. An increasing number accept bookings on the internet. ▶▶ *For contact details of national bus companies, see Lima Transport, page 119.*

With the better companies you will get a receipt for your luggage, it will be locked under the bus and you shouldn't have to worry about it at stops because the storage is not usually opened. On local buses there will be lots of people getting on and off the buses, loading and unloading bags, so it's best to watch your luggage. It will provide you with a good excuse to get off the bus and stretch anyway. Do not put your day bag above your head or on the floor inside the bus; keep it on your lap or beside you. It is too easy for someone to grab your bag and get off without your realizing. If you decide to get off the bus at a stop, take all your carry-on items with you. If you want to buy a return ticket from Lima, it is quite often cheaper to wait and buy the return portion when you arrive at your destination. This isn't always the case, but on the major lines things seem to cost more from the capital.

For long journeys be sure to take water and possibly a bit of food, although it is always possible to buy food at the stops along the way. See the warning under Safety, page 58, about not accepting food or drinks from fellow passengers. For mountain routes, have a blanket or at least a jacket handy as the temperature at night can drop quite low. Once you get off the beaten track, the quality of buses and roads deteriorates and you should stick to day buses. If your bus breaks down and you have to get on another bus, you will probably have to pay for the ticket, but keep your old ticket as some bus companies will give refunds. The back seats tend to be the most bumpy and the exhaust pipe is almost always on the left-hand side of the bus.

It is best to try to arrive at your destination during the day; it is safer and easier to find accommodation. Prices of tickets are raised by 60-100% during Semana Santa (Easter), Fiestas Patrias (Independence Day – July 28 and 29), Navidad (Christmas) and special local events. Prices will usually go up a few days before the holiday and possibly remain higher a few days after. Tickets also sell out during these times so if travelling then, buy your ticket as soon as you know what day you want to travel.

Car

Toll roads in Peru include: Aguas Verdes-Tumbes, many on the Pan-American Highway between Tumbes and Lima, many on the road from Chiclayo to Tarapoto, Pativilca–Huaraz, Lima–Pucusana, Ica–Nazca, Lima (highway around city), and Variante–Pacasmayo; these vary from US$1.35 to US$2.60. Ecuador to Chile/Bolivia on main roads comes to about US$30. Motorcycles are exempt from road tolls; use the extreme right-hand lane at toll gates.

You must have an international driving licence and be over 21 to drive in Peru. If bringing in your own vehicle you must provide proof of ownership. Officially you cannot enter Peru with a vehicle registered in someone else's name, but it is possible with a notarized letter of authorization and insurance documents stating that Peru is incorporated. On leaving Peru there is no check on the import of a vehicle as there is no evidence in your passport. There are two recognized documents for taking a vehicle into South America: a *carnet de passages* issued jointly by the Fedération Internationale de l'Automobile (FIA-Paris) and the **Alliance Internationale de Tourisme** (AIT-Geneva), and the *Libreta de Pasos por Aduana* issued by the **Federación Interamericana de Touring y Automóvil Clubs** (FITAC). Officially, Peru requires one or the other, but it is seldom asked for. Nevertheless, motorists seem to fare better with one than without it.

Insurance for the vehicle against accident, damage or theft is best arranged in the country of origin, but it is getting increasingly difficult to find agencies who offer this service. It is very expensive to insure against accident and theft, especially as you should take into account the value of the car increased by duties calculated in real (ie non-devaluing) terms. If the car is stolen or written off you will be required to pay very high import duty on its value. Get the legally required minimum cover, which is not expensive, as soon as you can, because if you should be involved in an accident and are uninsured, your car could be confiscated. If anyone is hurt, do not pick them up (you may become liable). Seek assistance from the nearest police station or hospital if you are able to do so.

The **Touring y Automóvil Club del Perú** ⓘ *Av Trinidad Morán 698, Lince, T01-614 9999, www.touringperu.com.pe*, offers help to tourists and particularly to members of the leading motoring associations. Good maps are available (see Maps, page 38).

Fuel 84 octane petrol/gasoline costs US$3.95/gallon; 90 octane, US$4.20; 95 octane, US$5.15; 98 octane, US$5.40. Diesel costs US$4. Unleaded fuel is available in large cities and along the Panamericana, but rarely in the highlands.

Car hire The minimum age for renting a car is 25. If renting a car, your home driving licence will be accepted for up to six months. Car hire companies are given in the text. Prices reflect high costs and accident rates. Hotels and tourist agencies will tell you where to find cheaper rates, but you will need to check that you have such basics as spare wheel, toolkit and functioning lights, etc.

Combis, colectivos and trucks

Combis operate between most small towns in the Andes on one- to three-hour journeys. This makes it possible, in many cases, just to turn up and travel within an hour or two. On rougher roads, combis are minibuses (invariably Japanese), while on better roads there are also slightly more expensive and much faster car colectivos, often called *autos*, or *cars*. They usually charge twice the bus fare and leave only when full. They go almost anywhere in Peru. Most firms have offices. If you book one day in advance, they will pick you up at your hotel or in the main plaza. Trucks are not always much cheaper than buses. They charge about 75% of the bus fare, but are wholly unpredictable. They are not recommended for long trips, and comfort depends on the load.

Hitchhiking

Hitchhiking in Peru is neither easy, owing to the lack of private vehicles, nor entirely risk-free. For obvious reasons, a lone female should not hitch by herself. Besides, you are more likely to get a lift if you are with a partner, whether they are male or female. The best combination is a male and female together. Positioning is also key. Freight traffic in Peru has to stop at the police *garitas* outside each town and these are the best places to try (also toll points, but these are further out of town).

Drivers usually ask for money but don't always expect to get it. In mountain and jungle areas you usually have to pay drivers of lorries, vans and even private cars; ask the driver first how much he is going to charge, and then recheck with the locals.

Motorcycling and cycling

Motorcycling The motorcycle should be off-road capable. A road bike can go most places an off-road bike can go. Get to know the bike before you go, ask the dealers in your country what goes wrong with it and arrange a link whereby you can get parts flown out to you. Get the book for international dealer coverage from your manufacturer, but don't rely on it. They frequently have few or no parts for modern, large machinery. An Abus D or chain will keep the bike secure. A cheap alarm gives you peace of mind if you leave the bike outside a hotel at night. Most hotels will allow you to bring the bike inside (see accommodation listings for details). Look for hotels that have a courtyard or more secure parking and never leave luggage on the bike overnight or while unattended. Passport, international driving licence and bike registration document are necessary. Riders fare much better with a *carnet de passages* than without it.

Cycling Unless you are planning a journey almost exclusively on paved roads – when a high-quality touring bike would suffice – a mountain bike is strongly recommended. The good-quality ones (and the cast-iron rule is never to skimp on quality), are incredibly tough and rugged, with low gear ratios for difficult terrain, wide tyres with plenty of tread, V brakes, sealed hubs and bottom bracket and a low centre of gravity for improved stability. A chrome-alloy frame is a desirable choice over aluminium as it can be welded if necessary. Although touring bikes, and to a lesser extent mountain bikes and spares are available in the larger cities, remember that most locally manufactured goods are shoddy and rarely last. (Shimano parts are generally the easiest to find.) Buy everything you possibly can before you leave home.

Remember that you can always stick your bike on a bus, canoe or plane to get yourself nearer to where you want to go. This is especially useful when there are long stretches of major road ahead, where all that awaits you are hours of turbulence as the constant stream of heavy trucks and long-haul buses zoom by. It is possible to rent a bike for a few days, or join an organized tour for riding in the mountains. You should check, however, that the machine you are hiring is up to the conditions you will be encountering, or that the tour company is not a fly-by-night outfit without back-up, good bikes or maintenance.

South American Explorers have valuable cycling information that is continuously updated. Visit **www.warmshowers.org** for a hospitality exchange for touring cyclists. A related organization is **Cyclo-Camping International** ① *25 rue Ramus, 75020 Paris, France, T01-4797 6218, www.cci.asso.fr.*

Taxi

Taxi prices are fixed in urban areas and cost US$0.75-1.20. In Lima prices range from US$2-4, but fares are not usually fixed. Ask locals what the price should be and always agree the fare before setting off. Remise taxis have a central office which you call to book a cab in advance. In some cases, like at airports, the company will have a desk at which you book your taxi. They are more expensive than taxis hailed on the street, but safer.

Taxis at airports are often a bit more expensive, but taxi drivers have been known to charge three times the correct price, so check in advance what the fare should be. Many taxi drivers work for commission from hotels and will try to convince you to go to that hotel. Feel free to choose your own hotel and go there. If you walk away from the Arrivals gate a bit, the fares should go down to a price that is reasonable.

Another common form of public transport is the *mototaxi*, or *motocarro*. This is a three-wheel motorcycle with an awning covering the double-seat behind the driver. In some places, like Iquitos and Tarapoto, they are ubiquitous and the only way to get around. Fares are about US$1.

Maps

It is a good idea to get as many as possible in your home country before leaving. A recommended series of general maps is that published by **International Travel Map Productions (ITM)** ① *345 West Broadway, Vancouver BC, V5Y 1P8, Canada, T604-879 3621, www.itmb.com*, compiled with historical notes by the late Kevin Healey. Relevant to this handbook are *South America North West* (1:4M) and *Amazon Basin* (1:4M). Another map series that has been mentioned is that of **New World Edition** ① *Bertelsmann, Neumarkter Strasse 18, 81673 München, Germany*, which includes *Südamerika Nord* and *Südamerika Sud (both 1:4M)*.

Good maps are available from street sellers in the centre of Lima, or in better bookshops (published by **Lima 2000**, T01-440 3486, www.lima2000.com.pe). Lima 2000's *Mapa Vial del Perú* (1:2,200,000) is probably the best and most correct road map available for the country. The **Instituto Geográfico Nacional** in Lima sells a selection of good, accurate country and regional maps (see page 113). **South American Explorers**, who will give good advice on road conditions (see page 66), stock an excellent collection of maps. In the UK, **Stanfords** ① *12-14 Longacre, London, WC2E 9LP, T020-78361321, www.stanfords. co.uk*, with a branch in Bristol, stocks an excellent range.

The **Touring y Automóvil Club del Perú**, see page 36, sells a road map at US$5 (*Mapa Vial del Perú*, 1:3,000,000, Ed 1980) and route maps covering most of Peru (*Hojas de Ruta, North, Centre* and *South*, US$1.65 each, available as pdf on their website).

Sleeping

Accommodation is plentiful throughout the price ranges and finding a hotel room to suit your budget should not present any problems, especially in the main tourist areas and larger towns and cities. The exception to this is during the Christmas and Easter holiday periods, Carnival, Cuzco in June and Independence celebrations at the end of July, when all hotels seem to be crowded. It's advisable to book in advance at these times and during school holidays and local festivals, see page 44.

Hotels, hostales, pensiones and hospedajes

There are many top-class hotels in Lima and Cuzco and in the main tourist centres, such as Arequipa, Iquitos and Trujillo. In less-visited places the choice of better-class hotels is more limited. Accommodation is more expensive in Lima, but the number of budget hotels is increasing year-by-year. The best-value accommodation can be found in the busiest tourist centres, especially Cuzco, which is full of excellent-value hotels throughout the range. Accommodation also tends to be more expensive in jungle towns such as Iquitos and Puerto Maldonado and in the north compared with the south, especially on the coast. If you want a room with air conditioning expect to pay around 30% extra.

All hotels in the upper price brackets charge 19% general sales tax (IGV) and 10% service on top of prices (foreigners should not have to pay the sales tax on hotel rooms; neither tax is included in prices given in the accommodation listings, unless specified). The more expensive hotels also charge in dollars according to the rate of exchange at midnight.

Sleeping price codes

LL over US$200	**L** US$151-200	**AL** US$101-150
A US$66-100	**B** US$46-65	**C** US$31-45
D US$21-30	**E** US$12-20	**F** US$7-11
G US$6 and under		

Prices given are for two people sharing a double room with bathroom (shower and toilet), unless the establishment charges per person, including taxes. If travelling alone, it's usually cheaper to share with others in a room with three or four beds. Prices are for the busy seasons (May- September, Christmas-February and Holy Week). During the low season, when many places may be half empty, it's often possible to bargain the room rate down. Note that the dollar/soles exchange rate can fluctuate substantially.

LL, L, AL and **A** Hotels in these categories are usually only found in the largest cities and main tourist centres. They should offer extensive leisure and business facilities, plus restaurants and bars. Most will provide a safe box in each room. Credit cards are usually accepted.

B and **C** These hotels range from very good to functional. You can expect breakfast, your own bathroom, a/c in tropical areas, plenty of hot water and towels, soap, shampoo, cable TV, a sitting area and a comfortable room.

D and **E** These are the most common categories and some offer very good value for money. Expect cleanliness, a private bathroom, hot water in the highlands, a/c or fan in the tropics, TV, maybe a simple breakfast, but no other frills.

F and **G** A room in these price ranges is small and consists of little more than a bed and walls. The bathroom is shared and soap, towels, toilet paper or a toilet seat are seldom supplied. In the highlands they may not have enough blankets, so take a sleeping bag. In the lowlands insects are common, use the mosquito net or bring your own, and ignore the cockroaches – they're harmless.

In shared rooms expect to pay from **G** to **E** pp, depending on the number of people sharing and the type of hostel. These range from the very basic to the 'boutique'. Many places offer single-sex dormitories. Some shared rooms have their own bath, others use communal showers. Almost all provide lockers for your belongings.

By law all places that offer accommodation now have a plaque outside bearing the letters **H** (Hotel), **Hs** (Hostal), **HR** (Hotel Residencial) or **P** (Pensión) according to type. A hotel has 51 rooms or more, a *hostal* 50 or fewer, but the categories do not describe quality or facilities. Generally speaking, though, a *pensión* or *hospedaje* will be cheaper than a hotel or *hostal*. Most mid-range hotels have their own restaurants serving lunch and dinner, as well as breakfast. Many budget places serve breakfast – almost invariably continental breakfast. Most places are friendly and helpful, irrespective of the price, particularly smaller *pensiones* and *hospedajes*, which are often family-run and will treat you as another member of the family.

The cheapest (and often the nastiest) hotels can be found around bus and train stations. If you're just passing through and need a bed for the night, then they may be acceptable. The better-value accommodation is generally found on and around the main plaza (though not always).

The electric showers used in many hotels (basic up to mid-range) are a health and safety nightmare. Avoid touching any part of the shower while it is producing hot water and always get out before you switch it off.

Youth hostels

The office of the Youth Hostel Association of Peru, Asociación Peruana de Albergues Turísticos Juveniles and Administradora Peruana Hostelling International ① *Av Casimiro Ulloa 328, Miraflores, Lima T01-446 5488, www.hostellingperu.com.pe or www.limahostell.com.pe*, has information about youth hostels. For information about International Student Identity Cards (ISIC) and lists of discounts available contact Intej, see Student travellers, page 59.

Camping

This normally presents no problems in Peru. There can, however, be problems with robbery when camping close to a small village. Avoid such a location, or ask permission to camp in a backyard or *chacra* (farmland). Most Peruvians are used to campers, but in some remote places, people have never seen a tent. Be casual about it, do not unpack all your gear, leave it inside your tent (especially at night) and never leave a tent unattended.

Obey the following rules for 'wild' camping: arrive in daylight and pitch your tent as it gets dark; ask permission to camp from the parish priest, the fire chief or the police, or a farmer regarding his own property; never ask a group of people – especially young people; never camp on a beach (because of sandflies and thieves). Also avoid camping at sea level, on riverbeds or on or below bluffs when El Niño rains are forecast as flash floods can occur; tidal waves may also follow earth tremors. If you can't get information from anyone, camp in a spot where you can't be seen from the nearest inhabited place, or road, and make sure no one saw you go there.

Camping gas in little blue bottles is available in the main cities. Those with stoves designed for lead-free gasoline should use *ron de quemar*, available from hardware shops (*ferreterías*). White gas is called *bencina*, also available from hardware stores. If you use a stove system that requires canisters make sure you dispose of the empty canisters properly; the same goes for all rubbish. Keep in mind as well that you are responsible for the trash that your group, guide or muledriver may drop and it is up to you to say something and pick up the rubbish. Often the rubbish that is on the trails is blamed on locals and this is not usually the case; low-impact travel is everyone's responsibility and while you are picking up your own trash, pick up other people's too.

Eating

Food

Not surprisingly for a country with such a diversity of geography and climates, Peru boasts the continent's most extensive menu. Its cuisine varies from region to region, but basically can be divided into coastal, highland and tropical. Peru also prides itself on its new, fusion cuisine, claiming for itself the title 'gastronomic capital of South America'. Many if the dishes include native ingredients and pre-Hispanic recipes which are combined with better-known ingredients in innovative and delicious ways. The commonly applied term for this type of food is Novo Andino. Chefs such as Gastón Acurio, who has opened Peruvian restaurants in many countries, are gaining a worldwide reputation for Peruvian food.

Coastal cuisine

With a coastline of more than 1800 km, the fruits of the sea are almost limitless. Sea bass, flounder, salmon, red snapper, sole and shellfish are all in abundance. The best coastal dishes are those with seafood bases, with the most popular being the jewel in the culinary crown, *ceviche*. This delicious dish of raw white fish marinated in lemon juice, onion and hot peppers can be found in neighbouring countries, but Peruvian is best. Ask for '*sin picante*' if you don't want it hot. Traditionally, *ceviche* is served with corn-on-the-cob, *cancha* (toasted corn), yucca and sweet potatoes. Another mouth-watering fish dish is *escabeche* – fish with onions, hot green pepper, red peppers, prawns (*langostinos*), cumin, hard-boiled eggs, olives, and sprinkled with cheese. For fish on its own, don't miss the excellent *corvina*, or white sea bass. You should also try *chupe de camarones*, which is a shrimp stew made with varying and somewhat surprising ingredients. Other fish dishes include *parihuela*, a popular bouillabaisse that includes *yuyo de mar*, a tangy seaweed, and *aguadito*, a thick rice and fish soup said to have rejuvenating powers.

Fish isn't the only thing eaten on the coast. A favourite northern coastal dish is *seco de cabrito*, roasted kid (baby goat) served with beans and rice, or *seco de cordero*, which uses lamb instead. Also good is *ají de gallina*, a rich and spicy creamed chicken, and duck is excellent.

People on the coast are referred to as *criollos* (see page 663) and *criollo* cooking can be found throughout the country. A dish almost guaranteed to appear on every restaurant menu is *lomo saltado*, a kind of stir-fried beef with onions, vinegar, ginger, chilli, tomatoes and fried potatoes, served with rice. Other popular examples are *cau cau*, made with tripe, potatoes, peppers and parsley, served with rice, and *anticuchos*, which are shish kebabs of beef heart with garlic, peppers, cumin seeds and vinegar. *Rocoto relleno* is spicy bell pepper stuffed with beef and vegetables, *palta rellena* is avocado filled with chicken or Russian salad, *estofado de carne* is a stew that often contains wine and *carne en adobo* is a cut and seasoned steak. Two good dishes that use potatoes are *causa* and *carapulca*. On coastal menus *causa* is made with mashed potato wrapped around a filling, which often contains crabmeat. On other occasions, *causa* has yellow potatoes, lemons, pepper, hard-boiled eggs, olives, lettuce, sweet cooked corn, sweet cooked potato, fresh cheese, and served with onion sauce.

Highland cuisine

The staples of highland cooking, corn and potatoes, date back to Inca times and are found in a remarkable variety of shapes, sizes and colours. A popular potato dish is *papa a la huancaína*, which is topped with a spicy sauce made with milk and cheese. The most commonly eaten corn dishes are *choclo con queso*, corn on the cob with cheese, and *tamales*, boiled corn dumplings filled with meat and wrapped in a banana leaf. Most typical of highland food is *pachamanca*, a combination of meats (beef, lamb, pork, chicken), potatoes, sweet potatoes, corn, beans, cheese and corn *humitas*, all slow-cooked in the ground, again dating back to Inca times.

Meat dishes are many and varied. *Ollucos con charqui* is a kind of potato with dried meat, *sancochado* is meat and all kinds of vegetables stewed together and seasoned with ground garlic and *lomo a la huancaína* is beef with egg and cheese sauce. Others include *fritos*, fried pork, usually eaten in the morning, *chicharrones*, deep fried chunks of pork ribs

Eating price codes

and chicken, and *lechón*, suckling pig. And not forgetting that popular childhood pet, *cuy* (guinea pig), which is considered a real delicacy.

Very filling and good value are the many soups on offer, such as *caldos* (broths): eg *de carnero*, *verde*, or *de cabeza*, which includes a sheep's head cooked with corn and tripe. Also *yacu-chupe*, a green soup that has a base of potato, with cheese, garlic, coriander leaves, parsley, peppers, eggs, onions, and mint, and *sopa a la criolla* containing thin noodles, beef heart, bits of egg and vegetables and pleasantly spiced. And not to be outdone in the fish department, *trucha* (trout) is delicious, particularly from Lake Titicaca.

Tropical cuisine

The main ingredient in much jungle cuisine is fish, especially the succulent, dolphin-sized *paiche*, which comes with the delicious *palmito*, or palm-hearts, and the ever-present yucca and fried bananas. *Tocacho* is green banana, cooked and ground to a chunky paste, usually served with pork (*cecina*) and sausage (*chorizo*). *Juanes* are a jungle version of *tamales*, stuffed with chicken and rice. A common dish to start the day is *chapo*, banana porridge, delicious with evaporated milk.

Desserts and fruits

The Peruvian sweet tooth is evident in the huge number of desserts and confections from which to choose. These include: *cocada al horno* – coconut, with yolk of egg, sesame seed, wine and butter; *picarones* – frittered cassava flour and eggs fried in fat and served with honey; *mazamorra morada* – purple maize, sweet potato starch, lemons, various dried fruits, sticks of ground cinnamon and cloves and perfumed pepper; *manjar blanco* – milk, sugar and eggs; *maná* – an almond paste with eggs, vanilla and milk; *alfajores* – shortbread biscuit with *manjar blanco*, pineapple, peanuts, etc; *pastelillos* – yuccas with sweet potato, sugar and anise fried in fat and powdered with sugar and served hot; and *zango de pasas*, made with maize, syrup, raisins and sugar. *Turrón*, the Lima nougat, is worth trying. *Tejas* are pieces of fruit or nut enveloped in *manjar blanco* and covered in chocolate or icing sugar – delicious.

The various Peruvian fruits are wonderful. They include bananas, the citrus fruits, pineapples, dates, avocados (*paltas*), eggfruit (*lúcuma*), the custard apple (*chirimoya* – the 'sweet of the gods' in Quechua) which can be as big as your head, quince, papaya, mango, guava, passion-fruit (*maracuyá*), prickly pear (*tuna*) and the soursop (*guanábana*). These should be tried as juices or ice cream – an unforgettable experience.

Eating out

The high-class restaurants and hotels serve both the much-vaunted modern Peruvian cuisine and international food. The range of food offered by mid-range restaurants differs from city to city, with greater variety in centres where more international visitors congregate (Cuzco, Arequipa). Native food at its best is found in the taverns (*chicherías*) and the local restaurants (*picanterías*).

Lunch is the main meal, and apart from the most exclusive places, most restaurants have one or two set lunch menus, called *menú ejecutivo* or *menú económico*. The set menu has the advantage of being served almost immediately and it's usually cheap. The *menú ejecutivo* costs US$2 or more for a three-course meal with a soft drink and it offers greater choice and more interesting dishes than the *menú económico*, which costs US$1.50-2.50. Don't leave it too late, though, most Peruvians eat lunch around 1230-1400. There are many Chinese restaurants (*chifas*) that serve good food at reasonable prices, and the *comedores populares* found in the markets of most cities offer a standard three-course meal for as little as US$1 (but keep an eye on cleanliness and hygiene). Buying food on the street is generally best left until your stomach has acclimatized, but avoid hamburgers sold at stalls anywhere in Peru (guaranteed to upset even the hardiest of constitutions).

For those who wish to eschew such good value, the menu is called *la carta*. An à la carte lunch or dinner costs US$5-8, but can go up to an expensive US$80 in a first-class restaurant, with drinks and wine included. Middle and high-class restaurants may add 10% service, but do include the 19% sales tax to the bill (which foreigners do have to pay). This is not shown on the price list or menu, so check in advance. Lower-class restaurants charge only tax, while cheap, local restaurants charge no taxes. Dinner in restaurants is normally about 1900 onwards, but choice may be more limited than lunchtime. Peruvians tend to ask guests for dinner at 2000.

The situation for **vegetarians** is improving, but slowly. In tourist centres you should have no problem finding a vegetarian restaurant (or a restaurant that has vegetarian options), especially Cuzco and Arequipa and, of course, Lima. Elsewhere, choice is limited and you may find that, as a non-meat eater, you are not understood. Vegetarians and people with allergies should be able to list (in Spanish) all the foods they cannot eat. By saying '*no como carne*' (I don't eat meat), people may assume that you eat chicken and eggs. If you do eat eggs, make sure they are cooked thoroughly. Restaurant staff will often bend over backwards to get you exactly what you want but you need to request it.

Drink

Peru's most famous drink is *pisco*, a grape brandy used in the wonderful pisco sour, a deceptively potent cocktail that also includes egg whites and lemon juice. The most renowned brands come from the Ica Valley. Other favourites are *chilcano*, a longer refreshing drink made with *guinda*, a local cherry brandy, and *algarrobina*, a sweet cocktail made with the syrup from the fruit of the carob tree, egg whites, evaporated milk, pisco and cinnamon.

Some Peruvian wines are good, others are acidic and poor. The best are the Ica wines Tabernero, Tacama (especially its Selección Especial and Terroix labels), Ocucaje and Santiago Queirolo (in particular its Intipalka label). Red, white and rosé, sweet and dry varieties can be found. Prices for a reasonable bottle start at around US$4.75, rising to US$18 for the best wines. Note that some Peruvian bodegas import Argentine wines and bottle them under their own label.

Peruvian beer is good, especially the *Cusqueña* and *Arequipeña* brands (lager) and *Trujillo Malta* (porter). In Lima *Cristal* and *Pilsen* are readily available. Other brands, including some Brazilian beers, are coming onto the market. Look out for the sweetish 'maltina' brown ale, which makes a change from the ubiquitous pilsner-type beers.

Chicha de jora is a strong but refreshing maize beer, usually homemade and not easy to come by, and *chicha morada* is a soft drink made with purple maize. Coffee in Peru is usually brought to the table in a small jug accompanied by a mug of hot water to which you add the coffee essence. If you want coffee with milk, a mug of milk is brought. The number of cafés serving good, fresh coffee is growing rapidly. There are many different kinds of herb tea: the commonest are *manzanilla* (camomile), *hierbaluisa* (lemongrass) and *mate de coca*. Although a stimulant, the latter is frequently served in the highlands to stave off the discomforts of altitude sickness. Try tea from another herb from the sierras, *muña*, instead, which is a relaxant and may be more effective.

Festivals and events

At any given time of the year there'll be a festival somewhere in Peru, drawing people from miles around. Check the websites of **PromPerú** and **South American Explorers**, see Tourist information, page 65. For a detailed list of local festival dates, see under each town in the travelling text. For more information on the historic roots behind Peru's festivals, see page 674.

Festivals

Jan Marinera festival, Trujillo. An opportunity to see Marinera dancers.
1st week of Feb Fiesta of the **Virgen de la Candelaria**, along the shores of Lake Titicaca near the Bolivian border and features dance groups from around the region.
Feb/Mar/Apr Carnaval is held over the weekend before Ash Wednesday, and **Semana Santa** (Holy Week), which ends on Easter Sunday. Carnaval is celebrated in most of the Andes and Semana Santa throughout Peru. Accommodation and transport is heavily booked and prices rise considerably. Book tickets and make hotel bookings early.
1 May Fiesta de la Cruz is held over much of the central and southern highlands and on the coast.
Jun Andinismo, Huaraz, a week-long festival held at the beginning of the month. In Cuzco, the entire month is one huge fiesta, culminating in **Inti Raymi**, on 24th. One of Peru's prime tourist attractions. This date is also celebrated for **San Juan** in the jungle lowlands.
29 Jun Many places on the coast celebrate San Pedro y San Pablo.
30 Aug Santa Rosa de Lima, in Lima.

Sep Spring festival, in Trujillo. An opportunity to see Marinera dancers.
Oct Señor de los Milagros, Lima, held on several dates throughout the month.
1 Nov Todos los Santos (All Saints)
8 Dec Festividad de la Inmaculada Concepción.

Public holidays

Most businesses such as banks, airline offices and tourist agencies close for the official holidays, while supermarkets and street markets may be open. Sometimes holidays that fall during mid-week will be moved to the following Mon to make a long weekend. If you are going to spend a holiday in a certain area, find out what the local customs and events are. Often there are parades, processions, special cuisine or traditions that characterize the event. The main public holidays are:
1 Jan New Year.
6 Jan Bajada de Reyes.
1 May Labour Day.
28-29 Jul Independence (Fiestas Patrias).
7 Oct Battle of Angamos.
24-25 Dec Christmas (Navidad).

Shopping

Almost everyone who visits Peru will end up buying a souvenir of some sort from the vast array of arts and crafts (*artesanía*) on offer. The best, and cheapest, place to shop for souvenirs, and pretty much anything else in Peru, is in the street markets that can be found absolutely everywhere. The country also has its share of shiny, modern shopping centres, especially in the capital, but remember that the high overheads are reflected in the prices.

What to buy

It is possible to find any kind of **handicraft** in the capital. The prices are often the same as in the highlands, and the quality is high. Good buys are: silver and gold handicrafts; hand-spun and hand-woven textiles; manufactured textiles in indigenous designs; llama and alpaca wool products such as ponchos, rugs, hats, blankets, slippers, coats and sweaters; **arpilleras** (appliqué pictures of Peruvian life), which are made with great skill and originality by women in the shanty towns; and fine leather products that are mostly handmade. Another good buy is **clothing** made from high-quality Pima cotton, grown in Peru.

The **mate burilado**, or engraved gourd found in every tourist shop, is cheap and one of the most genuine expressions of folk art in Peru. These are cheaper if bought in the villages of Cochas Grande or Cochas Chico near Huancayo in the Central Highlands. The Mantaro Valley is generally renowned for its folk culture, including all manner of *artesanía*, see Huancayo page 554.

Alpaca clothing, such as sweaters, hats and gloves, is cheaper in the sierra, especially in Puno. Another good source is Arequipa, where alpaca cloth for suits, coats, etc (mixed with 40% sheep's wool) can be bought cheaply from factories. However, although Lima is more expensive, it is often impossible to find the same quality of goods elsewhere. Genuine alpaca is odourless wet or dry, wet llama stinks.

One of the best places in Peru to look for *artesanía* is Ayacucho in the Central Highlands. Here you'll find excellent woven textiles, as well as the beautifully intricate **retablos**, or Saint Mark's boxes, see page 671. Cuzco is one of the main weaving centres and a good place to shop for textiles, as well as excellent woodcarvings, see page 157. Also recommended for textiles is Cajamarca. The island of Taquile on Lake Titicaca is a good place to buy **ch'uspas** (bags for coca leaves), **chumpis** (belts) and **chullos** (knitted hats). For a more detailed look at Peruvian arts and crafts, see page 668.

Bargaining

Sooner or later almost everyone has to bargain in Peru. Only the rich and famous can afford to pay the prices quoted by taxi drivers, receptionists and self-proclaimed guides. Most Peruvians are honest and extremely hard working, but their country is poor and often in turmoil, the future is uncertain and the overwhelming majority of people live below the poverty line. Foreigners are seen as rich, even if they are backpackers or students. In order to bring prices down, it is extremely helpful to speak at least some Spanish and/or to convince locals that you live, work or study in Peru and therefore know the real price.

You will not have to bargain in restaurants, department stores, expensive hotels or airline offices. However, almost all the rest is negotiable. Almost all better-class hotels have 'corporate' rates. Just say that you work for some company, that you are a journalist (they never check ID), or you are a researcher. This way you can usually get a reduction. If you think a lower price is appropriate in a cheaper hotel, ask for *una rebajita, por favor* ('a discount, please'). You can negotiate the price of a tour booked through a travel agency, but not an aeroplane, bus or train ticket. In fact, you will probably get a better price directly from the airline ticket office.

Bargaining is expected when you are shopping for artwork, handicrafts, souvenirs, or even food in the market. Remember, though, that most of the handicrafts, including alpaca and woollen goods, are made by hand. Keep in mind, these people are making a living and the 50 centavos you save by bargaining may buy the seller two loaves of bread. You want the fair price not the lowest one, so bargain only when you feel you are being ripped off. Remember that some Peruvians are so desperate that they will have to sell you their goods at any price, in order to survive. Please don't take advantage of it.

Responsible travel

Sustainable or ecotourism has been described as "ethical, considerate or informed tourism where visitors can enjoy the natural, historical and social heritage of an area without causing adverse environmental, socio-economic or cultural impacts that compromise the long-term ability of that area and its people to provide a recreational resource for future generations and an income for themselves". Peru is a beautiful, fascinating country but also a living, working landscape and a fragile place. By observing certain guidelines outlined in the box opposite and behaving responsibly, you can help to minimize your impact and protect the natural and cultural heritage of this wonderful country.

Environmental legislation plays its part in protecting tourist destinations. CITES (Convention on International Trade in Endangered Species of Wild Fauna and Flora) aims to control the trade in live specimens of endangered plants and animals and also "recognizable parts or derivatives" of protected species. If you feel the need to purchase souvenirs derived from wildlife, it would be prudent to check whether they are protected. Importation of CITES-protected species can lead to heavy fines, confiscation of goods and even imprisonment.

While the authenticity of some ecotourism operators' claims need to be interpreted with care, there is clearly both a huge demand for this type of activity and also significant opportunities to support worthwhile conservation and social development initiatives. If you are concerned about the application of the principles of ecotourism, in Peru as elsewhere, you need to make an informed choice by finding out in advance how establishments such as jungle lodges cope with waste and effluent disposal, whether

How big is your footprint?

- Where possible choose a destination, tour operator or hotel with a proven ethical and environmental commitment – if in doubt, ask.
- Spend money on locally produced (rather than imported) goods and services, buy directly from the producer or from a 'fair trade' shop, and use common sense when bargaining – the few dollars you save may be a week's salary to others.
- Use water and electricity carefully – travellers may receive preferential supply while the needs of local communities are overlooked.
- Learn about local etiquette and culture – consider local norms and behaviour and dress appropriately for local cultures and situations.
- Protect wildlife and other natural resources – don't buy souvenirs or goods unless they are clearly sustainably produced and are not protected under CITES legislation.
- Always ask before taking photographs or videos of people.
- Consider staying in local accommodation rather than foreign-owned hotels; the

economic benefits for host communities are far greater, and there are more opportunities to learn about local culture.
- Make a voluntary contribution to Climate Care, www.co2.org, to help counteract the pollution caused by tax-free fuel on your flight.

Further information
The following organizations have begun to develop and/or promote ecotourism projects and destinations; their websites are an excellent source of information:
- **Conservation International**, T703-341 2400, www.ecotour.org.
- **International Ecotourism Society**, T001-202-506 5033, www.ecotourism.org.
- **Planeta**, www.planeta.com.
- **Tourism Concern**, T44-20-7133 3800, www.tourismconcern.org.uk.
- Organizations such as **Earthwatch**, www.earthwatch.org, and **Discovery Initiatives**, www.discoveryinitiatives. co.uk, offer opportunities to participate directly in scientific research and development projects in the region.

they create the equivalent of 'monkey islands' by obtaining animals in the wild and putting them in the lodge's property, what their policy is towards employing and training local staff, and so on. See also Voluntourism, page 68.

Local customs and laws

Codes of conduct

Politeness – even a little ceremoniousness – is much appreciated in Peruvian society. Men should always remove any headgear and say *'con permiso'*, when entering offices, and shake hands with other men. Women or men meeting women usually greet each other with one kiss on the cheek. When introduced, Peruvians will probably expect to greet visitors in the same way. Always say *'buenos días'* (until midday) or *'buenas tardes'* and wait for a reply before proceeding further. Business cards are commonly used.

When dealing with officials, always remember to be friendly and courteous no matter how trying the circumstances. Never be impatient and do not criticize situations in public (the officials may know more English than you think and they can certainly interpret gestures and facial expressions). In some situations, however, politeness can be a liability. Most Peruvians are disorderly queuers. In commercial transactions (buying a meal, goods in a shop, etc) politeness should be accompanied by firmness, and always ask the price first.

Politeness should also be extended to street traders. Saying 'no, gracias' with a smile is better than an arrogant dismissal. Whether you give money to beggars is a personal matter, but your decision should be influenced by whether a person is begging out of need or trying to cash in on the tourist trail. In the former case, local people giving may provide an indication. Giving money to children is a separate issue, upon which most agree: don't do it. There are occasions where giving some healthy food may be appropriate, but first inform yourself of local practice.

In Peru it is common for locals to throw their rubbish, paper, wrappers and bottles into the street. Sometimes when asking a local where the rubbish bin is, they will indicate to you that it is the street. This does not give you the right to apply the 'when in Rome' theory. There are rubbish bins in public areas in many centres and tourists should use them.

Dress

Most Latin Americans, if they can afford it, devote great care to their clothes and appearance. It is appreciated if visitors do likewise. How you dress is mostly how people will judge you. This is particularly important when dealing with officials. Women should pack at least one medium- to long-length skirt and men might want to consider bringing a smart sweater or jacket. Wool sweaters and shawls can be easily purchased in Peru and make good additions to your wardrobe.

In general, clothing is less formal in the tropical lowlands, where men and women do wear shorts. In the highlands, people are more conservative, though wearing shorts is acceptable on hiking trails. Men should not be seen bare-chested in populated areas.

Essentials A-Z

Accident and emergency

Ambulance T01-225 4040 in Lima.
Emergency medical attention T117.
Fire T116, www.bomberosperu.gob.pe.
Police T105, www.pnp.gob.pe (PNP, Policía
Nacional del Perú), for police emergencies
nationwide. **Tourist police** Jr Moore 268,
Magdalena, 38th block of Av Brasil, Lima,
T01-460 1060, daily 24 hrs; for public
enquiries, etc, Av España con la Av Alfonso
Ugarte, Lima, and Colón 246, Miraflores,
T01-243 2190. Go there if you have had
property stolen. They are friendly, helpful
and speak English and some German.
Consumer Protection Bureau (Indecopi)
hotline for travellers' complaints T/F01-224
7777, outside Lima T0800-44040 (not from
pay phones), daily 0830-1630, www.indecopi.
gob.pe. This body (with offices, kiosks and
information stands in every town) will help
with complaints regarding customs, airlines,
travel agencies, accommodation, restaurants,
public authorities or if you have lost, or had
stolen, documents.

Children

Travel with children can bring you into closer
contact with local families and, generally,
presents no special problems – in fact the
path may even be smoother for family
groups. Officials are sometimes more
amenable where children are concerned and
they are pleased if your child knows a little
Spanish. For more detailed advice, see *Travel
with Kids* by William Gray (Footprint, 2007)
and **www.babygoes2.com**.

Bus travel Remember that a lot of time
can be spent waiting for and riding buses.
You should take reading material with you
as it is difficult to find and expensive. Also
look for the locally available comic strip
Condorito, which is popular and a good way

for older children to learn a bit of Spanish.
On long-distance buses you pay for each
seat, and there are no half fares. For shorter
trips it is cheaper, if less comfortable, to seat
small children on your knee. Sometimes there
are spare seats which children can occupy
after tickets have been collected. In city
buses, small children generally do not pay
a fare, but are not entitled to a seat when
paying customers are standing. On most
domestic flights, children under 12 pay less
than adults, the exact discounts vary. Make
sure that children accompanying you are fully
covered by your travel insurance policy.

Food This can be a problem if the
children are not adaptable. It is easier to take
food with you on longer trips than to rely
on meal stops where the food may not be
to taste. Avocados are safe, readily available,
easy to eat and nutritious; they can be fed
to babies as young as 6 months and most
older children like them. Best stick to simple
things like bread, bananas and tangerines
while you are actually on the road. Biscuits,
packaged junk food and bottled drinks
abound. A small immersion heater and
jug for making hot drinks is invaluable,
but remember that electric current is 220 v
in Peru and Bolivia, 110 v in Ecuador. In
restaurants, you can try to order a *media
porción* (half portion), or divide a full-sized
helping between 2 children.

Customs and duty free

On arrival Customs inspection is carried
out at airports after you clear immigration.
Customs are uncommon at land borders
but there may be spot checks further into
a country.

When travelling into Peru you can bring
20 packs of cigarettes (400 cigarettes),
50 cigars or 500 g of tobacco, 3 litres of
alcohol and new articles for personal use

of gifts valued at up to US$300. There are certain items that cannot be brought in duty-free: these include computers (but laptops are OK). The value-added tax for items that are not considered duty-free but are still intended for personal use is generally 20%. Personal items such as laptops, cameras, bicycles, hiking and climbing equipment and anything else necessary for adventure sports are exempt from taxes and should be regarded as personal effects that will not be sold or left in Peru. All customs agents should be satisfied by this and allow you to pass. Anything that looks like it's being brought in for resale, however, could give you trouble.

Goods shipped to you Except for documents, customs duties must be paid on all goods shipped to Peru. Better to bring anything you think you will need with you when you travel, rather than having it sent later on.

On departure All airline baggage is inspected by security personnel and sniffed by dogs for drugs. Never transport anything you have not packed yourself, as you will be held responsible for the contents. It is also prohibited to take any archaeological pieces or specimens of wild plants or animals without a permit.

Disabled travellers

As with most underdeveloped countries, facilities for the disabled traveller are sadly lacking. Wheelchair ramps are a rare luxury and getting a wheelchair into a bathroom or toilet is well nigh impossible, except for some of the more upmarket hotels. The entrance to many cheap hotels is up a narrow flight of stairs. Pavements are often in a poor state of repair (even fully able people need to look out for uncovered manholes and other unexpected traps). Visually and hearing-impaired travellers are similarly poorly catered for as a rule, but experienced guides can often provide tours with individual attention.

Disabled Peruvians obviously have to cope with these problems and mainly rely on the help of others to get on and off public transport and generally move around.

The Ministerio de la Mujer y Desarrollo Social (Ministry for Women and Social Development) incorporates a Consejo Nacional de Integración de la Persona con Discapacidad, **CONADIS** (National Council for the Integration of Disabled People, www.conadisperu.gob.pe – in Spanish). CONADIS, together with **PromPerú**, private businesses, **SATH** (see next paragraph) and **Kéroul** of Québec, has been involved in a project called **Peru: Towards an Accessible Tourism** and the *First Report on Accessibility in Peru for Tourists with Disabilities* was published in 2001. The report identifies many challenges in a number of major tourist sites. For instance, archaeological sites such as Machu Picchu and Chan Chán, being World Heritage Sites, may not be altered for accessibility although the latter, apart from soft sand in places, is almost entirely accessible. Specially trained personnel, however, can provide assistance to those with disabilities in these cases. The project can be accessed through the PromPerú website www.peru.info, click on *Turismo acesible*/Accessible tourism.

Some travel companies are beginning to specialize in exciting holidays, tailor-made for individuals depending on their level of disability. The **Global Access Disabled Travel Network Site**, www.globalaccessnews.com, is dedicated to providing information for 'disabled adventurers' and includes a number of reviews and tips from members of the public. Another informative site, www.sath.org, belongs to the **Society for Accessible Travel and Hospitality (SATH)**, and has lots of advice on how to travel with specific disabilities, plus listings and links. Also see **www.access-able.com**. One company in Cuzco that offers tours for disabled people is **Apumayo**, see Cuzco Activities and tours, page 168.

Drugs

Illegal drugs are the most common way for foreigners to get into serious trouble in this part of the world. Some people come specifically to consume or buy drugs and may have the false impression that the country is currently permissive in this regard. This is not the case. While drugs are easily available, anyone caught in possession will be assumed to be a trafficker. Drug use or purchase is punishable by up to 15 years' imprisonment and the number of foreigners in Peruvian prisons on drug charges is still increasing. If arrested on any charge the wait for trial in prison can take up to a year and is particularly unpleasant. Be wary of anyone approaching you in a club and asking where they can score – the chances are they'll be a plain-clothes cop. If you are asked to have your bags searched, insist on having a witness present at all times. Never respond to offers by anyone selling drugs on the street anywhere, as they may be a plain-clothes officer.

Electricity

220 volts AC, 60 cycles throughout the country, except Arequipa (50 cycles). Most 4- and 5-star hotels have 110 volts AC. Plugs are either American flat-pin or twin flat and round pin combined.

Embassies and consulates

Australia, 40 Brisbane Av, Barton, ACT 2600, Canberra, T02-6273 7351, www.embaperu.org.au.
Austria, Mahlerstrasse 7/22, A-1010, Vienna, T1-713 4377, www.embaperuaustria.at.
Belgium (consulate), rue de Praetere 2, 1050 Brussels, T32-2-641 8760, consulate.peru@conperbruselas.be.
Bolivia (consulate), Av 6 de Agosto 2455, of 402, Sopocachi, La Paz, T591-2-244 0631, conperlapaz@acelerate.com.

Canada, 130 Albert St, Suite 1901, Ottawa, Ontario K1M 1W5, T1-613-238 1777, www.embassyofperu.ca.
France, 50 Ave Kleber, 75116 Paris, T33-1-5370 4200, www.amb-perou.fr.
Germany, Mohrenstrasse 42, 10117 Berlin, T49-30-229 1455, www.embaperu.de.
Israel, 60 Medinat Hayehudin St, Herzliya Pituach, T972-9-9957 8835, consuladop@hotmail.com.
Italy, Via Siacci 2B, 2nd floor, 00197 Roma, T39-06-8069 1510, www.ambasciataperu.it.
Japan, 4-4 -27 Higashi Shibuya-Ku, Tokyo 150-0011, T081-3-3406 4243, www.embajadadelperuenjapon.org.
Netherlands (consulate), Amsteldijk 166-7E 1079 LH, Amsterdam, T31-20-622 8580, http://consuladoperuamsterdam.com.
New Zealand, Level 8, 40 Mercer St, Cigna House, Wellington, T64-4-499 8087, frojas@embassyofperu.org.nz.
South Africa (consulate), 200 Saint Patricks Street, Muckleneuk Hill, Pretoria, T27-12-440 1030, embaperu6@telkomsa.net.
Spain, C Príncipe de Vergara 36, 5to Derecha, 28001 Madrid, T34-91-431 4242, www.embajadaperu.es.
Sweden, Brunnsgatan 21 B, 111 38 Stockholm, T46-8-440 8740, www.peru embassy.se. Also for Denmark and Norway.
Switzerland, Thunstrasse No 36, CH-3005 Berne, T41-31-351 8555, www.embajadaperu.ch.
UK, 52 Sloane St, London, SW1X 9SP, T020-7235 1917, www.peruembassy-uk.com.
USA, 1700 Massachusetts Av NW, Washington DC 20036, T1-202-833 9860, www.peruvianembassy.us.

Health

Medical services, including hospitals, are listed in the Directory sections of the relevant town. You can also contact the embassy or consulate on arrival and ask where the recommended clinics (those used by diplomats) are.

See your GP or travel clinic at least 6 weeks before departure for general advice on travel risks and vaccinations. Try phoning a specialist travel clinic if your own doctor is unfamiliar with health in the region. Make sure you have sufficient medical travel insurance, get a dental check, know your own blood group and, if you suffer a long-term condition such as diabetes or epilepsy, obtain a **Medic Alert** bracelet (www.medicalalert.co.uk).

Vaccinations and anti-malarials
Confirm that your primary courses and boosters are up to date. It is advisable to vaccinate against polio, tetanus, typhoid, hepatitis A and, for more remote areas, rabies. Yellow fever vaccination is obligatory for tropical lowland areas but not the Pacific coast, nor the highlands. Specialist advice should be taken on the best anti-malarials to take before you leave.

Health risks
The major risks posed in the region are those caused by insect disease carriers such as mosquitoes and sandflies. The key parasitic and viral diseases are malaria, dengue fever, and in some areas South American trypanosomiasis (Chagas' disease). **Malaria** is a danger throughout the lowland tropics and coastal regions. **Dengue fever** is particularly hard to protect against as the mosquitoes can bite throughout the day as well as night (unlike those that carry malaria). Try to wear clothes that cover arms and legs and also use effective mosquito repellent. Mosquito nets dipped in permethrin provide a good physical and chemical barrier at night. **Chagas' disease** is spread by faeces of a bug called the *vinchuca* or *chirimacha* which occurs in the north-central highlands and, with a much greater prevalence, in southwestern Peru. Sandflies spread **leishmaniasis**, a serious skin disease; it is called *uta* in northern Peru.

Some form of **diarrhoea** or intestinal upset is almost inevitable, the standard advice is always to wash your hands before eating and to be careful with drinking water and ice. If you have any doubts about the water then boil it or filter and treat it. In a restaurant buy bottled water or ask where the water has come from. Food can also pose a problem. Be wary of salads if you don't know whether they have been washed or not, undercooked meat, reheated foods or food that has been left out in the sun having been cooked earlier in the day. There is a simple adage that says 'wash it, peel it, boil it or forget it'. The key treatment for diarrhoea is rehydration. Try to keep hydrated by taking the right mixture of salt and water. This is available as oral rehydration salts (ORS) in ready-made sachets, or can be made up by adding a teaspoon of sugar and half a teaspoon of salt to a litre of clean water. If diarrhoea persists for several days or you develop additional symptoms, see a doctor.

There is a constant threat of **tuberculosis** (TB) and although the BCG vaccine is available, it is still not guaranteed protection. It is best to avoid unpasteurized dairy products and try not to let people cough and splutter all over you.

One of the most common problems for travellers in the region is **altitude sickness**. Acute mountain sickness can strike from about 3000 m upwards and in general is more likely to affect those who ascend rapidly (for example by plane) and those who over-exert themselves. Smokers and those with underlying heart and lung disease are often hardest hit. The sickness presents with headache, lassitude, dizziness, loss of appetite, nausea and vomiting. Insomnia is common and often associated with a suffocating feeling when lying down in bed. If the symptoms are mild, the treatment is to rest from your trip, take it easy for the first few days and drink plenty of water. Should symptoms be severe and prolonged it is best to descend to a lower altitude immediately and re-ascend, if necessary, slowly and in stages.

It is essential to get acclimatized to the thin air of the Andes before undertaking long treks or arduous activities. No one should attempt to climb over 5000 m until they have spent at least a week at around 3000 m and then a couple of nights at 4000 m. Agencies who offer 2-day climbs without adequate acclimatization are not to be trusted.

The altitude of the Andes also means that strong **protection from the sun** is always needed, regardless of how cool it may feel. Always use sunblock and a hat. Mountaineers should use glasses that provide 100% UV protection. In fact a good pair of sunglasses and a high-factor sunscreen are recommended in all parts of Peru.

If you plan to **dive** make sure that you are fit to do so. The **British Sub-Aqua Club (BSAC)**, Telford's Quay, South Pier Rd, Ellesmere Port, Cheshire CH65 4FL, UK, T01513-506200, www.bsac.com, can put you in touch with doctors who will carry out medical examinations. Check that any dive companies you use are reputable and have the appropriate certification from the **Professional Association of Diving Instructors (PADI)**, www.padi.com, which has offices and centres worldwide.

Further information
Websites
Centres for Disease Control and Prevention (USA), www.cdc.gov.
Department of Health advice for travellers, www.dh.gov.uk/en/Policyandguidance/Healthadvicefortravellers/index.htm.
Fit for Travel (UK), www.fitfortravel.scot.nhs.uk, a site from Scotland providing a quick A-Z of vaccine and travel health advice requirements for each country.
National Travel Health Network and Centre (NaTHNaC), www.nathnac.org.
Prince Leopold Institute for Tropical Medicine, www.itg.be.
World Health Organisation, www.who.int.

Books
Dawood, R, editor, *Travellers' health*, 3rd ed, Oxford: Oxford University Press, 2002.
Johnson, Chris, Sarah Anderson and others,

Oxford Handbook of Expedition and Wilderness Medicine, OUP 2008.
Wilson-Howarth, Jane. *Bugs, Bites and Bowels: the essential guide to travel health*, Cadogan 2009.

Insurance

We strongly recommend that you invest in a good insurance policy that covers you for theft or loss of possessions and money, the cost of medical and dental treatment, cancellation of flights, delays in travel arrangements, accidents, missed departures, lost baggage, lost passport and personal liability and legal expenses. Also check on inclusion of 'dangerous activities' if you plan on doing any. These generally include climbing, diving, skiing, horse riding, parachuting, even trekking. You should always read the small print carefully. Not all policies cover ambulance, helicopter rescue or emergency flights home.

There are a variety of policies to choose from, so it's best to shop around. Your travel agent can advise on the best deals available. Reputable student travel organizations often offer good-value policies. Travellers from North America can try the **International Student Insurance Service (ISIS)**, which is available through **STA**, T800-7814040, www.statravel.com. Companies worth trying in Britain include **Direct Line Insurance**, T0845-246 8704, www.directline.com, and the **Flexicover Group**, T0800-093 9495, www.flexicover.net. Some companies will not cover those over 65. The best policies for older travellers are through **Age UK**, T0845-600 3348, www.ageuk.org.uk.

Internet

You can find internet access everywhere. Centres with high tourism have internet cafés on every corner; many of them have net2phone. Internet cafés are incredibly cheap to use, normally about US$0.60-1 per hr. When they first open in the morning is often a good time to use cyber cafés, as they are less busy then. Access is generally quick. Internet is more expensive in hotel business centres and in out-of-the-way places.

Language

The official language is Spanish. Quechua, an Andean language that predates the Incas, has been given some official status and there is much pride in its use, but despite the fact that it is spoken by millions of people in the sierra who have little or no knowledge of Spanish, it is not used in schools. Another important indigenous language is Aymara, used in the area around Lake Titicaca. The jungle is home to a plethora of languages but Spanish is spoken in all but the remotest areas. English is not spoken widely, except by those employed in the tourism industry (eg hotel, tour agency and airline staff).

Language courses are listed in the directories of cities and towns. AmeriSpan, 1334 Walnut St, 6th floor, Philadelphia PA 19107, USA, T1-800-879 6640 (USA and Canada), T215-751 1100 (worldwide), SKYPE: amerispan, www.amerispan.com, organizes programmes throughout Latin America. They also have lots of information about travelling in the region. Languages Abroad.com, 386 Ontario St, Toronto, Ontario, Canada, M5A 2V7, T1-800-219 9924, in UK T0800-404 7738, www.languages abroad.com, offer Spanish and Portuguese programmes in most South American countries. They also have language immersion courses throughout the world. Similarly, there is Cactus, in the UK T0845-130 4775, www.cactuslanguage.com, and Spanish Abroad, 3219 East Camelback Rd No 806, Phoenix, AZ 85018, USA, T1-888-722 7623, or T602-778 6791 (UK T0800-028 7706), www.spanishabroad.com.

LGBT (lesbian, gay, bisexual, transgendered) travellers

Movimiento Homosexual de Lima (MHOL), C Mcal Miller 828, Jesús María, T01-433 5314, www.mhol.org.pe, is a great contact for the gay community in Lima. Online resources for gay travellers in Peru are http://lima.queer city.info/index.html (a good site, in English, with lots of links and information), www.de ambiente.com/web and www.gayperu.com (both in Spanish). The latter also has a tour operator in Miraflores, T01-447 3366, www.gayperutravel.com.

In the Lima section we include the names of gay-friendly establishments. There are also gay-friendly places in Cuzco, but the scene is not very active there. This does not mean, however, that there is hostility towards gay and lesbian travellers. As a major tourist centre that welcomes a huge variety of visitors, Cuzco is probably more open than anywhere in Peru.

Media

Newspapers and magazines

Lima has several daily papers. The most informative are *El Comercio*, www.elcomercio peru.com.pe, and *La República*, www.la republica.com.pe. Also with an online edition is *Expreso*, www.expreso.com.pe. *Gestión*, www.gestion.com.pe, is a business daily. Very popular are the sensationalist papers, written in raunchy slang and featuring acres of bare female flesh on their pages. The main provincial cities have at least 1 newspaper each. There are a number of websites that provide regular news updates, including www.yachay.com.pe and www.peru.com.

The most widely read magazine is the weekly news magazine *Caretas*, www.caretas.com.pe, which gives a very considered angle on current affairs and is often critical of government policy.

Money matters

Low-value US dollar bills should be carried for changing into soles if arriving in the country when banks or casas de cambio are closed. They are also useful for shopping. In larger establishments in cities that receive many tourists, dollars are accepted instead of soles. If you are travelling on the cheap it is essential to keep in funds; watch weekends and public holidays carefully and never run out of local currency. Take plenty of local currency, in small denominations, when making trips in the provinces. Try to break down notes whenever you can as there is a countrywide shortage of change (or so it seems) and it will make life much simpler. It is difficult to get change in shops and museums and sometimes impossible from street vendors or cab drivers.

Radio

Radio is far more important in imparting news to Peruvians than newspapers, partly due to the fact that limited plane routes make it difficult to get papers to much of the population on the same day. There are countless local and community radio stations that cover even the most far-flung places. A popular station is *Radioprogramas del Perú* (www.rpp.com.pe), which features round-the-clock news.

A shortwave radio will allow you to absorb local culture, as well as pick up the **BBC World Service** (www.bbc.co.uk/worldservice) or the **Voice of America** (www.voa.gov).

Money → *Exchange rates: £1=S/.4.42, US$1 = S/. 2.83, 1 euro = S/.3.70 (Dec 2010).*

Currency

For up-to-the-minute exchange rates visit www.xe.com.

The **nuevo sol** (new sol, S/.) is the official currency of Peru. It is divided in 100 *céntimos* (cents) with coins valued at S/.5, S/.2, S/.1 and 50, 20, 10 and 5 *céntimo* pieces although the latter is being phased out as it is virtually worthless. Notes in circulation are S/.200, S/.100, S/.50, S/.20 and S/.10.

Prices of airline tickets, tour agency services, non-backpacker hotels and hostels, among others, are almost always quoted in dollars. You can pay in soles or dollars but it is generally easiest to pay dollars when the price is in dollars and in soles when the price is in soles. This will save you from losing on exchange rates. In major tourist centres such as Lima, Cuzco and Arequipa dollars are frequently accepted.

Almost no one, certainly not banks, will accept dollar bills that are ripped, taped, stapled or torn. Do not accept damaged dollars from anyone; simply tell them you would like another bill. Likewise, ask your bank at home to give you only nice, crisp, clean dollars and keep your dollars neat in your money belt or wallet so they don't accidentally tear.

Forgeries of dollars and soles are not uncommon. Always check the sol notes you have received, even at the bank. Money changers, especially at borders, mix fake notes with genuine bills when giving wads of soles for other currencies. Information on notes and coins in circulation, including forgeries, can be found on **www.bcrp. gob.pe**, under **Billetes y Monedas**. Hold the bills up to the light to check the watermark and that the colours change according to the angle of the light. The line down the side of the bill in which the amount of the money is written should appear green, blue and pink at different angles; fake bills are only pink and have no hologram properties. There should be tiny pieces of thread in the paper (not glued on). Check to see that the faces are clear. Also, the paper should not feel smooth like a photocopy but rougher and fibrous. Try not to accept brand-new notes, especially if changing on the street, slightly used notes are less likely to be forgeries. There are posters in public places explaining what to look for in forged sol notes. In parts of the country, forged 1- and 5-sol coins are in circulation. They are slightly off-colour, the surface copper can be scratched off and they tend to bear a recent date.

Banks and ATMs

BCP opens Mon-Fri 0900-1800 and Sat 0900-1300, changes US$ cash to soles. Cash advances on Visa in soles only. VíaBCP ATM for Visa/Plus, MasterCard/Cirrus, Amex. **BBVA Continental** changes US$ cash to soles, US$12 commission per transaction for TCs at selected branches. B24 ATM for Visa/Plus. **Interbank**, open Mon-Fri 0900-1815, Sat 0900-1230, changes US$ cash and TCs to soles, TCs to US$ cash for US$5 per transaction up to US$500. GlobalNet ATM (see below). **Scotiabank**, open Mon-Fri 0915-1800, Sat 0915-1230, changes US$ cash to soles, cash advances on MasterCard, ATM for Cirrus, Visa, MasterCard, Maestro. There are also **Global Net** and **Red Unicard** ATMs that accept Visa, Plus and MasterCard, Maestro and Cirrus (the former makes a charge per transaction). ATMs usually give US$ if you don't request soles and their use is widespread. Maximum allowed per transaction is US$140. It is safest to use ATMs during banking hours. At night and on Sun there is more chance of the transaction going wrong, or false money being in the machine. The compatibility of ATMs across Peru is increasing all the time. Your card has to be pretty obscure not to be able to obtain cash from an ATM, but availability decreases outside large towns. In smaller towns, take some cash.

Credit cards

Visa (by far the most widely accepted card in Peru), **MasterCard**, **Maestro**, **American Express** and **Diners Club** are all valid. There may be an 8-12% commission for all credit card charges. Often, it is cheaper to use your credit card to get money (dollars or soles) out of an ATM rather than to pay for your purchases. Of course, this depends on the interest rate for cash advances on your credit cards – ask your bank or card provider about this. Other options are to put extra money on your credit cards and use them as a bank card, or to take a prepaid currency card. There are many on offer, from, for example, **Caxton**, **FairFX**, **Travelex**, banks and other organizations. It pays to check their application fees and charges carefully.

Businesses displaying credit card symbols are unlikely to take foreign cards. Make sure you carry the phone numbers that you need in order to report your card lost or stolen. In addition, some travellers have reported problems with their credit cards being 'frozen' by their bank as soon as a charge from a foreign country occurs. To avoid this problem, notify your bank that you will be making charges in Peru (and other countries).

Credit card companies

American Express, Travex SA, Av Santa Cruz 621, Miraflores, Lima, T01-710 3900, info@travex.com.pe. For ATM locations: www.americanexpress.com.
Diners Club, Canaval y Moreyra 535, San Isidro, T01-615 1111, www.dinersclub.com.pe..
MasterCard, Porta 111, p 6, Miraflores, T01-311 6000, T0800-307 7309, www.mastercard.com/pe/gateway.html. For ATM locations: www.mastercard.com.
Visa Travel Assistance, T0800-890 0623. For ATM locations: www.visalatam.com.

Exchange

All banks' exchange rates are considerably less favourable than *casas de cambio* (exchange houses). Long queues and paperwork may be involved. US$ and euro are the only currencies that should be brought into Peru from abroad (take some small bills). There are no restrictions on foreign exchange. Few banks change euro but *casas de cambio* will do so. Always count your money in the presence of the cashier. Street changers give much the same rates for changing small amounts of US$ or euro cash as *casas de cambio*, but avoiding paperwork and queuing. Take care: check your soles before handing over your US$, check their calculators, etc, and don't change money in crowded areas. If using their services think about taking a taxi after changing, to avoid being followed. Street changers congregate near an office where the exchange 'wholesaler' operates; the office will probably offer better rates than on the street.

Soles can be exchanged into dollars at the banks and exchange houses at Lima airport, and you can change soles for dollars with street changers and at any border. Dollars can also be bought at the borders.

American Express will sell traveller's cheques to cardholders only, but will not exchange cheques into cash. They are also very efficient in replacing stolen cheques, though a police report is needed. Travellers have reported great difficulty in cashing traveller's cheques in the jungle area, even Iquitos, and other remote areas. Always sign traveller's cheques in blue or black ink or ballpen.

Cost of living

Living costs in the provinces are 20-50% below those in Lima, although Cuzco is a little more expensive than other, less touristy provincial cities. For a lot of low-income Peruvians, many items are simply beyond their reach.

Cost of travelling

The approximate budget is US$35-50 per person per day for living comfortably, with transport, or US$15-20 a day for low-budget travel. Your budget will be higher the longer you stay in Lima and will depend on on how many flights you take. Accommodation rates range from US$5 per person for the most basic *alojamiento* to US$15-30 for mid-range places, to over US$90 for top-of-the-range

hotels (more in Lima and Cuzco). For the price of eating out, see page 42.

Opening hours

Banks See under Money, above. Outside Lima and Cuzco banks may close 1200-1500 for lunch. **Government offices** Jan-Mar Mon-Fri 0830-1130; Apr-Dec Mon-Fri 0900-1230, 1500-1700, but these hrs change frequently. **Offices** Mon-Fri 0900-1700. Most close on Sat. **Shops** 0900 or 1000-1230 and 1500 or 1600-2000. In the main cities, supermarkets do not close for lunch, some in Lima open 24 hrs. Some are closed on Sat and most on Sun.

Post

The postal system is **Serpost**. Correo Central on the Plaza de Armas in Lima is the best place for postage (open Mon-Fri 0800-1800). Sending packages out of Peru is incredibly expensive and is not really worth it but letters are much more reasonable; rates are US$2.30 to South America and US$2.50 to North and Central America, US$2.70 to Europe and US$3.12 to Australia. Postcards cost US$1.90. You can also send letters registered at extra cost. Stamps, envelopes and cloth sacks (to send bigger parcels in) can all be bought at the central post office in Lima. Cuzco is also efficient for sending parcels. Don't put tape on envelopes or packages; wait until you get to the post office and use the glue they have. For emergency or important documents, use Serpost's own **EMS** service, or **DHL** and **Federal Express** in Lima and major cities.

To receive mail, letters can be sent to Poste Restante/General Delivery (*lista de correos*), your embassy, or, for cardholders, American Express office in Lima. Members of the **South American Explorers** can have post sent to them at either of the Peruvian offices. Try not to have articles sent by post to Peru – taxes can be 200% of the value.

Safety

The following notes on personal safety should not hide the fact that most Peruvians are hospitable and helpful. Peru is not a highly dangerous country to travel in, but it is by no means crime free. By being aware of the possible problems you may confront and by using a mixture of common sense and vigilance you can minimize the risks.

You need to take care everywhere but particularly in poor areas of cities, as this is where most theft takes place. While you should take local advice about being out at night, do not assume that daytime is safer than nighttime. If walking after dark, walk in the road, not on the pavement. You should also be on your guard during festivals, at markets and when streets are crowded. Care should be taken at all times and in most parts of Lima. Over the past couple of years there has been an alarming increase in aggressive assaults in centres along the 'gringo trail'. Places like Arequipa, Puno and Cuzco have, at times, been plagued by waves of strangle muggings.

Check with **South American Explorers** for a current summary of the situation and how to keep safe. A friendly attitude on your part, smiling even when you've thwarted a thief's attempt, can help you out of trouble. Be especially careful when using ATMs and when arriving at or leaving from bus and train stations, when you have a lot of important belongings with you. Do not set your bag down without putting your foot on it, even just to double check your tickets. Be wary of accepting food, drink, sweets or cigarettes from unknown people on buses or trains; they may be drugged.

Keep all documents secure and hide your main cash supply in different places or under your clothes. Keep cameras in bags, take spare spectacles and don't wear wristwatches or jewellery. If you wear a shoulder-bag, carry it in front of you. Small personal alarms are a good idea. Backpacks can be covered with a sack (a plastic one

will also keep out rain and dust) with maybe a layer of wire netting between. Make photocopies of important documents and give them to family or friends. Alternatively send yourself an email containing all important details, addresses, etc which you can access in an emergency. Where there is no safe or locker in your room, you should be able to leave valuables in the hotel's safe-deposit box. But keep a record of what you have deposited. If none of these options is available, lock everything in your pack and secure that in your room (some people take eyelet-screws for padlocking cupboards or drawers). If you lose your valuables, always report it to the police and note details of the report for insurance purposes. Double check that all reports written by the police actually state your complaint. The **tourist police** in Lima are excellent and, if you can, report any incidents to them (see Accident and emergency, page 49).

If someone spits, smears mustard, or sprays paint or shampoo on to your clothes, walk on to a safe, private place to clean yourself up. Similarly, ignore strangers' remarks like 'what's that on your shoulder?' or 'have you seen that dirt on your shoe?'. Furthermore, don't bend over to pick up money or other items in the street. These are all ploys intended to distract your attention and make it easy for an accomplice to rob you. If someone follows you when you're in the street, let him catch up with you and 'give him the eye'. Ruses involving 'plainclothes policemen' are infrequent, but it is worth knowing that the real police only have the right to see your passport (not your money, tickets or hotel room).

Until 2008 the activities of the terrorist groups Sendero Luminoso and MRTA had seemed to be a thing of the past, but neither organization was completely non-functional. Reports indicate that Sendero Luminoso was mobilizing again in the areas where its remants had gone to ground, the drug-growing zones of the Huallaga Valley and the jungle east of Ayacucho. In 2010 it was still safe to travel to all parts of Peru except those just mentioned, but it is important to inform yourself of the latest situation before going.

While in Lima or Cuzco, you can check in at **South American Explorers**, for the latest travel updates (Lima T01-444 2150, Cuzco T084-245484). Also check with the tourist police, your embassy or consulate.

Never offer a bribe unless you are fully conversant with local customs. Wait until the official makes the suggestion, or offer money in a form that is apparently not bribery, eg 'In our country we have a system of on-the-spot fines (*multas de inmediato*). Is there a similar system here?' Do not assume that an official who accepts a bribe is prepared to do anything else that is illegal. You bribe him to persuade him to do his job, or to persuade him not to do it, or to do it more quickly, or more slowly. You do not bribe him to do something which is against the law. If an official suggests that a bribe must be paid before you can proceed on your way, be patient and he may relent.

Many places in the Amazon and in Cuzco offer experiences with **Ayahuasca** or **San Pedro**, often in ceremonies with a shaman. These are legal, but always choose a reputable tour operator or shaman. Do not go with the first person who offers you a trip. Single women should not take part. There are plenty of websites for starting your research.

Students travellers

If you are in full-time education you will be entitled to an **International Student Identity Card**, which gives you special prices on all forms of transport (air, sea, rail, etc), and access to a variety of other concessions and services. If you need to find the location of your nearest ISIC office contact: **The ISIC Association**, www.isic.org.

Students can obtain very few reductions in Peru with an international student card,

except in and around Cuzco, at museums and Instituto Nacional de Cultura sites. To be any use in Peru, it must bear the owner's photograph. An ISIC card can be obtained in Lima from **Intej**: Av San Martín 240, Barranco, T01-247 3230. Also: Portal de Panes 123, of 304, Cuzco, T084-256367; Santo Domingo 123, of 401, Arequipa, T054-284756 ; Calle José Sabogal 913, Cajamarca, T076-362522; Av Mariscal Castilla 3909-4089, El Tambo, 7mo piso del Edificio de Administración y Gobierno de la UNCP, anexo 6056, Huancayo, T064-481081; Av Jorge Basadre Grohmann s/n, Pocollay, 4to piso del Edificio Facultad de Ciencias Empresariales (FACEM), Campus Capanique de la Universidad Privada de Tacna (UPT), Tacna, T051-981 084038, www.intej.org.

Tax

General sales tax of 19% is automatically added to the bill. There is also a departure tax when flying, see page 30.

Telephone → *Country code +51.*

The main service provider is **Telefónica**, www.telefonica.com.pe (or **Telser** in Cuzco), which has offices in all large and medium-sized towns. **Telefónica** offices are usually administrative and phones are provided on the street outside. Local, national and international calls can be made from public phone boxes with prepaid phone cards that can be bought at **Telefónica** offices or the many private phone offices called *locutorios*. Also, there are cards for a number of other carriers for long-distance calls. Their rates are very competitive and there are usually special offers. Collect calls are possible to almost anywhere by ringing the international operator (T108). This is also the number for directory enquiries and for international directory options (they speak English). Your home telephone company can give you the number to call as well. **Net Phones** are popular; costs and service vary. SKYPE can also be used.

The numbering system for mobile/cellular phones is as follows: for Lima mobiles, add 9 before the number, for the departments of La Libertad 94, Arequipa 95, Piura 96, Lambayeque 97; for other departments, add 9 – if not already in the number – and the city code (for example, Cuzco numbers start 984). Note also that some towns are dominated by **Claró**, others by **Movistar** (the 2 main mobile companies). As it is expensive to call between the 2 you should check, if spending some time in 1 city and using a mobile, which is the best account to have.

Red Privada Movistar (RPM) and **Red Privada Claró (RPC)** are operated by the respective mobile phone companies. Mobile phone users who subscribe to these services obtain a 6-digit number in addition their 9-digit mobile phone number. Both the 6- and 9-digit numbers ring on the same physical phone. The RPM and RPC numbers can be called from anywhere in Peru without using an area code, you just dial the 6 digits, and the cost is about 20% of calling the 9-digit number. This 80% discount usually also applies when calling from *locutorios*. Many establishments including hotels, tour operators and transport companies have both RPM and RPC numbers.

Time → *Peru is 5 hrs behind GMT.*

Peruvians, as with most Latin Americans, have a fairly relaxed attitude towards time. They will think nothing of arriving an hour or so late on social occasions. If you expect to meet someone more or less at an exact time, you can tell them that you want to meet *en punto* or specify *la hora inglesa* (English time).

Tipping

In most of the better restaurants a 10% service charge is included in the bill, but you can give an extra 5% as a tip if the service is good. The most basic restaurants do not include a tip in the bill, and tips are not expected. Taxi drivers are not tipped – bargain the price down, then pay extra for good service if you get it. Tip cloakroom attendants and hairdressers (very high class only), US$0.50-1; railway or airport porters, US$0.50; car wash boys, US$0.30; car 'watch' boys, US$0.20. If going on a trek or tour it is customary to tip the guide, as well as the cook and porters.

Toilets

Most Peruvian toilets are adequate but the further you go from main population and tourist centres, the poorer the facilities, so you may require a strong stomach and the ability to hold your breath for a long time. Almost without exception used toilet paper or feminine hygiene products should not be flushed down the pan, but placed in the receptacle provided. This applies even in quite expensive hotels. Not doing so will block the pan or drain, which can be a considerable health risk. It is quite common for people to stand on the toilet seat, as they do in Asia.

Tour operators

UK and Ireland
Adventure Peru Motorcycling, Coldharbour Barn, Battle Rd, Dallington, Nr Heathfield, East Sussex TN21 9LQ, T 01424-838618, www.perumotorcycling.com. In Peru based in Cajamarca, T0051-76-366630. Motorcycling adventure tours from 10 days to 4 weeks throughout the country, bikes provided, full back-up team, run by experienced bikers.

Amazing Peru, 9 Alma Rd, Manchester M19 2FG, T0800-520 0309, T1-800-216 0831 (Canada), T1-800-704 2915 or 1-800-704 2949 (USA), www.amazingperu.com. Professional and well-organized tours to Peru, with knowledgeable guides.

Amazing Voyages, 52 Brook St, London W1K 5DS, T020-7268 2053, www.amazingvoyages. co.uk. Luxury travel specialist.

Andean Trails, The Clockhouse, Bonnington Mill Business Centre, 72 Newhaven Rd, Edinburgh EH6 5QG, T0131-467 7086, www.andeantrails.co.uk. For mountain biking, trekking and other adventure tours.

Andes, 37a St Andrews St, Castle Douglas, Kirkcudbrightshire DG7 1EN, Scotland, T01556-503929, www.andes.org.uk. For climbing trips in Peru and all South America.

Audley Latin America, New Mill, New Mill Lane, Witney, Oxfordshire, OX29 0SX, T01993-838000, www.audleytravel.com.

Austral Tours, 20 Upper Tachbrook St, London SW1V 1SH, T020-7233 5384, www.latinamerica.co.uk. Tailor-made tours, flights and accommodation in Latin America.

Breast Cancer Care, T0845-092 0805 (UK), www.breastcancercare.org.uk/events. Machu Picchu treks to raise money to support people living with breast cancer. Treks leave on 29 Apr 2011, 16 Sep 2011, 13 Apr 2012 and 7 Sep 2012.

Chimu Adventures, www.chimuadventures. com. Web-based company providing tours, treks, active adventures and accommodation throughout South America and the Antarctic.

Condor Journeys and Adventures, 2 Ferry Bank, Colintraive, Argyll PA22 3AR, T01700-841318, www.condorjourneys-adventures.com. Eco and adventure tourism with specially designed tours to suit your requirements.

Dragoman, Camp Green, Debenham, Suffolk IP14 6LA, T01728-861133,

www.dragoman.com. Overland camping and/or hotel journeys throughout both South and Central America.

Exodus Travels, Grange Mills, 9 Weir Rd, London SW12 0NE, T020-8675 5550, www.exodus.co.uk. Experienced in adventure travel, including cultural tours and trekking and biking holidays.

Explore, Nelson House, 55 Victoria Rd, Farnborough, Hampshire GU14 7PA, T0845-0131537, www.explore.co.uk. Highly respected operator. They offer 2- to 5-week tours in more than 90 countries worldwide, including Peru. Small groups. Well executed.

Galapagos Classic Cruises in conjunction with **Classic Cruises** and **World Adventures**, 6 Keyes Rd, London NW2 3XA, T020-8933 0613, www.galapagoscruises.co.uk, specialize in individual and group travel including cruises, scuba-diving and land-based tours to the Galapagos, Peru and Bolivia.

Guerba Expeditions, Wessex House, 40 Station Rd, Westbury, Wiltshire BA13 3JN, T01373-828303/T0203-147 7777, www.guerba.com. Adventure holidays, from trekking safaris to wilderness camping.

High Places, Globe Centre, Penistone Rd, Sheffield S6 3AE, T0845-257 7500, www.highplaces.co.uk. Trekking and mountaineering trips.

Journey Latin America, 12-13 Heathfield Terr, Chiswick, London W4 4JE, T020-8622 8464, www.journeylatinamerica.co.uk. The world's leading tailor-made specialist for Latin America, running escorted tours throughout the region; they also offer a wide range of flight options.

KE Adventure Travel, 32 Lake Rd, Keswick, Cumbria CA12 5DQ, T017687-73966, www.keadventure.com. Specialist in adventure tours, including 3-week cycling trips in and around Cuzco.

Kumuka Expeditions, 40 Earls Court Rd, London W8 6EJ, T020-7937 8855, www.kumuka.com. Overland tour operator for small groups, both escorted or truck-based. Offices in Ireland, Germany, USA, Canada, Australia, New Zealand, South Africa and UAE.

Last Frontiers, The Mill, Quainton Rd, Waddesdon, Bucks HP18 0LP, T01296-653000, www.lastfrontiers.com. South American specialists offering tailor-made itineraries plus family holidays, honeymoons, and Galápagos cruises.

Latin American Travel Association (LATA), 46 Melbourne Rd, London SW19 3BA, www.lata.org. For useful country information and listing of all UK tour operators specializing in Latin America.

Llama Travel, Oxford House, 49A Oxford Rd, London N4 3EY, T020-7263 3000, www.llamatravel.com. Tours throughout Peru.

Naturetrek, Cheriton Mill, Cheriton, Alresford, Hampshire SO24 0NG, T01962-733051, www.naturetrek.co.uk. Birdwatching tours throughout the continent, also botany, natural history tours, treks and cruises.

Oasis Overland, The Marsh, Henstridge, Somerset BA8 0TF, T01963-363400, www.oasisoverland.com. Small-group trips in Peru and overland trips across South America.

Reef and Rainforest Tours, Dart Marine Park, Steamer Quay, Totnes, Devon TQ9 5AL, T01803-866965, www.reefandrainforest.co.uk. Specialists in tailor-made and group wildlife tours.

Select Latin Amercia (incorporating Galapagos Adventure Tours), 3.51 Canterbury Court, 1-3 Brixton Rd, Kennington Park Business Centre, London SW9 6DE, T020-7407 1478, www.selectlatinamerica.co.uk. Quality tailor-made holidays and small-group tours.

South American Experience, Welby House, 96 Wilton Rd, Victoria, London SW1V 1DW, T0845-2773366, www.southamericanexperience.com. Flights and accommodation bookings as well as tailor-made trips since 1987.

Steppes Latin America, 51 Castle St, Cirencester, Glos GL7 1QD, T01285-880980, www.steppestravel.co.uk. Tailor-made itineraries for destinations throughout Latin America.

Sunvil Latin America, Sunvil House, Upper Sq, Old Isleworth, Middlesex TW7 7BJ, T020-8568 4499, www.sunvil.co.uk. Small groups or individual tours.

The Adventure Company, Cross and Pillory House, Cross and Pillory Lane, Alton, Hampshire, GU34 1HL, T0845-450 5316, www.adventurecompany.co.uk.

To Escape To, 8 Thames Reach, Purley on Thames, Reading RG8 8TE, T020-7060 6747, www.toescapeto.com. Adventurous tailor-made trips, specialists in family travel.

Tribes Travel, 12 The Business Centre, Earl Soham, Woodbridge, Suffolk IP13 7SA, T01728-685971, www.tribes.co.uk. Has an associated charitable foundation that aims to relieve poverty in indigenous communities.

Trips Worldwide, 14 Frederick Pl, Clifton, Bristol BS8 1AS, T0800-840 0850,

www.tripsworldwide.co.uk. Tailor-made tours to South America.

Tucan Travel, 316 Uxbridge Rd, Acton, London W3 9QP, T020-8896 1600, Av del Sol 616, oficina 202, AP 0637, Cuzco T51-84-241123, and 217 Alison Rd, Randwick, NSW 2031, Sydney, T02-9326 6633, www.tucantravel.com.

Veloso Tours, ground floor, 34 Warple Way, London W3 0RG, T020-8762 0616, www.veloso.com.

Continental Europe

Nouveaux Mondes, Rte Suisse 7, CH-1295 Mies, Switzerland, T+41-22-950 9660, www.nouveauxmondes.com.

South American Tours, Stephanstrasse 13, D-60313, Frankfurt/M, Germany, T+49-69-405 8970, www.southamericantours.de. For holidays, business travel, or special packages. Has an office at Calle Bolognesi 381, Miraflores 18, Lima, T01-446 7799, and in New York, Tokyo, Montevideo, Quito, Rio de Janeiro, Santiago de Chile and Buenos Aires.

North America

Discover Latinamerica, 6205 Blue Lagoon Drive, suite 310, Miami, FL 33126, T305-266 5827, www.discoverlatinamerica.com.

eXito, 108 Rutgers St, Fort Collins, CO 80525, T1-800-655 4053, www.exito-travel.com.

GAP Adventures, 19 Charlotte St, Toronto, M5V 2H5, Canada, T1-800-708 7761 (in North America), 40 Star St, London W2 1QB, T0870 999 0144, T1-416-260 0999 (outside North America and UK), www.gapadventures.com.

Ladatco, 3006 Aviation, Suite 3A, Coconut Grove, FL 33133, USA, T1-800 327 6162, www.ladatco.com. 'Themed' explorer tours based around the Incas, mysticism, etc.

Myths and Mountains, 976 Tee Court, Incline Village, NV 89451, T775-832 5454, www.mythsandmountains.com.

Peru For Less, T1-877-269 0309 (USA toll free) T0203-002 0571 (UK), www.peruforless.com. Customized tours to Peru and the rest of Latin America, price and service guaranteed. Based in Texas, offices in Lima and Cuzco.

Puchka Peru, www.puchkaperu.com. Specializes in textiles, folk art and market tours.

Tambo Tours, USA, T1-888-2-GO-PERU (246-7378), www.2GOPERU.com. Long-established adventure and tour specialist with offices in Peru and the US. Customized trips to the Amazon and archaeological sites of Peru, Bolivia and Ecuador.

Tropical Nature Travel, PO Box 5276, Gainesville, FL 326270 5276, T1-877-827 8350, www.tropicalnaturetravel.com. Ecotour company with itineraries to Peru.

Wildland Adventures, 3516 NE 155 St, Seattle, WA 98155-7412, USA, T206-365 0686, T800-345 4453, www.wildland.com. Specializes in cultural and natural history tours to the Andes and Amazon.

South America

Aracari Travel Consulting, Schell 237 No 602, Miraflores, Lima, T01-651 2424, www.aracari.com. Regional tours in Peru.

Condor Travel, Armando Blondet 249, San Isidro, Lima 27, T01-615 3000, www.condor travel.com. In USA T1-877-236 7199. A full range of tours, including custom-made, and services in Bolivia, Ecuador and Peru (offices in each country), with a strong commitment to social responsibility.

Kolibri Expeditions, contact Gunnar Engblom, Lima, T01-273 7246, www.kolibri expeditions.com. Trip reports, recent sightings, travel tips, travel partners, range extensions, identification help, www.birding-peru.com. **Birding Peru** e-group: birdingperu-subscribe@yahoo groups.com.

Navimag, Naviera Magallanes SA, Angelmó 2187. Puerto Montt, Chile, T56-2-442 3120, www.navimag.com.

SouthAmerica.travel, www.southamerica. travel. Internet-based tour operator with offices in Peru (Jr Elías Aguirre 141, of 313, Miraflores, Lima, T01-719 7792), Germany (Hauptstr 131, D-70563 Stuttgart, T+49-711-856 6972), USA (322 SE Park Hill Dr, Chehalis WA 98532, T1-800-747 4540) and in Rio de Janeiro and Buenos Aires. Covering every type of travel throughout South America.

Surtrek, Av Amazonas 897 y Wilson, Quito, Ecuador, T593-2-250 0530, www.surtrek.com. Customized private group and individual adventure tours throughout South America.

Rest of the world

Adventure World, Level 20, 141 Walker St, North Sydney NSW 2060, T02-8913 0755, and Level 9, 40 St Georges Terrace, Perth 6000, T08-9226 4524, www.adventure world.com.au. Escorted group tours, locally escorted tours and packages to Peru and all of Latin America.

Tourist information

Tourism promotion and information is handled by **PromPerú**, Edif Minceutur, C Uno Oeste 50, p 13, urb Córpac, San Isidro, T01-224 3131, www.peru.info. They produce promotional material but offer no direct information service to individual tourists. The website does carry plenty of background and other information. PromPerú runs an information and assistance service, **iperú**, T01-574 8000 (24 hrs). Main office: Jorge Basadre 610, San Isidro, Lima, T01-421 1627, iperulima@promperu.gob.pe, Mon-Fri 0830-1830. Also a 24-hr office at Jorge Chávez airport; and throughout the country.

There are tourist offices in most towns, either run by the municipality, or independently. **Indecopi**, in Lima T01-224 7800, www.indecopi.gob.pe, is the government-run consumer protection and tourist complaint bureau. This body (with offices, kiosks and information stands in every town) will help with complaints regarding customs, airlines, travel agencies, accommodation, restaurants, public authorities or if you have lost, or had stolen, documents. For information on national parks and protected areas, see **El Servicio Nacional de Áreas Naturales Protegidas por el Estado (SERNANP)**, C Diecisiete 355, Urb El Palomar, San Isidro, Lima, T01-717 7500, www.sernanp.gob.pe.

Outside Peru, tourist information can be obtained from Peruvian embassies and consulates, see page 51.

With regard to security, it is better to seek advice before you leave from your own consulate than from travel agencies. Also contact: **British Foreign and Commonwealth Office**, Travel Advice Unit, T0845-850 2829 (travel advice), T020-7008 1500 (consular assistance from abroad). Footprint is a partner in the Foreign and Commonwealth Office's **Know before you go** campaign, www.fco.gov.uk/en/travel-and-living-abroad/. **US State Department's Bureau of Consular Affairs**, Overseas Citizens Services, T1-888-407 4747 (from

overseas: T202-501 4444), www.travel.
state.gov. **Australian Department of
Foreign Affairs**, T+61-2-6261 3305,
www.smartraveller.gov.au/.

South American Explorers,
www.saexplorers.org, is a non-profit,
educational organization that functions
primarily as an information network for Peru
and South America and is the most useful
organization for travellers in the continent.
They have offices in Lima, Cuzco, Quito,
Buenos Aires and the USA. Full details
are given in the Lima and Cuzco sections,
see pages 74 and 129.

Useful organizations

Agotur (Asociación de Guías Oficiales de
Turismo), Av La Paz 678, Miraflores, Lima,
www.agotur.com. With a full list of associated
guides and access to the Ley de Guía.
Apavit (Asociación Peruana de
Agencias de Viaje y Turismo), Antonio
Roca 121, Santa Beatriz, Lima, T01-433
1111, www.apavitperu.org.
Apotur (Asociación Peruana de Operadores
de Turismo), C San Fernando 287, Miraflores,
Lima 18, T01-446 4076, www.apoturperu.org.
Aptae (Asociación Peruana de Operadores
de Turismo de Aventura y Ecoturismo),
Bolognesi 125, of 703, Miraflores, Lima 18,
T01-447 8476, www.aptae.org.

Useful websites

www.aboutcusco.com, **www.cuscoon
line.com** and **www. cusco.net** Among
many websites about Cuzco, in Spanish,
English and other languages.
www.machu-picchu.info All about
Machu Picchu.
www.arequipa-tourism.com Site about
Arequipa in Spanish and English.
www.yachay.com.pe/especiales/nasca
Nazca lines (in Spanish).
www.andeanexplorer.com For Huaraz and
the Callejón de Huaylas, available in English.
www.xanga.com/TrujilloPeru Mainly for
the north of the country.
www.adonde.com For general information.

www.andeantravelweb.com/peru
Andean adventure travel, with advice,
links and more (English and Spanish).
www.livinginperu.com Informative guide
in English for people living in Peru.
www.minam.gob.pe Ministerio del
Ambiente (Spanish).
www.planeta.com Ron Mader's website
containting masses of useful information
on ecotourism, conservation, travel, news,
links, language schools and articles.
www.rree.gob.pe Ministry of Foreign
Affairs, for consular information, etc.
www.terra.com.pe Click on Turismo
to get to the travel page (in Spanish).
www.traficoperu.com Online agent with
lots of information (in Spanish and English).
www.yachay.com.pe Red Científica
Peruana, click on Turismo.
www.leaplocal.org Recommends good-
quality local guides, helping communities
benefit from socially responsible tourism.

Visas and immigration

Tourist cards No visa is necessary for
citizens of countries in the European Union,
most Asian countries, North and South
America and the Caribbean, or for citizens
of Andorra, Belarus, Croatia, Iceland, Israel,
Liechtenstein, Macedonia, Moldova, Norway,
Russian Federation, Serbia and Montenegro,
Switzerland, Ukraine, Australia, New Zealand
and South Africa. A tourist card (**TAM** – Tarjeta
Andina de Migración) is free on flights arriving
in Peru, or at border crossings for visits of up to
183 days. The form is in duplicate, the original
given up on arrival and the copy on departure.
A new tourist card must be obtained for each
re-entry. If your tourist card is stolen or lost, get
a new one at **Migraciones**, Digemin, Av España
730, Breña, Lima, T01-417 6900/433 0731,
www.digemin.gob.pe, Mon-Fri 0800-1300.
Tourist visas For citizens of countries not
listed above, tourist visas cost £20.70 (about
US$32.50) or equivalent, for which you
require a valid passport, a departure ticket

from Peru (or reservation showing arrival and departure dates), 1 colour passport photo, 1 application form, hotel reservation or package tour confirmation and proof of economic solvency.

Under Decree 1043 of Jun 2008, once in Peru tourists may not extend their tourist card or visa. It's therefore important to insist on getting the full number of days to cover your visit on arrival (it's at the discretion of the border official). If you exceed your card or visa, you'll pay a US$1-per-day fine.

All foreigners should be able to produce on demand some recognizable means of identification, preferably a passport. You must present your passport when reserving tickets for internal as well as international travel. An alternative is to photocopy the important pages of your passport – including the immigration stamp, and have it legalized by a 'notario público' (US$1.50). We have received no reports of travellers being asked for an onward ticket at the borders at Tacna, Aguas Verdes, La Tina, Yunguyo or Desaguadero. Travellers arriving by air are not asked for an onward flight ticket at Lima airport, but it is possible that you will not be allowed to board a plane in your home country without showing an onward ticket.
Business visas A visitor who is going to receive money from Peruvian sources must have a business visa: requirements are a valid passport, 1 colour passport photo, return ticket or reservation and a letter from an employer stating the nature of business, length of stay and guarantee that any Peruvian taxes will be paid and proof of solvency of the company. The visa costs £20.70 (about US$32.50) and allows the holder to stay 183 days in the country. On arrival business visitors must register with the **Dirección General de Contribuciones** for tax purposes.
Student visas To obtain a student visa you must enter the country as a tourist and then apply at **Migraciones** in Lima (address above). In addition to completing the general visa

form you must have proof of adequate funds, affiliation to a Peruvian body, and a letter of consent from parents or tutors if you are a minor. The cost is US$20. Full details are on the Digemin website (in Spanish). See above.

Weights and measures

Metric.

Women travellers

Generally women travellers should find visiting Peru an enjoyable experience. However, machismo is alive and well here and you should be prepared for this and try not to overreact. When you set out, err on the side of caution until your instincts have adjusted to the customs of a new culture.

It is easier for men to take the friendliness of locals at face value; women may be subject to much unwanted attention. To minimize this, do not wear suggestive clothing and do not flirt. By wearing a wedding ring, carrying a photograph of your 'husband' and 'children', and saying that your 'husband' is close at hand, you may dissuade an aspiring suitor. If politeness fails, do not feel bad about showing offence and departing. When accepting a social invitation, make sure that someone knows the address and the time you left. Ask if you can bring a friend (even if you do not intend to do so).

If, as a single woman, you can befriend a local woman, you will learn much more about the country you are visiting as well as finding out how best to deal with the barrage of suggestive comments, whistles and hisses that will invariably come your way.

There is a very definite 'gringo trail' that you can join, or follow, if seeking company. This can be helpful when looking for safe accommodation, especially if arriving after dark (which is best avoided).

Working and volunteering in Peru

Voluntourism

There are many opportunities for volunteer work in Peru (**South American Explorers** has an extensive database). Most volunteers do not need a visa for Peru, but you must check with a Peruvian consulate that this applies to you. The site www.trabajovoluntario.org helps volunteers and organizations to get in touch and browse for opporutnities. Likewise, www.volunteersouthamerica.net, a continent-wide directory of low-cost to zero-cost programmes, offers several opportunities in Peru. In Cuzco, **Hope Foundation** (at Marani Hotel, see page 145) and **Amauta Spanish School** (see page 172) accept volunteers. In Cajamarca, **I-Dev International**, Jr Amazonas 775, T01-992-705660, http://idevinternational.com, has a number of projects and offers "Doing development in..." programmes. In Huaraz, **Seeds of Hope**, Jr Damaso Antunez 782, Huaraz, T043-396305, www.peruseeds.org, aims to get children away from work on the street or in the fields and into education. With a similar mission is **Luz de Esperanza**, Av Eternidad 316, Huancayo, T064-439913, www.peruluz deesperanza.com. For information outside Peru on voluntary work and working abroad, try www.idealist.org for community organizations, volunteer opportunities and non-profit careers.

There is some overlap between volunteering and gap-year or career-break tourism as many people who make this type of trip are going to do some form of work. There is an increasing amount of help for students on a gap year and the career-break market is growing fast. The websites www.gapyear.com, www.lattitude.org.uk, www.thecareerbreaksite.com and www.yearoutgroup.org cater for that year away. For a range of other options, try www.i-to-i.com, www.handsup holidays.com for project vacations, www.madventurer.com, www.thepod site.co.uk (Personal Overseas Development) and www.visionsserviceadventures.com, www.projects-abroad.co.uk, for teaching-based projects and other activities. The website www.amerispan.com is principally concerned with language learning and teaching but also has a comprehensive list of volunteer opportunities.

Contents

Footprint features

Lima & around

At a glance

☺ **Getting around** After flying in, by public bus or taxi.

◎ **Time required** From just a few days to a full week.

☼ **Weather** Damp and misty May-Oct, hot and sunny Nov-Apr.

✕ **When not to go** There is no time when Lima should be avoided.

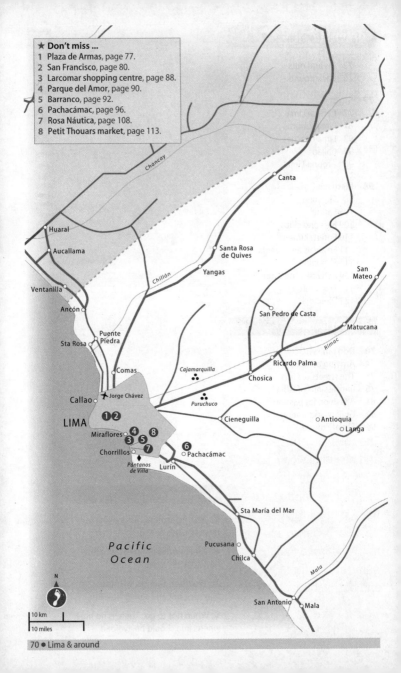

Chancay

Canta

Huaral

Aucallama

Santa Rosa
de Quives

Ventanilla

San
Mateo

Chillón

Yangas

Ancón

San Pedro de Casta

Matucana

Sta Rosa

Puente
Piedra

Rímac

Comas

Cajamarquilla

Ricardo Palma

Callao

Jorge Chávez

Puruchuco

Chosica

LIMA

Cieneguilla

Antioquía

Miraflores

❹ ❽

Langa

❸ ❺

Chorrillos

❼

❻ Pachacámac

Pántanos
de Villa

Lurín

Sta María del Mar

Pacific
Ocean

Pucusana

Chilca

Mala

N

10 km

10 miles

San Antonio

Mala

It is a well-established cliché to call Lima a city of contradictions and a rapid glance only reinforces that view. Here you'll encounter grinding poverty and conspicuous wealth in abundance. The hardships of the poor in this sprawling metropolis of 8.2 million inhabitants are all too evident in the lives of those struggling to get by in the crowded streets. Bus lanes are frantic and cars and taxis struggle to make progress on the congested thoroughfares. The drive from the airport to the city centre passes an array of urban landscapes, from the rubbish-strewn to the elegant, while the shanty towns on the outskirts emphasize the vast divisions within society. Most visitors, though, have the option of heading for Miraflores, San Isidro or Barranco, where smart restaurants and plush hotels rub shoulders with pre-Inca pyramids, and neat parks and the cliff-top Larcomar shopping centre overlook the ocean. Lima's image as a place to avoid or quickly pass through is enhanced by the thick grey blanket of cloud that descends in May and hangs around for the next seven months. Wait until the blanket is pulled aside in November to reveal bright blue skies and suddenly all Limeños descend on the city's popular coastal resorts. Weekends then become a raucous mix of sun, sea, salsa and *ceviche*. Lima can also entertain, excite and inform. It boasts some of the finest historical monuments and museums in the country. The colonial centre, with its grand Plaza de Armas, fine churches and beautiful wooden balconies, is one of Peru's 10 UNESCO World Heritage Sites and strenuous efforts are being made to refurbish the historical districts. The city's cuisine has earned it the title 'Gastronomic Capital of the Americas' and the bars, discos and *peñas* of Barranco and Miraflores ring to the sounds of everything from techno to traditional music. Scratch beneath that coating of grime and traffic fumes and you'll find one of the most vibrant and hospitable cities anywhere.

Getting there → *Phone code: 01. Population: 8.2 million.*

All **international flights** land at Jorge Chávez Airport, some 16 km from the centre of the city. It is a little further to Miraflores and Barranco. Transport into town is easy if a bit expensive. Remise taxis have desks outside International Arrivals and National Arrivals: **Taxi Green** ⓘ *T01-484 4001, www.taxigreen.com.pe*, US$8 to San Miguel, US$13 to the city centre, US$11.50 to San Isidro, US$15 to Miraflores and Barranco; **Mitsui** ⓘ *T01-349 7722, remisse@mitsuiautomotriz.com*, US$27 to centre, US$31 to San Isidro and Miraflores, US$36 to Barranco; and **CMV** ⓘ *T01-422 4838, cmv@exalmar.com.pe*, a little cheaper. There are many taxi drivers offering their services outside Arrivals with similar or higher prices (more at night). The **Bus Super Shuttle** ⓘ *T01-517 2556, www.supershuttle airport.com*, runs six-seater minibuses from the airport to San Miguel, the centre, San Isidro, Miraflores and Barranco for US$15 (six people sharing), or US$25 private hire. Alternatively, you can contact a taxi driver to meet you in advance, such as perufrienddrivers@hotmail.es, which offers fair prices and drivers who speak English.

1 Lima

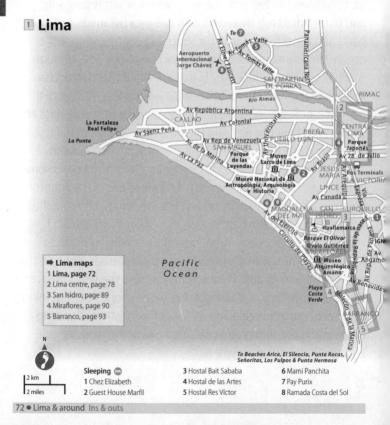

➡ **Lima maps**
1 Lima, page 72
2 Lima centre, page 78
3 San Isidro, page 89
4 Miraflores, page 90
5 Barranco, page 93

Pacific Ocean

To Beaches Arica, El Silencio, Punta Rocas,
Señoritas, Los Pulpos & Punta Hermosa

2 km
2 miles

Sleeping ⊜
1 Chez Elizabeth
2 Guest House Marfil

3 Hostal Bait Sababa
4 Hostal de las Artes
5 Hostal Res Víctor

6 Mami Panchita
7 Pay Purix
8 Ramada Costa del Sol

Note To get to Miraflores by combi, take the 'Callao-Ate' with a big red 'S' ('La S'), the only direct connection between the airport and Miraflores. You catch it outside the airport, on Avenida Faucett, US$0.45. This is not a safe option, however. You should definitely not take the cheapest, stopping buses to the centre along Avenida Faucett. They are frequently robbed. Nor go to the car park exit and find a taxi outside the perimeter. Although much cheaper than those inside, they are not safe either.

The airport is the best and most cost-effective place to arrange car hire. The larger international chains – Avis, Budget, Dollar, Hertz, Localiza, National – are usually cheaper and tend to have better-maintained vehicles than local firms. If hiring a car at the airport with the intention of driving to a hotel in the city, be aware that driving in Lima requires patience, forcefulness and nerves of steel.

If arriving in Lima by **bus** from the north and heading for the airport, you do not need to go into the centre: ask to be let out at 'Fiori' (look for the sign on top of a building on the left-hand side of the highway). This is by the junction of the Panamericana and Avenida Tomás Valle, which leads almost to Jorge Chávez. Take a taxi from Fiori.

If staying in Lima after arriving by **bus**, you may arrive at one of the company terminals around Jirón Carlos Zavala, just south of the historic centre of Lima. Take a taxi to your hotel even if it's close, as this area is not safe day or night. Some of the high-class bus companies have terminals in safer areas, so check with the bus company where their Lima terminal is and try to get your bearings before you arrive. ▶▶ See Transport, page 117.

Getting around

Downtown Lima can be explored on foot in the daytime, but take all the usual precautions. The central hotels are fairly close to the many of the tourist sites. At night taxis are a safer option. Many of the better hotels and restaurants are located in San Isidro, Miraflores and Barranco.

The Lima public transport system, at first glance very intimidating, is actually quite good. There are three different types of vehicle that will stop whenever flagged down: buses, combis, and colectivos. They can be distinguished by size: big and long; mid-size and minivans; or cars, respectively. The flat-rate fare for the first two types of vehicle is US$0.35, the third costs a little more. On public holidays, Sunday and from 2400 to 0500 every night, a small charge is added to the fare. Always try to pay with change to avoid hassles, delays and dirty looks from the *cobrador* (driver's assistant). Termini of public transport vehicles are posted above the windscreens, with the

SAN JUAN DE LURIGANCHO

Cerro San ▲ Cristóbal

Av Independencia

SANTA ANITA

Cerro El Agustino ▲

ATE

Av N Ayllón

Av México

Av Nicolás Arriola

Vía de Evitamiento

To Puruchuco

SAN BORJA

Museo de la Nación ⊞

LA MOLINA

Av Javier Prado Este

Hipódromo de Monterrico

Av Panamericana Sur

MONTERRICO

Av Aviación

Av Primavera

Av Alonso de Molina

Museo de Oro del Perú

Av Tomás Marzano

To Chorrillos

9 Tambopacaya

Metropolitano bus line ––––

Arriving at night

Barring delays, there are usually no flight arrivals between 0100 and 0530. (There are money-changing facilities and information services to meet all flights.) However, as check-in time is three hours before an international flight, and many flights depart from 0600 onwards, the airport starts to wake up at 0300 or 0400. No matter what time of night or day, though, there are people offering taxi rides into town. There is one hotel within the airport perimeter, but if you don't want to stay there, you must take some form of transport to get a bed and stow your bags.

Your best bet is to decide on a hotel before you even get to Lima. Most will arrange to pick you up from the airport, either free as part of the room rate, or for a fee of between US$12 and US$20 (depending on the category of hotel and how many people are in the vehicle). If you haven't arranged a room, don't leave the airport perimeter to find a public taxi or bus in the dark. The expensive remise services or the official taxis are the safest option. If you wish to stay in the airport until first light, it has seating areas and is safe.

route written on the side. However good the public transport system or smart your taxi, one thing is unavoidable, the amount of traffic. Lima's roads are congested almost throughout the whole day. Allow plenty of time to get from A to B and be patient. A new **Metropolitano** bus service runs from Chorrillas in the south to the Estación Central outside the Sheraton, continuing to Comas in the north. A **tren eléctrico** will link various eastern districts, including San Borja, in 2011 and a new coastal **autopista** is also under construction. ▸▸ *See Transport, page 117.*

Best time to visit

Only 12° south of the equator, you would expect a tropical climate, but Lima has two distinct seasons. The winter is from May to October, when a damp *garúa* (sea mist) hangs over the city, making everything look greyer than it is already. It is damp and cold, 8-15°C. The sun breaks through around November and temperatures rise as high as 30°C. Note that the temperature in the coastal suburbs is lower than in the centre because of the sea's influence. You should protect yourself against the sun's rays when visiting the beaches around Lima, or elsewhere in Peru.

Tourist information

iperú has offices at **Jorge Chávez International Airport** ① *T01-574 8000, daily 24 hrs;* at **Casa Basadre** ① *Av Jorge Basadre 610, San Isidro, T01-421 1627, Mon-Fri 0830-1830;* and at **Larcomar shopping centre** ① *Módulo 10, Plaza Principal, Miraflores, T01-445 9400, Mon-Fri 1100-1300, 1400-2000.* There is a **Municipal tourist kiosk** on Pasaje Ribera el Viejo, behind the Municipalidad, near the Plaza de Armas, www.munlima.gob.pe. Ask about guided walks in the city centre. There are eight kiosks: Parque Central; Parque Salazar; Parque del Amor; González Prada y Avenida Petit Thouars; Avenida R Palma y Avenida Petit Thouars; Avenida Larco y Avenida Benivides; Huaca Pucllana; and Ovalo Gutiérrez.

South American Explorers ① *Piura 135, Miraflores, T01-444 2150, T800-274 0568 (USA), www.saexplorers.org, Mon-Fri 0930-1700 (Wed until 2000 for events) and Sat 0930-1300. Headquarters in the USA: 126 Indian Creek Rd, Ithaca, NY, 14850, T1-607 277 0488,* is a non-profit educational organization that functions as a travel resource centre for South

Several blocks, with their own names, make up a long street, which is called a *jirón* (often abbreviated to Jr). You will be greatly helped by corner signs that bear the name of both the *jirón* and the block.

New and old names of streets are used interchangeably: remember that Colmena is also Nicolás de Piérola, Wilson is Inca Garcilaso de la Vega, and Carabaya is also Augusto N Wiese.

America and is widely recognized as the best place to get the most up-to-date information regarding everything from travel advice to volunteer opportunities. A yearly membership is currently US$60 per person and US$90 per couple. Services include access to member-written trip reports, a full map room for reference, an extensive library in English and a book exchange. Members can store luggage as well as valuables in their very secure deposit space. SAE sells official maps from the Instituto Geográfico Nacional, SAE-produced trekking maps, used equipment and a wide variety of Peruvian crafts. They host regular presentations on various topics ranging from jungle trips to freedom of the press. Discounts are available for students, volunteers and nationals. If you're looking to study Spanish in Peru, hoping to travel down the Amazon or in search of a quality Inca Trail tour company, they have the information you'll need to make it happen. South American Explorers, apart from the services mentioned above, is simply a great place to step out of the hustle and bustle of Lima and delight in the serenity of a cup of tea, a magazine and good conversation with a fellow traveller. SAE has other clubhouses in Cuzco and Quito (Ecuador), Buenos Aires (Argentina) and Ithaca (New York State).

Background

Lima, originally named 'La Ciudad de Los Reyes' (City of Kings), in honour of the Magi, was founded on Epiphany in 1535 by Francisco Pizarro. From then until the independence of the South American republics in the early 19th century, it was the chief city of Spanish South America. The name Lima, a corruption of the Quechua name *Rimac* (speaker), was not adopted until the end of the 16th century.

At the time of the Conquest, Lima was already an important commercial centre. It continued to grow throughout the colonial years and by 1610 the population was 26,000, of whom 10,000 were Spaniards. This was the time of greatest prosperity. The commercial centre of the city was just off the Plaza de Armas in the Calle de Mercaderes (first block of Jirón de la Unión) and was full of merchandise imported from Spain, Mexico and China. All the goods from the mother country arrived at the port of Callao, from where they were distributed all over Peru and as far away as Argentina.

At this time South American trade with Spain was controlled by a monopoly of Sevillian merchants and their Limeño counterparts who profited considerably. It wasn't until the end of the 18th century that free trade was established between Spain and her colonies, allowing Peru to enjoy a period of relative wealth. Much of this wealth was reinvested in the country, particularly in Lima where educational establishments benefited most of all.

After Francis Drake made a surprise attack on Callao on the night of 13 February 1579, plans were made to strengthen the city's defences against the threat from English pirates. However, an argument raged during the following century between Spain and Lima as to

Impressions of Lima

Ever since the earthquake of 1746 all but razed the city to the ground, descriptions of Lima have tended towards the unfavourable. Take the German naturalist and traveller, Alexander Von Humboldt, for instance, who considered life in the city to be tedious with its lack of diversions, and described touring round the capital in 1802 thus: "The filthyness of the streets, strewn with dead dogs and donkeys, and the unevenness of the ground make it impossible to enjoy." Charles Darwin, who made a short visit in 1839 during his historic research trip on the *Beagle*, was no less graphic in his appraisal. He found it "in a wretched state of decay; the streets are nearly unpaved and heaps of filth are piled up in all directions where black vultures pick up bits of carrion."

Rather more complimentary was Jean Jacques Tschudi, the Swiss naturalist. He wrote: "The impression produced at first sight of Lima is by no means favourable,

for the periphery, the quarter which the stranger first enters, contains none but old, dilapidated and dirty homes; but on approaching the vicinity of the principal square, the place improves so greatly that the miserable appearance it presents at first sight is easily forgotten."

The French feminist, Flora Tristan, who was Paul Gauguin's grandmother, came to Peru in 1834. She travelled extensively in the country and wrote a fascinating account of her experience, *Peregrinaciones de una Paria*, in which she painted Lima in a most favourable light: "The city has many beautiful monuments", she wrote: "The homes are neatly constructed, the streets well marked out, are long and wide." Paul Gauguin himself spent his formative years in Lima, where he was brought by his parents who were fleeing Napoleon Bonaparte's France. Towards the end of his life Gauguin wrote a collection of memoirs in which he included his impressions of Lima.

what form the defences should take and who should pay. Finally, it was agreed to encircle the city with a wall, which was completed by 1687.

Life for the white descendants of the Spaniards was good, although *criollos* (Spaniards born in the colonies) were not allowed to hold public office in Peru. The indigenous people and those of mixed blood were treated as lesser citizens. Their movements were strictly controlled. They weren't allowed to live in the city centre; only in areas allocated to them, referred to as *reducciones*.

There were few cities in the Old World that could rival Lima's wealth and luxury, until the terrible earthquake of 1746. The city's notable elegance was instantly reduced to dust. Only 20 of the 3000 houses were left standing and an estimated 4000 people were killed. Despite the efforts of the viceroy, José Manso de Velasco, to rebuild the city, Lima never recovered her former glory. During the 19th century man-made disasters rather than natural ones wreaked havoc on the capital and its people. The population dropped from 87,000 in 1810 to 53,000 in 1842, after the wars of Independence, and the city suffered considerable material damage during the Chilean occupation that followed the War of the Pacific.

Lima was built on both banks of the Rímac river. The walls erected at the end of the 17th century surrounded three sides while the Rímac bordered the fourth. By the time the North American railway engineer, Henry Meiggs, was contracted to demolish the city walls in 1870, Lima had already begun to spread outside the original limits. Meiggs reneged on his contract by leaving much of the wall intact in the poor area around Cercado, where the ruins can still be seen.

By the beginning of the 20th century the population had risen to 140,000 and the movement of people to the coastal areas meant that unskilled cheap labour was readily available for the increasing numbers of factories. Around this time, major improvements were made to the city's infrastructure in the shape of paved streets, modern sanitation, new markets and plazas. For the entertainment of the middle classes, a modern racetrack was opened in what is now the Campo de Marte, as well as the municipal theatre, the Teatro Segura. At the same time, the incumbent president, José Pardo, dramatically increased government expenditure on education, particularly in Lima.

Large-scale municipal improvements continued under the dictatorship of Augusto Leguía and the presidency of Oscar Benavides, who focused on education for the masses, housing facilities for workers and low-cost restaurants in the slum areas that were growing up around Lima.

Lima, a city of some 8.2 million people, continues to struggle to live up to its former reputation as the City of Kings. This has involved drastic changes in the last few years. The commercial heart has moved away from the centre of town and has taken root in more upmarket districts such as Miraflores and San Isidro. After suffering serious decline, the old centre is benefiting from great efforts to clean it up and is re-establishing itself as a place to visit. The city can, however, be seriously affected by smog at certain times of the year. It is also surrounded by *pueblos jóvenes*, or shanty settlements of squatters who have migrated from all parts of Peru looking for work and education (see box, page 94).

Sights

When Alberto Andrade Carmona became Mayor of Lima in 1995, he began a campaign to return the historic centre to its original beauty. This meant ejecting the ambulantes *(street sellers), cleaning the streets and pavements, and rehabilitating the Plaza de Armas and Plaza San Martín. He also mounted a security force called Serenazgo to enforce public safety and order, whose members are recognizable by their dark jump-suits, long night sticks and riot gear. At least until 2010, when Mayor Luis Castañeda Cossio was to step down, these efforts have continued. An increasing number of buildings in the centre are being restored and the whole area is being given a new lease of life as the architectural beauty and importance of the Cercado (as it is known) is recognized.*►► *For listings, see pages 98-124.*

Central Lima

Plaza de Armas
One block south of the Río Rímac lies the Plaza de Armas, which has been declared a World Heritage Site by UNESCO. The plaza used to be the city's most popular meeting point and main market. Before the building of the Acho bullring in the 1760s, bullfights were traditionally held here.

Around the great Plaza de Armas stand the **Palacio de Gobierno**, the **cathedral**, the **Archbishop's Palace**, the **Municipalidad** and the **Club Unión**. In the centre of the plaza is a bronze fountain dating from 1650. The flower beds are planted with blooms whose colours reflect the city's celebrations, eg red and white at Independence in July, purple at El Señor de los Milagros in October.

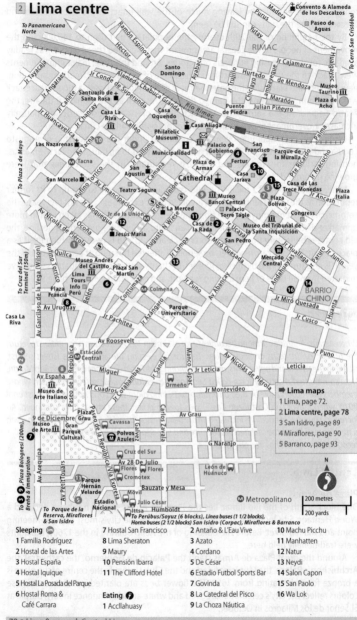

Sleeping 🛏️

1 Familia Rodríguez
2 Hostal de las Artes
3 Hostal España
4 Hostal Iquique
5 Hostal La Posada del Parque
6 Hostal Roma &
  Café Carrara

7 Hostal San Francisco
8 Lima Sheraton
9 Maury
10 Pensión Ibarra
11 The Clifford Hotel

Eating 🍴

1 Acclluasuay

2 Antaño & L'Eau Vive
3 Azato
4 Cordano
5 De César
6 Estadio Futbol Sports Bar
7 Govinda
8 La Catedral del Pisco
9 La Choza Náutica

10 Machu Picchu
11 Manhatten
12 Natur
13 Neydi
14 Salon Capon
15 San Paolo
16 Wa Lok

Palacio de Gobierno

ⓘ *Plaza de Armas, T01-311 3908. Tours in Spanish and English Mon-Fri 0830-1300, 1400-1700, 45 mins, free; book 2 days in advance at the Oficina de Turismo, of 201 (ask guard for directions); foreigners must take passport. Shorts may not be worn.*

The Government Palace stands on the site of the original palace built by Pizarro. When the Viceroyalty was founded, it became the official residence of the representative of the crown. Despite the opulent furnishings inside, the exterior remained a poor sight throughout colonial times, with shops lining the front facing the plaza. The façade was remodelled in the second half of the 19th century, then transformed in 1921, following a terrible fire. In 1937, the palace was totally rebuilt. The changing of the guard is at 1200 daily.

The cathedral

ⓘ *Plaza de Armas, T01-427 9647. Mon-Fri 0900-1700, Sat 1000-1300. Entry to cathedral US$3.65, ticket also including Museo Arzobispado US$11.*

The cathedral stands on the site of two previous buildings. The first, finished in 1555, was partly paid for by Francisca Pizarro on the condition that her father, the *Conquistador*, was buried there. A larger church, however, was soon required to complement the city's status as an archbishopric. In 1625, the three naves of the main building were completed while work continued on the towers and main door. The new building was reduced to rubble in the earthquake of 1746 and the existing church, completed in 1755, is a reconstruction on the lines of the original.

The interior is immediately impressive, with its massive columns and high nave. Also of note are the splendidly carved stalls (mid-17th century), the silver-covered altars surrounded by fine woodwork, mosaic-covered walls bearing the coats of arms of Lima and Pizarro and an allegory of Pizarro's commanders, the 'Thirteen men of Isla del Gallo'. The remains of Francisco Pizarro, found in the crypt, lie in a small chapel, the first on the right of the entrance. Notices give details of the bio-archaeological evidence proving the authenticity of the bones. There is a **Museo de Arte Religioso** in the cathedral, with sacred paintings, portraits, altar pieces and other items, as well as a café and toilets.

Next to the cathedral is the **Palacio Arzobispal** (Archbishop's Palace), rebuilt in 1924, with a superb wooden balcony. It also has a museum of religious art, **Museo Arzobispado** ⓘ *T01-427 6463, www.palacioarzobispaldelima.com, opening times as for cathedral.*

Around the Municipalidad

Just behind the Municipalidad de Lima is **Pasaje Ribera el Viejo**, which has been restored and is now a pleasant place, with several good cafés with outdoor seating. The **Museo Filatélico** ⓘ *central post office (correos) off Plaza de Armas, daily 0815-1300, 1400-1800, free*, contains an incomplete collection of Peruvian stamps and information on the Inca postal system. There is a stamp exchange in front of the museum every Saturday and Sunday, 0900-1300. You can buy stamps here too, particularly commemorative issues.

Casa Aliaga ⓘ *Unión 224, T01-427 7736, www.casadealiaga.com, Mon-Fri 0900-1700, US$11, knock on the door and wait to see if anyone will let you in, or contact in advance for tour operators who offer guided visits*, is still occupied by the Aliaga family and is open to the public. Don Jerónimo de Aliaga was one of the 13 commanders to arrive with Francisco Pizarro, all of whom were given land around the main square to build their own houses when Lima was founded in 1535. It contains what is said to be the oldest ceiling in Lima and is furnished entirely in the colonial style. All the rooms on view are lovingly kept, from the private chapel to reception rooms and bedrooms.

Santo Domingo

ⓘ *Church and monastery on the 1st block of Jr Camaná, T01-427 6793, Mon-Sat 0900-1230, 1500-1800, Sun and holidays, mornings only, US$1.65.*

Built in 1549, the church is still as originally planned with a nave and two aisles covered by a vaulted ceiling, though the present ceiling dates from the 17th century. The cloister is one of the most attractive in the city and dates from 1603. The second cloister is much less elaborate. A chapel, dedicated to San Martín de Porres, one of Peru's most revered saints, leads off from a side corridor. Between the two cloisters is the Chapter House (1730), which was once the premises of the Universidad de San Marcos (1551). In the covent is a magnificent cedarwood ceiling. Beneath the sacristy are the tombs of San Martín de Porres and Santa Rosa de Lima (see page 84). In 1669, Pope Clement presented the alabaster statue of Santa Rosa in front of the altar. The Basílica de La Veracruz is open at lunchtime. The main hall has some interesting relics.

Behind Santo Domingo is **Alameda Chabuca Granda**, named after one of Peru's greatest singers and composers. In the evening there are free art and music shows and you can sample food and sweets from all over Peru.

A couple of blocks beyond Santo Domingo is **Casa de Osambela Oquendo** ⓘ *Conde de Superunda 298, T01-427 7987.* It is said that José de San Martín stayed here after proclaiming independence from Spain. The house is typical of Lima secular architecture with two patios, a broad staircase leading from the lower to the upper floor, fine balconies and an observation tower. It is now the Centro Cultural Inca Garcilaso de la Vega and headquarters of various academies. Ask Lizardo Retes Bustamante (lizardo-retes@ hotmail.com) if you can visit.

San Francisco and around

ⓘ *Church and monastery stand on the 1st block of Jr Lampa, corner of Ancash, T01-427 1381, daily 0930-1645, guided tours only, US$1.65, US$0.50 children.*

The baroque church, which was finished in 1674, was one of the few edifices to withstand the 1746 earthquake. The nave and aisles are lavishly decorated in the Moorish, or Mudéjar, style. The choir, which dates from 1673, is notable for its beautifully carved seats in Nicaraguan hardwood and its Mudéjar ceiling. There is a valuable collection of paintings by the Spanish artist, Francisco de Zubarán (1598-1664), which depict the apostles and various saints.

The monastery is famous for the Sevillian tilework and panelled ceiling in the cloisters (1620). The 17th-century *retablos* in the main cloister are carved from cedar and represent scenes from the life of San Francisco, as do the paintings. A broad staircase leading down to a smaller cloister is covered by a remarkable carved wooden dome (nicknamed *la media naranja* – the half orange) dating from 1625. Next to this smaller cloister is the Capilla de la Soledad where a café is open to the public. The library contains 25,000 volumes. In the refectory, see the painting of the Last Supper in which Christ and his disciples are seated at a round table. Look for the devil at Judas Iscariot's shoulder. The catacombs under the church and part of the monastery are well worth seeing. This is where an estimated 25,000 Limeños were buried before the main cemetery was opened in 1808.

Parque de la Muralla ⓘ *open 0900-2000*, on the south bank of the Rímac behind San Francisco, incorporates a section of the old city wall, fountains, stalls and street performers. There is a cycle track, toilets and places to eat both inside and near the entrance on Calle de la Soledad. At the corner of this little street and Ancash is the **Caja Metropolitana** exhibition space in the Casa de las Trece Puertas.

A fashion for passion

A unique form of women's dress worn by Lima's upper-class *mestizas* (women born in the colonies of Spanish origin) in the 18th century was the *saya* and *manto*. Both were of Moorish origin. The *saya* was an overskirt of dark silk, worn tight at the waist with either a narrow or wide bottom. The *manto* was like a thick black veil fastened by a band at the back of the waist where it joined the *saya*. It was brought over the shoulders and head and drawn over the face so closely that only a small, triangular space was left uncovered, sufficient for one eye to peep through. This earned them the title '*las tapadas*', or 'the covered ones'.

The fashion was created by Lima's *mestizas* in order to compete in the flirting stakes with their Spanish-born counterparts, whose tiny waists and coquettish fan-waving was turning men's heads. The *tapadas*, though veiled, were by no means modest. Their skirts were daringly short, revealing their appealingly tiny feet, and necklines plunged to scandalously low levels. The French feminist, Flora Tristan, was much taken with this brazen show. She commented: "I am sure it needs little imagination to appreciate the consequences of this time-honoured practice."

One consequence of this fashion, which ensured anonymity, was that Lima's *mestizas* could freely indulge in romantic trysts with their lovers. Often, however, they were content with flirting – sometimes with their unwitting husbands. Another consequence of their anonymity was political. Many *tapadas* used their afternoon strolls to pass notes and messages to the organizers of the independence movement. This romantic and political intrigue usually took place on the Paseo de Aguas, a walkway of pools and gardens built by the viceroy.

Opposite the San Francisco church is a historic mansion worth visiting, the late 16th-century **Casa de Jarava** or **Pilatos** ① *Jr Ancash 390*. Two blocks beyond is **Casa de las Trece Monedas** ① *Jr Ancash 536*, built in 1787 by counts from Genoa. It still has the original doors and window grilles.

Plaza Bolívar

Wedged between Avenida Abancay and Jirón Ayacucho is Plaza Bolívar, from where General José de San Martín proclaimed Peru's independence. The plaza is dominated by the equestrian statue of the Liberator. Behind lies the Congress building, which occupies the former site of the **Universidad de San Marcos**, the first university in the Americas. Founded by the Dominicans in 1551, students first began to use this building in 1574. The university now occupies other premises away from the city centre.

Museo del Tribunal de la Santa Inquisición ① *Jr Junín 548, near the corner of Av Abancay, T01-311 7777, www.congreso.gob.pe/museo.htm, daily 0900-1700, free*, has a main hall with a splendidly carved mahogany ceiling that remains untouched. The Court of Inquisition was first held here in 1584, after being moved from its first home opposite the church of La Merced. From 1829 until 1938 the building was used by the Senate. In the basement there is an accurate recreation in situ of the gruesome tortures. The whole tour is fascinating, if a little morbid. A description in English is available at the desk and students will offer to show you round for a tip.

Guilt by inquisition

Established by Royal Decree in 1569, the Court of Inquisition was soon to prove a particularly cruel form of justice, even in the context of Spanish rule.

During its existence, the Church meted out many horrific tortures on innocent people. Among the most fashionable methods of making the accused confess their 'sins' were burning, dismemberment and asphyxiation, to name but a few. The most common form of punishment was public flogging, followed by exile and the not so appealing death by burning. Up until 1776, 86 people are recorded as having been burned alive and 458 excommunicated.

Given that no witnesses were called except the informer and that the accused were not allowed to know the identity of their accusers, this may have been less a test of religious conviction than a means of settling old scores. This Kafkaesque nightmare was then carried into the realms of surreal absurdity during the process of judgement. A statue of Christ was the final arbiter of guilt or innocence but had to express its belief in the prisoner's innocence with a shake of the head. Needless to say, not too many walked free.

The Inquisition was abolished by the viceroy in 1813 but later reinstated before finally being proscribed in 1820.

Jirón Ucayali

The **Museo Banco Central de Reserva** ① *Jr Ucayali at Jr Lampa, T01-613 2000 ext 2655, http://museobcr.perucultural.org.pe, Tue-Fri 1000-1630, Wed 1000-1900, Sat-Sun 1000-1300, free*, has a large collection of pottery from the Vicus or Piura culture (AD 500-600) and gold objects from Lambayeque, as well as 19th- and 20th-century paintings. Both modern and ancient exhibitions are highly recommended. Photography is prohibited. It also contains the **Museo Numismático del Perú**.

The city's best surviving specimen of secular colonial architecture is **Palacio Torre Tagle** ① *Jr Ucayali 363, access to the patio only Mon-Fri during working hours*, which was built in 1735 for Don José Bernardo de Tagle y Bracho, to whom King Philip V gave the title of First Marquis of Torre Tagle. The house remained in the family until it was acquired by the government in 1918. Today, it is still used by the Foreign Ministry, but visitors are allowed to enter courtyards to inspect the fine, Moorish-influenced woodcarving in the balconies, the wrought ironwork and a 16th-century coach, complete with commode.

Opposite, **Casa de la Rada**, or **Goyoneche** ① *Jr Ucayali 358*, is an extremely fine mid-18th-century town house in the French manner, which now belongs to a bank. The patio and first reception room are occasionally open to the public.

The church of **San Pedro** ① *on the 3rd block of Jr Ucayali, Mon-Sat 0930-1145, 1700-1800*, finished by Jesuits in 1638, has an unadorned façade, different from any other in the city. In one of the massive towers hangs a five-tonne bell called *La Abuelita* (the grandmother), first rung in 1590, which sounded the Declaration of Independence in 1821. The contrast between the sober exterior and sumptuous interior couldn't be more striking. The altars are marvellous, in particular the high altar, attributed to the skilled craftsman, Matías Maestro. The church also boasts Moorish-style balconies and rich, gilded woodcarvings in the choir and vestry, tiled throughout. The most important paintings in the church are hung near the main entrance. In the monastery, the sacristy is a beautiful example of 17th-century architecture. Also of note are La Capilla de Nuestra Señora de la O and the penitentiary. Several viceroys are buried below.

Jirón de la Unión

The Jirón de la Unión, the main shopping street, runs from the Plaza de Armas. It has been converted into a pedestrian precinct that teems with life.

La Merced ① *Plazuela de la Merced, Unión y Miró Quesada, T01-427 8199, Mon-Sat 0800-1245, 1600-2000, Sun 0700-1300, 1600-2000; monastery daily 0800-1200 and 1500-1730*, was the first church to be built in Lima, and it is said that it was the site where the first Mass took place. At Independence, the Virgin of La Merced was made a marshal of the Peruvian army. The restored colonial façade is a fine example of baroque architecture. Inside are magnificent altars and some notable tilework on the walls. A door from the right of the nave leads into the monastery where you can see 18th-century religious paintings in the sacristy. The cloister dates from 1546.

A couple of blocks further on, the 18th-century **Jesús María** ① *on the corner of Jr Moquegua and Jr Camaná, T01-427 6809, Mon-Sat 0900-1200, 1500-1700*, contains some of the finest paintings and gilded baroque altars in all of Lima.

South of Jirón de la Unión, the **Plaza San Martín** has a statue of the eponymous hero in the centre. The square has been remodelled with flowerbeds and trees and is now a nice place to relax. Taxis and colectivos line the north side, while Pasaje Quilca on the west side is lined with food stalls. Also on the plaza is the Gran Hotel Bolívar.

The two blocks of Jirón de la Unión south of Plaza San Martín are known as Calle Belén, on which is the **Museo Andrés del Castillo** ① *in the Casa Belén, Unión 1030, T01-433 2831, www.madc.com.pe, Wed-Mon 0900-1800, US$3.65, students half price*, with a collection of Peruvian minerals, especially crystals, Chancay ceramics and pre-Hispanic textiles.

San Agustín and around

The 1720 façade of **San Agustín** ① *Jr Ica 251, west of the Plaza de Armas, T01-427 7548, 0830-1130, 1630-1900 (ring for entry)*, is a splendid example of Churrigueresque architecture. There are carved choir stalls and effigies, and a sculpture of Death, said to have frightened its maker into an early grave. Since being damaged in the last earthquake the church has been sensitively restored, but the sculpture of Death is in storage (to protect tourists of a more nervous disposition).

Museo Teatral ① *Teatro Segura, Jr Huancavelica 265, T01-426 7189, 0900-1300, 1400-1700*, contains a collection of mementos and photographs of people who have appeared on the Lima stage.

AAA Theatre (Amateur Artists' Association) ① *Jr Ica 323*, is in a lovely 18th-century house with an *azaguán*, a covered area between the door and patio, a common feature in houses of this period. Further along Ica is **Casa La Riva** ① *Jr Ica 426*, which has an 18th-century porch and balconies, and a small gallery with some 20th-century paintings. It is run by the Entre Nous Society.

Las Nazarenas

① *Av Tacna, 4th block, T01-423 5718, daily 0700-1200 and 1600-2000.*

This 18th-century church was built around an image of Christ crucified painted by a liberated slave in the mid-16th century. In the earthquake of 1655, the church collapsed but the painting on the wall remained intact. This was deemed a miracle and the painting became the most venerated image in Lima. Together with an oil copy of *El Señor de los*

Milagros (Lord of Miracles), the image is encased in a gold frame and carried on a silver litter – the whole weighing nearly a ton – through the streets on 18, 19, and 28 October and again on 1 November (All Saints' Day). The whole city is decked out in purple. *El Comercio* newspaper and local pamphlets give details of times and routes.

Santuario de Santa Rosa

ⓘ *Av Tacna, 1st block, T01-425 1279, daily 0930-1300, 1500-1800, free entry to the grounds.*

Santa Rosa is the first saint of the Americas and patron saint of Lima. Born on 20 April 1586, Rosa of Lima became a member of the third order of St Dominic and established an infirmary in her family home for destitute children and old people. She died at the age of 31 on 23 August 1617 and was beatified on 16 December 1668. Her day is 30 August. The small but graceful church was built in 1728 and contains the 'Little doctor' image of Jesus who helped Rosa cure the sick. Beyond the church is a sanctuary where she was born and lived. There is a tiny room where she would allow herself only two hours' sleep each night on a bed of two tree trunks with stones as pillows. A chapel was later built on the site.

The hermitage in the garden was built by Rosa herself and she would retire there to pray alone. The well, into which she threw the key to the padlocked chain around her waist, now receives thanksgivings and petitions for forgiveness from the faithful.

Southwest of the centre

Plaza Dos de Mayo is just over a kilometre west of the Plaza de Armas. All the buildings around it are painted blue. About 1 km due south of this again is the circular **Plaza Bolognesi**, from which many major *avenidas* radiate.

San Marcelo ⓘ *Av de la Emancipación, 4th block*, is another church worth seeing for its two beautiful colonial doors. The interior is also remarkable, particularly the 18th-century gold-leaf high altar and pulpit and the religious paintings sited above attractive Sevillian tiles.

Museo Nacional de la Cultura Peruana ⓘ *Av Alfonso Ugarte 650, T01-423 5892, http://museodelacultura.perucultural.org.pe, Tue-Fri 1000-1700, Sat 1000-1400, US$1.10, students US$0.70, free guide in Spanish*, has an extraordinary mock Tiahuanaco façade and houses a rather disjointed collection of pre-Columbian and modern artefacts, including *mate burilado* (carved gourds), *retablos*, textiles, *keros* and *huacos* (pottery finds or artefacts). There are examples of ceramics and cloth from Amazonian tribes and a set of watercolours by Pancho Fierro, the 19th-century *costumbrista* artist.

South of the centre

South of the Plaza San Martín, the **Museo de Arte Italiano** ⓘ *Paseo de la República 250, T01-423 9932, Tue-Fri 0900-1900, Sat-Sun 1100-1700, US$1*, is in a wonderful neoclassical building, given by the Italian colony to Peru on the centenary of its independence. Note the remarkable mosaic murals on the outside. It consists of a large collection of Italian and other European works of art, including sculpture, lithographs and etchings. The museum now also houses the **Instituto de Arte Contemporáneo**, which has many exhibitions.

The **Gran Parque Cultural de Lima** (daily 0800-2030) was inaugurated in January 2000 by both the mayor of Lima, Alberto Andrade, and the then-president Alberto Fujimori. It has a medium-sized outdoor amphitheatre, Japanese garden, food court and children's activities. Relaxing strolls through this green, peaceful and safe oasis in the centre of Lima are recommended. Within the park is the **Museo de Arte** ⓘ *9 de Diciembre (Paseo Colón) 125, T01-423 4732, http://museoarte.perucultural.org.pe, Thu-Tue 1000-1700, US$3.65, free* *guide, signs in English*, which was built in 1868 as the Palacio de la Exposición. The building was designed by Alexandre Gustave Eiffel. There are more than 7000 exhibits, giving a chronological history of Peruvian cultures and art from the Paracas civilization up to today. They include excellent examples of 17th- and 18th-century Cuzco paintings, a beautiful display of carved furniture, heavy silver and jewelled stirrups and also pre-Columbian pottery. A *filmoteca* (cinema club) is on the premises and shows films almost every night; consult the local paper for details, or look in the museum itself.

In **Parque de la Reserva** ① *block 8 of Av Arequipa and going up towards the centre, Santa Beatriz, www.circuitomagicodelagua.com.pe, Wed-Sun and holidays 1600-2200, US$1.40*, is the **Circuito Mágico del Agua**, a display of 13 fountains, the highest reaching 80 m, enhanced by impressive light and music shows four times a night, great fun and very popular. It has featured in the *Guiness Book of Records* as the largest fountain complex in the world.

Further southwest again is the **Museo de Historia Natural** ① *Av Arenales 1256, Lince, T01-471 0117, Mon-Fri 0900-1500, Sat-Sun 0900-1300, US$1.20*. The museum belongs to the Universidad de San Marcos and its exhibits comprise Peruvian flora, birds, mammals, butterflies, insects, minerals and shells.

Northeast of the Plaza de Armas

From the Plaza de Armas, passing the Government Palace on the left, the **Desamparados Station** of the Central Railway lies straight ahead. The name, meaning 'the helpless ones', comes from the orphanage and church that used to be nearby.

Puente de Piedra, behind the Palacio de Gobierno, is a Roman-style stone bridge built in 1610. Until about 1870 it was the only bridge strong enough to take carriages across the river Rímac to the district of the same name. Though this part of the city enjoyed great popularity in colonial times, it can no longer be considered fashionable today.

Alameda de los Descalzos was designed in the early 17th century as a restful place to stroll and soon became one of the city's most popular meeting places. People of all social classes would gather here for their Sunday walk, some going up to the cross at the top of **Cerro San Cristóbal**. Today, however, you would be ill-advised to follow in their footsteps, as this is a dangerous area to wander around alone. Robberies are common in Rímac district and on Cerro San Cristóbal, so do not walk up; take a taxi (US$5). Worth visiting on the Alameda de los Descalzos, though, is the **Convento de los Descalzos** ① *T01-481 0441, Wed-Mon 1000-1300, 1500-1800, US$1, by guided tour only, 45 mins in Spanish, worth it*. Founded in 1592, it now contains over 300 paintings of the Cuzco, Quito and Lima schools, which line the four main cloisters and two ornate chapels. The chapel of El Carmen was constructed in 1730 and is notable for its baroque gold-leaf altar. A small chapel dedicated to Nuestra Señora de la Rosa Mística has some fine Cuzqueña paintings. Opposite, in the chapel dedicated to La Señora de los Angeles, Admiral Grau made his last confession before the Battle of Angamos. The museum shows the life of the Franciscan friars during colonial and early republican periods. The cellar, infirmary, pharmacy and a typical cell have been restored. The library has not yet been incorporated into the tour (researchers may be permitted to see specific books on request). Near the Alameda is the **Paseo de Aguas**, which was also popular for a Sunday stroll in days gone by.

Tours by minibus (Camaná y Conde Superunda, daily 1000-2100, one hour, US$2), depart from in front of Santo Domingo church. They go through the old *barrio* of Rímac, then pass the Alameda de los Descalzos before climbing through one of the city's oldest shanty towns with its brightly painted houses to the top of **Cerro San Cristóbal**. About half the tour is spent going to the summit, where there is a café, a small museum and a spectacular view of Lima. The other half is a historical tour. Check the cloud level first, otherwise you will see very little. **Urbanito** buses (T01-424 3650, www.urbanito.com.pe, three hours, weekends and holidays), also run from the Plaza de Armas on a tour of central Lima, which includes Cerro San Cristóbal.

Plaza de Acho, on Jirón Hualgayoc, is the bullring, famous for once being the largest in the world and the first in Spanish America. It was inaugurated on 20 January 1766. Limeños have always been great enthusiasts of bullfighting and in 1798 a royal decree had to be passed forbidding fights on Sundays as people were failing to attend Mass. July is the month when the most famous fighters come from Spain for the **Fiestas Patrias**. The season also runs from October to the first week of December. Famous *toreros* practise in the Lima ring and fighting bulls are of Spanish stock. Next to the bullring is the **Museo Taurino** ① *Hualgayoc 332, T01-482 3360, Mon-Sat 0800-1600, US$1, students US$0.50, photography US$2.* Apart from matadors' relics, the museum contains good collections of paintings and engravings, some of the latter by Goya. This, too, is in a dangerous area.

Barrio Chino

East of the historic centre of Lima in the district of Barrios Altos, next to the Mercado Central, is Lima's Chinatown (*Barrio Chino*). Peru is home to the largest population of first-generation Chinese in all of Latin America. Chinese people born in Peru (referred to as 'Tu-San') number more than a million. Some of the first immigrants arrived at the port of Callao in 1849 from the Chinese provinces of Canton and Fukien to work the coastal fields, replacing the black slaves given their freedom by then-president Ramón Castilla in 1851. More Chinese began to arrive, settling in the north in Chiclayo, Trujillo and the jungle town of Iquitos.

On the seventh block of Jirón Ucayali is the locally famous **Portada China**, the arch that stretches across the street and is the gateway to Chinatown. It was a gift from the Chinese government, officially inaugurated by Lima mayor Alberto Andrade in July 1997.
▸▸ *For authentic Chinese cuisine in this area, see Eating, page 105.*

Museo de la Nación

① *Javier Prado Este 2465, San Borja, T01-476 9933, Tue-Sun 0900-1700, closed major public holidays, 4-hr tours available, US$2.50, 50% discount with ISIC card. See http://inc. perucultural.org.pe/agenda.asp for details of temporary exhibitions. It is cold in the museum.* This is the anthropological and archaeological museum for the exhibition and study of the art and history of the aboriginal races of Peru. There are good explanations in Spanish and English on Peruvian history, with ceramics, textiles and displays about many ruins in Peru. It is arranged so that you can follow the development of Peruvian pre-colonial history through to the time of the Incas. A visit is recommended before you go to see the archaeological sites themselves. There are displays on the tomb of the Señor de Sipán, artefacts from Batán Grande near Chiclayo (Sicán culture), reconstructions of the friezes found at Huaca La Luna and Huaca El Brujo, near Trujillo, and of Sechín and other sites. Temporary exhibitions are held in the basement, where there is also an Instituto de Cultura bookshop. The museum also has a cafeteria.

To get to the museum from downtown Lima, take a combi with a window sticker that says 'Javier Prado/Aviación' from Avenida Garcilaso de la Vega. Get off at the 21st block of Javier Prado at Avenida Aviación. To get there from Miraflores, take a bus down Avenida Arequipa to Avenida Javier Prado (27th block), then take a bus with a window sticker saying 'Todo Javier Prado' or 'Aviación'. A taxi from downtown Lima or from the centre of Miraflores costs US$3.20.

South and east of San Borja

South and east of San Borja are the districts of **Santiago de Surco** and **Monterrico**, upper and middle-class residential districts. Avenida Angamos Este and its continuation, Avenida Primavera, forms the boundary between San Borja and Surco. **Primavera** has become a new gastronomical centre in the city. ▸▸ *For recommendations, see Eating, page 105.*

The **Museo de Oro del Perú** ⓘ *Alonso de Molina 1100, Monterrico, Surco (between blocks 18 and 19 of Av Primavera), Lima 33, T01-345 1292, www.museoroperu.com.pe, daily 1130-1900, US$11.55, children under 11 US$5.60, multilingual audioguides,* houses an enormous collection of Peruvian gold, silver and bronze objects, together with an impressive international array of arms and military uniforms from Spanish colonial times to the present day and textiles from Peru and elsewhere. Allow plenty of time to appreciate all that is on view. It is directed by the **Fundación Miguel Mujica Gallo** (named after the businessman, diplomat and collector who created the museum) which, following a controversy over the authenticity of a number of pieces, is now conducting an inventory and registration of the collection with the **Instituto Nacional de Cultura**. The museum remains a popular call on the capital's tourist circuit and 167 of its pieces can be seen in the **Sala Museo Oro del Perú**, in Larcomar (see below).

Lima suburbs

Pueblo Libre

Museo Nacional de Antropología, Arqueología e Historia ⓘ *Plaza Bolívar, not to be confused with Plaza Bolívar in the centre, T01-463 5070, http://museonacional.peru cultural.org.pe, Tue-Sat 0900-1700, Sun and bank holidays 0900-1600, US$4, students US$1.20, guides available for groups,* is the original museum of archaeology and anthropology. On display are ceramics of the Chimú, Nazca, Mochica and Ichma (Pachacámac) cultures, various Inca curiosities, works of art and interesting textiles. The museum houses the Raimondi Stela and the Tello obelisk from Chavín (see page 390) and a reconstruction of one of the galleries there. It also has a model of Machu Picchu.

Next door is the **Museo Nacional de Historia** ⓘ *Plaza Bolívar, T01-463 2009, Tue-Sat 0900-1700, Sun and holidays 0900-1600, US$3.65,* housed in a mansion built by Viceroy Pezuela and occupied by San Martín (1821-1822) and Bolívar (1823-1826). The exhibits comprise colonial and early republican paintings, manuscripts, portraits, uniforms, etc.

To get to both museums from the centre, take any public transport on Avenida Brasil with the window sticker 'Todo Brasil.' Get off at the 21st block and walk about five blocks down Vivanco. The museums will be on your left. From Miraflores, take bus SM 18 Carabayllo–Chorrillos, marked 'Bolívar, Arequipa, Larcomar', get out at block eight of Bolívar, by the Hospital Santa Rosa, and walk down Avenida San Martín five blocks till you see the 'blue line'; then turn left. Taxi from downtown Lima US$3; from Miraflores US$4.

A faded 'blue line' marked on the pavement links the Museo Nacional de Antropología, Arqueología e Historia to the **Museo Larco de Lima** ⓘ *Av Bolívar 1515, T01-461 1312, www.museolarco.org, daily 0900-1800, US$11 (half price for students); texts in 6 languages, guides, tours in Spanish, English and French can be booked, there is disabled access; photography is not allowed,* a 15-minute walk. Located in an 18th-century mansion built on a seventh-century pre-Columbian pyramid, this museum houses the collection of the archaeologist Rafael Larco Herrera, which gives world-class overview of the development of Peruvian cultures through their pottery and other objects. It has the world's largest collection of Moche, Sicán and Chimú pieces. There is a five-room Gold and Jewels Gallery, a magnificent textile collection and a fascinating erotica section. Don't miss the storerooms with their overwhelming array of pottery, unlike anything you'll see elsewhere. There is a library and computer room for your own research and the museum published its own fully-illustrated book on the collection. It is surrounded by flower-filled gardens, has a new entrance and park outside, a new boutique and the **Café del Museo** (see Eating, page 106).

To get there, take any bus to the 15th block of Avenida Brasil. Then take a bus down Avenida Bolívar. Or, from Miraflores, take the SM 18 Carabayllo-Chorrillos, see above, to block 15 of Bolívar. A taxi from downtown, Miraflores or San Isidro takes 15 minutes and costs US$4.

The plain exterior of the church of **Santa María Magdalena**, on Jirón San Martín, conceals some fine ornamentation and art inside. **Parque de las Leyendas** ① *La Mar, T01-464 4282, 0900-1730, US$2*, is arranged to represent the three regions of Peru: the coast, the mountainous sierra and the tropical jungles of the *selva*, with appropriate houses, animals and plants and a children's playground. It also contains a *huaca* from the Maranga culture, AD 500. The park gets very crowded at weekends. To get there from 24th block of Avenida de La Marina in **San Miguel**, take Avenida Parque Las Leyendas. Bus 23 will get you there or take a colectivo from Avenida Abancay, or bus 135A or colectivo from Avenida La Vega. Just to the east of the park is the **Universidad Católica del Perú**.

San Isidro

The district of San Isidro combines some upscale residential areas, many of Lima's fanciest hotels and restaurants and important commercial zones with a huge golf course smack in the middle. Along Avenida La República is **El Olivar**, an old olive grove planted by the first Spaniards, which has been turned into a beautiful park. It's definitely worth a stroll either by day or night.

Between San Isidro and Miraflores, is **Huallamarca** ① *C Nicolás de Rivera 201 and Av Rosario, T01-222 4124, 0900-1700, closed Mon, US$1.75, take bus 1 from Av Tacna, or minibus 13 or 73 to Choquechaca, then walk*. This adobe pyramid of the Maranga culture is also known as the Pan de Azúcar and dates from AD 100-500. There is a small site museum.

Miraflores

Miraflores, apart from being a nice residential part of Lima, is also home to a busy mercantile district full of fashionable shops, cafés, discos, fine restaurants and good hotels and guesthouses. As in the centre, there is a security force patrolling the streets, in trucks, on motorbikes or on foot.

In the centre of Miraflores is the beautiful **Parque Central de Miraflores** (**Parque Kennedy**) located between Avenida Larco and Avenida Oscar Benavides (locally known as Avenida Diagonal). This extremely well-kept park has a small open-air theatre with performances Thursday-Sunday, ranging from Afro-Peruvian music to comedy to rock'n'roll. Towards the bottom of the park is a nightly crafts market open 1700-2300.

At the end of Avenida Larco and running along the promenade is the renovated **Parque Salazar** and the very modern shopping complex called **Centro Comercial Larcomar**. The shopping centre's terraces, which have been carved out of the cliff, contain expensive shops, hip cafés and restaurants, an open-air internet café and discos.

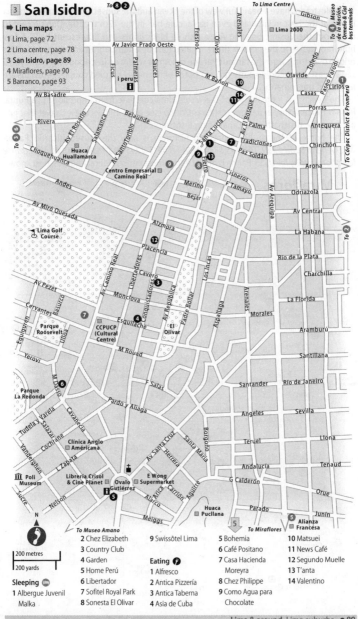

3 San Isidro

➡ Lima maps
1 Lima, page 72.
2 Lima centre, page 78
3 San Isidro, page 89
4 Miraflores, page 90
5 Barranco, page 93

Sleeping 🛏
1 Albergue Juvenil
  Malka
2 Chez Elizabeth
3 Country Club
4 Garden
5 Home Perú
6 Libertador
7 Sofitel Royal Park
8 Sonesta El Olivar
9 Swissôtel Lima

Eating 🍴
1 Alfresco
2 Antica Pizzería
3 Antica Taberna
4 Asia de Cuba
5 Bohemia
6 Café Positano
7 Casa Hacienda
  Moreyra
8 Chez Philippe
9 Como Agua para
  Chocolate
10 Matsuei
11 News Café
12 Segundo Muelle
13 T'anta
14 Valentino

The balustrades have a beautiful view of the ocean and the sunset. The 12-screen cinema is one of the best in Lima and even has a 'cine-bar' in the 12th theatre. Don't forget to check out the Cosmic Bowling Alley with its black lights and fluorescent balls. A few hundred metres to the north is the renovated **Parque Champagnat** and then, across the bridge over the gorge, the famous **Parque del Amor** where on just about any night you'll see at least one wedding party taking photos of the newly married couple. Peruvians are nothing if not romantic.

The beach has a great view of the whole Lima coastline from Chorrillos to La Punta. **Rosa Náutica**, a very expensive restaurant/disco (see page 108), occupies a pier that juts out from the beach: this is a Lima dining institution.

The home of the author, poet and historian is now the **Museo Ricardo Palma** ① *C General Suárez 189, T01-445 5836, Mon-Fri 0915-1245 and 1430-1700, small entrance fee; photography fee US$3.* Palma is one of Peru's most famous literary figures, best known

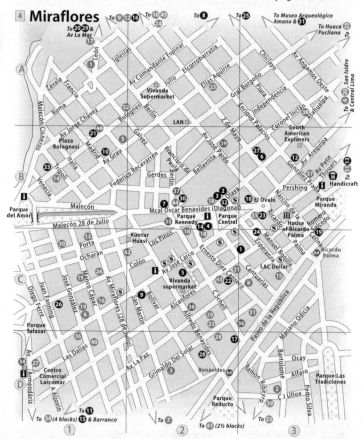

Miraflores

for his work *Tradiciones peruanas*, which covers the country's colonial period, see Literature, page 677.

Huaca Pucllana ① *at the intersection of Gral Borgoño y Tarapacá, near the 45th block of Av Arequipa, T01-445 8695, http://pucllana.perucultural.org.pe/, Wed-Mon 0900-1600, US$2.50, includes a good 45-min tour in Spanish or English*, is a fifth- to eighth-century AD ceremonial and administrative centre of the pre-Inca Lima culture. The pyramid of small adobe bricks is 23 m high. Evidence of occupation of the site by the Wari culture has been found. It has a site museum, with some objects from the site itself, an area growing crops and raising animals, and a souvenir shop. See also Eating, page 107.

Museo Arqueológico Amano ① *C Retiro 160 near the 11th block of Av Angamos Oeste, T01-441 2909, www.fundacionmuseoamano.org.pe, open by appointment only Mon-Fri 1500-1700, free, photography prohibited*, is a very fine private collection of artefacts from the Chancay, Chimú and Nazca periods, owned by the late Mr Yoshitaro Amano. It boasts

100 metres
100 yards

➡ **Lima maps**
1 Lima, page 72.
2 Lima centre, page 78
3 San Isidro, page 89
4 **Miraflores, page 90**
5 Barranco, page 93

one of the most complete exhibits of Chancay weaving and is particularly interesting for pottery and pre-Columbian textiles, all superbly displayed and lit. To get there, take a bus or colectivo to the corner of Avenida Arequipa y Avenida Angamos and another one to the 11th block of Avenida Angamos Oeste. Alternatively a taxi from downtown costs US$3.20 or from Parque Kennedy US$2.25.

One of the best private collections of colonial paintings, silver, cloth and furniture in Peru is displayed in the **Poli Museum** ① *Almte Cochrane 466, T01-422 2437, tours cost US$15 per person irrespective of the size of the group, allow 2 hrs, call in advance to arrange tours*. It also has a fine collection of pre-Columbian ceramics and gold, including material from Sipán. Guided tours are given in Spanish only and delivered rapidly by Sr Poli or his son, whose views are often contrary to long-held opinions about the symbolism of Peruvian cultures.

Barranco

South of Miraflores is Barranco, which was already a seaside resort by the end of the 17th century. During Spanish rule, it was a getaway for the rich who lived in or near the centre. Nowadays, Barranco is something of an intellectual haven, with artists' workshops and chic galleries.

The attractive public library, formerly the town hall, stands on the delightful plaza. Nearby is the interesting *bajada*, a steep path leading down to the beach, where many of Lima's artists live. The **Puente de los Suspiros** (Bridge of Sighs), leads towards the Malecón, with fine views of the bay.

Barranco is a quiet suburb during the day but comes alive at night when the city's young flock here to party at weekends. Squeezed together into a few streets are dozens of good bars and restaurants.

An antique train that discontinued its Barranco–Lima service in 1965 now offers a pleasant, albeit very short ride (six blocks) down Avenida Pedro de Osma to the door of the museum of the same name. There is a video on board describing the train's history. It runs Tuesday-Sunday from 0900 to 1700, depending on the number of passengers. Tickets can be bought at the **Electricity Museum** ① *Av Pedro de Osma 105, T01-477 6577, http://museoelectri.perucultural.org.pe, US$0.70*.

Museo de Arte Colonial Pedro de Osma ① *Av Pedro de Osma 421, T01-467 0141, www.museopedrodeosma.org, Tue-Sun 1000-1800, open by appointment public holidays, 1½-hr guided visits from 1030, US$3.50, students US$1.75*, has a private collection of colonial art of the Cuzco, Ayacucho and Arequipa schools.

Chorrillos

This district, beyond Barranco, has a redesigned, fashionable beachfront with mosaics and parks. In 2010 the Malecón was also being redesigned. It has always been a popular resort and is a good place to go to find fish restaurants. **Playa Herradura** is a little further on and is well-known for surfing. From Chorrillos you can get to some of the sites, such as Pachacámac and Pántanos de Villa, which are south of the city.

Lima beaches

Lima sits next to an open bay, with its two points at La Punta (Callao; see page 96) and Punta La Chira (Chorrillos). During the summer (December to March), beaches get very crowded on weekdays as much as at weekends, even though all the beaches lining the

5 Barranco

➡ **Lima maps**
1 Lima, page 72.
2 Lima centre, page 78
3 San Isidro, page 89
4 Miraflores, page 90
5 Barranco, page 93

Pacific Ocean

100 metres
100 yards

Sleeping
1 Barranco's Backpackers Inn
2 Casa Barranco
3 Domeyer
4 Hosp La Casona de Barranco
5 Safe in Lima
6 San Mart Inn
7 The Point

Eating
1 Antica Trattoria
2 Canta Rana
3 Expreso Virgen de Guadalupe

4 Istanbul
5 La Cía
6 La Costa Verde
7 La Fonda de los Suspiros
8 Las Mesitas
9 Sóngoro Cosongo
10 Tío Mario

Bars & clubs
11 Ayahuasca
12 Déjà Vu
13 Del Carajo
14 De Rompe y Raja
15 El Dragón
16 Juanitos

17 La Candelaria
18 La Estación de Barranco
19 La Noche
20 La Posada del Angel
21 La Posada del Mirador
22 Las Terrazas
23 Mochileros
24 Santos Café & Espirituosos
25 Sargento Pimienta

Ⓜ Metropolitano

Shanty towns

Known as *asentamientos humanos* or *pueblos jóvenes*, the shanty towns of Lima are monumental reminders of racial division and social inequality, and of the poverty in which more than half of the capital's population lives. Millions of people have no access to clean drinking water. Most of the Peruvians living in these settlements came from the provinces, escaping misery and the civil war of the 1980 and 1990s. They simply took the land on the hills surrounding Lima, only trying later to legalize their property.

There are old, 'established' shanty towns, like **Villa El Salvador**, with almost one million inhabitants, as well as new, rapidly expanding ones, like **Mi Perú** in Ventanilla, 20 km behind the Jorge Chávez airport. Some shanty towns, such as **Lurigancho** and **Canto Grande**, were controlled by Shining Path during the civil war. Others (around the Central Highway that leads towards the Andes) became famous for sheltering delinquents and drug addicts. There is even one shanty town housing Cuban exiles who escaped from the island looking for 'freedom' and a better life (now they wish they had stayed at home). Some settlements consist of bamboo shacks without roofs; others already have sound infrastructure, including markets, shops, small restaurants and cafés.

Divisions in Peruvian society run very deep. Most of the shanty town dwellers don't even know of the existence of posh neighbourhoods like San Isidro and Miraflores. Needless to say, most inhabitants of the rich parts of Lima never visit shanty towns.

Some voyeuristic visitors feel a fascination for Lima's poorest districts. Villa El Salvador, one of the oldest and biggest shanty towns, is the only one that can be visited without much danger. The only safe way to travel is by hiring a taxi (round trip from Miraflores including an hour wait can be arranged for US$11.50). If you must go, travel only by day, wear modest clothes and, if you walk, stick to the main street. It is not recommended that you visit any other shanty towns. Almost without exception, they are dangerous, especially after dark. Every week, there are countless cases of robbery, stabbing, burglary and rape. Murder is not uncommon. Under no circumstances should you travel by public transport. If you are planning to take a bus out of Lima, you will see many shanty towns along the highway.

Lima coast have been declared unsuitable for swimming. Most beaches have very strong currents and extreme caution should be exercised. Lifeguards are not always present. A stroll on the beach is pleasant during daylight hours but, when the sun goes down, the thieves come out and it becomes very dangerous. Needless to say, camping on the beach is a very bad idea.

The beaches of Miraflores, Barranco and Chorrillos are very popular and sand and sea can get dirty. It's much better to take a safe taxi 40 km south to **Punta Rocas**, **Señoritas** or **El Silencio**. **Punta Hermosa** has frequent surfing and volleyball tournaments. If you really want the height of fashion head to **Asia**, Km 92-104, which boasts some 20 beaches (mostly private) with boutiques, hotels, restaurants and condos (see page 302).

There is no separation between Lima and Callao; the two cities run into each other and the road between the two is lined with factories. But Callao is a city in its own right, the second largest in Peru with over one million inhabitants (many more if you include shanty town dwellers). Callao (not Lima) is the location of **Jorge Chávez International Airport** and is the most important Peruvian port, handling 75% of the nation's imports and some 25% of its exports. Shipyards far from sea load newly built fishing vessels on to huge lorries to be launched into the ocean here. Most parts of the city are ugly, unkempt, poor and dangerous. However, if you are willing to use some imagination and, if you like ports, Callao is worth visiting. Some attempts are being made to restore the historic centre and port area.

Background
Founded in 1537, Callao used to be one of the most important cities in South America, the only seaport on the continent authorized to trade with Spain during the 16th and 17th centuries. During much of the 16th century Spanish merchants were plagued by threats from English pirates such as Sir Francis Drake and Richard Hawkins who were all too willing to relieve the Spanish armada of its colonial spoils. The harbour was fortified in 1639 in order to prevent such attacks. In 1746, the port was completely destroyed by a massive wave, triggered by the terrible earthquake of that year. According to some sources, all 6000 of Callao's inhabitants were drowned. The watermark is still visible on the outside of the 18th-century church of **Nuestra Señora del Carmen de la Legua**, which stands near the corner of Avenida Oscar Benavides and the airport road, Avenida Elmer Faucett. In 1850, the first railway in South America was opened between Lima and Callao. It was used not only as a passenger service but also, more importantly, for the growing import-export trade, transporting ore from the mines in the Central Highlands and manufactured goods from incoming ships.

Sights
The most elegant area of Callao proper is **Plaza Grau**. It is well maintained and from here you can see a large part of the port and the **Palomino Islands** (inhabited by birds, seals and other marine species), including **Isla San Lorenzo**. This island has an underwater military bunker, where two famous prisoners were incarcerated, Abimael Guzmán, founder of Sendero Luminoso, and Víctor Polay, leader of MRTA. Trips to the islands by **Vientosur** and other agencies can be arranged from the pier next to Plaza Grau; ask around, as departures are mostly unscheduled.

Several houses surrounding the **Iglesia Matriz** have been restored, but generally the centre is in a state of permanent decay. **Museo Naval del Perú** ⓘ *Av Jorge Chávez 121, Plaza Grau, T01-429 4793, Tue-Sat 0900-1600, Sun 0900-1700, US$1,* has models of Peruvian and foreign ships, weapons, uniforms, torpedoes and other relics. There are also interesting photographs. It's recommended if you are in the area. **La Fortaleza Real Felipe** and **Museo del Ejército** ⓘ *T01-429 0532, www.regioncallao.gob.pe, Tue-Sun 0930-1600, US$2.20, students half price, no cameras allowed,* is an enormous Spanish castle in the heart of the city. It is still used by the Peruvian armed forces,but you should be allowed in to the museum and the areas open to the public. These include various areas and buildings within the fort, the museum itself, the fortifications and plenty of cannons.

La Punta

Founded in 1555, La Punta is a green peninsula next to Callao. It has only 6800 permanent residents and enjoys the relaxed, nostalgic atmosphere of a beach resort, good local seafood restaurants, pleasant walks, friendly people and great views. It's an interesting place to come for lunch, but the ride back to Lima, even in a taxi, can be dangerous at night, as you have to drive through Callao proper.

La Punta's main artery, **Avenida Coronel Bolognesi**, is lined with impressive old villas. There is a well-maintained Malecón parallel to Bolognesi, a lovely walk and great views of the islands, sailing boats and Callao port. On the corner of El Malecón and Jirón García y García is the **Club de Regatas Lima**, with a nice café and view from the second floor (open sporadically). Nearby is the **Club de Regatas Unión**. Along El Malecón is a pebble beach, but the water is not very clean, due to the proximity of Callao port. **Plaza Grau** has been well restored, with a library inside the municipality building. It has no tourist pamphlets, but you can get information about the past and the present of La Punta there. At Plaza Grau bright pleasure boats, complete with life jackets, take trippers out to the end of La Punta beach and back. The journey takes about 25 minutes and costs US$1.50. See also **Ecocruceros**, page 115.

Around Lima → *For listings, see pages 98-124.*

Pántanos de Villa

① *Daily 0900-1700, US$2, guides available for groups of 15 (free), unofficial website www.lospantanosdevilla.com.*

In the district of Chorrillos is the 396-ha wildlife sanctuary, Pántanos de Villa, an ecological wetland reserve with brackish water and abundant emergent vegetation. It provides the habitat for waterfowl typical of coastal Peru, including 17 species of migratory shorebirds. There are several species of fish, four types of reptile and over 50 species of water plant.

The visitor centre has lots of information in Spanish. Allow up to two hours for a visit and take binoculars if you have them. Access is by the road that goes to the seaside district of La Villa; the nearest public transport stops about 1 km away, so it's best to take a taxi from Barranco, US$4.

Pachacámac

① *Lurín Valley, 31 km from Lima, T01-430 0168, http://pachacamac.perucultural.org.pe/ and www.ulb.ac.be/philo/ychsma, Tue-Sun 0900-1700, open on public holidays by appointment, US$2.10 including the small site museum, students US$0.70, guides US$6.*

When the Spaniards arrived, Pachacámac was the largest city and ceremonial centre in coastal Peru. It was a vast complex of palaces and temple-pyramids, to which pilgrims paid homage, and where they obtained divinations from the oracle Pachacámac. A replica of the wooden statue of the god (a two-faced staff) is in the site museum. Hernando Pizarro came to Pachacámac in 1533, having been sent by his brother to speed the delivery of gold from the coast for Atahualpa's ransom. However, great disappointment awaited Pizarro as there was no store of riches. In their desperate search for the promised gold the Spaniards destroyed images, killed the priests and looted the temples. The ruins encircle the top of a low hill, whose crest was crowned with a **Temple of the Sun**, a large pyramid built in 1350 of sun-baked bricks, now partially restored. Slightly apart from the main group of buildings and hidden from view is the reconstructed **House of the Mamaconas**, where the 'chosen women' were taught to weave and spin fine cloth for the Inca and his court. Various other temples and palaces can be seen. Further to the north the Temple of Urpi-Huachac, who was reputed to be the wife of Pachacámac, is in a state of total ruin. The museum has a model of the city; there is also a café and toilets. An impression of the scale of the site can be gained from the top of the Temple of the Sun, or from walking or driving the 3-km circuit (the site is large and it is expected that tourists will be visiting by car – there are six parking spots).

Cieneguilla

Cieneguilla, 20 km east of the centre of Lima, is a country town on the Lurín river, an easy escape from the city and its cloud cover. It is a popular place on Sunday, with restaurants with gardens and swimming, all of which open daily for lunch, recreation centres and cabins for longer stays. Take a combi running east on Avenida Prado Este. It takes 30-45 minutes and costs US$0.50.

Puruchuco and around

In the eastern outskirts of Lima, near the stadium of La U football club, is **Puruchuco** ① *End of Av Javier Prado Este, T01-494 2641, museopuruchuco.perucultural.org.pe. Tue-Sun 0900-1600, US$1.75,* the reconstructed palace of a pre-Inca Huacho noble. There is a very good site museum, Jiménez Borja, with ceramics and textiles from the lower Rímac or Lima Valley. The palace is labyrinthine. This is also the site of a major archaeological find, announced in 2002. Under a shanty town called Túpac Amaru, over 2000 mummy bundles have been uncovered in an Inca cemetery known as **Puruchuco-Huaquerones**. The cemetery itself is not a new discovery, but the quantity and completeness of the mummies, plus the tens of thousands of accompanying objects, should reveal a wealth of information about the last century of Inca society before the Spanish conquest. It is clear that some of the mummies are of the Inca élite and all are well preserved. Archaeologists estimate that only 40% of the burials at the site have come to light. To see the tombs, ask the guards on Saturday morning if you can visit the archaeologists at work.

Also in the eastern suburbs, the vintage car collection of Jorge Nicolini is open to the public as the **Museo del Automóvil Antiguo** ① *Av La Molina cuadra 37, esq Totoritas, Urb Sol La Molina, Lima 12, T01-368 0373, www.museodelautomovilnicolini.com.* Cars from 1901-1973 are on display. You can also visit the workshop where the cars are restored and can get involved in the restoration process.

Ancón

Ancón, 30 km northwest of Lima, is reached by a double-lane asphalted highway. In the 19th and early 20th centuries, this was the smart seaside resort in Peru, but has now been deserted by the wealthy and in summer is crowded with day trippers. It has a mix of elegant 19th-century houses with wooden balconies and modern apartment blocks. There are tennis courts and a yacht club. The beaches are small and crowded during January-March holidays, but bathing is safe with no currents. Beyond Ancón is a **Chancay cemetery**, the source of weaving and pottery, as seen in the Museo Arqueológico Amano (see page 91).

Canta → *Colour map 3, B4. Altitude: 2837 m.*

Canta is a popular small town on the fringes of the high Andes less than three hours from Lima by paved road. After 1½ hours, by which time the *garúa* has been left behind, you pass through **Santa Rosa de Quives**, the birthplace of the patron Saint of Lima. Her house and the adjoining sanctuary can be visited. After two hours the petrogylphs of **Checta** are reached. Numerous small, complex drawings cover the surface of boulders spread across a hillside 15 minutes' steep walk from the road. The path is marked.

Canta itself was founded by the Spanish in 1535. It lies on one of the initial main routes down from the mines of the sierra to Lima. It is not especially attractive, but there are good day walks and significant ruins nearby. On the main street is the **tourist office** ① *T01-244 7013, Sat and Sun 1000-1600 only*.

The pre-Inca ruins of **Cantamarca** (3600 m) were probably built by the Chancay culture. They consist of large *chullpas* (burial towers) made from finely cut stone, many with roofs still supported by stone pillars. Take a steep trail from 5 km up the road to La Viuda. Allow two to three hours for the climb and carry water.

A few kilometres beyond Canta is Huaros (3587 m) from which a long day walk can be made to the **Parque Arqueológico de Huischo** and the **Bosque de Puyos Raimondis** (4050 m). Beyond Huaros the road continues to the beautiful Lake Chuchun below the 14 snow-capped peaks of the Cordillera de La Viuda.

Obrajillo

At weekends Limeños flock to this village set in beautiful countryside criss-crossed by fast-flowing streams. Eat in the main plaza or try the trout *chicharrones* and *pachamanca* at riverside restaurants. You can visit the waterfall, or go riding. A one-hour walk runs up the south side of the valley, on the opposite side to the waterfall, to **Santa Rosa de Acochaca** where there is a restaurant and shop. Returning on the opposite side of the valley a detour can be made to **San Miguel** (one hour), giving a bird's eye view of Obrajillo, before descending a steep path to the village (15 minutes).

● Lima and around listings

Hotel prices

LL over US$200	**L** US$151-200	**AL** US$101-150
A US$66-100	**B** US$46-65	**C** US$31-45
D US$21-30	**E** US$12-20	**F** US$7-11
G US$6 and under		

Restaurant prices

¶¶¶ over US$12	¶¶ US$7-12	¶ US$6 and under

● Sleeping

All hotels in the upper price brackets charge 19% state tax (IVA) and a service charge on top of prices. In hotels foreigners pay no IVA and the amount of service charged is up to the hotel. Neither is included in prices below, unless indicated otherwise.

The central colonial heart of Lima is not as safe at night as the more upmarket areas of San Isidro, Miraflores or Barranco. If you are only staying a short time in the city and want to see the main sights, the centre is convenient, but do take care. San Isidro is the poshest district, while Miraflores has a good

mix of places to stay, great ocean views, bookstores, restaurants and cinemas. From here you can commute to the centre by bus (30-45 mins) or by taxi (20-30 mins). Barranco, which is more bohemian, is a little further out.

Near the airport *map p72*
L Ramada Costa del Sol, Av Elmer Faucett s/n, T01-711 2000, www.ramada.com. Within the airport perimeter. Offers day rates as well as overnights if you can't get into the city.
B-D Hostal Residencial Víctor, Manuel Mattos 325, Urb San Amadeo de Garagay, Lima 31, T01-569 4662, hostalvictor@terra.com.pe. 5 mins from the airport by taxi, or phone or email in advance for free pick-up, large comfortable rooms, with bath, hot water, cable TV, free luggage store, free internet and 10% discount for Footprint book owners, American breakfast, evening meals can be ordered locally, 2 malls with restaurants, shops, cinemas, etc nearby, very

helpful. See also **La Catedral del Pisco**, page 106. For information, contact Víctor Melgar Morales, victortravelservice@terra.com.pe.

C Pay Purix, Av Bertello Bolatti, Mz F, Lote 5, Urb Los Jazmines, 1ra Etapa, Callao, T01-484 9118, www.paypurix.com. 3 mins from airport, can arrange pick-up (taxi US$6, US$2 from outside airport). Hostel with doubles and dorms (**E** per person), convenient, with breakfast, Wi-Fi, washing machine, English spoken, CDs, DVDs, games and use of kitchen.

Central Lima *p77, map 78*

LL-AL Lima Sheraton, Paseo de la República 170, T01-315 5000, reservas@sheraton.com.pe. A 5-star hotel located on the edge of downtown Lima in an imposing building, with the **Real Plaza** shopping centre next door. It has all the facilities associated with this international name. Rooms are good. Check for special offers.

B The Clifford Hotel, Parque Hernán Velarde 27, near 2nd block of Av Petit Thouars, Sta Beatriz, T01-433 4249, www.thecliffordhotel.com.pe. A nicely converted republican townhouse in a quiet and leafy park. Also has suites (**A**), includes breakfast, a welcome drink and airport transfer, good value, has a bar and conference room.

B Maury, Jr Ucayali 201, T01-428 8188, http://ekeko2.rcp.net.pe/hotelmaury. The most luxurious hotel in the historical centre, fancy, secure, breakfast included. The bar, all wood panels, is reputed to be the home of the first-ever pisco sour.

C La Posada del Parque Hostal, Parque Hernán Velarde 60, near 2nd block of Av Petit Thouars, Santa Beatriz, between centre and San Isidro, T01-433 2412, www.incacountry.com. A charmingly refurbished old house in a safe area, excellent bathrooms, cable TV, safe in room, breakfast US$2 extra, airport transfer 24 hrs, US$17 for up to 3 passengers, no credit cards, free internet 0830-2200. Always check the website for special offers and gifts. The owners speak good English. Recommended as excellent value.

D Hostal Iquique, Jr Iquique 758, Breña (discount for SAE members), T01-433 4724, www.hostal-iquique-lima.com. Rooms on top floor at the back are best, well-kept if a bit noisy and draughty, use of kitchen, warm water, storage facilities, safe, internet. Repeated recommendations.

D Hostal Roma, Jr Ica 326, T/F01-427 7576, www.hostalroma.8m.com. **E** without bath, cheaper in low season, hot water, basic, often full, internet extra, motorcycle parking. **Roma Tours** arranges city tours but shop around if you want to, flight reservations, Errol Branca speaks English.

E Hostal de las Artes, Jr Chota 1460, T01-433 0031. **F** without bath and for longer stay, safe, nice colonial building, solar hot water system, no breakfast or internet. Jr Chota is to be renovated. The hostal is very near PNP police headquarters.

F Hostal España, Jr Azángaro 105, T01-427 9196, www.hotelespanaperu.com. **E** with private bath (3 rooms), **G** per person in dorm,

fine old building, shared bathroom, hot showers, French and English spoken, internet, motor-cycle parking, luggage store (free), laundry service, don't leave valuables in rooms, roof garden, good café, can be very busy.

F Hostal San Francisco, Jr Azángaro 127, T01-426 2735, hostalsf@lanpro.com.pe. Dormitories with and without bathrooms, safe, Italian/Peruvian owners, good service, internet and café.

G pp **Familia Rodríguez**, Av Nicolás de Piérola 730, p 2, T01-423 6465, jotajot@ terra.com.pe. Breakfast, popular, some rooms noisy, will store luggage, also has dormitory accommodation with only 1 bathroom (same price), transport to airport US$10 per person for 2 people, US$4 per person for 3 or more, good information, secure.

G Pensión Ibarra, Av Tacna 359, p 14-16, T/F01-427 8603 (no sign), pensionibarra@ ekno.com. Breakfast US$2, discount for longer stay, use of kitchen, balcony with views of the city, very helpful owner, hot water, full board available (good small café next door).

Lima suburbs

Pueblo Libre *p87, map p72*

F pp **Guest House Marfil**, Parque Ayacucho 126, at the 3rd block of Bolívar, T01-463 3161, cosycoyllor@yahoo.com. English spoken, breakfast, kitchen facilities and laundry free of charge, internet, Spanish classes arranged, family atmosphere.

F pp **Hostal Bait Sababa**, Av San Martín 743, near the hospital, T01-261 4990, www.bait sababa.com. Home of a Jewish family who also speak Spanish and English, very helpful, Fri evening meal provided, restaurants, laundry, internet and phone nearby.

San Miguel and Magdalena del Mar

C Hostal Mami Panchita, Av Federico Gallessi 198 (ex-Av San Miguel), T01-263 7203, www.mami panchita.com. Dutch/Peruvian-owned, English, French, Dutch, Spanish and German spoken, includes breakfast and welcome drink, comfortable rooms with bath, hot water, living room and bar, patio, email service, book exchange, **Raymi Travel** agency (good service), 15 mins from airport, 15 mins from Miraflores, 20 mins from historical centre. Frequently recommended.

E Tambopacaya, Manco Capac 212 (block 31 of Av Brasil), T01-261 6122, www.tambopacaya.com. **F** in dorm, hot water, private rooms have bath, use of kitchen, internet, luggage store, laundry, convenient for airport and centre.

San Isidro *p88, map p89*

LL Country Club, Los Eucaliptos 590, T01-611 9000, www.hotelcountry.com. Excellent hotel offering fine service, luxurious rooms, safes in rooms, cable TV, free internet for guests, good bar and restaurant, classically stylish.

LL Libertador Hotels Peru, Los Eucaliptos 550, T01-518 6300, www.libertador.com.pe (reservations: Las Begonias 441, office 240, T01-518 6500). Overlooking the golf course, full facilities for the business traveller, large comfortable rooms in this relatively small hotel, fine service, good restaurant. Member of a hotel group with recommended properties throughout Peru.

LL Sonesta El Olivar, Pancho Fierro 194, T01-712 6000, www.sonesta.com/lima. One of the top 5-star hotels in Lima. Looking out onto El Olivar park, this first-rate modern hotel boasts many superb eating options. Very attentive staff, quiet, fine rooms with all amenities, bar, swimming pool, popular. Warmly recommended.

LL Swissôtel Lima, Vía Central 150, Centro Empresarial Real, T01-421 4400, www.lima.swissotel.com. Beautiful hotel with excellent 5-star service, 3 superb restaurants including **Le Café** and **Gourmet Deli**, and full business facilities.

L Sofitel Royal Park, Av Camino Real 1050, T01-215 1616, www.sofitel.com. Another recommended hotel at the top of the range, excellent rooms, charming, part of the French group, prices can be negotiated.

AL Garden, Rivera Navarrete 450, T01-442 1771, www.gardenhotel.com.pe. Includes breakfast, good beds, small restaurant, ideal for business visitors, convenient, free internet, good value.

D Chez Elizabeth, Av del Parque Norte 265, San Isidro, T01-998 007557, http://chezeliza beth.typepad.fr. Family house in residential area 7 mins' walk from Cruz del Sur bus station. Shared or private bathrooms, TV room, laundry, luggage storage, Wi-Fi, breakfast included, airport transfers US$17.50 for 3.

F Albergue Juvenil Malka, Los Lirios 165 (near 4th block of Av Javier Prado Este), San Isidro, T01-442 0162, hostelmalka@terra. com.pe. Youth hostel, 20% discount with ISIC card, dormitory style, 4-8 beds per room, English spoken, cable TV, laundry, kitchen, climbing wall, nice café.

Miraflores *p88, map p90*

LL Casa Andina Private Collection, Av La Paz 463, T01-213 4300, www.casa-andina.com. Top of the range hotel in this recommended Peruvian chain, modern, well-appointed large rooms with safe, cable TV, Wi-Fi, good bathrooms. Fine food in **Alma** restaurant and good value café, **Sama**, 1st-class service, bar, pool and gym.

LL JW Marriott, Malecón de la Reserva 615, T01-217 7000, www.marriott.com. Buffet breakfast is included. Across from **Larcomar** shopping centre, wonderful views from its towers, pool, fitness centre and health club, 2 restaurants, tennis court.

LL Miraflores Park, Av Malecón de la Reserva 1035, T01-610 4000, www.miraflourespark.com. An **Orient Express** hotel, excellent service and facilities, beautiful views over the ocean, top class. Rooftop, open-air, heated pool and spa which looks out over the ocean, open to the public when you buy a spa treatment. Check with the hotel for monthly offers. Highly recommended.

LL-L Sol de Oro, Jr San Martín 305, T01-610 7000, www.soldeoro.com.pe. Price includes buffet breakfast. Secluded but convenient for the centre of Miraflores, very pleasant, with jacuzzi, sauna, room service, and laundry.

L-AL La Paz Apart Hotel, Av La Paz 679, T01-242 9350, www.lapazaparthotel.com. Apartments with bath, kitchen, lounge, cable TV, convenient, very clean and comfortable, helpful staff. Recommended.

L-A Mansión San Antonio, Av Tejada 531, T01-445 9665, www.mansionsanantonio. com. Bed and breakfast, 7 suites of varying standards on 3 floors in a quiet residential area, safe, bar, coffee shop, Wi-Fi in public areas, swimming pool, stylish, gay-friendly.

L-A Sonesta Posadas del Inca, Alcanfores 329, T01-241 7688, www.sonesta.com/ miraflores. Part of renowned chain of hotels, convenient location, cable TV, a/c, restaurant.

AL-A Antigua Miraflores, Av Grau 350 at C Francia, T01-241 6116, www.peru-hotels -inns.com. A small, elegant hotel in a quiet but central location, very friendly service, tastefully furnished and decorated, gym, cable TV, good restaurant. Recommended.

AL-A Casa Andina, Av 28 de Julio 1088, T01-241 4050, www.casa-andina.com. Also at Av Petit Thouars 5444, T01-447 0263, in Miraflores. These Classic hotels in this chain have similar facilities and decor (others in the Cuzco area, Puno and Lake Titicaca, Arequipa, Colca, Chincha and Nazca). Very neat, with many useful touches, comfortable beds, free internet and Wi-Fi, a/c, fridge, safe, laundry service, buffet breakfast, other meals available. Check website for discounts.

A José Antonio, 28 de Julio 398 y C Colón, T01-445 7743, www.hotelesjoseantonio.com. Good in all respects, including the restaurant, huge rooms, jacuzzis, internet, swimming pool, business facilities, helpful staff speak some English.

A San Antonio Abad, Ramón Ribeyro 301, T01-447 6766, www.hotelsanantonio abad.com. Secure, quiet, helpful, tasty breakfasts, 1 free airport transfer with reservation, justifiably popular and frequently recommended.

A-B Casa de Baraybar, Toribio Pacheco 216, T01-441 2160, www.casadebaraybar.com. 1 block from the ocean, discounts for cash and long stay, extra long beds, breakfast included, TV, 24-hr room service, laundry, airport transfers free for stays of 3 nights. Bilingual staff, internet. Recommended.

A-B Hostal El Patio, Diez Canseco 341, T01-444 2107, www.hostalelpatio.net. Includes breakfast, reductions for cash and long stays. The patio has a fountain, lots of flowers and bird cages; terraces for sitting outside. Very nice suites and rooms, comfortable, English and French spoken, convenient, *comedor*, gay-friendly. Airport pick-up available.

B Alemán, Arequipa 4704, T01-241 1500, www. hotelaleman.com.pe. No sign, comfortable, quiet, garden, excellent breakfast included, enquire about laundry service, smiling staff, free internet, Wi-Fi.

B Esperanza, Esperanza 350, T01-444 2411, www.hotelesperanza-pe.com. Modern, convenient, good hot water, very helpful staff and manager, café, bar, secure, good value.

B Hostal La Castellana, Grimaldo del Solar 222, T01-444 4662, lacastellan@terra.com.pe. Pleasant, good value, nice garden, safe, expensive restaurant, laundry, English spoken, special price for SAE members.

B Sipán, Paseo de la República 6171, T01-447 0884, www.hotelsipan.com.pe. Breakfast and tax included, very pleasant, in a residential area next to the Vía Expresa (which can be heard from front rooms), TV, fridge, security box, internet access. Free airport transfers available.

C El Carmelo, Bolognesi 749, T01-446 0575, www.hostalelcarmelo.com.pe. With TV, great location a couple of blocks from the Parque del Amor, small restaurant downstairs serving *criolla* food and *ceviche*, price includes breakfast, good value, comfortable.

C La Casa Nostra, Av Grimaldo del Solar 265, T01-241 1718, www.lacasanostraperu.com. Variety of rooms (**E** per person in 4-bed room), good service, convenient, with breakfast, internet, safe, money exchange, laundry, tourist information. Popular.

C Señorial, José González 567, T01-445 0139, www.senorial.com. With breakfast, comfortable, nice garden, Wi-Fi, restaurant, good services. Recommended.

C-D pp Eurobackpackers, Manco Cápac 471, T01-654 4339, www.eurobackpackers.com. Under new management. Doubles with and without bath, dormitories including girls only **F** per person, breakfast included, kitchen, comfortable, internet, Wi-Fi (free). Airport (US$15) and bus terminal (US$8.50) transfers.

C-D Flying Dog, Diez Canseco 117, T01-445 6745, www.flyingdogperu.com. Also at Lima 457 and Olaya 280, all with dorms **F** per person. At Pershing 155 is a house for monthly rentals and they have hostels in Cuzco and Arequipa. All on or near Parque Kennedy, with kitchen, internet, lockers, but all with different features.

C-F Lion Backpackers, Grimaldo del Solar 139, T01-447 1827, www.lionbackpackers.com.

3 blocks from Parque Kennedy, doubles (**C**) and dorms (**E-F** per person), the hostal has a good atmosphere, clean rooms if a bit small, helpful staff, safe, use of kitchen, Wi-Fi.

D Inka Frog, Gral Iglesias 271, T01-445 8979, www.inkafrog.com. **E** with SAE discount. Renovated hostel, self-styled 'Exclusive B&B', comfortable, nice decor, lounge with huge TV, all rooms with bath and cable TV, rooftop terrace. Breakfast included, great value.

D The Lighthouse, Cesareo Chacaltana 162, T01-446 8397, www.thelighthouseperu.com. **F** in shared dorm. Near Plaza Morales Barros, British/Peruvian run, relaxed, small dorm or private rooms with shared bath. Free internet and Wi-Fi, use of kitchen, small indoor patio. Breakfast included. Recommended.

D-E Casa Rodas, Av Petit Thouars 4712, T01-447 5761, and Tarapacá 250, T01-242 4872, www.casarodas.com. Both locations provide clean rooms for 2, 3 or 4, good beds, hot water, breakfast included, use of kitchen, cable TV and DVD player, free internet, Wi-Fi available, helpful staff.

D-E Friend's House, José González 427, T01-446 3521, friendshouse_peru@ yahoo.com.mx. Very popular, reserve in advance. Near **Larcomar** shopping centre, plenty of good information and help, family atmosphere, includes breakfast, use of kitchen, cable TV, internet and Wi-Fi. Highly recommended. They have another branch at Jr Manco Cápac 368, T01-446 6248, with dormitory accommodation with shared bath and hot water, **F** per person. Neither branch is signed, except on the bell at No 427. (Do not confuse with a signed hostel of the same name on J González, near Porta.)

D-E Home Perú, Av Arequipa 4501 (no sign), T01-241 9898, www.homeperu.com. In a 1920s mansion with huge rooms, with breakfast, **E-F** per person with shared bath, group discounts, very welcoming and helpful, use of kitchen, luggage store, English spoken, laundry service, internet. Can help with bus and plane tickets, connected to other *hostales* in Peru.

D-F Hitchhikers B&B Backpackers Hostel, Bolognesi 400, T01-242 3008, www.hhikers peru.com. Close to the ocean, dorms (including female only) and private rooms with bath, kitchen, nice patio, Wi-Fi, plenty of parking.

E pp **Inka Lodge**, Elias Aguirre 278, T01-242 6989, www.inkalodge.com. Rooms and dormitories for males and females (**F** per person), convenient, excellent breakfast included, internet, laundry, very helpful.

E-F pp **Perú Backpackers Miraflores Guesthouse**, José González 526, T01-447 7044, www.backpackersperu.com. **C** in double room, has a girls-only dorm, good breakfast included, good service, cooking facilities, internet, DVD, safe, book exchange.

E-F pp **Stop & Drop Backpacker Hotel & Guesthouse**, Berlín 168, p2, T01-243 3101, www.stopandrop.com. **C-D** Double rooms with private bath. Backpacker hotel and guesthouse, also surf and Spanish school. Bar, kitchen facilities, luggage store, laundry,

TV, movies, internet, games, comfy beds, safe, hot showers 24 hrs, adventure sports (including diving, horse riding) and volunteer jobs. Airport pick-up.

F pp **Adventures House**, Jr Alfredo Leon 234, T01-241 5693, www.adventures house.com. Rooms for up to 4, also has doubles (**D**), with bath and hot water, free internet, national calls, pleasant, quiet, a short walk from all facilities, airport transfer, kitchen, bike rental US$15 per day. Associated with **Fly Adventure**, see Paragliding, page 115.

F pp **Albergue Turístico Juvenil Internacional**, Av Casimiro Ulloa 328, San Antonio, T01-446 5488, www.limahostell. com.pe. Dormitory accommodation, **C** in a double private room, basic cafeteria, travel information, cooking (minimal) and laundry facilities, swimming pool often empty, extra charge for kitchen facilities, safe, situated in a nice villa; 20 mins' walk from the beach. Bus No 2 or colectivos pass Av Benavides to the centre; taxi to centre, US$2.50.

F pp **Albergue Verde**, Grimaldo del Solar 459, T01-445 3816, www.albergue verde.com. Nice small hostal, comfortable beds, **D** per person in double, friendly owner, breakfast included, airport transfers US$15, bus terminal transfer US$4.

F pp **Condor's House**, Martín Napanga 137, T01-446 7267, www.condorshouse.com. Award-winning hostel in a quiet part of Miraflores, shared rooms with lockers, good bathrooms, also a twin and a matrimonial (**C**), with breakfast, good meeting place, TV room with films, book exchange, internet, Wi-Fi, kitchen, *almuerzo criollo* and *parrillada* prepared once a week, bar, not a party hostel. Helpful manager, Arturo Luna, and staff; friendly dog, Chévere.

F pp **Dragonfly**, Av 28 de Julio 190, T01-654 3226, www.dragonflyhostels.com. Shared rooms with lockers, without bath, double room **D**, breakfast included, internet, Wi-Fi, kitchen, can arrange surfing, papapenting and other sports and tours, best to reserve a bed in advance.

F pp **Explorer's House**, Av Alfredo León 158, by 10th block of Av José Pardo, T01-241 5002, explorers_ house@yahoo.es. No sign, but plenty of indications of the house number, with breakfast, dorm with shared bath, or double rooms with bath, hot water, use of kitchen, laundry service, Spanish classes, English spoken, very welcoming.

F pp **HQ Villa**, Independencia 1288, T01-221 3221, info@hqvilla.com. Peruvian/British owned hostel with mixed and girls-only dorms and doubles (**C**) in a modern house, garden, lounge, double kitchen, receptionists speak 3 languages, airport pick-up, with breakfast, internet, Wi-Fi, spacious, nice atmosphere.

F pp **Lex Luthor's House**, Porta 550, T01-242 7059, www.thelexluthorshouse.com. Dormitories and doubles (**D** with and without bath), breakfast included, pleasant family house, small, clean, use of kitchen, book exchange, internet, Wi-Fi, good value. In the same entrance, owned by a cousin, is **The Angels Inn**, No 540, T01-241 4614, www.theangelsinnperu.com, rooms with and without bath, bunk rooms, kitchen, Wi-Fi, reserve in advance.

F pp **Loki Backpackers**, José Galvez 576, T01-651 2966, www.lokihostel.com. In a quiet area, the capital's sister to the party hostel of the same name in Cuzco, **D** in double room, good showers, with breakfast (cooked breakfast extra), Fri barbecues, use of kitchen, free internet, lockers, airport transfer extra.

F Pariwana, Av Larco 189, T01-242 4350, www.pariwana-hostel.com. New in 2009, party hostel with dorms and shared bath, individual lockers with power outlets so you can leave your gadgets charging in a safe place.

F pp **Pirwa**, González Prada 179, T01-444 1266 and Coronel Inclán 494, T01-242 4059, www.pirwahostelsperu.com. Members of a chain of hostels in Peru (Cuzco, Arequipa, Puno, Nazca); G Prada branch has shared rooms with shared bath, Inclán branch is B&B with bath, **D**. Prices include breakfast, lockers, internet, Wi-Fi, use of kitchen, transfers, bike rental.

G pp **Blue House**, José González 475, T01-445 0476, www.bluehouse.com.pe. A true backpacker hostel, most rooms with bath including a double (**F**), basic but good value for the location, breakfast included, internet, Wi-Fi, use of kitchen, *terraza* with *parrilla*, films to watch.

G pp **Casa del Mochilero**, Cesareo Chacaltana 130A, T01-444 9089, pilaryv@hotmail.com. Ask for Pilar or Juan, dorms or **E** in double room on terrace, all with shared bath, breakfast and internet extra, hot water, Wi-Fi, use of kitchen. lots of information. Not to be confused with *Mochilero's Inn* at No 136, which also has dorms in **G** range.

Barranco p92, map p93

C Domeyer, C Domeyer 296, T01-247 1413, www.domeyerhostel.net. Friendly and clean, **E** in shared room, hot water 24 hrs, laundry service, secure and gay-friendly.

E pp **Barranco's Backpackers Inn**, Malecón Castilla 260, T01-247 1326. Ocean view, colourful rooms, all en suite, shared and private rooms (with cable TV), free internet with Wi-Fi, kitchen facilities. Breakfast included. Discount for **SAE** members.

E Casa Barranco, Av Grau 982, T01-477 0984, www.lacasabarranco.8m.com. There is no sign on the street, so just ring the bell. All rooms have shared bath, dormitory costs **F**, also monthly rentals available. Has kitchen, DVD room, cable TV and PS1. Helpful owner, Felipe. Discount for SAE members.

E pp **Hospedaje La Casona de Barranco**, Av Bolognesi 271, T01-247 8835. By Bulevar metropolitano stop. With bath, hot water, cable TV, comfortable and safe, no breakfast or internet. Next door is **La Vieja Taberna** restaurant with lunch *menú*.

E Safe in Lima, Alfredo Silva 150, T01-252 7330, www.safeinlima.com. Quiet, Belgian-run hostal with family atmosphere, with breakfast, very helpful, airport pick-up US$16.50, good value, reserve in advance, lots of information for travellers. Also a travel agency and tour operator, see page 117.

F pp **The Point**, Malecón Junín 300, T01-628 7952, www.thepointhostels.com. Rooms range from doubles to large dormitories, all with shared bath, very popular with backpackers (book in advance at weekends), breakfast included, internet, cable TV, laundry, kitchen facilities, gay-friendly, party atmosphere most of the time, **The Pointless Pub** open 2000 till whenever, weekly barbecues, therapeutic massage next door, can arrange bungee jumping, flight tickets and volunteering. Also has hostels in Arequipa, Cuzco, Máncora and Puno.

F pp **San Mart Inn**, Av San Martín 135, T01-247 1522, www.sanmart-inn.com. Backpacker hostel, also has doubles (**D**, cheaper with shared bath), hot water, with breakfast, Wi-Fi.

❷ Eating

19% state tax and 10% service will be added to your bill in middle- and upper-class restaurants. Chinese is often the cheapest at around US$5 including a drink.

Central Lima p77, map p78

₩ Wa Lok, Jr Paruro 864, Barrio Chino, T01-427 2656. Good dim sum, cakes and fortune cookies (when you pay the bill). English spoken, very friendly. Also at Av Angamos Oeste 700, Miraflores, T01-447 1329.

₩ Antaño, Ucayali 332, opposite the Torre Tagle Palace, T01-426 2372. Good, typical Peruvian food, nice patio. Recommended.

₩ La Choza Náutica, Jr Breña 204 and 211 behind Plaza Bolognesi, Breña, T01-483 8087. Good *ceviche* and friendly service, with 2 branches on this street, consistently recommended.

₩ L'Eau Vive, Ucayali 370, also opposite the Torre Tagle Palace, T01-427 5612. Mon-Sat, 1230-1500 and 1930-2130. Run by nuns, fixed-price lunch menu, Peruvian-style in interior dining room, or à la carte in either of dining rooms that open onto the patio, excellent, profits go to the poor, *Ave María* is sung nightly at 2100.

Ψ Manhatten, Jr Miró Quesada 259. Mon-Fri 0700-1900. Low-end executive-type restaurant, local and international food from US$5-10, good.

Ψ Salon Capon, Jr Paruro 819. Good dim sum, at this recommended *chifa*. Also has a branch at **Larcomar** shopping centre, which is ΨΨΨ, elegant and equally recommended.

ΨΨ-Ψ De César, Ancash 300, T01-428 8740. Open 0700-2300. Old-fashioned atmosphere, apart from the 3 TVs. Offers breakfasts, snacks, seafood, including *ceviche* and *chicharrones de marisco*. Meat dishes, pastas, pizza, juices, coffees and teas. Good food.

ΨΨ-Ψ San Paolo, Ancash 454, T01-427 4600. Open 0600-2400. Peruvian food, also has a good *menú diario* for US$3-4.

Ψ Azato, Av Arica 298, 3 blocks from Plaza Bolognesi, Breña, T01-423 4369. Excellent and cheap Peruvian dishes.

Ψ Cordano, Jr Ancash 202. Typical old Lima restaurant/watering hole, slow service and a bit grimy but full of character. Definitely worth the time it takes to drink a few beers.

Ψ Govinda, Av Garcilaso de la Vega 1670, opposite Gran Parque de Lima. Vegetarian food and natural products, good.

Ψ Machu Picchu, Jr Ancash 312. Closed for breakfast. Huge portions, grimy bathrooms, yet very popular.

Ψ Natur, Moquegua 132, 1 block from Jr de la Unión, T01-427 8281. The owner, Humberto Valdivia, is also president of the SAE's board of directors; the casual conversation, as well as his vegetarian restaurant, is certainly recommended.

Ψ Neydi, Puno 367. Daily 1100-2000. Good, cheap seafood, popular.

Cafés

Acllahuasy, Jr Ancash 400. Daily 0700-2300. Around the corner from **Hostal España**, good Peruvian dishes.

Café Carrara, Jr Ica 330, attached to Hostal Roma. Open daily from breakfast until 2300, pancakes, sandwiches.

La Catedral del Pisco, Av Uruguay 114, T01-330 0079, lacatedraldelpisco@hotmail.com.

Open 0800-2200 for *comida criolla*, drinks, free Peruvian coffee or pisco sour (both excellent) for Footprint guide owners, live music at night. See also **Victor Travel Service**, page 117, travel agency and information service, includes online facilities for visitors.

Lima suburbs

Pueblo Libre *p87, maps p72 and p89*
ΨΨ Café del Museo at the Museo Larco, Av Bolívar 1515, Pueblo Libre, T01-462 4757, www.cafedelmuseo.com. Daily 0900-1800. Seating inside and on the terrace. Specially designed interior, selection of salads, fine Peruvian dishes, pastas and seafood, a tapas bar of traditional Peruvian foods, snacks, desserts and cocktails. Highly regarded.

ΨΨ-Ψ Antigua Taberna Quierolo, Av San Martín 1090, 1 block from Plaza Bolívar. Atmospheric old bar with glass-fronted shelves of bottles, marble bar and old photos, owns bodega next door. Serves simple lunches, sandwiches and snacks, good for wine, does not serve dinner.

San Isidro *p88, map p89*
ΨΨΨ Alfresco, Santa Lucía 295 (no sign), T01-422 8915. Best known for its tempting seafood and *ceviche*, also pastas and rice dishes, expensive wines.

ΨΨΨ Antica Pizzería, Av Dos de Mayo 728, T01-222 8437, www.anticapizzeria.com.pe. Very popular, great ambience, excellent food, Italian owner. Also **Antica Trattoria** in Barranco at Alfonso Ugarte 242, and an excellent bar, **Antica Taberna**, with a limited range of food at Conquistadores 605, San Isidro, very good value, fashionable, get there early for a seat.

ΨΨΨ Asia de Cuba, Conquistadores 780, T01-222 4940. Popular, serving a mix of Asian, Cuban and Peruvian dishes. It also has a reputation for its bar and nightclub; try the martinis.

ΨΨΨ Casa Hacienda Moreyra, Av Paz Soldán 290, T01-444 4022, www.casahacienda moreyra.com. Closed Sun and 1600-1900.

A beautifully restored colonial house offering a fabulous *criolla* food.

Matsuei, C Manuel Bañón 260, T01-422 4323, www.matsueiperu.com. Sushi bar and Japanese dishes, very popular, among the best Japanese in Lima.

Valentino, Manuel Bañón 215, T01-441 6174. One of Lima's best international restaurants, formal, look for the tiny brass sign.

Bohemia, Av Santa Cruz 805, Ovalo Gutiérrez, T01-446 5240, www.bohemia cafe.com. Large menu of international food, great salads and sandwiches. Also at Av Alfredo Mendiola 3698, Tda 126, p 2, Mega Plaza, Lima Norte, T01-386 5681.

Chez Philippe, Av 2 de Mayo 748, T01-222 4953, www.chez-philippe.net. Pizza, pasta and crêpes, wood oven, rustic decor (same owners as **Pizza B&B** in Huaraz).

Como Agua Para Chocolate, Pancho Fierro 108, T01-222 0297, aguapachocolat @terra.com.pe. Dutch-Mexican owned restaurant, specializing in Mexican food as the name suggests, also has a very amusing Dutch night once a month. **SAE** members get a discount.

Segundo Muelle, Av Conquistadores 490, T01-421 1206, and Av Canaval y Moreyra (aka Corpac) 605. Excellent *ceviche* and other seafood, popular with the younger crowd.

Cafés
Café Positano/Café Luna, Miguel Dasso 147. Popular with politicians, café and bistro.

News Café, Av Santa Luisa 110. Great salads and desserts, popular and expensive.

T'anta, Pancho Fierro 115 (1 block from Hotel El Olivar). Huge selection of entrées and desserts, very smart with prices to match.

Miraflores *p88, map p90*
C San Ramón, known as 'Pizza Street' (across from Parque Kennedy), is a pedestrian walkway lined with outdoor restaurants/bars/discos open until the wee small hrs. It's very popular, with good-natured touts trying to entice diners and drinkers with free offers.

Astrid y Gaston, Cantuarias 175, T01-242 5387, www.astridygaston.com. Exceptional local/Novo Andino and international cuisine, one of the best in Lima, owners are Gastón Acurio and his wife Astrid. Also has a bar.

Café Voltaire, Av Dos de Mayo 220, T01-447 4807. Closed Sun. International cuisine with emphasis on French dishes, beautifully cooked food, pleasant ambience, good service.

Coco de Mer, Av Grau 400, T01-243 0278. Open daily from 1200 till whenever. Run by Englishwoman Lucy Ralph, popular, Mediterranean and Peruvian dishes, cocktails, events.

El Kapallaq, Av Petit Thouars 4844, T01-444 4149, www.elkapallaqrestaurant. blogspot.com. Mon-Fri 1200-1800. Prize-winning Peruvian restaurant specializing in seafood and fish, excellent *ceviches*.

El Rincón Gaucho, Av Armendáriz 580, T01-447 4778, www.rincongauchoperu.com. Renowned for its steaks.

El Señorío de Sulco, Malecón Cisneros 1470, T01-441 0183, www.senoriodesulco. com. Overlooking a clifftop park, with ocean views from upstairs. Forget the Footprint grading, this is a '5-fork' restaurant that some believe is the best in Lima, all Peruvian food, à la carte and buffet, piscos, wines, piano music at night.

Huaca Pucllana, Gral Borgoño cuadra 8 s/n, alt cuadra 45 Av Arequipa, T01-445 4042, www.resthuacapucllana.com. Facing the archaeological site of the same name, contemporary Peruvian fusion cooking, very good food in an unusual setting, popular with groups.

La Mar, Av La Mar 770 at 8 de Octubre, T01-421 3365. Tue-Sun 1230-1700. Another Gastón Acurio establishment which does not take bookings. Highly recommended for *ceviche* and other seafood dishes.

Las Brujas de Cachiche, Av Bolognesi 460, T01-447 1883, www.brujasde cachiche.com.pe. An old mansion converted into bars and dining rooms, traditional food (menu in Spanish and English), best *Lomo Saltado* in town, live *criollo* music.

¶¶¶ La Trattoria, Manuel Bonilla 106, 1 block from Parque Kennedy, T01-446 7002. Italian cuisine, popular, good desserts. Has another branch, **La Bodeguita**, opposite entrance to Huaca Pucllana.

¶¶¶ Panchita, Av 2 de Mayo 298, T01-242 5957. Another Gaston Acurio restaurant, specialising in *anticuchos* and *tamales*. Very good and popular, be prepared to queue as you cannot book in advance. Closed Sun.

¶¶¶ Pescados Capitales, Av La Mar 1337, at the edge of Miraflores, T01-421 8808. Daily 1230-1700. One of the very best *cevicherías* and fish restaurants on this avenue.

¶¶¶ Rosa Náutica, Espigón No 4, Circuito de Playas, T01-445 0149, www.larosanautica.com. Daily 1230-0200. Built on old British-style pier, in Lima Bay. Delightful opulence, finest fish cuisine, experience the atmosphere by buying an expensive beer in the bar at sunset.

¶¶¶ Sí Señor, Jr Bolognesi 706, T01-445 3789, www.sisenor.org. Mexican food, cheerful, interesting decor, huge portions.

¶¶¶-¶¶ Las Tejas, Diez Canseco 340, T01-444 4360. Daily 1100-2300. Good, Peruvian food, vegetarian dishes, recommended for *ceviche*.

¶¶ Café Tarata, Pasaje Tarata 260, T01-446 6330. Good atmosphere, family-run, good varied menu including Argentine steaks.

¶¶ Dalmacia, San Fernando 401, T01-445 7917. Spanish-owned, casual gourmet restaurant, excellent.

¶¶ El Huarike, Enrique Palacios 140, T01-241 6086, www.elhuarike.com. Rub shoulders with Miraflores high-fliers at this hip, gourmet restaurant which serves delicious combinations of *ceviche* and sushi.

¶¶ Il Postino, Colina 401, T01-446 8381. Great Italian food.

¶¶ Lobo del Mar - Octavio Otani, Colón 587, T242-1871. The basic apperance of this small seafood restaurant is deceptive. One of the oldest *cevicherías* in Miraflores, Octavio Otani makes a mean *ceviche* – and a good selection of other seafood dishes. Choose your own fish from the display counter if you want to.

¶¶ Mama Olla, Pasaje Tarata 248. Charming café on a pedestrian walkway, with huge menu and big portions. There are several other places to eat on this street.

¶¶-¶ Café Beirut, Mártir Olaya 204. Excellent Middle Eastern restaurant, close to the centre of Miraflores, enthusiastic waiters, superb falafel and Arabic favourites, both sweet and savoury. Also a good selection of international dishes.

¶¶-¶ Shehadi, Av Diagonal 220. Facing Parque Kennedy, US-owned, brightly lit restaurant specializing in pizza but also serving typical Peruvian fare. Good-value daytime menus. Popular with locals and foreigners.

¶ El Parquetito, Diez Canseco 150. Good cheap menu, serves breakfast, eat either inside or out.

¶ Govinda, Schell 630. Vegetarian, from the Hare Krishna foundation, lunch *menú* US$3.

¶ Madre Natura, Chiclayo 815. Closes 2100. Natural foods shop and eating place, good.

¶ Pardo's Chicken, Av Benavides 730. Chicken and chips, very good and popular (branches throughout Lima).

¶ Sandwich.com, Av Diagonal 234. Good, cheap sandwiches with interesting combinations of fillings.

Cafés

Café Café, Martín Olaya 250, near the Parque Kennedy roundabout on the corner with Av Diagonal 598, T01-444 5579. Good atmosphere, over 100 different blends of coffee, good salads and sandwiches, very popular with 'well-to-do' Limeños, has Wi-Fi. Also in Larcomar.

Café de la Paz, Lima 351, middle of Parque Kennedy. Good outdoor café right on the park, expensive, great cocktails.

Café La Máquina, Alcanfores 323. Friendly small café and bar with good cocktails, interesting sandwiches and great cakes. To while away the time there are hundreds of Rubik's cubes to set straight.

Café Zeta, Mcal Oscar R Benavides 598 y José Gálvez. American owned, excellent Peruvian coffee, teas, hot chocolate, and the best home-made cakes away from home, cheap.

C'est si bon, Av Cdte Espinar 663. Excellent cakes by the slice or whole, best in Lima.
Chef's Café, Av Larco 763. A smart place for a wide selection of sandwichs and light lunches, with good coffee.
Haiti, Av Diagonal 160, Parque Kennedy. Open almost round the clock daily, great for people watching, good ice cream.
La Tiendecita Blanca, Av Larco 111 on Parque Kennedy. One of Miraflores' oldest, expensive, good people-watching, very good cakes, European-style food and delicatessen.
Le Rendez-Vous, Av Petit Thouars 5411, at one of the entrances to the Mercado Inca. Sells Peruvian coffee, if you need a pick-me-up and break from all that craft shopping.
San Antonio, Av Angamos Oeste 1494, also Vasco Núñez de Balboa 770, Rocca de Vergallo 201, Magdalena del Mar and Av Primavera 373, San Borja, www.pasteleria sanantonio.com. Fashionable *pastelería* chain, good, not too expensive.

Barranco *p92, map p93*
🍴 **Canta Rana**, Génova 101, T01-247 7274. Sun-Mon 1200-1800, Tue-Sat 1200-2300. Good *ceviche*, expensive, small portions, but the most popular local place on Sun.
🍴 **La Costa Verde**, on Barranquito beach, T01-441 3086. Daily 1200-2400. Excellent fish and wine, expensive but recommended as the best by Limeños. Sun buffet.
🍴-🍴 **La Fonda de los Suspiros**, Pedro de Osma 102. Restaurant/bar by the Plaza, serving meat, pasta, fish and seafood dishes, with good reports.
🍴-🍴 **Tío Mario**, Jr Zepita 214, on the steps to the Puente de Suspiros. Excellent *anticuchería*, serving delicious Peruvian kebabs, always busy, fantastic service, varied menu and good prices.
🍴 **Las Mesitas**, Av Grau 341, T01-477 4199. Open 1200-0200. Traditional tea rooms-cum-restaurant, serving Creole food and traditional desserts which you won't find anywhere else, lunch *menú* served till 1400, US$3.
🍴-🍴 **Expreso Virgen de Guadalupe**, San Martín y Ayacucho. Vegetarian buffet in an old

railway carriage, also seating in the garden, more expensive at weekends, has Wi-Fi.
🍴-🍴 **Sóngoro Cosongo**, Ayacucho 281, T01-247 4730, at the top of the steps down to Puente de Suspiros. Good value *comida criolla*, 'un poco de todo'.

Cafés
Istanbul, Grau 310. Turkish café, new in 2010, with Wi-Fi.
La Cía, Grau 320. Colourful murals, young and trendy scene, friendly, good food such as lunch *menú* and desserts. Turns into a bar later at night.

🎵 Bars and clubs

Central Lima *p77, map p78*
The centre of town, specifically Jr de la Unión, has many discos. It's best to avoid the nightspots around the intersection of Av Tacna, Av Piérola and Av de la Vega. These places are rough and foreigners will receive much unwanted attention.
For latest recommendations for gay and lesbian places, check out http://lima.queer city.info/index.html, www.deambiente. com/web and www.gayperu.com.
El Rincón Cervecero, Jr de la Unión (Belén) 1045. German pub without the beer, fun.
Estadio Futbol Sports Bar, Av Nicolás de Piérola 926 on the Plaza San Martín, T01-428 8866. Beautiful bar with a disco, football theme, with life-sized models of famous footballers, with whom you can have a drink! Good international and Creole food.
Piano Bar Munich, Jr de la Unión 1044 (basement). Small and fun.
Yacama Arte & Rock Bar, Jr de la Unión 892, T01-427 7897. Unpretentious rock bar on 2nd floor, serves cheap beer.

Miraflores *p88, map p90*
Bartinis, in Larcomar, T01-241 1299, www.bartini-larcomar.com. Good cocktails, trendy crowd, expensive.

La Tasca, Av Diez Canseco 117, very near Parque Kennedy, part of the **Flying Dog** group and underneath one of the hostels (see Sleeping, above). Spanish-style bar with cheap beer (for Miraflores). Attracts an eclectic crowd including ex-pats, travellers and locals. Gay-friendly. Small and crowded.

Media Naranja, Schell 130, at the bottom of Parque Kennedy. Brazilian bar with typical drinks and food.

Murphy's, Schell 619, T01-447 1082. Open Mon-Sat from 1600. Happy hours every day with different offers, lots of entertainment, very popular.

The Old Pub, San Ramón 295 (Pizza St), www.oldpub.com.pe. Cosy, with live music most days.

Treff Pub Alemán, Av Benavides 571-104, T01-444 0148, www.treff-pub-aleman.com (hidden from the main road behind a cluster of tiny houses signed "Los Duendes"). A wide range of German beers, plus cocktails, good atmosphere, darts and other games.

Voluntarios Pub, Independencia 131, T01-445 3939, www.voluntariospub.com.pe. All staff are volunteers from non-profit organizations who benefit by receiving 90% of the profits made. Good atmosphere, music and drinks; it's nice to know that other people are benefiting from your partying.

Barranco p92, map p93
Barranco is the capital of Lima nightlife. The following is a short list of some of the better bars and clubs. Pasaje Sánchez Carrión, right off the main plaza, used to be the heart of it all. Watering holes and discos line both sides of this pedestrian walkway. Av Grau, just across the street from the plaza, is also lined with bars, eg **Las Terrazas**, Av Grau 290, **Déjà Vu**, No 294. Many of the bars in this area turn into discos later on.

Ayahuasca, San Martín 130. In the stunning Berninzon House from the Republican era, chilled out lounge bar with several areas for eating, drinking and dancing. Food is expensive and portions are small, but go for the atmosphere.

El Dragón, N de Piérola 168, T01-797 1033, www.eldragon.com.pe. Popular bar and venue for music, theatre and painting.

El Grill de Costa Verde, part of the **Costa Verde** restaurant on Barranco beach. Young crowd, packed at weekends.

Juanitos, Av Grau, opposite the park. Open from 1600-0400. Barranco's oldest bar, where writers and artists congregate, a perfect spot to start the evening.

La Noche, Bolognesi 307, at Pasaje Sánchez Carrión. A Lima institution and high standard, live music, Mon is jazz night, all kicks off at around 2200.

La Posada del Angel, 3 branches, Pedro de Osma 164 and 218 and Av Prol San Martín 157, T01-247 5544. These are popular bars serving snacks and meals.

La Posada del Mirador, near the Puente de los Suspiros (Bridge of Sighs). Beautiful view of the ocean, but you pay for the privilege.

Mochileros, Av Pedro de Osma 135. Good pub in a beautiful house, weekend events.

Santos Café & Espirituosos, Jr Zepita 203, just above the Puente de Suspiros, T01-247 4609. Mon-Sat 1700-0100. Favourite spot for trendy young professionals who want to drop a few hundred soles, relaxed, informal but pricey.

Sargento Pimienta, Bolognesi 755. Live music, always a favourite with Limeños.

⊙ Entertainment

Lima p77, maps p72, p78, p89, p90 and p93,
Cinema

The newspaper El Comercio lists cinema information in the section called Luces. Tue is reduced price at most cinemas and Mon and Wed are cheaper than Thu-Sun. Most films are in English with subtitles and cost US$2 in the centre and around US$4-5 in Miraflores. The best cinema chains in the city are **Cinemark, Cineplanet** and **UVK Multicines**. **Cinematógrafo de Barranco**, Pérez Roca 196, Barranco, T01-264 4374, www.elcinemato

grafo.com. Independent film club showing a wide range of international films.

Peñas

De Cajón, C Merino 2nd block, near 6th block of Av del Ejército, Miraflores. Good *música negra*.

Del Carajo, San Ambrosio 328, Barranco, T01-241 7977, www.delcarajo.com.pe. All types of traditional music.

De Rompe y Raja, Manuel Segura 127, Barranco, T01-247 3271, www.derompey raja.net. Popular, Thu, Fri, Sat for music, dancing and *criolla* food.

La Candelaria, Av Bolognesi 292, Barranco, T01-247 1314, www.lacandelariaperu.com. Fri-Sat from 2130. A good Barranco *peña*,

La Estación de Barranco, at Pedro de Osma 112, Barranco, T01-477 5030, www.laestaciondebarranco.com. Open from Thu. Good, family atmosphere, varied shows.

Las Brisas de Titicaca, Pasaje Walkuski 168, at 1st block of Av Brasil near Plaza Bolognesi, T01-332 1901, www.brisasdeltiticaca.com. A Lima institution.

Sachun, Av del Ejército 657, Miraflores, T01-441 0123, www.sachunperu.com. Great shows on weekdays as well.

Theatre

Most professional plays are staged at **Teatro Segura**, Jr Huancavelica 251, T01-427 9491. There are many other theatres in the city, some of which are related to Cultural centres (see page 122). The press gives details of performances. Theatre and concert tickets booked through **Teleticket**, T01-610 8888, Mon-Fri 0900-1900, www.teleticket.com.pe. Also in **Wong** supermarkets.

⊕ Festivals and events

Lima *p77, maps p72, p78, p89, p90 and p93*
18 Jan Founding of Lima. Semana Santa, or Holy Week, a colourful spectacle.

28-29 Jul Independence, with music and fireworks in the Plaza de Armas on the evening before.
30 Aug Santa Rosa de Lima.
Mid-Sep Mistura, www.mistura.pe, a huge gastronomy fair in Parque Exposición, with Peruvian foods to try, celebrity chefs, workshops and more. Fast gaining a reputation as one of the best food fairs in South America.
Oct The month of Our Lord of the Miracles; see Las Nazarenas church, page 83.

○ Shopping

Lima *p77, maps p72, p78, p89, p90 and p93*
Alpaca and cotton
There are bargains in high-quality Pima cotton. Shops selling alpaca items include:
Alpaca 859, Av Larco 859, Miraflores. Good-quality alpaca and baby alpaca products.
Da Capo, Aramburú 920, dpto 402, San Isidro, T01-441 0714. Beautiful alpaca scarves and shawls in new designs.
Kuna by Alpaca 111, Av Larco 671, Miraflores, T01-447 1623, www.kuna.com.pe. High-quality alpaca, baby alpaca and vicuña items. Also at Av Jorge Basadre Grohmann 380, San Isidro, T01-440 2320, in **Larcomar** shopping centre, Local 1-07, at the airport, and in the Museo Larco Herrera.

Art galleries
Many cultural centres (see page 122) have art galleries, cinemas and theatres.
Artco, Rouad y Paz Soldán 325, San Isidro, T01-221 3579, www.artcogaleria.com. Mon-Fri 1100-2000, Sat 1030-1330, 1530-1950.
Galería San Francisco, Plaza San Francisco 208, Barranco, T01-477 0537. A gallery in a pleasant building on a small plaza a little way from the centre of Barranco.
La Casa Azul, Alfonso Ugarte 150, Miraflores, T01-446 6380, T01-9807 1661. Marcia Moreno and Jorge Rengifo offer advice and sales of contemporary art and antique objects, handicrafts and furniture.

Manos Peruanas, Jr J Moore 199, Miraflores, T01-430 0901, www.raymisa.com. Entry by appointment only, US$1.75. A large collection of contemporary Peruvian folk art, also has temporary exhibitions and a shop selling handicrafts. In conjunction with **Asociación Civil Inti Raymi** NGO and **Raymi Tours**, www.raymitours.com.

Wu, Paseo Sáenz Peña 129, Barranco, T01-247 4685, www.wuediciones.com. Mon-Fri 1000-1300, 1400-2000, Sat 1100-1300, 1630-2000. Frances Wu's studio is also a gallery of engravings, etchings and other graphics, with an emphasis on Peruvian artists.

Bookshops

Crisol, Ovalo Gutiérrez, Av Santa Cruz 816, San Isidro, T01-221 1010, below Cine Planet. Large bookshop with café, titles in English, French and Spanish. Also in **Jockey Plaza Shopping Center**, Av Javier Prado Este 4200, Surco, T01-436 0004, and other branches, www.crisol.com.pe.

Epoca, Av Cdte Espinar 864, Miraflores, T01-241 2951. Great selection of books, mostly in Spanish.

Ibero Librerías, Av Oscar R Benavides 500, T01-242 2798, Larco 199, T01-445 5520, and in **Larcomar**, Miraflores, www.iberolibros. com. Stocks Footprint books as well as a wide range of other titles.

Special Book Services, Av Angamos Oeste 301, Miraflores, T01-241 8490, www.sbs. com.pe. Holds stock of international books in several languages. Has a branch in Larcomar and others around the country.

Virrey chain has a great selection, but few in English: Pasaje Los Escribanos 107-115, Lima centre behind the Municipalidad, T01-427 5080, and Miguel Dasso 147, T01-440 0607, San Isidro, www.elvirrey.com.

For magazines, whether in downtown Lima or Miraflores, almost all street kiosks sell magazines in English. In front of **Café Haiti** by Parque Kennedy, men sell newspapers taken from arriving international flights; bargain hard.

Camping equipment

It's better to bring all camping and hiking gear from home. Camping gas (the most popular brand is **Doite**, which comes in small blue bottles) is available from any large hardware store or bigger supermarket, about US$3.

Alpamayo, Av Larco 345, Miraflores at Parque Kennedy, T01-445 1671. Mon-Fri 1000-1330, 1430-2000, Sat 1000-1400. Sleeping mats, boots, rock shoes, climbing gear, water filters, tents, backpacks, etc, very expensive but top-quality equipment. Owner speaks fluent English and offers good information.

Altamira, Arica 880, Parque Damert, behind Wong on Ovalo Gutiérrez, Miraflores, T01-445 1286. Sleeping bags, climbing gear, hiking gear and tents.

Camping Center, Av Benavides 1620, Miraflores, T01-242 1779, www.camping peru.com. Mon-Fri 1000-2000, Sat 1000-1400. Selection of tents, backpacks, stoves, camping and climbing gear.

El Mundo de las Maletas, Preciados 308, Higuereta-Surco, T01-449 7850. Open 0900-2200 daily for suitcase repairs.

Minex, Gral Borgoño 394 y Piura, Miraflores, T01-445 3923 (ring bell). Quality camping gear for all types of weather, made-to-order products as well.

Tatoo, CC Larcomar, locs 123-126, T01-242 1938 and CC Jockey Plaza loc 127, Av Javier Prado 4200, T01-436 6055, www.tatoo.ws. For top-quality imported ranges and own brands of equipment.

Todo Camping, Av Angamos Oeste 350, Miraflores, near Av Arequipa, T01-447 6279. Sells 100% deet, blue gas canisters, lots of accessories, tents, crampons and backpacks.

Handicrafts

Since so many artisans have come to Lima, it is possible to find any kind of handicraft in the capital. Miraflores is a good place for high-quality, expensive handicrafts; there are many shops on and around Av La Paz.

Agua y Tierra, Diez Canseco 298 y Alcanfores, Miraflores, T01-444 6980. Fine crafts and indigenous art.

Arte XXI, Av La Paz 678, Miraflores, T01-447 9777. Gallery and store for Peruvian handicrafts.

Artesanía Santo Domingo, Plaza Santo Domingo, by the church of that name, in centre, T01-428 9860. Good Peruvian crafts.

Centro Comercial El Alamo, corner of La Paz y Diez Canseco, Miraflores. *Artesanía* shops with good choice.

Cuy Arts & Crafts, Av Larco 929, Miraflores, T01-447 7652, http://cuy-arts.com. Slightly more unusual souvenirs, T-shirts, even Paddington Bears.

Dédalo, Paseo Sáenz Peña 295, Barranco, T01-477 0562. A labyrinthine shop selling furniture, jewellery and other items, as good as a gallery. It also has a nice coffee shop and has cinema shows.

Kuntur Huasi, Ocharan 182, Miraflores, opposite **Sol de Oro** hotel, look for the sign above the wall, T01-447 7173, kunturh@speedy.com.pe. English-speaking owners are very knowledgeable about Peruvian textiles; often have exhibitions of fine folk art and crafts.

La Casa de la Mujer Artesana, Juan Pablo Ferandini 1550 (Av Brasil cuadra 15), Pueblo Libre, T01-423 8840, www.casadelamujerartesana.com. Mon-Fri 0900-1300, 1400-1700. A cooperative run by the Movimiento Manuela Ramos, excellent quality work mostly from *pueblos jóvenes*.

Las Pallas, Cajamarca 212, Barranco, T01-477 4629. Mon-Sat 0900-1900. Very high-quality handicrafts, English, French and German spoken.

Luz Hecho a Mano, Berlín 399, Miraflores, T01-446 7098, www.luzhechoamano.com. Lovely handmade handbags, wallets and other leather goods including clothing that lasts for years and can be custom-made.

Jewellery

On C La Esperanza and on C La Paz, Miraflores, dozens of shops offer gold and silverware at very reasonable prices.

Ilaria, Av 2 de Mayo 308, San Isidro, T01-221 8575. Jewellery and silverware with interesting designs. There are other branches in Lima, Cuzco and Arequipa. Recommended.

Maps

Instituto Geográfico Nacional (IGN), Av Aramburú 1190, Surquillo, T01-618 9800, ext 119, www.ign.gob.pe. Mon-Fri 0800-1730. It has topographical maps of the whole country, mostly at 1:100,000, political and physical maps of all departments and satellite and aerial photographs. They also have a new series of tourist maps for trekking, eg of the Cordillera Blanca, the Cuzco area, at 1:250,000. You may be asked to show your passport when buying these maps. **South American Explorers** (see page 74) also stocks a selection of the most popular maps.

Lima 2000, Av Arequipa 2625, Lince (near the intersection with Av Javier Prado), T01-440 3486, www.lima2000.com.pe. Mon-Fri 0900-1300 and 1400-1800. Has an excellent street map of Lima (the only one worth buying), US$10, or US$14 as booklet. Provincial maps and a country road map as well. Good for road conditions and distances, perfect for driving or cycling. **South American Explorers** also stocks these maps.

Markets

Av Petit Thouars, in Miraflores. At blocks 51-54 (near Parque Kennedy, parallel to Av Arequipa) is a crafts market area, popularly called Museo Inca, but made up of several sections, each named after a pre-Hispanic civilization. This is the largest crafts arcade in Miraflores. All are open 7 days a week until late(ish).

Parque Kennedy, the main park of Miraflores, hosts a daily crafts market open 1700-2300.

Polvos Azules, on García Naranjo, La Victoria, just off Av Grau in the centre of town. This is the official black market of Lima. The normal connotations of a black market do not apply here as this establishment is an accepted part of Lima society, condoned by the government and frequented by people of all economic backgrounds. It's good for cameras, hiking boots, music and personal stereos. This is not a safe area, so be alert and put your money in your front pockets.

Supermarkets

Supermarket chains include E Wong, Metro, Plaza Vea, Tottus and the upmarket Vivanda. They are all well stocked and carry a decent supply of imported goods.

▲ Activities and tours

Lima p77, maps p72, p78, p89, p90 and p93

Cycling

See www.ciclismoperu.com.
Best Internacional, Av Cdte Espinar 320, Miraflores, T01-446 4044. Mon-Sat 1000-1400, 1600-2000. Leisure and racing bikes, also repairs, parts and accessories.
Biclas, Av Conquistadores 641, San Isidro, T01-440 0890. Mon-Fri 1000-1300, 1600-2000, Sat 1000-1300. Knowledgeable staff, tours possible, good selection of bikes, repairs and accessories, cheap airline boxes.
BikeMavil, Av Aviación 4023, Surco, T01-449 8435. Mon-Sat 0930-2100. Rents mountain and racing bikes, repairs, tours.
Bike Tours of Lima, Bolívar 150, Miraflores, T01-445 3172, www.biketoursoflima.com. Offer a variety of day tours through the city of Lima by bike, also bicycle rentals.
Casa Okuyama, Manco Cápac 590, La Victoria, T01-330 9131. Mon-Fri 0900-1300, 1415-1800, Sat 0900-1300. Repairs, parts, try here for 28-in tyres, excellent service.
Cycloturismo Peru, Jr Emilio Fernández 640, Santa Beatriz; T01-433 7981, www.ciclo turismo peru.com. Offers good-value cycling trips around Lima and beyond, as well as bike rental. The owner, Aníbal Paredes, speaks good English, is very knowledgeable and is the owner of **Mont Blanc Gran Hotel**.
Perú Bike, T01-260 8225, www.perubike. com. Experienced agency leading tours,

professional guiding, mountain bike school and workshop.
Willy Pro (Williams Arce), Av Angamos Este 2485, San Borja, T9-9919 2514. Mon-Sat 0800-2000. Selection of specialized bikes, helpful staff.

Diving

Peru Divers, Santa Teresa 486, Chorrillos, T01-251 6231, www.perudivers.com. Mon-Fri 0900-1900, Sat 0900-1700. Owner Lucho Rodríguez is a certified PADI instructor who offers certification courses, tours and a wealth of good information.

Horse racing

Hipódromo Monterrico. Tue and Thu evenings (1900) and Sat and Sun (1400) in summer, and Tue evening and Sat and Sun afternoons in winter.
National Paso Association, Bellavista 546, Miraflores, T01-447 633, www.ancpcpp. org.pe. For Caballos de Paso, which move in 4-step amble, extravagantly paddling their forelegs.

Mountaineering

Asociación de Andinismo de la Universidad de Lima, Universidad de Lima, Javier Prado Este s/n, T01-437 6767. Meetings on Wed 1800-2000, offers climbing courses.
Base Camp Perú, E Diez Canseco 234, T01-243 3628, Miraflores, www.basecamp peru.com. Open climbing gym and climbing excursions.
Club de Montañeros Américo Tordoya, Francisco Graña 378, Magdalena, T01-460 6101, www.clubamericotordoya.org. Meetings at 2000 on Thu, contact Gonzalo Menacho. Climbing excursions ranging from easy to difficult.
Club de Montañismo Camycam, see www.camycam.org for contact numbers. Expeditions, climbing, trekking, courses, guiding and help with community projects.
Trekking and Backpacking Club, Jr Huáscar 1152, Jesús María, Lima 11, T01-423 2515,

T01-99-773 1959 (mob), www.angelfire.com/mi2/ tebac. Sr Miguel Chiri Valle, treks arranged, including in the Cordillera Blanca.

Paragliding

Andean Trail Perú, T01-99-836 3436 (mob), www.andeantrailperu.com. For parapenting tandem flights, US$53, and courses, US$600 for 10 days. They also have a funday for US$120 to learn the basics of parapenting. Parapenting, trekking and kayaking in the Cuzco area can be arranged. Recommended.
Fly Adventure, Alfredo León 234, of 202, Miraflores, T01-241 5693, T99-754 2011, www.flyadventure.net. 15-min tandem flights over the cliffs, 1-day course and 7-day course. Also offer paragliding tours. Recommended.

Surfing

Focus, Leonardo Da Vinci 208, San Borja, T01-475 8459. Shaping factory and surfboards, know about local spots and conditions, rents boards.
Klimax, José González 488, Miraflores, T01-447 1685. New and second-hand boards, knowledgeable.

To buy Aussie-made boards, all sizes, contact **Segundo**, T99-902 7112 (mob), segundodurangarcia@hotmail.com.

Tour operators

Do not conduct business anywhere other than in the agency's office and insist on a written contract. Bus offices or the airport are not the places to arrange and pay for tours. You may be dealing with representatives of companies that either do not exist or who fall far short of what is paid for.

Most of those in Lima specialize in selling air tickets, or in setting up a connection in the place where you want to start a tour. Shop around and compare prices; also check all information carefully. It is best to use a travel agent in the town closest to the place you wish to visit; it is cheaper and they are more reliable.

Andean Tours, Schell 319, of 304-305, Miraflores, T01-241 1222, www.andean-tours.com. Recommended for bespoke arrangements.
AQP (Travex), Av Santa Cruz 621, Miraflores, T01-710 3900, www.saaqp.com.pe. Comprehensive service, tours offered throughout the country.
Aracari Travel Consulting, Schell 237, of 602, Miraflores, T01-651 2424, www.aracari.com. Regional tours throughout Peru, also 'themed' and activity tours, has a very good reputation.
Class Adventure Travel (CAT), San Martín 800, Miraflores, T01-444 1652, www.cat-travel.com/peru/information. Dutch-owned and run, CAT has offices in several Latin American countries and offers tailor-made travel solutions throughout the continent. Highly recommended.
Coltur, Av Reducto 1255, Miraflores, T01-615 5555, www.coltur.com.pe. Helpful, well- organized and experienced tours.
Condor Travel, Armando Blondet 249, San Isidro, T01-615 3000, www.condortravel.com. Peruvian HQ of highly-regarded, South America-wide travel company, offices in Cuzco, Arequipa, commitment to social responsibility with Misminay Project near Cuzco, and others.
Dasatariq, Jr Francisco Bolognesi 510, Miraflores, T01-513 4400, www.dasatariq.com. Also in Cuzco. Well-organized, helpful, with a good reputation.
Domiruth Travel Service, Av Petit Thouars 4305, T01-610 6022, www.domiruth.com.pe. Tours throughout Peru, from the mystical to adventure travel. See also **Peru 4x4 Adventures**, part of Domiruth, T01-610 6000, www.peru4x4adventures.com, for exclusive 4WD tours with German, English, Spanish, Italian and Portuguese-speaking drivers.
Ecocruceros, Av Arequipa 4964, of 202, Miraflores, T01-226 8530, www.islas palomino.com. Daily departures at 1000 from Plaza Grau in Callao to see the sea lions at Islas Palomino, 30-40 mins wet-suit swimming with guide, snack lunch, US$35

(take ID). Transfer from Lima US$12 (US$24 for 1 person).

Explorandes, C San Fernando 320, Miraflores, T01-715 2323, www.explorandes.com. Award-winning company. Offers a wide range of adventure and cultural tours throughout the country. Also offices in Cuzco and Huaraz.

Fertur Peru Travel, C Schell 485, Miraflores, T01-445 1760, and Jr Junín 211, Plaza de Armas, T01-427 1958 (USA/Canada T1-877-247 0055 toll free, UK T020-3002 3811), www.fertur-travel.com. Open 0900-1900. Siduith Ferrer de Vecchio, CEO of this agency, is highly recommended; she offers up-to-date, correct tourist information on a national level, but also great prices on national and international flights, discounts for those with ISIC and Youth cards and SAE members. Other services include flight reconfirmations, hotel reservations and transfers to and from the airport or bus stations. Also tours.

Il Tucano Peru, Elías Aguirre 633, Miraflores, T01-444 9361, 24-hr number T01-975 05375. Personalized tours for groups or individuals throughout Peru, also 4WD overland trips, 1st-class drivers and guides, good service. Recommended.

Info Perú, Jr de la Unión (Belén) 1066, of 102, T01-431 0117, www.infoperu.com.pe. Mon-Fri 0900-1800, Sat 0930-1400. Run by a group of women, ask for Laura Gómez, offering personalized programmes, hotel bookings, transport, free tourist information, sale of maps, books and souvenirs, English and French spoken.

InkaNatura Travel, Manuel Bañón 461, San Isidro, T01-203 5000, www.inkanatura.com. Also in Cuzco and Chiclayo, experienced

company offering good tours with knowledgeable guides, special emphasis on both sustainable tourism and conservation, especially in Manu and Tambopata, also birdwatching, and on the archaeology of all of Peru. Very helpful. Recommended.

Lima Mentor, T01-275 2986, www.lima mentor.com. Contact through web, phone or through hotels. An agency offering cultural tours of Lima using freelance guides in specialist areas (eg gastronomy, art, archaeology, Lima at night), entertaining, finding different angles from regular tours. Half-day tours US$50-55, full day US$90-110. Recommended.

Lima Tours, Jr Belén 1040, T01-619 6900, www.limatours.com.pe. Recommended for tours in the capital and around the country; new programmes include health and wellness tours.

Masi Travel Sudamérica, Porta 350, Miraflores, T01-446 9094, www.masitravel. com. Tours throughout Peru, plenty of information on the website. Contact Verónika Reategui for an efficient service.

Peru For Less, ASTA Travel Agent, Luis Garcia Rojas 240, Urb Humboldt, US office: T1-877-269 0309; UK office: T+44-203-002 0571; Peru (Lima) office: T273 2486, Cuzco T084-254800, www.peruforless. com. Will meet or beat any published rates on the internet from outside Peru. Good reports.

Peru Rooms, Av Dos de Mayo 1545, of 205, San Isidro, T422 3434, www.perurooms.com. Internet-based travel service offering 3- to 5-star packages throughout Peru, cultural, adventure and nature tourism. Often recommended.

Rutas del Peru SAC, Av Enrique Palacios 1110, Miraflores, T01-445 7249, www.rutasdelperu.com. Bespoke trips and overland expeditions in trucks.

Safe in Lima, Alfredo Silva 150, Barranco, T01-252 7330, www.safeinlima.com. Tailor-made trips for individuals and groups. Also a friendly hostel of the same name, see page 105.

Viajes Pacífico (Gray Line), Av La Mar 163, T01-610 1900, www.graylineperu.com. Expanded service with tours throughout Peru and within South America.

Víctor Travel Service, Jr de la Unión 1100, esq Av Uruguay 114, T01-332 1064, or T01-999 583303/T01-993 350095, www.victortravelservice.com. Tours throughout Peru, hotel, bus and air reservations, English spoken, very helpful with information, maps and plans (free), daily 0800-2000. Víctor Melgar Morales also acts as a private guide, contact on T01-782 0104, or through the above phone numbers, or victormelgarmorales@hotmail.com. See also **La Catedral del Pisco**, page 106.

Viracocha, Av Vasco Núñez de Balboa 191, Miraflores, T01-445 3986, peruviantours@ viracocha.com.pe. Very helpful, especially with flights, adventure, cultural, mystical and birdwatching tours.

Private guides
The **MITINCI** (Ministry of Industry Tourism, Integration and International Business) certifies guides and can provide a list. Most are members of **AGOTUR** (Asociación de Guías Oficiales de Turismo), Av La Paz 678, Miraflores (for correspondence only), www.agotur.com. Book in advance. Most guides speak a language other than Spanish.

◉ Transport

Lima and around *p77, maps p72, p78, p89, p90 and p93*
Air
Arrivals or departures flight information T01-511 6055, www.lap.com.pe. **Jorge Chávez Airport**, 16 km from the centre of Lima.

Global Net ATMs (accepting American Express, Visa, MasterCard and the Plus, Cirrus and Maestro systems), *casas de cambio* (money-changing kiosks) and a bank can be found in many parts of arrivals and departures. The exchange rates are marginally poorer than outside the terminal.

There are public telephones around the airport and a **Teléfonica** *locutorio*, daily 0700-2300. Internet facilities are more expensive than in the city. There are postal services.

The airport has offices of **iperú**, T01-574 8000, daily 24 hrs. Information desks can be found in the national foyer, the international foyer and on the 1st floor. There are also helpful desks in the international and national arrivals halls. There are many smart shops, places to eat and drink, including Starbucks, and, in international arrivals, mobile phone rentals. See listings above for hotels near Jorge Chávez.

For Transport to and from the airport, see Ins and outs, page 72.

Internal air services There are daily flights to most destinations (most options are given in the text below) but flights may be cancelled in the rainy season.

Airline offices

Domestic LAN, Av José Pardo 513, Miraflores, T01-213 8200, www.lan.com. **LC Busre**, Los Tulipanes 218, San Eugenio-Lince, T01-619 1300, www.lcbusre.com.pe. **Peruvian Airlines**, Av José Pardo 495, Miraflores, T01-716 6000, www.peruvian airlines.pe. **Star Perú**, Av Cdte Espinar 331, Miraflores, T01-705 9000, www.starperu.com. **Taca Perú**, Av Cdte Espinar 331, Miraflores, T01-511 8222, www.grupotaca.com.

International Aerolíneas Argentinas, Carnaval y Moreyra 370, p 1, San Isidro, T01-513 6565, ventasperu@aerolineasargentinas.com.pe. **Air France-KLM**, Av Alvarez Calderón 185, p 6, San Isidro, T01-415 0923, www.klm.com. **American Airlines**, Las Begonias 471, San Isidro, and Av Pardo 392 y Jr Independencia, T01-211 7000. **Avianca**, Av José Pardo 140, Miraflores, T01-445 6895 or T0800-51936. **Continental**, Av V A Belaúnde Via Principal 110 of 101, Edificio Real 5, San Isidro, and in the Hotel Marriott, Av Larco 1325, Miraflores, T01-712 9230 or T0800-70030. **Copa**, Canaval y Moreyra y Los Halcones, Centro Empresarial Torre

Chocavento of 105, T01-610 0810. **Delta**, Av V A Belaúnde 147 Via Principal 180, Edif Real 3, of 701, San Isidro, T01-211 9211. **Iberia**, Av Camino Real 390, p 9, San Isidro, T01-411 7800. **Lacsa**, Av 2 de Mayo 755, Miraflores, T01-444 7818. **LAN**, see above. **Lufthansa**, Av Jorge Basadre 1330, San Isidro, T01-442 4455, lufthansa@hansaperu.com. **Tame**, Av La Paz 1631, Miraflores, T01-422 6600.

Bus
Local

Av Arequipa runs 52 blocks between downtown Lima and Parque Kennedy in **Miraflores**. There is no shortage of public transport on this avenue; they have 'Todo Arequipa' on the windscreen. When heading towards downtown from Miraflores the window sticker should say 'Wilson/Tacna'. To get to Parque Kennedy from downtown look on the windshield for 'Larco/Schell/Miraflores', 'Chorrillos/Huaylas' or 'Barranco/Ayacucho'.

Lima's only urban freeway, Vía Expresa, runs from Plaza Grau in the centre of town, to the northern tip of **Barranco**. This 6-lane thoroughfare, locally known as *El Zanjón* (The Ditch), with the **Metropolitano** bus lane in the middle, is the fastest way to cross the city. Buses downtown for the Vía Expresa can be caught on Av Tacna, Av Wilson (also called Garcilaso de la Vega), Av Bolivia and Av Alfonso Ugarte.

The **Metropolitano** is a system of articulated buses running on dedicated lanes of the Vía Expresa/Paseo de la República (T01-203 9000, www.metro politano.com.pe). The **Estación Central** is in front of the **Sheraton** hotel. The southern section runs to Matellini in Chorrillos (estimated journey time 32 mins). For Miraflores take stations between Angamos and 28 de Julio; for **Barranco** the Bulevar station is 170 m from the plaza. The northern branch runs to Naranjal in Comas, a 34-min journey. Stations Estación Central to Ramón Castilla serve the city centre. Tickets are prepaid and rechargeable, from

S/.5-100, each journey is S/.1.50 (US$0.55). Buses run from 0600-2150 daily. From 0700-0930, 1700-2030 Mon-Fri an express service between Estación Central and Matellini calls at just 10 stations. Buses are packed in rush hour.

Long distance

There are many different bus companies, but the larger ones are better organized, leave on time and do not wait until the bus is full. For approximate prices, frequency and duration of trip, see destinations. Also see Getting around in Essentials, page 31, for general points on bus travel. **Note** In the weeks either side of 28/29 Jul (Independence), and of the Christmas/New Year holiday, it is practically impossible to get bus tickets out of Lima, unless you book in advance. Bus prices double at these times.

Companies with nationwide coverage include: Cruz del Sur, T01-311 5050 (telephone sales), www.cruzdelsur.com.pe. The main terminal is at Av Javier Prado 1109, La Victoria, T01-225 6163, with *Cruzero* and *Cruzero Suite* services (luxury buses) and *Imperial* service (quite comfortable buses and periodic stops for food and bathroom breaks, a cheap option with a quality company) to most parts of Peru. Another terminal is at Jr Quilca 531, Lima centre, T01-431 5125, for *Imperial* and *Ideal* (economy) services to **Arequipa**, **Ayacucho**, **Chiclayo**, **Cuzco**, **Huancayo**, **Huaraz**, and **Trujillo**. There are sales offices throughout the city, eg on Av 28 de Julio.

Ormeño and its affiliated bus companies depart from and arrive at Av Carlos Zavala 177, Lima centre, T01-427 5679; also Av Javier Prado Este 1059, Santa Catalina, T01-472 1710, www.grupo-ormeno.com.pe. **Ormeño** offers *Royal Class* and *Business Class* service to certain destinations. These buses are very comfortable with bathrooms, hostess, etc. They mostly arrive and depart from the Javier Prado terminal, but the Carlos Zavala terminal is the best place to get information and buy any Ormeño ticket. **Cial**, República de

Panamá 2469, T01-265 8121, and Paseo de la República 646, T01-717 8322, www.expresocial.com, has national coverage. **Flores**, with terminals at Av Paseo de le República y Av 28 de Julio, Av Paseo de le República 627, T01-423 6069, and Av 28 de Julio 1204 y J Gálvez, T01-332 1212, has departures to many parts of the country, especially the **south**. Some of its services are good quality.

Other companies include: **Oltursa**, Aramburú 1160, San Isidro, T01-708 5000, www.oltursa.pe, a reputable company offering top-end services to **Nazca**, **Arequipa** and destinations in **northern Peru**, mainly at night. **Tepsa**, Javier Prado Este 1091, La Victoria, T01-202 3535, www.tepsa. com.pe, also at Av Paseo de la República 151-A, T01-427 5642, and Av Carlos Izaguirre 1400, Los Olivos, T01-386 5689 (not far from the airport, good for those short of time for a bus connection after landing in Lima), offers services to the north as far as **Tumbes** and the south to **Tacna**.

Transportes **Chanchamayo**, Av Manco Cápac 1052, La Victoria, T01-265 6850, to **Tarma**, **San Ramón** and **La Merced**. **Ittsa**, Paseo de la República 809, T01-332 1665, good service to the north, **Chiclayo**, **Piura** and **Tumbes**. Transportes León de Huánuco, Av 28 de Julio 1520, La Victoria, T01-424 3893, daily to **Huánuco**, **Tingo María** and **Pucallpa**. **Línea**, Paseo de la República 959, Lima centre, T01-424 0836, www.transportes linea.com.pe, also has a terminal at Av Carlos Izaguirre 1058, Los Olivos (see above under Tepsa), T01-522 3295, offers among the best services to destinations in the **north**. **Horna**, Paseo de la República 1045, to **Trujillo**, **Cajamarca**, **Cajabamba** and **Huamachuco**. **Móvil**, Av Paseo de La República 749, Lima Centre near the national stadium, T01-716 8000 (has a 2nd terminal at Los Olivos), www.moviltours. com.pe, to **Huaraz** and **Chiclayo** by *bus cama*, and **Chachapoyas** (should you want to go straight through). **Soyuz**, Av México 333, T01-205 2380, www.soyuz.com.pe, to **Ica** every 7 mins, well-organized. To **Huaraz**, there are various levels of bus service: **Cavassa**, Raimondi 129, Lima Centre, T01-421 3200. Also **Julio César**, José Gálvez 562, La Victoria, T01-424 8060, www.transportes juliocesar.com (sales office at Av Larco 101, **CC Caracol**, Miraflores, T01-241 6839). It is recommended to arrive in Huaraz and then use local transportation to points beyond.

Cromotex, Av Nicolás Arriola 898, Santa Catalina, Av Paseo de La República 659, T01-424 7575, www.cromotex.com.pe, offers services to **Cuzco** and **Arequipa**.

For bus or colectivo to **Pachacámac** from Lima: from the Pan American Highway (southbound) take a combi with a sticker in the window reading 'Pachacámac/Lurín' (US$0.85). Let the driver know you want to get off at the ruins. A taxi will cost approximately US$5.50, but if you don't ask the driver to wait for you (an extra cost), finding another to take you back to Lima may be a bit tricky. **Mirabús**, T01-242 6699, www.mirabusperu.com, goes from Parque Kennedy Tue-Sun at 1000 to Pachacámac and back with a stop at Pántanos de Villa wildlife sanctuary, US$19, 3½-hr tour. **Mirabús** runs other, open-top bus tours of the city. For other organized tours, contact one of the tour agencies listed above.

Warning The area around the bus terminals is very unsafe; thefts and assaults are more common in this neighbourhood than elsewhere in the city. You are strongly advised either to take a bus from a company that has a terminal away from the Carlos Zavala area (eg **Cruz del Sur**, **Oltursa**), or to take a taxi to and from your bus. Make sure your luggage is well guarded and put on the right bus. It is also important not to assume that buses leave from the place where you bought the tickets. Finally, always check your change very carefully when paying in cash.

Car rental

Most companies have an office at the airport, where you can arrange everything and pick up and leave the car. It is recommended to test-drive before signing the contract as quality varies. It can be much cheaper to rent a car in a town in the sierra for a few days than to drive from Lima; also companies don't have a collection service. Cars can be hired from: **Avis**, T01-434 1111, www.viperu.com; **Budget**, T01-204 4400, www.budget peru.com; **Hertz**, www.hertz.com; **Localiza**, T01-447 7474, www.localiza.com; **National**, T01-578 7878, www.nationalcar.com.pe. **Paz Rent A Car**, Av Diez Canseco 319, of 15, Miraflores, T01-446 4395, T01-9993 9853 (mob), www.perupaz consortium.com. Prices range from US$35 to US$85 depending on type of car. Make sure that your car is in a locked garage at night.

Taxi

The following are taxi fares for some of the more common routes, give or take a sol. **From downtown Lima to:** Parque Kennedy (Miraflores), US$3.55; San Isidro, US$3.20; Museo de la Nación, US$3.20. South American Explorers, US$3.55. Barranco, US$4.25.

From Miraflores (Parque Kennedy) to: Museo de la Nación, US$2.50; Archaeology Museum, US$3.20; Barranco, US$4.

By law, all taxis must have the vehicle's registration number painted on the side. They are often white or yellow, but can come in any colour, size or make. Licensed and phone taxis are safest, but if hailing a taxi on the street, local advice is to look for an older driver rather than a youngster. There are several reliable phone taxi companies, which can be called for immediate service, or booked in advance; prices are 2-3 times more than ordinary taxis; eg to the airport US$12.50-15, to suburbs US$9-10. Some are **Moli Taxi**, T01-479 0030; **Taxi Real**, T01-470 6263, www.taxireal.com; **Taxi Seguro**, T01-241 9292, www.taxiseguro.com.pe; **Taxi Tata**, T01-274 5151; **TCAM**, run by Carlos Astacio, T99-983 9305, safe, reliable. If hiring a taxi by the hour, agree on price beforehand, eg US$7-9.

Recommended, knowledgeable drivers: **César A Canales N**, T01-436 6184, T99-687

3310 (mob) or through **Home Perú** (see Sleeping, page 103), only speaks Spanish, reliable. **Hugo Casanova Morella**, T01-485 7708 (he lives in La Victoria), for city tours, travel to the airport, etc. **Mónica Velásquez Carlich**, T01-425 5087, T99-943 0796 (mob), vc_monica@hotmail.com. For airport pick-ups, tours, Speaks English, most helpful. **Note** Drivers don't expect tips; give them small change from the fare.

Train

Service on the Central Railway to **Huancayo** has been revived as a tourist route. Details are given under Huancayo, page 556.

⊕ Directory

Lima and around *p77, maps p72, p78, p89, p90 and p93*

Banks

Main banks' services are given in Essentials, under Money (see page 55). **BCP**, Jr Lampa 499, Lima centre (main branch), Av Larco at Pasaje Tarata, Miraflores, and others. **BBVA Continental**, corner of Av Larco and Av Benavides, Miraflores, and corner of Av Larco and Pasaje Tarata (this branch changes TCs), Jr Cusco 286, Lima centre near Plaza San Martín. **Banco Financiero**, Av Ricardo Palma 278, near Parque Kennedy (main branch). Cash only, GlobalNet ATM. **Banco Santander Central Hispano (BSCH)**, Av Augusto Tamayo 120, San Isidro (main branch), Av Pardo 482 and Av Larco 479, Miraflores. ATM for Visa/Plus and MasterCard. **Citibank**, Av Javier Prado Oeste 127, Miraflores, Mon-Fri 0900-1800, Sat 0930-1300. Red Unicard and GlobalNet ATMs; cash withdrawals on Visa cards and changes cash. **HSBC**, 28 de Julio y Av Larco, Miraflores, T01-616 4722, Mon-Fri 0900-1800, Sat 0900-1230, changes cash, Red Unicard ATM. **Interbank** has agencies everywhere, open Mon-Fri till 1800, and these will exchange TCs, including in **Vivanda** supermarkets, open till 2100. **Scotiabank**,

Av Diagonal 176 on Parque Kennedy, Av José Pardo 697, Miraflores, and others, for MasterCard cash withdrawals.

In Barranco there are branches of **Interbank**, **BBVA** and **Scotiabank** on Av Grau, with ATMs, and there is a **Scotiabank** ATM in the Municipalidad.

Exchange houses

There are many *casas de cambio* on and around Jr Ocoña off the Plaza San Martín. On the corner of Ocoña and Jr Camaná is a large concentration of *cambistas* (street changers) with huge wads of US$, euro and soles in one hand and a calculator in the other. They should be avoided. Changing money on the street should only be done with official street changers wearing an identity card with a photo. This card doesn't automatically mean that they are legitimate but you're less likely to have a problem. Around Parque Kennedy and down Av Larco in Miraflores are official *cambistas* with an ID card and a green vest. In 2010 there was no real advantage in changing money on the street. There are a few places on Jr de la Unión at Plaza San Martín that will accept worn, ripped and old bills, but the exchange will be terrible. A repeatedly recommended *casa de cambio* is **LAC Dolar**, Jr Camaná 779, 1 block from Plaza San Martín, p 2, T01-428 8127, also at Av La Paz 211, Miraflores, T01-242 4069. Open Mon-Sat 1000-1800, helpful, safe, fast, reliable, 2% commission on cash and TCs (Amex, Citicorp, Thomas Cook, Visa), will come to your hotel if you're in a group. Another recommended *casa de cambio* is **Virgen P Socorro**, Jr Ocoña 184, T01-428 7748. Open daily 0830-2000, safe, reliable and friendly. In Miraflores, *casas de cambio* include: Av Larco 657 (with internet, phones and Western Union); **Finserva**, Javier Prado Oeste 142; **MSB**, Av Larco y San Martín.

For credit card companies, see Essentials, page 56. **Moneygram**, Ocharan 260, Miraflores, T01-447 4044. Safe and reliable agency for sending and receiving money.

Locations throughout Lima and the provinces. Exchanges most world currencies and TCs.

Cultural centres

Alianza Francesa, Av Arequipa 4595, Miraflores, T01-446 5524, www.alianz afrancesalima. edu.pe. Various cultural activities, library. **Casa de la Literatura Peruana**, Ancash 207, behind Palacio de Gobierno, T01-426 2573, www.casadela literatura.gob.pe. Library, exhibitions, readings and cultural events related to Peruvian writers. **CCPUCP** (cultural centre of the Universidad Católica), Camino Real 1075, San Isidro, T01-616 1616, http://cultural.pucp. edu.pe. Excellent theatre (tickets US$7.15), European art films (US$1.45 Mon-Wed), galleries, good café and a bookshop selling art and literature titles. Recommended. **Centro Cultural Peruano Japonés**, Av Gregorio Escobedo 803, Jesús María, T01-463 0606, postmast@ apjp.org.pe. Has a concert hall, cinema, galleries, museum of Japanese immigration, cheap and excellent restaurant, lots of activities. Recommended. **Goethe Institute**, Jr Nazca 722, Jesús María, T01-433 3180, www.goethe.de. Mon-Fri 0800-2000, library, German papers. **Instituto Cultural Peruano-Norteamericano**, Jr Cusco 446, Lima Centre, T01-706 7000, with library. Central office at Av Angamos Oeste 160, Miraflores, www.icpna. edu.pe. Theatre productions, modern dance performances, etc. Also Spanish lessons; see Language schools, below.

Embassies and consulates

During the summer, most embassies open only in the morning. **Australia**, Av Víctor Andrés Belaúnde 147, Vía Principal 155, Ed Real 3, of 1301, San Isidro, Lima 27, T01-222 8281, info.peru@austrade.gov.au. **Austria**, Av República de Colombia 643, p 5, San Isidro, T01-442 0503, lima-ob@bmeia.gv.at. **Belgian Consulate**, Angamos Oeste 380, Miraflores, T01-241 7566, www.diplomatie.

be/lima. Bolivian Consulate, Los Castaños 235, San Isidro, T01-442 3836, embajada@boliviaenperu.com, 0900-1330, 24 hrs for visas (except those requiring clearance from La Paz). **Brazil**, José Pardo 850, Miraflores, T01-512 0830, www.embajadabrasil.org.pe, Mon-Fri 0930-1300. **Canada**, Libertad 130, Casilla 18-1126, Lima, T01-444 4015, lima@ dfaitmaeci.gc.ca. **Chilean Consulate**, Javier Prado Oeste 790, San Isidro, T01-710 2211, embchile@mail.cosapidata.com.pe, open 0900-1300, need appointment. **Ecuadorean Consulate**, Las Palmeras 356, San Isidro (6th block of Av Javier Prado Oeste), T01-212 4161, embajada@mecuador peru.org.pe. **French Embassy**, Arequipa 3415, San Isidro, T01-215 8400, www.ambafrance-pe.org. **Germany**, Av Arequipa 4202, Miraflores, T01-212 5016, emergency number T99-927 8338, www.lima.diplo.de. Israel, Natalio Sánchez 125, p 6, Santa Beatriz, T01-418 0500, http://lima.mfa. gov.il. **Italy**, Av Giusepe Garibaldi 298, Jesús María, T01-463 2727. **Japan**, Av San Felipe 356, Jesús María, T463 0000. **Netherlands Consulate**, Torre Parque Mar, Av José Larco 1301, p 13, Miraflores, T01-213 9800, info@nlgovlim.com, open Mon-Fri 0900-1200. **New Zealand Consulate**, Los Nogales 510, p 3, San Isidro, T01-422 7491, alfonsorey1@gmail.com, open Mon-Fri 0830-1300, 1400-1700. **Spain**, Jorge Basadre 498, San Isidro, T01-212 5155, open 0900-1300. **Sweden**, C La Santa María 130, San Isidro, T01-442 8905, konslima@ speedy.com.pe. **Switzerland**, Av Salaverry 3240, Magdalena, Lima 17, T01-264 0305, www.eda.admin.ch/lima. **UK**, Torre Parque Mar, p 22, T01-617 3000, www.british embassy.gov.uk/peru, open 1300-2130 (Dec-Apr to 1830 Mon and Fri, and Apr-Nov to 1830 Fri), good for security information and newspapers. **USA**, Av Encalada block 17, Surco, T01-618 2000, for emergencies after hours T01-434 3032, http://lima.usembassy. gov. The consulate is in the same building.

Emergencies
See page 49 in Essentials.

Immigration
Migraciones, Digemin, Av España 730, Breña, Lima, T01-417 6900/433 0731, www.digemin.gob.pe, Mon-Fri 0800-1300. Immigration procedures are described on page 66. Provides new entry stamps if passport is lost or stolen.

Internet
Lima is completely inundated with internet cafés, so you will have absolutely no problem finding one regardless of where you are. An hour will cost you US$0.60-0.90.

Language schools
Conexus, Av Paseo de la República 3195, of 1002, San Isidro, T01-421 5642, www.conexusinstitute.com. Reasonably priced and effective. **El Sol School of Languages**, Grimaldo del Solar 469, Miraflores, T01-242 7763, http://elsol. idiomasperu.com. US$20 per hr for private tuition, also small groups. Family homestays and volunteer programmes available. **Hispana**, San Martín 377, Miraflores, T446 3045, www.hispanaidiomas. com. 5-day travellers' programme and other courses, afternoon cultural activities. **Instituto Cultural Peruano-Norteamericano**, see Cultural centres, above. Classes Mon-Fri from 0900 to 1100, US$80 per month, no private classes offered. **Instituto de Idiomas** (Pontífica Universidad Católica del Perú), Av Camino Real 1037, San Isidro, T01-442 8761. Classes Mon-Fri 1100-1300, private lessons possible. Recommended.

Independent teachers
Enquire about rates: **Srta Susy Arteaga**, T01-534 9289, T99-989 7271 (mob), susyarteaga@hotmail.com, or susyarteaga@ yahoo.com. Recommended. **Srta Patty Félix**, T01-521 2559, patty_fel24@yahoo.com. **Luis Villanueva**, T01-247 7054, www.acspanish classes.com. Flexible, reliable, helpful.

Laundry
There are *lavanderías* (laundromats) all over Lima. Some charge by piece (expensive), others by weight. Many have a self-service option. Next-day service is the norm if you've left laundry for them to wash. Most of the hotels in the higher price range offer laundry but tend to be very expensive.

Medical services
It is worth contacting your consulate for recommendations for the type of medical attention you need.

Hospitals and clinics
Backpackers Medical Care, T99-735 2668, backpackersmc@yahoo.com. The 'backpackers' medic', Dr Jorge Bazán, has been recommended as professional and good value, about US$13 per consultation. **Centro Anti-Rabia de Lima**, Jr Austria 1300, Breña, T01-425 6313. Open Mon-Sat 0830-1830. **Clínica Anglo Americano**, Av Salazar 3rd block, San Isidro, a few blocks from Ovalo Gutiérrez, T01-616 8900, www.clinanglo americana.com.pe. Stocks Yellow Fever and Tetanus. **Clínica del Niño**, Av Brasil 600 at 1st block of Av 28 de Julio, Breña, T01-330 0066, www.isn.gob.pe. **Clínica Internacional**, Jr Washington 1471 y Paseo Colón (9 de Diciembre), downtown Lima, T01-619 6161. Good, clean and professional, consultations up to US$35, no inoculations. **Clínica Padre Luis Tezza**, Av El Polo 570, Monterrico, T01-610 5050, www.clinicatezza. com.pe. Clinic specializing in a wide variety of illnesses/disorders, etc, expensive; for stomach or intestinal problems. **Clínica Ricardo Palma**, Av Javier Prado Este 1066, San Isidro, T01-224 2224, www.crp.com.pe. For general medical consultations, English spoken. **Instituto de Medicina Tropical**, Av Honorio Delgado near the Pan American Highway in the Cayetano Heredia Hospital, San Martín de Porres, T01-482 3903, www.upch.edu.pe/tropicales/s. Good for check-ups after jungle travel. Recommended. **Instituto Médico Lince**, León Velarde 221,

near 17th and 18th blocks of Av Arenales, Lince, T01-471 2238. **International Health Department**, at Jorge Chávez airport, T01-517 1845. Open 24 hrs a day for vaccinations.

Pharmacies

Pharmacy chains are modern, well-stocked, safe and professional. They can be found throughout the city, often in or next to supermarkets. Some offer 24-hr delivery service. Among the most prominent chains are **Boticas Fasa**, T01-619 0000 for delivery, www.boticasfasa.com.pe; **Boticas Arcángel**, **Boticas BTL**, **Inkafarma** and **Salud**.

Post

The central post office is on Jr Camaná 195 in the centre of Lima near the Plaza de Armas. Open Mon-Fri 0730-1900 and Sat 0730-1600. Poste Restante is in the same building but is considered unreliable. In Miraflores the main post office is on Av Petit Thouars 5201 (same hours). There are many small branches around Lima, but they are less reliable. For express service: **EMS**, next to central post office in downtown Lima, T01-533 2020, is Serpost's courier service. **DHL**, **UPS** and **Federal Express** have branches throughout the city. When receiving parcels from other countries that weigh in over 1 kg, they will be automatically sent to one of Lima's 2 customs post offices. Take your passport and a lot of patience as the process can (but not always) take a long time: Teodoro Cárdenas 267, Santa Beatriz (12th block of Av Arequipa); and Av Tomás Valle, Los Olivos (near the Panamerican Highway). **Note** Long trousers must be worn when going to these offices.

Prison visits

Visits to the **Establecimiento Penitenciario de Mujeres Chorrillos Santa Mónica** (women's prison) in the district of Chorrillos are easy and much appreciated by the inmates, both Peruvian and foreign. You must bring your passport and give the name of someone you're visiting (for the current list, check with your embassy for prisoners from your own country, or ask at **South American Explorers**, who have some details). You are permitted to bring food (up to 1 kg of fruit, but none that ferments), toiletries, magazines, books, etc. Visiting times are 0900-1300 and 1400-1600 on Sat for men and Wed and Sun for women. Shoes that have any kind of heel are not permitted (nor are boots) and women must wear skirts below the knee which, if you don't have one, can be rented across the street from the prison. Men must wear long trousers. Visits are also possible to the men's prisons of **Callao** and **Lurigancho**.

Telephone

Easiest to use are the many independent phone offices, *locutorios*, all over the city. They take phone cards, which can be bought in *locutorios*, or in the street nearby. There are payphones all over the city. Some accept coins, some only phone cards and some both.

Contents

Footprint features

At a glance

⊖ **Getting around** On foot,
on horseback, by bus and taxi,
by train to Machu Picchu.

◎ **Time required** 1 week minimum
to 4 weeks for the whole zone.

☼ **Weather** Wettest months are
Nov-Apr; Jun-Sep is clear and sunny
by day, cold at night; Apr-May is
very pleasant.

⊗ **When not to go** If you don't
like crowds avoid high season in
Jun-Sep. Don't try to hike the Inca
Trail in Feb – it's closed.

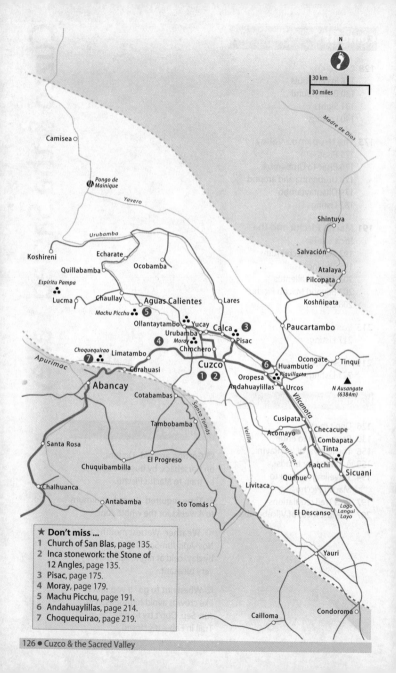

★ **Don't miss ...**
1 Church of San Blas, page 135.
2 Inca stonework: the Stone of
   12 Angles, page 135.
3 Pisac, page 175.
4 Moray, page 179.
5 Machu Picchu, page 191.
6 Andahuaylillas, page 214.
7 Choquequirao, page 219.

Cuzco stands at the head of the Sacred Valley of the Incas and is the jumping-off point for the Inca Trail and famous Inca city of Machu Picchu. It's not surprising, therefore, that this is the prime destination for the vast majority of Peru's visitors. In fact, what was once an ancient Inca capital is now the 'gringo' capital of the entire continent. And it's easy to see why. There are Inca ruins aplenty, as well as fabulous colonial architecture, stunning scenery, great trekking, river rafting and mountain biking, beautiful textiles and other traditional handicrafts – all within easy reach of the nearest cappuccino or comfy hotel room.

The Spaniards transformed the centre of a magnificent Inca civilization into a jewel of colonial achievement. Yet the city today is not some dead monument; its history breathes through the stones. The Quechua people bring the city to life, with a combination of pre-Hispanic and Christian beliefs, and every visitor is made welcome.

Starting your visit to the Cuzco region outside the city has many advantages. Staying a day or two in the valley of the Urubamba river will give you time to acclimatize to the shortage of oxygen at these altitudes. And, as nowhere is very far from the city, you can easily nip into town for any necessities. At Ollantaytambo and Pisac you will see Inca ruins and terraced hillsides without the overlay of the Spanish conquest. Then, when you are fit and ready, you can make your own assault on Cuzco and all its churches, museums, pubs, clubs and shops, not to mention the many festivals that are held throughout the year. If city life is not for you, there is no shortage of adventure. The huge influx of visitors has encouraged the opening of new trails, some for walking, some for biking, the latest hot spot being the 'lost city' of Choquequirao.

Cuzco city

→ *Colour map 5, A5. Population 275,000. Altitude 3310 m.*

Since there are so many sights to see in Cuzco city, not even the most ardent tourist would be able to visit them all. For those with limited time, or for those who want a whistle-stop tour, a list of must-sees would comprise: the combination of Inca and colonial architecture at Qoricancha; the huge Inca ceremonial centre of Sacsayhuaman; the paintings of the Last Supper and the 1650 earthquake in the cathedral; the main altar of La Compañía de Jesús; the pulpit of San Blas; the high choir at San Francisco; the monstrance at La Merced; and the view from San Cristóbal. If you have the energy, catch a taxi up to the White Christ and watch the sunset as you look out upon one of the most fascinating cities in the world. If you visit one museum make it the Museo Inka; it has the most comprehensive collection. ▶▶ *For listings, see pages 140-174.*

Ins and outs

Getting there

Most travellers arriving from Lima will do so by air. No flights arrive in Cuzco at night. The airport is at Quispiquilla, near the bus terminal, 1.6 km southeast of the centre. For airport information T084-222611/601. You can book a hotel at the airport through a travel agency, but this is not really necessary. Many representatives of hotels and travel agencies operate in the baggage retrieval area, offering transport to the hotel with which they are associated. If you haven't booked in advance, take your time to choose your hotel, at the price you can afford. Also in baggage retrieval are mobile phone rentals, ATMs, **LAC Dollar** money exchange, an **Oxyshot** oxygen sales stand and an **iperú** office. There are phone booths, restaurant and cafeteria at the airport. There is also a Tourist Protection Bureau desk. Do not forget to pay the airport tax at the appropriate desk before departure. A taxi to and from the airport costs US$2-3.50 (US$7.25 from official taxi desk). Colectivos to the centre cost US$0.30 from outside the airport car park.

All long-distance buses arrive and leave from the Terminal Terrestre, Avenida Vallejo Santoni, block 2 (Prolongación Pachacútec), in Ttio district. A colectivo from the centre costs US$0.30; a taxi US$1. Platform tax US$0.35. Transport to your hotel is not a problem as bus company representatives are often on hand.

There is one train station in Cuzco, **Estación Wanchac** ① *C Pachacútec, T084-581414,* for the **PerúRail** service to Juliaca and Puno. The office here offers direct information and ticket sales for all **PerúRail** services. When arriving in Cuzco, a tourist bus meets the train to take visitors to hotels. Machu Picchu trains do not leave from the city, but from **Poroy** (PerúRail), over the hill from Cuzco on the road to Urubamba, or from Ollantaytambo (see page 179), **Inca Rail** ① *Av Sol 613, T084-233030, www.incarail.com.pe,* **Machu Picchu Train** ① *Av Sol 576, T084-221199, www.machupicchutrain.com,* and **PerúRail** services. There is a sales office for **PerúRail** ① *Plaza de Armas, Portal de Carnes 214, T084-260809, cuscoplaza@perurail.com.* ▶▶ *See Transport, page 169. For trains to Machu Picchu, see page 194.*

Getting around

The centre of Cuzco is small and is easily explored on foot. Bear in mind, however, that at this altitude walking up some of the city's steep cobbled streets may leave you out of breath, so you'll need to take your time. It is even possible to walk up to Sacsayhuaman, but a better idea is to take a combi to Tambo Machay and walk back downhill to town via

Qenqo and Sacsayhuaman. Combis are the main form of public transport in the city: well-organized, cheap and safe. Taxis are also cheap and recommended when arriving by air, train or bus. If you wish to explore this area on your own, Road Map (*Hoja de ruta*) No 10 is excellent. You can get it from the **Touring y Automóvil Club del Perú**, see page 171. There are very few good maps of Cuzco available. ▸▸ *See Transport, page 169.*

Tourist information

Official **tourist office** ① *Portal Mantas 117-A, next to La Merced church, T084-263176, daily 0800-1830, closed Sun afternoon.* There are also **iperú tourist information desks** ① *airport, T084-237364, open when flights arrive and depart; Av Sol 103, of 102, Galerías Turísticas, T084-252974, daily 0830-1930.* **Dircetur** ① *Plaza Túpac Amaru Mz 1 Lte 2, Wanchac, T084-223761, Mon-Fri 0800-1300,* gives out a good map. **South American Explorers** ① *Cusco Clubhouse, Atocsaycuchi 670, T084-245484, www.saexplorers.org, Mon-Fri 0930-1700, Sat 0930-1300,* is an excellent resource for the traveller. It's worth making the climb up the steps to the large new clubhouse which has a garden. They provide great information on the Cuzco area including a comprehensive map of the city and area, an extensive English-language library, expedition reports, weekly events, local discounts and free internet for members, phone and mail service and equipment storage. They also have a recycling centre, rooms for rent, practical advice on responsible tourism and a volunteer resource centre. Their leaflet *Enjoy Cusco Safely* is invaluable (for more advice see page 58). They are also in Lima, see page 74.

Safety

If you need a *denuncia* (a report for insurance purposes, available from the Banco de la Nación), the **tourist police** ① *C Saphi 510, T084-249665/221961,* will type it out. Always go to the police when robbed, even though it will take a bit of time. Police patrol the streets, trains and stations, but one should still be vigilant. On no account walk back to your hotel after dark from a bar or club, as muggings do occur. For safety's sake, pay the US$1 taxi fare, but not just any taxi. Ask the club's doorman to get a licensed taxi for you (see Taxis, page 171).

Other areas in which to take care include Santa Pedro market, the San Cristóbal area and at out-of-the-way ruins. **Indecopi (Consumer Protection Bureau)** ① *Av Manco Inca 209, Wanchac, T084-252987, mmarroquin@indecopi.gob.pe, toll free T0800-44040 (24-hr hotline, not available from pay phones),* protects the consumer rights of all tourists and helps with any problems or complaints. They can be helpful in dealing with tour agencies, hotels or restaurants.

Permission to enter

A combined entry ticket to 16 of the main historical and cultural sites in and around Cuzco, called the **Boleto Turístico del Cusco (BTC)**, costs US$45/€33.50 (S/.130) and is valid for 10 days. It is payable in soles only. The 16 sites are: Municipal Exposición de Arte Contemporáneo, Museo Histórico Regional (Casa Garcilaso), Museo de Arte Popular, Museo de Sitio Qoricancha (but not Qoricancha itself), Centro Qosqo de Arte Nativo and Monumento Pachacútec in Cuzco city; the archaeological sites of Sacsayhuaman, Qenqo, Puka Pukara and Tambo Machay; the archaeological sites of Pisac, Ollantaytambo, Chinchero and Moray in the Sacred Valley; and the archaeological sites of Tipón and Piquillacta, southeast of Cuzco. A two-day ticket, costing US$24/€18 (S/.70), allows entry to Sacsayhuaman, Qenqo, Puka Pukara and Tambo Machay, or Pisac, Ollantaytambo, Chinchero and Moray. No individual tickets are available, except to Moray, Tipón and Piquillacta, which cost US$3.60 (S/.10) each.

The BTC can be bought at the **OFEC office** (Casa Garcilaso), Plaza Regocijo, esquina Calle Garcilaso, T084-226919, Monday-Saturday 0800-1600, Sunday 0800-1200, or **Cosituc**, Av Sol 103 of 102 (Galerías Turísticas of the Municipalidad), T084-261465, www.cosituc.gob.pe, Monday-Saturday 0800-1800, Sunday 0800-1300, or at any of the sites included in the ticket. For students with a green ISIC card, the BTC costs US$24 (S/.70), which is only available at the OFEC office (Casa Garcilaso) upon presentation of the student card. Take your ISIC card when visiting the sites, as some may ask to see it.

Entrance tickets for Museo Inka (Palacio del Almirante), Santo Domingo/ Qoricancha and La Merced are sold separately, while the cathedral (including the churches of El Triunfo and La Sagrada Familia), La Compañía, Templo de San Blas and the Museo de Arte Religioso del Arzobispado are included on a religious buildings ticket costing US$17.75 (S/.50), valid for 10 days. Each of these sites may be visited individually.

All sites are crowded on Sundays. Photography is not allowed in the churches and museums.

Machu Picchu ruins and Inca Trail entrance tickets are sold at the **Instituto Nacional de Cultura (INC)**, Av de la Cultura in ex-Hotel Fiori, T084-236061, Monday-Friday 0700-1600, Saturday 0700-1300, or, as of late 2010, online: www.inc-cusco.gob.pe (site under construction in October 2010).

Background

The ancient Inca capital is said to have been founded around AD 1100. According to the central Inca creation myth, the Sun sent his son, Manco Cápac, and the Moon sent her daughter, Mama Ocllo, to spread culture and enlightenment throughout the dark, barbaric lands. They emerged from the icy depths of Lake Titicaca and began their journey in search of a place to found their kingdom. They were ordered to head north from the lake until a golden staff they carried could be plunged into the ground for its entire length. The soil of the altiplano was so thin that they had to travel as far as the valley of Cuzco where, on the mountain of Huanacauri, the staff fully disappeared and the soil was found to be suitably fertile. This was the sign they were looking for. They named this place Cuzco, meaning 'navel of the earth' according to popular legend (there is no linguistic basis for this).

Today, the city's beauty cannot be overstated. It is a fascinating mix of Inca and colonial Spanish architecture: churches, monasteries and convents and pre-Columbian ruins are interspersed with hotels, bars and restaurants that have sprung up to cater for the hundreds of thousands of tourists. Almost every central street has remains of Inca walls, arches and doorways and many are lined with Inca stonework, now serving as the foundations for more modern dwellings.

Cuzco has developed into a major commercial centre of 326,000 inhabitants, a large proportion of whom are Quechua. While the city is spreading over the hills that surround it, its heart, laid out much as it was in Inca times, is still discernible. The Incas conceived their capital in the shape of a puma and this can be seen from above, with the Río Tullumayo forming the spine, Sacsayhuaman the head, and the main city centre the body. The best place for an overall view of the Cuzco Valley is from the puma's head – the top of the hill of Sacsayhuaman.

Sights

Plaza de Armas and around

The heart of the city in Inca days was *Huacaypata* (Place of Tears) and *Cusipata* (Place of Happiness), divided by a channel of the Río Saphi. Today, Huacaypata is the Plaza de Armas and Cusipata is Plaza Regocijo. This was the great civic square of the Incas, flanked by their palaces, and was a place of solemn parades and great assemblies. Each territory conquered by the Incas had some of its soil taken to Cuzco to be mingled symbolically with the soil of the Huacaypata, as a token of its incorporation into the empire. As well as the many great ceremonies, the plaza has also seen its share of executions, among them the last Inca, Túpac Amaru, the rebel *conquistador*, Diego de Almagro the Younger, and the 18th-century indigenous leader, Túpac Amaru II.

On the northeast side of the square, the early 17th-century baroque **cathedral** ① *entry US$9, students half price, or by religious buildings ticket; open daily 1000-1800, Quechua Mass at 0500-0600,* forms part of a three-church complex: the cathedral itself, **Iglesia de la Sagrada Familia** (1733) on the left as you look at it and **El Triunfo** (1533) on the right. There are two entrances; the cathedral doors are used during Mass but the tourist entrance is on the left-hand side through the Sagrada Familia. The cathedral itself was built on the site of the Palace of Inca Wiracocha (*Kiswarcancha*) using stones from Sacsayhuaman.

The gleaming, renovated gilded main altar of the **Iglesia Jesús y María** draws the eyes to the end of the church. However, take the time to look up at the colourful murals that have been partially restored. The two gaudy, mirror-encrusted altars towards the front of the church are also hard to miss.

Walking through into the cathedral's transept, the oldest surviving painting in Cuzco can be seen. It depicts the 1650 earthquake. It also shows how, within only one century, the Spaniards had already divided the main plaza in two. *El Señor de los Temblores* (Lord of the Earthquakes) can be seen being paraded around the Plaza de Armas, while fire rages through the colonial buildings with their typical red-tiled roofs. Much of modern-day Cuzco was built after this event. The choir stalls, by a 17th-century Spanish priest, are a magnificent example of colonial baroque art (80 saints and virgins are exquisitely represented), as is the elaborate pulpit. On the left is the solid-silver high altar. At the far right-hand end of the cathedral is an interesting local painting of the Last Supper (there is another in the Museo de Arte Religioso, see page 134). But this is the Last Supper with a difference, for Jesus is about to tuck into a plate of *cuy*, washed down with a glass of *chicha*!

Entering **El Triunfo** there is a stark contrast between the dark, heavy atmosphere of the cathedral and the light, simple structure of this serene church. Built on the site of *Suntur Huasi* (The Roundhouse), El Triunfo was the first Christian church in Cuzco. The name *El Triunfo* (The Triumph) came from the Spanish victory over an indigenous rebellion in 1536. It was here that the Spaniards congregated, hiding from Manco Inca who had besieged the city, almost taking it from the invaders. The Spaniards claim to have witnessed two miracles here in their hour of need. First, they were visited by the Virgin of the Descent, who helped put out the flames devouring the thatched roofs, then came the equestrian saint, James the Greater, who helped kill many indigenous people. The two

Cuzco

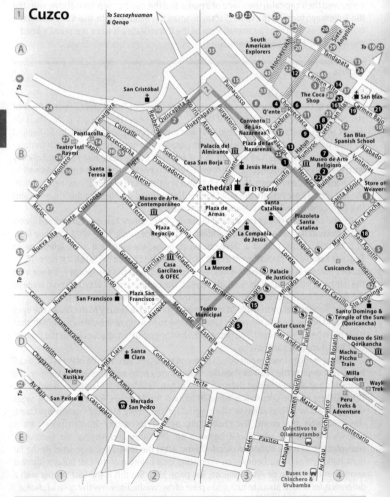

divinities are said to have led to the Spanish victory; not only was it the triumph of the Spaniards over the Incas, but also of the Catholic faith over the indigenous religion. The fine granite altar of El Triunfo is a welcome relief from the usual gilding. Here, the statue of the Virgin of the Descent resides and, above her, is a wooden cross known as the Cross of Conquest, said to be the first Christian cross on Inca land brought from Spain.

On the southeast side of the plaza is the beautiful church of **La Compañía de Jesús** ⓘ *entry US$3.55, or by religious buildings ticket, open daily 0900-1750*, built on the site of the Palace of the Serpents (*Amarucancha*, residence of the Inca Huayna Cápac). The original church was destroyed in the earthquake of 1650 and the present-day building

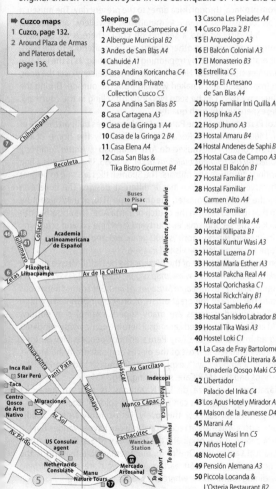

➡ Cuzco maps
1 Cuzco, page 132.
2 Around Plaza de Armas and Plateros detail, page 136.

Buses to Pisac

To Piquillacta, Puno y Bolivia

Academia Latinoamericana de Español

Plázoleta Limacpampa

Av de la Cultura

Av Garcilaso

Indecopi

Inca Rail
Star Perú
Taca
Centro Qosco de Arte Nativo
Migraciones

Manco Cápac

Av Sol

Pachacútec

US Consular agent

Wanchac Station

To Bus Terminal

To Airport & Airport

Netherlands Consulate

Manu Nature Tours

Mercado Artesanal

N

100 metres
100 yards

took 17 years to construct. It was inaugurated in 1668. The altarpiece is resplendent in gold leaf: it stands 21 m high and 12 m wide. It is carved in the baroque style, but the indigenous artists felt that this was too simple to please the gods and added their own intricacies. Gold leaf abounds in the many *retablos* and on the carved pulpit.

North and northeast of the Plaza de Armas

Palacio del Almirante, just north of the Plaza de Armas, is one of Cuzco's most impressive colonial buildings and houses the interesting **Museo Inka** ① *Cuesta del Almirante 103, T084-237380, Mon-Fri 0800-1900, Sat 0900-1600, US$3*, which exhibits the development of culture in the region from pre-Inca, through Inca times to the present day. The museum has a good combination of textiles, ceramics, metalwork, jewellery, architecture, technology, photographs, 3-D displays and a section on coca. There is an excellent collection of miniature turquoise figures and other objects made as offerings to the gods. The display of skulls, deliberately deformed by trepanning is fascinating, as is the full-size tomb complete with mummies stuck in urns. Note the pillar on the balcony over the door, showing a bearded man from inside and a naked woman from the outside. During the high season, local Quechuan weavers can be seen working and selling in the courtyard. The weavings are for sale; expensive but high quality.

Two blocks northeast of Plaza de Armas, the **Palacio Arzobispal** was built on the site of the palace occupied in 1400 by the Inca Roca and was formerly the home of the Marqueses de Buena Vista. It contains the **Museo de Arte Religioso** ① *Hatun Rumiyoc y Herrajes, 0800-1800, included on the religious buildings ticket, or US$5.35*, which has a fine collection of colonial paintings, furniture and mirrors. The Spanish tiles are said to be over 100 years old and each carved wooden door has a different design. The collection includes the paintings by the indigenous master, **Diego Quispe Tito**, of a 17th-century Corpus Christi procession that used to hang in the church of Santa Ana. They now hang in the two rooms at the back of the second smaller courtyard (see Fine art and sculpture, page 681). The throne in the old dining room is 300 years old and was taken up to Sacsayhuaman for the Pope to sit on when he visited in 1986.

In the Casa Cabrera, on the northwest side of the plaza, is the beautiful **Museo de Arte Precolombino** ① *Plaza de las Nazarenas 231, www.map.org.pe, 0900-2200, US$7, US$3.50 with student card; under same auspices as the Larco Museum in Lima*. Set around a spacious courtyard, it is dedicated to the work of the great artists of pre-Colombian Peru. Within the expertly lit and well-organized galleries are many superb examples of pottery, metalwork (largely in gold and silver) and wood carvings. There are some vividly rendered animistic designs, giving an insight into the way Peru's ancient peoples viewed their world and the creatures that inhabited it. Most of the pieces originate from the Moche, Chimú, Paracas, Nazca and Inca empires, with explanations in English and Spanish. The museum has high-class shops and the MAP Café, see Eating, page 151.

Convento de las Nazarenas, on Plaza de las Nazarenas, is now an annex of **El Monasterio** (see Sleeping, page 142). You can see the Inca-colonial doorway with a mermaid motif, but ask permission to view the lovely 18th-century frescos inside. **El Monasterio** itself is well worth a visit – ask at reception if you can have a wander. Built in 1595 on the site of an Inca palace, it was originally the **Seminary of San Antonio Abad** (a Peruvian National Historical Landmark). One of its most remarkable features is the baroque chapel, constructed after the 1650 earthquake. If you are not disturbing mealtimes, check out the dining room. This is where the monks used to sing.

San Blas

The San Blas district, called **Tococache** in Inca times, has been put on the tourist map by the large number of shops and galleries that sell local carvings, ceramics and paintings, see page 157. Even though it's a bit of climb from the Plaza de Armas, it has also become a popular place to stay and eat, with lots of choice and nothing too expensive. The **Templo de San Blas** ① *Carmen Bajo, 0800-1800, on the religious buildings ticket, or US$5.35*, is a simple rectangular adobe building whose walls were reinforced with stone after the 1650 and 1950 earthquakes. It houses one of the most famous pieces of wood carving in the Americas, a beautiful mestizo pulpit carved from a single cedar trunk.

East and southeast of the Plaza de Armas

The magnificent church, convent and museum of **Santa Catalina** ① *Arequipa at Santa Catalina Angosta, Sat-Thu 0900-1200 and 1300-1700, Fri 0900-1200, 1300-1600, joint ticket with Santo Domingo US$6, guided tours by English-speaking students (tip is expected), church daily 0700-0800*, is built upon the foundations of the *Acllahuasi* (House of the Chosen Women), whose nobility, virtue and beauty permitted them to be prepared for ceremonial and domestic duties – some were chosen to bear the Inca king's children. Today the convent is a closed order where the nuns have no contact with the outside world. The church has an ornate, gilded altarpiece and a beautifully carved pulpit. The museum, refurbished in 2009, has a wonderful collection of Cuzqueño school paintings spanning the decades of Spanish rule – a good guide can point out how the style changes from the heavy European influence to the more indigenous style.

Much original Inca stonework can be seen in the streets, particularly in the **Callejón Loreto**, running southeast past La Compañía de Jesús from the main plaza. The walls of the *Acllahuasi* are on one side, and of the *Amarucancha* on the other. There are also Inca remains in Calle San Agustín, east of the plaza. The famous **Stone of 12 Angles** is in Calle Hatun Rumiyoc, halfway along its second block, on the right-hand side going away from the plaza. The finest stonework is in the celebrated curved wall beneath the west end of Santo Domingo. This was rebuilt after the 1950 earthquake, when a niche that once contained a shrine was found at the inner top of the wall. Excavations have revealed Inca baths below here, and more Inca retaining walls. Another superb stretch of late-Inca stonework is in **Calle Ahuacpinta**, outside Qoricancha, to the east or left as you enter. True Inca stonework is wider at the base than at the top and features ever-smaller stones as the walls rise. Doorways and niches are trapezoidal. The Incas clearly learnt that the combination of these four techniques helped their structures to withstand earthquakes. This explains why, in two huge earthquakes (1650 and 1950), Inca walls stayed standing while colonial buildings tumbled down.

If you continue down Arequipa from Santa Catalina you come to Calle Maruri. Between this street at Santo Domingo is **Cusicancha** ① *US$1.75, Mon-Fri 0730-1600, sometimes open at weekends*, an open space showing the layout of the buildings as they would have been in Inca times. Recovered from what was a barracks are Inca walls and niches and a colonial arch. There is an exhibition space and alpacas and vicuñas wandering around the grassy areas.

Qoricancha at Santo Domingo

① *Mon-Sat 0830-1730, Sun 1400-1700 (except holidays), US$3.55, or joint ticket with Santa Catalina US$6 (not on the BTC visitor ticket). There are English-speaking guides outside who expect a tip of US$2-3.*

This is one of the most fascinating sights in Cuzco. Behind the walls of the Catholic church are remains of what was once the centre of the vast Inca society. The Golden Palace and Temple of the Sun was a complex filled with such fabulous treasures of gold and silver it took the Spanish three months to melt it all down. The Solar Garden contained life-sized gold sculptures of men, women, children, animals, insects and flowers, placed in homage to the Sun God. On the walls were more than 700 gold sheets weighing about 2 kg each. The *conquistadores* sent these back intact to prove to the King of Spain how rich their discovery was. There would also have been a large solar disc in the shape of a round face with rays and flames. This disc has never been found.

The first Inca, Manco Cápac, is said to have built the temple when he left Lake Titicaca and founded Cuzco with Mama Ocllo. However, it was the ninth Inca, Pachacútec, who transformed it. When the Spaniards arrived, the complex was awarded to Juan Pizarro, the younger brother of Francisco. He in turn willed it to the Dominicans who ripped much of it down to build their church.

Walk first into the courtyard then turn around to face the door you just passed through. Behind and to the left of the paintings (representing the life of Santo Domingo Guzmán) is Santo Domingo. This was where the Temple of the Sun stood, a massive structure 80 m wide, 20 m deep and 7 m in height. Only the curved wall of the western end still exists and

2 Around Plaza de Armas

will be seen (complete with a large crack from the 1950 earthquake), when you later walk left through to the lookout over the Solar Garden. Still in the baroque cloister, close by and facing the way you came in, turn left and cross to the remains of the Temple of the Moon, identifiable by a series of niches. Beyond this is the so-called Temple of Venus and the Stars. Stars were special deities used to predict weather, wealth and crops. In the Temple of Lightning on the other side of the courtyard is a stone; stand on it and you will appreciate how good the Incas were as stonemasons: all three windows are in perfect alignment.

Museo de Sitio Qoricancha ① *Mon-Sat 0900-1200, 1300-1700, Sun 0800-1400, entry with BTC visitor ticket, guided tour in Spanish, but please give a tip*, formerly the Museo Arqueológico, is now housed in an underground site on Avenida Sol, in the gardens below Santo Domingo. It contains a limited collection of pre-Columbian artefacts, a few Spanish paintings of imitation Inca royalty, dating from the 18th century, and photos of the excavation of Qoricancha.

South and southwest of the Plaza de Armas
Originally built in 1534, the church of **La Merced** ① *C Márquez, monastery and museum 1430-1700, church Mon-Fri 0800-1700, Sat 0900-1600, US$1*, was razed in the 1650 earthquake and rebuilt by indigenous stonemasons in the late 17th century. The high

Plateros detail

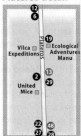

Sleeping 🛏
1 Andean Wings *A1*
2 Casa Andina Catedral *C3*
3 Casa Andina Plaza *C2*
4 Del Prado Inn *B3*
5 EcoPackers *A1*
6 El Procurador del Cusco *A2*
7 Emperador Plaza *C3*
8 Hospedaje Hatun Tumi *A1*
9 Hostal Corihuasi *A2*
10 Hostal Qosqo *C2*
11 Hostal Resbalosa *A3*
12 Hostal Royal Frankenstein *B1*
13 Hostal Turístico Plateros *Plateros detail*
14 La Casona Inkaterra *B3*
15 Loreto Boutique Hotel *C2*
16 Marqueses *B1*
17 Pariwana *C1*
18 Picoaga *A1*
19 Pirwa *B3*
20 Sonesta Posadas del Inca *B2*
21 The Point *C1*

Eating 🍴
1 Al Grano *C3*
2 Amaru *Plateros detail*
3 Bembos *C2*
4 Bistrot 370 *C3*
5 Café El Ayllu *B3*
6 Café Halliy *Plateros detail*
7 Café Perla *C3*
8 Chicha, El Truco & Taberna del Truco *B1*
9 Cicciolina *C3*
10 Dolce Vita *C3*
11 El Encuentro *A2, C3*
12 El Fogón *Plateros detail*
13 Fallen Angel restaurant & Guesthouse *B3*
14 Fusiones *C2*
15 Incanto & Greens Organic *C3*
16 Inka Grill *B2*
17 Kusikuy *B3*
18 La Bondiet *C1*
19 La Cosa Nostra *Plateros detail*
20 La Retama *B3*
21 Limo *B3*
22 Los Candiles *Plateros detail*
23 Maikhana *C2*
24 MAP Café *B3*
25 Pachacútec Grill & Bar *B2*
26 Paloma Imbis *A2*
27 Pucará *Plateros detail*
28 The Muse *Plateros detail*
29 The Real McCoy *Plateros detail*
30 Trotamundos *B2*
31 Tunupa *B2*
32 Tupananchis *C1*
33 Víctor Victoria *A2*
34 Witches Garden *C2*
35 Yaku Mama *A2*

Bars & clubs 🍸
36 Cross Keys Pub *A2*
37 El Garabato Video Music Club *B2*
38 Extreme *B3*
39 Indigo *A2*
40 Kamikaze *B2*
41 Los Perros *A2*
42 Mama Africa *B2*
43 Mythology *B3*
44 Norton Rat's Tavern & Hostal Gocta Cusco *C3*
45 Paddy's Pub *C3*
46 Roots *A2*
47 Rosie O'Grady's *C3*
48 Ukuku's *Plateros detail*

altar is neoclassical with six gilded columns. There are a further 12 altars. Inside the church are buried Gonzalo Pizarro, half-brother of Francisco, and the two Almagros, father and son. Attached is a fine monastery. The first cloister is the most beautiful, with its two floors, archways and pillars. The pictures on the first floor depicting the Saints of the Order and other religious subjects form part of the Museo del Convento de La Merced. One of its most prized possessions is the Custodia de Oro, weighing 22 kg and encrusted with diamonds and other precious stones, including a river pearl in the shape of a mermaid, La Sirena, considered the second largest in the world.

Museo Histórico Regional ① *Casa Garcilaso, C Garcilaso y Heladeros, daily 0730-1700, BTC visitor ticket, guide recommended,* shows the evolution of the Cuzqueño school of painting. It also contains Inca agricultural implements, a mummy from Nazca, complete with 1-m-long hair, colonial furniture and paintings, a small photographic exhibition of the 1950 earthquake and mementos of more recent times.

Three blocks southwest of the Plaza de Armas, the austere church of **San Francisco** ① *Plaza San Francisco, daily 0600-0800, 1800-2000,* reflects many indigenous influences, but it has a wonderful monastery, cloister and choir. Although at the time of writing the monastery was not officially open to the public, it is possible to visit. Approach the door to the left of the church and knock on it. The cloister is the oldest in the city, built in the Renaissance style, but with diverse influences. The ground floor has several crypts containing human bones. The high choir contains 92 carvings of martyrs and saints.

West and northwest of the Plaza de Armas

Above Cuzco, on the road up to Sacsayhuaman, is the church of **San Cristóbal**, built to honour his patron saint by Cristóbal Paullu Inca. The church's atrium has been restored and there is access to the Sacsayhuaman Archaeological Park (see below). North of San Cristóbal, you can see the 11 doorway-sized niches of the great Inca wall of the **Palacio de Colcampata**, which was the residence of Manco Inca before he rebelled against the Spanish and fled to Vilcabamba. **Cristo Blanco**, arms outstretched and brilliantly illuminated at night, stands over the town and is clearly visible if you look north from the Plaza de Armas. He was given to the city as a mark of gratitude by Palestinian refugees in 1944. A quick glance in the local telephone directory reveals there is still a large Arab population in Cuzco.

Sacsayhuaman

① *Daily 0700-1730. You can get in earlier if you wish; definitely try to get there before 1200 when the tour groups arrive. Entry with BTC visitor ticket. Free student guides available, but you should tip them. Lights to illuminate the site at night, which is a 30-min walk from the town centre; walk up Pumacurco from Plaza de las Nazarenas. Taxi US$1.50.*

There are some magnificent Inca walls in the ruined ceremonial centre of Sacsayhuaman, on a hill in the northern outskirts. The Inca stonework is hugely impressive. The massive rocks weighing up to 130 tons are fitted together with absolute perfection. Three walls run parallel for over 360 m and there are 21 bastions.

Sacsayhuaman was thought for centuries to be a fortress, but the layout and architecture suggest a great sanctuary and temple to the Sun, rising opposite the place previously believed to be the Inca's throne – which was probably an altar, carved out of the solid rock. Broad steps lead to the altar from either side. Zigzags in the boulders around the 'throne' are apparently '*chicha* grooves', channels down which maize beer flowed during festivals. Up the hill is an ancient quarry, the Rodadero, now used by children as a rock slide. Near it are many seats cut perfectly into the smooth rock.

The hieratic, rather than the military, hypothesis was supported by the discovery in 1982 of the graves of priests, who would have been unlikely to be buried in a fortress. The precise functions of the site, however, will probably continue to be a matter of dispute, as very few clues remain, due to its steady destruction.

The site survived the first years of the conquest. Pizarro's troops had entered Cuzco unopposed in 1533 and lived safely at Sacsayhuaman, until the rebellion of Manco Inca, in 1536, caught them off guard. The bitter struggle that ensued became the decisive military action of the conquest, for Manco's failure to hold Sacsayhuaman cost him the war, and the empire. The destruction of the hilltop site began after the defeat of Manco's rebellion. The outer walls still stand, but the complex of towers and buildings was razed to the ground. From then until the 1930s, Sacsayhuaman served as a kind of unofficial quarry of pre-cut stone for the inhabitants of Cuzco.

Other sites near Cuzco

Along the road from Sacsayhuaman to Pisac, past a radio station at 3600 m, is the temple and amphitheatre of **Qenqo** ① *on the BTC visitor ticket*. These are not exactly ruins, but are the finest examples of Inca stone carving in situ, especially inside the large hollowed-out stone that houses an altar. The rock is criss-crossed by zigzag channels that give the place its name and which served to course *chicha*, or perhaps sacrificial blood, for purposes of divination. The open space that many refer to as the 'plaza' or 'amphitheatre' was used for ceremonies. The 19 trapezoidal niches, which are partially destroyed, held idols and mummies.

Known as an Inca fortress, **Puka Pukara** ① *about 6 km from Qenqo, BTC visitor ticket* , whose name translates as 'Red Fort', was more likely to have been a *tambo*, a kind of post-house where travellers were lodged and goods and animals were housed temporarily. It is worth seeing for the views alone.

A few hundred metres up the road is the spring shrine of **Tambo Machay** ① *also on the BTC visitor ticket*, still in excellent condition. There are many opinions as to the function of this place. Some say it was a resting place for the Incas and others that it was used by Inca Yupanqui as a hunting place. There are three ceremonial water fountains built on different levels. It is possible that the site was a centre of a water cult. Water still flows via a hidden channel out of the masonry wall, straight into a rock pool, traditionally known as the Inca's bath.

It is possible to walk from Sacsayhuaman to Tambo Machay, via Qenqo, then **Cusilluchayoc** (Templo de los Monos, or Monkey Temple), an area of rocks and galleries with the remains of a fountain, then on a section of the Inca Cuzco–Pisac road to **Laqo** (Templo de la Luna, or Temple of the Moon), with sculptures in caves and an observatory, Chilcapuquio and Puka Pukara.

Taking a guide to the sites mentioned above is a good idea and you should visit in the morning for the best photographs. You can visit the sites on foot. It's a pleasant walk through the countryside requiring half a day or more, though remember to take water and sun protection, and watch out for dogs. An alternative is to take the Pisac bus up to Tambo Machay (US$0.35) and walk back. Other excellent ways to see the ruins are on horseback, arranged at travel agencies, or by bicycle. Rent a bike for US$25 for a full day; it's a 45-minute to one-hour ride from the city. An organized tour (with guide) will include the sites for US$15 per person, not including entrance fees (see page **160**). A taxi will charge about US$30 for three to four people.

⊕ Cuzco city listings

For Sleeping and Eating price codes and other relevant information, see pages 38-44.

⊜ Sleeping

You should book more expensive hotels well in advance through the internet or a good travel agency, particularly for the week or so around **Inti Raymi** (page 156), when prices are much higher. Hotel prices, especially in the mid to upper categories, are often lower when booked on the internet. Always check for special offers as, when there are fewer tourists, hotels may drop their prices by as much as half. Be wary of unlicensed hotel agents for mid-priced hotels, who are often misleading about details; their local nickname is *jalagringos* (gringo pullers), or *piratas* (pirates). Taxis and tourist minibuses meet arriving trains and take you to the hotel of your choice for US$0.75-1, but be insistent. Many hotels and *hostales* can arrange tours: don't be pressured into buying, but compare services with outside agencies for best value.

It is cold at night in Cuzco and many hotels do not have heating. It is worth asking for an *estufa*, a heater, which some places will provide for an extra charge. When staying in the big, popular hotels, allow plenty of time to check out if you have a plane or train to catch; front desks can be very busy. Assume that hotels have free luggage storage and 24-hr hot water in pre-heated tanks, unless otherwise stated. The city can suffer from water shortages. Cuzco's low-power electric showers often do a poor job of heating the very cold water and their safety is sometimes questionable.

Plaza de Armas and around
p131, maps 132 and p136

LL-L Andean Wings, Siete Cuartones 225, T084-243166, www.andeanwingshotel.com. In a restored 17th-century house, 5-star boutique hotel, each room, whether suite or standard, is of a good size and individually decorated, one with disabled access, some with jacuzzi, intimate and welcoming. Restaurant in covered patio, bar, Wi-Fi, laundry service. Artworks for sale and has a spa. In the same group as **Casas de la Gringa** and **Another Planet** (see below).

LL-L Picoaga, Santa Teresa 344 (2 blocks from the Plaza de Armas), T01-711 2000 ext 849/850, www.picoagahotel.com. Price includes buffet breakfast. Originally the home of the Marqués de Picoaga, this beautiful colonial building has large original bedrooms set around a shady courtyard and a modern section, with a/c, at the back. Cable TV, minibar and safe. Pleasant staff.

AL Del Prado Inn, Suecia 310, T084-224442, www.delpradoinn.com. A very smart hotel just off the plaza. 24-hr room service available, and closed-circuit TV in the public areas for additional security, Wi-Fi. Suites with jacuzzi cost US$135-145.

AL Ruinas, Ruinas 472, T084-260644, www.hotelruinas.com. A comfortable hotel conveniently located close to the plaza, good facilities (TV, Wi-Fi, minibar, etc) and comfortable beds, helpful staff, price includes buffet breakfast.

AL Sonesta Posadas del Inca, Portal Espinar 108, T084-227061, www.sonesta.com. Price includes buffet breakfast. Warmly decorated rooms with heating, safe and cable TV. Some rooms on 3rd floor have view of the plaza. Very helpful staff who speak English, restaurant serves Andean food, excellent service, business centre available.

AL-A Casa Andina Plaza, Portal Espinar 142, T084-231733, www.casa-andina.com. 1½ blocks from the plaza, this hotel has 40 rooms with cable TV, bath, safety deposit box, heating, duvets on the beds, Wi-Fi, ATM, restaurant and all the features common to this bright, cheerful chain. Equally recommendable are the **Casa Andina Koricancha**, San Agustín 371, T084-252633, the **Casa Andina Catedral**, Santa Catalina Angosta 149, T084-233661, and the **AL** Casa Andina San Blas, Chihuampata 278, San Blas, T084-263694, all of which are in the same vein (but the last 3 do not have an ATM).

AL-A Marqueses, Garcilaso 256, T084-264249, www.hotelmarqueses.com. Restored in Spanish-colonial style, with suitable artwork and 2 lovely courtyards. Prices include buffet breakfast. Some rooms have bath, others are a little dark. Discounts on **SAS Travel** (see Activities and tours, page 163).

A Emperador Plaza, Santa Catalina Ancha 377, T084-227412, www.emperadorplaza. com. Price includes buffet breakfast and airport transfer. A modern, light, airy hotel with friendly and helpful English-speaking staff. Cable TV, hairdryer, gas-heated showers and electric radiators.

A Hostal Gocta Cusco, Santa Catalina Angosta 116, nortonrats@yahoo.com. Reached through **Norton Rat's Tavern** (see page 154), with same owner. 6 rooms with good baths decorated with historic photographs, hot water, room service from the bar, cable TV, Wi-Fi. New in 2010.

A Loreto Boutique Hotel, Pasaje Loreto 115, Plaza de Armas, T084-226352, www.loreto boutiquehotel.com. Price includes buffet breakfast. Great location; 12 spacious rooms with original Inca walls, upgraded to "boutique" status. Laundry service, will help organize travel services including guides and taxis, free airport pick-up.

A-B Hostal Corihuasi, C Suecia 561, T084-232233, www.corihuasi.com. Price includes continental breakfast and airport pickup. A tough climb up from the northernmost corner of the Plaza de Armas, tranquil, popular with tour groups. Friendly, some rooms with good views, cable TV, solar heating, Wi-Fi. Recommended.

B-C Hostal Qosqo, Portal Mantas 115, near the Plaza de Armas, T084-252513, www.suqosqohostal.com. Bargain hard for a discount. Price includes continental breakfast, a heater and cable TV. The state of decor and quality of mattress varies from room to room but most stay here for its proximity to the plaza. Clean, friendly and helpful.

C Goldie's Guest House, Saphie 456, T511-242 5534, www.goldiesguesthouse.com. Self-contained accommodation (preferably long-term for a week or a month) in a pleasant and safe environment right in the centre of Cuzco (250 m from Plaza de Armas).

D Hostal Resbalosa, Resbalosa 494, T084-224839, www.hostalresbalosa.com. **E** with shared bath. Breakfast is US$1.45 extra; laundry service, internet. Superb views of the Plaza de Armas from a sunny terrace. Owner Georgina is very hospitable. Best rooms have a view, others may be pokey. Most guests love this place; it's often full.

D Hostal Turístico Plateros, Plateros 348, T084-236878, plateroshostal@hotmail.com. Price includes continental breakfast.

Clean, good-value *hostal* in a great location, pleasant communal area with cable TV. The best rooms overlook the street.

D-E El Procurador del Cusco, Coricalle 440, Prolongación Procuradores, at the end of Procuradores, T084-243559, http://hostel procuradordelcusco.blogspot.com. **G** per person without bathroom, price includes use of the basic kitchen (no fridge) and laundry area. Basic rooms and the beds somewhat hard, but upstairs is better. Staff are very friendly and helpful, good value. Recommended.

D-E Hostal Royal Frankenstein, San Juan de Dios 260, 2 blocks from the Plaza de Armas, T084-236999, www.hostal-frankenstein.net. This unforgettable place, with its ghoulish theme, has good services: fully equipped kitchen, cable TV in the living room, safe, laundry facilities and service, Wi-Fi, excellent mattresses but few rooms have outside windows, heaters for hire. German owner. Recommended.

E-F EcoPackers, Santa Teresa 375, T084-231800, www.ecopackersperu.com. Dorms for 4-18 people, also private rooms with bath **C-D**. With restaurant, bar, cable TV, Wi-Fi, safe, colonial atmosphere and well spoken-of.

E-F Hospedaje Hatun Tumi, Siete Cuartones 245, 2 blocks from Plaza de Armas, T084-253937, www.hatuntumi.com. Rooms for 1-3 people, price includes airport transfer, with luggage store, safe, coffee shop and laundry. Colonial house, clean rooms around a sunny courtyard, some with shared bath. Friendly, popular, good value; bargain for longer stays. Offers tours.

F pp Pariwana, Mesón de la Estrella 136, T084-233751, www.pariwana-hostel.com. Also doubles (**C-D**, cheaper without bath), in a converted colonial mansion, restaurant, bar/lounge, with breakfast, kitchen, internet and Wi-Fi, lockers, English spoken, lots of activities.

F Pirwa, Suecia 300, T084-244315, www.pirwahostelscusco.com. This is the bed-and-breakfast branch of this chain of hostels. They also have **Posada del Corregidor**, Portal de Panes 151 (Plaza de Armas), **Backpacker Familiar**, Carmen Alto

283, and **Backpacker Colonial**, Plaza San Francisco 360. With dorms and private rooms with bath, breakfast included, internet, use of kitchen, 24-hr reception.

F The Point, Mesón de la Estrella 172, T084-252266, www.thepointhostels.com. Price is per person in dormitory, also has doubles (**E** per person), includes breakfast, free internet and Wi-Fi, good beds, hot showers, clean, bar with good party atmosphere and nightly events. Has a travel centre which can arrange trips, see general note, page 140.

North and northeast of the Plaza de Armas *p134, maps p132 and p136*

LL Casa Cartagena, Pumacurco 336, T084-261171, www.casacartagena.com. In a converted monastery and national heritage building, super-deluxe facilities with Italian design and colonial features, 4 levels of suite from US$700 to US$1800 a night, **La Chola** restaurant, extensive **Qoya** spa, enriched oxygen system, Wi-Fi, and all services to be expected in a boutique hotel.

LL El Monasterio, Palacios 136, Plazoleta Nazarenas, T084-604000, www.monasterio hotel.com. This 5-star, beautifully restored Seminary of San Antonio Abad is central and is one of the best in town for historical interest (see page 134); it is worth a visit even if you can't afford the price tag. Soft Gregorian chants follow you as you wander through the baroque chapel, tranquil courtyards and charming cloisters, admiring the excellent collection of religious paintings. Rooms have all facilities and many offer an oxygen-enriched atmosphere to help clients acclimatize, for an additional fee. Staff, who all speak English, are very helpful and attentive. The price includes a great buffet breakfast (available to non-residents) that will fill you up for the rest of the day. The restaurant serves lunch and dinner à la carte.

LL Fallen Angel, Plazoleta Nazarenas 221, T084-258184, www.fallenangelincusco.com. The small luxury guesthouse above the restaurant of the same name, see page 151. Each of the 4 rooms is decorated in its own lavish style to create a distinct atmosphere, very comfortable and a far cry from the usual adaptation of colonial buildings elsewhere in the city. With all amenities, including Wi-Fi and use of the restaurant below. Excellent service and helpful staff.

LL La Casona Inkaterra, Plaza Las Nazarenas 113, T084-234010, www.inkaterra.com. Another hotel in a building with a long history, being in a converted 16th-century mansion, built on the site of Manco Cápac's palace. This 1st-class private, colonial-style boutique hotel has 11 exclusive suites, all facilities, concierge service with activities and excursions. Guests are given individual attention in the height of luxury. Breakfast is included, lunch and dinner are available, plus many other services including spa. In the **Relais & Chateaux** group.

LL Novotel, San Agustín 239, T084-581033, www.novotel.com/gb/hotel-3254-novotel-cusco/. 4-star, cheaper in modern section; price includes buffet breakfast. Converted from the home of *conquistador* Miguel Sánchez Ponce, it was remodelled after the 1650 earthquake with lovely stone archways and paintings of the saints on the grand stairway. Beautiful courtyard, roofed in glass, with sofas, coffee tables and pot plants around the central stone fountain. The modern 5-storey rear extension has excellent airy and bright rooms. Rooms in the colonial section are not much different but have high, beamed ceilings and huge beds. There are 2 restaurants and a French chef.

AL El Arqueólogo, Pumacurco 408, T084-232522, www.hotelarqueologo.com. Price includes buffet breakfast. Services include oxygen, a library and hot drinks. A colonial building on Inca foundations, this has rustic but stylish decor. Lovely sunny garden with comfy chairs and a small restaurant that serves interesting Peruvian food and fondue. French and English spoken. Recommended. Also has a bed and breakfast *hostal* at Carmen Alto 294, T084-232760, **A-B**, and **Vida Tours**, Ladrillo 425, T084-227750, www.vidatours.com. Traditional and adventure tourism.

AL Rumi Punku, Choquechaca 339, T084-221102, www.rumipunku.com. A genuine Inca doorway leads to a sunny, tranquil courtyard. 20 large, clean, comfortable rooms, helpful staff and safe. Highly recommended.

AL-A Piccola Locanda, Resbalosa 520, T084-252551, www.piccolalocanda.com. This colourful Peruvian/Italian run B&B is a steep walk up from the Plaza de Armas. Rooftop terrace has 360-degree views. It boasts the excellent restaurant **L'Osteria**, a TV/DVD room, pleasant courtyard. Rooms in individual style, some without bath. Associated with **Perú Etico** tour company and 2 children's projects. Recommended.

A-B Cusco Plaza 1, Plaza Nazarenas 181 (opposite **El Monasterio**), T084-246161, www.cuscoplazahotels.com. Price includes continental breakfast. Situated on a lovely small plaza in the town centre, clean rooms all with cable TV. Room 303 has the best view.

C Casa Elena, Choquechaca 162, T084-241202, www.casaelenacusco.com. French/Peruvian hostel, very comfortable and friendly, breakfast included. Highly recommended.

C Hostal María Esther, Pumacurco 516, T084-224382, http://hostalmariaesther.free.fr/. Price includes continental breakfast; heating extra. This very friendly, helpful place has a lovely garden, a lounge with sofas and a variety of rooms. There is also car parking. Recommended.

E El Balcón Colonial, Choquechaca 350, T084-238129, balconcolonial@hotmail.com. Accommodation for 11 people in this family house. Basic rooms with foam mattresses but hospitality is exceptional. Free airport pick-up. Continental breakfast and hot showers extra, use of the kitchen and laundry extra.

San Blas *p135, map p132*

Note that *hostales* on Calles Atocsaycuchi and Siete Angelitos and some of the streets above Plaza San Blas do not have vehicular access right to the door.

L-AL Casa San Blas, Tocuyeros 566, just off Cuesta San Blas, T084-237900, www.casasanblas.com. An international-standard boutique hotel with bright, airy rooms decorated with traditional textiles. Breakfast, served in the **Tika Bistro** downstairs, and Wi-Fi are included. Pleasant balcony with good views, very attentive service.

AL Los Apus Hotel y Mirador, Atocsaycuchi 515, corner with Choquechaca, T084-264243, www.losapushotel.com. Price includes buffet breakfast and airport pick-up; laundry US$1 per kg. Swiss-owned, very clean and smart with beamed bedrooms fitted with cable TV and real radiators! Disabled facilities.

A Casona Les Pleiades, Tandapata 116, T084-506430, www.casona-pleiades.com. Small guesthouse in renovated colonial house, cosy and warm, generous hosts, gas-heated water, buffet breakfast included, cable TV, Wi-Fi, roof terrace, video lounge and book exchange, café, free airport pick-up with reservation, lots of information for guests.

A-B Hostal Tika Wasi, Tandapata 491, T084-231609, www.tikawasi.com. Price includes breakfast and all rooms are heated. A family-run *hostal* with a lovely garden overlooking the city. Very stylish, softly lit rooms, great views. Comfortable beds and spotless bathrooms make this a good choice. Supports social projects.

B Hostal Casa de Campo, Tandapata 296-B (at the end of the street), T084-244404, www.hotelcasadecampo.com. Price (10% discount for Footprint readers on presentation of the book) includes continental breakfast and free airport/rail/bus transfer with reservations. Bedrooms have fabulous views but it's quite a climb to get to them! Safety deposit box, laundry,

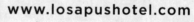

meals on request and a sun terrace. Dutch and English spoken; take a taxi there after dark. Soon to open new apartments for families and honeymooners at Casa Valer.

B Marani, Carmen Alto 194, T084-249462, www.hostalmarani.com. Breakfasts available. Book exchange and information on Andean life and culture. Large rooms with heaps of character, set around a courtyard. The **Hope Foundation** (www.stichtinghope.org) is run from here: Walter Meekes and his wife, Tineke, have built 20 schools in poor mountain villages and barrios, established a programme to teach teachers and set up a 30-bed burns unit in Cuzco general hospital. Good value, a great cause and highly recommended.

B Pensión Alemana, Tandapata 260, T084-226861, www.cuzco.com.pe. Price includes American breakfast; laundry and heating extra. Car parking available. Swiss-owned, modern European decor with a comfy lounge area, free internet, lovely garden with patio furniture. Recommended.

B-C Hostal Amaru, Cuesta San Blas 541, T084-225933, www.amaruhostal.com. (**D** with shared bathroom). Price includes breakfast and airport/train/bus pick-up. Services include oxygen, kitchen for use in the evenings only, laundry and free book exchange. Rooms around a pretty colonial courtyard, good beds, pleasant, relaxing, some Inca walls. Rooms in the 1st courtyard are best. Recommended. Also has **B Hostal Amaru II**, Chihuampata 642, San Blas, www.amaruhostal2.com, and **Hostería de Anita**, Alabado 525-5, T084-225933, amaruhostal3@speedy.com.pe, with bath, safe, quiet, good breakfast. Also the **Amaru Valle Hotel** in Urubamba.

C Andes de San Blas, Carmen Alto 227, T084-242346, www.andesdesanblas.com. Very friendly, family run hostel in an excellent location mid-way along Carmen Alto. Great views of Cuzco, Sacsayhuaman and Cristo Blanco from the small rooftop terrace and some rooms. Basic breakfast, living room with sofas and TV, internet access downstairs. The family can arrange tours; see general note, page 140. Rooms are clean and pleasant with basic decoration and comfy beds. Generally good.

C Hostal Kuntur Wasi, Tandapata 352-A, T084-227570, www.kunturws.com. Cheaper without bath, services include a safe, use of the kitchen and laundry (both extra), Wi-Fi. Great views from the terrace where you can breakfast. Very welcoming, helpful owners; a very pleasant place to stay.

C-D Hostal Sambleño, Carmen Alto 114, T084-262979, www.barnmed.com/hostalsambleno/index.htm. A lovely jumble of staircases overlooks a central courtyard. Rooms of varying quality, all with bath and hot water, breakfast available, laundry service. Beds are comfy, showers are electric.

D Hospedaje Jhuno, Carmen Alto 281, T084-233579, jhunohostel@hotmail.com. A small family-run *hospedaje*, clean rooms, family lounge. Breakfast is not included but guests can use the tiny kitchen.

D Hostal Pakcha Real, Tandapata 300, T084-237484, www.hostalpakchareal.com. Price includes airport/train/bus pick-up; rooms with bath (**E** without); breakfast, heaters and use of kitchen extra. Family-run with the comforts of home. Laundry service, spotless rooms, friendly and relaxed, but confirm booking if arriving late.

D-E Hostal Familiar Mirador del Inka, Tandapata 160, off Plaza San Blas, T084-241804, www.miradordelinka.info. This *hostal* was redeveloped in a very stylish way, with its Inca foundations and white colonial walls. Bedrooms with bath are spacious and some have great views. Price includes breakfast. The owner's son Edwin runs trekking trips and has an agency on site.

E pp Casa de la Gringa 1, Tandapata y Pasñapacana 148, T084-241168, www.casa delagringa.com. Individually decorated rooms, hot water, cable TV, use of kitchen, Wi-Fi, with a relaxed atmosphere. Also **E** per person **Casa de la Gringa 2**, Carmen Bajo 226, T084-254387, rooms with and without bath, breakfast included, internet. See **Another Planet** (Tour operators), below.

E Hospedaje Inka, Suytuccato 848, T084-231995, http://hospedajeinka.weebly.com. Taxis leave you at Plaza San Blas, walk steeply uphill for 5-10 mins, or phone the *hostal*. Price includes bath (cheaper without) and breakfast. Wonderful views, spacious rooms, very helpful owner, Américo.

F The Blue House, Kiskapata 291 (there are 2 Kiskapatas – this one runs parallel to and above Tandapata), T084-242407, www.aschisite02.activesbs.co.uk. Price per person. Snug little *hostal*, excellent value, with reductions for longer stays. Breakfast is included, DVD room, shared kitchen and great views with a small park in front.

F Hospedaje El Artesano de San Blas, Suytucato 790, T084-2639689, manosandinas@yahoo.com. Many clean, bright and airy rooms. As with the **Hospedaje Inka**, you need to walk up from San Blas.

F Hospedaje Familiar Inti Quilla, Atocsaycuchi 281, T084-252659. Breakfast not included and no facilities for making food. Colourful rooms around a little court-yard, quiet (on pedestrian street so taxis cannot drop you at the door). Good value.

F Hostal Familiar Carmen Alto, Carmen Alto 197, first on the right down steps (no sign), T084-224367, carmencitadelperu@hotmail.com. If there's no answer when ringing the bell, go to the shop next door, it's run by the same family. Basic rooms with great charac- ter (in one case, constructed around a huge tree). Tranquil, family-run, use of kitchen and washing machine. Carmen will make you a very good breakfast for US\$2. All rooms with shared bath, electric showers. Recommended.

East and southeast of the Plaza de Armas *p135, map p132*

LL Casa Andina Private Collection Cusco, Plazoleta de Limacpampa Chico 473, T084-232610, www.casa-andina.com. In a 16th-century mansion with 3 courtyards, this hotel is one of the recommended **Casa Andina** chain's upmarket establishments, with even higher standards of services and comfort than those listed above. Nice

location. It has all the main facilities, plus a gourmet restaurant, **Alma**, serving local cuisine and a bar with an extensive pisco collection. Attentive staff.

LL Libertador Palacio del Inka, in the Casa de los Cuatro Bustos, at Plazoleta Santo Domingo 259, T084-231961, www.libertador.com.pe. Splendid 5-star, award-winning hotel built on Inca ruins (the walls can be seen in the restaurant and bar), set around courtyards. 254 well-appointed rooms; the attention to detail is so great there are even Nazca Lines drawn in the sand of the ashtrays! Enjoy Andean music and dance over dinner in the excellent **Inti Raymi** restaurant. Recommended.

AL Munay Wasi Inn, Av Tulumayo 418, T084-240283, www.munaywasi.com. In the restored Casa del Reloj, 4 blocks from the Plaza de Armas, price includes buffet breakfast, restaurant and bar.

AL-A Sonesta Hotel Cusco, Av Sol 954, T084-224322, www.sonesta.com/cusco/. Sonesta has refurbished the old Hotel Savoy, with modern, comfortable rooms, cable TV, Wi-Fi, restaurant and bar.

D Maison de la Jeunesse (affiliated to Hostelling International), Av Sol, Cuadra 5, Pasaje Grace, Edificio San Jorge (down a small side street opposite Qoricancha), T084-235617, www.hostellingcuscoperu.com. Price is for a double room and includes bath and breakfast. A bed in a dorm with shared bath is **F**, breakfast included; HI discount. Very friendly hostel, TV and video room, internet, Wi-Fi, lockers, cooking facilities and very hot water.

F Albergue Casa Campesina, Av Tullumayo 274, T084-233466, reservas@apu.cbc.org.pe. Price includes breakfast, shared bathrooms only. A lovely place, set up to support the work of the **Casa Campesina** organization (www.cbc.org.pe/casacampesina/), which is linked to local *campesina* communities. On the same site is the **Store of the Weavers** (see Shopping, page 158). The money that people pay for accommodation goes to this good cause. 23% discount for **SAE** members. On the same avenue is Hotel La Casa de Fray

Bartolomé, Tullumayo 465, T084-233472, adm.fray@apu.cbc.org.pe, which is more expensive than the Albergue, 21 rooms with bath, restaurant and bar. Also **La Familia Café Literaria** and **Panadería Qosqo Maki**.
F Estrellita, Av Tullumayo 445, parte Alta, T084-234134. Price includes breakfast and tea and coffee all day. TV, video and old stereo in the tiny communal sitting area, basic kitchen for guests. Rooms are multiples with shared bath, plus 2 with private bath. Basic but excellent value. It is about a 15-min walk from the centre. When you arrive ring the bell several times and wait; you will be given your own keys when you register. Safe parking for cars and bikes. Recommended.

West and northwest of the Plaza de Armas *p138, map p132*

AL-A Hostal El Balcón, Tambo de Montero 222, T084-236738, www.balconcusco.com. Price includes breakfast. Lovingly restored 1630 colonial house with rooms set around a beautiful garden, homely atmosphere. Ask for a TV if you want one. Restaurant and kitchen for guests, laundry service. Recommended.
A Cusco Plaza 2, Saphi 486, T084-263000, www.cuscoplazahotels.com. Under same management as the **Cusco Plaza 1** (see page 143). The 24 nicely decorated rooms are set around 3 charming covered patios. Price includes American breakfast, and all rooms have cable TV and heating.
A Hostal Andenes de Saphi, Saphi 848, T084-227561, www.andenesdesaphi.com. Price includes continental breakfast and all rooms have heaters. Very friendly little hostel with a cosmopolitan atmosphere. Each room is decorated in a different style; the 4-bed family room is very nice. Lovely entertainment/games room, and a small but pleasant garden.
A-B Cahuide, Saphi 845, T084-222771, www.hotelcahuide-cusco.com. Price (negotiate for a discount, especially for longer stays) includes American breakfast. Cable TV in all rooms, ask for a heater. A modern hotel with 1970s furniture, plain white walls and comfy beds. Helpful staff.

B-C Hostal San Isidro Labrador, Saphi 440, T084-226241, labrador@qnet.com.pe. Continental breakfast included in the price. Pleasant 3-star hostal with elegant but simple decor, colonial arches and lovely patios. Plenty of hot water and heating.
C Hostel Loki, Cuesta Santa Ana 601, T084-243705, www.lokihostel.com/en/cusco. (From **F** per person). Huge, ultra-funky hostel in a restored viceroy's residence on the super-steep Cuesta Santa Ana. Dorms and rooms are set around a beautiful courtyard, and the view alone makes the climb well worth the effort. The beds have comfortable duvets, there's plenty of hot water, free internet access and lots of chill-out areas. A great place to meet other travellers.
C Niños Hotel, Meloc 442, T084-231424, www.ninoshotel.com. Price does not include the excellent breakfast. Services include the cafeteria and laundry service, Dutch, English, German and French spoken. Spotless, beautiful rooms in a 17th-century colonial house funding a fantastic charity, *Niños Unidos Peruanos*, established by Jolanda van den Berg. Also has **Niños 2** (same price), on C Fierro, a little further from the centre, 20 nicely decorated, clean and airy rooms, surrounding the central courtyard, and apartments in the same price range, also on C Fierro. Also **AL-A** Niños Hacienda in the village of Huasao, with bungalows, rooms, pool, horse riding. Contact the main hotel for reservations and for weekend packages.
C-D Hostal Qorichaska, Nueva Alta 458, T084-228974, www.qorichaskaperu.com. Price includes breakfast, use of well-equipped kitchen, internet and safe. Also has dorms, mixed and women only, **F** per preson without breakfast. Laundry service. Rooms are clean and sunny; ask for the older rooms – they're bigger and have traditional balconies. Friendly and recommended.
E Hostal Familiar, Saphi 661, T084-239353. Popular *hostal* in a colonial house 3 blocks from the central plaza. Most beds are comfy, hot water all day. Luggage deposit costs US$2.85 a day for a big pack.

E Hostal Killipata, Killichapata 238, just off Tambo de Montero, T084-236668, www.cusco.net/killipata/. **F** per person in shared rooms. Very clean, family-run lodging with good showers, hot water and fully equipped kitchen. Breakfast is US$2 extra. Recommended.

E Hostal Rickch'airy, Tambo de Montero 219, T084-236606. **F** without bath. Backpackers' haunt with views from the garden. Owner Leo has tourist information and will collect guests from the station.

E Suecia II, Tecseccocha 465 (no bell – knock!), T084-239757, www.hostalsuecia2 cusco.com (it is wise to book ahead). **F** without bath, breakfast extra from 0500. In a beautiful building, rooms are set around a glass-covered colonial courtyard and are warm. Beds have thick foam mattresses, water not always hot or bathrooms clean, can be noisy and the luggage store is closed at night, otherwise a good meeting place.

F Albergue Municipal, Kiskapata 240, near San Cristóbal, T084-252506, albergue@ municusco.gob.pe. Private rooms with double beds and dormitories in this very clean, helpful youth hostel. Nice communal area with cable TV and video. No rooms have bath. Great views, cafeteria and laundry facilities (laundry service US$0.75 per kg). Showers are electric, but there is no kitchen.

F Hostal Luzerna, Av Baja 205, near San Pedro train station (take a taxi at night), T084-232762. Price includes breakfast. A nice family-run *hostal*, hot water, good beds, clean, safe to leave luggage. Recommended.

Away from the centre

A Residencial Torre Dorada, C los Cipreses N–5, Residencial Huancaro, T084-241698, www.torredorada.com.pe. In a tranquil suburb to the west of the airport, this sparklingly clean modern hotel makes up in service for anything it might lose in location. Good size rooms with very comfortable beds, heating and plenty of hot water in the well-appointed en suite bathrooms. Buffet breakfast is included, as is free transportation to and from the airport/bus/train station, and daily to the historical centre of Cuzco. Internet access and Wi-Fi are also available. An excellent option for people looking to stay in a quieter part of town. Highly recommended.

🍴 Eating

Plaza de Armas and around
p131, maps p132 and p136

Procuradores and Plateros are 2 streets that lead off the northwest side of the Plaza de Armas. Procuradores, or **Gringo Alley** as the locals call it, is good for a value feed; its menus take the hungry backpacker from Mexico to Italy, Spain and Turkey. None is dreadful, many are very good indeed, especially for the price. Parallel with Gringo Alley, Plateros also has good-value places to eat. It is also lined with a great many tour operators, so you can wander up and down checking what deals are on offer.

Bistrot 370, Triunfo 370, p 2, T084-224908. Lima chef Rafael Osterling's Cuzco restaurant. 'Fusion' cuisine, blending Peruvian classics with Oriental touches, smart and highly regarded, well-stocked bar and a good wine list, cosy seating areas.

Chicha, Plaza Regocijo 261, p 2 (above El Truco), T084-240520, reservacionescusco@ chicha.com.pe. Daily 1200-2400. 1 of a group of 3 restaurants, the others in Arequipa and, yet to open, in Trujillo, which specialise in dishes of the region using recipes created by Gastón Acurio (see under Lima, Eating). There are also lighter meals if you prefer. The food here is of the highest standard in a renovated colonial house, at one time the royal mint, tastefully decorated, open-to-view kitchen, excellent selection of cocktails based on pisco, good service. Warmly recommended.

Cicciolina, Triunfo 393, 2nd floor, T084-239510, www.cicciolinacuzco.com. Sophisticated restaurant focusing largely on Italian/Mediterranean cuisine. It also has a tapas bar and a boutique bakery; the kitchens are open to view. The impressive wine list draws from across the globe but the emphasis is on Latin American produce. Good atmosphere, fine decor and great for a treat. Ask about their **Catering** scheme: a gourmet picnic will be taken to the location of your choice, with chef, waiters and all the trimmings (best for groups).

ŦŦŦ El Truco, Plaza Regocijo 261. Excellent local and international dishes, used a lot by tour groups, buffet lunch 1200-1500, nightly folk music at 2045, next door is **Taberna del Truco**, which is open 0900-0100.

ŦŦŦ Fusiones, Av El Sol 106, T084-233341. Open 1100-2300. In the new commercial centre La Merced, 2nd floor, very close to Plaza de Armas. Novo Andino and international cuisine, fine wines. Accepts credit cards.

ŦŦŦ Incanto, Santa Catalina Angosta 135, T084-254753, incanto@cuscorestaurants. com. Open daily 1100-2400. Under same ownership as **Inka Grill** and with the same standards, this new restaurant has Inca stone work and serves pastas, grilled meats, pizzas, desserts, accompanied by an extensive wine list. There is also a Peruvian delicatessen on the premises. Upstairs is **Greens Organic**, T084-243379, greens@cuscorestaurants.com, exclusively organic ingredients in fusion cuisine and a fresh daily buffet.

ŦŦŦ Inka Grill, Portal de Panes 115, T084-262992, www.inkagrillcusco.com. Daily 1100-2300. According to many the best food in town is served here, specializing in Novo Andino cuisine (the use of native ingredients and 'rescued' recipes) and innovative dishes, also home-made pastas, wide vegetarian selection, live music, excellent coffee and home-made pastries 'to go'. A good place to spoil yourself. Recommended.

ŦŦŦ Kusikuy, Suecia 339, T084-292870. Mon-Sat 0800-2300. Some say this serves the best *cuy* (guinea pig, US$20) in town and the owners say if you give them an hour's warning they will produce their absolute best. Many other typical Cuzco dishes on the menu. Set lunch is US$7. Also has live music.

ŦŦŦ La Retama, Portal de Panes 123, 2nd floor, T084-226372. Excellent Novo Andino food and service. There's a balcony, an enthusiastic music and dance group and art exhibitions.

ŦŦŦ Limo, Portal de Carnes 236, T084-240668, www.cuscorestaurants.com. On 2nd floor of a colonial mansion overlooking the Plaza de Armas, creative Peruvian cuisine with strong emphasis on fish and seafood, all prepared to the highest of standards. It has a pisco bar, good service and atmosphere. A good choice for a special occasion.

ŦŦŦ Maikhana, Av El Sol 106, T084-252044, www.maikhana.net. Authentic Indian restaurant in a mini-mall, serving filling curry, Indian breads, unlimited rice and lassies. Also has a coffee house and sports bar, free internet and phone.

ŦŦŦ Pachacútec Grill and Bar, Portal de Panes 105, www.pachacutecrestaurant.com. International cuisine including seafood and Italian specialities, also features folk music shows nightly.

ŦŦŦ Tunupa, Portal Confiturías 233, 2nd floor. One of the finest restaurants on the plaza (often used by tour groups). Also has the longest (glassed-in) balcony but this is narrow and best for couples only. Food is international, traditional and Novo Andino; wine list is limited. Also an excellent buffet that includes a pisco sour and a hot drink. In the evenings there is an excellent group playing 16th- and 17th- century-style Cuzqueñan music of their own composition, with dancers. Recommended.

ŦŦŦ Tupananchis, Portal Mantas 180, T084-245159/976 4494, tupananchis_ rest_cusco@hotmail.com. Tasty, beautifully presented Novo Andino and fusion cuisine in a smart, sophisticated atmosphere. Try the alpaca curry, river fish *ceviche* or stuffed chicken supreme. There is a café next door. Highly recommended.

ŦŦŦ-ŦŦ La Cosa Nostra, Plateros 358A, p 2, T084-232992. Open 1200-2300. Sicilian/ Peruvian-owned Italian place with good food and service, à la carte, wine list, unpretentious and intimate.

¶ Al Grano, Santa Catalina Ancha 398, T084-228032. Mon-Sat 1000-2100. Lunchtime menu US$3 is a good option if you are fed up with other menus. Evening serves 5 authentic Asian dishes for US$6, menu changes daily. Without doubt some of the best coffee in town, vegetarian choices and breakfasts, including 'Full English'. Recommended.

¶ A Mi Manera, Triunfo 393, T084-222219, www.amimaneraperu.com. Remodelled in 2006, imaginative Novo Andino cuisine with open kitchen. Both great hospitality and a good atmosphere.

¶ Pucará, Plateros 309. Mon-Sat 1230-2200. Peruvian and international food – no language skills required as a sample plate of their daily menu is placed in the window at lunchtime. Japanese owner does very good *aji de gallina* (garlic chicken) and cream of potato soup, pleasant atmosphere. Recommended.

¶ The Real McCoy, Plateros 326, p 2, T084-261111, http://www.bookingbox.org/realmccoy/index.html. A fabulous retreat for homesick Brits and Aussies. There's a good-value breakfast buffet, with PG Tips and Heinz Baked Beans, and a huge Full English. On offer for dinner are some English classics: roast beef with Yorkshire pudding, or try roast alpaca for a twist, chicken pie, bangers and mash, to name but a few. Finish it all off with banoffee pie or apple crumble with custard and cream, or a chocolate fondue if you can manage it. Wi-Fi and comfy sofas and well-stocked book exchange.

¶ Witches Garden, Loreto 125, T084-244077, www.witchesgarden.net. Good Novo Andino, Québécois and international cuisine served in this warmly decorated little restaurant; the chicken and beef dishes, the Montreal Classic Combo and the desserts are recommended. There's TV and video, with a selection of movies, available for patrons. French- Canadian owned.

¶ Bembos, Portal Comercio 153. Peru's answer to MacDonalds. Originally from San Isidro, Lima, Bembos has grown from sandwiches sold from the back of a bicycle

to a chain in Lima and this one in Cuzco. Burgers and sandwiches are based on traditional Peruvian fare, such as *uchucuta* and *cecina con tacacho*. Very popular. Also has a coffee shop and internet on the 2nd floor.

¶ El Encuentro, Santa Catalina Ancha 384, T084-247977, Choquechaca 136, T084-225496, and Tigre 130, www.restaurantel encuentro.blogspot.com. One of the best-value eateries, 3 courses of good healthy food and a drink will set you back US$2, very busy at lunchtime, especially at Santa Catalina.

¶ El Fogón, Plateros 365. Huge local *menú del día*, good solid food at reasonable prices. Very popular.

¶ Los Candiles, Plateros 323. Good set lunch.

¶ Paloma Imbis, Procuradores 362. The *rollo mixto* comes in delicious home-baked bread. Has doner kebabs. For vegetarians the *rollo de falafel y queso* is a tasty option.

¶ Víctor Victoria, Tecsecocha 466, T084-252854. Israeli and local dishes, highly recommended for breakfast, good value.

Cafés, delis and panaderías

Amaru, Plateros 325, 2nd floor, T084-246976. Limitless coffee, tea, great bread and juices served, even on non-buffet breakfasts. Colonial balcony; also a pub serving pizzas, etc. Recommended.

Café El Ayllu, Almagro 133, T084-232357, and Marqués 263, T084-255078, www.inkaworld.org/cafeayllu. The new locations of one of Cuzco's oldest cafés (it used to be on the Plaza de Armas). Fantastic breakfasts (have the special fruit salad, sandwiches, coffee and classical music as well as wonderful apple pastries. The *ponche con pisco* is an excellent way to end a cold evening. Superb service.

Café Halliy, Plateros 363. Popular meeting place, especially for breakfast, good for comments on guides, has good snacks and *copa Halliy* (fruit, muesli, yoghurt, honey and chocolate cake), also serves vegetarian dishes.

Café Perla, Santa Catalina Ancha 304, on the plazoleta. Extensive menu of light meals, coffee, including beans for sale roasted on the premises. Popular.

Dolce Vita, Santa Catalina Ancha 366 (with another branch on Márquez). 1000-2100. Delicious Italian ice cream, this *heladería* is an absolute must.

La Bondiet, Av Márquez y Heladeros. Clean, simple café with a huge selection of sweet and savoury pastries, good sandwiches, juices and coffee.

The Muse Too, Tandapata 917, above the Plazoleta San Blas. This is a new location, back in San Blas. The other location on Plateros has closed, and is moving to Triunfo 338, 2nd floor, just up from Paddy's Bar. A funky little café with a cosy feel and great views over the plaza. Fresh coffee locally grown in Quillabamba, good food, including vegetarian lasagne, chicken curry, carrot cake and the best smoothies in town. There's often live music in the afternoons/evenings with no cover charge. English owner Clair is very helpful. The Muse will refill water bottles for a small charge in an attempt to minimize plastic waste in Cuzco.

Trotamundos, Portal Comercio 177, 2nd floor. Mon-Sat 0800-2400. One of the most pleasant cafés in the plaza if a bit pricey. Has a balcony overlooking the plaza and a warm atmosphere especially at night with its open fire. Good coffees and cakes, safe salads, *brochetas*, sandwiches and pancakes as well as computers with internet access.

Yaku Mama, Procuradores 397. Good for breakfast; unlimited fruit and coffee. Service can be slow.

North and northeast of the Plaza de Armas *p134, map p132*

🍴🍴🍴 **Fallen Angel**, Plazoleta Nazarenas 320, T084-258184, www.fallenangelincusco.com. Mon-Sat 1100 till whenever (bar closes at midnight, kitchen at 2300), Tue and Sun opens at 1500. Like nowhere else. This is the 2nd venture of Cuzco native Andrés Zúñiga (the other being **Macondo** – see below). The menu features steaks and some innovative pasta dishes. Cocktails are excellent. Live DJ at night. Regular parties/fashion shows

are always events to remember. Free Wi-Fi. Always phone to reserve.

🍴🍴🍴 **MAP Café**, Plaza de las Nazarenas 231, a glass structure in the **Museo de Arte Precolombino**, T084-242476. Operates as a café 1000-1830 and a restaurant 1830-2200. Serves excellent Peruvian-Andean cuisine and international food, with an innovative children's menu. It has a very good list of wines and piscos. After your museum visit, this is an ideal place for tea or coffee or a sophisticated meal.

🍴🍴🍴 **Baco**, Ruinas 465, T084-242808, bacorestaurante@yahoo.com. Wine bar and bistro-style restaurant with same owner as **Cicciolina**. Specializes in *degustación* meals for groups, with barbecued and grilled meats, vegetarian dishes, interesting pizzas, and good wines. Unpretentious but comfortable, with a wide range of prices.

🍴🍴🍴 **Justina**, Palacios 110. Open Mon-Sat from 1800. Good value pizzería, with wine bar. It's at the back of a patio.

🍴🍴🍴 **L'Osteria della Locanda**, Quiskapata 215, T084-252551, riserve@osteriadellalocanda. com. Mon-Sat, evenings only; book in advance if possible. In the same group as Piccola Locanda and an Italian/Peruvian-run tour company. Excellent handmade Italian food, fresh pasta, pizza and lasagna created as you wait with imported olive oil and parmesan. US$0.50 per table goes towards 2 family-run children's projects in the area.

🍴🍴-🍴 **Yanapay**, Ruinas 415, p 2. Good café serving breakfast, lunch and dinner. Run by a charity which supports children's homes (www.aldeayanapay.org). They welcome volunteers.

Cafés, delis and panaderías

Café Punchay, Choquechaca 229. German-owned café with speciality coffees, cocktails, pastas, sandwiches, cakes, garden and big screen for live sports broadcasts.

Chocolate, Choquechaca 162, T084-984 752172 (mob). Good for coffee and cakes but the real highlights are the fresh gourmet chocolates (up to European standards) and deliciously rich hot chocolate with marshmallows.

San Blas p135, map p132

Pachapapa, Plazoleta San Blas 120, opposite church of San Blas, T084-241318. Open 1130-2200. A beautiful patio restaurant in a wonderful old colonial house, with resident harp player. Under same ownership as Inka Grill. Very good Cuzqueña dishes, including *pachamanca* (previous reservation required for 6 people). At night, diners can sit in their own private colonial dining room. Recommended.

Jack's Café, on the corner of Choquechaca and San Blas. T084-806960. Opens at 0630 for great-value English breakfast. Excellent varied menu with generous portions, all in a light and relaxed atmosphere. Fabulous American-style pancakes and freshly ground local coffee. Lunchtime can be very busy, expect to queue outside in the high season.

La Bodega, Carmen Alto 146. Snug Dutch- and Peruvian-owned café/restaurant serving hot chocolate by candlelight in the afternoons and with evening meals. Dishes come with a trip to the salad bar, American breakfast and a good-value lunch menu. Highly recommended.

Macondo, Cuesta San Blas 571, T084-229415. www.macondoincusco.com. A bit pricier than others in this range but fantastic. A casual, cosy, arty and comfortable restaurant that's been redecorated under a change of ownership. Serves an exotic menu with jungle and Novo Andino food. It also has an art gallery. Popular, and a steep 3-block walk from the plaza. Happy hour 1500-1800. Visa attracts a 10% surcharge. Recommended.

Tika Bistro Gourmet, Tocuyeros 566, T084-237900, www.casasanblas.com/tikabistro. A snug, beautifully decorated little eatery, underneath the Casa San Blas, offers an eating experience on par with London or Paris. Dishes range from filling and beautifully presented stuffed meats with spicy risottos, through to oriental plates of spicy beef wantons and spring rolls of various flavours, served with a variety of mouth-watering sauces. The wine list, largely Latin American, is excellent, as is the service.

Granja Heidi, Cuesta San Blas 525, T084-238383. Offers 3- or 4-course *menú del día* in a clean and relaxed environment. There are usually vegetarian options; superb yoghurt, granola, ricotta cheese and honey and other breakfast choices.

Inka...fé, Choquechaca 131-A, T084-258073, www.inkafe.com.pe. Good coffee, set breakfasts and good-value lunch menus. Their signature dishes are Inka..fé chicken or risotto; excellent main meals at a good price. Range of sandwiches in French bread and good desserts. English spoken. They have a delicatessen opposite at No 140.

Cafés, delis and panaderías

Juanito's Sandwich Café, Qanchipata 596. Cuzco's answer to a university greasy spoon burger bar. Great grilled veggie and meaty burgers and sandwiches with titles like 'La Cabaña' and the '4 x 4'. Coffee, tea and hot chocolate. Juanito himself is a great character, staff are friendly, and the café stays open late, a classic post-club/party retreat.

Panadería El Buen Pastor, Cuesta San Blas 579. Very good bread and pastries, excellent meat and chicken *empanadas*. The proceeds go to a charity for orphans and street children. Very popular with backpackers. Recommended.

East and southeast of the Plaza de Armas *p135, map p132*

¶¶ **El Baton del Inka**, Hatun Rumiyoc 487, 2nd floor, T084-601304. Specializes in Peruvian food but also good international and vegetarian menu.

¶¶ **Inkanato**, San Agustín 280, T084-222926, www.perou.net. Good food, staff dressed in Inca outfits and dishes made only with ingredients known in Inca times.

¶¶ **Los Toldos**, Almagro 171 y San Andrés 219. If you're feeling peckish, on a budget and fancy being served by waiters in a bow tie, try their great chicken *brocheta*. Comes with fries, a trip to the salad bar and is enough for 2 people at just US$2.30. Also *trattoria* with home-made pasta and pizza, delivery T084-229829.

¶ **Chifa Sipan**, Quera 251 (better than their other branch for tourists in Plateros). Owner Carlos may not sound Chinese but he is and joins in the cooking at this excellent restaurant. There is no great ambience but it's busy at lunchtimes with locals, which speaks volumes. Skip to the back of the menu for better deals.

South and southwest of the Plaza de Armas *p137, map p132*

¶ **San Pedro market**, to eat really cheaply, and if your stomach is acclimatized to South American food, head for the market 5 blocks southwest of the Plaza de Armas and eat at one of the many stalls. Food will cost no more than US$0.70 and 3-fruit juices are just US$0.45. Otherwise, look for the set *menús*, usually served 1200- 1500, although they are no good for vegetarians.

Cafés, delis and panaderías

Manu Café, Av Pardo 1046. Good coffee and good food too in a jungle decor. It would be a sin to miss one of their liqueur coffees.

Moni, San Agustín 311, T084-231029, www.moni-cusco.com. Peruvian/English-owned, good fresh food and breakfast, British music, magazines, bright, clean and comfy.

⏻ Bars and clubs

Cuzco city *p128, maps p132 and p136*
Bars
Bar 7, Tandapata 690, San Blas, T084-506472. Good food and drinks in a trendy bar specializing in local ingredients.

The Cross Keys, Triunfo 350 (upstairs), T084-229227, www.cross-keys-pub-cusco-peru.com. 1100-0130. Run by Barry Walker

CROSS KEYS

Pub & Restaurant

Calle Triunfo 350
Cusco - Peru
Tel: +51 (84) 229227
www.cross-keys-pub-cusco-peru.com
CrossKeys@ManuExpeditions.com

of **Manu Expeditions,** a Mancunian and ornithologist, this Cuzco institution moved from the Plaza de Armas in 2009 into its new, cosier location on Triunfo. Darts, cable sports, pool, bar meals, plus daily half-price specials Sun-Wed, great pisco sours, very popular, with a great atmosphere. The only English-style pub in Cuzco.

Indigo, Tecseccocha 2, p 2, T084-260271. Shows 3 films a day, also has a lounge and cocktail bar and serves Asian and local food. A log fire keeps out the night-time cold.

Km 0 (Arte y Tapas), Tandapata 100, San Blas. Lovely Mediterranean-themed bar tucked in behind San Blas. Good snacks and tapas (of course), affordable, and with live music every night (around 2200 – lots of acoustic guitar, etc).

Los Perros Bar, Tecseccocha 436, above Gringo Alley (Procuradores). A great place to chill on comfy couches listening to excellent music. There's a book exchange, English and other magazines and board games. Opens 1100 for coffee and pastries; kitchen opens at 1300; very good vegetarian lunch, closes 0100. Occasionally hosts live music and special events. Opened a take-out only branch in 2009 at Suecia 368 which operates from midnight to 0600 for good quality, post-club food.

Marcelo Batata, Palacios 121, 3rd floor, T084-222424, www.cuzcodining.com. Bar/restaurant offering sandwiches and international food. The service is slow, but it's worth going to sit on the rooftop for the great 360-degree panorama and enjoy the Cuzco sunshine.

Norton Rat's Tavern, Santa Catalina Angosta 116, nortonrats@yahoo.com. Opens at 0700 for breakfast, and through the day till 0230. This pub has a fine, sunny balcony overlooking the corner of the Plaza de Armas. Pleasant, popular, with a pool table, dart boards and other games, cable TV and lots of flags and pictures of motorbikes. Owner Jeffrey Powers loves the machines and can provide information for bikers. Serves burgers, etc and a full Mexican menu, with a good selection of beers. See **Hostal Gocta Cuzco,** above.

Paddy's Pub, C Triunfo 124, corner of the plaza, 1300-0100. An Irish theme pub, deservedly popular. Good seating and great food – the jacket potatoes, shepherd's pie and baguettes are all highly recommended.

Rosie O'Grady's, at Santa Catalina Ancha 360, T084-247935. Open 1100 till late (food served till midnight, happy hours 1300-1400, 1800-1900, 2300-2330). Has good music, tasty food. English and Russian spoken.

Clubs

Before your evening meal don't turn down flyers being handed out around the Plaza de Armas. Each coupon not only gives you free entry, it is worth a *cuba libre*. On the back of this tour you will be able to check out which club most suits your tastes. Sadly, the free entry-and-drink system doesn't appear to apply to Peruvians who are invariably asked to pay, even if their tourist companions get in for free. This discrimination should be discouraged. Also note that free drinks are made with the cheapest, least healthy alcohol; always watch your drink being made and obviously never leave it unattended. If you fancy learning a few Latin dance steps before hitting the dancefloor, many of the clubs offer free lessons. Ask at the door for details or look out for flyers.

El Garabato Video Music Club, Espaderos 132, 3rd floor. Daily 1600-0300. Dance area, lounge for chilling, bar with saddles for stools, tastefully decorated in a colonial setting, with live shows 2300-0300 (all sorts of styles) and a large screen showing music videos. Recommended.

Extreme, on Suecia, next door to **Magtas Bar.** An old Cuzco staple. Movies are shown late afternoon and early evening, but after midnight this place really gets going with an eclectic range of music, from 60s and 70s rock and pop to techno and trance. This place seems to give out more free drinks than most, so it's a good option for kicking off a big night on the town!

Kamikaze, plaza Regocijo 274, T084-233865. Peña at 2200, good old traditional rock music, candle-lit cavern atmosphere, entry US$2.50 but usually you don't have to pay.

Mama Africa, Portal de Panes 190. Cool music and clubbers' spot. Serves good food from a varied menu, happy hour until 2300, good value.

Mythology, Portal de Carnes 298, p 2. Tucked in the corner of the plaza. A popular spot but don't expect cutting-edge tunes. It's more an early 80s and 90s combination of cheese, punk and classic. They also show movies in the afternoons. Food in served in the jungle themed **Lek Café**.

Roots, Huaynápata 194 (just of Suecia). Plays mostly reggae, but there are other styles too, good atmosphere and popular.

Siete Angelitos, Siete Angelitos 638. Tiny hole-in-the-wall bar, just a couple of rooms really, but spectacular cocktails and good food (especially the pasta dishes and steaks), a friendly owner by the name of Walter and an awesome atmosphere when things get going. Often hosts guest DJs, ranging from Latin to trance.

Ukuku's, Plateros 316. US$1.35 entry or free with a pass. This is somewhat different to the other clubs as every night there is a live band that might play anything from rock to salsa. The DJ then plays a mixture of Peruvian and international music but the emphasis is on local. It has a good mix of Cuzqueños and tourists. Videos are shown here at 1600 and 1800. Films are free with any purchase.

✪ Entertainment

Cuzco city *p128, maps p132 and p136*
Centro Qosqo de Arte Nativo, Av Sol 604, T084-227901. There's a regular nightly folklore show here 1900-2030, entrance on the BTC visitor ticket.

Teatro Inti Raymi, Saphi 605. Music nightly at 1845, US$4.50 entry and well worth it.

Teatro Kusikay, Unión 117, T084-255414, www.kusikay.com (tickets from the theatre Mon-Sat 0900-2100 or, out of hours, **Inka Grill** or **Incanto** restaurants, or at the **Mayu Café** at Ollantaytambo train station). Mon-Sat 1930. US$35, thrilling show with spectacular dances based on the Mamacha Carmen festival of Paucartambo, with lavish costumes, special effects and a troupe of 30.

Teatro Municipal, C Mesón de la Estrella 149 (T084-227321 for information 0900-1300 and 1500-1900). This is a venue for plays, dancing and shows, mostly Thu-Sun. Ask for their programmes. They also run classes in music and dancing Jan-Mar that are great value.

✪ Festivals and events

Cuzco city *p128, maps p132 and p136*
20 Jan A procession of saints in the San Sebastián district of Cuzco.

Feb/Mar Carnival in Cuzco is a messy affair with flour, water, cacti, rotten fruit and manure thrown in the streets. Be prepared.

Mar/Apr Easter Mon sees the procession of El Señor de los Temblores (Lord of the Earthquakes), starting at 1600 outside the cathedral. A large crucifix is paraded through the streets, returning to the plaza de Armas around 2000 to bless the tens of thousands of people who have assembled there.

2-3 May The Vigil of the Cross takes place at all mountaintops with crosses on them, is a boisterous affair.

Jun Corpus Christi, on the Thu after Trinity Sunday, when all the statues of the Virgin and of saints from Cuzco's churches are paraded through the streets to the cathedral. This is a colourful event. The Plaza de Armas is surrounded by tables with women selling *cuy* (guinea pig) and a mixed grill called *chiriuchu* (*cuy*, chicken, tortillas, fish eggs, water-weeds, maize, cheese and sausage) and lots of Cusqueña beer.

The festival of Inti Raymi

The sun was the principal object of Inca worship and at their winter solstice, in June, the Incas honoured the solar deity with a great celebration known as Inti Raymi, the sun festival. The Spanish suppressed the Inca religion, and the last royal Inti Raymi was celebrated in 1535.

However, in 1944, a group of Cuzco intellectuals, inspired by the 'indigenist' movement, revived the ceremony in the form of a pageant, putting it together from chronicles and historical documents. The event caught the public imagination, and it has been celebrated every year since then on 24 Jun, now a Cuzco public holiday. Hundreds of local men and women play the parts of Inca priests, nobles, chosen women, soldiers (played by the local army garrison), runners, and the like. The coveted part of the Inca emperor Pachacuti is won by audition, and the event is organized by the municipal authorities.

It begins around 1000 at the Qoricancha (page 135) – the former sun temple of Cuzco – and winds its way up the main avenue into the Plaza de Armas, accompanied by songs, ringing declarations and the occasional drink of chicha. At the main plaza, Cuzco's presiding mayor is whisked back to Inca times, to receive Pachacuti's blessing and a stern lecture on good government. Climbing through Plaza Nazarenas and up Pumacurcu, the procession reaches the ruins of Sacsayhuaman at about 1400.

Before Pachacuti arrives the Sinchi (Pachacuti's chief general) ushers in contingents from the four Suyus (regions) of the Inca empire. Much of the ceremony is based around alternating action between these four groups of players. A Chaski (messenger) enters to announce the imminent arrival of the Inca and his Coya (queen). Men sweep the ground before him and women scatter flowers. The Inka takes the stage alone and has a dialogue with the sun. Then he receives reports from the governors of the four Suyus. This is followed by a drink of the sacred chicha, the re-lighting of the sacred fire of the empire, the sacrifice (faked) of a llama and the reading of auguries in its entrails. Finally the ritual eating of sankhu (corn paste mixed with the victim's blood) ends the ceremonies. The Inca gives a last message to his assembled children, and departs. The music and dancing continues until nightfall. See also Festivals and events, below.

Jun Qoyllur Rit'i (Snow Star Festival), held at a 4700-m glacier north of Ocongate (Ausangate), 150 km southeast of Cuzco. It has its final day 58 days after Easter Sunday. Getting there involves a 2-hr walk up from the nearest road at Mawayani, beyond Ocongate, then it's a further exhausting climb up to the glacier. It's a good idea to take a tent, food and plenty of warm clothing. Many trucks leave Cuzco, from Limacpampa, in the days prior to the full moon in mid-Jun; prices from US$2 upwards. This is a very rough and dusty overnight journey lasting 14 hrs, requiring warm clothing and coca leaves to fend off cold and exhaustion. Several agencies offer tours, see page 160.

24 Jun Inti Raymi, the Inca festival of the winter solstice (see box, above) is enacted at the fortress of Sacsayhuaman. The spectacle starts at 1000 at the Qoricancha (crowds line the streets and jostle for space to watch), then proceeds to the Plaza de Armas. From there performers and spectators go to Sacsayhuaman for the main event, which starts at 1300. It lasts 2½ hrs and is in Quechua. Tickets for the stands can be bought in advance from the **Emufec** office, Santa Catalina Ancha 325, and cost US$80 (less if bought Mar-May). Travel agents can arrange the whole day for you, with meeting points, transport, reserved seats and packed lunch. Don't believe anyone who tries to persuade you to buy a ticket for the right to film or take photos. On the night before **Inti Raymi**, the Plaza de Armas is crowded with processions and food stalls. Try to arrive in Cuzco 15 days before Inti Raymi. The atmosphere in the town during the build up is fantastic and something is always going on (festivals, parades, etc).

Late Aug/early Sep The Huarachicoy Festival at Sacsayhuaman is a spectacular re-enactment of the Inca manhood rite, performed in dazzling costumes by boys of a local school.

8 Sep Day of the Virgin, when there's a colourful procession of masked dancers from the church of Almudena, at the southwest edge of Cuzco, near Belén, to the Plaza de San Francisco. There is also a fair at Almudena, and a bullfight the following day.

8 Dec Cuzco Day, when churches and museums close at 1200.

24 Dec Santuranticuy, 'the buying of saints'. This is a huge celebration of Christmas shopping with a big crafts market in the Plaza de Armas, which is very noisy until the early hrs of the 25th.

O Shopping

Cuzco city *p128, maps p132 and p136*
Arts and crafts
Cuzco has some of the best craft shopping in all Peru. In the Plaza San Blas and the surrounding area, authentic Cuzco crafts still survive and woodworkers can be seen in almost any street. A market is held on Sat. The main market for artisans' stalls is at the bottom of Av Sol. There are also small markets of 10 or so permament stalls dotted around the city that offer goods made from alpaca as well as modern materials.

Cuzco is also the weaving centre of Peru and excellent textiles can be found at good

value; but watch out for sharp practices when buying gold and silver objects and jewellery. Note that much of the wood used for picture frames, etc, is *cedro*, a rare timber not extracted by sustainable means.

Agua y Tierra, Plazoleta Nazarenas 167, and also at Cuesta San Blas 595, T084-226951. Excellent quality crafts from lowland rainforest communities, largely the Shipibo and Ashaninka tribes from the Selva Central whose work is considered to be among the finest in the Amazon Basin.

Alpaca 3, Ruinas 472. Quality alpaca items.

Alpaca Golden, Portal de Panes 151, T084-251724, alpaca.golden@terra.com.pe. Also at Plazoleta Nazarenas 175. Designer, producer and retailer of fine alpaca clothing.

Apacheta, San Juan de Dios 250, T084-238210, www.apachetaperu.com. Replicas of pre-Inca and Inca textiles, ceramics, alpaca goods, contemporary art gallery, and books on Andean culture.

Arte Vivo del Cusco al Mundo, on the right-hand side in Capilla San Ignacio, Plaza de Armas. Open 1030-1300, 1530-2100. The outlet for 2 cooperatives of weavers.

Calas, Siete Angelitos 619-B, San Blas. Handmade silver jewellery in interesting designs and alpaca goods from the community of Pitumarca.

Center for Traditional Textiles of Cusco, Av Sol 603-A, T084-228117, www.textiles cusco.org. A non-profit organization that promotes the weaving traditions of the area. Tours of workshops in Chinchero and beyond, also weaving classes. In the Cuzco outlet you can watch weavers at work. Excellent quality textiles at prices reflecting the fact that over 50% goes direct to the weaver. Recommended.

Hilo, Carmen Alto 260, T084-254536. Fashion gear for ladies and gents. Each item in this tiny little shop is designed separately and hand-made on-site. Influences seem to range from Inca to Heidi and back to Madonna's finest hour. Run by Eibhlin Cassidy, who can adjust and tailor designs and sometimes offers 'The best *chai* this side of Mumbai' to customers.

A market for beads

The huge variety of multicoloured beads for sale are called Inca beads, although this is, in fact, something of a misnomer. The Incas were talented potters who used detailed geometric motifs, but they are not known to have made beads. These have become popular relatively recently.

They used to be rolled individually by hand and were very time-consuming to produce. Now, in a major concession to consumerism, they are machine-made and produced in quantity, then hand-painted and glazed.

Today, the beads are produced in countless, often family-run, workshops in Cuzco and Pisac. Some are made into earrings, necklaces and bracelets, other are sold loose.

Ilaria, Portal Carrizos 258, T084-246253, and in hotels **Monasterio**, **Libertador** and at the airport. Branches of the recommended jewellery and silver stores from Lima.

Inka Treasure, Triunfo 375, T084-227470, www.inkatreasure.com.pe. With branches at Av Pardo 1080, Plazoleta Nazarenas 159 and Portal de Panes 163. Also at the airport and the airport in Juliaca. Fine jewellery including goldwork, mostly with pre-Columbian designs, and silver with the owner's designs. Tours of workshops at Av Circunvalación, near Cristo Blanco. The stores also incorporte the work of famed jeweller Carlos Chakiras.

Inkantations, Choquechaca 200. Radical baskets made from natural materials in all sorts of weird and wonderful shapes. Also ceramics and Andean weavings. Interesting and original.

Josefina Olivera, Portal Comercio 173, Plaza de Armas. Open daily 1100-2100. She sells old ponchos and antique *mantas* (shawls), without the usual haggling. Her prices are high, but it is worth it to save pieces being cut up to make other items.

Kuna by Alpaca 111, Plaza Regocijo 202, T084-243233. High-quality alpaca clothing, with shops also in hotels **Monasterio**, **Libertador** and Machu Picchu Sanctuary Lodge, and at the airport.

La Mamita, Portal de Carnes 244, Plaza de Armas, sells the ceramics of **Seminario-Behar** (see page 178), plus cotton, basketry, jewellery, etc.

La Pérez, Urb Mateo Pumacahua 598, Huanchac, T084-232186. A big cooperative with a good selection. They will arrange a free pick-up from your hotel.

Maky Artesanías, Carmen Alto 101, T084-653643. Individually designed ceramics. Ask for discounts if buying several pieces.

Mullu, Triunfo 120, T084-229831. Open Mon-Sat 1000-2100. Silver jewellery with semi-precious stones and cotton clothing with interesting designs.

Pedazo de Arte, Plateros 334B. A tasteful collection of Andean handicrafts, many designed by Japanese owner Miki Suzuki.

Primitiva, Hatun Rumiyoc 495, T084-260152, San Blas, www.coscio.com. Excellent Peruvian contemporary art gallery, largely featuring the work of Federico Coscio.

Spondylus, Cuesta San Blas 505 y Plazoleta San Blas 617, T084-226929, spondylus cusco@mixmail.com. Interesting jewellery in gold and silver, also using semi-precious stones and shells. They also sell T-shirts featuring Inca and pre-Inca designs.

Store of the Weavers (Asociación Central de Artesanos y Artesanas del Sur Andino Inkakunaq Ruwaynin), Av Tullumayo 274, T084-233466, www.cbc.org.pe/tejidosandinos. A store administered by 6 local weaving communities, some of whose residents you can see working on site. All profits go to the weavers themselves. Most of the work utilizes traditional dyes and the fine quality of the *mantas* and other textiles on sale makes this store well worth a visit.

Taki Museo de Música de los Andes, Hatunrumiyoq 487-5. Shop and workshop selling and displaying musical instruments, knowledgeable owner, who is an ethnomusicologist. Recommended.

Books

Centro de Estudios Regionales Andinos Bartolomé de las Casas, Av Tullumayo 465, T084-233472, www.cbc.org.pe. Mon-Sat 1100-1400, 1600-1900. Good books on Peruvian history, archaeology, etc. Head office is at Pampa de La Alianza 164, T084-245415.
Jerusalem, Heladeros 143, T084-235408. English books, guidebooks, music, postcards, book exchange (3 for 1).
Puro Perú, Heladeros 167. For new books, book exchange and music.
SBS (Special Book Services), Av Sol 781-A, opposite the post office, T084-248106. Mon-Fri 0830-1330, 1530-1930, Sat 0830-1300.
The Sun, Plazoleta Limacpampa Chico 471. This café/restaurant has the best book exchange, 1 for 1, run by an Australian.

Camping and outdoor equipment

There are several places on Plateros that rent out equipment but check it carefully as it is common for parts to be missing. A deposit of US$100 is asked, plus credit card, passport or plane ticket. Check stoves carefully. White gas (*bencina*) costs US$1.50 per litre and can be bought at hardware stores, but check the purity. Stove spirit (*alcohol para quemar*) is available at pharmacies. Blue gas canisters (US$5), can be found at some hardware stores and at shops that rent gear. You can also rent equipment through travel agencies.
Cordillera Cuzco, Garcilaso 210, T084-244133, www.cordillerastore.com. Boutique camping store. Footwear, clothing and accessories from top outdoor brands.
Edson Zuñiga Huillca, Mercado Rosaspata, Jr Abel Landeo P-1, T084-802831, T084-984 937243 (mob). 3 mins from Plaza de Armas, for repair of camping gear and footwear, also equipment rental, open 24 hrs a day, 7 days a week, English and Italian spoken.

Tatoo Adventure Gear, C del Medio 130, T084-254211, www.tatoo.ws. Adventure gear, high-quality hiking, climbing and camping gear, big brand names: Colombia, Gore-Tex, Polartec, etc. The house brand, Tatoo, produces good trousers, thermals, fleeces and jackets. Imported hiking boots. Tatoo also has branches in Lima and Huaraz.

Food and natural products

Casa Ecológica Cusco, Triunfo 393 and Portal de Carnes 236, interior 2, Plaza de Armas. Organic foods, wild honey, coffee, granola. Also offers natural medicines, indigenous art and weavings. They claim to pay fair prices when dealing with local suppliers.
The Coca Shop, Carmen Alto 115, San Blas, T084-260774, www.thecocashop.com. A tiny shop selling an interesteing selection of sweets and chocolates made using coca leaf flour. There is also plenty of information about the nutritional values of coca leaves.
La Cholita, Portal Espinar 142-B and at airport. Extra-special chocolates made with local ingredients.
Tik'a, www.tikasoapperu.com. Eco-friendly soaps, oils and beauty products made from local ingredients by Fiona Cameron and Carmen Pedraza.

Markets

San Jerónimo, just out of town, is the wholesale Sat morning fruit and vegetable market, but food that's just as good and not much more expensive (and washed) can be bought at the markets in town: **Wanchac**, Av Garcilaso (not C Garcilaso), or **San Pedro**, opposite Estación San Pedro, which sells a variety of goods. The best value is at closing time or in the rain. Take care after dark. Sacks to cover rucksacks are available in the market for US$0.75. Both Huanchac and San Pedro open every day from 0700.

El Molino, under the Puente Grau, is for contraband goods brought in from abroad without duty or tax being paid, but it is tolerated by the authorities. Everything from computers to trekking boots, to wine can be bought here (take a taxi for US$0.60). It is clean and safe (but take the usual common sense precautions about valuables) and is open daily 0600-2030.

Supermarkets

D'Dinos Market, Av La Cultura 2003, T084-252656 for home delivery. Open 24 hrs, well supplied, takes credit cards.
Gato's Market, Portal Belén 115.
La Canasta, Av La Cultura 2000 block. Very well stocked, accepts credit cards, ATM outside.
Mega Market, Matará 271, Av Garcilaso at Plaza Tupac Amaru and Av La Cultura in Magisterio. Daily 0700-2200, credit cards accepted. US-style market.

▲ Activities and tours

Cuzco city *p128, maps p132 and p136*
There are a million and one tour operators in Cuzco. The sheer number and variety of tours on offer is bewildering and prices for the same tour can vary dramatically. You should only deal directly with the agencies and seek advice from visitors returning from trips. Agencies listed below are included under the field in which they are best known. City tours cost about between US$7-15 and last 4 hrs; check what sites are included (either too few or too rushed) and that the guide is experienced. 1-day Sacred Valley tours cost from US$20. Beware of tours that stop for long lunches at pricey hotels. Check if there are cancellation fees. Students will normally receive a discount on production of an ISIC card.

You could also consider hiring a private guide. As most of the sights do not have any information or signs in English, this can really improve your visit. Either arrange this before you set out or grab one of those hanging around the sights' entrances (this is much easier to do in the low season). A tip is expected at the end of the tour. Set prices: tours of the city or Sacred Valley cost US$50 for half-day, US$65 full day; a guide to Machu Picchu charges US$80 per day. A list of official guides is held by **Agotur Cusco**, C Heladeros 157, of 34-F, p 3, T084-233457, www.agoturcusco.org.pe. **Leap Local,** www.leaplocal.org, is a website that recommends good quality local guides.

There are also many Cuzco-based operators offering trips and tours to see Manu Biosphere Reserve. For full details of these operators and all the tours on offer, see page 635.

City, Inca Trail and general tours
Only a restricted number of agencies are licensed to operate Inca Trail trips. SERNANP, Av José Gabriel Cosio 408, Urb Magisterial, 1 etapa, T084-229297, www.sernanp.gob.pe, verifies operating permits. Other agencies will sell Inca Trail trips, but pass clients on to the operating agency in a pooling system. This can cause confusion and booking problems at busy times.

Inclusion in our list does not guarantee that the company is licensed to operate the Inca Trail (2010). All those listed below have been recommended for their services (except for any reservations noted). Many agencies, and the alternatives they offer, plus a list and contact details for recommended local guides, can be found in the trip reports of **South America Explorers**, Atocsaycuchi 670, www.saexplorers.org (for members only).

Note that many companies offer treks as alternatives to the Inca Trail and its variations to Machu Picchu. Unlike the Inca Trail, these treks are unrelegated. You should check that the trekking company does not employ the sort of practices (such as overloading porters, not clearing up rubbish) which are now outlawed on the trails to Machu Picchu.

Amazing Peru, C Yepez Miranda C-6, Magisterio, www.amazing peru.com. Professional and well-organized, recommended as providing the "perfect tour", knowledgeable guides.

Amazon Trails Peru, Tandapata 660, Cuzco, T084-437374, T084-984 714148, www.amazon trailsperu.com. Trekking tours around the area, including the Inca Trail, Salkantay and Choquequirao. Also trips to Manu.

Andean Treks, Av Pardo 705, T084-225701, www.andeantreks.com. Mon-Fri 0900-1300, 1500-1800, Sat 0900-1300. Manager Tom Hendrickson uses high-quality equipment and satellite phones. The company organizes interesting itineraries, from 2 to 15 days, with a wide variety of activities in this area and further afield.

Andina Travel, Treks and Eco-Adventures, Plazoleta Santa Catalina 219, T084-251892, www.andinatravel.com. Eco-agency with more than 10 years operating all local treks. Has a reputation in Cuzco for local expertise and community projects.

Big Foot, Triunfo 392 (of 213), T084-238568, www.bigfootcusco.com. Specialists in tailor-made hiking trips, especially in the remote corners of the Vilcabamba and Vilcanota mountains. Also the more conventional Inca Trail routes.

Breast Cancer Care, T0845-092 0805 (UK), www.breastcancercare.org.uk/events. Machu Picchu treks to raise money to support people living with breast cancer. Treks leave on 29 Apr 2011, 16 Sep 2011, 13 Apr 2012 and 7 Sep 2012.

Ch'aska, Calle Garcilaso 265, p 2 of 6, T084-240424, www.chaskatours.com. Dutch-Peruvian company that has quickly acquired a solid reputation offering cultural, adventure, nature and esoteric tours. They specialize in the Inca Trail, but also llama treks to Lares and recommended trips to Choquequirao and beyond.

Culturas Peru, Tandapata 345A, T084-243629, www.culturasperu.com. A Swiss-Peruvian company offering adventure, cultural, ecological and spiritual tours. They specialize in alternative Inca trails.

Destinos Turísticos, Portal de Panes 123, of 101-102, Plaza de Armas, T084-228168, www.destinosturisticosperu.com. The owner speaks Spanish, English, Dutch and Portuguese and specializes in package tours from economy to 5-star budgets. Individuals are welcome to come in for advice on booking jungle trips to renting mountain bikes. Ask in advance if you require guides with specific languages. Informative and helpful.

EcotrailPeru, Av El Sol 106, p 2, No 205, T084-233357, www.ecotrailperu.com. Operates treks, tours and adventure trips throughout Peru for all fitness levels. Committed to sustainable travel.

Enigma Adventure, Jr Clorinda Matto de Turner 100, Magisterio 1a etapa, T084-222155, www.enigmaperu.com. Adventure tour agency run by Spaniard Silvia Rico Coll. Has an excellent reputation for well-organized and innovative trekking expeditions. In addition to the regular Inca Trail, she offers, for example, a 7-day programme to the remote and beautiful Laguna Sibinacocha, in the Vilcanota Mountains, or a 3-night trek into the Lares Valley. Set departures and fixed prices on some routes, but on the more remote excursions prices depend on group numbers. Also cultural tours to traditional weaving communities, Ayahuasca therapy and can arrange climbing and biking itineraries on demand. Enigma also offers a luxury trekking service.

Explorandes, Av Garcilaso 316-A (not to be confused with C Garcilaso in the centre), T084-238380, www.explorandes.com. Experienced high-end adventure company. Their main office is in Lima, but trips can be arranged from Cuzco. Vast range of trips available in both Peru and Ecuador, easily booked through their well-organized website. Also arranges tours across Peru for lovers of orchids, ceramics or textiles. Award-winning environmental practices.

Fertur, Procuradores 341, p 1 int F, T084-221304, www.fertur-travel.com. Mon-Fri 0900-1900, Sat 0900-1200. Cuzco branch of the Lima tour operator.

Gatur Cusco, Puluchapata 140 (a small street off Av Sol 3rd block), T084-223496, www.gaturcusco.com. Esoteric, ecotourism, and general tours. Owner Dr José (Pepe) Altamirano is knowledgeable in Andean folk traditions. Excellent conventional tours, bilingual guides and transportation, helpful. Guides speak English, French, Spanish and German. They can also book internal flights.

Hiking Peru, Portal de Panes 109, office 6, T084-247942/ T084-984 651414 (mob), www.hiking peru.com. Concentrates on the less-beaten paths, eg 8-day treks to Espíritu Pampa, 7 days/6 nights around Ausangate, 4 days/3 nights Lares Valley Trek.

Inca Explorers, Ruinas 427, T084-241070, www.incaexplorers.com. Specialist trekking agency with a good reputation for small group expeditions executed in socially and environmentally responsible manner. More demanding, adventurous trips include a 2-week hike in the Cordillera Vilcanota (passing Nevado Ausangate), and Choque-quirao to Espíritu Pampa, again for 2 weeks.

InkaNatura Travel, Ricardo Palma J1, T084-255255, www.inkanatura.com. Offers tours with special emphasis on sustainable tourism and conservation. Knowledgeable guides.

Liz's Explorer, Medio 114B, T084-246619, www.lizexplorer.com. For the Inca Trail and other trips. Inca Trail 4-day/3-night (minimum group size 10, maximum 16), other length of trips available. Liz gives a clearly laid out list of what is and what is not included. Down and fibre sleeping bags can be hired. If you need a guide who speaks a language other than English let her know in advance. Also city tours and the Sacred Valley. Feedback on trip is good, less so for the office.

Llama Path, San Juan de Dios 250, T084-240822, www.llamapath.com. A wide variety of local tours, specializing in Inca Trail and alternative treks, the company is involved in environmental campaigns and porter welfare. Many good reports received.

Machete Tours, Nueva Alta 432, int B, T084-224829, T084-984 631662 (mob), www.machetetours.com. Founded by born-and-bred jungle hand Ronaldo and his Danish partner Tina, **Machete** offer many

innovative trekking trips, for example a 9-day traverse of the Cordillera Vilcabamba from the Apurímac Canyon and Choquequirao across the range to Machu Picchu itself. They also offer expeditions to Espíritu Pampa, Ausangate and the Inca Trail. They have a new rainforest lodge on the remote Río Blanco, south of the Manu Biosphere Reserve and have set up camps deep in the forest. These jungle trips are focused more on hiking and rustic 'adventure' than those of the classic Manu operators. All the staff speak English. Eric is a recommended guide for Choquequirao.

Manu Nature Tours, Av Pardo 1046, T084-252721, www.manuperu.com. Trips to Manu Biosphere Reserve. Owned by Boris Gómez Luna, English spoken.

Perú Planet, Suecia 318, T084-251145, www.peru-planet.net. Peruvian/Belgian-owned agency offering tours of the Inca Trail, other treks around Cuzco and packages within Peru. Also Bolivia and Patagonia.

Peru Treks and Adventure, Av Pardo 540, T084-222722, www.perutreks.com. Trekking agency set up by Englishman Mike Weston and his wife Koqui González. They pride themselves on good treatment of porters and support staff and have been consistently recommended for their professionalism and customer care. A portion of profits goes to community projects (school supplies and clothing accepted at office). Treks include Salkantay, the Lares Valley and Vilcabamba Vieja. Mike also runs the **Andean Travel Web**, www.andeantravel web.com, which focuses on sustainable tourism in the region.

Q'ente, Choquechaca 229, p 2, T084-222535, www.qente.com. Their Inca Trail service is recommended and they offer a great variety of treks in the Cuzco area. They also offer traditional tours and longer packages. Prices depend on group size. Very good, especially with children.

SAS Travel, Garcilaso 270, Plaza San Francisco, T084-249194, www.sastravel peru.com. Discount for students. Inca Trail 4-day/3-night US$540 (can rent down bags for US$20). SAS offers a variety of alternatives to the classic Inca Trail. Before setting off you are told everything that is included and given advice on what personal items should be taken. Also Manu, family tours, mountain bike, horse riding and rafting trips can be organized. All guides speak English (some better than others). They can book internal flights at much cheaper rates than booking from overseas.

Sky Travel, Santa Catalina Ancha 366, interior 3-C (down alleyway near **Rosie O'Grady's** pub), T084-261818, www.skyperu.com. Open Mon-Sat. English spoken. General tours around city and Sacred Valley. 4-day/3-night Inca Trail in good-sized double tents and a dinner tent. The group is asked what it

Manu Cloud Forest Lodge

Cock-of-the Rock Dance Company
Performances: Twice daily, year-round

manu nature tours
Manu National Park tour operators since 1985

Manu Lodge, Manu National Park

You would not be yawning if you saw this kitty!
Picture by: R. Quirmbach. German tourist

Avenida Pardo 1046, Cusco-Perú. T (+5184) 252721 or (+5184) 252521
F+ 5184 234793 info@manunaturetours.com www.manuperu.com

would like on the menu 2 days before departure. Other trips include Vilcabamba and Ausangate (trekking only), Colca and Misti (Arequipa) and Titicaca.

Tambo Tours, 4405 Spring Cypress Rd, Suite 210, Spring, TX 77388, USA, T1-888-2-GO-PERU (246-7378), T001-281 528 9448, www.2GOPERU.com. Long-established adventure and tour specialist with 20 years' experience in Peru. Offices in Peru and USA. Customized trips for families, individuals and groups to the Amazon and archaeological sites of Peru, Bolivia and Ecuador, including Machu Picchu.

Trekperu, Av República de Chile B-15, Parque Industrial, Wanchac, T084-261501, www.trekperu.com. Experienced trek operator as well as other adventure sports and mountain biking. Offers 'culturally sensitive' tours. 5-day/4-night Cuzco Biking Adventure visits Tipón ruins, Huacarpay Lake, Huanca, Pisac, Urubamba and Moray. Includes support vehicle and good camping gear. Need sleeping bag.

Tucan Travel, T084-241123, cuzco@tucan travel.com. Offer adventure tours and overland expeditions.

United Mice, Plateros 351, T084-221139, www.unitedmice.com. Inca Trail and alternatives via Salkantay and Santa Teresa. Good English-speaking guides; Salustio speaks Italian and Portuguese. Discount with student card, good food and equipment. Also city tours in Spanish and English, Sacred Valley Tours in Spanish and English. They offer treks to Choquequirao for 5 days/4 nights.

Wayki Trek, Av Pardo 510, T084-224092, www.waykitrek.net. Budget travel agency, recommended for their Inca Trail service. Owner Leo grew up in the countryside near Ollantaytambo and knows the area very well. They run treks to several little-known Inca sites. Leo offers many interesting variations on the 'classic' Inca Trail and runs a programme where clients can visit porters communities before starting treks. Wayki also run treks to Ausangate, Salkantay and Choquequirao.

X-Treme Tourbulencia, Plateros 358, T084-222405, www.x-tremetourbulencia. com. They run the 'Classic Inka Trail' and alternative Inka treks, Ausangate, city tours and jungle trips.

Cultural and shamanic tours

Among the many forms of spiritual tourism offered in the Cuzco region, one that attracts much attention is shamanic and drug experiences. (The following list is not restricted to this type of tourism.) San Pedro and Ayahuasca have been used since before Inca times, mostly as a sacred healing experience. The plants are prepared with special treatments for curative purposes; they have never been considered a drug. If you choose to experience these incredible healing/teaching plants, only do so under the guidance of a reputable agency or shaman and always have a friend with you who is not partaking. If the medicine is not prepared correctly, it can be highly toxic and, in rare cases, severely dangerous. Never buy tours off the streets, never buy from someone who is not recommended and never try to prepare the plants yourself.

Another Planet, Tandapata y Pasñapacana 148, San Blas, T084-241168, or T084-974 790411, www.anotherplanetperu.net. Run by Lesley Myburgh, who operates mystical and adventure tours in and around Cuzco, and is an expert in San Pedro cactus preparation. She arranges San Pedro sessions for healing at physical, emotional and spiritual levels in the beautiful garden of her house outside Cuzco. Tours meet at La Casa de la Gringa, see Sleeping, above. This a good place to stay if you are looking for this kind of experience.

Milla Tourism, Av Pardo 689, T084-231710, www.millaturismo.com. Mon-Fri 0800-1300, 1500-1900, Sat 0800-1300. A wide variety of tours, including traditional, historical, educational and cultural. Also private tours arranged to Moray agricultural terracing and Maras salt mines in Sacred Valley. Guide speaks only basic English. They also arrange cultural and environmental lectures and courses.

Eleana Molina, T084-984 751791, misticanativa@yahoo.com. For Ayahuasca ceremonies.

Mountain biking

Cuzco offers a multitude of rides to suit all abilities. All ideally require a guide as its very easy to get lost in the Andes. Some options are: a half-day tour of nearby **Inca ruins** (Tambo Machay, Qenqo and Sacsayhuaman) exploring the very best of the single-track options. Each trip is customized to individual abilities. Don't forget your combined entrance ticket. **Chinchero–Moray–Maras–Las Salinas–Urubamba:** one of the finest 1-day trips in Peru, best done with a guide and support vehicle. It includes almost 1000 m of descent on a mix of dirt trails and donkey tracks as well as the Moray circular terraces and an amazing downhill through the spectacular saltpans. The **Lares Valley** offers some incredible downhill and uphill options on 2- to 3-day circuits including a relaxing soak in the beautiful Lares hot springs. Various descents from the sierra to the jungle: **Abra Málaga:** from 4200 m, an 80-km descent to the jungle, now know as part of the 'Inca Jungle Trail' (see page 202); **Tres Cruces to Manu,** a 250-km, beautiful dirt road ride offering big climbs and an even bigger (2-day) descent; and **Cuzco–Puerto Maldonado,** formerly a great Trans-Andean Challenge on a bike, now almost all tarmac. With a support vehicle this can be done in a 2-3 days of mainly downhill cycling, a good way to get to the jungle town of Puerto Maldonado from where jungle tours to lodges can be organized.

A wonderful new route takes cross-country riders from the shores of Lake Titicaca, through Juliaca, Lampa, Tinajani canyon and on dirt roads through the Andes to Cuzco in 8 days of tough but incredibly beautiful riding. Overnight riders camp and stay with local families and at an experimental alpaca farm. See **KE Adventure** in Tour operators in Essentials (www.keadventure.com) for details.

There is a growing downhill mountain biking community in and around Cuzco and competitions are run most months on a series of world-class courses. To find out about and experience these rides, talk to the experts and rent a bike and guide for the day for a truly unforgettable day out. See Sports tour operators, page 167, for mountain biking companies.

Paragliding and ballooning

Magnificent scenery, soaring close to snow-capped mountains makes this an awesome experience. 45 km from Cuzco is **Cerro Sacro** (3797 m) on the Pampa de Chincheros with 550 m clearance at take-off. It is the launch site for cross-country flights over the Sacred Valley, Sacsayhuaman and Cuzco. Particularly good for parapenting is the **Mirador de Urubamba,** 38 km from Cuzco, at 3650 m, with 800-m clearance and views over Pisac. Note that the Sacred Valley offers exciting but challenging paragliding so if wind conditions are bad, flights may be delayed till the following day. Beware pilots offering suspiciously cheap flights; their experience and equipment is unlikely to be appropriate for the Sacred Valley's conditions. **Globos de los Andes,** Aero Sports Club of the Sacred Valley, www.globosperu.com. Hot-air ballooning in the Sacred Valley and expeditions with balloons and 4WD lasting several days.

Rafting

The Cuzco region is probably the rafting capital of Peru, with more whitewater runs on offer than anywhere else in the country. When looking for an operator please consider more than just the price of your tour. Competition between companies in Cuzco is intense and price wars can lead to compromises in safety as corners are cut or less experienced (and therefore cheaper) guides are hired. Bargaining the price down will have the same effect. A 1-day rafting trip on the Vilcanota river will cost US$40 for a cheap trip, pooled by various agencies, with up to 30 other tourists. Expect to pay US$75-100 per person for a small group of, on average, 4 people with experienced guides, quality equipment, a safety kayaker and good food. A 3-day Apurímac rafting trip will cost US$200 for a pooled tour with 25-35 participants and no guarantee on equipment, guides, or safety record. Pay around US$450-600 for a safe, high-quality, environmentally-friendly small group trip. On a large and potentially dangerous river like the Apurímac, and when any of the rivers are high, this can make all the difference (fatalities occur, most recently in 2010 on the Río Urubamba). See Rafting, page 277, for more advice.

Urubamba Perhaps the most popular day run in the whole country, but try to avoid the sections heavily affected by pollution below Cuzco and from the towns of the Sacred Valley, especially around Ollantaytambo, as the waters contain raw sewage and have only average-quality rapids. Clean-up campaigns are organized periodically, but they just touch the surface of the problem. Further upriver from Cuzco, on the Chuquicahuana and Cusipata sections, the river is generally cleaner and the rapids are more fun. There is also a beautiful section called Piñipampa, just 45 mins drive from Cuzco, where inflatable kayaking (or "duckies" as they are called locally) is practised. Paddling your canoe through some fun, but not-too-frantic rapids in a beautiful canyon for half, or a whole day is suitable for anyone looking to try the next thing after rafting. This trip can be combined with a trip to visit Pisac market, or the ruins of Tipón and Pikillacta. There are various stretches of rafting on the river, from Grade I to Grade V+. Some are available all year, others depend on the season. Grade I, II and III rafting with children can also be organized, but check the operator has equipment (wetsuits, booties, life-jackets, etc) suitable for children and that they have experience in dealing with such groups. Ask a reputable operator for recommendations

to suit your ability and always heed advice if the river is running high.

Apurímac Technically the true source of the Amazon, the Apurímac cuts a 2000-m-deep gorge through incredible desert scenery and offers probably some of the finest whitewater rafting sections on the planet. Some are rarely run, such as **The Abyss** or **Choquequirao** (consult an agency which caters for experts), but most popular for a multi-day trip is **Puente Hualpachaca-Puente Cunyac** (May-Nov, Grade IV-V): 3 days (better in 4) of non-stop whitewater through an awesome gorge just 5 hrs drive from Cuzco. Wildlife includes condors, otters, foxes, deer and, if you are very lucky, pampas cats and pumas. Again, book with the experts to get you through rapids with names like *U-first*, *Toothache* and *Last laugh*. A new section of the Río Apurímac for rafting is called the **Black Canyon**. A spectacular 4-hr drive from Cuzco takes you to the village of Naihua from where it is 4 days of fairly relaxed, wilderness rafting with Grade III-IV+ rapids and a couple of portages around the trickiest rapids. There are hikes to waterfalls, pristine beaches for camping and the sense of being in the middle of nowhere for 3-4 days. The return from Hualpachaca to Cuzco takes approximately 4 hrs. See below for rafting companies. Cuzco rafting companies usually organize trips further afield. These include the **Río Tambopata**, slicing its way through the Bahuaje-Sonene National Park all the way to Puerto Maldonado. After a 4WD drive from Lake Titicaca, this 9-day adventure includes Grade III-IV+ rapids and some of the best wildlife viewing in the Amazon Basin. Possibly the very best run in Peru is on the **Río Cotahuasi**, reached from Arequipa: over 8 days/120 km of world-class Grade IV and V whitewater rapids, in the deepest canyon. Every night camp is set up on beaches beside Inca ruins. It is best run May-Jun only. Both trips are made infrequently, so book in advance.

Mayuc, Portal Confiturias 211, Plaza de Armas, T084-242824, www.mayuc.com; also www.perurafting.com. One of the longest-running rafting adventure companies in Cuzco.

Sports tour operators

The following operators offer a range of adventure sports and activities.

Amazonas Explorer, Av Collasuyo 910, Miravalle, PO Box 722, www.amazonas-explorer.com. Experts in rafting, inflatable canoeing, mountain biking, horse riding and hiking; used by BBC. English owner Paul Cripps has great experience, but takes most bookings from overseas (in UK, T01874-658125, Jan-Mar; T01437-891743, Apr-Dec). However, he may be able to arrange a trip for travellers in Cuzco preferably with advanced notice. Rafting and inflatable canoeing includes Río Urubamba (1 day), Río Apurímac (3-4 days), Río Tambopata (14 days including Lake Titicaca), Cotahuasi (14 days out of

Arequipa). Specialist kayaking trips can be organized on request. Also 5-day/4-night Inca Trail trip of the highest quality, and alternatives to the Inca Trail and Choquequirao to Machu Picchu. Amazonas offer an excellent variation of the Ausangate Circuit, featuring an extension to the little-visited Laguna Singrenacocha and an opportunity for ice-climbers to tackle the remote Campa Peak with experienced guides. New for 2011 is a trek to Espíritu Pampa, the last city of the Incas. Multi-activity and family trips are a speciality, catering for all ages, but juniors in particular. Mountain biking trips all use state-of-the-art, full-suspension Kona mountain bikes, expert guides and support vehicles where appropriate. All options are at the higher end of the market and are highly recommended. **Amazonas Explorer** are also the first company to join www.onepercentfortheplanet.org, donating 1% of their turnover to a tree-planting project in the Lares watershed.

Apumayo, Jr Ricardo Palma N-5, Santa Mónica, Wanchaq, T084-246018, www.apumayo.com. Mon-Sat 0900-1300, 1600-2000. Urubamba and Apurímac rafting; Inca Trail trekking. Also mountain biking, eg Maras and Moray in Sacred Valley, or 5-day epic biking from Cuzco to Quillabamba, horse riding, multi-activity and cultural tours. This company also offers tours for disabled people, including rafting.

Apus Peru, Cuichipunco 366, T084-232691, www.apus-peru.com. Conducts most business by internet and specializes in alternatives to the Inca Trail. It has a strong commitment to sustainability and runs well-organized adventure trips. The agency is associated with **Threads of Peru**, www.threadsofperu.com, an NGO which helps weavers in the Lares Valley. Visits can be arranged through Apus Peru.

Camp Expeditions, Triunfo 392, of 202, T084-431468, www.campexpedition.net. All sorts of adventure tours, but specialists in climbing, for which they are recommended as most reliable, and trekking.

Cusco Adventure Team, Santa Catalina Ancha 398 (under Al Grano), T084-228032, www.cuscoadventureteam.com. Utilizing the experience of **Amazonas Explorers**, CAT offer half-day to 3-day bike rides and rafting and canoe trips for small groups or individuals, state of the art equipment, adventurous, safe and environmentally aware. Part of **Grupo Inca**, www.grupo-inca.com (see **Amazonas Explorer**, above).

Eric Adventures, Urb Santa María A1-6, San Sebastián, T084-272862, www.eric adventures.com. Specialize in many adventure activities. They clearly explain what equipment is included in their prices and what you will need to bring. They also rent motorcross bikes (US$70-90 per day), mountain bikes and cars and 4WDs. Prices are more expensive if you book by email, you can get huge discounts if you book in the office. A popular company.

Instinct, Av de la Cultura 1318, Wanchaq, T084-233451, www.instinct-travel.com. Run by the very experienced Juan and Benjamín Muñiz, this company now largely operates through web-based bookings, arranging both multi-week expeditions and shorter adventures for those already in the Cuzco area. Instinct offers activities as diverse as surf safaris on Peru's north coast to multi-day horseriding tours in the Sacred Valley.

Manu Expeditions, C Clorinda Matto de Turner 330, Urb Magisterial, primera etapa, T084-225990, www.manuexpeditions.com. As well as Manu trips (see page 620), also runs tailor-made bird trips in cloud- and rainforest around Cuzco and Peru, as well as butterfly watching, and has horse riding and a 9-day/8-night trip to Machu Picchu along a different route from the Inca Trail, rejoining at the Sun Gate. Barry Walker runs horse-supported treks to Choquequirao, starting from Huancacalle. Highly recommended.

The Medina Brothers, contact Christian or Alain Medina on T084-225163 or T084-984 653485/984 691670 (mob). Friendly family-run rafting company with good equipment and plenty of experience. They usually focus on day rafting trips in the Sacred Valley, but services are tailored to the needs of the client. Reasonable prices dependent on client numbers. Recommended.

Pachatusan Trek, Psje Esmeralda 160, Santiago, T084-231817, www.pachatusantrek.com. Offers a wide variety to treks, as alternatives to the Inca Trail, professional and caring staff.

River Explorers, C Garcilaso 210, int 128, T084-260926 or T084-984 909249, www.riverexplorers.com. An adventure company offering mountain biking, trekking and rafting trips (on the Apurímac, Urubamba and Tambopata). Experienced and qualified guides with environmental awareness. Apurímac rafting trips from US$385.

Terra Explorer Peru, T084-237352, www.terraexplorerperu.com. Offers a wide range of trips from high-end rafting in the Sacred Valley and expeditions to the Colca and Cotahuasi canyons, trekking the Inca Trail and others, mountain biking, kayaking (including on Lake Titicaca) and jungle trips. All guides are bilingual.

⊖ Transport

Cuzco city *p128, maps p132 and p136*
Air
To **Lima**, 55 mins, daily flights with Taca, Star Perú, Peruvian Airlines and Lan. Flights are heavily booked in school holidays (May, Jul, Oct and Dec-Mar) and national holidays. To **Arequipa** and to **Puerto Maldonado**, 30 mins each daily with Lan. Star Perú also flies to Puerto Maldonado. To/from **La Paz** with Aero Sur, 3 times a week.

    Airline offices Aero Sur, Av Sol 948, CC Cusco Sol Plaza, of 120, T084-254691, www.aerosur.com. Lan, Av Sol 627-B, T084-225552. **Peruvian Airlines**, Del Medio 117, T084-254890. **Star Perú**, Av Sol 679,

of 1, T084-262768. **Taca**, Av Sol 602, T084-249921, good service.

Bus

Local Combis run 0500-2200 or 2300, US$0.30, to all parts of the city, including the bus and train stations and the airport, but are not allowed within 2 blocks of the Plaza de Armas. Stops are signed and the driver's assistant calls out the names of stops. By law all passengers are insured. After 2200 combis may not run their full route; demand to be taken to your stop, or better still, use a taxi late at night.

El Tranvía de Cusco is actually a motor coach that runs on the route of the original Cuzco tramway system. The route starts in the Plaza de Armas (except Sun morning) and ends at the Sacsayhuaman Archaeological Park. There is a 10-min stop at the mirador by the Cristo Blanco before descending to the Plaza de Armas. Departures start at 1000 daily, 1 hr 20 mins, with explanations of the city's history, architecture, customs, etc; US$2, US$1.40 for students with ID. For group reservations, call T084-740640.

Long distance Almost all direct buses to **Lima** (18-20 hrs) go via **Abancay**, 195 km, 5 hrs (longer in the rainy season), and **Nazca**, on the Panamerican Highway. This route is paved, but floods in the wet season can damage sections of the highway. If prone to car sickness, be prepared on the road to Abancay, there are many, many curves, but the scenery is magnificent (it also happens to be a great route for cycling). At Abancay, the road forks, the other branch going to **Andahuaylas**, a further 138 km, 10-11 hrs from Cuzco, and **Ayacucho** in the Central Highlands, another 261 km, 20 hrs from Cuzco. On both routes at night, take a blanket or sleeping bag to ward off the cold. All buses leave daily from the Terminal Terrestre.

Molina, who also have an office on Av Pachacútec, just past the railway station, has buses on both routes. They run 3 services a day to **Lima** via **Abancay** and **Nazca**, and 1, at 1900, to **Abancay** and **Andahuaylas**.

Cruz del Sur's service leaves for **Lima** via Abancay at 0730 and 1400, while their more comfortable services depart at 1500 and 1600. Celtur and Los Chankas have buses to **Abancay**, **Andahuaylas** and **Ayacucho**. Turismo Ampay and Turismo Abancay go 3 times a day to Abancay, and **Expreso Huamanga** once. Bredde has 5 buses a day to Abancay. Fares to **Abancay** US$10, **Andahuaylas** US$14, **Nazca** up to US$28.50-46, **Lima** also US$28.50-46 for a reliable service; eg Flores or Cromotex (T084-249573, www.cromotex.com.pe). Cruz del Sur charges US$49-57 (*Cruzero* and *VIP* classes; same fares to Nazca and Ica). In Cuzco you may be told that there are no buses in the day from Abancay to Andahuaylas; this is not true – **Señor de Huanca** does so. If you leave Cuzco before 0800, with luck you'll make the onward connection at 1300, which is worth it for the scenery.

Ormeño has a service from Cuzco to Lima via Arequipa which takes longer than the Abancay route (22 hrs), but is a more comfortable journey.

To **Lake Titicaca and Bolivia**: To **Juliaca**, 344 km, 6 hrs, US$5-12. The road is fully paved, but after heavy rain buses may not run. To **Puno**, via Juliaca, US$5-12; direct US$8.50 (*bus cama* US$12) 6 hrs. First Class and Inka Express, Av La Paz C-32, Urb El Ovalo, Wanchac, T084-247887, www.inkaexpress.com, have a service calling at Andahuaylillas church, Raqchi, La Raya, Sicuani and Pucará en route (lunch, but not entrance tickets, is included), US$30. Travel agencies sell this ticket. **Note** It is safest to travel by day on the Cuzco–Juliaca–Puno route.

To **Arequipa**, 521 km, US$21; Cruz del Sur use the direct paved route via Juliaca and have a *Cruzero suite* service at 2000 and a *Cruzero/VIP* service at 2030, 10 hrs, US$33/40. Other buses join the new Juliaca–Arequipa road at Imata, 10-12 hrs (eg Carhuamayo, 3 a day). To **Tacna**, San Martín, T084-805729, at 1430, US$20. To **Puerto Maldonado**, Móvil

(Terminal Terrestre, T084-238223) at 1800, 1945, US$16.

Car

Touring y Automóvil Club del Perú, Av Sol 349, T084-224561, cusco@touringperu. com.pe. A good source of information on motoring, car hire and mechanics.

Taxi

Taxis have fixed prices: in the centre US$0.60 (US$0.90 after 2200); and to the suburbs US$0.85-1.55 (touts at the airport and train station will always ask much higher fares). In town it is advisable to take municipality-authorized taxis that have a sticker with a number on the window and a chequerboard pattern on the side. Safer still are licensed taxis, which have a sign with the company's name on the roof, not just a sticker in the window. These taxis are summoned by phone and are more expensive, in the centre US$1.25 (**Aló Cusco** T084-222222, Ocarina T084-247080).

Taxi trips to **Sacsayhuaman** cost US$10; to the ruins of **Tambo Machay** US$15-20 (3-4 people); a whole-day trip costs US$40-70. For US$50 a taxi can be hired for a whole day (ideally Sun) to take you to **Chinchero**, **Maras**, **Urubamba**, **Ollantaytambo**, **Calca**, **Lamay**, **Coya**, **Pisac**, **Tambo Machay**, **Qenqo** and **Sacsayhuaman**.

To organize your own **Sacred Valley** transport, try one of these taxi drivers, recommended by **South America Explorers**: **Manuel Calanche**, T084-227368, T084-984 695402 (mob); **Carlos Hinojosa**, T084-251160; **Ferdinand Pinares Cuadros**, Yuracpunco 155, Tahuantinsuyo, T084-225914, T084-984 681519 (mob), speaks English, French and Spanish; **Eduardo**, T084-231809, speaks English. Also recommended are: **Angel Marcavillaca Palomino**, Av Regional 877, T084-251822, amarcavillaca@yahoo.com, helpful, patient, reasonable prices; **Movilidad Inmediata**, T084-984 623821 (mob), runs local tours with an English-speaking guide.

Angel Salazar, Marcavalle I-4 Wanchac, T084-224679 (leave a message), is English-speaking and arranges good tours, very knowledgeable and enthusiastic; **Milton Velásquez**, T084-222638, T084-984 680730 (mob), is also an anthropologist and tour guide and speaks English.

Train

See Ins and outs, page 128 for details of the train companies out of Cuzco. For trains to Aguas Calientes for Machu Picchu, see page 194.

The train to **Puno** leaves at 0800, on Mon, Wed, Fri and Sat, arriving in Puno at 1800 (sit on the left for the best views). The train makes a stop to view the scenery at La Raya. Between Nov-Mar there is no train on Fri. There is only 1 class, *Andean Explorer*, US$220, includes lunch, afternoon tea, and luxury seating. Tickets can be bought in advance. The ticket office at Wanchac station is open Mon- Fri 0700-1700, Sat, Sun and holidays 0700-1200. The **PerúRail** office at Portal de Carnes 214 is open Mon-Fri 1000-2200, Sat, Sun and holidays 1400-2300. You can buy tickets on www.perurail.com, or through a travel agent.

❶ Directory

Cuzco city *p128, maps p132 and p136*
Banks All the banks along Av Sol have ATMs from which you can withdraw dollars or soles at any hour. Whether you use the counter or an ATM, choose your time carefully as there can be long queues at both. Most banks are closed 1300-1600. All branches offer the same services as elsewhere in the country. BCP, Av Sol 189. **Banco de la Nación**, Av Sol y Almagro. **Interbank**, Av Sol y Puluchapata. Next door is **Banco Continental**, Av Sol 459. **Scotiabank**, Maruri y Arequipa. There are ATMs around the Plaza de Armas, in San Blas and on Av La Cultura.

Many travel agencies and *casas de cambio* change dollars. Some change TCs as well, but charge 4-5% commission. There are many *cambios* on the west side of the Plaza de Armas (eg Portal Comercio) and on the west side of Av Sol, most change TCs (best rates in the *cambios* at the top of Av Sol). **LAC Dólar**, Av Sol 150, T084-257762, Mon-Sat 0900- 2000, with delivery service to central hotels, cash and TCs, is recommended. The street changers hang around Av Sol, blocks 2-3, every day and are a pleasure to do business with. Some of them will also change TCs. In banks and on the street check the notes. **Embassies and consulates** Belgium, Av Sol 954, T084-224322. Mon-Fri 0900-1300, 1500-1700. France, Jorge Escobar, C Micaela Bastidas 101, 4th floor, T084-233610. Germany, Sra Maria-Sophia Júrgens de Hermoza, San Agustín 307, T084-235459, acupari@terra.com.pe. Mon-Fri 1000-1200, appointments may be made by phone, it also has a book exchange. Ireland, Charlie Donovan, Santa Catalina Ancha 360 (Rosie O'Grady's), T084-243514. Italy, Sr Fedos Rubatto, Av Garcilaso 700, T084-224398. Mon-Fri 0900-1200, 1500-1700. Netherlands, Sra Marcela Alarco, Av Pardo 827, T084-241897, marcela_alarco@ yahoo.com. Mon-Fri 0900-1500. Spain, Sra Juana María Lambarri, Av Pardo (Paseo de los Héroes) 1041, T084-984 650106. Switzerland, Av Regional 222, T084-243533. UK, Barry Walker, Av Pardo 895, T084-239974, bwalker@amauta. rcp.net.pe. US Agent, Dra Olga Villagarcía, Av Pardo 845, T084-231474, coreses@state.gov. **Immigration** Av Sol, Local Prefectural, p 1, T084-222741. Mon-Fri 0800-1300. Reported as not very helpful. **Internet** You can't walk for 2 mins in Cuzco without running into an internet café, and new places are opening all the time. Most have similar rates, around US$0.50 per hr. **Language classes** Academia Latinoamericana de Español, Plaza Limacpampa 565, T084-243364, www.latinoschools.com. The same company also has schools in Ecuador (Quito) and in Bolivia (Sucre). They can arrange courses that include any combination of these locations using identical teaching methods and materials. Professionally run with experienced staff. Many activities per week, including dance lessons and excursions to sites of historical and cultural interest. Good homestays. Private classes US$170 for 20 hrs, groups, with a maximum of 4 students US$125, again for 20 hrs. **Acupari**, San Agustín 307, T084-242970, www.acupari.com. The German-Peruvian Cultural Association offers Spanish classes. **Amauta Spanish School**, C Suecia 480, T084-262345, www.amautaspanish.com. Spanish classes, 1-to-1 or in small groups, also volunteer work, Quechua classes and workshops on Peruvian culture, US$10.50 per hr 1-to-1, but cheaper and possibly better value for group tuition (2-6 people), US$98 for 20 hrs. They have pleasant accommodation on site, as well as a free internet café for students, and can arrange excursions and can help find voluntary work. They also have a school in Urubamba and can arrange courses in the Manu rainforest, in conjunction with **Pantiacolla Tours SRL**. **Amigos Spanish School**, Zaguán del Cielo B-23, T084-242292, www.spanishcusco.com. Certified, experienced teachers, friendly atmosphere. All profits support a foundation for disadvantaged children. Private lessons for US$8 per hr, US$108 for 20 hrs of classes in a small group. Comfortable homestays and free activities available, including a 'real city tour' through Cuzco's poor areas. **Cusco Spanish School**, Garcilaso 265, of 6 (2nd floor), T084-226928, www.cuscospanish school.com. US$175 for 20 hrs private classes, cheaper in groups. School offers homestays, optional activities including dance and music classes, cookery courses, ceramics, Quechua, hiking and volunteer programmes. They also offer courses on an hacienda at Cusipata in the Vilcanota valley, east of Cuzco. **Excel**, Cruz Verde 336, T084-235298, www.excel-spanishlanguage programs-peru.org. Very professional, US$7 per hr for private 1-to-1 lessons.

US$229 for 20 hrs with 2 people, or US$277 with homestay, 1-to-1 for 20 hrs. **Fairplay Spanish School**, Pasaje Zavaleta C-5, Wanchac, T084-984 789252, www.fairplay-peru.org. This relatively new NGO teaches Peruvians who wouldn't normally have the opportunity (Peruvian single mothers, for example) to become Spanish teachers themselves over several months of training. The agency then acts as an agent, allowing these same teachers to find work with visiting students. Classes with these teachers cost US$4.50 or US$6 per hr, of which 33% is reinvested in the NGO, the rest going direct to the teachers. Can also arrange volunteer work and homestay programmes. **La Casona de la Esquina**, Purgatorio 395, corner with Huaynapata, T084-235830. US$5 per hr for 1-to-1 classes. Recommended. **Mundo Verde**, Coviduc H-14, San Sebastián, T084-274574, www.mundoverdespanish.com. Spanish lessons with the option to study in the rainforest and the possibility of working on environmental and social projects while studying. Some of your money goes towards developing sustainable farming practices in the area. US$250 for 20 hrs tuition with homestay. **San Blas Spanish School**, Carmen Bajo 224, T084-247898, www.spanishschoolperu.com. Groups, with 4 clients maximum, US$90 for 20 hrs tuition (US$130 1-to-1).

Laundry There are several cheap laundries on Procuradores, Suecia and Tecseccocha. **Adonai**, Choquechaca 216-A, San Blas.

Good hole-in-the-wall laundry, US$0.60 per kg for wash and dry, friendly and usually reliable, small book exchange. **Dana's Laundry**, Nueva Baja y Unión. US$2.10 per kg, takes about 6 hrs. **Lavandería**, Saphi 578. Mon-Sat 0800-2000, Sun 0800-1300. Good, fast service, US$1 per kg. String markers will be attached to clothes if they have no label. **Lavandería Louis**, Choquechaca 264, San Blas. US$0.85 per kg, fresh, clean, good value. **Lavandería T'aqsana Wasi**, Santa Catalina Ancha 345. Same-day service, they also iron clothes, US$2 per kg, good service, speak English, German, Italian and French, Mon-Fri 0900-2030, Sat 0900-1900. **Splendid Laundry Service**, Carmen Alto 195. Very good, US$0.75 per kg, laundry sometimes available after only 3-4 hrs.

Massage and therapies Casa de la serenidad, Santa María P-8, San Sebastián, T084-792224, T084-948 671867, www.shamanspirit.net. A shamanic therapy centre run by Lilo Ccoyllor, a healer and Reiki Master who uses medicinal 'power' plants. It also has bed and breakfast and has received very good reports. **Healing Hands**, based at Loki Hostel, faeryamanita@hotmail.com. Angela is a reiki, shiatsu and craniosacral therapist. Very relaxing and recommended.

Medical services Clínica Panamericana, Urb Larapa Grande C-17, T084-270000, T084-984 785303 (mob), www.cuscohealth.com. 24-hr emergency and medical attention. **Clínica Pardo**, Av de la Cultura 710, T084-240387, www.clinicapardo.com. 24-hr

emergency and hospitalization/medical attention, international department, trained bilingual personnel, handles complete medical assistance coverage with international insurance companies, free ambulance service, visit to hotel, discount in pharmacy, dental service, X-rays, laboratory, full medical specialization. The most highly recommeded clinic in Cuzco. **Hampi Land Clínica del Viajero**, Av Huáscar 105 A-26, T084-240768, www.hampiland.com. Professional medical care for tourists, with pharmacy, vaccinations, diagnostics, etc, also has ambulance and evacuation service. **Hospital Regional**, Av de la Cultura, T084-227661, emergencies T084-223691. **Dr Ilya Gomon**, Pasaje Santa Cruz de Peñalva 288 (Huayna Ccapac), Wanchac, T084-965 1906, www.perucuzco.com/chiropractic_cusco/. Canadian chiropractor, good, reasonable prices, available for hotel or home visits. **Dr Gilbert Espejo** and **Dr Boris Espejo**

Muñoz, both in the Centro Comercial Cusco, of 7, T084-228074 and T084-231918 respectively. If you need a yellow fever vaccination (for the jungle lowlands, or for travel to Bolivia or Brazil where it is required), it is available at the paediatric department of the **Hospital Antonio Lorena**, Plazoleta Belén 1358, T084-226511, from 0830 on Mon, Wed and Fri; they are free and include the international vaccination certificate. **Dentists**: Dr Eduardo Franco, Av de la Cultura, Edif Santa Fe, of 310, T084-242207, T084-984 650179 (mob). 24-hr.

Post Central office, Av Sol at the bottom end of block 5, T084-225232. Mon-Sat 0730-2000, 0800-1400 Sun and holidays. Poste restante is free and helpful. Sending packages from Cuzco is not cheap.

Telephone There are independent phone offices in the centre. **Telefónica**, Av del Sol 386, T084-241111. For telephone and fax, Mon-Sat 0700-2300; 0700-1200 Sun and holidays.

The Urubamba Valley

The Río Urubamba cuts its way through fields and rocky gorges beneath the high peaks of the Cordillera. Brown hills, covered in wheat fields, separate Cuzco from this beautiful high valley, which stretches from Sicuani (on the railway to Puno) to the gorge of Torontoi, 600 m lower, to the northwest of Cuzco. That the river was of great significance to the Incas can be seen in the number of strategic sites they built above it: Pisac, Ollantaytambo and Machu Picchu among them. Upstream from Pisac, the river is usually called the Vilcanota; downstream it is the Urubamba.
▶▶ For listings, see pages 182-190.

Ins and outs

Getting there The road from Cuzco that runs past Sacsayhuaman and on to Tambo Machay (see page 139) climbs up to a pass, then continues over the pampa before descending into the densely populated Urubamba Valley. This road then crosses the Río Urubamba by a bridge at Pisac and follows the north bank to the end of the paved road at Ollantaytambo. It passes through Calca, Yucay and Urubamba, which can also be reached from Cuzco by the beautiful, direct road through Chinchero, see page 178. ▶▶ *See Cuzco Activities and tours, page 160, and Transport, page 189.*

Getting around Paved roads, plentiful transport and a good selection of hotels and eating places make this a straightforward place to explore. You can choose either a quick visit from the city or, better still, linger for a few days. Don't hurry; most organized tours are too fast. A regular day tour costs US$14.50, not including entry tickets. Explore it on foot, by bike or on horseback. Using public transport and staying overnight in the Valley allows much more time to see the ruins and markets.

Best time to to visit April to May or October to November. The high season is from June to September, but the rainy season, December to March, is cheaper and pleasant enough.

Pisac → *For listings, see pages 182-190. Colour map 5, A5.*

Only 30 km north of Cuzco is the little village of Pisac, which is well worth a visit for its superb Inca ruins, perched precariously on the mountain, above the town. They are considered to be among the finest Inca ruins in the valley. Strangely, however, most visitors don't come to Pisac for the ruins. Instead, they come in droves for its Sunday morning market and growing number of shopping outlets. Pisac is usually visited as part of a tour from Cuzco but this often allows only 1½ hours here, not enough time to take in the ruins and splendid scenery.

Pisac village and market

The market contains sections for the tourist and for the local community. Traditionally, Sunday is the day when the people of the highlands come down to sell their produce (potatoes, corn, beans, vegetables, weavings and pottery). These are traded for essentials such as salt, sugar, rice, noodles, fruit, medicines, plastic goods and tools. The market comes to life after the arrival of tourist buses around 1000, and is usually over by 1700. However, there is also an important ceremony every Sunday, in which the *Varayocs* (village mayors) from the surrounding and highland villages participate in a Quechua Catholic Mass in **Pisac**

church. It is a good example of the merging of, and respect for, different religious cultures. This aspect of the traditional Pisac Sunday market is still celebrated at 1100 sharp. Pisac has other, somewhat less crowded, less expensive markets on Tuesday and Thursday morning; in each case, it's best to get there before 0900.

On the plaza, which has several large *pisonay* trees, are the church and a small interesting **Museo Folklórico**. The town, with its narrow streets, is worth strolling around, and while you're doing so, look for the fine façade at Grau 485. The **Museo Comunitario Pisac** ① *Av Amazonas y Retamayoc K'asa, museopisac@gmail.com, daily 1000-1700, free but donations welcome* was opened in 2009, with a display of village life, created by the people of Pisac. There are many souvenir shops on Bolognesi.

Inca ruins

① *Daily 0700-1730. If you go early (before 1000) you'll have the ruins to yourself. Entry is by BTC visitor ticket (see box, page 130). Guides charge US$5, but the wardens on site are very helpful and don't charge anything to give out information.*

The ruins of Inca Pisac stand on a spur between the Río Urubamba to the south and the smaller Chongo to the east. It provides an ideal vantage point over the flat plain of the Urubamba, the terraces below and the terraced hillsides. This is one of the largest Inca ruins in the vicinity of Cuzco and it clearly had defensive, religious and agricultural functions, as well as being an Inca country estate.

To appreciate the site fully, allow five or six hours on foot. Even if going by car, do not rush as there is a lot to see and a lot of walking to do. Walking up, although tiring, is recommended for the views and location. It's at least one hour uphill all the way, but the descent takes 30 minutes. Horses are available for US$5 per person. Road transport approaches from the Kanchiracay end. The drive up from town takes about 20 minutes. Combis charge US$0.75 per person and taxis US$4 one way up to the ruins from near the bridge. Then you can walk back down (if you want the taxi to take you back down negotiate a fare and pick-up time). Overnight parking is allowed in the car park.

The walk up to the ruins begins from the plaza, passing the Centro de Salud and a control post. The path goes through working terraces, giving the ruins a context. The first group of buildings is **Pisaqa**, with a fine curving wall. Climb up to the central part of the ruins, the **Intihuatana** group of temples and rock outcrops in the most magnificent Inca masonry. Here are the **Reloj Solar** (Hitching Post of the Sun) – now closed because thieves stole a piece from it – palaces of the moon and stars, solstice markers, baths and water channels. From Intihuatana, a path leads around the hillside through a tunnel to **Q'Allaqasa** (military area). Across the valley at this point, a large area of Inca tombs in holes in the hillside can be seen. The end of the site is **Kanchiracay**, where the agricultural workers were housed. At dusk you will hear, if not see, the *pisaca* (partridges), after which the place is named, and you may see deer too.

Pisac to Urubamba → *For listings, see pages 182-190.*

Calca and around

Near **Lamay**, the second village on the road from Pisac towards Urubamba, are warm springs, which are highly regarded locally for their medicinal properties. **Calca**, 18 km beyond Pisac at 2900 m, is a busy hub in the valley, with a plaza that is divided into two. Look out for the *api* sellers with their bicycles loaded with a steaming kettle and assortment of bottles, glasses and tubs. There are mineral baths at **Machacancha**, 8 km east of Calca.

These springs are indoors, warm and will open at night for groups. They are half an hour by taxi from town. About 3 km beyond Machacancha are the Inca ruins of **Arquasmarca**.

The ruins of a small Inca town, **Huchuy Cuzco** ① *US$7.15 for trek and entry*, are reached across the Río Urubamba and after a stiff three- to four-hour climb. Huchuy Cuzco (also spelt Qosqo), which in Quechua means 'Little Cuzco', was originally called Kakya Qawani, 'from where the lightning can be seen'. It is dramatically located on a flat esplanade almost 600 m above the villages of Lamay and Calca in the Sacred Valley. The views are magnificent. The ruins themselves consist of extensive agricultural terraces with high retaining walls and several buildings made from finely wrought stonework and adobe mud bricks.

A road has been built to the ruins from Calca. Alternatively, a steep trail goes to the site from behind the village of Lamay, which is reached by crossing the bridge over the river. Another longer route leads to Huchuy Cuzco from Tambo Machay near Cuzco, a magnificent one- or two-day trek along the route once taken by the Inca from his capital to his country estate at Huchuy Cuzco; some sections of the original Inca highway remain intact.

Valle de Lares

To the north of Urubamba and Calca, beyond the great peaks that tower above the Sacred Valley, lies the valley of **Lares**, an area famed for its traditional Quechua communities and strong weaving traditions. The mountainous territory that lies between these two valleys and, indeed, the valleys themselves offers a great deal for the ambitious trekker. The entire Urubamba range is threaded with tracks and the remains of ancient Inca trails and, as you might expect, the variety of trekking routes is almost endless. One of these options is presented below.

The four-day trek from **Huarán** (6 km west of Calca) to **Yanahuara** (beyond Urubamba on the road to Ollantaytambo) goes via the village of Lares through ancient native forests and past some of the Cordillera Urubamba's greatest snow peaks, their waters feeding jewelled lakes and cascades below. It provides an insight into the communities that inhabit this rugged and challenging land. Halfway you can have a good soak in the hot springs at Lares. Many of the locals may offer to sell weavings or *mantas* along the route, at prices a fraction of those in Cuzco. Remember if you bargain that many of these works take weeks, or perhaps a month or more to complete, so always give a fair price; at least here all the money goes to the weavers themselves.

Lares is also a perfect example of Peru's fabulous mountain biking opportunities and it has something for everyone, suiting all levels of daring and technical ability. In two days you can freewheel from chilly mountain passes, past llamas and traditional Quechua communities, on unpaved but drivable roads, or down technical single-track routes following old Inca trails and through precipitous canyons alongside rushing mountain torrents. The area is firmly established with Cuzco agencies for trekking and cycling tours, often as an alternative, or add-on to the Inca Trail.▸▸ *See Cuzco Activities and tours, page 160.*

Yucay

A few kilometres east of Urubamba, Yucay has two large, grassy plazas divided by the restored colonial church of **Santiago Apóstol**, with its oil paintings and fine altars. On the opposite side from Plaza Manco II is the **adobe palace** built for Sayri Túpac (Manco's son) when he emerged from Vilcabamba in 1558.

Urubamba → *Colour map 5, A5. Altitude: 2863 m.*

Like many places along the valley, Urubamba has a fine setting, with views of the Chicón snow-capped peaks and glaciers, and enjoys a mild climate. The main plaza has a fountain capped by a maize cob. Calle Berriózabal, on the west edge of town, is lined with pisonay trees. The large market square is one block west of the main plaza. Market days are Wednesday and Friday. The main road skirts the town and the bridge for the road to Chinchero is just to the east of town.

Seminario-Behar Ceramic Studio ⓘ *C Berriózabal 405, a right turning, signed, off the main road to Ollantaytambo, T084-201002, www.ceramicaseminario.com, open every day, just ring the bell,* was founded in 1979. Pablo Seminario has investigated the techniques and designs of pre-Columbian Peruvian cultures and has created a style with strong links to the past. Each piece, both utilitarian and artisitic, is handmade and painted, using ancient glazes and minerals, before firing. The resulting pieces are very attractive and Seminario has exhibited in US museums. Visitors may purchase items, tour the workshops to see the different techniques and watch a video (also on YouTube). Tours are given in Englsih and Spanish. As well as the Centro de Arte and shop, there is a small collection of Andean animals. Seminario-Behar also has a shop on the Plaza de Armas in Cuzco.

Chinchero → *Colour map 5, A5. Altitude: 3762 m.*

ⓘ *0700-1730. Entry with BTC visitor ticket (see box, page 130).* Chinchero is northwest from Cuzco, just off a direct road to Urubamba. The streets of the village wind up from the lower sections to the **plaza**, which is reached through an archway. The great square appears to be stepped, with a magnificent Inca wall separating the two levels. Let into the wall is a row of trapezoidal niches, each much taller than a man. From the paved lower section, another arch leads to an upper terrace, upon which the Spaniards built a **church**. The ceiling, beams and walls are covered in beautiful floral and religious designs. The altar, too, is fine. The church is open on Sunday for mass and at festivals. Opposite the church is a small local museum. Excavations have revealed many Inca walls and terraces.

Chinchero attracts few tourists, except on Sunday. The local produce **market** on Sunday morning is fascinating and very colourful, and best before the tour groups arrive. It's on your left as you come into town. There's also a small handicraft market on Sunday, up by the church. On the main road, a new Municipio and park were built in 2010. The town celebrates the **Day of the Virgin**, on 8 September.

Salinas

Five kilometres west of Urubamba is the village of **Tarabamba** (Km 77 on the Sacred Valley road), where a bridge crosses the Río Urubamba. If you turn right after the bridge you'll come to **Pichingoto**, a tumbled-down village built under an overhanging cliff. Just over the bridge and before the town to the left of a small, walled cemetery is a salt stream. Follow the footpath beside the stream and you'll come to **Salinas**, a small village below which are a mass of terraced pre-Inca **salineras (salt pans)** ⓘ *US$1.80, payable at whichever point you enter, top or bottom,* which are still in production after thousands of years. There are 3200 pools and 480 cooperative members. They only work the pans from May to October, during the dry season. These are now a fixture on the tourist circuit and can become congested with buses.

It's a 45-minute walk from Urubamba to the salt pans. The climb up from the bridge, on the right side of the valley, is fairly steep but easy, with great views of Nevado Chicón. The path passes by the cascade of rectangular salt pans, taking up to 1½ hours to the top. From the summit of the cliff above the salt pans, walk to **Maras**, about 45 minutes. Focus on the white, **colonial church** ① *US$1.50*, and visit it when you get there; it has been beautifully renovated. Take water as it can be very hot and dry here.

Moray

① *Entry with the BTC visitor ticket (see box, page 130), or US$3.60; allow an hour for a full visit.*
This remote but beautiful site lies 9 km by road to the west of the little town of Maras. There are three 'colosseums', used by the Incas, according to some theories, as a sort of open-air crop nursery, known locally as the laboratory of the Incas. The great depressions do not contain ruined buildings, but are lined with fine terracing. Each level is said to have its own microclimate. It is a very atmospheric place, which, some claim, has mystical power. The scenery around here is absolutely stunning, especially in the late afternoon when the light is wonderful. For photography, though, it's best to arrive in the morning. The road eventually arrives at the guardian's hut, but there is little indication of the scale of the colosseums until you reach the rim.

The most interesting ways to get to Moray are on foot from Urubamba via the *salineras* (see above), or a day-long cycle trip, starting in Chinchero (see above) and ending at the foot of the *salineras* (a challenging descent; go with a specialist agency or guide).
➤ See also Chinchero Transport, page 189.

Ollantaytambo → For listings, see pages 182-190. Colour map 5, A5. Altitude: 2800 m.

The attractive town of Ollantaytambo, at the foot of some spectacular Inca ruins and terraces, is built directly on top of the original Inca town, or Llacta. Tourist facilities are growing now that most Machu Picchu trains terminate here.

Ins and outs

Getting there Ollantaytambo can be reached by bus from Cuzco, Urubamba and Chinchero. It is also one of the principal stations for catching the train to Machu Picchu; see page 194 for details. ➤ See also Transport, page 190.

Getting around Ollantaytambo is small enough to walk around. The station is 15 minutes downhill from the Plaza. There are *hostales*, restaurants and shops everywhere, including in the original part of town.

Tourist information The **Municipalidad** on the Plaza de Armas has a tourist office with leaflets and booklet (US$1.80), www.muniollantaytambo.gob.pe.

The fortress

① *Daily 0700-1730. Admission is by BTC visitor ticket (see box, page 130), which can be bought at the site. There are guides at the entrance. If possible arrive very early, 0700, before the tourists. Avoid Sun afternoons, when tour groups from Pisac descend in their hundreds. Allow 2-3 hrs to explore the ruins fully.*
When Manco Inca decided to rebel against the Spaniards in 1536, he fell back to Ollantaytambo from Calca to stage one of the greatest acts of resistance to the *conquistadores*. Hernando Pizarro led his troops to the foot of the Inca's stronghold and, on seeing how well-manned and fortified the place was, described it as "a thing of

horror". Under fierce fire, Pizarro's men failed to capture Manco and retreated to Cuzco, but Manco could not press home any advantage. In 1537, feeling vulnerable to further attacks, he left Ollantaytambo for Vilcabamba.

When you visit Ollantaytambo you will be confronted by a series of 16 massive, stepped terraces of the very finest stonework, after crossing the great high-walled trapezoidal esplanade known as 'Mañariki'. Beyond these imposing terraces lies the so-called **Temple of Ten Niches**, a funeral chamber once dedicated to the worship of Pachacútec's royal household. Immediately above this are six monolithic upright blocks of rose-coloured rhyolite, the remains of what is popularly called the **Temple of the Sun**. The dark grey stone is embellished today with bright orange lichen.

You can either descend by the route you came up, or follow the terracing round to the left (as you face the town) and work your way down to the **Valley of the Patacancha**. Here are more Inca ruins in the small area between the town and the temple fortress, behind the church. Most impressive is the **Baño de la Ñusta** (Bath of the Princess), a grey granite rock, about waist high, beneath which is the bath itself. The front of the boulder, over which the water falls, was delicately finished with a three-stepped pyramid, making a relief arch over the pool.

Ollantaytambo

Sleeping	
1 Apu Lodge	
2 Don Ascencio B&B & Orishas bar/restaurant	
3 El Albergue	
4 El Bosque & Wayra's	

5 Hostal Chaska Wasi	15 Pakaritampu
6 Hostal Iskay II	16 Sol Ollantay
7 Hostal KB Tambo	17 Tunupa Lodge
8 Hostal K'uychipunku	
9 Hostal Munay T'ika	**Eating**
10 Hostal Ollanta	1 Alcázar Café
11 Hostal Sauce	2 Blue Puppy
12 Hostal Tambo	3 Café Perla & other cafés
13 Las Orquídeas	4 Calicanto Café
14 Las Portadas	5 El Chasqui

| 6 Heart's Café |
| 7 Huatucay |
| 8 Il Cappuccino & Kusicoyllor |
| 9 Inka Bucks |
| 10 Inka's Park |
| 11 La Ñusta |
| 12 Mayupata |
| 13 Panaka |
| 14 Ripoka |

The town

Entering Ollantaytambo from Urubamba, the road is built along the long **Wall of 100 Niches**. Note the inclination of the wall towards the road. Since it was the Incas' practice to build with the walls leaning towards the interiors of the buildings, it has been deduced that the road, much narrower then, was built inside a succession of buildings. The road leads into the Plaza de Armas (under repair in 2010). The road from the northwest corner of the plaza looks up to the Inca temple, but to get there you have to cross the bridge over the river and go down to the colonial church of Santiago Apóstol with its *recinto* (enclosure). The original colonial bridge was washed away in 2010; a temporary bridge spans the river. Beyond is a grand plaza, Araccama, full of handicraft stalls and soft drinks sellers, and the entrance to the archaeological site.

The original Inca town is behind the north side of the Plaza de Armas. The *canchas* (blocks of houses) are almost entirely intact and can be clearly seen. It's an impressive sight and it is worth wandering through the narrow alleys and streets to get a glimpse of the interiors of the blocks. All the streets have canals running down them which used to be used in the houses.

At the junction of K'uychipunku and Calle La Convención is the **Bio Museo** ① *T084-204181, T084-984 962607, www.biomuseo.org, Tue-Sun 0930-2030, US$1.80 requested as a donation*, created by Maribel Torres León. It houses a comprehensive collection of native herbs, potatoes and grains. Working with a network of communities (**Inkaq Kusi Kausaynin**, www.tourrural.net) to preserve local foods and traditions, the museum not only shows the plants but offers essential oils, teas, etc for sale and demonstrates how plants are used as dyes. There are weaving, sculpture and medicinal workshops three days a week. Visitors can learn how to make *chicha*, grind and brew coffee in a traditional kitchen and, in the evening, there are storytelling sessions with music (at 1930, one hour, US$3.60).

El Museo Catcco (Centro Andino de Tecnología Tradicional y Cultural de las Comunidades de Ollantaytambo) ① *Casa Horno, Patacalle, 1 block from the plaza, T084-204024, open intermittently in 2010*, which houses a fine ethnographical collection. Outside the museum, Catcco runs non-profit cultural programmes, temporary exhibitions, concerts, lectures and guided walks to ruins.

An Ollantaytambo-based, non-profit organization, **Awamaki** ① *Urb Pillcohuasi D-4, shop just before Plaza Araccama, T084-204149, www.awamaki.org*, runs trips to communities in the **Patacancha** valley to visit the weavers. Trips include transport, a weaving demonstration and the chance to buy items direct from the makers. This is an initiative to revitalise the weaving tradition in the area and empower the women weavers. Weavings are also sold in the shop, where you can obtain all information and ask about volunteering opportunities.

At **Pinkulluna**, west of Ollantaytambo, looking across the town to the Fortress, is an impressive collection of storehouses, or *colcas*. They are clearly visible from below and a marked path leads up from the end of Calle de las Rosas/T'ika K'ikllu in the Inca town. It's a relatively straightforward climb up steep steps. After 10 minutes the path divides, right to the buildings on a promontory and left to the colcas, a further 20-25 minutes. The views are best seen in the morning, but are impressive at any time.

A two-dimensional '**pyramid**' has been identified on the west side of the main ruins of Ollantaytambo. Its discoverers, Fernando and Edgar Elorietta, claim it is the real Pacaritambo, from where the four original Inca brothers emerged to found their empire (this alternative Inca creation myth, the Inn of Origin, tells of four brothers and four sisters emerging from a cave in a cliff). Whether this is the case or not, it is still a first-class piece of engineering with great terraced fields and a fine 750-m wall creating the optical illusion of a pyramid. The wall is aligned with the rays of the winter solstice, on 21 June. People gather at mid-winter dawn to watch this event. The mysterious 'pyramid', which covers 50-60 ha, can be seen properly from the other side of the river. This is a pleasant, easy one-hour walk, west from the Puente Inca, just outside the town. You'll also be rewarded with great views of the Sacred Valley and the river, with the snowy peaks of the Verónica massif as a backdrop.

Around Ollantaytambo

The stone quarries of **Cachiccata** are some 9 km from Ollantaytambo. Standing to the left of the six monolithic blocks of the Temple of the Sun, you can see them, looking west-southwest across the valley. The stones that the Inca masons chose here had to be quarried, hewn into a rough shape and hauled across the valley floor and up to the temple by means of a ramp, which can still be seen. Between the ruins and the quarries more than 50 enormous stones that never reached their destination lie abandoned. They are known as the '*las piedras cansadas*', or 'the tired stones'. It takes about a day to walk to the Inca quarries on the opposite of the river and return to Ollantaytambo.

◉ The Urumbamba Valley listings

For Sleeping and Eating price codes and other relevant information, see pages 38-44.

⊜ Sleeping

Pisac *p175*

A Royal Inca Pisac, Carretera Ruinas Km 1.5, T084-267236, www.royalinkahotel.com/hpisac.html. In the same chain as the **Royal Incas I** and **II** in Cuzco, this hotel can be reached by the hotels' own bus service. It is a short distance out of town, on the road that goes up to the ruins, a taxi ride after dark. Price includes taxes and breakfast. Camping is available for US$5 per person. A guide for the ruins can be provided. The rooms are comfortable, in a number of blocks in the grounds of a converted hacienda. There is an olympic-sized pool (day use US$3.50), sauna and jacuzzi (guest use only), tennis court, horse riding and bicycle rental. The restaurant is good and there is a bar. The hotel is popular with day-trippers from Cuzco. Staff are very helpful and accommodating.

B Paz y Luz, T084-203204, www.pazyluzperu.com. 10-15 mins' walk from Pisac Plaza, close to the river. American expat Diane Dunn owns this hotel with a pleasant garden, nicely designed rooms, all with private bath and breakfast included in the price. Good place to chill and admire the rural surroundings and impressive mountain landscapes that rise dramatically above Pisac. Diane also offers healing from many traditions (including Andean), sacred tours, workshops and gatherings. Recommended.

B Pisac Inn, at the corner of Pardo on the plaza, T084-203062, www.pisacinn.com. Bright and charming local decor and a pleasant atmosphere, clean and friendly, all rooms with private bath and hot water, around a flower-filled patio. Massage can be arranged, laundry service. Good breakfast, afternoon tea. See restaurant, **Cuchara de Palo**, below, also has a sidewalk café. The **Inn** supports the Kusi Kawsay school initiative, www.kusikawsay.org.

C Hostal Varayoc, Mariscal Castilla 380, T084-223638, luzpaz3@hotmail.com. Renovated hotel around a colonial courtyard with working bread oven. Decor is smart and bathrooms are modern.

F Residencial Beho, Intihuatana 642, 50 m up the hill from the plaza, T/F084-203001. Ask for a room in the main building. They serve a good breakfast for US$1. The *hostal* has a shop selling local handicrafts including masks. The owner's son will act as a guide to the ruins at the weekend.

Pisac to Urubamba *p176*

LL Aranwa, between Calca and Urubamba (office Av Manuel Olguin 901, Monterrico-

Surco, Lima 33, T01-434 1452), www.aranwa hotels.com. First of a new chain of spa hotels in Peru, 5-star, luxury accommodation with a full range of facilities and treatments at the Hacienda Yaravilca near Huayllabamba.

L-AL Sonesta Posadas del Inca, Plaza Manco II de Yucay 123, Yucay, T084-201107, www.sonesta.com. A converted 300-year-old monastery is now a hotel that is like a little village with plazas, lovely gardens, a chapel and 69 comfortable, heated rooms. The price includes buffet breakfast, but not taxes. **Inkafe** restaurant is open to all, serving Peruvian, fusion and traditional cuisine with a US$15 buffet. Lots of activities can be arranged – canoeing, horse riding, mountain biking, etc. There is a conference centre. Highly recommended. Also have hotels in Lima, Cuzco, Puno and Arequipa.

L-AL Urubamba Villas, in the hamlet of Higuspurco, between Urubamba and Yukay, T01-221 6691, www.urubamba-villas.com. Price is per person in 1 of 2 self-contained villas in spacious gardens, fully equipped, breakfast and dinner included, lunch optional, courtesy bottle of wine. Has a bar, access to excursions and activities with car and driver available.

AL La Casona de Yucay, Plaza Manco II 104, Yucay, T084-201116, www.hotelcasona yucay.com. Colonial house where Simón Bolívar stayed during his liberation campaign in 1824. The price includes taxes and breakfast. The rooms have heating and, outside, there are 2 patios and gardens. **Don Manuel** restaurant is good, also has bar. Helpful staff.

B The Green House, Km 60.2 Huarán, T084-984 770130 (mob), www.thegreenhouse peru.com. A charming retreat, only 4 rooms (1 with 4 beds), plenty of common areas with a comfy lounge with fireplace and dining room, beautiful garden. No TV in rooms, but there are DVDs to watch, restricted internet and no Wi-Fi, quiet area for meditation, small kitchen for guests' use. Dinner is available for US$13. Owners Gabriel and Bryan can provide information about independent walks and day trips in the area. Warmly recommended.

C Hostal Y'Llary, Plaza Manco II 107, Yucay, T084-201112, www.hostalyllary.com. A hostal in a remodelled building fronting the plaza, with gardens. Price includes bathroom and breakfast, nice garden.

Urubamba *p178*

LL Río Sagrado (Orient Express), Km 76 Carretera Cuzco–Ollantaytambo, T084-201631, www.riosagrado.com. 4 km from Urubamba, set in beautiful gardens overlooking the river with views of surrounding mountains. Rooms and villas, Mayu Wilka spa, restaurant and bar, offfers various packages including *Hiram Bingham* train to Machu Picchu.

LL Sol y Luna, west of town, T084-201620, www.hotelsolyluna.com. Attractive bungalows and brand-new suites set off the main road in lovely gardens, pool, excellent buffet in restaurant, has an on-site spa and a varied wine cellar (wine tasting sessions can be arranged). French/Swiss-owned. Also

arranges adventure and cultural activities and traditional tours.

LL Tambo del Inka, Av Ferrocarril s/n, T084-581777, www.luxurycollection.com/vallesagrado. A Luxury Collection resort and spa on the edge of town, in gardens by the river. Completely remodelled with a variety of rooms and suites, fitness centre, swimming pools, **Hawa** restaurant, bar, business faciliteis and lots of activities arranged.

LL-AL Casa Andina Private Collection Sacred Valley, 5° paradero, Yanahuara, between Urubamba and Ollantaytambo, T084-984 765501, www.casa-andina.com. In its own 3-ha estate, with all the facilities associated with this chain, plus a gym, organic garden and restaurant with Novo Andino cuisine. Adventure activities can be arranged here. It also has a spa offering a range of massages and treatments and a planetarium and observatory, showing the Inca view of the night sky.

L K'uychi Rumi, Km 73.5 on the road to Ollantaytambo, 3 km from town, T084-201169, www.urubamba.com. 6 cottages for rent with 2 bedrooms, fully equipped, fireplace, terrace and balcony, surrounded by gardens. Price is for 1-2 people, each house can accommodate 6. Book in advance.

L San Agustín Monasterio de la Recoleta, Jr Recoleta s/n, T084-201004, www.hotelessanagustin.com.pe. In a converted monastery (the earliest in Cuzco) east of town, this hotel has suites and standard rooms with heating and all facilities, **San Isidro** restaurant. From the main road take Jr Hortencia Lorena from the Primax service station, otherwise 9 de Noviembre and C Recoleta from town centre.

A San Agustín Urubamba, Ctra Cuzco–Pisac Km 69, T084-201444, www.hotelessanagustin.com.pe. An upgraded hotel in a lovely setting just out of Urubamba, with suites and standard rooms, pool, sauna, massage and jacuzzi, **Naranjachayoc's** restaurant and bar.

B Posada Las Tres Marías, Zavala 307, T084-201006, www.posadatresmarias.com. A little way from the centre, quiet. Comfortable

rooms with hot water and no TV, lovely garden and shady terrace, breakfast included (can be early), laundry service, welcoming hosts. Recommended.

D Hospedaje Los Jardines, Jr Convención 459, T084-201331, www.hospedajelosjardines.blogspot.com. An attractive guesthouse with comfortable rooms with bath and hot water, non-smoking, delicious breakfast US$3.25 extra (vegans catered for), safe, lovely garden, laundry. Discounts for long stays. **Sacred Valley Mountain Bike Tours** also based here.

D pp Las Chullpas, 3 km west of town in the Pumahuanca Valley, T084-201568, www.uhupi.com/chullpas. Very peaceful, includes excellent breakfast, vegetarian meals, English and German spoken, Spanish classes, natural medicine, treks, horse riding, mountain biking, camping US$3 with hot shower. Mototaxi from town US$0.85, taxi (ask for Querocancha) US$2.

E Hostal Buganvilla, Jr Convención 280, T084-205102, T084-984 618900. Sizable rooms with bath, hot water, TV, breakfast on request, quiet, clean.

E Hostal Indigo, Jr Roca Fuerte 1, T084-509716, www.cusco-peru.de. On the edge of town on the road to Yucay, modern hostal, with bath, hot water, breakfast, garden, family-run.

E Hostal Urubamba, Bolognesi 605, T084-201062. Basic but clean, pleasant rooms with bath and cold water, TV, cheaper without bath, no breakfast.

Chinchero p178

C La Casa de Barro, T084-306031, www.lacasadebarro.com. New, modern hotel, price includes American breakfast, with hot water, bar, restaurant, tours arranged.

Ollantaytambo p179, map p180
Hospedajes and *hostales* are opening up all over town, including in the Inca town and on Av Ferrocarril (eg from the new **B Tunupa Lodge**, No 50, T084-204025, tunupalodgehtl@hotmail.com, to **Wayra's**,

50 m from the station, T084-204019, and **El Bosque**, T084-204148, with restaurant and internet, both **D**). There are other places to stay along the Calle de las Cien Ventanas/C Principal, leading into town. Closest to the centre is **Las Portadas**, T084-204008, hsjlasportadas05@yahoo.es.

AL Pakaritampu, C Ferrocarril s/n, T084-204020, www.pakaritampu.com. The price includes breakfast and taxes. This modern, 3-star hotel has 37 rooms with bath and views. It is owned by a former Peruvian women's volleyball star. There is a TV room, restaurant and bar, internet and Wi-Fi for guests, laundry, safe and room service, all set in beautiful gardens. Adventure sports and tours can be arranged. Buffet lunch and dinner are extra. Excellent quality and service.

A Hostal Sauce, C Ventiderio 248, T084-204044, www. hostalsauce.com.pe. Modern hotel in the centre. Smart, simple decor and views of the ruins from some rooms.

A Ñustayoc Mountain Lodge and Resort, 5 km west of Ollantaytambo, just before Chillca and the start of the Inca Trail, T01-275 0706, www.nustayoclodge.com. Large and somewhat rambling lodge in a wonderful location with great views of the snowy Verónica massif and other peaks. There's a lovely flower-filled garden and grounds. Nicely decorated, spacious rooms, all with private bath. Price includes continental breakfast served in the large restaurant area.

A-B Apu Lodge, C Lari, T084-797162, www.apu lodge.com. On the edge of the old Inca town, great views of the ruins and surrounding mountains. Run by Scot Louise Norton and husband Arturo, good service, can help organize tours and treks. They work with **Leap Local** (www.leaplocal.org) guides project.

A-B El Albergue, within the railway station gates, T084-204014, www. elalbergue.com. Owned by North American artist Wendy Weeks, the *albergue* has 16 rooms with bath, Wi-Fi, some with safe. Price includes breakfast; also has **Café Mayu** on the station and a good open-plan restaurant and kitchen for lunch and dinner. The rooms are full of

character and are set in buildings around a courtyard and lovely gardens. Great showers and a eucalyptus steam sauna. The whole place is charming, relaxing and homely. Books for sale and exchange, also handicrafts and **Matacuy** digestif. It's very convenient for the Machu Picchu train and a good place for information. Private transport can be arranged to nearby attractions, also mountain-biking, rafting and taxi transfers to the airport. Highly recommended.

C Hostal Iskay II, Patacalle s/n, T084-204004, www.hostaliskay.com. In the Inca town, overlooking the Fortress from the garden and terrace. Car access is difficult. Only 6 rooms, price includes buffet breakfast, bath, hot water, internet and Wi-Fi. There is a video and music room, free tea and coffee, use of kitchen. A pleasant place with good reports.

C Hostal K'uychipunku, K'uychipunku 6, T084-204175, www.kuychipunku.com. Very close to Plaza Araccama, rooms with bath and hot water, breakfast included, modern, some with view, courtyard, internet and Wi-Fi, new in 2009.

C Hostal Munay T'ika, Av Ferrocarril 118, T084-204111, www.munaytika.com. Price includes breakfast and bath. Dinner is served by arrangement. Sauna costs US$5 with prior notice. Also has a nice garden, internet and Wi-Fi. Recommended. Also owns the **Tawa Chaki** restaurant/pizzería on the corner of Plaza Araccama, with *menú turístico* and à la carte, indoors and garden dining.

C Sol Ollantay, C Ventiderio s/n by the bridge between the 2 plazas, T084-204130, www.sol-ollantay.com. Tastefully renovated in 2009 with new bathrooms, hot water. Price includes breakfast, no other, meals. Good views from most rooms.

C-D Don Ascencio B&B, Av Ferrocarril s/n, T084-204178, garitho@hotmail.com. New in 2010, with bath and breakfast, TV, heaters if needed. Beside it is **Orishas** bar/restaurant, ¶¶¶-¶¶, with Wi-Fi, serving the popular tourist selection (see below), but a bit more upmarket and with a good café.

C-D Las Orquídeas, at the top of Av Ferrocarril, T084-204032, www.hostallas orquideasollantaytambo.com. A good choice. Price includes breakfast, hot water, Wi-Fi, fairly small but nice rooms, flower-filled patio. May be used by tour groups.

C-E pp Hostal KB Tambo, C Ventiderio between the main plaza and the ruins, T084-204091, www.kbtambo.com. Spacious, comfortable rooms, suites, garden view or standard, hot water, Wi-Fi, flower-filled garden, very good restaurant (𝄐), breakfast extra. Reserve in advance. Also offers adventure tours.

F pp Hostal Chaska Wasi, Calle del Medio s/n, T084-204045, www.hostalchaskawasi.com. Cheaper with shared bath, with continental breakfast, rooms for up to 4 sharing. For a private room reserve in advance. A B&B snuggled away in the small alleys behind the plaza, bar and terrace, lunch and dinner on request, clean, simple, use of small kitchen, internet, laundry service. Owner Katy is very friendly.

F Hostal Ollanta, on the south side of the plaza, T084-204116. Basic and clean, but with a great location. All rooms with shared bath.

F pp Hostal Tambo, C Horno, north of the plaza, T084-773262 or T084-984 489094, paula1_79@hotmail.com. Cheaper for groups, breakfast extra. Once past the brown door you emerge into a garden full of fruit trees and flowers. Small, rooms for up to 3 people, basic, shared bath, hot water. Paula is very friendly.

Camping

Restaurant Huatucay, at the edge of the Inca town, between Patacalle and the road to Patacancha, has camping for US$3.60 per person. There are toilets, a minimarket and the restaurant serves typical food.

❷ Eating

Pisac p175

𝄐𝄐-𝄐𝄐 Cuchara de Palo, in Pisac Inn, on the Plaza. "Gourmet Andean cuisine". Serves meals using fresh, local ingredients as well as pizza on Sun market day. It also has a bar with various styles of pisco sour, cocktail hour, charming atmosphere.

𝄐𝄐-𝄐 Miski Mijuna Wasi, on the Plaza de Armas, T084-203266. Serves very tasty local food, typical Novo Andino and international dishes. Has a *pastelería* also.

𝄐𝄐-𝄐 Mullu, Mcal Castilla 375, T084-208182. Tue-Sun 0900-1900. Café/restaurant related to the Mullu store in Cuzco, also has a gallery promoting local artists.

𝄐 Doña Clorinda, on the plaza opposite the church. A very friendly place. It doesn't look very inviting but cooks tasty food, including vegetarian options.

𝄐 Valle Sagrado, Av Amazonas 116 (the main street where buses go towards Urubamba). Good quality, generous portions and a lunchtime buffet that includes vegetarian options. Go early before the tour groups arrive. **Valle Sagrado II** is due to open in 2010.

Cafés

Bakery, Av Mcal Castilla 372, sells excellent cheese and onion *empanadas* for US$0.25, suitable for vegetarians, and good wholemeal bread. The oven is tremendous.

Blue Llama Café, corner of the plaza opposite **Pisac Inn**, T084-203135, www.bluellamacafe.com. A cute, colourful café with a huge range of teas, good coffee, breakfasts and daily menus.

Ulrike's Café, Plaza de Armas 828, T084-203195, ulrikescafe@terra.com.pe. This comfortable café is renowned for its apple crumble with ice cream, to say nothing of great coffee, smoothies and a wide range of international cuisine. Also serves a good value, 3-course daily *menú*. A good place to chill after a hard day exploring the market and ruins.

Urubamba p178

𝄐𝄐𝄐 Tunupa, Km 77, on left side of the road on the riverbank, in a renovated colonial hacienda (same ownership as **Tunupa** in Cuzco), zappa@terra.com.pe. Excellent food served indoors or outdoors, bar, lounge, library, chapel, gardens, stables and an alpaca-jewellery shop. Outstanding exhibition of pre-Columbian objects and colonial paintings. **Seminario**'s ceramics feature in the decor. People on valley tours are served a varied buffet including Novo Andino cuisine; buffet lunch 1200-1500. Dinner (1800-2030) is à la carte.

♥♥♥-♥♥ El Huacatay, Arica 620, T084-201790, http://elhuacatay.com. Open Mon-Sat. A small restaurant with a reputation for fine, creative fusion cuisine (local, Mediterranean, Asian).

♥♥ El Fogón, Parque Pintacha, T084-201534. Traditional Peruvian food, large servings, nice atmosphere. Recommended.

♥♥ El Maizal, on the road before the bridge, T084-201454. Country-style restaurant with a good reputation, buffet service with a variety of typical Novo Andino dishes, plus international choices, beautiful gardens with native flowers and fruit trees. Recommended. They also have a hotel of the same name.

♥♥ Quinta los Geranios, on the main road before the bridge, T084-201043. Regional dishes, excellent lunch with more than enough food.

♥ La Chepita, Av 1 de Mayo, M6, in a small plaza. The place to go on Sun for regional food in the biggest portions you have ever seen. Get 1 plate between 2.

♥ Pizza Wasi, Av Mcal Castilla 857, T084-434751 for delivery. Good pizzas and pastas. Mulled wine served in a small restaurant with nice decor, also has eating upstairs. Clean, good value. Recommended. Has another branch on Plaza Araccama in Ollantaytambo.

Cafés
Café Plaza, Bolívar 440, on the plaza. Serves breakfasts, meals, desserts, teas and coffee and has a pottery shop next door.

Misky Sonq'o, Comercio 337. For coffee, breakfast, juices, burgers, toasties and snacks.

Ollantaytambo *p179, map p180*
There are restaurants all over town offering *menú turístico*, pizzas, pastas, snacks, juices and hot drinks, just the stuff before boarding the train to Machu Picchu. Several can be found on the Plaza de Armas, others on Av Ferrocarril.

♥♥♥-♥♥ Panaka, Plaza de Armas corner of Chaupi Calle, T084-204047, www.panakagrill.com. More upmarket place for Peruvian dishes, *parrillas*, pizza and pasta. The bar has a wide range of drinks. Also has a daily *menú* for US$9.

♥♥ Blue Puppy, C Horno at the plaza, T084-630464, www.cuzcodining.com. Restaurant and lounge in the same group as **Marcelo Batata** in Cuzco. Open for breakfast, lunch and dinner, serving Tex-Mex, local dishes, pizzas, soups, salads, and desserts. Also has a bar, sports and DVDs on the screen, new in 2010.

♥♥ El Chasqui, C Ventiderio y Av Ferrocarril, T084-204143. Peruvian dishes and the popular fare mentioned above. 3 eating areas, OK. Also has a shop and a **Hostal**, hostalchasqui@hotmail.com, rooms with bath and hot water.

♥♥ Heart's Café, on Plaza de Armas, T084-204078, www.livingheartperu.org. Open 0700-2100. Mainly wholefood restaurant serving international and Peruvian dishes, including vegetarian, box lunch and take-away available, good coffee. Owned by Sonia Newhouse, who directs all profits to education and self-help projects in the Sacred Valley. Bright and run by villagers. Deservedly popular and recommended.

♥♥ Il Cappuccino and **Kusicoyllor**, Plaza Araccama. Offers the best cappuccino in town, in fact great coffee generally. Good continental and American breakfasts. Also serves *menú turístico*, lunch and dinner, desserts, juices and light meals.

♥♥ Mayupata, Jr Convención s/n, across the bridge on the way to the ruins, on the left, T084-204083. It opens at 0600 for breakfast, and serves lunch and dinner. Serving international choices and a selection of Peruvian dishes, pizzas, desserts, sandwiches and coffee. The bar has a fireplace; river view, relaxing atmosphere.

♥♥-♥ Alcázar Café, Chaupi Calle (C del Medio s/n), 50 m from the plaza, T084-204034, alcazar@ollantaytambo.org. Mostly vegetarian restaurant, also offering fish and meat dishes, pasta specialities. Offers excursions to traditional Andean communities.

ᵀᵀ-ᵀ La Ñusta, Plaza de Armas corner of Chaupi Calle, ask here about their *hospedaje*. Popular, good food, snacks, soups, salads and juices available.

Cafés

Calicanto, on the righthand side just before the bridge leading to Plaza Araccama. For coffees and light meals, etc, overlooking the river that divides the town.

Inca Bucks, Plaza Araccama. Serves a wide variety of coffees and teas, also iced varieties, milkshakes and cold drinks.

Inca's Park, Plaza de Armas. Friendly, central café which also has *hospedaje* in the **E** range (with bath and hot water). Meals are not included in the lodging price.

Ripoka, K'uychipunku y La Convención. Tucked away opposite the Bio Museo, small café that also sells handicrafts from the rainforest.

⊕ Festivals and events

Pisac *p175*
15 Jul A local fiesta in Pisac.

Pisac to Urubamba *p176*
15-16 Aug Fiesta de la Virgen Asunta, Coya.
15 Aug Lamay hosts a festival.

Urubamba *p178*
May and Jun Harvest months, with many processions following mysterious ancient schedules.
1st week of Jun Urubamba's main festival, El Señor de Torrechayoc.

Ollantaytambo *p179, map p180*
5-8 Jan Bajada de Reyes Magos (the Magi), with traditional dancing, a bull fight, local food and a fair.
17 Feb Chutanacuy, a tug-of-war between groups from the 2 halves of town, with dancing also.
End May-early Jun Pentecost, 50 days after Easter, is the Fiesta del Señor de

Choquekillca, patron saint of Ollantaytambo. There are several days of dancing, weddings, processions, masses, feasting and drinking (the last opportunity to see traditional *cuzqueño* dancing).
29 Jun Following **Inti Raymi** in Cuzco, there is a colourful festival, the **Ollanta-Raymi**, at which the Quechua drama, *Ollantay*, is re-enacted.
29 Oct Aniversario de Ollantaytambo, a festival with dancing in traditional costume and many local delicacies for sale.

▲▲ Activities and tours

Pisac to Urubamba *p176*
Munaycha, Km 60.2 Carretera Pisac-Urubamba, Huarán, T084-984 770108, www.munaycha.com. Near **The Green House**. Duilio and Andrea Vellutino, specialists in kayaking, mountain biking, trekking and other sports, half- and 1-day trips as well as longer adventures. Also traditional tours in the Sacred Valley.

Urubamba *p178*
Agrotourism
Chichubamba, Casa de ProPerú, Jr Rejachayoc, Urubamba, T084-201562, www.agrotourismsacredvalley.com.
A community tourism project that lets visitors take part in a number of traditional activities (culinary, horticulture, textiles, ceramics, beekeeping, etc, US$3 per person, cheaper for groups), hiking US$10, lodging (**E** per person) and local meals. It's about 10 mins' walk from Urubamba; follow the signs.

Horse riding
Perol Chico, 5 km from Urubamba at Km 77, T084-974 798890/974 780020 , www.perolchico. com. Owned and operated by Eduard van Brunschot Vega (Dutch/ Peruvian), 1- to 14-day trips out of Urubamba, good horses, riding is Peruvian Paso style; 1-day trip to Moray and the salt pans costs US$110 (minimum 2 people, starting in Cuzco). Recommended.

Trekking

Haku Trek, contact Javier Saldívar or Yeral Quillahuman, T084-984 613001 (mob). A cooperative tourism project in the Chicón valley (the mountain valley above Urubamba), run by residents of the community. 3 different hiking trips are offered: two 1-day hiking options (US$20 per person including food and accommodation) and a third, 2-day hike up to the Chicón Glacier itself (US$45 all inclusive). Hikes are based at a simple, but beautifully located eco-lodge in the valley and profits are used to fund reforestation of native forest in the area.

Peru Alive, Av Convención 210, Urubamba, T084-401395, T084-984 698232 (mob), www.perualive.com. Agency run by the group **Ayni Kallpa** for treks such as Choquequirao, small, good value, all proceeds go to local people.

Ollantaytambo p179, map p180

On the south side of the Plaza de Armas trips to local sites, horse riding and more are offered by various tour operators, including **KB Tours**, T084-204133 (separate from **Hostal KB Tambo**, above). These, and other agencies on Av Ferrocarril offer 'free tourist information'.

⊖ Transport

To organize your own Sacred Valley transport, try one of the taxi drivers listed on page 171.

Pisac p175
Bus

To Cuzco From C Puputi on the outskirts of Cuzco, near the Clorindo Matto de Turner school and Av de la Cultura. 32 km, 1 hr, US$0.85. Colectivos, minibuses and buses leave when full, between 0600 and 1600; also trucks and pickups. Buses returning from Pisac are often full. The last one back leaves around 2000. Taxis charge about US$20 for the round trip. To **Pisac**, **Calca** (18 km beyond Pisac) and **Urubamba**, buses leave from Av Tullumayo 800 block, Huanchac, US$1.

Urubamba p178
Bus

The bus and combi terminal is just west of town on the main road. To **Calca**, **Pisac** (US$1, 1 hr) and **Cuzco** (2 hrs, US$1.80), from 0530 onwards. Also buses to Cuzco via **Chinchero**, same fare.

Colectivos to **Cuzco** can be caught outside the terminal and on the main road, US$1.80. Combis run to **Ollantaytambo**, 45 mins, US$0.50. There are also buses from here to **Quillabamba**.

Chinchero p178

Bus from Cuzco Combis and colectivos for Chinchero leave from 300 block of Av Grau, **Cuzco**, 1 block before crossing the bridge. 23 km, 45 mins, US$0.75; and for **Urubamba** a further 25 km, 45 mins, US$0.75.

To Maras There is a paved road from the main road between Chinchero and Urubamba to the village of Maras, 4 km, and from there an unmade road in good condition leads to Moray, 9 km. Ask in Maras for the best route to walk, other than on the main road. Any bus between Urubamba and Cuzco via Chinchero passes the clearly marked turning to Maras, 20 mins from Chinchero. From the junction taxi colectivos charge US$1.50 per person to Maras, or you can walk (30 mins). There is public transport from Chinchero to Maras and regular pickup trucks that carry people and produce in and out. Transport stops running between 1700 and 1800; it costs between US$0.60 and US$1. Hitching back to **Urubamba** is quite easy, but there are no hotels at all in the area, so take care not to be stranded.

Taxis wait at the Maras/Moray junction on the Urubamba/Chinchero road. They charge US$20 to go to Salinas and then on to Moray, with a 1-hr wait at each. Radio taxi: **Aló Urubamba**, T084-201010, reliable, will pick up anywhere, supposedly 24 hrs, US$20-25 to Cuzco.

Ollantaytambo p179
Bus

The main colectivo stop is outside the market, near the Plaza de Armas. There is a direct bus service to Ollantaytambo from Av Grau, **Cuzco**, at 0745 and 1945 direct (or catch a bus to Urubamba from Av Grau). From Ollantaytambo to Cuzco at 0715 and 1945; the fare is US$2.85. Direct taxi colectivo service from C Pavitos, Cuzco, leaves when full US$3.60 to Ollantaytambo. Minibuses and taxis leave the small Terminal de Transportes just up from Ollantaytambo station at train times for **Urubamba** and **Cuzco**, US$3.60 shared to either place, but they may try to charge US$24 as a private service only. Say you'll go to the colectivo terminal and they may reduce the price. Transfers and tours with **Aló K'antuyoc**, at the hostel of that name on Av Ferrocarril, T084-204147, kantuyoc@hotmail.com.

Train

See page 194. The station is 15 mins' walk from the plaza down Av Ferrocarril (turn left just before the bridge that leads to the ruins). There are colectivos and mototaxis at the Plaza for the station when trains are due. You won't be allowed on the station unless you have previously bought a ticket for the train (unless you are staying at **El Albergue**); the gates are locked and only those with tickets can enter. Trains pull in and out from about 0530 until after 2200 and things get pretty chaotic at the station and on Av Ferrocarril at arrival and departure times.

Perú Rail and Inca Rail have parking lots and ticket offices on Av Ferrocarril. **Inca Rail** office open 0545-0745, 0945-1245, 1445-1745. Between their offices and the station are several café/restaurants (**Tawa's**, **Miski Unu**, **Café Perla**, **Café d'Paris** – the last 2 serve real coffee), a cambio, internet, toilets, minimarket and grocery stalls.

❶ Directory

Pisac p175

Banks Money excange at the **Blue Llama Café** on the plaza. There is an ATM on the plaza next to **Ulrike's Café** (sometimes hard to find behind the market stalls!). To change TCs, try at the shop on M Castilla, heading away from the plaza, near where the road bends. **Internet and telephone** On the same side of the plaza as the museum is the municipal building with a computer centre (internet for US$0.75 per hr, closed Sun morning); also a public phone booth.

Pisac to Urubamba p176

Internet In Calca, the municipal library has internet connection. In Yucay, there are several places.

Urubamba p178

Banks Banks in the town centre on Comercio. ATM on the plaza at **Caja Municipal Arequipa**, Visa and MasterCard. Also **GlobalNet** on main road at the Pecsa service station, junction of M Castilla. **Internet and telephone** There are locutorios around the centre, not many and sometimes not well-signed. **Medical services** Casa del Bienestar, Plaza Manco Capac II s/n, Yucay, T084-201446 or T084-984 273539, Mario Orihuela. Recommended for massage and other treatments. **Hampi Land Traveller's Clinic**, C Cien Ventanas s/n, T084-797164, www.hampiland.com. Has ambulance and evacuation service and professional medical care. **Post** Serpost, post office, Plaza de Armas.

Ollantaytambo p179, map p180

Banks BCP ATM at C Ventiderio 248, between the Plaza and Av Ferrocarril, in Hotel Sauce. **Globalnet** on north side of Plaza. **Internet** Several places in town, many with call centres. **Medical services** Hampi Land Traveller's Clinic on the Plaza de Armas, T084-797164, www.hampiland.com. Medical centre, as above.

Machu Picchu and the Inca trails

There is a tremendous feeling of awe on first witnessing this incredible sight. The ancient citadel of Machu Picchu, 42 km from Ollantaytambo by rail, straddles the saddle of a high mountain with steep terraced slopes falling away to the fast-flowing Río Urubamba snaking its hairpin course far below in the valley floor. Towering overhead is Huayna Picchu, and green jungle peaks provide the backdrop for the whole majestic scene.

If you take the Inca Trail to Machu Picchu, following in the footsteps of its creators, you are making a true pilgrimage and the sweat and struggle is all worth it when you set your eyes on this mystical site at sunrise from the Inca sun gate above the ruins. That way you see Machu Picchu in its proper context. Afterwards you can recover in Aguas Calientes and soothe those aching limbs in the hot springs. The introduction of strict regulations for walking the Inca Trail in 2001 opened up additional options for trekking to Machu Picchu, some shorter, some longer than the old route. So if you fancy widening the perspective of how the Incas walked to their sacred city, ask your chosen tour operator to show you the alternatives.▸▸ For listings, see pages 208-212.

Ins and outs

Getting there There are two ways to get to Machu Picchu. The easy way is by train from Poroy (over the hill from Cuzco), or Ollantaytambo, with a bus ride for the final climb from the rail terminus at Aguas Calientes to the ruins (see Transport, page 211, for the times). The walk up from Aguas Calientes takes 1½ to two hours, following the Inca path. Walking down to Aguas Calientes, if staying the night there, takes between

The excitement grows while we get closer to know Machu Picchu.

30 minutes and one hour. The ruins are quieter after 1530, but don't forget that the last bus down from the ruins leaves at 1730. The strenuous, but most rewarding way to Machu Picchu is to hike one of the Inca trails, the 'classic' example of which is described in its own section (see page 196).

Visitor information Tickets for Machu Picchu must be purchased in advance from the Instituto Nacional de Cultura (INC) ① *Av Pachacútec cuadra 1, Aguas Calientes, 0500-2200, in Cuzco, or online (see page 130), www.inc-cusco.gob.pe.* At the time of writing, the online sales system was not fully operational and the website was not working so you are advised to check in Cuzco about new procedures. The agency officially responsible for the site is **Unidad Gestión de Machu Picchu** ① *C Garcilaso 223, Cuzco, T084-242103.* It is an excellent source of information on Machu Picchu and this is the place to which any complaints or observations should be directed. **iperú** ① *in the INC office, as above, of 4, T084-211104, iperumachupicchu@promperu.gob.pe, daily 0900-1300 and 1400-2000,* can provide general information.

Machu Picchu ruins → *For listings, see pages 208-212. Colour map 5, A5. Altitude: 2380 m.*

① *Daily 0600-1730. Entrance fee is US$44.55 (S/.126), to be purchased in advance from the INC, see above. Students with a valid ISIC card pay US$22.30. It is only possible to pay in soles. You cannot take backpacks into Machu Picchu; leave them at the entrance for US$1. Guides are available at the site, they are often very knowledgeable and worthwhile. The official price for a guide is US$80 for a full tour for 1-10 people.*

For centuries Machu Picchu was buried in jungle, until Hiram Bingham stumbled upon it in July 1911. It was then explored by an archaeological expedition sent by Yale University. Machu Picchu was a stunning find. The only major Inca site to escape 400 years of looting and destruction, it was remarkably well preserved. And it was no ordinary Inca settlement. It sat in an inaccessible location above the Urubamba Gorge, and contained so many fine buildings that people have puzzled over its meaning ever since. **Historical note** Research published in 2008 by Carlos Carcelen, Paolo Greer and others shows that Bingham was not the first non-Peruvian to know Machu Picchu. A German explorer and trader, Augusto Berns, ran a sawmill and had a concession to mine in what is now Aguas Calientes and clearly knew about and looted the ruins.

Once you have passed through the ticket gate you follow a path to a small complex of buildings that now acts as the **main entrance** (1) to the ruins. It is set at the eastern end of the extensive **terracing** (2) that must have supplied the crops for the city. Above this point, turning back on yourself, is the final stretch of the Inca Trail leading down from **Intipunku** (Sun Gate), see page 201. From a promontory here, on which stands the building called the **Watchman's Hut** (3), you get the perfect view of the city (the one you've seen on all the postcards), laid out before you with Huayna Picchu rising above the furthest extremity. Go round the promontory and head south for the **Intipata** (Inca bridge), see page 196. The main path into the ruins comes to a **dry moat** (4) that cuts right across the site. At the moat you can either climb the long staircase that goes to the upper reaches of the city, or you can enter the city by the baths and Temple of the Sun.

The more strenuous way into the city is by the former route, which takes you past quarries on your left as you look down to the Urubamba on the west flank of the mountain. To your right are roofless buildings where you can see in close up the general construction methods used in the city. Proceeding along this level, above the main

1 Machu Picchu

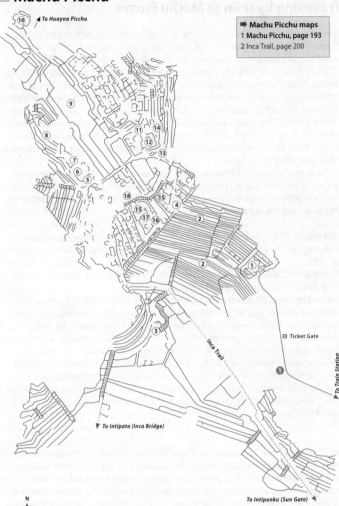

➡ Machu Picchu maps
1 Machu Picchu, page 193
2 Inca Trail, page 200

To Huayna Picchu

To Train Station

Inca Trail

Ticket Gate

To Intipata (Inca Bridge)

To Intipunku (Sun Gate)

N

50 metres
50 yards

Main entrance **1**
Terracing **2**
Watchman's Hut **3**

Dry moat **4**
Temple of the Three
  Windows **5**
Principal Temple **6**
Sacristry **7**
Intihuatana **8**
Main Plaza **9**
Sacred Rock **10**

Living quarters &
  workshops **11**
Mortar buildings **12**
Prison Group &
  Condor Temple **13**
Intimachay **14**
Ceremonial baths
  or Fountains **15**

Principal Bath **16**
Temple of the Sun **17**
Royal Sector **18**

Sleeping
Machu Picchu
Sanctuary Lodge **1**

Cuzco & the Sacred Valley **Machu Picchu & the Inca trails • 193**

Travelling by train to Machu Picchu

Three companies operate along this route: **PerúRail** (Avenida Pachacútec, Wanchac Station, T084-581414, www.perurail.com) runs to Machu Picchu from Poroy, near Cuzco, and from Ollantaytambo. **Inca Rail** (Avenida El Sol 611, Cuzco, T084-233030, or Lima T01-613 5288, www.incarail.com.pe) runs from Ollantaytambo to Machu Picchu. **Machu Picchu Train** (Avenida Sol 576, T084-221199, www.machupicchutrain.com) also runs from Ollantaytambo. All trains run to **Aguas Calientes** (the official name of this station is 'Machu Picchu'). **PerúRail** and **Inca Rail** also have ticket offices near the station in Ollantaytambo. The station for the tourist trains at Aguas Calientes is on the outskirts of town, 200 m from the Pueblo Hotel and 50 m from where buses leave for Machu Picchu ruins. There is a paved road in poor condition between Aguas Calientes and the start of the road up to the ruins.

There are four classes of **PerúRail** tourist train. Note that timetables and prices are subject to frequent change. Tickets for all trains may be bought at Wanchac station and the sales office on Portal de Carnes, Plaza de Armas, in Cuzco, at travel agencies, or via **PerúRail**'s website, www.perurail.com.

Vistadome (US$71 one way) departs from Poroy daily at 0653, arriving at Aguas Calientes (Machu Picchu) at 1038. It returns from Machu Picchu at 1600, reaching Poroy at 1942.
Expedition (US$48 single) departs Poroy daily at 0742, reaching Aguas Calientes at 1151. It returns at 1703, getting back to Poroy at 2101.
Hiram Bingham (US$334 one way) is a super-luxury train with dining car and bar. It leaves Poroy Monday to Saturday at 0910 with brunch on board, reaching Aguas Calientes at 1309. It leaves Aguas Calientes at 1807, cocktails, dinner and live entertainment on board, arriving in Poroy at 2159 with a bus service back to Cuzco hotels. The cost includes all meals, buses and entry to the ruins.
Ollantaytambo Vistadome (US$43, 53 and 60 one way: the more expensive trains arrive at Machu Picchu at peak times) leaves Ollantaytambo five times a day from 0659 to 1615, returning from Aguas Calientes at 1322 to 2020; journey time is about two hours. Tickets include food in the price. These trains have toilets, video, snacks and drinks for sale.

plazas, you reach the **Temple of the Three Windows** (5) and the **Principal Temple** (6), which has a smaller building called the **Sacristy** (7). The two main buildings are three-sided and were clearly of great importance, given the fine stonework involved. The wall with the three windows is built onto a single rock, one of the many instances in the city where the architects did not merely put their construction on a convenient piece of land. They used and fashioned its features to suit their concept of how the city should be tied to the mountain, its forces and the alignment of its stones to the surrounding peaks. In the Principal Temple, a diamond-shaped stone in the floor is said to depict the constellation of the Southern Cross.

Continue on the path behind the Sacristy to reach the **Intihuatana** (8), the 'hitching-post of the sun'. The name comes from the theory that such carved rocks (*gnomons*), found at all major Inca sites, were the point to which the sun was symbolically

Ollantaytambo Backpacker (US$31 and 34 one way) departs four times a day from 0602-2312, returning from Aguas Calientes 0505-2230. Seats can be reserved even if you're not returning the same day.

Ollantaytambo Expedition (US$43) leaves at 0910, arriving at Aguas Calientes at 1118, returning at 1924, reaching Ollantaytambo at 2115. An *autovagón* service from Ollantaytambo at 0815 has a connecting bus from Wanchac station in Cuzco (US$60). It returns from Aguas Calientes at 1845.

Inca Rail has three trains a day Ollantayambo–Machu Picchu (*Yllari* at sunrise, *Waala* in the morning and *Tutayay* at sunset), with fares at US$50 one way executive class, US$75 one way 1st class. Coaches have a/c and heating, snacks are available.

Machu Picchu Train also has three trains a day Ollantayambo–Machu Picchu (*The Lost City Traveller* at 0720, returning 1612, *Cusco Imperial* and *Sunrise* – at the time of writing the last two were awaiting schedules). *The Lost City Traveller* fare is US$59. Journey time is 1 hour 25 minutes. Coaches have been specially designed for the service.

Local trains

Tourists are not permitted to travel on the local train from Cuzco to Machu Picchu, but you can avoid the train services altogether. Take a bus from Cuzco towards Quillabamba at 1900, US$6 (other buses in the day may not connect with onward transport). Get out at Santa María (about seven hours) where minibuses wait to go to Santa Teresa, two hours, US$2.10. You'll reach Santa Teresa by sunrise in time to buy breakfast. From Santa Teresa you have to cross the Río Urubamba by the new bridge and walk 6 km to the Central Hidroeléctrica, a nice, flat road, or take a combi, US$10-15. From the Hidroeléctrica train station it's 40 minutes on the local train to Aguas Calientes at 1520, US$8 for tourists, or you can walk along the railway in two-three hours (at Km 114.5 is F per person **Hospedaje Mandor**, about 2 km from bridge to Machu Picchu). To return, at 0600 walk from Aguas Calientes to Santa Teresa to catch a bus at 1000 to Santa María, arrive at 1200. At 1300 take a bus back to Cuzco, arriving between 1900-2000. Or take the local train from Aguas Calientes to Santa Teresa at 1210, stay in a hostal, then take the 1000 bus to Santa María. If using this route, don't forget to buy your ticket for Machu Picchu in Cuzco, unless you want to buy it in Aguas Calientes.

'tied' at the winter solstice, before being freed to rise again on its annual ascent towards the summer solstice. The steps, angles and planes of this sculpted block appear to indicate a purpose beyond simple decoration, and researchers have sought the trajectory of each alignment. Whatever the motivation behind this magnificent carving, it is undoubtedly one of the highlights of Machu Picchu.

Climb down from the Intihuatana's mound to the **Main Plaza** (9). Beyond its northern end is a small plaza with open-sided buildings on two sides and on the third, the **Sacred Rock** (10). The outline of this gigantic, flat stone echoes that of the mountains behind it. From here you can proceed to the entrance to the trail to Huayna Picchu (see below). Returning to the Main Plaza and heading southeast you pass, on your left, several groups of closely packed buildings that have been taken to be **living quarters** and **Workshops** (11), **Mortar Buildings** (12; look for the house with two discs let into the floor) and the

Prison Group (13), one of whose constructions is known as the **Condor Temple**. Also in this area is a cave called **Intimachay** (14).

A short distance from the Condor Temple is the lower end of a series of **ceremonial baths** (15) or fountains. They were probably used for ritual bathing and the water still flows down them today. The uppermost, **Principal Bath** (16), is the most elaborate. Next to it is the **Temple of the Sun** (17), or Torreón. This singular building has one straight wall from which another wall curves around and back to meet the straight one, but for the doorway. From above it looks like an incomplete letter P. It is another example of the architecture being at one with its environment as the interior is taken up by the partly worked summit of the outcrop onto which the building is placed. All indications are that this temple was used for astronomical purposes. Underneath the Torreón a cave-like opening has been formed by an oblique gash in the rock. Fine masonry has been added to the opposing wall, making a second side of a triangle, which contrasts with the rough edge of the split rock. But the blocks of masonry appear to have been slotted behind another sculpted piece of natural stone, which has been cut into a four-stepped buttress. Immediately behind this is a two-stepped buttress. This strange combination of the natural and the man-made has been called the Tomb or Palace of the Princess. Across the stairway from the complex which includes the Torreón is the group of buildings known as the **Royal Sector** (18).

The famous Inca bridge – **Intipata** – is about 30 minutes along a well-marked trail south of the Royal Sector. The bridge, which is actually a couple of logs, is spectacularly sited, carved into a vertiginous cliff-face. The walk is well worth it for the fine views, but the bridge itself is closed to visitors. Not only is it in a poor state of repair, but the path before it has collapsed.

Note Camping is not allowed at Intipunku, or anywhere else at the site; guards may confiscate your tent. There is, however, a campsite at Puente Ruinas (see below).

Huayna Picchu

ⓘ *Visitors are given access for 2 departure times daily, 0700 and 1000, latest return time 1500. Maximum 200 people per departure. Check with the INC in Aguas Calientes or Cuzco for current departure times and to sign up for a spot.*

Synonymous with the ruins themselves is Huayna Picchu, the verdant mountain overlooking the site. There are also ruins on the mountain itself, and steps to the top for a superlative view of the whole magnificent scene, but this is not for those with vertigo. The climb takes up to 90 minutes but the steps are dangerous after bad weather and you shouldn't leave the path. You must register at a hut at the beginning of the trail. The other trail to Huayna Picchu, down near the Urubamba, is via the Temple of the Moon: two caves, one above the other, with superb Inca niches inside, sadly blemished by graffiti. To reach the **Temple of the Moon** from the path to Huayna Picchu, take the marked trail to the left; it is in good shape. It descends further than you think it should. After the Temple you may proceed to Huayna Picchu, but this path is overgrown, slippery when wet and has a crooked ladder on an exposed part about 10 minutes before the top (not for the faint-hearted). It is safer to return to the main trail to Huayna Picchu, but this adds about 30 minutes to the climb. The round trip takes about four hours.

The Inca Trail → For listings, see pages 208-212.

The wonder of Machu Picchu has been well documented over the years. Equally impressive is the centuries-old Inca Trail that winds its way from the Sacred Valley near

Inca Trail regulations

Tourists should be aware of the following regulations:

- All agencies must have a licence to work in the area.
- Groups of up to seven independent travellers who do not wish to use a tour operator are allowed to hike the trail accompanied by an independent, licensed guide, as long as they do not employ any other support staff, such as porters or cooks.
- A maximum of 500 visitors per day are allowed on the trail.
- Operators should pay US$15 for each porter and other trail staff; porters are not permitted to carry more than 15 kg, plus 5 kg of personal items (less scrupulous agencies find ways to circumvent these requirements).
- Littering is banned. Plastic water bottles may not be carried on the trail; only canteens are permitted.
- Pets and pack animals are prohibited, although llamas are allowed as far as the first pass.
- Groups have to use approved campsites; on the routes from Km 82, Km 88 and Salkantay, the campsites may be changed with prior authorization.
- The Inca Trail is closed each February for maintenance.

Ollantaytambo, taking three to four days. What makes this hike so special is the stunning combination of Inca ruins, unforgettable views, magnificent mountains, exotic vegetation and extraordinary ecological variety. The government acknowledged all this in 1981 by including the trail in a 325-sq-km national park, the Machu Picchu Historical Sanctuary. Machu Picchu itself cannot be understood without the Inca Trail. Its principal sites are ceremonial in character, apparently in ascending hierarchical order. This Inca province was a unique area of elite access. The trail is essentially a work of spiritual art, like a Gothic cathedral, and walking it was formerly an act of devotion.

Ins and outs

Entrance tickets and tours An entrance ticket for the trail or its variations must be bought at the **Instituto Nacional de Cultura (INC)** office in Cuzco; no tickets are sold at the entrance gates. Furthermore, tickets are only sold on presentation of a letter from a licensed tour operator on behalf of the visitor, with full passport details. Tickets are

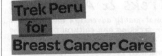

non-refundable and cannot be changed so make sure you provide accurate passport details to your tour operator. There is a 50% discount for students, but note that officials are very strict, only an ISIC card will be accepted as proof of status. Tickets are checked at Km 82, Huayllabamba and Wiñay-Wayna.

On all hiking trails (Km 82 or Km 88 to Machu Picchu, Salkantay to Machu Picchu, and Km 82 or Km 88 to Machu Picchu via Km 104) adults must pay US$86, students and children under 15 US$43. On the **Camino Real de los Inkas** from Km 104 to Wiñay-Wayna and Machu Picchu (see page 201) the fee is US$51 per adult, US$28 for students and children; Salkantay to Huayllabamba and Km 88 is US$51. The **Salkantay trek** (see page 201) is subject to a US$45 trekking fee.

Travel agencies in Cuzco arrange transport to the start, equipment, food, etc, for an all-in price. Prices vary from about US$450 to US$540 per person for a responsible four-day, three-night trek (similar prices are charged for the Salkantay trek). Remember that you get what you pay for and bear in mind that prices lower than those above suggest that corners are being cut, with less attention paid to the environment and the porters. This respect is, after all, the goal of the 2001 legislation.

There is a quota for agencies and groups to use the Trail, but some agencies make block bookings way in advance of departure dates. This makes it much harder for other agencies to guarantee their clients places on the Trail. Consequently, current advice is to book your preferred dates as early as possible, between two months and a year in advance depending on the season you want to go, then confirm nearer the time. There have been many instances of disappointed trekkers whose bookings did not materialize: don't wait till the last minute and always check your operator's cancellation charges.

You can save a bit of money by arranging your own transport back to Ollantaytambo in advance, either for the last day of your tour, or by staying an extra night in Aguas Calientes and taking the early morning train, then a bus back to Cuzco. If you take your own tent and sleeping gear, some agencies give a discount. Make sure your return ticket for the tourist train to Cuzco has your name on it, otherwise you have to pay for any changes.

Advice and information Although security has improved in recent years, it's still best to leave all your valuables in Cuzco and keep everything else inside your tent, even your shoes. Avoid the July/August high season and the rainy season from November to April (note that this can change, so check in advance). In the wet it is cloudy and the paths are very muddy and difficult. Also watch out for coral snakes in this area (black, red, yellow bands). Please remove all your rubbish, including toilet paper, or use the pits provided. Do not light open

fires as they can get out of control. The **Annual Inca Trail Clean-up** takes place usually in September. Many agencies and organizations are involved and volunteers should contact **South American Explorers** in Cuzco (see page 129) for full details of ways to help.

If you feel that your porters have been neglected or abused on the trek, express this to your agency, inform the **South American Explorers** and please also drop us a line at Footprint (go to www.footprinttravelguides.com or send us a letter to our Bath address in the UK). We read all your letters and agencies who repeatedly mistreat their porters will be removed from our publications.

Equipment It is cold at night and weather conditions change rapidly, so it is important to take strong footwear, rain gear and warm clothing (this includes long johns if you want to sleep rather than freeze at night): dress in layers. Also take food, water, water purification tablets, insect repellent, sunscreen, a hat and sunglasses, a supply of plastic bags, coverings (blankets, ponchos, etc), a good sleeping bag, a torch and a stove for preparing hot food and drink to ward off the cold at night. It is worth paying extra to hire a down sleeping bag if you haven't brought your own. A paraffin (kerosene) stove is preferable, as fuel can be bought in small quantities in markets.

A tent is essential, but if you're hiring one in Cuzco, check carefully for leaks. Caves marked on some maps are little better than overhangs and are not sufficient shelter to sleep in. You could also take a first-aid kit; if you don't need it, the porters probably will, given their rather basic footwear. It is forbidden to use trekking poles because the metal tips are damaging the trail. Instead, buy a carved wooden stick on sale in the main plaza in Ollantaytambo or at the trail head. Many will need this for the steep descents on the path.

All the necessary equipment can be rented in Cuzco, see page 159. Good maps of the trail and area can be bought from **South American Explorers** in Lima or Cuzco, see pages 74 and 129. If you have any doubts about carrying your own pack, porters/guides are available through Cuzco agencies. Always carry a day-pack, though, with water and snacks, in case you walk at a faster or slower pace than the porters. Take enough cash to ensure that your group tips a minimum of US$10 per porter, plus the tips for the guides and cook, and for your purchases at the end of the trail.

The trek

Day 1 The trek to the sacred site begins either at Km 82, **Piscacucho**, or at Km 88, **Qorihuayrachina**, at 2600 m. In order to reach Km 82, hikers are transported by their tour operator in a minibus on the road that goes to Quillabamba. From Piri onwards the road follows the riverbank and ends at Km 82, where there is a bridge. You can depart as early as you like and arrive at Km 82 faster than going by train. The Inca Trail equipment, food, fuel and field personnel reach Km 82 (depending on the tour operator's logistics) for the Sernanp staff to weigh each bundle before the group arrives. When several groups are leaving on the same day, it is more convenient to arrive early.

Km 88 can only be reached by train, subject to schedule and baggage limitations. The train goes slower than a bus, but you start your walk nearer to Llaqtapata and Huayllabamba.

The first ruin is **Llaqtapata**, near Km 88, the utilitarian centre of a large settlement of farming terraces that probably supplied the other Inca Trail sites. From here, it is a relatively easy three-hour walk to the village of **Huayllabamba**. Note that the route from Km 82 goes via **Cusichaca**, the valley in which Ann Kendall worked, rather than Llaqtapata.

A series of gentle climbs and descents leads along the Río Cusichaca, the ideal introduction to the trail. The village is a popular camping spot for tour groups, so it's a better idea to continue for about an hour up to the next site, **Llulluchayoc** – 'three white stones' – which is a patch of green beside a fast-flowing stream. It's a steep climb but you're pretty much guaranteed a decent pitch for the night. If you're feeling really energetic, you can go on to the next camping spot, a perfectly flat meadow, called **Llulluchapampa**. This means a punishing 1½-hour ascent through cloudforest, but it does leave you with a much easier second day. There's also the advantage of relative isolation and a magnificent view back down the valley.

Day 2 For most people the second day is by far the toughest. It's a steep climb to the meadow, followed by an exhausting 2½-hour haul up to the first pass – aptly named **Warmiwañusqa** (Dead Woman) – at 4200 m. The feeling of relief on reaching the top is immense. After a well-earned break it's a sharp descent on a treacherous path down to the Pacamayo Valley, where there are a few flat camping spots near a stream if you're too weary to continue.

Day 2/3 If you're feeling energetic, you can proceed to the second pass. Halfway up comes the ruin of **Runkuracay**, which was probably an Inca *tambo* (post-house). Camping is no longer permitted here. A steep climb up an Inca staircase leads to the next pass, at 3850 m, with spectacular views of Pumasillo (6246 m) and the Vilcabamba range. The trail descends to **Sayacmarca** (Inaccessible town), a spectacular site over the Aobamba Valley. Just below Sayacmarca lies **Conchamarca** (Shell town), a small group of buildings standing on rounded terraces.

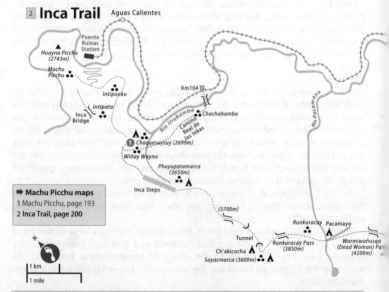

2 Inca Trail

➡ **Machu Picchu maps**
1 Machu Picchu, page 193
2 Inca Trail, page 200

Day 3 A blissfully gentle two-hour climb on a stone highway leads through an Inca tunnel and along the enchanted fringes of the cloudforest, to the third pass. This is the most rewarding part of the trail, with spectacular views of the entire Vilcabamba range. Then it's down to the extensive ruins of **Phuyupatamarca** (Cloud-level town), at 3650 m, where Inca observation platforms offer awesome views of nearby Salkantay (6270 m) and surrounding peaks. There is a 'tourist bathroom' here, where water can be collected, but do purify it before drinking.

From here, an Inca stairway of white granite plunges more than 1000 m to the spectacularly sited and impressive ruins of **Wiñay-Wayna** (Forever Young, entry US$5.75), offering views of agricultural terraces at **Intipata** (Sun place). A trail, not easily visible, goes from Wiñay-Wayna to the terracing. There is a youth hostel at Wiñay-Wayna (see Sleeping, page 208) and there are spaces for a few tents, but they get snapped up quickly. After Wiñay-Wayna there is no water, and no place to camp, until Machu Picchu. A gate by Wiñay-Wayna is locked between 1530 and 0500, preventing access to the path to Machu Picchu at night.

Day 4 From Wiñay-Wayna it is a gentle hour's walk through another type of forest, with larger trees and giant ferns, to a steep Inca staircase that leads up to **Intipunku** (Sun Gate), where you look down, at last, upon Machu Picchu, basking in all her glory. Your aching muscles will be quickly forgotten and even the presence of the functional hotel building cannot detract from one of the most magical sights in all the Americas.

Camino Real de los Inkas

The Inca Trail from Km 104 This short Inca Trail is used by those who don't want to endure the full hike. It starts at Km 104, where a footbridge gives access to the ruins of **Chachabamba** and the trail ascends to the main trail at Wiñay-Wayna. Half way up is a good view of the ruins of **Choquesuysuy**. The first part is a steady, continuous three-hour ascent (take water) and the trail is narrow and exposed in parts. About 15 minutes before Wiñay-Wayna is a waterfall where fresh water can be obtained (best to purify it before drinking).

Salkantay treks

Four hours' drive west of Cuzco is **Mollepata**, starting point for two major alternatives to the 'classic' Inca Trail. The road from Cuzco is good-quality tarmac until the turn off just beyond Limatambo, in the Río Colorado valley floor. A dirt road then winds steeply up to Mollepata. Both treks pass beneath the magnificent glacial bulk of **Salkantay**, at 6271 m the loftiest peak of the Vilcabamba range.

Santa Teresa trek The first four-day trek takes the northwestern pass under Salkantay, leading into the high jungles of

Km 88 Qorihuayrachina (2600m)

To Chillca

Wayna Q'Ente

Llaqtapata (2288m)

Río Cusichaca

Llulluchapampa

Llulluchayoc (3 White Stones)

Huayllabamba (2950m)

To Salkantay

the Santa Teresa valley and eventually down to the town of Santa Teresa itself at the confluence with the Río Urubamba, from where Aguas Calientes and Machu Picchu are accessible. **Cruzpata** (3100 m) is the starting point for the trek, which goes via **Soraypampa** and **Salkantay Pampa**, the 4500-m **Huamantay Pass**, the villages of **Chaullay** and **Colcanpampa** and the meeting of the Río Totora with the Quebrada Chalán to form the **Río Santa Teresa**. After the village of **La Playa** you can choose to go to the Hidroeléctrica railway station, via the ruins of **Patallacta**, or to the village of Santa Teresa. The restrictions on the Inca Trail quickly turned the Santa Teresa Trek into the most popular alternative to the 'classic' Trail, but the INC has ruled that this trek may only be done with an agency and trekkers are charged US$89 when they pass through Soraypampa.

High Inca Trail The second route, often referred to as the High Inca Trail, follows the same route up to the base of Salkantay before turning east across the **Inca Chiriasca Pass** at approximately 4900 m. This route then descends via **Sisaypampa**, from where you trek to **Pampacahuana**, an outstanding Inca ruin. The remains of an Inca road then go down to the singular Inca ruins of **Paucarcancha**. Paucarcancha is also an important camping site on the Ancascocha trek, described below. On the third day you join the 'classic' Inca Trail at **Huayllabamba** (see page 199), before continuing to Machu Picchu. Because the route follows the Km 88 trail in its second half, permits are required and thus booking in advance is highly recommended. It is not possible to trek this route without a registered Peruvian guide. There is also an obligatory change from animals to porters before you reach Huayllabamba.

If you don't want to join up with the classic Inca Trail, an alternative is to go to Huayllabamba, then down to Km 88, from where you can take the train to Aguas Calientes, or back to Cuzco. It is also possible to walk the 30 km from Km 88 to Aguas Calientes, but the authorities are not keen on this, especially from Aguas Calientes to Km 88. There is an entrance fee of US$51 for this hike, but it does not include the entrance to Machu Picchu. If you combine this route with the short Inca Trail from Km 104, you have to pay the US$51 trail fee (see above for full details on prices).

Ancascocha

Named after a tiny but beautifully situated community in the Cordillera Vilcabamba's remote eastern fringe, this is a little-known, but worthy addition to the growing list of alternative Inca trails. It starts in the village of Huarocondo (near the Cuzco–Aguas Calientes railway line). Crossing three fairly steep passes, it offers fabulous views of some of the region's best-known snow peaks, Salkantay and La Verónica foremost among them. An added bonus is the impressive Nevado Huayanay, which towers above a landscape laced with icy lakes and cascades. Along with the natural attractions you'll pass interesting ruins, fragmented sections of Inca trail and friendly pastoral communities. Ancascocha can easily be combined with the classic Inca Trail (given the timely reservation of permits), or longer routes into the heart of the Vilcabamba range. For those with more limited time, transport direct to either Aguas Calientes or Cuzco can be obtained from the trail's end. The Ancascocha trail finishes at several points: you can link up with the Salkantay treks at Paucarcancha; you can link up with the Inca Trail at Huayllabamba and continue to Machu Picchu; or you can end up at Km 88 or Km 82 on the railway line.

Inca Jungle Trail

This is offered by several tour operators in Cuzco: on the first day you cycle downhill from Abra Málaga to Santa María, 80 km of mainly downhill riding through changing scenery which includes Inca ruins, coffee plantations and lush high jungle and cloud forest. Be aware, though, that this is the main Quillabamba–Cuzco highway with speeding vehicles inattentive to cyclists on the road. As ever, you get what you pay for and cheap tours will have bikes with poor or no brakes or gears, no safety or luggage-carrying backup. The second day is a hard seven-hour trek from Santa María to Santa Teresa. It involves crossing three adventurous bridges and bathing in the beautifully refurbished hot springs at Santa Teresa (US$1.65 entry). The third day is a six-hour trek from Santa Teresa to Aguas Calientes and the final day is a guided tour of Machu Picchu. Find out what equipment, support and standards are offered by tour operators before paying.

Aguas Calientes → *For listings, see pages 208-212. Colour map 5, A5. Phone code: 084.*

Only 1.5 km back along the railway from Puente Ruinas, this is a popular resting place for those recovering from the rigours of the Inca Trail. It is named Aguas Calientes (or just Aguas) after the hot springs above the town. It is also called the town of Machu Picchu. Most activity is centred around the old railway station, on the plaza, or on Avenida Pachacútec, which leads from the plaza to the **thermal baths** ⓘ *daily 0500-2030, US$3.15*. They consist of a communal pool, which smells a bit sulphurous, 10 minutes' walk from the town by the banks of the river amid rich cloud forest vegetation. You can rent towels and bathing costumes for US$3 at several places on the road to the baths, or buy them if you prefer. There are basic toilets, changing facilities and showers. Take soap and shampoo and keep an eye on your valuables. The new **Museo Manuel Chávez Ballon** ⓘ *Carretera Hiram Bingham, Wed-Sun 0900-1600, US$6*, displays objects found at Machu Picchu.

Beyond Machu Picchu → *For listings, see pages 208-212.*

The lower reaches of the Río Urubamba beyond Machu Picchu are the gateway to regions that are very different from the highlands of Cuzco, yet intimately linked to it by history. The most important town is Quillabamba, from where you can set out to the mysterious last stronghold of the Incas, Vilcabamba, or to the Pongo de Mainique, frequently described as one of the most beautiful places on earth.

Ins and outs

As no trains run beyond Aguas Calientes, the only route to Quillabamba is by road from Cuzco via Ollantaytambo. Beyond here, there are buses to Ivochote, for boats down river, and to Huancacalle for the hike to Vilcabamba. After leaving Ollantaytambo, the road passes through Peña, a place of great beauty. Once out of **Peña**, the road climbs on endless zigzags, offering breathtaking views, to reach the **Abra Málaga Pass**, just below the beautiful glaciated peak of Verónica. The patches of *polylepis* woodland here, with their endemic bird species, have become a prime site for birdwatching. At Chaullay, the road meets the old railway to Quillabamba, Machu Picchu and Cuzco and continues up the east bank of the river.

Quillabamba and around → *Colour map 5, A5.*

'La Ciudad de Eterno Verano' (City of Eternal Summer), as it is known, was once a prosperous town from the sale of coffee. It has now become the overnighting spot for people going to Vilcabamba, Espíritu Pampa and the Pongo de Mainique. This delightful market town survives on the export of fruit, coffee, honey and other produce to Cuzco.

Aguas Calientes

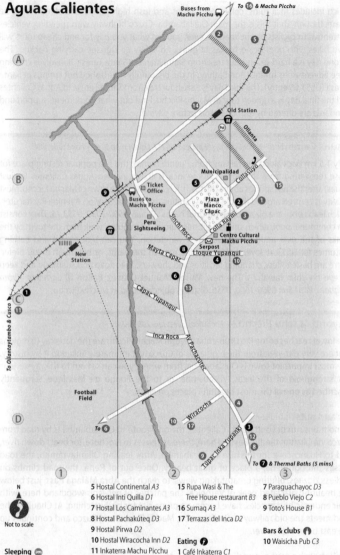

Sleeping 🛏
1 Gringo Bill's
   (Hostal Q'oñi Unu) B3
2 Hatuchay Tower A2
3 Hospedaje Las Bromelias B3
4 Hospedaje Quilla D3

5 Hostal Continental A3
6 Hostal Inti Quilla D1
7 Hostal Los Caminantes A3
8 Hostal Pachakúteq D3
9 Hostal Pirwa D2
10 Hostal Wiracocha Inn D2
11 Inkaterra Machu Picchu
   Pueblo C1
12 La Cabaña D3
13 Machu Picchu Inn C2
14 Presidente &
   Hostal Machu Picchu A2

15 Rupa Wasi & The
   Tree House restaurant B3
16 Sumaq A3
17 Terrazas del Inca D2

Eating 🍴
1 Café Inkaterra C1
2 Discovery Café B3
3 Govinda D3
4 Indio Feliz C2
5 Inka's Pizza Pub B2
6 Inka Wasi C2

7 Paraguachayoc D3
8 Pueblo Viejo C2
9 Toto's House B1

Bars & clubs 🍸
10 Waisicha Pub C3

N
Not to scale

The tourist season is from June to July, when Peruvian holidaymakers descend on the place. Although Quillabamba has plenty to offer, it's normally overlooked because of the incredibly bumpy, but beautiful ride to get there.

For the weary traveller one of the biggest attractions, about 1.5 km from Quillabamba, is **Sambaray** ① *US$0.20, transport by combi costs US$0.20, taxi US$0.60*, a recreation area with an outdoor swimming pool, restaurant, volleyball and football field. As Sambaray is situated on the Río Alto Urubamba, you can also swim in the river, or, if you're feeling brave, tube down it. Ask locals for the best place to start, as the river can be quite rapid. **Siete Tinajas** (Seven Small Baths) is a beautiful waterfall some 45 minutes by combi from town (take the bus from Paradero El Grifo, US$1). It is well worth the trip for the photos, although be careful when climbing to the top, as it can be very slippery.

Pongo de Mainique and beyond
Before the Río Urubamba enters the vast plain of the Amazon Basin it carves its way through one last wall of foothills and the result is spectacular. The Pongo de Mainique is a sheer rainforest canyon, hundreds of metres deep with the Urubamba surging through its centre and many small waterfalls tumbling in on either side. The Machiguenga people who live in the area believe this to be a portal to the afterlife. They are, however, very private people and do not take kindly to uninvited strangers; if you wish to visit them on their reserve take someone who has contact with them.

To get to the Pongo de Mainique, take a bus from Quillabamba's northern bus 'terminal' (a dusty outdoor affair with many food stalls and the occasional ticket booth) to **Ivochote**, via a new road into the jungle. The road can be in terrible condition in places. En route you'll pass **Kiteni**, a rapidly expanding jungle town. Ivochote is the end of the road, literally, but it develops a party atmosphere on Saturday, which is market day in the jungle. Due to the **Camisea Natural Gas Project** downriver, boat traffic is fairly intense. *Lanchas* (boats) head downstream early in the morning on most days during the dry season. In the wet season (roughly December to April) the river may be too dangerous to navigate, especially the rapids in the Pongo itself. Depending on your bargaining ability, passage downriver to the Pongo or to **La Casa de los Ugarte** (see Sleeping, page 210) will set you back about US$10, providing the captain has trading business downstream. Hiring a boat independently will cost you a lot more. To return upstream, prices are roughly one third higher, owing to the increased amount of gasoline required to motor against the current. Two to three hours downstream from the **Casa de los Ugarte**, on the right-hand bank of the river, you pass the Machiguenga community of **Timpia**.

Beyond the Pongo a day's boat travel will bring you to **Malvinas**, centre of the hugely controversial **Camisea Natural Gas Project**, and on to **Camisea** itself. If you wish to stay here, you must ask the *Presidente* of the community first. Another day downriver and you'll reach **Sepahua**, a largely indigenous village on the edge of the Alto Purus region. It has a few *hostales* and you can buy pretty much anything you need. Those with time and an adventurous spirit can continue downriver to **Pucallpa** via Atalaya (see page 574). To go all the way to Iquitos means, overall, a journey of 2500 km by boat, an incredible opportunity to see the Peruvian jungle.

Huancacalle and around
At **Chaullay**, the historic **Choquechaca Bridge**, built on Inca foundations, allows drivers to cross the river to Huancacalle, a two-street village (no restaurants, but a few shops) between four and seven hours from Quillabamba. Huancacalle is the best base for exploring

the nearby Inca ruins of Vitcos and is the starting point for the trek to Espíritu Pampa. At **Vitcos** ① *entry US$11*, is the palace of the last four Inca rulers from 1536 to 1572, and **Yurac Rumi**, the sacred White Rock of the Incas (also referred to as **Chuquipalta**). The White Rock, once the most sacred site in South America, is large (8 m high and 20 m wide), with intricate and elaborate carvings. Lichens now cover its whiteness.

You can also hike up to **Vilcabamba La Nueva** from Huancacalle. It's a three-hour walk through beautiful countryside with Inca ruins dotted around. There is a missionary building run by Italians, with electricity and running water, where you may be able to spend the night.

Huancacalle to Espíritu Pampa → *Colour map 5, A4/5.*
① *The INC charge for this trek is US$38.20 (students US$19), not including entry to the archaeological site, US$11.*

In 1536, three years after the fall of the Inca Empire to the Spanish *conquistadores*, Manco Inca led a rebellion against the conquerors. Retiring from Cuzco when Spanish reinforcements arrived, Manco and his followers fell back to the remote triangle of Vilcabamba, where they maintained the Inca traditions, religion and government outside the reach of the Spanish authorities. Centuries after the eventual Spanish crushing of Inca

Vilcabamba

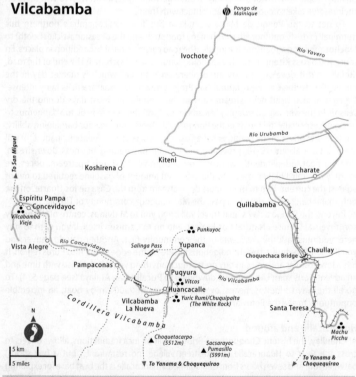

The last Incas of Vilcabamba

After Pizarro killed Atahualpa in 1532, the Inca empire disintegrated rapidly, and it is often thought that native resistance ended there. But, in fact, it continued for 40 more years, beginning with Manco, a teenage half-brother of Atahualpa.

In 1536, Manco escaped from the Spanish and returned to lead a massive army against them. He besieged Cuzco and Lima simultaneously, and came close to dislodging the Spaniards from Peru. Spanish reinforcements arrived and Manco fled to Vilcabamba, a mountainous forest region west of Cuzco that was remote, but still fairly close to the Inca capital, which he always dreamed of recapturing.

The Spanish chased Manco deep into Vilcabamba but he managed to elude them and continued his guerrilla war, raiding Spanish commerce on the Lima highway, and keeping alive the Inca flame. Then, in 1544, Spanish outlaws to whom he had given refuge murdered him, ending the most active period of Inca resistance.

The Inca line passed to his sons. The first, a child too young to rule named Sayri Túpac, eventually yielded to Spanish enticements and emerged from Vilcabamba, taking up residence in Yucay, near Urubamba in 1558. He died mysteriously – possibly poisoned – three years later.

His brother Titu Cusi, who was still in Vilcabamba, now took up the Inca mantle. Astute and determined, he resumed raiding and fomenting rebellion against the Spanish. But in 1570, Titu Cusi fell ill and died. A Spanish priest was accused of murdering him. Anti-Spanish resentment erupted, and the priest and a Spanish viceregal envoy were killed. The Spanish Viceroy reacted immediately, and the Spanish invaded Vilcabamba for the third and last time in 1572.

A third brother, Túpac Amaru, was now in charge. He lacked his brother's experience and acuity, and his destiny was to be the sacrificial last Inca. The Spanish overran the Inca's jungle capital, and dragged him back to Cuzco in chains. There, Túpac Amaru, the last Inca, was publicly executed in Cuzco's main plaza.

The location of the neo-Inca capital of Vilcabamba was forgotten over the centuries, and the search for it provoked Hiram Bingham's expeditions, and his discovery of Machu Picchu. Bingham also discovered Vilcabama the Old, without realizing it, but the true location at Espíritu Pampa was only pinpointed by Gene Savoy in the 1960s, and wasn't confirmed irrefutably until the work of Vincent Lee in the 1980s.

resistance, it was difficult to locate and identify Manco's capital of Vilcabamba. See box, above, for more information.

The trek to Espíritu Pampa from Huancacalle takes three days, but would be a more comfortable undertaking in four. Espíritu Pampa itself is quite a large site, and further groups of buildings may still be awaiting discovery in the densely forested mountains surrounding the valley. Give yourself at least a day at the site to soak up the atmosphere before continuing a further six hours to Chanquiri, the starting point for transport to Kiteni and Quillabamba. The best time of year is from May to November, possibly December. Outside this period it is very dangerous, as the trails are very narrow and can be thick with mud and very slippery. Insect repellent is essential; there are millions of mosquitoes. Also take painkillers and other basic medicines; these will be much appreciated by the local people should you need to take advantage of their hospitality.

An excellent guide is Jesús Castillo Alveres who can be contacted through the *hospedaje* **Sixpac Manco** in Huancacalle (see page 210). Many members of the Cobos family also guide. A good rate of pay for guides/mule drivers is US$8 per day, plus expenses, and US$6 per mule or horse used (in some seasons, the trail is unsuitable for horses). Before you leave be very clear about your exact itinerary and expectations; some guides have been known to leave clients in Espíritu Pampa, half a day's hike from the roadhead in Chanquiri. Always provide sufficient food and a waterproof tent by way of accommodation for your guide on the trail. If you enjoy your trip, give your guide a tip; it will be appreciated. Remember, *arrieros* (mule drivers) based in Huancacalle have to walk all the way back along the route, a journey of at least 2½ days, and for this they don't charge. Always take all plastic and non-biodegradable rubbish back to Cuzco for more efficient disposal. All supplies must be brought from Huancacalle as even basic supplies are scarce on the trail.

◉ Machu Picchu & the Inca trails listings

For Sleeping and Eating price codes and other relevant information, see pages 38-44.

● Sleeping

Machu Picchu ruins *p192, map p193*
LL Machu Picchu Sanctuary Lodge, Carretera Hiram Bingham Km 7.5, under the same management as the **Hotel Monasterio** in Cuzco, T084-984 816956, www.sanctuary lodge.net. This hotel, at the entrance to the ruins, has some environmentally friendly features. The rooms are comfortable, the service is good and the staff helpful. Electricity and water available 24 hrs a day. Food in the restaurant is well cooked; the restaurant is for residents only in the evening, but the buffet lunch is open to all. The hotel is usually fully booked well in advance; if struggling for a booking try Sun night as other tourists find Pisac market a greater attraction.

The Inca Trail *p196, map p200*
G pp **Youth Hostel**, at Wiñay-Wayna, with bunk beds, showers and a small restaurant. It is often fully booked. You can sleep on the floor of the restaurant more cheaply, but it is open for diners until 2300. There are also spaces for a few tents, but they get snapped up quickly too. The hostel's door is closed at 1730.

Salkantay treks *p201*
Machu Picchu Lodge to Lodge, T084-243636 (Lima T01-421 6952), www.mountainlodgesof

peru.com. **Mountain Lodges of Peru** have set up a series of lodges on the Santa Teresa trek to Machu Picchu. 7-day fully-guided tours go from lodge to lodge, which are at Soraypampa (**Salkantay Lodge and Adventure Resort**), Huayraccmachay (**Wayra Lodge**), Collpapampa (**Colpa Lodge**) and Lucmabamba (**Lucma Lodge**). Contact Mountain Lodges of Peru for rates, departure dates and all other details.
F pp **Hospedaje Mollepata**, Mollepata, T084-832103, or Cuzco T084-245449. Just above the plaza, behind the solid, elegant church. Hot-water electric shower, nice courtyard with café and **ÑanTika** restaurant attached. Swings in the courtyard are a real bonus!

Aguas Calientes *p203, map p204*
Some hotels in Aguas Calientes have increased their prices in response to the rising costs of train services and excursions on the Inca Trail. Be sure to bargain hard for good-value accommodation and book in advance from Cuzco.
LL Inkaterra Machu Picchu Pueblo.
Reservations: Andalucía 174, San Isidro, Lima, T01-610 0400; in Cuzco at Plaza las Nazarenas 167, T084-245314, www.inkaterra.com. Beautiful colonial-style bungalows have been built in a village compound surrounded by cloudforest 5 mins' walk along the railway from the town. The hotel has lovely gardens in which there are many species of birds, butterflies and orchids. There is a pool, spa and an expensive restaurant. It offers tours to

Machu Picchu, several guided walks on the property and to local beauty spots. The buffet breakfasts are great. It also has the **Café Inkaterra** by the railway line. The hotel is involved in a project to rehabilitate spectacled bears and release them back into the wild. Recommended, but there are a lot of steps between the public areas and rooms.

LL Sumaq, Av Hermanos Ayar Mz 1, Lte 3, T084-211059, www.sumaqhotelperu.com. An impressive 5-star hotel near the Urubamba river with on-site spa, bar and restaurant.

LL-L Hatuchay Tower, Ctra Puente Ruinas block 4, T084-211201, www.hatuchaytower.com. This smart, modern hotel is below the old station. Buffet breakfast and all taxes are included. There are standard rooms and luxury suites with hot water.

AL La Cabaña, Av Pachacútec M20-3, T084-211048, www.lacabanamachupicchu.com. Price includes bathroom and continental breakfast. Rooms have hot water. There is a café, laundry service and a DVD player and TV (with a good selection of movies) for clients in the lounge. The staff are helpful and can provide information on interesting local walks. The hotel is popular with groups.

AL Machu Picchu Inn, Av Pachacútec 101, T084-211057, mapiinn@peruhotel.com.pe. The price includes bathroom and breakfast. A modern hotel, with a functional atmosphere.

AL-A Gringo Bill's (Hostal Q'oñi Unu), Colla Raymi 104, T084-211046 (Cuzco office Av El Sol 520, T084-223663), www.gringobills.com. From deluxe to standard rooms, price includes bathroom and continental breakfast. An Aguas Calientes institution, it's friendly, relaxed, with a lot of coming and going, hot water, good beds, luggage store, laundry and money exchange. Good but expensive meals are served in the restaurant; breakfast starts at 0530 and they offer a packed lunch to take up to the ruins. Sadly for Gringo Bill's the monstrous new municipal building has been plonked right in front of the hotel and obscures the views from rooms which once looked out over the plaza.

AL-A Rupa Wasi, C Huanacaure 180, T084-211101, www.rupawasi.net. Rustic 'eco-lodge',

located up a small alley off Collasuyo. The lodge and its owners have a very laid-back, comfortable style, there are great views from the balconies of the 1st-floor rooms and purified water (so you don't have to buy more plastic). Birdwatching and other treks available. Breakfast is included and half-board is available: gourmet cuisine in the recommended restaurant. Cookery classes are offered, too.

A Presidente, at the old station, T084-211034 (Cuzco T084-244598), www.hostal presidente.com. Next to **Hostal Machu Picchu**, see below, this is the more upmarket half of the establishment. Rooms without river view are cheaper, but the price includes breakfast and taxes. There seems to be only minimal difference between this and **Machu Picchu**, which represents much better value for money.

B Hostal Continental, Av Imperio de los incas 127, near the old train station, T084-211065, http://hostalcontinentalperu.com. Very clean rooms with good beds, hot showers. This renovated *hostal* is in the same group as the **Presidente** and **Hostal Machu Picchu**.

C Hostal Machu Picchu, at the old station, T084-211065, sierrandina@gmail.com. Price includes breakfast and taxes. A clean, functional establishment, which is quiet and friendly (especially Wilber, the owner's son). There is hot water, a nice balcony over the Urubamba, a grocery store and travel information is available. Recommended.

C Hostal Pachakúteq, up the hill beyond Hostal La Cabaña, T084-211061. Rooms with bathroom and 24-hr hot water. Breakfast is included, quiet, family-run. Recommended.

C Hostal Wiracocha Inn, C Wiracocha, T084-211088, www.wiracochainn.com. Rooms with bath and hot water. Breakfast included. There is a small garden at this very friendly and helpful *hostal*. Some rooms have been converted into suites and are offered at a higher price. It's popular particularly with European groups.

D Hospedaje Las Bromelias, Colla Raymi, T084-211145. Just off the plaza before

Gringo Bill's, this is a small place that has rooms with bath and hot water. Accommodation is cheaper without bath.
D Hospedaje Quilla, Av Pachacútec, T084-211009, between Wiracocha and Túpac Inka Yupanki. Price includes breakfast, bath and hot water. Rents bathing gear for the hot springs if you arrive without it.
E Hostal Inti Quilla, Calle Aymuraypa Tikan s/n, Urb Las Orquídeas, T084-211096, hostalintiquillamapi@hotmail.com. On the other side of the river from most hotels. Private bath and hot water, laundry, friendly, clean, good value.
E Hostal Los Caminantes, Av Imperio de los Incas 140, by the railway just beyond the old station, T084-211083. Price per person for a room with bathroom. Hot water but breakfast extra. Basic but friendly and clean.
E Hostal Pirwa, C Túpac Inka Yupanki, www.pirwahostelscusco.com. With breakfast, TV, bath and luggage store, this hostel is in the same group as in Cuzco, Lima and elsewhere.
E Terrazas del Inca, Calle Wiracocha s/n, T084-211113, www.terrazasdelinca.com. Safety deposit box, rooms with private bath, continental breakfast included, use of kitchen. Friendly and helpful staff. Recommended.

Camping
The only official campsite is in a field by the river, just below Puente Ruinas station, it has toilets and showers, US$3.50 per person. Do not leave your tent and belongings unattended.

Quillabamba p203
C Hostal Quillabamba, Prolongación M Grau 590, just behind the main market, T084-281369, http://hostalquillabamba.com. Highly kitsch design, one of the largest hostels in Quillabamba, all rooms have private bath, TV (local channels only) and telephone, swimming pool (which occasionally has water in it), restaurant, parking. Less appealing is the small zoo. They also have a cockfighting school for the championship, which is held every year in late Jul.

C-D Hostal Don Carlos, Jr Libertad 566, T084-281150, www.hostaldoncarlosquilla bamba.com. Clean and simple, all rooms have private shower with generally hot water. There is a bar and restaurant.
D-E Hostal Alto Urubamba, Jr 2 de Mayo 333, T084-281131, altourub@ec-red.com. Rooms with shared bath cheaper. Spotlessly clean, pleasant hotel, 1 block from the Plaza de Armas. Staff are friendly and knowledge-able. Small local restaurant attached and there are great views over the town from the roof. Highly recommended.

Pongo de Mainique and beyond p205
F Hostal La Casa de los Ugarte, just beyond the Pongo, on the left bank of the river (if heading downstream). The small hacienda of Ida and Abel Ugarte. They are very helpful and will let you camp on their land for a small fee. They have a modest general store and basic supplies, fruit and very fresh eggs are available. The forest behind the hacienda is rich in wildlife and the family may be able to arrange expeditions in the jungle, given time to make the arrangements.
F Hostal Pongo de Mainique, Ivochote, just behind **F Señor de Huanca**, Ivochote, on the right once over the footbridge. The former is the nicer of the 2, although both are basic.
F Hostal Vanessa, Sepahua. On the main street close to the port, very pleasant.
Sabeti Lodge, Timpía, www.sabetilodge. com, or contact the Centro para el Desarrollo del Indígena Amazónico (CEDIA), T01-420 4340. The lodge founded by the Machiguenga community, CEDIA and Perú Verde. Offers 4- and 5-night packages for eco and eco-mystical tourism with guided tours (contact them directly for prices). With restaurant and bar.

Huancacalle and around p205
Villagers will accept travellers in their very basic homes (take a sleeping bag).
F Sixpac Manco, managed by the Cobos family, this hostel is fairly comfortable and has good beds.

🍴 Eating

Aguas Calientes *p203, map p204*
Pizza seems to be the most common dish in town, but many of the pizzerías serve other types of food as well. The old station and Av Pachútec are lined with eating places. Check if tax is included as Aguas Calientes is the only place in Peru where it is often added to the published price.

🍴🍴🍴 **Café Inkaterra**, on the railway, just below Inkaterra Machu Picchu. US$15 for a great lunch buffet with scenic views of the river.

🍴🍴 **Indio Feliz**, C Lloque Yupanqui, T084- 211090, www.indiofeliz.com. Great French cuisine, excellent value and service, set 3-course meal for US$10, good pisco sours. Expanded to include a bar area with elaborate decor and great atmosphere. Highly recommended.

🍴🍴 **Inka's Pizza Pub**, on the plaza. Good pizzas, changes money and accepts TCs.

🍴🍴 **Inka Wasi**, Av Pachacútec, www.inkawasi restaurant.com. A very good place to eat. Atmospheric and warm because of the open fire in the centre. Full Peruvian and international menu including pizza and pasta.

🍴🍴 **Pueblo Viejo**, Av Pachacútec, near the plaza. Good food in a spacious but warm environment. Price includes salad bar.

🍴🍴 **Toto's House**, Av Imperio de los Incas, on the railway line. Same owners as **Pueblo Viejo**. Good value and quality *menú*. Also serves a buffet from 1130 to 1500 every day.

🍴 **Discovery Café**, Plaza de Armas, T084-211355. Without a doubt both the best internet connection and coffee in Aguas Calientes. Several computers and Wi-Fi.

🍴 **Govinda**, Av Pachacútec y Túpac Inka Yupanki. Vegetarian restaurant with a cheap set lunch. Recommended.

🍴 **Paraguachayoc**, Av Pachacútec, at the top near the baths. Charming little restaurant with trout farm where you can catch your own dinner. US$5 for a whole trout with chips and drink.

🍴 **The Tree House**, Jr Huancarane (at **Rupa Wasi Eco-Lodge**) T084-211101. Restaurant serving gourmet organic food.

Quillabamba *p203*
Quillabamba's a great place for freshly squeezed fruit juices – head for the 2nd floor in the main market. **Gabbi's Juice Stall**, on the far right-hand side, is especially good.

🍴 **El Gordito**, on Espinar. A good place for chicken.

🍴 **Pizzería Venecia**, Jr Libertad 461, on the Plaza de Armas, T084-281582. Decent pizza, delivery available.

🍴 **Pub Don Sebas**, Jr Espinar 235 on Plaza de Armas. Great sandwiches, run by Karen Molero who is very friendly and always ready for a chat.

🍸 Bars and clubs

Aguas Calientes *p203, map p204*
Waisicha Pub, C Lloque Yupanqui. For good music and atmosphere.

⛰ Activities and tours

Aguas Calientes *p203, map p204*
Peru Sightseeing, www.perusightseeing. com. The only agency in Aguas Calientes, they offer guided trips to Machu Picchu with audio tours as well as a local guide. You can book a whole 2 or 3 day package in advance, or just the Machu Picchu tour. Also half-day tours in the area to Mandor and the Machu Picchu musuem. Can make onward travel arrangements.

🚌 Transport

Aguas Calientes *p203, map p204*
Bus
To **Machu Picchu** every 30 mins from 0630 to 1300, US$14 return, US$7 single, valid for 48 hrs. Buses return from the ruins 1200-1730. It is also possible to take a bus down 0700-0900. The ticket office is opposite the bus stop, which is 50 m from the railway station. Tickets can also be bought in advance at **Consetur**, Santa

Catalina Ancha, Cuzco, to save queuing when you arrive in Aguas Calientes.

Train
See box, page 194.

Quillabamba *p203*
Bus
Most buses leave **Cuzco** for Quillabamba from the Terminal Terrestre de Santiago between 1800 and 2000. Journey time is about 8 hrs, although expect 14 hrs or more in the rainy season, because of landslides. 4 bus companies on this route are: **Valle de los Incas**, T084-244787, **Ben Hur**, T084-229193, **Ampay**, T084-245734, and **Selva Sur**, T084-247975. Selva Sur has 2 buses on the route, one of which is quite comfortable, with good reclining seats, perhaps the best bus for the journey. Buy tickets in advance, US$6. **Ampay** also runs from **Ollantaytambo** to Quillabamba. The bus station in Quillabamba is on Av 28 de Julio and buses depart for **Cuzco** daily, with buses leaving in the morning around 0700 and evening. There are extra services at weekends. Taxi colectivos provide a faster service to Quillabamba from outside the Almudena cemetary in Cuzco, they leave when full and make the journey in 6 hrs.

From **Quillabamba** buses take 10 hrs to reach **Ivochote** and cost around US$4. Ask locals for their opinions on the best companies for this route. Buses (combis) leave Quillabamba for **Huancacalle** daily from Jr San Martín, near Plaza Grau, at 0900 and 1200, US$3.30. The journey takes 4-7 hrs. On Fri they go all the way to **Vilcabamba La Nueva**.

Pongo de Mainique and beyond *p205*
Boat
For boats beyond Ivochote, you may have to wait a few days for a boat downstream, but try to get as far as Bajo Pongo or **Timpia**, 4 hrs, US$10. It's a further 4 hrs, US$10 to

Camisea. After **Sepahua** boats are larger, boats more frequent and distances greater. To **Atalaya** you can take an express, 10 hrs, US$15, or a delivery boat, up to 2 days. From here boats go to **Pucallpa**.

Huancacalle to Espíritu Pampa *p206*
From Chanquiri, at the end of the Espíritu Pampa trail, trucks and buses leave for **Kiteni** and **Quillabamba**, Wed and Sun, 8-12 hrs, US$2.50.

❶ Directory

Aguas Calientes *p203, map p204*
Banks There are several ATMs in town and a branch of **BCP** for changing TCs, which also has an ATM. It is not uncommon for ATMs to run out of cash at weekend. **Internet** Many internet shops, average price US$1 per hr; slow connection. **Discovery Café** (see Eating) has the best connection. Ask also at **Peru Sightseeing** if their satellite link has been installed. **Medical services** Hampi Land, C Hermanos Ayar, Lote 6 Mz 10, T084-782641, www.hampiland.com. Professional, 24-hr medical care for tourists, with emergency rescue and ambulance services, pharmacy, oxygen. **Urgent Medical Center**, Av de Los Incas 119, T084-211005, 084-984 761314 (mob). Good care at affordable prices. **Post** Serpost agencies, just off the plaza, between the Centro Cultural Machu Picchu and Galería de Arte Tunupa, and on the railway line. **Telephone** Oficina on C Collasuyo, and there are plenty of phone booths around town.

Quillabamba *p203*
Banks BCP, Jr Libertad, good for TCs. Banco Continental, Av F Bolognesi, accepts Visa and Cirrus. **Internet** Ciber Master, Jr Espinar, plaza.

East of Cuzco

Along or near the main road from Cuzco to Lake Titicaca and Peru's major southern city, Arequipa, are archaeological sites, fascinating colonial churches, beautiful lakes and the majestic Ausangate massif, where you can do some serious high-altitude trekking. Off this route is also the gateway to Peru's southeastern jungle in the Department of Madre de Dios. ➤➤ *For listings, see pages 217-218.*

Ins and outs

A paved road runs southeast from Cuzco to Sicuani, at the southeastern edge of the Department of Cuzco. It continues to Puno, on the shores of Lake Titicaca, then on to the border with Bolivia. Combis run every 15-20 minutes between Cuzco and Sicuani, and more frequently to the villages and towns in between.

To Huambutío and Paucartambo

Tipón ruins ① *between Saylla and Oropesa, on the BTC visitor ticket, see box page 130, or US$3.60*, are extensive and include baths, terraces, irrigation systems and a temple complex, accessible from a path leading from just above the last terrace, all in a fine setting. From Tipón village it's an hour's climb to the ruins; or take a taxi. At the Tipón ruins, if you head to the left at the back, there is a trail round to where you will see more small ruins. From there you will find an amazing Inca road with a deep irrigation channel, which can be followed to Cerro Pachatusan. Nearby, **Oropesa** is known as the national capital of bread; try the delicious sweet circular loaves known as *chutas*. Most buses will slow down when passing through so that people can buy through the windows.

At **Huambutío**, north of Huacarpay, the road divides: northwest to Pisac (see page 175) and north to Paucartambo, on the eastern slope of the Andes. Huambutío and its surroundings were badly damaged by floods in 2010. The road from Huambutío northwest to Pisac (about 20 km) is unpaved and poor. This is an access road for the first river-rafting section on the Río Urubamba, which also connects with another rafting route from Piñipampa. In the rainy season, and for less experienced rafters, the Huambutío (Piñipampa) to Pisac river section is safer to run. The rafting trip is 30 to 35 km long with spectacular views of the Urubamba valley that are not seen in a conventional valley tour. This part of the river offers views of the **Sanctuary of El Señor de Huanca**, an image painted on a rock around which the church has been built. The rock and surroundings date back to pre-Inca times as a *huaca*, or sacred place. The month of pilgrimage to El Señor de Huanca is September, with the 14th being the main day.

Paucartambo

This once remote town, 80 km east of Cuzco, is on the road to Pilcopata, Atalaya and Shintuya. This is now the overland route used by tour companies from Cuzco into Manu Biosphere Reserve (see page 620). It has a famous 17th-century stone bridge, built on the orders of King Carlos III of Spain. The town is famous for the annual **Fiesta of the Virgen del Carmen** held on 15-17 July, in which dance groups from the surrounding villages compete in dance in honour of the Virgin. Masked participants enact rituals and folk tales in the streets. In the small park in the plaza bronze statues represent the characters from the traditional dances.

From Paucartambo, in the dry season, you can go 44 km to **Tres Cruces**, along the Pilcopata road, turning left after 25 km. Tres Cruces gives a wonderful view of the sunrise in June and July: peculiar climactic conditions make it appear as if three suns are rising. Tour operators in Cuzco, see page 160, can arrange transport and lodging.

Piquillacta Archaeological Park

ⓘ *Daily 0700-1730, by BTC visitor ticket, see box page 130, or US$3.60. Buses to Urcos from Av Huáscar, Cuzco drop you at the north side entrance, though this is not the official entry.*

The Piquillacta Archaeological Park is 30 km southeast of Cuzco, with an area of 3421 ha. Its nucleus is the remains of a lake, the Laguna de Huacarpay, around which are many pre-Columbian archaeological remains, the principal of which are Piquillacta and Rumicolca. The lake is a favourite birdwatching destination and it's good to hike or cycle round it. The Huari ruins of **Piquillacta** (which translates as the City of Fleas) are extensive, with some reconstruction in progress. It was an administrative centre at the southern end of the Huari Empire. The whole site is surrounded by a wall, encompassing many enclosed compounds with buildings of over one storey; it appears that the walls were plastered and finished with a layer of lime. Going with a guide is recommended as the more interesting structures are not easy to find. Tiny turquoise figurines found at the site are on display in the Inka Museum in Cuzco.

The huge gateway of **Rumicolca** is on the right of the main road to Sicuani, shortly after the turn-off to Piquillacta. You can walk around it for free. This was a Huari aqueduct, built across this narrow stretch of the valley, which the Incas clad in fine stonework to create this gateway. If you look at the top you can see the original walls, four tiers high.

Andahuaylillas

Continuing southeast towards Urcos you reach Andahuaylillas, 32 km from Cuzco, with a fascinating 17th-century church. This is a simple structure, but it has been referred to as the Andean Sistine Chapel because of its beautiful frescoes and internal architecture. Go in and wait for your eyes to adjust to the darkness, in order to see, on the right of the splendid door, the path to heaven, which is narrow and thorny, and, on the left, the way to hell, which is wide and littered with flowers. Above is the high choir, built in local wood, where there are two organs. The main altar is gilded in 24-carat gold leaf and has symbols from both the Quechua and Christian religions. Sr Eulogio is a good guide, but speaks Spanish only. Tour groups visit at around 100 and 1600 daily.

Huaro and Urcos

At the quiet village of Huaro, the church on the ugly plaza is stunning inside. The walls are plastered with frescoes. Grinning skeletons compete with dragons and devils ushering the living into the afterlife and punishing them thereafter. They are now mostly in a sad state of repair. Beyond Huaro is **Urcos**. There are lodgings here, but they're basic. The **Laguna de Urcos** is a popular picnic spot and makes for a pleasant day out from Cuzco. There is a clear path from the town to the Laguna which can be seen from the road. A spectacular road from Urcos crosses the Eastern Cordillera to Puerto Maldonado in the jungle (see page 624).

Cordillera Vilcanota → *Colour map 5, A6.*

East of Cuzco lies the Cordillera Vilcanota, the greatest concentration of mountains and glaciers in southern Peru. With at least four great peaks towering above 6000 m in densely packed icy masses, this area is reminiscent of the Cordillera Huayhuash further to the north. Viewed from the ruins of Sacsayhuaman above Cuzco, **Ausangate**, at 6384 m the range's loftiest member, is impressive even from a distance of nearly 100 km, but in the Vilcanota mountains Ausangate is just the beginning. Unlike both the Cordilleras of Vilcabamba and Urubamba, which plunge precipitously from sheer glaciers into lush subtropical valleys, the Vilcanota rises from the northern altiplano; treks into the region rarely, if ever, drop below 4000 m. Life is harsh for the communities who live in the shadow of these great peaks. Knowledge of Spanish is often limited or non-existent and the people's respect for ancient ways and the power of the *apus* (mountain spirits), runs strong. Survival is eked from a meagre diet of potatoes, *cuy* (guinea pig) and the meat and wool of the large herds of domesticated llamas and alpacas that roam the valleys.

The road to Puerto Maldonado Some 82 km from Urcos, at the base of Nevado Ausangate, is the town of **Ocongate**, which has two hotels on the Plaza de Armas. The small town of **Tinqui**, further east, is the traditional starting point for treks into the region and is a good place to find local guides and *arrieros* (mule drivers). Forty-seven kilometers after passing the snow-line **Hualla-Hualla Pass**, at 4820 m, the super-hot thermal baths of **Marcapata** ① *173 km from Urcos, US$0.10,* provide a relaxing break. Beyond this point, what is arguably the most spectacular road in Peru descends the eastern flank of the Andes towards Puerto Maldonado (see page 624).

Ausangate circuit This is the most popular trekking route and involves four to six days of fairly tough hiking around the peak itself, featuring icy mountain vistas, high passes (including two over 5000 m) and some beautiful turquoise lakes. As an added bonus, there are two geothermal springs, **Upis** and **Pacchanta**, to thaw out in at the beginning and end! In addition to 'The Circuit' there is a great variety of other options, including treks around the range's northern peaks and routes to the magnificent **Laguna Sibinacocha**, a stunning 15-km long lake set at 4800 m in remote territory to the east of Ausangate.

A standard fee for locals hired independently is US$8 per day for an *arriero* and US$6 per horse per day. You are also expected to provide sufficient food and a tent for the *arriero*. Tiofilo is a recommended guide/*arriero* who can be contacted through Tinqui's radio station, located just of the town's main plaza. The IGN 1:100,000 Ocongate map (available at **South American Explorers** in Cuzco) covers all trekking areas described below and is fairly accurate. Note that as you leave Tinqui you will be charged a community fee for using the Ausangate trail of about US$4.

An alternative to the classic circuit is a new five-day trek that includes four mountain lodges for each night. The start of the Camino del Apu Ausangate is reached from Checacupe, where a side road goes to Pitumarca and the start of the trail near Chillca. Two indigenous communities of llama and alpaca herders have helped design the route with Auqui Mountain Spirit tour operator. For more details, **Andean Lodges** ① *José Gabriel Cosio 307, Urb Magisterial, Cuzco, T084-251578, www.andeanlodges.com.*

Acomayo and the Inca bridge
Between Cusipata and **Checacupe** a road branches west, soon becoming a dirt road. At the first fork, just before a beautiful mountain lake, **Lago Pomancanchi**, turn right to travel past a small community and on to **Acomayo**, a pretty village that has a chapel with mural paintings of the 14 Incas. From Acomayo, you can walk to the canyons of the upper Apurímac, vast beyond imagination, and to Inca ruins in astonishing locations.

If you turn left at Lago Pomancanchi the road passes three more beautiful lakes. Stop a while by the fourth. Set against the pale green grass banks, serene waters reflect the red soil of the hills behind. The only sound is the occasional splash and hoot of a white-beaked Andean coot. The air is thin, clear and crisp.

The road continues to **Yanaoca**, where you'll find basic accommodation and restaurants. From here it is possible to continue on to Sicuani, but a side trip to **Qeswachaka** and the grass Inca bridge 30 km away is well worth the effort. Turn right just before you leave the village to join a road which, at times, is very rough. The way is marked with kilometre signs and you must turn right just after Km 22 where another road begins, marked with a Km 0. You will find steps down to the bridge shortly before Km 31, two bends from the bright orange road bridge. The footbridge has been rebuilt every year for the past 400 years during a three-day festival. This starts on 10 June and is celebrated by the three communities who use the bridge. It is built entirely of *pajabrava* grass, woven and spliced to make six sturdy cables which are strung across the 15-m chasm. The work lasts five months, after which the fibres deteriorate and you should not attempt to cross.

Raqchi → Colour map 5, B6.
① Entrance to the site is US$3.55. There is a basic shop at the site.
About 120 km southeast of Cuzco, in a fertile tributary valley of the Vilcanota, is the colonial village of **San Pedro de Cacha**, which stands within one of the most important archaeological sites in Peru, Raqchi. A few hundred metres beyond the village are the principal remains, the once great **Temple of Viracocha**, the pan-Andean creator of all living creatures. This is one of the only remaining examples of a two-storey building of Inca architecture. It was 90 m long and 15 m high and was probably the largest roofed building ever built by the Incas. Above walls of finely dressed masonry 3- to 4-m high rise the remains of another 5- to 6-m high wall of adobe brickwork of which only isolated sections remain. Similarly, of the 22 outer columns, which supported great sloping roofs, just one or two remain complete, the others being in various states of preservation. There are numerous other constructions, including *acllahuasi* (houses of chosen women), granaries, reservoirs, baths and fountains. The burial site includes round *chullpa* tombs of the sort found around Lake Titicaca. Much of it was damaged and demolished in search of treasure during or after the Spanish conquest.

The village of Raqchi is also well known for its distinctive pottery featuring simple designs of animals and fish from the area. The daily market in the plaza now sells mostly mass-produced pottery brought from Cuzco, but if you ask for ceramics *al estilo Raqchi* you may be able to purchase pieces, or be taken to a local workshop.

Raqchi has also become something of a centre for **residential tourism projects** where tourists stay in the homes of local families, usually for one month, and share in their daily lives, including helping out with agricultural work. To get involved ask for the current leader of the *proyecto turismo vivencial*. You will need to speak at least some Spanish to get the most out of this experience.

Sicuani → Phone code: 084. Colour map 5, B6. Altitude: 3690 m.
Sicuani is an important agricultural centre and an excellent place for items of llama and alpaca wool and skins. They are sold at the railway station and at the excellent Sunday morning market. Around the plaza are several shops selling local hats. For places between Sicuani and Juliaca, see page 248.

For Sleeping and Eating price codes and other relevant information, see pages 38-44.

⬤ Sleeping

Andahuaylillas *p214*
E La Casa del Sol, close to the central plaza at Garcilaso 514. Relaxing, clean and bright hostal. Well-decorated rooms set around a courtyard, excellent value. Owned by Dr Gladys Oblitas, the hostal funds her project to provide medical services to poor campesinos. While staying you can take a course on natural and alternative medicine. She has a practice in Cuzco, T084-227264. Make reservations in Cuzco before going to Andahuaylillas as the *hostal* does not operate year round.

Cordillera Vilcanota *p214*
F Ausangate, Tinqui, very basic but warm, friendly atmosphere. Sr Crispin (or Cayetano), the owner, is knowledgeable and can arrange guides, mules, etc. He and his brothers can be contacted in Cuzco on F084-227768. All have been recommended as reliable sources of trekking and climbing information, for arranging trips and for being safety conscious.
F Hostal Tinqui Guide, on the right-hand side as you enter the village, friendly, meals available, owner arranges guides and horses.

Acomayo and the Inca bridge *p215*
There are many places to camp wild by the lakes. Take warm clothing for night time and plenty of water. At **Qeswachaca** there's good camping downstream, but take water.

Sicuani *p216*
E Hotel Obada, Jr Tacna 104, T084-351214. At the new end of the bridge. Has seen better days. Large, clean rooms with hot showers.
E Royal Inti, Av Centenario 116, T084-352730. Modern, clean and friendly.
F pp José's Hostal, Centenario 143, T084-351254. Rooms with bath, clean.

F Samary, Av Centenario 138 (next to **Royal Inti**), T084-352518. Offers good-value rooms with bathrooms.

⊘ Eating

Sicuani *p216*
⬤ **El Fogón**, C Zevallos, the main drag down from the plaza. Good chicken and chips.
⬤ **Mijuna Wasi**, Jr Tacna 146. Closed Sun. 1 of several *picanterías* that prepares typical dishes such as *adobo* served with huge glasses of *chicha* in a dilapidated but atmospheric courtyard. Recommended.
⬤ **Pizzería Bon Vino**, 2 de Mayo 129, 2nd floor, good for an Italian meal.

⊛ Festivals and events

Paucartambo *p213*
15-17 Jul Fiesta of the Virgen del Carmen, see above.

Acomayo and the Inca bridge *p215*
10 Jun Festival to celebrate the rebuilding of the Inca footbridge at **Qeswachaka**.

Raqchi *p216*
24-29 Jun The **Wiracocha** festivities. Dancers come to Raqchi and, through music and dance, illustrate everything from the ploughing of fields to bull fights. This leads into the feast of **San Pedro and San Pablo** on 29 Jun.

⊝ Transport

Paucartambo *p213*
Private car hire for a round trip from Cuzco on 15-17 Jul costs US$30. A minibus leaves for Paucartambo from Av Huáscar in Cuzco, every other day, US$4.50, 3-4 hrs; alternate days Paucartambo–Cuzco. Trucks and a

private bus leave from the Coliseo, behind Hospital del Seguro in Cuzco, 5 hrs, US$2.50.

Andahuaylillas p214

To Andahuaylillas take a taxi, or the **Oropesa** bus from Av Huáscar in Cuzco, via Tipón, Piquillacta and Rumicolca. Taxi colectivos leave from block 17 of Av La Cultura, opposite the university in Cuzco.

Huaro and Urcos p214

Transportes Vilcanota depart from the terminal on Av de la Cultura, Cuzco, at the Paradero Hospital Regional (on a side street), and run to **San Jerónimo**, **Saylla**, **Huasao**, **Tipón**, **Oropesa**, **Piquillacta/ Huacarpay**, **Andahuaylillas** and on to **Urcos**. These buses run 0500-2100, fare US$0.75 to Urcos.

Cordillera Vilcanota p214

Buses leave for **Tinqui** from Av Tomasatito Condemayta, at the corner of the Coliseo Cerrado in Cuzco, Mon-Sat 1000, 6-7 hrs, US$3.50. **Huayna Ausangate** is a recommended company; they have a ticket office near the Coliseo Cerrado .

Acomayo and the Inca bridge p215

To get to **Acomayo**, take the **Unancha** bus from Calle Huáscar. They have services from 0500-0800, book in advance. Also you can take a combi from Cuzco to Sicuani (US$1.25, 1½ hrs), then a truck or bus to Acomayo (3 hrs, US$1). Alternatively, get off at Checacupe and take a truck on to Acomayo. To visit the 4 beautiful mountain lakes and Inca bridge, it's worthwhile renting a 4WD for 2 days. Giving locals a lift is fun and they will make sure you take the right road. Alternatively, hire a vehicle with a driver. It is just as feasible by combi. The bridge can also be reached from **Combapata** on the main Cuzco–Sicuani road. Combis and colectivos leave for the 30-km trip when full from the plaza for **Yanaoca** (US$0.50). Then hitchhike to **Quehue** (no accommodation), a 1½-hr walk from Qeswachaka, or to **Qeswachaka** itself, on the road to Livitaca. Be prepared for long waits on this road. On Wed and Sat there are direct buses to **Livitaca** from Cuzco with the **Warari** and **Olivares** companies that pass the site, returning on Mon and Thu.

Raqchi p216

There are frequent combis to and from **Cuzco** on the Sicuani route.

Sicuani p216

Combis run every 15-20 mins between **Cuzco** and Sicuani (137 km, US$1.25). It is 250 km to **Puno**. 38 km beyond the town is La Raya pass (4321 m), which marks the divide between Cuzco Department and the altiplano that stretches to Lake Titicaca.

West of Cuzco

West of Cuzco is the road to Abancay (195 km from Cuzco), where the principal overland route to Lima, via Nazca, heads west and another road continues through the highlands to Ayacucho. There are enough Inca sites on or near this road in the Department of Cuzco to remind us that the empire's influence spread to all four cardinal points. Add to this some magnificent scenery, especially in the canyon of the Río Apurímac, and you have the makings of some fascinating excursions away from the centre. One, to the ruins of Choquequirao, is a tough but rewarding trip; getting there requires an expedition of four days or more. ›› *For listings, see pages 221-222.*

Anta to Curahuasi → *Colour map 5, A5.*
The Cuzco–Machu Picchu train follows the road west from the city through the Anta canyon for 10 km, and then, at a sharp angle, the Urubamba canyon, and descends along the river valley, flanked by high cliffs and peaks. In the town of **Anta**, felt trilby hats are on sale.

Some 76 km from Cuzco, beyond Anta on the Abancay road, and 2 km before Limatambo, are the ruins of **Tarahuasi** ① *US$3.55.* A few hundred metres from the road there is a very well-preserved Inca temple platform, with 28 tall niches, and a long stretch of fine polygonal masonry. The ruins are impressive, enhanced by the orange lichen that give the walls a beautiful honey colour. It was near here that the *conquistadores*, en route to the Inca capital of Cuzco, suffered what could have been a major setback. Had it not been for the arrival of Spanish reinforcements, they may well have been routed by the Inca army at Vilcaconga.

One hundred kilometres from Cuzco along the Abancay road is the exciting descent into the **Apurímac Canyon**, near the former Inca suspension bridge that inspired Thornton Wilder's *The Bridge of San Luis Rey* (see Books, page 695). The bridge itself was made of rope and was where the royal Inca road crossed the river. When the *conquistadores* reached this point on the march to Cuzco, they found the bridge destroyed. But luck was again on their side since, it being the dry season, the normally fierce Apurímac was low enough for the men and horses to ford. In colonial times the bridge was rebuilt several times, but it no longer exists.

Choquequirao → *Colour map 5, A5.*
① *Entry US$13, students US$6.25.*
Choquequirao is another 'lost city of the Incas', built on a ridge spur almost 1600 m above the Apurímac. Its Inca name is unknown, but research has shown that it was built during the reign of Inca Pachacútec. Although only 30% has been uncovered, it is believed to be a larger site than Machu Picchu, but with fewer buildings. The stonework is different from the classic Inca construction and masonry, simply because the preferred granite and andesite are not found in this region. A number of high-profile explorers and archaeologists, including Hiram Bingham, researched the site, but its importance has only recently been recognized. Now that the tourist industry has caught on, following the introduction of regulations to cut congestion on the Inca Trail, Choquequirao is being promoted as a replacement for the traditional hike. The INC may introduce a fee to trek to the ruins, but it was not included in their 2010 prices.

The main features of Choquequirao include the **Lower Plaza**, considered by most experts to be the focal point of the city. Three of the main buildings were two-storey structures. The **Upper Plaza**, reached by a huge set of steps or terraces, has what are possibly ritual baths. A beautiful set of slightly curved agricultural terraces run for over 300 m east-northeast of the Lower Plaza. The *usnu* is a levelled hilltop platform, ringed with stones and giving awesome 360-degree views. Perhaps it was a ceremonial site, or was used for solar and astronomical observations. The **Ridge Group**, still shrouded in vegetation, is a large collection of buildings some 50 to 100 m below the *usnu*. Unrestored, with some significant hall-like structures, this whole area makes for great exploring. The **Outlier Building**, isolated and surrounded on three sides by sheer drops of over 1.5 km into the Apurímac Canyon, possesses some of the finest stonework within Choquequirao. The significance of this building's isolation from other structures remains a mystery, like so many other questions regarding the Incas and their society. **Capuliyoc**, nearly 500 m below the Lower Plaza, is a great set of agricultural terraces, visible on the approach from the far side of the valley. These terraces enabled the Incas to cultivate plants from a significantly warmer climate in close geographical proximity to their ridge-top home. Opened to the public in 2008, a section of the terracing decorated with llamas in white stone is the highlight.

Cachora to Choquequirao There are three ways to reach Choquequirao; none is a gentle stroll. The shortest way is from **Cachora**, a village in a magnificent location on the south side of the Apurímac, reached by a side road from the Cuzco–Abancay highway, near Saywite (see page 564). It is four hours by bus from Cuzco to the turn-off, then a two-hour descent from the road to Cachora (from 3695 m to 2875 m). Combis run from Abancay to Cachora. Accommodation, guides (Celestino Peña is the official guide) and mules are available in Cachora (about US$12 a day for guide and mule).

From Cachora take the road heading down, out of the village, through lush cultivated countryside and meadows. There are many trails close to the village; if uncertain of the trail, ask. After 15 minutes, a sign for Choquequirao points to a left-hand path, initially following the course of a small stream. Follow the trail and cross a footbridge to the other side of a large stream. From here the trail becomes more obvious, with few trails diverging from the main route. After 9 km, two to 2½ hours from the start of the trek, is the wonderful mirador (viewpoint) of **Capuliyoc**, at 2800 m, with fantastic vistas of the Apurímac Canyon and the snowy Vilcabamba range across the river (this also makes a great day-hike from Cachora). With a pair of binoculars it's just possible to recognize Choquequirao, etched into the forested hills to the west. Condors are sometimes seen in this area. Beyond Capuliyoc the trail begins to descend towards the river. Further down the valley lies **Cocamasana**, a rest spot with a rough covered roof. From this point the river is clearly visible. At Km 16 is **Chiquisca** (1930 m), a lovely wooded spot. It has two camping areas and has become an official campsite with running water and basic toilets. There is a small shop selling chocolate bars, matches, camping gas (most likely refilled canisters) and sometimes avocados and fruit grown in the area. If you don't want to continue any further on the first day, this is a good campsite at US$1.50 per person. Another one-hour descent leads to the suspension bridge crossing the Río Apurímac. On the other side the path ascends very steeply for 1½ hours. **Santa Rosa**, a good area for camping near the property of a local family, is just after the Km 21 sign. Clean water is available. If this area is occupied, another larger site is available 10 minutes further up the hill. Ask residents for directions. The family at Santa Rosa also has a small shop and brew their own chicha, which your *arrieros* may be interested in! From Santa Rosa continue uphill on a steep zigzag for two hours to the mirador of **Marampata**, where the family sells hot meals. Trom here the trail flattens out towards Choquequirao. After 1½ hours you enter some beautiful stretches of cloudforest, before a final short climb and arrival at Choquequirao itself. If coming from Santa Rosa you should have the afternoon free to explore the complex, but it is highly recommended that you allow one full day to explore the ruins (in other words, at least five days for the trek). To return to Cachora, simply retrace the route, possibly camping at Chiquisca, which would nicely break the two-day return trek.

Other treks The second and third routes take a minimum of eight days and require thorough preparation. Both cross the watershed of the Cordillera Vilcabamba between the Urubamba and Apurímac rivers. The second hike uses the same route from Cachora as the first trek, then continues from Choquequirao to the **Yanama** river valley before continuing to **Santa Teresa** or **Machu Picchu** itself. The third route splits from the second in the Yanama valley and goes to **Huancacalle** (see page 205), via the pass of **Choquetacarpo**, 4600 m high. From Huancacalle it's possible to continue on to **Espíritu Pampa** on the edge of the rainforest (see page 206). Either route can be undertaken in reverse. Both pass the mines of La Victoria and both involve an incredible number of strenuous ascents and descents. En route you are rewarded with fabulous views of the Sacsarayoc massif (also called Pumasillo), Salkantay, other snow peaks, and the deep canyons of the Río Blanco and the Apurímac. You will also see condors and meet very friendly people, but the highlight is Choquequirao itself. More detailed information and trekking maps can be obtained from South American Explorers in Cuzco. Ask for Miguel Jove, an excellent guide.

◉ West of Cuzco listings

For Sleeping and Eating price codes and other relevant information, see pages 38-44.

● Sleeping

Anta to Curahuasi *p219*
F Hostal Central, Jirón Jaquijahuanca 714, Anta. A basic, friendly place with motorbike parking; beware of water shortages.
F Hostal Rivera, near the river, at *Limatambo*. An old stone house built around a courtyard, clean, quiet and full of character.
F Hostal San Cristóbal, Curahuasi. Clean, nice decor, courtyard, shared bath, cold shower (new bathroom block being built).

Choquequirao *p219*
B pp Los Tres Balcones, Jr Abancay s/n, Cachora, www.choquequirau.com. Hostel designed as start and end-point for the trek to Choquequirao. Breakfast included, comfortable, hot showers, restaurant and pizza oven, camping. Shares information with the town's only internet café. They run a 5-day trek to Choquequirao, US$550, with camping gear (but not sleeping bag), all meals and lunch at the hostel afterwards, entrance to the ruins, horses to carry luggage (US$650 including transport from Cuzco and bilingual tour guide).
D pp Casa de Salcantay, Prolongación Salcantay s/n, T084-984 397336, www.salcantay.com. Price includes breakfast, dinner available if booked in advance. Dutch-run hostel with links to community projects, comfortable, small, Dutch, English, German spoken, can help with arranging independent treks, or organize treks with tour operator.
F pp La Casona de Ocampo, San Martín 122, T084-237514, lacasonadeocampo@yahoo.es. With hot shower all day, free camping, owner Carlos Robles is friendly and knowledgeable, rents camping equipment, organizes treks to Choquequirao and beyond.

🍴 Eating

Anta to Curahuasi *p219*

🍴 **La Amistad**, Curahuasi. The best restaurant in town, popular, with good food and moderate prices, but poor service.

🍴 **Tres de Mayo**, Anta. Very good and popular, with top service.

🚌 Transport

Choquequirao *p219*

From Cuzco take the 1st Abancay bus of the morning with **Bredde** which leaves the Terminal Terrestre at 0600. Buy your ticket the night before to make sure you get a seat. From Cachora to **Abancay**, buses at 0630 and 1100, 2 hrs, US$1.50; also colectivo taxis.

Contents

Footprint features

Border crossings

At a glance

⊖ **Getting around** By bus and by boat on the lake.

◉ **Time required** 1 to 2 weeks.

☼ **Weather** In Jun-Aug it is very cold at night. The wet months are Nov-Apr.

✗ **When not to go** There's no time to avoid, but if you don't enjoy crowded festivals don't go during Fiesta de la Candelaria, in the first 2 weeks of Feb, or over 4-5 Nov.

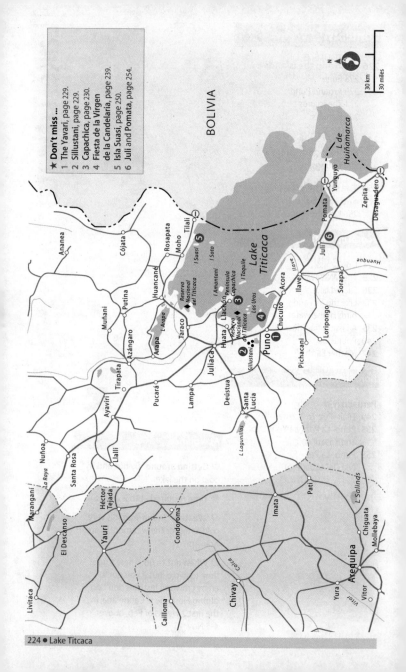

BOLIVIA

L de Huiñamarca

Lake Titicaca

Ananea

Cójata

Rosapata

Moho

Tilali

I Suasi

I Soto

Yunguyo

Zepita

Desaguadero

Huancané

Putina

Muñani

Reserva Nacional del Titicaca

L Arapa

I Amantani

I Soto

I Taquile

Peninsula Capachica

Llachón

Huata

Reserva Nacional del Titicaca

Pomata

Juli

Huenque

Sorapa

Azángaro

Arapa

Taraco

Los Uros

Acora

Ilave

Ilave

Juliaca

Sillustani del Titicaca

Puno

Chucuito

Pichacani

Loripongo

Tirapata

Lampa

Deústua

Santa Lucía

Pucará

L Lagunillas

Ayaviri

Llalli

Llalli

La Raya

Santa Rosa

Nuñoa

Marangani

El Descanso

Yauri

Héctor Tejada

Condoroma

Imata

Pati

L Salinas

Livitaca

Cailloma

Chivay

Colca

Imata

Yura

Vitor

Chiguata

Mollebaya

Arequipa

Vitor

30 km
30 miles

N

Straddling Peru's southern border with landlocked Bolivia are the deep, sapphire-blue waters of mystical Lake Titicaca, everyone's favourite school geography statistic. This gigantic inland sea covers up to 8500 sq km and is the highest navigable lake in the world, at an average 3810 m above sea level. Its shores and islands are home to the Aymara, Quechua and Uros peoples. Here you can wander through old traditional villages where Spanish is a second language and where ancient myths and beliefs are still held.

The main city on the lake is Puno, where chilled travellers gather to stock up on warm woollies to keep the cold at bay. The high-altitude town is the departure point for the islands of Taquile and Amantaní, as well as the floating reed islands of Los Uros. But while the latter may not be to everyone's taste, having acquired a reputation for tourism overkill, a trip to Taquile and Amantaní provides a real insight into traditional Andean life, especially during one of the festivals. Apart from the obvious attraction of the lake's islands, Puno is also well placed to visit the remarkable funeral towers of Sillustani. Even if you're feeling a bit ruined-out by this stage in your Peruvian odyssey, Sillustani is well worth the effort. For community-based tourism, the Capachica Peninsula is similar to the islands, but quieter, and you don't have to take a boat to get there. When it is time to move on, there is the beautiful but expensive train ride from Puno to Cuzco, and the opportunity to reach the parts of Peru that other travellers rarely get to, by exploring the remote eastern shore of the lake, an area that is only just beginning to welcome curious visitors.

Puno and the islands

→ *Colour map 6, B2.*

On the northwest shore of Lake Titicaca, at 3855 m, Puno is a major folklore centre and a great place to buy handicrafts, particularly those amazingly tactile alpaca jumpers and hats. It also has a rich tradition of music and dance and is a good place to enjoy a number of Andean festivals, some wild, some solemn. Puno is capital of its department and, while it isn't the most attractive of cities, it has a certain vitality, helped by the fact there is a large student population. ▶▶ *For listings, see pages 235-244.*

Puno

Sleeping
1 Balsa Inn *C2*
2 Camino Real *B2*
3 Casa Andina Plaza *B2*
4 Casa Andina Private
  Collection Puno *A4*
5 Casa Andina Tikarani *B2*

6 Casona Plaza *C2*
7 Colón Inn *centre*
8 Conde de Lemos *C2*
9 Eco Inn *A4*
10 El Buho *centre*
11 Hosp Res Margarita *B2*
12 Hostal Europa *centre*
13 Hostal Illampu &
  Hostal Q'oñi Wasi *B3*
14 Hostal Imperial &
  Los Uros *B3*
15 Hostal Los Pinos *B2*
16 Hostal Monterrey *centre*
17 Hostal Pukara *centre*

18 Hostal Rubi
  'Los Portales' *C3*
19 Hotel Italia *B2*
20 Inka's Rest *B3*
21 Intiqa *B2*
22 Julio César *centre*
23 La Hacienda Puno *centre*
24 Libertador
  Lago Titicaca *A4*
25 Manco Cápac Inn *centre*
26 MN Yavari B&B
  & ship/museum *A4*
27 Munay Tambo *centre*
28 Ollanta Inn *B3*

29 Plaza Mayor *centre*
30 Posada Don Giorgio *B2*
31 Puno Plaza *C2*
32 Qelqatani *A4*
33 Royal Inn *C2*
34 Sillustani *centre*
35 Sol Plaza Puno *C2*
36 Sonesta
  Posadas del Inca *A4*
37 Tambo Real *B2*
38 The Point *C1*

Ins and outs

Getting there The railway station for trains from Cuzco is quite central and within walking distance of the centre, but if you've got heavy bags, it's a good idea to hire a three-wheel cycle cart (*trici-taxi*), which costs about US$0.35 per km per person. The train halts for guests at the hotels **Libertador** and **Sonesta**. The bus station and the depots for local buses are further away, southeast of the centre, but *trici-taxis* and conventional taxis serve this area.

Getting around The centre of town is easy to walk around, but as said above, a *trici-taxi* can make life a lot easier, even if this is not your first stop at high altitude. Colectivos (buses) in town have different colours and numbers to help you find the right one and charge US$0.50 per person.

Puno centre

Best time to visit Being so high up, Puno gets bitterly cold at night, generally not below -5°C, but in June-August the temperature at night can plummet to -25°C. Days are bright and the midday sun is hot, but you can never be quite sure what weather is going to come off the lake. The first two weeks in February, when the Fiesta de la Candelaria takes place, and 4-5 November, the pageant of the emergence of the founding Incas, are good times to visit, but crowded, too.

Tourist information iperú ⓘ *Lima y Deústua, T051-365088, near Plaza de Armas, daily 0830-1930.* They are friendly, speak English and helpful with general information and they provide all maps and information free. The **Dircetur office** ⓘ *Ayacucho 684, T051-364976, puno@mincetur.gob.pe, and has a counter at the Terminal Terrestre, www.punored.com is a portal for the Puno area,* has limited services for tourists. Puno is gaining a reputation for scams; keep your wits about you and don't be fooled by changes to prices or menu items in restaurants, by claims that entry tickets have expired or that your return boat ticket is in fact a single. Note also that some hotels are full of dubious street tour sellers. Others are linked to tour operators that may or may not belong to them, so are not above pressurized tour selling (see Tour operators, page 241).

Eating 🍴
1 Casa del Corregidor *C2*
2 Casa Grill La Estancia *centre*
3 Chifa Nan Hua *B2*
4 Coca Kintu *centre*
5 Don Piero *centre*
6 Govinda *centre*
7 IncAbar *centre*
8 Internacional *centre*
9 Keros *centre*
10 La Choza de Oscar *centre*
11 La Hostería *centre*
12 La Plaza *C2*
13 Los Balcones de Puno *centre*

14 Mojsa *C2*
15 Pizzería-Trattoria El Buho *centre*
16 Remembranzas *centre*
17 Ricos Pan *centre, C2*
18 Tradiciones del Lago *centre*
19 Tulipans *centre*
20 Ukukus *centre*
21 Vida Natural *centre*

Bars & clubs 🍸
22 Pub Ekeko's *centre*

Puno sits on a bay at the northwest end of the lake. The Bahía de Puno is only 3 m deep and a channel is dredged to the exit into the open water of Titicaca. The port and lakeside quarters are several blocks from the centre, whose focus is the Plaza de Armas and the pedestrianized Jirón Lima. The impressive baroque exterior of the **cathedral** ① *Mon-Fri 0800-1200, 1500-1800, Sat-Sun 0800-1200, 1500-1900*, completed in 1657, belies an austere interior. Just across the street from the cathedral is the famous **Balcony of the Conde de Lemos**, on the corner of Deústua and Conde de Lemos, where Peru's viceroy stayed. Today it houses the Puno office of the INC and a small **art gallery** ① *Mon-Fri 0800-1600*. Also here is the **Museo Municipal Carlos Dreyer** ① *Conde de Lemos 289, www.museodreyer.com, Mon-Sat 1030-2200, Sun 1600-2200, US$5 includes 45-min guided tour*. The museum combines municipal collections with the private collection of pre-Columbian artefacts bequeathed to the city by their owner, Sr Carlos Dreyer, including gold pieces found at the nearby Sillustani funerary towers. In the same block is the **Casa del Corregidor** ① *Deústua 576, T051-365603, www.casadelcorregidor.pe, Tue-Fri 1000-2200, closed for lunch on Sat*. One of Puno's oldest buildings, it has been converted into Puno's most important cultural centre, check website for exhibitions. It also has a great café (see page 239), a fair trade shop selling handicrafts and the **All Ways Travel office**, see below.

A short walk up Independencia leads to the **Arco Deústua**, a monument to those killed in the battles of Junín and Ayacucho. Nearby is a mirador giving fine views over the town, the port and also the lake beyond. The walk from Jirón Cornejo following the Stations of the Cross up a nearby hill, with fine views of Lake Titicaca, has been recommended, but be careful and don't go alone. The same applies to all the hills around Puno: Huajsapata is known for music and folklore gatherings; Azoguine and Cancharani are higher, with good views and sacred associations. To get to Azoguine you go through Barrio Las Cruces, which is very dangerous.

Avenida Titicaca leads to the port, from where boats go to the islands. From its intersection with Avenida Costañera (a new, coastal road) towards the pier, one side of the road is lined with the kiosks of the Artesanos Unificados de Puno, selling crafts. Closer to the port are food kiosks. On the opposite side of the road is a shallow lake where you can hire **pedal boats** ① *US$0.70 per person for 20 mins*. At the pier are the ticket counters for transport to the islands. On the way from the centre to the port is the **Museo Naval** ① *Av El Puerto y Av Sol, Mon-Fri 0830-1230, 1430-1700, free*. Here you can find a small exhibit on navigating on Lake Titicaca. The **Malecón Bahía de los Incas**, a lovely promenade along the waterfront, extends to the north and south; it is a pleasant place for a stroll and for birdwatching with views of the lake. The section to the north connects the port with Av Floral at the north end of the bay and continues on to Huaja, a district housing several of the more up-market resort-style hotels. The section to the south follows the bay to the Terminal Terrestre and the suburb of Salcedo, 4 km from the port. The bay by Puno is very polluted but several plans to build a sewage treatment plant have foundered.

Hull (UK)-built **MS Ollanta**, sailed the lake from 1926 to the 1970s. PerúRail has restored the vessel with a view eventually to starting cruises, but it is not currently open to the public. Berthed next to it is another old ship, the **MN Colla** ① *Barrio Guaje, beyond the Hotel Sonesta Posada del Inka, T051-368156, daily 0800-1700*, built in Scotland and launched on the lake in 1892. Its museum is similar to that of the Yavari. Its restaurant serves Peruvian specialities, set menu US$7, buffet US$8, if they have dinner reservations they stay open in the evening.

The MN Yavari

The **MN Yavari** ① *0815-1715, then illuminated till 2230 for 'Happy Hour' run by Hotel Sonesta Posada del Inka, entry free in daytime, but donations of US$6 encouraged to help with maintenance costs,* is the oldest ship on Lake Titicaca. It was restored in the port of Puno and turned into a museum, before being moved to its present location in 2002. The iron-hulled ship, now painted in her original livery of black, white and red, was built in England in 1862 and, together with her twin, the *Yapura* (now the Peruvian Navy's Hospital ship and called the *BAP Puno*), was shipped in kit form to Arica. From Arica, the two ships went by rail to Tacna from where the 2766 pieces were carried by mule to Lake Titicaca. The journey took six years. The *Yavari* was eventually launched on Christmas Day 1870 and on 14 June 1871 sailed on her maiden voyage. From after the War of the Pacific until the nationalization of the Railways and Lake Fleet in 1975, the *Yavari* was operated as a passenger/cargo vessel by the London-based Peruvian Corporation. The ship was bought in 1987 and has been restored by an Anglo-Peruvian Association. Visitors are very welcome on board the *Yavari* and will be shown over the ship and its exhibition of archival documentation and memorabilia on the Lake Fleet by the Captain, Carlos Saavedra, or a volunteer. You can also stay overnight, see Sleeping, below. The *Yavari* is berthed near the entrance to the **Hotel Sonesta Posada del Inca** (see below). You have to go through the hotel to get to the ship. To get there you can go by taxi, bus or *trici-taxi*, but the most charming way is by boat from the port, about US$2 return, including wait. **Project addresses** ① *61 Mexfield Rd, London, SW15 2RG, England, T44-20 8874 0583, yavarilarken@talktalk.net; in Puno: La Asociación Yavari, T051-369329, www.proyecto.perucultural.org.pe.* For general information, volunteering, donations, etc, visit www.yavari.org.

Around Puno → *For listings, see pages 235-244.*

Sillustani → *Colour map 6, B2.*

① *US$1.90. Take an organized tour, which lasts about 3-4 hrs and leaves at 1430, US$8.50-10. Tours usually stop at a Colla house on the way to see local products, alpacas and guinea pigs. Alternatively, take a Juliaca bus to the Sillustani turn-off (US$0.35); from here a 15-km paved road runs across the altiplano to the ruins. Moto-taxis and some combis run to Atuncolla (4 km away with a lovely colonial church), US$0.40, or US$0.85 to Sillustani (out of season you may have to walk the 4 km from Atuncolla). Go early to avoid tour groups at the site. A taxi from Puno costs about US$12, including wait. Camping possible outside the museum (tip the guardian).*

A highly recommended trip is to the *chullpas* (pre-Columbian funeral towers) of Sillustani in a beautiful setting on a peninsula in **Lago Umayo** (3890 m), 32 km from Puno on an excellent road. According to expert John Hemming, these are burial towers of the Aymara-speaking Colla tribe and most of them date from the period of Inca occupation in the 15th century. As Hemming also states: "The engineering involved in their construction is more complex than anything the Incas built – it is defeating archaeologists' attempts to rebuild the tallest 'lizard' *chullpa*. Two are unfinished: one with a ramp still in place to raise blocks; the other with cut stones ready to go onto a very

Sacred lake

Lake Titicaca has played a dominant role in Andean beliefs for over two millennia. This, the highest navigable body of water in the world, is the most sacred lake in the Andes.

From the lake's profound, icy depths emerged the Inca creator deity, Viracocha. Legend has it that the sun god had his children, Manco Cápac and his sister, Mama Ocllo, spring from the its waters to found Cusco and the Inca dynasty.

The name Titicaca derives from the word *titi*, an Aymara mountain cat and the Quechua word *caca* meaning rock. The rock refers to the Sacred Rock on the Isla del Sol (on the Bolivian side), which was worshipped by the pre-Inca people on the island. The mountain cat inhabited the shores of the lake and is said to have visited the Isla del Sol occasionally.

The link between the rock and the cat comes from the legend that the ancient indigenous people saw the eyes of a mountain cat gleaming in the Sacred Rock and so named it Titicaca, or Rock of the Mountain Cat. It was this that gave rise to the idea of the sun having its home there.

The *titi* has characteristics – such as its aquatic ability and the brilliance of its eyes – that conceptually link it with a mythological flying feline called *ccoa*. The role of the *ccoa* was (and in some parts still is) important throughout the Andes. It is believed to have thrown lightning from its eyes, urinated rain (hence the expression), spit hail and roared thunder. It was associated with the gods that controlled the weather.

Among indigenous people today, the *ccoa* is believed to be one of the mountain god's servants and lives in the mountains. It is closely involved in their daily life and is considered the most feared of the spirits as it uses lightning and hail.

ambitious corbelled false dome. A series of stone circles to the east of the site are now thought to be the bases of domed thatch or peat living huts, rather than having any religious meaning. The quarry near the towers is also worth seeing." Other Inca remains can be seen in the shape of square buildings, a temple of the Sun and a temple of the Moon. Underground burials at the site predating the Colla have been found from the Pukara and Tiahuanaco periods.

There is a museum, and handicraft sellers in traditional costume wait at the exit. Guides are also available here. Photographers will find the afternoon light best, though this is when the wind is at its strongest and can kick up a mini-sandstorm. It's also best not to wear contact lenses. The scenery is barren, but nonetheless impressive. The island in Lago Umayo is a nature reserve. On the lake before the ruins there are flamingos and ducks. Take warm clothing, water and sun protection.

Capachica Peninsula

The pretty farming villages of **Llachón**, **Santa María** and **Ccotos**, at the eastern end of the Península de Capachica, have become a focus of community-based tourism. The sandy beaches, pre-Inca terracing and trees and flowers dotted around, make the peninsula a charming place to visit. You'll be welcomed with a necklace of cantuta flowers and then invited to share in local activities; 70% of all produce served is from the residents' farms. The peninsula is also good for hiking and mountain biking and sailing boats can be hired. After all that activity, take in the sunset from the **Auki Carus** hill; reckoned to be better even than from Taquile. Neither Taquile nor Amantaní are far away and can be seen from the top of the hill. **Capachica** is the main town and crossroads of the peninsula. It has a colourful Sunday market, two very basic *hospedajes* and simple *comedores*. There is a small cultural centre at Jr Trucos 305 set up by a foundation for children's education called **Wawa Marca**. It has a collection of stone amulets found in the area. Nearby is **Playa Chifrón**, popular with locals. Throughout the peninsula the dress of the local women is very colourful, with four-cornered hats called *monteros*, matching waistcoats and colourful *polleras*.

There are currently six different community-tourism organizations, each with a dozen or more families and links to different tour operators in Puno, Cuzco or abroad. Families offer accommodation on a rotational basis, see page 237. The atmosphere is pleasant and low key. The peninsula is a great place to start a visit to Lake Titicaca, especially if you are flying in. It is closer to come here directly from Juliaca and you can go to the islands or to Puno by boat.

Other sights
Another place where *chullpas* can be seen is **Cutimbo**, 34 km south of Puno in the district of Pichacani, between Puno and Laraqueri on the old road to Moquegua. Here the funeral towers are round and square and stand on a table-top mountain. There are rock paintings on the mountainside. A road goes part of the way up. A taxi there costs US$19, including wait, three hours in total.

Some 8 km from Puno, just off the Puno–Juliaca road, is **Fundo Chincheros** ① *T051-355694, www.casadelcorregidor.com.pe, or go to Jr Deústua 572, for more information, US$7 includes guided tour; US$13.50 for half-day stays including lunch (available for groups of 5 or more)*, an old hacienda open to the public. The colonial house with its own chapel is in the middle of fields. Llamas, alpacas and vicuñas are on site as well as horses for riding. The wild flowers, cactus and views make this a worthwhile trip.

The islands → *For listings, see pages 235-244.*

Los Uros → *Colour map 6, B2.*
① *Entry US$1.70*
Of the estimated 40 floating islands, only about 15 are regularly visited by tourists, and today we can talk about two kinds of Uros people; those close to the city of Puno and easily accessible to tourism, and those on islands that remain relatively isolated. The Uros islanders fish, hunt birds and live off the lake plants, most important of which are the totora reeds they use for their boats, houses and the very foundations of their islands (see box, page 232). Their diet is very rich in fats. This, plus the high red corpuscle content, leads to the saying that they have black blood. On those more far-flung islands, reached via narrow channels through the reed beds, the Uros do not like to be photographed and continue to lead relatively traditional lives outside the monetary economy. They hunt and fish and still depend on trade with the mainland for other essentials. There are opportunities to stay overnight in reed houses on some of the Uros islands, for example at Kamisaraki and Kantati. There are also native guides, some who speak English, offering two-hour tours for US$3.40. Organized tour parties are usually given a boat-building demonstration and the chance to take a short trip in a reed boat (US$0.70 per person).

Visitors to the floating islands encounter more women than men. These women wait every day for the tour boats to sell their handicrafts. The few men one does see might be building or repairing boats or fixing their nets. The rest are to be found out on the lake, hunting and fishing. The Uros cannot live from tourism alone, and the extra income they glean from tourists merely supplements their more traditional activities.

Like the fish and birds of the water

Titicaca's waters nourished great civilizations like the Tiahuanaco and Pukará and drew the Incas south in search of new lands and the origin of their own creation legend. But very little is known about a third people who made Titicaca their home. They were the Uros, the people of the floating islands. The ephemeral nature of their totora reed constructions and the watery world they inhabit make archaeological study impossible, and only their myths remain.

In their oral histories, the Uros say that their forefathers came from the south. We cannot know for certain when the Uros first arrived at Lake Titicaca, but it is thought that a great drought around 1200 AD provoked a series of massive migrations of entire peoples across the altiplano. In a scenario similar to the one predicted for parts of the world in the 21st century, conflicts arose as competition increased for water and fertile land.

The Uros found the fertile shores of the great lake occupied by other, much larger ethnic groups. According to Uro tradition, facing defeat by their established rivals, the Uros escaped to the reed beds. It is said that they hid in the water among the reeds. Tired and cold, they cut the totora and, by binding the reeds together, made a number of rafts on which they slept.

Legend has it that when the Inca Pachacútec arrived to conquer the lake region he asked the Uros who they were. These people who had hunted and fished in the same way for generations replied as they always had, saying: "We are the founders of the world, the first inhabitants of the planet. Our blood is black and we cannot drown. We are like the fish and birds of the water."

With the arrival of the Spanish in the 16th century, the Uros isolated themselves even more from the mainland. Persecuted by the invaders, they began to meld themselves more than ever to their lake environment and their only outside contact was with other ethnic groups onshore, with whom they exchanged fish and birds for agricultural products.

Recalling their childhood, some old Uros islanders still remember when the first tourists arrived. Fearing that the Spanish had returned, their grandparents told them to run and hide.

Times have changed on some of the floating islands. There the Uros smile, pose for photographs, and then ask for a tip. After generations of intermarriage with their Aymara neighbours, what was once one of South America's most ancient tribal groups is in fact now ethnically extinct. The last Uro died in 1959, and the Uros language died with her.

Many tourists find that, although the people are friendly, they are very poor and a few subject visitors to a hard-sell approach for handicrafts. The islands visited by tour boats are little more than 'floating souvenir stalls' while boatloads of tourists are sometimes greeted with a song and some islanders will pose for photos. However, it is better to buy handicrafts or pay for services than just to tip, although they appreciate gifts of pens, paper, etc for their two schools. All the same, this form of tourism on the Uros Islands is now well-established and, whether it has done irreparable harm or will ultimately prove beneficial, it takes place in superb surroundings.

Note There is no drinking water on the floating islands and you need to be careful where you walk, as the surface can be unsteady underfoot.

A lasting tradition

One of the most enduring textile traditions in Peru is found among the people of Taquile. Each family possesses at least four different types of costume: for work, leisure, weddings and festivals.

For weddings, which all take place on 3 May, when the planet Venus – Hatun Chaska – is visible, the bridegroom wears a red poncho provided by the best man. As a single man he wore a half red, half white cap, but to signify his married status he wears a long red hat and a wide red wedding belt, or *chumpi*. His bag for coca leaves, *ch'uspa*, is also filled.

The bride wears a wide red hat (*montera*) and her hands are covered with a ritual cloth (*katana-oncoma*). A *quincha*, a small white cloth symbolizing purity, is hidden in her skirt. With her red wedding blouse (*gonna*), she wears a gathered skirt (*pollera*), made from 20 different layers of brightly coloured cloth. She also wears a belt (*faja*) and black cloak known as a *chukoo*.

The wool used for weaving is usually spun by the women, but on Taquile men spin wool, as well as knitting their conical hats (*chullos*). In fact, only the men on Taquile know how to knit. By the age of 10, a boy can knit his own Chullo Santa María, which is white-tipped to show single status. When he marries, or moves in with a woman, he adopts the red-tipped *chullo*, which is exclusive to the island. Today, much of the wool for knitting is bought ready-spun from factories in Arequipa.

Taquile

Isla Taquile, some 45 km from Puno, has numerous pre-Inca and Inca ruins, and Inca terracing. At the highest point is a ruin from which to view the sunset (the path is signed). The island is quiet and hospitable, but at the height of the season and at Sunday lunchtime it gets busy and touristy (about 50 boats a day in high season).

The island is only about 1 km wide and 6-7 km long. On the north side of the island is the warmest part of Lake Titicaca. Ask for the (unmarked) **Museum of Traditional Costumes** ① *on the plaza, free,* and also where you can see and photograph local weaving. There is a cooperative shop on the plaza that sells exceptional woollen goods that are not cheap, but of very fine quality. They are much cheaper in the market at Puno but the artisans may not have received such a fair price for their work. You need to spend a night on Taquile to appreciate fully its beauty and, therefore, it may be better to travel independently and go at your own pace.

Every Sunday, the island's four *suyos* (districts) coordinate their activities with a reunion in the main plaza after Quechua Mass. Numerous **festivals** take place on the island (see page 240), with many dances in between. Weddings are celebrated each May and August. The priest comes from Puno and there is a week-long party. The book, *Encuentro con los hijos del sol/Encounter with the Children of the Sun/Rencontre avec les fils du soleil*, by Christian Nonis of the Colón Inn, has been recommended.

The influx of tourists unfortunately prompts persistent requests by children for sweets or to have their photo taken. They whisper, quite politely, *caramelo* (sweet) or *foto* (photo). When you arrive, boys tie friendship bracelets to your wrist, or give you *muña* (a herb used for infusions) for a sol. Recordings of traditional music have been made and are on sale as an additional source of income for the islanders. Buy their handicrafts instead of handing out sweets indiscriminately. Gifts of fruit, sugar, salt, spices, torches (there is no electricity), moisturizer or sun block (the children suffer sore cheeks) are appreciated.

You are advised to take some food, particularly fruit, bread and vegetables, water, plenty of small-value notes, candles and a torch/flashlight. Take precautions against sunburn and seasickness. If staying the night, take warm clothes, a sleeping bag and a hot water bottle. The same applies to Amantaní. Tourism to both islands is community based: the community has set fees so the difference between prices of tours relates to the quality of tour (what boat they use, the guide, the food on offer) and the profit the agency makes. Native guides in Taquile, some speaking English and/or German, charge US$3.40 for two-hour tours.

There are two main entry points. The Puerto Principal at the south end has a very steep climb up many steps; the northern entry is longer but more gradual (remember you are at 3800 m). Visitors pay US$0.60 to land. Plentiful accommodation can be found in private houses and it is worth spending a night on Taquile to observe the daily flurry of activity when boatloads of tourists arrive, the demonstrations of traditional dress and weaving techniques, the preparation of trout to feed hungry tourists. When the boats leave, the island breathes a gentle sigh and the people slowly return to their more traditional activities. ▶▶ *See Sleeping, page 238.*

Amantaní → *Colour map 6, B2.*

Another island well worth visiting is Amantaní. It is very beautiful and peaceful, and many say is less spoiled, more genuine and friendlier than Taquile (about 10 boats visit a day in high season). Visitors pay US$1 to land. There are six villages (population about 4000) and ruins on both of the island's peaks, **Pacha Tata** and **Pacha Mama**, from which there are excellent views. There are also temples and on the shore there is a throne carved out of stone, the **Inkatiana**. It is rather eroded from flooding. It's a 30-minute walk west of **El Pueblo**, the village on the north end. Turn right down the steep slope after the last house on the right. If staying overnight the Jefe can find you accommodation with a family. Often folklore shows will be arranged in the Municipalidad when there are groups of tourists.

Several fiestas are celebrated on Amantaní (see page 240) and islanders arrange dances for tour groups (independent travellers can join in); visitors dress up in local clothes and join the dances. Small shops sell water and snacks, but are more expensive than those in Puno.

The residents make beautiful textiles and sell them at the **Artesanía Cooperativa**, at the east end of El Pueblo. They also make basketwork and stoneware. The people are Quechua speakers, but understand Spanish.

Anapia and Yuspique

In the Peruvian part of the Lago Menor are the islands of Anapia, a friendly, Aymara-speaking community, and Yuspique, on which are ruins and vicuñas. The community has organized committees for tourism, motor boats, sailing boats and accommodation with families (**All Ways Travel** arranges tours, see Activities and tours, page 241). Visitors are involved with community projects during their visit and there is always a celebration at the end of the stay. It's highly worthwhile. On the island ask for José Flores, who is very knowledgeable about Anapia's history, flora and fauna. He sometimes acts as a guide.
▶▶ *See Transport, page 243, on how to get to the islands in the lake.*

For Sleeping and Eating price codes and other relevant information, see pages 38-44.

⊙ Sleeping

Puno *p228, map p226*

Prices vary according to the season. Check if breakfast is included. A number of luxury hotels are opening in and around the city (see for example **Titilaka**, under Chucuito, page 256). Many touts try to persuade tourists to go to a hotel not of their own choosing, even when reservations have been booked. Be firm. Do not believe the stories they tell you.

L-AL Royal Inn, Jr Ayacucho 438, T051-364574, www.royalinnhoteles.com. Luxury hotel with glossy wooden decor, ample rooms and suites with large beds, heating, *frigobar*, safe, bathtub, internet, restaurant, bar.

AL Libertador Lago Titicaca Hotel, Isla Esteves s/n, Lago Titicaca, on an island linked by a causeway 5 km northeast of Puno (taxi US$3, or red colectivo No 16, or white Nos 24 and 33), T051-367780, www.libertador.com.pe. Built on a Tiahuanaco-period site, the hotel is spacious with good views. Bar, good restaurant, disco, good service, electricity and hot water all day, parking.

AL-A Sonesta Posadas del Inca, Av Sesquicentenario 610, Huaje, 5 km from Puno on the lakeshore (same transport as for **Libertador Lago Titicaca Hotel**), T051-364111, www.sonesta.com/laketiticaca/. 62 large rooms with heating, in similar vein to other hotels in this group but with local touches, such as the textile decorations and the Andean menu in the **Inkafé** restaurant. Has facilities for the disabled, fine views, attractive, good service, folklore shows.

A Casa Andina Private Collection Puno, Av Sesquicentenario 1970, Huaje, T051-363992, www.casa-andina.com. Part of this chain's luxury range, on the lakeshore.

A Eco Inn, Av Chulluni 195, Huaje (same transport as for **Libertador Lago Titicaca Hotel**), T051-365525, www.ecoinnhotels.com.

Price includes taxes and buffet breakfast. Comfortable, brightly decorated rooms with bath, safe, luggage store, internet, parking, nice view of the lake from the front. Has alpacas in the grounds.

A Intiqa, Jr Tarapaca 272, T051-366900, www.intiqahotel.com. New, stylish hotel with professional staff built around a sunny courtyard with good restaurant. Rooms have heaters, phone, Wi-Fi.

A Puno Plaza, overlooking Plaza de Armas, T051-351424, www.punoplaza.com. Tastefully decorated modern hotel, includes buffet breakfast, comfortable rooms, all non-smoking, with bathtub or jacuzzi, hairdryer, heater, safety box, coffee/tea kettles, internet in lobby, good restaurant.

A-B Casona Plaza, Jr Arequipa 655, 1 block from Plaza de Armas, T051-365614, www.casonaplazahotel.com. Has buffet breakfast, nice ample, modern rooms with heater, bathtub, internet in lobby, Wi-Fi, café.

A-B La Hacienda Puno, Jr Deústua 297, T/F051-356109, www.lahaciendapuno.com. Price includes buffet breakfast. Refurbished colonial house, comfortable warm and cosy rooms with bath and hot water, TV, café, internet on ground floor. Rooms facing the front have private balconies and some top floor rooms have lake view. Recommended.

A-B Plaza Mayor, Deústua 342, T051-366089, www.plazamayorhotel.com. Price includes buffet breakfast. Comfortable, well appointed and decorated, very close to the plaza. The rooms have good big beds, hot water and TV. There is a laundry, safe and a restaurant serving local and European food. Recommended.

A-B Qelqatani, Tarapacá 355, T051-366172, www.qelqatani.com. A hotel in colonial style, central, clean, spacious rooms, heating on request, good option in this price range.

A-B Sol Plaza Puno, Jr Puno 307, T051-352658, www.solplazahotel.com. Includes buffet breakfast, small modern rooms with heater, bathtub, restaurant.

B Balsa Inn, Cajamarca 555, T051-363144, www.hotelbalsainn.com. With breakfast (no other meals except for groups by arrangement). See the nativity collection on display; comfortable lobby. Rooms are comfy, too, with big bathrooms, hot water, TV, safe, heating. Very helpful.

B Camino Real, Deza 328, T051-367296, www.caminoreal-turistico.com. Good central hotel, price includes buffet breakfast, cable TV, 24-hr room service, internet. Recommended.

B Casa Andina Plaza, Jr Grau 270, T051-367520, www.casa-andina.com. Includes breakfast and 10% service charge. One of this chain's modern hotels, a block from the plaza, rooms with bath, TV and heating, non-smoking rooms, clean, safe and central. Business centre with internet for guests, parking.

B Casa Andina Tikarani, Independencia 185, T051-367803, www.casa-andina.com. Similar in most respects to the **Casa Andina Plaza**, but further from the centre.

B Colón Inn, Tacna 290, T051-351432, www.coloninn.com. Price includes tax and buffet breakfast. Colonial style, good rooms with hot shower, good service, safe, Wi-Fi internet in rooms, restaurant **Sol Naciente** and pizzería **Europa**, the Belgian manager Christian Nonis is well known, especially for his work on behalf of the people on Taquile island. Recommended.

B Conde de Lemos, Jr Puno 675, T051-369898, www.condelemosinn.com. Well-positioned comfortable hotel in colonial style. Breakfast, washing machine, internet, Wi-Fi, elevator, wheelchair friendly, heating, restaurant.

B El Buho, Lambayeque 142, T/F051-366122, www.hotelbuho.com. Breakfast included. Hot water, nicely decorated rooms with heaters, TV, restaurant, safe, special discount to Footprint readers, travel agency for excursions and flight reconfirmations. Recommended.

B Sillustani, Jr Tarapaca 305, corner with Lambayeque, T051-351881, www.sillustani.com. Price includes breakfast and taxes. Hot water, cable TV, safety deposit, heaters, internet, very good, long-established, popular with tour groups, reservations advised.

B Tambo Real, Jr Santiago Giraldo 362, T051-366060, www.tamborealtitikaka.com. A few blocks from the Plaza de Armas, good value, clean, bright rooms, good bathrooms, hot water, Wi-Fi, 2 computers for guests' use, price includes breakfast, tea and coffee in lobby all day, family-owned, professional and helpful staff. Recommended.

B-C Munay Tambo, Jr Lambayeque 127, T051-364373, www.munaytambo.com. Private bathroom, hot water, TV, internet, coffee shop.

C Hostal Pukara, Jr Libertad 328, T/F051-368448, pukara@terra.com.pe. Includes good American breakfast. Popular, with bath, hot water and heating. English spoken, central, quiet, free coca tea in evening. Recommended.

C Hotel Italia, Theodoro Valcárcel 122, T051-367706, www.hotelitaliaperu.com. 2 blocks from the station. With good breakfast, cheaper in low season. Good, safe, hot water, good food, free tea and coffee, small rooms, staff helpful, internet. Recommended.

C pp MN Yavari, Muelle del Hotel Sonesta Posada del Inka, T051-369329 (in Lima T01-2557268), reservasyavari@gmail.com. Bed and breakfast is now available on board, where there are 3 twin rooms with shared bathroom. Dinner served on request downstairs in the Victorian saloon, ⊪.

C-E Hostal Monterrey, Lima 441, T051-351691. Price includes breakfast and cable TV. Cheaper rooms have shared bath, better rooms with showers, hot water, restaurant, laundry, secure for luggage, motorcycle parking US$0.50. In town centre, can be noisy.

D Hostal Imperial, Teodoro Valcárcel 145, T051-352386, www.hostalimperial.com. **E-F** (low season), breakfast extra, US$1.85 (good coffee). With good shower, hot water, helpful, stores luggage, comfortable if basic, safe, ask for extra blanket if it's cold.

D Julio César, Tacna 336, T051-366026, www.juliocesarhoteles.com. Very clean, hot water, price includes breakfast, some staff speak English.

D Ollanta Inn, Jr Ilo E-1, 2a cuadra Jr Los Incas, T051-366743, ollanta_inn@ hotmail.com. Modern, just behind station, hot water 24 hrs, pleasant, clean, helpful owner, fan heater and TV extra, breakfast included.

D Posada Don Giorgio, Tarapacá 238, T051-363648, www.posadadongiorgio.com. Breakfast included. Large, comfortable, pleasantly decorated rooms with bath, hot water, TV, parking US$1.50 extra.

D-E Hostal Rubi 'Los Portales', Jr Cajamarca 152-154, T/F051-353384, www.mancocapa cinn.com/i_rubilodge_espanol.htm. Breakfast US$2 extra, hot water, safe, TV, tours arranged. Recommended.

D-E Manco Cápac Inn, Av Tacna 227, T051-352985, www.mancocapacinn.com/ i_mancocapac_espanol.htm. With bath and hot water, luggage store, safe, average breakfast extra, as are heating and cable TV.

E Hospedaje Residencial Margarita, Jr Tarapacá 130, T051-352820, www.hostal margaritapuno.com. Large building, family atmosphere, hot water most of the day, stores luggage, tours can be arranged. Recommended.

E Hostal Nesther, Deústua 268, T051-363308. Also has triples, with bath, hot water 0600-0900, 1800-2100, clean, simple rooms.

E-F Hostal Illampu, Av La Torre 137-interior 9, T051-353284, illampu97@hotmail.com. With bath and warm water, breakfast and TV extra. Has a café, laundry, safe, exchanges money, arranges excursions (ask for Santiago).

E-F Hostal Los Pinos, Tarapacá 182, T/F051-367398, hostalpinos@hotmail.com. Cheaper without bath. Family-run, electric showers, breakfast US$2, clean, safe, luggage store, laundry facilities, helpful, cheap tours organized. Recommended.

E-F Hostal Q'oñi Wasi, Av La Torre 119, opposite the rail station, T051-365784, qoniwasi_lourdes@hotmail.com. Cheaper without bath and in low season. Heating is extra, but hot water available all day, laundry facilities and service, luggage store, breakfast included

from 0600-0900, lunch on request, kitchen facilities, safe, very helpful. Recommended.

E-F Los Uros, Teodoro Valcárcel 135, T051-352141, www.losuros.com. Cheaper without bath and in low season. Hot water, plenty of blankets, breakfast is available (at extra cost), quiet at the back, good value. They make a small charge to leave luggage, laundry, often full. Recommended.

F Hostal Europa, Alfonso Ugarte 112, near the train station, T051-353026, heuropa@ terramail.com. Popular, cheaper without bath, luggage may be stored, but don't leave your valuables in the room, hot water sometimes, garage space for motorcycles.

F pp The Point, Av Circunvalación Norte 278, Huajsapata, T051-351427, www.thepointhostels.com. Latest addition to The Point's chain of party hostels in Peru, 3 long blocks from main plaza, with the regular facilities such as dorms for 3 to 12 people, twin rooms, hot water, **The Pointless Bar**, travel centre, free internet, kitchen, restaurant.

Youth hostels

F pp Inka's Rest, Pasaje San Carlos 158, T051-368720. Includes breakfast, several apartments each with shared sitting area and bath, hot water, free internet, rooms a bit small, cooking and laundry facilities, a place to meet other travellers, reserve ahead.

Capachica Peninsula *p229*
Llachón

Families offer accommodation on a rotational basis and, as the community presidents change each year, the standard of facilities changes from year to year and family to family. All hosts arrange boat transport to Amantaní. Among those who offer lodging (**F** per bed, meals extra) are Tomás Cahui Coila, Centro Turístico Santa María Llachón, T051-951 923595 (mob), www.exploretiticaca.com; Primo Flores, Santa María, T051-951 821392/951 680040/951 410901 (mob), primopuno@hotmail.com; Valentín Quispe, T051-951 821392 (mob), llachon@yahoo.com.

The islands *p231*
Los Uros
Armando Suaña, T051-951 341374. A local guide offering accommodation in Kantati.
Oscar Coyla Coila, T051-951 824378 (mob), is the Uros community representative. Accommodation **F** per person, meal packages available.
René Coyla Coila, T051-951 743533 (mob), is an official tour guide who can advise on lodging.

Taquile
D-E pp, full board. On arrival, you are greeted by a *jefe de alojamiento*, who oversees where you are going to stay. You can either say where you are going, if you (or your guide) know where you want to stay, or the *jefe* can find you a room. It is worth asking which families are in need of a visit as some have become favourites of tour groups and consequently have better facilities while those less popular have remained more basic. **Leucario Huata Cruz**, T051-951 830433 (mob) is the *Presidente del Comité Turístico de Taquile*.

Instead of staying in the busy part around the main square, the Huayllano community, on the south side of the island, is hosting visitors. Contact **Alipio Huata Cruz**, T051-951 668551 or T051-951 615239 (mob) or you can arrange a visit with **All Ways Travel** (see Tour operators, below).

Amantaní
The *Presidente del Comité Turístico de Amantaní* is **Señón Tipo Huatta**, T051-951 832308 (mob). Ask your boat owner where you can stay; families living close to the port tend to receive tour company business and more tourists. If you walk to one of the communities further away, you might get a better price and you are helping to share the income. Accommodation **D-E** per person, full board. This includes 3 meals of remarkable similarity and generally poor quality (take bread and fruit). It's good value for visitors, but the prices have been forced down to unrealistically low levels, from which the islanders benefit hardly at all. Some contacts for accommodation are:

Ambrosio Mamani, j.mamani.cari@eudoramail.com, skipper of the *Barco Atlántico*, good lodging and food.
Familia Victoriano Calsin Quispe, Casilla 312, Isla Amantaní, T051-360220 (Irma) or T051-363320 (Puno contact).
Hospedaje Jorge Cari, basic, but nice family, great view of lake from room.
Kantuta Lodge, T051-789290, T051-951 636172, www.kantutalodge.com.

❶ Eating

Puno *p228, map p226*
Very cheap places on Jr Deústua serve lunch or dinner. There are many places on Jr Lima, too many to list here, which cater for the tourist market, they usually have good atmosphere and very good food.
❡ **Coca Kintu**, Jr Lima 401, T051-365566, mendelmar@hotmail.com. Novo Andean cuisine.
❡ **IncAbar**, Lima 348, T051-368031. Open for breakfast, lunch and dinner, interesting dishes in creative sauces, fish, pastas, curries, café and couch bar, nice decor.
❡ **Internacional**, Moquegua 201, T051-352502, h_internacional@latinmail.com. Very popular particularly with locals, excellent trout, good pizzas, recommended.
❡ **Keros**, Lambayeque 131, T051-364602. Fancy, bar/restaurant catering for the tourist market, mostly Peruvian food, good service, pleasant surroundings, good drinks.
❡ **La Choza de Oscar**, Jr Libertad 340, T051-9751185, www.lachozadeoscar.com. Novo Andean cuisine, folklore show every evening, popular with groups.
❡ **La Hostería**, Lima 501, T051-365406. Good set meal and à la carte dishes including local fare like alpaca and guinea pig, pizza, music in the evening, open from 1700.
❡ **La Plaza**, Puno 425, Plaza de Armas. Good food and service, international dishes and *comida nueva andina* (or Novo Andean cuisine).
❡ **Los Balcones de Puno**, Libertad 345, T051-365300, www.losbalconesdeperu.com.

Peruvian and international food, daily folklore show 1900-2100.

♔♔ **Mojsa**, Jr Lima 635 p 2, Plaza de Armas, T051-363182, www.mojsarestaurant.com. Good international and *comida nueva andina* dishes, also has an arts and crafts shop. Recommended.

♔♔ **Tradiciones del Lago**, Jr Lima 418, T051-368140. Wide selection of Peruvian food, buffet or à la carte.

♔♔ **Tulipans**, Jr Lima 394, T051-351796, tulipans_restaurant@hotmail.com. Sandwiches, juices and a lunchtime *menú*. Pleasant outdoor seating in a colonial courtyard.

♔♔-♔ **Don Piero**, Lima 360. Huge meals, live music, try their 'pollo coca-cola' (chicken in a sweet and sour sauce), slow service, popular, tax extra.

♔♔-♔ **Pizzería-Trattoria El Buho**, Lima 349 and at Jr Libertad 386, T051-356223. Open 1800 onwards. Excellent pizza, lively atmosphere.

♔ **Casa Grill La Estancia**, Jr Libertad 137, T051-365469. Salad bar, huge steaks, grilled meat and Peruvian food. Very popular with locals for big lunches and a few beers.

♔ **Chifa Nan Hua**, Arequipa 378. Tasty, big portions of Chinese food.

♔ **Govinda**, Deústua 312. Closes at 2000. Cheap vegetarian lunch menus.

♔ **Remembranzas**, Jr Moquegua 200. Open 0630-2200. Pizzas as well as local food.

♔ **Ukukus**, Jr Libertad 216 and Pje Grau 172, T051-367373. Good combination of Andean and Novo Andino cuisine as well as pizza and some Chinese *chifa* style.

♔ **Vida Natural**, Tacna 141. Open for breakfast, lunch and dinner, veggie meals, salads, fruits, yoghurts.

Cafés
Cafetería Mercedes, Jr Arequipa 144, T051-354904. Good *menú* US$1.50, also breads, cakes, snacks, juices and tea.
Casa del Corregidor, Deústua 576, aptdo 2, T051-355694. In restored 17th-century building, sandwiches, good snacks, coffee, good music, great atmosphere, nice

surroundings with patio. Fair trade shop selling handicrafts.
Ricos Pan, Arequipa 332 and Moquegua 326, T051-351024. Open 0600-2300, closed Sun. Café and bakery, great cakes, excellent coffees, juices and pastries, good breakfasts and other dishes, reasonable prices, great place to relax. Branches of their panadería at Jr Arequipa cuadra 3 and Moquegua 330.

The islands *p231*
Taquile
There are many small restaurants around the plaza and on the track to the Puerto Principal (eg Gerardo Huatta's **La Flor de Cantuta**, on the steps; **El Inca** on the main plaza). Meals are generally fish, rice and chips, omelette and *fiambre* – a local stew. Meat is rarely available and drinks often run out. Breakfast consists of pancakes and bread. Shops on the plaza sell film, postcards, water, chocolate bars and dry goods.

Amantaní
One restaurant, **Samariy**.

🌙 Bars and clubs

Puno *p228, map p226*
Dómino, Libertad 443. 'Megadisco', happy hour Mon-Thu 2000-2130, good.
Positive, Jr Lima 378 esq Jr Libertad, T051-951 310615. Drinks, large screen TV, modern music, occasional heavy metal rock groups.
Pub Ekeko's, Jr Lima 355, p 2. Live music every night, happy hour 2000-2200.

⊛ Festivals and events

Puno *p228, map p226*
It is difficult to find a month in Puno without some sort of celebration.
Feb The very colourful **Fiesta de la Virgen de la Candelaria** takes place during the first 2 weeks in Feb. Bands and dancers from all the local towns compete in this *Diablada*, or Devil

Pot luck

One of the most intriguing items for sale in Andean markets is Ekeko, the god of good fortune and plenty and one of the most enduring and endearing of the Aymara gods and folk legends.

He is a cheery, avuncular little chap, with a happy face to make children laugh, a pot belly, because of his predilection for food, and short legs so he can't run away.

His image, usually in plaster of Paris, is laden with sacks of grain, sweets, household tools, baskets, utensils, suitcases, confetti and streamers, rice, noodles and other essentials. Dangling from his lower lip is the ubiquitous lit cigarette. Believers say that these little statues only bring luck if received as gifts, not purchased.

Dance, with the climax coming on Sun. The festival is famous for its elaborate and grotesque masks, which depict characters in local legends as well as caricatures of former landowners and mine bosses. The festivities are better at night on the streets than the official functions in the stadium. Check in advance on the date because Candelaria may be moved if pre-Lenten carnival coincides with it. This festival is great fun and shouldn't be missed if you're here around this time.

Mar/Apr On Good Fri there's a candlelit procession through darkened streets, with bands, dignatories and statues of Jesus.

3 May Festividad de las Cruces, celebrated with masses, a procession and the Alasita festival of miniatures.

29 Jun San Pedro, is a colourful festival of with a procession at Zepita (see page 255).

4-5 Nov There's an impressive pageant dedicated to the founding of Puno and the emergence of Manco Cápac and Mama Ocllo from the waters of Lake Titicaca. The royal couple sail from a point on the lake (it varies annually) and arrive at the port between 0900 and 1000. The procession from the lake moves up Av Titicaca to the stadium where a ceremony takes place with dancers from local towns and villages. If you buy an entrance ticket, US$0.60, you can watch from the top tier as the float carrying the Incas, followed by the local dancing groups, enters the stadium. Many of the groups continue dancing outside. This is not the best time to visit Taquile and Amantaní since many of their

inhabitants are at the festival. This date coincides with the anniversary of the founding of Puno, celebrated with parades at night and a full military parade on the Sun.

The islands *p231*
Taquile
Mar/Apr Semana Santa.
Jun Pentecost.
25 Jul-2 Aug Fiesta de Santiago, the main festival, held over 2 weeks.

Amantaní
15-20 Jan San Sebastián, or Pago a la Tierra is celebrated on both hills. The festivities have been reported as spectacular, very colourful, musical and hard-drinking.
9 Apr Aniversario del Consejo (of the local council), which might not be as boring as it sounds.
8-16 Aug Feria de Artesanías.

O Shopping

Puno *p228, map p226*
Puno is the best place in Peru to buy **alpaca wool** articles; bargaining is appropriate. Along the avenue leading to the port is the large **Mercado Artesanal Asociación de Artesanos Unificados**, daily 0900-1800. Closer to the centre are **Mercado Coriwasi**, Ugarte 150, daily 0800-2100, and **Central Integral de Artesanos del Perú (CIAP)**, Jr Deústua 756, Mon-Sat 1000-1800. The **Mercado Central**,

in the blocks bound by Arbulú, Arequipa, Oquendo and Tacna, has all kinds of food, including good cheeses (especially those made at nearby Ayaviri) as well as a few crafts.

Consorcio Casa Parodi, Lima 394. T051-363551, alpacas@terra.com.pe. Another expensive, high-quality alpaca store.

Kuna by Alpaca 111, Lima 218-224, T051-366050, www.kuna.com.pe. A very good-quality alpaca shop at the high end of the price range.

La Casa de Wiracocha, Tarapaca 260. Select Peruvian handicrafts, associated with **Hotel Intiqa**.

▲ Activities and tours

Puno *p228, map p226*

Agencies organize trips to the Uros floating islands and the islands of Taquile and Amantaní, as well as to Sillustani, and other places. Make sure that you settle all details before embarking on the tour. Alternatively, you can easily go down to the lake and make your own arrangements with the boatmen. Each island has its ticket office at the port, where fares are sold at set rates. Watch out for the many unofficial street tour sellers – or *jalagringos* – who offer hotels and tours at different rates, depending on how wealthy you look. Once you realize they have charged more than the going rate, they'll be gone. They are everywhere: train station, bus offices, airport and hotels. Ask to see their guide's ID card. Only use agencies with named premises and compare prices. Companies that offer transport to the airport also offer hire vehicles with driver for touring.

Tour operators

The following have been recommended:

All Ways Travel, Casa del Corregidor, Deústua 576, p 2, T/F051-353979, and at Tacna 285, of 104-2042, T/F051-355552, www.titicacaperu.com. Very helpful, kind and attentive to visitors' needs but office closed at lunchtime. Reliable, staff speak German,

French, English and Italian. They offer a unique cultural tour to the islands of Anapia and Yuspique in Lake Wiñaymarka, beyond the straits of Tiquina, 'The Treasure of Wiñaymarka', departures Thu and Sun. You can contribute to owner Víctor Lazo's educational project by donating children's books for schools. They also have a speed boat for 40 passengers. Also do an alternative visit to Taquile going to the south of the island to visit the Huayllano community; this is a lot less touristy then the regular Taquile visit.

Amazing Peru, Jr Lambayeque 274, www.amazingperu.com. Well-organized tours with knowledgeable guides.

Arcobaleno, Jr Tarapaca 391, T051-364068, www.titicacalake.com. Local tours, Western Union representative and coordinator for **Crillon Tours** of La Paz, Bolivia. Receptive tour agency and not so helpful for walk-in tourists.

Cusi Expeditions, Jr Theodoro Varcárcel 164, T051-369072, reservascusi@terra.com.pe. Taquile, Amantaní, Sillustani, Uros. They own most of the boats which operate the standard tours of the islands. You will very likely end up on a Cusi tour so it's best to buy from them directly to get the best price and the most accurate information.

Edgar Adventures, Jr Lima 328, T/F051-353444 , www.edgaradventures.com. Run by Edgar Apaza and Norka Flórez who speak English, German and French, very helpful and knowledgeable, expanding repertoire of off-the-beaten-track tours in the area, including kayaking tour of Llachon. Promotes community benefits and responsible tourism. Recommended.

Käfer Viajes, Arequipa 179, T051-354742, www.kafer-titicaca.com. Efficient and helpful.

Kontiki Tours, Jr Melgar 188. T051-355887, www.kontikiperu.com. Receptive tour agency specializing in special interest excursions. Recommended.

León Tours, Ayacucho 148-152, T051-352771. Run catamarans on Lake Titicaca. Peruvian representative for Bolivian company, see **Transturin**, page 257.

Nayra Travel, Jr Lima 419, of 105. T051-

337934, www.nayratravel.com. Small agency with very helpful staff, offering local tours and a variety of options in Llachón. Off-the-beaten-track excursions for a minimum of 2 people. Recommended.

Peru Up to Date, Arequipa 340, T051-951 921549 (mob), www.peruuptodate.com. New, offers tours in the Puno and Titicaca area.

Pirámide Tours, Jr Rosendo Huirse 130, T051-366107, www.titikakalake.com. Out of the ordinary and classic tours, flexible, personalized service, modern fast launches, very helpful, but works only via internet and overseas clients.

Titikaka Explorers, Jr Puno 633, of 207, T051-368903, www.titikaka-explorer.com. Good service, helpful.

⊖ Transport

Puno *p228, map p226*
Air
Airline offices: Lan, Tacna y Libertad, T051-367227; Star Perú, Libertad 300 y Tacna, T051-364615, www.starperu.com. The nearest airport is at Juliaca, see page 252. Airport transfers US$3.40 per person with Camtur, Tacna 336, of 104, T051-967652 and Rossy Tours, Tacna 308, T051-366709, www.rossytours.tk. Some of the upmarket hotels include airport transfers in their price. Taxi to the airport US$17-20. If taking regular public transport to Juliaca and a taxi to the airport from there, allow extra time as the combis might drive around looking for passengers before leaving Puno.

Boat
Boats to the islands leave from the terminal in the harbour; *trici-taxi* from centre, US$1.

Bus
All long-distance buses, except some Cuzco services and buses to La Paz (see below), leave from the **Terminal Terrestre**, which is at 1 de Mayo 703 y Victoria, by the lake, southeast of the centre, T051-364733. It has a **Dircetur** information office, tourist police, internet, snack bars and toilets. Platform tax US$0.35. Bus prices to Cuzco and La Paz have seasonal variations.

Daily buses to **Arequipa**, 5-6 hrs via **Juliaca**, 297 km by paved road, US$5-7 with **Cruz del Sur, Destinos, Julsa, Señor de Milagros**, or **Sur Oriente**; most have a morning and evening bus – better quality buses go at night but there have been some problems with luggage theft on night buses. **4M Express** to **Arequipa** (US$30), **Chivay** (0630, US$40), **Moquegua** (US$4.50-6), **Tacna** (US$10, 10 hrs), and **Lima** (1011 km, 21 hrs, US$27-51); all buses go through Arequipa, sometimes with a change of bus.

To **Cuzco**, 388 km, 5-7 hrs. If you wish to travel by bus and cannot get on a direct bus, it is no problem to take separate buses to Juliaca, then to Sicuani, then to Cuzco, but obviously this takes longer. It is advisable not to take night buses to Cuzco because of theft. There are 3 levels of service: regular, via Juliaca, US$5-7, 7 hrs (**Libertad**, 4 a day, **Cisnes**, 2 a day, and others); direct, non-stop, with **Tour Perú**, 0800, US$8.50, and 2130, US$10, 6 hrs (*bus cama*); and tourist service, 0730, 10 hrs, with a good lunch stop at Sicuani (included in price) and visits to Pukará, La Raya, Raqchi and Andahuaylillas en route, US$30 plus museum entry fees (US$7), with **Inka Express** (may pick up at hotel on request) and with **First Class** or **Turismo Mer**. In high season try to book 2 days in advance.

Small buses and colectivos/combis for local destinations leave from the **Terminal Zonal**, Av Bolívar between Carabaya and Palma. They leave throughout the day as they fill. To **Juliaca**, 44 km, 45 mins, bus US$0.70, combi US$0.85. Buses and combis to Juliaca also leave from several other locations, the most central being a lane off Av Tacna between Melgar and Deústua. To **Ilave**, US$0.70, 1 hr. To **Juli**, US$1.20, 1½ hrs. To **Pomata**, US$1.70, 2 hrs (take a combi going to Yunguyo). To **Desaguadero**, US$2, 2½ hrs. To **Yunguyo**, US$1.70, 1½ hrs.

To **La Paz** or **Copacabana** (Bolivia), the best direct services are with **Tour Perú**, leaving Puno daily at 0700 and 0730 respectively, also **Panamericano** and **Litoral** (cheaper, although thefts reported on night buses). For **Yunguyo** and the **Bolivian border**, see page 255.

Bus companies 4M Express, Jr Arequipa 736, T051-364887, www.4m-express.com. Cisnes, at Terminal C-17, T051-368674. Cruz del Sur, Terminal C-10, T051-368524. First Class, Jr Tacna 280-300, T051-364640, firstclass@terra. com.pe. Inka Express, Tacna 346 and at the Terminal Terrestre, T051-365654, www.inkaexpress.com. Julsa, Terminal C-33, T051-364080. Libertad, at Terminal C-15, T051-363694. Ormeño, Terminal C-11, T051-368176, neryzp@hotmail.com. Sur Oriente, Terminal C-1, T051-368133. Tour Perú, Jr Tacna and Terminal C-1, T051-352991, www.tourperu.com.pe. Turismo Mer, Jr Tacna 336, T051-367223, www.turismomer.com.

Train

The railway runs from Puno to **Juliaca** (44 km), where it divides, to **Cuzco** (381 km) and **Arequipa** (279 km; no passenger service). The train from Puno to **Cuzco** leaves at 0800, on Mon, Wed, Fri and Sat, arriving at 1800 or later (same journey time each way, no stop in Juliaca, try to sit on the right-hand side for the views). The train makes a stop to view the scenery at La Raya. Between Nov-Mar there is no train on Fri. There is only 1 class, *Andean Explorer*, US$220, includes lunch, afternoon tea, luxury seating and entertainment. The railway station is at Av La Torre 224, T051-369179, www.perurail.com, open 0700-1700 Mon-Fri, 0700-1200 Sat, Sun and holidays. It is well-guarded by police and sealed off to those without tickets.

Around Puno *p229*
Bus
From Puno to **Capachica**, minibuses from Jr Talara, block 1, opposite Mercado Bellavista (known as El Contrabando), 0700-1600, US$1.35, 1½ hrs. Capachica to **Juliaca**, US$1, leave when full from the Plaza de Armas (likewise to Puno). Minibuses from Capachica to **Llachón** 0800-1400, US$0.70, 30 mins. Tour operators in Puno arrange visits, about US$25 per person staying overnight, in groups of 10-15.

Boat
Only 1 weekly public boat from **Llachón** to **Puno**, Fri 0900, returning to Llachón Sat 1000, US$1.20, 3½ hrs. The daily 0800 boat from Amantantí can drop you off at **Colata** (at the tip of the peninsula), a 1-hr walk from Llachón, or a minibus ride to Capachica; confirm details in advance. Returning to Puno, you can try to flag down the boat from Amantaní that passes Colata between 0830 and 0930. All fares US$3 one way. In Santa María (Llachón), boats can be hired for trips to Amantaní (40 mins) and Taquile (50 mins), US$20 return, minimum 10 passengers.

The islands *p231*
Asociación de Transporte los Uros, at the port, T051-368024, aeuttal@hotmail.com, 0800-1600. Motorboats charge US$3.40 per person to take tourists to the **Uros** islands for a 2-hr excursion. Boats leave from the harbour in Puno about every 30 mins from around 0600-1600, or whenever there are 10 or more people to fill the boat. The earlier you go the better, to beat the crowds of tourists. Almost any agency going to the other islands in the lake will stop first at Los Uros. Just to Los Uros, agencies charge US$7-10.

Centro de Operadores de Transporte Taquile, at the port, T051-205477, 0600-1100, 1400-1800. In high season, boats leave Puno harbour for **Taquile** daily at 0730 and 0800, returning 1400 and 1430 (only 1 daily boat in low season), US$3.40 one way. The journey takes 3 hrs. 1 day doesn't leave enough time to appreciate the island fully. Organized tours can be arranged for about US$10-16 per person, but only give you about 2 hrs on the island. Make sure you and the boatman know exactly what you are paying for.

Transportes Unificados Amantaní, at the port, T051-369714, 0800-1100. Boats for **Amantaní** from the harbour in Puno leave at 0815 daily, and return to Puno at 0800 the following day. The journey takes 4-5 hrs – take water. There are 2 boats, 1 of which stops at Uros. They return at 0800 the next day, 1 direct to Puno, the other stops at Taquile. The trip costs US$3.40 one way direct, US$10 return with stops at Uros and Taquile. Amantaní–Taquile costs US$1.70. If you stop in Taquile on the way back, you can continue to Puno at 1200 with the Amantaní boat or take a Taquile boat at 1400 (also 1430 in high season). Purchasing one-way tickets gives you more flexibility if you wish to stay longer on the islands. Several tour operators in Puno offer 2- to 3-day excursions to Amantaní, Taquile and a visit to the floating islands. These cost from US$12 per person upwards, including meals, depending on the season and size of group. This gives you 1 night on Amantaní and 3-4 hrs on Taquile. There is little difference in price visiting the islands independently or on a tour, but going independently means that the islanders get all the proceeds, with no commission paid to Puno tour companies, you can stay as many nights as you wish and you will be able to explore the islands at your own pace. When not taking a tour, do not buy your boat ticket from anyone other than the boat operator at the harbour, do not believe anyone who says you can only visit the islands on a tour and do not be pressurized by touts.

To visit **Anapia** independently, buses Sun, Tue, Thu, US$3 one way. Or take a colectivo from Yunguyo to Tinicachi and alight at Punta Hermosa, just after Unacachi. Boats to Anapia leave Punta Hermosa on Sun and Thu at 1300 (they leave Anapia for Yunguyo market on the same days at 0630). It's 2 hrs each way by boat.

Boats can be hired from Puno or the islands to the private island of **Isla Suasi** and the **Casa Andina** hotel (see below), US$270, 6-7 hrs from Puno, 3½ hrs from Amantaní, they will stop at other islands on request. If you are staying at the hotel transport is included. There may be high waves on the open lake and this can be a rough crossing in bad weather.

ⓘ Directory

Puno p228, map p226
Banks BCP, Lima 510. Changes TCs before 1300 without commission, cash advance on Visa and Visa ATM. **Banco Continental**, Lima 444-411, Visa ATM. **Scotiabank**, Lima esq Deústua, at Plaza de Armas. **Interbank**, Lima 444, changes TCs morning and afternoon, 0.5% commission, Visa ATM. For cash go to the *cambios*, the travel agencies or the better hotels. Best rates with money changers on Jr Lima, many on 400 block, and on Tacna near the market, eg Arbulu y Tacna. Check your Peruvian soles carefully. Exchange rates from soles to bolivianos and vice versa are sometimes better in Puno than in Yunguyo; check with other travellers.
Consulates Bolivia, Jr Arequipa 136, T051-351251. Issues a visa in 48 hrs, price varies according to nationality, Mon-Fri 0830-1400. **Immigration** Ayacucho 280, T051-357103, Mon-Fri 0800-1300, 1500-1700. For renewing entry stamps, etc. You must fill in 2 application forms at a bank, but there's nothing else to pay. **Internet** There are offices everywhere in the centre, upstairs and down. Average price is US$0.30-0.45 per hr. Choz@net, Jr Lima 339, p2, has fast computers and a small snack bar.
Laundry Don Marcelo, head office at Ayacucho 651, T051-352444, has agencies in several places in the centre, including on Lima 427, will collect and deliver laundry. US$1.50 per kg. **Police** Policía de Turismo, Jr Deústua 558, T051-354764, daily 0600-2200, for report in case of theft. **Post** Jr Moquegua 268, open Mon-Sat 0800-2000.
Telephone *Locutorios* everywhere.

Juliaca to the northeastern shore

The opposite shores of Lake Titicaca are quite different. Between Puno and Desaguadero at the lake's southeastern tip, the plain is intensively worked. The tin roofs of the communities glint everywhere in the sun. Heading north from Puno, the road crosses a range of hills to another coastal plain, which leads to Juliaca. North of Puno is the first sector (29,150 ha) of the Reserva Nacional del Titicaca. The smaller, Ramis sector (7030 ha) is northeast of Juliaca, at the outflow of the Río Ramis that floods in the wet season. The reserve protects extensive totora reed beds in which thousands of birds live. On the flat, windy altiplano between Juliaca and Huancané you will see small, square houses with conical roofs, all made of blocks of earth, putukus de champa. After Huancané, the lakeshore becomes mountainous, with cliffs, bays and fabulous vistas over the water.
▶▶ *For listings, see pages 250-253.*

Ins and outs

Heading north and west, Juliaca is a major transport hub for paved roads to Cuzco and Arequipa and also has the only airport in the region. Transport along the north shore is less frequent, but that should not discourage you from travelling here. For information in Spanish, see www.juliacavirtual.com/version1/indexj.htm. **Dircetur regional tourist office** ① *Jr Noriega 191, p 3, T051-321839, ceturjuliaca@yahoo.es, Mon-Fri 0730-1530.*

Juliaca → *Colour map 6, B2. Population: 134,700. Altitude: 3825 m.*

As the commercial focus of an area bounded by Puno, Arequipa and the jungle, Juliaca has grown very fast into a chaotic place with a large impermanent population, lots of contraband and more trici taxis (*taxicholos*) than cars. Monday, market day, is the most disorganized of all. On the positive side, Juliaca provides access to the north side of the Lake as well as various other worthwhile attractions. It is less of a tourist town than Puno and is an alternative base for independent travellers who want to explore Titicaca beyond the gringo trail. It's freezing cold at night, so make sure you're wrapped up well in your recently purchased alpaca clothing.

You can buy wool and alpaca goods at the large Sunday **market**, La Dominical, near the exit to Cuzco. Another good place to find cheap alpaca sweaters is the **Galería Artesanal Las Calceteras**, on Plaza Bolognesi. **Túpac Amaru market**, on Moquegua, seven blocks east of the railway line, is a cheap black market that's great value. The **Plaza de Armas** is mostly lined with modern buildings. On it stands the grey-stone cathedral, Santa Catalina, sombre inside and lit by candles and the yellow light through the windows. In the Municipalidad there is a cultural centre with a small museum.

To get an overview of town and the surrounding altiplano, climb one of the hills that rise to the west. Follow the steps at the south end of Ayacucho to the hill with the antennae, from there you can continue along the stations of the cross to the Cristo Blanco statue. It is not safe to go in the evening.

Around Juliaca

A highly recommended trip is 34 km northwest of Juliaca to the unspoiled little colonial town of **Lampa**, known as the 'Pink City'. The patron saint of Lampa is La Virgen Inmaculada, whose fiesta is held 6-15 December. There is a splendid church, built 1675-1685, called Santiago Apóstol, containing a copy of Michelangelo's *Pietà* (the story goes that when the original in Rome was damaged, they came to Lampa to see how the repairs should be done). A guided tour of the church, including catacombs and an impressive crypt, is available for US$1.70; see the note on the church door or ask around for the guide. In addition to the replica of the *Pietà* there are many excellent paintings of the Cuzco School and an elaborately carved wooden pulpit. Also of interest is the **Kampac Museo** ① *Jr Ayacucho esq Alfonso Ugarte, T051-951 820085, flexible hours, ask at shop opposite, free tour but contributions appreciated*, a small, private museum of Profesor Jesús Vargas, with an eclectic collection of sculptures and ceramics from the Lampa and Juli areas as well as other Peruvian cultures. The museum is visited by groups with the various companies offering a tourist bus service between Puno and Cuzco at around 0900 and 1400 daily. The façade of the Municipalidad has large murals depicting local history. The building houses a second *Pietà* made of plaster. The two plazas in the town with native

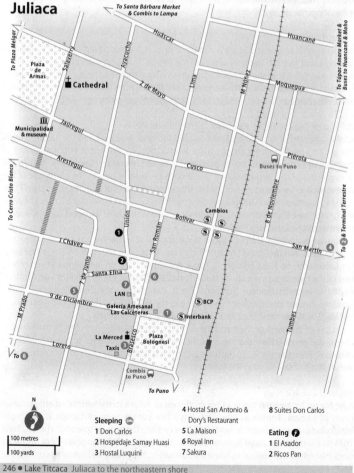

Juliaca

N
100 metres
100 yards

Sleeping
1 Don Carlos
2 Hospedaje Samay Huasi
3 Hostal Luquini
4 Hostal San Antonio & Dory's Restaurant
5 La Maison
6 Royal Inn
7 Sakura
8 Suites Don Carlos

Eating
1 El Asador
2 Ricos Pan

Mother Earth

Pachamama, or Mother Earth, occupies a very privileged place in Aymara culture because she is the generative source of life. The Aymara believe that man was created from the land, and thus he is fraternally tied to all the living beings that share the earth. According to them, the earth is our mother, and it is on the basis of this understanding that all of human society is organized, always maintaining the cosmic norms and laws.

Women's and men's relationship with nature is what the Aymara call ecology, harmony and equilibrium. The Aymara furthermore believe that private land ownership is a social sin because the land is for everyone. It should be shared and not used for the benefit of a few.

Vicenta Mamani Bernabé of the Andean Regional Superior Institute of Theological Studies states: "Land is life because it produces all that we need to live. Water emanates from the land as if from the veins of a human body, there is also the natural wealth of minerals, and pasture grows from it to feed the animals. Therefore, for the Aymaras, the Pachamama is sacred and since we are her children, we are also sacred. No one can replace the earth, she is not meant to be exploited, or to be converted into merchandise. Our duty is to respect and care for the earth. This is what white people today are just beginning to realize, and it is called ecology. Respect for the Pachamama is respect for ourselves as she is life. Today, she is threatened with death and must be liberated for the sake of her children's liberation."

quenual trees are very well kept. It also has a small Sunday market. Cars (US$0.65), and combis (US$0.50), leave Juliaca when full throughout the day from Jirón Huáscar esquina Ricardo Palma, one block from Mercado Santa Bárbara, 30 minutes. There are a number of places of interest around Lampa, the surrounding hills offer fine walking amid ancient terracing, small lakes are rich in bird-life including flamingos. Nearby are three Inca fortresses. A few kilometres away is the **Cueva del Toro** with petroglyphs, further afield is a forest of Puya Raymondi.

The town of **Pucará** lies 63 km to the north, with pre-Inca ruins and its pottery. The ceramic bulls which can be seen on the roofs of houses throughout the southern Peruvian Andes, placed there to bring fertility and health to the homes they stand on, originate here. Ask in the market for *torritos de Pucará*. There are some restaurants along the main road. The sheep farm of San Antonio, between Ayaviri and Chiquibambilla, owned by the Prime family, who are descendants of British emigrants, can be visited.

Some 71 km northeast of Juliaca is the old town of **Azángaro** with a famous church, La Asunción, which is filled with *retablos* and paintings of the Cuzco school. There are good thermal springs at the village of **Putina**, 84 km northeast of Juliaca, 5½ hours by bus or truck, US$2.50.

Some tours from Cuzco to Lake Titicaca have the Isla Suasi (see below) as their initial destination. The route taken goes through Pucará, Azángaro and Muñani and two nights are spent at **Mallkini** ① *Juan de la Torre 101, San Lázaro, Arequipa (head office), T054-202525, www.mallkini.com.pe.* This is an alpaca farm at over 4000 m, owned by the Michell family, the largest alpaca textile group in Peru. If you wish to see an altiplano farm, this is a first-class set-up. Guests are well-looked after and can take part in various activities such as riding, trekking with llamas and off-roading. You can also go independently and take advantage of Mallkini's packages; the ranch has six rooms and camping facilities.

Juliaca to Cuzco

The Puno–Juliaca–Cuzco road is now fully paved and in good condition. Bus services are consequently an acceptable alternative to the train, which runs at an average altitude of 3500 m. There is much to see on the way, but neither the daytime buses nor the trains make frequent stops. You would have to use your own transport, or take buses from town to town to sample what the places en route have to offer, or alternatively take one of the tourist bus services which stop at several places of interest. The road climbs steadily after Juliaca, passing Pucará (see above) then running through the villages of Ayaviri and Santa Rosa (where knitted alpaca ponchos and pullovers and miniature llamas are sold, rooms are available). It then rises further, up to the pass at La Raya. **Ayaviri** is a lively town with a daily market selling the local cheese, the best in the area, creamy and similar to a mild cheddar. It is sold in large round moulds for about US$4 per kilo. In the pleasant plaza are two puya raimondi plants.

The road and railway cross the altiplano, climbing to **La Raya**, the highest pass on the line; 210 km from Puno, at 4321 m. Enterprising locals have set up a market at La Raya and there are public toilets (US$0.20). Up on the heights breathing may be a little difficult, but the descent along the Río Vilcanota is rapid. To the right of **Aguas Calientes**, 10 km from La Raya, are steaming pools of hot water in the middle of the green grass; a startling sight. The temperature of the springs is 40°C, and they show beautiful deposits of red ferro-oxide. Several communal bathing pools and a block of changing rooms have been opened. Entrance US$0.15. At **Marangani**, the river is wider and the fields greener, with groves of eucalyptus trees. At Km 147, next to a colonial house, is the **Maranganí Fábrica Tejidos** ① *T084-352215*, a textile manufacturer using alpaca wool. Although little more than 10 years old, some of the machines are much older than that and all use punch cards (no computerization here). The textiles are exported all over the world. The administrator, Sr Walter Chung Valdez, is happy to show interested travellers around.

The Vilcanota plunges into a gorge, but the train winds above it and round the side of the mountain. At **Huambutío** the railway turns left to follow the Río Huatanay on the final stretch to Cuzco. The Vilcanota here widens into the great Urubamba canyon, flanked on both sides by high cliffs, on its way to join the Ucayali, a tributary of the Amazon. For more information about places between La Raya and Cuzco, see page 213.

Northeast coast of Lake Titicaca

The crossing from Peru to Bolivia via Huancané and Moho is the most remote, but nevertheless a highly recommended route between the two countries. As the road leaves Juliaca, it crosses a single-track bridge, which can get congested if opposing drivers do not give way. To Huancané the road is paved across the altiplano.

Huancané (56 km from Juliaca, altitude 3825 m) is known as *tierra de chirihuanos*, for the wind instrument (like a *zampoña*) that is played here. It has a massive adobe church by a nice plaza. The town suffers from water shortages. There are good birdwatching possibilities 10 km southwest of town where the road crosses the Río Ramis, part of the Reserva Nacional del Titicaca. Ten kilometres east of Huancané, 1 km off the road to Moho, is the small town **Vilque Chico**, from where a road goes northeast to Cojata on the Bolivian border (Ulla Ulla on the Bolivian side). Several undeveloped archaeological sites can be visited from here; **Cotañi** with one *chullpa* is one hour's walk away and the more

Border essentials: Peru–Bolivia

Tilali–Puerto Acosta

The last Peruvian settlement before the border is **Tilali**, a small town with a large Plaza de Armas with topiary. It is a sleepy place except on Wednesday and Saturday, market days at the border. There are a couple of basic, cheap *hospedajes* on or near the plaza. The main fiesta in honour of Virgen de los Remedios is held from 19-21 November.

Customs and immigration There is a Peruvian customs post 2 km past Tilali but no immigration service here, so you must get your exit stamp ahead of time in Puno. The border is a further 2-km steep climb along a very poor dirt track. An obelisk marks the international frontier at Cerro Janko Janko, on a promontory high above the lake with magnificent views. Here are hundreds of small stone storerooms, deserted except during the busy Wednesday and Saturday smugglers' market. From the border it is about 10 km to Puerto Acosta, Bolivia, where you must get a preliminary entry stamp at the police station on the plaza. Get the definitive entry stamp at Migración in La Paz. Puerto Acosta it is a nice town with a large plaza and several simple places to stay and eat.

Transport Difficult and unreliable. Walking 10-15 km with all your luggage at 3800 m above sea level may be necessary. Transport to the border from Juliaca is abundant on Tuesday and Friday starting 2000, but it is not considered safe: buses are crowded, you arrive in the middle of the night, there is nowhere to stay and it is bitterly cold. The best option is to take an early morning bus from Juliaca to Tilali which, on Wednesday and Saturday, usually goes on to the border. Confirm all details in advance in Juliaca. It is very difficult to get transport from Tilali to the border on other days. You can try to arrange a private vehicle, but there are few in town. It is even more difficult to arrange transport from Tilali all the way to Puerto Acosta; expect to pay about US$25 if you can find something. From the border to Puerto Acosta, you can try to get a ride (45 minutes) with the trucks returning to La Paz on market days. Daily buses from Puerto Acosta–La Paz at about 1400, more frequent service on Sunday, five hours, US$3.75. If you are in a hurry and miss the bus, ask the truck to drop you off 25 km further in Escoma, from where there are frequent minivans to La Paz. Travelling from Bolivia to Peru is equally challenging. Buses leave La Paz–Puerto Acosta at 0600 daily, from Reyes Cardona 772, Cancha Tejar (cemetery district), T02-238 2239. Transport past Puerto Acosta only operates on market days and is mostly cargo lorries. There are daily buses from Tilali to Juliaca, departing around 0100, plus a morning bus (about 0800-1000) on Sunday, Tuesday and Friday.

Note Bolivian time is one hour ahead of Peru.

---

extensive **Quiñalata**, two hours' walking; ask for directions or hire a taxi in town. There are no lodgings in Vilque Chico, only a couple of very basic eateries. Combi from Huancané US$0.30, 15 minutes. Past Vilque Chico, the views are especially beautiful.

At Jipata, the road splits, giving two ways of getting to **Moho** (40 km; public phones T051-832300/01/02): inland, over the hills, the route the buses take as it is shorter; or clinging to the lakeshore, with lots of bends, but beautiful views. Moho is known as the 'Garden of the Altiplano'. Maximizing the climatic benefits of the lake, they grow roses and many other flowers. The plaza has rose bushes, topiary hedges and a colourful fountain. The large, green Consejo Municipal is totally out of keeping with the rest of the plaza. Buses for Juliaca collect on the plaza. The main fiesta in honour of **Señor de la Exaltación** is held 13-16 September, celebrated with dances, bands, bullfights, etc. On a ridge top, two hours' climb from Moho is **Merka Marka** or 'old city', an impressive, undeveloped pre-Inca archaeological site, with gorgeous views of the lake and the altiplano, all the way to the glaciers on the Cordillera Apolobamba.

Conima, a pleasant small town in a lovely setting overlooking the lake, has a nice plaza with a fountain, colourful flower beds and an old stone church tower. The main fiesta, **San Miguel Arcángel**, runs from 28-30 September. A 30-minute walk through worked fields leads down to a nice beach. Nearby is the Península de Huata with a stone monolith on the rigetop. **Cambria**, a village 2 km north of Conima is the access point for **Isla Suasi**, the only tourist project on the north shore. A fine, get-away-from-it-all hotel is the only house on this tiny, tranquil, private island. The microclimate allows for beautiful terraced gardens, which are at their best from January to March. The non-native eucalyptus trees are being replaced by native varieties. You can take a community rowing boat around the island to see birds (US$1.50) or paddle yourself in one of the hotel's canoes. The island has six vicuñas, a small herd of alpacas and various domestic animals. The sunsets from the highest point are out of this world.

Rinconada

At 5200 m, Rinconada is a cold, isolated town near Ananea and Culijón mountain. Its population of about 25,000 is involved entirely in gold mining and the mines are all under a glacier. A glacier lake below the town is marred by the rock and sand dug out of the mines. You can see all the processes in extracting, refining and selling the gold (which can be found pretty cheaply in the local shops). There's no infrastructure for tourists: just four or five basic *hostales*, countless basic restaurants serving good food and, apart from gold, shops sell mainly mining equipment. Wrap up warm as it is cold by day and bitter at night (it's hard to sleep in the thin air).

◉ Juliaca to the northeastern shore listings

For Sleeping and Eating price codes and other relevant information, see pages 38-44.

◉ Sleeping

Juliaca *p245, map p246*
There are water problems in town, especially in the dry season.
L-AL Royal Inn, San Román 158, T051-321561, www.royalinnhoteles.com/juliaca. Decent accommodation with rooms and suites, breakfast included, hot water, jacuzzi, TV, heaters in rooms, safe, laundry, internet, good restaurant.
A Don Carlos, Jr 9 de Diciembre 114, Plaza Bolognesi, T051-323600, www.hotelesdon carlos.com. Breakfast included. Comfortable,

modern facilities, hot water, TV, heater, restaurant and room service. Recommended.
A Suites Don Carlos, Jr M Prado 335, T051-321571, www.hotelesdoncarlos.com. 45 rooms, including a presidential suite, *frigobar*, good facilities, breakfast included.
C La Maison, Jr 7 de Junio 535, T051-321444. Carpeted rooms, hot water, 1 room has jacuzzi, restaurant, Wi-Fi, parking.
E Hostal Luquini, Jr Brasesco 409, T051-321510. Comfortable, reliable hot water in morning only, helpful staff, patio, motorcycle parking. Owner has 4WD vehicle for hire.
E-F Hostal San Antonio, Jr San Martín 347, T051-331803. Simple rooms with or without bath, hot shower extra, basic, parking.

E-F Sakura, San Román 133, T051-322072, hotelsakura@hotmail.com. Rooms with private or shared bath and hot water all day, TV, breakfast included. Cheaper, basic rooms in older section in the back. Cafeteria, internet available for extra charge.

F Hospedaje Samay Huasi, Jr San Martín 1220, T051-323314. Very basic, family-run, friendly, helpful, clean, round the corner from the Cruz del Sur office. Private rooms with shared bath upstairs with hot water and TV. Dorm rooms on ground floor used by locals.

Around Juliaca p245

C Hostal La Casona de Lampa, Tarapaca 271, Plaza de Armas, Lampa, T051-832325, lacasonalampa@yahoo.com. Nicely refurbished old house decorated with antiques, breakfast included, other meals US$7, 8 rooms all with private bath, hot water, heater in room and hot-water bottles, advance booking required, caters for groups, interesting tours.

F Hospedaje La Estrella, Jr Municipal 540. Simple rooms, with or without private bath, hot water.

F Hospedaje Milan, Jr Juan José Calle 513, T051-794266. Shared bath, electric shower, basic but hospitable owner.

Juliaca to Cuzco p248

F Paraíso, Jr Leoncio Prado 254 (about 3 blocks from the plaza), Ayaviri, T051-863024. Hot showers, clean, friendly.

Northeast coast of Lake Titicaca p248

LL Hotel Isla Suasi, T051-95131 0070, Casa Andina Private Collection hotel, www.casa-andina.com. Price is full board. Facilities are spacious, comfortable and solar-powered. Rooms have lake view, bath and hot water and hot-water bottles are put between your sheets at bedtime, very attentive service. The food is excellent and innovative (Andean *nouvelle cuisine*), lots of vegetables, all locally produced. Canoes. Warmly recommended.

F Hotel Moho, at the Consejo Municipal, Plaza de Armas, Moho. Becoming run down, some rooms small, solar-heated water (best shower in the early afternoon), friendly.

G Hospedaje Huancané, Jr Lima 309 at Plaza de Armas, Huancané (no phone). Basic, shared bath, cold water, nice courtyard, friendly. A couple of other places at the entrance to town from Juliaca.

G Hostal Moheño, Arequipa behind the church, Moho. Shared bath, cold water, very basic, friendly.

G Hotel Don Raúl, at a corner shop on the Plaza de Armas (no sign), Conima. Basic but reasonably clean and friendly, shared crouch toilet, no running water.

🍴 Eating

Juliaca p245, map p246

🍴 **Dory's**, San Martín 347. Sun-Thu 0800-2000, Fri 0800-1400. Simple vegetarian.

🍴 **El Asador**, Unión 119. Open 1800-2400. Chicken, grill and pizza, good food and service, pleasant atmosphere.

🍴 **Ricos Pan**, San Román 177 y Chávez. A good bakery with café, very popular. Recommended.

Juliaca to Cuzco p248

🍴 **Restaurante La Mundial**, Jr Tacna 465, Ayaviri, T051-863375. Serves cheap local food, including lamb, a speciality, friendly place.

Northeast coast of Lake Titicaca p248

All the main towns along this route have simple *comedores*.

🎉 Festivals and events

Juliaca p245, map p246

Feb/Mar Carnival is unusually celebrated on the week starting Ash Wed, with over 50 groups dancing *morenada* and *diablada*.
23-24 Sep Virgen de las Mercedes is celebrated with brass bands, *morenada* and fireworks (*castillos*).

⊖ Transport

Juliaca p245, map p246

Air

The airport is small but well organized, airport tax US$4.20. There are daily flights to/from **Lima** (2¼ hrs) with LAN, direct, via **Arequipa** (30 mins), or **Cuzco**, and StarPerú once a day via Arequipa. Minibus 1-B on Núñez, US$0.15; from airport to town, they take you to your hotel. Beware overcharging for transport from Juliaca airport. If you have little luggage, combis stop just outside the airport parking area. Taxi from Plaza Bolognesi, US$1.75, taxi from airport US$3.40. For transfers to/from Puno, see page 242.

Airline offices LAN, San Román 125, T051-322228 (airport 324448), Mon-Fri 0800-1900, Sat and Sun 0800-1800. StarPerú, San Román 175, T051-327478.

Bus

The Terminal Terrestre at the east end of San Martín (cuadra 9, across Av Circunvalación) was not being used in 2010. Most bus companies have their offices nearby on San Martín. Lots of companies (including **Cruz del Sur**, **Julsa**, **Power** and **Ormeño**) serve **Arequipa** (4 hrs, US$6.50-13.50), **Lima** (20 hrs, US$27-44) and **Cuzco** (5-6 hrs, US$5-12). To **Cuzco**, 344 km, 5-6 hrs, with **Tour Perú**, day and night buses, prices as from Puno (see page 242 for warning about night buses to Cuzco). First Class and Inka Express have Pullman tourist buses that stop for sightseeing and lunch, with guide, see under Puno. The road is paved and in good condition. Buses from Puno will stop in Juliaca on the way to Cuzco. To **Puno**, 44 km, 1 hr, US$0.65; small buses leave when full throughout the day from Piérola y 18 de Noviembre. Combis to Puno and the faster, more comfortable 'sprinters' (minibuses), run by **Virgen de Fátima**, leave from inside courtyard on Loreto by Plaza Bolognesi, US$0.85. Buses to **Capachica** for Llachón from Cerro Colorado Market, leave when full 0500-1700, 1½ hrs, US$0.65. To **Puerto**

Maldonado, 16-18 hrs, US$17, along a rough but dramatic road via the San Gabán gorge and Mazuco; buses leave from M Núñez cuadra 11 by the exit to Cuzco; with **Tambopata**, M Núñez 1130, daily at 1600, and **Aguilas/Tahuamanu**, M Núñez 1130, T051-323840, daily 1200, 1600. The journey takes much longer in the wet season. To **La Paz** take a sprinter to Puno and change there. **Bus companies** Cruz del Sur, T051-322011, www.cruzdelsur.com.pe. Inka Express, www.inkaexpress.com. Julsa, T051-331952. Ormeño, T051-326994. Tour Perú, tourperu@mixmail.com.

Train

The station at Juliaca is the junction for services between **Arequipa** (no passenger services), **Puno** and **Cuzco**. See under Puno (page 243) and Cuzco (page 171) for more information. Fares to Cuzco are the same as from Puno, but no tickets are sold in Juliaca. You can get on the train in Juliaca but only if you have purchased your ticket in advance in Puno. "At Juliaca, the track runs down the middle of the main market street, which is hurriedly cleared as the train approaches and rebuilt as soon as it passes, great place for camera shots." (Martin Steer)

Northeast coast of Lake Titicaca p248

Bus

From **Juliaca**: combis to **Huancané** (on the north side of Lake Titicaca), 51 km, 40 mins, from Grifo San Juan del Oro, Sucre y Ballón, US$0.45, 1 hr. From Hunacané, combis leave for Juliaca when full throughout the day. Buses to **Moho**, 31 km beyond Huancané, from Moquegua y Ballón, past Túpac Amaru market, 4 daily, 2-2½ hrs, US$1.50. From Moho to Juliaca, buses leave at 0130, 0800 and 1300 daily. Buses to **Conima**, Municipal bus Mon 1300, Thu 1300, Sun 0800, 2½-3 hrs, US$1.80. Buses to **Tilali**, Transportes Lucero, 1 or 2 daily in early morning, **Aguila del Sur**, 1 daily in morning, both from Circunvalación y Lambayeque, 4 hrs, US$2.50. Also several buses around 2000 Tue and Fri from Jr

Huancané y El Maestro, but usually crowded with *contrabandistas* and reported unsafe at night. For **Isla Suasi**: take a Tilali or Conima bus and alight in Cambría, about 20 mins past Moho (walk down to the shore and take a rowing boat to Suasi, 10 mins, US$1.50 per person). Private boats from Puno to **Isla Suasi** are expensive and take 4-6 hrs (2½ hrs by fast boat, US$450 up to 15 passengers), but you can call at the islands or Llachón en route. A car for 4 people will cost US$75.

Rinconada *p250*
Bus
Buses leave Juliaca at 0600-0700, taking 5-6 hrs, the road deteriorates after Huancané. Buses return from Rinconada at 0500-0700, taking about 30 mins less on the downhill journey; US$3.50 one way.

⬤ Directory

Juliaca *p245, map p246*
Banks Interbank, M Núñez 231. With Red Activa 24 ATM for Visa/Plus, MasterCard/ Cirrus and Amex. **BCP**, M Núñez entre Chávez y 9 de Diciembre, changes cash and TCs but has no ATM. Many *cambios* and street changers at Núñez y Bolívar, cash US dollars and soles. **Milenium**, Bolívar y Núñez, change bolivianos, but don't always have small bills. **Internet** There are many places in the centre, all charging US$0.30 per hr.

The southwestern shore and into Bolivia

The road from Puno towards Bolivia runs along the western shore of Lake Titicaca, so the villages described below are easily reached by public transport. Anybody interested in religious architecture should visit these villages. They are all on the main road except Zepita, which is beyond the turn-off to Yunguyo. ›› *For listings, see pages 256-258.*

Chucuito

An Inca sundial can be seen near the village of Chucuito (19 km), which has an interesting church, **La Asunción**, and houses with carved stone doorways. Visits to Chucuito usually include the Templo de la Fertilidad, **Inca Uyo**, which boasts many phalli and other fertility symbols. The authenticity and original location of these objects is the subject of debate. The locals tend to expect a tip for anything and everything. Nearby, are cave paintings at **Chichiflope**.

Ilave

On the road to Juli is Ilave, where the old road for Tacna branches off. It is typical of a gaunt altiplano town, with a good Sunday market where you can buy woven goods. It is growing rapidly and is an important commercial centre, a small version of Juliaca. This town received a lot of press in 2004 when the local population lynched the corrupt mayor and besieged the police station.

Juli

The main road then bypasses the little town of Juli, 83 km southeast, a pleasant town. Known as the 'Rome of Peru', it is built on a saddle surrounded by seven hills, which offer good walking with lovely views of the lake. The town has some fine examples of religious architecture in its four churches. **San Pedro Cathedral** ① *0630-1130, 1400-1600, except Tue when only for Mass at 0700 and Sun for Mass at 0730, 1100 and 1800, free, but donations appreciated*, on the plaza, is the only functioning church and has been extensively restored. It contains a series of paintings of saints, with the Via Crucis scenes in the same frame, and gilt side altars above which some of the arches have baroque designs. The other churches are museums. **San Juan Letrán** ① *daily 0800-1600, US$1.20*, has two sets of 17th-century paintings of the lives of St John the Baptist and of St Teresa, contained in sumptuous gilded frames. San Juan is a museum. It also has intricate mestizo carving in pink stone. A long flight of shallow steps leads past the Centro Comunal and schools to the **church of Santa Cruz**, which was destroyed by lightning and is closed to visitors, but there is a view of the lake from the plaza in front. The fourth museum church, **La Asunción** ① *daily 0800-1630, US$1.20*, has been restored in recent years. The great nave is empty, but its walls are lined with colonial paintings with no labels. The original painting on the walls of the transept is fading. Its fine bell tower was damaged by earthquake or lightning. Outside is an archway and atrium which date from the early 17th century. Needlework, other weavings, handicrafts and antiques are offered for sale in town. Near Juli is a small colony of flamingos. Many other birds can be seen from the road.

Pomata

A further 20 km along the lake is Pomata (US$0.50 from Juli, US$1.70 from Puno), a quiet, attractive town overlooking the lake. If the colectivo does not enter town, get out by the barracks (*cuartel*) and walk up. The **church of Santiago Apóstol** ① *0700-1200, 1330-1600,*

Border essentials: Peru–Bolivia

There are two principal routes across the border, both of which are fairly straight-forward. The one listed first is by far the more popular. There is a third and rarely travelled route (see page 249) and, finally, it is possible to cross the border by hydrofoil or catamaran as part of a tour. For more detailed information on transport to the borders, see page 257.

Puno–La Paz via Yunguyo and Kasani

The Peruvian immigration office at Kasani, the village right at the frontier, is five minutes' drive from Yunguyo and 100 m from the Bolivian post. It is open 0800-1900 (Peruvian time) and Bolivian immigration is open 0830-1930 (Bolivian time). Peruvian time is one hour behind Bolivian time.

When leaving you must get an exit stamp before crossing the border and an entry stamp on the other side. Leaving Peru, you must first go to the Policía Judicial, then to Peruvian immigration for your exit stamp. Entering Peru, after you get your Bolivian exit stamp, you need to go only to Peruvian immigration (no need to go to the police at this border). A 90-day visa is normally given when entering Peru (30 days for Bolivia). Be aware of corruption at customs and look out for official or unofficial people trying to charge you a fee on either side of the border (say that you know it is illegal and ask why only gringos are approached to pay 'embarkation tax').

Puno–La Paz (via Desaguadero)

The most direct road route, which continues 41 km beyond the turn-off to Yunguyo, all paved for the 150 km to the border. Desaguadero is a scruffy, unscrupulous place. There is no need to stop over as, if you leave La Paz, Moquegua or Puno early enough, you should be at your destination before nightfall.

Peruvian immigration is beside the bridge closest to the lake (there are two). It is open daily 0700-2000 (Peruvian time). Bolivian immigration is open daily 0830-2030 (Bolivian time). A 30-day visa is normally given on entering Bolivia, ask for more if you need it, or get an extension in La Paz. This border crossing allows you to stop at the archaeological site of Tiahuanaco (US$11), en route. It is possible to do a round trip to the site from Puno in about 12-13 hours. Take an early colectivo to Desaguadero, cross the border and take another colectivo towards La Paz. Pay the full fare, but ask to be let out at the junction for Tiahuanaco; walk or hitch the 1.5 km to the ruins.

US$0.70 for foreign tourists, get a ticket from the guardian if he is there, otherwise leave your donation on the table just inside the door, is built of striking red sandstone (1532, started by the Jesuits, finished by the Dominicans). It stands on a promontory above the main road and has wonderful carvings in Andean mestizo baroque of vases full of tropical plants, flowers and animals in the window frames, lintels and cornices. The windows and font are of alabaster. The beautiful interior contains statues, painted columns, a Spanish tiled floor, paintings of the Cuzqueña school and a cupola decorated with figures whose florid, stylized bodies have linked arms. Beneath the Altar of El Señor del Sepulcro is an altarpiece covered in all the tools used in the construction. At **Zepita**, near Desaguadero, the 18th-century Dominican church is also worth a visit.

For Sleeping and Eating price codes and other relevant information, see pages 38-44.

● Sleeping

Chucuito *p254*

LL Titilaka, Comunidad de Huencalla s/n, on a private peninsula near Chucuito, www.titilaka.com. Opened in 2008, luxury boutique hotel offering all-inclusive packages in an exclusive environment on the edge of the lake. Plenty of activities available.

A Taypikala Hotel & Spa, 18 km south of Puno on the road to Desaguadero, T051-792252, www.taypikala.com. Built in 'Inka' style with lots of indoor plants, new-age feel, lovely gardens, most rooms have view of the lake. Good restaurant, bar, spa, store, disco, meditation room, popular with tour groups.

C Las Cabañas, Jr Tarapaca 538, Chucuito, T051-368494, 051-951 751196 (mob), www.chucuito.com. Great little rooms and cottages, private bathroom, fireplace, hot water, breakfast included, other meals available, will collect you from Puno if you phone in advance. A very good choice.

Juli *p254*

Water supply is limited to the early morning.

F Alojamiento 8 de Diciembre, Jr Cuzco 531, T051-951 923964. Shared bath, squat toilet, cold water, clean, basic, nice yard, parking, friendly.

G Alojamiento Mini, Jr Loyola 227, T051-554127. Shared bath, cold water, very basic.

Pomata *p254*

F Hospedaje Municipal, Plaza de Armas. Shared bath, cold water, nice on the outside but not well cared for nor clean, basic, restaurant downstairs.

Border with Bolivia *p255*

There is also accommodation on the Bolivian side. Most places have rooms for sleeping and lock-ups to store your bags.

E-G Hostal Corona, Av Panamericana 248, Desaguadero, T051-851120. The best hotel of a poor lot, cheaper without bath, TV, hot water, parking, luggage store, no meals.

G San Carlos, Desaguadero. Without bath, extra for hot shower, basic, tiny rooms.

F Hostal Isabel, San Francisco 110, Plaza de Armas, Yunguyo, T051-951 794228. Shared or private bathroom, electric shower, nice rooms and courtyard, parking, friendly.

F Hostal San Andrés, 2 de Mayo 516, Plaza 2 de Mayo, Yunguyo, T051-556009. Simple, adequate rooms, private bathroom with electric shower or shared bathroom with cold water.

● Eating

Juli *p254*

Not much to choose from here, keep an eye on hygiene.

♥ **Pollería**, Jr Ilave, 1½ blocks downhill from the Plaza de Armas. Adequate.

Border with Bolivia *p255*

There are several restaurants in Desaguadero, mostly *pollerías*. On the Peruvian side **Panamericano**, **Así Es Mi Tierra** and **Perú Criollo** advertise a bit more variety.

♥ **Rosita**, Jr Bolognesi at Plaza de Armas, Yunguyo. Decent set meals and à la carte.

▲ Activities and tours

The southwestern shore and into Bolivia *p254*

Crillon Tours, PO Box 4785, Av Camacho 1223, La Paz, Bolivia, T591-2-233 7533, www.titicaca.com. Also see **Arcobaleno**, page 241; Crillon have an operational office in Puno at Cajamarca 393 esq Lima, Edif Ramos p 2, of 21, T051-951 542442. In the USA, 1450 South Bayshore Dr, Suite 815 Miami, Fl 33131, T305-358 5353, darius@titicaca.com. Run a hydrofoil service on Lake Titicaca with bilingual guides. Tours stop at their Andean Roots cultural complex at Inca Utama. **Transturin**, Av Arce 2678, La Paz, T591-2-242 2222, www.transturin.com. Also have an office in Puno: **León Tours**, Ayacucho 148-152, T051-352771. Run catamarans on Lake Titicaca either for sightseeing or on the La Paz–Puno route.

See below for details of both **Crillon Tours'** and **Transturin's** services.

⊝ Transport

llave *p254*
Many buses and colectivos run between llave and **Puno**, US$0.70, 1 hr.

Juli *p254*
Colectivos from **Puno** to Juli cost US$1.20. They stop in the main plaza before going to the *paradero* outside market, at llave 349, 3 blocks downhill from Plaza de Armas from where they return to Puno and northwestern destinations. Colectivos going southeast towards the border leave from a small terminal on Jr Lima, 1½ blocks from Plaza de Armas. To **Pomata**, US$0.50, 30 mins; to **Chaca Chaca**, where the road divides to Yunguyo and Desaguadero, US$0.70. 45 mins; no direct transport to Yunguyo, change at Chaca Chaca from where it is US$0.50, 30 mins to Yunguyo; to **Desaguadero**, US$1.20, 1 hr.

Pomata *p254*
To **Puno**, US$1.70, 2 hrs. Most transport does not go up to town, take the steps down to the highway and wait by the army barracks.

Border with Bolivia *p255*
Puno–La Paz via Yunguyo and Kasani
From Puno Terminal Terrestre to Copacabana, US$5, 3 hrs, continuing to La Paz, US$8.50-10 (from Puno), 7 hrs. The best direct service is with **Tour Perú**, Tacna 282, T051-206088, leaving Puno for Copacabana at 0730 and for La Paz at 0700 daily. **Panamericano**, Tacna 245, T051-369010, at 0730 and **Litoral** (Terminal Terrestre, cheaper but theft reported on night buses). You can purchase the service just to Copacabana or through to La Paz, which involves a stop for a meal (not included) in Copacabana and changing buses to a Bolivian company that may be of inferior standard to those in Peru. You only need to change money into bolivianos for lunch on this route. There are minibuses and combis from the Terminal Zonal in Puno to Yunguyo 0600-1900, 2½ hrs, US$1.80, returning from Jr Cuzco esq Arica, 1 block from Plaza 2 de Mayo. From Yunguyo to the border (Kasani) from Jr Titicaca esq San Francisco, 1 block from Plaza de Armas, colectivos charge US$0.15 per person, mototaxis US$0.35, taxis US$1, 5 mins. From the border it is a 20-min drive to Copacabana. Colectivos and minibuses leave from just outside Bolivian

immigration, US$0.35 per person, shared taxi US$0.40, taxi US$2, 20 mins. Taxi from Kasani to La Paz US$47, 3 hrs. Entering Peru, don't take a taxi from Yunguyo–Puno without checking its reliability first, the driver may pick up an accomplice to rob passengers.

Puno–La Paz via Desaguadero

Trici-taxis carry people and their baggage around for US$0.30, but they'll probably ask for more at some point in the ride. To Desaguadero, from the Terminal Zonal in **Puno**, combis and minibuses 0600-1900, 2½ hrs, US$2. The last bus from the border to Puno leaves at 1930. Taxis between Puno and Desaguadero charge US$30, 1½ hrs. **Flores, Julsa** and **Ormeño** have a bus service direct to **Tacna**, US$7, 7 hrs, **Arequipa**, US$7-17, 7 hrs, and **Lima**, US$27-37, 24 hrs. Frequent transport from the Bolivian side (4 blocks from bridge) to **La Paz** (105 km from Desaguadero), daily 0500-2000, 2 hrs, US$1.35 minivan, US$2.70 shared taxi. See page 334 for the road from **Moquegua**. **Mily Tours**, Av Panamericana 321, run colectivos to Moquegua, US$10, 3½ hrs. There are buses from Desaguadero to **Arequipa** via Puno, eg **Julsa**, at 2000, US$7-8.50, 8 hrs, also Desaguadero to **Tacna**, via the old road, Julsa at 0730 and 2030, US$13.50, 13 hrs.

To La Paz by hydrofoil or catamaran

There are luxury services from Puno to La Paz by **Crillon Tours'** hydrofoil and **Transturin's** catamarans. Crillon's services can be booked at their office at **Arcobaleno Tours**, their head office in La Paz – see addresses, page 256, or all Puno travel agents have details. The Puno office will take care of all documentation for crossing the border into Bolivia. The main itinerary is: Puno–Copacabana by bus or hydrofoil; Copacabana–Isla del Sol–Isla de la Luna–Huatajata (Bolivia) by hydrofoil; Huatajata–La Paz by bus; 12 hrs.

More budget tours can be requested with less navigation or to other islands such as Pariti, Kalauta and/or the floating Urus-Iruitos Islands. Ask for full-day extensions from Puno to Islas del Sol and de la Luna (round trip). Visits to their

establishments can be incorporated into **Crillon's** tours with many options available. These include overnight possibilities in their Huatajata or Isla del Sol hotels. **Crillon** also has a sustainable tourism project with Urus-Iruitos people from the Río Desaguadero area which will be of interest to anyone who has visited the Urus of the Bahía de Puno.

Similar services, by more leisurely catamaran, are run by **Transturin**, whose dock is at Chúa, Bolivia. Bookings can be made through **Transturin's** offices in La Paz and Puno (see page 256 for addresses).

The main route is Puno to Copacabana by bus with stops at places of interest along the way, Copacabana to the Isla del Sol (including a land tour) and on to Chúa by catamaran, then bus to La Paz. The trip can be done in one day, or with a night on board the catamaran, moored at the Isla del Sol. It is also possible to go Puno (depart 0630)–Isla del Sol–Puno (arrive 1930). **Crillon** and **Transturin** road services between Peru and Bolivia do not involve a change of vehicle at the border.

❶ Directory

Border with Bolivia *p255*

Banks Best rates for US$ cash and bolivianos at **Farmacia Loza**, Jr Bolognesi 567, Plaza 2 de Mayo. Also *casas de cambio* on Plaza de Armas, and street changers who deal in US$, bolivianos and euro. There are a couple of *casas de cambio* on the Peruvian side of the border offering slightly lower rates than in Yunguyo, but better rates than the shops on the Bolivian side. US$ cash and soles can also be exchanged at *cambios* in Copacabana. No ATMs in Copacabana.

Consulates Bolivian Consulate, Jr Grau 339, T051-856032, near the main plaza in Yunguyo. Mon-Fri 0830-1500, for those who need a visa. Some nationalities have to pay, the fee varies depending on nationality.

Contents

Footprint features

Arequipa & around

At a glance

⊖ **Getting around** On foot, by public bus and by taxi.

◉ **Time required** 1 to 2 weeks.

☼ **Weather** The sun shines 360 days a year.

✕ **When not to go** Can be visited at any time. In the Colca Canyon it rains Jan-Apr; not the best time to see condors.

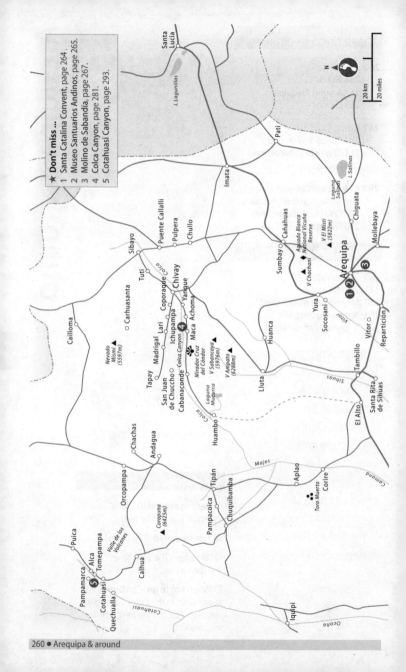

Don't miss ...
★ Santa Catalina Convent, page 264.
1 Museo Santuarios Andinos, page 265.
2 Molino de Sabandía, page 267.
3 Colca Canyon, page 281.
4 Cotahuasi Canyon, page 293.

The distinctive volcanic sillar used in the building of the city of Arequipa has given it its nickname of 'White City'. Spanish churches, mansions and the 19th-century Plaza de Armas all shine with this stonework. In contrast, the city's most famous colonial jewel, the Santa Catalina Convent, is painted in bright colours, a gorgeous little city within a city. This is only one attraction in a region of volcanoes, deep canyons and terraced valleys. The perfect cone of El Misti and its companions Chachani and Pichu-Pichu overlook Arequipa itself. Active Sabancaya and frequent earth tremors are reminders that this is a very unstable region.

Two famous canyons are within relatively easy reach. To arrive at these great gorges, you must take rough roads at high altitudes. Cotahuasi Canyon is the deepest in the world at 3354 m, but it has not yet achieved the same popularity as its neighbour, Colca. And it was only recently that the ancient peoples here, the Cabana and Collagua, had their villages and farms exposed to the gaze of tourism. There is excellent trekking and riding on the terraces of Colca, accommodation includes some of the finest four- and five-star hotels in Peru and the calendar is full of festivals. Above all, Colca also happens to be the best place in the whole world to get a close-up view of the majestic condor rising on the morning thermals. On the altiplanos of this region there are herds of alpaca and vicuña and, at the World Heritage Site of Toro Muerto, the largest field of petroglyphs in the world.

There's an individual feeling to this southwestern corner of Peru which, in part, stems from the stubborn pride of its people who have continuously attempted to gain more independence from Lima. Fellow Peruvians will jokingly refer to this region as the 'Independent Republic of Arequipa'.

Arequipa

→ *Colour map 5, C6. Phone code: 054. Population: 1 million. Altitude: 2380 m.*

The city of Arequipa stands in a beautiful valley at the foot of El Misti volcano, a snow-capped, perfect cone, 5822 m high, guarded on either side by the mountains Chachani (6057 m) and Pichu-Pichu (5669 m). The city was re-founded on 15 August 1540 by an emissary of Pizarro, but it had previously been occupied by the Aymara and the Incas. It has since grown into a magnificent city – fine Spanish buildings and many old and interesting churches built of sillar (a pearly white volcanic material almost exclusively used in the construction of Arequipa) exude an air of intellectual rigour and political passion. Among its famous sons and daughters are former President Fernando Belaúnde Terry and the Nobel Prize winner Mario Vargas Llosa (see page 680). Now, Arequipa is the main commercial centre for the south and its fiercely proud people resent the general tendency to believe that everything is run from Lima. ▶▶ *For listings, see pages 269-281.*

Ins and outs

Getting there **Aeropuerto Rodríguez Ballón** ① *7 km from town, information T054-443464*, has two desks offering hotel reservations and free transport to town and car rentals. The journey from airport to town takes 30-40 minutes depending on the traffic. Transport to the airport may be arranged when buying a ticket at a travel agency, but it's not always reliable. Local buses and combis go to about 500 m from the airport, look for ones marked 'Río Seco', 'Cono-Norte' or 'Zamacola'.

All buses use one of the two terminals south of the city centre. The older terminal is called **Terminal Terrestre** ① *Av Andrés A Cáceres s/n, Parque Industrial, opposite Inca Tops factory; 15 mins by colectivo US$0.35, or 10 mins by taxi US$1.50*, which contains a tourist office, shops and places to eat. The newer terminal is **Terrapuerto**, the other side of the car park, also with a tourist office (which makes hotel reservations, with free transfers to affiliated hotels, and its own *hostal*, T054-421375, **E** without breakfast). Theft is a serious problem in the bus station area. Take a taxi to and from the bus station and do not wander around with your belongings. No one is allowed to enter the terminal between 2100-0500, so new arrivals cannot be met by hoteliers between those hours; best not to arrive at night. ▶▶ *See Transport, page 278.*

Getting around Arequipa is a compact city with the main places of interest and hotels within a few blocks of the Plaza de Armas. Take a bus or taxi if you want to the visit the suburbs. Taxis (can be shared) charge US$5-6 from the airport to the city. Fares around town are US$0.85-1. A cheap circular tour of the city, down Calles Jerusalén and San Juan de Dios, can be made in a Vallecito bus: 1½ hours for US$0.35. Alternatively an open-top bus tours the city and nearby attractions from Portal San Agustín, Plaza de Armas daily at 0900 and 1400, US$8 for 2½ hours, US$12 for 4½ hours. **Bus Tour** ① *T054-203434, www.bustour.com.pe*, and **Tour Class Arequipa** ① *T054-220551, tourclassarequipa@hotmail.com.*

Tourist information iperú has three offices in Arequipa: the **central office** ① *in the Plaza de Armas at Portal de la Municipalidad 110, T054-223265, iperuarequipa@promperu.gob.pe, Mon-Sat 0830-1930, Sun 0830-1600*, and **Casona Santa Catalina** ① *C Santa Catalina 210, T054-221227, daily 0900-1900*. The third is at the airport, in the **arrivals hall** ① *T054-444564*, but only open when flights are arriving. All the iperú offices are helpful and have free maps of the city and the region with points of interest marked, as well as leaflets with information about the main attractions of the area. Also **Municipal tourist office** ① *Municipalidad, south side of the Plaza de Armas, No 112 (next to the iperú office), T054-211021, www.arequipa-tourism.com*; **Dircetur (regional tourist office)** ① *C Jacinto Ibáñez, 450, Parque Industrial, T054-213044, arequipa @mincetur.gob.pe, 0800-1615*; **Indecopi (tourist protection bureau)**

1 Arequipa

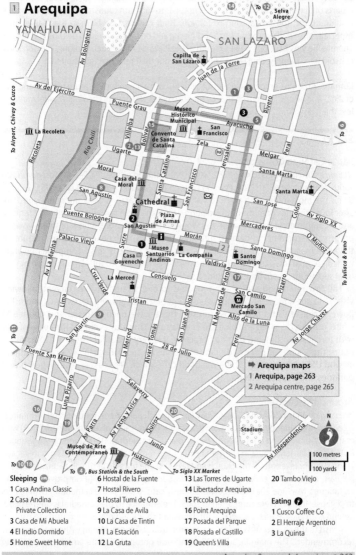

➡ **Arequipa maps**
1 Arequipa, page 263
2 Arequipa centre, page 265

Sleeping
1 Casa Andina Classic
2 Casa Andina Private Collection
3 Casa de Mi Abuela
4 El Indio Dormido
5 Home Sweet Home
6 Hostal de la Fuente
7 Hostal Rivero
8 Hostal Tumi de Oro
9 La Casa de Avila
10 La Casa de Tintin
11 La Estación
12 La Gruta
13 Las Torres de Ugarte
14 Libertador Arequipa
15 Piccola Daniela
16 Point Arequipa
17 Posada del Parque
18 Posada el Castillo
19 Queen's Villa
20 Tambo Viejo

Eating
1 Cusco Coffee Co
2 El Herraje Argentino
3 La Quinta

① *Hipólito Unanue 100-A, Urb Victoria, T054-212054, mlcornejo@indecopi.gob.pe*; and the tourist police ① *Jerusalén 315, T054-201258, open 24 hrs*, very helpful dealing with complaints or giving directions.

Security There has been an increase in street crime in Arequipa since 2006, with many reports of taxi drivers in collusion with criminals to rob both tourists and locals. Ask hotels, restaurant, etc, to book a safe taxi for you. Theft can be a problem in the market area, especially after dark, in the park at Selva Alegre and on Calles San Juan de Dios and Alvarez Thomas. Be very cautious walking south of the Plaza de Armas area at night. The police are conspicuous, friendly, courteous and efficient, but their resources are limited.

Climate Arequipa enjoys a wonderful climate, with a mean temperature before sundown of 23°C, and after sundown of 14.5°C. The sun shines 360 days of the year. Annual rainfall is less than 150 mm.

Sights

Santa Catalina Convent

① *Santa Catalina 301, T054-608282, www.santacatalina.org.pe, 0900-1700 (last admission 1600), high season 0800-1700, evening visits on Tue and Thu, 1900 until 2000, US$12.*

By far the most interesting place to visit is the Santa Catalina Convent, opened in 1970 after four centuries of mysterious isolation. This is the most remarkable sight in Arequipa and a complete contrast to what you would expect from nuns who had taken vows of poverty. The convent has been beautifully refurbished, with period furniture, pictures of the Arequipa and Cuzco schools and fully equipped kitchens. It is a complete miniature walled colonial town of over 2 ha in the middle of the city. About 450 nuns lived here in total seclusion, except for their women servants.

The few remaining nuns have retreated to one section of the convent, allowing visitors to see a maze of cobbled streets and plazas bright with geraniums and other flowers, cloisters and buttressed houses. These have been restored and painted in white, orange, deep red and blue. On Tuesday and Thursday evenings the convent is lit with torches, candles and blazing fireplaces; it is very beautiful. There are tours of 1½ hours; there's no set price and many of the guides speak English or German (a tip of around US$6 is expected). There is a good café, which sells cakes, sandwiches, baked potatoes and a special blend of tea.

Around the centre

The elegant **Plaza de Armas**, beautifully laid out with palm trees, gardens and fountain, is faced on three sides by arcaded colonial buildings (rebuilt after an earthquake in 1863) with many restaurants, and on the fourth by the massive **cathedral**. The cathedral was founded in 1612 and largely rebuilt in the 19th century. It is remarkable for having its ornate façade along the whole length of the church and takes up one full side of the plaza. Inside is a fine Belgian organ and elaborately carved wooden pulpit. Despite improved building techniques, the June 2001 earthquake famously caused one of the cathedral's twin towers to collapse. Repairs were completed in 2003. The entrance to the cathedral is on the plaza. Behind is an alley, Pasaje Catedral, with handicraft shops and places for tourists to eat.

A visit to the church and cloister of **La Compañía** at General Morán y Alvarez Thomas, is recommended. The main façade (1698) and side portal (1654) are striking examples of

② Arequipa centre

Arequipa maps
1 Arequipa, page 263
2 Arequipa centre, page 265

50 metres
50 yards

the florid Andean mestizo style. There are two adjoining cloisters now given over to attractive shops. Also of note is the **Capilla Real (Royal Chapel)** ① *to the left of the sanctuary, Mon-Fri 0900-1230, 1500-1930, Sat 1130-1230, 1500-1800, Sun 0900-1230, 1700-1800, with Mass every day at 1200, free entrance but there is a donations box by the main altar*, and its San Ignacio chapel with a beautiful polychrome cupola. The stark cloister is impressive.

The Universidad de San Agustín has an **archaeological museum** ① *Alvarez Thomas y Palacio Viejo, T054-288881, Mon-Fri 0815-1700*, with an interesting collection of ceramics and mummies. It traces the region's history from pre-Colombian times to the Republican era.

Also worth seeing, west of the plaza, are the recently restored church of **San Agustín** ① *San Agustín y Sucre, Mon-Sat 0800-1200, 1700-1900*, and **La Casona Chávez de la Rosa** ① *San Agustín 104*, part of the Universidad San Agustín, which holds art and photography exhibitions.

Firmly established as one of the major sites in Arequipa, **Museo Santuarios Andinos** ① *La Merced 110, T054-215013, www.ucsm.edu.pe/santury, Mon-Sat 0900-1800, Sun 0900-1500, US$6, discount with student card*, contains the frozen mummies found on Ampato volcano. The mummy known as 'Juanita' is particularly fascinating (see page 283). From January to April, Juanita is often jetting round the world, and is replaced by other child sacrifices unearthed in the mountains. Admission to the museum includes a 20-minute video of the discovery in English, followed by an hour-long guided tour in English, French, German, Italian or Spanish (tip the guide).

Museo de Arte Textil ① *Patio del Ekeko, Mercaderes 141, Mon-Sat 1000-2030, Sun 1000-1530*, has an interesting collection of textiles and shows short documentaries about Arequipa. The 16th-century church of **San Francisco** also has a convent and

library ⓘ *Zela 103, US$1.65*, and opposite is the interesting **Museo Histórico Municipal** ⓘ *Plaza San Francisco 407, Mon-Fri 0900-1700, US$0.70*, with much war memorabilia and impressive photos of the city in the aftermath of several notable earthquakes.

Arequipa is said to have the best preserved colonial architecture in Peru, outside Cuzco. Several fine seignorial houses with large carved tympanums over the entrances can be seen in the city centre. They are one-storey structures, and so have mostly withstood the earthquakes that regularly pound this city. They are distinguished by their small patios with no galleries, flat roofs and small windows, disguised by superimposed lintels or heavy grilles. Since many of these buildings are now banks and have heavy security it can sometimes be difficult to get inside for a good look around.

One of the best examples is the 18th-century **Casa Tristán del Pozo**, better known as the **Gibbs-Ricketts house** ⓘ *San Francisco 108, Mon-Sat 0915-1245, 1600-1800*, with its fine portal and puma-head waterspouts. It is now the main office of Banco Continental. Other good examples are the **Casa del Moral**, or **Williams House** ⓘ *C Moral 318 y Bolívar, Mon-Sat 0900-1700, Sun 0900-1300, US$1.80 or US$1 for students*, with a museum, in the Banco Industrial. **Casa de la Moneda** ⓘ *Ugarte y Villalba*, is behind Santa Catalina Convent and has now been converted to a hotel, the **Casa Andina Private Collection**. **Casa Goyeneche** ⓘ *La Merced 201 y Palacio Viejo*, is now an office of the Banco Central de la Reserva. Ask to see the courtyard and fine period rooms. In the next block south is the early 17th-century church of **La Merced** ⓘ *La Merced 303*.

The church of **Santo Domingo** ⓘ *Santo Domingo y Piérola*, dates from the 17th century. In its fine door, an indigenous face can be seen amid the flowers and grapes. The central **San Camilo market** ⓘ *between Perú, San Camilo, Piérola and Alto de la Luna*, is worth visiting.

South of the centre in the old railway station, is the **Museo de Arte Contemporáneo** ⓘ *Tacna y Arica 201, T054-221068, Tue-Fri 1000-1700, Sat-Sun 1000-1400, US$1*. This new museum is dedicated to painting and photography from 1990 onwards. The building is surrounded by gardens and has a Sunday market. Also in this area, east of the railway station, is the Siglo XX market, worth visiting.

La Recoleta
ⓘ *Jr Recoleta 117, T054-270966, Mon-Sat 0900-1200, 1500-1700, US$1.50.*
La Recoleta, a Franciscan monastery built in 1647, stands on the other side of the river. A seldom-visited hidden gem, it contains a variety of exhibits. As well as several cloisters and a religious art museum, the pre-Columbian art museum contains ceramics and textiles produced by cultures who inhabited the Arequipa area. Most impressive however, are the museum of Amazon exploration, featuring many artefacts as well as photos of early Franciscan missionaries in the Amazon, and the library, containing many antique books. The library is available for supervised visits at 45 minutes past the hour for 15 minutes when the museum is open. In the other rooms expect to go around turning the light switches on and off as you go. It is well worth visiting.

San Lázaro
The oldest district in the city is San Lázaro, a collection of tiny climbing streets and houses quite close to the Hotel Libertador, where you can find the ancient **Capilla de San Lázaro**. At **Selva Alegre** there is a shady park in front of the **Hotel Libertador**, which is within easy walking distance of all the famous churches and main plaza (but see Security, page 264).

Northwest

Some 2 km northwest of the city (cross Puente Grau and turn right along Avenida Bolognesi) is the district of **Yanahuara**, where there is a 1750 mestizo-style church (opens 1500), with a magnificent churrigueresque façade, all in sillar. The church stands on a plaza, at the end of which is a mirador and a fine view of El Misti with the city at its feet. There's live music at **Peña El Moro**, on Parque Principal. A score of *picanterías* specialize in piquant foods such as *rocoto relleno* (hot stuffed peppers), *cuy chactado* (seared guinea-pig), *papas con ocopa* (boiled potatoes with a hot spicy yellow sauce) and *adobo* (pork stew). The **Museo Pre-Inca de Chiribaya** ① *Miguel Grau 402, www.museochiribaya.org, Mon-Sat 0830-1900, Sun 0900-1500,* has a good collection of vessels and well-preserved textiles from before the Incas arrived in Arequipa.

In the hillside suburb of **Cayma**, 3 km northwest of the city, is a delightful 18th-century church ① *open until 1700,* and many old buildings associated with Bolívar and Garcilaso de la Vega. Many local buses go to Cayma.

Beyond the airport, at **Las Canteras de Sillar**, you can see the quarries where the sillar blocks are cut for buildings in the city. They are worth a brief visit if passing, but not a special detour.

Southeast

Most of the attractions in the southeast can be reached on an open top bus tour, see Getting around, above. Entry fees are not included in the tour price. **Tingo** has a very small lake and three swimming pools. You should visit on Sunday for local food such as *anticuchos* and *buñuelos*. (Take bus No 7, US$0.35.) Three kilometres past Tingo, beside the Sabandía river on the Huasacache road, is **La Mansión del Fundador** ① *0900-1700, US$2.50,* with a cafeteria and bar. Originally built by the founder of Arequipa, Don Garcí Manuel de Carbajal, in 1540, it has been open to the public since 1897 and restored as a museum with original furnishings and paintings. Nearby is the **Mirador Sachaca** ① *US$0.35; take a bus marked 'Sachaca' from C La Merced.* It has fine panoramic views, best between 0630 and 0730 before the smog obscures the view. In the district of Sachaca, 4 km from the centre, is the **Palacio Goyeneche**.

Molino de Sabandía ① *US$1.50, ring the bell for admission,* is 8 km from Arequipa. A round trip by taxi costs US$6. This was the first stone mill in the area, built in 1621. It has been fully restored and the guardian diverts water to run the grinding stones when visitors arrive. The well-kept grounds have old willow trees and the surrounding countryside is pleasant; a worthwhile trip. Adjoining Sabandía is **Yumina** ① *tourist fee of US$6, which may be asked for on the bus to Chivay,* with many Inca terraces that are still in use. Between Sabandía and Arequipa is **Paucarpata**, with an old church and views of terraces, El Misti and Chachani. The **thermal baths of Jesús** ① *0500-1230,* are 30 minutes by car, on the slopes of Pichu-Pichu.

Yura → *Colour map 5, C6.*

Yura, is a pleasant town, 29 km from Arequipa in a small, interesting valley on the west slopes of Chachani. It is popular with Arequipeños for its **thermal baths** ① *Tue-Sat until 1500, US$2.* A bus leaves from Calle San Juan de Dios in Arequipa, every three hours (US$0.40); alight on the main road by the Yura Tourist Hotel, which serves meals, and then walk down to the river. The first set of baths contains four small pools that are not suitable for swimming; follow the river to the next one, which is bigger. Note that the water is not very hot. To return to Arequipa, catch a colectivo on the main road by the hotel.

El Misti and Chachani
At 5822 m, **El Misti** volcano offers a relatively straightforward opportunity to scale a high peak. There are three routes for climbing the volcano; all take two days.

The northeast route starts from the Aguada Blanca reservoir, reached by 4WD, from where a four-hour hike takes you to the Monte Blanco camp at 4800 m. Then it's a five- to six-hour ascent to the top. Two hours takes you back down to the trail.

The southwest route involves taking a 4WD vehicle to the trailhead at Pastores (3400 m), followed by a hike of five to six hours to a camp at 4700 m. A five-hour climb takes you to the summit, before a three-hour descent to the trail.

A southern route (Grau) also starts at 3400 m, with a camp at 4610 m, followed by a five-hour hike to the summit and a two-hour descent.

In all cases contact an experienced guiding agency in Arequipa. Be prepared for early starts and climbing on loose scree. Take plenty of water, food and protection against the weather. Favoured months are May to September.

In recent years climbing the peak of **Chachani**, just to the northwest of El Misti, has also become popular. In the January to April rainy season, when El Misti has a full covering of snow, they say he is wearing his poncho. But in recent years the sight of snow crowning El Misti's summit has become increasingly rare, especially in the drier winter months. Chachani, in contrast, still retains its icy covering, though this too is fast disappearing. The fact that Chachani tops the magic 6000-m mark (6057 m) has led to a growing number of climbers on the mountain.

Remember that both summits are at very high altitude and that this, combined with climbing on scree and sometimes ice, makes it hard going for the untrained; take your time to acclimatize. Proper equipment (crampons, walking pick, etc) is required on Chachani and reports of armed hold-ups make it inadvisable for you to climb alone; join a group or take a guide. Further information is available from travel agencies and professional guides. For a description of **Nevado Mismi**, see page 283.

Laguna Salinas
In this area, it is possible to see many of the specialities that inhabit the arid scrub and Polylepis woodland of the Andean west slope. The best road for birdwatching is the one heading east of Arequipa to Laguna Salinas. This large salt lake regularly holds three species of flamingo: Chilean, Andean and puna. It is also a good place to see Andean avocet and puna plover. In the dry season, you may have to hike out towards the middle of the lake, but do not forget your sunglasses as the glare from the salt is fierce. Between Arequipa and Laguna Salinas, birding the Polylepis-clad slopes and arid scrub can reveal various earthcreepers and *canasteros* not found elsewhere; this is one of only two places for tamarugo conebill.

For Sleeping and Eating price codes and other relevant information, see pages 38-44.

⊙ Sleeping

Arequipa *p262, maps p263 and p265*
When arriving by bus, do not believe taxi drivers who say the hotel of your choice is closed or full. This applies to many of the popular hotels; drivers will try to take you to another hotel to get themselves commission. Ring the door bell and check for yourself.

LL-L Casa Andina Private Collection, Ugarte 403, T054-226907, www.casa-andina.com. Luxury hotel in a restored 18th-century mansion and former Casa de la Moneda. 5 large suites in colonial building, 36 rooms in modern extension off 2nd courtyard. Gourmet restaurant, room service, business centre, Wi-Fi, roof terrace with views.

LL-L Libertador Arequipa Hotel, Plaza Bolívar, Urb Selva Alegre, T054-215110, www.libertador.com.pe. Safe, large comfortable rooms, good service, swimming pool (cold), gardens, good meals, pub-style bar, cocktail lounge, squash court.

L-A Sonesta Posadas del Inca, Portal de Flores 116, T054-215530, www.sonesta peru.com. On the Plaza de Armas, all the services associated with this chain, **Inkafé café and bar** (daily 0530-2230) with good views, restaurant, tiny outdoor pool, business centre with internet.

AL-B Casa Andina Classic, C Jerusalén 603, T054-202070, www.casa-andina.com. Part of the attractive Casa Andina chain, with breakfast, comfortable and colourful, central, modern, good restaurant, safe, cable TV, phones, friendly staff, car parking.

A Los Tambos, Puente Bolognesi 129, T054-600900, www.lostambos.com.pe. Modern hotel, fireplace in lobby, concierge, elevator, Wi-Fi.

A-C Queen's Villa, Luna Pizarro 512, Vallecito, T054-235233, www.queensvillahotel.com. Variety of rooms and suites overlooking pool of garden, smoking and non-smoking, Wi-Fi, minibar, restaurant, safe, parking, laundry.

B Casa de Mi Abuela, Jerusalén 606, T054-241206, www.lacasademiabuela.com. Very clean, friendly, safe, hot water, laundry, cable TV, swimming pool, rooms at the back are quieter and overlook the garden, **E** without bath, self-catering if desired, English spoken, internet access US$3 per hr, Wi-Fi, mini bar, games room, laundry, tours and transport organized in own agency (**Giardino**, T054-221345, www.giardino tours.com), which has good information, small library of European books. Breakfast or evening snacks on patio or in beautiful garden, parking, full restaurant behind the pool for evening meals, lots of tour groups. Recommended.

B La Gruta, La Gruta 304, Selva Alegra, T054-224631, www.lagrutahotel.com. Nice environment, some rooms have fireplace, minibar, Wi-Fi, breakfast included, cable TV.

B Los Balcones de Moral y Santa Catalina, Moral 217, T054-201291, www.balcones hotel.com. Convenient, 1 block from Plaza de Armas and close to Santa Catalina, large rooms, comfortable beds, with bath, hot water, laundry, café, tourist information.

B-C La Casa de Margott, Jerusalén 304, T054-229517, www.lacasademargott.com. Bright with a massive palm tree in patio, spacious, convenient, small bar/café, cable TV, phone, security box, Wi-Fi, renovated 2010. Recommended.

B-C Posada el Castillo, Pasaje Campos 105, Vallecito, T054-201828, www.posadael castillo.com. Dutch-owned hotel in colonial style 15 mins' walk south of Plaza de Armas. Variety of rooms and suites, some with balcony and view of El Misti, free internet, TV, pool, wonderful breakfast, expensive laundry. Parking for 2 vehicles. Recommended.

C Casablanca Hostal, Puente Bolognesi 104, a few m from the Plaza de Armas, T054-221327, www.casablancahostal.com. Super-stylish hostal, lovely minimalist rooms in a colonial building. Ambient lighting,

8 rooms with private bath (hot water), internet, laundry, tourist information.

C Hostal de la Fuente, Urb Campiña Paisajista D-14A, San Lázaro, T054-203996, delafuente_hostal@hotmail.com. In a residential district some distance east of the Plaza de Armas, with breakfast, family-style, welcoming, comfortable rooms, with bath, 24-hr hot water, cable TV, internet, laundry, café, bar, safe boxes.

C Hostal Solar, Ayacucho 108, Cercado, T/F054-241793, hostalsolar.com. Nice colonial building, TV, bath, hot water, includes good breakfast served in nice patio, sun lounge on roof, Wi-Fi, luggage store, book exchange, very secure, quiet. Warmly recommended.

C La Casa de Avila, San Martín 116, T054 213177, www.casadeavila.com. All rooms with bathroom and hot water, price includes good breakfast, spacious, sunny garden, guests' kitchen, internet, can arrange airport/bus station pickup, Spanish courses (which are recommended) and other activities.

C La Casa de Tintin, Urbanización San Isidro F1, Vallecito, T054-284700, www.hotel tintin.com. 15 mins' walk, 5 mins by taxi from the Plaza de Armas. Belgian/Peruvian owned, hot water, cable TV, garden, terrace, sauna, laundry service, restaurant, café, bar, internet, mountain bike hire, pleasant and comfortable, breakfast included. Recommended.

D Casa de Melgar, Melgar 108, T/F054-222459, www.lacasademelgar.com. Delightful 18th-century building, excellent rooms, all different, with bathroom, hot water all day (solar panel), safe, clean, friendly, nice courtyard, good breakfast in café open in the morning and 1730-2100, book exchange, luggage store. Can arrange good taxi tours with driver, Angel. Recommended.

D Las Torres de Ugarte, Ugarte 401-A, T/F054-283532, hostaltorresdeugarte@star.com.pe. Round the corner from Santa Catalina convent, some rooms bungalow-style in colonial part at the back, hot water, cable TV, roof terrace, laundry service, reflexology, parking, safe, luggage store, helpful staff, price includes breakfast served in a sunny room.

D-E La Estación, Loreto 410, Umacollo, T054-273852. Unusual dormitory accommodation in 2 train carriages, includes breakfast, hot water, restaurant next door, friendly, clean and fresh. 10 mins' walk from Plaza, ask directions for '*El Ovalo del Vallecito*', English spoken.

D-E Lula's B&B, in Cayma, T054-272517, T959-992995, www.bbaqpe.com. Same owner as **Ari Quipay** language school, Lula speaks English, German and French, discount for long stay, with breakfast and airport/bus terminal pick-up, modern, charming, free internet, quiet, meals available.

D-G Tambo Viejo, Av Malecón Socabaya 107, IV Centenario, 5 blocks south of the plaza near the rail station, T054-288195, www.tamboviejo.com. Rooms vary and range from double with bath to dormitory, quiet, attractive, clean, good facilities: walled garden, hot water, breakfast extra, vegetarian, English and Dutch spoken, laundry service, cable TV, safe deposit, coffee shop, bar, book exchange (2 for 1), money changed, tourist information for guests, internet, phone for international calls, bike rental, luggage store extra, tours and volcano climbs arranged. For a small fee, you can use the facilities if passing through. Telephone the hostel and they will pick you up free of charge from 0500-2100 from the bus terminal; US$5 from the airport.

E Colonial House Inn, Puente Grau 114, T/F054-223533, colonialhouseinn@hotmail. com. Hot water, quieter rooms at the back, laundry facilities and service, kitchen facilities, roof terrace, good choice of breakfasts, owners speak English.

E Home Sweet Home, Rivero 509A, Cercado, T054-405982, www.homesweethome-peru.com. Run by María and daughter Cathy, who runs a travel agency and speaks Spanish, English, Italian, French, very helpful, warm and inviting atmosphere, substantial fresh breakfast included. Private or shared bath, hot water all day, simple rooms.

E Hospedaje El Caminante Class, Santa Catalina 207-A, 2nd floor, T054-203444, www.elcaminanteclass.com. With bathroom, cheaper without, hot water, TV, clean, laundry service and facilities, sun terrace, very helpful owners. Recommended.

E Hostal La Reyna, Zela 209, T054-286578, hostalreyna@yahoo.com. With or without bath, 2 more expensive rooms at the top of the house (very good), hot water 24 hrs, clean, the daughter speaks English, laundry, breakfast for US$1.15, rooftop seating, can arrange Spanish classes, will store luggage and arrange trips to the Colca Canyon and volcanoes, especially Misti and Chachani. Opposite Arequipa nightlife and popular with young backpackers so can be noisy at night.

E Hostal Regis, Ugarte 202, T054-226111, regis@gnet.com.pe. Colonial house, French-style interior, clean, hot water all day, use of fridge and laundry facilities, sun terrace with good views, street-facing rooms with sound-proofed windows, safe deposit, luggage store, video rental, guidebooks and English-language magazines for reference, tours arranged, poor breakfast.

E Hostal Tumi de Oro, San Agustín 311A, 2½ blocks from the Plaza de Armas, T/F054-281319. With bathroom, French and English spoken, hot water, roof terrace, book exchange, tea/coffee facilities, safe.

E La Posada del Cacique, Puente Grau 219 and at Jerusalén 404, T054-202170, posadadel cacique@yahoo.es. At Puente Grau is an old house with tall ceilings, remodelled in 2008, teeny patio, sun terrace, friendly, good hot water, English spoken, family atmosphere, **F** without bath, also dorm accommodation, safe storage facilities, laundry service, will pick up from airport and bus terminal. Jerusalén 404 has a roof terrace and bar, café/restaurant, Wi-Fi. Recommended.

E La Posada del Virrey, Puente Grau 103, T054-224050, www.usuarios.multimania.es/posadavirrey/. Spacious rooms with and without bath (**F**), dorms (**G** pp), hot water, kitchen and laundry facilities, helpful, café-bar, small patio; free internet for guests.

E Lluvia de Oro, Jerusalén 308, T054-214252, lluvia_de_oro@hotmail.com. Cheaper without bath, English-speaking, breakfast US$2, good views, laundry service, friendly,

beautiful colonial house with cheery, colourful decor.

E Los Andes Bed & Breakfast, La Merced 123, T054-330015, losandesaqp@hotmail.com. A good-value option just off the Plaza de Armas with free internet, kitchen use, breakfast included, hot water, 2 shared TV rooms, cheaper rates for long stays. Recommended.

E-F Hostal Rivero, Rivero 420, T054-229266, hostal_rivero@yahoo.com. Cheaper with shared bath, hot water, cable TV extra, medical assistance, laundry facilities, very helpful, good value.

E-F Hostal Santa Catalina, Santa Catalina 500, T054-243705, www.hostalsantacatalinaperu. com. Comfy rooms arranged around a court-yard, with or without bath, roof terrace with great views, charming and helpful staff. Can arrange trips and accommodation in other cities.

E-F Piccola Daniela, Bolívar 400, T054-405727, piccoladanielaaqp@hotmail.com. Includes breakfast, cheaper without bath, good value, cable TV, hot water, tiny patio, no English.

E-F pp The Point Arequipa, Lima 515, Vallecito, T054-286920, www.thepointhostels.com. In a relaxed suburb, free airport/bus station pickup. Nice building with big garden, private or shared rooms, great place to meet other travellers, lots of services (free internet, laundry, DVDs) and a big party pad. Other **Points** are located in Lima, Cuzco and Máncora.

F pp El Indio Dormido, Av Andrés Avelino Cáceres B-9, T054-427401, the_sleeping_indian@yahoo.com. Close to bus terminal, free transport to centre, some rooms with bath, **E**, TV, clean, very helpful.

F La Casita de Ugarte, Ugarte 212, T054-204363. English/Peruvian-run, large basic rooms, colonial building, good value.

F La Fiorentina, Puente Grau 110, T054-202571, lafiorentinahostal@hotmail.com. Cheaper without bath, hot water, comfortable, family atmosphere, tours arranged, laundry facilities, café bar and shared TV room.

F Posada del Parque, Deán Valdivia 238-A, T054-212275. Opposite Parque de la Madre, comfortable, private or shared rooms, hot water, Wi-Fi, cable TV, breakfast on roof terrace.

🍴 Eating

Arequipa *p262, maps p263 and p265*
Several restaurants overlook the Plaza de Armas; their staff may pounce on you good-naturedly as you pass. For typical Arequipeño food, head to Av Arancota, in the Tingo District, by the Río Chili. Typical food is also available at the San Camilo market. A good local speciality is Mejía cheese. You should also try the *queso helado*, which is frozen fresh milk mixed with sugar and a sprinkling of cinnamon. The local chocolate is excellent: La Ibérica, in Patio del Ekeko, Mercaderes 141, is top quality, but expensive. The toffee and the fruit drinks called *papayada* and *tumbada* are also local specialities in the market and restaurants.
🍴🍴🍴 La Quinta, Jerusalén 522. Excellent local food, large portions but limited menu, some veggie dishes, attentive service, quiet garden, aimed primarily at the tourist market. Also has a *peña*, mainly at weekends, US$1.50 cover.
🍴🍴🍴 Tradición Arequipeña, Av Dolores 111, Paucarpata, T054-246467. Restaurant serving excellent food, popular with tourists and locals alike, also dance hall. There are many other restaurants and discos on this avenue, some distance from the centre.
🍴🍴🍴 Wayrana, Santa Catalina 200, T054-285641. Traditional Arequipeño dishes with a modern twist, specializing in seafood, *cuy* and alpaca. Beautiful colonial building with stylish interior design, worth a visit.
🍴🍴🍴 Zig Zag, Zela 210, T054-206020. In a colonial house, European (including Swiss) and local dishes, excellent meats include ostrich and alpaca, top class. Advance booking essential.
🍴🍴🍴-🍴 El Cebillano, C Misti 110, Yanahuara, T054-484866. Excellent *cebichería* in Yanahuara suburb, with good seafood, attentive service and long queues at weekends.
🍴🍴 Ary Quepay, Jerusalén 502. Open 1000-2400. Excellent local meat and vegetarian dishes, very touristy, but fun.
🍴🍴 Café-Restaurante Bóveda San Agustín, Portal San Agustín 127-129, T054-243596. Attractive, opens at 0700 for good-value

breakfasts, lunches and evening specials. Downstairs it has a bar-type atmosphere, and upstairs is a balcony overlooking the Plaza de Armas.
🍴🍴 Crepísimo, Santa Catalina 208, T054-206620, www.crepisimo.com. Excellent variety of sweet and savoury crepes, good-value set lunch, also snacks, cocktails, great coffee. Magazines and board games.
🍴🍴 El Turko II, San Francisco 315. Excellent Turkish, local and international food, has a lovely courtyard. Recommended.
🍴🍴 Qochamama, Ugarte 300 2nd floor, T054-231407. 'Pre-inka sea cuisine' inspired by the traditional Peruvian cooking style using hot stones: the marine branch of Soccollay. More of a bar in the evenings with an interesting mixture of cocktails including the 'macho' with hot pepper-flavoured pisco.
🍴🍴 Sonccollay, Portal de San Agustín 149, T054-959 673517. Serving 'Inca and Pre-Inca' dishes, this restaurant gives a new twist to 'traditional' food. Stone-cooked alpaca steaks and meats are a speciality, ask to see the kitchen to see how the meat is roasted on huge stone slabs. Hosted by an entertaining owner, plenty of home-made *chicha* and very generous servings of pisco sour.
🍴🍴-🍴 El Asador, Zela 201, opposite Zig Zag, T054-223414. Good value for alpaca steaks, *parrillada*, pleasant atmosphere, good music.
🍴 Bruno Pizzeria, Jerusalén with Santa Marta/San Francisco, Delivery T054-4420. Pizzas and pastas with good lunch and dinner menus.
🍴 El Herraje Argentino, Puente Bolognesi 127. Argentine restaurant, *parrilladas* and grilled chicken. Very good value menus with salad bar included.
🍴 El Turko, San Francisco 216-A. Open 0700-2200. Kebabs, coffee, breakfasts, good sandwiches. El Turko III is at the airport.
🍴 Fez, San Francisco 229 and Istanbul, San Francisco 231-A. More upmarket restaurants run by the same company as El Turko. Delicious falafel, Middle Eastern fast food and coffee, friendly, courtyard.
🍴 Lakshmivan, Jerusalén 402, T054-228768. Vegetarian wholefood restaurant, set

breakfast, lunch and dinner options for under US$2, pleasant courtyard, good value and healthy food, but slow service.

Mandala, Jerusalén 207, T054-229974, mandala26@correoweb.com. Good-value vegetarian, breakfast, 3 set menus for lunch, buffet, dinner, friendly staff. Recommended.

Pizza Golosa, Portal San Agustín 13, T054-772177. You can make up your own pizza, also has a delivery service.

Ras El Hanout y los 40 Sabores, San Francisco 227, T054-227779, raselhanout40@hotmail.com. Morrocan 'resto-lounge'. Breakfast, tagines, keftas, salads, juices, world music.

Cafés

Antojitos de Arequipa, Jerusalén 120, Gen Morán 125-A, Portal Flores 144. An Arequipeño institution, Antojitos sells traditional sweets from Arequipa. They also serve a decent lunch and dinner menu in their restaurant next door

Café Capriccio, Mercaderes 121. Not that cheap, but excellent coffee, cakes, etc. Very popular with local business people, free internet upstairs in lounge for customers, as well as Wi-Fi. Recommended.

Café Manolo, Mercaderes 107 and 113. Great cakes and coffee, also cheap lunches, pastas, sandwiches and juices.

Café Valenzuela, Morán 114. Fantastic coffee, locals' favourite. Also sells coffee beans and ground coffee.

Cusco Coffee Co, La Merced 135 with Palacio Viejo, T054-281152. Good variety of coffees to drink in or take away. Great cakes, average sandwiches, comfy sofas, modern coffee shop atmosphere, Wi-Fi.

La Canasta, Jerusalén 115. Bakes excellent baguettes twice daily, also serves breakfast and delicious apple and brazil nut pastries.

Salchichería Alemana, San Francisco 137. More sausages than you can wave a knackwurst at, plus some very good *empanadas* and sandwiches. Good value and popular.

Suri Cafetería, Portal de Flores 128, T054-237202. The best chicken pie in Arequipa and more. Great for a cheap, quick snack while you look out onto the Plaza.

Bars and clubs

Arequipa *p262, map p265*
There are many good dancing spots on Av Ejército in Yanahuara, but most night-owls head to Av Dolores, a short taxi ride away (US$1), which can get rowdy, or the popular San Francisco, packed full of bars and clubs.

Casona Forum, San Francisco 317, www.forumrockcafe.com. Opens 1800 everyday. Huge complex hosting the **Retro Bar**, **Zero** pool bar, **Forum Rock café**, **Chill Out** sofa bar on the top floor and swanky **Terrasse** lounge. With live music, underground club with huge imitation waterfall and top-floor classy restaurant with great views of the city.

Déjà Vu, San Francisco 319-B. Open 2000-2400. Café, restaurant and bar, good food, relaxing terrace, DJ evenings and live music, shows movies, has rooftop bar and often live music, weekend drink specials, popular. Recommended.

Farren's, Pasaje La Catedral. Friendly Irish bar with local and imported (expensive) beer. Pool table.

Las Quenas, Santa Catalina 302. T054-281115, call to reserve. Mon-Fri 2100. For *peña* music, traditional food and live show.

Festivals and events

Arequipa *p262, maps p263 and p265*
6 Jan El Día de los Reyes in the district of Tiabaya is traditionally celebrated by shaking the fruit from pear trees.

10 Jan Sor Ana de Los Angeles y Monteagudo, a festival for the patron saint of Santa Catalina monastery.

2-3 Feb Fiesta de la Virgen de la Candelaria is celebrated in the churches of Cayma, Characato, Chiguata and Chapi with masses, processions of the Virgin through the streets, and fireworks.

3 Mar Fiesta de La Amargura is a movable feast in Paucarpata, during which the Passion Play is enacted in the main plaza. **Domingo de Cuaresma**, in the district of Tiabaya, is also dedicated to Jesus Christ. Residents gather in the plaza and carry the cross from there up to a nearby hilltop, crossing the Río Chili.

Mar/Apr Semana Santa celebrations in Arequipa are carried out Sevillano style, with the townsfolk turned out in traditional mourning dress. There are huge processions every night, culminating in the burning of an effigy of Judas on **Easter Sun** in the main plazas of Cayma and Yanahuara, and the reading of his 'will', containing criticisms of the city authorities. Afterwards, people retire to the *picanterías* to partake of a little Adobo a la Antaño with some *pan de tres puntas*.

May Known as the **Month of the Crosses**, during May there are ceremonies on hilltops throughout the city.

1 May Fiesta de la Virgen de Chapi is a great pilgrimage to the sanctuary of Chapi and one of the most important religious ceremonies in the region.

15 May The popular fiesta of **San Isidro Labrador** takes place in Sachaca, Chuquibamba and other towns and villages in the valley, and lasts for 7 days.

13 Jun A remembrance of **San Antonio de Padua**, patron of hopeless cases, is held in the churches of Tingo Grande and San Francisco, among others.

29 Jun In Yanahuara, the **Fiesta de San Juan**, the local patron saint, is held with mass and fireworks.

6-31 Aug Fiesta Artesanal del Fundo del Fierro, a sale and exhibition of artesanía from all parts of Peru, taking place near Plaza San Francisco. At the same time, **6-17 Aug** is the celebration of the **city's anniversary**; various events are held, including music, dancing and exhibitions. On the eve of the actual day, the 15th, there is a splendid firework display in the Plaza de Armas and a decorated float parade. For a short time it feels like Rio Carnival with music everywhere, no space to move and parties continuing until morning. There is also a mass ascent of El Misti from the Plaza de Armas. It is virtually impossible to find a hotel room during the celebrations.

30 Aug El Día de Santa Rosa is celebrated in the churches of Tomilla, Cayma and Huancarqui in the Majes Valley.

Nov In Arequipa, this is the month of the traditional **guaguas**, which are *bizcochos* (sponge cakes) filled with *manjar* (caramel made from boiling milk and sugar).

O Shopping

Arequipa *p262, maps p263 and p265*
Alpaca goods, textiles and clothing
Arequipa is an excellent place to buy top-quality alpaca knitwear.

Alpaca 21, Jerusalén 115, of 125, T054-213425. Recommended.

Colca Trading Company, Santa Catalina 300B, T054-242088 (Lima T01-254 1885), info@peru naturtex.com. Sells a wide variety of naturally coloured ecological and organic cotton and alpaca clothing for both adults and children.

Kuna by Alpaca 111, in the Patio del Ekeko (see below), Casona Santa Catalina, Santa Catalina 210, Local 1-2, T054-282485, in the **Hotel Libertador**, T054-223303, www.kuna.com.pe. Recommended for high-quality alpaca and wool products. See also www.incalpaca.com.

Michell y Cia, Juan de la Torre 101, T054-202525, www.michell.com.pe. Factory outlet, excellent place for alpaca yarn, also a clearance room for baby and adult alpaca yarn. They also sell other types of wool. Alpaca garments for sale. 1920s machinery on display. Michell has another outlet, **Sol Alpaca**, Santa Catalina 210 (inside La Casona Santa Catalina) T054-221454, with branches in Lima and Cuzco, for their latest lines in alpaca and pima cotton clothing. Also part of the Michell Group is **Mundo Alpaca**, Alameda San Lorenzo 101, T054-202525, www.mundoalpaca.com.pe. Helpful staff, informative on all aspects of alpaca fibre production, good quality.

Millma's Baby Alpaca, Pasaje Catedral 117, T054-205134, millmas@hotmail.com. 100% baby alpaca goods, run by Peruvian family, high quality, beautiful designs, good prices.

Ancient apparel

Four thousand years before the Spanish conquistadores set foot on Peruvian soil, the indigenous peoples excelled at the textile arts. Cotton was cultivated on the arid coast but, up on the high Andean plain, there was a ready supply of fibre in the shape of the native camelids – llamas, alpacas, vicuñas and guanacos. Alpacas and llamas were domesticated as early as 4000 BC and the wild camelids (guanacos and vicuñas) were used as clothing even further back, by hunters who roamed the bleak, high Andean plateau. By 1500-1000 BC llamas were being used for ritual burial offerings, indicating their prestige.

Camelid fibre is easy to spin and dye and allowed the ancient weavers to develop extraordinarily fine spinning techniques. The pre-Columbian peoples prized the silky soft fibre of the alpaca, in particular. Living at altitudes of 4000 m, where temperatures can drop to -15°C, these animals have developed a coat that not only has thermal properties but is also soft and resistant. Production of alpaca fibre remains low because more than 75% of Peru's alpacas are in the hands of small breeders and peasant communities who still herd and manage their animals in much the same way as their ancestors.

Patio del Ekeko, Centros Comerciales Turísticos SA, C Mercaderes 139-141, T054-215861, www.patiodelekeko.com. A shopping, entertainment and cultural centre. Shops include **Kuna** for alpaca and vicuña, **Ilaria** for fine jewellery and silverware, **La Ibérica** for chocolates and **Artesanías del Ekeko**. There is also a restaurant, the **Café del Ekeko**, which has internet, as well as sandwiches, desserts, coffee and a bar (**Centro del Pisco**), and an art gallery.
Sombrería El Triunfino, N de Piérola 329-331. A good selection of hats, but pricey.

Bookshops

For international magazines, look along San Francisco, between Mercaderes and San José.
Librería El Lector, San Francisco 221. Wide selection, including Peruvian authors and Footprint titles, book exchange in various languages (2 for 1).
Librerías San Francisco has branches at Portal de Flores 138, San Francisco 102-106 and 133-135. Books on Arequipa and Peru, some in English.
SBS Book Service, San Francisco 125, T054-205317. Good selection of travel books, etc.

Handicrafts

Arequipa is noted for its leather work. The main street of saddlers and leather workers is Puente Bolognesi. The handicraft shop in the old prison opposite San Francisco is particularly good for bags. There are markets that are good for general handicrafts. The covered market opposite the Teatro Municipal on Mercaderes is recommended for knitted goods, bags, etc. Also worth a try is the market around Valdivia and Nicolas de Piérola. The large **Fundo del Fierro** handicraft market behind the old prison on Plaza San Francisco is also worth a visit. Shop 14 sells alpaca wool handicrafts from Callalli in the Colca Canyon.

Supermarkets

El Super, on the south side of Plaza del Armas. Buy supplies for trekking here.

▲▲ Activities and tours

Arequipa *p262, maps p263 and p265*
Climbing and trekking
International recommendations are for a 300 m per day maximum altitude gain. Be wary of agencies wanting to sell you trips with very fast ascents.

Recommended climbing guides include **Julver Castro** at **Mountrekk**, T054-601833, julver_mountrekk@hotmail.com, an experienced guide and full of energy.
Carlos Zárate Aventuras, Santa Catalina 204, of 3, T054-202461/263107, www.zarate adventures.com. Run by Carlos Zárate of the Mountaineering Club of Peru. Good family-run business that always works with qualified mountain guides. A specialist in mountaineering and exploring, with a great deal of information and advice and some equipment rental. Carlos also runs trips to the source of the Amazon, Nevado Mismi, as well as trekking in the Cotahuasi canyon and climbing tougher peaks such as Coropuna.
Colca Trek, Jerusalén 401 B, T054-206217, www.colcatrek.com.pe. Run by the English-speaking Vlado Soto, this company is recommended for climbing, trekking and mountain biking in the Colca Canyon. Vlado is one of the best guides for the Cotahuasi Canyon. He also rents equipment and has topographical maps. Recommended.
Naturaleza Activa, Santa Catalina 211, T054-204182, naturactiva@yahoo.com. Experienced guides, knowledgeable, climbing and trekking. Good-quality mountain biking and safety equipment. They also offer paragliding and rafting trips.
Sacred Tours, Jerusalén 400, T054-330408, sacred_road@hotmail.com. Arranges hiking and rock climbing in the Colca Canyon and elsewhere. Experienced guides, equipment available.
Selern Services, Urb Puerta Verde F13, José LB y Rivero, Arequipa, T054-348685, www.selernexpediciones.com. Trekking in Colca and Cotahuasi canyons, adventure tourism, volcano and rock climbing.
Volcanyon Travel, C Villalba 414, T054-205078, mario-ortiz@terra.com.pe. Trekking and some mountain-bike tours in the Colca Canyon, also volcano climbing.

Rafting
Río Chili (year-round, Grade II-IV): just outside Arequipa but highly water dependent and relying on dam releases to make it worthwhile. A fun half-day out if you need a break from the heat.
Río Colca (Jun, Grade IV-V): possibly even harder than the Cotahuasi, this rarely run expedition river has had its fair share of casualties in the past. Be prepared for rocks falling off the cliffs almost continuously, sandflies, storms and out-of-this-world whitewater. Recent seismic activity around Arequipa has caused major changes to several rapids; definitely book with the local experts.
Río Cotahuasi (May-Jun, Grade IV-V): this is a total expedition, including a long drive past Corupuna mountain, a 2-day trek around the spectacular Sipia Falls (where the river drops 150 m into an impenetrable gorge), followed by 6 days of non-stop technical whitewater. The scenery is out of this world, including pre-Inca Huari culture terracing and ruins all in an incredibly deep desert canyon. Probably the best whitewater river on offer in Peru, only a handful of operators offer this trip and only 1 or 2 depart each year. Book early and only with companies who have plenty of experience.
Río Majes (all year, Grade II-III): where the Colca emerges from its gorge it becomes the Río Majes and some day trips can be organized directly from Arequipa. Good freshwater shrimp make up for the pretty average whitewater.

Tour operators
These agencies have been recommended as helpful and reliable. Most run tours to the Colca Canyon (page 281). Many agencies on Jerusalén, Santa Catalina and around Plaza de Armas sell air, train and bus tickets and offer tours of Colca, Cotahuasi, Toro Muerto and the city. Prices vary greatly so shop around. As a general rule, you get what you pay for, so check details of the cheapest tours carefully and make sure that there are enough people for the tour to run. Many tourists prefer to contract tours through their hotel. If a travel agency puts you in touch with a guide, make sure he or

Staying safe when rafting

As the sport of rafting has increased in popularity over the last few years, so too have the number of accidents (including fatalities). The introduction of a new regulatory body in 2010 will, it is hoped, bring greater safety on what are some of the best whitewater runs anywhere in South America, if not the whole world. Nevertheless rafting is an inherently dangerous sport so there are certain precautions you should observe.

New legislation demands that Grade IV+ guides hold the internationally recognized qualifications of Swift Water Rescue Technician and hold current first-aid certificates. All rafting equipment will be checked regularly to ensure it meets basic safety standards. At present there are a number of guides with the relevant qualifications, but you will only find them at companies who operate the longer, multi-day trips.

As with many of Peru's adventure options, it simply boils down to 'you get what you pay for'. If price is all that matters to you, bear in mind the following: the cheaper the price, the less you get, be it with safety cover, experience of guides, quality of equipment, quantity and wholesomeness of food, emergency back up and environmental awareness (including proper disposal of waste, human or otherwise).

Often on trips you will be required to show proof that your travel insurance will cover you for whitewater rafting. If you are unsure about it, it is worth checking with your insurance company before you leave, as some policies have an additional charge. Very few policies cover Grade V rafting - read the small print. When signing up you should ask about the experience and qualifications of the guides or even, if possible, meet them. Find out their command of English (or whatever language – there are a few German-speaking guides available), essential if you are going to understand their commands. Find out their experience. How many times have they done this particular stretch of river? Many Peruvian guides have worked overseas in the off-season, from Chile to Costa Rica, Europe and New Zealand. The more international experience your guide has, the more aware he will be of international safety practices. All guides should have some experience in rescue techniques. All guides must have knowledge of whitewater rescue and wilderness first aid. Ask when they last took a course and what level they are at.

Good equipment is essential. If possible ask to see some of the gear provided. Basic essentials include self-bailing rafts for all but the calmest of rivers. Check how old your raft is and where it was made. Satellite phones are essential on long trips in remote areas. Paddles should be of plastic and metal construction. Wooden paddles can snap, but a few companies use locally made ones that can be excellent. Helmets should be provided and fit correctly. Life jackets must be of a lifeguard-recognized quality and be replaced regularly. Wetsuits should be provided, or, at the very least, quality Splash jackets. Ask to see the first aid kit and find out what is in there and, most importantly, do they know how to use it? On the longer trips, are sound tents provided? Also ask about the dry bags they use - how old are they? Do they leak? There is nothing worse than a soggy sleeping bag at the end of a hard day's rafting.

she is official. It is not advisable to book tours to Machu Picchu here; make all these arrangements in Cuzco.

A l Travel Tours, Miguel Fernández and Saskia Tegels, Santa Catalina 203, of 1, Cercado, T054-222052, www.aitravel tours.com. Peruvian-Dutch tour operator. Tours and trekking to Colca Canyon, as well as tours throughout Peru for groups and individuals. Book exchange.

Andina Travel Service, Jerusalén 309-402, T054-225082, www.andinatravelaqp.com. Good for tours of the Colca Canyon, guide Gelmond Ynca Aparicio is very enthusiastic.

Cusipata, Jerusalén 408, T054-203966, www.cusipata.com. Recommended as the best local operator, run 6-day trips on the Río Colca. May-Dec, Río Chili 1-day kayak courses, also trekking and mountain bike tours.

Holley's Unusual Excursions, T/F054-258459 (home) daily 1700-0700, or all day Sat and Sun, or T054-222525 from Mon-Fri 0800-1600 and leave a message, angocho@ terra.com.pe. Expat Anthony Holley runs trips in his Land Rover to El Misti, Toro Muerto, the desert and coast.

Land Adventure, Santa Catalina 118-B, T054-204872, www.landadventures.net. 'Sustainable' tour operator with good guides for communities in the Colca, trekking, climbing and downhill biking.

Pablo Tour, Jerusalén 400-AB-1, T054-203737, www.pablo tour.com. Family-run agency that owns several *hostales* in Cabaconde (**Valle del Fuego**, etc, see page 289); they know the area well. Free tourist information, sells topographical maps, hotel and bus reservations. Son Edwin Junco Cabrera can sometimes be found in the office, he speaks fluent French and English. The family are keen to promote 'mixed adventure tours': several days exploring the region with combinations of biking (safety equipment provided), horse riding, trekking and rafting – many options available. Good for a challenge!

Peru Adventure Tours, Jerusalén 410, T054-221658, www.peruadventurestours.com.

Downhill mountain biking, start at 0700 with 4WD 3-hr trip into Misti and Chachani mountains, stopping along the way for sightseeing. Cycle ride starts at Azufrero (5000 m), finishing in Arequipa at 1600 m. All equipment, oxygen and snack provided. English-speaking guide.

Santa Catalina Tours, Santa Catalina 219-223, T054-284292, www.santacatalinatours.com. Daily 0800-1900. Offer unique tours of Collagua communities in the Colca Canyon.

Transcontinental Arequipa, Puente Bolognesi 132, oficina 5, T054-213843, transcontinental-aqp@terra.com.pe. Cultural and wildlife tours in the Colca Canyon.

Vita Tours, Jerusalén, T054-284211, www.vita tours.com.pe. Tours in the Arequipa area, down to the coast and in the Colca Canyon, where they have a hotel, **La Casa de Lucila**.

⊖ Transport

Arequipa *p262, maps p263 and p265*
Air
Several flights daily to and from **Lima**, with **LAN, Peruvian Airlines** and **Star Perú**. LAN also to **Juliaca** and **Cuzco**. Peruvian Airlines to **Tacna**.

Airline offices Most tour agencies sell air tickets. Prices are quoted in dollars but payment is in soles so check exchange rate carefully. A&R, Moral 212, T054-285050, Iberia representative, reconfirmation and sales. LAN, Santa Catalina 118-C, T054-201100. Star Perú, Santa Catalina 105a, T054-221896.

Bus
For details of the terminals, see Ins and outs, page 262. A terminal tax of US$0.30 must be paid on entry to the platform. Check which terminal your bus will leave from as it may not depart from the terminal where you bought your ticket. All the bus companies have their offices in the **Terminal Terrestre** and several also have offices in **Terrapuerto**. Some tour operators also make bus reservations for a small fee.

To **Lima**, 1011 km, 16-18 hrs, several daily. **Cruz del Sur**, the most expensive company, quotes prices of economy service US$12, US$30 (video, toilet, meals, comfortable seats, blankets), *bus-cama* US$40-48. **Enlaces**, T054-430333, office 39-40 in Terrapuerto; **Tepsa**, T054-608079; **Cruz del Sur**, T054- 427728; **Flores**, T054-238741/431717; **Oltursa**, T054-423152; and **Cromotex**, T054-421555 in Terminal Terrestre, T054-509910 in Terrapuerto, www.cromotex.com.pe; and **Ormeño**, T054-424187, are recommended. The road is paved but drifting sand may prolong the trip. Buses will stop at the major cities en route, but not always Pisco. The desert scenery is stunning.

To **Nazca**, 566 km, 9 hrs, US$10, US$32-46 *bus-cama*, several buses daily, mostly at night and most buses continue to Lima. Some bus companies charge the same fare to Nazca as to Lima. To **Chala**, 8 hrs, US$7.25. To **Moquegua**, 213 km, 3 hrs, US$4-8, several buses and colectivos daily. To **Tacna**, 320 km, 6-7 hrs, US$9-15, many buses daily, most with **Flores**, but some with the recommended Cruzero service from Cruz del Sur.

To **Cuzco**, all buses now go via Juliaca or Puno, US$21-23, US$32-39 with **Cruz del Sur**, 10 hrs. Most companies use double-decker buses (toilet, TV, hostess, etc) and go overnight, eg **Enlaces**, **Cial**, **Ziva** and **Ormeño**, running 1 morning and, some companies, 1 afternoon bus. There is a new, quick paved road to **Juliaca**, via Yura and Santa Lucía, cutting the Arequipa–Juliaca journey time to 4 hrs, US$6.50-13.50, and **Puno**, 6 hrs, US$5-7 (US$20-30 Cruz del Sur *bus-cama*). Most buses and colectivos continue to Puno. **Flores**, **Sur Oriente** and **Julsa** are recommended.

Transportes Milagros (T054-430612), La Reyna (T054-531115, recommended) and Andalucia (T054-694060) have almost hourly departures daily from Arequipa to **Chivay** (for the Colca Canyon) with some continuing to **Cabanaconde**; a further 75 km, 2 hrs, US$1. La Reyna has the quickest service at about 6 hrs, US$5; others US$4. Buy a ticket in advance to ensure a seat (many agencies can buy them for you for a fee).

Car and taxi
Car hire Avis, Ugarte 216, T054-224727, or at the airport T054-443576. **Transjesa**, also at the airport, counter 1, T054-460403. Good value and new vehicles. **Genesis**, Jerusalén y Puente Grau, T054-223918. Rents 4WDs in good condition, can also arrange drivers. Owner of Hostal Reyna, see Sleeping, can arrange cars, vans and 4WDs with drivers. Recommended. **Radio taxis** Alo 45, T054-454545; Taxi 21, T054-212121; **Taxitel**, T054-452020; Turismo Arequipa, T054-458888.

Train
The railway goes from Arequipa to **Juliaca**, where it divides, 1 line going north to **Cuzco**, the other south to **Puno**. With the opening of the new Arequipa–Juliaca highway, the decreased demand for rail travel has led to the suspension of regular passenger services on this route. PerúRail, www.perurail.com, runs trains for private charter for groups of over 40.

⊕ Directory

Arequipa *p262, maps p263 and p265*
Banks ATM Globalnet cash machines everywhere, eg on the Plaza, at iperú offices. Many give cash in soles or US$ and they accept a wide range of cards: Visa, Plus, Diners Club, Amex, Maestro, Cirrus and many Peruvian cards. **Interbank**, Mercaderes 217, also **Interbank Direct cambio** in the Portal de Flores, main plaza, open 0800-2200. **BCP**, San Juan de Dios 125, also at Santo Domingo y Jerusalén. **BBV Continental**, San Francisco 108. **HSBC**, Plaza de Armas on the corner of La Merced and Puente Bolognesi. Change money at *cambios* on Jerusalén and San Juan de Dios, and several travel agencies. **Sergio A del Carpio D**, Jerusalén 126, T054-242987, good rates for dollars. **Via Tours**, Santo

Domingo 114, good rates. **Casa de Cambio**, San Juan de Dios 109, T054-282528, good rates. It is almost impossible to change TCs on Sat afternoon or Sun; try to find a sympathetic street changer. Better rates for cash dollars in banks and *casas de cambio*.

Consulates Belgium, Francisco de la Rosa Calle 13, Mza 1, lote 2, Parque I, T054-285508. **Bolivia**, Rivero 408, Edif Cáceres of 5-6, Cercado, T054-213391, and at Coronel Zavala 171, Mollendo, T054-533848. **Chile**, Mercaderes 212, p 6, Galerías Gameza, T054-251421, entrance to lift 30 m down passageway down Mercaderes on left. Mon-Fri 0900-1300, present passport 0900-1100 if you need a visa. **France**, Edif Magnus 1301 esq Av Cayma, T054-270257. **Germany**, Colegio Max Uhle, Sachaca, T054-218669. **Italy**, Los Cerezos 110, Cayma, T054-254686, 1130. **Spain**, Ugarte 218, p 2, T054-214977, Mon-Fri 1100-1300, Sat 0900-1300. **Sweden**, Quezada 107, Yanahuara, T054-255494, Mon-Fri 0830-1300, 1500-1730. **Switzerland**, Av Miguel Forga 348, Parque Industrial, T054-232723. **UK**, Mr Roberts, Tacna y Arica 156, T054-241340, gerencia@grupo roberts.com, Mon-Fri 0830-1230, 1500-1830, reported as friendly and helpful. **Cultural centres** Alianza Francesa, Santa Catalina 208, T054-215579, www.afarequipa.org.pe. Centro Cultural Peruano-Norte Americano, Casa de los Mendiburo, Melgar 109, T054-391020, www.cultural.edu.pe, has an English library. Instituto Cultural Peruano Alemán, Ugarte 207, T054-228130, www.icpa.org.pe. Instituto Nacional de Cultura, Alameda San Lázaro 120, T054-213171. **Internet** Everywhere, often charging less than US$0.30 per hr. Best services are constantly changing, so hunt around. **Language courses** Carlos Rojas Núñez, Filtro 405, T054-285061, carlrojas@mixmail.com. Private or group lessons for all levels, encourages conversation, knowledgeable on culture and politics. Recommended. Cecilia Pinto Oppe, Hostal La Reyna, Puente Grau 108, T959 961638, www.cepesmaidiomasceci.com. Good-value

lessons, held in a café that helps orphaned children. **Centro de Intercambio Cultural Arequipa (CEICA)**, Los Arces 257-A, Cayma, T054-221165, T95-991 0196 (mob), www.ceica-peru.com. Individual classes US$136 for 20 hrs' tuition, US$102 for groups of 3 or more, rooms with families, (US$95 per week for a single room with breakfast, US$120 half board, US$140 full board), also dance lessons, history and cultural classes, excursions. **Escuela de Español Ari Quipay (EDEAQ)**, T054-272517, T95-999 2995 (mob), www.edeaq.com. Peruvian/Swiss-run, experienced, multilingual staff, recognized by Ministry of Education, in a colonial house near the Plaza de Armas, 1-to-1 and group classes, home stay available (Lula's B&B in Cayma, T054-272517, www.bbaqpe.com, Lula speaks English, German and French, discount for long-stay, meals available, free internet, charming and quiet, in our **E** range). Liz and Edwin Pérez, T054-264068, edwinett @mixmail.com. US$5 per hr 1-to-1 tuition, will go to your hotel. Llama Education, Casabella, lote A6, Cerro Colorado, T054-274069, www.arequipaspanish.com/index.html. Professional, with personal attention, owner María Huaman is very helpful, individual and small-group tuition, home stays and cultural exchanges. **Silvana Cornejo**, 7 de Junio 118, Cerrito Los Alvarez, Cerro Colorado, T054-254985, silvanacor@yahoo.com. US$6 per hr, negotiable for groups, recommended. Her sister Roxanna also teaches Spanish. Classes also available at the **Centro Peruano-Norte Americano** (US$10 per hr) and Instituto Cultural Peruano Alemán (US$4 per hr). **Medical services** Ambulance: San Miguel, T054-283330 (24 hrs). **Hospitals and clinics:** Regional Honorio Delgado, Av A Carrión s/n, T054-238465/233812/231818 (inoculations). Central del Sur, Filtro y Peral s/n, T054-214430 in emergency. **Clínica Arequipa SA**, esq Puente Grau y Av Bolognesi, T054-599000, www.clinicaarequipa.com.pe. Fast and efficient with English-speaking doctors and all hospital facilities. **Paz Holandesa**, Villa

Continental, C 4, No 101, Paucarpata, T054-432281, www.pazholandesa.com. Dutch foundation dedicated to helping the impoverished (potential volunteers should see their website), with a travel clinic for tourists. Dutch and English spoken, 24-hr service, also a dentist. Highly recommended. Only use reputable hospitals or clinics, not practitioners who advertise independent services. **Pharmacy: Farmacia Libertad,** Piérola 108. Owner speaks English.

Post Central office is at Moral 118, Mon-Sat 0800-2000, Sun 0800-1400. **DHL,** Santa Catalina 115, T054-234288, for sending documents and money. Western Union representative. **Telephone** Alvarez Thomas y Palacio Viejo. *Locutorios* and internet cafés offer international calls from US$0.25 per min.

Colca Canyon

→ *Colour map 6, B1.*

Twice as deep as the Grand Canyon and once thought to be the deepest canyon in the world (until the nearby Cotahuasi Canyon was found to be all of 163 m deeper), the Colca Canyon is an area of astounding beauty. Giant amphitheatres of pre-Inca terracing become narrow, precipitous gorges, and in the background looms the grey, smoking mass of Sabancaya, one of the most active volcanoes in the Americas, and its more docile neighbour, Ampato (6288 m). Unspoiled Andean villages lie on both sides of the canyon, inhabited by the Cabana and Collagua peoples. The Río Colca snakes its way through the length of this massive gorge, 3500 m above sea level at Chivay (the canyon's main town) falling to 2200 m at Cabanaconde, at the far end of the canyon. Now, the Colca Canyon is best known for its associations with some rather large birds. Visitors flock here for a close encounter with the giant Andean condor at the aptly named Cruz del Cóndor and, for many, this is the final destination in the canyon. Rather than hurrying back to Arequipa, continue to Cabanaconde, as good a base for exploring as Chivay, with many new options opening up. ▸▸ *For listings, see pages 288-292.*

Ins and outs

Getting there and around Most buses from Arequipa take the new road via Yura and Cañahuas, following the railway, which is being developed as a route to Cuzco. This is longer, but quicker, than the old route through Cayma. In the rainy season it is better to travel by day as the road can get slippery at night. Buses all leave from the main terminal in Arequipa (see page 262), or reservations can be made through some of the tourist agencies on Santa Catalina and Jerusalén. Buses and colectivos run from Chivay to the villages in the canyon. And, naturally, there are numerous trekking possibilities to consider. ▸▸ *See Transport, page 292.*

Entry ticket A fee of US$24 is charged for a tourist ticket (usually valid for up to a week) granting entrance to the Cruz del Cóndor, trekking and tourist areas in the Colca and valley of the volcanoes, plus Nevado Mismi and the Aguada Blanca y Salinas reserve. This cost is not included in agency prices and most visitors buy the ticket at a checkpoint before entering Chivay. Keep the ticket with you while in the Colca area.

Best time to visit January to April is the rainy season, but this makes the area green, with lots of flowers. This is not the best time to see condors. May to December is the dry, cold season when there is more chance of seeing the birds.

The name Colca derives from the Inca practice of storing harvested crops in sealed vaults, called colcas, which were carved into the canyon walls.

Chivay and around → *For listings, see pages 288-292.*

Chivay is the gateway to the canyon and the overnight stopping point for two-day tours run by agencies in Arequipa. There is a road bridge over the river here (others are at Yanque and Lari).

Arequipa to Chivay → *Colour map 5, B/C6.*

From Arequipa there are two routes to Chivay, the first village on the edge of the Canyon: the old route, via the suburb of **Cayma**, and the new route following the railway, through **Yura**, which is longer but quicker. It can be cold, reaching 4825 m on the Pata Pampa Pass, north of Cañahuas, but the views are worth it. Cyclists should use the Yura road, as it's in better condition and has less of a climb at the start.

   The old dirt route runs north from Arequipa, over the altiplano. About an hour out of Arequipa is the **Aguada Blanca National Vicuña Reserve**. If you're lucky, you can see herds of these rare and timid camelids near the road. If taking a bus to the reserve to vicuña-watch, there should be enough traffic on the road to be able to hitch a ride back to Arequipa in the evening. This route affords fine views of the volcanoes Misti, Chachani, Ampato and the active Sabancaya.

   From Chivay, a road heads northeast to **Tuti** (for the start of the Nevado Mismi trek, see page 283), where there is a small handicrafts shop, and **Sibayo**, with a pensión and grocery store. A long circuit back to Arequipa heads south from Sibayo, passing through **Puente Callalli** (where Arequipa buses can sometimes be caught for Cuzco), **Chullo** and **Sumbay**. This is a little-travelled road, but the views of fine landscapes with vicuña, llamas, alpacas and Andean duck are superb. Another road from Sibayo goes northwest, following the northern side of the Colca mountain range to **Cailloma**, **Orcopampa** and **Andagua** (see page 294). Water from the Colca river has been diverted through a series of tunnels and canals to the desert between Repartición and Camaná, to irrigate the Majes pampa.

Chivay → *Colour map 5, B6. Altitude 3600 m.*

There is a helpful **tourist office** ① *open Mon-Fri*, in the Municipalidad on the west side of the plaza that gives away a useful map of the valley. The tourist police, also on the plaza, can give advice about locally trained guides. A reconstructed *chullpa* on the hilltop across Puente Inca gives good views over the town. The **Maria Reiche Planetarium and Observatory** ① *Casa Andina hotel, 6 blocks west of the Plaza between Huayna Capac and Garcilazo, www.casa-andina.com, US$6, discounts for students*, makes the most of the Colca's clear southern hemisphere skies with a powerful telescope and two 55-minute presentations per day at 1830 (Spanish) and 1930 (English).

   The hot springs of **La Calera** ① *US$3.50*, are 4 km from Chivay. To get there take one of the regular colectivos (US$0.25) from beside the market or it's a pleasant hour-long walk. There are several large hot pools and showers but only two pools are usually open to tourists. The hot springs are highly recommended after a hard day's trekking, with good facilities and a beautiful setting. A small cultural museum on site is included in the price. From La Calera you can trek through the Canocota canyon to Canocota (four to five hours); alternatively take a colectivo to Canocota and hike to La Calera; it's a beautiful trip, but ask directions.

Appeasing the gods

To the Incas, Nevado Ampato was a sacred god who brought water and good harvests and, as such, claimed the highest tribute: human sacrifice.

In September 1995, Johan Reinhard of Chicago's Field Museum of Natural History, accompanied by Peruvian climber, Miguel Zárate, whose brother Carlos is a well-known mountain guide, were climbing Ampato when they made a startling discovery. At about 6000 m they found the perfectly preserved mummified body of an Inca girl, wrapped tightly in textiles. They concluded that she had been ritually sacrificed and buried on the summit.

Mummies of Inca human sacrifices had been found before on Andean summits, but the girl from Ampato, nicknamed Juanita, is the first frozen Inca female to be unearthed and her body may be the best preserved of any found in the Americas from pre-Columbian times. The intact tissues and organs of naturally mummified, frozen bodies are a storehouse of biological information. Studies reveal how she died, where she came from, who her living relatives are and even yield insights about the Inca diet.

Juanita's clothes are no less remarkable. The richly patterned textiles will serve as the model for future depictions of the way noble Inca women dressed. Her *lliclla* – a bright red and white shawl beneath the outer wrappings – has been declared "the finest Inca woman's textile in the world".

Ampato was described as one of the principal deities in the Colca Canyon region. The Incas appeased the mountain gods with the sacrifice of children. The Cabana and Collagua people even bound their children's heads to make them look like the mountains from which they believed they were descended.

A subsequent ascent of Ampato revealed a further two mummies at the summit. One is a young girl and the other, though badly charred by lightning, is believed to be a boy. If so, it may mean that these children were sacrificed together in a symbolic marriage.

Nowadays, villages in the Colca continue to make offerings to the mountain gods for water and good harvests, but thankfully the gods have modified their tastes, now preferring *chicha* to children.

From Chivay you can hike to **Coporaque** (1¾ hours) and **Ichupampa** (a further 1½ hours). Half an hour above Coporaque are interesting **cliff tombs** and, just beyond the village, are the Huari ruins of **Ullu Ullu**. West beyond Ichupampa are **Lari**, **Madrigal** (where a footbridge connects to Maca) and **Tapay** (connected by a footbridge to Cabanaconde). Between Coporaque and Ichupampa, foot and road bridges cross the river to **Yanque** (one hour), from where it's an 8-km hike back to Chivay. Follow the road or you'll end up lost in a maze of terraced fields. If you feel too tired to walk back to Chivay, catch a colectivo from the plaza in Yanque for US$0.25.

Nevado Mismi: trek to the source of the Amazon

Although not the greatest mountain in the region, Nevado Mismi, a rugged 5597-m peak roughly 15 km north of Ichupampa and the Río Colca, is special for a couple of reasons that might be worth remembering at 0300, when it's -15°C and you're huddled inside a sleeping bag, counting the hours to daylight.

A source of controversy

So, how do we know that the source of the Amazon is on Nevado Mismi? In 1971 a *National Geographic*-sponsored expedition, led by acclaimed explorer Loren McIntyre was the first to speculate that this might be longest of the river's many tributaries. Unfortunately, McIntyre possessed neither the technology nor the resources to prove this beyond doubt.

In 1985/1986 an 11-man international team set out to prove the river's length and kayak it from the source to the mouth. Dogged by accidents, illness and a leadership crisis, only four of the 11 made it to the Atlantic six months later, among them American journalist Joe Kane, author of the highly entertaining account, *Running the Amazon*.

In 2000, Andrew Pietowski led a 22-man *National Geographic* expedition and confirmed Nevado Mismi as the source, using state-of-the-art GPS technology, also giving the length of the river at 6275 km.

First, it provides an adventurous trek to the source of what, in terms of volume, number and scale of tributaries, perhaps even legendary status, is the greatest river system on the planet (see box, above). Below the mountain to the east, tropical forest stretches uninterrupted to the Atlantic Ocean. Second, the region's extreme remoteness means that wildlife, extinct in other parts of the Andes, is present here. It's not unusual to see vicuñas, viscachas, many species of Andean water birds and, perhaps, the occasional condor in the mountains to the north of Tuti. Pumas and the spectacularly rare Andean mountain cat, prey on the tough herbivores of these undeveloped hills. Cultural aspects long vanished elsewhere also cling to existence close to the Amazon's beginning. The area north of the Colca Canyon has some of Peru's last traditional llama- and alpaca-herding communities. Living a nomadic existence, these remarkable folk live a life dedicated to the needs of their animals and the growth of the tough grasses that form their staple diet.

On a practical level, this is one of harder areas in the Peruvian Andes to get to with public transport, so a professional guide or, at a bare minimum, a local *arriero* (mule driver) is highly recommended. Several established agencies in Arequipa offer itineraries in the area. Carlos Zárate (see page 276) is very knowledgeable regarding the region's possibilities and has backed up TV companies in the zone. Without a guide you must be totally self-sufficient. There are many interesting hiking routes in this region. A good one requiring four to five days is outlined below. Make sure you're well acclimatized before you start treks in the area; much of the land lies at 5000 m or higher and you must be prepared for rapidly changing weather conditions.

Day 1 With Chivay as a starting point it's fairly easy to hire a taxi as far as **Tuti**, a pleasant rural community and a good spot to begin your trek. Beyond Tuti the road continues a few kilometres to the northeast before one branch turns to the north, gaining height in switchbacks on the route towards Mismi and the Amazon source. The route, now mainly heading northwest, passes some beautiful alpine lakes, excellent for bird watching, and the lovely 17th-century church and colonial *reduction* of **Ran Ran**, before emerging onto the bare moonscape of the altiplano. At **Aquenta**, 4800 m, there's a site with good water where it's possible to camp for the first night. If required, a 4WD can reach just beyond this point, as far as the **Carhuasanta** valley in the dry season. In the rainy season the entire region becomes a mud bath and vehicular access is practically impossible.

Day 2 Crossing into the Carhuasanta valley and following the stream south to its source, takes you to the Amazon watershed. Carhuasanta is a beautiful, windswept and empty valley, stained with the reds and browns of metals and other minerals. Scrambling up some boulders brings you to the base of a dark cliff, where the source itself is marked with a cross carved into the rock. This is the place where the ice melts and the water's journey of over 6000 km begins. For real perfectionists the small **Laguna McIntyre**, and indeed the summit of Mismi itself, lie only a couple of hundred metres higher. Glacial retreat means that, for most of the year, crampons aren't necessary. Give yourself a couple of days to explore the picturesque vicinity of the source and summit of Mismi but remember that nights spent here above 5000 m are truly chilling. From this point onwards you can either retrace your steps via Tuti and Chivay, or, in a couple more days, complete a circuit of Mismi, crossing the 5200-m **Apacheta Pass** (and the Atlantic/Pacific watershed) and descending via the Qollpa/Callumayo valley to Lari and the Colca Canyon. On this far side of Apacheta you will encounter the remains of an Inca, possibly pre-Inca highway.

Chivay to Cabanaconde → *For listings, see pages 288-292.*

From Chivay, the main road goes west along the Colca Canyon. The first village, after 8 km, is **Yanque**, where there's an interesting church and a bridge to the villages on the other side (see page 283). Beside the renovated Inca bridge, a 20-minute walk from Yanque plaza, is a large, warm thermal **swimming pool** ① *US$0.75*. The next village after Yanque is **Achoma**, 30 minutes from Chivay along the Cabanaconde road. There is an old settlement where you can camp. The road continues to **Maca**, which barely survived an earthquake in November 1991. Then comes the tiny village of **Pinchollo**, with **Hospedaje Refugio del Gayser** (Calle Melgar s/n, behind the municipality, T054-959 007441/958 032090), basic with good local information. There are no restaurants but you can eat at the *comedor popular*. From here it is a 30-minute walk on a dirt track to visit the geyser Hatun Infiernillo. You can walk from Pinchollo to the **Sabancaya** geyser in approximately seven hours. Boys will offer to guide you there. For information, ask for Eduardo, who acts as a guide. He lives next to the plaza.

Cruz del Cóndor → *See Ins and outs, page 281, for entry fees.*

From Pinchollo the road winds its way on to the Mirador, or Cruz del Cóndor, where you may be asked to show your tourist ticket, at the deepest point of the canyon. The view from here is wonderful but people don't just come for that. This is where the immense Andean condor can be seen rising on the morning thermals. The reason this particular spot is so unique is that the condors swoop by in startling close up, so close, in fact, that you feel you can reach out and touch them. It is a breathtaking and very humbling experience.

The best time to arrive in the morning is a matter of some dispute, although the consensus is around 0900. Arrive by 0800 for a good spot, any earlier and you may be faced with a long, chilly wait; this may be unavoidable if you're travelling by public transport. Milagros' 0630 bus from Chivay stops here very briefly at around 0800 (ask the driver to stop), or try hitching with a tour bus at around 0600. Buses from Cabanaconde plaza at 0630 (Andalucía) or 0800 (Reyna) take about 30 minutes. Or you can walk along the road, which takes about three hours. Horses can be hired to save you the walk; arrange the night before in Cabanaconde.

The condors fly off to look for carrion on the higher slopes of the surrounding peaks at 0900-1000. The condors can also be seen returning from the day's food searching at around 1600-1800. Just below the Mirador is a rocky outcrop, which allows a more peaceful viewing but take great care on the loose scree. Binoculars are recommended. Snacks and drinks are available but camping here is officially forbidden, although if you ask the tourist police in Chivay, they may help.

Unfortunately, the peace of the Cruz del Cóndor has been disrupted by road-building projects, ironically to improve access for tourist buses. The projects have been carried out without an environmental impact assessment and have been decried by locals and tour operators alike. For now, it's not known what consequences the bulldozers and explosives blasts will have on future condor populations, but it is feared that the birds' breeding cycles may have been badly affected by the disturbances.

Cabanaconde → Colour map 5, B5 .

From the Mirador it's a 40-minute bus ride to this friendly village at 3287 m, the last in the Colca Canyon. To walk from the Mirador to Cabanaconde (three hours), follow the road until Cabanaconde is in sight, then turn off the road 50 m after a small reservoir down a walled track. After about 1 km turn left onto an old Inca road and continue down to rejoin the road into Cabanaconde.

The indigenous people of this part of the canyon are **Cabanas**. Cabanaconde plaza is brimming with life. Women squat on their haunches, selling bruised fruit and a few knobbly root crops. Their distinctive flower-patterned hats, voluminous skirts and intricately embroidered blouses bring a splash of colour to the uniform brown adobe buildings. Children tend sheep, goats and llamas; old men lead burdened mules while pigs laze in the sun and chickens peck at the ground. At dusk, large groups of animals wander back into the village to the corrals adjoining most houses.

The views into the canyon are excellent and condors can be seen from the hill just west of the village, a 15-minute walk from the plaza. From here, you'll also see the amazing terraces to the south of the village, arguably the most attractive in the valley. The hill is surrounded by a 2-km-long Huari wall, which is 6 m high and 4 m wide in places. It also encompasses the village football field where it is possible to see condors flying over a late-afternoon game.

Cabanaconde provides an excellent base for visiting the region. Interesting trekking and climbing lies all around the village, and local guides are beginning to see new opportunities for biking and horse riding in this amazing landscape. Many locals are keen to encourage respectful tourism in the area. There's a tourist information office attended by friendly locals willing to give plenty of advice, if not maps, T054-280212. It's a good place to find trekking guides and muleteers.

It takes two days to walk from Chivay to **Cabanaconde** (70 km) but you can camp along the route. You will have to walk all day in the sun – there is no shade – so you'll need plenty of drinking water and sun block. Mule hire is US$30 a day including guide (ask if they have a saddle). You can hike for three days through the local villages and return by bus as an alternative to a two-day tour.

Trekking from Cabanaconde

There are many hikes in the area. Make sure to take enough water as it gets very hot and there is not a lot of water available. Sun protection is also a must. Some treks are impossible if it rains heavily in the wet season, but most of the time the rainy season is dry; check beforehand. Ask locals for directions as there are hundreds of confusing paths going into the canyon. Buy food for longer hikes in Arequipa. Topographical maps are available at the **Instituto Geográfico Nacional** in Lima (IGN 1:100,000 Huambo and Chivay sheets give the best coverage), from **Colca Trek** or **Pablo Tour** in Arequipa (see page 276), and good information can be obtained from **South American Explorers**.

Two hours below Cabanaconde is **Sangalle**, a beautiful oasis of palm trees and swimming areas, where there are three campsites with basic bungalows and toilets. The three sites from top to bottom are: Eden, US$3, the first site you come to, nice huts; Oasis Paradise, US$5, but often free entry if you stay at Valle del Fuego, run by Pablo Tour, lots of space; finally, closest to the river is El Paradaiso, US$6, cheaper out of season, the most aesthetically pleasing site, pools and waterfalls built into huge natural boulders. It takes up to 4½ hours to climb back up but horses can be hired to carry your bag, US$6; ask for the best route in both directions.

A popular hike from Cabanconde involves walking east on the Chivay road to the **Mirador de Tapay** (before Cruz del Cóndor), then descending to the river on a steep track (four hours, take care). Cross the bridge to the north bank. At the village of **San Juan de Chuccho** you can stay and eat at a basic family hostel, of which there are several. **Hostal Roy** and Casa de Rebelino (F) are both good and US$2 will buy you a decent meal. From here pass **Tapay**, where it is also possible to camp and the small villages of Malata and Cosnirhua, all the time heading west along the north side of the Río Colca; take a guide or ask local directions as there are many different trails. After about three hours' walking, cross another bridge to reach **Sangalle** on the south bank of the Río Colca, follow signs to the oasis, spend the night and return to Cabanaconde on the third day. This route is offered by many Arequipa and local agencies. More good hiking and a further extension of this 'Oasis' trek heads up a **Quebrada** to the north-northwest, leading to an impressive waterfall above the settlement of **Fure** (accommodation available, **F**). Again, ask locally for details.

A longer hike from Cabanaconde goes to **Chachas** and takes four or five days. Follow a small path to the west, descending slowly into the canyon (three hours); ask locals for

Trekking around Cabanaconde

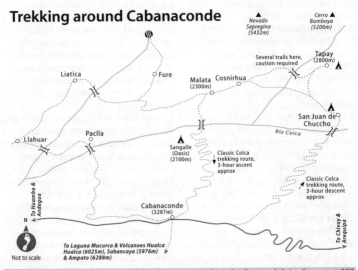

directions to **Choco**. Cross the Río Colca by the Puente Colgado (an Inca bridge) and ascend to Choco, 2473 m (five to six hours). From Choco climb high above the village to the pass at 4500 m and then down to Chachas, at 3100 m (eight to 12 hours). There is a minibus daily at 1300 from Chachas to **Andagua** in the valley of the volcanoes (see page 294). Otherwise it is a day's hike. This is a superb walk through untouched areas and villages but you'll need camping equipment, food and lots of water, as there is hardly any on this trek.

South of Cabanaconde

Fifteen kilometres to the south on rough trails is **Laguna Mucurca**, an 8-km long lake that offers good birdwatching, especially in June to October when its resident group of flamingos are present; please don't disturb their feeding. Reigning supreme above the lake is the volcanic chain of **Ampato** (6288 m), **Sabancaya** (5976 m – caution required, this is the most active volcano in Peru) and **Hualca Hualca** (6025 m, the most northerly of the three). A minimum of two days is required to make the most of this area and qualified guides are essential if you want to climb any of the peaks, all of which were sacred *Apus*, or gods, for the Incas.

◉ Colca Canyon listings

For Sleeping and Eating price codes and other relevant information, see pages 38-44.

● Sleeping

Chivay and around *p282*
Ask if your hotel can provide heating. Many of the better hotels are used by tour groups. There are several other hotels and family homes where you can stay; ask around.
AL Estancia Pozo del Cielo, C Huascar B-3, Sacsayhuaman-Chivay, over the Puente Inca from Chivay amid pre-Inca terraces, T054-531041, www.pozodelcielo.com.pe. Very comfortable, friendly, warm rooms, good views, good service and restaurant. Recommended.
A Casa Andina, Huayna Cápac s/n, T054-531020, www.casa-andina.com. Attractive cabins with hot showers and a cosy bar/ dining area, another member of this recommended hotel chain, heating, internet, parking. Also here (not directly owned by Casa Andina) is the Maria Reiche Planetarium and Observatory, see page 282.
C Colca Inn, Salaverry 307, T054-531111, www.hotelcolcainn.com. A good mid-range option, modern, spick and span, hot water, with a decent restaurant.

C Cóndor Wasi, on the road to La Calera hot springs, 1 km from Chivay, T95-944 4956, condorwasi@hotmail.com. Rustic accommodation with rooms with private bath, hot water, very tranquil.
D Posada del Colca, Salaverry 325, T054-531032, posadachivay@hotmail.com. Central, clean and friendly, good rooms, hot water, breakfast included.
D Wasi Kolping, Siglo XX s/n, 10 blocks south of the town, opposite the Plaza de Toros, T054-531076, www.hoteleskolping. net/colcawasi. Comfortable cabins with hot shower, very clean and quiet, good views.
E La Casa de Lucila, M Grau 131, T054-607086. With bath, comfortable, coffee, guides available.
E La Pascana, Puente Inca y Calle Siglo XX 106, T054-531001, hrlapascana@hotmail.com. On the northwest corner of the plaza. Excellent value with spacious en suite rooms, spotless showers with hot water, most rooms overlook a pleasant garden. Price includes breakfast, there is parking and a good restaurant.
E-F Hospedaje Restaurant Los Portales, Arequipa 603, T054-531164, www.losportales chivay.com. Good-value accommodation, though beds have rather floppy mattresses, breakfast included. Restaurant downstairs.

F Hostal La Casa de Anita, No 607, on the north side of the plaza, T054-531114. Clean, with bathroom, rooms look onto a small garden, friendly. Recommended.

G pp **Rumi Wasi**, C Sucre 714, 6 blocks from plaza (3 mins' walk), T054-531114. Good rooms, breakfast included (insist on it), hot water, bike hire (in poor condition).

Chivay to Cabanaconde *p285*
Yanque

LL Las Casitas del Colca, Parque Curiña s/n, T054-959 672480, www.lascasitasdel colca.com. An **Orient Express** hotel with luxury bungalows made of local materials. Has a restaurant, vegetable garden and farm, offers cookery courses, the **Samay Spa** offers a variety of treatments, swimming pool.

LL-L Colca Lodge, across the river between Coporaque and Ichupampa at Fundo Puye-Yanque-Caylloma, T054-531191, office at Mariscal Benavides 201, Selva Alegre, Arequipa, T054-202587, www.colca-lodge.com. Very relaxing, with beautiful hot springs and eco-spa beside the river, spend at least a day to make the most of the activities on offer. Day pass US$22 per person, overnight packages include some meals. Recommended.

A Collahua, Av Collahua cuadra 7, in Arequipa at Mercaderes 212, Galerías Garnesa, T054-226098, www.hotelcollahua. com. Modern bungalows just outside Yanque, with heating, solar-powered 24-hr hot water and plush rooms.

C Tradición Colca, on main road. In Arequipa C Argentina 108, Urb Fecia JL Bustamante y Rivero, T054-424926/T054-935 7117 (mob) for reservations, www.tradicioncolca.com. Price is per unit, **D** in low season, includes breakfast, with gardens, restaurant, bar, games room, guided hiking tour to Ullu Ullu, also has a travel agency in Arequipa. Recommended.

D Yavari Hostal-Restaurant, Plaza de Armas 604, T054-489109, www.yavarigourmet. com.pe. Small rooms but with modern installations and stylish decor, ask for a

2nd-floor room with plaza view. Cable TV, hot water, breakfast included.

E Casa Bella Flor Sumaq Wayta Wasi, Cuzco 303, T054-253586, www.casabellaflor.com. Charming small lodge run by Sra Hilde Checca, flower-filled garden, tasteful rooms, good meals (also open to non-residents), Hilde's uncle, Gregorio, guides visitors to pre-Colombian sites.

F La Posada del Cóndor, Av Salaverry 202, T084-488618, laposada_delcondor@ hotmail.com. Simple accommodation near the main plaza, cable TV, laundry, popular lunchtime buffet in the ground floor restaurant.

F Luchos Hostal, Calle Arequipa 116, T054-531262. Good location, modern building and reasonably clean. All rooms with private bath, hot water, laundry service, breakfast included. Good value and popular with Peruvian tourists – expect to be able to hear nearby rooms' TV sets in the evenings.

Cabanaconde *p286*

B Kuntur Wassi, C Cruz Blanca s/n, on the hill above the plaza, T054-812166, www.arequipacolca.com. Excellent 3-star hotel with parking, **D** in low season, breakfast included and fine traditional meals on request. Creative design with rooms spaced between rock gardens and waterfalls. 'Viewing tower' and conference centre above. Good views of the valley everywhere, and owners Walter and María very welcoming and knowledgeable about local hikes. Recommended.

C Posada del Conde, C San Pedro a couple of blocks from the plaza, T054-440197, www.posadadelconde.com. Smart hotel and a lodge. Cheaper in low season, with hot shower, excellent value, very good food.

E Majestic Colca, Miguel Grau s/n near C San Pedro, T958-962129, www.majesticcolca. com. Modern, hot water, roof-top terrace and restaurant, includes breakfast.

E-F Hostal Valle del Fuego, 1 and 2 blocks from the plaza on C Grau and Bolívar, T054-830032, www.pablotour.com. Good rooms with comfortable beds, all with private bath and hot water, plus free laundry facilities. They have 2 places, both with restaurants serving meals for around US$3. The Junco family – Pablo, Edwin and Jamil, among others – are a wealth of information having built up a small family 'empire', including the Arequipa agency **Pablo Tour**, the **Oasis Paradise** in Sangalle (discounts for clients of Valle del Fuego) and a bar, the **Casa de Pablo Club** (see below) at the end of the street. They usually meet the incoming buses. Good-value choice for backpackers, but keep in mind the 'family' nature of the business.

F Villa Pastor, Main Plaza, T054-630171, T01-993 375 0497. All rooms with private bath, hot water, laundry, cable TV, internet access for guests.

F Virgen del Carmen, Av Arequipa s/n, T054-832159, 5 blocks from the plaza. Clean, hot showers, friendly, may offer you a welcoming glass of *chicha*. Recommended.

F-G Pachamama Home, San Pedro 209, T054-253879/T959-316322, www.pachamamahome.com. Backpacker hostel, with and without bath, family atmosphere, with breakfast, hot water, lots of information, good bar'/pizzería next door, you can help with teaching and activities for village children. Recommended.

❷ Eating

Chivay and around *p282*
Several restaurants serve buffet lunches for tour groups, US$5 per person, also open to the general public. Of the few that open in the evening, most have folklore shows and are packed with tour groups. For local cheeses and dairy products, visit **Productos del Colca**, Av 22 de Agosto in the central market.

†† El Balcón de Don Zacarías, Av 22 de Agosto 102, on plaza, T054-531108.

Breakfast, the best lunch buffet in town, à la carte menu, *novo andean* and international cuisine. Recommended.

††-† Lobos Pizzería, on the plaza. Good pizzas and pasta, fast service, bar, popular. Has mountain biking information and **Isuiza Turismo y Aventura** agency, T959-860870.

††-† McElroy's Irish Pub, on the plaza. Bar run by a Peruvian and an Irishman, friendly, good selection of drinks (sometimes including pricey Guinness), pizza, pasta, sandwiches and music. Mountain bikes for hire. Accepts Visa.

††-† Witete, Siglo XX 328. Good international food and some local dishes.

† Innkas Café-Bar, main plaza No 706, T054-531209. Coffee, sandwiches, *menú*, pizza, pool table, nice atmosphere.

† La Pascana, near the Plaza de Armas. Good value, tasty local food. Also has good lodging in our **D** range.

† Ruadhri Irish Pub, Av Salaverry 202. Nothing Irish about it, but still a popular hang-out offering pizzas, pasta and sandwiches, has happy hour and a pool table.

Cabanaconde *p286*
††-† Casa de Pablo Club, C Grau. Jamil Junco runs this comfortable bar just beyond **Valle del Fuego**. Excellent fresh juices and pisco sour, cable TV (football!), small book exchange and equipment hire.

† Don Piero, signposted just off main plaza. Excellent choice and good information.

† Las Brisas del Colca, main plaza, T054-631593. Pleasant, serves breakfast, tourist menu, à la carte dishes, juices and sandwiches. Recommended.

† Limeño, just to the north of the plaza. Excellent-value breakfasts, friendly service.

† Pizzería Bar Bon Appetit, Jorge Chávez s/n, main plaza, T054-630171. Pizzas, pasta, breakfast and vegetarian.

† Rancho del Colca, on the plaza. Serves mainly vegetarian food.

✷ Festivals and events

Colca Canyon *p281*
This is a region of wild and frequent festivals.
20-25 Jan El Día de San Sebastián is
celebrated over 5 days in Pinchollo.
2-3 Feb Virgen de la Candelaria is
celebrated in the towns of Chivay and
Cabanaconde, with dancing in the plaza,
and over 5 days in Maca and Tapay.
Mar/Apr Semana Santa is celebrated
with particular gusto in the villages.
27 Apr Celebration of the apostle Santiago.
Apr/May Many festivals are held in the Colca
Canyon at this time of year. La Cruz de Piedra
is celebrated over 5 days in May in the main
plaza in Tuti, near Chivay.
13 Jun San Antonio is celebrated in the
villages of Maca, Callalli and Yanque.
14 Jun In Sibayo and Ichupampa the
Fiesta de San Juan is held over 5 days.
21 Jun Anniversary of the district of
Chivay in Cailloma.
14-17 Jul Fiesta de la Virgen del Carmen
is held in Cabanaconde and Pampacolca,
when folk dancing takes place in the streets.
Of particular interest is the dance of Los
Turcos, which represents the indigenous
peoples' struggle against the conquistadors.
This fiesta is also held in the churches of Yura,
Carmen Alto, Congata, Tingo Grande and the
Convent of Santa Teresa in Arequipa city.
25 Jul Fiesta de Santiago Apostol in
Coporaque and Madrigal, in the canyon.
26 Jul-2 Aug Various religious ceremonies,
accompanied by dancing, are held in honour
of the Virgen Santa Ana in Maca.
15 Aug In Chivay, fiesta of the Virgen de la
Asunta, the town's patron saint, lasts 8 days.
Sep In Tisco, the fiesta of the Virgen de la
Natividad is held over 5 days.
8 Dec The fiesta of the Inmaculada
Concepción is held in Chivay and Yanque
lasting 5 days. Groups of musicians and dancers
present the traditional dance, the Witite.
25 Dec The Witite is a festival lasting 6 days
in Yanque.

⚠ Activities and tours

It is not always possible to join a tour in
Chivay; it is best to organize it in Arequipa
and travel with a group.
Travel agencies in Arequipa (see page 276)
arrange a 1-day tour to the Cruz del Cóndor
for US$20-25. They leave Arequipa at 0400,
arriving at the Cruz del Cóndor at 0800-0900,
followed by an expensive lunch stop at
Chivay and back to Arequipa by 2100.
For many, especially for those with altitude
problems, this is too much to fit into 1 day
(the only advantage is that you don't
have to sleep at high altitude). It's also
more dangerous since drivers get tired
on the way back.
2-day tours start at US$25-30 per person
with an overnight stop in Chivay or Yanque;
more expensive tours range from US$45
to US$90 with accommodation at the top
of the range. Most agencies will have a
base price for the tour then different prices
depending on which hotel you book. Allow
at least 2-3 days, more if you are planning
to do some trekking in the Colca Canyon.
Travel agents frequently work together
in a 'pooling' system to fill buses (even the
more expensive agencies may not have
their own transport) and there are lots of
touts. This can mean that a busload of
tourists will come from different agencies,
all paying different prices, but all expecting
the same level of service. On occasion the
company providing the transport may
not have the same high standards as the
operator through which the tour was
booked. **Note** Don't forget that the
compulsory entry ticket (see Ins and outs,
page 281) is rarely included in agency prices.

Chivay and around *p282*
Ampato Adventure Sports, Plaza de Armas
(close to **Lobos Pizzería**), Chivay, T054-
531073, www.ampatocolca.com. Offer
information and rent good mountain bikes,
but rarely open.

Colca Explorer, Mariscal Benavides 201 Selva Alegre, T054-202587, www.colca-explorer.com. Agency associated with **Amazonas Explorer** in Cuzco, with many options in Colca and southern Peru: from classic local tours to horse riding, mountain biking, fishing in remote lakes, mountain climbing (eg 'Three Peaks in Two Weeks'), treks and visiting alpaca farms on the altiplano. The general manager, Julver Eguilez, is a UAIGM mountain guide.

Colca-Turismo, Av Salaverry 321, Chivay, T054-503368, and guide Zacarías Ocsa Osca, zacariasocsa@hotmail.com, seem to offer a professional service.

Cabanaconde *p286*

Chiqui Travel & Expeditions, San Pedro s/n, T054-958 063602, chiquitravel_expeditions@hotmail.com. Small, but professional and reliable, organizes trekking, biking and horse riding.

Guías Locales Aproset, T054-958 099332, cabanatours@hotmail.com. Association of local guides, can organize mules and muleteers for independent treks.

Henry López Junco, T054-280367. A guide in Cabanaconde.

⊖ Transport

Chivay and around *p282*
Bus Trans Milagros, T054-531115; La Reyna, T054-430612; and **Andalucia**, T054-694060; have almost hourly departures daily from Arequipa to Chivay, some continuing to Cabanaconde, a further 75 km, 2 hrs, US$1.

La Reyna has the quickest service, about 6 hrs, US$5, others US$4. Buses return to **Arequipa** from the bus station in Chivay, 3 blocks from the main plaza, next to the stadium.

Combis and colectivos leave from the new terminal in Chivay to any village in the area including **Achoma** (every 30 mins), **Maca** (every hr), **Ichupampa** (every hr) and **Puente Callalli** (every hr); ask the drivers for details.

To **Puno**, with 4M Express, www.4m-express.com, 5¾ hrs, US$40, at 1330, it is difficult to go to **Cuzco** from Chivay: you can take a colectivo to Puente Callalli, but the police there are unwilling to let passengers wait for a passing Cuzco-bound bus, which may not stop anyway. Best to go back to Arequipa.

Cabanaconde *p286*
See under Chivay for buses on the Arequipa–Chivay–Cabanaconde route. Milagros, Andalucía and La Reyna buses leave Cabanaconde for **Arequipa** between 0730 and 1500, always from the Plaza de Armas, US$6 (usually a wait in Chivay).

❶ Directory

Chivay and around *p282*
Banks TCs and credit cards are seldom accepted so take plenty of cash in soles, not dollars. There is a **Globalnet** ATM close to the plaza. **Medical services** Traveller's Medical Center (TMC), Ramón Castilla 232, T054-531037, tmc.colcaperu@hotmail.com.

Cotahuasi Canyon

→ *Colour map 5, B5.*

A road heads northwest off the Panamericana between Camaná and Repartición towards Corire, Aplao and the Cotahuasi Canyon. It passes the Toro Muerto petroglyphs and traverses the western slopes of Nevado Coropuna, Peru's third-highest peak at 6425 m, before winding down into Cotahuasi. Considered one of the most beautiful canyons in the world, as well as the deepest (about 1850 m deeper than the Grand Canyon in the USA), Cotahuasi has several traditional communities where ancient customs persist. The river, cutting its way through steep walls, is the focus of some tremendous scenery and top-quality rafting or kayaking. Once part of an Inca route from the coast to Cuzco, it is now a great place for hiking, with no end of ruins, hot springs, cascades and rivers to explore. ▸▸ For listings, see pages 296-298.

Ins and outs

The only way into the canyon is by road; there are bus services from Arequipa. Tour operators run to Toro Muerto and can arrange trips to Cotahuasi. Accommodation and services are basic. The most knowledgeable contact for trekking and exploring is Vlado Soto of **Colca Trek**, see page 276.

Background

The canyon, in the northwest of the Department of Arequipa, has been cut by the Río Cotahuasi, whose waters are formed by the Río Huayllapaña flowing from the north, above Pampamarca, and the Río Huarcaya from the west, above Tomepampa. The river cuts its way westwards and then southwards through the deepest parts of the canyon, below Quechualla. It flows into the Pacific as the Río Ocuña, having joined with the Río Marán along the way. At its deepest, at Ninochaca (just below the village of Quechualla), the canyon is 3354 m deep, 163 m deeper than the Colca Canyon and the deepest in the world. From this point the only way down the canyon is by kayak and it is through kayakers' reports since 1994 that the area has come to the notice of tourists. It was declared a Zona de Reserva Turística in 1988 and there is pressure to make parts of it into a national park. The vertiginous gradient of the canyon walls and the aridity of its climate allow little agriculture but there are several charming citrus-growing villages downstream, among them **Chaupa**, **Velinga** and **Quechualla**.

In Inca times the road linking Puerto Inca on the Pacific coast and Cuzco ran along much of the canyon's course. It was used for taking fish to the ancient Inca capital. Parts of the road are still intact and there are numerous remains of *andenes*, or terraces, which supported settlement along the route. There are also Huari and other pre-Inca ruins.

Northwest from Arequipa → *For listings, see pages 296-298.*

Toro Muerto

ⓘ *US$2; entrance 10 mins' drive from the petroglyphs.*

The world's largest field of petroglyphs at Toro Muerto is near **Corire** (about three hours by road from Arequipa). There are several restaurants around the plaza in Corire and a BCP. You can make a return day trip from Arequipa, if you leave really early, but it's better to allow two days, or combine it with a trip to the Cotahuasi Canyon.

To reach the petroglyphs, there's a turn-off on the right heading back out of Corire; it's about a one-hour walk. Alternatively, ask to be let off the bus at the big sign to 'Toro Muerto' beside a small church. A track leads through the fields; at the end, turn right. Ask directions en route. Just before the site is a tiny settlement of wattle-and-daub huts. From here follow the most worn track, which veers right between the hills. There are two signposts on the track leading into the desert valley.

The higher you go, the more interesting the petroglyphs, though many have been ruined by graffiti. The designs range from simple llamas to elaborate human figures and animals and local sources estimate that there are some 6000 petroglyphs. The sheer scale of the site is awe-inspiring (it's on the UNESCO World Heritage list) and the view back down the arid desert valley against the backdrop of the distant lush, green irrigated fields is wonderful. Go early to allow several hours to appreciate the place fully and take plenty of water and protection against the fierce sun, including sunglasses. Also take insect repellent if crossing the fields on foot. A guide is recommended if you're short of time because they take you to some of the more interesting carvings.

Towards the Valle de los Volcanes

A road goes north from **Aplao** on the Cotahuasi road to **Andagua**, a village lying at the head of the Valley of the Volcanoes. No fuel is available here. **Transportes Reyna**'s Arequipa-Andagua bus goes on to **Orcopampa**, from which the thermal springs of Huancarama can be visited.

From Andagua there is a road to **Chachas**, a picturesque little village on the edge of a lake. The area is heavily cultivated and there are perfect views of the valley from the top of the hill above Chachas. It is possible to hike from Chachas to Choco and on to Cabanaconde via the Río Colca in four or five days (see page 287). If you have a 4WD vehicle, this is a superb area for driving some rough roads: for instance, a circuit: Arequipa–Aplao–Andagua–Orcopamba–Cailloma–Chivay–Arequipa.

Cotahuasi and around → *For listings, see pages 296-298.*

Cotahuasi → *Population: 3200. Altitude: 2600 m.*

Cotahuasi town nestles in a sheltered hanging valley beneath Cerro Huinao, several kilometres away from the erosive action of the Río Cotahuasi. Though above the citrus zone itself, it has fertile, irrigated environs. The name derives from the Quechua words 'Cota' (union) and 'Huasi' (house), literally translating as united house or close-knit community.

It is a peaceful, colonial town of narrow streets and whitewashed houses with gently subsiding balconies. The main street, Jirón Arequipa, becomes a part of the plaza on busy Sunday mornings. The only traffic seen is the occasional glimpse of the mayor's car, the odd tractor and the infrequent comings and goings of the two buses and occasional combi (see Transport, page 297).

From Cotahuasi, routes split in a 'Y': southwest along the Río Cotahuasi to the Cataratas de Sipia, Quechualla and beyond; north up the Río Huayllapaña to Pampamarca, and northeast to Tomepampa, Alca, Puica and its environs. You can purchase expensive fuel in these places. It is possible to raft or kayak from a point on the Upper Cotahuasi, just past the town, almost to the Pacific, a descent of 2300 m (boats are usually taken out of the water at the village of Iquipi). The season is May to June; rapids Grade IV to V; some portaging is unavoidable.

Around Cotahuasi

Pampamarca, two bumpy hours by combi north of Cotahuasi, is a quaint, small village well-known for rugmaking. It is set on a plateau at 3200 m. From here, you can trek up to the **Bosque de Piedras** (three hours), to the hot springs of **Josla** (3.5 km), or down to the 50-m waterfall of **Uskuni** (under an hour). There's a mirador with beautiful views of the waterfall and the valley (15 minutes). Ask at the Municipio for directions. Some local women can prepare food given warning; ask for Señora Julia to the right of the Municipio. There are also a few rudimentary shops.

Following the Río Cotahuasi to the northeast up the valley, you come to the villages of **Tomepampa** (10 km), the hot springs of **Luicho** (18 km) and **Alca** (20 km), all connected by buses and combis from Cotahuasi. Tomepampa is a neat little hamlet at 2700 m, with painted houses and a handsome chapel. A day's walk beyond Tomepampa is the spectacular rock forest of **Santo Santo**. The recently rehabilitated and attractive hot springs of **Luicho** ① *24 hrs, 33-38°C, US$1.50*, are a short walk from the road, across a bridge. The small village of Alca has one *hostal* (see Sleeping, page 296). Above Alca are the small ruins of Kallak, Tiknay and a 'stone library' of rock formations. Head out of Alca by climbing the stone stairs for the village of Cahuana.

Puica is the last village of any significance in the valley, hanging on a hillside at nearly 3700 m and connected to Alca by combi (three hours, US$1.50). Facilities are basic, but it's an ideal springboard for nearby attractions: for Churca and a vast prairie of Puya Raimondi cacti; the Ocoruro geysers; the ruins of Maucallacta; and the Laguna de Igma. Horses can be hired for US$3 a day, and locals can act as guides. Puica's fiesta is on the 28 July.

About 4 km out of Cotahuasi on the road to Tomepampa, a bridge crosses over to **Taurisma**, from where it's a two-hour walk northeast to the village and pre-Inca ruins of **Huaynacotas**. At the village of **Toro** you can find the thermal springs of Sirhua and Siringay. There are ruins nearby and, from the village, you get fantastic views of the Solimana glacier. To get to Toro, take a combi from Cotahuasi back up the main road towards Chuquibamba, then fork west (around two hours).

Trekking in the Cotahuasi Canyon

One of the main treks in the region follows the Inca trade road from Cotahuasi to **Quechualla** (two days each way).

The path starts next to the football pitch beside the airstrip in Cotahuasi. It heads downhill to **Piro**, which is almost a satellite of Cotahuasi and the gateway to the canyon (the path heads round to the right of the village, just above it). The path then crosses the river twice as it follows its course to **Sipia** (three hours), near which are the tremendously powerful, 150-m-high **Cataratas de Sipia**. Climb to the bluff just beyond the mouth of the black hole and you'll have a superb view downriver. Take extreme care near the falls if it's windy. Water is a problem further down the canyon, so if continuing, fill up your water bottles near the falls. You can get to within an hour's walk of the Cataratas by combi from Cotahuasi; they leave 0600 and 1930, return 0900 and 1400. It's best to visit at midday.

The next three-hour stretch to **Chaupo** is not for those of a nervous disposition as the path is barely etched into the canyon wall, 400 m above the river in places. The towering cliffs are magnificent reds and browns and dissected by near vertical water channels. You can camp at Chaupo, which lies on the pampa, 100 m above the river. Water is available, but ask permission.

Next is **Velinga**, a village that was almost wiped out by Chagas disease. Now only six families remain. Take the path down to the river before the village and cross over the bridge to the right bank. Half a kilometre further on you may need to wade for about 15 m at the foot of a cliff to regain the path. Stay on the same side of the river. If it rains, Quechualla can be cut off for days, as sections of river become too deep and treacherous to wade through (eg just past Velinga).

Before Quechualla are the extensive ruins of **Huña**. They are dilapidated but the remains of terraces and houses give a good idea of the importance of this route in pre-Columbian times. There is an almost intact 100-m stretch of Inca road above a bend in the river on the approach to Quechualla. It can be a bit scary in parts but the alternative is to wade waist deep through the river.

Quechualla is a charming village and, although it is populated by only eight families, it is the administrative capital of the district. It sits up on a cliff above the river. The church and school overlook the wooden bridge and the short climb up to the citrus groves. Trellised vines provide some welcome shade in the street. You may be able to sleep in the schoolhouse; ask Señor Carmelo Velásquez Gálvez for permission. Below the village, on the opposite side of the river, are the ruined terraces of **Maucullachta**. A 16-km hike continues to the ruins of **Marpa**, which are in better condition. The canyon walls, however, are too steep to continue along the river. You need to climb 8 km, on a path at right angles to the river, to Huachuy, then descend a further 8 km to the ruins near the river. There is no water en route; allow four more days to get there.

⊙ Cotahuasi Canyon listings

For Sleeping and Eating price codes and other relevant information, see pages 38-44.

⊜ Sleeping

Toro Muerto *p293*
F El Mirador, Lima 304, Chuquibamba, T054-489279. New, good showers, clean, friendly owner, good views, use of kitchen.
F Hostal Willys, Av Progreso 400, before the Plaza de Armas, Corire, T054-472046. Clean and helpful.
G Hostal Rodríguez, on main plaza in Chuquibamba, T054-489206. Primitive.

Towards the Valle de los Volcanes *p294*
There are several hotels in **Andagua**; Casa Grande is recommended. On the plaza, Restaurant Sarita will cook good, cheap meals for you. In **Chacas**, a woman in the village will let you sleep in a spare room next to her house; she also provides an evening meal. The cost is not fixed and is left up to you – around US$2 per person should be OK.

Cotahuasi *p294*
D Hotel Valle Hermoso, Tacna 108-110, T054-581057, www.hotelvallehermoso.com. Nice cosy environment, beautiful views of the canyon, comfortable rooms, friendly.
E Hostal Alcalá II, Arequipa 116, T054-581090. Run by same family as **Hostal Alcalá** in Alca. Very good, 24-hr hot showers, excellent beds, doubles and triples, friendly, a bit small. Recommended.
F-G Alojamiento Chávez, Jr Cabildo 125, T0554-581028. Has basic rooms around a pleasant, flower-filled courtyard, friendly, Sr José Chávez is helpful on places to visit.
F-G Hostal Fany Luz, Independencia 117, T054-581002. Opposite **Hostal Villa**, basic but amenable, with shared hot showers, double room available with cold water only.
F-G Hostal Villa, Independencia 118, just off the plaza, T054-581018. Basic, shared bathroom is miles from the rooms.

Around Cotahuasi *p295*
E-F Hostal Alcalá, Alca, T054-280450. One of the best *hostales* in the valley. 2 bedrooms with private showers, others

shared, very clean, plenty of hot water, restaurant, good food. Prices vary, sometimes wildly, according to season and demand.
F-G Hostal Primavera, C Unión 112, Tomepampa, n Arequipa, Calle Cruz Verde 300-B, T054-779928/634142, www.cotahuasi-peru.com. On the main street, accommodation with the local school teacher, Señora Irma Sanabria, with hot water and pretty rooms.
G Hostal Uskuni, the only *hostal* in Pampa-marca, off the main square, T054-812189, uskuni@aedes.com.pe. Run by the Vargas family, very basic, cold water, friendly.
G Wasi Punko, T054-266941. Simple accommodation near the turn off for the Luicho baths.

The Municipio in **Puica** has decrepit rooms for guests and can give information, T054-280458. Better accommodation is with the Señora who runs the shop opposite the Municipio, 3 rooms, shared cold water baths, nice views.

🍴 Eating

Toro Muerto *p293*
Recommended restaurants in Corire include **El Fogón** and **La Sirena**, both on Av Progreso. Try the local speciality of *camarones* from the Río Majes.

Cotahuasi *p294*
There are 3 small restaurants/bars on Jr Arequipa offer basic fare; the best is **BuenSabor**, opposite **Hostal Alcalá II**. There are many well-stocked *tiendas*, selling fruit, vegetables and local wine.
🍴 **El Pionero**, Jr Centenario. Clean, with a good *menú*.
🍴 **Las Quenas** and **Las Delicias**, both on main square, have decent menus.

▲▲ Activities and tours

Cotahuasi Canyon *p293*
Several recommended tour operators in Arequipa run 4-day trips to the Cotahuasi Canyon, which take in the highlights of the Sipia falls and the Puya Raimondi Cacti forest. They can also organize adventure sports activities.
Cotahuasi Trek, www.cotahuasitrek.com. Specialist adventure company based in Cotahuasi, owned by Marcio Ruiz, a locally renowned guide.

🚌 Transport

Toro Muerto *p293*
To reach the petroglyphs take the **Empresa Del Carpio** bus to **Corire** from Arequipa main terminal (hourly from 0500, 3-4 hrs, US$4) and ask to be let out at the beginning of the track to Toro Muerto. You can also hire a taxi from the plaza in Corire to the petroglyphs, US$10, including a 2-hr wait.

Towards the Valle de los Volcanes *p294*
La Reyna services from Arequipa to **Andagua** continue to **Orcopampa**. Trebol (T054-425936) and **Reyna** (T054-420770) both depart Arequipa at 1600. Buses return from Andagua to **Arequipa** early afternoon, arriving in the very early morning but you can sleep on the bus until daybreak. There is a daily minibus service Chacas to **Andagua** at 1300 and a truck at around 1000, usually on Sat, Tue and Thu; ask when it's leaving.

Cotahuasi and around *p294*
Alex and La Reyna buses leave Alca for **Arequipa** around 1400 daily. They depart from the plaza in Cotahuasi at 1530 (**Alex**) and 1600 (**La Reyna**), 11-12 hrs, US$12. All companies stop for refreshments in **Chuquibamba** where the paved road begins, about halfway to Arequipa. There are also combis between Cotahuasi and **Alca**.

❶ Directory

Cotahuasi *p294*

Banks There is no place to change money.
Maps Some survey maps are available in the **Municipalidad** and PNP; ask for Richard Posso, T054-581012. They may let you make photocopies at the shop on the corner of the plaza and Arequipa. Sr Chávez has photocopies of the sheets covering Cotahuasi and surroundings. The **Lima 2000** map of the Colca and Cotahuasi canyons is 1:225,000 and has information about the small villages throughout the canyon as well as about interesting places to visit. **Police** The PNP are on the plaza; it is advisable to register with them on arrival and before leaving.

Contents

Footprint features

Border crossings

South Coast

At a glance

◉ **Getting around** Bus.

◉ **Time required** 1 to 2 weeks; a few days if only stopping in Nazca en route to elsewhere.

☼ **Weather** Summer months are Dec-Apr. There may be sea mists May-Oct.

✗ **When not to go** The coast is very dry. There is no time to avoid, unless you don't want to be in the fog. The Nazca Lines are far enough inland not to be covered in mist.

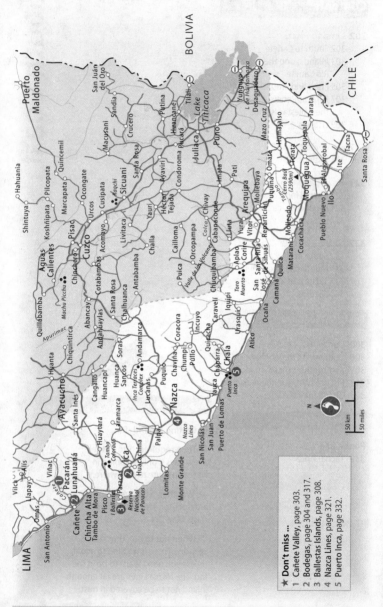

★ **Don't miss ...**
1 Cañete Valley, page 303.
2 Bodegas, page 304 and 317.
3 Ballestas Islands, page 308.
4 Nazca Lines, page 321.
5 Puerto Inca, page 332.

The Pan-American Highway runs all the way south from Lima to the Chilean border and the desert coast has some distinctive attractions. The most famous, and perhaps the strangest, are the enigmatic Nazca Lines, whose origin and function continue to puzzle scientists. More designs on the desert, plus tomb finds at neighbouring Palpa are casting new light on the mystery. Paracas Peninsula is one of the world's great marine bird reserves and was home to one of Peru's most important ancient civilizations. As you bob in a boat to the Ballestas Islands to watch the seabirds, look for the giant Candelabra, drawn on the cliffs by unknown hands.

Further south, the Ica Valley with its wonderful climate, is home to that equally wonderful grape brandy known as pisco. South of Nazca, on a small bay, is Puerto Inca, the seaport and fishing harbour for Cuzco in pre-colonial times. The road from here through the canyons to the sierra was a major Inca artery. That route may have fallen into disuse, but new roads are making it much easier to climb up from the coast with its ramshackle fishing villages and brief flashes of green irrigated valleys. One is the paved highway from Nazca to Abancay, which passes the Pampas Galeras vicuña reserve. Further south, also paved, the stunning road from the port of Ilo to Lake Titicaca can be picked up in the oasis town of Moquegua.

Another route from coast to sierra which is a must to explore is the road which starts in the Cañete Valley, not far south of Lima, and climbs through the Yauyos to Huancayo. There is stunning scenery of rivers and waterfalls in the Nor Yauyos-Cochas Reserve, miles of pre-Columbian agricultural terracing and culturally fascinating villages where ancient languages are spoken. Here, sandwiched between the main Pacific highway and one of the principal commercial centres of the Central Highlands, you will find a way of life quite different from mainstream Peru.

Lima to Pisco

South to Cañete → *For listings, see pages 309-316. Colour map 5, A1/2.*

The first 60 km south from Lima are dotted with a series of seaside resort towns and clubs that come alive in the summer months of December to March. Note that most beaches have very strong currents and can be dangerous if swimming. If you're unsure, ask the locals. The first popular beach is **El Silencio**, at Km 34, which is good for a day trip from Lima. The beach is lined with *cebicherías*, all offering fresh seafood, but go early to get an umbrella and lounge chair (you will be expected to buy food or drinks if using these facilities). Just before El Silencio is a spectacular rock formation a short distance out to sea consisting of two islands known as **La Ballena** (the whale). The next notable beach is **Punta Hermosa** at Km 39, which is a popular summer retreat for Limeños. There are many summer houses here and some nice hostels for those looking to soak up some sun or to surf. Fresh seafood restaurants line the boardwalk of Punta Hermosa. The next beach from Punta Hermosa is **Punta Negra**, Km 47, a popular spot for surfers, well known for having the most consistent surfing break south of Lima. **San Bartolo** is 49 km south from Lima. It is very busy from New Year's Eve to March, but at other times is quiet and relaxing. There are plenty of cheap places to eat. A further 2 km is **Santa María**.

Next comes the charming fishing village of **Pucusana**, 57 km south of Lima (combis from Surco). There are excellent views from the cliffs above the village. It is a working harbour with summer houses for Limeños. You can hire a boat for an hour's trip with **Julián Durán**, T01-998 074829, or **Cóndor**, for US$14, to see Humboldt penguins, sea cat otters, Inca terns, gulls, pelicans, red-legged and Guanay cormorants, shags, boobies, surf birds and Peruvian seaside cinclodes. Don't sail in the direction of the smelly factory, but to the rocks where you can see seabirds close at hand.

The small beach resort of **Chilca**, 14 km south of Pucusana, is 30 minutes by colectivo from the market place. There isn't much to see, but a long, deserted beach does present camping possibilities. You can walk along the beach from Chilca to Salinas (5 km), which has mineral baths. There are a few restaurants and *pensiones*. In summer (December-February), these places fill up with holidaymakers from Lima. Chilca is famous for its figs; roadside stalls sell delicious fig ice cream.

Asia, from Km 92 to Km 104 south of Lima, is an exclusive resort for wealthy Limeños, marked by a great wall. The 20 or so beaches are private, but the commercial centre adjoining the Panamericana with its smart restaurants and summer-opening only **Wong** supermarket is open to all who can afford it.

Chepeconde Beach is reached by a dirt road from Km 120 of the Panamericana. It has fine sand and rocky outcrops that divide it into three sections. The northernmost is the safest and most visited. It's very popular with Peruvian campers in summer.

A few kilometres before Cañete, there is a turning to **Cerro Azul**, an uncrowded beach village, with good surfing and hotels and restaurants on the shore (see below; **Don Satu** is another good option for fresh seafood platters). At this point the dual carriageway ends, but work is continuing to dual the Panamercana to Chincha.

Cañete

About 150 km south of Lima, on the Río Cañete, is the prosperous market centre of **San Vicente de Cañete** (commonly called **Cañete**). All the main services are within a couple of blocks of the plaza. The town hosts a festival in the last week of August, a good opportunity to hear black coastal music and see dance troupes such as Perú Negro.

Inland along the Río Cañete → *For listings, see pages 309-316.*

Ins and outs

Direct buses from Lima for the Cañete Valley leave daily around 1500 with **San Juan de Yauyos**, whose terminal is in the dodgy Grau area of the city. The buses go to various destinations in the valley on different days of the week. Most pass through **Catahuasi**, the stop for Tupe, and on Thursday go direct to **Laraos**. Otherwise go to Cañete and ask about the service with **ETAS/Angoma** to **Huancayo**, via **Catahuasi**, **Chavín**, **Yauyos** and **Llapay**.
▶▶ *See Transport, page 315. For ETAS services in the opposite direction, see page 556.*

Quebrada de Lunahuaná → *Phone code: 01.*

From Cañete, a paved road runs inland, mostly beside the Río Cañete, through **Imperial**, which has a market on Saturday, Sunday and Monday (good for every type of household item), and Nuevo Imperial to the **Quebrada de Lunahuaná**.

Lunahuaná consists of a town and several districts (*anexos*) strung along the valley. They are totally dependent on the Río Cañete for irrigation and for the tourist attractions of rafting and kayaking. Beyond the reach of the water, the surrounding countryside is completely barren but not without its own appeal. In early morning and at dusk the hills are painted in infinite shades of grey, pink and brown, framed by the clear blue sky, fertile green valley and rushing water.

Eight kilometres before Lunahuaná is **Incawasi**, the ruins of an Inca city. A new road cuts right through the middle of the site, which dominates the valley and *quebradas* that run down into it. Incawasi is said to have been a replica of Cuzco, with its divided trapezoidal plaza. The site was built outside the fertile zone of the valley and its rough walls blend in perfectly with the barren hills.

Paullo is the first *anexo* reached after Incawasi. Here stand the ruins of the first church of Lunahuaná. In summer, when the river is high, rafting trips start from just below the plaza. In the low river season a temporary footbridge crosses the river to **Lúcumo**. Two kilometres further on is **San Jerónimo**, the area's whitewater rafting centre; there are several agencies to choose from. Other adventure tourism activities include paragliding and there is an artificial wall for climbing. There is a campsite at Km 33.

Lunahuaná town (40 km from Cañete) has an 18th-century church on the plaza. Opposite the west door, at the top of the plaza, are the Banco de la Nación and Municipalidad, in which is the **tourist office** ① *T01-284 1006, mlunah@mixmail.com*. There are several restaurants in town and in the surrounding *anexos*, some offering rafting. Freshwater shrimp is a local speciality. On Sunday the town is full of life with pisco tastings from the valley's bodegas, food and handicrafts for sale in the plaza and lots of rafting, abseiling and other activities round and about. After the town of Lunahuaná (40 km from Cañete), the road continues unpaved to **Huancayo** up in the sierra, see page 546. Beyond **Condoray** and **Uchupampa** it crosses the Río Cañete to **Catapalla**. A little further on is a *puente colgante* (suspension bridge). Across the road bridge turn right to the village or left to the pre-Inca remains of **Cantagallo**. The site is not signposted; ask directions.

Bodegas

It is interesting to visit the bodegas (wine cellars) in the valley and try the wine. The best known is **Los Reyes** (T01-284 1206) in Condoray, where you can try pisco, wine, manzanilla and *arope* (a grape juice concentrate). A good time to visit is during February and March when you can see the traditional methods of treading the grapes by foot to the beat of the drum. Other bodegas in Condoray include: **Viña Santa María** (T01-437 8892), beside Hostal Río Alto; **Del Valle**, by La Laguna restaurant, and **Viñas del Sur** (T01-437 3187). Also try **El Olimpo** (T01-460 7698) in Uchupampa, beside the Hotel Embassy and bodegas **Reina de Lunahuaná**, in Catapalla, a five-minute walk from the suspension bridge. This last is the most rustic and authentic bodega in the valley and produces an excellent pisco. It offers a free tour and has a restaurant, open at weekends. Recommended.

The Yauyos

Beyond Lunahuaná the road ascending the Cañete Valley leaves the narrow flood plain and runs through a series of *retama*-lined gorges. It passes through **Pacarán** (town of 'eternal spring', also with good pisco) and Zuñiga, where the road narrows, until the paving ends at the San Jerónimo bridge. Here the road divides. A poor but dramatic unpaved road runs 41 km up to the small Andean village of **Viñac** (3190 m). On the way it passes the village of **Huangáscar** and in parts of the valley wall you can see extensive stretches of pre-Columbian agricultural terracing. From January to mid-March the road is impassable after Huangáscar.

The other branch of the road goes to **Catahuasi** (for access to Tupe, see below) and **San Lorenzo de Putinza** before entering the **Reserva Paisajística Nor Yauyos-Cochas** (for information contact Juan Carlos Pilco, specialist in rural community tourism at SERNANP, pilco_traveler@hotmail.com; regional office RPNYC ① *Av Huancavelica 3113, Covica, El Tambo, Huancayo, T064-243888, http://rpnycperu.blogspot.com*. The market town of **Yauyos**, with basic accommodation, is 5 km off this road. The next village is **Llapay**, a good base for exploring the area. There is a basic *hostal* with a restaurant here and you may be able to catch transport to other villages with workers from the **Instituto Valle Grande AECI**. If you have your own car, you can go wherever you want, but the roads are poor and you should seek the advice of someone who knows the region well. The people are friendly but you need to speak Spanish. Two hours' walk west from Llapay (one hour by car) is the village of **Carania**, from where a further two hours' trekking leads to the pre-Inca ruins of **Huamanmarca**.

Further upstream, the valley narrows to an exceptionally tight canyon, with a hair-raising road squeezed between nothing but rock and rushing water. At **Alís** the road forks: north, following the Río Cañete deeper into the reserve to **Huancaya** and **Vilca**, and east, where a steep climb leads to mine workings near the 4600-m pass, beyond which the road drops to Huancayo. For information see www.huancaya.lim.md.gob.pe, the website of the **Municipalidad Distrital of Huancaya**, T01-810 6085, www.huancaya.com, or contact the president of the **Comité de Turismo Rural** in Alís, Jorge Sandoval Varillas, josava_5@hotmail.com.

North of Alís, the upper valley is one of the most beautiful and amazing of all Peru's coastal river valleys, on a par with the Colca Valley. Above Huancaya the river passes through high Andean terrain and descends through a seemingly endless series of incredibly attractive, absolutely clear, turquoise pools and lakes, interrupted by cascades and whitewater rapids. In some pools, huge clumps of tortora reed sway gently and in all there are prolific numbers of trout and abundant birdlife. Large parts of the valley are inaccessible in this section but marvellous day walks can be made upriver from Huancaya and 30 km further on at **Vilca**. At both there are also attractive old colonial bridges across the river.

Culturally, the valley is fascinating for its dying indigenous languages and perhaps the best pre-Columbian terracing anywhere in Peru. **Tupe**, reached on a six-hour walk from Catahuasi, is home to the Jaqaru people, distant cousins to the Aymara of Bolivia and southern Peru. Astonishingly, the Jaqaru have managed to keep alive their traditions and language, which may be the key to unravelling the ultimate origins of the Aymara languages. Tupe's older women still wear traditional red and black dress, though a modern tartan-style variant is taking over among most younger women. Dark red headscarves also abound, and for festivals they still wear *tupus* (traditional dress pins), identical to those depicted on colonial drawings of Inca women's dress. The village is overlooked by the almost sheer rock-face of Tupinachaka, complete with ancient rock paintings.

Laraos is also a linguistic final refuge. A very few aged speakers of the local form of Quechua are to be found in a beautiful, old village of steep streets. Some houses here have the same structure as the reconstructed Inca houses at Machu Picchu, with steeply sloping thatched roofs much longer and lower on one side than on the other. Good times to visit are for the fiestas at **Carnival** (beware the water bombs and flour or talcum powder attacks!), for the irrigation channel cleaning in May, or for the town fiesta in August. The valley's sides are covered with *andenes* in a sweeping curve of several kilometres. There are scenic hikes further up the valley beyond the seasonal lake below the village. Laraos is a 1½-hour walk from Llapay, or there is a daily combi from Llapay at 1100.

Pisco and around → *For listings, see pages 309-316.*

Chincha Alta → *Colour map 5, A2. Population: 110,016.*
After Cañete the highway leaves the green river valley and approaches **Chincha**. On the way is the large development of the **Perú LNG srl** natural gas works at Melchorita. In the surrounding desert towns for the workers are growing up, such as **El Trébol del Pacífico** and **Nuevo Ayacucho**. Arriving at Chincha you pass battery chicken farms and truckstops.

Some 35 km north of Pisco, near Chincha Baja, is **Tambo de Mora**, the old port, with nearby archaeological sites at Huaca de Tambo de Mora, La Centinela, Chinchaycama and Huaca Alvarado. **Chincha** itself still has a thriving negro/criollo culture (for more details, see page 663). It is a good place to sample locally produced wine and pisco. One of the best bodegas is the **Naldo Navarro** ① *Pasaje Santa Rosa, Sunampe, 100 m west of the Panamericana, T056-271356, http://vinosnaldonavarro.com, free guided tours, including tasting*. Founded in 1897 and now run by the fourth generation of the Navarro family, the old cellars are being converted into a museum and the whole bodega is being refurbished. Other bodegas also have guided tours and the third Saturday in September is national pisco day.

Pisco → *Phone code: 056. Colour map 5, B2. Population: 82,250.*
Despite being christened as San Clemente de Macera by the Spanish in 1640, the town had already been unofficially named after the famous local brandy and would always be known as Pisco. Now the largest port between Callao and Matarani, 237 km south of Lima, it serves a large agricultural hinterland.

The town was originally divided into two: **Pisco Pueblo**, with its colonial-style homes, patios and gardens; and **Pisco Puerto**, which, apart from fisheries, has been replaced as a port by the deep-water Puerto General San Martín, beyond Paracas. The two have now

Textiles and trepanation

The Paracas Necropolis culture, which inhabited this region between 1300 BC and AD 200, is renowned for its finely woven textiles, in particular mantos, large decorated cloths, embroidered with anthropomorphic, zoomorphic and geometric designs. These *mantos* were used to wrap mummified bodies in their funerary bundles. Their discovery by anthropologists and archaeologists provided vital clues to this civilization. The bodies were often found to have trepanned skulls. Trepanation was a form of brain surgery performed by the Paracas people in which metal plates were inserted to replace broken sections of skull – a common injury among warring factions at that time. In addition, the Paracas culture practised the intentional deformation of infants' skulls for aesthetic reasons.

expanded into one fairly unattractive town. Avenida San Martín runs from the Plaza de Armas to the sea. It is not recommended to walk on or near **Pisco Playa** at night, as there are many reports of tourists being robbed while walking to the beach; take a taxi or mototaxi. It is best not to carry important items such as plane tickets, passports or anything flash, while out at night.

In August 2007, an earthquake measuring 7.9 on the Richter scale struck the coast of Peru south of Lima, killing 519 people, with 1366 injured and 58,500 homes destroyed. Hardest hit was the province of Ica. In the city of Pisco almost half of all buildings were levelled, while the Chincha area was also heavily damaged. The days following the earthquake showed a remarkable level of solidarity as aid poured in both domestically and from abroad. Schools, supermarkets, even the national stadium were used as collection points for such donations as clothing, dried goods and bottled water. Many people made humanitarian runs, in whatever transport they could get their hands on, to the affected areas to distribute what they had collected. International humanitarian organizations arrived soon afterwards and in a few weeks Pisco had become a tented city. Three years later and many people are still without permanent homes and are living in shacks on the outskirts of town. As far away as the Yauyos you can still see the wooden modular buildings given by the EU still in use, while in Pisco such buildings are hidden behind high brick walls.

Rebuilding is slow for a number of reasons: the high cost of seismic-resistant building materials and designs, a shortage of construction workers and materials and because of difficulties in establishing who owns the land on which rebuilding is planned. There are new buildings going up around the main plaza, with several banks in operation, but the church remains destroyed. The main pedestrian walkway has also been repaired. But Pisco also suffers from its relative isolation. While the road from the Panamericana into the town was being restored as a dual carriageway so that buses can make it into the centre, many bus companies and, more recently, tourist agencies set up their offices at the Pisco turning on the Panamericana. Government support, after an initial surge, is hard to come by for families, but some NGOs are working to rebuild communities. If you wish to lend a hand, contact an organization such as **Pisco Sin Fronteras** ① *Av Las Américas, Asociación San Pedro Mz B, Lt 19, Pisco, T056-534970, www.piscosinfronteras.org*, or **South American Explorers** in Lima. From the tourism point of view almost all activity has moved to Paracas.

Inland from Pisco

From San Clemente on the Pan-American Highway near Pisco, a paved road runs 317 km up to Ayacucho in the sierra, with a branch to Huancavelica. At Castrovirreyna the road reaches 4600 m. The scenery on this journey is superb.

One of the best-preserved Inca ruins in coastal Peru is **Tambo Colorado**, 38 km from San Clemente. It includes buildings where the Inca and his retinue would have stayed. Many of the walls retain their original colours. On the other side of the road is the public plaza and the garrison and messengers' quarters. The caretaker will act as a guide and has a small collection of items found on the site. Wait at his house for transport back to Pisco.

At **Huaytará**, four hours by bus from Pisco, the whole side of the church is a perfectly preserved Inca wall with niches and trapezoidal doorways. Twenty minutes from town are the ruins of Incahuasi with thermal baths. On 24 June is the **Fiesta of San Juan Bautista**.

Paracas Peninsula and the Ballestas Islands → For listings, see pages 309-316.
Colour map 5, B2.

Fifteen kilometres down the coast from Pisco Puerto is the bay of Paracas sheltered by the Paracas Peninsula. It is named after the Paracas winds – sandstorms that can last for three days, especially in August. The wind gets up every afternoon, peaking at around 1500. The whole peninsula, a large area of coast to the south and the Ballestas Islands, are all part of a national reserve, created in 1975, which covers a total of 335,000 ha. It is one of the most important marine reserves in the world, with the highest concentration of marine birds. The region is also economically important, being a major producer of guano (see box, page 309).

Ins and outs

Getting there and around Most visitors explore the reserve on an organized tour from Paracas or Pisco but, if you're travelling independently, it can be reached along the coast road from Pisco and San Andrés, passing the fishing port, an oil refinery and a large proportion of Peru's fishmeal industry. Alternatively, go down the Pan-American Highway for 14.5 km beyond the Pisco turning and take the road to Paracas across the desert. After 11 km turn left along the coast road and, 1 km further on, fork right to Paracas village. Return to the main road for the entrance to the reserve, where you pay and can ask for a map.

From the park entrance, it takes about 50 minutes to get to Lagunilla by private transport, 45 minutes to La Mina and an hour to Mirador de los Lobos. Make sure your car is in good condition and never leave it unattended. It's safest to stay close to tour groups.
▶▶ For details of tours, see page 315.

Paracas

Since the 2007 earthquake, Paracas has developed into a busy little place, providing all the services that visitors need for getting to the national reserve and the Islas Ballestas. There are plenty of tour operators, *hostales*, restaurants and handicraft shops based around the plaza and the Malecón while, to the south of town, holiday homes for Limeños stretch round the bay to a couple of luxury resorts.

Paracas National Reserve

ⓘ *Daily 0900-1700, US$1.75, www.sernanp.gob.pe*
The entrance to the reserve is just south of the town of Paracas on the main paved road at a control booth (*garita*). Nearby is the **Julio Tello Site Museum** (undergoing refurbishment in

2010). Its exhibits are from the burial sites discovered in 1925 under the Paracas desert by the Peruvian archaeologist, Julio C Tello. However, the best examples of textiles and funerary bundles can be found in Lima at the Museo de la Nación (see page 86) and at the archaeological museum, Pueblo Libre. The wildlife on view includes a wide variety of sea mammals and rare and exotic birds. Condors can even be seen in February and March from the rough road to Laguna Grande. These massive birds feed on the ready supply of sea lion carcasses. Rather more delicate are the flamingos that tend to feed at Mendieta bay, between Laguna Grande and Playa Supay. You will need binoculars for the best view. Note that from January to March the birds head for the sierra.

A network of roads, reasonably well signed, crosses the peninsula. From the entrance the road is paved to the Zarcillo mirador (look-out) over **La Catedral**. This used to be the main landmark of the reserve, an arch carved in the cliffs by the sea, until it was destroyed in the 2007 earthquake. An explanatory sign shows what people used to look at, but the view over the ocean, with seabirds flying around the cliffs, is still worth seeing. Near here is the mirador over Playa Supay to the south. Nearby, a monument marks the spot where San Martín landed in Peru, on 8 September 1820, after liberating Argentina. Soon after, a shipload of British troops, led by Lord Cochrane, arrived to help General San Martín plan his strategy to break the Spanish stranglehold in the region. Tours usually head north from here to **Yumaque** bay and then towards the fishing village of **Lagunillas**, 5 km from the museum. It has beaches that are free from stingrays, but not very clean. There are eating places here but they are poor value (watch out for prices in dollars) and unhygienic.

Heading west from Lagunillas 6 km around the peninsula, you reach **Mirador de los Lobos** at Punta El Arquillo, which looks down on a raucous mob of sea lions. On the north side of the peninsula, about 14 km from the entrance, a pre-Columbian drawing known as **El Candelabro** (the candelabra) is traced into the hillside. At least 50 m long, it is best seen from the sea. Approaching it by land is not a good idea as disturbance of the sand around it is beginning to destroy the monument; some idiots have even driven over it. There are differing theories as to its exact purpose. Some believe it to be linked to the Nazca Lines (see page 321), 200 km to the south, others that it is related to the Southern Cross constellation and was used to help guide ancient sailors. Still others contend that it represents the cactus used by the ancient high priests for its hallucinogenic powers. A few cruel cynics have even suggested that it was the work of some opportunistic local guides.

Extended tours are available which go through the desert in the southern portion of the reserve. Details of walking routes are available from the visitor centre or ask for the 'Hoja 28-K' map at **Instituto Geográfico Nacional** in Lima. It is not safe to walk alone and it is easy to get lost in the hot, wide desert area.

Ballestas Islands

The Ballestas islands, dubbed the poor man's Galápagos by many, are nonetheless spectacular in their own right and well worth visiting. They are eroded into numerous arches and caves, hence their name – *ballesta* means bow, as in archery. These arches provide shelter for thousands of seabirds, some of which are very rare, and countless sea lions. A former guano factory can be seen on one of the islands and several others have installations. The book *Las Aves del Departamento de Lima* by Maria Koepcke is useful (see also www.avesdelima.com/playas.htm).

Boat trips to the islands leave from the jetty in Paracas town. They usually go in the morning to avoid rougher seas in the afternoon and last two hours; tours may be cancelled entirely if the sea is too choppy. Most boats are speedboats with life jackets, but

An economic mess

The islands lying off the coast of Peru are the breeding grounds for millions of sea birds, whose droppings have accumulated over the centuries. These piles of mineral-rich excrement were turned into piles of cash during the last century.

Though the ancient Peruvians knew of the benefits of guano – the name given to the natural fertilizer – and used it on their crops, it wasn't until 1840 that vast deposits of the stuff were exploited for commercial purposes. It was at this time that Peru began to trade abroad, particularly with France and England. Almost simultaneously, guano began to replace rare metals as the country's main export.

However, with the economy heavily based on the sales of bird droppings, Peru was caught in a vicious circle of borrowing money on future sales, then having to repay loans at vastly inflated rates. This unhealthy state of affairs was exacerbated in 1864 when Spain decided to occupy the guano islands of Chincha, thereby leaving the Peruvian government really up to its neck in it.

The main producers of guano are the guanay cormorant and the Peruvian booby. They gather in colonies on the islands, attracted by the huge shoals of anchovy that feed on the plankton in the cold water of the Humboldt current.

some are very crowded. Wear warm clothing, but also take protection against the sun and wear sunglasses. You will see, close up, sea lions, guano birds, pelicans, penguins and, if you're lucky, dolphins swimming in the bay. The boats pass Puerto San Martín and the Candelabra (see above) en route to the islands but they do not go to see the flamingos and few tours include Isla San Gallán, where there are thousands of sea lions.

After the 2007 earthquake seabirds and sea lions migrated in great numbers to the islands off Lima and Callao. By 2010, many had returned to Paracas.

◉ Lima to Pisco listings

For Sleeping and Eating price codes and other relevant information, see pages 38-44.

◉ Sleeping

South to Cañete *p302*
Many hotels advertise that they have swimming pools. If they do indeed have them, they are only likely to be full during the summer, Dec-Mar/Apr.

Punta Hermosa
A-D Casa Barco, Av Punta Hermosa 340, T01-230 7081, www.casabarco.com. This is a funky little hotel with a pool, decorated with great artwork, very clean and offers double rooms with private bathroom, sea views and cable TV or a bed in a shared room with shared bathroom. It also has luxury suites. Meal plans available, breakfast is included. It's a short walk from where buses drop passengers off.
D-E La Rotunda, Av Bolognesi 592, T01-440 2529. This is a quaint little hostel above a restaurant of the same name. Large rooms, great views, above the boardwalk, cable TV.
E La Isla, T01-230 7146. Also right on the boardwalk, not as charming as the others, but cheaper in a dorm. Breakfast is included.

Punta Negra
E Hostal Hamacas, T01-231 5498, surfresortperu@terra.com.pe. Right on the beach, but the lodgings are basic.

San Bartolo
A Peñascal Surf Hotel, Av Las Palmeras 258, T01-430 7436, www.surfpenascal.com. Price is for full board, including welcome drink, yoga and Spanish lessons, hot water and laundry; rooms with private bathroom, kitchen, surf specials. Relaxing spot, with balconies overlooking the surf – a good place to chill for a couple of days.
B Hostal 110, next door to **Posada del Mirador**, Malecón San Martín. Rents apartments and rooms with great views, some with chimney, all with fridge, pool, very comfortable.
B Posada del Mirador, Malecón San Martín 105, T01-9964 88169. Price for a bungalow is **AL**, breakfast included, a/c, TV, pool, bikes, tennis, but mainly for surfers. Remodelled and landscaped on the beachfront.

Pucusana
E El Mirador – Centro Turístico Belvedere, T01-430 9228, elmirador depucusana@ hotmail.com. Owned by hospitable Adolfo del Campo, on hill overlooking the village and harbour, a cheap haven for travellers. Adolfo cooks whatever is available when the boats come in.

Cerro Azul
B Las Palmeras, Panamericana Sur Km 132, on the beach, T01-284 6005. Said to be the best in town, with TV and pool.
C Hostal Juanito, on seafront, T01-335 3710, juanito_cerroazul@hotmail.com. This *hostal* has a restaurant with delicious fresh seafood.

Cañete *p302*
E Hostal Colibrí, Urb Los Libertadores, Mz A, Lote 9, T01-581 1309. A clean hotel.
E Hostal Edwar's, Benavides 150, T01-581 3632. Clean, friendly, rooms with TV and bath, quieter rooms at the back.
E Hostal Rec, Urb Los Libertadores, Mz A, Lote 7, T01-581 2623. A comfortable hotel with wooden floors and cable TV.
F Hostal San Francisco, Santa Rosa 739, 2 blocks north of the plaza, T01-581 2409.

Rooms with bathroom, clean, friendly, quiet. Recommended.

Quebrada de Lunahuaná *p303*
B Río Alto, just outside Lunahuaná, T01-284 1125, www.rioaltohotel.com. Rooms with bathroom or bungalows for 7, hot water. Also pool, restaurant, disco, rafting, very nice.
B-C Embassy Jardín, Uchupampa, T01-472 3525. Price drops in low season. All facilities, restaurants, disco, gardens, rafting, large property, good, popular with families. In same group but slightly more expensive is **Embassy Río**, same phone, riverside location.
B-C Regina, Condoray, T/F01-472 2370. Price drops in low season. Hot water, TV, swimming pool, cafeteria, attractive, with good views over the valley.
E El Refugio, Jr Bolognesi 179, Lunahuaná, T01-284 1020. A pleasant, serviceable *hostal* near the plaza, with TV, clean.
F Hostal Casuarinas, Grau 295, Lunahuaná, T01-284 1045. Near the plaza, a clean, basic *hostal*, with TV, bath and hot water.

The Yauyos *p304*
Yauyos
AL-A pp Viñak-Reichraming, (Refugios del Perú), near Santiago de Viñac, 77 km from Lunahuaná; Emilio Cavenecia 225, of 321, Lima, T01-421 6952, www.refugiosdelperu.com. A purpose-built lodge with a marvellous view down the valley. Rooms and a bungalow suite, full board with good meals, open fires, a tempting outdoor hot tub, internet, TV room with DVDs, kind service. Activities include top-class horse riding, mountain biking and trekking, all included in the price. A great place to escape from Lima for a couple of days – there is no point in trying to go for 1 night, the journey is too long and you'll need a bit of time to acclimatise to the altitude. Closed Jan to mid-Mar. Recommended.

Llapay
G Hostal Llapay, Llapay. Basic, very friendly, with restaurant. They will open the door even if you arrive in the middle of the night.

Huancaya

In Huancaya there are several *hospedajes*, including: **La Posada de Don Pedro**, Familia Reinoso Zárate, on the Plaza, T01-348 9013 (in Lima, ask for Lucia Lastarria), with hot water; **Los Rosales**, Familia Fernández, T01-459 9489, with hot water, has guides for local excursions; **Mi Tradición**, Familia Salazar Rodríguez, T064-212090, and **G Familia Torres**, T01-534 5860, basic but clean and friendly. All offer accommodation and meals. T01-810 6086/7, municipal phone, to ask for details.

Vilca

There is 3 basic *hospedajes* in Vilca, an **Albergue Turístico**, **Brisas de Papacocha** and **Hospedaje Restaurante Vilca** (all **G** pp, T01-810 0301 for all of them).

Tupe

In Tupe accommodation hardly exists, but there is a basic municipal *hostal*, and you should always be able to find someone willing to put you up and cook you a basic meal. There are also flat grazing areas with streams immediately below and above the village where a tent could be pitched.

Laraos

In Laraos is a municipal hotel with a restaurant (**G** pp), basic but good; you can pay a little extra for a hot shower.

Chincha Alta *p305*

Along the Panamericana in Chincha itself there are many hotels and *hostales*, especially near the **Soyuz** bus terminal.
AL-A Casa Andina Classic, Panamericana Km 197.5, T056-262451, www.casa-andina. com. A modern hotel on the outskirts of Chincha Alta, with gardens, swimming pool, buffet breakfast included, Wi-Fi and all other facilities in this recommended chain's style.

Casa Andina has taken over the famous **Hacienda San José**, 9 km south of town in El Carmen district, turn off at Km 203, to turn it into a **Private Collection** hotel. A 17th-century sugar and cotton estate

ranch-house, with beautiful buildings, pool, garden, small church, colonial crafts, it was severely damaged in 2007. Tunnels run from the basement and are believed to link up with Tambo de Mora in order to facilitate the contraband trade in black slaves from Africa. The catacombs, where many of those slaves were interred, can be visited.

Pisco *p305*

Despite the earthquake damage, there is a wide choice of hotels in Pisco. If arriving by bus and getting out at the turn-off for Pisco on the Panamericana, do not be bullied by taxi drivers who tell you that your preferred hotel in Pisco or Paracas is closed/too expensive/no good. Stick to your decision and go to the place of your choice. Then make your own mind up. Mosquitoes are a problem in the summer.
C La Hostería del Monasterio, Av Bolognesi 326, T056-531383, sister hotel of **Posada Hispana**. Fairly new; 3 triples and 8 doubles, hot water, cable TV, breakfast terrace.
C Posada Hispana Hotel, Bolognesi 222, T056-536363, www.posadahispana.com. Rooms each with loft and bathroom, also rooms with shared bath, hot water, can accommodate groups, comfortable, has **Café de Posada** (lunch US$2), information service, English, French, Italian and Catalan spoken. Recommended.
C-D Hostal San Isidro, San Clemente 103, T/F056-536471, www.sanisidrohostal.com. With bath, **F** without, hot water, safe, clean and welcoming, very nice pool and cafeteria, free laundry facilities, games room, English spoken, parking. Breakfast not included, new kitchen to offer restaurant services. Arranges dune buggy tours. Recommended.
C-D Residencial San Jorge, Jr Barrio Nuevo 133, T056-532885, www.hotelsanjorge residencial.com. Cable TV, hot water, internet, secure parking, breakfast is not included in room price but there is a restaurant on site serving breakfast, lunch and dinner, swanky by Pisco standards and spacious, café/bar in the garden.

D Hostal El Candelabro, Callao y Pedemonte, T056-532620, hostalelcandelabro@hotmail.com. Modern, pleasant, all rooms with bath, fridge, cable TV.

D Hostal Los Inkas Inn, Prol Barrio Nuevo Mz M, Lte 14, Urb San Isidro, T056-536634, www.losinkasinn.com. Affordable, rooms have safes, rooftop games area, internet, **G** pp in dorm, small pool. Soon to open Inkas Inn II on the other side of the road with bar/disco on top floor.

D Hostal Tambo Colorado, Av Bolognesi 159, T056-531379, www.hostaltambo colorado.com. Welcoming, helpful owners are knowledgeable about the area, hot water, cable TV, small café/bar.

Paracas *p 307*

LL Doubletree Guest Suites Paracas, Lote 30-34, Urb Santo Domingo on the outskirts, T01-617 1000, www.doubletree.com. Low rise luxury rersort at the far south end of the town on a sheltered bay. It has clean lines and is of a comfortable size, built around a lovely pool. On the beach, with water sports, spa, all mod cons including Wi-Fi and kitchenette, and popular with families.

LL Hotel Paracas Luxury Collection Resort, Av Paracas 173, T056-581333, www.libertador.com.pe. The reincarnation of the famous **Hotel Paracas**, as a resort with spa, pools and excellent rooms in cottages around the grounds. It has access to beach, a choice of restaurants and a bar. Even though it is in town, it is secluded behind a high wall.

L La Hacienda Bahía Paracas, Lote 25, Urb Santo Domingo, T01-213 1000, www.hotel eslahacienda.com. Next to **Doubletree** but not connected to it, with rooms and suites, some with access straight to the pool, with a spa, a choice of restaurants and bar.

B Posada del Emancipador, Av Paracas 25, T056-532818, www.posadadelemancipador. com. Modern, with rooms, suites and bungalows, restaurant **Wayra**, swimming pool, bar, breakfast included, Wi-Fi and parking.

B-C El Mirador, just outside town at the turn-off to El Chaco, T056-545086, www.elmiradorhotel.com. A relaxing place with tranquil gardens, rooms have hot water, good service, boat trips arranged, meals available, large outdoor pool.

C Santa María, Av Paracas s/n, T056-545045, www.santamariahostal.com. Smart rooms, hot water, internet and ¶ **El Chorito** restaurant, mainly serving fish and seafood.

D Hostal El Amigo, El Chaco, T056-545042, hostalelamigo@hotmail.com. Simple, hot water, breakfast not yet available, good reports. Also arranges tours to Islas Ballestas and the national reserve.

D Los Frayles, Av Paracas Mz D lote 5, T056-545141, www.hostallosfrayles.com. A variety of simple, well-kept rooms, breakfast extra, free internet for 30 mins, roof terrace, tourist information.

D Mar Azul, Alan García Mz B lote 20, T056-534542, hmarazulparacas@hotmail.com. Family run, all female staff, comfortable, also dorm **F** per person, hot water, breezy

Pisco: a history in the making

A visit to Peru would not be complete without savouring a pisco sour. Peruvians are mighty proud of their national tipple, which has turned out to be one of the few positive results of conquest.

Peru was the first conquered territory in Spanish America to produce wines and brandies. The cultivation of grapes began with the import of vinestalks from the Canary Islands, which were planted on the outskirts of Lima. The crop later reached Cuzco and Ayacucho in the Andes but it was in Ica that the enterprise really took off, owing to the region's exceptional climate.

A hundred years after the conquest, the wine and pisco trade had grown considerably. Ica sent its wine to Huamanga, Cuzco, Lima and Callao. And ships left from Pisco for ports in Central America, as well as Valparaíso and Buenos Aires.

Royal bans tried to halt the expansion of Peruvian vineyards because it endangered the Spanish wine industry. In 1629, the prohibition included the transport of Peruvian wines aboard Atlantic-bound ships. But despite the restrictions, the industry continued to expand during the 17th and 18th centuries.

Though a few firms utilize modern procedures to manufacture and market larger quantities, pisco is still mostly made by small, independent producers. The grapes are crushed by foot and the fermented grape juice is emptied into traditional Peruvian stills, called *falcas*, which are crucial to the process of true pisco production. More conventional wineries still rely on wood from the carob tree, a slow-burning fuel whose constant source of heat makes for a finer flavour, rather like food cooked over a charcoal fire.

Another important factor is the type of grape used. The Quebranta, brought to the Americas by the Spaniards, lends its unique characteristics to the making of renowned 'pure' pisco. There are also fragrant piscos from Moscatel and Albilla varieties, 'Creole' piscos made with prime fragrant grapes and 'green' piscos made with partially fermented grape juice.

The Ica valley is still Peru's foremost producer of pisco, followed by the valleys of Pisco, Chincha, Lunahuaná and Moquegua. Other centres include Vitor in Arequipa, Locumba in Tacna and Surco in Lima.

---

roof terrace for breakfast (included in the price), helpful owner Yudy Patiño. Also owns **Ballestas Expeditions** for local tours.

❼ Eating

South to Cañete *p302*

♈-♈ **Bahía**, Billinghurst 225, Pucusana, at the end of the cul-de-sac leading off the port. Serves good seafood and has a *hospedaje*.
♈-♈ **El Sol**, Billinghurst 220, Pucusana, T01-430 9072. Probably the best restaurant, good for fish and seafood.

Cañete *p302*

There are also several good Chinese restaurants near the plaza. Try **Panadería Valentino** for baked *empanadas* and sweet treats.
♈ **Cevichería Muelle 56**, Bolognesi 156. Recommended restaurant serving seafood.
♈ **El Piloto**, Km 137 on the Panamerican Highway just before entering Cañete. This is a great restaurant serving breakfasts, fresh seafood and other Peruvian dishes, guaranteed to satisfy. There is also a Pecsa service station and good toilets.
♈ **Magdalena**, Bolognesi 135. Serves a good *menú*, including dishes such as pork cooked in wine and butter beans.

♥ **Marinas Chicken** on 2 de Mayo, 2 blocks from the plaza, T01-581 1358. Welcoming with great chicken and other Peruvian food.

Quebrada de Lunahuaná p303
♥♥-♥ **El Pueblo**, Grau 406, Lunahuaná. Specializes in *camarones*. The *chupe de camarones* is recommended.
♥♥-♥ **Pizzería de Camarones**, Condoray. Open weekends only. Serves huge pizzas.
♥♥-♥ **Refugio de Santiago**, C Real 33, T01-436 2717, Paullo. Sat and Sun only. Excellent restaurant with a fine view, herb garden and orchard. Try the *criollo* buffet.
♥ **Cremoladas Josefina**, Jita. Delicious, refreshing *cremoladas* of crushed ice (boiled water used) mixed with fruit pulp; grape and *lúcuma* varieties are especially good.

Pisco p305
♥♥-♥ **As de Oro**, San Martín 472, T056-532010, www.asdeoros.com.pe. Closed Mon. Good food, not cheap but always full at lunchtime, swimming pool.
♥ **Café Pirata**, Callao 104, T056-534343, cafepiratapisco@gmail.com. Open Mon-Sat 0630-1500, 1800-2200. Desserts, pizzas, sandwiches, coffee and lunch menu.
♥ **Chifa Lisen**, Av San Martín 325, T056-535527. Open 1230-1530, 1800-2200. Chinese food.

Paracas p307
There are several eating places on the Malecón by Playa El Chaco, all with similar menus and prices (in our ♥♥ range) and open for breakfast, eg **Bahía** (T056-532384); **Brisa Marina** (T056-545125), varied menu, mainly seafood, good; **Johnny y Jennifer** (T056-545006), which also serves vegetarian.

⊛ **Festivals and events**

Quebrada de Lunahuaná p303
Feb Festival of adventure sports.
Mar Fiesta de la Vendimia, the grape harvest festival on the 1st weekend.

Late Sep/early Oct The lively Fiesta del Níspero (medlar fruit harvesting festival).

The Yauyos p304
2 Feb Tupe's main annual festival celebrates the Virgen de la Candelaria.
17 Jul Festival Nor-Yauyina held in Llapay, attended by many people including Limeños.

Chincha Alta p305
Among other things (eg olives) Chincha is famous for its many festivals.
6 Jan Celebración del Nacimiento de la Beata Melchorita Saravia.
End Feb Verano Negro, or Black Summer. During this time the black culture of the area, repressed for so many centuries, is freely expressed in the dancing competitions, though black participation in the festival is still somewhat limited.
Mar Festival de la Vendimia, grape harvest festival is celebrated in the 2nd week.
Mid-Jul Festival de la Virgen del Carmen.
Late Oct/early Nov Tourist Week.
Nov Festival de Danzas Negras, held in the black community of El Carmen, 10 km south.
4 Dec Peregrinación a la Ermita de la Beata Melchorita.

Pisco p305
End Jun Fiesta de San Pedro.
Sep Tourist Week in the 2nd week.
21 Nov Peregrinación a la Hermita de la Beata de Humay (Pilgrimage to the Sanctuary of the Beate de Humay). The little church in which the bust of the Saint is kept was destroyed in the 2007 eathquake, but the devotion continues, see www.beatitadehumay.com.

▲ **Activities and tours**

South to Cañete p302
Entre Mares, Manzana E, Lote 27, Urb La Planicie, Punta Hermosa, T01-230 4078, www.peru-surf.com. Surfing, classes and equipment rental, bungalows and bunk rooms

for 2 to 8, hot water, meals available, airport transfers, internet, living room with cable TV. **Peru Adventure Lodge**, Manzana Ñ, Lote 1, Urb La Planicie, Punta Hermosa, T01-230 8351, www.peruadventure.com. Offers accommodation, surfing, spearfishing, diving, fossil hunting and more.

Quebrada de Lunahuaná *p303*

Several places in **San Jerónimo** and **Paullo** offer rafting and kayaking. In Nov-Apr, when the river is high (highest from Dec), white-water rafting is at Grades IV-V. May-Oct is the low-water season when only boat trips are possible (Grades I-II). There's excellent kayaking 2½ hrs upriver. Rafting costs US$15 per person for 1½ hrs. Annual championships and a festival of adventure sports are held every Feb.

Hemiriver Adventures, Av Grau 255, Lunahuana, T01-534 2339, www.hemiriver. com. Rafting, mountain biking, trekking, ATV trips, rappel, kayak courses and horseriding.
Río Cañete Expediciones, Camping San Jerónimo, Carretera Cañete-Lunahuaná Km 33, T01-284 1271, www.riocanete.com.pe. Longest-established company in Lunahuaná, for hiking, sport climbing, rafting, camping, with an outdoor restaurant.
Xtreme Raft, Jr Grau 329, Lunahuaná, T01-284 1264, www.extremeraft.com. Offers rafting, mountain biking, trekking, ATV trips, rappel and kayak courses. Also tours to Huancaya in the Reserva Paisajística Nor Yauyos-Cochas.

Paracas *p307*

There are agencies all over town offering trips to the Islas Ballestas, the Paracas reserve, Ica, Nazca and Tambo Colorado. A 2-hr boat tour to the islands costs US$12-14 per person. Usually, agencies will pool clients together in 1 boat. A private boat trip costs US$25-30, minimum 2 people. To visit Isla San Gallán you have to rent a boat for about US$230 for 20 passengers, plus US$35 if Ballestas are included. Bicycles can be hired in town for US$7.25. Only deal with agencies. Do not book tours on the street. An agency that does not pool clients is **Huacachina**, based in Ica, with an office in Paracas, T056-215582, www.huacachinatours.com.

Zarcillo Connections, Independencia A-20, Paracas, T056-536636, www.zarcillo connections.net. With 15 years' experience for trips to the Paracas National Reserve, Tambo Colorado, trekking and tours to Ica, Chincha and the Nazca Lines and surrounding sites. Agent for **Cruz del Sur** buses. Also has its own hotel, **Zarcillo Paradise**, in Paracas.

Transport

Cañete *p302*

The main bus stop in San Vicente de Cañete is on the highway; wait for the service you want going north or south and hope there are free seats. To **Lima**, frequent, with Soyuz/PerúBus (2 de Mayo block 7 y Panamericana), 2 hrs, US$3. To **Pisco**, 2 hrs, US$2.

To **Huancaya** direct, Sat night only, but a more frequent service is planned, following road improvements. Other options include taking a bus to Yauyos or Alís and looking for onward traffic from there.

To **Huancayo**, via the Cañete Valley, with ETAS/Angoma (opposite the AEDO service station), T01-287 8831, T9771 1254, US$7.55.

Quebrada de Lunahuaná *p303*

To reach **Lunahuaná**, take a Soyuz combi from Cañete for US$1.85, or a taxi (more from the Panamericana than from centre). Alternatively take a colectivo from 2 de Mayo block 1 (US$0.75) to **Imperial** and then a colectivo from Av La Mar, 30 mins, US$0.90, or combi, 45 mins, US$0.75. For **Condoray** or **Uchupampa**, take a taxi, US$1-2. Turismo Viñac, Av La Mar, runs from Imperial to **Viñac**, Mon, Wed, Sat, 5 hrs, US$3.50. You can get from Lunahuaná to **Yauyos** in the upper Cañete Valley, daily 1900-2200; ask for the shop where the bus stops and get the shopkeeper to stop the bus.

The Yauyos *p304*

Bus services through the valley are provided by San Juan de Yauyos to and from **Lima**, and by ETAS in **Cañete** and **Huancayo**. If you visit **Laraos**, you may be lucky and get a direct bus back to Lima from Laraos itself (usually Thu, about 1000) but on other days your best bet is to hitch or hike back down to **Llapay** for the ETAS bus from Huancayo as it passes through. A bus goes from Yauyos at 0100-0230, passing **Llapay** 0200-0400 en route to **Huancayo**, where it arrives 0900. There may also be a few buses a week from Huancayo to Yauyos with San Juan de Yauyos. There is little regular traffic north of Alís to **Huancaya** and **Vilca**.

Pisco and around *p305*

Bus Buses drop passengers at San Clemente on Panamericana Sur, known as **El Cruce**; many bus companies and tour agencies have their offices here. It's a 10-km taxi ride from the centre, US$5, US$8 to Paracas. Colectivos leave from outside the Banco Continental in the Plaza for El Cruce when full, US$2. To **Lima**, 242 km, 4 hrs, US$4. The best companies are: Ormeño, Cruz del Sur, 2 a day each, and Soyuz, every 7 mins. Ormeño has an office in Pisco plaza and will take you to El Cruce to meet their 1600 bus. Flores is the only company that goes into Pisco town, from Lima and Ica, but buses are poor and services erratic. To **Ica**, US$0.90 by bus, 45 mins, 70 km, with Ormeño, also colectivos. To **Nazca**, 210 km, take a bus to Ica and then change to a colectivo. To **Ayacucho**, 317 km, 8-10 hrs, US$7.55-15.15, several buses daily, leave from El Cruce, book in advance to ensure seat and take warm clothing as it gets cold at night. To **Tambo Colorado** from San Clemente colectivos charge US$1.50 per person. Alight 20 mins after the stop at Humay; the road passes right through the site. Return by bus to Pisco in the afternoon. For transport back to Pisco wait at the caretaker's house. Taxi from Pisco US$25. Tours from Pisco agencies US$10-15 with guide, minimum 2 people.

Paracas *p307*

Cruz del Sur, Oltursa and Ormeño buses between Lima and Nazca stop at the Double Tree Hotel near Paracas, Cruz del Sur 4 a day (office at Zarcillo Connections, see above), US$20-26 from **Lima**, US$12-15 to **Nazca**. Others have 1-2 a day, US$19-22.

Taxi

From **Pisco** to Paracas about US$2.50-3; combis when full, US$0.50, 25 mins.

❶ Directory

Pisco *p305*

Banks ATMs at banks on Plaza, Visa and Globalnet. Also **BCP** on Fermín Tangüis in a Repsol service station. **Internet and telephone** In the town centre.

Ica and around

→ *Colour map 5, B2. Phone code: 056. Population: 161,406. Altitude: 410 m.*
Ica is Peru's main wine centre. The city is on the Río Ica, which is almost permanently dry and rubbish-strewn but the waters of the Choclacocha and Orococha lakes at 4570 m are tunnelled for 9 km from the Andes into the Ica Valley and irrigate 30,000 ha of land. As well as wine, the city is famous for its tejas, a local sweet of manjarblanco. It suffered less damage than Pisco in the 2007 earthquake, but one side of the Plaza de Armas collapsed. Most travellers spend little time in Ica itself, preferring to stay at the oasis at Huacachina. Here you will find a lake surrounded by towering sand dunes, which are great for racing up and down on dune buggies and learning the skills of sandboarding. Increasingly popular are trips into the desert to experience the mysteries of this barren landscape. ▸▸ *For listings, see pages 318-320.*

Ins and outs

Getting there and around Buses from Lima travel along the Avenida Municipalidad nearly into the centre of town. Most bus offices are on Lambayeque blocks one and two and Salaverry block three. Look after your bags when transferring between buses to or from Nazca, Pisco or Lima; pickpockets and bag-snatchers operate here. The majority of hotels are on the far side of the Plaza de Armas from the bus offices, or increasingly in out-of-town residential neighbourhoods. You will need a taxi to get around especially if you intend to visit the bodegas.

Tourist information Regional information is available from **Dircetur** ① *Av Grau 148, T056-238710, ica@mincetur.gob.pe.* See also www.helloica.com. Some tourist information is available at travel agencies. Also try **Touring y Automóvil Club del Perú** ① *Camino a Huacachina s/n, T056-235061, ica@touringperu.com.pe.*

Sights

Southwest of the centre is the **Museo Regional** ① *Av Ayabaca, block 8, T056-234383, Mon-Wed 0800-1900, Thu-Sun 0900-1800, US$4, students US$2.15, tip guides US$4-5, bus No 17 from the Plaza de Armas (US$0.50).* It houses mummies, ceramics, textiles and trepanned skulls from the Paracas, Nazca and Inca cultures. There's a well-displayed collection of Inca *quipus* and clothes made of feathers. It also has informative displays with maps of all sites in the department. Behind the building is a scale model of the Nazca Lines with an observation tower. The kiosk outside sells copies of motifs from ceramics and textiles.

Bodegas around Ica

There are several wine bodegas you can visit. **Bodega El Carmen** is on the right-hand side when arriving from Lima. This pisco distillery has an ancient grape press made from a huge tree trunk and is worth a visit. **Bodega La Caravedo** ① *Panamericana Sur 298, T511-9833 4729,* with organic production and sophisticated presentation. Ten kilometres outside Ica, in the district of Subtanjalla, is **Bodega El Catador** ① *Fondo Tres Esquinas 102, T056-962629, elcatadorcristel@yahoo.es, daily 1000-1800, good tours in Spanish, take a combi from the 2nd block of Moquegua, 20 mins, US$0.40, taxi, 10 mins, US$1.50.* It has a shop selling home-made wines and pisco, plus traditional handicrafts associated with winemaking. There is also a restaurant-bar serving lunch, with dancing and music in the evening. The best time to visit is during harvest – late February to early April – when wine and pisco tasting is usually possible. Try Cachina, a very young white wine 'with a strong yeasty taste', which is drunk about two weeks after the grape harvest. Nearby is **Bodega Alvarez**, whose owner, Umberto Alvarez, is very hospitable. Ask about their *pisco de mosto verde* and the rarer, more expensive, *pisco de limón*, which will set you back US$40 per bottle.

In **Ocucaje**, 30 km south of Ica, Señor Luis Chipana's **bodega** ① *Mon-Fri 0900-1200, 1400-1700, Sat 0900-1200*, makes a very good, strong Moscatel, sold in unlabelled bottles. He is always short of bottles so it's best to take your own. A visit is recommended, but you'll need good Spanish. Señor Chipana lives on the main plaza beside his bodega; ask for him in the bar on the plaza. The town is a popular excursion from Ica for tours of the **Ocucaje winery** ① *Panamericana Sur, Km 335.5, T01-251 4570, www.ocucaje.com*, which makes wines and pisco.

Huacachina

This attractive oasis and summer resort is 5 km from Ica, set around a palm-fringed lake and amid impressive sand dunes. Its green sulphur waters are said to possess curative properties. Increasingly, the resort has become a hang-out for people seeking a change from the archaeology and chill of the Andes. Plenty of cheap hostels and bars have opened, playing pop and grunge as opposed to pan-pipe music. Paddleboats can be rented for US$3 for 30 minutes of boating around the lake. Sandboarding on the dunes has become a major pastime, attracting fans from Europe and elsewhere. Board hire is US$2 per hour. For the inexperienced, note that sandboarding can be dangerous. Dune buggies also do white-knuckle, rollercoaster tours for US$15-20 (plus a municipal fee of US$1.05), most start between 1600 and 1700 for sunsets, some at 1000, 2½ hours. In the town is the **Biblioteca de Abraham Valdelomar** ① *Mon-Sat 0900-1300, 1500-1800, take a taxi from Ica for US$1.*

◉ Ica and around listings

For Sleeping and Eating price codes and other relevant information, see pages 38-44.

◉ Sleeping

Ica *p317*
Hotels are fully booked during the harvest festival and prices rise greatly. If taking a taxi, insist on going to the hotel of your choice.
LL-L Las Dunas, Av La Angostura 400, T056-256224, www.lasdunashotel.com. (Lima office: Av Vasco Núñez de Balboa 259, Miraflores, Lima, T01-213 5000). Prices are reduced on weekdays. There are also more expensive suites and *cabañas*. Complete resort with restaurant, swimming pool, many sporting activities and full-day programmes. Recommended.

B Villa Jazmín, Los Girasoles Manzana C-1, Lote 7, Res La Angostura, T056-258179, www.villajazmin.net. Modern hotel in a residential area near the sand dunes, 8 mins from the city centre, solar-heated water, restaurant, pool, Wi-Fi, tours, airport and bus transfers, helpful staff, tranquil and very good.
D La Florida Inn, Residencias La Florida B-01, Urb San Luís, T056-237313. Not easy to find, 16 rooms, cheaper without bath, restaurant.
D Princess, Urb Santa María D-103, T/F056-215421, hotel_princess@yahoo.com. A taxi ride from the main plaza, small rooms, hot water, TV, pool, helpful, peaceful neighbourhood, very good.
E Arameli, Tacna 239 T056-239107. One block from the Plaza de Armas, has cable TV and is a nice place to stay, good value.

E-F Hostal El Paraíso, Bolívar 418, T056-227582. Clean, hot water, cable TV, affordable and basic accommodation.

Huacachina *p318*

AL-A Hotel Mossone, at the eastern end of the lake, T056-213630, mossone@dematour hoteles.com. An elegant hacienda-like hotel, full board available, with bath, pool, bicycles and sandboards for guests' use. Offers 3-day, 2-night packages. End the day with a *Perú libre* in the majestic bar/restaurant with a fantastic view over the lake. On quiet days and at the hotel staff's discretion you can pay S/.10 to use the large, very clean swimming pool.

A-B Hostería Suiza, Malecón 264, T056-238762, hostesuiza@terra.com.pe. Airy house with a huge terrace overlooking the lake, lovely grounds, quiet, friendly, clean, includes breakfast, safe parking. Recommended.

B-C Hostal Huacachinero, opposite Hostal Salvatierra, T056-217435, http://elhuaca chinero.com. Breakfast US$3, comfortable, nice atmosphere, pool, outside bar and restaurant only for guests, parking, offers tours and buggy rides.

F Carola del Sur (also known as **Casa de Arena II**), Av Perotti s/n, T056-215439. Basic rooms, popular with back packers, small pool, restaurant/bar, hammocks, access to Casa de Arena's bigger pool.

F Casa de Arena, Av Perotti s/n, T056-215274, casadearena@hotmail.com. Basic rooms, cheaper without bath, bar, small pool, laundry facilities, board hire, popular with backpackers, can be noisy and grubby, check your bill and change carefully, don't leave valuables unattended.

F Hostal del Barco, Balneario de Huacachina 180. A very relaxed place with hammocks on the front terrace, basic rooms, bar, use of kitchen, can arrange tours.

F Hostal Rocha, T056-222256, kikerocha@ hotmail.com. Rooms with bath (cheaper without), hot water, family-run, kitchen and laundry facilities, board hire, small pool, nice grounds, popular with backpackers, a bit run down, not on the waterfront.

F Hostal Salvatierra, T056-232352, hospedajesalvatierra@hotmail.com. Though not on the waterfront, this is a charming *hostal* in a grand old building. It has a great pool, relaxing courtyard, all rooms with bath, rents sandboards at a good price. Good value.

F Hostal Titanic, T056-229003. Small rooms, pool, café, clothes washing, board hire, good value for lodging and set meals.

⑦ Eating

Ica *p317*

♥♥-♥ **Anita**, Libertad 133, Plaza de Armas. Local dishes, no set breakfast, a bit expensive for what is offered.

♥♥-♥ **Carne y pescao**, Av Juan José Elias 417, T056-228157. For sea food and, at night, grilled chicken and *parrilladas*.

♥♥-♥ **El Peñoncito**, Bolívar 255, harryhernandez@yahoo.com. Peruvian and international cuisine, open for breakfast, lunch and dinner.

♥♥-♥ **Huarango Grill**, Av San Martín y Abraham Valdelomar 611, T056-221649. Grilled chicken, *parrilladas*, international food and karaoke.

♥♥-♥ **Las Carnes**, Av San Martín, some distance from centre. Peruvian fare, emphasis on chicken, US$5 all-day *menú*, popular with locals.

♥♥-♥ **Plaza 125**, Lima 125, Plaza de Armas, T056-211816. Serving regional and international food as well as breakfast.

♥♥-♥ **Rokys**, Lima 149, Plaza de Armas. National grilled chicken chain restaurant, also selling pankakes, a variety of breakfasts and sandwiches.

Cafés

D'lizia, Lima 155, Plaza de Armas, T056-237733, www.delizia.com.pe. Also in the Patio de comidas at **Plaza Vea** mall and in **Urb Moderna**. Modern and bright, for breakfasts, lunches, sandwiches, snacks, ice cream, cakes and sweets, juices and drinks.

Tejas Helena, Cajamarca 137. This is the place for the best *tejas*.

Huacachina *p318*

†-† **La Casa de Bamboo Café-bar**, Av Perotti s/n, next to **Hostería Suiza**, T056-776649, www.bookingbox.org/lacasadebamboo. British/Peruvian-owned place with a garden. They serve English and other breakfasts (including marmite) and a wide range of dishes and snacks, including Thai curry, falafel, vegetarian and vegan options and coffee. Also TV, book exchange and games.

†-† **Moroni**, T056-238471. Open 0800 till late. The only restaurant right on the lake shore, serving a variety of Peruvian and international food.

⊛ Festivals and events

Ica *p317*

Early Mar Festival Internacional de la Vendimia (wine harvest festival) and the Concurso Nacional de Marinera.
Early May Fiesta de la Cruz in the 1st week.
Late May Día Internacional del Pisco celebrated on 3rd Sun.
Jun Ica Week is the 3rd week.
Early Oct The image of El Señor de Luren, in a fine church in Parque Luren, draws pilgrims from all Peru, and there are all-night processions throughout the first fortnight.

▲ Activities and tours

Ica *p317*

In Ica, agencies offer city tours, Nazca Lines, Paracas, Islas Ballestas, buggies and sand boarding and bodega tours. For example, **AV Dolphin Travel**, C Municipalidad 132, of 4, T056-256234, www.av-dolphintravel peru.com. And **Desert Travel**, Lima 171, inside Tejas Don Juan, Plaza de Armas, T056-227215, desert_travel@hotmail.com.

Ica Desert Trip, Bolívar 178, T056-237373, www.icadeserttrip.com. Roberto Penny Cabrera (speaks Spanish and English) offers 1-, 2- and 3-day off-road trips into the desert, focusing on archaeology, geology, etc. Maximum 4 people per trip, email in advance. Take something warm for the evening, a long-sleeved loose cotton shirt for the day, long trousers and toilet paper. Recommended but "not for the faint-hearted".

Huacachina *p318*

Desert Adventures, T056-228458, www.desertadventure.net. Frequently recommended for sandboarding and camping trips into the desert by 4WD and buggies, French, English and Spanish spoken. Also tours to virgin beaches, Isla Ballestas and Nazca Lines flights.
Over Sand Adventures, T056-956-757601/ 956-357402, ruben1985_6@hotmail.com. Buggie, sandboarding and beach tours .

⊖ Transport

Ica *p317*

To **Pisco** (70 km), several daily, 45 mins, US$1 with **Ormeño** and colectivos. To **Lima** (302 km), 4 hrs, US$5-10, several daily including **Soyuz** (Av Manzanilla 130, T056-224743, has a **hostal** here) every 8 mins, 0600-2200, **Ormeño** (Lambayeque 180) and Flores. To **Nazca**, 140 km, 2 hrs, minimum US$1.50; several buses and colectivos daily, including **Ormeño**, **Flores**, 4 daily, and **Cueva** (José Elias y Huánuco), hourly on the hour 0600-2200. To **Arequipa** the route goes via Nazca (see page 330).

⊕ Directory

Ica *p317*

Banks Banks include BCP. **Post** At Callao y Moquegua.

Nazca and around

→ *Colour map 5, B3. Phone code: 056. Population: over 50,000. Altitude: 598 m.*
Set in a green valley surrounded by mountains, Nazca would be just like any other anonymous desert oasis (the sun blazes for much of the year by day and the nights are crisp) were it not for the 'discovery' of a series of strange lines etched on the plains to the north. Tourists in their thousands now flock to the town to fly over the famous Nazca Lines, whose precise purpose still remains a mystery. Overlooking the town, 10 km southeast, is Cerro Blanco (2078 m), the highest sand dune in the world; it's popular for sandboarding and paragliding. ▸▸ *For listings, see pages 327-331.*

Ins and outs

Getting there and around There is no central bus station in Nazca, but offices are at the western end of town, close to the Panamericana Sur after it has crossed the Río Tierras Blancas. Most of the hotels are on Jirón Lima and around the Plaza de Armas, within easy walking distance of the bus stations. ▸▸ *See Activities and tours, page 329, for details on tours, and Transport, page 330.*

Sights

As most of Nazca's attractions lie on the outskirts, the town itself is quite functional. The large **Museo Antonini** ① *Av de la Cultura 600, at the eastern end of Jr Lima, ring the bell to get in, T056-523444, cahuachi@terra.com.pe, daily 0900-1900, US$3, including a local guide,* is worth a visit for a perspective on the area. A video is shown in the Conference Room. It is a 10-minute walk from the plaza, or a short taxi ride. It houses the discoveries of Professor Orefici and his team from the huge pre-Inca city at Cahuachi (see page 325), which, Orefici believes, holds the key to the Nazca Lines. Many tombs survived the *huaqueros* and there are displays of mummies, ceramics, textiles, amazing *antaras* (panpipes) and photos of the excavations and the Lines. In the garden is a pre-Hispanic aqueduct. Recommended.

The **Maria Reiche Planetarium** ① *Hotel Nasca Lines, T056-522293, shows usually at 1900 and 2115 in English, 2000 in Spanish, US$6 (half price for students),* was opened in May 2000 in honour of Maria Reiche (see box, page 323). Stimulating lectures are given every night about the Nazca Lines, based on Reiche's theories, which cover archaeology and astronomy. The show lasts about 45 minutes (commentary in English), after which visitors are able to look at the moon, planets and stars through sophisticated telescopes.

Nazca Lines → *Colour map 5, B3.*

Cut into the stony desert are large numbers of lines, not only parallels and geometrical figures, but also a killer whale, a monkey, birds (one with a wing span of over 100 m), a spider and a tree. The lines, which can best be appreciated from the air, are located above the Ingenio valley on the Pampa de San José, about 22 km north of Nazca, and across the Ingenio river, on the plain around Palpa. The Pan-American Highway passes close to, even through, the Lines.

Background

The Nazca Lines were etched on the pampa sands by the Nazca people. It's estimated that they were begun around 400 BC and continued to be made for perhaps another thousand years. Since they were first spotted from the air 70 years ago, their meaning, function and origin have tormented scientists around the world. Dr Paul Kosok, a North American scientist, gave the first explanation in 1941, when he observed a line pointing towards the place where the sun would have risen on the mid-winter solstice in ancient Nazca times. So impressed was he, that he described the Nazca pampa as "the biggest astronomy book in the world".

By the 1950s Maria Reiche, inspired by Kosok, was mapping the area and discovered giant animals too vast to be appreciated from the ground. Her many years of research led her to the conclusion that the Lines were a huge astronomical calendar. (Reiche's book, *Mystery on the Desert*, is on sale for US$10 – proceeds to conservation work – in Nazca.)

There are those who disagree with the German mathematician's hypothesis. The International Explorers Society, for example, was convinced that the desert artists would not have drawn something they themselves could not see. They set out to prove that the ancient Peruvians could fly, based on the fact that the lines are best seen from the air, and that there are pieces of ancient local pottery and tapestry showing balloonists as well as local legends of flying men. In 1975, they made a hot-air balloon of cloth and reed, called it *Condor I* and attempted to fly it for 15 minutes over the pampa. Unfortunately for them, the flight lasted only 60 seconds, thereby leaving the issue unresolved.

Some of the competing theories as to the function of the Nazca Lines are rather far-fetched. Erich Von Daniken, in his book *Chariots of the Gods*, posited that the pampa was an extraterrestrial landing strip. This idea, however, only succeeded in drawing to the site thousands of visitors who tore across the lines on motorbikes, 4WD, horses and whatever else they could get their hands on, leaving an indelible mark. It is now an offence to walk or drive on the pampa, punishable by heavy fine or imprisonment

Nazca

200 metres
200 yards

Sleeping
1 Alegría
2 Casa Andina Classic
3 El Mirador de Nasca
4 Friends House
5 Hostal Alegría
6 Internacional
7 Las Líneas
8 Maison Suisse
9 Majoro
10 Nasca
11 Nasca Lines
12 Nido de Cóndor
13 Paredones Inn
14 Perugia Hostal
15 Posada Guadalupe
16 Sol de Nasca
17 The Walk On Inn

Eating
1 Chifa Guang Zhou
2 Coffee Break
3 Concordia
4 El Huarango &
   Travel Service
5 El Portón
6 Fuente de Soda Jumbory
7 Kañada
8 La Carreta
9 La Choza
10 La Taberna
11 Los Angeles
12 Panadería
13 Picante's
14 Plaza Mayor
15 Rico Pollo
16 Vía La Encantada

Guardian of the lines

The greatest contribution to our awareness of the lines is that of Maria Reiche, who lived and worked on the pampa for over 50 years. The young German mathematician arrived in Peru in the early 1930s and would dedicate the rest of her life to removing centuries of windswept debris and painstaking survey work. She even used to sleep on the pampa.

Maria Reiche's years of meticulous measurement and study of the lines led her to the conclusion that they represented a huge astronomical calendar. She also used her mathematical knowledge to determine how the many drawings and symbols could have been created with such precise symmetry. She suggested that those responsible for the lines used long cords attached to stakes in the ground. The figures were drawn by means of a series of circular arcs of different radius. Reiche also contended

that they used a standard unit of measurement of 1.30 m, or the distance between the fingertips of a person's extended arms.

As well as the anthropomorphic and zoomorphic drawings, there are a great many geometric figures. Reiche believed these to be a symbolic form of writing associated with the movements of the stars. In this way, the lines could have been used as a kind of calendar that not only recorded celestial events but also had a practical day-to-day function such as indicating the times for harvest, fishing and festivals.

Whatever the real purpose of the Nazca lines was, one fact remains indisputable: that their status as one of the country's major tourist attractions is largely due to the selfless work of Maria Reiche, the unofficial guardian of the lines. Maria Reiche died in June 1998.

(undeterred, trucks avoiding a toll post near the lines have driven over the site; just one of many threats to this remarkable plain).

Other theories are that the Nazca designs were part of a giant running track (George A Von Breunig – 1980; also proposed by the English astronomer Alan Sawyer). Another suggestion is that they represent weaving patterns and yarns (Henri Stirlin), or that the plain is a map demonstrating the Tiahuanaco Empire (Zsoltan Zelko). Dr Johan Reinhard brings together ethnographic, historical and archaeological data, including the current use of straight lines in Chile and Bolivia, to suggest that the Lines conform to fertility practices throughout the Andes.

Recent research The BBC series *Ancient Voices* pointed to yet another theory. The clues to the function of the lines are found in the highly advanced pottery and textiles of the ancient Nazcans. Some pots and tapestries show a flying being emitting discharge from its nose and mouth. This is believed to portray the flight of the shaman. The shaman consumes certain psycho-active drugs that convince him he can fly and so enter the real world of spirits in order to rid sick people of evil spirits. In this way, the lines were not designed to be seen physically from above, but from the mind's eye of the flying shaman. This also explains the presence of incongruous creatures such as a monkey or killer whale. They were chosen because they possess the qualities admired and needed by the shaman in his spirit journeys.

But this does not explain the spectacular geometric figures. These straight lines are a feature of ancient Peruvian ritual behaviour, much like ley lines in Europe. They represent invisible paths of perceived energy. The pampa's most remarkable features are the trapezoids, which are thought to have been ritual spaces where offerings were made to the gods, in the hope of favours in return.

Scientists have discovered evidence of a terrible 40-year drought around AD 550 or 600. This coincides not only with the abandonment of the nearby Cahuachi temples (see page 325) but also with a period of increased bloody warfare and greater line-making in the desert sands. This would seem to indicate that the Nazcans grew more and more desperate in the face of continued drought, abandoned traditional religious practices and, instead, intensified their sacrificial offerings to the gods.

The results of eight years' work by Peruvian archaeologist Johny Isla and Markus Reindel of the Swiss-Liechtenstein Foundation threw new light on the Lines in 2002. Their findings tie together some of the earlier ideas and discredit both the astronomical calendar and extraterrestrial theories. Working at La Muña and Los Molinos, near Palpa (see page 325) with photogrammetry (mapping using aerial photographs), they have deduced that the lines on both the Palpa and Nazca plains are offerings dedicated to the worship of water and fertility. These two elements were of paramount importance to the coastal people in this arid environment; they expressed their adoration not only in the desert, but also on their ceramics and on the engraved stones of the Paracas culture. Isla and Reindel believe that the Palpa lines predate those at Nazca and that the lines and drawings themselves are scaled-up versions of the Paracas drawings, made at a time when the Nazca people were becoming independent of Paracas. In addition, objects in the shape of drops of water, whales and chillies, found in grave sites, are repeated in the desert. In 2005, drawings similar to those at Palpa were uncovered by the Paracas winds near the Río Ingenio in Nazca. This new research proposes the theory that the Nazca culture succumbed not to drought, but to heavy rainfall, probably during an El Niño event.

Viewing and understanding the Nazca Lines

In 1976 Maria Reiche had a 12-m **Mirador** put up at her own expense, 17 km north of Nazca. From here three of the huge designs can be seen – the Hands, the Lizard and the Tree, although some travellers suggest the view from the hill 500 m back to Nazca is better. The Mirador is included on some arranged tours but enquire with your agency to be sure. If you're travelling independently, go early as the site gets very hot; better still, take a taxi (US$5-7 per hour) and arrive at 0745 before the tour buses; make sure it will wait for you and take you back.

In January 1994 Maria Reiche also opened a small **museum** ⓘ *5 km from Nazca, Km 416, US$1; take micro from in front of Ormeño terminal, US$0.75.* Viktoria Nikitzhi, a colleague of Maria Reiche, gives one-hour lectures about the Nazca Lines at **Dr Maria Reiche Center** ⓘ *US$5, Av de los Espinales 300, 1 block from Ormeño bus stop, T056-969 9419, viktorianikitzki@hotmail.com.* She also organizes tours in June and December to see the sun at the solstice striking the Lines (phone in advance to confirm times) and has many original documents and objects; see also the Planetarium, page 321. ➤➤ *For details of aerial tours over the Lines, see Activities and tours, page 329.*

Around Nazca → *For listings, see pages 327-331.*

Palpa → *Population: 15,000.*

Known as the 'Capital de la Naranja' (the Capital of Oranges), Palpa is a hospitable town 43 km northwest of Nazca, 97 km south of Ica. The climate is hot and dry (average annual temperature 21.4°C) and the main crops, besides oranges, are other fruits (such as plums, bananas) and cotton. There is also fishing for shrimp in the river.

The Plaza de Armas, on which the Municipalidad and church stand, is bordered by arches. Also on the plaza is the **Municipal Museum** ① *daily 0900-1700, free*, which contains aerial photos of the area, models and ceramics. Information is displayed in English and Spanish. Some colonial-style buildings survive.

Around Palpa

There are several archaeological sites, of different periods, not far from Palpa. The **Ciudad Perdida de Hualluri**, on the west side of the Panamericana Sur, 16 km from Palpa, 5 km from the Highway (Distrito Santa Cruz), is a ruined pre-Inca city. At the entrance to the site is a *huarango* tree that's over 1000 years old. In Sector Sacramento, 2 km from the Highway, is the **Puente Colgante del Inca**, built during the reign of Pachacútec. At **Chicchitara** is a vast area of petroglyphs thought to date from the Formative Period, 3000 to 500 BC (Chavín and Paracas cultures).

On the desert near Palpa there are drawings similar to those found at Nazca: a sun dial, the Reloj Solar, measuring 150 m across, a whale (35 m), a pelican (45 m), the so-called Familia Real, a man, woman and child (30 m tall) and another 1000 or so lines and figures. Two Nazca culture centres have been excavated at **La Muña**, which has the largest Nazca tombs, and **Los Molinos**. Ceramics, necklaces, spondylus sea shells and gold objects have been found, despite earlier sacking by grave robbers. Los Molinos is a monumental complex where more burials have been uncovered. See page 324 for the relationship of these markings on the desert with those at Nazca. For further information, visit the Consejo Municipal in Palpa or ask tour operators in Nazca, see page 330.

West of Nazca

The Nazca area is dotted with over 100 cemeteries and the dry, humidity-free climate has preserved perfectly invaluable tapestries, cloth and mummies. A good cemetery, with mummies still to be seen, is in the valley of **Jumana**, one hour west of Nazca in the river bed. Gold mining is one of the main local industries and a cemetery tour usually includes a visit to a small family processing shop where old-fashioned techniques are still used.

West of the Nazca Lines, **Cahuachi** ① *US$17 per person on a tour, US$12-15 by private taxi, minimum 2 people* comprises some 30 pyramids and is believed to have been a sacred centre for the exclusive use of artists and priests whose symbols were given expression in the lines on the desert. It is currently being excavated by a team of Italian archaeologists. A site called 'El Estaquería', with a series of wooden pillars, is thought to have been a place of mummification, where dead bodies were dried. Tours of the ruins of Cahuachi sometimes include a visit to the **Museo Antonini** (see page 321).

East of Nazca

The ruins of **Paredones** ① *just east of Nazca on the Puquio road, US$3, ticket also includes Acueducto Ocongalla, Cantalloc, El Telar and Las Agujas, taxi US$12 round-trip or tour US$12 per person*, also called Cacsamarca, are Inca on a pre-Inca base. They are not well-preserved but the cool, underground aqueducts, or *puquios*, built 300 BC to AD 700, still provide water for the local people: 33 aqueducts irrigate 20 ha each and, to this day, local farmers have the job of cleaning the section for which their group has been responsible for as long as they can remember. The aqueducts are beautifully built and even have S-bends to slow down the flow of water.

Up to one hour on foot from Paredones, through Buena Fe, are markings on the valley floor at **Cantalloc**. These consist of a triangle pointing to a hill and a *tela* (cloth) with a spiral depicting the threads; climb the mountain to see better examples. There are also aqueducts here. Visits to Catalloc are best done with a guide, or by car. A round-trip by taxi (with a wait at the site) will cost US$8; arranged tours cost US$12 per person, minimum two people.

South of Nazca

Some 30 km south of Nazca on the Panamericana Sur, then a further 12 km left off the highway (unsigned) is the cemetery site of **Chauchilla**. Grave-robbing *huaqueros* have ransacked the tombs and left remains all over the place: bones, skulls, mummies and pottery shards litter the desert. A tour is worthwhile and takes about two hours. It should cost about US$12 per person, plus the cost of entrance to the cemetery, with a minimum of two people. The area has been cordoned off and has clean bathrooms. There are other cemeteries in the vicinity. Some, like **Poroma**, have been so desecrated that there is nothing left to see.

Ninety kilometres south of Nazca is **Sacaco**, which has a museum built over the fossilized remains of a whale excavated in the desert. The keeper lives in a house nearby and is helpful. To get there, take a morning bus from Calle Bolognesi in Nazca (check times in advance) towards Chala (see page 332); ask the driver where to get off and be ready for a 2-km walk in the sun. Return to the Pan-American Highway no later than 1800 for a bus back. Do not go two to three days after a new moon as a vicious wind blows at this time.

Nazca to Cuzco

The highway from Nazca to Cuzco is paved and safe; fuel is available in Puquio and Chalhuanca. Two hours out of Nazca (80 km) is the **Reserva Nacional Pampas Galeras** at 4100 m. The Reserve covers 12,000 ha and contains 8000 vicuñas. Shearing takes place May to October and is celebrated during a three-day annual round-up and shearing ceremony in June, known as the *chaccu*. At Km 89 is the reserve office and a free museum containing stuffed Andean animals.

At Km 155 is **Puquio**, a small highland town at 3200 m from which the impressive Inca terraces at Andamarca and the sierra towards Cotahuasi to the south are accessible. The principal fiesta is on 7 October. There is a **Banco de la Nación** on the Plaza de Armas, open weekdays 0800-1730 and Saturday morning. Combis depart from Puquio when full for the journey to the steep terraced valley of **Andamarca** (3450 m), three hours, US$3. The Incas' complex underground drainage system has survived and has ensured that the Andamarca terraces have remained the most extensively and continuously used agricultural terraces anywhere in Peru since Inca times. They are at their greenest and most beautiful in May and June, covered with traditional crops such as quinua, maize, kiwicha and alfalfa. The nearby village of Sondondo was the birthplace of the great Inca chronicler Felipe Guaman Poma (see page 677).

After another 185 km **Chalhuanca** is reached. There are wonderful views on this stretch, with lots of small villages, valleys and alpacas. Across the river from Chalhuanca in the village of **Chiquinga**, whose beautiful 17th-century church has extensive frescos. A further 5 km and 200 m above the valley floor are the thermal baths (47.8°C) of **Pinahuacho** ① *US$0.75, taxi from Chalhuanca US$5, including a 1-hr wait.*

⊙ Nazca and around listings

For Sleeping and Eating price codes and other relevant information, see pages 38-44.

⊙ Sleeping

Nazca and around *p321, map p322*
If arriving by bus beware of touts who tell you that the hotel of your choice (notably **Alegría**) is closed, or full, and no longer runs tours. If you phone or email the hotel they will pick you up at the bus station free of charge day or night.

AL Maison Suisse, opposite the airport, T/F056-522434, www.aeroica.net.
Nice, comfortable, safe car park, expensive restaurant, pool, suites with jacuzzi, accepts Amex, shows video of Nazca Lines. Also has camping facilities. Ask for packages, including flights over Nazca Lines.

AL Nazca Lines, Jr Bolognesi 147, T056-522293, www.dematourshoteles.com.
Large with a/c, comfortable, rooms with private patio, hot water, peaceful, price includes American breakfast, restaurant, good but expensive meals, safe car park, pool (US$4.50 for non-guests, or free if having lunch), they can arrange package tours that include 2-3 nights at the hotel plus a flight over the lines and a city tour, US$167 per person. Recommended.

AL-A Majoro, Panamericana Sur Km 452, T056-522490, www.hotelmajoro.com.
A charming old hacienda at Majoro about 5 km from town past the airstrip, beautiful gardens, pool, restaurant, quiet and homely, attentive service, serene surroundings, good arrangements for flights and tours. Offers 3-day/2-night packages.

A Alegría, Jr Lima 166, T056-522497, www.hotelalegria.net. Continental breakfast, bus terminal transfers, left-luggage service and Wi-Fi included. Rooms with bathroom, carpet and a/c, hot water, cafeteria, pool, garden, English, Hebrew, Italian and German spoken, laundry facilities, book exchange, restaurant, ATM, parking, massages, activities,

very popular. Also has a tour agency and guests are encouraged to buy tours (see page 330), flights and bus tickets arranged.

A Casa Andina Classic, Jr Bolognesi 367, T056-523563, www.casa-andina.com.
This recommended chain of hotels' Nazca property, offering standardized services in distinctive style. Bright, modern decor, clean, a/c, pool, friendly, TV, internet, restaurant.

A Nido del Cóndor, opposite the airport, Panamericana Sur Km 447, T056-522424, www.nidodelcondornasca.com. Large rooms, hot water, good restaurant, bar, shop, videos, swimming pool, camping US$3, parking, English, Italian German spoken, free pick-up from town, reservation advised.

A Paredones Inn, Lima 600, T056-522181, www.paredonesinn.com. 1 block from the Plaza de Armas, pleasant, ample rooms with cable TV, clean bathrooms, minibar, modern, great views from rooftop terrace, laundry service, bar, suites with jacuzzi and microwave, helpful staff. Good.

D El Mirador de Nasca, Tacna 436, T056-523121, www.activeb.es/hotelmiradordenasca. On main plaza, comfortable rooms with shower, hot water, good breakfast, TV downstairs, internet and Wi-Fi in lobby, modern, clean.

D Internacional, Av Maria Reiche 112, T056-522744. With bathroom, hot water, garage, café and very nice bungalows.

D-E Las Líneas, Jr Arica 299, T056-522488. Cheaper without bath, clean, spacious, restaurant. Recommended, but ask for a room away from the street.

E Nasca, C Lima 438, T056-522085, marionasca13@hotmail.com. Cheaper without bathroom, hot water, noisy, clean, nice lawn area, new annexe at the back, clothes washing facilities, luggage store, safe motorcycle parking.

E Perugia Hostal, Arica 520, T056-521484, perugiahostal@hotmail.com. Hot water, cable TV, internet and tours around Nazca.

F Friends House, C Juan Matta 712, T056-524191, www.friendshousenazca.com. Popular backpackers' hang out, single and shared rooms, also has a cheap dorm room, rooftop rest area with hammocks, open kitchen, breakfast provided, internet, buggie rides and more.

F pp Hostal Alegría, Av Los Incas 117, opposite Ormeño bus terminal, T056-522497. More basic than **Alegría** (above) to which it is unrelated, hot water, clean, hammocks, nice gardens, camping permitted, restaurant.

F Posada Guadalupe, San Martín 225, T056-522249. Family-run, basic, **G** without bath, hot water, good breakfast, relaxing (touts who try to sell tours are nothing to do with hotel).

F Sol de Nasca, Callao 586, T056-522730, reservasnazca@hotmail.com. Rooms with and without hot showers, TV, also has a restaurant, pleasant, don't leave valuables in luggage store.

F pp The WalkOn Inn, JM Mejía 108, 3 blocks from Plaza de Armas, T/F056-522566, www.walkoninn.com. Rooms with bathroom, **G** per person in dorm, hot water, family atmosphere, small swimming pool, TV room, excellent and cheap restaurant on top floor for breakfast and salads, very helpful staff, internet, Wi-Fi, luggage store, works with **Nasca Trails** for flights and tours, information given. Also has *hostales* in Puno and Cuzco. Recommended.

Palpa *p324*

F San Francisco, Lima 181, T056-404043. Basic accommodation.

Other hotels include the **Palpa**. There are also several *pensiones*, including **Villa Sol**, Lima 200, T056-404149, which has really basic accommodation.

Nazca to Cuzco *p326*

F Hostal Jousef, Ayacucho 246, Puquio, T066-407415. Clean, hot water, private bath, TV, clothes washing possible. Recommended.

F Hostal Los Andes, 9 de Diciembre 286, Puquio, T066-452323. The best alternative, in an older house, hot water, private bath.

🍴 Eating

Nazca and around *p321, map p322*
There are many restaurants near the Plaza de Armas and along Bolognesi as well.

₸₸-₸ Concordia, Lima 594. Good, also rents bikes at US$1 an hr.

₸₸-₸ El Portón, Moresky 120, in front of **Hotel Nazca Lines**. A popular stopover with tours, and well worth the visit. Specializes in Peruvian food, has a great indoor/outdoor setting with wood decor. Can cater to large groups with advanced notice.

₸₸-₸ La Carreta, Bolognesi, next door to **Los Angeles**. New, look for Novo Andino dishes made using traditional Andean ingredients, rustic, lively atmosphere, stage for live music. Good.

₸₸-₸ La Choza, Bolognesi 290. Nice decor with woven chairs and thatched roof, all types of food, live music at night. Single women may be put off by the crowds of young men hanging around the doors handing out flyers.

₸₸-₸ La Taberna, Jr Lima 321, T056-521411. Excellent food, live music, popular with gringos, it's worth a look just for the graffiti on the walls.

₸₸-₸ Plaza Mayor, on the plaza. Rustic atmosphere. Specializes in barbecues of all types, roasted chicken, steaks, *anticuchos* and great salads. Large portions, nice staff. Highly recommended.

₸ Chifa Guang Zhou, Bolognesi 297, T056-522036. Very good Peruvian/Chinese food.

₸ El Huarango, Arica 602. National and international cuisine. Relaxed family atmosphere and deliciously breezy terrace.

₸ Kañada, Lima 160, nazcanada@yahoo.com. Cheap *menú*, excellent pisco sours, nice wines, popular, display of local artists' work, email service, English spoken, owner Juan Carlos Fraola is very helpful.

₸ Los Angeles, Bolognesi 266. Good, cheap, try *sopa criolla*, and chocolate cake.

₸ Rico Pollo, Lima 190, a few doors down from **Hotel Alegría**. Good local restaurant with great chicken dishes, cheap.

¶ Vía La Encantada, Bolognesi 282, www.vialaencantada.com. Restaurant/bar with a good variety of dishes and strong coffee, nice enviroment, with balcony, Wi-Fi.

Cafés
Coffee Break, Bolognesi 219. Sun-Fri 0700-2300. For real coffee.
Fuente de Soda Jumbory, near the cinema. Good *almuerzo*.
Panadería, Bolognesi 387.
Picante's, Av Bolognesi 464. Delicious real coffee and cakes. Owner, Percy Pizzaro, is knowledgeable about the Nazca Lines.

Palpa *p324*
¶ Claudia, Grau 291. Good for *camarones*.

⊛ Festivals and events

Nazca and around *p321, map p322*
29 Aug-10 Sep Festival de la Virgen de la Guadalupe.

Palpa *p324*
Mar/Apr Fiesta de la Ciruela y Vendimia (plum and wine harvest festival).
Last week of Jul The town's **Tourist Week**.
30 Jul-17 Aug Fiesta de la Naranja is part of the main fiesta; 15 Aug is the main day.

○ Shopping

Nazca and around *p321, map p322*
There is a market at Lima y Grau; the **Mercado Central** is between Arica and Tacna.

▲▲ Activities and tours

Nazca and around *p321, map p322*
All guides must be approved by the Ministry of Tourism and should have an official identity card. Touts (*jaladores*) operate at popular hotels and the bus terminals using false ID cards and fake hotel and tour brochures. They are all rip-off merchants who overcharge and mislead those who arrive by bus. Always head straight to a hotel and find an official agency to handle your flights and tours. Taxi drivers usually act as guides, but most speak only Spanish. It is not dangerous to visit the outlying sites with a trustworthy person but do not take just any taxi on the plaza, as they are unreliable and can lead to robbery. Taxis will charge from US$5-7 per hr to wait for you at the sites and bring you back to the city.

Aerial tours
Stop press In view of the number of fatal plane crashes during flights over the Nazca Lines, many overseas governments have issued safety warnings. Tourists should check with their insurer that they are covered for accidents on Nazca flights. Many companies withdrew cover in 2010.

Flights over the Nazca Lines last 30-35 mins and are controlled by air traffic personnel at the airport to avoid congestion. Small planes take 3-5 passengers. The price for a flight range from US$40-80 per person depending on season (special deals are sometimes available; touts charge more). You also have to pay US$3 airport tax. It is best to organize and reserve a flight direct with the airlines at the airport rather then through an agency or tout. Accidents do occur (2 in 2010), so make sure you ask for a company's safety record, clarify everything before getting on the plane and ask for a receipt. Also let them know in advance if you have any special requests. Note that some airlines work with large tour operators who book up flights, which may lead to individual passengers being bumped off the flight for which they have paid. Taxi to airport US$3.35, bus US$0.10, but transport to the airport is usually included in the tour price.

Flights are bumpy and many people are airsick, so it may be best to avoid food and drink. Best times to fly are 0800-1000 and

1500-1630 when there is less turbulence and better light (assuming there is no fog, in which case chaos may ensue).

Aero Ica, in Jr Lima, at Maison Suisse and at the airport, T01-446 3026 (Lima), www.aeroica.net. Offers flights over Nazca and Palpa, US$105, full-day packages from Pisco, US$209, and from Lima with lunch at Maison Suisse plus flight over the lines, US$599, but book 48 hrs in advance.

Alas Peruanas, T056-522444, www.alas peruanas.com. Experienced pilots fluent in English. Often include other features in their 35-min flight over the Lines, such as the spiral ventilation holes of the aqueducts. Also 1-hr flights over the Palpa and Llipata areas (US$100 per person, minimum 3) and Nazca and Palpa combined (US$200). See the website for promotional offers. All flights include the BBC film. Can be booked at Hotel Alegría (see page 327).

Tour operators

Air Nasca Travel, Jr Lima 185, T056-521027, guide Susi recommended. Very helpful and friendly staff, very competitive prices. Can do all types of tours around Nazca, Ica, Paracas and Pisco. Recommended.

Alegría Tours, Lima 168, T056-522444 (24 hrs). Tours to Palpa, Puerto Inca, Sacaco and the San Fernando Reserve, also to Chauchilla, Cantalloc, Ica, Paracas and the Ballestas Islands. Guides with radio contact and maps can be provided for hikes to nearby sites. They have guides who speak English, German, French and Italian. Birdwatching in the high Andes, visits to Pampas Galeras vicuña reserve, the village of Andamarca and downhill mountain biking trips. Also sandboarding on Cerro Blanco. Alegría runs a bus from Nazca to Pisco daily 1000 via Ica, Huacachina and bodegas. Bus and flight tickets can be arranged, as well as packages to other parts of Peru.

Félix Quispe Sarmiento, El Nativo de Nazca, Fedeyogin5@hotmail.com. He has his own museum, Hantun Nazca, Panamericana Sur 447 and works with the Instituto Nacional de Cultura. Tours off the beaten track, can arrange flights, knowledgeable, ask for him at Kañada restaurant. Recommended.

Fernández family, who run the Hotel Nasca, also run local tours. Ask for the hotel owners and speak to them directly. They will arrange taxis to outlying sites.

Huarango Travel Service, Arica 602, T056-522141, huarangotravel@yahoo.es. Tours around Paracas, Ica, Huacachina, Nazca and Palpa.

Jesús Erazo Buitrón, Juan Matta 1110, T056-523005. Very knowledgeable. He speaks a little English and his Spanish is easy to follow. Recommended.

Mystery Peru, Ignacio Morsesky 126, Parque Bolognesi, T056-522379/956-691155 (mob), www.mysteryperu.com. Owned by Enrique Levano Alarcón, based in Nazca, with many local tours, also packages throughout Peru.

Nanasca Tours, Jr Lima 160, T/F056-522917/ 956-622054, nanascatours@yahoo.com. Very helpful.

Nasca Trails, Bolognesi 550, T056-522858, nascatrails@terra.com.pe. Juan Tohalino Vera speaks English, French, German and Italian. Recommended.

◉ Transport

Nazca and around *p321, map p322*
Bus
It is worth paying extra for a good bus because of reports of robbery on the cheaper services. Overbooking is common.

Local To Palpa, colectivos leave when full, 20 mins, US$0.75. Colectivos to Chala, 2 hrs, daily in the morning, US$3.50 per person. To Puerto de Lomas, 1½ hrs, US$1.75. Nazca to Puquio, combis, 4 hrs, US$3, and colectivos, 3 hrs, US$4.50. Most depart, in both directions, in the early morning from the market. They will drop visitors off at the Pampas Galeras vicuña reserve en route, 2 hrs, US$1.50 by combi, or 1½ hrs, US$2.50 by colectivo.

Long distance To **Ica**, 2 hrs, US$1.50, 4 daily, with **Ormeño**. To **Pisco**, 210 km, 3 hrs, see under Pisco transport, page 316. Note that buses to Pisco don't go into the centre, but stop 5 km outside town; change to a colectivo or in Ica for direct transport.

To **Lima** (446 km), 7 hrs, several buses and colectivos daily. Recommended companies include: **Civa**, Av Guardia Civil, T056-523019, normal service at 2300; **Cruz del Sur**, Lima y San Martín, T056-523713, 4 daily via Ica and Paracas, US$13-31.50 (luxury service). **Oltursa**, Av Lima 105, T056-522265, reliable, comfortable and secure. **Ormeño**, T056-522058, Royal Class from Hotel Nazca Lines, Jr Bolognesi, at 0530 and 1330, US$24, normal service from Av Los Incas, 6 a day, US$13.

To **Arequipa**, 565 km, 9 hrs, US$10, or US$30-46 *bus cama* services, with **Ormeño**, from Av Los Incas, or Royal Class at 2130, 8 hrs; **Cruz del Sur**, 2200; also **Civa**, 8 hrs. Delays are possible out of Nazca because of drifting sand across the road or mudslides in the rainy season. Travel in daylight. Book your ticket on previous day.

To **Cuzco**, 659 km, 13 hrs, via **Chalhuanca** and **Abancay**. The highway from Nazca is paved and is safe for bus travellers, drivers of private vehicles and motorcyclists. To Cuzco with **Ormeño**, US$46.

❶ Directory

Nazca and around *p321, map p322*
Banks BCP, Lima y Grau. Globalnet ATM on Bolognesi. Some street changers will change TCs, but at 8% commission.
Internet Many places on Jr Bolognesi.
Medical services Hospital: Callao entre Morsesky y Castillo. Open 24 hrs.
Police Tourist police, Av Los Incas, cuadra 1, T056-522105, T105 for emergencies.
Post Fermín de Castillo 379, T056-522016.
Telephone Telefónica for international calls with coins on Plaza Bolognesi. Also on Plaza de Armas and at Lima 359.

Nazca to Chile

From Nazca to the Chilean border the coastal desert continues, broken by the occasional irrigation scheme. In places the dunes are otherworldly. There are a few ports, old ones such as Puerto Inca, which served Imperial Cuzco, and new ones like Matarani. If you head south on the Panamericana, instead of turning off at the junction to Arequipa and the sierra, you reach the fruitful valley of Moquegua. This town has many historical associations and is the start of a great road up to Lake Titicaca. Nearby Ilo will soon be connected to Brazil by the Interoceanic Highway. On the border with Chile is the city of Tacna, seemingly a long way from anywhere else in Peru.
▶▶ For listings, see pages 340-344.

South of Nazca → For listings see pages 340-344.

Lying on the coast, 98 km from Nazca and 7 km off the Pan-American Highway, is **Puerto de Lomas**, a fishing village with safe beaches which are popular in February and March. From here, the Panamericana heads south through the **Yauca Valley**, which is almost entirely devoted to olive trees; have a few *soles* ready to buy some when the bus stops.

Chala and Puerto Inca → Phone code: 054.
Chala, 173 km from Nazca, is a fishing village with nice beaches, although it is only safe to swim near the harbour. The town has expanded greatly in recent years on the back of gold-mining in the nearby hills. It now consists of **Chala Sur**, where the fishing pier, better hotels and restaurants are located; and **Chala Norte**, a bit seedier, where buses stop and miners congregate around video bars. Fresh fish is available in the morning and it may be possible to go out with the local fishermen. There are dozens of restaurants, most catering for passing buses. Try *chicharrones de pulpo* (octopus) and *lenguado* (fried fish). **Chala Viejo** is a separate village, 11 km inland.

Ten kilometres north of Chala are the large pre-Columbian ruins of **Puerto Inca** on the coast in a beautiful bay. On its discovery in the 1950s, the site was misunderstood and thus neglected but it is now recognized that this was the port for Cuzco. The site is in excellent condition: drying and store houses can be seen as holes in the ground (be careful where you walk); there's a cemetery on the right side of the bay and a temple of resurrection on the hill; the Inca road from the coast to Cuzco is also clearly visible. The road was 240 km long and had a staging post every 7 km; with a change of runner at every post, fish for the Inca's table and messages could be sent to Cuzco in 24 hours.

The water in the two small bays is usually calm and clear and the fishing and diving are excellent. In winter, though, coastal fog can take away much of the bay's atmosphere. There is a good two-hour walk back from Puerto Inca to Chala. Take one of the paths going up behind the ruins on the south side of the bay and swing slightly inland to cross a deep *quebrada*. The path then continues through spectacular rock formations with dramatic views of the coast towards the Panamerica.

Camaná heading inland → Phone code 054. Population 40,000.
South of Chala the Pan-American Highway passes **Atico**, where there is a basic *hostal*, and **Ocaña** before reaching **Camaná**, 222 km south of Chala and 5 km inland from the sea. It has a modern church and plaza, as well as a short pedestrian boulevard. There is an archaeology museum at **La Inmaculada High School** ① *Av Samuel Pastor 1201, north end*

of town, free but contributions appreciated. It's a small well-presented collection of ceramics and textiles, including Nazca, Tiahuanaco, Wari and Inca. There are few other attractions in the town itself but various beaches to the south are visited by *arequipeños* from January to March. Camaná has a range of hotels, restaurants and other services; bus agencies are concentrated on the 300 block of Av Lima.

The Pan-American Highway swings inland from Camaná to **El Alto** where a road branches left off the Pan-American Highway and leads to **Corire**, **Aplao** and the valley of the Río Majes (see page 293). The Pan-American Highway, meanwhile, runs along the top of a plateau with strange ash-grey sand dunes. These are unique in appearance and formation. All are crescent shaped and of varying sizes, from 6 m to 30 m across and from 2 m to 5 m high, with the points of the crescent on the leeward side. The sand is slowly blown up the convex side, drifts down into the concave side, moving the dunes about 15 m a year. If plans to extend the Majes project are completed, the irrigation of a further 60,000 ha of land will destroy a large portion of these unique sand dunes.

Mollendo → *Colour map 6, C1. Phone code: 054. Population: 30,000.*

Since Matarani, 14.5 km to the northwest, has replaced it as a port, Mollendo depends partly upon the summer attraction of its beaches. Hotels can be full during the high season, which starts on 6 January, the first day of summer and anniversary of the district, and lasts until March. Out of season Mollendo is pleasant and tranquil. The town has lots of character, with an abandoned castle perched high on bluffs above the sea, brightly painted old wooden houses, a wrought-iron market and many well-maintained parks. People are friendly and the authorities are trying to foster tourism. There is a tourist complex on the beach near the old railway with a swimming pool, tennis courts and popular bar, which has live music at weekends in high season and blasts out loud cumbia music during the day. The side of the beach is full of stalls selling *ceviche* and beers out of cool boxes. The atmosphere is good, but be mindful of hygiene.

Playa Catarindo, in a small bay 2 km north of town, is reportedly good for bathing. There are many others but mind the powerful undertow. Three sandy beaches stretch south of town, of which the small one nearest town is the safest for swimming. The swimming pool on the beach is open January to March. Out of season the beaches are littered with rubbish.

On the coast, a few kilometres southeast by road is a national reserve based around lagoons at **Mejía** ① *visitor centre at entrance, T054-835001, daily 0700-1700, US$1.50; US$0.40 by colectivo from Mollendo.* Part of the Ramsar Convention on Wetlands, the reserve has 92 resident species of birds and 83 visiting species. Arrive early in the morning to see the birdlife at its best. A 7.5-km trail runs parallel to the wild seashore; it can be flooded so be prepared to wade and take insect repellent, hat, sun screen, water, etc.

The road out of Mollendo goes through the fertile **Valle de Tambo**, which is full of rice paddies, sugar cane and fields of peppers and onions. Tambo is famous for its *alfajores de Tambo*, small round pastries filled with cane syrup or *manjar blanco*. The very best are made in **La Curva**, 10 km from Mollendo, eg at **Alfajorería Vildoso**, Calle Las Mercedes 121. Take any combi toward Cocachacras and ask for directions.

Moquegua and around → *For listings, see pages 340-344. Colour map 6, C2.*
Phone code: 053. Population: 110,000. Altitude: 1412 m.

Moquegua is a peaceful town in the narrow valley of the Moquegua River and enjoys a sub-tropical climate. Strategically placed near the intersection of the Pan-American Highway and the paved road to Lake Titicaca and Bolivia, it offers a full range of services and is a more tranquil alternative to Tacna for breaking a journey through this area. The town was formerly known as Santa Catalina de Guadalcazar but reverted to its original name, which means 'silent place' in Quechua. The Inca emperor, Mayta Capac, sent his captains to carry out a pacifying occupation of the fertile valleys around Moquegua. They founded two settlements, Moquegua and Cuchuna, which is thought to be the site of present-day Torata. Today, most of the valley below the city grows grapes and the upper part grows avocados (*paltas*), wheat, maize, potatoes, some cotton and fruits. Northeast from Moquegua is Cuajone, one of the most important copper mines in Peru.

Ins and outs
Getting there and around There is no bus station. All bus companies are on Avenida Ejército, two blocks north of the market, at Grau, except **Ormeño**, which is on Avenida La Paz casi Balta. The road into town runs along Avenida La Paz. It joins the main street (Avenida Balta) at the large roundabout. Avenida Balta runs two blocks north of the Plaza de Armas. On Saturday nights Jirón Moquegua, west from the plaza to Jirón Piura, becomes the centre of activity in this compact town. Taxi in town costs US$0.60 or US$0.85 outside the city.

Moquegua

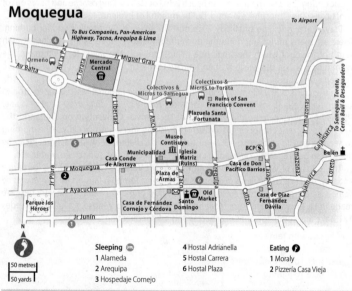

Sleeping	**4** Hostal Adrianella	**Eating**
1 Alameda	**5** Hostal Carrera	**1** Moraly
2 Arequipa	**6** Hostal Plaza	**2** Pizzería Casa Vieja
3 Hospedaje Cornejo		

Tourist information Information is available from the **Dircetur office** ① *Ayacucho 1060, T053-462236, moquegua@mincetur.gob.pe, Mon-Fri 0800-1630*. Pamphlets and useful information about the archeological sites are available from **Museo Contisuyo** (see below).

Sights

Moquegua is not a pretty sight from the Pan-American Highway, but the old centre, a few blocks above Avenida Balta, is well worth a look for its quiet, winding cobbled streets and historic buildings. The **Plaza de Armas**, with its mix of ruined and preserved churches, colonial and republican façades and fine trees, is one of the most interesting small-town plazas in the country. The fountain is said to have been designed by Eiffel, though there is some debate on the matter. **Museo Contisuyo** ① *Plaza de Armas, T053-461844, http://bruceowen.com/contisuyo/museoe.html, Wed-Mon 0800-1300, 1430-1730, Tue 0800-1200, 1600-2000, US$0.45*, is within the ruins of the Iglesia Matriz, which was rebuilt after many earthquakes over the centuries, but finally left as a ruin in 1868. It covers the cultures that thrived in the Moquegua and Ilo valleys, including the Huari, Tiahuanaco, Chiribaya and Estuquiña, who were conquered by the Incas. Artefacts from the area are well-displayed and all the exhibits are labelled in Spanish and English.

The decadent statuary of the fountain in front of the **Santo Domingo** church is seen by some as a challenge to the traditional Catholic religious iconography inside, where the body of the city's saint, Fortunata, lies in a glass-sided casket. She died in the 17th century but her hair and nails are reputed to continue to grow miraculously. The old market beside Santo Domingo has a fine entrance but not much inside.

The roofs of many of the old houses in Moquegua are built with sugar-cane thatch and clay and are of an unusual design, with semi-rounded gables, a little reminiscent of 18th-century Dutch gables. This type of construction is called *mojinete* and is also found in the Valle de Tambo. The houses' sculpted door surrounds are particularly notable, as are the balconies, for example on 700 block of Moquegua.

There are several interesting colonial houses that make a good, short walking tour. Some are private, but the owners may allow entry. **Casa de Regidor Perpetuo de La Ciudad** or **Casa Conde de Alastaya**, at Jirón Moquegua 404-414, is an 18th-century house, although just the portal remains after the earthquake of 2001. **Casa de Fernández Cornejo y Córdova** (La Casa Tradicional de Moquegua) at Jirón Ayacucho 540, beside the post office on the plaza, has a fine 18th-century wooden balcony; visitors are welcome. Also on the south side of the plaza is the office of the INC (corner of Ancash). **Casa de Díaz Fernández Dávila**, Jirón Ayacucho 828, has a collapsed interior but baroque elements can be seen in the ornate portal. Also worth seeing is **Casa de Don Pacífico Barrios** at Jirón Moquegua 820-848 and, opposite, the façade at No 831. On Jirón Lima, between Callao and Tacna, are the ruins of the convent of San Francisco. There is little to see and nothing inside except an open-air church with an awning roof.

Moquegua is famous for its pisco; **Biondi** is the best known brand. Outside town in the direction of the airport are some interesting bodegas, such as **Bodega Villegas** at the corner of Jirón Ayacucho and Puno. You can also find wine from Omate in town.

To the southeast of town is the **Chen Chen** archaeological site, a Tiahuanaco settlement with remains of houses, a cemetery and geoglyphs carved into a hillside. **Samegua**, 4.5 km from Moquegua, is known as 'avocado town', and has many restaurants. To get there take a micro from Avenida Balta, between Tacna and Ancash; it should take 10 minutes.

Omate → *Population: 3000. Altitude: 2160 m.*

Omate is a small town, 146 km north of Moquegua on an unpaved road and 129 km south of Arequipa (five hours). The town is important for its famed **Semana Santa processions**. It is also known for growing grapes, *damascos* and other fruits, and for its shrimp farms. Nearby are the thermal baths at **Ulucán**.

Torata and around

Torata is 24 km northeast of Moquegua. It's a quiet, small town with a shaded plaza. Above the town, on a hill, are two crosses and the Huari ruins of **Torata Alta**, a 30-minute walk away. The ruins are in a poor state but you can get an idea of the shape and size of the houses from the low surviving walls. The site enjoys good views over to **Cerro Baúl**, 2590 m, which can be combined with the ruins at Torata to make a full day's excursion. The mountain is like a *tepuy*, with sheer sides and flat top, hence its name, which means trunk. Covering the entire summit, which is 1.5 km long and 200 m wide, are hundreds of modern arrangements of stones and miniature houses, which, together with looting, are destroying the original look of the place. In the seventh century AD Cerro Baúl was a Huari citadel; there are extensive Huari ruins at the end nearest the path. The mountain became famous in legend as the place of refuge for the Cochunas, who resisted the peaceful invasion of the Incas and whose children regularly made nocturnal food raids into the Inca camps below. The Cochunas were eventually starved off the mountain.

To get to Torata, take a micro or colectivo from Avenida Balta in Moquegua, between Jirón Arequipa y Tacna, US$1.70, 30 minutes. To reach Cerro Baúl get off at the crossroads at the top of the pass beneath the northern end of the mountain. The path leads up the gradual slope from the road. There is a steep section for the last 200 m, on which cement steps have been built. It takes an hour or so from the road to the top. The path leads to a Christian shrine (two crosses). Take water and sun protection.

Moquegua to Desaguadero

The Carretera Interoceánica, from Ilo on the coast to La Paz, has a breathtaking stretch from Moquegua to Desaguadero at the southeastern end of Lake Titicaca. It skirts Cerro Baúl and climbs through zones of ancient terraces at Camata to its highest point at 4755 m. At 4610 m is lonely **Restaurant Humajalso**. On the *altiplano* there are herds of llamas and alpacas, watery *bofedales*, lakes with waterfowl, strange mountain formations and snow-covered peaks. At **Mazo Cruz** there is a PNP checkpoint where all documents and bags are checked. As you approach Desaguadero, the Cordillera Real of Bolivia comes into view. The road is fully paved but should only be taken in daylight.

Ilo → *Phone code: 053. Population: 65,000.*

Located near the mouth of the Río Osmore, 90 km southwest of Moquegua (two hours by bus), Ilo is the southernmost port of Peru. It hopes to become the Pacific terminus of **La Interoceánica** connecting Peru, Bolivia, Paraguay and Brazil, once the paving of this route is complete. Ilo is a functional place with air pollution from a copper smelter. It has a *malecón* (oceanfront promenade) but few other attractions. **Dircetur tourist office** ① *Av Venecia 222, T053-481347, Mon-Fri 0800-1630*. At **Algarrobal** along the road to Moquegua is an archaeological site of the Chiribaya culture with on-site museum. A coastal road (an alternative to the Pan-American Highway), served by buses, runs northwest to Mollendo (unpaved, 3½ hours) and southeast to Tacna (paved, 2½ hours; customs checkpoint at Vila Vila).

Footprint Mini Atlas
Peru

Map 1

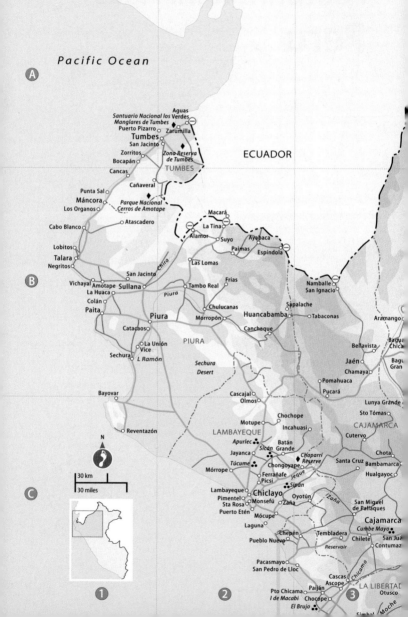

Pacific Ocean

A

ECUADOR

Aguas Verdes
Santuario Nacional los
Manglares de Tumbes
Puerto Pizarro ○ Zarumilla
Tumbes
San Jacinto
Zorritos ○ Zona Reserva
Bocapán ○ de Tumbes
Cancas ○ **TUMBES**
Cañaveral

Punta Sal ○
Máncora ○ Parque Nacional
Los Organos ○ Cerros de Amotape
Cabo Blanco ○ Atascadero

Macará ○
La Tina
Alamor ○ Suyo
Paimas ○ Ayabaca
Espindola

Lobitos ○
Talara ○
Negritos ○ Las Lomas
Vichayal ○ Amotape San Jacinto
La Huaca **Sullana** Frias
Colán ○ Chira Tambo Real
Paita ○ Piura
Catacaos ○
La Unión **Piura** Chulucanas
Vice Morropón ○ **Huancabamba** ○ Tabaconas
Sechura ○ L Ramón Canchaque
PIURA

Namballe
San Ignacio

Sapalache

Aramango

Bellavista ○ Bagu
Chica

Jaén ○ Bagu
Chamaya ○ Gran

Sechura
Desert

Bayovar ○

Pomahuaca ○
Pucará ○

Reventazón ○

Cascajal ○
Olmos ○

Motupe ○ Chochope
LAMBAYEQUE Incahuasi
Apurlec Batán
Jayanca Sicán Grande
Túcume Chongoyape
Mórrope ○ Ferreñafe
Picsi
Lambayeque ○ **Chiclayo**
Pimentel Monsefú Oyotún
Sta Rosa Zaña
Puerto Etén
Mócupe

Laguna ○
Chepén ○ Tembladera
Pueblo Nuevo ○ Reservoir

Pacasmayo ○
San Pedro de Lloc

Lunya Grande ○
Sto Tómas ○

CAJAMARCA

Cutervo ○

Chota ○
Santa Cruz Bambamarca ○
Hualgayoc ○

Chaparrí
Reserve

Sipán

San Miguel
de Pallaques

Cajamarca

Cumbe Mayo
Chilete San Jua
Contumaz

Cascas ○ Chicama
Ascope ○
Pto Chicama **LA LIBERTAD**
Paiján Otusco
I de Macabi Chocope ○
El Brujo Moche

N

30 km
30 miles

1   **2**   **3**

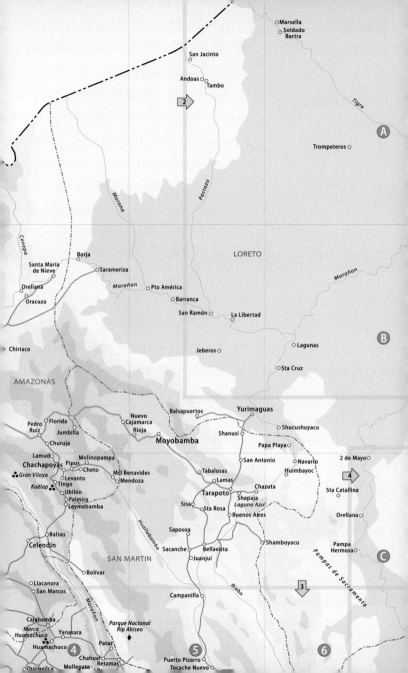

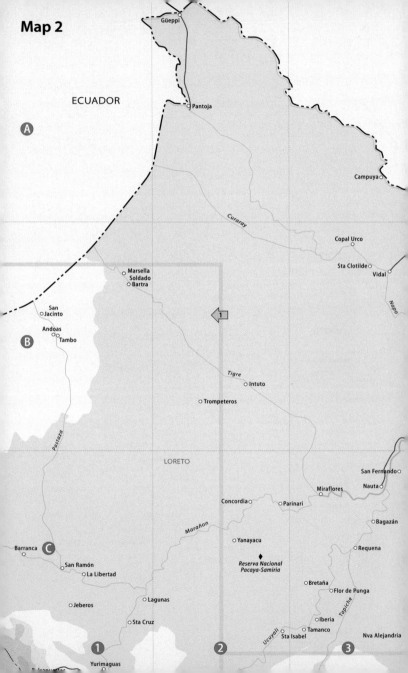

Map 2

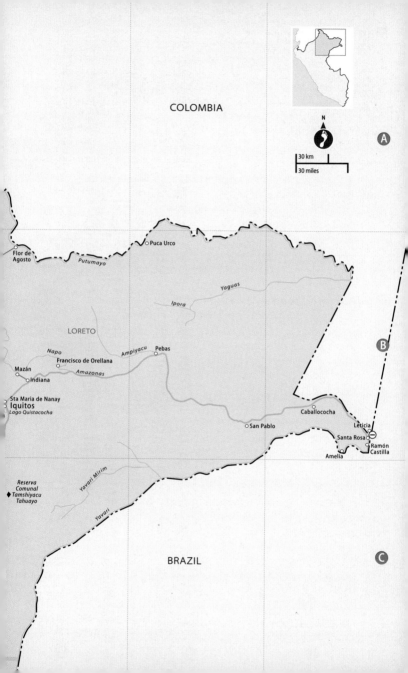

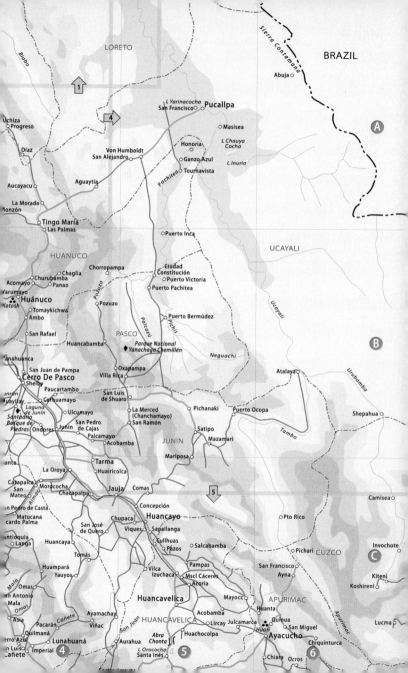

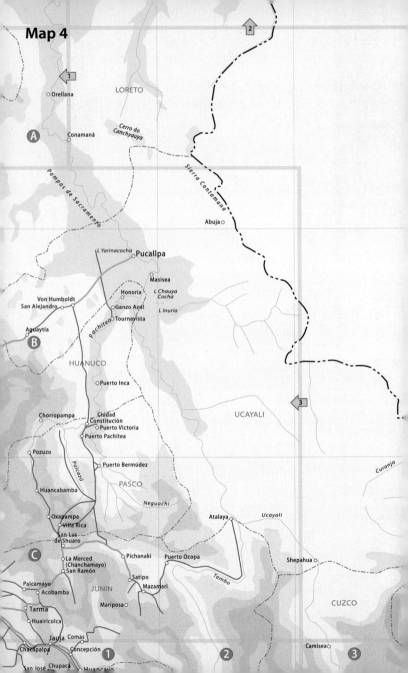

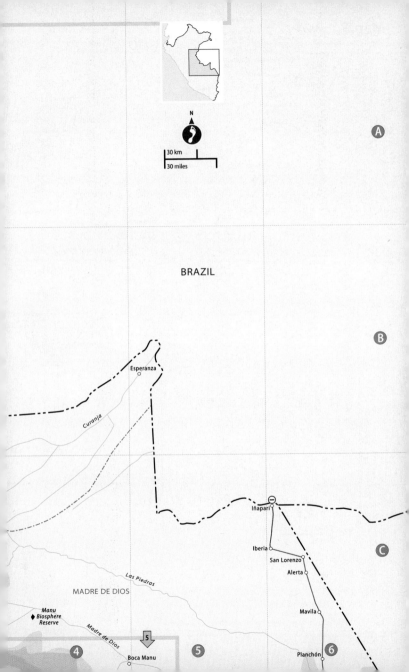

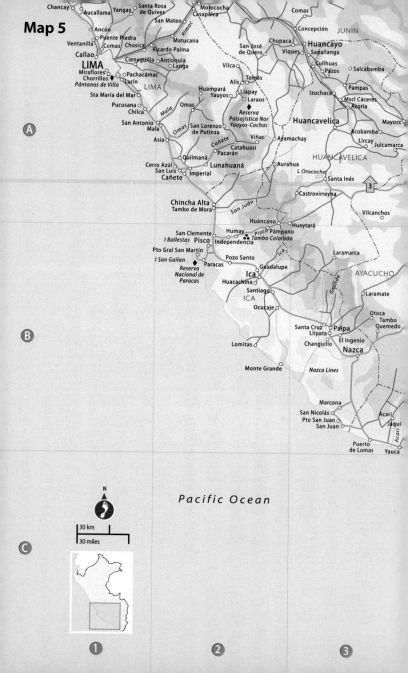

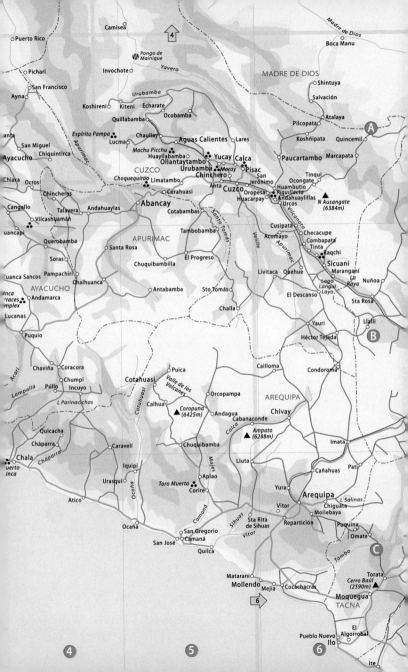

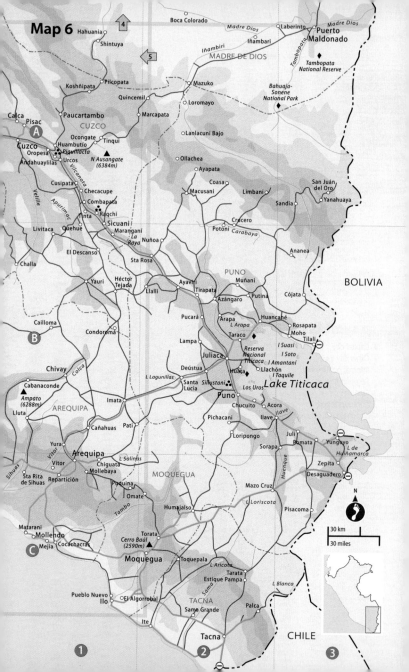

Distance chart

	Arequipa	Ayacucho	Cajamarca	Cuzco	Chachapoyas	Chiclayo	Huancayo	Huaraz	Ica	Lima	Piura	Puerto Maldonado	Puno	Tacna	Trujillo
Ayacucho	1078														
Cajamarca	1860	1394													
Cuzco	515	597	1957												
Chachapoyas	2195	1729	335	2292											
Chiclayo	1773	1307	260	1870	622										
Huancayo	1308	257	1150	854	1485	1063									
Huaraz	1417	951	857	1514	1192	770	707								
Ica	706	372	1154	803	1489	1067	602	711							
Lima	997	556	856	1153	1186	763	299	517	303						
Piura	1982	1516	496	2079	831	209	1272	979	1276	973					
Puerto Maldonado	1048	1130	2490	533	2825	2403	1387	2047	1336	1637	2612				
Puno	326	986	2186	389	2573	2099	1243	1743	1032	1542	2308	922			
Tacna	284	1306	2144	799	2479	2057	1592	1701	990	1293	2266	1332	610		
Trujillo	2022	1100	294	1663	629	207	856	563	860	557	416	2196	1892	1850	
Tumbes	2265	1799	750	2362	1114	492	1555	1262	1559	1299	283	2895	2591	2549	699

Distances in kilometres   1 kilometre = 0.62 miles

Map symbols

- □ Capital city
- ○ Other city, town
- ⌇ International border
- ⌇ Regional border
- ⊖ Customs
- ◎ Contours (approx)
- ▲ Mountain, volcano
- ⇆ Mountain pass
- � Escarpment
- � Glacier
- Salt flat
- Rocks
- Seasonal marshland
- Beach, sandbank
- ◊ Waterfall
- ⌁ Reef
- ═══ Motorway
- ─── Main road
- ─── Minor road
- ─ ─ ─ Track
- ······ Footpath
- ─── Railway
- ⊷■ Railway with station
- ✈ Airport
- ⛟ Bus station
- Ⓜ Metro station

- - - - - Cable car
- +++++ Funicular
- ⛴ Ferry
- Pedestrianized street
- ⟆ ⟅ Tunnel
- → One way-street
- Steps
- ⇌ Bridge
- Fortified wall
- Park, garden, stadium
- ● Sleeping
- ● Eating
- ● Bars & clubs
- ■ Building
- ■ Sight
- ◫◫ Cathedral, church
- 🏮 Chinese temple
- 🛕 Hindu temple
- Meru
- Mosque
- Stupa
- ✡ Synagogue
- ℹ Tourist office
- 🏛 Museum
- ✉ Post office
- Ⓟ Police

- Ⓢ Bank
- @ Internet
- ☎ Telephone
- ⛟ Market
- ⛑ Medical services
- Ⓟ Parking
- ⛽ Petrol
- Golf
- ⚶ Archaeological site
- ◆ National park, wildlife reserve
- ⚘ Viewing point
- ▲ Campsite
- ⌂ Refuge, lodge
- 🏰 Castle, fort
- Diving
- 🌴 Deciduous, coniferous, palm trees
- ⌂ Hide
- Vineyard, winery
- Distillery
- Shipwreck
- ⚔ Historic battlefield
- 1 Detail map
- 1 Related map

Index

Join us online...

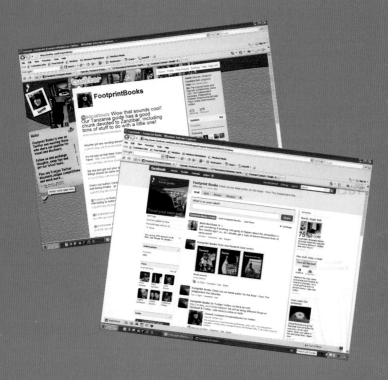

Follow us on **Twitter** and **Facebook** – ask us questions, speak to our authors, swap your stories, and be kept up to date with travel news and exclusive discounts and competitions.

Upload your travel pics to our **Flickr** site – inspire others on where to go next, and have your photos considered for inclusion in Footprint guides.

And don't forget to visit us at

Tacna and around → *For listings, see pages 340-344.*

→ *Colour map 6, C2. Phone code: 052. Population: 174,366. Altitude: 550 m.*

Tacna was in Chilean hands from 1880 to 1929, when its people voted by plebiscite to return to Peru. It is an important commercial centre and has a free-trade zone. There are good schools, housing estates, a stadium to seat 10,000 people, an airport, many military posts and a hospital. Chileans cross the border for cheap medical and dental treatment, to shop and to play the slot machines. Around the city the desert is gradually being irrigated. The local economy includes olive groves, vineyards and fishing. The waters of **Laguna Aricota**, 80 km north, are now being tapped for further irrigation and hydroelectric power for industry.

Ins and outs

Getting there Tacna is 156 km south of Moquegua by the Pan-American Highway, 36 km from the Chilean frontier and 56 km from the international port of Arica, to which there is a railway. It is 1292 km from Lima by road. As this is the nearest town to Chile,

400 metres
400 yards

Sleeping
1 Camino Real
2 Copacabana
3 Dorado
4 El Mesón
5 Gran Hotel Tacna
6 Hostal Anturio
7 Hostal Bon Ami
8 La Posada del Cacique
9 Maximo's
10 Roble 18 Residencial

Eating
1 Café Zeit
2 Cusqueñita
3 Da Vinci
4 El Conquistador
5 Fu-Lin
6 Il Pomodoro
7 Koyuki
8 Un Limón
9 Verdi

Bars & clubs
10 Genova

transport links are good. The airport (T052-314503) is at Km 5 on the Panamericana Sur, on the way to the border. A taxi from the airport to town and the bus terminal costs US$2-3. It is also possible to take a taxi from the airport to Arica, US$30, but the cheapest way is either to take a taxi to Tacna bus station, then take a colectivo, or to call the bus terminal and request a colectivo to pick you up on its way to the border, US$4. ➨See Transport, page 343.

Getting around Many hotels, restaurants and cafés are in the city centre, within easy walking distance. Otherwise the town is quite spread out and you will need to catch a bus or taxi to see much. City bus costs US$0.15; taxi minimum US$0.60.

Tourist information A city map and regional information is available from **Dircetur** (tourist office) ① *Blondell 50, p 3, T052-422784, banyuosa@mincetur.gob.pe, Mon-Fri 0730-1530; also at the Centro Cultural Miculla, corner Blondell y Francisco Lazo, Mon-Fri 0800-1300, Spanish only.* There are also helpful, friendly information booths at the **Terminal Terrestre Nacional** ① *T052-427007, daily 0600-2200;* and at the **Terminal Internacional** ① *Mon-Fri 0800-1500, Sat 0800-1200,* both of which can provide a city map and a list of official taxi rates to different destinations. There is an **iperú** desk at the airport in the arrivals hall which is usually manned when flights are scheduled to arrive. See also www.hellotacna.com.

Safety The city centre is generally safe and pleasant, but be careful outside banks and *cambios* and watch for pickpockets in markets. Drug smuggling is rife in this border area, so only ever transport your own possessions. If they are just passing through, visitors can leave their bags with the **Tourist police** ① *Pasaje Calderón de la Barca 353, inside the main police station;* who will also escort groups on request.

Sights
The **cathedral**, designed by Eiffel, faces the **Plaza de Armas**, which contains huge bronze statues of Admiral Grau and Colonel Bolognesi. They stand at either end of the **Arca de los Héroes**, the triumphal arch that is the symbol of the city. The bronze fountain in the plaza is said to be a duplicate of the one in the Place de la Concorde (Paris) and was also designed by Eiffel.

Parque de la Locomotora, on Avenida Grau near the city centre, has a British-built locomotive, which was used in the War of the Pacific. There is also a very good railway museum further north at the station: **Museo Ferroviario** ① *Coronel Albarracín, daily 0700-1700, US$0.30; ring the bell by the gate on Jr 2 de Mayo for entry.* The **Teatro Municipal** ① *Pasaje Calderón de la Barca y 2 de Mayo, knock on second door on 2 de Mayo, free,* built in the 1870s, is well preserved and worth a visit. There are occasional performances, enquire in advance. The house of Francisco Zela, who gave the 'Cry of Independence' on 20 July 1811 now houses the **Museo de Zela** ① *Zela 542, Mon-Sat 0830-1230, 1530-1900, free.* Avenida Bolognesi is a main commercial street with several markets, including at 721 the **Feria Caplina**, a shopping mall-cum-market selling jewellery, musical instruments but mostly clothes. **Mercado Central** is at Bolognesi y Pallardelli. If you have half a day to spend in Tacna, consider taking a **Tranvía Tour** ① *www.tranviatour.com, 2 departures daily 0845 and 1245, 4 hrs, US$12 per person* on an open-top double-decker bus. It covers the highlights of the city centre and the valley around Tacna.

Border essentials: Peru–Chile

Tacna–Arica

It is 30 minutes from Tacna to the Peruvian border post at Santa Rosa, open from Sunday-Thursday 0800-2300 (Peruvian time), and Friday-Saturday 24 hours.

Customs and immigration You need to obtain a Peruvian exit stamp and a Chilean entrance stamp. All luggage is X-rayed in both directions. No fruit or vegetables are allowed across the border. This is a busy border and there may be long queues but the crossing is otherwise straightforward.

If you're travelling by bus or colectivo, the driver will hustle you through all the procedures (don't give him your passport). If you need a Chilean visa, you will have to get it in Tacna beforehand (see Directory, page 344). Those leaving Peru by car will need to buy official forms, known as *relaciones de pasajeros* (US$0.45) from the kiosk at the border or from a bookshop; you will need four copies. Next, hand in your tourist card, visit the PNP office, return the vehicle permit and finally depart through the checkpoints. A short distance beyond is the Chilean post at Chacalluta, where again the bus driver will show you what to do. All formalities take about 30 minutes. It's a further 15 minutes to Arica.

Transport From Tacna to Arica (56 km) takes one to two hours, depending on waiting time at border; buses charge US$1.80 and colectivo taxis US$4-5 per person. All leave from the international terminal in Tacna throughout the day.

As you approach the terminal you will be grabbed by a driver or his agent and told that the car is "just about to leave". This is hard to verify as you may not see the colectivo until you have filled in the paperwork. It is best to deal with the company's office, rather than a driver/agent. Either way, at the company's office your passport will be taken from you and the details filled out on a Chilean entry form. You can change your remaining soles at the bus terminal while this is being done.

Arica is 20 km south of the border. It has road links with La Paz, Bolivia, and with the rest of Chile. If travelling onwards into Chile, buy bus tickets in Arica, where they are cheaper than in Tacna.

Note Peruvian time is one hour behind Chilean time March-October; two hours behind from September/October-February/March (varies annually).

 Some 8 km above the city, just off the Panamericana Norte, is the Campo de la Alianza, scene of a battle between Peru and Chile in 1880.

Around Tacna

To the northeast is the fruit-growing valley of the **Río Caplina**, known as Valle Viejo, where *tacneños* go for *comida típica* at weekends. It is 23 km to the thermal baths at **Calientes** ① *open 24 hrs, US$1 for pool, US$2.50 per person for tubs*, which has clean individual hot tubs and a tepid outdoor pool, popular with locals and crowded at weekends. There's a restaurant and simple accommodation (**D**) on site. One hour's walk through the desert from Calientes is the archeological site of **Miculla** ① *daily 24 hrs, entry US$0.30*, set in the rocky valley of the Río Palca. Many excellent petroglyphs from various periods may be seen as well as two rope suspension bridges over the river (rebuilt with a steel cable core) and a fragment of ancient road. It's a good spot for stargazing at night from June to September. There is a caretaker at the entrance but the site itself is vast and desolate; do not take valuables or go alone.

Along the Tacna seashore are several fishing villages and beaches, popular with locals from January to March. **Playa Los Palos** to the south, as well as **Pozo Redondo**, **Tres Cuevas** and **Punta Brava** further north, are among the favourites; beware of strong undertow. Transport leaves from the Terminal Bolognesi.

◉ Nazca to Chile listings

For Sleeping and Eating price codes and other relevant information, see pages 38-44.

● Sleeping

South of Nazca *p332*
C Hostal Capricho de Verano, Los Jazmines s/n, Puerto de Lomas, T056-210282. Beautifully situated on the cliffs, bungalows with bathroom, clean, very friendly, special rates for young travellers. Recommended.

Chala and Puerto Inca *p332*
Chala
In Chala, all the better hotels are in Chala Sur, rather than Chala Norte.
D Turistas, Comercio s/n, Chala Sur, T054-551111. With breakfast and bath (**E** without), large rooms, good beds, friendly, hot water, restaurant, sea view, showing its age but best in town.
E Hostal Camino Real, Av Prolongación Comercio Mz 17, Lote 10, T054-505601, Chala Norte, near bus agencies. With private bath, **F** with shared bath, good value.
F Hostal 2 de Enero, 2 de Enero, 2 blocks from the Panamericana. Shared bath, cold water, small rooms, basic, clean and friendly.
F Hostal Evertyth, Comercio 705, Chala Sur, T054-551095. Clean, with bath, cold water, simple, friendly, rooms facing the ocean, secure parking.

Peru to Inca
A Puerto Inka, signposted 2 km along a side road from Km 610 on the Panamericana, T054-778458, www.puertoinka.com.pe. A great place to relax, on a superb beach, boats and diving equipment for hire, disco, hammocks, recommended but used by tour groups and busy in summer, low season

discounts. Price reflects the location. Camping US$5 per person.

Mollendo *p333*
Low season prices are given below, they increase by 50% or more Jan-Mar.
D La Villa, Av Mcal Castilla 366, away from centre, T/F054-532700. Grand old wooden house in front with modern comfortable rooms at back. Restaurant and bar, nice terrace and small pool, parking.
E Hostal Cabaña, Comercio 240, T054-534671. A wooden building with huge balconies, rooms with bath, hot water, faded glory but still OK.
E Hostal California, Blondel 541, T054-533675. With private electric shower, **F** with shared bath, breakfast available, family run, friendly, best rooms at top.
E Hostal D'Manuel, Deán Valdivia 416, T054-535511. With bath, solar hot water best during daytime, modern, good value.

Moquegua *p334, map p334*
D Alameda, Junín 322, T053-463971. Includes breakfast, large comfortable rooms, friendly service.
E Arequipa, Arequipa 360, T053-461338, javierhotelarequipa@hotmail.com. Clean, hot water sometimes, pleasant.
E Hostal Adrianella, Miguel Grau 239, T/F053-463469. Hot water, TV, safe, helpful, close to market and buses, adequate.
E Hostal Plaza, Ayacucho 675, T053-461612. Modern and comfortable, good value.
F Hospedaje Cornejo, Tarapacá 281-A, T053-507681. With bath, electric shower, basic but clean.
F Hostal Carrera, Jr Lima 320 (no sign), T053-462113. With private or shared bath, solar hot water best in afternoon, small patio,

clean, friendly, good value, laundry facilities on roof. Recommended.

Tacna *p337, map p337*
There are a great many hotels and rooms are usually easy to find, except perhaps before Christmas. There are several simple places by the bus terminals, but it makes more sense to stay in the centre.

A Gran Hotel Tacna, Av Bolognesi 300, T052-424193, www.granhoteltacna.com. Modern, 3-star hotel. Includes breakfast, internet, gardens, 2 pools (open to non-guests who spend min US$8 in restaurant or bar), safe car park, English spoken.

B Dorado, Arias Araguez 145, T052-415741, www.doradohoteltacna.com. Includes breakfast, restaurant, modern and comfortable.

C El Mesón, Unánue 175, T052-425841, www.mesonhotel.com. With breakfast, TV, central, modern, comfortable, safe, Wi-Fi in rooms.

C Maximo's, Arias Araguez 281, T052-242604. With breakfast, modern rooms with *frigobar*, Wi-Fi, sauna.

D Camino Real, Av San Martín 855-857, T052-242010. Rooms with cable TV and fridge, restaurant, bar, coffee shop and Wi-Fi.

D Copacabana, Arias Araguez 281 y 2 de Mayo, T052-421721, www.copahotel.com. Includes breakfast, good rooms.

D Roble 18 Residencial, Hipólito Unánue 245, T052-241414, roble18@gmail.com. Internet, Wi-Fi, cableTV, hot water, English, Italian and German spoken.

E Hostal Anturio, 28 de Julio 194 y Zela, T052-244258. Cafeteria downstairs, breakfast extra, clean, modern and good value.

E La Posada del Cacique, Arias Araguez 300-304, T052-247424, laposada_hostal@hotmail.com. Antique style in an amazing building built around a huge spiral staircase.

F Hostal Bon Ami, 2 de Mayo 445, T052-244847. Private bath, cheaper with shared bath, solar hot water best in afternoon, simple but clean and adequate, secure.

❶ Eating

Mollendo *p333*
Several restaurants including **Cevichería Teo**, Comercio 208, excellent, cheap set meals, and **Pizzería Golosa**, Plaza de Armas, part of a chain which is growing in southern Peru, pizza, garlic bread and drink, wide variety of toppings, bright, diner-style ambiance, popular. Others can be found on Comercio (eg **Marco Antonio**, plus several *chifas* and *pollerías*).
Heladería Venezia, Comercio 118. Ice cream made on the premises.

Moquegua *p334, map p334*
The best-known local dish is *cuy chactado*, pan-fried guinea pig. 2 famous places to try it are **Samegua** and **Los Angeles**, both a few kilometres out of town (taxi US$0.50, or combi, 10 mins), with several restaurants in each town. *Damascos*, a type of small, yellow plum, can be found both stewed and *remojado*, steeped in pisco (delicious). *Chicha de jora* and *chicha morado* can be found in the market; the latter is served with most *menús* at lunchtime. Local spirits and other liqueurs can be bought at **La Tranquita**, Piura 148 (no sign). All foodstuffs can be bought at the market (bounded by Grau, Torata, Av Balta and Libertad) and the streets around.
ᵀᵀ-ᵀ Pizzería Casa Vieja, Moquegua 326. Mon-Sat 1830-2300. Pizza and Italian dishes.
ᵀ Moraly, Lima 398 y Libertad. Mon-Sat 1000-2200, Sun 1000-1600. Good-sized portions, moderate prices, best in town, *menú del día*, good lunches.

Tacna *p337, map p337*
ᵀᵀ Da Vinci, San Martín 596 y Arias Araguez, T052-744648. Mon-Sat 1100-2300. Pizza and other dishes, nice atmosphere, bar upstairs Tue-Sat 2000-0200.
ᵀᵀ Il Pomodoro, Bolívar 524 y Apurimac. Closed Sun evening and Mon midday. Upscale Italian, set lunch Tue-Fri, pricey à la carte in the evening, attentive service.
ᵀ Café Zeit, Pasaje Vigil 51, www.cafezeitperu. com. A German-owned coffee shop offering

cultural events and live music as well as good quality coffee and cakes. The closest thing in Tacna to a swanky coffee shop. Also at Deústua 150.

ɬ Cusqueñita, Zela 747. 1100-1600, excellent 4-course lunch, large portions, good value, variety of choices. Recommended.

ɬ El Conquistador, Av San Martín 884, T052-412496. Grills and *anticuchos*.

ɬ Fu-Lin, Arias Araguez 396 y 2 de Mayo. Mon-Sat 0930-1600. Vegetarian Chinese.

ɬ Koyuki, Bolívar 718. Generous set lunch daily, seafood and other à la carte in the evening, closed Sun evening. Several other popular lunch places on the same block.

ɬ Un Limón, Av San Martín 843, T052-425182, www.unlimon.net. Best known for *ceviches* and variety of seafood .

ɬ Verdi, Pasaje Vigil 57. Simple place for set lunch, excellent *empanadas* and sweets.

⟟ Bars and clubs

Mollendo *p333*
El Observatorio, Comercio y Deán Valdivia. A massive semi-open-air disco, "has to be seen to be believed", no cover charge.

Tacna *p337, map p337*
Genova, Av San Martín 649 y Pasaje Libertad. Mon-Sat 1100-0200, Sun 1200-2300. Trendy bar/café/restaurant with sidewalk seating.
Jethro's Pub, Arias Araguez 131 y San Martín. Popular.

⊛ Festivals and events

Moquegua *p334, map p334*
14 Oct Santa Fortunata.
25 Nov Día de Santa Catalina, anniversary of the founding of the colonial city.

Tacna *p337, map p337*
Jun 23-24 Noche de San Juan y Caravana al Valle Viejo combines the Christian festival with a tribute to the *Pachamama*.

Aug 28 Reincorporación de Tacna al Perú, week-long celebrations with parades, cultural events and a fair.

⊖ Transport

Chala and Puerto Inca *p332*
Buses stop in **Chala Norte**, a 10-min walk from the Chala Sur hotels. Night buses from Lima arrive 0600-0700; there are others in the early evening. To **Lima**, 9 hrs, US$11, with **Flores**, 6 daily from 1200, *bus cama* at 2215; also 6 daily with **Cruz del Sur**, 1330 and late at night. To **Arequipa**, 7½ hrs, US$7.25, with **Flores**, **Llamosa** and **Caminos del Inca**, all around 2000; also **Caminos del Inca** at 1330. To **Puerto Inca**, get a colectivo just north of the town as far as the turn-off for Puerto Inca, Km 610, about US$1 per person, beware overcharging; a taxi costs US$5.

Mollendo *p333*
Bus station at north end of town, usage fee US$0.30, taxi from centre US$0.60. To **Arequipa**, 129 km, buses and colectivos daily, 2½ hrs, US$2. **Santa Ursula** has buses every hour between Arequipa and Mollendo from their terminal just opposite the main Terminal Terrestre in Arequipa. To **Moquegua**, 156 km, 2 hrs, US$2-3, buses and colectivos daily. To **Tacna** (315 km) Transportes Moquegua Turismo twice a day via Moquegua. Alternatively, take a colectivo from the obelisk at the top end of Av Mcal Castilla to **Cocachacra**, 40 min, US$1; then another to **El Fiscal**, 20 min, US$0.60; catch a south-bound bus from there. No direct service to **Lima**: take an Arequipa-bound bus to '48', on the Pan-American Highway, 1½ hrs, US$1.50; buses pass frequently en route to Lima, 13 hrs, US$11.

Moquegua *p334, map p334*
All bus companies are on Av del Ejército, 2 blocks north of the market at Jr Grau, except **Ormeño**, Av La Paz casi Balta. To **Lima**, many companies with executive and regular

services, 15 hrs, US$15-30. To **Tacna**, 159 km, 2 hrs, US$3, hourly buses with **Flores**, Av del Ejército y Andrés Aurelio Cáceres. To **Arequipa**, 3½ hrs, US$4-8, several buses daily. Colectivos for these 2 destinations leave when full from Av del Ejército y Andrés Aurelio Cáceres, almost double the bus fare – negotiate. To **Desaguadero** and **Puno**, 4 a day, 6 hrs, US$7.50; the 2130 bus continues to **Cuzco**; to Cuzco direct at 1100, 13 hrs, US$13.50. **Mily Tours**, Av del Ejército 32-B, T053-464000, colectivos to **Desaguadero**, 4 hrs, US$15. To **Mollendo**, **Transportes Moquegua Turismo** twice a day, or take an Arequipa-bound bus to El Fiscal, see Mollendo transport, above.

Tacna *p337, map p337*
Local To **Calientes**, take Ruta 12 minibus from the Centro Comercial Tacnacentro, Av Leguía cuadra 9, every 15 mins throughout the day, 45 mins to Calientes, US$0.60. For **Miculla**, get off at the fork 2 km before Calientes and walk 2 km along a paved road to the archaeological site. Taxis charge US$12 to both sites with 1-hr wait.

Air
The airport (T052-314503) is at Km 5 on the Panamericana Sur, on the way to the border. To go from the airport directly to Arica, call the bus terminal (T052-427007) and ask a colectivo to pick you up on its way to the border, US$4. Taxi from airport to Tacna centre US$2-3. To **Lima**, 1½ hrs, daily with LAN (San Martín 259, T052-428346). Also Peruvian Airlines (Av San Martín 670, p 2, T052-412699) have flights from Tacna to **Arequipa** and Lima.

Bus
There are 2 bus terminals on Hipólito Unánue (T052-427007), 1 km from the plaza (colectivo US$0.25, taxi US$0.60 min). 1 terminal is for international services (ie Arica), the other for domestic, both are well-organized, local tax US$0.30, baggage store, easy to make connections to the

border, Arequipa or Lima. Tickets can be purchased several days before departure. Beware of touts selling tickets at inflated prices; only buy tickets at company offices. Ormeño has its terminal on Arias Araguez by the petrol station.

Heading north, note that luggage is checked at a customs complex at **Tomasiri**, 35 km north of Tacna, whether you've been out of the country or not. There is also a police control checking passports 10 km after the **Camiara** bridge (near a military base), just before the Tacna/ Moquegua departmental border, 59 km from Tacna, 61 km from Moquegua. Sernanp have a post where any fruit will be confiscated in an attempt to keep fruit flies out of Peru. Don't agree to carry anything on the bus for anyone else, just your own belongings.

To **Moquegua**, 159 km, hourly with Flores (Av Saucini behind the Terminal Nacional, T052-426691), US$3, 2½ hrs. Transportes Moquegua Turismo have direct services to **Mollendo**, **Moquegua** and **Arequipa** in comfortable *bus cama* from 1030 to 2130 daily. Otherwise, catch one of the frequent buses to **El Fiscal** (US$4, 4 hrs, see Mollendo Transport, above), then a colectivo to Mollendo. To **Arequipa**, 6 hrs, US$9-15, several buses daily, most with Flores. Cruz del Sur has a *cruzero* service once a day. To **Nazca**, 793 km, 12 hrs, about US$3 less than to Lima. Several companies daily to **Lima**, 1239 km, 21-26 hrs, regular US$15-20, *bus cama* US$32-52, eg Flores, Cruz del Sur and Ormeño.

To **Desaguadero**, **Puno**, and **Cuzco**, from Terminal Collasuyo (T052-312538), Av Internacional in Barrio Altos de la Alianza neighbourhood; taxi to centre US$0.75. San Martín-Nobleza (T052-952 4252) is recommended, 4 daily to Desaguadero, US$13.50 and Puno, US$10, 8-10 hrs, the 1900 bus continues to **Juliaca** and **Cuzco**; to Cuzco direct at 0830, US$20, 15 hrs, or change in Moquegua.

Bus travel to **La Paz**, Bolivia, is quickest and cheapest via Moquegua and Desaguadero, involving 1 less border crossing than via Arica and Tambo Quemado.

Car
Explorer Tacna Rent a Car, T052-421753, explorer tacna@viabcp.com. Car hire.

Train
The station is on Av Albaracín y 2 de Mayo, ticket office daily 0800-0900 and 1430-1600; for the morning train it's best to buy tickets the day before as they sell out. *Autoferro* to **Arica**, Mon-Sat 0600 and 1600 (returning from Arica at 0900 and 2000 Peruvian time), US$1.50, 1½ hrs, customs and immigration at railway stations.

❶ Directory

Moquegua *p334, map p334*
Banks BCP, Moquegua y Tarapacá, the only bank that changes TCs, will advance money on Visa. Open daily 0915-1315, 1630-1830, Telebanco 24 Horas ATM (Visa). There are street changers at the **Mercado Central**.
Internet Many places all over town,

US$0.35 per hr. **Post** On the Plaza de Armas in a colonial house. **Telephone** All over town.

Tacna *p337, map p337*
Banks BCP, San Martín 574. Scotiabank, San Martín 476. Several *casas de cambio* at San Martín y Arias Araguez and at the international bus terminal, all offering good rates for US$; also euro, pesos chilenos (best rates) and bolivianos. Street changers stand outside the **Municipalidad. Embassies and consulates** **Post** Bolivia, Av Bolognesi 1721 y Piura, T052-715125. Open Mon-Fri 0900-1500. **Chile**, Presbítero Andía block 1, T052-723063. Open Mon-Fri 0800-1300, closed holidays. **Immigration** Av Circunvalación s/n, Urb El Triángulo, T052-243231. **Internet** Many on San Martín, several open 24 hrs. Others around the centre, average US$0.35 per hr.
Laundry Lavandería Tacna, Zela 374. US$1.50 per kg, open Mon-Sat 0800-1300, 1500-2000. **Post** Av Bolognesi 361. Open Mon-Sat 0800-2000. **Telephone** Public *locutorios* everywhere. Shop around for the best prices.

Contents

Footprint features

Cordilleras Blanca & Huayhuash

At a glance

⊖ **Getting around** On foot (trekking), by bus.

◉ **Time required** 1 to 3 weeks.

☼ **Weather** May-Sep is the dry season and best for trekking. Nov-Apr can be wet.

✖ **When not to go** Outside the dry season, views may be restricted by cloud and paths muddy.

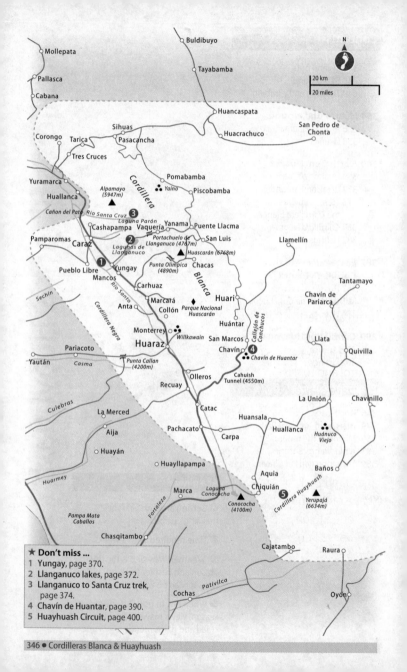

★ **Don't miss ...**
1 Yungay, page 370.
2 Llanganuco lakes, page 372.
3 Llanganuco to Santa Cruz trek,
  page 374.
4 Chavín de Huantar, page 390.
5 Huayhuash Circuit, page 400.

The Cordillera Blanca is a region of jewelled lakes and sparkling white mountain peaks that attracts mountaineers, hikers, cyclists and rafters in their thousands. Here stand the highest mountains in South America, with some 30 snow-crested peaks over 6000 m, including Huascarán, the highest mountain in Peru at 6768 m. From the region's main centre, Huaraz, several of these giants can be seen. This area contains the largest concentration of glaciers found in the world's tropical zone: a source of both beauty and danger.

The turquoise-coloured lakes (*cochas*) that form in the terminal moraines are the jewels of the Andes and you should hike up to at least one during your stay. Laguna Churup is a day's walk from Huaraz, Lago Parón is close to Caraz, while the beautiful twin lakes of Llanganuco are within easy reach of Yungay and are on the route of the long-distance Santa Cruz trek. The tranquility of these glacial lakes masks a frightening history. They have caused much death and destruction when dykes have broken, sending tons of water hurtling down the canyons, wiping out everything in their path. The levels of some have been artificially lowered for flood control and to feed the huge Cañón del Pato dam. Earthquakes, too, have scarred the high valleys and the mass grave that was once the old town of Yungay is a very humbling place.

Southeast of Huaraz, the Cordillera Huayhuash is an area that more than equals the Cordillera Blanca in beauty and majesty. It is rapidly gaining a reputation among long-distance trekkers and climbers. Even the archaeologist is catered for here in the shape of the ruins of Chavín de Huantar. This fortress-temple belonged to one of the earliest and most influential cultures in pre-Inca Peru and it has some fine carvings and stonework.

Ins and outs → *Colour map 3, B3.*

Getting there

It is possible to fly from Lima to the small airport at Anta, just north of Huaraz, with LC Busre. There are three main overland routes to reach the Cordillera Blanca. Probably the easiest is the paved road that branches east off the Pan-American Highway north of Pativilca at Km 209, see page 409. Further north, a second route is via the Callán Pass from Casma to Huaraz, see page 410, a rough but beautiful trip through the heart of the Cordillera Negra. The third option is from Chimbote to Caraz via the Cañón del Pato, see page 413, also a very scenic journey, with magnificent views of this spectacular canyon. The main access to the Cordillera Huayhuash is from Huaraz. Cajatambo, the southern access point, can be reached from Lima by bus and the area can also be reached by bus on the Huánuco–La Unión–Huaraz route. ► *See Transport, page 367.*

Getting around

In the Cordillera Blanca minibuses run between most of the towns on a regular basis, while more remote places have less frequent services. Several roads have been improved to cope with mining traffic. Of course, on some routes, you can always walk!

Best time to visit

The dry season (May-October) is the best time to visit the region and the only time for climbing most summits. Trekking is also possible at other times of the year, but conditions are less amenable and the views are less rewarding. Christmas to New Year is a popular time for foreigners seeking an exotic location to spend the holidays.

Background

The snow-capped Cordillera Blanca runs north to south for almost 200 km. Alongside it to the west lies its alter ego, the bare and dry **Cordillera Negra**, which rises to 4600 m. The valley of the **Río Santa**, known as the **Callejón de Huaylas**, separates the two ranges. The Santa rises in **Laguna Conococha**, at the south end of the two mountain chains and flows due north between them, before turning west to enter the spectacular **Cañón del Pato** and making its way to the Pacific.

To the east of the Cordillera Blanca lies another set of valleys, the **Callejón de Conchucos**, containing the archaeological treasures of **Chavín de Huantar**, see page 390. Callejones de Huaylas and Conchucos are both well-populated areas with lovely little villages of narrow cobblestone streets and houses with odd-angled roofs. Their inhabitants grow potatoes and barley at the higher altitudes and maize, alfalfa, fruits and flowers lower down. These valleys also provide road access to the region's wonders. Many excellent trekking routes and approaches to climbers' base camps cross from one *callejón* to the other, over the high passes of the Cordillera Blanca. Communities are close to each other in the Callejón de Huaylas, so there is little sense of isolation until you are right up in the mountains, or in the more remote areas beyond this valley.

Huaraz, undoubtedly at the heart of things, has become very tourist-oriented, catering for the adventure sports market with all the requisite services and facilities. Only an hour northwest, **Caraz** has the same mix of engineers (for the hydroelectric scheme) and tourism, but on a much smaller scale. However, the waters coming off the mountains make this a fertile area and it is agriculture, above all, that dictates the pace of life.

Huascarán National Park

Established in July 1975, the park encompasses the entire Cordillera Blanca above 4000 m. It covers a total area of 3400 sq km: 180 km from north to south and 20 km from east to west. It is a UNESCO World Biosphere Reserve and part of the World Heritage Trust. The park's objectives are to protect the unique flora, fauna, geology, archaeological sites and extraordinary scenic beauty of the Cordillera. Please take all your rubbish away with you.

Park administration is at Jirón Federico Sal y Rosas 555, by Plazuela Belén, Huaraz, T043-722086, pnh@terra.com.pe. Open Monday-Friday 0830-1300 and 1430-1700, it is principally administrative. Fees for visiting the national park are collected at rangers posts at **Quebrada Llanganuco** (see page 372) and **Huascarán** (see page 374) for the Llanganuco to Santa Cruz trek, at **Collon** on the way up the **Quebrada Ishinca** (see page 357) and at **Pitec** (see page 357). It costs S/.5 or US$1.65 for a day visit. For visits of up to two weeks (ie for trekking and climbing trips) a permit costing S/.70 or US$26 (in 2010) must be bought.

Sernanp (Servicio Nacional de Areas Naturales Protegidos por el Estado, www.sernanp.gob.pe) implements regulations governing the national park similar to those governing the Inca trails at Machu Picchu. Local guides are mandatory for everywhere except designated 'Recreation Zones' (areas accessible by car). Tourists must hire a licensed tour operator for all activities and those operators may only employ licensed guides, cooks, *arrieros* and porters. Anyone wishing to trek, climb or ski in Huascarán should seek advice from Sernanp or a local tour operator and climbers attempting difficult climbing routes will have to be accompanied by a local climbing guide.

Further south lie the cordilleras Huayhuash and Raura, offering more spectacular climbing and hiking in a less visited area, see page 399.

Trekking and climbing

The Cordillera Blanca offers the most popular – and some of the best – trekking and climbing in Peru, with a network of trails used by the local people and some less well-defined mountaineers' routes. There are numerous possibilities for day hikes, trekking and climbing. Of these, only a very few routes are currently used by most visitors, and so they have accumulated rubbish and other signs of impact. While these favourite treks – notably Santa Cruz–Llanganuco (see page 374) and the Alpamayo circuit (see page 376) – are undeniably interesting, you should consider the various excellent alternatives if you want to enjoy a less crowded experience and help conserve the area's great natural beauty. For details of access and permits, see box, above.

Trekking options

The many other options include: **Laguna Parón**, with its impressive cirque of surrounding summits (access from Caraz, see page 374); **Hualcayán to Pomabamba**, traversing the northern end of the Cordillera Blanca with fine views of Alpamayo and many other peaks (access from Caraz; see page 376); **Laguna 69** at the end of Llanganuco Valley (access from Yungay; see page 371); the **Ulta Valley** and **Laguna Auquiscocha**, between the

Mining in the mountains

The Department of Ancash contains important mineral deposits including copper, zinc, silver, gold and perhaps uranium (the latter is not discussed openly). In the Cordillera Negra alone, 12,000 different sites have been prospected. An open pit mine and smelter, 12 km north of Huaraz, has brought major changes to the Callejón de Huaylas. The US/Canadian consortium operating the mine promised to minimize environmental impact, yet there are conflicting claims as to the extent of environmental damage. There has, however, been an undeniable impact on some of the finest natural areas of the Peruvian Andes. Mining companies have built their own neighbourhoods and camps, while many new roads continue to be made by and for the mines.

Similar developments are taking place east of San Marcos, near Chavín in the Callejón de Conchucos, where a huge underground mine and concentrator at Antamina has come on stream. Hundreds of kilometres of good roads, thousands of jobs for Peruvians and a resident ex-pat community near Huaraz have undoubtedly had a significant effect on the local economy.

In the Cordillera Huayhuash, a Japanese corporation has a major mining project in the vicinity of Pocpa and Laguna Jahuacocha, the jewel of the entire region. Other mines are under consideration. Local communities have rejected the proposal that the area be made a national park as it would restrict their ability to levy fees on tourists passing through their lands.

massifs of Huascarán, Ulta and Hualcán (access from Carhuaz, see page 369); to name but a few. There remains a good deal to be discovered in the area and your creativity in choosing a route is certain to be rewarded.

There are two traditional trekking routes in the **Huayhuash**: a complete loop around the range (see page 400); and a half-circuit, starting from the trail head at Cuartel Huain and ending in Cajatambo. These are but two of very many excellent options and hikers are urged to be creative in choosing their routes and campsites – both to enjoy more pristine surroundings and to allow over-used areas to recover.

Advice to climbers

The height of the mountains in the Cordillera Blanca and nearby ranges and their location in the tropics create conditions different from the Alps or even the Himalayas. Fierce sun makes the mountain snow porous and the glaciers move more rapidly. Deglaciation is rapidly changing the face of the Cordillera, so older maps do not provide a reliable indication of the extent of glaciers and snow fields (according to some studies 15% of the range's glaciers have disappeared since the 1970s); local experience is important. Climbers should not assume that their experience on other ranges will be sufficient for the Cordillera Blanca and first-timers here should take a guide for safety.

The British Embassy advises climbers to take at least six days for acclimatization, to move in groups of four or more, reporting to a reliable fellow climber, an agency, your hotel or embassy before departing, giving the date at which a search should begin, and leaving the telephone number of your embassy with enough money to make a phone call.

The **Departamento de Salvamento de Alta Montaña (DEPSAM)** ① *Jr Bolognesi 410, Caraz, T043-391163/391669, http://www.huaraz.info/usam/index.html*, has a 35-member rescue team in Yungay, with 24-hour phone service and vhf/uhf radio dispatch. They have trained search-and-rescue dogs and a Peruvian army helicopter. At present, they will rescue anyone – climbers, trekkers, tourists – without asking for cash up front; insured climbers will be billed but rescues are currently free for uninsured climbers, although this policy is likely to change. DEPSAM will only take the injured person as far as Caraz or Huaraz hospitals, from where additional costly medical evacuation may be required. It therefore remains imperative that all climbers carry adequate insurance; it cannot be purchased locally. Be well-prepared before setting out on a climb. Wait or cancel your trip when weather conditions are bad. Every year climbers are killed through failing to take weather conditions seriously. Climb only when and where you have sufficient experience.

Advice to hikers and trekkers

Most circuits can be hiked in five days. Although the trails are easily followed, they are rugged and the passes are very high – between 4000 m and nearly 5000 m – so you should be fit and properly acclimatized to the altitude, and carry all necessary equipment. In the Cordillera Huayhuash you must be entirely self-sufficient. Evacuation in the event of illness or accident may require several days. Essential items are a tent, warm sleeping bag, stove and protection against wind and rain (climatic conditions are quite unreliable here and you cannot rule out rain and hail storms even in the dry season). Trekking with mules or donkeys demands less stamina, since equipment is carried for you. Nobody should trek entirely on their own. Something as minor as a sprained ankle can become a disaster if there is no one to assist you or go for help. In accordance with the British Embassy advice to climbers above, you should always inform trusted friends or associates where you plan to hike and the latest date you plan to return.

Safety and conduct

Before heading out on any route, trekkers and climbers must always enquire locally about public safety. Following hold-ups of trekking parties in the Cordillera Huayhuash in recent years, an entrance fee is now paid at the Huascaran park office, of which some goes to the local communities in a bid to reduce the attacks on tourists. The Cordillera Blanca is generally quite safe, but muggings have taken place on the way to Laguna Churup, to the Mirador Rataquena above Huaraz, the Mirador above Monterrey, and at Wilkawain. The eastern side of the Huayhuash/Raura range, in the Department of Huánuco, has a reputation for more aggressive behaviour; be especially cautious in this area.

On all treks in this area, respect the locals' property, leave no rubbish behind, do not give sweets or money to children who beg (a serious problem on popular routes) and remember your cooking utensils, tent, etc, would be very expensive for a *campesino*, so be sensitive and responsible. Do not leave your gear unattended at any time and stow everything in your tent overnight. Some camping areas in the Huayhuash charge a fee for trekkers, US$55 for the full loop; insist on a numbered ticket or receipt from each community you pass through.

You will encounter many cattle with dogs guarding them; it's best to give both a wide berth. Carrying a walking stick or crouching to pick up a stone will usually discourage the canines but throwing stones has been known to provoke an attack.

Rubbish is a significant problem at the usual campsites and you should personally pack out everything you bring in; you cannot trust muleteers in this regard. Much of the area is above the tree line; the remainder has been badly deforested. Make sure you have a reliable stove and enough fuel for cooking and resist the temptation to use what little firewood remains. Camp fires spreading out of control have caused huge damage in critical areas of the Andes. Improper disposal of human waste is also a problem. Exercise great care in this fragile environment.

Hiring guides and muleteers

The **Dirección de Turismo** issues qualified guides and *arrieros* (muleteers) with a photo ID. Always check for this when making arrangements; note down the name and card number in case you should have any complaints. Prices for specific services are set, so enquire before hiring someone. You should also make your priorities clear to the muleteer in advance of the trek (pace, choice of route, campsites, etc) or else you will be led around with the line, 'all the gringos do this'. Some guides speak English and are friendly but lack technical expertise; others have expertise but lack communicative ability. You may have to choose between the former and the latter. There are several associations of local **arrieros Humacchuco – Llanganuco Association** (for porters and cooks) ① *T043-943 786497 (mob), victorcautivo@hotmail.com;* **Pashpa Arrieros Association** ① *T043-830540, Musho Arrieros T043-814416;* and **Collon Arrieros Association** (for llama trekking) ① *T043-833417.* Avoid 'private' guides who seek you out on the street.

Prices in 2010 for both Cordilleras Blanca and Huayhuash were as follows: *arriero*, US$10 per day; donkey or mule US$6 per day; trekking guides US$40-50 per day (more for foreign guides); climbing guides US$70-120 per day (more for foreign guides), depending on the difficulty of the peak; cooks US$25-30 per day. You are required to provide or pay for food and shelter for all porters, guides, cooks and *arrieros*. Tour operators in Huaraz (see page 364) offer a range of treks in the Huayhuash, from US$570 for a basic service, five-person minimum, nine-day trek, to US$700 for 10 people for 11 days with full service including guide/cook, food, equipment, mules and driver, and public transport. Three tour operators in Caraz (see page 385) also offer treks in the Huayhuash. Other small operators on Avenida Luzuriaga offer treks as low as US$25 a day for Huayhuash, but they are very basic and you must get a printed agreement stating what is included and what is not, as there are a lot of hidden costs. Tours without guide cost US$160 per person: you have to cook your own food and feed the mule driver, do your own setting up of tents, etc.

For the Cordillera Huayhuash treks, it is sometimes a problem in the high climbing/trekking season to hire mules straightaway. This is because all the ones at the northern end are kept at Llamac and Pocpa and it may take a day to bring the mules to your starting point. The muleteers are a mixed bunch, ranging from excellent to irresponsible. Get a recommendation from someone who has recently returned from a trek; otherwise call ahead to **Hostal San Miguel** or ask at **Restaurant Yerupajá** or **Panadería Santa Rosa** (see Chiquián Sleeping and Eating, page 402).

Mountain shelters

There are four shelters: **Refugio Perú Pisco** (4765 m, 80 beds, meals, two hours from Llanganuco), **Refugio Don Bosco Huascarán** (4675 m, 60 beds, meals, four hours from Musho), **Refugio Ishinca** (4350 m, 60 beds, meals, three hours from Collon) and **Vivaque Giordano Longoni** at Ishinca (5000 m, 18 beds, no meals, five hours from Collon). They are operated by **Operazione Mato Grosso** ① *Marcará, Carhuaz, T043-443061, www.rifugi-omg.org, US$35 per person including breakfast and supper or US$49 full board; for Giordano Longoni, US$10 per bed per night, you must collect the keys from Ishinca,* and are open in high season only. In the rainy season there is a guard but no cooks.

Provisions and equipment

Huaraz is the region's supply centre and all but the most specialized items may be obtained here (see page 363). Check all camping and climbing equipment very carefully before hiring or buying it. Hired gear is of variable quality and most is second hand, left behind by others. Also note that some items may not be available, so it's best to bring your own. All prices are standard, but not cheap, and all require payment in advance, passport or air ticket as deposit and will not usually give you any money back if you return gear early. Many trekking agencies sell camping gas cartridges. White gas (*bencina*) is available from *ferreterías*, but shop around to avoid overcharging. It should cost about US$1.50 per litre. Expensive, imported, freeze-dried meals can be bought in Lima and Huaraz. Better to buy abroad or purchase the local, cheaper brands of freeze-dried *locros* and *tarwi* dishes.

In the Huayhuash, Chiquián's shops are usually well stocked with basic supplies, including locally produced butter and cheese, although prices may be a bit higher here. Almost nothing is available in the hamlets along the route, but fresh trout may be purchased by some of the lakes and a very few items (mostly beer, soft drinks and potatoes) might be purchased in Llamac, Pocpa, Carhuacocha, Huayllapa and Pacllón. Take coins and small notes as there is seldom any change. Bring a fishing line and lure to supplement your diet.

Maps and information

Casa de Guías ① *Plaza Ginebra 28-g, Huaraz, T043-421811, casa_de_guias@hotmail.com www.casadeguias.com.pe, Mon-Sat 0900-1300, 1600-2000*, is the climbers' and hikers' meeting place. It has information, books, maps, arrangements for guides, *arrieros*, mules, and so on. There is a noticeboard, postcards and posters for sale. The Casa de Guías has a full list of all members of the **Asociación de Guías de Montaña del Perú (AGMP)** throughout the country. Originally non-profit, the Casa de Guías now sells its information, which is geared towards you buying one of their tours.

A good tourist map of the Callejón de Huaylas and Cordillera Huayhuash, by **Felipe Díaz** (edition 2008-2009, US$6), is available in many shops in the region and at **Casa de Guías** in Huaraz (see above); it's not accurate enough for hiking the less-travelled trails. **Alpenvereinskarte Cordillera Blanca Nord 0/3a** and **Alpenvereinskarte Cordillera Blanca Süd 0/3b at 1:100,000** are easily the best maps of the Cordillera Blanca; they are available in Huaraz for US$24 each (also in Lima). Stocks locally are small, so it's best to get it before you arrive. **Instituto Geográfico Nacional** has mapped the area with its 1:100,000 topographical series. These are more useful to the mountaineer than hiker, however, since the trails marked are confusing and inaccurate. **South American Explorers** publishes a good map with additional notes on the popular Llanganuco to Santa Cruz loop. See page 400 for a recommended Cordillera Huayhuash map. ▸▸ *For guide books, see Books page 695.*

Huaraz and around

→ Colour map 3, B3. Phone code 043.

The main town in the valley, with a population of 80,000, Huaraz is expanding rapidly as a major tourist centre but it is also a busy commercial hub, especially on market days (Monday and Thursday). The region is both a prime destination for hikers and international climbers, as well as a vacation haven for Peruvian urbanites seeking clean mountain air and a glimpse of the glaciers.

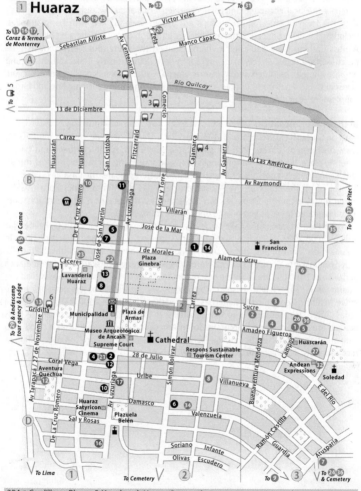

School groups flock to the city from mid-September to mid-December (the 'época de promociones colegiales'). The city was half destroyed in the earthquake of May 1970 so don't expect red-tiled roofs or overhanging eaves. What the reconstructed city lacks in colonial charm, it makes up for with its spectacular setting at 3091 m between the mountains of the cordilleras Blanca and Negra. The peaks of Huamashraju, Churup, Rima Rima and Vallunaraju loom so close as to seem almost a part of the architecture while, in the distance, the giants Huascarán and Huandoy can also be seen.
▶▶ *For listings, see pages 358-368.*

200 metres

200 yards

Sleeping 😴
1 Albergue Churup *C3*
2 Alojamiento El Jacal *C3*
3 Alojamiento Marilla *C3*
4 Alojamiento Nemy's *C3*
5 Alojamiento Soledad *C3*
6 Alpes Huaraz *C3*
7 Andino Club *D3*
8 Angeles Inn *D2*
9 Apu Wasi *D3*
10 Backpackers *B1*
11 Baños Termales
    Monterrey *A1*
12 Benkawasi *D1*
13 Casa Jaimes *C1*
14 Casa Jansy's *C2*
15 Edward's Inn *B1*
16 Edward's Inn *A1*
17 El Patio *A1*
18 Hatun Wasi *A1*
19 Hostal Alfredo *A2*
20 Hostal Colomba *A2*
21 Hostal Continental *C1*
22 Hostal Estoico *C1*
23 Hostal Quintana *C1*
24 Hotel Santa Cruz *D3*
25 Jo's Place *A2*
26 La Cabaña *C3*
27 La Casa de Zarela *C3*
28 Lazy Dog Inn *B3*
29 Lodging Caroline *C1*
30 Lodging Casa Sucre *C3*
31 Lodging House
    Ezama *A3*
32 Olaza Guesthouse *D3*
33 Pastoruri *A2*
34 Residencial NG *D2*
35 San Sebastián *B3*

36 Steel Guest House *D3*
37 The Way Inn Lodge *B3*

Eating 🍴
1 Bistro de los Andes *C2*
2 Café El Centro *C1*
3 Cafetería y Jugería *C2*
4 California Café *C1*
5 Fuente de Salud *B1*
6 Huaraz Querido *D2*
7 Las Puyas *B1*
8 Pachamama *C1*
9 Panadería La Alameda *B1*
10 Panadería Montserrat *D1*
11 Pepe's Place *B1*
12 Pizza Bruno *D1*
13 Salud y Vida *C1*
14 Siam de Los Andes *C2*

Bars & clubs 🍸
15 Chacraraju/Chill-Out *C2*
16 La Cascada *D1*
17 X-treme *D1*

Transport 🚌
1 Sandoval Chavín
    Express *C1*
2 Combis to Caraz *A1, A2*
3 Combis to Wilcawain *A2*
4 Julio César *B2*
5 Móvil Tours *A1*
6 Terminal de Transportistas
    Zona Sur *C1*
7 Trans Huandoy *A2*

➡ **Huaraz maps**
1 Huaraz, page 354
2 Huaraz centre, page 356

Ins and outs

Getting there and around The bus offices are in the centre of town and are conveniently close to many of the hotels and hostels. The city is small enough to get around by foot, providing sensible precautions are taken, especially at night. Huaraz has its share of crime, especially since the arrival of mining in the area (see box, page 350) and during the high tourist season. On no account should women go to surrounding districts and sites alone. ▶▶ *For safety while trekking or climbing, see page 351.*

Tourist information Information is provided by **iperú** ① *Pasaje Atusparia, of 1, Luzuriaga on Plaza de Armas, T043-428812, iperuhuaraz@promperu.gob.pe, Mon-Sat 0800-1830, Sun 0830-1400.* On the second floor of same building, **Policía de Turismo** ① *T043-421341, ext 315, Mon-Fri 0900-1300, 1600-1900, Sat 0900-1300,* is the place to report all crimes and mistreatment by tour operators, hotels, etc. There is also an **iperú** tourist information booth ① *Jr San Martín Cuadra 6 s/n, daily 0800-1100,* opposite where the tourist buses park, and in the airport open when flights arrive.

Sights

The **Plaza de Armas** has been rebuilt, with a towering white statue of Christ, and a new cathedral is being constructed. **Museo Arqueológico de Ancash** ① *Instituto Nacional de Cultura, Plaza de Armas, Mon-Sat 0900-1700, Sun 0900-1400, US$1.80,* contains stone monoliths and huacos (pottery artefacts) from the Recuay and other cultures. The exhibits are well labelled and laid out. The **Sala de Cultura SUNARP** ① *Av Centenario 530, Independencia, T043-421301, Mon-Fri 1700-2000, Sat 0900-1300, free*, often has interesting art and photography exhibitions by local artists.

The main thoroughfare, **Avenida Luzuriaga**, is bursting at the seams with travel agencies, climbing equipment hire shops, restaurants, cafés and bars. Within a block or two you can find a less frantic ambience, but a good alternative for those seeking peace and quiet is the **La Soledad** neighbourhood, six blocks uphill from the Plaza de Armas on Avenida Sucre. Here, along Sucre as well as Jirón Amadeo Figueroa, every second house seems to rent rooms, most without signs. We list but a few, see page 358. There are several decent neighbourhood eateries nearby, plus many shops, internet cafés and other facilities.

Around Huaraz → *For listings, see pages 358-368.*

Willkawain
① *8 km northeast of Huaraz. Entrance to the site is US$1.50. Take a combi from 13 de Diciembre y Comercio, US$0.55 direct to Willkawain. Alternatively, the purple city bus (line 2B) will take you to Marian, a 15-min walk from the ruins.*

The Willkawain archaeological site near Huaraz dates from AD 700-1000. This was the second and imperial phase of the Huari empire, when Huari influence spread north from the city of the same name near Ayacucho. The Huari empire was remarkable for the strong Tiahuanaco influence (see page 645) in its architecture and ceramics, and for introducing the concept of a great walled urban centre.

The site consists of one large three-storey structure with intact stone slab roofs and several small structures. The windowless inner chambers can be explored as electric light has been installed. All the rooms are accessible and a few have been opened up to reveal a sophisticated ventilation system and skilful stone

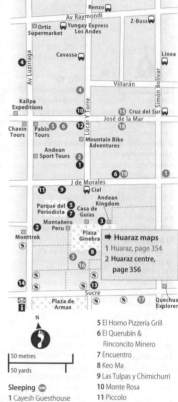

Huaraz centre

➡ **Huaraz maps**
1 Huaraz, page 354
2 Huaraz centre, page 356

Sleeping
1 Cayesh Guesthouse
2 Familia Meza
3 Hostal Gyula
4 Hostal Tany
5 Monte Blanco
6 Oscar's Hostal

Eating
1 Café Andino
2 Chifa Jim Hua
3 Chilli Heaven
4 Créperie Patrick
5 El Horno Pizzería Grill
6 El Querubín & Rinconcito Minero
7 Encuentro
8 Keo Ma
9 Las Tulpas y Chimichurri
10 Monte Rosa
11 Piccolo
12 Pizza B&B
13 Pizzería Landauro
14 Sabor Salud

Bars & clubs
15 '13 Buhos' & Makondo's
16 Amadeus
17 Monttrek Disco
18 Taberna Tambo
19 Vagamundo

craftsmanship. About 500 m past Willkawain is **Ichiwillkawain** with several similar but smaller structures.

Even if you're not an archaeology buff, the trip is worth it for a fascinating insight into rural life in the valley. Taking a colectivo up to the ruins and then walking back down to Huaraz is thoroughly recommended. If walking up, go past the **Hotel Huascarán**. After crossing a small bridge, take a second right (well- signposted), from where it's about a two-hour uphill walk. Ask frequently as there are many criss-crossing paths. Take a torch if you are likely to be late. Beware of dogs (and begging children). A good grasp of Spanish will greatly enhance the pleasure of this experience as the locals are very welcoming.

Baños Termales Monterrey → *Colour map 3, B3.*
① *6 km along the road to Caraz. Upper pool closed Mon for cleaning. Lower pool US$0.85, upper pool US$1.35, individual and family tubs US$1.35 per person for 20 mins. City buses from Av Luzuriaga until 1900, US$0.22. Taxi US$2-3.*
North of Huaraz, Monterrey makes a good day trip or an alternative place to stay for those seeking peace and quiet, although it gets crowded at weekends and holidays. The baths are run by the **Hotel Baños Termales Monterrey** and, owing to the high iron content, the water is dark brown but not too dirty. The upper pool is the nicest. There are also individual and family tubs.

Laguna Churup
① *US$20 payable to local cooperative in Pitec, only for groups with pack animals. Colectivo from Caraz y Comercio early in the morning to Llupa, 40 mins, US$0.60.*
To the east of Huaraz, off the road between Unchus and Pitec is a trail to Laguna Churup, which makes a good one-day excursion from Huaraz. The trail starts at **Llupa**, from where it's a one-hour hike to the national park ranger post at **Pitec**. From there, it's a further three hours up to the lake, which is surrounded by high mountains. The last part involves scrambling over rocks (dangerous when raining). It's about three hours back to Llupa, where colectivos run until about 1800.

From **Pitec** there are three-day hikes up the Quebrada Quillcayhuanca to Cayesh or to Lagunas Tullpacocha and Cuchilacocha. From the latter you can cross a pass to the Cojup Valley (see below) and descend to Llupa (a further two days). You have to pay a national park entrance fee in Pitec to do these treks.

Quebrada Ishinca
A good place for acclimatization and trekking at high altitude is the Ishinca hut at 4350 m in the Quebrada Ishinca. To get there, take a bus towards Paltay and then a colectivo to **Collon**; a taxi from Huaraz costs US$20. From Collon it's a nice four-hour walk to the hut; donkeys can be arranged in Collon, ask for Lorenzo. It costs US$10 to sleep at the hut, breakfast and dinner are US$10 each; you can also camp here. It's very popular with climbers. The easiest nearby climbs are Urus, 5420 m, and Ishinca, 5530 m. It is also possible to make a circuit back to Huaraz via Quebrada Cojup in three days, going over 5000 m. This is a good trek with great views.

Punta Callan
① *A taxi to Punta Callan will cost about US$25 and take about 1 hr, or take a Casma bus and get off at the pass.*
This walk in the Cordillera Negra makes an excellent day trip from Huaraz, with superb views of almost the whole of the Cordillera Blanca and some nice rural scenery. It is best to

leave Huaraz early in the morning, ideally about 0800, for the best light on the mountains. From the pass at 4200 m, walk northwards (the right-hand side of the road) to a small hill of 4600 m for the best views. Then head directly back down to Huaraz, which you'll see in the valley below you. Follow various trails and farm tracks, with several routes being possible. It takes about four hours' walking to reach the first places where you'll get return minibus transport. Add another hour or so to walk all the way back to Huaraz.

◉ Huaraz and around listings

For Sleeping and Eating price codes and other relevant information, see pages 38-44.

● Sleeping

Huaraz *p354, maps p354 and p356*
Hotels are plentiful (there are many more than those listed below) but fill up rapidly during the high season (May-Sep), especially during public holidays and special events (such as the **Semana de Andinismo** in Jun) when prices rise. Lodging in private homes is common during these periods.

Avoid touts at bus stations offering rooms and tours, some can be quite aggressive and often slander other hostels. Do not let them put you off your choice of lodging and try to ring in advance to confirm your booking. Unless otherwise stated, all hotels listed are recommended.

LL-AL Andino Club, Pedro Cochachín 357, some way southeast from the centre (take a taxi after dark), T043-421662, www.hotel andino.com. Good international standard hotel with restaurant, free internet for guests, lift, safe parking, Swiss-run, and friendly. 2nd-, 3rd- and 4th-floor rooms have balconies and views of Huascarán. Newly built section has suites and an apartment, which boast personal saunas, among other facilities. Not surprisingly these are more expensive. Breakfast and taxes included.

AL-A Pastoruri, Jr Corongo 145, across the bridge, several blocks north of the river, T043-427018, www.pastorurihotel.com. New 3-star business-style hotel with well-equipped, internet-enabled, spacious rooms and big bathrooms. Suites have jacuzzis into the bargain.

Breakfast, taxes and use of the top-floor gym are included.

A Hostal Colomba, Francisco de Zela 210, on Centenario across the river, T043-421501, www.huarazhotel.com. Lovely old hacienda, family-run, fabulous garden, safe car parking, gym and well-equipped rooms with cable TV, comfortable beds and internet access. All bathrooms have tub and jacuzzi.

A-B San Sebastián, Jr Italia 1124, T043-426960, www.sansebastianhuaraz.com. Elegant, modern hotel, rooms and junior suites, more expensive with mountain views, comfortable beds with duvets, parking available, internet connection in rooms. Very helpful, buffet breakfast included.

B Hotel Santa Cruz, Jr Gabino Uribe Mz 09 Lt 12Am, Pedregal, T043-396096, www.santa cruzperu.com. Full breakfast included, private bathroom, hot water, library, 25% discount for SAE members, good views.

C Steel Guest House, Alejandro Maguiña 1467, T043-429709, www.steelguest.com. Comfortable guesthouse, price includes breakfast. Excellent view of the major peaks from the roof terrace, although its location (close to **Andino Club**) entails a fair walk from the centre; a taxi is recommended late at night. Small but comfortable rooms with TV and private bathroom, a sauna, massages, kitchen for guests, internet access, good value. Table football, a full-size pool table, darts, plus a TV lounge with DVDs and a book exchange.

C-E Hostal Alfredo, Av Centenario 184, T043-421632, www.hostalalfredo.com. Variety of rooms and suites, TV, phones, room service 0600-2400, jacuzzi, bath with hydro massage, internet, tourist information, English and German spoken, cafeteria.

C-F Albergue Churup, Jr Figueroa 1257, T043-424200, www.churup.com. Rooms or dormitory, optional breakfast, hot water, nice fire in the attractive sitting room, roof terrace, great views, internet (including wireless) access in the private rooms, cafeteria, use of kitchen, roof terrace, lots of information, luggage store, laundry, book exchange, English spoken, Spanish classes, extremely helpful.

D Apu Wasi, Jr Federico Sal y Rosas 820, T043-426035, h_apuwasi@yahoo.com. Modern but simple hotel. All rooms have TV, private bathrooms and very comfortable beds. Standard price includes a basic breakfast. Discounts for longer stays.

D Monte Blanco, José de la Mar 620, T043-426384, http://monteblancohotel.com. Very comfortable, good hot showers, cable TV, helpful staff (no English spoken), great value, restaurant attached for breakfast which isn't included in the rates, roof terrace with superb views.

D Olaza Guesthouse, J Argüedas 1242, T043-422529, www.olazas.com. Run by Tito Olaza and recently upgraded with minimalist but very comfortable rooms with Wi-Fi internet access. Safe, stylish, luggage stored, nice terrace with views, breakfast included. Pick up from bus station with room reservation. Downstairs there's an office for Mountain Bike Adventures (see page 365), run by Julio Olaza. They have a 2nd office closer to the centre at Jr Lúcar y Torre 530.

D-E Alojamiento Soledad, Jr Amadeo Figueroa 1267, T043-421196, www.lodging soledad.com. Price includes breakfast and bath, some hard beds, hot water, kitchen, use of internet, family-run and friendly, secure, trekking information given. Higher prices in high season.

D-E Hostal Quintana, Jr Mcal A Cáceres 411, T043-426060, www.hostal-quintana.com. All rooms with bath and breakfast included, friendly, English, French, Italian and Spanish spoken, mountain gear rental, 2 of the owner's sons are certified guides and can arrange itineraries, laundry facilities, cafeteria, luggage store, popular with trekkers. Recommended.

D-E Residencial NG, Pasaje Valenzuela 837, T043-421831, www.residencialng.com. Breakfast included, various room sizes, hot water, TV, good value, helpful, restaurant, laundry, Wi-Fi, luggage storage.

E Alpes Huaraz, Jr Ladislao Meza 112, San Francisco, at east end of Alameda Grau, T043-428896, www.hostalalpeshuaraz.com. All rooms with private bathroom, hot showers (ask owner to switch them on), breakfast available, TV, laundry service.

E Angeles Inn, Av Gamarra 815, T043-422205, solandperu@yahoo.com. No sign, look for Sol Andino travel agency in same building (www.solandino.com). Kitchen and laundry facilities, small garden, hot water. Owners Max and Saul Angeles are official guides, helpful with trekking and climbing, equipment hire.

E Benkawasi, Parque Santa Rosa 928, 10 mins from centre, T043-423150, www.huaraz benkawasi.com. Rooms for 1-4 people or dorm beds for S/.10, hot water, breakfast S/.5, use of kitchen and laundry, games room, pickup from bus station. Owner Benjamín Morales also has Xtreme Bar, Andean Garden Club bar and restaurant, Infinite Adventures tour operator (Plazuela Belén 1035, T043-427304, www.infiniteadventuresperu. com) and a lodge at Playa Tortugas near Casma (arranges 5-hr downhill biking there from Huaraz).

E Edward's Inn, Bolognesi 121, T/F043-422692, www.edwardsinn.com. Cheaper without bath, clean, nice garden, laundry, friendly, breakfast extra, insist on proper rates in low season, popular. Edward speaks English and has 30 years' experience trekking, climbing and guiding in the area. He also rents gear.

E La Casa de Zarela, J Arguedas 1263, T043-421694, www.lacasadezarela.com. With bath, hot water, breakfast available, use of kitchen, laundry facilities, owner Zarela, who speaks English, organizes groups and is very knowledgeable, stores luggage, nice terrace.

E-F Hatun Wasi, Jr Daniel Villayzán 268, T043-425055, www.hatunwasi.net. Family-run, next door to Jo's Place. Clean, spacious rooms, all with private bathroom and hot water, cafeteria, laundry, luggage store. Pleasant roof terrace, ideal for breakfasts, with great views of the Cordillera.

F Alojamiento Nemy's, Jr Figueroa 1135, T043-422949. Secure, hot shower, breakfast available, good for climbers, luggage store.

F pp Andescamp Lodge, Jr Huáscar Mz 6 sub lote B-2, T043-799093/T043-943 563424 (mob), www.andescamp.com. Private rooms and dorm rooms with shared bath, hot showers, good mattresses, a big common room with a kitchen, laundry, internet and Wi-Fi, laundry service, tourist information. See **Andescamp** tour operator, below.

F Familia Meza, Lúcar y Torre 538, T043-426367, familiameza_lodging@hotmail.com. Shared bath, hot water, use of kitchen and laundry facilities, terrace with view, popular with trekkers, mountaineers and bikers.

F Hostal Estoico, San Martín 635, T043-422371. Cheaper without bathroom, friendly, clean, safe, hot water, laundry, good value.

F Hostal Gyula, Parque Ginebra 632, opposite the Casa de Guías, T043-421567, www.madeinhuaraz.com. With bathroom, hot water, cheaper in dorm-style rooms, very friendly and helpful, information on tours, stores luggage. Noisy at weekends.

F Hostal Tany, Lúcar y Torre 468A, T043-422534. With bathroom, cheaper without, hot water at night, spotless, money exchange, tours, café/restaurant.

F Jo's Place, Jr Daniel Villayzan 276, T043-425505, www.josplacehuaraz.com. Rooms with private or shared bathroom, dorm or camping in the garden. Safe, hot water at night, kitchen facilities, mountain views, garden, terrace, warm atmosphere, English owner Jo Parsons and his Peruvian partner Vicky are good sources of information with plenty of advice on trekking and climbing in the area. Popular meeting point for climbers. British Sunday papers. Highly recommended.

F La Cabaña, Jr Sucre 1224, T043-423428. Shared and double rooms, hot showers, cable TV, small breakfast included, laundry, kitchen, computer, DVD, very friendly, popular, safe for parking, bikes and luggage, English and French spoken, very good value.

F Lodging Caroline, Urb Avitentel Mz D – Lt 1, T043-422588, http://carolinelodging.com. Includes breakfast, 10-min walk from centre, free pick up from bus station (phone ahead), hot water, kitchen facilities, tourist information, laundry, helpful. Recommended, but compare tours offered here with those of established operators.

F Lodging Casa Sucre, Sucre 1240, T043-422264, filibertor@terra.com.pe. Private house, with bath, kitchen, laundry facilities, friendly, clean, hot water, English, French and German spoken. Mountaineering guide Filiberto Rurush can be contacted here.

F Oscar's Hostal, La Mar 624, T/F043-422720, cvmonical@hotmail.com. Bathroom, hot water, cheap breakfast next door, good beds, helpful, cheaper in low season.

F-G Alojamiento El Jacal, Jr Sucre 1044, T043-424612, reservaseljacal@yahoo.es. With or without shower, hot water, nice family, use of kitchen, internet café, garden, luggage store, laundry, good value, popular.

F-G Alojamiento Marilla, Sucre 1123, T043-428160, alojamaril@latinmail.com. Good views, modern, clean rooms with private or shared bath, dormitories, hot water, breakfast available, kitchen facilities, luggage store, knowledgeable, friendly owners.

F-G pp Backpackers, Av Raimondi 510, T043-421773, http://huaraz.com/backpackers. Breakfast not included. Dorm beds or private room with bathroom. Spacious, hot showers, good views, very friendly, a real bargain.

F-G Casa Jansy's, Jr Sucre 948. Hot water, meals, laundry, owner Jesús Rivera Lúcar is a mountain guide.

F-G pp Cayesh Guesthouse, Jr Julián de Morales 867, T043-428821. Comfortable hostel with good location, efficient solar hot-water system, kitchen and TV lounge with over 250 DVDs, internet. Owner is an enthusiastic climber and happy to provide advice on potential routes in the Cordilleras.

G pp Casa Jaimes, Alberto Gridilla 267, T043-422281, www.casajaimes.com. Friendly and cheap but noisy. 1 hr free internet use per day, laundry facilities and cheap laundry service, has maps and books of the region, equipment rental, use of kitchen, popular with Israelis.

G Hostal Continental, 28 de Julio 586, nr Plaza de Armas, T043-424171. With bath, clean, hot water, friendly, cafeteria serving good breakfasts. Avoid the rooms overlooking the street as there are 2 noisy *peñas* nearby.

G pp Lodging House Ezama, Mariano Melgar 623, Independencia, T043-423490, 15 mins' walk from Plaza de Armas (US$0.50 by taxi). Light, spacious rooms, hot water, safe, helpful.

Around Huaraz *p356*

AL-A El Patio, Av Monterrey, 250 m downhill from the Monterrey baths, T043-424965, www.elpatio.com.pe. Classy hotel with lovely gardens and comfortable rooms, some with balconies; also 4 bungalows with fireplaces. Restaurant for breakfast and dinner, bar, friendly, colonial-style. Recommended.

A-B The Lazy Dog Inn, close to the Quebrada Cojup and the boundary of Huascarán National Park, T043-943-789330, www.thelazydoginn. com. Eco-tourism lodge built with local materials, manpower and support. Actively involved in community projects. Beautifully designed in warm colours, each room with its own design. The lodge is constructed with adobe bricks and features water recycling systems and composting toilets. Great location gives access to several fabulous, little-visited mountain valleys. Friendly owners Wayne and Diana can organize horse-riding and hiking trips into the mountains. High altitude (3650 m) can be tricky if just arrived in Peru. Excellent home cooking, breakfast and dinner included in rates. 4.5 km from Huaraz via Marian, 12 km via Wuillcahuain, a better road (US$10 by taxi).

A-G The Way Inn Lodge, at 3712 m, close to the border of Huascarán National Park, 15 km up the road to Pitec, address in town Jr Buenaventura Mendoza 821, T043-943-466219, www.thewayinn.com. Rooms in bungalows, dorm rooms and camping, breakfast included, other meals available. Many activities available.

C-D Baños Termales Monterrey, Av Monterrey, at the top of the hill in Monterrey,

T/F043-427690, realhotelmonterrey@ yahoo.com. Slightly run down but classic old spa, beautiful garden and use of pools, restaurant, bar. Good location for walking. There is a rock face behind the hotel that's used for climbing practice. Very good value.

E El Nogal, Jr Los Libertadores 106, close to El Patio and the Baños Termales Monterrey, T043-425929. New friendly hotel with good-value, pleasant rooms, especially on 2nd floor.

🍴 Eating

Huaraz *p354, maps p354 and p356*
For local dishes, such as *pachamanca*, go to C José Olaya at the weekend, where stalls are set up.

🍴🍴 **Crêperie Patrick**, Luzuriaga 422. Tasty crêpes, fish, quiche, spaghetti and good wine.

🍴🍴 **Monte Rosa**, J de la Mar 661. Open 1000-2300. Pizzería, also fondue and other Swiss dishes. Swiss owner is Victorinox representative, offering knives for sale and repair also climbing and trekking books to read, excellent postcards for sale.

🍴🍴 **Pizza Bruno**, Luzuriaga 834. 1600-2300. Excellent pizzas, crêpes and pastries, good service. French owner Bruno Reviron also has a 4WD with driver for hire.

🍴🍴 **Siam de Los Andes**, Gamarra corner J de Morales. Authentic Thai cuisine, but tasty and with a wide range of dishes, as mild or spicy as you desire. There is a nice fireplace, too.

🍴 **Bistro de los Andes**, J de Morales 823 and Plaza de Armas 2nd floor, T/F043-426249. Good food, owner speaks English, French and German. Plaza branch has a nice panoramic view of the plaza. Very wide range of dishes including breakfasts, meats, pastas and curries – even Peruvian dishes if you look hard enough.

🍴 **Chilli Heaven**, Parque Ginebra, just up from the Casa de Guías, T043-396085. Run by a British biker. Great curries, Indian, Thai, or otherwise and filling burritos, chillies – the works. In fact anyone who appreciates a bit of spice will enjoy this snug, very popular restaurant. Good pizza and the desserts are mouth-watering as well. Imported beers overpriced. Book exchange.

El Horno, Pizzería Grill, Parque del Periodista, T043-424617. Good atmosphere, fine grilled meats and nice location overlooking the Parque del Periodista.

El Rinconcito Minero, Je de Morales 757. Breakfast, good value at lunchtime (including vegetarian), coffee and snacks, popular for good food and service, also has video bar.

Fuente de Salud, J de la Mar 562. Vegetarian, also meat and pasta dishes, good soups, excellent fruit salads and smoothies, breakfasts. Recommended.

Huaraz Querido, Bolívar 981. Open for lunch only, very popular place for great ceviche and other fish dishes.

Pachamama, San Martín 687. Bar, café and restaurant, concerts, art gallery, garden, nice place to relax, good toilets, pool table and table tennis, information on treks, Swiss-owned. Recommended.

Pepe's Place, Raymondi 624. Good pizza, chicken, meat, warm atmosphere.

Piccolo, J de Morales 632. Pizzería, very popular with gringos.

Pizza BB, La Mar 674, T043-421719, www.chez-philippe.net. Pizza is excellent, as is their dessert specialty *tarte flambée*, wood oven, pleasant decor and atmosphere, attentive service. Recommended.

Pizzería Landauro, Sucre, on corner of Plaza de Armas. Closed 1200-1800 and on Sun. Good for pizzas, Italian dishes, sandwiches, breakfasts, nice atmosphere.

Sabor Salud, Luzuriaga 672, upstairs. Restaurant and pizzería specializing in vegetarian and Italian food.

Chifa Jim Hua, Luzuriaga 645, upstairs. Mon-Sat 0900-1500, 1800-2400, Sun 1800-2200. Large, tasty portions, *menú* US$1.15 and a wide variety of other Peruvian-Chinese dishes.

Encuentro, Parque Ginebra, off Luzuriaga cuadra 6. Open 0700 for breakfast, serves good lunches and dinners, very busy, try the fillet mignon.

Salud y Vida, San Martín y Jr Mariscal Cáceres. Serves a vegetarian set menu.

El Querubín, J de Morales 767. Clean, friendly, good breakfast and set meals (high season only), also vegetarian, snacks and à la carte, very good, decorated with nice regional paintings.

Keo Ma, Parque Ginebra 626 , T043-428915. Pizza, pasta and good sandwiches.

Las Puyas, Morales 535. Popular with gringos, serves an excellent *sopa criolla* and very good trout, also serves breakfast.

Cafés

Café Andino, Lúcar y Torre 538, T043-421203, cafeandino@hotmail.com. American-run café and book exchange, great coffee and food, including very good curries, extensive lending library in many languages, a nice place to relax and write postcards, great atmosphere, and a good meeting place. The café's owner, Chris, organizes treks in cordilleras Blanca and Huayhuash, lots of advice offered.

Café El Centro, 28 de Julio 592. Good breakfast for US$1.30-2, great chocolate cake and apple pie.

Cafetería y Juguería, Sucre 806. Cheap café just above the Plaza. Serves excellent yogurt and honey drinks, among other treats.

California Café, Jr 28 de Julio 562, T043-428354, http://huaylas.com/californiacafé/ california.htm. A rival to **Café Andino** in all but the view, California offers perhaps the best breakfast in town, great coffee and chocolate cake that can only be described as dangerous! There's also a book exchange, library, games and some comfortable sofas into the bargain.

Las Tulpas y Chimichurri, J de Morales 756, between Luzuriaga y Bolívar. Open 0730-2300. Good breakfasts and good-value lunchtime menu, keen to promote Peruvian cuisine with Western standards of presentation. Good fish, excellent *lomo saltado*, nice garden.

Panadería La Alameda, Juan de La Cruz Romero 523 near market. Excellent bread and sweets.

Panadería Montserrat, Av Luzuriaga 928, T043-426260. Bakery and café, pleasant atmosphere, lots of cakes and *empanadas*, sausage rolls, etc. Good for a snack.

Around Huaraz *p356*

There are several country-style restaurants in Monterrey that are popular with locals and busy at weekends, serving trout, *pachamanca* and other regional specialities. There are several cheaper restaurants and stands along Av Monterrey.

† **El Cortijo**, Monterrey, along the Huaraz–Caraz road at Km 6.5. Serves very good food, eg chicken and barley stew, and *anticuchos*.

☊ Bars and clubs

Huaraz *p354, maps p354 and p356*

13 Buhos Bar, José de la Mar 2nd floor, just above Makondo's. Funky, popular bar with good range of tunes, snacks and games. Owner is Lucho, physically tall and big on personality … with a hat like Indiana Jones.
Amadeus, Parque Ginebra, bar-disco.
Chacraraju/Chill-out Bar, Jr Sucre 959, next of the agency of the same name. Good pizzas, good atmosphere, and, on occasion, a good DJ or 2.
La Cascada, Luzuriaga 1276. Disco tavern.
Makondo's, José de la Mar opposite Cruz del Sur bus station. Bar, restaurant and nightclub, safe, popular.
Monttrek Disco, Sucre just off Plaza de Armas, in a converted cinema, reasonable prices.
Taberna Tambo, José de la Mar 776. Daily 1000-1600 and 2000 till late. Folk music and disco. Full-on, non-stop dance mecca. Very popular with both locals and gringos, although the music can lack variety.
Vagamundo, J de Morales 753. Popular bar with snacks and football tables.
X-treme, Jr Gabino Uribe near Luzuriaga. 1900-0200. Upstairs bar, popular with gringos, soft music.

⊙ Entertainment

Huaraz *p354, maps p354 and p356*
Cinema
Huaraz Satyricon, Luzuriaga 1036, T043-955 7343. American-run café and movie theatre, big screen, comfortable sofas, chocolate chip cookies and falafel sandwiches, US$1.20. Movies range from 1960s' classics to cutting-edge Latin American, plus occasional showings of *Touching the Void*, the film set and partially shot in the Huayhuash.

⊛ Festivals and events

Huaraz *p354, maps p354 and p356*
Mar/Apr Semana Santa (Holy Week) is widely celebrated, colourful and lively.
3 May El Señor de la Soledad, the town's patron saint's day, marks the start of a week of parades, dancing, music, fireworks and much drinking.
Jun Semana del Andinismo is an international climbing and skiing week.
Last week of Jun San Juan and San Pedro are celebrated throughout the region. On the eve of San Juan fires are lit throughout the valley to burn the chaff from the harvest. The following day the valley is thick with smoke.
Aug Inkafest Mountain Film, www.inkafest.com, is an annual film festival with competitions, workshops, movies, exhibitions, speakers and tours, organized by climbers and documentary makers.

○ Shopping

Huaraz *p354, maps p354 and p356*
Climbing and trekking equipment
For equipment rental, see Activities and tours, below.
Tatoo, on Parque Ginebra, T043-422966, www.tatoo.ws. Good shop for climbing and outdoor clothes and gear, locally produced and international brands.

Food and drink

The central market offers a wide variety of canned and dry goods, including nuts and dried fruit, as well as fresh fruit and veg. Be sure to check expiry dates. Leave all valuables in a safe place when shopping in the market; pickpockets abound.

Ortiz, Luzuriaga 401 corner Raymondi. A well-stocked supermarket with a good selection of items, but expensive.

Rosa Rosita, Jr San Martín, half a block from Morales. Local cheese and *manjarblanco*.

Handicrafts

Local sweaters, hats, gloves, ceramics and wall hangings can be bought from stalls on Pasaje Mcal Cáceres just off Luzuriaga, in the stalls off Luzuriaga between Morales and Sucre, on Bolívar cuadra 6 and elsewhere.

Andean Expressions, Jr J Arguedas 1246, near La Soledad church, T043-422951, www.andeanexpressions.com. Open 0800-2200. Run by Lucho, Mauro and Beto Olaza, and recommended for hand-printed T-shirts and sweatshirts with unusual motifs. The family also runs the **Andean Explorer** agency and produces a free guidemap of the Huaraz area.

La Perla, Sr Enrique Salazar Salas, Jr San Martín 574. Handmade cowboy-style boots can be made to fit in 3 days for about US$80.

Photography

Foto Galería Andes, at Pasaje Cayetano Requena, near the market. Good for camera repairs. Sells professional photos of the Cordillera Blanca.

▲▲ Activities and tours

Huaraz *p354, maps p354 and p356*
Huaraz is overflowing with agencies and quality varies. Try to get a recommendation from someone who has recently returned from a tour, climb or trek, or see **South American Explorers'** recommendations in the Lima office. Avoid unlicensed guides at

hotels. All agencies run conventional tours to **Llanganuco** (US$12 per person, very long day) and **Chavín** (8-10 hrs, US$14 per person), entry tickets not included. Many hire equipment and also offer climbing and trekking tours as well as ski instruction.

Equipment hire

For general information, see page 353. The **Casa de Guías** (see page 353) rents equipment and sells dried food. The following agencies are also recommended for hiring gear: **Andean Kingdom**; **Andean Sport Tours**, Luzuriaga 571, T043-421612; **Galaxia Expeditions**, **Monttrek**; **Kallpa**. Also try **Skyline**, T043-427097, www.sladventure school.com; **Montañero Peru**, Parque Ginebra 30-B, T043-426386, www.trekking peru.com, and **MountClimb**, Jr Mcal Cáceres 421, T043-426060, mountclimb@yahoo.com.

Horse riding

Posada de Yungar, at Yungar (about 20 km on the Carhuaz road), T043-421267, T94367 9836 (mob). Swiss run. Ask for José Flores or Gustavo Soto. US$4.50 per hr on nice horses; good 4-hr trip in the Cordillera Negra with fabulous views.

Sr Robinson Ayala Gride, T043-423813. Contact him well in advance for half-day trips (enquire at **El Cortijo** restaurant, page 363). He is a master *paso* rider.

Mountain biking

The Callejón de Huaylas offers superb variety for mountain bikers, from 1-day routes to popular attractions to longer trails through agricultural land, over bridges and into traditional villages. More demanding are the routes over the Cordillera Negra to the Pacific coast and, toughest of the lot, the energy-sapping, highly exhilarating climbs over 5000-m passes beneath the snow peaks of the Cordillera Blanca. A typical circuit is Huaraz–Recuay–Chavín–Huari–San Luis–Chacas–Punta Olímpica, which lasts 2 days; or returning through Quebrada Llanganuco, lasting 6 days.

Montañero Peru, www.trekkingperu.com, offer tours of up to 26 days in the Cordillera Blanca. Camping gear is needed. Local tour and trekking agencies can supply bikes, guides and full backup, including driving you up some of the steepest bits if your leg muscles can't cope. Also has a comfortable hostal at this address (**D**).

Mountain Bike Adventures, Lúcar y Torre 530, T043-424259, www.chakinaniperu.com. Contact Julio Olaza. US$20 for 5 hrs, various routes. Julio speaks excellent English and also runs a book exchange, sells topo maps and climbing books. Recommended for its 2-wheeled exploits and excellent standard of equipment.

Guides

For further information, visit the **Casa de Guías** (see page 353). The guides listed below are not necessarily members of AGMP but they are recommended for their mountaineering expertise.

Aritza Monasterio, through **Casa de Guías**. Speaks English, Spanish and Euskerra.

Augusto Ortega, Jr San Martín 1004, T043-424888. The only Peruvian to have climbed Everest.

Christopher Benway, La Cima Logistics, T043-421203, cafeandino@hotmail.com. Organizes treks in the Huayhuash. Chris is the owner of **Café Andino**, so it's usually easy to track him down, plus he's very friendly and helpful.

Filiberto Rurush Paucar, Lodging Casa Sucre, Sucre 1240, T043-422264. Speaks English, Spanish and Quechua.

Genaro Yanac Olivera, T043-422825. Speaks good English and some German, also a climbing guide.

Hugo Sifuentes Maguiña, Siex (Sifuentes Expeditions), Jr Huaylas 139, T043-426529, www.siexperu.com. Trekking, rock climbing and less adventurous tours.

Koky Castañeda, T043-421694 (or through La Casa de Zarela or Café Andino). Speaks English and French, AGMP certified.

Max and Saul Angeles, T043-422205 (Sol Andino travel agency), speak some English, know the Huayhuash well.

Ted Alexander, Skyline Adventures, T043-427097, www.skyline-adventures.com. American Outward Bound instructor, very knowledgeable, lots of information, works with highly qualified and experienced staff.

Tjen Verheye, Jr Carlos Valenzuela 911, T043-422569, is Belgian and speaks Dutch, French, German and reasonable English, runs trekking and conventional tours and is knowledgeable about the Chavín culture.

Vladimiro and Máximo Hinostrosa, at Mountain Shop Chacraraju, T043-969 2395, trekking guides with knowledge of the entire region.

Parapenting and hang gliding

Launch sites near Huaraz are the Puca Ventana near the Mirador, or from Churup-Pitec.

River rafting and canoeing

Rafting on the Río Santa (US$15 for half a day) year round, Grade II-III, not particularly special, but in a pretty setting. Most agencies provide food, transport, mules and guides. Prices tend to be 20% less during low season, Oct-Apr.

Trekking and climbing

Trekking tours cost US$40-70 per person per day; climbing US$90-140 per person per day. Prices vary a great deal. Many companies close in low season. Ask tour agencies, independent guides and the Casa de Guías about rock-climbing courses at Monterrey (behind Hotel Baños Termales Monterrey, see page 357), Chancos, Recuay and Huanchac (30 mins' walk from Huaraz), and about ice climbing on Vallanaraju (for example). Jatun Machay in the Cordillera Negra is another fabulous spot for rock climbing and bouldering, be it at beginner level or if you are an experienced climber looking for a serious challenge.

Active Peru, Av Gamarra 699, T043-423339, www.activeperu.com. Friendly agency offering the classic treks, climbing, plus tours to Chavín and Llanganuco, among others.

Andean Footsteps, Carretera Huaraz-Caraz Km 14, Paltay, and Jr José Olaya 103, Huaraz,

T043-943-318820, www.andeanfootsteps. com. British/Peruvian operation (Yvonne Danson and David Maguiña), specializing in treks, climbs and tours with a commitment to using local personnel and resources. Local projects are sponsored.

Andean Kingdom, Parque Ginebra, next to Casa de Guías, T043-425555, www.andean kingdom.com. Free information, maps, rock and ice climbing, including multi-day courses, treks, equipment rental, very helpful, English spoken, can be very busy. The company has a Refugio de Montaña, **Hatun Machay (F)**, near the excellent rock-climbing site of Hatun Machay in the Cordillera Negra, with kitchen facilities and heating, transport arranged.

Andescamp, Jr Huáscar Mz 6 sub lote B-2, T043-799093/T043-943563424, www.andes camp.com. Popular, especially with budget travellers. Only qualified guides used for climbing trips. Variety of treks, mountaineering expeditions and courses, rafting, paragliding and other adventure sports. Also has a lodge, see page 360.

Aventura Quechua Peru, Av 27 de Noviembre 777, T043-423375, www.aventura quechua.com. Offer private transfer between Huaraz-Queros/Llamac, also special trek around Alpamayo and Santa Cruz.

Chacraraju Expeditions, Jr José de Sucre No 959, T043-426271, www.chacraraju expedition.com. Tours and equipment for hire, plus a small climbing wall and a 24-hr **Climbers' Pub** with fireplace and music.

Cordillera Blanca Adventures, Los Nogales 108, T043-421934, www.cordillerablanca.org. Run by the Mejía Romero family. Experienced, quality climbing and trekking trips, good guides and equipment.

Galaxia Expeditions, Parque del Periodista, T043-425355, www.galaxia-expeditions.com. Reputable agency with the usual range of tours, climbing, hiking, biking, equipment hire, etc.

Huascarán, Jr Pedro Campos 711, Soledad, T043-424504, www.huascaran-peru.com. Contact Pablo Tinoco Depaz, one of the brothers who run the company. 4-day Santa Cruz trip recommended. Good food and equipment, professional and friendly service, free loan of waterproofs and pisco sour on last evening. Recommended.

Kallpa, José de la Mar 579 y Luzuriaga, p 2, T043-427868, www.kallpaexpeditions.com. Organizes treks, rents gear, arranges *arrieros* and mules, very helpful.

Montañero, Parque Ginebra 30-B, T043-426386, www.trekkingperu.com. Run by veteran mountain guide Selio Villón, German, French and English spoken.

Monttrek, Luzuriaga 646, upstairs, T043-421124, monttrek@terra.com.pe. Good trekking and climbing information, advice and maps, ice and rock-climbing courses (at Monterrey), tours to Laguna Churup and the

'spectacular' Luna Llena tour; they also hire out mountain bikes, run ski instruction and trips, and river rafting. Helpful, conscientious guides. Next door in the pizzeria is a climbing wall, good maps, videos and slide shows. For new routes and maps contact Porfirio Cacha Macedo, 'Pocho', at **Monttrek** or at Jr Corongo 307, T043-423930.

Peruvian Andes Adventures, José Olaya 532, T043-421864, www.peruvianandes.com. Run by Hisao and Eli Morales, with an agency in New Zealand, use professional, registered mountain and trekking guides. All equipment and services for treks of 3-15 days, climbing technical and non-technical peaks, or just day walks. Vegetarians catered for.

Quechua Explorer, Jr José de Sucre 705 of 4, T043-422886, www.quechuaexplorer.com. Hiking mountaineering, rock and ice climbing, rafting, biking, cultural and ecological tourism, experienced and friendly guides.

Respons Sustainable Tourism Center, Jr 26 de Julio 821, T043-427949, www.respons.org. Sustainable tourism initiatives, community based, with trekking, homestays, tours, volunteering and other responsible travel ideas.

Tour operators
Amazing Peru, Jr Sucre 1214, www.amazingperu.com. UK-managed tours with knowledgeable guides.
Chavín Tours, Luzuriaga 502, T043-421578, www.chavintours.com.pe. Local tours, long-standing national agency.
Pablo Tours, Luzuriaga 501, T043-421145, www.pablotours.com. Local tours, with many years of operation.

⊖ Transport

Huaraz p354, maps p354 and p356
Air
The airport for Huaraz is at Anta, just north of town. LC Busre flies daily to/from **Lima**, 1hr, US$134 one way. Office at Av Toribio de Luzuriaga 904, Belén, T043-424734.

Bus
Many bus companies have offices selling tickets in the centre, but buses leave from the edge of the centre. Several buses and minivans run daily 0500-2000 to **Caraz**, 1¼ hrs, US$1.50, stopping at all the places in between. They depart from the parking area under the bridge on Fitzcarrald and from the open space beside the bridge on the other side of the river (beware of thieves here).

To **Chavín**, 110 km, 2 hrs (sit on left side for best views), US$3. Service provided by Sandoval/Chavín Express, Mcal Cáceres 338, 0830, 1430, 2030, and by Trans Río Mosna, Jr Mcal Cáceres 265, T043-426632, daily 0800, 1400 and 2000, US$3.30. Both have buses that go on to **Huari**, 4 hrs on paved but pot-holed road, US$4.10, and **Llamellín**, 8 hrs, US$7.

To **Chacas**, US$3.75, and **San Luis**, US$5.75, at 0700 with Virgen de Guadalupe, Caraz 607. El Veloz, Av Raymondi 827, T043-221225, daily at 0630 and 1400 to **Chacas**, US$6, **San Luis**, US$6.70 and **Yauya**, US$8.30. Renzo, Raymondi 821, T043-425371, runs to **Chacas** daily (0615, 1400, US$6), **Piscobamba** and **Pomabamba** (0630, best, and 1900, US$8.25). Los Andes, same office as Yungay Express, T043-427362, daily 0630 to **Yungay**, US$0.75, **Lagunas de Llanganuco**, US$3.45, **Yanama**, US$3.45, **Piscobamba**, US$5.20 and **Pomabamba**, US$6, 8 hrs. This route is also served by La Perla de Alta Mayo, daily 0630, 8 hrs to **Pomabamba**, US$6. To **Sihuas**, also Sandoval/Chavín Express, Tue and Fri 0800; Perú Andino, 1 a week, 8 hrs, US$7.

Colectivos to **Recuay**, US$0.45, **Ticapampa** and **Catac**, US$0.55, leave daily 0500-2100, from Gridilla, just off Tarapacá (Terminal Terrestre Transportistas Zona Sur).

To **Chiquián** for the Cordillera Huayhuash, 120 km, 3½ hrs: El Rápido, at Bolognesi 216, T043-422887, at 0500 and 1330, and Chiquián Tours, on Tarapacá behind the market.

To **Huallanca** (Húanuco), along a paved road through Conococha, Chiquián and Aquia to Huansala, then good dirt road to

Huallanca and **La Unión** (the road is being paved). Departs Huaraz twice daily (1 at 1330), 4½ hrs, US$4.80, with **Trans El Rápido**, Bolognesi 216, T043-422887. Frequent daily service from Huallanca to Huánuco.

To **Lima**, 420 km, 7-8 hrs, US$10-29. The road is in good condition. There is a large selection of buses to Lima, both ordinary service and luxury coaches, with departures throughout the day. Many of the companies have their offices along Av Raymondi and on Jr Lúcar y Torre. Remember to take care of your belongings when loading onto and off the bus at both ends of the journey. Some recommended companies are: **Cavassa**, Jr Lúcar y Torre 446, T043-425767; **Cial**, J de Morales 650, T043-429253; **Cruz del Sur**, Bolívar Mz C Lote 12 , T043-728726; **Empresa 14**, Fitzcarrald 216, T043-421282, terminal at Bolívar 407; **Julio César**, Prol Cajamarca s/n, cuadra 1, T043-396443; **Móvil Tours**, Av Confraternidad Internacional Oeste 451, T043-422555, www.moviltours.com.pe; **Z-Buss**, Av Raymondi, T043-428327.

To **Casma** via the Callán Pass and Pariacoto, 150 km, 7 hrs, US$7.50, the lower section of the road is very poor, landslides and closures are common (sit on the left for best views, as long as you don't mind precipices): Transportes Huandoy, Fitzcarrald 261, T043-427507 (terminal at Caraz 820), daily 0800, 1000 and 1300; **Yungay Express**, Raymondi 930, T043-424377, 3 a day, continuing to **Chimbote**, 185 km. To **Chimbote** via Caraz, the Cañón del Pato and Huallanca (sit on the right for the most exciting views), with **Yungay Express**, daily 0715, US$9, 10 hrs (also picks up passengers from Caraz). Other companies go to **Chimbote**, 7 hrs, via **Pativilca**, 160 km, 4 hrs, and most continue to **Trujillo**, 8-9 hrs, US$10; all buses depart at night: **Línea**, Simón Bolívar 450, T043-726666; **Empresa 14** and **Móvil Tours**, addresses above.

Taxi
The standard fare for a taxi in town is about US$0.60, US$0.70 at night. The fare to **Monterrey** or **Huanchac** is US$1.45. Radio taxis T043-421482 or T043-422512.

ⓓ Directory

Huaraz *p354, maps p354 and p356*
Banks BCP, on the Plaza de Armas, closed 1300-1630, same services as elsewhere in Peru, but there may be very long queues for cash advances on Visa, 2 ATMs (Visa). Interbank, on Plaza de Armas. **Casa de Cambio Oh Na Nay**, across the street from Interbank, good rates for US$, but poor for other currencies. There are several other *casas de cambio* and many street changers (be careful) on Luzuriaga. **Internet** Ubiquitous, US$0.30 per hr. Cafés usually offer video phones, scanning, CD burning and printing services. Since equipment is constantly changing it is best to find your own favourite spot; you should have plenty of choice. Phonecalls to Europe or North America are sometimes possible from US$0.15 per min. **Laundry** B & B, La Mar 674. US$1.20 per kg, special machine for down garments and sleeping bags, French run. Recommended. Huaraz, on the plaza on Mcal Cáceres, next to Galaxia Mountain Shop. Lavandería Liz, Bolívar 711, US$2 per kg, also at the Casa de Guías (see page 353). Laundry Express at JM Expediciones, between Luzuriaga and Plaza Ginebra. Takshar, Jr Bolívar 617, next-day service, US$1 per kg. **Medical services** Clínica San Pedro, Jr Huaylas 172, Independencia, T043-428811/428805. Policlínico Niño Jesús de Praga (Travellers' Clinic), 28 de Julio 602 y Luzuriaga. T043-428384, www.simonkomori.com. Open 24 hrs daily. **Post** Serpost is on Luzuriaga 702, Mon-Sat 0800-2000. **Telephone** Telefónica, Sucre y Bolívar, corner of Plaza de Armas. National and international phone and fax, daily 0700-2300. Private calling centres along Luzuriaga. Many coin phones.

North from Huaraz

The road north out of Huaraz goes through the beautiful Callejón de Huaylas, giving access to some wonderful treks that go up into, or over the mountains of the Cordillera Blanca. Caraz, the focus of the northern end of the valley, is less hectic than Huaraz, but is just as good a place to stay. It is definitely worth spending some time in this area. ▶▶ *For listings, see pages 382-386.*

Huaraz to Caraz → *For listings, see pages 382-386. Colour map 3, B2/3.*

There are frequent small buses running up and down the Callejón from Huaraz and in between the towns en route. The main road north from Huaraz through the **Callejón de Huaylas** goes to **Taricá** (not to be confused with Tarica at the north end of the Cordillera Blanca), where there is a home pottery industry. Good-value purchases can be made from Francisco Zargosa Cordero.

Marcará and the Huandoy Valley

The next town is **Marcará**, 26 km from Huaraz (one hour, US$0.45), where there are a couple of hotels, basic restaurants and shops. Pickups and colectivos go east from Marcará along a branch road 3 km to **Chancos**, a little settlement with hot baths. There is an uninviting lukewarm pool (US$0.45) here, as well as some none-too-clean private tubs (US$0.90) and very popular natural steam baths in caves (US$1.35 per person). The caves are interesting and worth a try, with locked changing rooms (cave five is the smallest and hottest). Just before the hot springs, on the left-hand side of the road, is a very good 10-m climbing wall (free), with bolts and anchor chains in place. There is accommodation in the shape of two very basic *alojamientos* and there are also several basic restaurants and food stalls.

From Chancos the road and transport continue to **Vicos**, 3 km further up the Huandoy valley. Vicos is 7 km from Marcará (US$0.30) in superb surroundings, with views of Nevados Tocllaraju and Ranrapalca. To hike from Chancos to Vicos takes about two hours up the valley through farmland. A trail leads from Vicos to Laguna Lejíacocha, taking four hours. There are archaeological sites nearby at **Copa**, **Kekepampa** and **Joncopampa**. The last named is considered to be second only to Chavín in the region. From Vicos, cross the river on a footbridge, and it's about one hour further to Joncopampa. From Vicos, you can also walk through the Quebrada Honda, over the Portachuelo de Honda Pass at 4750 m, to **Chacas**, an excellent, not difficult hike, which takes about four days.

Carhuaz → *Colour map 3, B2.*

Carhuaz, a friendly, quiet mountain town with a pleasant plaza with tall palm trees and lovely rose bushes is 7 km further on from Marcará. There is very good trekking in the neighbourhood (outlined below). There's a market on Wednesday and another larger market on Sunday, when *campesinos* bring their produce to town. Good peaches are grown locally, among other crops. The locals are renowned for their lively celebrations, hence the town's nickname, '*Carhuaz alegría*'.

Treks from Carhuaz

Trek 1: to Yanama The trek up to the **Ulta Valley** over the Punta Yanayacu Pass to Yanama is little used but offers impressive views of Huascarán and other peaks. It takes three days. If you catch a truck up the valley to where the road begins to zigzag up to the pass, it will shorten the trek by one day (see Transport, page 385). If not, start hiking from Shilla, 13 km east of Carhuaz, or from Huaypan. There are combis to Shilla when full (early morning) from Jirón 9 de Diciembre y La Merced, one block northeast of the plaza in Carhuaz, US$0.30. A taxi to Shilla costs US$3 (sharing possible). Return transport to Carhuaz is scarce. Combis go to Huaypan on Wednesday and Sunday, US$0.50, one hour.

Trek 2: to hot springs Seven kilometres east of Carhuaz, near the village of Hualcán, are the **Baños de Pariacaca**, which were badly damaged by a landslide in 1993. The hot springs can be seen bubbling between the rocks by the river's edge and there are some small rock pools in which the enthusiastic can bathe. From the plaza in Carhuaz follow Comercio to the top of the hill, turn right as far as Cinco esquinas (five corners), turn left and follow the road uphill. When you reach the bridge, cross it left to Hualcán and ask directions from there. There is transport to Hualcán leaving from the plaza in Carhuaz on Wednesday and Sunday.

Trek 3: to Laguna 513 Half an hour beyond Baños de Pariacaca (see Trek 2 above) is the village of **Pariacaca** (no facilities) from where a trail continues into the mountains. In three hours you can reach **Laguna Rajupaquinan** and, 45 minutes beyond, the imaginatively named **Laguna 513**, with beautiful views. If you continue, you will see the Auquiscocha lakes, which you can reach in another three hours. Laguna 513 can also be reached directly from Hualcán in about four hours, along the north side of the river. This latter trail has fewer rocks to negotiate. Take adequate gear and a map if you plan to go beyond Pariacaca.

Mancos and around → Colour map 3, B2.
From Carhuaz it is a further 14 km to Mancos, at the foot of Huascarán. (From here, climbers can go to **Musho** to reach the base camp.) You can also do a strenuous 30-km, one-day walk from Mancos that gives great views of Huascarán. Follow the road east and take the branch for Tumpa, about 13 km away; ask directions as the road branches several times. Continue north to Musho for about 1 km, then descend via Arhuay to **Ranrahirca**, which is between Mancos and Yungay on the main road. There are daily colectivos from Mancos to Musho; transport to Ranrahirca and Arhuay is on Wednesday and Sunday only.

Cueva Guitarreros is a cave, west of Mancos in the Cordillera Negra, which contains rock paintings dating back some 12,000 years. Access is either through Mancos, from where it is about 30 minutes' walk along an overgrown trail (with many spines!), or through Tingua and Shupluy further south, from where it takes about one hour. The thermal springs at **Chirpas**, which have a high lithium content (used in the treatment of manic depression), are near the caves. There are good views of Huascarán from this area.

Yungay → Colour map 3, A2. Altitude 2500 m.
Yungay is 8 km north of Mancos on the main road. The original town of Yungay was completely buried during the 1970 earthquake by a massive mudslide, caused when a piece of Huascarán's glacier was prised loose by the quake and came hurtling towards the town. 20,000 people lost their lives. The earthquake and its aftermath are remembered by many residents of the Callejón de Huaylas and the scars remain part of the local psyche.

The original site of Yungay, known as **Yungay Viejo** ① *off the Huaraz–Yungay road, officially open daily 0800-1800, US$0.75*, has been consecrated as a *camposanto* (cemetery). It is a haunting place, with flower beds and paths covering the 8-12 m of soil under which the old town lies. Of the four palm trees from the old Plaza de Armas that protrude through the landslide, only one remains alive. Five pine trees and a monument mark the site where five policemen died. Nearby, on top of a hill, is the old cemetery with a large statue of Christ, where a handful of residents managed to escape the disaster. Many of the town's children also escaped as they were in the stadium watching the circus. There's a café, toilets and shops at the main entrance.

The **new settlement** is on a hillside just north of the old town, and is growing gradually. It has a pleasant modern plaza and a concrete market, busiest on Wednesday and Sunday, which is good for stocking up on supplies. The predominant colour in the town is *celeste* (sky blue). One part of town is called the **Barrio Ruso**, where typical, Russian wooden houses, erected temporarily in the 1970s as a gift from the USSR, are still in use. There's a **tourist office** ① *on the corner of the Plaza de Armas, Mon-Fri 0800-1300, 1400-1800.*

Around Yungay

A day walk from Yungay to **Mirador de Atma** gives beautiful views of Huascarán, Huandoy and the Santa Valley. From town, follow a dirt road east for 3 km (about one hour). You can return via the Quebrada Ancash road that runs further north, between the Río Ancash and Cerro Pan de Azúcar. This will bring you to the Yungay–Caraz road about 1 km north of Yungay. It is about a three-hour round trip.

Yungay

Matacoto, 6 km from Yungay in the Cordillera Negra at 3000 m, has excellent views of Huascarán, Huandoy and other major peaks. The turn-off is at Huarazcucho (Km 251), 3 km south of new Yungay. It is another 3 km from here, across the bridge over the Río Santa to Matacoto. (Matacoto can also be reached in three hours from Mancos.) Colectivos from Yungay run daily 0700-1300, US$0.50; taxis charge US$3.30.

Laguna 69 can also be visited in a day from Yungay. Take a combi from Yungay past the Llanganuco lakes (see below; US$2.45-3). After about 90 minutes get off the bus at a bend called Curva Pisco. Keep to the right of the river along the valley bottom. You will see the gentle zigzags going up to the right to a col with a small lake. Pass this and you come to a large plateau: keep to the right-hand side. There is a signpost in the middle pointing right to a glacier and straight ahead to Laguna 69, heading to a large wall of rock. The path zigzags steeply up to the left of this rock face to the lake, near glaciers and the snow line. It takes three to four hours for the 7-km hike and 750-m climb and some two to three hours to walk back down to the road. There are superb views of waterfalls, glaciers and Huascarán. A new trail now leads from Laguna 69 to the Refugio Perú

Sleeping ⌂
1 COMTURY
2 Hostal Gledel
3 Hostal Mery
4 Hostal Sol de Oro

5 Hostal Yungay

Eating ❶
1 Alpamayo
2 Café Pilar

or Pisco Base Camp, taking about two to three hours. Ask the combi to return for you at about 1630, the latest time to get back to Yungay for a combi back to Huaraz.

Lagunas de Llanganuco

The Lagunas de Llanganuco are two lakes nestling 1000 m below the snowline beneath Huascarán and Huandoy. From Yungay, the first you come to is **Laguna Chinancocha** at 3850 m, followed by **Laguna Orconcocha** at 3863 m. The story goes that in times gone by, when the water levels were higher, the day's snow melt and rainfall would raise Orconcocha sufficiently for it to flow into Chinancocha each evening; by dawn they had separated again. Hence the lakes' other names: Laguna Macho (male – Orconcocha) and Laguna Hembra (female – Chinancocha). A nature trail, **Sendero María Josefa** (sign on the road), leads for 1½ hours to the western end of Chinancocha where there is a control post, descriptive trail and boat trips on the lake (a popular area for day trippers). Walk along the road beside the lake to its far eastern end for peace and quiet among the *quenoal* trees. These trees (polylepis, or paper bark) are the symbol of the Huascarán national park and provide shelter for 75% of the birdlife found in the park. The lakes themselves are superb areas for observing water birds, with yellow-billed, blue and mountain ducks commonly seen, as well as Andean geese, puna ibis and a variety of gulls. Hunting birds such as caracas and American kestrels make an appearance. If you're lucky, you may even catch a glimpse of the rare torrent duck, swimming up Grade V rapids in classic style.

🌑 *According to legend, the rise and fall of the waters in Lagunas de Llanganuco is also related to the tears of Huáscar and Huandy, the prince and princess of enemy tribes whose forbidden love was discovered, causing them to be turned into the mountains Huascarán and Huandoy.*

Caraz and around → *For listings, see pages 382-386. Colour map 3, A2. Altitude: 2290 m.*

The pleasant town of Caraz is a good centre for walking and the access point for many excellent treks and climbs. It is increasingly popular with visitors as a more tranquil alternative to Huaraz. In July and August the town has splendid views of Huandoy and Huascarán from its lovely plaza, which is filled with jacarandas, rose bushes and palms. In other months, the mountains are often shrouded in cloud. Caraz has a milder climate than Huaraz and is more suited to day trips. The sweet-toothed will enjoy the locally produced *manjar blanco*, from which the town derives its nickname, 'Caraz dulzura'. Market days are Wednesday and Sunday. The **tourist office** ① *Plaza de Armas, T043-391029, Mon-Fri 0745-1300, 1430-1700*, has limited information. There is a new museum on San Martín, a block up from the plaza.

The ruins of **Tunshukaiko** are 1 km from the Plaza de Armas, in the suburb of Cruz Viva. This is a poor area so be discreet with cameras, etc. There are seven platforms from the Huaraz culture, dating from around 2000-1800 BC, between the Galgada and Chavín periods. Excavations have uncovered structures 300 m in diameter, 25 m high. They are on a promontory with a view of the farms, fields, eucalyptus and other trees between the Cordilleras Blanca and Negra. To get there, from the plaza in Caraz follow San Martín uphill, turn left on 28 de Julio, continue about 400 m past the bridge over the Río Llullán. Look for a wide track between houses on your left (about 300 m before the turnoff for Lago Parón).

Cañón del Pato

The road out of the Callejón de Huaylas heads north from Caraz, en route to Chimbote on the coast. At Km 22 at a point called Bocatoma, the road enters the very narrow and spectacular **Cañón del Pato**. You pass under tremendous walls of bare rock and through 35 tunnels, but the flow of the river has been greatly reduced by the hydroelectric scheme, which takes the water into the mountain at Bocatoma.

The canyon can be visited on a half-day trip from Caraz. Take a colectivo from near the market to Huallanca (a few go towards Yuramarca, see Transport page 386). Sit in the front or on the right for great views. Get off at Huallanca and get on the next bus going back, sitting in the front or on the left. Ask the driver to drop you off at the yellow footbridge where the canyon is narrowest (ask for Cañón del Pato). Walk back north through one small tunnel. In the second tunnel, take the first side tunnel to the right that leads to a very precarious footpath that goes along the edge of the canyon at its narrowest point. Walking back south you come to a dam and the hydroelectric plant with water pouring over the dam wall. Pick up another bus going back to Caraz. Take great care on the path in the canyon and in the tunnels as they are narrow and have no places to retreat if a large vehicle comes through. Take a torch. The trip is best at midday when the sun shines directly into the gorge.

Treks from Caraz in the Cordillera Blanca

Cerro San Juan
This is a six- to seven-hour walk with views of Huandoy and Huascarán. It follows the foothills of the Cordillera Blanca, south from Caraz. Leave town on Bolognesi, continuing up to 28 de Julio; turn right, go past the **2 de Mayo (Markham) High School** and climb

Sleeping
1 Alojamiento Caballero
2 Caraz Dulzura
3 Chamanna
4 Chavín
5 Cordillera Blanca
6 Hostal La Casona
7 La Alameda
8 La Perla de los Andes
9 La Perla de los Andes Annex
10 Los Pinos
11 O'Pal Inn
12 Ramírez
13 Regina
14 Tunshukaiko

Eating
1 El Turista
2 Esmeralda
3 Heladería Caraz Dulzura
4 Jeny
5 La Punta Grande
6 Oasis
7 Panificadora La Alameda
8 Venezia

Bars & clubs
9 El Tabasco Taberna
10 Taberna Disco Huandy

Transport
1 Cavassa
2 Combis to Huallanca
3 El Huaralino
4 Expreso Ancash
5 Móvil
6 Yungay Express

Cerro San Juan; about 45 minutes. Continue south to the main local summit in an area known as **Ticrapa** (two hours). Head down to **Pata-Pata**, from where a track goes down beside the Río Ancash to **Puente Ancash** on the Caraz–Yungay road (two to three hours), where you can take transport back to Caraz. The hike can be done the other way by getting out of a combi from Huaraz or Caraz at Puente Ancash. The tourist office and **Pony's Expeditions** (see page 385) have a map of this trek.

Laguna Parón

From Caraz a narrow, rough road goes east 32 km to Laguna Parón (US$3.50), in a cirque surrounded by several, massive snow-capped peaks, including Huandoy, Pirámide Garcilazo and Caraz. The gorge leading to it is spectacular and the lake is really beautiful, well worth a visit.

It is a long day's trek from Caraz for acclimatized hikers (25 km) up to the lake at 4150 m, or a four- to five-hour walk from the village of **Parón**, which can be reached by combi. Where possible follow the walking trail, which is much shorter than the road. By climbing up the slippery moraine to the south of the lake towards Huandoy, you get a fine view of Artesonraju. Camping is possible next to the **Duke Energy** refuge. A trail follows the north shore of the lake to a base campon the north side of the inflow, about two hours past the refuge. Beyond this point, the trail divides: one branch goes towards **Pirámide Garcilazo** (5885 m) and **Pisco** (5752 m); another to **Laguna Artesoncocha** at the base of an enormous glacier, and a third towards **Artesonraju** (6025 m). You will need a map if you are going past Laguna Parón.

There are camping possibilities along these trails. Try to find shelter in the *quenoal* stands or behind a ridge, as the wind can be very strong and the nights are cold. The views are magnificent as you are always surrounded by many beautiful peaks. When you ford a river, remember that the flow increases in the afternoon with the meltdown, so make sure you can get back to your camp early. On the route to Artesonraju there is a morraine camp, just before reaching the glacier.

A taxi from Caraz to Laguna Parón costs US$25 for four, with two hours' wait. **Pony's Expeditions** (Caraz) have a pool of well-trained drivers that make daily departures to Parón at 0800, US$33 for four, US$30 for two or three passengers, including a two-hour visit to the lake and a walk downhill to the bridge, where the driver will pick up the group. Extra hours cost US$3.30. You can also hire a bicycle (US$15) and use these transport services one way (US$6) and cycle back down.

Santa Cruz Valley

This loop is one of the finest and most heavily used walks in the Cordillera Blanca. It usually takes three to five days depending on your starting point. It is considered easier in the direction Santa Cruz to Llanganuco, requiring four to five days, depending where you finish. **Please take all your rubbish with you.**

Day 1 Caraz to Llamacorral (3850 m) Taking a combi to **Cashapampa** covers the first 600 m and one hour, 20 minutes of the trip (see Caraz Transport, page 386). Services in Cashapampa include shops, campsites and transport; *arrieros* and their mules can be hired. (The local community charge a fee of 10 soles for every trekker on the Santa Cruz hike. In addition to the fees for hiring an *arriero* and a mule, donkey or horse, you have to pay for one full day for return from Vaquería or Llanganuco and two days if ending at Quebrada Ulta. You also pay for food and tent if hired in Cashapampa.) A recommended *arriero* is

Mellan Leiva Pariachi (Caserío de Shuyo, Cashapampa). From here it's a 10-km, 900-m climb to the Llamacorral campsite (four hours).

Day 2 Llamacorral to Taullipampa (4250 m) This is an easy day, perfect for acclimatizing (a total of 12 km, climbing about 400 m). The trail leads to the Ichiccocha and Jatuncocha lakes, both providing shelter for many water birds and exotic plants. Beyond the lakes there is a *quisuar* forest, providing perfect shade for lunch. A side trip to the north (left) of the main valley takes a series of switchbacks to the famous **Alpamayo Base Camp** (see page 378). After 45 minutes and climbing some 200 m, the circle of glaciers and snow peaks comes into full view. Go no further unless you plan to camp here. If returning to the main trail, look on the left of the trail (east) for a tiny path that will take you to **Taullipampa**, the next campsite. It's only 3 km to the camp, which is one of the most beautiful in the whole region, surrounded by snow peaks, a silent river and incredible plants.

Treks from Yungay & Caraz

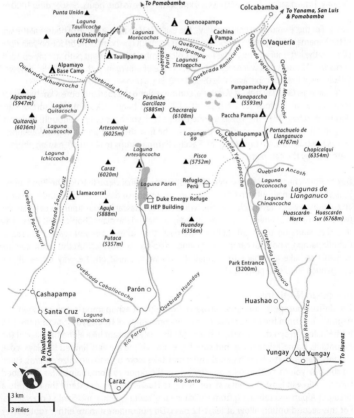

Day 3 Taullipampa to Huaripampa (3750 m) Make an early start for the **Punta Unión Pass**, the highest point on the trail, at 4750 m. The 4-km trail makes a series of switchbacks, but at a gentle pace you will reach this point in two to three hours. From the campsite the pass seems to be just a notch on the rock ridge right of Taulliraju (5850 m) but once there, the view is a 360° panorama of the snow peaks. The descent starts steeply, then traverses the granite slabs close to the ridge, before another series of switchbacks drive to the far left of the valley to descend on the lake below, another nice spot for lunch. Now the trail becomes slippery, crossing grass-like meadows towards **Quebrada Huaripampa**. After about two hours, a granite tower on your left is your sign to look for the bridge to cross the river. Now, with the river on your right, you will reach the **Quebrada Paría**. This is a good campsite, with great views of Paría mountain. It's usually crowded in July and August so, for more privacy, continue 2 km down the valley to camp at **Quenoapampa**. This is a spot at the end of the *quenoal* forest and a great campsite, despite the mosquitoes before sunset. For most travellers, the next campsite, some 3 km away, known as **Cachina Pampa** (3750 m), is a better option as it makes a shorter fourth day to catch the early buses back to Yungay. Total distance from the pass is 9 km, some three to four hours, descending 1000 m.

Day 4 For those who have only four days, the exit is at **Vaquería**, a group of houses at the side of the Yanama to Yungay road. Descend for 4 km in about one hour to the bridge on your right, climb to the left until you meet the fork to Colcabamba, take the right path steeply upwards and after 1½ hours you will meet the road. In case of emergency, there is a solar-powered telephone at Colcabamba, available 0900-1800. Buy a phone card for *teléfono rural*.

If making a five-day trek, at Vaquería, continue along the road for some 4 km to a green meadow, a toilet block (or what is left of it) and a huge rock forming a sort of cave (**Pampamachay**, 3870 m). This is a good campsite. If you have energy enough, and want to gain on the next day, continue by taking the first short cut on the right. Walk uphill across the trail through bushes to the **Paccha Pampa** campsite (4120 m), named after the waterfalls by the campsite.

Day 5 Portachuelo to Llanganuco lakes (3850 m) A final climb reaches the Portachuelo Pass at 4767 m, in about two hours. You can see, on a clear day, more snow peaks than on any of the previous days, including the twin peaks of Huascarán, four summits of Huandoy, two of Pisco, two of Chacraraju, three of Yanapaccha and the giant Chopicalqui. The trail to the lakes starts on the south (left) of the pass, then after 5 km you reach the area of **Cebollapampa**, a popular campsite for climbers going to Cerro Pisco. At this point, cars are available to take you back to Yungay. If you wish, pause on the way down at the Llanganuco lakes (see page 372).

Alpamayo North trek

This difficult but spectacular trek can begin from either **Cashapampa** (recommended, see page 374), or from the more remote, smaller community of **Hualcayan**. Starting the trek from Hualcayan avoids 2½ to three hours' (7 km) fairly pleasant hike along the base of the mountains from Cashapampa, but supplies in this village are very limited (cookies, cola, candles, better to stock up in Caraz) and it may take more time to organize *arrieros*. Once on the trek you can either hike directly across the range to **Pomabamba** (as described below – allow at least seven days), returning to Huaraz by bus, or extend the trek into a circuit of Alpamayo returning from Huilca via the Yanta Quenua and Santa Cruz valleys. For this second option allow at least 12 days. Do not underestimate either route. They take in spectacular, constantly changing mountain vistas, including picture-postcard views of Alpamayo, Quitaraju and the Pucajirca range. They cross three major, very steep mountain passes over 4700 m, plus an assortment of smaller challenges.

Day 1 Cashapampa to Hualcayan (four to 4½ hours) After 20 minutes' hiking north along the main route from Cashapampa, the **Baños Termales Huancarhuas** come into view in the valley below. These are passed after one to 1½ hours of easy walking, first crossing a rushing stream in the valley floor. Beyond the baths the route climbs gently uphill, following the trail beneath the mountains. You pass through traditional villages and fields. Cacti, spider plants, bromeliads and flowers are everywhere, not to mention the ubiquitous stands of eucalyptus. Views of the Cordillera Negra include a rich agricultural tapestry of small holdings and villages. After about three hours, the trail turns a little to the north, crossing a steep *quebrada*, just before a final one-hour steep climb to **Hualcayan** (3139 m). If you ask politely, you may be able to camp next to the football pitch and beneath the ancient terraces that rise above the village, US$1.75. US$1.50 per person was the community charge for park entry and trail maintenance in 2008. A receipt is given by Sr Erasmo Ramírez.

Day 2 Hualcayan to Huishcash (2½ hours) Heading east into the mountains you soon leave the 'road', following a zigzag trail as it climbs steeply, heading towards a waterfall. A red signpost showing a trekking figure confirms you're on the correct route. Quickly gaining height, the trail keeps to the south of the waterfall for the first hour before crossing an adobe bridge to the north bank above the cascade. Views of the Cañón del Pato below, not to mention the Cordillera Negra across the valley, become increasingly more impressive as you climb above Hualcayan. After two hours, the path begins taking a more direct route, slowly climbing north towards a small patch of polylepis woodland. A red sign board marks the limit of Parque Nacional Huascarán at 3710 m. Thirty minutes later, heading north, you begin crossing a large landslide area and just beyond that you reach the beautiful remnant of polylepis woodland just mentioned. Beyond the forest there's an open pasture area, which makes a good stopping point for lunch and also a very good camping spot. (Note that the next potential campsite is by Laguna Cullicocha (see below), 3½ hours away: very high and cold.) If you decide to stay at **Huishcash** you could explore **Laguna Yanacocha**, 1.65 km away; a sign just beyond Huishcash points the way.

Alpamayo North trek

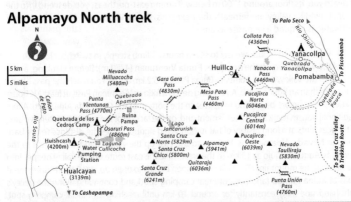

Day 3 Huishcash to Quebrada Vientunan (5½ to six hours) At the sign to Laguna Yanacocha, walk up the winding trail heading away from the direction in which the sign is pointing, straight up the hill in front of you. Fifteen minutes later you cross a small stream on an adobe bridge passing a small 'walking man' trail sign. This sign also names this pampa as Huishcash (4200 m), as well as listing various prohibitions: no fires, no fishing, no booze, no rubbish, etc. Some 1½ hours after the Huishcash lunch/camping spot, a sign indicates 2.7 km to Laguna Cullicocha and, in another direction, 7 km to Laguna Yanacocha. On the left is a black, canyon-like feature, full of dense native vegetation below, but barren on exposed ridges and faces. Not far beyond the last signpost the path runs just to the left, underneath a black hill on top of the pass and in between the two black mountains above the dark valley. Lots of polylepis woodland covers the inaccessible parts of this gorge.

Roughly 3½ hours after leaving Huishcash you come to the water-pumping micro-hydro station and the potential campsite in front of **Laguna Cullicocha**. This station is always staffed. Before arriving at the station, follow the steep right-hand side of the gorge, passing (but not following) a water drainage channel. The campsite itself is set in a landscape of smooth sculpted rocks backed by spectacular views of the Laguna Cullicocha and, behind the lake, the icy walls of the Santa Cruz massif: **Santa Cruz Norte** (5829 m), **Chico** (5800 m) and **Santa Cruz Grande** (6241 m, also referred to as **Pucaraju**). The rocks and high altitude make for an uncomfortable campsite but, if you are very polite, the pumping station attendant may let you stay in the station's spare accommodation. The next good campsite is a couple of hours' hike further, on the far side of one of the trek's major passes.

Head north, following trail markers just to the west of the Cullicocha pumping station, with great views again of the Santa Cruz mountains and the lakes below. After about 15 minutes the trail begins to swing more to the east towards Santa Cruz Norte and begins to zigzag higher above the lakes towards the pass. Thirty to 40 minutes after the station, the route starts to turn north through a jagged rocky area, heading up towards the pass. From here you have a good view down into the glacial moraine of Santa Cruz. Fifty minutes after Cullicocha, a knife-edge ridge on the top of the first pass, **Osoruri** (4860 m), is reached. A great vista of the mountains of the **Milluacocha** massif opens up, with the trail twisting into the valley below you on your right. Condors may be seen here. Between Osoruri and Nevado Milluacocha the valley of the **Quebrada Alpamayo** plunges beneath you, its floor around 1700 m below. Turning east-northeast you descend into the steep, bowl-like valley, underneath the next pass, **Punta Vientunan**. This, with shelter and water, is as good a campsite as any.

Day 4 Vientunan to Alpamayo (six to seven hours) Climb steeply in switchbacks on the far wall of the valley to reach the next pass, **Punta Vientunan** (4770 m). Before climbing, at the bottom of the valley, a sign points to Ruina Pampa, 5.2 km away. You reach the pass after a little more than an hour's climb. A very long descent follows Vientunan Pass, at least 1¼ hours of knee stress, before beginning to approach the bottom of the Quebrada Alpamayo. A few traditional houses mark a small settlement and, on the far side of the valley, an extensive area of terraces hints at a long history of habitation. A red signpost gives the distance to the base camp at **Nevado Alpamayo** as 10.5 km to the east up the valley, and the distance to the Ruinas de Auquis Puquio as 13 km to the west. Take the east route up the valley deeper into the heart of the mountains. The valley floor soon begins to open up, passing the unrestored walls of **Ruina Pampa** (another potential camping spot) and continuing along the valley's right-hand side fairly constantly for around 10 km until reaching an official camping spot, marked by another red/orange board. Surrounded by magnificent mountains on all sides, the site is positioned just before the turn to the south where the valley swings towards Lago Jancarurish and the glacial moraines. In good weather the classic northwest face of **Alpamayo** is visible, but for the best views of the mountain, leave yourself some time the following day and ascend the moraine to the south.

Day 5 Alpamayo viewpoint (optional) Heading south up the valley, a brief climb to the summit of the moraine affords fabulous views of the turquoise **Lago Jancarurish**, vast cliffs and a spectacular cascade pouring from Alpamayo and its glacier above. Glance to the west and you'll find views of **Santa Cruz** and her sister peaks, perhaps from their most striking angle. Hiking further up the valley on the right-hand side will bring you to the climbers' base camp, and the beauty and potential risk that the world of ice and snow entails.

Day 6 Alpamayo to Huillca (6½ to seven hours) From the official campsite near Lago Jancarurish, cross to the north side of the Quebrada Alpamayo, then bear left, heading north towards the Gara Gara Pass, but zigzagging up on the left-hand (west) side of the valley. The initial climb is steep but offers increasingly panoramic views of the surrounding peaks, including **Quitaraju** to the south, an impressive mountain often hidden by rocky outcrops from the valley floor. After about an hour of climbing, the trail leads into a flatter valley, with a small lake on its right-hand side. Beyond this flatter section, the final push up to the pass is a steep scree slope, almost a scramble in the last moments. It should take a couple of hours to reach the chilly, windswept **Gara Gara Pass** (4830 m). There's not a lot of room to manoeuvre up there, but with awe-inspiring peaks all around, Gara Gara offers perhaps the most jaw-dropping vista on the trek.

On the far side of the pass, descend roughly east-to-northeast, following the trail down through steep rocky ground. This valley appears to have a slightly wetter climate than Quebrada Alpamayo, with cushion mosses and many flowers. A couple of small ruins are passed in the higher sections of the valley. The descent from the pass is fairly steep for the first 45 minutes, then flattens out into a damp puna environment, with thick ichu grass everywhere and occasional boggy patches. Follow the left flank of the valley to the northeast. A couple of hours after the pass, the trail reasserts its easterly course, crossing to the right-hand side of the valley and climbing towards the small Mesapata Pass. At the same time the Quebrada Mayobamba swings sharply to the north, away from your route. After another hour (five hours after starting out) you reach the summit of **Mesapata** (4460 m), to be rewarded by yet another imposing range, the ice-bound peaks of the **Pucajirca** massif. Below you lies the **Quebrada Tayapampa** and, on the river's left-hand bank, a rough road heading northeast. Descend into the valley and follow the road until it crosses the river and opens up into the wide valley of **Huillca**. Here you'll find a traditional, almost totally self-sufficient settlement of three Quechua families, all carving a rugged existence from animal herding, with large groups of pigs, alpacas and horses. With permission from these families, it's possible to camp on the eastern side of the valley, beyond the Yanta Quenua stream. The inhabitants of the valley are often interested in trading food (cooked potatoes, eggs, etc) for products difficult to obtain locally: matches, lighters, pens, etc. Always treat the inhabitants of this valley, and their extraordinary culture, with respect. At the same make sure you store all valuables inside your tent.

At Huillca, you have the choice of either continuing east to the far side of the mountains and **Pomabamba** (described in detail below), or turning southeast up the **Yanta Quenua Valley**. This route, if followed for a couple of days over the 4610-m

Yanacon Pass, then through the Quebradas Yanajanca and Tuctubamba will bring you to the classic Santa Cruz trekking route (see page 374), close to the small Laguna Huecrucocha. Heading west from here will lead you in two or three days over the spectacular Punta Unión Pass (see page 376) and through the Santa Cruz Valley, completing what's generally termed the **Alpamayo Circuit**.

Day 7 Huillca to Quebrada Yanajanca (five to six hours) The trail to Pomabamba starts in the Huillca valley's southeast corner, zigzagging up the hill to the northeast before swinging more to the north. The top of the first pass is reached after around 50 minutes, the route commanding spectacular views of the Pucajirca snow peaks and passing through a small patch of polylepis woodland. Reaching the top of the pass (there's no name on the Alpenverin Map, but let's call it **Punta Shuitucocha** for clarity) you are presented with a view of a second valley to the east. This valley has two lakes, the more southerly, larger of which is **Laguna Shuitucocha**. The trail now follows a route between the two lakes, then up the hill to the far side, taking a generally east-northeasterly course along the left-hand edge of the hills. After around 2½ hours you'll reach the bleak 4360-m **Collota Pass**, crowned by a large cross.

A steep descent to the east leads towards a trail/rough road. A long descent down this valley on the left (north) bank leads into a lush, jungle-like landscape. The valley becomes increasingly heavily populated, the trail crossing over onto the right bank of the river, passing some small shops, before re-crossing the river and heading through the main part of the **Yanacollpa** village. Some families in the village and slightly beyond it will allow you to camp or rent a room for a small fee. Keep a close eye on your gear when staying close to the village. Alternatively, camp before crossing the bridge just before Yanacollpa to avoid fees and locals hanging around your tent asking for goods, medicine, money, matches, candies, etc.

Day 8 Yanacollpa to Pomabamba Just a few hours' trek this morning, first crossing the river, following its course down the right-hand bank of the Yanacollpa until it meets the Río Shiula, then following the water downstream to the southeast to your destination. Make certain that just before **Pomabamba** you cross the river to the north side; this route will take you right into the town centre. If you want to relax after the trek, there are some good thermal baths close to Pomabamba (see page 393).

Cordillera Negra

Torreón Andino

West of Caraz is **Huata** at 2700 m, where there is a religious sanctuary and a dirty hotel (**F**); a truck leaves from Caraz market daily at 1000. Some 6 km down a track off the Caraz–Huata road are the Inca ruins of **Chonta**. From Huata you can climb to the **Quebrada de Cochacocha** (3500 m), at the top of which is the Inca ruin of Cantu (excellent views), and on to the Inca lookout, **Torreón Andino** (5006 m). Take water, food and a tent. Allow three days for the hike, as there are lagoons near the peak. Refer to the late Professor Bernardino Aguilar Prieto's *Torreón Andino Information* book before climbing it.

Pueblo Libre

A good day hike from Caraz with nice views of the Cordillera Blanca is to Pueblo Libre. Follow Jirón D Villar west across the Río Santa bridge and turn south to **Tunaspampa**, an interesting desert area with cacti and hummingbirds. Continue through the villages of

A blooming century

The giant *Puya Raimondi*, named after Antonio Raimondi, the Italian scholar who discovered it, is a rare species, considered to be one of the oldest plants in the world.

Often mistakenly referred to as a cactus, it is actually the largest member of the bromeliad family and is found in only a few isolated areas of the Andes. One of these areas is the Huascarán National Park, particularly the Ingenio and Queshque gorges, the high plateaus of Cajamarquilla, along the route leading to Pastoruri in the Pachacoto gorge and by the road from Caraz to Pamparomas.

At its base, the *Puya* forms a rosette of long, spiked, waxy leaves, 2 m in diameter. The distinctive phallic spike of the plant can reach a height of 12 m during the flowering process. This takes its entire lifespan – an incredible 100 years – after which time the plant withers and dies.

As the final flowering begins, usually during May, the spike is covered in flowers. As many as 20,000 blooms can decorate a single plant. Groups of *Puya Raimondi* bloom together to create a spectacular picture against the dramatic backdrop of the Cordillera Blanca.

Shingal, Tocash and Rinconada on to **Pueblo Libre**. It is about a four-hour round trip, or you can take a colectivo back to Caraz.

Huinchus

Beyond Pueblo Libre, the road continues via Pamparomas and Moro to join the coastal highway between Casma and Chimbote. After 45 km (two hours) a large stand of *Puya Raimondi* (see above) can be seen at a place called **Huinchus**, with views stretching 145 km, east to the Cordillera Blanca and west to the Pacific. The flowers are usually in bloom in May or October. 'Huinchu', or 'Wincho', is the local name for the giant hummingbird, *Patagona gigas*, which has an 18-cm wingspan.

There are two possible routes by public transport from Caraz to the puyas at Huinchus: Caraz–Huata–El Cruce (from where it's a 2-km walk to the *puyas*), continuing to Pamparomas; or Caraz–Pueblo Libre–Huashtacruz–El Paso (from where it's a 15-minute walk to the *puyas*), continuing to El Cruce and Pamparomas. On the return to Caraz, you will have to walk 2 km to El Cruce to be sure to catch the returning transport between 1230 and 1300. This will not give you too much time at the *puyas*. Increasingly popular alternatives are to rent a bicycle (US$15), which you can take on public transport to the puyas (departing at 0800-0900; see Transport, page 386) and then ride back to Caraz in about four to five hours.

For Sleeping and Eating price codes and other relevant information, see pages 38-44.

⊜ Sleeping

Marcará and the Huandoy Valley *p369*
There are homestay opportunities in **Vicos**, contact the **Mountain Institute** in Huaraz, Ricardo Palma 100, Pedregal Alto, T043-423446, www.mountain.org.

Carhuaz *p369*
B-C COMTUCAR (Complejo Turístico Carhuaz), 200 m south of town on main road to Huaraz No 1099, T043-394051, www.qnet.com.pe/carhuaz. Functional hotel, includes breakfast, restaurant, pool, sauna, gardens.
C pp **Casa de Pocha**, 1.5 km out of town towards Hualcán at foot of Nevado Hualcán, ask directions in town, T943-961 3058 (mob, 1800-2000), www.socialwellbeing.org/lacasadepocha.htm. Advance bookings required. Nice country setting, price includes breakfast and dinner, solar- and wind-powered electricity, hot water, sauna and pool, home-produced food (vegetarian available), horses for hire, Spanish, Quechua, Portuguese, English, French and Italian spoken. Good base for hiking. Recommended.
C El Abuelo, Jr 9 de Diciembre 257 y Tumbes, T043-394456, www.elabuelohostal.com. Modern, pricey 3-star, comfortable, with restaurant and parking. Ask at **Heladería El Abuelo** on main plaza. Knowledgeable owner, Felipe Díaz, is the publisher of a useful tourist map of the cordilleras Blanca and Huayhuash, available widely in the area.
F Hostal Señor de Luren, Jr Río Buin 549, 30 m from Plaza de Armas, , T01-924-668806. Hot water, TV, safe motorcycle parking, very friendly.
    4 family-run *hospedajes* (**F**) have been built as part of a community development project. All have private bath and hot water.

The better 2 are the modern **Hospedaje Robri**, Jr Comercio 935, T043-394505, and **Alojamiento Las Torresitas**, Jr Amazonas 603, T043-794213. The latter is a nice place with friendly *señora* and pretty courtyard. Rooms with TV and bath.
G Alojamiento Turístico, Río Santa with 28 de Julio, near Colegio San Martín, T043-394128. Quiet and pleasant, single and double rooms with private bath and hot water.
G Hostal La Merced, Ucayali 724, T043-394241 (in Lima T01-442 3201). 'Like going back to the 1950s', clean, friendly, hot water (usually), some rooms with private bathroom, luggage store.

Mancos *p370*
There's a nice dorm at **La Casita de mi Abuela**, Barrio Huascarán, Pukio, Jr Comercio 110, and **La Plazza**, on the Plaza de Armas, can provide meals. Also some basic shops and restaurants.

Yungay *p370, map p371*
D COMTURY, Complejo Turístico Yungay, Prolongación 2 de Mayo 1019, 2.5 km south of the new town, 700 m east of the main road in Aura, the only part of old Yungay that survived, T043-788656, http://comtury.com. Nice bungalows with single rooms, doubles and 2-bedroom units, in a pleasant country setting, hot water, fireplace, friendly, restaurant with regional specialities, camping is also possible.
F Hostal Gledel, Av Arias Grazziani, north past the plaza, T043-793048, rugamboa@viabcp.com. Owned by Sra Gamboa, who is hospitable and a good cook, very clean but tiny rooms, shared bathroom, warm water, no towels or soap, cheap meals prepared on request, nice courtyard.
F Hostal Sol de Oro, Calle 7 lote B Urb, Santo Domingo 07, T043-393116. Private bath, hot water, comfy and good value. The best in town.

F Hotal Yungay, Jr Santo Domingo, on the plaza, T043-393053. Private bath with hot water, laundry, clean and basic.
G Hostal Mery, 28 de julio s/n, T043-303107. Simple but OK, hot water, rooms at the front can be noisy.

Caraz and around *p372, map p373*
AL-C O'Pal Inn, 3 km south of Caraz, T/F043-391015, www.opalsierraresort.com. This scenic hotel is outside town, set back from road. Bungalows and rooms, which have private bath, swimming pool. Recommended.
D-E Chamanna, Av Nueva Victoria 185, 25 mins' walk from centre, T043-943 784841/943-535279 (mob), www.chamanna.com. Clean cabañas in a beautiful garden, with or without private bath, hot water, secure, excellent French and international cuisine in pricey restaurant. Recommended.
D-F Los Pinos, Parque San Martín 103, 5 blocks from plaza, T043-391130, lospinos @apuaventura.com. Rooms with and without private bath and TV, hot water, airy and comfortable, garden open to all travellers, camping US$2.50, use of internet US$0.50 per hr, use of kitchen US$3, laundry service, clean, safe, book exchange, information and travel agency **Apu-Aventura** (see page 385). Breakfast and dinner are available, bar with movies every night. Recommended.
E Caraz Dulzura, Sáenz Peña 212, about 10 blocks from the town centre, T043-391523, hostalcarazdulzura@hotmail.com. Modern building in an old street, 6 double rooms, hot water, with or without bathroom and TV, comfortable, great service, very helpful owner (Carlos), clean and airy rooms, breakfast extra, very good food available. Recommended.
E La Alameda, Av Noé Bazán Peralta 262, T043-391177, www.hotellaalameda.com. Hot water. Comfortable rooms, breakfast, parking, gardens. Recommended.
E La Perla de los Andes, Plaza de Armas 179, T/F043-392007. Comfortable rooms with bath, hot water, TV, helpful, fair restaurant.

Has a large new, cheaper annex 1 block up San Martín. Recommended.
E Tunshukaiko, Jr Melgar 114, T043-792212. Private bath, hot water, balconies, nice garden, sitting room with fireplace.
F Chavín, San Martín 1135 just off the plaza, T043-391171, hostalchavin@hotmail.com. With bathroom, warm water, good service but a bit grubby and dark, breakfast extra, guiding service, can arrange transport to Lago Parón.
F Cordillera Blanca, Grau 903, T043-391938. Modern concrete building opposite market, rooms with private bath, hot water and TV.
F Regina, Los Olivos Manzana B-Lote 4 y Gálvez, 1 block west of road to Yungay, T043-391520. Modern, with bath, clean, quiet, good value.
G Alojamiento Caballero, D Villar 485, ask at **Pony's Expeditions**. Shared bathroom, hot water, washing facilities, stores luggage, basic, family run.
G Hostal La Casona, Raymondi 319, 1 block east from the plaza, T043-391334. Most rooms without bathroom, hot water, clean, lovely little patio, basic but good.
G pp Ramírez, D Villar 407, T043-588254. Basic, clean, shared bathroom, limited hot water.

🍴 Eating

Carhuaz *p369*
🍴 **El Abuelo**, Plaza de Armas, T043-394149. Local and international fare. Produce from their garden, including natural ice cream.
🍴 **El Mirador**, off the main highway, 10 mins outside Carhuaz. An upscale tourist restaurant with Andean and Peruvian food, good value.
🍴 **La Cabaña**, at Acopampa, 3 km south of town. Specialities are regional dishes, including *cuy*. Nice garden, friendly owner.

Yungay *p370, map p371*
🍴 **Alpamayo**, Av Arias Grazziani s/n, T043-393090. Open lunch only. Best in town serving excellent-value local dishes such

as trout, *cuy*, *tamales* and *pachamanca* at weekends.

Ψ Café Pilar, on the main plaza. Good for juices, cakes and snacks.

Around Yungay *p371*
The only tourism infrastructure in **Matacoto** is the **Almawasi** restaurant, serving European home cooking at reasonable prices on a breathtaking terrace facing the snow peaks.

Caraz and around *p372, map p373*
ΨΨ La Punta Grande, D Villar 595, 10 mins' walk from centre. Best place for local dishes, good, open for lunch only till 1700.
Ψ Esmeralda, Av Alfonso Ugarte 404. Good set meal, breakfast, friendly, recommended.
Ψ Heladería Caraz Dulzura, D Villar on plaza, next to Perla de los Andes. Excellent home-made ice cream, good value meals, pastries.
Ψ Jeny, Daniel Villar on the plaza between cathedral and phone office. Good food at reasonable prices, also *pollería*.
Ψ Oasis, Raymondi, just off the plaza. Meals for about US$1-1.50, also has rooms (**E**).
Ψ Venezia, Av Noé Bazán Peralta, 1 block east of the Colegio 2 de Mayo. Open Thu-Tue, 1000-2200. Good grilled meat and pasta.

Cafés
Good *manjar blanco* is sold by the Lúcar family, Villa Luisa brand, in a house next to the phone office on Raymondi.
Café de Rat, Sucre 1266, above Pony's Expeditions. Breakfast, vegetarian and meat dishes, pizzas, drinks and snacks, darts, travel books, free Wi-Fi, nice vibe. Recommended.
El Turista, San Martín 1117. Open morning and evening. Popular for breakfast; ham omelettes and sandwiches are specialities.
Establo La Alameda, D Villar 420. Excellent *manjar blanco*, cakes and sweets.
Panificadora La Alameda, D Villar y San Martín. Very good bread and pastries, ice cream, popular with locals.

🎵 Bars and clubs

Caraz and around *p372, map p373*
El Tabasco Taberna, ½ block north of D Villar. Disco, Latin and other music.
Taberna Disco Huandy, Mcal Cáceres 119. Fri and Sat only. Reasonable prices, good atmosphere, young crowd, Latin music.

✺ Festivals and events

Carhuaz *p369*
14-24 Sep Fiesta in honour of the **Vírgen de las Mercedes**, rated as the best in the region.

Yungay *p370, map p371*
28 Oct The anniversary of the founding of the town: parades, fireworks and dances.

Caraz and around *p372, map p373*
20 Jan Virgen de Chiquinquirá.
Mar/Apr Semana Santa (Holy Week) features processions and streets carpeted with flower petals.
Last week in Jul Semana Turística, sports, canoeing, parasailing and folkloric events.

🛒 Shopping

Caraz and around *p372, map p373*
Shop for camping supplies, such as fresh food, in the market.

▲ Activities and tours

Yungay *p370, map p371*
Cycle World, Arias Graziani 3ra cuadra, near bridge at south end of Yungay, T043-303109. Bike rentals at US$10 per day including helmet and gloves. For US$3 a combi will take you and your rented bike to Llanganuco. The ride down is beautiful and exhilarating, but cold. Recommended.

Caraz and around *p372, map p373*
Horse riding
La Alameda, 4 km south of Caraz, 5 mins by combi towards Yungay, T043-391935. A variety of horse-riding routes through fields, across the Río Santa and in to the Cordillera Negra to give fine views of the peaks, US$5 per hr, with guide. Horses for both novice and experienced riders are available.

Mountain biking
Llanganuco is a popular 1-day ride from Caraz, as is **Lago Parón**, the **Cañón del Pato** and the **Puya Raimondii** plants at **Winchus**. The **Santa Cruz Valley** forms part of another long circuit.

Parasailing
Parasailing is practised 9 km on the road to Huaraz but you must supply your own equipment. **Cayasbamba**, near Caraz, is a good launch site at 3000 m.

Rock climbing
Rocodromo Pachar-Shuply, Mancos, access from Tingua, 22 km S of Caraz. 3 zones, red, green, yellow, with 12, 4 and 4 routes respectively. Gear hire from **Pony's Expeditions**.

Tour operators
All 3 tour operators in Caraz can sell the Huascarán Park admission tickets, avoiding the need to go to Huaraz to get them.
Apu-Aventura, based at Hotel Los Pinos (see page 383), www.apuaventura.com. Adventure sports and equipment rental.
Pony's Expeditions, Sucre 1266, near the Plaza de Armas, T/F043-391642, www.ponyexpeditions.com. Mon-Sat 0800-2200. English, French and Quechua spoken, reliable information about the area. Owners Alberto and Aidé Cafferata are very knowledgeable about treks and climbs. They arrange local tours, trekking and transport (US$30 for up 4 people) for day excursions, and have a bulletin board where people who want to share transport for local excursions leave their name and contact details. Maps

and books for sale, also equipment for hire, mountain bike rental (US$15 for a full day). Some dried camping food is available, also camping gas canisters and white gas. Agents for **Cruz de Sur** buses and **LC Busre** air tickets Lima–Huaraz. Highly recommended.
Summit Peru, Sucre 1106, T043-791958, www.summitperu.com. Trekking, climbing and day trips.

Trekking
Mariano Araya is a trekking guide who is also keen on photography and archaeology. Ask at the municipality.

● Transport

Carhuaz *p369*
All transport leaves from the main plaza. To **Huaraz**, colectivos and buses 0500-2000, US$0.75, 40 mins. To **Caraz**, 0500-2000, US$0.75, 1 hr. Buses from Huaraz to **Chacas** in the Cordillera Blanca (see page 367), 87 km, 4-5 hrs, US$3.75, pass through Carhuaz about 40 mins after leaving Huaraz. The road works its way up the Ulta valley to **Punta Olímpica** from where there are excellent views. The dirt road is not in a very good condition owing to landslides every year (in the wet season it can be closed). The trucks continue to **San Luis**, a further 10 km, 1½ hrs. In addition, **Trans Huandoy** does the return trip from Carhuaz to **Chacas**, Thu only, US$6 one way, 5 hrs.

Yungay *p370, map p371*
Most transport leaves from Jr 28 de Julio. Buses and colectivos run all day to **Caraz**, 12 km, US$0.30, and to **Huaraz**, 54 km, 1½ hrs, US$1. To **Lagunas Llanganuco**, combis leave when full, especially 0700-0900, from Av 28 de Julio 1 block from the plaza, 1 hr, US$1.50, otherwise it's US$9 to hire a vehicle (or US$12 with 2-hr wait).
To **Yanama**, via the Portachuelo de Llanganuco Pass, 4767 m, 3½ hrs, US$3; stopping at María Huayta, after 2 hrs, US$2.
To **Pomabamba**, via Piscobamba, Trans

Los Andes, daily 0700- 0730 (only company with a ticket office in Yungay); La Perla de Altamayo buses from Huaraz, 0730, stop if they have room, 6-7 hrs, US$6. After passing the Llanganuco lakes and crossing the Portachuelo the buses descend to Puente Llacma, where it is possible to pick up buses and combis heading south to San Luis, Chacas and Huari.

Caraz and around p372, map p373
Local
To Huaraz, frequent combis, daily 0400-2000, 1¼ hrs, US$1.35, the road is in good condition. They leave from a terminal on the way out of town, where the south end of Sucre meets the highway. By combi to Yungay, 12 km, 15 mins, US$0.30. To the village of Parón (for trekking in Laguna Parón area) combis leave from the corner of Ramón Castilla y Jorge Chávez, close to the market, Mon-Sat 0400 and 1300, Sun 0300 and 1300, 1 hr, US$1.20; they return from Parón at 0600 and 1400. To Cashapampa (the corner of Ramón Castilla y Jorge Chávez) buses from Santa Cruz y Grau, hourly 0600-1530, 1 hr 20 mins, US$1.50; taxis charge US$7.55. To Huallanca (Caraz) and Yuramarca for the Cañón del Pato, combis and cars leave from Córdova y La Mar, 0700-1730, US$1.50. Combis to Hualcayan for the Alpamayo Valley trek from Ramón Castilla y Jorge Chávez, 0400, 0700, 1100 and 1300, US$2.45, 2 hrs. To Huata for the Cordillera Negra, combis and cars leave from the Parque del Maestro (Córdova y Santa Cruz), 0700, 1000, 1200, 1 hr. For the Puya Raimondi at

Huinchus, take a combi from Ramón Castilla y Jorge Chávez around 0900, 2 hrs, US$2 (get there at about 0800 as they often leave early), or hire a combi for US$42.50 for 8 people, plus US$7.20 for a guide.

Long distance
Most Lima–Huaraz buses continue to Caraz. To Lima, 470 km, via Huaraz and Pativilca; several companies on D Villar and Jr Córdova, daily, 10-11 hrs, US$7: El Huaralino, Expreso Ancash, T043- 391509, Móvil, Cavassa.

To Chimbote, with Yungay Express (D Villar 318), via Cañón del Pato, 0830, US$8, 8 hrs; with Movil Tours, daily at 1900; sit on the right for best views. To Trujillo, via Huaraz and Pativilca, with Chinchaysuyo (Córdova 830, T791903), daily 1845, US$13.50, 11-12 hrs, stops in Casma and Chimbote; with Movil Tours, daily at 1930.

❶ Directory

Caraz and around p372, map p373
Banks BCP, D Villar 217, Mon-Fri 0930-1600, Sat 1000-1300. Banco de la Nación, Jr Raimondi, has an ATM that accepts Visa cards, Mastercard and American Express debit and credit cards and dispenses both US and Peruvian currencies. Importaciones América, Sucre 721, T043- 391479, offers good rates and service, open weekends and evenings. For large amounts of cash it is better to exchange in Huaraz. **Internet and telephone** Many places; internet US$0.30. **Post** At San Martín 909.

Eastern flank of the Cordillera Blanca

A trip to Chavín de Huantar is a must if you are in the area, as it is one of the most important archaeological sites in the country. At the height of its power, Chavín's influence was felt over a vast area. Along the east side of the Cordillera Blanca, which is known as the Callejón de Conchucos, runs a good, but narrow, dirt road, subject to rapid deterioration when it rains. The region has seen fewer foreign tourists than the Callejón de Huaylas, so some discretion, as well as responsible behaviour, is called for. ▸▸ *For listings, see pages 394-398.*

Ins and outs

Many people only go as far as Chavín de Huantar, taking a tour with a Huaraz company. If you decide to go north from Chavín all, or part way up the eastern side of the Cordillera Blanca, note that public transport is less frequent and less reliable here than in the Callejón de Huaylas, with some towns getting only two buses per week, direct from Lima. Private vehicles, usually large trucks, are few and far between, although there are some buses running across the passes back to the Callejón de Huaylas. ▸▸ *See Transport page 396.*

Huaraz to Chavín → *For listings, see pages 394-398.*

Olleros and around

The main road south to Pativilca passes the turn-off for **Olleros** at 3450 m, the starting point for the spectacular three-day hike to Chavín, along a pre-Columbian trail (see below). Some basic meals and food supplies are available here. An alternative trek from Olleros is to **Quebrada Rurec** via **Huaripampa**, a small village with a few bodegas that will sell or prepare food. Public transport is available to Huaripampa. There are granite walls of up to 600 m at Rurec, the highest in the Cordillera Blanca, which are recommended for rock climbing. The trek itself is also worthwhile.

Further south on the main road (27 km, 30 minutes from Huaraz) is **Recuay**, one of the few provincial capitals to have survived the 1970 earthquake and retained its colonial features. There is a sizeable cave with stalagmites and stalagtites on the main road (free entry). On 11-16 September the town celebrates the **Festividad Señor de Burgos de Recuay**.

Olleros to Chavín trek

The trek begins at the village of **Canrey Chico** and follows an impressive pre-Inca road with several unexplored ruins along the way. There are combis to Canrey Chico from Parque PIP or Avenida Tarapacá in Huaraz, starting early, but with no reliable schedule (US$1.50); better to take a taxi, 30 minutes, US$4.

This lovely and relatively easy three- to four-day trek has become less popular with agencies and groups in recent times, perhaps because of persistent begging on the Chavín side. Hence there is is an opportunity for independent trekkers to fill the gap and try to remedy the social situation. Never give money, medicines or sweets, which will do more harm than good. Consider sharing other food, if you feel it is appropriate, otherwise offer only a polite smile. There are also dogs along the route, generally raucous but inoffensive. The route follows the south (right) shores of the Río Negro, Quebrada Uquián, Quebrada Shongo, and Quebrada Huachecsa all the way to the Chavín archaeologic site.

The route (Numbers in the text refer to numbers on the map, below.) When you reach **Canrey Chico** (1), turn right to keep on the road that follows the Río Negro. Keep the river on the left. The track is perfectly clear and there is a large Parque Nacional Huascarán sign. At this point a track branches off to the left into the **Quebrada Rurec** (see above); continue straight ahead. A small sign marks the intersection (2). **Quebrada Uquian** (3) becomes flatter here and the river more sinuous. By some stone corrals, you see a lateral morraine on your right, evidence of old glacial activity. To avoid the boggy valley floor, you can climb along the crest of the morraine (4) to more corrals and straw-thatched stone huts. Here you begin to see the large flat top of the valley.

Sacrapampa (5), marked with a large sign, is a convenient spot to camp before starting the climb to the pass. At the top of the valley, it divides into four valleys. The path swings right to avoid the marsh then heads up the second valley on the left, often with a ridge between the path and the river, to the highest point. It is quite easy to lose the track here, but keep heading in the direction of the pass and you'll pick it up eventually. It's a slow, gradual climb to the pass. There are stone cairns and several small ponds at **Punta Yanashallash** (6; 4700 m), and great views of the surrounding summits. The trail then follows the ancient road over impressive zigzags making light work of what would otherwise be a difficult 400-m descent.

Shongo (7), also called Shongopampa and marked with a large sign, is a good camping spot; the last before entering populated areas where begging is a problem. At **Lluchucaca** (8; bare cliff) the trail crosses a narrow ledge. This is safe in dry weather but can be avoided by descending to the river. Fifteen minutes ahead is a wooden bridge over Quebrada Shongo. Cross to the north side if you wish to make a side-trip to Jato and explore the valleys up from there. Otherwise, stay on the south side of Quebrada Shongo and follow the trail through the hamlet of **Chichucancha**. Head down into the **Quebrada Huachecsa** (9) till you reach Punta Huancayo where you can see the ruins of **Chavín de Huantar** (10). Go through the village of Nueva Florida to reach the road. The town of Chavín is on the left and the archaeological ruins are straight ahead.

Catac to Chavín → *Colour map 3, B3.*

The main road continues 11 km south from Recuay to **Catac**, where a road branches east for Chavín (all paved). From Catac to Chavín is a magnificent, scenic journey, if frightening

Olleros to Chavín trek

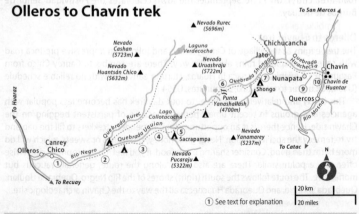

① See text for explanation

20 km
20 miles

The stone gods of Chavín

Archaeologists have learnt very little about the Chavín culture, whose architecture and sculpture had a strong impact on the artistic and cultural development of a large part of the coast and central highlands of Peru. Based on physical evidence from the study of this 17-acre site, the temple of Chavín de Huantar is thought to have been a major ceremonial centre.

What first strikes visitors is the quality of the stonework. The sculptures have three functions: architectural, ornamental and cultist. Examples include the Lanzón, the Tello obelisk and the Raimondi stela; the latter two currently grace the Museo Nacional de Antropología, Arqueología e Historia in Lima (see page 87).

At 5 m high, the **Lanzón** is the crowning glory of the Chavín religion and stands at the heart of the underground complex. Its Spanish name comes from the lance-, or dagger-like shape of the monolith which appears to be stuck in the ground. Carved into the top of the head are thin, grooved channels; some speculate that animals, or even humans, may have been sacrificed to this god. Others suggest that the Lanzón was merely the dominant figure for worship.

Named after the Peruvian scientist, Julius C Tello, the **Tello obelisk** belongs to the earliest period of occupation of Chavín (c 100 BC). It represents a complex deity – perhaps a caiman-alligator – connected with the earth, water and all the living elements of nature. Carved on the body are the people, birds, serpents and felines that the divine beast has consumed.

The **Raimondi stela** was named after the Italian naturalist, who also gave his name to the famous plant (see page 381). It shows a feline anthropomorphic divinity standing with open arms and holding a staff in each hand.

Together, the stone figures at Chavín indicate that the resident cult was based principally on the feline, or jaguar, and secondarily on serpents and birds.

---

at times. Beyond Laguna Querococha, there are good views of the Yanamarey peaks and, at the top of the route, the road is cut through a huge rock face, entering the **Cahuish Tunnel** at 4550 m. (If cycling through the Cahuish Tunnel, make sure you have a strong light so that trucks and buses can see you.) The road through the tunnel is now two lanes. A small stream, up to 30-cm deep, runs inside. On the other side the road descends into the Tambillo Valley, then the Río Mosna gorge before reaching Chavín.

A good spot to see Puya Raimondi plants is the Queshque Gorge. Follow the Río Queshque from Catac; it's easy to find.

Southern Cordillera Blanca

Several kilometres south of Catac is **Pachacoto** from where a road goes to **Huallanca** (Huánuco) on the other side of the Cordillera Blanca (133 km, 4½ hours; see page 588), not to be confused with the town of the same name by the Cañón del Pato. Buses to Huallanca no longer take this route but go on the paved road via Chiquián.

In this southern part of the *cordillera* there are few high, snow-covered peaks, but the glacier of **Pastoruri** is the only skiing area in Peru. It is nothing compared with other skiing areas in South America – there aren't even ski lifts – but it is a place to get in a little practice. Basic ice-climbing skills can also be learnt here. The glacier is receding rapidly and a famous ice cave has melted away to almost nothing. Daily tours from Huaraz to the Pastoruri valley were suspended in 2008 after the local indigenous community decided to close their lands to visitors, but normally tours run via the **Pumapampa Valley**, a good place to see the impressive Puya Raimondi plants. You can hike up the 14-km gravel road from Pachacoto to the Huascarán National Park entrance at 4200 m, in 2½ hours. There's an office here and you can spend the night. Walking up the road beyond this point, you will see more gigantic Puya Raimondi plants. The glacier is a steep one-hour walk up from the car park. Take extra clothing.

Chavín de Huantar → *Colour map 3, B3.*

ⓘ *Daily 0800-1700; some areas are closed to visitors. US$3, US$5 for a group with Spanish-speaking guide; recommended. All galleries open to the public have electric lights. There's a small museum at the entrance, with carvings and Chavín pottery.*

The famous ruins of Chavín de Huantar lie just to the south of the town of Chavín. This fortress temple, built about 800 BC, is the only large structure remaining of the Chavín culture which, in its heyday, is thought to have held influence in a region between Cajamarca and Chiclayo in the north to Ayacucho and Ica in the south. It is a pyramidal structure with several levels of galleries, underground galleries and chambers, many of them in complete darkness. In 1985, UNESCO designated Chavín a World Heritage Site.

The site is in good condition despite the effects of time and nature. The easternmost building was damaged in 1993, when the Río Mosna burst its banks, while in 1945, a major landslide along the Río Huachecsa completely covered the site with mud. It took many years to remove the rubble and some structures remain hidden. Ongoing investigations suggest an extensive tunnel system beyond the boundaries of the current site and research is being carried out by Stanford University. The Huaraz road, which cuts across this area, may have to be moved to the other side of the valley some time in the future in order for excavations to continue.

The main attractions are the marvellous carved stone heads, the designs in relief of symbolic figures (see box, page 389) and the many tunnels and culverts that form an extensive labyrinth throughout the interior of the structures. The carvings are in excellent condition, though many of the best sculptures are in Huaraz and Lima. The famous Lanzón dagger-shaped stone monolith of 800 BC is found inside one of the temple tunnels. Excavations in 2001 uncovered a collection of 20 *pututos* (wind instruments) dating from the site's origins.

Day tours from Huaraz are offered by many agencies; it's a long but worthwhile trip, but check how many hours you get at the site. In high season, the site is busy with

Chavín

Sandoval/Chavín Express

Librería Aquarius @

Municipalidad

Plaza de Armas

To San Marcos & Huari

Pol

Combis to San Marcos & Huari

Inca Roca

Tupac Yupanqui

Mayta Capac

Río Huachecsa

17 de Enero

Wiracocha

San Martín

Julio Tello

To Olleros

Chavín Ruins

To Thermal Baths (2 km) & Huaraz

N

Not to scale

Sleeping 🛏
1 Hostal Chavín
2 Inca
3 La Casona
4 R'ickay

Eating 🍴
1 Buongiorno
2 Chavín Turístico
3 La Portada
4 La Ramada

tourists all day long. You will receive an information leaflet in Spanish at the entrance. The guard also sells other reference material including *Chavín de Huantar* by Willhelm and Nancy Hoogendoorn, an English/Spanish guide to the ruins, which includes a description of each building and an historical overview.

Chavín → *Colour map 3, B3. Altitude: 3160 m.*

The town of Chavín is the commercial centre for the nearby potato- and corn-growing area. The local fiesta takes place on 13-20 July. It has a pleasant plaza with palm and pine trees, and several good, simple hotels and restaurants, the quality of which has improved because of the prosperity brought by the local mining industry. The town is painted in 'colonial yellow' and white, and streets are paved. The shops are well stocked with basic supplies, and carved stone replicas are produced for the tourist trade. There is also a small market. Gasoline is available at the north end of town but there is nowhere to change money. The paved road from Huaraz is much damaged so the trip to Chavín takes about three hours, short enough for a day trip. The **Baños Termales de Chavín** ① *Quercos, Km 68, 2 km south of Chavín, US$0.60*, are hot sulphur baths, consisting of one small, quite cool pool and four individual baths in a pleasant setting by the Río Mosna. You may have to queue and clean the bath yourself. Camping is possible here. The main museum for the area ① *1 km north of town on the road to San Marcos, closed Mon, US$3.75*, has a collection of items not exhibited before, gathered from several deposits and museums.

Callejón de Conchucos → *For listings, see pages 394-398.*

The road north from Chavín descends into the dry Mosna river canyon. This is the start of the route to Pomabamba and beyond. If you plan to travel in this area, allow plenty of time, especially in the rainy season, as the bus service is infrequent.

San Marcos → *Altitude: 2960 m.*

After 8 km is San Marcos, a small, friendly town with a nice plaza and a fancy modern church. It is known as 'City of the Magnolias', but there are few in evidence around the town. Gasoline is available 24 hours. Combis run from San Marcos to the large Canadian-run mine, high on the puna, at **Antamina**, two hours. (Unfortunately, the impressive mine road from Antamina, via Huallanca (Huánuco), to Conococha is privately owned and it is not possible to travel direct from Chavín to Huallanca without returning to Huaraz at present.)

Twenty kilometres beyond San Marcos, at the junction of the Huari and Mosna rivers, is the village of **Pomachaca** (Las Tunas), where a road branches northeast to **Llamellín**. The main road continues north and climbs, criss-crossing the Huari river amid dry hills, to reach Huari 12 km further on.

Huari and around → *Colour map 3, B3. Altitude: 3150 m.*

The town (population: 9000), perched on a hillside at 3120 m, has steep streets with good views of the mountains. The Plaza de Armas and cathedral are modern, having been rebuilt after the 1970 earthquake. Two blocks uphill is the attractive Parque Vigil. There is a nice mirador along the north edge of town, with great views of the mountains and valleys. A pleasant one-hour walk up a stone path from the end of Jr Lima takes you to a large concrete cross at Chullín, with more lovely views. The town has a small fruit and vegetable market, which is quite busy on Sunday, and well-stocked shops. The water supply can be intermittent. Buses leave from the new Terminal Terrestre on Avenida

Circunvalación Baja. The local fiesta of **Nuestra Señora del Rosario** is held during the first two weeks of October, 7 October being the principal day. **Fundación Kuntur** ① *Jr Facundo Villacís 485, T043-753077, kunturhuari@peru.com*, is working to develop community tourism along the Inca Road in this area.

There is a spectacular two- to three-day walk from Huari to Chacas via **Laguna Purhuay**. Muleteers and guides are readily available. The route is clearly shown on the IGM map, sheet 19. The walking is very easy, crossing over a 4500-m pass and through the beautiful Purhuay Valley, at 3500 m. The valley has its own microclimate and the animals, insects and flowers are more like those found in a tropical jungle. At the northern end of Purhuay there's a *quenoal* forest and orchids. There's plenty of running water and lots of good places for camping. There are several tourist activities at the Laguna Purchuay including boat rides and kayak rental (US$3). The pre-Inca remains at LLamacorral are a short walk east from the lake, and have some interesting structures.

A day walk to Laguna Purhuay can be done by those who don't want the longer walk to Chacas, but there is not really enough time to walk the steep paths that go round and above the lake. To get to Laguna Purhuay, climb the stairs at the end of Jirón Luzuriaga in Huari to the main road; turn north, and walk for about 3 km to the village of **Acopalca**, which has a fish farm where you can buy trout. Turn left after crossing the bridge (ask directions), from where it's a 1½-hour walk up to the lake. The path to Chacas forks left just before the lake, while another good trail crosses the outflow and climbs above the eastern shore to a lookout, where it divides: the left fork descends to the inflow, which is a narrow gorge called La Cola (the tail); the right fork climbs to the village of Cachitzinan (no facilities). There are no good trails along the shore of the lake.

Chacas → *Colour map 3, A3. Altitude: 3360 m.*

Ten kilometres south of San Luis, on a new road, is Chacas, with its fine church. The local *fiesta patronal*, Virgen de la Asunción, is on 15 August, with bullfights, a famous *carrera de cintas* (belt race) and fireworks. There are shops, restaurants, a small market and several *hostales*. Seek out the **Taller Don Bosco**, a woodcarving workshop run by an Italian priest.

It is a two-day hike from Chacas to **Marcará** (see page 369) via the Quebradas Juytush and Honda (lots of condors to be seen). The latter is known as the 'Paraíso de las Cascadas' because it contains at least seven waterfalls.

San Luis and around → *Colour map 3, A3. Altitude: 3130 m.*

From Huari the road climbs to the Huachacocha Pass at 4350 m and descends to San Luis at 3130 m. There is basic and cheap accommodation at Hostal Rotta, also a few basic restaurants, shops and a market. To continue north from San Luis, you may have to hire a minibus (US$15 for the vehicle) to take you the 28 km to **Puente Llacma**, the junction of the roads for Yanama and Pomabamba, from where you can hitchhike. The road that branches left at Puente Llacma goes to **Yanama**, 45 km from San Luis, at 3400 m. The village is beautifully surrounded by snow-capped peaks. Three are gold and silver mines to visit as well as several treks. A two-hour walk uphill takes you to the Pupash Pass, from where you get a 270° view of the Cordillera Blanca, including the southeast face of Mount Alpamayo. A day's hike to the ruins above the town affords superb views. There are lodgings and food is available. From Yanama, you can return to Huaraz via Yungay (see page 370).

Piscobamba → *Colour map 3, A3. Altitude: 3290 m.*

A large sanctuary to **Nuestro Señor de Pumayukay**, built by Italian priests, is a 15-minute ride from San Luis towards Pomabamba and then a turn-off to the east. The main road through the Callejón de Conchucos continues north for 62 km to **Piscobamba** ('pampa of the birds', from the Quechua 'Pishco Pampa'). It has a pleasant plaza and spectacular views across the heavily wooded valley to the Cordillera Blanca, stretching from the Alpamayo massif in the north to beyond Huascarán in the south. Hostales **San Pedro** and **Yomara** are both basic. There are also a few shops and small restaurants.

Pomabamba → *Colour map 3, A3. Altitude: 2950 m.*

Known as 'City of the Cedars', though only two very old specimens remain in the centre of the plaza, surrounded by roses and jacarandas, Pomabamba ('pampa of the pumas', Quechua 'Puma Pampa') is 22 km beyond Piscobamba. The main plaza has been rebuilt and there is a small museum and tourist office at Huaraz 515, with variable opening hours. A five-minute walk down a steep path from the plaza and across the river are very hot natural springs and three different bathing establishments, all with private baths (US$0.30 per person, no time limit). Ask for the baths to be cleaned before you use them. The main festival is 24 June.

Treks from Pomabamba

Several good walks into the Cordillera Blanca start from near Pomabamba. You can hike up either the Yanacollpa or Jancapampa valleys, from where you can go on, if you're fit enough, to **Nevado Alpamayo**, dubbed 'the most beautiful mountain in the world', with an incredible glacier. A complete description of this route is given on page 376.

For the less energetic, a good day trip can be made to the quite extensive, though sadly dilapidated, Huari ruins of **Yaino**, on top of a very steep mountain and visible from the main plaza of Pomabamba. The walls are beautifully built and there are two very large buildings, a square one and a circular one. The site commands excellent views of the many peaks of the Cordillera. To get there take a combi to Huaychó, one hour, US$1. Take the path to Garhuay (two hours), a set of smaller Huari ruins, and continue upwards to Yaino (two hours). An alternative return route is to walk down to Huayllan, on the Pomabamba–Huaychó road, and catch a combi (30 minutes). Take food and lots of water, as you can get very dehydrated by climbing and perspiring in the thin dry air. It's also very cold when the sun goes in, so take warm, waterproof clothes.

Another good day walk leaves Pomabamba for the Inca Road: climb from the **Curayacu** fountain to the hamlet of **Cushurú** and then up along the ridge on your right. You can follow the road south and return to Pomabamba via Pajash. There are several unexplored ruins along the Inca Road. To the north is **Mesa Rumi** (two hours), a remarkably precise and unique metre-square block of Inca stone with ceremonial holes in its upper surface.

A shorter walk (three to four hours) begins from the bridge over the river and runs up a side valley, past a trout farm, to the beautiful **Jancapampa Valley** below the Alpamayo massif. Camping is possible there.

Sihuas and beyond → *Colour map 3, A2. Altitude: 2730 m.*

From Pomabamba a dusty road runs up the wooded valley crossing the puna at **Palo Seco**, 23 km. The road then descends steeply into the desert-like Sihuas Valley, passing through the village of **Sicsibamba**. The valley is crossed half an hour below Sihuas.

The small town of Sihuas itself, in a deep valley between high ridges, is divided into three sections spreading over a kilometre up the valley. The lowest district is the oldest with a fine colonial interior to the church. All the bus company offices, hotels and restaurants are in the middle district. The town is a major connection point between the Callejón de Conchucos, Callejón de Huaylas, the upper Marañón and the coast but although you may stop over while travelling between these areas, there is little to do in the immediate surrounding area. The town suffers from water shortages.

The trip from Sihuas to the coast or the Callejón de Huaylas is spectacular, but not for those with a fear of heights. For over an hour the bus climbs steeply along the narrow dirt road winding its way directly above town, to reach the mining town of Pasacancha (3560 m) and a pass at 4100 m. Then it drops to the village of Tarica (3350 m), and down, down, down, to a bridge over the Río Santa at 1200 m, where it joins the Chimbote–Cañón del Pato–Huaraz road.

From Sihuas it is now possible to travel, via Huancaspata, Tayabamba, Retamas and Chahual, to **Huamachuco** along a road which is very poor in places and involves crossing the river Marañón twice. The building of a new bridge over the river means that it is now possible to travel by public transport all the way from Cuzco to Quito through the Andes, without going down to the Pacific Lowlands. The journey is best undertaken in this direction (south–north) though the road may be almost impassable in the wet season. A detour up the Marañón Valley leads to **Huacrachuco**, where there are several basic *hostales*. The significant Inca ruins of **Mamahuagay** are nearby and a five-day walk down to Uchiza in the Huallaga Valley can be made.

◉ Eastern flank of the Cordillera Blanca listings

For Sleeping and Eating price codes and other relevant information, see pages 38-44.

◉ Sleeping

Olleros and around *p387*
D Altas Montañas, Av Puyhuan s/n, T043-422569, www.altasmontanas.com/index9.htm. Small 3-star lodge, Belgian-run, with hot showers, good breakfast included, dinner available, bar, birdwatching, guided treks, information, laundry, recommended for start or end of trek to Chavín, phone 24 hrs in advance, preferably at 2000, to arrange free pickup from Huaraz.

Chavín *p391, map p390*
E Hotel Inca, Wiracocha 170, T043-454021, www.huaraz.com/hotelinca. In a renovated house, with or without bath, good beds, hot water on request, nice garden, friendly.
E La Casona, Wiracocha 130, Plaza de Armas, T043-454116, lacasonachavin@ peru.com.

In an old house with attractive courtyard, private bathroom, cheaper with shared bath, insufficient hot water, friendly, one room with a double bed, motorcycle parking.
E Gran Hotel R'ickay, on 17 de Enero 172N (north), T043-454027, www.hotelrickay.com. Set around two patios, modern, pricey, all rooms with private bathroom and TV, hot water, restaurant (see below).
F Hostal Chavín, Jr San Martín 141-151, half a block from the plaza, T/F043-454055. Set around a pleasant courtyard, hot water, provides breakfast for groups, best of the more basic hotels, friendly and helpful, but poor beds.

Camping
Camping inside park gates at Chavín de Huantar is possible for vehicles, with permission from the guard.

San Marcos *p391*
A pp Konchukos Tambo, 2 km from San Marcos, T043-454631, T043-943 709772 (mob)

in Huaraz, daniela@konchukostambo.com.
A lodge in the Conchucos Valley, about 12 km
from Chavín. Price includes full board and
transport from Huaraz. Bungalow complex,
rooms with stove, bath and hot water.
Gardens, dining room and bar. Activities
include visits to Chavín, hikes, horse riding,
biking and fishing.
G La Rinconada, La Merced 325.
Best of the several basic *hostales*.

Huari and around p391

F Tang Premium, Jr Guzmán Barron 325 y
San Martín, 1 block from Parque Vigil,
T043-797779, T01-992 655429 (Lima mob).
Multistorey building, small bright rooms,
plenty of hot water in morning, clean,
friendly, best in town.
F-G Paraíso, Bolívar 263 y San Martín, 1 block
from Plaza de Armas, T043-453029. Basic,
small rooms, small courtyard, friendly.

Chacas p392

E Alameda, Jr Lima s/n, T043-782838,
hospedajealameda@yahoo.com. Run by
Samuel Obregón and Ana Olórtegui, who
offer 21 double rooms with bath.
E Asunción, Jr Bolognesi s/n, T043-778813,
hospedajeasuncion@yahoo.com. Small
hospedaje run by Samuel Zaragoza and Zelinda
Balmaceda, double rooms with bathroom.
E Carina, Jr Buenos Aires s/n, T043-782722,
ramorchacasino@yahoo.com. Double rooms
with bathroom, comfortable, excellent beds,
breakfast can be arranged the night before,
run by Ernesto Mariluz and Eddy Cafferata.

San Luis and around p392

B-E Andes Lodge Peru, Jr Gran Chavín,
Yanama, 2 blocks from plaza, T043-943-
847423, www.andeslodgeperu.com. Price
depends on season and whether food (good,
home-cooked) is included. Great beds, down
duvets, 24-hr hot water, shared or private
bathroom, good quality new hostel, run
by friendly young local Peruvian, very
knowledgeable. Off the beaten track in
traditional village, good walking, lakes

and ruins nearby, close to National Park
and starting point for Santa Cruz trek.
E Hostal Puñuri, Jr Ramón Castilla 151,
San Luis, T043-830408. Private bathroom,
hot water, clean and friendly.
F Hostal El Pino, Yanama. Clean, with good
views and a small restaurant. Recommended.

Pomabamba p393

F Albergue Turístico Vía, Jr Primavera 323,
T043-741052, verladicho@hotmail.com.
Family run, breakfast available, rooms with
bath and shared bath, cold water, friendly.
Also private bath-house at thermal baths.
G Anny, Jr Moquegua y Jorge Gálvez, barrio
El Convento, T043-751125. Some rooms
with private bath, cold water.
G Hostal Estrada Vidal, Huaraz 209, T043-
804615. Run by friendly Sra Estrada Vidal,
rustic, rooms around a pleasant courtyard,
clean, cold water, good value. Recommended.
G Hostal Pomabamba, Jr Huamachuco 338
on Plaza de Armas, T043-751276. With private
bath, even cheaper without, cold water,
basic but OK.

Sihuas and beyond p393

F-G Hostal Lilian, Jr Ramón Castilla 125 y
Ricardo Palma, T043-441247. Small, simple
rooms, plenty of hot water at night and in
early morning, private or shared bath, laundry
facilities, friendly and helpful, good value.
F-G Hostal Milagritos, Ramón Castilla s/n,
down the hill from Av 28 de Julio, T043-
441163. Ample rooms, some a bit bare,
hot water, private or shared bath, same
management as **Hostal Lilian**.
G Hostal Francesca, Jr Ancash y Raymondi,
1 block from Av 28 de Julio, T043-441329.
Small, basic rooms.

🍴 Eating

Chavín p391, map p390
In the better restaurants, specialities include
rabbit stew, trout *ceviche* and *llunca*, a solid,
wheat-based soup.

R'ickay, see Sleeping, above. Pasta and pizza dishes in the evenings.

Buongiorno, in front of the ruins, just across the bridge. Good trout, cakes and set menu.

Chavín Turístico, 17 de Enero 439. Overpriced and mediocre *menú*, but good à la carte, delicious apple pie, clean, nice courtyard. Beware of overcharging.

La Portada, 17 de Enero 311. In an old house with tables set around a garden.

La Ramada, 17 de Enero. Regional dishes, also trout and set lunch.

San Marcos *p391*

Las Magnolias and Crillón Chico, in the main plaza, are the best of several basic, cheap restaurants.

Huari and around *p391*

El Milagro, San Martín 589 y Bolívar, 1 block from Plaza de Armas. Open daily 0700-2030. Good set meals and à la carte.

Luchito, Jr Bolívar 530, near Plaza de Armas. Open daily 0700-2100. One of several simple places with good set meals or à la carte.

Rinconcito Huaracino, Bolívar 530. Open till 2100. Good *menú*.

Chacas *p392*

Amor Chacasino, Jr Lima s/n, T043-782836, ramorchacasino@yahoo.com. Open daily 0900-2100. Good service, good food and great view.

El Mirador, Jr Lima s/n, Barrio Alameda, T043-782968, miradordechacas@yahoo.com. Open 0900-2100. Great breakfast, good dinner (pasta), awesome view, friendly service, some souvenirs on show and for sale.

Pomabamba *p393*

There is a limited choice of places to eat and most close by 2100.

Davis-David, Huaraz 269. Offers the best *menú* and can prepare soups to order.

Las Piedras, Jr Arica 350. *Menú* and à la carte, including trout.

Los Cedros, Huaraz 531. Good for breakfast.

Sihuas and beyond *p393*

Chosas Náuticas is a basic *comedor* with set meals, also good for breakfast. There are other similar places along Av 28 de Julio.

Sheyla, Jr Ramón Castilla, next to Hostal Lilian. Good set meals.

Transport

The long-distance bus route to the Eastern Cordillera is Lima–Huaraz–Chavín–Huari, with some going on to **San Luis**, a further 61 km, 3 hrs; **Piscobamba**, a further 62 km, 3 hrs; and **Pomabamba**, a further 22 km, 1 hr; other buses from Lima and Huaraz terminate in **Llamellín**, 120 km from Huari, 4 hrs.

Chavín *p391, map p390*
Bus

It is much easier to get to Chavín by bus than it is to leave it. To **Huaraz**, 110 km, 2 hrs, US$3. All buses to Huaraz originate in Huari or beyond. They pass through Chavín at irregular hours and may not have seats available. Buying a ticket at an agency in Chavín does not guarantee you will get a seat or even a bus. Sandoval/Chavín Express passes through around 1200, 1600 and 1700 daily; Río Mosna around 0430, 1600, 1800, 2000, and 2200 daily. All schedules are subject to change during road construction and improvements in the area.

To **Lima**, 438 km, 12 hrs, US$9, with Trans El Solitario and Perú Andino daily. Most companies use older, uncomfortable buses and many locals prefer to travel first to Huaraz and then take one of the more reputable companies from there (see page 367).

To other destinations in the Callejón de Conchucos it is necessary either to use buses coming from Huaraz or Lima, or to hop on and off combis that run between each town. Combis to **San Marcos**, every 20 mins from the Plaza de Armas, 25 mins, US$0.50; to **Huari**, 2 hrs , US$1.50.

Huari and around p391
Bus

Bus companies have their offices around Parque Vigil. To **Huaraz** with Sandoval/Chavín Express, 4 hrs on paved but pot-holed road, daily 1100, 1500, 2200, US$4.10. Buses heading north pass through Huari on their way to San Luis, Piscobamba and Pomabamba, but not every day. To **San Luis**, Tue and Sat, 0600 with El Solitario, 0830 with Perú Andino. To **Pomabamba**, El Solitario coming from Lima passes through Wed, Sat, Sun about 1800, 9 hrs, US$6.50; Turismo Andino on Wed, Sun, 0600. To **Lima**, daily 1900, 12 hrs, US$11, with Turismo Huari, or with Turismo Andino different times daily. On Mon, Tue and Sat buses bound for Lima originating further north pass Huari 1000-1200.

San Luis and around p392
Bus

From San Luis to **Chavín** Wed and Sun, 5 hrs, US$6. To **Huaraz**, via Yanama and the pass at 4730 m under Huascarán, 8 hrs, but public transport is scarce on this route (**Virgen de Guadalupe** buses go to Huaraz via Chacas; **Renzo** buses daily at 0600, 1400, 2000, US$4.40, 5½ hrs, via Carhuaz and Shilla). From Yanama to **Yungay**, 3½ hrs, US$3, several combis daily 0600-0700, passing over the 4767 m Portachuelo de Llanganuco and through Vaquería (on the Santa Cruz trek). Also several in the other direction, especially in the early morning and late afternoon, continuing to **Pomabamba**. The El Pino service has been recommended.

Piscobamba p393

Combis to **Pomabamba** from the Plaza de Armas, hourly 0700-1800, 1 hr, US$1.20. There are no combis from Piscobamba to San Luis.

Pomabamba p393

All transport leaves from the Plaza de Armas. To **Piscobamba**, combis hourly, 1 hr, US$1.20. To **Sihuas**, combis at 0200 daily but best to reserve your seat by arriving at least an hour before, 4 hrs, US$3.80. To **Huaraz**,

combis leave mid-morning, 7 hrs, US$6, via **Yungay**, 6 hrs, US$6. Additional departures with **Renzo** at 1300 and 1945 daily; Los Andes at 1945 daily.

To **Lima**, 18 hrs, US$11, via **San Luis**, 4 hrs, US$3; **Huari**, 6 hrs, US$4.50; and **Chavín**, 9 hrs, US$6, with El Solitario, Sun, Mon and Thu 0800. To **Lima**, 16 hrs, US$11, via Yungay and Huaraz with La Perla del Alto Mayo, Wed, Thu, Sat, Sun.

Sihuas and beyond p393

To **Pomabamba**, combis daily at around 1100, 4 hrs, US$3.80; no office, be out on the street early to get a seat. To **Huaraz**, via Huallanca, with Cielo Azul, daily 0830, 10 hrs, US$8 (Jr Caraz 833, Huaraz), **Trans Chavín Express**, Wed and Sat, and Perú Andino, Tue 1100, 8 hrs, US$7. To **Tayabamba**, for the Marañón route north to Huamachuco and Cajamarca, with **Andía** (en route from Lima) Sat and Sun 0100-0200, 8 hrs, US$8, or La Perla del Alto Mayo (also from Lima), Tue and Thu, 2400-0200; also Garrincha Wed, Sun 0800; the beginning of a long wild ride. To **Huacrachuco**, Trans Andina, daily 1000; Andía (en route from Lima) passes Wed, Sat about 0100, US$3.20, 4 hrs, returning same days at 1000. To **Chimbote**, La Perla del Alta Mayo Tue, Thu and Sun, 10 hrs, US$9; Corvival, Wed, Thu, Sun in the morning, 9 hrs, US$6.50, returning Wed, Fri, Sun. To **Lima** via Chimbote, with Andía Tue and Sun 0200, Wed, Sat 1600, 19 hrs, US$14.40; Amanecer Pampino, Fri 1800; Rosario, Mon 0800; La Perla del Alto Mayo, Mon, Fri 1800; confirm all times locally. To **Trujillo** via Chimbote, Garrincha Mon and Thu 2200, 12 hrs, US$12.50.

ⓘ Directory

Chavín p391, map p390

Internet At Librería Aquarius, 17 de Enero y Túpac Yupanqui, US$1 per hr. **Post** At 17 de Enero 365N (north). 0630-2200. **Telephone** Pay phones all over town.

Huari and around *p391*

Bank Banco de la Nación, Jr San Martín y Guzmá Barron, 1 block from Parque Vigil, Mon-Fri 0900-1730, Sat 0900-1300, US$ cash only, no TCs, ATM or cash advances. Some shops may change US$ cash at poor rates. **Internet** Many places, US$0.30 per hr.

Sihuas and beyond *p393*

Bank Banco de la Nación, Plaza de Armas, US$ cash only at fair rates, Mon-Fri 0800-1730, Sat 0900-1300, no TCs, ATM or cash advances. Hostel owners change US$ cash at poor rates. **Internet** Several places, US$0.50 per hr.

Cordilleras Huayhuash and Raura

→ *Colour map 3, B3/4*

Lying south of the Cordillera Blanca, the Cordillera Huayhuash has been dubbed the 'Himalayas of America' and is perhaps the most spectacular in Peru for its massive ice faces that seem to rise sheer out of the contrasting green of the puna. Azure trout-filled lakes are interwoven with deep quebradas and high pastures around the hem of the range. You may see tropical parakeets in the bottom of the gorges and condors circling the peaks.

Although the area may well have been inhabited for thousands of years, the Huayhuash only became known to the outside world following a plane crash on the southeast face of Jirishanca in 1954. Since then, the number of visitors has grown steadily, with a hiatus during the era of insurgency in the 1980s. The mountain range's renown increased following Joe Simpson and Simon Yates' near-tragic climbing expedition in 1985, as recounted in Simpson's book and the subsequent hit film, Touching the Void. *Although less touristy than some popular routes in the Cordillera Blanca, it nonetheless receives significant numbers of trekkers and climbers every year.*

The area is rugged and traditional, with local villagers generally surviving as herdsmen, tending flocks of cattle, sheep and alpacas. Having said that, tourism, large-scale mining interests and the relentless advance of paved roads has significantly affected the area, its people and environment, not always for the better. ▶▶ *For listings, see page 402.*

Ins and outs

Getting there Both the Huayhuash and Raura ranges can be approached from **Chiquián** in the north; from **Oyón**, with links to Cerro de Pasco to the southeast; from **Churín** in the south, or from **Cajatambo** to the southwest. Coming from Huaraz, the road is now paved beyond Chiquián as far as **Huansala**, on the road to Huallanca (Huánuco). Whereas only five years ago it was necessary to hike from Chiquián through semi-desert canyons for a couple of days before reaching the peaks, now you can drive directly to the base of the cordillera and the trailhead close to the settlements of **Matacancha** and **Rondoy**. In the south, surfaced roads from Cajatambo now push as far as the breathtaking **Punta Cuyoc**, situated between the Cordilleras Huayhuash and Raura.

Trekking Trekking in the Cordillera Huayhuash is generally considered difficult and certainly requires stamina, with up to eight passes over 4600 m, depending on the route. Ten to 12 days are required for the complete loop, but the trails are good and most gradients are relatively gentle. Moreover, due to improving road access (see below), many Huaraz-based tour agencies (see page 364) now offer shortened eight-day itineraries.

Safety and practicalities The roads and increasing popularity have brought significant waste-disposal issues and problems with aggressive behaviour and armed robbery. Local communities now provide an armed escort service for all trekking groups in between Huayhuash and Viconga lake. Each community charges an obligatory fee for protection on its land before handing responsibility over to the next village. Make sure you hang on to **all** receipts/tickets and know exactly what you are paying for. Once you arrive at any campsite, licensed members of the corresponding community will show up with tickets. Once you pay for you and your pack animals this covers your camping fees, use of pastures, security and cleaning up of the trails and campsites. Camping fees in 2008 were US$32 for Llamac to Cajatambo and US$50 for the full loop. Obtain full details on arrival in the area.

Maps The 2nd edition of Brad Johnson's 1:50,000 topographic map (revised 2004) is highly recommended, if not essential, for adventures in the Huayhuash. It can be obtained internationally through map specialists such as **Stanfords** in London, several locations in Huaraz (eg **Café Andino**; see page 362), or from branches of **South American Explorers** in Lima and Cuzco.

Chiquián → *Phone code: 043. Altitude: 3400 m.*

Chiquián is a little town of narrow streets and overhanging eaves. An interesting feature is a public television mounted in a box on a pedestal that sits proudly in the Plaza de Armas, around which folks gather every evening. There is a **Semana Turística** during the first week of July and the local fiesta is celebrated on 30 August in honour of Santa Rosa.

Cajatambo → *Phone code: 043. Altitude: 3380 m.*

The southern approach to the Cordillera Huayhuash is a small, developing market town, with a beautiful 18th-century church and a lovely plaza. Note that the road out of Cajatambo is not for the fainthearted. For the first three to four hours it is no more than a bus-width, clinging to the cliff edge.

Huayhuash Circuit

(Figures in the text and on the map indicate the most usual camping sites.) The trail head is at **Cuartel Huain (1)**, between Matacancha and the **Punta Cacanan Pass** (the

Cordilleras Huayhuash & Raura

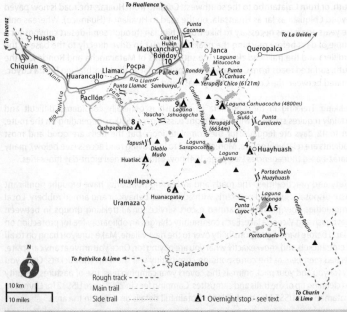

continental divide at 4700 m). This northernmost point on the trek gives access to the village of Janca, to Laguna Mitucocha (2) and to the eastern flank of the Cordillera. A very steep short cut on scree takes you through the gap in the northern spur of the range above Matacancha and Janca village on the other side. This could save two or three hours.

The eastern side of the Cordillera is a chain of passes, lakes and stunning views of Jirishanca Chico, Yerupajá Chico, Yerupajá (Peru's second highest peak at 6634 m) and Siulá Grande. From Janca, a small side valley leads off Quebrada Mitucocha to Punta Carhuac (4650 m) and beyond to Laguna Carhuacocha, with magnificent camping (3) and views. Following on from there are Punta Carnicero (4600 m) – a section of Inca road and petroglyphs are found nearby – the twin lakes of Azulcocha and Atoqshaico (just beyond the pass) and Huayhuash village (4 – one house).

This is the regular route, but a new route is also open, following round Laguna Carhuacocha, passing Laguna Siulá and emerging on the regular route just before Huayhuash village. This trail has gained popularity thanks to *Touching the Void*; there are no maps and it is for experienced trekkers only. A guide is recommended as the weather can change very suddenly.

The next pass, Portachuelo Huayhuash (4750 m, the continental divide), overlooks the superb southward line of pyramidal peaks and rounded ice caps of the Cordillera Raura. A path leads from Laguna Viconga below (5 – near the dam), over a pass and hugs the western flank of the Raura all the way to Oyón. (Transportes Javier run a daily bus from Raura to Cerro de Pasco, seven hours, US$5.50; there are also daily buses from Oyón.) Four hours away from Oyón is Churín, which boasts the 'best thermal baths in Peru'. There is also a small thermal pool 1 km past the outflow of Viconga, along the trail to Cajatambo. Note that water is released from the Viconga dam daily 0500-1100, and you cannot ford the outflow during this time. If you are bailing out at Cajatambo (6), it is downhill all the way from Laguna Viconga, apart from a short sting in the tail at the end.

Those continuing the circuit must cross the Punto Cuyoc (5000 m), sometimes snowbound, with outstanding 360° views. This is the highpoint of the circuit in every sense of the word. There follows a long, gentle descent into the Quebrada Huanacpatay (6 on the full circuit) and an optional one-day side trip up the valley of the Río Huayllapa to Laguna Jurau and Laguna Sarapococha, both beautiful lakes.

The route continues downhill to the village of Huayllapa (with shop and basic lodging and meals); just before town it turns north to begin climbing to the Tapush Pass (4800 m) below the summit of Diablo Mudo (also known as Suerococha), via Huatiac (7).

After the pass you reach Cashpapampa (8), from where you head east to the Yaucha Pass (4800 m, outstanding views), then north, by way of the Quebrada Huacrish, to Laguna Jahuacocha, which lies beneath Yerupajá and *nevados* Jirishanca and Rondoy. The lake offers the most idyllic campsite (9) in the Cordillera. It can also be reached from Llamac, by crossing over the Punta Llamac Pass at 4300 m, southeast of that town: first head southwest along a path just beneath the cemetery and zigzag up above the town. Llamac is also used as a starting point for the trek. You can camp on the football pitch (US$1.50 per night) and drinking water is available from the water source that is 200 m on the trail north to Pocpa; ask locals.

The 4800-m Sambunya Pass, beneath Rondoy, leads to the descent to the town of Rondoy (10), Matacancha and the trail head.

Cordilleras Huayhuash and Raura listings

For Sleeping and Eating price codes and other relevant information, see pages 38-44.

Sleeping

Chiquián *p400*
E Gran Hotel Huayhuash, 28 de Julio 400 esq Figueredo, T043-447049, www.hotel huayhuash.com. Private bathroom, hot water, TV, restaurant, laundry, parking, modern, great views, information and tours.
F Hostal San Miguel, Jr Comercio 233, Chiquián, T043-447001. Nice courtyard and garden, clean, many rooms, popular.
G pp Los Nogales, Jr Comercio 1301, T043-447121 (in Lima T01-460 8037), hotel_nogales_chiquian@yahoo.com. With bath, hot water, cable TV, laundry, internet, cafe, parking. Recommended.

Cajatambo *p400*
G Hostal Cajatambo, on the plaza 315, T043-244 2036. Basic, cheap, not for the squeamish as the courtyard is a chicken slaughterhouse.
G Hostal Miranda, Jr Tacna 141. Homely, friendly, cold shower, basic. Recommended.
G Hostal Tambomachay, Jr Bolognesi 110, T043-244 2046. Nice courtyard and restaurant.
G Hostal Trinidad, Jr Raimondi 141. Basic.

Eating

Chiquián *p400*
❖ **El Refugio de Bolognesi**, Tarapacá 471. Offers basic set meals.
❖ **Panificadora Santa Rosa**, Comercio 900, on the plaza. For good bread and sweets.
❖ **Yerupajá**, Jr Tarapacá 351. For basic set meals and information.

Cajatambo *p400*
❖ **Restaurant Andreita**, Av Grau 440.

Activities and tours

Chiquián *p400*
Sr Delao Callupe is a guide for the Huayhuash. Ask for him in Chiquián.

Transport

Chiquián *p400*
To **Huaraz**, Chiquián Tours leave from the plaza daily 0500, US$1.75; **El Rápido**, T043-747049, leaves from Jr Figueredo 216, daily 0500 and 1330, US$3.65. Also colectivo Chiquián–Huaraz 1500, 3 hrs, US$2.45 per person. To **Llamac**, 0900 and 1700 (returning 0800 and 1200), 1½ hrs, US$2; book as early as possible. Llamac to Huaraz, with a change in Chiquián, 1130, arrive 1630.

There is also a connection from Chiquián to **Huallanca** (Huánuco) with buses coming up from Lima in the early morning and combis during the day, which leave when full, 3 hrs, US$2.50. From Huallanca there are regular combis on to **La Unión**, 1 hr, US$0.75, and from there transport to **Huallanca** (Huánuco).

Cajatambo *p400*
Buses to **Lima** leave daily 0600, US$8.80, with Empresa Andina (office on plaza next to Hostal Cajatambo) and **Tour Bello**, one block off the plaza. The only way back to **Huaraz** is via Pativilca on the coast, a long detour. Buses from Cajatambo arrive in **Pativilca** around midday; wait for Lima–Huaraz buses to pass between 1330 and 1400 and arrive in Huaraz about 1700. Turismo Cajatambo, Jr Grau 120 (in Lima, Av Carlos Zavala 124 corner of Miguel Aljovin 449, T01-426 7238, in Barranca, Prologación Sáenz Peña 139).

Contents

Footprint features

Border crossings

North Coast

At a glance

⊖ **Getting around** Plane and bus.

◉ **Time required** 1 to 3 weeks, depending on how many centres you choose to visit.

☼ **Weather** Summer months are Dec-Apr. There may be sea mists from May-Oct, more so the further south you are.

✕ **When not to go** There is no time to avoid the North Coast, but keep an eye on weather predictions for El Niño events, which tend to affect the North Coast worse than elsewhere.

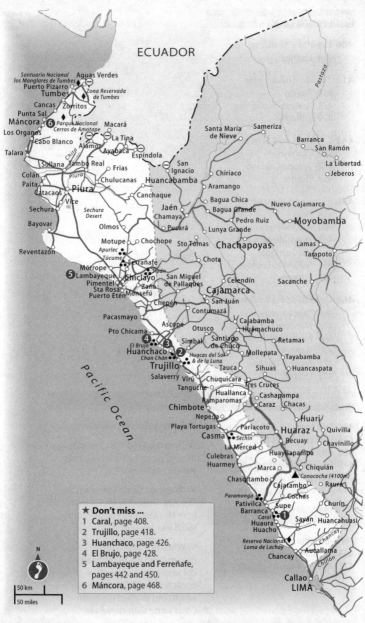

ECUADOR

Santuario Nacional
los Manglares de Tumbes · Aguas Verdes
Puerto Pizarro
Tumbes · Zona Reservada
Cancas · de Tumbes
Punta Sal · Zorritos
Máncora · Parque Nacional
Los Organos · Cerros de Amotape
Cabo Blanco · Macará
Talara · Alamor · Ayabaca
Sullana · Tambo Real
Colán · Frias · Espíndola
Paita · Chulucanas · San Ignacio
Catacaos · Piura · Canchaque · Chiriaco
Sechura · Vice · Aramango
Bayovar · Sechura · Jaén · Bagua Chica · Nuevo Cajamarca
Desert · Chamaya · Bagua Grande · Moyobamba
Olmos · Pucará · Pedro Ruiz · Lamas
Reventazón · Motupe · Chochope · Sto Tomas · Chachapoyas · Tarapoto
Apurlec · Chota · Sacanche
Mórrope · Túcume · Ferreñafe · Celendín
Lambayeque · Sipán · San Miguel · Cajamarca
Pimentel · Chiclayo · de Pallaques
Sta Rosa · Zaña · Monsefú · San Juan
Puerto Etén · Chepén · Contumazá · Cajabamba
Pacasmayo · Ascope · Otusco · Huamachuco
Pto Chicama · Santiago · Retamas
El Brujo · Simbal · de Chuco · Tayabamba
Huanchaco · Huacas del Sol · Mollepata · Huancaspata
Chan Chán · & de la Luna
Trujillo · Tauca · Sihuas
Salaverry · Viru · Chuquicara · Tres Cruces
Tanguche · Huallanca · Cashapampa
Chimbote · Pamparomas · Caraz · Chacas
Nepeña · Pariacoto · Huari
Playa Tortugas · Huaraz · Quivilla
Casma · Sechín · Recuay · Chavinillo
La Merced · Huayllapampa
Culebras · Marca · Chiquián
Huarmey · Chasqitambo · Conococha (4100m) · Rauré
Paramonga · Cochas · Churín
Pativilca · Supe
Barranca · Caral · Sayán · Huancahuasi
Huaura
Huacho
Reserva Nacional
Loma de Lachay · Chancay · Aucallama
Callao
LIMA

Pacific Ocean

Pastaza

Santa María · Samериza
de Nieve · Barranca · San Ramón
La Libertad · Jeberos

Huancabamba

★ Don't miss ...

1 Caral, page 408.
2 Trujillo, page 418.
3 Huanchaco, page 426.
4 El Brujo, page 428.
5 Lambayeque and Ferreñafe,
 pages 442 and 450.
6 Máncora, page 468.

N

50 km
50 miles

Peru's north coast could well be described as the Egypt of South America. This is a region of numerous monumental ruins, built by the many highly skilled pre-Inca cultures that once thrived here. The recent, ground-breaking discovery at Caral is now open to visitors. Not far from Trujillo, Chan Chán was the capital of the Chimú Kingdom; its crumbling remains still represent the largest adobe city in the world. The Huaca de la Luna and the Huaca Cao Viejo of the Moche Empire are revealing fabulous, multicoloured friezes of gods from the first millennium AD. At the latter, at El Brujo, north of Trujillo, the mummy of a tattooed woman has also been found. Further north, near Chiclayo, the adobe brick pyramids of Túcume, Sipán and Sicán rise massively from the coastal plains. The wealth from some of their tombs is now displayed in new, state-of-the-art museums.

But it's not all pyramids and royal tombs. The elegant city of Trujillo is one of the finest examples of colonial architecture in the country. There are charming towns such as Huanchaco, with its bizarre-looking reed fishing rafts, and Chulucanas, with its famous pottery. Lambayeque Department has umpteen festivals; you can visit witchdoctors or simply buy their potions; up and down the coast the seafood is wonderful and the hospitality unrivalled. In addition, the northern seaboard enjoys a rain-free climate all year, and sports Peru's finest beaches for bathing and surfing. Around Tumbes, the most northerly provincial capital, three reserves protect mangroves, equatorial dry scrub and rainforest, each of which contains endangered species, from crocodiles to eagles.

Lima to Chimbote

Between Lima and Pativilca there is a narrow belt of coastal land deposited at the mouths of the rivers and, from Pativilca to the mouth of the Río Santa, north of Chimbote, the Andes come down to the sea. The Pan-American Highway parallels the coast all the way to the far north, and feeder roads branch from it up the various valleys. ▸▸ *For listings, see pages 414-417.*

Pasamayo sand dune

Just north of Ancón, see page 97, the Pasamayo sand dune, stretching for 20 km, comes right down to the seashore. The old road that snakes above the sea is spectacular, but is now closed except to commercial traffic and buses. The new toll road, which goes right over the top, is safe and gives spectacular views over the nearby coast and valleys.

Chancay Valley → *Colour map 3, C3.*

Though the Chancay Culture once extended across many valleys to the north of Lima and much evidence of ceramic artefacts can be seen in museums, there are no significant remains in the valley. There are, however, two curiosities to distract the traveller. As the old coastal road descends into the valley a complex of strange, decorated, conical structures made of adobe comes into view (Km 63). **Eco Truly Park** ① *Eco Truly Tours, Javier Prado Este 185, Lima, T01-421 0016, www.ecotrulypark.org,* is run by the Hare Krishna movement and consists of a temple complex, vegetarian restaurant, organic farm and rustic accommodation for visitors in the *trulys* (conical constructions, **C-E**, depending on whether meals and yoga are included). Weekend visits cost US$23.75-29 for one day to US$49 for two days, with guided tours. Yoga lessons cost US$5.50 on Sunday and other therapies and courses are run regularly. **Chancay 'castle'** ① *entrance and tour US$1.50,* built by a bohemian descendant of the last viceroy in the 1920s, is located on the cliff tops in Chancay town. Once visited by the elite of Lima, it is now a decaying recreational centre with restaurants, bars, pools and a museum containing many Chancay culture artefacts.

Just inland from the coastal town of Chancay is **Huaral**, which gives access to the Chancay Valley, up which are the extraordinary, little-visited ruins of **Chiprac**, **Rupac** and **Añay**. Chiprac is a 2½-hour climb from **Huascoy** (see below). The Salvador family has accommodation and Carlos is a recommended guide for the ruins, though a guide is not strictly necessary. It is a good day's walk there and back with time to take photographs and eat. Huascoy celebrates the **Fiesta de San Cristóbal** in the week before Independence (28 July), with a procession, masses, dancing, fireworks and football matches. **Rupac** is best reached from La Florida. Its ruins are the best preserved of the group, though less extensive than Chiprac. All the ruins have complete roofs, which is unique in Peru. For **Añay**, go to Huaral as for the other ruins, then get transport to Huayopampa (basic accommodation) or La Perla from where the ruins can easily be reached. Get a guide to take you there from either village.

Reserva Nacional de Lachay

① *Tue-Sun 0830-1730, US$1.85 (children half price), T01-377 1621.*

Just north of the southern turn-off to Sayán is a track signposted to the **Lomas de Lachay** (5070 ha). Lima–Huacho buses (see Transport, below) drop off/pick up visitors from Km 105. It is 3 km, a one-hour walk, up to the guard post.

This small reserve is a typical example of 'loma' habitat, and it holds several important species. Loma vegetation is formed during the winter months, when fog caused by the Humboldt Current drives inland, rises and condenses, and forms a dew on the surrounding landscape. This dew is sufficient to sustain the seasonal loma or 'fog vegetation' that is the home of birds such as the endemic Raimondi's yellow-finch and thick-billed miner. Within just 5 km the landscape changes from barren desert to a green carpet, resonating with the sound of birdcalls. In September and October the plants are in bloom and very beautiful. There is a visitor centre, trails and picnic areas. Camping is permitted at the visitor centre in the heart of the reserve, 2 km beyond the guard post, US$3.70 per night, bring all food and water, especially in the dry season (January-March). The reserve is very popular with Lima residents at the weekend.

Huacho → Colour map 3, B3. Population: 35,900.

At Km 101 is Huacho, where you can turn off the Pan-American and head west to Puerto Huacho, which is the outlet for cotton and sugar grown in the rich Huaura Valley. There are cotton-seed oil and other factories. The port and sea are sometimes alive with huge jellyfish. There are several basic hotels at Huacho (none at the port). A turn-off at Km 135 leads to **El Paraíso**, where endless, empty beaches and calm, clear waters attract campers in summer. There is good fishing and windsurfing. Birdwatchers should go to the nearby lagoon, formed by run-off from an irrigation project, where over 100 species have been recorded.

Huacho to Churín

The journey inland from Huacho, up the Huaura Valley, is spectacular. **Sayán**, 30 km inland, is an attractive agricultural town at the base of the Andean foothills. It would be a nicer place to stay en route to Churín than the coastal towns, if there were more choice in the way of hotels. Combis go every half hour to Huacho from Avenida Balta. Buses from Lima for Churín stop at the bridge.

Churín → Colour map 3, B3. Population: 2000. Altitude: 2080 m.

Beyond Sayán the road follows the Huaura Valley which narrows almost to a gorge before climbing steeply to Churín, one of Peru's best-known spas, with hot, sulphurous springs used to cure a number of ailments. The climate is dry, with temperatures ranging from 10°C to 32°C. The area is famous for cheese, yoghurt and other natural products. Churín is popular with Limeños. Accommodation and buses are fully booked at holiday times.

A highly recommended excursion can be made up a side valley, 5 km below Churín, to **Huancahuasi**. The new Huancahuasi baths include a pool that ex-President Fujimori swam in (hot, US$1 per person), while on the opposite side of the river the new **Picoy** baths include excellent private pools carved out of the rock (hot, US$0.50 per person). Snacks such as *pachamanca* are available at riverside stalls. The trip includes a stop-off at Picoy, which has a remarkable colonial church with a highly carved façade, and at **Chiuchin**. Chiuchin baths ⓘ *US$0.50 per person for pool; US$0.75 per person for private baths*, are now rather neglected and run down. Combis leave from beside the church in Churín for the two-hour trip 0800-0900, returning 1500-1700. A round trip costs US$3.50.

Huacho to Barranca

The town of **Huaura,** on the north bank of the Río Huaura, has grown little over the last 200 years but remains hugely significant in the annals of Peruvian Independence. It was here that General San Martín first proclaimed the country's independence from Spain, eight months prior to the official declaration of Independence in Lima. The house with the balcony from which he made the proclamation is now a small **museum** ① *0900-1700, US$1*. Stand on the balcony yourself and re-enact the declaration.

The road passes from the valley of Mazo through the irrigated valley of San Felipe. There is more desert and then the cotton-fields of San Nicolás lead to **Supe** at Km 187, and nearby Puerto Supe, a busy port shipping fishmeal, cotton, sugar and minerals. At **El Aspero**, near Supe, is one of the earliest pre-historic sites in Peru, see page 643.

At **Barranca** (Km 195, by-passed by the Highway), 1 km below the town, lies the long, sandy Chorrillos beach, which is windy but popular with surfers.

Caral

① *Open 0900-1700, all visitors must be accompanied by an official guide, US$7 per group, in the car park is the ticket office, toilets and handicrafts stalls. Visitors can stay or camp at the Casa del Arqueólogo. For details, Proyecto Especial Caral, Av Las Lomas de la Molina 327, Urb Las Lomas, Lima 12, T205 2500 ext 517, www.caralperu.gob.pe. It is a UNESCO World Heritage Site.*
A few kilometres before Barranca, a turning to the right (east) at Km 184 leads to Caral, a city 26 km from the coast whose date (about 2600 BC) and monumental construction are overturning many of the accepted theories of Peruvian archaeology. It appears to be easily the oldest city-state in South America. Tours operate from Lima; also see page 416.

The dry, desert site lies on the southern fringes of the Supe Valley, along whose flanks there are many more ruins, 19 out of 32 of which have been explored. On the coast the fishing port of Bandurria is believed to be the place from where the people of Caral traded. It is possible to visit Bandurria and have a community tour. Caral itself covers 66 ha and contains eight significant pyramidal structures. To date seven have been excavated by archaeologists from the University of San Marcos, Lima. One remains unexcavated, a rounded mound of stone and sand showing no discernible sign of its likely inner contents. The seven pyramids investigated reveal a stone and mortar construction with a yellow and white wash being the most common finish, small areas of which remain visible. Archaeologists are undertaking careful restoration upon the existing foundations to re-establish the pyramidal tiers. It is possible to walk around the pyramids. A viewpoint provides a panorama across the whole site. **Pirámide de Anfiteatro** (11 m high), on the north side of the small pyramid, is a large amphitheatre from which a series of ceremonial rooms rise. **Pirámide de la Huanca** (12 m high) is constructed in three tiers with a 23-step staircase leading up to the ceremonial platform. It takes its name from the large stone obelisk (*huanca*) in the centre of the plaza, which it overlooks. The residence of the elite, a complex of well-built adobe rooms, abuts the pyramid. **Pirámide de la Galería** (the gallery pyramid, 17 m high) has a nearly 7-m-wide stairway leading up to a room sunk into the ceremonial platform lined with huarango wood and containing eight huge whalebone vertebrate seats. **Pirámide Menor** (7.5 m high) is the smallest of the pyramids. **Pirámide Mayor** (the great pyramid, 153.5 by 110 by 28 m) is the largest pyramid with a sunken circular plaza on its south side. Two *lanzones* (obelisk-sized stones) frame the two entrances to the plaza and a further *lanzón* sits atop the pyramid which is reached by an impressive 9-m-wide stairway from the plaza. **Pirámide de la Cantera** (the quarry pyramid, 13.5 m high) is the only pyramid partly straddling a rock outcrop, much of which was used in its construction. A 4.2-m-wide stairway with 32 steps ascends to the summit, on which is a round, walk-in altar with an outer wall 8 m in diameter and an inner wall 3.7 m in diameter, inside which there was a central fireplace. In addition, there is a long building containing 18 internal niches along each facing wall. **El Templo de Altar Circular**

(4 m high) consists of at least 13 rooms in at least two groupings. Inside one square room there is a 2.7-m-diameter walk-in altar with a central fireplace. Some later adobe ruins of the Chancay era fringe the site. Detailed, illustrated Spanish information panels are located around the site, which is well organized, criss-crossed by paths that must be adhered to. Allow at least two hours to visit the site.

Pativilca to Huaraz

The straggling town of Pativilca (Km 203), has a small museum and a good, cheap restaurant, **Cornejo**. Just beyond town, a good paved road turns east for Huaraz in the Cordillera Blanca, see page 354.

The road at first climbs gradually from the coast. At Km 48, just west of the town of **Chasquitambo (Restaurante Delicias)** it reaches Rumi Siki (Rump Rock), with unusual rock formations, including the one that gives the site its name. Beyond this point, the grade is steeper and at Km 120 the chilly pass at 4080 m is reached. Shortly after, **Laguna Conococha** comes into view, where the Río Santa rises. Delicious trout is available in Conococha village. A road branches off from Conococha to **Chiquián** (see page 400) and the Cordilleras Huayhuash and Raura to the southeast. After crossing a high plateau the main road descends gradually for 47 km until **Catac** (see page 388), where another road branches east to Chavín and on to the **Callejón de Conchucos** (see page 391). **Huaraz** is 36 km further on and the road then continues north through the Callejón de Huaylas.

Four kilometres beyond the turn-off to Huaraz, beside the Pan-American Highway, are the well-preserved ruins of the Chimú **temple of Paramonga** ① *US$1.80*, set on high ground with a view of the ocean, the fortress-like mound is reinforced by eight quadrangular walls rising in tiers to the top of the hill. It is well worth visiting. No buses run to the ruins, only to the port (about 15 mins from Barranca), a taxi from Paramonga and return after waiting costs US$6, otherwise take a Barranca-Paramonga port bus, then it's a 3-km walk. The town of **Paramonga** is a small port, 3 km off the Pan-American Highway, 4 km from the ruins and 205 km from Lima.

Casma to Huaraz via Pariacoto

Between Pativilca and Chimbote the mountains come down to the sea. The road passes by a few very small protected harbours in tiny rock-encircled bays – **Huarmey**, **Culebras**

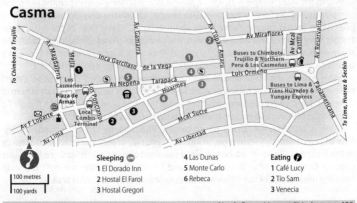

Casma

Sleeping		Eating
1 El Dorado Inn	4 Las Dunas	1 Café Lucy
2 Hostal El Farol	5 Monte Carlo	2 Tío Sam
3 Hostal Gregori	6 Rebeca	3 Venecia

and **Vesique**. Both Huarmey and Culebras have fine beaches. Between Paramonga and Huarmey there are restaurants at Km 223 and 248.

Largely destroyed by the 1970 earthquake, **Casma** has since been rebuilt, partly with Chilean help. It has a pleasant Plaza de Armas, several parks and two markets including a good food market. Sechín ruins are only 5 km away and it is a much nicer place to stay than Chimbote. The weather is usually sunny, hence its title Ciudad del Sol Eterno (City of Eternal Sun).

From Casma a road runs inland over the **Callán Pass** (4224 m) 150 km to Huaraz. It's a difficult but beautiful trip, and worth taking in daylight. Few buses take this route, so check before leaving (see Transport, page 416).

From Casma the first 50 km are paved, then a good dirt road follows for 20 km to **Pariacoto**. From here to the pass the road is rough, with landslides in the rainy season, but once the Cordillera Negra has been crossed, the wide, gravel road is better with spectacular views of the Cordillera Blanca. To catch the best views, before the Cordillera Blanca becomes covered in cloud (usually in the afternoon), take the earliest bus possible. Sit on the right-hand side of the bus.

Sechín → *Colour map 3, B2.*

ⓘ *Daily 0800-1800, www.xanga.com/sechin, US$1.80, children half price; the ticket is also valid for the museum and Pañamarca (see page 412). Frequent colectivos leave early in the morning from in front of the market in Casma, US$0.50 per person; otherwise take a mototaxi for US$1 per person.*

This is one of the most important ruins on the Peruvian coast. It consists of a large square temple completely faced with carved stone monoliths – probably over 500 of them – representing two lines of warriors marching towards the principal entrance from opposite sides. Between each warrior are carvings of men being eviscerated, heads with blood gushing from eyes or mouths, dismembered legs, arms, torsos, ears, eyes and vertebrae.

The mural is thought by some to narrate the results of a battle, with the fates of the conquerors and the conquered graphically depicted. Others believe it shows ritual rather than actual combat. Either way, the style is unique in Peru for its naturalistic vigour. The importance of the site lies in the fact that it is one of the oldest centres in the country to demonstrate war-like activity, ceremonial or otherwise, and the extent to which extreme violence was a part of life.

Within the stone temple is an earlier, pre-ceramic mud temple with painted walls. The complex as a whole forms a temple-palace associated with the development of the local pre-Chavín Sechín culture, dating from about 1600 BC. Three sides of the large stone temple have been excavated and restored. You cannot see the adobe buildings inside the stone walls, which belong to an earlier period. They were later covered up and used as a base for a second storey which, unfortunately, has been completely destroyed.

Some experts think the temple and surroundings were buried on purpose. Others believe it was engulfed by natural disaster. The latter theory is supported by finds of human skeletons. Tombs have been found in front and at the same level as the temple. A wall of a large adobe building under excavation runs round the sides and back of the temple.

There is an attractive, shady picnic garden. Photography is best around midday. **Max Uhle Museum** by the ruins has an interesting display of Sechín artefacts and a replica of the façade of the inner adobe temple. If you need a guide ask in advance for Wilder León or Carlos Cuy, who speaks English and French. Outside the museum is a map showing the location of the different archaeological sites in the Casma area.

Two kilometres further along is **Sechín Alto**, two pyramids of the late Chavín period, but these have not yet been extensively excavated. Follow the track to the west (left) at the Km 4 post past the first, smaller pyramid and the farmhouse. The second pyramid is huge, measuring 300 m x 250 m x 25 m, covering 50 ha, and once consisted of three levels. Though most of the stone façade has turned to rubble, small sections of the exterior wall and huge entrance stones on the north side are visible. Recent investigations have uncovered some storage chambers and adobe platforms built from unusual conical adobes atop the pyramid. At **Sechín Bajo** excavations have revealed a circular sunken plaza and other buildings which, archaeologists claim, date back to 3600 BC, the oldest construction in Peru.

Among numerous other sites in the area, there are two of particular interest, but a mototaxi is needed to visit them. At Km 15 on the Pariacoto road there are several lines and figures etched in the desert surface, as at Nazca. Though nowhere near as impressive as the Nazca Lines, the figure of a 'warrior' is clearly visible from a nearby hilltop. The lines are up to 25 m long, 20 cm wide and have been dated to 1000 BC. Archaeologists are uncertain as to their purpose.

Chanquillo, located off the Panamericana at Km 361, is a 2300-year-old structure on a hilltop. It consists of three concentric stone walls with rectangular and circular buildings inside the interior wall. Some of the original carob tree supports remain. Beyond the ruins, stretching for over 300 m along a ridge, are 13 towers (2-6 m high). Recent studies suggest a close solar alignment between the main ruins and the towers. Consequently, the site is by far the oldest known solar observatory in the Americas. Solar observations would have allowed the inhabitants of the surrounding valleys to receive important guidance for agricultural tasks. If driving there off the Panamericana, 4WD is recommended; otherwise ask for directions from the Sechín museum from the road to Huaraz.

Playa Tortugas

Located 2 km east of the Pan-American Highway at Km 391, 18 km north of Casma, Playa Tortugas is a fishing village on a nice bay with calm water and a rocky beach. Colectivos leave Casma when full from Plaza Poncianos between the Plaza de Armas and the market, 0500-2000, US$0.75, 15 minutes. From the north end of the bay the road continues to **Playa Huayuna**, a windy, closed bay with a sandy beach and a scallop farm. From the south end of Tortugas a road goes to **Rincón de Piños**, a beach with wild surf. To the south of Casma, at Km 345, are the sandy beaches of **La Gramita** and **Las Aldas**.

Chimbote → *Colour map 3, A2. Phone code: 043. Population: 296,600. See www.chimboteperu.com.*

Not only is Chimbote Peru's largest fishing port, it is also the smelliest city in the country, with the powerful reek of the fishmeal plant permeating every nook and cranny. But, in a Peruvian twist to Yorkshire's "Where there's muck, there's brass", where there's a stench there's money. There are no tourist attractions as such, although it has a spacious **Plaza de Armas** with the cathedral and the modern Municipal building, which has a small **art gallery** ① *0900-2000*. The best thing about the place is the Terminal Terrestre, 4 km south of the centre on Avenida Meiggs. When transferring from Trujillo, Huaraz, Casma or Lima, there is no need to leave the bus station.

Note Chimbote is not safe by day or night. Travellers are often attacked and robbed here. Take extra precautions. Although it's small enough to walk around, don't; take a taxi, except for going out to eat near your hotel. On no account walk from the bus station to town.

Nepeña Valley

About 25 km south of Chimbote, at Km 405 on the Pan-American Highway, a paved road leads east to the Nepeña Valley, where several pre-Columbian ruins including Cerro Blanco, Pañamarca and Paredones can be found. The valley is dominated by the vast San Jacinto sugar plantation. The village of Capellanía is 11 km from the crossroads. Just beyond are the ruins of **Pañamarca**. The site includes a two-storey stone structure, built on a hill, dating from the formative period (2000 BC-AD 100) and many adobe structures from the Moche period, including three pyramids. Remains of polychromatic murals and animal sculptures can also be seen. Twenty kilometres from Pañamarca, via the villages of San Jacinto and Moro, is the site of **Paredones**, a large stone structure, with 4-m-high granite walls and a very impressive gateway known as 'Portada de Paredones' or 'Puerta del Sol'. It is believed to have been a Chavín palace.

Chimbote to Huaraz

The route from Chimbote to Huaraz passes through the **Santa Valley** and the spectacular Cañón del Pato, one of the most thrilling bus trips in all of Peru. Just north of the smelly port, a road branches northeast off the Pan-American Highway and, joining another road from the town of Santa, goes up the Santa Valley following the route, including nearly 40 tunnels, of the old **Santa Corporation Railway**. This used to run as far as **Huallanca** (Ancash – not to be confused with the town of the same name southeast of Huaraz),

Chimbote

To Caraz, Trujillo & Northern Peru

Pacific Ocean

Sleeping
1 Cantón & Chifa Cantón
2 D'Carlo
3 Hostal Karol Inn & Chifa Jin Lon
4 Ivansino Inn
5 Res El Parque
6 San Felipe
7 Tany

Eating
1 Aquarius
2 Recutecu

50 metres
50 yards

140 km up the valley, but the track was largely destroyed by the 1970 earthquake. At Chuquicara, three hours from Chimbote, some 60 km before Huallanca, is **Restaurante Rosales**, a good place to stop for a meal (you can sleep here, too, but it's very rough). The road from Chimbote to Chuquicara is paved, but after that it becomes a track, very bumpy, stony and dusty (hard driving). The road goes between barren hills and passes poor mining camps. The geology is fantastic, with ravines, whorls, faults and strata at all angles to each other. The varying colours of the rock are also amazing. At the next village, **Yuramarca**, there is lodging, places to eat, fuel and a police station.

At Huallanca is an impressive hydroelectric plant, built into a mountain, which cannot be visited. There is accommodation at the **Hotel Huascarán**, which is good and friendly; also **Koki's Hostal**. Fuel is available. Everything closes early.

At the top of the valley by the hydroelectric centre, the road turns right to go through the **Cañón del Pato**. After this point the road is fully paved. Soon you reach the Callejón de Huaylas and the road south to Caraz and Huaraz (see pages 372 and 354).

An alternative road for cyclists (and vehicles with a permit) is the private road known as the 'Brasileños', used by the Brazilian company Odebrecht who have built a water channel for the Chavimochic irrigation scheme from the Río Santa to the coast. Permits are available (US$6.50) from the company HQ in San José de Virú, or from the guardian at the gate on Sunday. The turn-off is 35 km north of the Santa turning, 15 km south of the bridge in Chao, at Km 482 on the Pan-American Highway. It is a good all-weather road to Tanguche, 22 km from the turn-off, where it continues up the north bank of the Río Santa, crosses a bridge 28 km from Tanguche, to meet up with the public road.

North of Chimbote

The highway crosses the valleys of Chao and Virú and, after 137 km, reach the first great city of Northern Peru, Trujillo. The Virú Valley contains the largest single sand dune in South America, known as **Pur Pur**. Between Virú and Trujillo the desert is being turned 'green' with asparagus and other crops, thanks to the huge Chavimochic project. It is hard to believe that the irrigated land was once as lifeless as the desert that surrounds it. For different reasons, both Virú and Chavimochic are proposing to promote their tourist potential, the former for its little-known archaeological sites and adventure sports, the latter for its economic and social developments. There is basic lodging available and places to eat in both Chao and Virú.

For Sleeping and Eating price codes and other relevant information, see pages 38-44.

⊖ Sleeping

Huacho *p407*

D Centenario, Av 28 de Julio 836, T01-232 3731. Modern, clean, hot water, with outdoor pool, café, internet, negotiate price.

There are other places to stay on Av 28 de Julio.

Churín *p407*

Prices double at holiday periods.

C Las Termas, Av Larco Herrera 411, T01-237 3094. Has rooms with a pool in the town centre and others up at the La Meseta baths, gardens, restaurant and bar.

E Hostal La Cabaña, Av Larco Herrera 368, T01-237 3023. Clean, rooms with bath, hot water and TV, attractive courtyard, use of kitchen available.

Huacho to Barranca *p407*

D Chavín, Gálvez 222, Barranca, T01-235 2358. With bathroom, warm water, clean, good value, recommended, though front rooms are noisy; it also has a restaurant for lunch and dinner; breakfast bar and café opens onto the street by the main entrance.

F Jefferson, Lima 946, Barranca, T01-235 2184. Clean, friendly.

Casma to Huaraz via Pariacoto

p409, map p409

Huarmey

D La Posada de Huarmey, Panamericana 293, Huarmey, T043-600330. Small, with bath, TV, hot water, clean, good service, restaurant, noisy from road traffic.

F pp Jaime Crazy, Manuel Scorza 371 y 373, Sector B-8, Huarmey, T043-772388, www.jaimecrazyperu.com. A new hostel offering all sorts of activities as well as bed and board. **G** in dormitory, rooms with and without bath, trips to beaches for surfing,

archaeological sites, farming communities, biking, horse riding and trekking. Good reports received.

Casma

Most of the following hotels in Casma are on the Panamericana so rooms at the back will be quieter. The Panamericana is divided into 3 sections: Av Luis Ormeño, Av Tarapacá and Av Nepeña, which leads to the plaza.

B-C Hostal El Farol, Túpac Amaru 450, T043-411064, www.elfarolinn.com. Ask for the cheaper rate in the low season, with bathroom, breakfast extra, hot water, swimming pool, good restaurant, pleasant garden setting surrounded by a wall, parking, good local information.

C El Dorado Inn, Av Garcilazo de la Vega Mz J, Lt 37, T043-411795, www.eldoradoinn casma.com. 1 block from the Panamericana. Rooms with bath, fan, cable TV, internet and Wi-Fi, pool, restaurant and tourist information.

D Las Dunas, Ormeño 505, T/F043-711057. A converted, upgraded and enlarged family home, friendly.

E-F Hostal Gregori, Luis Ormeño 530, T043-711073. Cheaper without bathroom, clean, friendly, café downstairs.

E-F Monte Carlo, Nepeña 370, T043-411421. Clean, friendly, TV, internet, laundry, good value.

E-F Rebeca, Huarmey 377, T043-711258. Modern, hot water only at night, good.

Playa Tortugas *p411*

C El Farol Inn Tortugas, sister to the one in Casma, www.elfarolinn.com, open all year, **D** mid-Apr to mid-Dec.

C Las Terrazas, Av Antigua Panamericana Mz H, Lt 1, Caleta Norte, T043-943 619042 (mob), www.lasterrazas.com. Open Nov-Apr, rooms with bath and bay view, also has a restaurant and bar. Offers excursions to local sites of interest.

Chimbote *p411, map p412*

There are plenty of hotels in Chimbote so it is often possible to negotiate a lower rate. Note that the main street, Av Victor Raul Haya de la Torre, is commonly known as José Pardo.

B Cantón, Villavicencio 197, T043-344388. Modern hotel with a good but pricey *chifa* restaurant.

B Ivansino Inn, Haya de la Torre 738, T043-321811, ivansino@hotmail.com. Includes breakfast, comfortable, clean and modern, internet and Wi-Fi.

D D'Carlo, Villavicencio 376, on the plaza, T/F043-321047. Spacious, friendly, TV, minibar, restaurant.

D Hostal Karol Inn, Manuel Ruiz 277, T/F043-321216. Clean, with bathroom, hot water, a good place to stay, family-run, laundry service, cafeteria.

D San Felipe, Haya de la Torre 514, T043-323401. With bathroom, hot water, clean, friendly, comfortable, restaurant.

E Residencial El Parque, E Palacios 309, on the main plaza, T043-345572. A converted old home, with bathroom, hot water, clean, nice, secure, friendly, no breakfast.

E Tany, Palacios 553, T/F043-323411. Clean, friendly, TV, includes breakfast, good value.

E-F Hostal El Ensueño, Sáenz Peña 268, 2 blocks from Plaza Central, T043-328662. Cheaper rooms without bath, very good, safe, welcoming.

● Eating

Huacho *p407*

♥♥ **El Clásico**, C Inca s/n, near seafront, T01-232 6993. *Cevichería* open 1000-1800. Serves huge plates of seafood. Very good, takes credit cards.

♥ **La Estrella**, Av 28 de Julio 561. A good place to stop for coffee, breakfast and other meals.

Huacho to Churín *p407*

♥ **Jalisco**, Balta 342, Sayán. The best place to eat, sometimes has local river shrimp and wine on the menu.

Churín *p407*

Churín is full of restaurants offering healthy portions and a wide range of *dulces* (desserts). Local delicacies include honey, *alfajores*, *manjar blanca*, cheeses and *calabaza* (a delicious pudding made from squash).

Huacho to Barranca *p407*

♥♥ **Tacu Tato**, on Chorrillos beach. Has won national prizes for its *tacu tacu*, a Peruvian seafood paella.

♥ **Cevichería Fujino**, Arica 210, Barranca. Good for fish. Try the *tamales*.

Casma to Huaraz via Pariacoto
p409, map p409

Casma

There are several cheap restaurants on Calle Huarmey. The famous locally made ice cream, Caribe, includes some delicious flavours such as *lúcuma* and *maracuyá*. Available at the *panadería* at Ormeño 545.

♥ **Café Lucy**, Mejía 150. Opens early for breakfast, which includes fried fish and soups.

♥ **Tío Sam**, Huarmey 138. Decorated with photos of Sechín, this restaurant specializes in excellent fresh fish dishes, such as *lenguado sudado*.

♥ **Venecia**, Huarmey 204. Serves local dishes such as goat stew, popular with locals.

Playa Tortugas *p411*

♥♥ **Costa Azul**, on the seafront as you enter the settlement. One of the best seafood restaurants for fried fish or *ceviche*.

Chimbote *p411, map p412*

There are several cheap restaurants on Haya de la Torre by the plaza.

♥ **Aquarius**, Haya de la Torre 360. A vegetarian restaurant in the centre.

♥ **Chifa Jin Lon**, adjoining **Hostal Karol Inn**. Well-prepared Chinese food, popular.

♥ **Recutecu**, L Prado 556. Good set lunch with a wide choice.

Cafés and panaderías

Delca, Haya de la Torre 568, excellent bakery.

▲▲ Activities and tours

Casma to Huaraz via Pariacoto
p409, map p409

Sechín Tours, in Hostal Monte Carlo, Casma, T043-711421. Organizes tours in the local area. The guide, Renato, only speaks Spanish but has knowledge of local ruins and can be contacted on T043-712528, renatotours@yahoo.com.

⊖ Transport

Chancay Valley *p406*
Take a bus to **Huaral** from Plaza de Acho, by the bullring, in Lima (beware of thieves). Then take the Juan Batista bus, on Tue and Fri, to **Huascoy**, US$3, 2 km beyond San Juan, which is up beyond Acos, at 3500 m.

Huacho *p407*
América Móvil (Av Luna Pizarro 251, La Victoria, T01-423 6338; in Huacho T01-232 7631) and **Zeta** (Av Abancay 900, T01-426 8087; in Huacho T01-239 6176) run every 20-30 mins **Lima–Huacho**, from 0600 to 2000, 2½ hrs, US$2.55-3 (more expensive at weekends). Buses heading north usually arrive full. They can be caught at the round-about on the Panamericana. There are regular combis to **Sayán**. There is a toll post at El Paraíso Huacho.

Churín *p407*
Trans Estrella Polar, **Espadín** and **Beteta** each have several buses a day to **Lima**, 4-5 hrs, US$7. Some buses from Lima continue to **Oyón**, 1 hr. From Oyón it is possible to continue over the sierras to **Cerro de Pasco** on a very rough high-altitude road, **Trans Javier**, 0800, 5 hrs, US$6.

Huacho to Barranca *p407*
From **Lima** to Barranca takes 3½ hrs, US$4. Several bus companies serve the Lima–Barranca route such as **Trans América** and **Trans Paramonga**. As bus companies have

their offices in Barranca, buses will stop there rather than at Pativilca or Paramonga. Bus from Barranca to **Casma**, 155 km, several daily, 2½ hrs, US$3. To continue to **Huaraz** or northern coastal cities, take a colectivo to the service station (el grifo) at the northern end of Pativilca, where buses from Lima with space stop. There are also colectivos to **Huarmey**, 1¼ hrs, US$2.75, from where it is also possible to continue northward.

Caral *p408*
To **Caral**, Empresa Valle Sagrado Caral leave from terminal at Berenice Dávila, cuadra 2, Barranca, US$1.75 shared, or US$28 private service with 1½ hrs at the site. The ruins are 25 km along a road which runs up the Supe valley from Km 184 of the Panamericana (signed). Between Kms 18 and 19 of this road a track to the right crosses the river then leads across the valley, out of the agricultural zone to the ruins in the desert, 30 mins. The river may be impassable Dec-Mar. Tours from Lima usually allow 1½ hrs at Caral, with a 3-hr journey each way, stopping for morning coffee and for lunch in Huacho on the return.

Pativilca to Huaraz *p409*
By bus, Pativilca to **Huaraz** is US$7.25, 6 hrs, or US$11 by colectivo.

Casma to Huaraz via Pariacoto
p409, map p409
Bus Lima-**Huarmey** costs US$7.25. **Pativilca** to Huaraz is US$3.60 by colectivo.

There are half-hourly buses from **Lima** to Chimbote that can drop you off in Casma, 370 km, 6 hrs, US$16. If going to **Lima** many of the buses from Trujillo and Chimbote stop briefly opposite the petrol station, block 1 of Ormeño or, if they have small offices, along blocks 1-5 of Av Ormeño. Tepsa's office is at Av Huarmey 356, T01-9902 723337. To **Chimbote**, 55 km, it is easiest to take a **Los Casmeños** colectivo, which depart when full from in front of the petrol station, block 1 of Ormeño, or from Plaza Poncianos, 45 mins, US$1.65. To

Trujillo it is best to go first to Chimbote bus station and then take an **América Express** bus. To **Huaraz** (150 km), via Pariacoto, buses come from Chimbote, 6-7 hrs, US$7.50 (for a description of the route see above). Transportes Huandoy, Ormeño 166, T043-712336, departs at 0700, 1100 and 1400, while Yungay Express, Ormeño 158, departs at 0600, 0800 and 1400. Most Huaraz buses go via **Pativilca**, which is further but the road is better, see above, Móvil Tours and Trans Chinchaysuyo, all run at night.

Chimbote *p411, map p412*
Bus
Under no circumstances walk the 4 km from the bus station to the city centre. Some buses to/from places north of Chimbote stop in the centre, but not in a safe area. Likewise, colectivo taxis from Casma drop passengers near the market; ask to be let out at the bus terminal. Always go to the terminal even though there are no hotels nearby: a colectivo to town costs US$0.50, taxi US$1.25. If arriving from Caraz via the Cañón del Pato there is usually time to make a connection to **Casma** or **Trujillo/Huanchaco** and avoid over-nighting in Chimbote. If travelling to **Caraz**, take Línea 0600 or earlier bus from Trujillo to make the 0830 bus up the Cañón del Pato. If overnighting is unavoidable, Casma is near enough to stay in but you will need to buy your Caraz ticket the day before; the bus station is on the Casma side of Chimbote.

From **Lima** to Chimbote, 420 km, 6 hrs, US$12.35 (Línea) to US$18 with Tepsa (T043-350072), and US$22.50-30 Cruz del Sur (T043-321283) *cruzero* service. Frequent buses with many companies, including Trans Isla Blanca, Línea (T043-354000) and Oltursa (T043-353585). To **Trujillo**, 130 km, 2 hrs, US$3, América Express have buses every 20 mins until 2100, after which you must hope for Lima buses passing through with space. To **Huaraz** most companies, with the best buses, go the 'long way round', ie down the Panamericana to Pativilca, then up the paved highway, 7 hrs, US$8.30. The best companies are Móvil Tours, T043-353616, and Chinchaysuyo; both start in Trujillo, their buses continue on to **Caraz**. To **Huaraz** via Pariacoto, 7 hrs, US$8.30, Trans Huandoy (Etseturh, T043-354024), at 0600, 1000 and 1300, and Yungay Express at 0500, 0700 and 1300 (see above for a description of this route). To **Caraz** via Cañón del Pato, 7-8 hrs, US$8, Yungay Express at 0830 (for a description of this route see above). To guarantee a seat on this bus if coming from Trujillo or Casma, T043-321235 the evening before and they will meet your incoming bus and transfer you. To **Sihuas**, 10 hrs, US$8, Trans Andino is the only company with a daytime bus at 0800 on Wed, Fri and Sun.

Taxi
Radio taxis from T043-334433.

❶ Directory

Casma to Huaraz via Pariacoto
p409, map p409
Banks BCP, Bolívar 111, Casma. Dollars can be changed in Casma at Ormeño 529 and Nepeña 384. **Internet** Café on west side of plaza, Casma. 0900-2100. **Post** Fernando Loparte, ½ block from Plaza de Armas, Casma.

Chimbote *p411, map p412*
Banks BCP and Interbank, both on Bolognesi and M Ruiz. Casa Arroyo, M Ruiz 292. For cash only. There are other *casas* along M Ruiz between Bolognesi and VR Haya de la Torre. **Internet** Places in the centre. **Post** Serpost, Av J Pardo 294.

Trujillo and around

Trujillo, capital of the Department of La Libertad, disputes the title of second city of Peru with Arequipa. Founded by Diego de Almagro in 1534 as an express assignment ordered by Francisco Pizarro, the city was named after the latter's native town in Spain. There is enough here to hold the attention for several days. The area abounds in pre-Columbian sites, there are beaches and good surfing within easy reach and the city itself still has many old churches and graceful colonial homes, built during the reigns of the viceroys.

Perhaps Trujillo's greatest attractions are the impressive Pre-Inca ruins that surround it: the Moche pyramids of Huaca del Sol and de la Luna, Chan Chán and the more distant El Brujo. All can be reached by public transport, but if that sounds complicated, there are many tours available. You need at least an hour to gain a full explanation of Chan Chán and Huaca La Luna, but many tours only allow 20 minutes each. If you are all ruined-out, just a few minutes up the coast from Trujillo is the seaside town of Huanchaco, long a favourite of travellers for surfing, watching the fishermen on their reed boats and just hanging out. ▶▶ *For listings, see pages 429-441.*

Trujillo → *For listings, see pages 429-441. Colour map 3, A1. Phone code: 044. Population: 1,539,774.*

Ins and outs

Getting there The airport is to the west of town. You will enter town along Avenida Mansiche. There is no central bus terminal and none of the bus stations are in the centre. They are spread out on all four sides of the city, between the inner and outer ring roads, Avenidas España and América. Plenty of taxis can be found at the terminals to get you to your hotel. Insist on being taken to the hotel of your choice. Taxi drivers constantly say your hotel is too far/close, expensive/cheap, noisy/boring. They want to take you to the most distant/expensive/remote place to increase fare/commission/overcharging possibilities. ▶▶ *See Transport, page 438.*

Getting around With its compact colonial centre and mild, spring-like climate, Trujillo is best explored on foot. However, should you need a taxi, there are plenty of them. Always use official taxis, which are mainly yellow, or cooperative taxis, which have the company logo and telephone number on the side. The major sites outside the city, Chan Chán, the Moche pyramids and Huanchaco beach are easily reached by public transport or taxi, but care is needed when walking around. Beware of overcharging, check fares with locals. A number of recommended guides run expert tours to these and other places.
Note The very centre of Trujillo has confusing double street names; the smaller printed name is the one generally shown on maps, and in general use.

Tourist information iperú ⓘ *Diego de Almagro 420, Plaza de Armas, T044-294561, iperu trujillo@promperu.gob.pe, Mon-Sat 0900-1800, Sun 1000-1400.* Also useful: **Municipalidad de Trujillo, Sub-Gerencia de Turismo** ⓘ *Av España 742, T044-244212, anexo 119, sgturismo@ munitrujillo.gob.pe.* **Indecopi tourist complaints office** ⓘ *Santo Toribio de Mogrovejo 518, Urb San Andrés II etapa, T044-295733, toll free T0800-44040, sobregon@indecopi.gob.pe,* for complaints. **Gobierno Regional de La Libertad** ⓘ *Dirección de Turismo, Av España 1800, T044-296221,* with plenty of information, including on rural tourism, and helpful staff. Useful websites include www.xanga.com/trujilloperu and www.laindustria.com/industria (especially articles by Guido Sánchez Tafur, a university professor in the Tourism department).

Take care anywhere, especially beyond the inner ring road, Avenida España, as well as obvious places around terminals, walking to and from bus stops and at ATMs and internet cafés. Also be wary if going to the beaches south of Trujillo; though pleasant, they are quite deserted and there is always a risk of robbery. Tourists may be approached by vendors selling *huacos* and necklaces from the Chimú period. The export of these items is strictly illegal if they are genuine, but they almost certainly aren't.

Sights

Plaza de Armas The focal point is the pleasant and spacious Plaza de Armas. The prominent sculpture represents agriculture, commerce, education, art, slavery, action and liberation, crowned by a young man holding a torch depicting Liberty. Fronting it is the **cathedral** ⓘ *open 0700-1230, 1700-2000*, dating from 1666, with, next door, its museum of religious paintings and sculptures, **Museo Catedralicio** ⓘ *open Mon-Fri 0900-1300, 1600-1900, US$1.45, students US$0.75*. Also on the plaza are the **Hotel Libertador**, the colonial-style Sociedad de Beneficencia Pública de Trujillo and the Municipalidad.

The **Universidad de La Libertad**, second only to that of San Marcos at Lima, was founded in 1824. Two beautiful colonial mansions on the plaza have been taken over. The Banco Central de Reserva is in the colonial-style **Casa Urquiaga** (or **Calonge**) ⓘ *Pizarro 446, Mon-Fri, 0930-1500, Sat 1000-1330, free guided tour lasts 30 mins, take passport or a photocopy*. It contains valuable pre-Columbian ceramics and an exhibition of colonial coins. The other is **Casa Bracamonte** (or **Lizarzaburu**), at Independencia 441, with occasional exhibits. Opposite the cathedral on Independencia is the **Casa Garci Olguín** (**Caja Nuestra Gente**), recently restored but boasting the oldest façade in the city, baroque and rococo features and Moorish-style murals. The buildings that surround the plaza, and many others in the vicinity, are painted in bright pastel colours. Street lamps are on brackets, adding to the charm of the centre.

North and east of the Plaza de Armas In **San Francisco** ⓘ *on the corner of Gamarra and Independencia, 0800-1200, 1600-2000*, is the pulpit that survived the earthquake of Saint Valentine's Day in 1619. It has three golden altars and others inside. **Casa Ganoza Chopitea** ⓘ *Independencia 630 opposite San Francisco church, Mon-Fri 0915-1230, 1430-1630*, is architecturally the most representative house in the city and considered the most outstanding of the viceroyalty. It combines baroque and rococo styles and it is due to be restored as a cultural centre. Continuing up Independencia you come to the **Museo del Juguete** ⓘ *Independencia 705 y Junín, Mon-Sat 1000-1800, Sun 1000-1300, US$1.85, children US$0.70*, the toy museum, which contains examples from pre-historic times to 1950, collected by painter Gerardo Chávez. Downstairs is the **Espacio Cultural Angelmira** in a restored **casona** ⓘ *daily 0900-2300*, with a café bar. It's worth a visit. Turn off Independencia to **Santa Clara** ⓘ *Sun only*, on the fourth block of Junín. The next cross street is Pizarro. Turn left to **Plazuela El Recreo** at the north end of Pizarro. It was known as El Estanque during the colonial period as it housed a pool from which the city's water was distributed. A marble fountain by Eiffel now stands in the square, transferred from the Plaza de Armas.

If you head back to the Plaza de Armas, you pass the spacious 18th-century **Palacio Iturregui**, now occupied by the **Club Central** ⓘ *Jr Pizarro 688, to enter the patio is free*. This exclusive social centre of Trujillo houses a **private collection of ceramics** ⓘ *open 0830-1030, US$1.85*. **Casa de la Emancipación** ⓘ *Jr Pizarro 610, Banco Continental, Mon-Sat 0900-1300, 1600-2000*, is where independence from Spain was planned and was the first seat of government and congress in Peru. The first room on the right as you go in displays plans and the history of the building. There are exhibits on the life of the poet César Vallejo (1892-1938) and Bishop Martínez Compañón (1737-1797), whose circuits took him all around northern Peru. There are watercolours of life in the 18th century. Before you arrive back at the plaza you come to the restored 17th-century church of **La Merced** ① *Pizarro 550, 0800-1200, 1600-2000, free*, with picturesque moulded figures

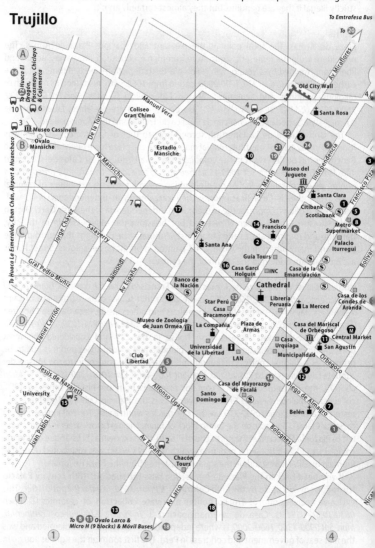

Trujillo

below the dome. It has a mock rococo organ above the choir stalls and *retablos* from the 17th century which, unusually, are still visible, painted on the walls, from the time before free-standing altars were used.

If you leave the plaza on Orbegoso, the **Casa del Mariscal de Orbegoso** ⓘ *Orbegoso 553, closed for refurbishment 2010*, is at the first junction. It was named after the

Map labels: To Huamachuco · La Unión · Av España · Plazuela El Recreo · Estete · El Carmen · Museo de Arqueología · San Lorenzo · Plaza de Toros · Old City Wall · Mercado Mayorista · Galvez · Suárez · Zela · Junín · Ayacucho · Gamarra · Grau · Atahualpa · Sinchi Roca · Lloque Yupanqui · Av Los Incas · España · Huayna Capac · Moche · Cahuide · Ejército · Amazonas

N · 200 metres · 200 yards

To Ovalo Grau & Micro H (5 blocks), Southern Bus Terminal, Linea, Chimbote & Lima · To 2 ex-president, General Luis José de Orbegoso, is the Museo de la República, owned by Interbank. Opposite is **San Agustín** ① *Bolívar 508, 0800-1200, 1600-2000*. Turn up Bolívar and go one block right for the **Museo de Arqueología** ① *Casa Risco, Junín 682 y Ayacucho, T044-249322, www.unitru.edu.pe/cultural/arq (mainly in Spanish), Mon-Fri 0830-1430, US$1.85, guided tours in Spanish available*. It houses a large collection of thematic exhibits from pre-Hispanic cultures of the area. Further up Bolívar is the church and monastery of **El Carmen** ① *Colón y Bolívar, open for mass Sun 0700-0730*. Described as the 'most valuable jewel of colonial art in Trujillo', El Carmen has five gilt altars, balconies and religious paintings, but it is rarely open. Next door is the Pinacoteca Carmelita, with more paintings. It includes a room on picture restoration.

At the southeastern edge of the city, Gerardo Chávez (see Museo del Juguete, above) has opened a **Museo de Arte Moderno** ① *3.5 km from the centre at the junction of Carretera Industrial and Av Villareal, El Bosque, T044-215668, open Mon-Sat 0930-1730, Sun 0930-1400, US$3.50 (students half price)*. To get there take a taxi US$1.75. It has some fine exhibits by European and Latin American masters, plus monumental works by Chávez himself, a colourful garden in summer with lots of birds and animals and friendly staff.

South and west of the Plaza de Armas The **Museo de Zoología de Juan Ormea** ① *Jr San Martín 368, T044-205011, Mon-Fri 0700-1850, US$0.70*, has interesting displays of Peruvian animals. **La Compañía**, the former Jesuit church near Plaza de Armas, is usually only open as an auditorium for cultural events, but its exterior is very photogenic. Other churches in this area are **Santo Domingo** ① *on the 4th block of Bolognesi*, and **Belén** ① *on the 6th block of Almagro*. The **Casa del Mayorazgo de Facalá** ① *Pizarro 314, entrance on Bolognesi, Mon-Fri 0915-1230*, which is now the **Scotiabank**, was once owned by Don Pedro de Tinoco whose wife embroidered the first Peruvian flag to be hoisted following Trujillo's independence from Spanish rule in 1820.

For a change of scene, you can walk from the old inner city along the fairly safe Avenida Larco to the new and very busy **Ovalo Larco** district. If you prefer, take a taxi down Avenida Larco, which is lined with residential districts. Here are many restaurants, grills, fast-food outlets, educational and professional institutions, supermarkets, café/bars, gift shops and beauty parlours. From Ovalo Larco it is easy to get a bus to anywhere you want.

Also southwest of the Plaza de Armas is the **Universidad Nacional de Trujillo (UNT)**, one of Peru's major universities. It is surrounded by high walls, one of which running along Avenida Juan Pablo II is covered by a 800-m-long mosaic depicting folkloric scenes, dances and traditions of northern Peru. This mural is said to be the longest mosaic mural in the world.

Northwest of the Plaza de Armas Heading northwest from plaza, you pass **Santa Ana** ① *on the 2nd block of Mcal Orbegoso*, one of the three 'iglesias menores' (lesser churches). The others were San Lorenzo and Santa Rosa. The street becomes Avenida Mansiche, which leads to the routes out of town. The basement of the **Cassinelli garage** ① *on the fork of the Pan-American and Huanchaco roads, Av N de Piérola 607, T044-231801, behind a petrol station, 1000-1300, 1430-1800, US$2.45*, contains a superb private collection of Mochica and Chimú pottery and is highly recommended.

Huacas del Sol and de la Luna

① *Open 0900-1600 (last entry, but site open till sunset), US$3.80 with guide, some of whom speak European languages (students US$2, children US$0.35), booklet in English or Spanish US$2.85. You have to go with a guide on a 1-hr tour in English, French or Spanish. Groups can be up to 25 people and quite rushed. See Proyecto Huaca de la Luna, Jr Junín 682, Trujillo, T044-297430, www.huacadelaluna.org.pe; also www.huacas.com.*

A few kilometres south of Trujillo a new 3.2-km access road leads to the huge Moche pyramids, the Huaca del Sol and Huaca de la Luna. The **Huaca del Sol** was once, before the Spanish diverted the nearby river and washed a third of it away in a search for treasure, the largest man-made structure in the Americas, reaching a height of 45 m. It consisted of seven levels, with 11 or 12 phases of construction over the first six centuries AD. Built from 143 million adobe bricks, it was the political centre of the site. The ceremonial platforms have been further eroded by the weather and visitors, but climbing on them is now prohibited. Today, about two thirds of the pyramid have been lost.

The **Huaca de la Luna**, 500 m away, was a 'religious pyramid'. It received relatively little attention compared to its larger neighbour until more than 8000 sq m of remarkable mural paintings and reliefs were uncovered in the 1990s. The yellow, white, blue, red and black paint has faded little over the centuries and many metres of the intricate geometric patterns and fearsome feline deities depicted are virtually complete. It has now been established that the pyramid once consisted of seven levels, each possibly pertaining to a different ruler-priest. When each priest died he was buried within the *huaca* and a new level was built covering up entirely the previous level. The highest mural is a 'serpent' that runs the length of the wall, beneath it there are repeated motifs of 'felines' holding decapitated heads of warriors, then repeated motifs of 'fishermen' holding fish against a bright blue background and, next, huge 'spider/crab' motifs. The bottom two levels show dancers or officials grimly holding hands and, below them, victorious warriors following naked prisoners past scenes of combat and two complex scenes, similar to those at Huaca

Around Trujillo

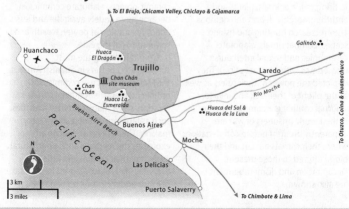

Masters of sculpture

One of the most remarkable pre-Inca civilizations was that of the Moche people, who evolved during the first century AD and lasted until around AD 750. Though these early Peruvians had no written language, they left a vivid record of their life and culture in beautifully modelled and painted ceramics.

Compared with the empires of their successors, the Chimú and Inca, the realm of the Moche was very small, covering less than 250 miles of coast from the valleys of Lambayeque to Nepeña, south of present-day Chimbote. Though a seemingly inhospitable stretch of coast, the Moche harnessed rivers spilling from the Andean cordillera, channelling them into a network of irrigation canals that watered the arid coastal valleys. The resultant lush fields produced plentiful crops, which, along with the sea's bountiful harvest of fish and seafood, gave the Moche a rich and varied diet. With the leisure allowed by such abundant food, Moche craftsmen invented new techniques to produce their artistic masterpieces. It is these ancient pottery vessels that have made the greatest contribution to our understanding of this great civilization.

These masters of sculpture used clay to bring to life animals, plants and anthropomorphic deities and demons. They recreated hunting and fishing scenes, combat rituals, elaborate ceremonies and sexual intercourse (sometimes with contraception). They depicted the power of their rulers as well as the plight of their sick and invalid.

Ritual combat is a common theme in their work; prisoners of war are apparently brought before congregations where their throats are cut and their blood offered to those present. Decapitation and dismemberment are also shown.

Moche potters were amazingly skilled at reproducing facial features, specializing in the subtle nuances of individual personality. In addition to these 3D sculptures, the Moche potter was skilled at decorating vessels with low-relief designs. Among the most popular scenes are skeletal death figures holding hands while dancing in long processions to the accompaniment of musicians. The potters also developed a technique of fine-line painting scenes on ceramic vessels. Over a period of several centuries the painters became increasingly skillful at depicting complex and lively scenes with multiple figures. Because of their complexity and detail, these scenes are of vital importance in reconstructing Moche life.

The early introduction of moulds and stamps brought efficiency to the production of Moche ceramics. By pressing moist clay into the halves of a mould, it was possible to produce an object much more rapidly than by hand. Similarly, the use of stamps facilitated the decoration of ceramic vessels with elaborate low-relief designs. Mould-making technology thus resulted in many duplications of individual pieces. Since there were almost no unique ceramic objects, elaborate ceramics became more widely available and less effective as a sign of power, wealth and social status of the élite.

Although among the most sophisticated potters in Spanish America, the Moche did not use ceramics for ordinary tableware. Neither do their ceramics show many everyday activities, such as farming, cooking and pottery making. This is because Moche art expresses the religious and supernatural aspects of their culture and little of everyday life is illustrated for its own sake. See also under History, on page 645.

Cao Viejo at El Brujo (see page 428). Below the bottom end of the north/south ramp the second level shows a 5-m-long reptile approaching a life-sized human figure apparently defending human figures holding hands. Combined with intricate, brightly painted two-dimensional motifs in the sacrificial area atop the *huaca*, Huaca de la Luna is now a truly significant site well worth visiting. The project was awarded an EU prize as the best in Latin America in 2006.

In 2010 two new areas were opened to the public. The **Templo Nuevo**, or Plataforma III, represents the period 600 to 900 AD and has friezes in the upper showing the so-called Rebellion of the Artefacts, in which weapons take on human characteristics and attack their owners. Also new is the **Museo Huacas de Moche** ① *5 mins' walk from Huaca de la Luna, daily 0900-1600, US$1.10, students US$0.75, children US$0.40, www.huacasdemoche.pe*, the site museum. Three halls display objects found in the *huacas*, including beautiful ceramics, arranged thematically around the Moche themselves, the cermonial complex, daily life, the deities of power and of the mountains and priests who worshipped them.

Between the two *huacas* lie the remains of a once sizeable settlement, maybe as large as 20,000 people, now mainly lost beneath the sands; excavations are taking place.

The visitor centre (T044-834901) has good toilets, a video/lecture hall, a café showing videos and souvenir shop selling modern ceramics, T-shirts, postcards, etc. Books and videos are sold at the ticket office. In an outside patio craftsmen reproduce ceramics in authentic designs from northern Peru. Good local food is prepared on Sunday in the nearby town of Moche.

Chan Chán → *Colour map 3, A1.*

① *Open 0900-1600, arrive well before that. A ticket covering the entrance fees for Chan Chán, the site museum, as well as Huaca El Dragón and Huaca La Esmeralda (for 2 days) costs US$3.80 (students US$2 with an official ISIC card, children US$0.35; tickets can be bought at any of the sites, except La Esmeralda). A guide at the site costs US$10 (the price is the same for a small group); they wait by the souvenir shops. A guide is recommended so you don't miss anything. There are police at the entrance to the site, but it is a 25-min walk to the ticket office. Taxis also wait at the entrance. Take care if not taking a car on this track; it is best to go in a group. On no account walk the 4 km from Chan Chán to, or on, Buenos Aires beach as there is serious danger of robbery and of being attacked by dogs.*

This crumbling imperial city of the Chimú is the largest adobe city in the world and lies about 5 km from Trujillo. Heavy rain and flooding in 1925 and 1983 damaged much of the ruins and, although they are still standing, nine palaces are closed to visitors. Thankfully, UNESCO donated US$100,000 and protection work ensured that the 1998 El Niño had little effect. Conservation work has uncovered more friezes and objects of high value since then, while new resoration methods both replicate and protect the original mouldings.

The ruins consist of ten great compounds built by Chimú emperors. The 11- to 12-m-high perimeter walls surrounded sacred enclosures with usually only one narrow entrance. Inside, as well as plazas and assembly rooms, are rows of storerooms which contained the agricultural wealth of the empire, which stretched 1000 km along the coast from near Guayaquil, in Ecuador, to the Carabayllo Valley, north of Lima.

Most of the compounds contain a huge walk-in well that tapped the ground water, raised to a high level by irrigation higher up the valley. Each compound also included a platform mound that was the burial place of the emperor, with his women and his treasure, presumably maintained as a memorial. The Incas almost certainly copied this system and transported it to Cuzco where the last Incas continued building huge

Absolute power

Chimú was a despotic state that based its power on wars of conquest. Rigid social stratification existed and power rested in the hands of the great lords. These lords were followed in the social scale by a group of urban courtiers who enjoyed a certain amount of economic power. At the bottom were the peasants. Prisoners for sacrifice belonged to yet another level.

The Chimú economy was based on agriculture supplemented by fishing, hunting and craft production. They were renowned metalsmiths, who, like the Moche, alloyed and plated copper with gold and silver. The burial mounds of the Chimú nobles at Chan Chán were despoiled of their gold and silver statuettes by the Spaniards.

enclosures. The Chimú surrendered to the Incas around 1471 after 11 years of siege and cutting off the irrigation canals.

The dilapidated city walls enclose an area of 28 sq km containing the remains of palaces, temples, workshops, streets, houses, gardens and a canal. Canals up to 74 km long kept the city supplied with water. What is left of the adobe walls bears either well-restored, or modern fibreglass fabrications of moulded decorations showing small figures of fish, birds, fishing nets and various geometric motifs. Painted designs have been found on pottery unearthed from the debris of a city ravaged by floods, earthquakes and *huaqueros*. Of the ten compounds, only the **Ciudadela of Nik-An** (formerly called Tschudi) is open to the public.

The **site museum** ① *US$1, 0830-1630*, on the main road, 100 m before the turn-off, has objects found in the area, displays and signs in Spanish and English.

> Sometimes a singer waits in the Plaza Principal of the Ciudadela to show the perfect acoustics of the square (she expects a tip).

Huacas El Dragón and La Esmeralda

The partly restored temple, **Huaca El Dragón** ① *daily 0900-1630*, dating from Huari to Chimú times (AD 1000-1470), is also known as **Huaca Arco Iris** (rainbow), after the shape of friezes that decorate it. It is on the west side of the Pan-American Highway in the district of La Esperanza. Take a combi from Avenida España y Manuel Vera marked 'Arco Iris/La Esperanza', from the Ovalo Mansiche, or, if on the east side of the city, from Huayna Cápac y Avenida Los Incas; a taxi costs US$2.

The poorly preserved **Huaca La Esmeralda** is at Mansiche, between Trujillo and Chan Chán, behind the church and near the Mall Aventura shopping centre. Buses to Chan Chán and Huanchaco pass the church at Mansiche.

Huanchaco → Colour map 3, A1. Phone code: 044.

A popular alternative to staying in Trujillo is the fishing and surfing town of Huanchaco, which is full of hotels, guesthouses and restaurants. Having been first developed with beach houses and homes for wealthy Trujillanos it is still expanding, with foreign as well as local investment in high-rise apartment buildings and hotels. It has great beaches to the south; to the north are reed beds good for birdwatching. The town is famous for its narrow pointed fishing rafts, known as *caballitos* (little horses), made of totora reeds and depicted on Salinar, Gallinazo, Virú, Moche, Lambayeque and Chimú pottery. These are still a familiar sight in places along the northern Peruvian coast. Unlike those used on Lake

Titicaca, they are flat, not hollow, and ride the breakers rather like surfboards. You can see the reeds growing in sunken pits at the north end of the beach, the Reserva Los Balsares de Huanchaco. Fishermen offer trips on their *caballitos* for US$1.75, be prepared to get

Huanchaco

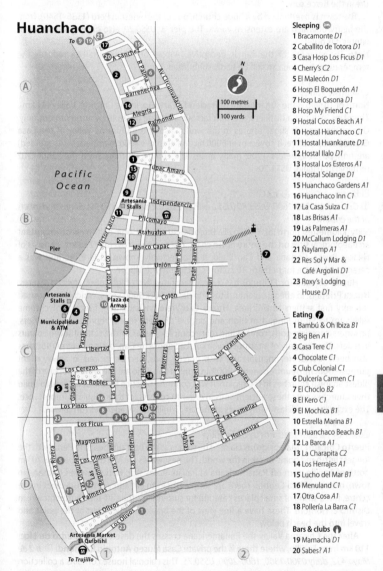

Sleeping
1 Bracamonte *D1*
2 Caballito de Totora *D1*
3 Casa Hosp Los Ficus *D1*
4 Cherry's *C2*
5 El Malecón *D1*
6 Hosp El Boquerón *A1*
7 Hosp La Casona *D1*
8 Hosp My Friend *C1*
9 Hostal Cocos Beach *A1*
10 Hostal Huanchaco *C1*
11 Hostal Huankarute *D1*
12 Hostal Ilalo *D1*
13 Hostal Los Esteros *A1*
14 Hostal Solange *D1*
15 Huanchaco Gardens *A1*
16 Huanchaco Inn *C1*
17 La Casa Suiza *C1*
18 Las Brisas *A1*
19 Las Palmeras *A1*
20 McCallum Lodging *D1*
21 Ñaylamp *A1*
22 Res Sol y Mar & Café Argolini *D1*
23 Roxy's Lodging House *D1*

Eating
1 Bambú & Oh Ibiza *B1*
2 Big Ben *A1*
3 Casa Tere *C1*
4 Chocolate *C1*
5 Club Colonial *C1*
6 Dulcería Carmen *C1*
7 El Choclo *B2*
8 El Kero *C1*
9 El Mochica *B1*
10 Estrella Marina *B1*
11 Huanchaco Beach *B1*
12 La Barca *A1*
13 La Charapita *C2*
14 Los Herrajes *A1*
15 Lucho del Mar *B1*
16 Menuland *C1*
17 Otra Cosa *A1*
18 Pollería La Barra *C1*

Bars & clubs
19 Mamacha *D1*
20 Sabes? *A1*

wet (groups can contact Luis Gordillo, El Mambo, T044-461092). Fishermen give demonstrations for US$3.50 (groups should give more). You can see fishermen returning to shore in their reed rafts at about 0800 and 1600 when they stack the boats upright to dry in the fierce sun.

The town is overlooked by a huge **church**, one of the oldest in Peru (1535-1540), from the belfry of which are extensive views. The **pier** ① *US$0.20*, also gives good views. In winter it is quiet.

Note The strength of the sun is deceptive. A cool breeze off the sea reduces the temperature, but you can still be badly sunburned.

Chicama Valley

North of Trujillo is the sugar estate of **Hacienda Cartavio**, in the Chicama Valley (43 km). The plant includes a distillery and rum factory. Visits are possible by appointment only. One of the biggest sugar estates in the world, also in the Chicama Valley, is the **Casa Grande cooperative**. It covers over 6000 ha and employs 4000 members. Visits (guided) are only possible before 1200; many buses and combis go there from the Santa Cruz terminal in Trujillo, US$1.10.

El Brujo → *Colour map 3, A1.*
① *Open daily 0900-1600, US$3.80 (US$2 with ISIC card, children US$0.35). Shops and toilets at the entrance.*

Sixty kilometres north of Trujillo, El Brujo is considered one of the most important archaeological sites on the entire north coast. The complex, covering 2 sq km, consists of Huacas Prieta, Cortada and Cao Viejo. It is collectively known as El Brujo and was a ceremonial centre for perhaps 10 cultures, including the Moche.

Huaca Cortada (or El Brujo) has a wall decorated with high-relief, stylized figures. **Huaca Prieta** is, in effect, a giant rubbish tip dating back 5000 years, which once housed the very first settlers to this area. **Huaca Cao Viejo** has extensive friezes, polychrome reliefs up to 90 m long, 4 m high and on five different levels, representing warriors, prisoners, sacrificer gods, combat and more complex scenes, with a total of seven colours in reliefs. The mummy of a tattooed woman, **La Señora de Cao**, dating from AD 450, has also been found. Her mausoleum, with grave goods, can be visited in an excellent purpose-built museum, opened in 2009. In front of Cao Viejo are the remains of one of the oldest Spanish churches in the region. It was common practice for the Spaniards to build their churches near these ancient sites in order to counteract their religious importance. The excavations will last many years at the site. Trujillo travel agencies run tours.

Coast of La Libertad north of Trujillo

Puerto Chicama (Malabrigo), is claimed by surfers as the best surf beach in Peru, with the longest left-hand point-break in the world. The best waves are March-October. It is 70 km north of Trujillo, turn off Panamericana at Paiján. Buses stop opposite the Comisaria in town, near the Plaza Central. There are simple places to eat and a few *hospedajes* in the centre, but a string of small places catering for surfers lines the cliff-top south of town, in Distrito El Hombre. These have a fine view of the breakers which start at the point and travel into the beach below.

After the Chicama Valley the Panamericana crosses the desert to **San Pedro de Lloc**, 110 km from Trujillo, where there is the private **Casa Museo Antonio Raimondi** ① *Jr 2 de Mayo 432, daily 0900-1300, 1600-2000, US$0.75*. This colonial house contains a collection of the work of the 19th-century Italian explorer. The nearby beaches at **Puémape** are good for surfing, but out of the summer season there is nowhere to stay or eat.

Pacasmayo (colour map 3, A1; population: 12,300) the port for the next oasis north, is 9 km north of San Pedro de Lloc. It has a nice beach front with an old Customs House and a very long pier. Resort El Faro is 1 km away, with surfing at the point and kite- and windsurfing closer to town. In the high season (January-February and Semana Santa) colectivos run to El Faro. There are maritime festivals at New Year and Semana Santa. Away from the front it is a busy commercial centre.

Some 20 km further north on the Panamericana is the main road connection from the coast to Cajamarca at a junction called **Ciudad de Dios**. The paved 175-km road branches off the Pan-American Highway soon after it crosses the Río Jequetepeque. The river valley has terraced rice fields and mimosas may often be seen in bloom, brightening the otherwise dusty landscape.

About 30-40 minutes from the Panamericana towards the ocean, near the Río Jequetepeque, are the ruins of Pacatnamú, comparable in size to Chan Chán. It consists of pyramids, a cemetery and living quarters of nobles and fishermen, possibly initiated in the Chavín period. There is evidence also of Moche and Chimú occupation. No excavations are taking place and the site is more or less abandoned. Likewise, where the Highway crosses the Jequetepeque, the signed ruins of Farfán are closed to the public. The city was separate from Pacatnamú, but probably of the same period. It has yielded important Inca burials.

The next town north is **Chepén**. The town itself is not particularly fascinating but **Cerro Chepén**, towering over it, is the site of an ancient fortress from the Middle Horizon (late Moche/Huari). The fortress contains the ruins of what may be a palace, surrounded by other buildings. The as yet unexcavated site could have been the main station in a chain of lookout posts along the north coast. A little further north is **San José de Moro** (70 km from Chiclayo), which does have an archaeological site open to the public, a ceremonial centre and cemetery of the late Moche and transitional Moche/ Lambayeque period. About 1000 tombs have been found, including those of priestesses. The site is a couple of blocks from the town's main plaza where there is a museum. The guardian of the site can open the museum. He also has his own workshop reproducing the pottery, characterized by fineline painting, found at the site (entry free, but please give a tip; see http://sanjosedemoro.pucp.edu.pe). Harvard University holds an annual field course here in the summer.

◉ Trujillo and around listings

For Sleeping and Eating price codes and other relevant information, see pages 38-44.

◉ Sleeping

Trujillo *p418, map p420*
LL-L Libertador, Independencia 485, Plaza de Armas, T044-232741, www.libertador.com.pe. Comfortable rooms in this luxury hotel at the heart of the city, excellent service, swimming

pool in a flower-filled patio, sauna, cafetería and restaurant, breakfast extra, excellent buffet lunch on Sun. Recommended.
L El Gran Marqués, Díaz de Cienfuegos 145-147, Urb La Merced, T044-249366, www.elgranmarques.com. Price includes breakfast. Modern, free internet connection in rooms, facilities include pool, sauna, jacuzzi, restaurant. Recommended.

AL Los Conquistadores, Diego de Almagro 586, T044-203350, losconquistadores@ viabcp.com. Includes American breakfast, internet, bar, restaurant, very comfortable.

A Paraíso, San Martín 240, opposite the Club Libertad, T044-200073, www.hotelesparaiso. com.pe. Friendly and helpful staff, cheaper without a/c, free internet and Wi-Fi, has roof terrace and pool. In same group as hotel of same name in Chiclayo.

A-B Recreo, Estete 647, T044-220055, www.hotelrecreo.com. Smart modern hotel with suites and rooms with bath and cable TV (jacuzzi in suites), lift, restaurant/bar, internet and Wi-Fi.

B Gran Bolívar, Bolívar 957, T044-222090, www.granbolivarhotel.net. Includes breakfast, in converted 18th-century house, internet, café, bar, parking.

B Hostal Malibú, Av Larco 1471, Urb La Merced, T044-284811, www.hostal malibu.com. Variety of rooms, restaurant, room service, Wi-Fi, minibar, laundry, massage, currency exchange. Also has a sister hotel of the same name at Av Larco 1000 in Huanchaco.

B Torre Norte, Av Miraflores 551, T044-235015, http://hoteltorrenorte.com. New hotel, with attentive staff, café/bar, price includes American breakfast, internet, Wi-Fi and cable TV.

C Chichikuna, San Martín 258 (next to Paraíso), T044-470339, www.chichicuna. com. New hotel with 7 rooms, with bath, a/c optional, hot water, Wi-Fi, Continental breakfast included.

C Colonial, Independencia 618, T044-258261, www.hostalcolonial.com.pe. Attractive but small rooms, hot showers, basic breakfast, good restaurant, especially for set lunch, has travel agency. Recommended.

C Continental, Gamarra 663, T044-241607, hotelcontinental@viabcp.com. Modern hotel opposite the market, with bath, hot water, good breakfast, helpful, safe.

C San Martín, San Martín 749, T044-252311, sanmartin@deperu.com. Attractive, TV, good for breakfast in cafeteria, Wi-Fi, can be noisy.

D Almagro, Jr Almagro 748, T044-223845. New hotel with cable TV, hot water, cafetería (breakfast extra), good.

D Chan Chán Inn, Av Ejército 307, T044-298583, chanchaninn@hotmail.com. Close to several bus terminals so noisy, includes breakfast (cheaper without), popular with backpackers, luggage store, café, laundry, internet, money exchange, information.

D Turismo, Gamarra 747, T044-244181. Includes continental breakfast, central, good services TV, restaurant, parking, travel agency.

E Hostería El Sol, Brillantes 224, Urb Santa Inés, T044-231933, near bus terminals on Av Nicolás de Piérola. With hot shower, restaurant, all meals available for US$2.60.

E Primavera, Av N de Piérola 872, Urb Primavera, T044-231915. Close to bus terminals. Hot water, restaurant, bar, pool.

E-F Beto's Guest House, Ollantay 310, Urb Santa María, T044-204067, www.betosguest house.com. Rooms with and without bath for 1-3 people, hot water, cable TV, on 4 floors of a modern building, use of kitchen, internet, safe parking for cars and motorbikes, airport pick-up US$15, laundry service, Spanish lessons. Several good reports.

E-F Mochica's B&B, La Arboleda E-19, T044-422006, www.mochicas.com. 5 mins by taxi from centre near Av América Sur and bus terminals. Shared rooms for 1, 2 or 4 with bath, safe residential area, quiet, very helpful, good breakfast, internet, TV and DVDs, use of kitchen, hot water.

F pp Casa de Clara, Cahuide 495, T044-243347, www.xanga.com/CasadeClara. Cheaper without bath, hot water, good food (breakfast US$0.90, lunch US$1.50, dinner US$2.10), very helpful, loads of information available, laundry US$1.50 per kg, meeting place and lots going on, internet and Wi-Fi, many languages spoken (see Clara Luz Bravo and Michael White, Activities and tours below). Restaurants nearby. Recommended.

F Residencia Vanini, Av Larco 237, outside Av España, T044-200878, enriqueva@ hotmail.com. Youth hostel in a converted private house, a good option but not in the centre, some rooms with bath, others with shared shower.

F-G pp **El Mochilero**, Independencia 887, T044-297842/992-305471, http://elmochilero.blogia.com. New in 2009, variety of dorms and rooms, only 1 with bath (**E**), electric showers, internet, Wi-Fi, breakfast US$1.75, fridge for guests' use. Tours arranged, information.

Huanchaco *p426, map p427*

The town is a good alternative for sleeping to Trujillo as it is quieter, less polluted, safer and cheaper. There are are many named and unnamed *hostales* in all ranges, especially on the seafront and there is also demand for economical long-stay apartments. Since 2008 street numbers have been changing; some places display the old and the new numbers.

A Caballito de Totora, Av La Rivera 348, T044-462636, reservas@hotelcaballitode totora.com.pe. Rooms and suites, price includes breakfast, cable TV, free internet and Wi-Fi, room service, pool, restaurant, cafeteria and bar, very clean. Same owners as **Continental** hotels in Cajamarca.

B Bracamonte, Los Olivos 503, T044-461162, www.hotelbracamonte.com.pe. Comfortable, good, all rooms with private bathroom, TV, Wi-Fi, pool, secure, good restaurant offers also lunch *menú* and some vegetarian dishes, English spoken, free internet, laundry service, gamesroom. Highly recommended.

B Hostal Huankarute, La Rivera 312, T044-461705, www.hostalhuankarute.com. On the seafront, with small pool, bar, sun terrace, friendly, English spoken; some rooms larger, more luxurious and more expensive. Has Wi-Fi and free internet, travel agency. Recommended.

B Las Palmeras, Av Larco 1624, sector Los Tumbos, T044-461199, www.laspalmeras dehuanchaco.com. A good option, rooms with terrace more expensive than those with view of pool; with breakfast, bath, TV, hot water, dining room has ocean view, lunch and dinner for guests on request, internet and Wi-Fi on 1st floor but not in rooms, pool and gardens.

C Residencial Sol y Mar, La Rivera 400, T044-461120, ctsolymar1@hotmail.com. Breakfast extra, TV (not all cable), with roof terraces, pool, restaurant (Pollería Xquisito) and beautiful gardens, has a good reputation.

D El Malecón, Av La Rivera 225, T044-461275, hostalelm@yahoo.com. Overlooking the sea, some rooms with terrace, clean, hot water, TV, internet and Wi-Fi, café, friendly staff.

D Hostal Huanchaco, Av Larco 287 on the plaza, T044-461272, www.huanchaco hostal.com. With bath, breakfast extra, TV, hot water, clean and friendly, pool, car park, adjacent cafeteria with home-made cakes and other good meals, video, pool table, back door is half a block from beach. Recommended.

D Huanchaco Inn, Los Pinos 185, T044-461158, www.huanchacoinn.net. Rooms with and without bath, 16 rooms, hot water, cable TV, internet cabins, use of kitchen, laundry service, small pool.

D La Casa Suiza, Los Pinos 308, T044-461285, www.lacasasuiza.com. One of Huanchaco's institutions has been bought and revamped by Frenchman Philippe Faucon, with a variety of rooms with and without bath (**F-G** per person), hot water, with small restaurant mainly serving pizza, breakfast extra, barbecue on the roof, free internet, Wi-Fi and book exchange. Owner has recently opened Los Faraones Hotel at Km 11 on the Trujillo–Huanchaco highway.

D Roxy's Lodging House, Los Olivos 122, T044-462646. Family-run, good place for families staying for a few days, breakfast served on small roof terrace with sea view, restaurant, small indoor pool for children.

D-E Hostal Cocos Beach, Av Larco 1500 Los Tumbos, T044-461023, www.hostelcocos beach.com. Opposite the beach, rooms with beds and bunks, hot water, restaurant, internet, surfing lessons, tours arranged.

D-E Huanchaco Gardens, Av Circunvalación 440, El Boquerón, T044-461194, www.huan chacogardens.com. Family-run, bungalows with kitchenette (**D**), cable TV, also shared dorms, camping (US$10 for 2) and parking for RVs, hot water, breakfast on request and other meals if ordered in advance, free luggage store, friendly and helpful, garden with 2 pools (1 for children), free internet and Wi-Fi, laundry US$1.75 per kg. Public transport passes in front. Frequently recommended.

D-E Ñaylamp, Prolongación Víctor Larco 1420, northern end of the seafront in El Boquerón, T044-461022, www.hostalnaylamp.com. Rooms set around a courtyard, a little more expensive in the new wing, with bath, dorms with shared bath (**G** per person), hammocks, nice garden, kitchen, clean, hot water 24 hrs, camping US$3.50 with own tent, US$4.65 with hired tent, laundry facilities, internet, luggage store, safe, good views of the sunset from the campsite and terrace restaurant, Italian food, good breakfasts. Recommended. When coming from Trujillo by bus, take the H-Corazón micro or A or B combi as they are the only ones which will drop you off near the *hostal*.

E Cherry's, Los Pinos 448, T044-462066, limjc160@hotmail.com. Owner Juan Carlos speaks English, **G** per person without bath, hot water, use of kitchen, shop, bar, roof terrace, laundry, even a small swimming pool.

E Hostal Los Esteros, Av Larco 618, T044-461300, huanchacoesteros@yahoo.com. Bathroom, hot water, cable TV, restaurant, friendly, safe car and motorcycle parking, can arrange surfing and *caballitos de totora* trips, popular with groups.

E Las Brisas, Raymondi 146, T044-461186, lasbrisas@hotmail.com. 20 rooms with bath, hot water, restaurant, cable TV, comfy.

E McCallum Lodging, Los Ficus 460, T044-501813. Private rooms and shared triples (**F**), hot water, use of kitchen, family atmosphere, highly considered by locals and tourists, especially for longer stays.

F pp Hostal Solange, Los Ficus 258, 1 block from the beach, T044-461410, hsolange@yahoo.es. With bathroom, hot water, dormitory with bunks **G** per person, breakfast US$2.15 and small restaurant, good

food, laundry facilities and laundry service US$1.75 per kg.

G pp Casa Hospedaje Los Ficus, Los Ficus 516, T044-461719. With bath, breakfast and laundry extra. Family-run, limited hot water, also has pricier rooms, use of kitchen.

G pp Hospedaje El Boquerón, R Palma 330, T044-461968, maznaran@hotmail.com. 1 block from beach, a modern house with shared bathrooms, hot water, fully equipped kitchen, good bakery, laundry facilities and service, clean, friendly landlady speaks French. Ask here about long-stay apartments.

G pp Hospedaje La Casona, Las Palmeras 449, T044-501898. Has a big garden, roof terrace, parking facilities, use of kitchen use, family atmosphere. They have a contract with the University of North Carolina to lodge students on archeological field course.

G Hospedaje My Friend, Los Pinos 533, T044-461080, myfriendhuanchaco@ hotmail.com. Popular place with surfers and foreigners, good for meeting others and for breakfast or a meal in the restaurant, *menú* US$2.75 (open 0800-1800), TV room, with bath and hot water (when the plumbing is functioning), erratic service. Tours arranged.

G Hostal Ilalo, La Orquídeas 312, T044-957 9753. Hot water, roof terrace, welcomes US and local visitors.

Coast of La Libertad north of Trujillo *p428*

Puerto Chicama

At Distrito El Hombre there are several places to stay, from the exclusive **AL Chicama Surf Resort**, www.chicamasurfresort.com, with surfing classes, boats to the waves, spa, restaurant,infinity pool, to the 3-star **A Chicama Beach**, www.chicamabeach.com, with restaurant, Wi-Fi (both open all year), and other humbler places such as **Hostal Long Wave** and **Los Delfines de Chicama** (several close out of season).

Pacasmayo

C La Estación, Malecón Grau 69, T044-521515, www.hotellaestacion.com.pe.

Restaurant on ground floor, all meals extra, 4 rooms with terrace overlooking sea, internet, fan, good beds.

C Libertad, Leoncio Pardo 1-D, T044-521937, www.hotellibertad.com.pe. 2 km from beach by petrol station, with breakfast, Wi-Fi and internet, safe, restaurant/bar, parking, efficient and nice.

C Pakatnamú, Malecón Grau 103, T044-522368, hotelpakatnamu@hotmail.com. Older building on seafront, 1 suite, new rooms have seaview, with breakfast.

D-E Duke Kahanamoku, Ayacucho 44, T044-521889, www.eldukepacasmayo.com. Surfing place, with classes and board rental, breakfast extra, hot water, Wi-Fi, free internet.

◗ Eating

Trujillo *p418, map p420*
A speciality is *shambar*, a thick minestrone made with gammon (pork), served on Mon. Look for it in the better class restaurants. On the westside of the Central Market (Pasaje San Augustín), there are several small restaurants, some open before 0700. On Calle Pizarro there are many eating places to suit all budgets and tastes. Most serve lunch at 1200.

Ħ Romano-Rincón Criollo, Estados Unidos 162, Urb El Recreo, 10-min walk from centre, T044-244207. Northern Peruvian cuisine, *menú* for US$5.60, smart.

Ħ-Ħ El Mochica, Bolívar 462. Typical restaurant with a good reputation, the food is among the best in town and, on special occasions, there's live music. Warmly recommended.

Ħ Chelsea, Estete 675, T044-257032, www.chelsea.com. Restaurant/bar, open 1145-1645, 1700-0100. Buffet *criollo* US$8.70 on Sun, special shows on Fri (live music, fee US$3.50) and Sat (*Marinera* dance show, US$5.25). Recommended.

Ħ Demarco, Pizarro 725. Popular at midday for lunchtime menus and for its cakes and desserts.

Ħ La Rústica, Bolívar 446 (next to El Mochica). Restaurant and disco/bar, open daily 1230-1600 for lunch with a buffet *criollo* for US$9. Night-time shows on Tue and Thu (fee US$5.50) and Fri and Sat (live music, same fee). On Mon there is no entrance fee.

Ħ Le Nature, Marcelo Corne 338, T044-209674. Open Mon-Thu 1000-2200, Fri, Sun 1000-1600, Sat 1900-2200. In a residential district off Av Larco, probably the best vegetarian food in town.

Ħ Pizzería Pizzanino, Av Juan Pablo II 183, Urb San Andrés, opposite University. Recommended for pizzas, pastas, meats, desserts, evening only.

Ħ Romano, Pizarro 747. International food, good *menú*, breakfasts, coffee, excellent milkshakes, cakes, has internet.

Ħ-Ÿ Cevichería Puerto Mori, Estete 482, T044-346752. Very popular, they serve only good seafood. At the same location are 2 more fish restaurants, but not of the same quality.

Ÿ Asturias, Pizarro 741. Nice café with a reasonable *menú*, good pastas, cakes and sandwiches.

Ÿ Café Oviedo, Pizarro 737. With vegetarian options, good salads and cakes, helpful.

Ÿ El Sol, Zepita 203, T044-345105. Open Mon-Sat 0800-2200, Sun 0800-1600. Vegetarian, lunch menú and à la carte.

Ÿ Juguería San Agustín, Bolívar 526. Good juices, good *menú*, popular, excellent value.

Ÿ Parnasillo, Gamarra 368, T044-234715, Mon-Sat 1300-1530. Restaurant and hotel school in a colonial building with marble-topped tables, good *menú* US$3.25-4, food nicely presented, good value. You can see through to the kitchen.

Ÿ Rincón de Vallejo, Orbegoso 303. Good *menú*, typical dishes, very crowded at peak times. So popular that a 2nd branch has opened at Av España 736.

Ÿ Sabor Supremo, Diego de Almagro 210, T044-220437. *Menú* US$1.75, also à la carte, vegetarian food, vegan on special request.

Ÿ Sal y Pimienta, Colón 201. Very popular for lunch, US$1 and US$1.85, close to buses for Huanchaco and Chan Chán.

Cafés

Café Amaretto, Gamarra 368. Smart, good selection of real coffees, "brilliant" cakes, sweets, snacks and drinks.

Dulcería Castañeda, Pizarro 722. Sells local specialities such as *alfajores* and *king kong* to take away. Among the best of many.

Dulcería Doña Carmen, San Martín 814. Also serves local specialities such as *alfajores*, *budin*, *king kong*, etc.

El Chileno, Ayacucho 408. Café and ice cream parlour, popular.

El Kluv, Junin 527 (next to Metro Market). Italian owned, fresh, tasty pizzas at noon and in the late afternoon.

Fitopán, Bolívar 406. Good selection of breads, also serves lunches.

Huanchaco *p426, map p427*

There are plenty of restaurants on the beachfront. Many close in low season and at night.

♥♥♥ Big Ben, Av Larco 1182, near A Sánchez, T044-461869, www.bigbenhuanchaco.com. Daily 1130-1730. Seafood and international menu, à la carte only, most expensive but very good.

♥♥♥ Club Colonial, La Rivera 514, on the beachfront, T044-461015. Open 1100-2300. A smart "lounge-gourmet-bar-restaurant". French-speaking Belgian owner. Also has 6 rooms for rent (**A-B**).

♥♥♥ El Mochica, Av Larco 700, T044-461963. Daily 1200-1800. Same owners and quality as this restaurant in Trujillo, very nice dining area and panorama.

♥♥♥ Huanchaco Beach, Av Larco 602, T044-461484, huanchacobeach@hotmail.com. One of the best for quality seafood in town, popular with tours and cruise passengers.

♥♥♥-♥♥ El Kero, Av La Ribera 612, T044-461184. Open 0800-2400. Very popular meeting place and good restaurant, reduced service in low season.

♥♥ Casa Tere, Plaza de Armas, T044-461197, casatere@yahoo.es. In a beautiful colonial building, for best pizzas in town, also pasta, burgers and breakfasts.

♥♥ Estrella Marina, Av Larco 740, T044-461850. Open 1100-2400. Family-run, great value for fish, serves chicken after 1800.

♥♥ La Barca, Raimondi 117, T044-461855. Open daily till late all year round. Very good seafood, well-run, popular.

♥♥ Los Herrajes, Av Larco 1020, T044-461397, www.losherrajes.com. Open daily 0900-1800. Excellent seafood and nice sea-view terrace, also has a low-priced *menú*. Recommended.

♥♥ Lucho del Mar, Av Larco 750. On seafront road, serves excellent seafood.

♥♥-♥ Menuland, Los Pinos 250, T044-773579. Managed by a German/Peruvian couple, English, German, Italian spoken. Peruvian and international dishes, breakfast, lunch *menú* for US$1.75. Also has 2 double rooms (**G** per person), book exchange.

♥♥-♥ Otra Cosa, Av Larco 1312, T044-461346, www.otracosa.info. Open 0830-2130. Dutch/Peruvian owners, best-known restaurant for vegetarian dishes, breakfast US$3.15, overlooking the sea, check their webiste and blog for volunteer opportunities.

♥ Bambú, Túpac Amaru 117. Open daily from 1630-2300 (longer in high season). Chinese food, salads, sandwiches and juices.

♥ El Dragón, Av Larco 630. Owner also has a restaurant of this name in Trujillo, serving chicken and Chinese food, economical.

♥ El Choclo (de Don Feliciano), Mar de Plata 235. A little remote, uphill next to the church, in front of Colegio Olaya. Take a mototaxi up and walk back down. Very modest and basic, but reputed to have the best *ceviche* in town.

♥ La Charapita, Huáscar 162. Modest but popular restaurant serving large portions.

♥ Pollería La Barra, Los Helechos 619. Open 2100-2300. Considered by locals as the best chicken restaurant. Also delivery service, convenient if staying in Los Pinos district.

Cafés

Argolini, Av Rivera 400, in the **Sol y Mar** building. Convenient for people staying in the Los Pinos/Los Ficus area for fresh bread, cakes, ice cream, coffee and juices. Reasonable prices.

Chocolate, Av Rivera 752, T044-462420. Open 0730-1900. Dutch/Peruvian management, very clean and well-run, serves breakfast, also some vegetarian food, coffee and cakes. Also offers bed and breakfast.
Dulcería Carmen, next to police station on Av Rivera. Popular for breakfast, or for a coffee, good value.
Sabor Divino, T044-696916. Vegetarian food, delivery service only.

◐ Bars and clubs

Trujillo p418, map p420
Nightlife is concentrated around Ovalo Larco, with lots of pubs and restaurants close to the Centro Comercial Vea and the UPAO university. There are still many places in the centre, some listed below, and several restaurants have shows, some listed above.
Bar/Café Juguete, Independencia 705. Old-style café, good coffee. Open until midnight. Good pasta restaurant attached.
Bar/Café Stradivarius, Colón 327. An attractive café with sofas, open in the evenings only.
Canana, San Martín 788, T044-232503. Bars and restaurant, disco, live music at weekends (US$1.50-3), video screens (also has travel agency). Recommended, but take care on leaving.
El Estribo, San Martin 809, T044-204053. Club open from Wed playing a different style of music every night. Attracts a mixed crowd.
Luna Rota, Av América Sur 2119. Good, has folk music on Thu and Sat night.
Tributo, Pizarro 389. Always busy, attracts a well-heeled crowd.

Huanchaco p426, map p427
El Balcón, Av Larco 810, T044-462441, rosenbergward@hotmail.com. Colombian owned, popular at night, offers seafood dishes, irregular hours but open late.
Mamacha, Las Gardenias entre Los Pinos y Los Ficus. Lounge, including some vegetarian dishes, and bar in a separate room. Bar opens at 2000.

Oh Ibiza, Túpac Amaru 105. Café, music and delicatessen with karaoke upstairs, Spanish owner, opens at 1900, being refurbished in 2010.
Sabes?, Av Larco 920, T044-461555, ysabes@yahoo.com. Opens at 2000. Pub with food, internet café, pool table, popular a good place for an early evening get-together.
Sunkella, next to El Quibishi complex. Restaurant and disco bar, in off-season only open on Fri night, sometimes has live music.

❁ Festivals and events

Trujillo p418, map p420
End Jan The National Marinera Contest lasts 2 weeks and consists of hundreds of couples competing in 6 categories, from children to seniors. This event is organized by the **Club Libertad** and has taken place since 1960.
19-22 Mar Feria de San José, an important festival held in Las Delicias.
18 Jun Festival de la Música.
Last week of Sep Festival Internacional de la Primavera, www.tuprimaveraen trujillo.com. Organized by the Club de Leones, it is a celebration of the arrival of spring and has grown over the years to become one of Peru's most important tourist events. The final parade (corso) has plenty to enjoy, with many local dancers, dog owners' clubs, schools parades and so on. Those who are strongly opposed to beauty pageants may want to give it a miss as there are floats with beauty queens from South and North America participating. Other days feature cultural events (some charitable), and, above all, Trujillo's famous **Caballos de Paso**, a fine breed of horses with a tripping gait that has made them renowned worldwide. These horses, a Spanish legacy, have been immortalized in Peruvian waltzes. Riders still compete in their own form of the Marinera dance and buyers congregate to see them shown at the Spring Festival (see www.rcp.net.pe/rcp/caballos).

Huanchaco *p426, map p427*
1st week of May Festival del Mar, a celebration of the disembarkation of Taycanamo, the leader of the Chimú period. A procession is made in *totora* boats.
29 Jun San Pedro, patron saint of fishermen. His statue is taken out to sea on a huge *totora*-reed boat.

There are also surf competitions (eg 29 Jan) and **Carnival** and **New Year** are especially popular.

O Shopping

Trujillo *p418, map p420*
Bookshops
Librería Peruana, Pizarro 505, just off the Plaza de Armas. Has the best selection in town, ask for Sra Inés Guerra de Guijón.
SBS, Jr Bolívar 714, in **Mall Aventura** shopping centre, Av Mansiche block 20, and in **Mall Real Plaza**, Prol Av César Vallejo (behind UPAO University), California (see below). Sells some Footprint titles.

Camera repairs
Fotolab, Av España 2755, T044-295590. Hugo Guevara repairs all makes.
Fotovisión Para Tí, Pizarro 523. Also repairs cameras.
Studio Osito, Orbegoso 756. Can repair a range of cameras and is centrally located.

Handicrafts
120 Artesanía por Descubrir, Las Magnolias 403, California, www.tienda120.blogspot. com. Art gallery designs and handmade crafts, near Real Plaza.
APIAT, craft market, Av España y Zela. The largest craft market in the city, good for ceramics, totora boats, woodwork and leather, competitive prices.
Artesanía del Norte, at Dulcería La Libertad, Jr Pizarro 758, and at the Huacas del Sol y de la Luna, www.artesaniadelnorte.com. Sells items mostly to the owner, Mary Cortijo's, design using traditional techniques.

Trama Perú, Pizarro 754, T044-287897, www.tramaperu.com. Mon-Fri 1000-2130. High-quality, handmade art objects, authorized Moche art replicas.

Leather and shoes
Trujillo is renowned for its leather and shoe industry. Prices for shoes are very attractive, but sizes over European 42 are hard to find. Try on both sides of blocks 18, 19 and 20 of **Av España**, blocks 6 and 7 of Grau, or block 7 of Jr Colón for all kinds of leather goods.

Markets
Sunday is the busiest day. **Mercado Central**, Gamarra, Ayacucho and Pasaje San Agustín. **Mercado La Hermelinda** in Florencio de Mora district is the biggest, but not in a safe area. **Mercado Mayorista** between Sinchi Roca and Av Los Incas, also an unsafe zone. **Mercado Unión**, between Av Santa and Av Perú, somewhat safer than other markets, also offers repairs on shoes, clothes and bags.

Supermarkets
Metro, Junín 700. **Tottus**, in the Mall Aventura, Av Mansiche blocks 20-22 (most convenient for Huanchaco). This Mall also has 14 fast food outlets, all kinds of shop and banks. **Vea**, Real Plaza Shopping Center, behind the UPAO university on Prolongación Av César Vallejo, California district (take taxi or the green California micro A which stops at one corner of the Mall. The Huanchaco micro A also passes nearby). **Wong**, Av Larco 857 (near Ovalo Larco).

Huanchaco *p426, map p427*
The main *artesanía* market, **El Quibishi**, is at the entrance to Huanchaco at the southern end of the beach and is divided into handicraft stalls, which close early evening, and a popular food section, mostly open at weekends. Some stalls also on the seafront adjoining the Municipalidad, **El Erizo**, Av La Rivera 735, **Wachake**, Av La Rivera 720 (opposite) and **Takaynamo**, Av Larco 620. No supermarkets (use those

in Trujillo) and food in the shops is a bit more expensive than Trujillo. There is a small fresh food market on Pilcomayo, ½ block from Deán Saavedra; there are also small restaurants on Pilcomayo (eg **La Marea** at No 320).

▲ Activities and tours

Trujillo *p418, map p420*
Billiards/pool
Pool halls near the UNT university, on block 2 of Av Juan Pablo II and block 3 of Av Jesús de Nazareth, are much visited by students and teachers. They also frequent the neighbouring restaurants **Charole's** and **Katty**.

Caballos de paso
La Asociación de Criadores de Caballos de Paso Peruanos, www.ancpcpp.org.pe, has an enclosure with plots for each member's house and stables on the Vía de Evitamiento, just north of its junction with Av Larco. Owners may be prepared to show visitors around.
El Palmar, stables, on the Vía de Evitamiento near **Hotel El Golf**, charges US$12 per person to see and maybe ride the horses at its stables. Book the day before at the office on Pizarro, on the Plaza de Armas.

For group visits to **Manucci** stables, just south of the Huaca del Sol, and **Vásquez Nacarino** at Paiján, contact Clara Bravo and Michael White, see Tour guides, below.

Football
The city team **César Vallejo** plays at the Mansiche stadium on the north side of the city centre. Entry US$3-6 (visitors should buy a more expensive seat).

Sandboarding
Sandboarding is possible on large dunes near Simbal, 1 hr up the Moche Valley, about US$10 with agencies, including board.

Swimming
Academia Berendson, Bolognesi 251. Heated pool, Mon-Fri 0600-2200, Sat 0700-1400.
Fiorella Spa and Fitness Club,
Jr Zepita 386, T044-205625.

There's an outdoor municipal swimming pool next to Mansiche stadium, entrance on Av España side, where buses arrive from Chan Chán and Huanchaco. Daily 0900-1300 and 1600-1800, entry US$0.50.

Tour operators
Prices vary and competition is fierce so shop around for the best deal. To **Chan Chán**, **El Dragón** and **Huanchaco**, 4-4½ hrs for US$8-9 per person. To **Huacas del Sol** and **de la Luna**, 2½-3 hrs for US$8-9 per person (effectively only Huaca de la Luna as the Huaca del Sol cannot be visited – operators on the plaza do not explain this). To **El Brujo**, US$27-34 per person, 5-8 hrs. **Caballos de paso**, US$8.50 per person, 2-2½ hrs, usually at 1330. **City tours** cost US$3.50 pp, 2-2½ hrs. Prices do not include entrance fees. Few agencies run tours on Sun and often only at fixed times on other days. Check exactly which sites are included, if transport, entry and guide are included, how many people will be in the group and whether guides speak your language.
Chacón Tours, Av España 106-112, T044-255212. Open Sat afternoon and Sun morning. Recommended for flights, etc, but offers few local tours.
Guía Tours, Independencia 580, T044-234856, guiatour@amauta.rcp.net.pe. Also Western Union agent. Recommended.

Tour guides
Many hotels work on a commission basis with taxi drivers and travel agencies. If you decide on a guide, make your own direct approach and always agree what is included in the price. The tourist police (see Directory) has a list of guides; average cost US$7 per hr. Beware of cowboy outfits herding up tourists around the plazas and bus terminals for rapid,

poorly translated tours. Also beware scammers offering surfing or salsa lessons and party invitations.

Clara Bravo, Cahuide 495, T949-243347, www.xanga.com/trujilloperu. An experienced tourist guide who speaks Spanish, English, German and understands Italian. She takes tourists on extended circuits of the region (archaeological tour US$20 for 6 hrs, city tour US$7 per person, US$53 per car to El Brujo, with extension to Sipán, Brüning Museum and Túcume possible – tours in Lambayeque involve public transport, not included in cost). Clara works with English chartered accountant **Michael White** (same address, microbewhite@yahoo.com, also speaks German, French and Italian), who provides transport. He is very knowledgeable about tourist sites. They run tours any day of the week; 24-hr attention, accommodate small groups.

Luis Ocas Saldaña, Jr José Martí 2019, T949-339593, guianorteperu@hotmail.com. Very knowledgeable, helpful, covers all of northern Peru. Recommended.

Gustavo Prada Marga, at Chan Chán, is an experienced guide.

Alfredo Ríos Mercedes, riosmercedes@ hotmail.com, T949-657978. Speaks English.

Jannet Rojas Sánchez, Alto Mochica Mz Q 19, Trujillo, T949-344844, jannarojas@hotmail. com. Speaks English, enthusiastic, works also for **Guía Tours**.

Celso Eduardo Roldán, celsoroldan@ hotmail.com. Helpful and informative guide.

José Soto Ríos, Atahualpa 514, dpto 3, T949-251489. He speaks English and French.

Huanchaco p426, map p427
Surfing
There are plenty of surf schools. Cost of equipment rental US$8.75 per day, 1 lesson US$14-15.50.

Indigan, Deán Saavedra 582 (next to soccer field), T044-462591, indigansurf@ hotmail.com. John and Giancarlos Urcía for lessons, surf trips and rentals. Also offer lodging at their home.

Muchik, Av Larco 650, T044-462535, www.escuela tablamuchik.com. Instructors Chico and Omar Huamanchumo are former surf champions and run trips to various surf sites. Also repairs.

Olas Norte, Los Ficus 450, olasnorte_rnm@ hotmail.com. Individual and group lessons, prices include full equipment.

Onechako, at the time of writing seeking new premises, escuelasurfonechako@ hotmail.com. Owner Tito Lescano. Also offer *caballito de totora* riding lessons. Surf trips to other surf beaches in the North.

Yenth Ccora, Av Larco 500, T044-949 403871, ycc_mar@hotmail.com. Surfing equipment manufacture, repair, rental and surfing school.

Tour operators
Huanchaco Tours, Av La Rivera Sur 312, T044-462383, www.huanchaco-tours.com. Part of **Huankarute** hotel, offers local tours and all-inclusive 2- to 4-day tours.

Ozelyne Robin, T044-94 8402471, ozelyne. robin@hotmail.com. Private tours in French, English or Spanish, call to arrange routes and prices, also does trips to rural areas.

⊖ Transport

Trujillo p418, map p420
Air
Airport T044-464013. There are daily flights to and from **Lima** with LAN and Star Perú. Most flights leave after dark so it is not safe to walk the 2 km from turn-off on the main road to the terminal. Wherever you are, take a taxi to the airport, US$4.

Airline offices LAN, Almagro 490, T044-221469. **Star Perú**, Independencia 463, T044-226948, open 0900-1930.

Bus
Local Micros (small buses with 25 or more seats) and combis (up to 15 passengers) cost US$0.30 in the urban area, US$0.35-0.45 to the outskirts; colectivos (cars carrying 6 passengers), US$0.40, tend to run on main

avenues starting from Av España. None is allowed inside an area bounded by Av Los Incas in the east to Ovalo Mansiche in the west and the north and south perimeters of Av España. If alone, take care in these shared vehicles. Some authorized colectivo taxi companies have strictly defined routes along main streets. The cars are generally black and show a sign with letters (A, B, C). The most important and most used are: the east-west route between the inner city and Buenos Aires, along Av Larco; the south–north routes from the Mercado Mayorista district along Av España (one on the east side, the other on the west) via Ovalo Mansiche to Esperanza district on Av Nicolás de Piérola.

Long distance A large new bus terminal for southbound buses is being built between Ovalos Grau and La Marina – no completion date has been set. Meanwhile, better bus companies maintain their own terminals. To and from **Lima**, 561 km, 7½ hrs in the upper range buses, average fare US$24-35, 10 hrs in the cheaper buses, US$10.50-17. There are many bus companies operating along this route, among those recommended are: **Cruz del Sur**, Amazonas 437 near Av Ejército, T044-261801; **Turismo Díaz**, Nicolás de Piérola 1079 on Panamericana Norte, T044-201237; **Línea**, Av América Sur 2857, T044-297000 (with an office opposite **Rincón de Vallejo** on Orbegoso), 3 levels of service, also to **Chimbote** hourly, **Huaraz**, 9 hrs, **Cajamarca** 5 a day, **Chiclayo**, hourly, US$4.75, from Carrión by Av Mansiche, T044-235847, on the hour, and **Piura**, 2300. Also **Flores**, Av Ejército 346, T044-208250. **Ittsa**, Av Mansiche 145, T044-251415; No 431 for northern destinations – good service, T044-222541. **Móvil**, Av América Sur 3959, T044-286538. **Oltursa**, Av Ejército 342, T044-263055, 3 *bus cama* services to Lima. **Tepsa**, Av La Marina 205, T044-205017. **TRC Express**, Av Jesús de Nazareth 1890, near Aventura Mall, T044-612122, offering VIP service to **Lima** and **Chiclayo** only, new buses with reclining seats with individual LCD screens.

Small **Pakatnamú** buses leave when full, 0400-2100, from Av N de Piérola 1092, T044-206594, to **Pacasmayo**, 102 km, 1¼ hrs, US$3.40. There is a similar service from beside the Ittsa northern terminal, Av Mansiche 431. To **Chiclayo**, 3 hrs from Trujillo, US$4.75, several companies. Among the best are **Emtrafesa**, Av Túpac Amaru 185, T044-471521, www.emtrafesa.com, on the half-hour every hour; also to **Jaén**, 1930, 9 hrs, US$10; **Piura**, 6 hrs, US$9.25 (Ittsa's 1330, or Línea's 1415 buses are good choices).

Direct buses to **Huaraz**, 319 km, via **Chimbote** and **Casma** (169 km), with **Línea** and **Móvil**, 8 hrs, US$12-20.50. There are several buses and colectivos to **Chimbote**, with **América Express** from Av La Marina 315, 135 km, 2 hrs, US$2.85, departures every 30 mins from 0530 (ticket sales from 0500); then change at Chimbote (see above – leave Trujillo before 0600 to make a connection from 0800). Ask Clara Bravo and Michael White (see Tour guides, above) about transport to Caraz avoiding Chimbote (a very worthwhile trip via the Brasileños road and Cañón del Pato).

To **Cajamarca**, 300 km, 7-8 hrs, US$7-29: with **Línea**, **Emtrafesa**, see above, at 2145, and **Horna**, Av N de Piérola 1249, T044-225303.

To **Huamachuco**, 170 km, 6 hrs, US$7-8.55, **Trans Horna**, 5 a day, also Tunesa, Prol Av Vallejo 1390, T044-210725.

To **Chachapoyas**, **Móvil's** Lima-Chiclayo-Chachapoyas service passes through Trujillo at 1600 and Chiclayo at 2000, US$22.

To **Tarapoto**, via Moyobamba, **Tarapoto Tours**, US$21-29, Av N de Piérola 1239, T044-470318, at 2230, and **Ejetur** Av N de Piérola 1238, T044-222228, at 1300, 1500, also to Yurimaguas at 0700, and to Jaén at 1700, US$10.

Taxi Town trip, US$0.85 within Av España and US$1.05 within Av América. To airport US$4. Beware of overcharging, check fares with locals. Taxi from in front of Hotel Libertador, US$10 per hr, about the same rate as a tour with an independent guide or travel agent for 1-2 people.

Huacas del Sol and de la Luna p423

Combis every 15 mins from Ovalo Grau and, less safe, Galvez y Los Incas. They leave you a long walk from the site. On the return go to Ovalo Grau for onward connections. US$0.40. Taxis about US$5; few at site for return, unless you ask driver to wiat.

Chan Chán p425

Take any transport between Trujillo and Huanchaco (see below) and ask to get out at the turn-off to Chan Chán, US$0.40. A taxi is US$3 from Trujillo to the ruins, US$0.85 from museum to ruins, US$2 to Huanchaco.

Huanchaco p426, map p427

2 combi routes run between Trujillo and Huanchaco, A and B, **Caballitos de Totora** company (white and black). 4 micros run between Trujillo and Huanchaco: A, B (also known as Mercado Mayorista), H (UPAO) and H-Corazón (with red heart, Mercado Hermelinda), **Transportes Huanchaco**, red, yellow and white. They run 0500-2030, every 5-10 mins. Fare is US$0.55 for the journey (25 mins by combi, 45-60 mins by microbus). The easiest place to pick up any of these combis or micros is Ovalo Mansiche, 3 blocks northwest of Av España in front of the Cassinelli museum. In Trujillo, combi A takes a route on the south side of Av España, before heading up Av Los Incas. Combi B takes the northerly side of Av España. Micro A from Huanchaco goes to the 28 de Julio/Costa Rica junction where it turns west along Prolongación César Vallejo, passing the UPAO university and Plaza Real shopping centre, continuing to the Av El Golf (the terminus for return to Huanchaco on almost the same route). From Huanchaco to the city centre on other routes, ask the *cobrador* to let you off near C Pizarro on Av España. For the **Línea, Móvil Tours** and southern bus terminals, take micro H. It also goes to Ovalo Grau where you can catch buses to the Huacas del Sol and de la Luna. For **Cruz del Sur, Ormeño, Flores, Oltursa**, etc, take combi or micro B from Huanchaco. Taxis US$4.10-5.10.

Puerto Chicama

Micros from Santa Cruz terminal, Av Santa Cruz, 1 block from Av America Sur, US$1.65. Also **Dorado** buses, Av N de Piérola 1062, T044-291778 (via Paiján), US$1.65, US$0.35 from Paiján, 16 km.

El Brujo p428

The complex can be reached by taking one of the regular buses from Trujillo to **Chocope**, US$1, and then a colectivo (every 30 mins) to **Magdalena de Cao**, US$0.50, then a mototaxi to the site, including wait, US$5, or a 5-km walk to the site.

Coast of La Libertad north of Trujillo p428

Bus from Pacasmayo to **Cajamarca**, US$5.75, 5 hrs; to **Chiclayo**, US$2.30, 2 hrs.

⊙ Directory

Trujillo p418, map p420
Banks . Banco de la Nación, Diego de Almagro 297. BBVA Continental, Pizarro 620. BCP, Gamarra 562. Citibank, Junín 468, T044-204353. Interbank, Pizarro y Gamarra. Scotiabank, Pizarro 314, Casa de Mayorazgo de Facalá; also opposite Metro supermarket, Pizarro y Junín. There are many *casas de cambio* and street changers on Gamarra block 5 and Bolívar blocks 5 and 6.
Consulates UK, Honorary Consul, Mr Winston Barber, Jr Alfonso Ugarte 310, T044-245935, winstonbarber@terra.com.pe. Mon-Fri 0900-1700. **Cultural centres** Alianza Francesa, San Martín 858-62, T044-231232, www.alianzafrancesa.org.pe, open Mon-Fri 0900-1300-1500-1730. Instituto Nacional de Cultura, Independencia 572, open Mon-Fri 0900-1300, 1500-1730. Instituto de Cultura Peruano Norte-americano, Av Venezuela 125, Urb El Recreo, T044-232512, www.elcultural.com.pe.
Immigration Av Larco 1220, Urb Los Pinos, T044-282217. Mon-Fri 0815-1230, 1500-1630, entrance at the back of the

building. Gives 30-day visa extensions, US$20 (proof of funds and onward ticket required), plus US$0.80 for *formulario* in Banco de la Nación (fixers on the street will charge more).

Internet There are internet offices all over the centre, in most hotels and *hostales*, US$0.35 per hr. Many internet offices also offer photocopying; the best places are in front of the main entrances to the universities. **Laundry** American dry cleaners, Bolognesi 784, ironing is charged extra. 24-hr service. **Laundry Room**, Indepedencia 316-A, T044-294037, same day delivery. **Lavanderías Unidas**, Pizarro 683, US$3 per kg. **Splash Clean**, Bolognesi 261, English spoken. **Medical services** Doctors: Dr César Aníbal Calderón Alfaro, T044-255591, T94-995 3606 (mob). Understands English. **Hospitals: Hospital Belén**, Bolívar 350, T044-245281, emergency entrance from Bolognesi. **Clínica Peruano Americana**, Av Mansiche 702, T044-231261. English spoken, good. **Clínica Sánchez Ferrer**, Los Laureles 436, Urb California, T044-284889. **Pharmacies:** Several pharmacy chains in the centre (on Pizarro and Gamarra) and others on either side of Belén hospital on Bolognesi.

Post Independencia 286 y Bolognesi, 0800-2000, Sun 0900-1300, stamps only on special request (better to go to Huanchaco psot office for stamps). DHL, Almagro 579. **Telephone** Locutorios are all over the centre. **Tourist police** Independencia 572, in the INC building, T044-291705, policia_turismo_tru@hotmail.com, daily 0800-2000. They provide useful information and can help with reports of thefts, etc. Some police speak English.

Huanchaco *p426, map p427*
Banks BBV ATM just south of pier next to Municipalidad. On the other side of the Municipalidad is a **GlobalNet** ATM. **Multiservice**, Av Rivera 770, offers exchange. **Internet** Many *hostales* and other places in town offer internet and Wi-Fi. On Los Pinos, Deán Saavedra and La Rivera. **Laundry** **Lavandería El Wayki**, Los Sauces 560, open daily 1000 to 2200. **Lavandería Mister Phil**, Los Helechos 619. Open daily 0900-1900, new machines, US$1.75 per wash, US$2 to dry. **Medical services** **Centro de Salud**, Jr Atahualpa 128, T044-461547. **Post** Manco Capac 304, Mon-Sat 1400-1800.

Chiclayo and around

Chiclayo, set up by Spanish priests in the 1560s as a rural Indian village, has long since outgrown other towns of the Lambayeque Department. It came to prominence after Zaña (see page 446) was abandoned in 1726. Sandwiched between the Pacific Ocean and the Andes, Lambayeque is one of Peru's principal agricultural regions, and its chief producer of rice and sugar cane. It is also the outlet for produce from the northern jungle, which comes by road over the comparatively low Porculla Pass. Chiclayo is the major commercial hub of the zone, but also boasts distinctive cuisine and musical tradition (Marinera, Tondero and Afro-Peruvian rhythms), a famous witchdoctors' market and an unparalleled archaeological and ethnographic heritage. The area is also growing in importance as a birdwatching destination. Chiclayo is dubbed 'The Capital of Friendship', and while that tag could equally apply to most of the north coast of Peru, there is an earthiness and vivacity about its citizens that definitely sets it apart. ▸▸ *For listings, see pages 452-457.*

Ins and outs

Getting there José Abelardo Quiñones González airport, T074-233192, is 1 km from the town centre; taxi from centre costs US$2.75. There is no bus terminal; most buses stop outside their offices, many on or around Bolognesi, which is south of the centre. Confusingly many of the buses leaving for the surrounding area are to the north of the centre.

Getting around Calle Balta is the main street but the markets and most of the hotels and restaurants are spread out over about five blocks from the Plaza de Armas. Mototaxis are cheap. They cost US$0.70 anywhere in city. The surrounding area is well served by public transport.

Tourist information Centro de Información Turística ① *Sáenz Peña 838, T074-205703, iperuchiclayo@ promperu.gob.pe, 0900-1900, Sun 0900-1300*; also at the airport (open daily). **Indecopi** ① *Los Tumbos 245, Santa Victoria, T074-206223, aleyva@indecopi.gob.pe, Mon-Fri 0800-1300, 1630-1930*, for complaints and consumer protection. The tourist police ① *Av Sáenz Peña 830, T236700, ext 311, 24 hrs a day*, are very helpful and may store luggage and take you to the sites themselves. There are tourist kiosks on the plaza and on Balta.

Chiclayo → *For listings, see pages 452-457. Colour map 1, C2. Phone code: 074. Population: 411,536.*

On the Plaza de Armas is the 19th-century neoclassical **cathedral**, designed by the English architect Andrew Townsend, whose descendants can still be identified among the town's principals. The private **Club de la Unión** is on the plaza at the corner of Calle San José. Where Avenida Balta meets Bolognesi, a **Paseo de Las Musas** has been built, with pleasant gardens, statues of the Greek muses and imitation Greek columns. A similar **Paseo de Los Héroes** is at the opposite end of town. Another newish plaza is **Parque Leonardo Ortiz**, with a statue of Ñaylamp, buildings in the Lambayeque style and fountains.

Around Chiclayo → *For listings, see pages 452-457.*

Lambayeque → *Colour map 1, C2.*

About 12 km northwest from Chiclayo is Lambayeque, its narrow streets lined by colonial and republican houses, many retaining their distinctive wooden balconies and wrought iron grill-work over the windows, but many in very bad shape. On Calle 2 de Mayo see especially **Casa de la Logia o Montjoy**, whose 64-m-long balcony is said to be the longest in the colonial Americas. It is being restored. At 8 de Octubre 345 is **Casona Descalzi**, which is well-preserved as a good restaurant (see below). It has 120 carved iguana heads on the ceiling. Opposite, at No 328, **Casona Cúneo**, and **Casona Iturregui Aguilarte**, No 410, are, by contrast, seriously neglected. Also of interest is the 16th-century **Complejo Religioso Monumental de San Francisco de Asís** and the

Chiclayo

N

100 metres
100 yards

Sleeping 🛏
1 América *B2*
2 Casa de la Luna *B1*
3 Costa del Sol *C3*
4 El Sol *B1*
5 Garza *C3*
6 Gran Hotel Chiclayo *B1*
7 Hosp Concordia *C3*
8 Hosp San Eduardo *C3*
9 Inti *B2*
10 Las Musas *C3*
11 Paraíso *A3*
12 Pirámide Real *C3*
13 Santa Rosa *B2*
14 Sicán *C2*
15 Sol Radiante *C2*

Eating 🍴
1 Boulevar *B2*
2 Café Astoria *C2*
3 D'Onofrio *C3*
4 El Huaralino *C1*
5 Fiesta *B1*
6 Hebrón *C3*
7 Kaprichos *A3*
8 La Panadería *B2*
9 La Parra *C3*
10 La Plazuela *B1*
11 Las Américas *B3*
12 Roma *C3*
13 Romana *C3*
14 Tradiciones *C3*

Transport 🚌
1 Brüning Express to Lambayeque *B1*
2 Cial *C1*
3 Civa *C3*
4 Colectivos to Lambayeque *A2*
5 Colectivos to Puerto Etén *A3*
6 Cruz del Sur *C3*
7 Emtrafesa *C3*
8 Línea *C2*
9 Móvil *C2*
10 Oltursa *B1*
11 Tepsa *C2*
12 Transportes Chiclayo *B1*

baroque church of the same name which stands on the **Plaza de Armas 27 de Diciembre**. The French neo-baroque **Palacio Municipal** is also on the plaza.

The reason most people visit is to see the town's two museums. The older of the two is the **Brüning Archaeological Museum** ① *0900-1700, US$3.50, a guided tour costs an extra US$2.75*, in a modern building, specializing in Mochica, Lambayeque/Sicán and Chimú cultures.

Three blocks east is the more recent **Museo de las Tumbas Reales de Sipán** ① *http://sipan.perucultural.org.pe, 0900-1700, closed Mon, US$3.45, mototaxi from plaza US$0.35*, shaped like a pyramid. The magnificent treasure from the tomb of 'The Old Lord of Sipán' (see page 447), and a replica of the Lord of Sipán's tomb are displayed here. A ramp from the main entrance takes visitors to the third floor, from where you descend, mirroring the sequence of the archaeologists' discoveries. There are handicrafts outside and a **tourist office** ① *Tue-Sun 1030-1400, 1500-1730*.

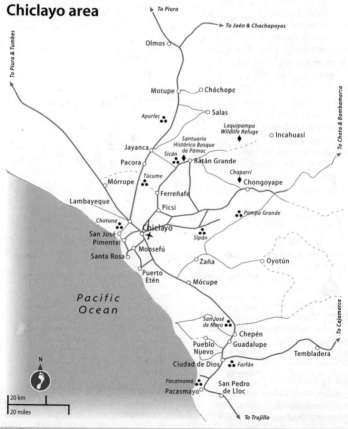

Chiclayo area

To Piura
To Jaén & Chachapoyas
To Piura & Tumbes
Olmos
Motupe
Chóchope
Apurlec
Salas
Laquipampa Wildlife Refuge
Incahuasí
Santuario Histórico Bosque de Pómac
Jayanca
Sicán
Batán Grande
To Chota & Bambamarca
Pacora
Túcume
Chaparrí
Chongoyape
Mórrope
Ferreñafe
Lambayeque
Picsi
Pampa Grande
Chotuna
Chiclayo
San José Pimentel
Sipán
Monsefú
Santa Rosa
Zaña
Oyotún
Puerto Etén
Mócupe
Pacific Ocean
To Cajamarca
San José de Moro
Chepén
Pueblo Nuevo
Guadalupe
Ciudad de Dios
Farfán
Tembladera
Pacatnamú
San Pedro de Lloc
Pacasmayo
N
20 km
20 miles
To Trujillo

Legend of Ñaylamp

Like much else along this stretch of the Peruvian coast, the exact origin of the people's forebears is something of a mystery. The Spaniard, Cabello de Balboa, in 1578, is said to be the first outsider to hear of a local folk legend referring to a person named Ñaylamp who arrived on the coast of Lambayeque along with his court, his servants and his many concubines in numerous balsa rafts.

He then constructed residential buildings near the coast and a temple called Chot, or Chotuna, where he placed an idol called Yampallec, from which Lambayeque is supposed to derive its name. (See below).

The name Ñaylamp came to occupy an important place in the religious imagery of later civilizations through the designs of *tumis*, or ceremonial knives, funerary masks and countless other objects. In the ancient Muchik language spoken by the Moche, *ñam* means bird and *lá* means water, and the figures on Moche ceramics, jewellery and temple walls often have bird-like features and eyes shaped like wings. On his death, the people were told that Ñaylamp had grown wings and flown away.

Ñaylamp had many children but only three are known of: Cium, Nor and Cala, who founded the present site of Túcume. This dynasty is said to have ended with the death of the last governor, Fempellec, as a result of his illicit relationship with a demon in the shape of a beautiful woman. With catastrophic consequences, she tricked him into moving Yampallec away from Chota.

Chotuna ① *Entry US$1.80*. A rough road running through fields towards San José leads 7 km to the archaeological site of Chotuna, where the legend of Ñaylamp was revealed. There are three main pyramids: Huaca Chornancap (100 m x 85 m x 25 m), where polychrome paintings have been found, Huaca Norte, which has been extensively excavated, and Templo de los Frisos; you may be able to see the friezes when archaeologists are at work, Monday-Friday. There is a viewpoint overlooking the site. The site museum contains models, paintings of Ñaylamp's story and a some objects.

Mórrope → *Colour map 1, C2.*
On the plaza in Mórrope, on the Pan-American Highway north of Chiclayo (20 km beyond Lambayeque), is one of the earliest churches in northern Peru, **San Pedro de Mórrope** (1545), an adobe and algarrobo structure (under reconstruction, ask for Carlos Tejada in the restuarant on the plaza, who has the key). The pillars and rafters were cut from the local carob tree, giving the church interior the appearance of the skeleton of some enormous beast. It contains the tomb of the cacique Santiago Cazusol. Next to it is the more modern parish church. Mórrope was famous for its craftsmen who produced pottery for the towns of northern Peru using pre-Hispanic techniques. With a *paletín* (paddle) the potter manipulated the coil of clay into shape. Sometimes the *paletín* had a pattern on it, which was transferred onto the clay. Nowadays, sadly, it is almost impossible to find a potter practising this art.

Monsefú, Pimentel, Santa Rosa and Puerto Eten → *Colour map 1, C2.*
The traditional town of **Monsefú**, 16 km to the southwest, is worth a visit. The town's **music** is nationally famous, and there are many popular orchestras. It is also known for **handicrafts** and has a good **market** on Avenida Venezuela, four blocks from the plaza. Handicraft stalls

open when potential customers arrive. **Feria de Monsefú**, at the end of September, has market stalls around the plaza selling *artesanía*, bread, plastic toys and ceramics. The town market covers one block, entered off the plaza (with your back to the church, on the left side). At the entrance are bread sellers with huge baskets of breads and buns.

There are three ports serving the Chiclayo area, all beyond Monsefú. **Pimentel**, 8 km from Chiclayo by a new highway, is the closest beach resort to the city. It gets very crowded on Sundays. The surfing between Pimentel and the Bayovar Peninsula is excellent, reached from Chiclayo (14.5 km) by road branching off from the Pan-American Highway. Sea-going reed boats (*caballitos de totora*) are used by fishermen and can be seen returning in the late afternoon. The old, decaying **pier** ⓘ *US$0.25*, from which huge quantities of cotton and sugar were once exported, can be visited to watch the fishermen unloading their catches. The pier is to be renovated and made into a tourist attraction. There is a **Casa/Museo** ⓘ *Quiñones 448*, dedicated to **José Quiñones**, hero of the 1942 war with Ecuador.

A more traditional fishing village is nearby **Santa Rosa**, where fishermen use two groups of boats *caballitos* and *bolicheros* – pastel-painted craft that line the shore after the day's fishing. Take a combi between the two towns – on no account walk. The most southerly is **Puerto Eten**, a quaint port with wooden buildings on the plaza, 24 km by road from Chiclayo. There are plans to redevelop its pier, too, and its old railway station is a national heritage site. On the adjacent beaches and reedbeds, there is good birdwatching for shore and marine birds, but go in a group with a guide as the beaches are risky places. In the adjacent roadstead, **Villa de Eten**, panama hats are the local industry.

Zaña→ *Colour map 1, C2.*
The ruined Spanish town of **Zaña** (also spelt Saña), lies 51 km south of Chiclayo. Zaña was destroyed by floods in 1726, and sacked by English pirates on more than one occasion. The ruins of five colonial churches and the convents of San Agustín, La Merced and San Francisco bear witness to the former splendour of this town which, at one time, was destined to become the country's capital.

Sipán → *Colour map 1, C2.*
ⓘ *http://sipan.perucultural.org.pe, site is open 0900-1700. Entrance is US$2.85, students half price. A guide at the site costs US$7 (may not speak English). Small boys offer to guide you (other kids hang around the handicraft stalls and pester for a tip for doing nothing). Allow 3-4 hrs. Take mosquito repellent.*

At this imposing twin-pyramid complex 35 km southeast of Chiclayo, excavations since 1987 in one of the three crumbling pyramids have brought to light a cache of funerary objects considered to rank among the finest examples of pre-Columbian art.

The Peruvian archaeologist Walter Alva, leader of the dig, continues to probe the immense mound that has revealed no less than 12 royal tombs filled with 1800-year-old offerings worked in precious metals, stone, pottery and textiles of the Moche culture (circa AD 1-750). In the most extravagant Moche tomb discovered, **El Señor de Sipán**, a priest was found clad in gold (ear ornaments, breast plate, etc), with turquoise and other valuables.

In another tomb were found the remnants of what is thought to have been a priest, sacrificed llama and a dog, together with copper decorations. In 1989 another richly appointed, unlooted tomb contained even older metal and ceramic artefacts associated with what was probably a high-ranking shaman or spiritual leader, called 'The Old Lord of Sipán' (see box opposite). Yet another elite tomb was discovered in 2007.

Old Lord of Sipán

The excavations at Sipán by the archaeologist Walter Alva have already revealed a huge number of riches in the shape of 'El Señor de Sipán'. This well-documented discovery was followed by an equally astounding find dating from AD 100. The tomb of the 'Old Lord of Sipán', as it has come to be known, predates the original Lord of Sipán by some 200 years, and could well be an ancestor of his.

Some of the finest examples of Moche craftsmanship have been found in the tomb of the Old Lord. One object in particular is remarkable; a crab deity with a human head and legs and the carapace, legs and claws of a crab. The gilded piece is over half a metre tall – unprecedented for a Moche figurine. This crab-like figure has been called Ulluchu Man, because the banner on which it was mounted yielded some of the first samples yet found of this ancient fruit.

The ulluchu fruit usually appears in scenes relating to war and the ritual offering of a prisoner's blood. One theory is that the ulluchu is part of the papaya family and has anticoagulant properties that are useful in preventing clotting before a man's blood is offered.

Three tombs are on display, containing replicas of the original finds. A site museum was opened in 1992 featuring photos and maps of excavations, technical displays and replicas of some finds. A new museum, **Museo de Sitio Huaca Rajada** ① *daily 0900-1700, US$2.85*, was opened in 2010. It concentrates on the finds at the site, especially Tomb 14 (the 'Sacerdote-Guerrero', or Priest-Warrior), the decorative techniques of the Moche and the roles that archaeologists and local communities play in protecting these pecious discoveries. You can wander around the previously excavated areas of the Huaca Rajada to get an idea of the construction of the burial mound and adjacent pyramids. For a good view, climb the large pyramid across from the excavated Huaca Rajada. A 4000-year-old temple, Ventarrón, was uncovered about 20 km from Sipán in 2007 by Walter Alva. It predates Sipán by some 2000 years and its murals are claimed to be the oldest in the Americas.

Around Sipán

Twenty-five kilometres from Sipán is **Pampa Grande**, a Mochica settlement dating from circa AD 550. This was the largest Moche complex 1400 years ago, at which time as many as 10,000 people may have lived here. Pampa Grande was a ceremonial centre, possibly including ritual offering of human blood as represented in the Sipán exhibits. These were presided over by a lord who also directed production and distribution, including precious materials to the artisans. Some experts believe that a prolonged drought around AD 562-594 displaced large groups of Moche people living to the south who moved to Pampa Grande, which became the centre of a state holding sway over the Lambayeque and Jequetepeque valleys.

The reason for the downfall of this once-powerful city remains in dispute. The structures associated with the rich and powerful ruling class appear to have been selectively burned and then abandoned leading some to conclude that a peasant revolution may have been the cause. Others (eg Moseley) believe that an earthquake, El Niño events and drought combined to lead to the demise of the Moche.

Chaparrí

A minor road runs to Chongoyape, a pleasant old town 70 km to the east (3 km before the city, turn left/west to the Chavín petroglyphs of Cerro Mulato). Nearby are the vast Taymi and Pampa Grande pre-Columbian and modern irrigation systems (the modern are also called Taymi). Also near Chongoyape are the aqueduct of Racarrumi, the hill fort of Mal Paso and the ruins of Majín (12-14 pyramids). In the district of Chongoyape is the **Chaparrí Private Conservation Area** ① *Comunidad Campesina Muchik Santa Catalina de Chongoyape, www.chaparri.org, US$11 for a day visit, see EcoLodge Chaparrí on page 453, if intending to stay overnight.* This community-owned project (the first of its kind in Peru) covers over 34,000 ha, extending from 1540 to 1350 m above sea level. The variety of habitats, including dry desert forest, harbours many bird and mammal species, some of which are extremely rare. Notable birds are the white-winged guan (see also Zoocriadero Bárbara d'Achille, page 451) and the Peruvian plantcutter, while there are also spectacled bears, Sechuran fox, puma and other cats. There are no dogs or goats in the area so the forest is recuperating. The Tinajones reservoir, good for birdwatching, is another reserve here. All staff and guides are locals. For every ten people you have to have a guide (this provides work and helps to prevent rubbish).

Túcume → *Colour map 1, C2.*

① *T074-835026, 0900-1700, US$3, students US$1, children US$0.30, guide US$7, www.museodesitiotucume.com.*

About 35 km north of Chiclayo, beside the old Panamericana to Piura, lie the ruins of this vast city built over a thousand years ago. This mysterious and evocative site is worth visiting around sundown, not only to avoid the fierce heat, but to add to the eerie thrill that the place induces.

A short climb to the two *miradores* on **Cerro La Raya**, or **El Purgatorio**, as it is also known, offers an unparalleled panoramic vista of 26 major pyramids, platform mounds, walled citadels and residential compounds flanking a ceremonial centre and ancient cemeteries. The entire complex covers well over 200 ha and measures 1.7 km from east to west and 2 km from north to south. One of the pyramids, Huaca Larga, where excavations are continuing, is the longest adobe structure in the world, measuring 700 m long, 280 m wide and over 30 m high.

There is no evidence of occupation of Túcume previous to the Sicán, or Lambayeque people (see below) who developed the site between AD 1050/1100 and 1375 until the Chimú came, saw and conquered the region, establishing a short reign until the arrival of the Incas in around 1470. The Incas built on top of the existing structure of **Huaca Larga** using stone from Cerro La Raya. Among the tombs excavated so far is one dating from the Inca period. It is thought to be that of a warrior, judging by the many battle scars. The body is heavily adorned and was interred along with two male compatriots and no less than 19 females aged between 10 and 30. Beside the Huaca Larga is the shrine known as the 'Templo de la Piedra Sagrada' (Temple of the Sacred Stone), which was clearly very holy to the Lambayeque, Chimú and Incas.

Among the other pyramids that make up this huge complex are: **Huaca El Mirador, Huaca Las Estacas, Huaca Pintada** and **Huaca de las Balsas**, which is thought to have housed people of elevated status such as priests.

Excavations at the site, led by the late Norwegian explorer-archaeologist, Thor Heyerdahl of *Kon-Tiki* fame, challenge many conventional views of ancient Peruvian culture. Some suspect that it will prove to be a civilization centre greater than Chan Chán.

A tale of demons and fish

Just one of the many legends that abound in this part of Northern Peru pertains to the hill that dominates the pyramids at Túcume and the precise origin of its name. The hill is known locally as 'El Purgatorio' (Purgatory), or more commonly, Cerro La Raya (Ray Hill).

The former name derives from the conquering Spaniards' attempts to convert the indigenous people to the Christian faith. The Spanish invaders encountered fierce local resistance to their religion and came up with the idea of convincing the people of Túcume that the hill was, in fact, purgatory. They told the locals that there lived on the hill a demon who would punish anyone not accepting the Roman Catholic faith.

In order to lend some credence to this tale, a group of Spaniards set out one dark, moonless night and built a huge bonfire at the foot of 'El Purgatorio', giving the appearance of an erupting volcano and frightening the townsfolk half to death. Thus they came to accept the Spaniards' assertion that any unbelievers or sinners would be thrown alive into the flames of this diabolical fire.

As if that wasn't enough to terrify the local populace, the Spanish also concocted the fiendish tale of 'El Carretón', or wagon. This was an enormous wagon pulled by four great horses that would supposedly speed forth from the bowels of 'El Purgatorio' on the darkest of nights. Driven by a dandily dressed demon boss, and carrying his equally dandy demon buddies, this hellish vehicle careered round the town of Túcume making a fearsome racket. Any poor unbelievers or sinners found wandering the streets would immediately be carted off and thrown into the flames of purgatory.

The alternative name of Cerro La Raya refers to the local legend of a manta ray that lived in a nearby lake. The local children constantly tormented the fish by throwing stones at it, so, to escape this torment, the poor creature decided to move to the hill and become part of it. The lake then disappeared and ever since, the hill has been enchanted.

There is also evidence, including art and remains of navigation gear, that the people of Túcume were intrepid seafarers. Not much of the site is open to view, only the miradores mentioned above and the walk through the site there, as lots of study is going on. There is a pleasant dry forest walk to Huaca I, with shade, bird- and lizard-watching.

The **site museum**, with three halls, is built from adobe and mezquite logs in pre-Hispanic style. The collections show architectural reconstructions, photographs and drawings, highlighting the finds, which include weaving paraphernalia, a ceremonial oar and a fabulous bas relief and mural depicting maritime scenes suggesting former sea trade and inter-regional contact. Traditional dishes and drinks are available.

The town of Túcume Viejo is a 20-minute walk from the site, or a US$1 mototaxi ride. Look for the side road in town heading towards a new park, opposite which is the ruin of a huge colonial church made of adobe and some brick. The surrounding countryside is pleasant for walks through mango trees and fields of maize. The present site of the town is not the original one but dates from 1720. Local legend has it that the town was moved following an apparition of the Virgin. The icon of the Virgin mysteriously disappeared but was later seen on top of Cerro Cueto, having her long hair combed by a native girl while gazing over pasture lands below. This was taken as a sign to relocate the church and the rest of the town with it. ▸▸ *See Festivals and events, page 454.*

Ferreñafe and Sicán → *Colour map 1, C2.*

The colonial town of Ferreñafe, 18 km northeast of Chiclayo, is worth a visit, especially for the **Museo Nacional Sicán** ① *T074-286469, http://sican.perucultural.org.pe, Tue-Sun 0900-1700, US$2.85, students US$1.10, guide (Spanish only) available at extra cost.* This excellent new museum is designed to house objects of the Sicán (Lambayeque) culture from near Batán Grande (fascinating exhibits, knowledgeable staff, but little English spoken). There's a helpful **Mincetur tourist office** ① *T074-282843, citesipan@mincetur.gob.pe*, on the Plaza de Armas.

The entrance to **El Santuario Histórico Bosque de Pómac**, which includes the ruins of **Sicán**, lies 16 km beyond Ferreñafe along the road to Batán Grande. There is another entrance from the Panamericana near Tucumé. Visiting the sanctuary is not easy because of the very arid conditions, lack of marked trails and distances involved, which mean that walking around the site is only for the intrepid and well prepared: it is 10 km to the nearest *huaca* (pyramid). At the **visitor centre** ① *free, dalemandelama@gmail.com, 0900-1700, a guide (Spanish only) can be hired with transport, US$3.45, horses US$6.* The two-hour tour of the area includes a mirador over the forest, some of the most ancient carob (*algarrobo*) trees and at least two *huacas*. Food and drinks are available at the centre and camping is permitted. Sicán has revealed several sumptuous tombs dating to the middle Sicán period, AD 900-1100. The ruins comprise some 12 adobe pyramids, arranged around a huge plaza, measuring 500 by 250 m, with 40 archaeological sites in total. They range in size with the largest reaching 40 m in height and approximately 100 m square. The site as a whole covers 45 sq km. A visit to the mirador affords a beautiful view across the emerald green tops of the carob forest with the enormous pyramids dramatically breaking through. The two main tombs discovered were located either side of the entrance ramp leading up the south face of **Huaca de Loro**. In one tomb 20 bodies were excavated and nearly a tonne of metal and other objects unearthed. Twenty more tombs were discovered in 2006. There is nothing to see on the ground now that both sites are completely overgrown with scrub. Here, some of the best examples of pre-Columbian gold artefacts were found, notably the oldest *tumi* (ceremonial knife) unearthed in Peru. *Tumis* so commonly found in other cultures are all later, which suggests that they were copied from Sicán. A Sicán *tumi* can be identified from the particularly feline, slanted form of the eyes, reflecting the iconografic representation of their principal deity. Many gold objects have been removed to private collections, such as the Gold Museum in Lima, but many are in the new Museo Nacional Sicán in Ferreñafe. The *huacas* were badly eroded by the rains of the 1998 El Niño and are now semi-protected by flimsy corrugated-iron 'roofs'.

Professor Izumi Shimada has worked here for more than 15 years researching a culture which has, to a large extent, been forgotten. It now seems that the origins of the Sicán culture lie with the Mochica (Muchik), though there are clear influences of other contemporary cultures: Wari and Pachacámac. Recent research suggests that when the Mochica religio-political centre based around Huaca Fortaleza, Pampagrande, collapsed in AD 700-750 the population was displaced. It moved 30 km north to Poma on the banks of Río La Leche, which was not then a dry river. The resulting culture extended across the Motupe valley to the north, La Leche valley, and Zaña and Lambeyeque valleys to the south. It is known today as the Sicán culture (some refer to it as Lambayeque), which reached its height in AD 900-1100. The city was probably moved to a new site at Túcume, 6 km west, following 30 years of severe drought and then a devastating El Niño-related flood in AD 1050-1100. These events appear to have provoked a rebellion in which many of the remaining temples atop the pyramids were burnt and destroyed. At the new Túcume site the Sicán culture continued to flourish for another 300 years until conquest by the Chimú.

Historical Sanctuary Bosque de Pómac, established in 2001, covers 5887 ha of carob forest either side of the river La Leche, which remains dry most years. It is the largest intact carob forest in the world, containing trees up to 1000 years old. Despite the dry, scrubby terrain the tree tops shimmer emerald green and there is prolific birdlife (47 species) as well as numerous reptiles and mammals, including an endangered species of wild cat.

Laquipampa Wildlife Refuge ① *rvslaquipampa@sernanp.gob.pe; see www.sernanp. gob.pe*, covering 8329 ha, is situated in a green and fertile high Andean valley. It is one habitat of the rare and critically endangered white-winged guan (*Penelope albipennis*, see below), the bearded guan and many other birds endemic to the Tumbesian zone, also the spectacled bear and rare flora in a dry forest belt ranging from 500-2500 m. It lies two hours beyond Sicán; take a passing bus for Incahuasi.

North to Piura

Sixty kilometres north of Chiclayo, beside the old Panamericana, is the site of **Apurlec**. It comprises a stone wall surrounding a hill and pyramids dating from the Tiahuanaco period, as well as irrigation canals and reservoirs. The system was enlarged during Moche, Chimú and Inca occupation of the site. The ruins are overgrown, but climb the Cerro Viejo to get an idea of the size. To get there from Chiclayo, take a bus from Pedro Ruiz block 5. The bus continues to Motupe (10 km).

Further north on the old Pan-American Highway, 885 km from Lima, is the peaceful town of **Olmos**. During the last week of June the **Festival de Limón** is celebrated here. At Olmos, a road runs east over the Porculla Pass for Jaén and Bagua, see page 528. The old Pan-American Highway continues from Olmos to Cruz de Caña and on to Piura.

Olmos is the best base for observing the white-winged guan, a bird thought extinct for 100 years until its rediscovery in 1977. On the outskirts is the white-winged guan captive breeding centre, **Zoocriadero Bárbara d'Achille** ① *Km 103, Olmos*, which also has an aviary of rescued birds, and the **Asociación Cracidae Perú** ① *Torres Paz 708, Chiclayo, T074-238748, cracidae@llampayec.rcp.net.pe; director Fernando Angulo Pratolongo*. Captive breeding started in 1979 and the first reintroduction into the wild was made in 2001 at Chaparrí (see page 448). One place where the guans can be seen in the wild is Quebrada Limón (or Frejolillo), where guides from the local community check on the guans' whereabouts in order to take visitors to see them in the early morning. Ask at the breeding centre for how to get there.

At Lambayeque the new Pan-American Highway, which is in good condition, branches off the old road and drives 190 km straight across the Sechura Desert to Piura. There is also a coast road, narrow and scenic, between Lambayeque and Piura, via Bayovar and the town of **Sechura**. The fine 17th-century cathedral has a lovely west front that's been under renovation for a long time and is normally closed to the public. There is a restaurant at the junction to Bayovar, where you can sleep.

Sechura Desert → *Colour map 1, B2.*

A large area of shifting sands separates the cities of Chiclayo and Piura. Water for irrigation comes from the Chira and Piura rivers, and from the Olmos and Tinajones irrigation projects that bring water from the Amazon watershed by means of tunnels (one over 16 km long) through the Andes to the Pacific coast.

The northern river – the Chira – usually has a super-abundance of water. Along its irrigated banks large crops of Tangüis cotton are grown. A dam has been built at Poechos on the Chira to divert water to the Piura valley. In its upper course the Piura – whose flow is far less dependable – is mostly used to grow subsistence food crops, but around Piura, when there is enough water, the hardy long-staple Pima cotton is planted.

In the 1870s, the government of Manuel Pardo decreed that all native cotton, including kapok, should be destroyed because it was believed that it gave parasites to the favoured, imported varieties. This was not the case and the value of Peruvian cotton is now recognized. It grows on a tall bush, unlike the short, Egyptian variety, and comes in seven colours, each of which was given a name by the Moche.

Solo cyclists should not cross the Sechura Desert as muggings have occurred. Take the safer, inland route. There are several restaurants between Km 845 and Km 848, and another midway between Mórrope and Piura, but there are no hotels. Do not camp out if possible, though heading south, strong headwinds may make camping unavoidable.

◉ Chiclayo and around listings

For Sleeping and Eating price codes and other relevant information, see pages 38-44.

▣ Sleeping

Chiclayo *p442, map p443*

AL Costa del Sol, Balta 399, T074-227272, www.costadelsolperu.com. Non-smoking rooms, smart, TV, good security, mall pool, sauna, jacuzzi, Wi-Fi, ATM. **Páprika** restaurant is good value with Sun buffets US$7.50, vegetarian options.

AL Gran Hotel Chiclayo, Villareal 115, T074-234911, www.granhotelchiclayo.com.pe. A 1st-class hotel. Price includes breakfast, a/c, pool, safe car park, changes dollars, jacuzzi, entertainments, restaurant. Warmly recommended.

AL-A Garza, Bolognesi 756, T074-228172, www.garzahotel.com. A/c, excellent bar/restaurant, pool, car park, airport transfers, Wi-Fi, close to bus stations so activity at all hours, remodelled in 2010. Recommended.

A Casa de la Luna, José Bernardo Alcedo 250, T074-270156, www.hotelcasadelaluna.com.pe. Good modern, business-class hotel, with a/c, excellent showers, internet, Wi-Fi, pool, restaurant, parking.

A Inti, Luis Gonzales 622, T074-235931, www.intihotel.com.pe. More expensive rooms with jacuzzi, family rooms available,

welcome cocktail, airport transfer included, with buffet breakfast, parking, Wi-Fi, a/c, safe and fridge in room, restaurant, helpful staff.

A Las Musas, Los Faiques 101, Urb Santa Victoria, T074-273445, lasmusas@terra. com.pe. Large rooms, affable service, TV, minibar, internet and Wi-Fi, good restaurant, holds karaoke and fiestas at weekends, which makes the hotel busy.

C El Sol, Elías Aguirre 119, T074-232120, hotelvicus@hotmail.com. Hot water, big rooms, restaurant, pool by car park, TV lounge, comfortable, good value.

C-D Paraíso, Pedro Ruiz 1064, T074-228161, www.hotelesparaiso.com.pe. Near the **Mercado Modelo**, comfortable and well appointed, but can be noisy. Recommended as the best of 3 in this street, the others are **Kalu**, No 1038, and **Paracas**, No 1046. It's not the safest of areas.

C-D Santa Rosa, L González 927, T074-224411, www.santarosahotelchiclayo.com. Hot water, fan, laundry, with breakfast, Wi-Fi, good value.

D América, Av L González 943, T074-229305, hotelamericasac@hotmail.com. Comfortable, restaurant, good value, breakfast included, Wi-Fi, frigobar. Recommended.

D-E Hospedaje Concordia, 7 de Enero Sur 235, Urb San Eduardo, T074-209423. Rooms on 2nd floor bigger than 3rd, modern, pleasant, discounts for long stays, TV, no meals, Wi-Fi, laundry service, view of Parque San Eduardo.

D-E Hospedaje San Eduardo, 7 de Enero Sur 267, Urb San Eduardo, T074-208668. No meals, colourful decor, modern bathrooms, fan, Wi-Fi, public phone, quiet, cable TV, hot water.

D-E Sol Radiante, Izaga 392, T074-237858. Hot water, comfortable, TV, pleasant, family-run, Wi-Fi, laundry, tourist information. Pay in advance.

E Pirámide Real, MM Izaga 726, T074-224036. Compact and spotless, good value, no meals, safe in room, TV, fan, Wi-Fi, very central.

E Sicán, MM Izaga 356, T074-208741, hsican@hotmail.com. With breakfast, hot water, TV, internet cabin, fan, comfortable, welcoming and trustworthy.

Lambayeque *p442*

B Hostería San Roque, 2 de Mayo 437, T074-282860, www.hosteriasanroque.com. In a fine, extensive 19th-century house, beautifully refurbished, helpful staff, bar, swimming pool, with breakfast, lunch on request. Recommended. The owners are also rebuilding **Hostería Santa Lucía**, 8 de Octubre y San Martín, with hotel, upmarket café, promises to be equally impressive.

D Hostal Libertad, Bolívar 570, T074-283561, www.hostallibertad.com. 1½ blocks from the plaza, big rooms, fridge, TV, meals extra, good, arranges tours.

E Posada La Norteña, Panamericana Norte Km 780, 3 blocks from town, T074-282602. Quiet, safe, hot water, fan, more expensive with TV, meals extra.

Chaparrí *p448*

AL-A EcoLodge Chaparrí, T084-984 676249 or T01-985 040907, www.chaparrilodge.com. A delightful oasis in the dry forest, 6 beautifully decorated cabins, built of stone and mud, nice and cool, solar power. Price is per person for all-inclusive package (including a guide for 1 day, but not horse

hire), 3-day/2-night packages available. 1st-class food and attention. Closely-tied to the Chaparrí Reserve and to sustainable and ecologically responsible principles; 3 trails and great wildlife watching. Sechuran foxes can be seen in the gardens; hummingbirds bathe at the pool at about 0600 every day; has a spectacled bear rescue centre. Recommended.

Túcume *p448*

C pp Los Horcones, beside the archaeological site, T01-996 837161 (in Lima T01-264 0968), www.loshorconesdetucume.com. A good hostel, rustic luxury in the shadow of the pyramids, with adobe and *algarrobo* rooms set in lovely garden with lots of birdlife. Includes breakfast, lunch and dinner extra. Horse riding can be arranged. Note that if rice is being grown nearby in Jan-May there can be a serious mosquito problem.

F pp Hospedaje Naylamp, 28 de Julio 117, opposite Centro de Educación Inicial 207, Pacora (just north of Túcume on the Panamericana), T074-691674. 10 rooms, 2 with bath (**E**), meals can be provided for a fee, TV room, pool, laundry facilities.

North to Piura *p451*

D El Remanso, San Francisco 100, T074-427158, elremansolmos@yahoo.com. Like a hacienda with courtyards, small pool, whitewashed rooms, colourful bedding, flowers and bottled water in room, hot water (supposedly). Price is full board, good restaurant. Charming owner.

⑦ Eating

Chiclayo *p442, map p443*
Local specialities include *ceviche* and *chingurito* (a *ceviche* of strips of dried guitar fish, which is chewy but good). For delicious and cheap *ceviche*, go to the *nativo* stall in the Mercado Central, a local favourite. *Cabrito* is a spiced stew of kid goat. *Arroz con pato* is a paella-like duck casserole. *Humitas* are

tamal-like fritters of green corn. *King kong* is a baked pastry layered with candied fruit and milk caramel, appealing to those with a very sweet tooth (San Roque is the best brand). *Chicha* is the fermented maize drink with delicious fruit variations.

♦♦♦ **El Huaralino**, La Libertad 155, Santa Victoria. Serves a wide variety of international and Creole dishes.

♦♦♦ **Fiesta**, Av Salaverry 1820 in 3 de Octubre suburb, T074-201970, www.restaurantfiesta gourmet.com. The place for gourmet local dishes, beautifully presented, excellent food, very good service, daily and seasonal specials, fabulous juices, popular business lunch place. Recommended.

♦♦ **Hebrón**, Balta 605. For more upmarket than average chicken, but also local food and *parrilla*, good salads. Also does an excellent breakfast and a good buffet at weekends.

♦♦ **Kaprichos**, Pedro Ruíz 1059, T074-232721. Chinese, delicious, huge portions.

♦♦ **Las Américas**, Aguirre 824. Open 0700-0200. Good service. Recommended.

♦♦ **Roma**, Izaga 706. Wide choice, open all day for breakfasts, snacks and meals.

♦♦ **Romana**, Balta 512,T074-223598. 1st-class food, usually good breakfast, popular with locals.

♦♦ **Tradiciones**, 7 de Enero Sur 105, T074-221192. Open daily 0900-1700. Good variety of local dishes, including *ceviche*, and drinks, nice atmosphere and garden, good service.

♦ **Boulevar**, Colón entre Izaga y Aguirre. Good, friendly, *menú* and à la carte.

♦ **Café Astoria**, Bolognesi 627. Open 0800-1200, 1530-2100. Breakfast, good value *menú*.

♦ **La Parra**, Izaga 746. Chinese and creole, *parrillada*, very good, large portions, cheerful place.

♦ **La Plazuela**, San José 299, Plaza Elías Aguirre. Good food, seats outside.

Cafés

D'Onofrio, Balta y Torres Paz. Good ice cream.

Greycy, Elias Aguirre y Lapoint. Good local ice cream.

La Panadería, Lapoint 847. Good choice of breads, including *integral*, snacks and soft drinks.

Lambayeque *p442*

♦♦-♦ **Casona Descalzi**, 8 de Octubre 345, T074-284341. Open 1100-1700 daily, serving *ceviches* and *tiraditos* in a historic setting.

♦♦-♦ **El Cántaro**, 2 de Mayo 180, http://restaurantelcntaro.com. Serves excellent traditional local dishes, both à la carte and has a good *menú*. Generally regarded as the best in town.

♦ **El Jordano**, Grau 400. *Pollo a la brasa*, reasonable, probably the best option in the centre at night.

⊛ Festivals and events

Chiclayo and around *p442, maps p443 and p444*

6 Jan Among the many festivals held in and around the city is **Reyes Magos** in Mórrope, Illimo and other towns. This is a recreation of a medieval pageant in which pre-Columbian deities become the Wise Men.

Feb Túcume celebrates the **Fiesta de la Purísima Concepción**, the town's Patron Saint, 8 days prior to Carnival in Feb, with music, dancing, fireworks, cockfights, sports events and, of course, much eating and drinking. During the **Dance of the Devils** (which is common in northern Peru), the participants wear horned masks, forked tails and long capes and are said to represent the diabolical drunken Spanish priests from colonial times. It also features a song and dance dedicated to the native girl who was seen combing the Virgin's hair.

14 Mar Festividad Señor Cautivo, Monsefú.

Mar/Apr Holy Week, many villages have traditional Easter celebrations.

1 May Fiesta de la Cruz is held in Pimentel.

1st week of Jun Divine Child of the Miracle, in Villa de Eten.

Last week of Jun Festividad de San Pedro in Morrope.

27-31 Jul Fexticum, in Monsefú, with traditional foods, drink, handicrafts, music and dance.

5 Aug Pilgrimage from the mountain shrine of Chalpón to Motupe, 90 km north of Chiclayo; the cross is brought down from a cave and carried in procession.

24 Sep Virgen de las Mercedes post-harvest festival in Incahuasi, 12 hrs by truck east of Chiclayo.

Dec At Christmas and New Year, processions and children dancers (*pastorcitos* and *seranitas*) can be seen in many villages, eg Ferreñafe, Mochumi and Mórrope.

O Shopping

Chiclayo *p442, map p443*
Bookshops
SBS, Luis Gonzáles 1336A, T074-223672, chiclayo@sbs.com.pe.

Markets
Mercado Central, in the city centre, is smaller than the Mercado Modelo.
Mercado Modelo, 5 blocks north of the main plaza on Balta. This is one of northern Peru's liveliest and largest daily markets. Don't miss the colourful fruits, handicrafts stalls (see Monsefú) and the well-organized section of ritual paraphernalia used by traditional curers and diviners (*curanderos*), which is just off C Arica on the south side. It is filled with herbal medicines, folk charms, curing potions, and exotic objects used by *curanderos* and *brujos* to cure all manner of real and imagined illnesses. The stallholders are generally very friendly and will explain the uses of such items as monkey claws, dried foetuses and dragon's blood. As in all markets, take good care of your belongings.
Paseo de Artesanías, Bolognesi y Colón. Stalls sell woodwork, basketwork and other handicrafts in a quiet, peaceful, custom-built open-air arcade.

▲ Activities and tours

Chiclayo and around *p442, maps p443 and p444*
The museums at Lambayeque, Sipán and Túcume can easily be visited by public transport. Local operators run 3-hr tours to Sipán; Túcume and Lambayeque (5 hrs); Sicán is a full-day tour including Ferreñafe and Pómac. Other tours go to Zaña and the coastal towns.
Inkanatura Travel, Gran Hotel Chiclayo, see page 452, T074-209948, www.inkanatura.net. Also in Lima. Open Mon-Fri 0915-1315, 1515-1915, Sat 0915-1315. Offers historical and nature tours throughout northern Peru. Good service and helpful staff.

Horse riding
Rancho Santana, in Pacora, T074-97971 2145, www.cabalgatasperu.com. Relaxing tours on horseback, half-day (US$15.50), 1-day (US$22.50) or 3-day tours, including to Santuario Bosque de Pómac, Sicán ruins and Túcume, Swiss-run (Andrea Martin), good horses. Frequently recommended.

⊖ Transport

Chiclayo *p442, map p443*
Air
Flights to and from **Lima** and **Piura** with LAN (M M Izaga 770), daily. In Nov 2010 StarPerú began commercial flights between Chiclayo and **Cuenca**, Ecuador.

Bus
There is no terminal terrestre; most buses stop outside their offices on Bolognesi. To **Lima**, 770 km, US$15-24 and US$28-42 for *bus cama*: Civa, Av Bolognesi 714, T074-223434; Cruz del Sur, Bolognesi 888, T074-225508; Ormeño, Haya de la Torre 242, 2 blocks south of Bolognesi, T074-234206; Ittsa, Av Bolognesi 155, T074-233612; Línea,

Bolognesi 638, T074-222221, *especial* and *bus cama* service; **Móvil**, Av Bolognesi 195, T074-271940 (goes as far as Tarapoto); **Oltursa**, ticket office at Balta e Izaga, T074-237789, terminal at Vicente de la Vega 101, T074-225611; **Tepsa**, Bolognesi 504-36 y Colón, T074-236981; **Transportes Chiclayo**, Av L Ortiz 010, T074-223632. Most companies leave from 1900 onwards. To **Trujillo**, 209 km, with **Emtrafesa**, Av Balta 110, T074-600660, almost hourly from 0530-2015, US$4.75, and **Línea**, as above.

To **Piura**, US$4.50, **Línea** and **Transportes Chiclayo** leave hourly throughout the day; also **Emtrafesa** and buses from the Cial/Flores terminal, Bolognesi 751, T074-239579. To **Sullana**, US$5.50. To **Tumbes**, US$6, 9-10 hrs; with **Cial**, **Cruz del Sur** or **El Dorado**. Some companies on the route northwards arrive full from Lima. Many buses go on to the **Ecuadorean border** at **Aguas Verdes**. Go to the *Salida* on Elías Aguirre, mototaxi drivers know where it is, be there by 1900. All buses stop here after leaving their terminals to try and fill empty seats, so discounts may be possible.

To **Cajamarca**, 260 km, US$6.25-15.50, eg **Línea**, 4 a day; others from Tepsa terminal, Bolognesi y Colón, eg **Días**, T074-224448. To **Chachapoyas**, US$11-16: **Civa** 1730 daily, 10-11 hrs; **Turismo Kuélap**, in Tepsa station, 1830 daily, **Móvil**, address above, at 2000. To **Jaén**, US$5.50-10: eg **Móvil**, and **Transcade** (Av Saenz Peña 106, T074-232552, also to **Bagua Grande** at 1000 and 2200, 7 hrs, US$8.50). To **Tarapoto**, 18 hrs, US$12.50-23, with **Móvil**, also **Tarapoto Tours**, Bolognesi 751, T074-636231.

Lambayeque *p442*
For **Lambayeque**, colectivos from Chiclayo charge US$0.50, 25 mins. They leave from Pedro Ruiz at the junction with Av Ugarte. Also **Brüning Express** combis from Vicente de la Vega between Angamos and Av L Ortiz, every 15 mins, US$0.50.

Monsefú *p445*
Combis cost US$0.50 from Balta y Pedro Ruiz, or Terminal Epsel, Av Quiñónez.

Pimentel, Santa Rosa and Puerto Eten *p446*
The ports of can all be visited on a pleasant ½-day trip from Chiclayo. Combis leave from Av L Ortiz y San José, Chiclayo, to **Pimentel**, US$0.50. Colectivos to **Eten** leave from 7 de Enero y Arica.

Sipán *p446*
Combis leave from Plaza Elías Aguirre, US$0.50, 1 hr. The way to the village is well signed through fields of sugar cane. Once you get to the village, the signs end: turn left, then right and go through the village to get to the site.

Chaparrí *p448*
To Chaparrí, take a public bus from the corner of Leoncio Prado and Sáenz Peña to **Chongoyape**, US$1.10, 1¼ hrs, then a mototaxi to Chaparrí, US$7.50.

Túcume *p448*
Combis go from Chiclayo, Av Leguía, 15 m from Angamos, US$0.75, 45 mins. A combi from Túcume to the village of **Come** passes the ruins hourly. You cannot miss the town of Túcume with its huge sign. Soon after the sign take a right turn on the paved road that leads to the museum and site. Don't be fooled by the pyramid close to the sign; it's part of the group, but some distance from the entrance. A combi from Túcume to **Lambayeque** is US$0.45 and takes 25 mins.

Ferreñafe and Sicán *p450*
Colectivos from **Chiclayo** to Ferreñafe leave every few mins from 8 de Octubre y Sáenz Peña, 15 mins, US$0.75, but only run to Ferreñafe town centre so take a mototaxi on to the museum, 5 mins, US$0.50. Alternatively, combis for **Batán Grande** depart from the Terminal Nor-Este, in Av N de Piérola in Chiclayo, and pass the museum every 15-20 mins, 20 mins, US$0.85.

⊙ Directory

Chiclayo *p442, map p443*
Banks Beware of counterfeit bills, especially among street changers on 6th block of Balta, on Plaza de Armas and 7th block of MM Izaga. BCP, Balta 630. Scotiabank, Bolognesi, opposite Cuglievan. Interbank, on Plaza de Armas. All open Sat morning.
Consulates Honorary German Consul, Armin Dietrich Bülow, José Francisco Cabrera Cdra 1 (Casa Comunal de la Juventud), T074-237442, abm@ddm.com.pe. **Cultural centres** Alianza Francesa, Cuglievan 644, T074-237571, www.universidadperu.com/alianza-francesa-de-chiclayo.php. Instituto de Cultura Peruano-Norteamericana, Av Izaga 807, T074-231241, icpnachi@mail.udep.edu.pe. Instituto Nacional de la Cultura, Av L González 375, T074-237261, occasional poetry readings, information on local archaeological sites, lectures, etc.
Internet Lots of places, particularly on San José and Elías Aguirre, average price US$0.60 per hr. **Medical services** Ambulance: Max Salud, 7 de Enero 185, T074-234032, maxsalud@telematic.edu.com.
Post On 1 block of Aguirre, 6 blocks from Plaza. **Telephone** Telefónica, headquarters at Aguirre 919; bank of phone booths on 7th block of 7 de Enero behind Cathedral for international and collect calls. Phone card sellers hang around here.

Piura and around

A proud and historic city, 264 km from Chiclayo, Piura was founded as San Miguel at Tangarará in 1532, three years before Lima, by the conquistadores left behind by Pizarro. It was relocated, first as Pirwa, then with its current name, in 1534. There are two well-kept parks, Cortés and Pizarro (with a statue of the conquistador, also called Plaza de las Tres Culturas), and public gardens. Old buildings are kept in repair and new buildings blend with the Spanish style of the old city. Close to the city are interesting towns on the coast and others specializing in handicrafts. Further afield is the culturally fascinating area of Las Guaringas and the more prosaic route to Ecuador through Sullana.
▶▶ *For listings, see pages 463-467.*

Ins and outs

Getting there A taxi to Capitán Guillermo Concha airport costs US$1.85 by day, more by night. Most bus companies are on Avenida Sánchez Cerro, blocks 11, 12 and 13 in the northwest of the town. There are some hotels in this area, but for central ones take a taxi.

Getting around From the Plaza de Armas, some of the hotels and bus companies are too far to walk, but many of the sights and places to stay can be reached on foot. Three bridges cross the Río Piura to Castilla, the oldest from Calle Huancavelica (Puente San Miguel), another from Calle Sánchez Cerro and the newest from Avenida Panamericana Norte, west of town. Taxis in town charge US$1, mototaxis US$0.50. Transport to nearby towns is easy to find, likewise buses going to Sullana and on to Ecuador. For Las Guaringas, expect a long journey.

Tourist information Information at the **tourist office** ⓘ *Ayacucho 377, T073-320249, iperupiura@promperu.gob.pe. Mon-Sat 0830-1900, Sun 0830-1400. Also at the airport. See www.munipiura.gob.pe/turismo/ in Spanish for information and links.* **Dirección Regional de Turismo** ⓘ *Av Fortunato Chirichigno, Urb San Eduardo, T073-308229, dir_turismo@region piura.gob.pe, at the north end of town, Mon-Fri 0730-1330, 1430-1630.* **Indecopi** ⓘ *Av Los Cocos 268, Urb Club Grau, T073-308549, dnavarro@indecopi.gob,* helpful when there are consumer and tourist protection problems.

Best time to visit The winter climate, May to September, is very pleasant although nights can be cold and the wind piercing, while December to March is very hot. It is extremely difficult to find a room in the last week of July because of Independence festivities. The city suffers from water shortages.

Piura → *For listings, see pages 463-467. Colour map 1, B1. Phone code: 073. Population: 377,500.*

Standing on the **Plaza de Armas** is the **cathedral**, with a gold-covered altar, and paintings by Ignacio Merino. A few blocks away at Lima y Callao is the **San Francisco** church, where the city's independence from Spain was declared on 4 January 1821, nearly eight months before Lima. The church was completely rebuilt in 2002.

The church of **María Auxiliadora** stands on a small plaza on Libertad, near Avenida Sánchez Cerro. Across the plaza is the **Museo de Arte Religioso**. **San Sebastián**, on Tacna y Moquegua, is also worth seeing. The birthplace of Admiral Miguel Grau, hero of the War of the Pacific with Chile, is **Casa Museo Grau** ⓘ *Jr Tacna 662, opposite the Centro Cívico,*

Mon-Fri 0800-1300, 1600-1900, free. It has been opened as a museum and contains a model of the *Huáscar*, the largest Peruvian warship in the War of the Pacific, which was built in Britain. It also contains interesting old photographs.

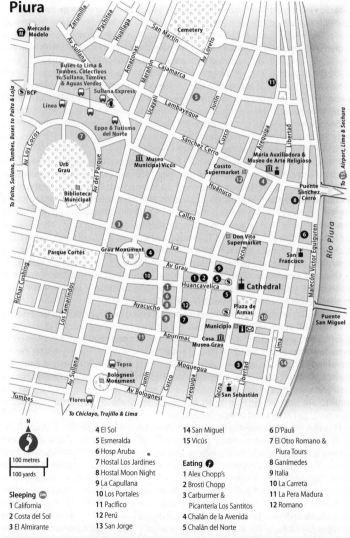

Piura

Sleeping
1 California
2 Costa del Sol
3 El Almirante
4 El Sol
5 Esmeralda
6 Hosp Aruba
7 Hostal Los Jardines
8 Hostal Moon Night
9 La Capullana
10 Los Portales
11 Pacífico
12 Perú
13 San Jorge
14 San Miguel
15 Vicús

Eating
1 Alex Chopp's
2 Brosti Chopp
3 Carburmer & Picantería Los Santitos
4 Chalán de la Avenida
5 Chalán del Norte
6 D'Pauli
7 El Otro Romano & Piura Tours
8 Ganímedes
9 Italia
10 La Carreta
11 La Pera Madura
12 Romano

The **Museo Municipal Vicús** ⓘ *Sullana, near Huánuco, Mon-Sat 0800-2200, Sun 0800-1200*, includes 60 gold artefacts from the local Vicus culture. It also has an art section. Local craftwork is sold at the **Mercado Modelo**. The market on Sánchez Cerro is good for fruit.

Around Piura → *For listings, see pages 463-467.*

Catacaos is a small town famous for its *chicha* (maize beer) – though be careful as the quality is not always reliable – and *picanterías*, which are local restaurants, some with music. The village is also noted for its *artesanía* such as tooled leather, gold and silver filigree jewellery, wooden articles and straw hats, though prices are relatively high and streets are lined with shops, including some jewellers more suited to a shopping mall. Inside the large church are vivid murals and, in 2000, a miracle was said to have occurred when an image of Christ appeared in the paintwork on an exterior wall. The village is also renowned for its celebrations in Holy Week, Good Friday especially (when all of Piura seems to be there). There is a procession at 1800 and the town centre is closed to traffic.

Two kilometres south of Catacaos is the Narihualá archaeological site. It includes a large adobe pyramid, 40 m high, from the Tallán culture that populated the Chira and Piura valleys before it was conquered by the Chimús.

The port for the area is **Paita**, 50 km from Piura. It exports cotton, cotton seed, wool and flax. It is a very old fishing port built on a small beach, flanked on three sides by a towering, sandy bluff and connected with Piura and Sullana by paved highways. Several colonial buildings survive, but they are in poor condition. Bolívar's mistress, Manuela Sáenz, lived the last 24 years of her life in Paita, after being exiled from Quito. She supported herself until her death in 1856 by weaving and embroidering and making candy after refusing the fortune left her by her husband. The house can be visited if you ask the people living in it, but there's not much to see. It is on the main road into town, after the market, just before and overlooking a petrol station. Fishing and fishmeal are prosperous industries.

On a bluff looming over Paita is a small colonial **fortress** built to repel pirates. Paita was a port of call for Spanish shipping en route from Lima to Panama and Mexico. It was a frequent target for attack, from Drake (1579) to Anson (1741).

Twenty-five kilometres up the coast is **Colán**, reached by driving down a large, sandy bluff (turn off at Km 989). Near the base is a striking and lonely colonial church, with breathtaking architecture and beautiful paintings in good condition. It is claimed by some to be the oldest church in Peru, if not in South America. The key-holder can be found by asking in the adjoining village of San Lucas de Colán. The seafront houses in the holiday resort stand on wooden stilts and are surrounded by palms. The seawater is clear and warm (but beware of stingrays – drag your feet when entering the water) and sunsets are spectacular; the town has excellent seafood restaurants. By public transport, go to Paita and change buses there.

Fifty kilometres northeast of Piura and 10 km off the old Pan-American Highway is the small town of **Chulucanas**, centre of the lemon- and orange-growing area. An ancient pottery technique has been discovered and revived here since the 1960s. The local potters formerly produced only large, utilitarian terracotta pots, until the 1960s when graverobbers brought to light examples of pottery from the Vicus and Tallane cultures dating from the second half of the first millennium BC. A group of Quechua pottery specialists researched and experimented with forms and techniques based on the pre-Columbian finds. These produce a very subtle and unusual effect. At first, the potters imitated the forms of the Vicus pieces but gradually they began to develop their own stylized figures. The most popular form is now the Chichera, a fat lady who makes and sells *chicha*. The most highly prized pieces are signed and sold in galleries and shops in Lima and abroad. Excellent ceramics can also be bought in the town, at a shop on the plaza and three others are within one block.

Huancabamba and Las Guaringas → *For listings, see pages 463-467. Colour map 1, B2.*

From Chulucanas the paved road heads southeast. A turn-off east to Morropán leads to a dirt road to **Canchaque**, a delightfully situated small centre for coffee, sugar-cane and fruit production (basic lodging). The difficult and tiring road, impossible for ordinary vehicles in the wet season, continues over a pass in the Andes of more than 3000 m for 69 km to Huancabamba. This very pretty town in a wonderful setting hosts a tourist week in early July and the Virgen del Carmen festival in mid-July. It has three claims to fame. First, the predominance of European features, due to the fact that it was an important Spanish settlement in colonial times. Second, it is called *la ciudad que camina*, 'the walking town', as it is built on irregularly slipping strata causing much subsidence. Evidence for this includes the fall of the bridge over the Río Huancabamba.

The third, and by far the most remarkable claim to fame, is that Huancabamba is the base for reaching **Las Guaringas**, a series of lakes at about 4000 m. Around here live the most famous witch doctors of Peru, to whom sick people flock from all over the country and abroad. The shamanic ceremony is definitely off the gringo trail and is an unforgettable trip. To take part in the ceremony, arrive in town and prepare to be approached almost immediately by a shaman's 'agent'. As dodgy as this sounds, this person can help you by doing all preparations. Go to the tourist centre in the plaza beforehand and double check if the agent's witch doctor is trustworthy. You'll then hop in a van, travel to the doctor's house, agree on a price and commence the ceremony immediately. It is an outdoor affair involving light hallucinogenic San Pedro cactus juice that is quite vile. The ceremony lasts all night and participants dance, reveal and predict the future. The entire ceremony is very mellow and most witch doctors have the disposition of concerned uncles. A spartan meal is provided so bring snacks. The next day involves a three-hour horse ride to a high mountain lagoon where near-skinny dipping and more ceremonies take place. You're back in Huancabamba (tired and cold) by late afternoon.

Horses to the lakes can be hired for US$6.50. There are also trips to the village of **San Antonio** below Lago Carmen, and the village of **Salalá** below Lago Shumbe. Ignacio León, who owns a *bodega* opposite **Hotel El Dorado** (see Sleeping, page 464), runs an early pick-up service to the outlying villages and takes trips at negotiable prices.

Sullana to Ecuador → *For listings, see pages 463-467.*

Sullana → *Colour map 1, B1. Population: 181,955.*
Sullana, 39 km north of Piura, is built on a bluff over the fertile Chira valley and is a busy, modern place. Avenida José de Lama, once a dusty, linear market, has a green, shady park with benches along the centre. Many of the bus companies have their offices along this avenue. San Martín is the main commercial street. Parks and monuments were added in 1994 to 1995, and have greatly improved the city's appearance. At the entrance, on the Pan-American Highway is an interesting mosaic statue of an iguana. There are lookouts over the Chira Valley at Plaza Bolognesi and by the arches near the Plaza de Armas. The local fiesta and agricultural fair is **Reyes**, held on 5-29 January. After

a few years of relative safety, the city appears to have reverted to its unsavoury past. Spend as little time here as possible. Preferably take some form of through transport. If this is not possible, don't arrive after dark.

At Sullana the Pan-American Highway forks. To the east it crosses the Peru-Ecuador border at La Tina and continues via Macará to Loja and Cuenca. The road is scenic and paved to the border, 128 km. **Macará**, which is 4 km from the border in Ecuador, is a dusty town in a rice-growing area. There are hotels and a few restaurants in town. See Border essentials, page 463, for details on this crossing into Ecuador.

Note The more frequently used route to the border is the coastal road that goes from Sullana north-west towards the Talara oilfields and then follows the coastline to Máncora and Tumbes, see page 468.

Ayabaca ➔ Colour map 1, B2. Altitude 2710 m.

Some 182 km northeast of Sullana in the highlands is the pleasant town of Ayabaca. The plaza is dominated by the large church of **El Señor Cautivo de Ayabaca** (the captured Christ on his way to crucifixion). Many devotees make pilgrimages to his shrine, the most famous in northern Peru, especially on 12 October.

Northeast of Ayabaca is the 1200-ha **Bosque de Cuyas** nature reserve, which protects a remnant of cloudforest. One hundred and twenty-one species of bird have been identified here. It is run by **Naturaleza y Cultura Internacional** ① T073-502431, Sullana, ayabaca@natureandculture.org; Ayabaca contact Angel Seminario, T073-471108. Access is along a road north starting at **Los Cocos**, 5 km from Ayabaca on the road to Espíndola. **Aypate**, an impressive archaeological site on a mountain-top, is part of what is believed to have been an important Inca settlement. Only two of over 100 ha have been cleared. The *usnu* (platform) and temple of the sun are especially beautiful and a mirador gives wonderful views. Access is along a poor road (impassable in the rainy season) from Yanchalá. Pickups from Ayabaca charge US$45 return with several hours' wait. It's a 20-minute walk from the end of the vehicle road to the ruins. There are cheaper ways to get there: a shared taxi to Yanchalá or Hualcuy from Prado y Bolognesi near the Ayabaca market, followed by three- or five-hour trails (enquire about safety before setting out). There is no lodging at Aypate but the caretakers may offer basic hospitality or you can camp. Take food, water and warm clothing.

A rough road goes via Yanchalá (34 km), Samanguilla (49 km), and El Toldo (57 km) to Espíndola. Near Samanguilla and

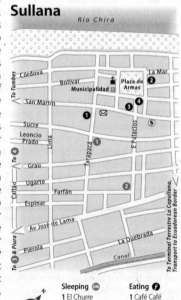

Sullana

Río Chira

Sleeping 😴
1 El Churre
2 Hosp San Miguel
3 Hostal La Siesta
4 Hostal Lion's Palace

Eating 🍴
1 Café Café
2 Chifa El Dorado
3 Due Torri
4 Monterrico

100 metres
100 yards

Border essentials: Peru–Ecuador

La Tina–Macará

Open 24 hours. Go to Peruvian immigration at the end of the bridge, get a stamp, walk across and then go to Ecuadorean immigration. When entering Peru, after getting your exit stamp from Ecuador, go to Peruvian immigration to get a form (*Tarjeta Andina*), fill it out, go across the street to the police (PNP) to get their stamp, then go back to immigration for the entry stamp. There are no money changers right at the bridge, only in Macará. At the border, there is only Banco Financiero on the Peruvian side, open Monday-Friday 0900-1600, changes US$ cash only. At the border, there is a *hospedaje* and several eating places on the road down to the bridge.
Transport From Sullana to the border combis leave from Terminal Terrestre La Capullana, off Avenida Buenos Aires, several blocks beyond the canal, to the international bridge. US$3.40 per person, 1¾ hours (US$24 for the whole car). Take a taxi or mototaxi to and from the terminal. From the border to Macará is 4 km: take one of the pickups that run from the border (10 minutes, US$0.30). Frequent buses leave the Ecuadorean side for Loja (six hours, US$6), so if you're not taking the through bus (see Piura transport, page 466) you can go from Sullana to Loja in a day. From border to Sullana, cars may leave before full (car to Piura US$30).

El Toldo are the **Samanga** petroglyphs. It is not possible to cross into Ecuador from Espíndola at the time of writing.

◉ Piura and around listings

For Sleeping and Eating price codes and other relevant information, see pages 38-44.

● Sleeping

Piura *p458, map p459*
AL Los Portales, Libertad 875, Plaza de Armas, T073-321161, www.hotelportales piura.com. Price includes breakfast, tax and welcome cocktail. This ex-government hotel, in the **Country Club** group, has been attractively refurbished and is the city's social centre, elegant, a/c, hot water, pleasant terrace and patio, nice pool.
AL-A Costa del Sol, Loreto 649, T/F073-302864, www.costadelsolperu.com. Luxury, pool, casino, internet facilities, restaurant.
A Esmeralda, Loreto 235, T/F073-331205, www.hotelesmeralda.com.pe. With bathroom, hot water, a/c (**B** with fan

and without breakfast), clean, comfortable, good, restaurant.
C San Miguel, Lima 1007, Plaza Pizarro, T073-305122. Modern, comfortable, with bath, TV, café.
C Vicús, Av Guardia Civil B-3, in Castilla 2 blocks across the river on the Sánchez Cerro bridge, T073-343201, http://hotelvicus.com. With bathroom, hot water, fan, clean, quiet, swimming pool, parking.
D El Almirante, Ica 860, T/F073-335239. With bathroom, fan, clean, modern, owner is knowledgeable about the area.
D El Sol, Sánchez Cerro 411, T073-324461. With bathroom, hot water, small pool, snack bar, parking, accepts dollars cash or TCs but won't change them. Recommended.
D San Jorge, Jr Loreto 960, T073-327514. With bathroom and fan, cheaper without cable TV, hot water, clean, a little overpriced.

E Hostal Los Jardines, Av Los Cocos 436, T073-326590. With bath, hot water, TV, laundry, parking, good value.

E Perú, Arequipa 476, T073-333919. With bathroom and fan, clean, safe, friendly, laundry service, cold water, modern small rooms, all meals in restaurant extra.

F Hostal Moon Night, Junín 899, T073-336174. Comfortable, modern, spacious, cheaper without bath/TV, clean, good value.

F La Capullana, Junín 925, T073-321239. With bath, some cheaper single rooms, welcoming.

F Pacífico, Apurímac 717, T073-303061. With bath, hot water and fan, simple and clean, recommended as good value.

G pp California, Junín 835, upstairs, T073-328789. Shared bath, own water tank, mosquito netting on windows, roof terrace, clean, brightly decorated, friendly owner. Recommended (some rooms rented by the hour, though).

G Hospedaje Aruba, Junín 851, T073-303067. Small rooms but clean and comfortable, shared bath, fan on request, very friendly. Recommended.

Around Piura *p460*

AL-A Bocatoma Resort, Av Costanera Norte Co99, Colán, T01-975 366833, http://bocatomahotelresort.com. Prices rise in high season and there is a variety of cabins for 2, 4 and 7 people. There are lalso packages available. Cabins on a spit of land between the ocean and lagoons, with restaurant, pool and sports facilities.

A-C Hotel Sol de Colán, on the promenade, Colán, T073-969 655455, www.elsoldecolan hotel.com. With pool, bar, games room, restaurant. Rooms with and without TV (**C**) and bungalow accommodation (**A-B**) with en suite facilities.

E Las Brisas, Av Ugarte, Paita, T073-611023. The best, with bathroom but little cold water, safe.

Huancabamba and Las Guaringas *p461*

F Hotel El Dorado, on the main plaza, Huancabamba. Good, clean hotel, informative owner, with restaurant.

Sullana *p461, map p462*

B Hostal La Siesta, Av Panamericana 400, T073-502264, at the entrance to town. Hot water, fan, cable TV, cheaper with cold water, pool, restaurant, laundry.

D El Churre, Tarapacá 501, T073-507006. With bath, TV, laundry, café. Recommended.

E Hospedaje San Miguel, C J Farfán 204, T073-502789. Cheaper without bathroom, all rooms open off a central passage-way, basic, helpful, good showers, staff will spray rooms against mosquitoes, cafeteria.

E Hostal Lion's Palace, Grau 1030, T073-502587. With bathroom, fan, patio, pleasant, quiet, no breakfast.

Ayabaca *p462*

D-E Hotel de Turistas Samanga, Tacna y Grau, Plaza de Armas, T073-471049. With bath, hot water, a bit run down but still best in town.

F Hospedaje Plaza, Cáceres at Plaza de Armas, T073-471085. Shared bath, electric shower, basic and friendly.

F Hostal Oro Verde, Salavery 381, 1 block from plaza, T073-499830, adac1277@ hotmail.com. Cheaper with shared bath, limited hot water (best in morning), meals on request, family-run, good value, noise every night from nearby.

🍴 Eating

Piura *p458, map p459*

Piura's special dishes include *majado de yuca* (manioc root with pork); *seco de chavelo* (beef and plantain stew); and *carne seca* (sun-dried meat). Its best-known sweet is the delicious natilla, made mostly of goats' milk and molasses. The local drink is *pipa fría*, chilled coconut juice drunk from the nut with a straw.

There is a concentration of restaurants on Ayacucho, several of which are also nightspots.

Carburmer, Libertad 1014, T073-332380. Very good lunches and dinners, also pizza.

Picantería Los Santitos, in the same precinct and same phone as **Carburmer**. Lunch only, wide range of traditional dishes in a renovated colonial house.

Alex Chopp's, Huancavelica 538, T073-322568. Seafood, fish, chicken and meats, beer, popular at lunchtime.

Brosti Chopp, Arequipa 780, T073-303753. Similar to **Alex Chopp's**, but with lunch menu for US$1.45.

El Otro Romano, Ayacucho 579, T073-803084. Tue-Sun 0900-1700. Same owner and same fare as **Romano**, across the street.

La Carreta, Huancavelica 726, T073-304231. One of the most popular places for roast chicken.

Romano, Ayacucho 580. Open Mon-Sat 0700-2300. Popular with locals, extensive menu, excellent set meal for US$1.55. Highly recommended.

Ganímedes, Lima 440, T073-329176. A good vegetarian restaurant, very popular set lunch, à la carte is slow but well worth it, try the excellent yoghurt and fruit.

Italia, Grau 172. For breakfasts, snacks, desserts and juices.

La Pera Madura, Arequipa 168, next to the Cine Municipal. Open daily 1700-2300. A good place for traditional snacks, eg turkey sandwiches and *tamales*.

Cafés

Chalán del Norte, Tacna 520, Plaza de Armas, Grau 173 and 452 (Chalán de la Grau). Several branches of this popular chain, for good sweets, cakes and ice cream.

D'Pauli, Lima 541. Also for sweets, cakes and ice cream, good.

Around Piura *p460*

La Chayo, San Francisco 439, Catacaos, T073-370121. Recommended for its local dishes and *chicha*. There are several other places to eat on and close to C San Francisco.

Chifa Hong Kong, Junín 358, Paita. Considered by locals to offer really authentic Chinese food.

Club Liberal building, 2nd floor, Jorge Chávez 161, Paita. This serves good fish, seafood and crêpes, and is good value.

Huancabamba and Las Guaringas *p461*

Local specialities include *rompope*, a rich and strong drink made of egg, spices and *cañazo* (sugar-cane spirit), roast *cuy* (guinea-pig) and local cheeses.

Sullana *p461, map p462*

Café Café, Tarapacá 484. Sandwiches, *tamales*, lunch menu US$1, juices and drinks.

Chifa El Dorado, on the plaza. One of the more authentic of several *chifas*.

Due Torri, E Palacios 122. Italian and regional, popular with locals.

Monterrico, Plaza de Armas. Set menu for US$1, popular.

Ayabaca *p462*

El Carbón, Tacna 1 block from Plaza de Armas. Peruvian and international dishes, upscale for where it is, pleasant atmosphere. There are other, limited, eating places.

⊛ Festivals and events

Piura *p458, map p459*
26-28 Jul Festival Internacional de Tunas.
27 Aug-2 Sep Semana Turística de Piura, tourism week.
7 Oct Festival Nacional de Marinera y Tondero, celebrating local dances.

▲ Activities and tours

Piura *p458, map p459*
Piura Tours, C Ayacucho 585, T073-326778,
piuratours@cpi.udep.edu.pe. The manager
Mario speaks very good English.

⊖ Transport

Piura *p458, map p459*
Air
Capitán Guillermo Concha airport is in
Castilla, 10 mins from the centre by taxi
(US$1.85). It has gift shops and 2 car
rental agencies. Daily flights with **LAN**
(Av Grau 140) to **Lima** via **Chiclayo**.

Bus
Most companies are on Av Sánchez Cerro,
blocks 11, 12 and 13 (see www.munipiura.
gob.pe/turismo/transporte.shtml). To **Lima**,
1038 km, 14-16 hrs, US$25-39, US$45 on
bus cama, eg **Cruz del Sur**'s *VIP* and Ittsa's
supercama services, on the Panamericana
Norte. Most buses stop at the major cities
on route; **Cruz del Sur, Ittsa, Línea, Oltursa,
Tepsa**. To **Chiclayo**, 190 km, 3 hrs, US$4.50,
several buses daily. To **Trujillo**, 7 hrs, 487 km,
US$9.25, several daily. To travel by day
change in Chiclayo. To **Talara**, US$2, 2 hrs,
with **Eppo**. To **Máncora**, US$3.15, 3 hrs, with
Eppo. To **Tumbes**, 282 km, 4½ hrs, US$5.50,
several buses daily, eg **Cruz del Sur** (also to
Lima), **El Dorado** and **Trans Chiclayo**; also
colectivos, 3½ hrs, leave when full, US$7. To
Paita, Trans Dora, every 20 mins, 1 hr, US$1;
also from Paita terminal on Av Gullman, just
off Sánchez Cerro. All services drop off and
collect passengers in the market area in
Paita. To **Catacaos**, colectivos leave Piura
from the far side of Puente San Miguel,
US$0.25, 15-20 mins; also combis from
the bus terminal, block 12 Av Sánchez
Cerro, US$0.25. For **Chulucanas** combis
from Piura charge US$1.50.

   To Ecuador To **Machala** and
Guayaquil, the fastest route if you are
heading directly to Quito, **CIFA**, 5 a day,
Machala US$6, 6 hrs, Guayaquil US$10, 9 hrs.
Ecuatoriana Pullman, on Av Loreto, 0830,
2030 to **Guayaquil** via Sullana, Tumbes and
Machala, US$9, 10 hrs. Otherwise, go to
Tumbes and travel on from there for the
Aguas Verdes crossing. To **Loja**, the best
option if you want to visit the southern or
central highlands of Ecuador, **Transportes
Loja**, 4 daily, US$8, 8 hrs, to **Macará** US$4.
Or **Unión Cariamanga**, at 1330 and 2000.
Alternatively take a bus to **Sullana**, 38 km,
30 mins (US$0.50), **Eppo, Sullana Express**
and **Turismo del Norte**, all on 1100 block
of Sánchez Cerro; also colectivos (US$1).
For **La Tina** on the Ecuadorean frontier,
a further 128 km, see box, page 463 and
under Sullana below.

   Bus companies **Cial**, Bolognesi 817,
T073- 304250. **CIFA**, Los Naranjos y Sánchez
Cerro (cuadra 11-12) opposite Emtrafesa,
T073-305925. **Cruz del Sur**, Av
Circunvalación 160, T073-337094.
Emtrafesa, Los Naranjos 255, T073-337093.
Eppo, Av Sánchez Cerro 1141, T073-304543.
Ittsa, Sánchez Cerro 1142, T073-308645.
Línea, Sánchez Cerro 1215, T073-327821.
Oltursa, Bolognesi 801, T073-326666.
Tepsa, Loreto 1195, T073-306345. **Trans
Dora**, Sánchez Cerro 1391. **Trans Loja**,
Sánchez Cerro 1480, T073-309407. **Unión
Cariamanga**, Sánchez Cerro y Av Vice,
Urb Santa Ana, T073-9699 00135.

Car rental
At the airport: **Ramos**, T073-348668,
www.ramosrentacars.com; **Vicús**, T073-
342051, http://vicusrentacar.com.pe/.

Taxis
Radio Taxis, T073-324509 or T073-324630.

Huancabamba and Las
Guaringas *p461*
To get to **Huancabamba**, take a bus from
Piura to Canchaque and Huancabamba,
which leaves daily at 0900 and 1000 (it
takes at least 10 hrs, US$9), from Av Ramón

Castilla 196. Buy your ticket early on the day before travelling. It returns from Huancabamba at 0700 and 1000. A truck costs US$11.50. If driving, take the Pan-American Highway south of Piura for 66 km where there is a signpost to Huancabamba. Buses to **Las Guaringas** lakes leave at 0400 from the main plaza in Huancabamba.

Sullana *p461, map p462*
There are frequent buses and colectivos from **Piura** to Sullana, 38 km, 30 mins (US$0.50), see above. To **La Tina** on the Ecuadorean frontier, is a further 128 km, 1¾ hrs, US$3.40. It's best to take an early bus to Sullana (start at 0430), then a colectivo. Try not to arrive in Sullana or Piura after dark, it's unsafe.

In Sullana several bus companies, including Ormeño, use the Terminal Terrestre. There are several daily buses to and from **Tumbes**, 244 km, 4-5 hrs US$5. If you have time, it is worth continuing to Piura rather than staying in Sullana. To **Chiclayo** and **Trujillo**, see under Piura. To **Lima**, 1076 km, 14-16 hrs, several buses daily, most coming from Tumbes or Talara; luxury overnight bus via Trujillo with Ittsa (T073-503705), Ormeño and Tepsa, José de Lama 236, T073-502120. To **Paita** colectivos leave from the market, 2 blocks from Av Lama, US$1, 1 hr. To **Talara**, Eppo and Emtrafesa, C Comercio, 1 block from Av Lama, each leave hourly. Eppo are faster but more expensive, 1 hr, US$1.25. To **Máncora**, Eppo, 5 a day, 2½ hrs, US$3, or travel to Talara and then on from there via Los Organos.

Taxis
Mototaxis in Sullana charge US$0.45 around town. Radio Taxis, T073-502210/504354.

Ayabaca *p462*
From Piura to Ayabaca, Trans Vegas is recommended, Av Panamericana frente al cementerio, Urb San Ramón, T073-308729, daily 0830, 1500, plus Sat 0800, Sun 2300. Also Poderoso Cautivo, Av Sullana Norte

next to Iglesia Cristo Rey, T073-309888, daily 0900, 1500, Sun also 2300. To **Piura**, both companies are on Cáceres at Plaza de Armas. Vegas, T073-471080, Tue-Sun 0830, 1500, Mon 0800, 0900, 1500. **Poderoso Cautivo**, T073-471247, daily 0830, 1500, Fri also 1530, 1630.

⏱ Directory

Piura *p458, map p459*
Banks BCP, Grau y Tacna. Banco Continental, Plaza de Armas. Interbank, Grau 170. *Casas de cambio* are at Arequipa 600 block and 722, and Ica 366, 456 and 460. Street changers can be found on Grau outside BCP. **Consulates** Honorary British Consul, c/o American Airlines, Huancavelica 223, T073-305990. Ecuador, Av Chirichigno 505, Urb El Chipe, T073-308027, consulado_de_ecuador@speedy.com.pe. Honorary German Consul, Dr Percy Cavero, La Ribera MZ B Lote 6, Urb La Ribera, T300243, percy.garcia@udep.pe. **Immigration** Av Integración Urbana esq Av Sullana, T073-335536. **Internet** Several internet and phone offices in the centre. 10 machines in the Biblioteca Municipal, Urb Grau, US$0.60 per hr, clean. **Laundry** Lavandería Liz-to, Tacna 785. Charges by weight. **Post** On the corner of Libertad and Ayacucho on Plaza de Armas is not too helpful, Mon-Sat, 0800-1600. Perhaps it's better going to Hotel Los Portales. **Telephone** Loreto 259, national and international phone and fax. Also at Ovalo Grau 483.

Sullana *p461, map p462*
Banks BCP, San Martín 685. There are *casas de cambio* and street changers on San Martín by Tarapacá. **Immigration** Grau 939. **Internet and telephone** Several in the centre, on San Martín and Av Lama. **Post** San Martín 778, Mon-Sat 0800-1930, Sun 0800-1300.

Coastal route to Ecuador

Although it leads to the tiresome border crossing of Aguas Verdes/Huaquillas, this road passes some of Peru's best and most popular beaches and to the area around Tumbes. The region also has national parks protecting habitats not found anywhere else in the country. ▸▸ *For listings, see pages 473-480.*

Talara and around → *For listings, see pages 473-480. Colour map 1, B1. Population: 87,620. Phone code: 073.*

Talara is the main centre of the coastal oil area, with a state-owned 60,000 barrel-a-day oil refinery and a fertilizer plant. Set in a desert oasis 5 km west of the Panamericana, the city is a triumph over formidable natural difficulties, with water piped 40 km from the Río Chira. A couple of kilometres from the town is La Peña beach, which is unspoilt. Other attractions in the area can be reached via paved highways that connect the town with the Negritos, Lagunitos, La Brea and other oilfields.

Of historical interest are the old tarpits at **La Brea**, 21 km inland from Punta Pariñas, south of Talara, and near the foot of the Amotape mountains. Here the Spaniards boiled the tar to get pitch for caulking their ships. Surfers will love the empty swell north and south of town, especially near Negritos where a gentle beach break and rolling thunder are separated by Punta Balcones, the westernmost point of South America. The impressive sea lion colony and the occasional dolphin make this an interesting spot.

Some 31 km north of Talara, is the small port of **Cabo Blanco**, famous for its excellent sea-fishing and surfing. The scenery has, unfortunately, been spoilt by numerous oil installations. The turn-off from the Pan-American Highway is at the town of **El Alto**, where many oil workers are housed. There are several basic hotels here. Camping is permitted free of charge at Cabo Blanco, on the beach or by the **Fishing Club** overlooking the sea, at least in the off-season, June to December. The film of Ernest Hemingway's *The Old Man and the Sea* was shot here. Marlin grew scarce in the late 1960s owing to commercial fishing and to climatic and maritime factors but in the last few years the marlin have returned. The old **Fishing Club** in Cabo Blanco, built in the 1950s, has been remodelled in the shape of the **Fishing Club Lodge Hotel**, which has a restaurant, pool, and offers watersports (it's likely to be full in the New Year period). A launch also provides all the necessary facilities for deep-sea fishing. Now, would-be Ernest Hemingways can return to Cabo Blanco in search of their dream catch.

Los Organos (www.losorganos.com), a small town and fishing port with a fine long sandy beach and easy surfing at its southern end, provides a quieter and cheaper alternative to Máncora. For those looking to relax, it's especially suitable at peak periods.

Máncora and around → *For listings, see pages 473-480. Colour map 1, B1.*

A small resort stretching along 3 km of the highway, Máncora is parallel to a long, attractive, sandy beach with safe bathing. It is a popular stop-off for travellers on the Peru–Ecuador route, even more so with Argentines and young *limeños* who arrive at weekends and holiday times. Consequently it has a very lively feel with numerous bars and music playing all night. Tourist office: **iperú** ① *Av Piura 250, Thu-Sun 1000-1700.* See www.vivamancora.com. The water here is warm enough for bathing and the town has some of the friendliest local surfers on the planet. Surfing is best November to March (boards and suits can be hired from several places along the southern blocks of Avenida Piura). This stretch of coast is famous for its excellent *mero* (grouper).

The Pan-American Highway runs through the centre of town and is the main street, called Avenida Piura. Most of the tourist facilities are south of the town centre and *artesanía* stalls line the avenue between the centre and south end. At peak times youngsters spill out from the concentration of bars bringing traffic to a complete standstill. At the north end of town the beach is inaccessible and dirty, and this is not a safe area. South of Máncora along the coastal road (old Pan-American Highway) are some excellent beaches that are being developed, for example **Las Pocitas**, a resort ideal for families, or just for relaxing, and **Vichayito**, a separate beach around a headland from Las Pocitas, better reached from Los Organos than Máncora.

Fresh water is piped into the area, producing the incongruous but welcome sight of green lawns and lush gardens between the sea and desert cliffs. There is a line of rocks parallel to the beach, which form interesting bathing pools at low tide, though these can be dangerous at high tide.

At **Las Arenas** resort, 4 km south of Máncora, the beach is unspoilt, with armies of small crabs and abundant bird life, including frigates and masked and brown pelicans.

East of Máncora are hot mud baths (*baños de barro*), which are nice after a day in the surf. There is no infrastructure, but the landscape, desert foothills and shrub lands, is beautiful. The access is north of town, at Km 1168, from where you head for Quebrada Fernández. Beyond is **El Angolo Game Reserve**, which extends as far south as the Río Chira. Take a mototaxi from Máncora, 20 minutes, and pay US$5.75 for the return journey and an hour's wait while you bathe.

North of Máncora → For listings, see pages 473-480.

At Km 1182 is an enormous customs house for checking southbound traffic. Twenty-two kilometres north of Máncora, at Km 1187 (El Arco – a large white arch), is the turn-off for **Punta Sal Grande**, a posh resort town at the southern end of beautiful Playa Punta Sal, a 3-km-long sandy beach, with calm surf. Its clientèle is more upmarket than Máncora. Accommodation options are therefore mostly of a very high standard (with prices to match) and there is no town centre or services such as restaurants independent of hotels. It is very quiet in the low season; a good option for those who want complete tranquility, or are travelling with private transport. The beach offers kilometres of golden sand, relatively warm turquoise water, interesting sea-life in the rock pools and huge schools of whales passing on the distant horizon at dusk. A pleasant walk can be made along the beach to **Punta Sal Chica**, allow at least three hours for the round trip and take water.

The fishing village of **Cancas** has a few shops, restaurants and a gas station. From Punta Mero (Km 1204) north, the beach is used by *larveros*, extracting shrimp larvae from the ocean for use in the shrimp industry, and is no longer considered safe for camping. Several new resorts are being built between Punta Mero and Tumbes.

Zorritos, 27 km south of Tumbes (US$0.55 by combi), is an important fishing centre, with a good beach. Several new hotels and resorts have been built. At **Caleta La Cruz** is the only part of the Peruvian coast where the sea is warm all year. The beach is 16 km southwest of Tumbes, one of two good beaches near the town. It is here that Pizarro landed in 1532. The original Cruz de Conquista was taken to Lima. Regular colectivos run back and forth from Tumbes, US$0.30 each way.

Tumbes → *For listings, see pages 473-480. Colour map 1, A2. Phone code: 072. Population: 94,750.*

Tumbes, about 141 km north of Talara, and 265 km north of Piura, is the most northerly of Peru's provincial capitals. It is not the most beautiful, but it does have some interesting historic wooden buildings in the centre. Tumbes is also a garrison town, so watch where you point your camera. Mosquito repellent is a must for the Tumbes area.

Ins and outs

Getting there A taxi to the airport costs US$2.50-3, 20 minutes. Combis charge US$1.50. Taxis meet flights to take passengers to the border for US$4.50-5. There are no combis from the airport to the border. Beware of overcharging. All the bus companies have offices on Avenida Tumbes.

Getting around Everything is fairly conveniently located close to the Plaza de Armas, although transport to the Ecuadorean border is a little bit further out. Hotels are mostly central to the north of the river either side of Avenida Tumbes and Bolívar.

Tourist information The tourist office is inside the local council offices, **Centro Cívico** ⓘ *Bolognesi 194, 2nd level, on the plaza, T072-524940, dirceturtumbes@gmail.com, open*

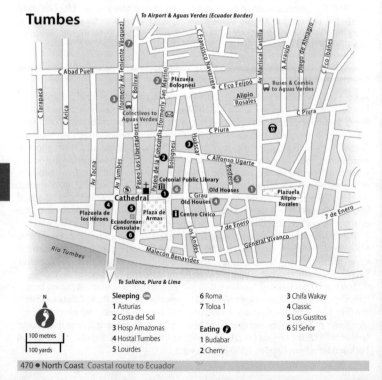

Sleeping ⬤	6 Roma	3 Chifa Wakay
1 Asturias	7 Toloa 1	4 Classic
2 Costa del Sol		5 Los Gustitos
3 Hosp Amazonas	**Eating** 🍴	6 Sí Señor
4 Hostal Tumbes	1 Budabar	
5 Lourdes	2 Cherry	

Mon-Fri 0730-1300, 1400-1630. Another source of specialized information about National Parks and resources in the area is **Pronaturaleza** ① *Bq 0B-14, 4 Etapa, Urb Casas Fonavi, T072-9935 83445, Tumbes representative María Lizbeth Alemán Peralta, www.pronaturaleza. org*, an NGO dedicated to the preservation of the natural environment and the development of sustainable tourism.

Sights

Tumbes is the transport hub for travel to and from Ecuador and most tourists only stop briefly to get transport connections to the beaches to the south, or to Ecuador to the north. If you find yourself with some time to kill in Tumbes there are a couple of points of interest in the town as well as some decent hotels and eateries. The first thing you notice about the city is the bright colours and cheery architecture of modern public buildings. The **Malecón Benavides** provides a walkway along the Río Tumbes, with rainbow-coloured archways and a monstrous statue called *El Beso* (the Kiss). The Plaza de Armas also sports a large structure of many colours and even the cathedral (1903, restored in 1985) has green and pink stripes. You can enter the cathedral when it opens for morning and evening mass every day. The paved streets of Bolívar and San Martín (**Paseo de la Concordia**) make for a pleasant wander and there is a small artesans' market at the top end of San Martín (approaching Plaza Bolognesi). Other points of interest are the tumble-down colonial houses on Calle Grau, many of which look like they might be about to fall down on top of you and are no longer in use.

The Río Tumbes forms a significant boundary between the dry, scrubby desert vegetation to the south and the more lush green landscape north of the river. The river was only bridged in 1930 and the long-term isolation of Tumbes from the rest of Peru is still reflected in the people and their approach to life today.

Around Tumbes → *For listings, see pages 473-480.*

The remains of the Cabeza de Vaca cult centre of the Tumpis people can be found at **Corrales**, 5 km south of Tumbes, but were heavily damaged by both the 1983 and 1997/1998 rains. The Incas built their fort of San Pedro on the site of the Tumpis settlement. The fort was visited by Pizarro on his way from the coast along the Inca coastal highway up to Cajamarca.

Three protected areas consisting of three distinct environments form the UNESCO Biosphere Reserve of northwest Peru. It is an area rich in wildlife and flora, but is little visited by travellers passing by en route between Peru and Ecuador. In a single day it is possible to visit all three areas and sample the rainforest, dry scrub and mangrove swamps.

Santuario Nacional los Manglares de Tumbes

This national reserve was created to protect the mangrove ecosystem in the northernmost part of the Peruvian coast. It extends between the border with Ecuador in the north and Puerto Pizarro (see below) in the south. Of the 4750 remaining hectares, 2988 are protected. There are five species of mangrove, the main one being the red mangrove on whose roots the *conchas negras* live. At least 200 bird species have been recorded, eight of which are endemic, including the mangrove eagle. The mangroves are under threat from fresh water brought down by the rivers during El Niño and the expanding shrimp farming industry, though at 3000 ha it's small compared to that of Ecuador. The Río Tumbes is navigable by small boat to the mouth of the river, an

Border essentials: Peru–Ecuador

Aguas Verdes–Huaquillas

The border is open 24 hours. In mid-2010, a new border complex with customs, immigration and Policía Nacional del Perú (PNP) was opened, a few metres from a new international bridge. The old complex at **Zarumilla**, 3 km from **Aguas Verdes**, was also operational. At the time of writing, it was possible to cross at either bridge. An Ecuadorean border complex was under construction near the new bridge. These details will likely change. Allow at least one hour for border formalities. The Huaquillas–Tumbes crossing has traditionally been harrowing, made worse by the crowds and heat. You must always watch your belongings carefully. In addition to cheating by money changers and cab drivers, this border is known for its thefts and con tricks on travellers. Those on direct buses from Piura or Tumbes to Guayaquil or Machala should have fewer hassles, otherwise it is best to cross in a group. Women are advised not to cross alone. Perhaps things will improve once the new border complex away from the busy towns of Huaquillas and Aguas Verdes is open. Those seeking a more relaxed crossing to or from Peru should consider La Tina–Macará or La Balsa.

Having obtained your exit stamp, proceed across the bridge into Huaquillas, a small city with a reasonable selection of hotels and other services. Passports are stamped 3 km north of town along the road to Machala. There's no urban transport; taxis charge US$1.50 from Huaquillas to immigration. When driving into Peru vehicle fumigation is not required, but there is one outfit who will attempt to fumigate your vehicle with water and charge US$10. Beware of officials claiming that you need a carnet to obtain your 90-day transit permit. This is not so; cite Decreto Supremo 015-87-ICTI/TUR (but check that rules have not changed). There are frequent road tolls between Tumbes and Lima, about US$2.65 each.

Transport From Tumbes to the border colectivos leave from block 3 of Avenida Tumbes. US$1.25 per person or US$8 to hire a car, and wait at the immigration office before continuing to the border, 30-40 minutes. Colectivos can cross the bridge, taxis cannot (so don't hire a Peruvian taxi to take you into Ecuador). Make sure the driver takes you all the way to the border and not just as far as the complex 4 km south of the bridge. Combis leave from the market area along Mcal Castilla across from Calle Alipio Rosales, US$0.75, luggage on roof. They leave passengers at the immigration office. Old, slow city buses ply the same route as combis, US$0.60.

Returning from the border, some colectivos leave from near the bridge, but charge more than others that leave two blocks down along main street by a small plaza opposite the church. Combis and buses return to Tumbes from an esplanade three blocks east of the colectivo stop, but don't wait at immigration. A mototaxi from the border to Zarumilla is US$0.75 per person. Taxi to Tumbes, including wait, US$8. Links to other parts of Ecuador (Machala – 80 km, one hour, also Quito, Guayaquil, Cuenca and Loja) are good.

interesting two-hour trip with fantastic birdlife and mangrove swamps. The mangrove swamps are full of pelicans; it's best to visit them at high tide. A few tame birds beg for fish on the beaches.

Puerto Pizarro

Puerto Pizarro, a small, rubbish-strewn fishing port 13 km northeast of Tumbes, is another access point for the mangroves. Worth visiting from here is the research station where the **Río Tumbes crocodile**, a UN Red-data species, is protected. The crocodile is found at the river's mouth, threatened by shrimp farming, and in the Río Tumbes' upper reaches, threatened by gold-mining.

Parque Nacional Cerros de Amotape

The Parque Nacional Cerros de Amotape was created to protect an area representative of the equatorial forest. It extends southeast from the south bank of the Tumbes river, towards the El Angolo game preserve northeast of Máncora. It covers 90,700 ha comprising seven different habitats, including the best-preserved area of dry forest on the Pacific coast. Species that may be sighted include the black parrot, white-backed squirrels, foxes, deer, tigrillos, pumas and white-winged guan. Permission to enter is needed from Sernanp, which Pronaturaleza can arrange. There is no entrance fee. All water must be carried, which is why most visitors choose to visit by tour.

Zona Reservada de Tumbes

The Zona Reservada de Tumbes (75,000 ha), lies to the northeast of Tumbes, between the Ecuadorean border and Cerros de Amotape National Park. It was created to protect dry equatorial forest and tropical rainforest. The wildlife includes monkeys, otters, wild boars, small cats and crocodiles. Access from Tumbes is via Cabuyal, Pampas de Hospital and El Caucho to the Quebrada Faical research station or via Zarumilla and Matapalo. The best accessible forest is around El Narango, which lies beyond the research station.

ⓒ Coastal route to Ecuador listings

For Sleeping and Eating price codes and other relevant information, see pages 38-44.

● Sleeping

Talara and around *p468*

All hotels have water-supply problems.
A Gran Pacífico, Av Aviación y Arica, Talara, T/F073-385450. The most luxurious in town, 4-star, suites, hot water, pool, restaurant, bar, parking.
E Residencial Grau, Av Grau 77, Talara, T073-382841, near the main plaza. Clean, friendly, possible to park 1 motorbike, owner changes dollars.

Los Organos

There are attractive places to stay on the beach. These include:
A-B Takaynamo, T073-257587, www.takaynamoperu.com. Rooms with

terrace and bath, some with hot water, restaurant and bar, swimming pool.
B Veleritos Bungalows, T073-257433, www.vivamancora.com/veleritos. Bungalows and rooms with hot water, TV, internet and Wi-Fi, restaurant/bar, pools, parking.
D Hostal La Perla, southern end of the beach, T073-257753, www.elaperla.com.pe. With pool and restaurant, clean and friendly, good value. Recommended.
E Hostal Roland Kent, Av Túpac Amaru 769, T073-257163, rolandkentperu@yahoo.com. Named after the owner and his favourite brand of cigarettes! Clean, friendly, TV, good value, best restaurant in town.

Máncora and around *p468*

In Máncora town the main strip of the Panamericana is known as Av Piura from the bridge for the 1st couple of blocks, then Av Grau to the end of town. The better hotels are at the southern end of town, with a small concentration of mid-range hotels just over the bridge. Hotels to the left look onto the beach directly in front of the best surf and often have beach entrances as well as road entrances. As the most popular with tourists, they are all quite noisy at night from nearby discos, which go until around 0200 week nights and 0600 at weekends. Prices can increase by up to 100% in high season (Dec-Mar). Many hotels have special rates for Christmas, New Year, Easter and Independence Day holidays when the resort is full to bursting with partying Limeños. Cheaper options in the centre of Máncora abound if you don´t mind a bit of grime in the bathroom and travel with your own sheets. Just look for the signs saying 'Hospedaje' along Av Piura. When checking into any hotel, expect to pay up front and make sure you get a receipt as you are likely to be asked to pay again the next time the receptionist sees you.

B Del Wawa, beachfront, T073-258427, www.delwawa.com. This relaxed and spacious hotel is popular with serious surfers.

B-C Las Olas, beachfront, T01-9826 8211, www.lasolasmancora.com. Smart, cabin-style rooms, hammocks and gardens, half- and full-board rates available.

B-C Punta Ballenas, south of Cabo Blanco bridge at the south entrance to town, T073-258136, www.puntaballenas.com. Price rise in high season, lovely setting on beach, garden with pool, includes breakfast, expensive restaurant.

D Loki del Mar, Av Piura 262, T073-258484, www.lokihostel.com. Latest addition to the Loki group, seafront, modern hostel, **F** per person in dorm, with breakfast, bar, pool, internet, surf board hire.

E Casa del Turista, Av Piura 224, T073-258126. Family-run, TV, roof terraces giving sea views. Recommended but all but the top-floor suites are noisy at night due to nearby Sol y Mar disco.

F Hospedaje Crillon, Paita 168, 1 block back from Panamericana in centre, T073-258001.

Basic rooms with 4 or more beds, shared bath, plenty of water. Recommended.

F pp Sol y Mar, beachfront, T073-258106, www.solymarmancora.com. One of the oldest hotels in Máncora, very popular with young travellers out for a good time. Prices rise in high season. Has the loudest disco in town, and offers basic but clean room with bath and fan. Mixed reports.

F pp The Point Máncora Beach, Playa El Amor, T073-706320, www.thepoint hostels.com/mancora.html. Price is for a bed in a dorm, also has cabins at **D**. Right on the beach, with travel centre, surfing and other games and sports, **Poto Blanco** bar and restaurant.

Quebrada Cabo Blanco

Crossing the bridge into Máncora, a dirt track leads downhill to the right, to the Quebrada Cabo Blanco, signed to La Posada Youth Hostel. The 4 hotels at the end of the track require better lighting for guests returning at night, but they are quiet and relaxing. Robberies have occurred so take a mototaxi at night (US$0.35).

B Kimbas Bungalows, T073-258373, www.kimbasbungalowsmancora.com. Chilled-out spot with charming thatched bungalows, central complex with restaurant and bar, and a small pool.

B La Quebrada, T073-258669, www.vivaman cora.com/laquebrada/index.html. Smart, modern, large rooms with glass patio doors and hammocks, shared kitchen and TV.

D-E El Pirata, T073-258459, www.vivaman cora.com/ elpirata. Impressive (if wobbly) bamboo rooms, large, airy, mosquito nets; downstairs rooms are sturdier but lack light and some are very small. Use of basic kitchen and BBQ. Staff are helpful.

Las Pocitas

South of Máncora, a stretch of beautiful beach with rocks on the shore, behind which little pools (or pocitas) form at low tide. Being developed with luxury resorts, popular with more upmarket tourists and families.

LL-AL La Casita de Sueños, T073-258389, www.mancora-peru.com. 3 luxury bungalows on the beach, fully equipped, secluded, self-catering, but a cook can be provided.

L Casa Del Muelle, Km 1215 Antigua Panamericana Norte, T01-9998 59080, www.casadelmuellemancora.com. Just before the pier, elegant, aimed at families. It has a well-equipped kitchen for guests to use. 4 spacious and airy rooms each sleep up to 5, all with views of the pool, beach and sea, large windows give the feeling of being on the beach, small covered terrace with comfortable chairs.

L Las Arenas de Máncora, old Panamericana norte 1213, T073-258240, www.lasarenasde mancora.com. Smart bungalow-style accommodation, hot water, cable TV, with central bar and restaurant which serves imaginative dishes, beautiful pool, palm-lined beach front, includes breakfast, etc, very romantic.

AL Grandmare, T073-258716, www.grandmaremancora.com. Beach bungalows around a central pool, rooms all have safes, a/c and cable TV, internet. Has 3- and 4-day packages on offer.

B Puerto Palos, along the old Pan-American Highway south of town (10 mins by mototaxi, US$1.45), T073-258199, www.puertopalos. com. Excellent, nice pool overlooking ocean, good but expensive restaurant.

D Mancoral, 1 km south of Máncora pier, T073-516107, www.vivamancora.com/ mancoral. Good budget option, basic but clean, small, hospitable. Best of all, it is built on a steep dune so rooms look over the sea stadium-style, many have private balconies.

Vichayito

AL-A Vichayito, on the beach at Km 1121 on the old Pan-American Highway, T01-434 1452, www.vichayito.com. Attractive, comfortable bungalows set among the dunes, with a beautiful pool, bar, restaurant and pool table. Includes breakfast. Recommended.

A-B El Refugio, on the beach, T073-671626, www.elrefugiodevichayito.com. Smart

bungalows around a pool and restaurant, includes breakfast. Prices rise in high season. Can arrange surfing an fishing trips, and horse riding.

B pp in high season (Dec-Mar, Easter and holidays) **La Siesta**, T01-9814 88453, www.lasiesta-bungalows.com. Bungalows and suites, Spanish-owned, **C** per person in low season. Very comfortable, personal service, good restaurant, swimming pool, jacuzzi. Recommended.

North of Máncora p469

L-AL Samana Chakra, T073-258604, www.samanachakra.com. A well-being retreat offering peaceful beachside bungalows, home-cooked food and yoga and meditation classes held in a specially built open-air yoga studio looking out over the pool and ocean. They also offer the location for beach-front weddings should you feel romantically inclined while in Máncora. In high season rates rise 35% and 3 and 5-night stays are expected.

D Laguna Surf Camp, T073-671727, www.vivamancora.com/lagunacamp. 100 m from the sea near new breakwater, thatched roofs, hammocks, cabins sleeping up to 6, helpful. Relaxed atmosphere, cabins surround small communal area with hammocks.

Punta Sal Grande

A pp **Caballito De Mar**, T072-540058, www.hotelcaballitodemar.com. Immaculate beach-front rooms and small bungalows built into the cliff behind the road, pool and bar area face the ocean. **C-D** in low season. Professional and helpful staff.

C pp **Hospedaje El Bucanero**, at the entrance to Playa Punta Sal, set back from the beach, T073-381125, www.elbucanero puntasal.com. **A** in high season. The most happening place in Punta Sal, popular with travellers, a variety of rooms, pool, restaurant, bar, gardens and billiards, great view.

E pp **Huá**, on the beach at the entrance to Playa Punta Sal, T072-540023, www.hua-puntasal.com. **C** per person in the high season, cheaper with cold water. A rustic old wooden building, pleasant terrace overlooking ocean, discount for IYHF card holders, camping permitted on the beach beside the hotel, meals available.

E pp Las Terrazas, opposite Sunset Punta Sal, T01-996 08288, lasterrazaspuntasal@ yahoo.com. One of the more basic and cheaper hotels in Punta Sal, restaurant has sea view, some rooms better than others, those with own bath and sea view twice the price. Helpful owners.

Zorritos

F pp Casa Grillo Centro Ecoturístico Naturista, Los Pinos 563, between Bocapán and Los Pinos, 30 km from Tumbes, T072-794830, www.casagrillo.net. Take colectivo from Tumbes market to Los Pinos, or get off bus on Pan-American Highway at Km 1236.5. **G** with shared bath, youth hostel, excellent restaurant including vegetarian, great place to relax, 6 rooms for up to 4, made of local materials, shared bath, hot water, laundry, surfing, scuba-diving, fishing, cycling, trekking, horse riding, camping available. Recommended.

Tumbes p470, map p470

There are many cheap hotels by the market. At holiday times it can be very difficult to find a vacant room.

A Costa del Sol, San Martín 275, T072-523991, www.costadelsolperu.com. The only high-class hotel in town featuring hot water, minibars, a/c, a good restaurant, a garden with pool, and great service. Parking is available for an extra fee. Avoid the rooms at the front that look onto the Plazuela Bolognesi as they are noisy.

C Asturias, Av Mcal Castilla 305, T072-522569, turismoasturiasrl@hotmail.com. Comfortable rooms with private bath, hot water, a/c, phone, cable TV, restaurant and bar and laundry. Accepts credit cards.

C Lourdes, Mayor Bodero 118, T072-522966. A friendly hotel with a very narrow corridor leading to small, cell-like rooms

that are actually plushly decorated with an incongruous mixture of antique and modern furniture. Good clean bathrooms and fans in each room.

D Roma, Bolognesi 425 Plaza de Armas, T072-524137, hotelromatumbes@ hotmail.com. The best of the budget hotels. Rooms are large, light and spacious (despite the dark corridors), all with bath, hot water, cable TV, phones and fans. A 2nd floor terrace looks out over the Plaza de Armas. Recommended.

E Hospedaje Amazonas, Av Tumbes 317, T072-525266. A large, noisy hotel with basic facilities, smallish dark rooms, but relatively clean and secure. Unreliable water supply in the mornings.

E Hostal Tumbes, Grau 614, T072-522203. Small, dark, basic, cleanish rooms with fan and private bathroom. A good cheap option.

F Toloa 1, Av Tumbes 436, T072-523771. No-frills *hostal* , standard rooms with private bath, fan and cable TV. Noisy as on the Panamericana, popular with businessmen, which may provide an uncomfortable environment for single women.

Around Tumbes p471

F pp Hospedaje Bayside, by the Malecón, Puerto Pizarro, T072-543045. Bungalows with bath, pool, food available.

F Hostal Francis, Av República del Perú 220, Aguas Verdes, T072-561177. OK option if you are stuck overnight in the border area. There are 4 hotels in Zarumilla, at Km 1290 on the Panamericana, 5 km south of Aguas Verdes.

🍴 Eating

Talara and around p468

The better restaurants are in the main hotels; cheaper restaurants are on the main plaza.

Several restaurants overlook the beach in Los Organos: **Bambú** is clean and prepares an excellent *ceviche* with fish freshly caught by the fishing boats bobbing in the bay.

Máncora and around p468

A small open-air commercial centre called **The Birdhouse** has some of the best eateries in town, including: **Green Eggs and Ham**, open 0730-1300 for great breakfasts at US$3.35, 8 options including waffles, pancakes or eggs and bacon, plus optional extra portions, juice or coffee included. **Papa Mo's** milk bar, directly underneath Green Eggs and Ham, with comfy seats practically on the beach and a selection of drinks. Along the main strip of the Panamericana:

♯ **Pizzería Chan-Chan**, Av Piura, udoliliana@ terraplus.com.pe. Good pizza and pasta, fairly expensive but delicious.

♯♯-♯ **El Faro**, Av Piura 233, elfarodemancora@ hotmail.com. One of the most popular restaurants, a large variety of seafood, chicken and meat dishes for lunch or dinner, as well as a cheap set menu at lunch times. In the evening becomes a crowded spot for drinks.

♯♯-♯ **El Tuno**, Av Piura 233. Probably the best restaurant in Máncora, gourmet food at everyday prices. Specialties are grilled tuna steaks and home-made pastas.

♯ **Angela's Place/Cafetería de Angela**, Av Piura 396, www.vivamancora.com/deangela. A great option for a healthy breakfast or lunch and heaven for vegetarians and wholefood lovers, home-made rye bread and whole grain bread featuring 10 grains, as well as natural yogurts, fresh fruit, etc. Free tourist information on the back of the menus.

♯ **Café La Bajadita**, has an impressive selection of delicious home-made desserts and cakes including cheesecake with a choice of 3 fruit toppings. Other food is disappointing – come here for the desserts. There are many cheaper restaurants further north along Av Piura and at the entrance to the beach, all offering *ceviche* and other popular local fish and seafood dishes. **La Espada** and **Don Pedro** are good choices for quality and quantity. Remember that beachfront restaurants don't have as high hygiene standards as the more established restaurants along the highway.

Tumbes p470, map p470

There are cheap restaurants on Plaza de Armas, Paseo de la Concordia and near the markets.

♯♯-♯ **Budabar**, Grau 309, T072-525 493, budabartumbes@hotmail.com. One-of-a-kind chill-out lounge, on the main plaza, offering traditional food and comfy seating with outdoor tables and cheap beer. Very popular in the evenings.

♯♯-♯ **Chifa Wakay**, Huáscar 413. A large and well-ventilated smart restaurant offering the usual *chifa* (Chinese/Peruvian-style) favourites. Open evenings only.

♯♯-♯ **Classic**, Tumbes 185. Look for it almost under the bridge over the river Tumbes heading south. Popular for local food. Recommended.

♯♯-♯ **Los Gustitos**, Bolívar 148. Excellent set menus and à la carte. Popular with locals and has a good atmosphere at lunchtimes.

♯ **Sí Señor**, Bolívar 119, on plaza. Good for snacks and offers cheap lunch menus.

Cafés

Fuente de Soda Cherry, San Martín 116. Open 0800-1400, 1700-2300. Tiny cafe offering an amazing selection of cakes and desserts that will satisfy even the sweetest of teeth! They also serve fresh juices, shakes, sandwiches, hot and cold drinks and the traditional *cremoladas* (fruit juice with crushed ice).

⊛ Festivals and events

Around Tumbes p471

Festival of San Pedro y San Pablo takes place on **29-30 Jun**.

▲ Activities and tours

Máncora and around p468

Iguanas Trips, Av Piura 245, T01-9853 5099, www.vivamancora.com/iguanastrips. Run by Ursula Behr, offers a variety of adventure tourism trips including whitewater rafting, horseriding and camping trips in the nearby national parks and reserve zones.

Tumbes p470, map p470

Day trips to the Manglares at Puerto Pizarro, US$25 per person (including entrance to the crocodile breeding centre), or to the Zona Reservada de Tumbes for US$30-50 per person (including Sernanp entrance fee). Day trip to Cerros de Amotape costs US$35-55 per person, including visits to ruins at Rica Playa. Also available is a 1-day Historical Tour, including the Huaca Gran Chilimasa and site museum, the place where petrol was first extracted, and hot springs (hervideros) and the beach at Puntal Sal, US$35 per person. **Rosillo Tours**, Tumbes 293, T072-523892, www.rosillotours.com. Operate all of the above tours and are equipped to handle large groups.

Around Tumbes p471

Boats from **Comité de Transporte Acuático**, Malecón Turístico, T072-543019, go to: **Isla de Amor** (bars, restaurants, camping, windsurfing, hammocks for rent, over-nighting 'homeless lovers', US$5); **Isla Hueso de Ballena** (open ocean and quiet bay, swimming, no services, US$6); **crocodile farm** (US$8), **Isla de los Pájaros** (best to see birds 1700-1800, US$9); full tour including mangroves, 2 hrs, US$15 (price per boat, maximum 8 people).

☉ Transport

Talara and around p468
Air

To/from **Lima**, Star Perú (T98-900 6864), via **Cajamarca**, Tue, Thu, Sun.

Bus

See under Sullana. To and from **Tumbes**, 171 km, 3 hrs, US$4, several daily. Most come from Piura and most stop at major towns

going north. To **Piura**, 111 km, 2 hrs, US$2. To **El Alto** (Cabo Blanco), 32 km, 30 mins, US$1. To **Máncora** take a combi from beside the Tepsa terminal (Av la Merino F21, Pariñas) to Los Organos (an oil workers town on the Panamericana with a windy beach and good seafood restaurants on the plaza), US$1, 1 hr; change combis there and continue to Máncora, 28 km, 20 mins, US$0.50. **Los Organos to/from Piura**, Eppo 3 hrs, US$4. Colectivos leave when full for **Máncora**, 15 mins, US$0.50, and **Tumbes**, 2 hrs, US$2. All transport leaves from the Panamericana in the town centre.

Máncora and around p468

To **Talara, Sullana and Piura** with Eppo, Grau 470, 1 block north of plaza, 5 a day, just over 3 hrs, US$4. Other buses stop en route from Tumbes in the main plaza. To **Tumbes** (and points in between), combis tour the length of Av Piura all day as far as the bridge until full, US$2, 2 hrs. **Tepsa** office, Grau 113, T073-258348, fare to **Lima** US$36. Emtrafesa, T073-411324.

North of Máncora p469

A taxi from Máncora is the quickest and easiest way to get to Punta Sal Grande, 20 mins, US$14, mototaxi 40 mins, US$10, otherwise take any combi going between Máncora and Tumbes and tell the driver you want to get out at Punta Sal. Look out for the arch marking the entrance, it takes about 30 mins to walk down to the beach. A mototaxi to/from El Arco and the hotels costs US$2.50, up to 10 mins. If popping in to Máncora for anything while staying at Punta Sal, it is best not to use passing buses for the short journey as they can be held up at the customs checkpoint; use combis instead.

Tumbes p470, map p470
Air

There are daily flights to **Lima** with **LAN**, Bolognesi 250.

Bus

Daily buses to and from **Lima**, 1320 km, 18-20 hrs, from US$31-40 (Cruz del Sur regular), US$50 (**Cruz del Sur** VIP) to US$57-67 on **CIVA**. Cheaper buses usually leave 1600-2100, more expensive ones 1200-1400. Except for luxury service, most buses to Lima stop at major cities en route. Tickets to anywhere between Tumbes and Lima sell quickly, so if arriving from Ecuador you may have to stay overnight. Piura is a good place for connections in the daytime.

To **Talara**, 171 km, US$4, 3 hrs. To **Sullana**, 244 km, 3-4 hrs, US$5, several buses daily. To **Piura**, 4-5 hrs, 282 km, US$5.50; with **Trans Chiclayo, Cruz del Sur, El Dorado**, (also to Máncora and Trujillo) 8 a day. **Comité Tumbes/Piura** colectivos costs US$7, fast cars, leave when full, 3½ hrs. To **Chiclayo**, 552 km, 6 hrs, US$6, several each day with Cruz del Sur, El Dorado. To **Trujillo**, 769 km, 10-11 hrs, US$10-19, Ormeño, Cruz del Sur, El Dorado and Emtrafesa. For transport to the border, see page 472.

Bus companies Comité Tumbes/Piura colectivos, Tumbes 308, T072-525977. Cruz del Sur, Tumbes Norte 319, T072-896163. El Dorado, Piura 459, T072-523480. Emtrafesa, Tumbes 596, T072-522894. Línea, Bolívar 914, T072-524857. Oltursa, Av Tumbes Norte 307, T072-523048. Ormeño, Av Tumbes s/n, T072-522228. Tepsa, Av Tumbes Norte 199, T072-522428. Trans Chiclayo, Tumbes 466, T072-525260.

Around Tumbes p471

The best access to **Santuario Nacional los Manglares de Tumbes** is via the Panamericana north as far as Zarumilla. Combis leave every few mins from Tumbes market, US$0.50, 20 mins. In Zarumilla hire a mototaxi for the 7 km run (20 mins, US$1.50) to the CEDECOM (Centro de Conservación para el Desarrollo de los Manglares), you must arrange for the bike to return to collect you. Standard tour price is US$15 for a boat taking up to 6 passengers, 2½ hrs, and includes the mangrove walkway

and a trip up several creeks, subject to tide levels. Book with **Pronaturaleza**, in Tumbes, who can also arrange a sanctuary visitors permit from Sernanp. There is no entry fee.

For **Puerto Pizarro**, take colectivo No 6 from the small plaza on C Piura in Tumbes; US$0.50, 20 mins.

Access to **Parque Nacional Cerros de Amotape** is via the road that goes southeast from the Panamericana at Bocapán (Km 1233) to Casitas and Huásimo, it takes 2 hrs by car from Tumbes, and is best done in the dry season (Jul-Nov). Also access via Quebrada Fernández from Máncora and via Querecotilo and Los Encuentros from Sullana.

For transport to the border, see page 472.

Directory

Máncora and around p468

Banks There are 2 ATMs in Máncora that accept all major cards. Several places change money, but exchange rates tend to be 1 to 2 points lower than in major cities, so change dollars before arriving in Máncora if you can. **Internet** Several places on Av Piura, relatively fast connection. More upmarket hotels also have internet and Wi-Fi connection for guests. **Medical services** 24-hr emergency clinic at Av Piura 306, T073-258712. Normal surgery hrs Mon-Sat 0800-1400, 1600-2100. Also has good lab for clinical tests. **Pharmacies:** Boticas BTL, Av Piura 621 (next to police station) part of a major chain with good stock. Open daily 0700-2300. Delivery within Máncora T073-258587. **Botica Mariluz** (next to Casa de Betty), 24-hr delivery T073-258214. **Telephone** Several places on Av Piura offer good rates for local, national and international calls, such as **Locutorio Conecta Perú** and **Bodega Locutorio Los Angeles**.

Tumbes p470, map p470

Banks There are several large banks on the Plaza de Armas, and 3 ATMS that accept Visa, MasterCard, Maesto, Cirrus, Visa Electron and

Plus. **Scotiabank**, Av Bolognesi 111, with ATM in the plaza. **BBV Continental**, Bolívar 121. **Cambios Internacionales**, Av Bolívar 259-A. Cash only, good rates, open 0800-1300, 1530-1900. Minimum amount to exchange is US$20. Money changers on the street (on Bolívar, left of the cathedral) give a much better rate than banks or *cambios*, but some are unscrupulous and don't accept the first offer you are given. None change TCs. Conterfeit money is a big problem; only use them if you are confident of being able to spot fakes. Rates offered at the airport are bad. If you're travelling on to Ecuador, it is better to change your soles at the border as the rate is higher. **Consulates** Ecuadorean Consulate, Bolívar 129, Plaza de Armas,

T072- 521739, consultum@speedy.com.pe. Mon-Fri 0900-1300 and 1400-1630.
Internet Widely available. **Laundry** Lavandería Flash, Piura 1000. Pay by weight.
Medical services 24-hr emergency clinic at Av Mcal Castilla 305, T072-525341. Consultancy hrs Mon-Fri 0800-1400. **Dentist:** Dr Carlos Feijoó, Grau 693, 0900-1300, 1600-2000. **Post** San Martín 208, on Paseo de la Concordia.

Around Tumbes p471

Banks Money can be changed on either side of the border. Ecuador uses the dollar as currency. Do not change money on the minibus in Aguas Verdes, very poor rates.

Contents

Footprint features

Border crossings

Northern Highlands

At a glance

◉ **Getting around** By bus, and some trekking.

◉ **Time required** 1 to 2½ weeks, depending on how many areas you choose to visit.

☼ **Weather** Nov-Apr is the wet season. The Chachapoyas area may be cloudy at any time of year. The further east you go, the more Amazonian the climate.

✖ **When not to go** Carnival in Cajamarca can be particularly messy and violent. Otherwise, as with many parts of the country, travel can be difficult during the wetter months.

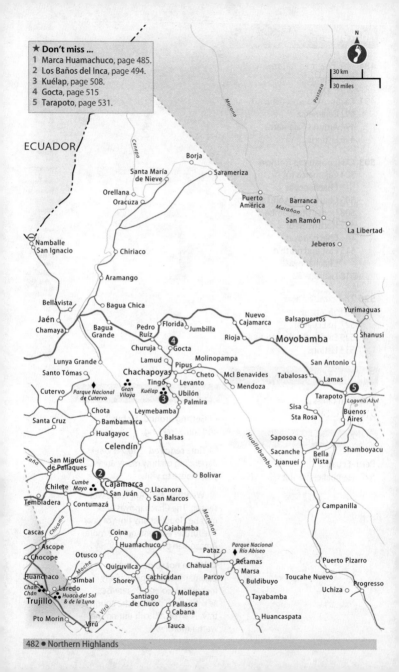

★ **Don't miss ...**
1 Marca Huamachuco, page 485.
2 Los Baños del Inca, page 494.
3 Kuélap, page 508.
4 Gocta, page 515
5 Tarapoto, page 531.

N

30 km
30 miles

ECUADOR

Borja
Santa María
de Nieve   Sarameriza
Orellana
Oracuza   Puerto
                 América   Barranca
Namballe   San Ramón   La Libertad
San Ignacio   Chiriaco   Jeberos
Bellavista
Jaén   Bagua Chica
Chamaya Bagua   Nuevo   Balsapuertos   Yurimaguas
         Grande Pedro Florida Jumbilla Cajamarca   Shanusi
Lunya Grande   Ruíz   Rioja   Moyobamba
                Churuja   Gocta   San Antonio
Santo Tómas   Lamud   Pipus Molinopampa   Tabalosas Lamas
         Chachapoyas   Cheto Mcl Benavides
Cutervo Parque Nacional Gran Tingo Levanto   Tarapoto
         de Cutervo Vilaya Kuélap Ubilón Mendoza Sisa Buenos
Santa Cruz Chota Bambamarca Palmira   Sta Rosa Aires
         Hualgayoc Leymebamba   Saposoa   Shamboyacu
         Celendín Balsas   Sacanche Bella
San Miguel   Juanueí   Vista
de Pallaques   Campanilla
Chilete Cumbe   Cajamarca Bolívar
         Mayo   Llacanora
Tembladera Contumazá San Juán
                       San Marcos
Cascas   Cajabamba
         Coina   Parque Nacional
Ascope   Huamachuco   Pataz   Río Abiseo   Puerto Pizarro
Chocope Otusco   Chahual Retamas
         Quiruvilca Cachicadan Marsa Toucahe Nuevo
Huanchaco Simbal Shorey Parcoy Buldibuyo   Progresso
Chán   Laredo   Mollepata Tayabamba Uchiza
Chán   Huaca del Sol Santiago Pallasca
Trujillo & de la Luna de Chuco Cabana Huancaspata
Pto Morin Virú   Tauca

This vast area stretches from the western foothills of the Andes across the mountains and down to the fringes of the Amazon jungle. It contains Peru's most spectacular pre-Columbian ruins, some of them built on a massive scale unequalled anywhere in the Americas. A good road rises from the coast to the city of Cajamarca, where the Inca Atahualpa was captured by the Spanish. Only one Inca building remains, the so-called Ransom Chamber, but the city has a pleasant colonial centre with comfortable hotels and good restaurants. Change is coming fast as a huge gold mine is bringing new investment, but also conflict, to the area. Close by are the hot springs where Atahualpa used to bathe, still very much in use today, and a number of pre-Inca sites. Beyond Cajamarca, a tortuous road winds its way east to the functional town of Chachapoyas. This is a friendly place, opening its doors to visitors as it lies at the centre of a region full of fantastic archaeological treasures whose mysteries are only just being uncovered. There are fortresses, mysterious cities and strange burial sites replete with mummies and giant sarcophagi.

From Chachapoyas there are three options: carry on eastwards on one of Peru's most beautiful roads to the tropical lowland town of Tarapoto passing waterfalls and high moors before dropping down to the jungle zone; return to the coast at Chiclayo; or head north to Ecuador on a new route via Jaén and San Ignacio for the crossing to Zumba and Vilcabamba. With new roads and bridges in operation, a great adventure is opening up. It's now possible to travel from Ecuador, through Chachapoyas and Cajamarca on to the Cordillera Blanca, even to Cuzco, without touching the coast, and all by public transport. It may be a slow route, but it will take some beating. All these possibilities are getting easier as the area becomes the focus of tourism development to rival the Lima–Cuzco–Arequipa axis.

The coast to Cajamarca

Cajamarca can be reached from the coast, directly northeast from Trujillo on a 180-km, paved road north of the port of Pacasmayo, midway between Trujillo and Chiclayo. The road branches off the Pan-American Highway soon after it crosses the Río Jequetepeque at Ciudad de Dios and takes about seven hours from either Trujillo or Chiclayo. Alternatively, you can take the old road via Huamachuco and Cajabamba, which still takes a couple of days by bus. The old road is more interesting, passing through sierra towns and over the bare puna before dropping into the Huamachuco Valley, where the archaeological site of Marca Huamachuco is one of the main attractions. ►► *For listings, see pages 488-490.*

Chilete and Kuntur Wasi → *Colour map 1, C3.*

Some 103 km east of Pacasmayo is the mining town of **Chilete**. Some 21 km from Chilete, on the road north to San Pablo, are the pyramid and stone monoliths of **Kuntur Wasi**. If you are rushing along the paved road, do try to pause here, it is a very fine pre-Inca site. Devoted to a feline cult, it is undergoing development under a Japanese archaeological team. Kuntur Wasi can be visited from Cajamarca with some local tour companies. It has an excellent on-site museum, making a visit worthwhile. There are a couple of hotels at Chilete but rooms are hard to find on Tuesday because of the Wednesday market. Further along the road to Cajamarca is Yonán, where there are petroglyphs.

    Contumazá ① *www.municontumaza.gob.pe*, 40 km south of Chilete, is considered an important cultural centre, with festivals and dances throughout the year and handicraft production. Near the village of Catan, 50 km from Contumazá, is the **Tantarica** archaeological site at 2834 m, showing some similarities with the Marca Huamachuco complex (see below). Contumazá can be reached by public transport from Chilete, or from Trujillo via Ascope in the Chicama Valley and Cascas.

Trujillo to Huamachuco

The paved road to Huamachuco goes first to **Otusco**, arguably the most accessible sierra town, in terms of proximity to the coast, anywhere in Peru. Being 1½ hours from Trujillo, it makes a pleasant half-day excursion. 'La Ciudad de la Fe', as it is known, is an attractive Andean town at 2200 m with some narrow cobbled streets. The modern church houses the important **Virgen de la Puerta**, which attracts devotees from all over Peru, especially during the big **festival** on 15 December. Adjoining it, in the old colonial church, is an amazing **museum** ① *Mon and Wed-Sat 0830-1230, 1400-1800, Sun 0830-1700, US$0.30*, filled with public gifts for the *Virgen*, including endless cabinets displaying elaborately embroidered capes, cheap jewellery and even shoes.

    From Otusco the paved road continues to **Shorey** and the **Quiruvilca** turn-off. The pollution in these mining towns is shocking. About 8 km east of Quiruvilca, Alto Chicama (the second largest opencast gold mine in Peru) was opened in 2005. In Shorey a road branches off to **Santiago de Chuco**, birthplace of the poet César Vallejo (see Literature, page 679), where there is the annual **festival of Santiago El Mayor** in the second half of July. The main procession is on 25 July, when the image is carried through the streets. Beyond Santiago de Chuco, one to 1½ hours, is **Cachicadan**, where there are good hot baths.

    A spectacular but rough road, with a superb *balcón andino* (viewpoint, after the pass) looking down in to the Alto Chicama Valley, continues beyond Otusco to **Usquil** (two hours). It then descends steeply down to **Coina** at 1200 m (two hours). Crowded combis pass through from Trujillo, US$2.50. Hikes can be made through fields of barley and *limón* orchards around Coina and along the picturesque Chicama Valley. Beyond Coina is **Chuquizongo** (one hour), famed for its fighting bulls, and **Huaranchal** (another hour), which has thermal baths (US$0.50). There are a couple of combis each day from Coina.

Huamachuco → *Colour map 3, A2. Phone code: 044. Altitude: 3180 m.*

The paved main road runs on to this colonial town, which was formerly on the Royal Inca road coming from Cajabamba. The centre of the town follows the original Inca town plan. The plaza was once twice the size with an *usnu* (platform) in the centre. The old church of San José now sits on top of the *usnu*. The town also has the largest main plaza in Peru, with fine topiary, and a controversial modern **cathedral**, likened by some to an aeroplane hangar, sitting on top of the remains of an Inca palace. There is a colourful **Sunday market**, with dancing in the plaza, and **Museo Municipal Wamachuko** ① *Sucre 195, Mon-Sat 0900-1300, 1500-1900, Sun 0900-1200, free*, displays artefacts found at Cerro Amaru and Marca Huamachuco, plus aerial photos of the latter. The main reason for visiting Huamachuco is to see the spectacular, but little-known ruins of **Marca Huamachuco**, which are located on the summit (3600 m) of one of the mountains northwest of town.

There is tourist information at **Infotur** ① *Jr Sucre cuadra 1 (Plazuela Tauricuxi), T044-441121.* See also the municipal website, www.munihuamachuco.gob.pe.

Marca Huamachuco

① *Open daily 0900-1700, US$1. A minimum of 2 hrs is needed, 4 hrs to really explore. Carry all food and drink with you. Access is along a poor vehicle road, off the road to Sanagorán. There is an archway at the turn-off, about 5 km from Huamachuco. In dry weather, 4WDs can make it to the top. It is much faster to walk on the mule trail that starts just after the archway. A mototaxi to the turn-off costs US$2. There are also combis to Sanagorán in the morning. Funds have been approved to improve the road and build a site museum.*

The Marca Huamachuco ruins surely rank in the top 10 archaeological sites in Peru. It is an extensive site, 3 km long, dating back to at least 300 BC though many structures were added later. Its most impressive features are: **El Castillo**, a remarkable circular structure with walls up to 8 m high located at the highest point of the site. This and other structures are the oldest-known buildings in Peru to extend to more than two storeys and may have reached five storeys. The outer defensive wall, which is accessible where it bisects the hill halfway along, also reaches up to 8 m in height. It consists of two parallel walls with gallery rooms in between. The **Convento** complex consists of five circular structures of varying sizes located towards the northern end of the hill. These are later constructions dating back to AD 600-800. The largest one has been partially reconstructed by the INC and provides an interesting insight into how they must once have appeared, with two or three parallel outer walls, gallery rooms between them and several other internal structures. It has been suggested that these buildings housed the privileged members of an elite class.

Some 3 km before the ruins you will pass the remarkable **Cerro Amaru** on the left. It would seem that the whole of this relatively small hilltop was adapted to store water by placing an impermeable layer of clay around it. Wells (**Los Chiles**) on the summit, which can still be viewed, then provided access to the water within. Almost certainly the hill acquired major religious and cultural significance within the Huari-Tiahuanaco Empire and became a place of pilgrimage and sacrifice in times of drought.

It seems likely that Marca Huamachuco existed for many centuries as the centre of an autonomous religious cult, separate from the activities of the Chachapoyans to the north and east. The site was certainly used as much as a ceremonial centre as it was for defensive purposes. Latest theories suggest that the Huari-Tiahuanaco culture (AD 600-1100) may have developed from the north out of places such as Marca Huamachuco and Yaino and then spread south, rather than the other way round. Apparently, the chronology of sites fits much better on this basis, but, if correct, this would require a complete reassessment of the Huari-Tiahuanuco culture.

Around Huamachuco

Wiracochapampa is an extensive Huari site, 3 km to the north of the town, a 45-minute walk. Much of the site is overgrown and poorly conserved, but walls up to 3 m high can still be found. It is believed that the complex was never completed, possibly because the principal builder was taken south to construct Piquillacta, near Cuzco, with which it has many similarities. It is on a plain opposite Marca Huamachuco and has very good views of the latter. A crafts cooperative across from the Wiracochapampa school sells woven goods made on back-strap looms.

Also worth seeing is **Laguna Sausacocha** (3150 m), a beautiful spot surrounded by low hills, along the road to Cajabamba. Here are several simple *comedores* (try *ceviche de trucha*). It is possible to go rowing on the lake.

The **Yanasara thermal baths** are a 30-minute walk from the village of El Pallar set in a beautiful valley at 2300 m. The hot, clean baths consist of a pool and four individual baths, all US$0.30 per person. Thermal baths can also be found at **El Edén** ① *free, 1½ hrs south of Huamachuco, take a combi for Sarin, US$1.50*. An open-air complex of four pools, you can sit beneath a mini-waterfall in one of them, and a warm river set among rock cliffs. Take food and drink.

Cushuro (4000 m), 10 km south of Huamachuco, is a vicuña breeding centre with a good stretch of the Royal Inca highway passing nearby.

A pleasant two-hour walk can be made up the Río Grande Valley to the hacienda of **Cochabamba**, once the Andean retreat of the owners of the Laredo sugar plantation.

South from Huamachuco → *Colour map 3, A2.*

It is now possible to travel, via Retamas and Tayabamba (see below), to Sihuas and the Cordillera Blanca along a road that's very poor in places and involves crossing the Río Marañón twice. The building of a new bridge over the river means that it is feasible to go from Cuzco to Quito entirely by public transport without going down to the Pacific coast, though few travellers have made this journey. The route from Cajamarca to Huaraz via Huamachuco and the upper Marañón Valley is considerably longer, more difficult and more expensive than going via Trujillo and Chimbote on the coast. The rewards, however, are incomparable views and a glimpse of everyday life in some of the country's most tranquil highland villages as well as its grimiest mining camps. For those with plenty of time, the route provides access to the wilds of Río Abiseo National Park. Along the way, vertiginous roads repeatedly traverse altitudes ranging from 4200 m to 1450 m, with vast changes in temperatures between the *puna* and Marañón Valley, and vertical drops of 1000 m from hairpin bends. The road may be impassable in the wet season.

From Huamachuco, follow the main road to Cajabamba as far as Sausacocha, where a turn-off goes down to Yanasara (see above). The Río Grande is then crossed before climbing to Chugay (3400 m, **Hospedaje Pérez** and basic *comedores*) and on to a pass at

3900 m. At Molino Viejo, three hours from Yanasara, where a side road forks to Sartimbamba, a small patch of woodland is home to the Purple-backed sunbeam, otherwise known as Alice's, hummingbird (*Aglaeactis aliciae*). It's one of the largest and rarest species of Andean hummingbird. From the pass just mentioned the road plummets 2450 m to **Chahual** (1450 m), a small hot settlement where a bridge spans the Río Marañón. The hillsides are covered in cactuses, mango and avocado trees.

At Chahual, right after the bridge, the road forks: left to Pataz, and right to climb 1000 m to the **Balcón del Diablo**, overlooking **Laguna Pías**. The town of Pías, down by the lake and reached via a turn-off from the main road, has an office for **Parque Nacional Río Abiseo** and a landing strip (for charter flights to Lima for mining companies; spare seats may be available). **Pataz** is a small gold-mining town, about 100 km from Huamachuco. From here you can reach the World Heritage site of **Pajatén**, with its circular pre-Inca ruins (it requires a 10-day trip with mules from Los Alisos, near Pataz). The ruins lie within the Río Abiseo National Park, and both Sernamp and INC permits are needed to visit. These are issued to archaeologists, researchers and 'adventure' tourists, though day passes to enter the park can also be obtained (check with both institutes). Pataz is one hour by road from Chahual. Your best chance of finding a *camioneta* going up is early in the morning.

The road continues to **Retamas** (2700 m), a rough-and-tumble mining town. To avoid sleeping in Retamas, take a shared taxi to **Llacuabamba** (15 minutes, US$0.75), which is more tranquil. You must return to Retamas for onward transport. Near Retamas is **Parcoy**, the original settlement in the area with a colonial church. After Retamas are more hectic and scarred mining communities, Marsa and Buldibuyo, bordering the Río Abiseo National Park. The road then drops down to **Tayabamba** (3300 m). This small, chilly Andean town is surrounded by scenic countryside. It has a large church and a rotating bronze angel in the neat plaza. The interesting annual fiesta is held in honour of **Santo Toribio**, 24-31 April.

North from Huamachuco

From Huamachuco the gravel road runs on 55 km past Laguna Sausacocha through some small highland villages, where roof tiles are baked in round ovens, to **Cajabamba** (www.cajabamba.com), which sits on a balcony overlooking the sugar-producing Condebamba Valley. The climate is mild for its altitude because of influence from this large warm valley. Founded in 1572, this is an especially friendly town with an attractive Plaza de Armas. The annual festival is **Virgen del Rosario**, starting the first weekend of October and featuring the *Danza de los Diablos*. The surrounding countryside offers good walking amid lakes, waterfalls and Inca road remnants, well worth taking a few days to explore.

The road continues from Cajabamba, much of it newly asphalted, through **San Marcos** (2400 m) to Cajamarca. There is a short section of asphalt road to the south of San Marcos, which is important for its Sunday cattle market. Both it and Cajabamba are on the Inca road. From San Marcos to Cajamarca (124 km) the road is paved (three hours by bus, US$2.50).

The Coast to Cajamarca listings

For Sleeping and Eating price codes and other relevant information, see pages 38-44.

Sleeping

Chilete and Kuntur Wasi *p484*
F Hospedaje Caribe, Miraflores 241, Chilete, T076-554103.
F Hospedaje Miraflores, Miraflores 232, Chilete, T076-554228.

Trujillo to Huamachuco *p484*
All hotels are full in mid-Dec.
E Hostal Silita Star, in Cachicadan. Rustic, hot water, TV and restaurant. Recommended.
E Los Portales, Santa Rosa 680, Otusco. Hot water, with bath, TV, clean, good value.
F Hospedaje San José, Tacna 672, Otusco, T044-323550. With hot water and TV.
F Hostal Coina, Av 28 de Julio s/n, Coina. Basic but clean and friendly.
G pp Hostería El Sol, 500 m above the town (before you enter arriving from Otusco), Coina, T044-231933 (see *hostería* of same name in Trujillo). Meals are prepared in the adjoining hospital canteen. Bungalows set among pines and palms, pool. Camping possible. The original owner – Dr Kaufmann – also founded the hospital.

Huamachuco *p485*
C Real, Bolívar 250, T044-441402, www.hotelrealhuamachuco.com. Clean, with bath, TV, sauna, internet, many of the fittings are of wood. Recommended.
D Hostal Santa Fe, San Martín 297, T044-441019, www.actiweb.es/luisnv83. Clean, TV, hot water, Wi-Fi. Recommended.
E Hostal Gran Colonial, Castilla 537, T044-441534, grancolonialhostal@hotmail.com. An attractive old colonial house, with bath, hot water, TV. Its restaurant is clean and good value. Recommended.
E Hostal Noche Buena, San Román 401 on the main plaza, T044-441435. Clean with hot showers, TV, laundry, overlooking the plaza.

E Huamachuco, Castilla 354, on the plaza, T044-441525. Clean, with hot showers, friendly, good value, has parking.

Around Huamachuco *p486*
D-E Hotel Yanasara, Yanasara, T044-441245. A large hotel owned by priests set among meadows and a 5-min walk from the thermal baths, with restaurant and a pool, booking may be required in peak periods. Camping is also permitted within the grounds.

South from Huamachuco *p486*
E Hostal Gemiles, Bolognesi 656, Tayabamba. Clean, with private bath, hot water all day. Recommended.
F Hostal Caballero, Bolognesi 649, Tayabamba, T044-330024. With private bath, hot water, basic but OK, water shortages.
F Hostal El Triunfo, Salaverry 227, Tayabamba. Near bus agencies. With private bath and electric shower, cheaper without, small rooms, basic and friendly, suffers from water shortages.
F Hostal Morillo, Llacuabamba. With private bath, hot water, parking, some short-stay couples, basic, OK for where it is.
F Hostal Oasis, Chahual. Clean and friendly and has a restaurant. There are a couple of simple *comedores* by the bridge.
F Hostal Paraíso, Huancaspata. Possibly best in town, but rustic, rooms around a courtyard, shared bath, hot water.
G Hostal Imperial Class, Retamas. Shared bath, basic, caters to short-stay couples.
G Hostal Roldán, Huancaspata. Also rustic with rooms around a courtyard, cold water and shared bath.

North from Huamachuco *p487*
D Sol Naciente, Jr Inclán 485, 1 block from Plaza de Armas, San Marcos, T076-558191. Rooms with bath and hot water; it's cheaper without.
E Hostal Flores, Leoncio Prado 137, on the Plaza de Armas, Cajabamba, T076-551086.

With electric shower, cheaper without bath, friendly and clean but rooms are gloomy, nice patio; no breakfast.

🍴 Eating

Trujillo to Huamachuco *p484*
🍴 **Milagros**, Tacna 790, Otusco. Good for *cuy*.
🍴 **Sagitario**, Tacna 769, Otusco. The best place in town for the delicious local speciality of *jamón con yuca*.

Huamachuco *p485*
🍴 **Café Somos**, R Castilla 670. Good coffee, large turkey/ham sandwiches and excellent cakes.
🍴 **La Casona**, Sánchez Carrión 294. Daily 0700-0900, 1200-1430, 1900-2030. Serves good-value and quality set meals and local dishes, popular.

South from Huamachuco *p486*
🍴 **Cosas Dulces**, next to church on the Plaza de Armas, Tayabamba. For sweets and hot drinks.
🍴 **Juan Baptista**, Bolognesi 461, Tayabamba. The only proper restaurant in town but has a limited menu. Closes at 2100, like most places in town. There's also an unnamed *comedor* at Bolognesi y Sucre. Good home cooking.
🍴 **La Huanuqueña**, Llacuabamba. Serves an adequate *menú*.
🍴 **Restaurant Kananga**, in Huancaspata. Apparently named after a Japanese cartoon character, this is the best place to eat and it serves an excellent *caldo*.

North from Huamachuco *p487*
🍴 **Cafetería La Otuscana**, Grau 929, Cajabamba. Daily 0730-2200. Good bakery, sweets and sandwiches.
🍴 **Don Lucho**, Jr Leoncio Prado 227, Cajabamba. Good local trout and other à la carte dishes.

🍴 **Fuente de soda Grau**, Grau 832, Cajabamba. Serving big fresh fruit salads and cakes.
🍴 **Quengococha**, Bolognesi 790, Cajabamba. Tasty local dishes served in earthenware pots.

✪ Festivals and events

Huamachuco *p485*
2nd Sun in Aug Waman Raymi, a major festival held in the ruins of Wiracochapampa (see page 486), a northern version of Inti Raymi in Cuzco.
10 Aug Los Wamachucos, another colourful festival, is held in the neighbourhood above the centre.
15 Aug Beginning of a week of festivities to mark the founding of Huamachuco which features spectacular fireworks and the remarkable Turcos – aggressive male dancers from a nearby village who wear at least 10 layered skirts when dancing. Huamachuco (founded in 1553) has made an effort to rescue its pre-Hispanic and pre-Inca traditions. Celebrations include many native themes and dances.

⊖ Transport

Trujillo to Huamachuco *p484*
Bus
To **Otusco** from Trujillo, **Emp Pacífico**, Prolongación Unión 1888, buses leave when full, 2 hrs, US$2.50. Car combis leave from opposite the **Pacífico** terminal when full, 1½ hrs, US$4. From Otusco to **Trujillo**, colectivos leave when full from the south side of town. To **Coina** from Trujillo with **Turismo Express**, Unión 1888, or **Coina Express**, Unión 1557, 6 hrs, US$7. Buses to **Santiago de Chuco** from Trujillo, **Horna**, N de Piérola 1279, T044-294880, 2100, 6 hrs, US$7, only at night; they continue to **Cachicadan**. Combis depart frequently, when full, from Santiago de Chuco to Cachicadan, US$2, 1½ hrs.

Huamachuco *p485*
Bus

To **Trujillo**, 170 km, improved road, US$7-8.50, 6 hrs: **Tunesa (Turismo Negreiros)**; Balta y Juárez, T044-441157, 0900 and 1300. Recommended. **Trans Horna**, San Martín 875, T044-440114, transporteshorna@yahoo.es, 4 a day including bus *cama* service. Recommended. (Also has 3 a day to **Lima**, US$18-23.) **Fuentes**, José Balta 1088, T044-440111, bus *cama* service. To **Cajabamba**, **Trans Los Andes**, Pasaje Hospital 109, has 3 combis a day, 3 hrs, US$4. Horna also has daily departures at 1600 and 2000, 3 hrs. To **Retamas**, **Trans Garrincha**, Garcilazo de la Vega s/n esq Román, T044-441594, Sun, Wed, Fri at 0600, 12 hrs, US$11. The bus passes through from Trujillo but seats may sometimes be booked in Huamachuco. Enquire in advance. Combis leave from near the hospital daily 0200-0600, depending on demand, 10 hrs, US$14. They are less comfortable than the bus but faster, and have an easier time negotiating the narrow winding road.

Around Huamachuco *p486*
To **Laguna Sausacocha**, combis take 30 mins, US$0.75. Combis and shared taxis go directly from Huamachuco to **Yanasara** (1½ hrs, US$2), from which the baths are a 15-min walk.

South from Huamachuco *p486*
Air
For **Chahual**, there is a small airport 5 km down the valley.

Bus
Buses arrive in **Chahual** after 8 hrs from Huamachuco, US$10.

From **Retamas**, Garrincha travel to **Huamachuco**, Mon 0800, Thu 2000, Sat 0400, 12 hrs, US$11, continuing to **Trujillo**, 19 hrs, US$20. To Retamas from **Trujillo**, Garrincha (Prolongación Vallejo 1250, T044-441594), Tue and Sat 2100, 22 hrs, US$25. You can also take combis to **Huamachuco** starting 1800 daily, 10 hrs, US$14. Combis and shared taxis to **Tayabamba**, 6 a day 0500-1700, 3 hrs, US$6; Tayabamba–Retamas 6 a day 0700-1630.

Most transport in **Tayabamba** leaves from Salaverry y Cahuide (behind the church), where their agencies are located, except as noted. To **Sihuas** for the Cordillera Blanca: **La Perla de Alto Mayo**, Grau y Sucre, Mon, Wed, Sat at 1930; **Andía**, Mon, Wed, Sat at 1900; **Garrincha**, Mon and Thu at 0800; **San Antonio de Padua**, Fri at 1900; all 7-8 hrs, US$9. Most buses continue to **Chimbote** (17 hrs, US$20) and some to **Trujillo** (20 hrs, US$17.50) or **Lima** (24 hrs, US$25).

North from Huamachuco *p487*
From **Cajabamba** to **Huamachuco**: Trans Los Andes, Grau 1170, buses leave from police station below the market, 3 hrs, US$4; **Horna**, Av L Martínez 405, at 0430 and 0900, 3 hrs. From **Cajabamba** to **Cajamarca**, combis 3 hrs, US$5. Companies include Rojas and Perú Bus, several daily, 4 hrs, US$4. Some continue to **Trujillo**, 10 hrs, US$12, and **Lima**, 18 hrs, US$20-25 (**Horna**).

❶ Directory

Huamachuco *p485*
Banks Caja Norperuano, Sánchez Carrión on Plaza de Armas, has good rates; cash only. Obtain soles elsewhere if relying on ATMs or TCs. *Casas de cambio* on Sánchez Carrión, block 7, offer poor rates. **Internet** All over town. Best places are in Castilla, block 3, in the plaza. **Post** Grau 454, Mon-Fri 0830-1230, 1400-1700.

Cajamarca and around

Cajamarca is a beautiful colonial town and the most important in the northern highlands. It sits at the edge of a green valley that is ideal for dairy farming. Around the Plaza de Armas are many fine old houses, which are being converted into tasteful hotels, restaurants and galleries to cater for engineers and incomers from the adjacent Yanacocha mining project. The airport has been expanded to cater for the mining personnel, but tourism has yet to catch on to this facility. The mine, now that it is fully operational and looking to expand, has provoked opposition from farmers and created worries over pollution, intruding on the provincial calm of a city once closely tied to its pastoral surroundings. It remains, though, a great place to buy handicrafts, but lest you forget where the money now lies, you can find soapstone carvings of miners with power drills alongside more traditional figures. Outside town are several good haciendas offering bed, board and rural pursuits, while at the Baños del Inca, just up the road, you can unwind as the steam from the thermal waters meets the cool mountain air. ▶▶ *For listings, see pages 496-502.*

Ins and outs

Getting there The **airport** ⓘ *5 km northeast of town, T076-342689*, is smart, with café, dairy shop, bookshop, good toilets; taxi US$4.20. To get there go down Calle 2 de Mayo (traffic goes downhill on this street, but uphill on Calle Del Batán) and follow the Avenida Hoyos Rubio, the highway to Otuzco, passing **El Quinde** shopping mall.

Bus ticket offices and terminals are on Avenida Atahualpa from block two to block six, a 20-minute walk from the Plaza de Armas; some are Avenida Independencia, blocks two and three.

Getting around All the main sights are clustered around the Plaza de Armas. With its many old colonial buildings it is an interesting town to wander around, although the climb up Santa Apolonia hill is quite demanding. The district around Plaza Francia (Amazonas y José Gálvez), the market area and east of Amazonas are not safe at night (prostitution and drugs). Buses in town charge US$0.25. Taxis US$1 within city limits. Mototaxis US$0.50. Combis run to the main places outside town, like Baños del Inca. Others, like Cumbemayo, are best reached on a tour, and some make good day walks.

Best time to visit Cajamarca has a pleasant climate year round, with warm days and chilly nights. The wettest months are December to March. Depending on your point of view, Carnival (February or March) is the time to be there, or the time to avoid – it is a riotous, messy affair. Hotels are also booked up at this time. More sedate festivals are Holy Week, especially Palm Sunday at nearby Porcón, and Corpus Christi in May. During October and November there are numerous school trips to this area, so most of the budget hotels are full at this time.

Tourist information Dirección Regional de Turismo and Instituto Nacional de Cultura ⓘ *in the Conjunto Monumental de Belén, Belén 631, T076-362601, www.regioncajamarca. gob.pe, www.inccajamarca.org, Mon-Fri 0900-1300, 1500-1730*. **Sub-Gerencia de Turismo of the Cajamarca Municipality** ⓘ *Cruz de la Piedra 635, T076-602233 ext 253, www.municajamarca.gob.pe*, will move in late 2010 to the new municipal Capac Ñan building, opposite UNC university on the road to Baños del Inca. The **University tourist school** ⓘ *Del Batán 289, T076-361546, Mon-Fri 0830-1300, 1500-2200*, offering free advice and leaflets. Another option for information is **Centro de Informacion y Cultura (CIC)** ① *Del Comercio 251, T076-340209, cic@yanacocha.com.pe, Mon-Fri 0800-1300, 1400-1800*, which is involved in many social and cultural affairs in Cajamarca province. See also http://cajamarcainfo.com. There is an **Indecopi office** ① *Apurímac 601, T076-363315, mcastillo@indecopi.gob.pe.*

Background

Before Cajamarca became an Inca religious centre and favoured haunt of the nobility in 1456, it had been at the heart of a culture known as Caxamarca, which flourished from AD 500 to 1000. The violent events of 1532-1533 are today belied by the city's provincial calm. It was named provincial capital in 1855 and Patrimonio Histórico y Cultural de las Américas by the Organization of American States in 1986. It is now seeking UNESCO World Heritage status. In addition to its historical associations, Cajamarca is best known for its dairy industry, textiles and intricately worked mirrors (see Shopping, page 500). Change is coming, though, in the form of the Circuito Turístico Nororiental, which is opening up the Chiclayo–Cajamarca–Chachapoyas tourist route, and in the effect on the town from the Yanacocha gold mine. This has brought many foreign mining engineers and economic benefits, but also serious debates and protests over ecological impact, compensation to *campesinos* and threats to the city's drinking water supply. Only groups are allowed to visit the mine, which has a **public relations office** ① *Av Evitamiento Norte 16719, in front of Hotel El Ingenio, T076-584000 ext 23759, www.yanacocha.com.pe.* A new mine at Michiquillay will inevitably bring a further influx of workers.

Cajamarca → *For listings, see pages 496-502. Colour map 1, C3. Phone code: 076. Population: 201,000. Altitude: 2750 m.*

Plaza de Armas

The main Plaza de Armas, where Atahualpa was executed, has a 350-year-old fountain, topiary and gardens. It was remodelled in 2006. The impressive **cathedral** ① *0800-1000, 1600-1800*, opened in 1776, is still missing its belfry, but the façade has beautiful baroque carving in stone. The altar is covered in original gold leaf.

On the opposite side of the plaza is the 17th-century **San Francisco Church** ① *Mon-Fri 0900-1200, 1600-1800*, older than the cathedral and with more interior stone carving and elaborate altars. A side chapel has an ornate ceiling. **Museo de Arte Colonial** ① *Mon-Sat 1430-1800, US$1, entrance is behind the church on Amalia Puga y Belén.* Tickets are sold from an unmarked office on the right of courtyard as you walk towards the church. Attached to San Francisco, the museum is filled with colonial paintings and icons. The guided tour of the museum includes entry to the church's spooky catacombs.

Complejo Belén

① *Tue-Sat 0900-1300, 1500-1800, Sun 0900-1300, US$1.55; tickets are valid for 2 days and include entry to the Cuarto de Rescate. A guide in Spanish for all the sites costs US$2.85 (US$5.75-8.50 for guides in other languages).*

This group of buildings comprises the **tourist office** and **Institute of Culture**, a beautifully ornate church, considered the city's finest, and two museums. The arches, pillars and walls of the nave of Belén church are covered in lozenges (*rombos*), a design picked out in the gold tracery of the altar. See the inside of the dome, where eight giant cherubs support an intricate flowering centrepiece. The carved pulpit has a spiral staircase and the doors are intricately worked in wood. In the same courtyard is the **Museo Médico Belén**, which has a collection of medical instruments. Across the street is a maternity hospital from the colonial era, now the **Archaeological and Ethnological Museum** ⓘ *Junín y Belén*. It has a wide range of ceramics from all regions and civilizations of Peru.

Cuarto de Rescate

ⓘ *Entrance is at Amalia Puga 750, Tue-Sat 0900-1300, 1500-1800, Sun 0900-1300.*

The Cuarto de Rescate shown to tourists is not the actual ransom chamber but in fact the room where Atahualpa was held prisoner. A red line on the wall is said to indicate where Atahualpa reached up and drew a mark, agreeing to have his subjects fill the room to the line with gold treasures. The chamber is roped off and can only be viewed from the outside. Pollution and weather have had a detrimental effect on the stone.

Other sights

Also worth seeing are **La Recoleta Church** ⓘ *Maestro y Av Los Héroes*, and **San Pedro** ⓘ *Gálvez y Junín*. The city has many old colonial houses with garden patios, and 104 elaborately carved doorways: see the **Bishop's Palace** across the street from the

Cajamarca

Sleeping	
1 Cajamarca	
2 Casa Blanca &	
La Casona del Inca	
3 Clarín	
4 Continental	
5 Costa del Sol	
6 El Cabildo	

7 El Cumbe Inn
8 El Ingenio
9 El Portal del Marqués
10 Gran Hotel Continental
11 Hosp Los Jazmines
12 Hostal Becerra
13 Hostal Los Pinos
14 Hostal Olympo
15 Hostal Pepe
16 Hostal Perú &
  Hostal Santa Apolonia

17 Los Balcones de
  La Recoleta
18 Posada Belén

Eating
1 Bella's Café Lounge
2 Casa Club
3 Cascanuez
4 De Buena Laya
5 Don Paco
6 El Pez Loco

7 El Zarco
8 Heladería Holanda
9 Las Tullpas
10 Natur Center
11 Om-Gri
12 Pascana
13 Pizzería El Marengo
14 Pizzería Vaca Loca
15 Querubino
16 Salas
17 Sanguchón.com

cathedral; the **Palace of the Condes de Uceda** ① *Jr Apurímac 719*, now occupied by BCP bank; and the **Casa Silva Santiesteban** ① *Junín y 2 de Mayo*.

Museo Arqueológico Horacio H Urteaga ① *Del Batán 289, Mon-Fri 0745-1445, free, donations accepted (under threat of closure)*, of the Universidad Nacional de Cajamarca, has objects of the pre-Inca Cajamarca and other cultures. The university maintains an experimental arboretum and agricultural station, the **Museo Silvo-agropecuario** ① *Km 2.5 on the road to Baños del Inca*, with a lovely mural at the entrance.

You can also visit the plaza where Atahualpa was ambushed and the stone altar set high on **Santa Apolonia hill** ① *US$0.60*. To get there, take bus marked 'Santa Apolonia/Fonavi', or micro 'A' or combis on Sabogal or Tarapacá. Here the Inca is said to have reviewed his subjects. There is a road to the top or, if you are fit, you can walk up from Calle 2 de Mayo, using the stairway. The view from the top, over red-tiled roofs and green fields, is worth the effort, especially very early in the morning for the beautiful sunrises. However, it's best not to go alone at this time of day.

Around Cajamarca → *For listings, see pages 496-502. Colour map 1, C3.*

Los Baños del Inca

① *0500-2000, entry US$0.70, T076-348385, www.ctbinca.com.pe. Take a towel; soaps are sold outside. Only spend 20 mins maximum in the water; obey instructions; many of the facilities allow bathers in shifts, divided by time and/or gender. Massage US$7; hydromassage US$8.75; sauna, 2 hrs, US$3.50; thermal tubs, 20-min bathing time, US$1.75-2.10; outdoor thermal swimming pool, shifts of 2 hrs, US$1.40; thermal showers, US$0.70. El Remanso recreational centre with playground, US$0.70, showers also US$0.70, open 0500-1900, at weekends entry limited to 1¾ hrs. Combis marked Baños del Inca and buses cost US$0.20, 15 mins, ask driver where to get off. The bus stop is just after crossing the Río Chonta on the right of bridge. Taxi from Cajamarca minimum US$2.30.*

Six kilometres southeast are the sulphurous thermal springs known as Los Baños del Inca, where there are baths of at least 72°C. It is a large municipal complex with lots of facilities and services, although you can still see the natural springs, bubbling rusty pools with sulphurous fumes, among the buildings of the complex. The baths have several medicinal benefits, including dermatological, gastric and anti-stress. Atahualpa tried the effect of these waters on a festering war wound and his bath is still there. The least crowded time to bathe is first thing in the morning. On the first shift the water is 100% thermal-medicinal, whereas later on it becomes diluted. The complex is regularly renewed, with gardens, recreational centres and two types of accommodation, a lodge and bungalows with private pools that are detailed in Sleeping below. There is also a unit for the elderly and the disabled. On the site are archaeological remains, a museum and a café.

The construction of luxury homes for upper echelon mining personnel has given Baños del Inca an increasingly suburban feel, complete with commuter traffic. There are two tourist offices, **Oficina de Turismo de Baños del Inca** at El Remanso open-air swimming pools and a **Dirección Regional de Turismo** booth next to the **Banco de la Nación** agency. There is also an ATM (Scotiabank) at **Hostal José Gálvez**.

Cumbe Mayo

① *Guided tour US$7.55 per person from 0930-1430, taxi US$15 (no buses). It may be possible to go with the milk truck leaving at 0400 from C Revilla 170; ask Sr Segundo Malca, Jr Pisagua 482.*

There's a small charge, dress warmly. To walk up takes 3-4 hrs (take a guide or tour, best time May-Sep).

Cumbe Mayo (3600 m), a *pampa* on a mountain range, is 20 km southwest of Cajamarca. It is famous for its extraordinary, well-engineered pre-Inca channels, running for 9 km across the mountain tops. It is said to be the oldest man-made construction in South America. The sheer scale of the scene is impressive and the huge rock formations of **Los Frailones** ('big monks') and others with fanciful names are strange indeed. It is worth taking a guided tour since the area has a lot of petroglyphs, altars and sacrificial stones from pre-Inca cultures. On the way to Cumbe Mayo is the **Layzón ceremonial centre** from 500-200 BC (7 km).

The trail to the site starts from the hill of Santa Apolonia (Silla del Inca), and goes to Cumbe Mayo, straight through the village and up the hill. At the top of the mountain, leave the trail and take the road to the right to the canal. The walk is not difficult and you do not need hiking boots. Take a good torch/flashlight. The locals use the trail to bring their goods to market.

Other sights near Cajamarca

Llacanora is a typical Andean village in beautiful scenery (13 km southeast). Nearby is **La Collpa**, a hacienda that is now a cooperative farm of the Ministry of Agriculture. It breeds bulls and has a lake and gardens. The cows are handmilked at 1400, not a particularly inspiring spectacle in itself, but the difference here is that the cows are called by name and respond accordingly.

Ventanillas de Otusco ① *0800-1800, US$1*, part of an old pre-Inca cemetery, has a gallery of secondary burial niches. A one-day round trip can be made: take a bus from Del Batán to Ventanillas de Otusco (30 minutes) or a colectivo leaving hourly from Revilla 170, US$0.15, then walk to Baños del Inca (1½ hours, 6 km). You can either follow the east shore of the Río Chonta, or take a higher route with better views through the village of

Around Cajamarca

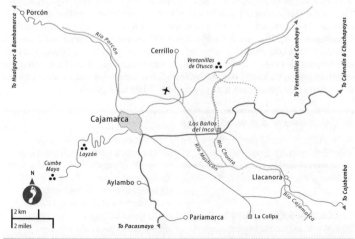

Puylucana. Ask for directions often and take a stick to fend off dogs. From Baños del Inca walk to Llacanora (one hour, 7 km), passing the caves and rock art at Callacpuma, and then a further hour to La Collpa.

Some 6 km upstream from Otusco village, in Luichupucro Bajo, is a project aimed at preparing inhabitants for sustainable tourism (*Proyecto turismo sostenible en la modalidad de turismo vivencial y aviturismo*), including workshops, reforestation, sponsored by Aprec (see page 501).

Another typical Andean village from which you can walk to Baños del Inca is **Pariamarca**. Take a micro from Ovalo Bolognesi heading towards the coast. Ask to be let out at the turn-off to Pariamarca and walk from there.

A road goes to **Ventanillas de Combayo**, some 20 km past the burial niches of Otusco. These are more numerous and more spectacular, being located in a rather isolated, mountainous area, and are distributed over the face of a steep 200-m-high hillside. There are occasional combis on weekdays, but more transport to the site on Sunday when a market is held nearby, one hour. Road conditions are to be improved, which will give greater access to this site. There are many other archaeological and rural tourism sites in the area which await development (enquire at the Baños del Inca tourist office).

Porcón, at 3400 m, a rural cooperative with its evangelical faith expressed on billboards, is a popular excursion, 30 km northwest of Cajamarca. It is tightly organized and has a bakery, cheese- and yoghurt-making facilities, and a zoo with many of the region's wild animals, including vicuñas. Its carpentry uses wood from extensive pine plantations. A good guide helps to explain everything and it may be possible to participate in many of these activities. Horse riding, fishing and hiking may also be available. If not taking a tour, contact **Cooperativa Agraria Atahualpa-Jerusalén** ① *Chanchamayo 1355, Fonavi 1, T/F076-825631*.

Parque Nacional de Cutervo was the first to be created in Peru in 1961. Despite its small size of only 8214 ha, divided into northern and southern sections, this fascinating area of cloudforest protects a wide variety of rare or endemic plants and animals in the Cordillera de los Tarros, including the mountain tapir, the spectacled bear and the Andean cock of the rock. The area is particularly well known for its caves that harbour colonies of rare oil birds (*Steatornis caripensis*). These large birds with a wingspan of nearly 1 m, use their screeching calls as a form of echo location to guide them through the pitch darkness. The caves also support a rare species of fish, the 'Bagre de las Cavernas' (*Astroblepus rosei*). The park is remote, about 260 km north of Cajamarca on twisting mountain roads. Combis leave Cajamarca for **Cutervo** (see Transport, page 502), and from here it's possible to reach the village of San Andrés de Cutervo. Check at the local police station regarding park entry regulations. From San Andrés it is about one hour's hike to the oil bird's (*guácharos*) cave. It may be possible to hire local guides.

◉ Cajamarca and around listings

For Sleeping and Eating price codes and other relevant information, see pages 38-44.

● Sleeping

Cajamarca *p492, map p493*
L-AL Costa del Sol, Cruz de la Piedra 707,
T076-344040, www.costadelsolperu.com.

Prominent location on the Plaza de Armas, part of a Peruvian chain, the place to see and be seen. Priced includes buffet breakfast from 0500; internet access, Wi-Fi available, ATM, luggage store, travel agency, casino, parking, airport transfer, welcome drink, restaurant and bars, pool and spa. The new cafetería on the 2nd floor has a panoramic view.

AL-A Posada del Puruay, 5 km north of city, T076-367928, www.posadapuruay.com.pe. 17th-century hacienda that's been converted into a 'hotel museum' with all rooms appointed to a high standard and containing beautiful pieces of colonial furniture. Good food and activities, including horse riding, are offered. All rooms en suite. Recommended.

A Continental, Jr Amazonas 760, T076-363063, hotelcontinental@terra.com.pe. Price includes breakfast. Very clean, hot water, modern, good restaurant (popular for set-menu lunch for US$3.75, specializes in *cuy frito*). The hotel caters more for the tourist market than its **Gran** partner at Jr Amazonas 781, T076-341030.

B Clarín, Amazonas 1025, T076-341275, hotel_clarin@hotmail.com. A modern, business-oriented hotel with pleasant decoration, rooms with bath, good beds, laptop connection, car park, restaurant (lunch *menú* US$2.50, *panadería* next door.

B El Ingenio, Av Vía de Evitamiento 1611-1709, T076-368733, www.elingenio.com. 1½ blocks from El Quinde shopping mall. With bathroom, solar-powered hot water, spacious, relaxed, internet in rooms, helpful, good restaurant, bar, parking. Highly recommended.

B El Portal del Marqués, Del Comercio 644, T/F076-368464, www.portaldelmarques.com. Price includes breakfast. Located in an attractive converted colonial house, all rooms carpeted, en suite, with TV, internet connection, laundry, safe, parking. A luxury matrimonial suite with jacuzzi is available (**A**) for those in need of pampering! Recommended. Leased restaurant **El Mesón del Marqués** also has a good lunchtime *menú*, 1200-1500.

B Hostal Los Pinos, Jr La Mar 521, T076-365992, www.lospinosinn.com. Includes breakfast, other meals on request. In a lovely colonial house (Patrimonio Nacional) with a new extension, all decorated in an extravagant style, comfortable, also has 2 apartments (**A**) on top floor with kitchen and fireplace.

B-C Casa Blanca, 2 de Mayo 446, Plaza de Armas, T/F076-362141. Price includes breakfast. Clean, safe, nice old building with garden, good view of the plaza. Also has café for breakfast.

C Cajamarca, 2 de Mayo 311, T076-362532, hotelcajamarca@gmail.com. 3-star hotel in beautiful colonial mansion, sizeable rooms, hot water, food excellent in *Los Faroles* restaurant, free calls to USA, Wi-Fi, TV, safe in room, luggage store, airport transfer, tours. Recommended.

C El Cabildo, Junín 1062, T/F076-827025, cabildoh@latinmail.com. Includes breakfast. In a historic monument with patio and modern fountain, full of character, elegant, local decorations, comfortable, breakfast served but no bar or restaurant, popular with European groups, friendly and helpful, internet and Wi-Fi. Recommended.

C El Cumbe Inn, Pasaje Atahualpa 345, T076-826858, www.elcumbeinn.com. Includes breakfast. A variety of comfortable rooms, with bath, hot water, cable TV, internet and Wi-Fi, personal service, 2 patios, small gym, well kept, will arrange taxis and tours, restaurant, evening meals on request, super friendly and helpful. Frequently recommended.

C Hostal Santa Apolonia, Amalia Puga 649, T076-367207, hostalsantapolonia@ hotmail.com. Reliable commercial hotel on the plaza, TV, Wi-Fi, safe, laundry, hot water, frigobar.

C La Casona del Inca, 2 de Mayo 458-460, Plaza de Armas, T076-367524, www.casona delincaperu.com. Upstairs in an old building, in traditional style, some rooms overlooking the plaza, some with interior windows, good beds, TV, Wi-Fi, breakfast in café on top floor, tours, luggage store, laundry.

C Los Balcones de la Recoleta, Amalia Puga 1050, T076-363302, hslosbalcones@ speedy.com.pe. A beautifully restored 19th-century house, with a pleasant courtyard full of flowers; some rooms with period furniture but all 12 are en suite with internet access, free Wi-Fi, breakfast extra, use of kitchen, helpful staff, some English spoken. Recommended.

C-D Posada Belén, del Comercio 1008, T076-340681, posadabelen@hotmail.com. Just off Plaza de Armas, hot water, TV, Wi-Fi, popular, laundry.

D Hospedaje Los Jazmines, Amazonas 775, T076-361812, hospedajelosjazmines@ yahoo.com. In a converted colonial house with courtyard, 14 snug, rustic rooms with bath, cheaper without. Restaurant, *menú* for US$2.85. All funds go to disabled children, some staff are disabled, guests can visit the project's school and help. Recommended.

D Hostal Becerra, Del Batán 195, T076-367867. With bath, hot water and TV, modern, pleasant, no breakfast, clean and friendly, they'll let you leave your luggage until late buses depart.

D Hostal Perú, Amalia Puga 605, on Plaza, T076-365568, hostal_peru@elzarco.org. With bath, hot water, Wi-Fi, functional rooms in old building around central patio used by El Zarco restaurant, wooden floors, credit cards taken.

Near the bus offices

E Gran Spyzzo, 244 Av Atahualpa, T076-362076, near Flores, hot water, TV.

E Hostal Olympo (no name shown), Av Atahualpa 439, opposite Volvo, T076-324105. 12 rooms, TV, internet room.

E-F Hostal Pepe, Av Atahualpa 343, T076-361887. Private or shared bathroom, hot water, no breakfast, noisy from all-night traffic.

F Hosp María Auxiliadora, No 304 (inside Transportes Rojas), cheaper without hot water, basic.

F Hostal Samari, Av Luis Rebajo 305, in quiet area, almost opposite the Cruz del Sur/Cial bus terminals, reported safe and formal.

Around Cajamarca *p494, map p495*
L-AL Laguna Seca, Av Manco Cápac 1098, Los Baños del Inca, T076-584300, www.lagunaseca.com.pe. In pleasant surroundings with thermal streams (atmospheric misty mornings), private

hot thermal baths in rooms, swimming pool with thermal water, Peruvian/International-style restaurant, bar, health spa with a variety of treatments, horses for hire, has seen better days. Rates include airport transfers and breakfast. Offers 4 day/3 night packages for US$515 double.

B Hostal Fundo Campero San Antonio, 2 km off the Baños road (turn off at Km 5 from Cajamarca), T/F076-348237, jc_luna@ viabcp.com. An old hacienda, wonderfully restored, with open fireplaces and gardens, 15 mins' walk along the river to Baños del Inca. All rooms en suite. The price includes breakfast and a ride on the hotel's *caballos de paso*. Restaurant serves the hotel's own dairy produce, fruit and vegetables, catch your own trout for supper; try the *licor de sauco* (elderberry). Recommended.

B-D Los Baños del Inca, see page 494, T076-348385, www.ctbinca.com.pe. Various accommodation: bungalows for 2 to 4 with thermal water, TV, fridge; **Albergue Juvenil**, not IYFH, hostel rooms with bunk beds or double rooms, private bath, caters to groups, basic and overpriced. Camping possible. Restaurant offers full board for US$7.25.

There are a few more *hostales* and *hospedajes* in **Baños del Inca** but only Hostal José Gálvez, Manco Capac 552, T076-348396, is worth considering (others cater for mining company personnel, or hourly clients).

🍴 Eating

Cajamarca *p492, map p493*
♦♦♦ Pascana, Av Atahualpa 947. Well-known and recommended as the best in town, near the new Capac Ñan Municipality. See **Taberna del Diablo** disco, below.
♦♦♦ Querubino, Amalia Puga 589, T076-340900. Mediterranean-style decoration, a bit of everything on the menu, including pastas, daily specials, breakfasts, cocktails, coffees, expensive wines, otherwise reasonable, popular.
♦♦ Casa Club, Amalia Puga 458-A, T076-340198. Open 0800-2300. *Menú*, including

vegetarian, and extensive selection à la carte, family atmosphere, slow but attentive service.

Don Paco, Amalia Puga 390, T076-362655. Opposite San Francisco. Typical dishes, including Novo Andino and international food on extensive à la carte menu, good value *menú ejecutivo* for US$2.85, vegetarian options, tasty food, desserts. Open for breakfast. Has a wine list and plenty of 'sour' cocktails. Popular.

El Pez Loco, San Martín 333. Recommended for fish dishes.

Las Tullpas, 2 de Mayo 390. Open 0730-2300. Local and international dishes, à la carte and 3 choices of *menú ejecutivo*.

Om-Gri, San Martín 360, near the Plaza de Armas. Good Italian dishes, small, informal, French spoken, opens 1300 (1830 Sun).

Pizzería El Marengo, Junín 1201. Good pizzas and warm atmosphere, T076-368045 for delivery.

Salas, Amalia Puga 637, on the main plaza, T076-362867. A Cajamarca tradition, open 0700-2200. Fast service, excellent local food (try their *cuy frito*), best *tamales* in town.

De Buena Laya, 2 de Mayo 343. With a rustic interior, popular with *hostales*, offers Novo Cajamarquino cuisine. Menu at lunchtime costs US$3.50.

El Zarco, Jr Del Batán 170, T076-363421. Open Sun-Fri 0700-2300. Very popular, also has a short *chifa* menu, good vegetarian dishes, excellent fish, popular for breakfast.

Natur Center, Amalia Puga 409. Open Sun-Thu 0800-1445, 1700-2045, Fri 0800-1445. New vegetarian place with a good selection of dishes.

Pizzería Vaca Loca, San Martín 330. Popular, regarded as the best pizzas in town.

Cafés

Bella's Café Lounge, Junín 1184, T076-345794. For breakfasts, sandwiches, great desserts and coffee from Chanchamayo, Wi-Fi, a place to linger, check emails and relax, owner Raúl speaks English. Popular with visitors to the city.

Cascanuez, Amalia Puga 554. Great cakes, extensive menu including *humitas*, breakfasts, ice creams and coffees, highly regarded.

Heladería Holanda, Amalia Puga 657 on the Plaza de Armas, T076-340113. Dutch-owned, easily the best ice creams in Cajamarca, 50 flavours (but not all on at the same time), try *poro poro*, *lúcuma* or *sauco*, also serves coffee. Four branches, including at Baños del Inca. Ask if it is possible to visit their factory. They assist deaf people and single mothers.

Panadería Campos, Jr del Comercio 661. Good for local cookies, best *rosquitas* in town. Also sells postcards by well-known local photographer, Sr Campos.

Panadería La Ideal, Amalia Puga 307. Good for bread.

Sanguchón.com, Junín 1137. Best burgers in town, sandwiches, also popular bar.

There is a good *pasteleria* at Jr Amazonas 747 and at El Quinde Shopping mall. Closed Sun.

Around Cajamarca *p494, map p495*
There are many cheap rancho-type restaurants near the Albergue at Los Baños del Inca. There are also 14 registered restaurants, mostly on the main street, Manco Cápac, and others on the parallel Sinchi Roca. Many people, after a bathe, go to the *pastelería* (opposite **Heladería Holanda**) for a good selection of cakes at great prices. The **Cremería** on the Plaza de Armas, serves ice cream, sandwiches and hamburgers.

🍸 Bars and clubs

Cajamarca *p492, map p493*
El Brujo Bar, Apurímac 519, on 2nd floor above Lo'Alfredo Grill. Disco bar, *peña*, karaoke, open daily with live shows, popular with younger set.
Full Skee, Amazonas 709. Lounge bar, open daily at 1900.
Gruta Cien, Silva Santiesteban 100 next to the Santa Apolonia stairways on Junín. Bar with open fireplace, music.

Los Frailones, Av Perú 701, T076-344272. Thu-Sat from 2030. Waiters dressed as monks.

Mamut Disco Bar, on Vía de Evitamiento s/n (ask for directions). Well-known and visited by younger people.

McCuy, Amalia Puga 774, close to Cuarto del Rescate. Popular bar, part Peruvian, part Irish, live music at weekends, with big TV for sports events.

De La Selva y Su Encanto, Av Atahualpa, in the UNC university district. Open mainly at weekends for live music and dance shows.

Peña Usha Usha, Amalia Puga 320. Well-known venue for live *música criolla*.

Taberna del Diablo, Av Atahualpa 947, opposite UNC university on road to Baños del Inca (see **Pascana** restaurant, above). The best disco bar in the city.

⊛ Festivals and events

Cajamarca *p492, map p493*

Feb Cajamarca is known as the Carnival capital of Peru. **Carnival week**, with many processions and dances, is a messy, raucous affair – the level of water, motor oil and paint-throwing would put Laurel and Hardy to shame. This is not for the faint-hearted. You have been warned!

May/Jun Corpus Christi is a solemn religious affair.

24 Jun San Juan in Cajamarca, Chota, Llacanora, San Juan and Cutervo.

1st Sun in Oct Festival Folklórico.

2nd week Oct The city's 'Tourist Week'.

Around Cajamarca *p494, map p495*

22-20 Jul An agricultural fair, **Feria Fongal**, is held at Baños del Inca. It coincides with **Fiestas Patrias** and besides agricultural displays, has *artesanía* and *caballos de paso*.

7-8 Sep Fiesta de Huanchaco in Baños del Inca, a festival organized by the local campesinos.

Mar/Apr Domingo de Ramos (Palm Sun) processions in Porcón are worth seeing.

O Shopping

Cajamarca *p492, map p493*
Food and drink

The area is renowned for its dairy produce. Many shops sell cheese, butter, honey, etc. Look out for *queso ahumado* (smoked cheese), sold at shops on 2 de Mayo, block 5, and Amazonas, blocks 5-8. Eucalyptus honey is sold in the market on Amazonas, block 7, and is said to be a cure for rheumatism. Also look out for local jams, especially *mermelada de sauco* (elderberry) and *mermelada de aguaymanto* (Peruvian physalis). Elderberry liqueur is also sold.

El Porcón, Cooperative Atahualpa-Jerusalén, Chanchamayo 1355 (1 block from Vía Evitamiento, 'Fonavi' combis, No 19, and micros 'A' pass). It sells *queso suizo* although quality is said to vary.

El Tambo, 2 de Mayo 576 and Amazonas, block 5, branches of the local Chugur dairy. Peruvians prefer a *queso fresco* for cooking, ask for a *queso maduro* if you want something for a sandwich.

Huacariz dairy shop, Amazonas 771 and Silva Santesteben 866. 1 of the 2 dairies providing cheese to supermarkets around Peru; pricey.

La Collpa, see page 495, has a shop at Romero 124, sells cheese and butter. Try the *queso mantecoso*, which is full-cream cheese, or sweet *manjar blanco*.

Los Alpes, Junín 965. Formerly Swiss-run, much more expensive than other brands. Their dairy is included in local tours.

Handicrafts

Cajamarca is famous for its gilded mirrors. The frames are not carved but decorated with patterns transferred onto pieces of glass using the silkscreen process. This tradition lapsed during the post-colonial period and present production goes back less than 20 years.

Cajamarca is also an excellent place to buy cheap, good-quality handicrafts. Specialities include cotton and wool saddlebags (*alforjas*), found at the **San Antonio market**, at the north end of Jr Apurímac. Handwoven woollen items can be made to order. Other items include painted ceramic masks and soapstone figures (including miners with power drills). The market on **Amazonas** is good for *artesanía*. There are stalls near the Belén complex (Belén and/or 2 de Mayo) and along the steps up to Santa Apolonia hill. At Jr El Comercio 1045, next to the police office, is a **Feria Artesanal**, as well as **El Molino** at 2 de Mayo. All offer a good range of local crafts. **Textiles y Artesanías Paredes**, 2 de Mayo 264, up the steps. Has a different selection from what you find in the streets.

Supermarkets
El Quinde, Av Hoyos Rubio, blocks 6 and 7, Fonavi. Shopping centre on the road to airport, with well-stocked supermarket. Good, local cheese and dairy products but prices for many goods are higher than in Trujillo. For many people it is not just a shopping mall, but also a popular meeting place and playground for children. It has the only cinema in Cajamarca and has a great number of fast-food restaurants, etc.

▲ Activites and tours

Cajamarca *p492, map p493*
Many travel agencies on or near the Plaza de Armas offer trips to local sites and further afield, trekking on Inca and other trails, cycling, climbing, riding *caballos de paso* and handicraft tours. 2010 prices: **Cumbe Mayo**, US$6.50-8.50, 4-5 hrs at 0930. **Porcón**, US$6.50-8.50, 4-5 hrs at 0930. **Otusco**, US$4.50-7, 3-3½ hrs at 1530; also includes the suspension bridge on the **Río Chonta**, **Jardín de las Hortensias** (hydrangeas) and **Los Alpes** dairy. City tour, US$7, 3 hrs at 0930 or 1530. There are many full-day tours, eg to **Kuntur Wasi**, **Combayo** burial site, the villages of **Namora**, **Pariamarca** and others. There are also 2 day/3 night tours to **Kuélap** and **Cutervo** **National Park**.

Asociación Civil para el Rescate del Ecosistema de Cajamarca (**Aprec**), Av Manco Cápac 1098, Baños del Inca, T076-894600. The association, sponsored by Pro Aves Perú, Hotel Laguna Seca and Yanacocha mines, aims to "restore the ecological health" of the Cajamarca region and specifically to protect the grey-bellied comet, a hummingbird endemic to the Cajamarca Valley and close to extinction. 4 Inca trail loops have been made accessible to hikers, including 1, to Sangal, which passes the hummingbird's habitat. Its office at Laguna Seca hotel is not often open.
Atahualpa Inca Tours, La Mar 435, T076-367014. Conventional tours and trekking (in Hostal El Mirador).
Cumbemayo Tours, Amalia Puga 635 on the plaza, T076-362938, cumbemayotours@ usa.net. Guides in English and French, all the standard tours.
Mega Tours, Amalia Puga 691 on the plaza, T076-341876, www.megatours.org. Conventional tours, full day and further afield, ecotourism and adventures.
Saelma Tours, Junín 1100, T076-341305. Conventional, full days and strong emphasis on trekking.

◉ Transport

Cajamarca *p492, map p493*
Air
To/from **Lima** daily with LAN (Cruz de la Piedra 657), **LC Busre** (Comercio 1024, T076-361098), and **Star Perú** (Junín 1300, T076-367243, no flight Sun). One-way fare US$120-144; schedules change frequently, book in advance.

Bus
To **Lima**, 870 km, 12-14 hrs, *económico* US$18-22, to *cama* US$35-46, and Super VIP, US$79, including Civa, Horna, Línea and Cruz del Sur's luxury service, several buses daily. To **Trujillo**, 295 km, 7 hrs, US$7-29, regular buses daily 0900-2230 most continue to

Lima. To **Chiclayo**, 265 km, 6 hrs, US$6.25-15.50, several buses daily; you have to change buses to go on to Piura and Tumbes. To **Celendín**, 107 km, 3½ hrs, US$3.45, usually 2 a day with CABA, Royal Palace's and Rojas. Móvil has a service to **Chachapoyas**, 336 km, 11-12 hrs, US$18, via **Leymebamba**, US$12.50, 9-10 hrs. **Horna**, Rojas and others go to **Cajabamba**, 75 km, US$4, 4 hrs, several daily; also combis, 3 hrs. Buses also go to **Bambamarca** US$3.50, **Chota** (6 hrs, US$5.25) and **Cutervo**.

Bus companies Ticket offices and terminals are located principally between the Plazuela Bolognesi and the Ovalo de Evitamiento on Av Atahualpa, cuadra 3. Until a new unified bus terminal is built (no date has been set for this), finding the bus you want is a complicated business. CABA, Atahualpa 299, T076-366665 (Celendín); Civa, Ayacucho 753, T076-361460 (Lima); Cruz del Sur, Atahualpa 664, T076-361737 (Lima); El Cumbe, San Martín de Porras 160, T076-363068; Emtrafesa, Atahualpa 315, T076-369663 (to Trujillo); Horna, Atahualpa 313, T076-363218 (Lima, Trujillo, Cajabamba, Huamachuco); Línea, Atahualpa 318, T076-363956, www.transporteslinea.com (Lima, Trujillo, Chiclayo); Móvil, Atahualpa 405, T076-340873, www.moviltours.com.pe (Lima, Chachapoyas); Rojas, Atahualpa 309, T076-340548 (to Cajabamba, buses not coming from Lima; Celendín); Royal Palace's, Reina Forje 130, T076-343063 (Lima, Trujillo, Celendín), has a ticket office on Atahualpa, but terminal is next to Tepsa; Tepsa, Sucre 594 y Reina Forje, T076-363306 (Lima); Turismo Días, Av Evitamiento s/n, T076-344322 (to Lima, Chimbote, Trujillo, Chiclayo). Note Atahualpa, Atahualpa 299, T076-363060 (Celendín, Cajabamba and other local destinations), once the dominant company in Cajamarca, is in financial difficulties and its services are in decline (2010).

Taxi

Radio taxi: El Sol, T076-368897, 24 hrs. Taxi Super Seguro, T076-507090, used by some mining companies. In ordinary taxis, ask for the price before boarding.

Directory

Cajamarca p492, map p493
Banks BCP, Apurímac 719. Mon-Fri 0900-1830, Sat 0900-1300. ATM accepts all cards. Scotia Bank, Amazonas 750, T076-367101. Mon-Fri 0915-1800, Sat 0930-1300. ATM accepts all cards. Interbank, 2 de Mayo 546, on plaza. Open 0900-1300, 1600-1815. In Cajamarca, ATMs appear to accept all cards. There is a Telebanco 24 Horas ATM (Visa) at the gas station next to Línea buses on Av Atahualpa. Dollars can be changed in most banks and travel agencies on east side of plaza, but euro are hard to change. *Casa de cambio* in Casa del Artefacto musical and electrical store at Amazonas 537. Good rates, cash only. *Casas de cambio* also at Jr del Comercio y Apurímac and at Amalia Puga 673. Street changers on Jr Del Batán by the Plaza de Armas and at Del Batán y Amazonas. **Internet** Everywhere; US$0.35 per hr. **Laundry** Lavandería Dandy, Jr Amalia Puga 545. Pay by weight. Lava Express, Jr Belén 678. Good service, US$1.50 per kg. **Medical services** Hospital: Clínica Limatambo, Puno 265, T076-364241. Private, recommended. Doctor Gurmandi speaks English. Clínica Los Fresnos, Jr Los Nogales 179, Urb El Ingenio, T076-824046. Mainly used by foreign companies and has some English-speaking staff. Clínica San Francisco, Av Grau 851, T076-362050. Private, recommended. Hospital at Av Mario Urteaga. **Post** Serpost, Apurímac 626. Mon-Sat 0800-2000. **Telephone** *Locutorio* and internet offices can be found all over the centre.

Chachapoyas Region

The Chachapoyas Region contains so many archaeological riches that you need at least a week to begin to appreciate the remarkable legacy of the Chachapoyans, also known as 'The Cloud People'. Great pre-Inca cities, immense fortresses such as Kuélap and ancient effigies that gaze over a dramatic landscape reward the visitor. There are many cities and burial sites scattered around the cloud-covered mountain slopes, often in inaccessible places. To reach them is an adventure in itself and the natural beauty of high plateaus, vertical escarpments and world-class waterfalls is as dramatic as the archaeology. ▶▶ *For listings, see pages 518-525.*

Ins and outs

Getting there The city of Chachapoyas is the best base for visiting this region. Air service here has not always been reliable, but the area can be reached overland from Chiclayo, Cajamarca or Tarapoto, or southern Ecuador via Jaén. From Chachapoyas a scenic paved road descends 54 km to Pedro Ruiz on the main Chiclayo–Yurimaguas highway (Carretera Marginal de la Selva). At El Cruce, 14 km from Chachapoyas, a narrow unpaved road branches south and follows the Río Utcubamba upriver to Leymebamba, then continues to Celendín and Cajamarca. **Móvil Tours** offer a bus service from Lima via Chiclayo, travelling Chiclayo to Chachapoyas by day. Buses starting in Chiclayo however, all involve an overnight journey, missing the fine scenery along the way. An alternative is to go by bus from Chiclayo to Jaén, continuing the next day to Chachapoyas via Bagua Grande and Pedro Ruiz, using shared taxis (*autos*). From Cajamarca, **Móvil Tours** has daily direct service to Chachapoyas via Celendín, crossing the Marañón at Balsas between descents and climbs of thousands of vertical metres. The journey is an entirely unforgettable experience in its own right, well worth doing in daylight. Also beautiful is the route from Tarapoto via Moyobamba and Pedro Ruiz, along the paved highway. It is possible to do this journey in one day, leaving Tarapoto in the morning.

Getting around Archaelogical and natural sites are spread out in a large area; the easiest way to reach them is on a tour. Public transport is not plentiful in this region. Most journeys are done by *autos* or combis, starting their routes in Chachapoyas, often before dawn. To reach the more remote archaeological sites you will have to do some walking, in one or two cases for several days.

Best time to visit The dry season is preferable (normally May to September), but the seasons are less stable than in the past; in the last few years it has been sunny and dry well into December. During the rains, roads may become impassable due to landslides and access to the more remote areas may be impossible, or involve weeks of delay. Likewise, trekking in the area can be very pleasant in the dry season, but may involve wading through waist-deep mud on some routes during the rainy season. Other places are still accessible in the wet, but rubber boots are essential. Good hiking gear is always a must, as well as a sleeping bag and tent.

Tourist information iperú ⓘ *Jr Ortiz 588, Plaza de Armas, Chachapoyas, T041-477292, iperuchachapoyas@promperu.gob.pe, Mon-Sat 0900-1300, 1400-1800, Sun 0900-1300.* **Dircetur (Dirección Regional de Turismo)** ⓘ *Jr Santa Ana 1162, T041-478355, Mon-Fri 0800-1300, 1400-1700.*

Background

Theories about the Chachapoyan Empire show that their cities, highways, terracing, irrigation, massive stonework and metal-craft were all fully developed. The culture began about AD 0 and covered an area bounded by the rivers Marañón and Huallaga, as far as Pataz in the south and Bagua in the north. Socially the Chachapoya were organized into chiefdoms, which formed war-alliances in the case of external aggression. Archaeologists claim that this region overwhelms even Machu Picchu and its neighbouring Inca sites in grandeur and mystery. By some counts, its 'lost' and uncharted cities, such as Pueblo Alto, near the village of Pueblo Nuevo (25 km from Kuélap) and Saposoa in the northeast of San Martín department, exceed three dozen. By far the majority of these cities, fortresses and villages were never discovered by the Spanish. In fact many had already returned to the jungle by the time they arrived in 1532.

The German ethnologist, Doctor Peter Lerche, of the Camayoc Foundation ⓘ http://camayocperu.com, and mayor of Chachapoyas (2006-2010), is the resident expert regarding Chachapoyan cultures and trekking. He is very knowledgeable, speaks English, sometimes guides groups and may be contacted for information on anthropology and history. In an article in *National Geographic*, September 2000, "Quest for the Lost Tombs of the Peruvian Cloud People", Doctor Lerche writes about the discovery of a Chachapoya tomb named the 'White House' and gives a good general introduction to the history and archaeology of the region (he has also provided information for this section).

This region is called 'La Ceja de la Selva' (eyebrow of the jungle). Its beautiful scenery includes a good deal of virgin cloudforest (although other sections are sadly deforested), as well as endless deep dry canyons traversed by hair-raisingly dangerous roads. The temperature is always in the 20°Cs during the day, but the nights are cool at around 3000 m. Many ruins are overgrown with ferns, bromeliads and orchids and easily missed.

The central geographic feature of the department, and its boundary with neighbouring Cajamarca, is the great Río Marañón, one of the major tributaries of the Amazon. Running roughly parallel to the mighty Marañón, one range to the east, is the gentler valley of the Utcubamba, home to much of the area's ancient and present population. Over yet another cordillera to the east, lie the isolated subtropical valleys of the province of Rodríguez de Mendoza, the origin of whose inhabitants, has been the source of much debate (see page 515).

Cajamarca to Chachapoyas → For listings, see pages 518-525.

East from Cajamarca, the route follows a road (paved as far as Encañada, about 50 minutes) through beautiful countryside; it is expected that more of the road will be paved soon because of mining projects in the area, reducing the time taken to visit Chachapoyas.

Celendín → Colour map 1, C4. Phone code: 076.

The first town of note is **Celendín**, whose residents are known as Shilicos. It is a clean and tranquil place, with warm friendly people but a decidedly chilly climate. The buildings around the plaza, including the cathedral, are painted predominantly blue. There is a fascinating **market** on Sunday which is held in three distinct areas. At 0630 the hat market is held by the Alameda, between Ayacucho and 2 de Mayo at Jorge Chávez. You can see the hats worn by local people at every stage of production, starting with the sale of the bundles of straw which comes from Rioja. Women buy the straw and make the basic shape. They then bring the unfinished hats to the Sunday market where wholesalers buy them. Men then finish the hats off in the various styles. *Sombrerías* such as **Artesanía y Sombrería Sánchez**, by the Alameda, then sell the finished hats. Other hat shops in town open sporadically. The market is over within an hour or so. Then at 0930 the potato market takes place at 2 de Mayo y Sucre and, at the other end of town, the livestock market on Túpac Amaru. Both are full of activity. Walk up the hill to the chapel of San Isidro Labrador for views of the town and its surroundings. The **Museo Cultural Huaco** ① *Bolívar 211, T076-552096 in the nearby village of Sucre, take colectivo from Jr Bolognesi block 2, US$0.70*, is interesting for local history (friendly curator).

Just over 20 km from Celendín and 800 m below in a beautiful river valley are the hot springs of **Llanguat** ① *US$0.75*. The hot bathing pools are basic square affairs, but apparently the medicinal quality of the waters is excellent and they are a less commercial alternative to Baños del Inca. Across the river are hot mud pools for bathing in, but at times of high water the river may be too fast-flowing and dangerous to cross. Taxi US$20-25, US$2.75 by limited public transport.

The rough road from Celendín to Chachapoyas (226 km) follows a winding course, crossing the wide and deep canyon of the Río Marañón at Balsas, at 950 m. It then climbs steeply, over countless hair-raising hairpin bends, with superb views of the mountains and the valleys below, to reach the Barro Negro pass at 3680 m, before descending to Leymebamba in the upper Utcubamba Valley (see page 511). The journey can be much longer and more dangerous when it rains.

Chachapoyas and around → *For listings, see pages 518-525. Colour map 1, C4.*
Phone code: 041. Population: about 30,000. Altitude: 2335 m.

Chachapoyas, or 'Chacha', as it is known among locals, is the capital of the Department of Amazonas. It was founded on 5 September 1538, but retains only some of its colonial character, in the form of large old homes with their typical patios and wooden balconies. The city's importance as a crossroads between the coast and jungle began to decline in the late 1940s, with the building of the road through Pedro Ruiz. However, archaeological and ecological tourism have grown gradually since the 1990s and there are hopes that these will bring increasing economic benefits to the region.

Chachapoyas
The modern cathedral (being rebuilt in 2010) faces a spacious plaza that fills with locals for the evening *paseo*. Other interesting churches are the **Capilla de la Virgen Asunta**, the city's patroness, at Asunción y Puno, and **Señor de Burgos**, at Amazonas y Santa Lucía. The **Instituto Nacional de Cultura (INC)** has a small **museum** ① *Ayacucho 904, Tue-Sat 0830-1230, 1345-1730, US$2*. It contains a few artefacts and mummies in display cases, with explanations in Spanish.

Housed in the first indigenous church of Chachapoyas, is **Museo Santa Ana** ① *Jr Santa Ana 1054, T041-790988, Mon-Fri 0800-1800, Sat-Sun 0900-1300, 1500-1800, US$2.50, opened in 2009*, with colonial religious art and pre-Hispanic ceramics and textiles. A lookout to the west of town offers fine views of the city. A decisive battle for independence from Spain took place at the **Pampas de Higos Urco**, at the east end of town, a 20-minute walk, with great views of lush Andes to the east.

Huancas

This picturesque village, stands on a hilltop north of Chacha. It's a two-hour walk starting on the airport road. There is some small-scale pottery at the community-run **Taller Artesanal La Cusana**. Walk 1 km uphill from plaza in town to the **Mirador** ① entry US$0.35, crafts on sale, for a magnificent view into the deep canyon of the Río Sonche, with tumbling waterfalls. There is good walking in the area, which also has Inca and pre-Inca ruins. At **Huanca Urco**, 5 km from Huancas, past the large prison complex, are remains of an Inca road and another mirador with more fine views including Gocta Waterfall in the distance. *Autos* for Huancas leave from Jirón Ortiz Arrieta 370 y Libertad, 0600-1800, US$1, 20 minutes.

Levanto → *Colour map 1, C4. Altitude: 2400 m.*

The Spaniards built this, one of the first of several capitals of the area, in 1538, directly on top of the previous Chachapoyan structures. Nowadays Levanto, due south of Chachapoyas, is a

Chachapoyas

To Museo Santa Ana & Capilla de la Virgen Asunta

To Airport

Jr Santa Ana

Quebrada Santa Lucia

Jr Libertad

Santo Domingo

Pasaje Reyes

Jr Salamanca

Isamax

INC

BCP
iPerú

Plaza
de Armas

Cathedral

Banco de
la Nación

Jr Chincha Alta

Jr Ortiz Arrieta

Jr Junín

Jr Grau

Jr Triunfo

Jr 2 de Mayo

Jr Amazonas

Jr La Merced

Jr Ayacucho

Jr Unión

Jr Recreo

To & Pedro Ruiz

N

200 metres

200 yards

Sleeping
1 Belén *A1*
2 Casa Vieja *A1*
3 Casona Monsante *B2*
4 El Dorado *A1*
5 Gocta *B2*
6 Gran Vilaya *B2*
7 Las Orquídeas *A1*

8 Puma Urco *B2*
9 Revash *B2*
10 Rumi Huasi *A1*
11 Villa París *B1*
12 Vista Hermosa *A1*

Eating
1 Dulcería Santa Elena *B2*
2 El Edén *A2*
3 El Tejado *A1*
4 Fusiones *A1*
5 Heladería San Antonio *B2*
6 La Real Cecina *B3*
7 La Tushpa *B1*

8 Mari Pizza *B2*
9 Matalaché *B3*
10 Panadería Café San José *B2*
11 Romana *A1*
12 Sabores del Perú *A2*

Transport
1 Cars to Huancas & Mendoza *A2*
2 Cars to Lamud & Luya *A1*
3 Combis to Pedro Ruiz *A1*
4 Trans Zelada *A2*
5 Cars to Celendín *A2*

6 Trans Rollers to María *A2*
7 Cars to Pedro Ruiz & Bagua Grande *A2*
8 Civa *A2*
9 Virgen del Carmen to Mendoza and Celendín *A2*
10 Karlita to Leymebamba *A2*
11 Trans Kuélap *A3*
12 Móvil Tours *B3*
13 GH Bus *B3*
14 Combis to Pizuquia *A2*

Sites around Chachapoyas

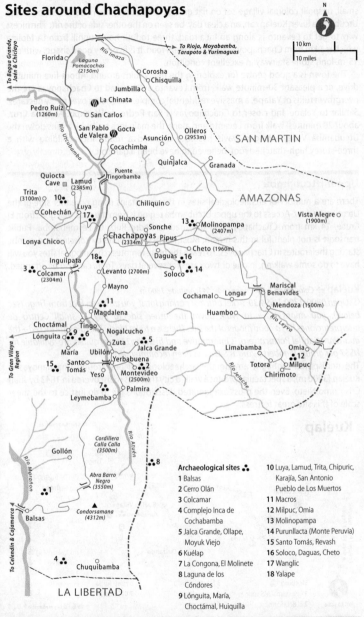

N

| 10 km |
| 10 miles |

To Bagua Grande, Jaén & Chiclayo

Florida

Laguna Pomacochas (2150m)

Corosha
Chisquilla

Jumbilla

To Rioja, Moyobamba, Tarapoto & Yurimaguas

La Chinata

Pedro Ruiz (1260m)

San Carlos

San Pablo de Valera   Gocta

Cocachimba

Olleros (2953m)

Asunción

SAN MARTIN

Puente Tingorbamba

Quinjalca   Granada

Quiocta Cave   Lamud (2345m)

Trita (3100m)   10

Cohechán   Luya   17

Chiliquin

AMAZONAS

Huancas   Sonche   13   Molinopampa (2407m)

Chachapoyas (2334m)   Pipus

Vista Alegre (1900m)

Lonya Chico

Inguilpata   18

Cheto (1960m)

3   Colcamar (2304m)

Levanto (2700m)   Daguas   16   14

Soloco

Mayno

Mariscal Benavides

Cochamal   Longar

Mendoza (1500m)

11

Magdalena

Huambo

Rio Leyva

Choctámal   Tingo
Lónguita   9   6   Nogalcucho

5
Zuta

María   Ubilón   Jalca Grande

15   Santo   Yerbabuena   2
Tomás
Yeso   Montevideo (2500m)

Limabamba   Omia
12
Totora   Milpuc
Chirimoto

7   Palmira

Cordillera Calla Calla (3500m)

To Gran Vilaya Region

Rio Utcubamba

Rio Imaza

Rio Urcubamba

Rio Leyva

Rio Jelache

Rio Atuén

Gollón

Rio Marañón

Abra Barro Negro (3550m)

Condorsamana (4312m)

1

Balsas

To Celendín & Cajamarca

4   Chuquibamba

LA LIBERTAD

8

Archaeological sites ∴

1 Balsas
2 Cerro Olán
3 Colcamar
4 Complejo Inca de Cochabamba
5 Jalca Grande, Ollape, Moyuk Viejo
6 Kuélap
7 La Congona, El Molinete
8 Laguna de los Cóndores
9 Lónguita, María, Choctámal, Huiquilla

10 Luya, Lamud, Trita, Chipuric, Karajía, San Antonio Pueblo de Los Muertos
11 Macros
12 Milpuc, Omia
13 Molinopampa
14 Purunllacta (Monte Peruvia)
15 Santo Tomás, Revash
16 Soloco, Daguas, Cheto
17 Wanglic
18 Yalape

small, unspoilt colonial village set on flat ground overlooking the massive canyon of the Utcubamba River. Kuélap can, on a clear day, be seen on the other side of the rift. The nicest way to get to Levanto is along an Inca road, three to four hours uphill from La Molina which is 5 km from Chachapoyas along the main road. It is in pretty good shape, with one 15-m-long stone stairway in excellent condition.

The town is a good centre for exploring the many ruins around. About five minutes' drive, or a pleasant 30-minute walk, from Levanto on the road to Chachapoyas are the overgrown ruins of **Yalape**, a massive residential complex extending over many hectares. Similar to Yalape and closer to Chachapoyas is **San Pedro de Wushpu**. At **Colla Cruz**, about 20 minutes' walk from Levanto and along the main Inca trail which runs down the Utcubamba Valley, Morgan Davis has reconstructed a round Inca building with a three-storey high-thatched roof, believed to have been a garrison.

Upper Utcubamba

There are a number of archaeological sites in the mountains rising on either side of the Utcubamba river. Access to the upper Utcubamba region is from the road that goes from El Cruce, 14 km from Chachapoyas on the road to Pedro Ruiz, to Leymebamba. Public transport is not plentiful in this region. Most journeys are done by *colectivo* and combi, starting their routes in Chachapoyas. To reach the more remote archaeological sites you will have to do some walking, in one or two cases for several days. Tours can also be arranged.

Kuélap → *Colour map 1, C4. Phone code: 041. Altitude: 1800 m.*
ⓘ *Open 0800-1700, US$4.30, ticket office at parking lot, if you arrive on foot from Tingo (see below), you might have to walk down the other side to pay. A small Centro de Interpretaciones has a good model of the site. There is a toilet block. The ruins are locked – the guardian, Gabriel Portocarrero, is informative and friendly; 11 local guides are available for US$7 per group; Rigoberto Vargas Silva has been recommended.*

The undisputed highlight among the archaeological riches around Chachapoyas is Kuélap (3000 m), a spectacular pre-Inca walled city that was rediscovered in 1843 by Juan Crisótomo Nieto. Even the most exaggerated descriptions fail to do justice to the sheer scale of this site great fortress.

Kuélap

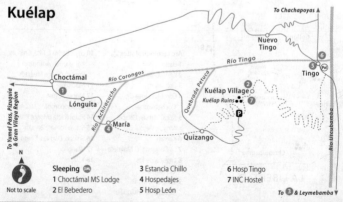

Sleeping
1 Choctámal MS Lodge
2 El Bebedero
3 Estancia Chillo
4 Hospedajes
5 Hosp León
6 Hosp Tingo
7 INC Hostel

Not to scale

Kuélap was built starting AD 500 and was under continuous development until it was abandoned. It contains three times more stone than the Great Pyramid at Giza in Egypt. The site lies sprawled along the summit of a mountain crest, more than a kilometre in length. It is divided into three parts: at the northwest end is a small outpost; at the southeast end of the ridge is a spread-out village in total ruin; and the cigar-shaped fortress lies between the two, 585 m long by 110 m wide at its widest. The walls are as formidable as those of any pre-Columbian city. They vary in height between 8 m and 17 m and were constructed in 40 courses of stone block, each one weighing between 100 and 200 kg. It has been estimated that 100,000 such blocks went into the completion of this massive structure.

The majority of the main walls on all four levels are original. Also original is the inverted, cone-shaped structure, long assumed to be a dungeon, although recent studies claim it to be a giant solar calendar, known as *el tintero* (the inkwell). There are a number of defensive walls and passageways as well as many houses. Some reconstruction has taken place, mostly of small houses and walls, but only one building has been completely restored. The remainder have been left in their cloudforest setting, the trees covered in bromeliads and moss, the flowers visited by hummingbirds. There are numerous petroglyphs and some structures are adorned with simple geometric friezes that represent the eyes of animals and birds. An interesting feature is that almost all the buildings (about 420 in number) are circular. Recent archaeological findings indicate that they were public spaces and served as kitchens, toilets and storage areas, rather than warriors' barracks as was first thought. It is estimated that up to 3500 people lived in Kuélap at its zenith. The site was never mentioned in Inca chronicles, meaning that by the time of the Inca invasion in the 1470s, it was of little significance to the Chachas. The five rectangular structures indicate that the Incas occupied the fortress.

Tingo (1800 m), about 37 km south of Chachapoyas along the road to Leymebamba, is the village from which you can reach Kuélap. A road climbs steeply from Tingo via Nuevo Tingo to **Choctámal**, where it divides. One branch goes west towards the Yumal Pass, Pizuquia and the Gran Vilaya region; the second branch climbs east to **Lónguita, María, Quizango** and Kuélap. Before Tingo, an alternative road goes up to Nuevo Tingo; most tour buses take this. Between this road and Tingo, look for the ruins of **Macros** above the east bank of the river. The ruins are accessed walking half an hour from the town of Magdalena, east of Tingo. Some tours visit Macros.

There are four options to reach Kuélap: **1** Take a tour from Chachapoyas with one of the operators (see page 522). Most hotels will organize tours to Kuélap and other archaeological sites when there are sufficient people. Expect to pay around US$15-25 per person for a full-day trip to Kuélap, including guide and in some cases also lunch. When booking a tour, request a guide who speaks English, if you so wish. Tours leave at 0830 and, after a spectacular, if not disconcerting, three-hour drive, you arrive at Kuélap. The tours usually allow a sufficient three to four hours for exploration before returning to Chachapoyas, with a possible stop along the way for a late lunch. **2** Hire your own vehicle with driver in Chachapoyas, US$35 per vehicle. **3** A less expensive option and, in many ways, the recommended one since it allows you to see Kuélap wrapped in early-morning mist, is to take a combi to Choctámal, María or Quizango (see Transport, page 523). You can spend the night in **Choctámal** or **María** (see Sleeping, page 520). The next day, it is a relatively gentle 19 km, four- to five-hour walk along the vehicle road from Choctámal to Kuélap or two to 2½ hours from María. It's best to visit the site at your leisure and spend the night here, then walk down the steep path (three to four hours) to Tingo the next day. **4** Take a combi from Chachapoyas to Tingo (see Transport, page 523). Either spend the night in Tingo and start climbing at dawn the next day, or hike straight up and spend the night in María. The strenuous four- to five-hour hike (with a 1200 m vertical gain) to Kuélap begins on the right-hand side of the bridge, past the police station. At first the track follows the west bank of the Utcubamba, before turning right and climbing steeply into the mountains. The route is intermittently marked with red arrows painted on the rocks. It can get very hot and there is no water whatsoever until the top, but the trail may be muddy in the rainy season. Take water, food, adequate clothing and footwear, etc. You reach the small village of Kuélap first, the walls of the fortress become visible only at the very end of the climb. It'll take about three hours to walk down. A shorter walk to Kuélap is from **Estancia Chillo** (see Tingo Sleeping, page 519).

Jalca Grande

South of Tingo and Kuélap there are many sights of interest on either bank of the Río Utcubamba. At **Ubilón**, a road goes east to the town of Jalca Grande (or La Jalca as it is known locally), at 2800 m. The town has the remains of a Chachapoyan roundhouse, a stone church and a small **museum** ① *entry US$1.80*, with ceramics and textiles. There is one very basic *hospedaje* one block from the plaza, past the church. Market day is Saturday. Half an hour west of the town are the ruins of **Ollape**, a series of platforms with intricate fretwork designs and wide balconies. A much larger site, though more primitive, is **Moyuk Viejo**, a 2½-hour walk to the north.

A strenuous but rewarding three- to four-day trek can be made from La Jalca to Huambo or Limabamba, over the cordillera and through cloudforests to the subtropical valleys. Part of the route follows an ancient road and there are undeveloped ruins along the way. Trekking experience and self-sufficiency are indispensable.

Revash

Further south is the town of **Yerbabuena**. Its Sunday market is the largest in the area, with animals, local produce, including cheeses, farming implements, etc, on sale or for barter. Here are **F Hospedaje La Fortaleza Kuélap**, basic, and **Restaurant Karina**.

From Yerbabuena a road goes west to **Puente Santo Tomás**, at the turn-off for the vivid burial *chullpas* of **Revash**, belonging to the Revash culture (around AD 1250) and on to the town of **Santo Tomás**. The tombs are roughly three hours' walk from Puente Santo Tomás. Follow the road towards Santo Tomás, then cross the wooden bridge on the right and take the dirt track towards the mountains; it is a steep climb up and takes 1½ to two hours from the bridge. Revash can also be reached from **San Bartolo**, a village 25-minutes' drive from Yerbabuena. The tombs are a 30- to 45-minutes' walk downhill from the village. As you approach, small adobe houses can be seen in the cliff face, covered by an overhang. The houses are buff coloured with red roofs and resemble tiny Swiss cottages with crosses in the form of bricked-up windows. They are, in fact, small tombs. There are lots of human bones lying around and cave paintings. The tombs have long since been looted. Observe the structures from below. Please do not climb on the houses as they are incredibly fragile. Examine the cliff face to the left of the houses and you'll notice several more tombs, peeking out from the limestone face.

Cerro Olán

South of Yerbabuena, a road leads east to **Montevideo**, with a basic *hospedaje*, and beyond to the small village of **San Pedro de Utac**. A 30-minute walk from the village is Cerro Olán, a Chachapoyan site. From the plaza a clear trail rises directly to the ruins in the hills to the east; they can be seen from the village. Here are the remains of towers which some archaeologists claim had roofs like medieval European castles. According to Morgan Davis this was a military installation and once a small city of considerable luxury, similar in construction to La Congona (see page 512) but on a grander scale. Past the turnoff for Montevideo, the main road passes through **Palmira**, just before Leymebamba.

Leymebamba → *Colour map 1, C4. Altitude: 2250, www.leymebamba.org*
This pleasant, friendly town derives its name from a visit in around 1475 by the Inca Túpac Yupanqui, who stayed to celebrate the **Fiesta de Inti-Raymi**. From that moment, the town came to be known as the Field of the Festival of The Sun, or Raymi-Pampa, which in turn became Leymebamba. The city was moved from its original location, 3 km south, following an epidemic of yellow fever in the 1600s. The local fiesta is held in honour of the **Virgen del Carmen** on the week preceeding 16 July.

The town's Saturday market is very limited, a better option is the one at Yerbabuena on Sunday morning. The Spanish priest, Padre Diego, who was involved in setting up the local museum (see below), is very helpful. Water is sporadic and notoriously dirty; drink only bottled water. If you should fall ill, the Centro de Salud is reportedly helpful.

Leymebamba is at the junction of the Atuén and Pomacochas rivers, the source of the Utcubamba. There is good walking along all the river valleys. The canyon of the Atuén is particularly scenic and condors might be spotted here. **Vilaya Tours** (see tour operators, page 522) offers trekking tours in this area.

Laguna de los Cóndores
In 1996 a spectacular site consisting of six burial *chullpas*, containing 219 mummies and vast quantities of ceramics, textiles, woodwork, *quipus* and everyday utensils from the late Inca period, was discovered at Laguna de los Cóndores, a beautiful lake in a jungle setting, south of Leymebamba.

In order to protect this major discovery from *huaqueros*, who had already done considerable damage, the material was moved to the excellent **Museo Leymebamba** ⓘ *outside San Miguel, on the road to Celendín, T041-816803, www.museoleymebamba.org, Tue-Sun 1000-1630, entry US$3.60, additional donations are welcome. Spanish, English and German explanations. Taxi from Leymebamba US$2.50.* From the town it's a pleasant 45-minute walk, 3 km south to San Miguel, the site of the original Leymebamba town; from there, take the footpath uphill (the road is much longer). A portion of the over 5000 artefacts discovered are on display, the great majority of them from the Laguna de los Cóndores site. There are artefacts from Chachapoya, Inca and other cultures. The museum and its materials were entirely made by hand, a true artisan construction. Across the road, in a lovely setting is **Kentikafe**, offering snacks, drinks and observation of 17 species of hummingbird (including the marvelous spatuletail) attracted to their many feeders; lodging was under construction in 2010, enquire at T041-816804.

The trip to Laguna de los Cóndores from Leymebamba takes nine to 10 hours each way on horseback (three days in all). It is not for the faint-hearted, but is generally agreed to be one of the trips of a lifetime. The route climbs to 3700 m before descending to the laguna where there is a basic lodge, US$7, run by **Hospedaje Laguna de los Cóndores** in Leymebamba. Bring a sleeping bag, warm clothes and all food and cook it there or pay the family to prepare it. Make sure your horse is in good condition as the track is often knee deep in mud. It is best done during the dry season (May to September). A US$3.60 fee is payable at the INC in Leymebamba. Guides can be arranged by Leymebamba hotels; the cost for guides, muleteers and horses is US$9-11 per day for each, plus food. Three-day tours with Chachapoyas agencies run at about US$120-130 per person. Unfortunately, the impressive funerary site overlooking the river has been stripped of artefacts and even some of its colourful plaster. Please do not climb on the houses or remove anything.

La Congona

There are numerous ruins around Leymebamba, many of which are covered in vegetation. The most spectacular is the Chachapoyan site of La Congona to the west.

The site is a brisk three-hour walk starting at the lower end of 16 de Julio. A vehicle road (under construction in 2010) and the remaining sections of the old path climb steeply from town to the village of Fila San Cristóbal. Continue straight on a trail past the football field (not the road to the right), it undulates before descending to the large flat pasture of Tío Pampa, about 30 minutes past the village. Turn left at the end of the pasture and follow a streambed with white sand, then climb to a ridge and follow it left. There are many structures spread on the hills here, aim for the middle of three peaks, covered in vegetation and identified by a white limestone cliff. The most impressive structures are clustered in a small area, impossible to see until you are right there. Turn right off the main trail and go through a gate to get there. If the landowner is there, he appreciates a contribution. The views are stupendous and the ruins worth the effort, allow one to two hours to explore them at leisure. There are some 30 decorated round stone houses (some with evidence of three storeys) and a watch tower. It is supposed to be the only site displaying all three Chacha friezes – zigzag, rhomboid and Greek stepped.

There are two other sites, **El Molinete** and **Pumahuanyuna**, nearby. All three can be visited in a day but a guide is advisable to explain the area and show the way to the ruins as it is easy to get lost. Archaeological sites to the south of Leymebamba include **La Petaca**, **La Joya** and **Diablo Huasi**. There are also caves with petroglyphs at **Chururco**, two and a half hours walk from Pomacochas (not to be confused with Pomacochas on the road to Tarapoto), reached by taxi for US$5.40.

Northwest of Chachapoyas → For listings, see pages 518-525.

There are more extraordinary archaeological remains, including strange sarcophagi in cliffs, with rewarding trekking possibilities in this area.

Luya, Karajía, Lamud and Pueblo de los Muertos

The village of **Luya** is on a turn-off from the road north to Pedro Ruiz at Caclic, 37 km from Chachapoyas. In a lush canyon, 1½ hours' walk from the road to Luya is **Wanglic** (also spelled Huanglic), a funeral site with large circular structures built under a ledge. Nearby is a beautiful waterfall, a worthwhile excursion. Three kilometres or 1½ hours' walk from Luya is **Chipuric**, a residential complex belonging to the Chachapoyas culture. The site consists of burial tombs set in a cliff face on a high ledge with circular stone buildings on the hill above. The tombs, which are 1 m high and look like beehives, have all been looted. Continue along the dirt road from Luya until it forks; take the higher road with the irrigation canal. At **Pueblo Molino** (a small cluster of houses and one shop), the cliff face and the burial tombs are visible. On the lower road that passes below the cliff on the other side of the river, is Chipuric town. The cliff is steep but it's possible to climb up to the tombs with some difficulty and quite a few scratches from the thorn bushes. There are great views from the top, though.

At Luya, the road divides, one branch goes north to Lamud (see below), the second one south and west to Cohechán and Cruzpata. The striking site of **Karajía**, is 2½ hours' walk from Luya or about 30 minutes' walk from **Cruzpata**; *autos* run from Luya to Cruzpata (0600-1700, US$2.90, one hour). In the Karajía Valley are the remarkable, 2.5-m-high sarcophagi, which date from AD 1200, set into an impressive cliff face. Just below these inscrutable figures are plenty of human bones, if you look carefully. Study the cliff face for a dozen more smaller sarcophagi. The viewpoint is 25 m below the sarcophagi; take binoculars for a closer look. The sarcophagi can also be seen from the villages of Trita and Shipata accross the valley. A visit to Karajía can be combined with with a longer trek in the Gran Vilaya region (see below).

Ten minutes north of Luya, 37 km northwest of Chachapoyas, is **Lamud**, a convenient base for several interesting archaeological sites. The local **fiesta of Señor de Gualamita** on 14 September is well-attended.

At **San Antonio**, half an hour from Lamud, is a sandstone cliff face with several groups of burial tombs high on a ledge. They are difficult to see unless you know what you're looking for (there are sarcophagi and other tombs, but you need binoculars to see them). The ruins, set on the hill above, are a residential complex, thought to form part of a group of people belonging to the Chipuric. The main nucleus is almost completely ruined, but the ruins are unusual in that the stucco is still in place. A guide is not necessary, but ask for directions. On the bottom of the hill, where the road ends, a colonial-era tunnel and water-wheel can be explored.

Ten kilometres north of Lamud are the mind-boggling ruins of **Pueblo de los Muertos**, circular stone houses overlooking the valley a thousand metres below. A road goes to within 40 minutes of the site and then you have a steep, 40-minute walk on loose rock. The view is spectacular and the ruins are difficult to find as they are overgrown. Since being brought to public attention by Gene Savoy in the mid-1960s, the site has been largely destroyed by local grave robbers. Despite this, it is unmatched for location and scenery in the area. Ask directions before setting out.

Northwest of Lamud, 25 minutes by car (taxi US$15) then 15 minutes' walk from the road is **Quiocta** ① *entry US$1.80*, a cave with impressive stalactites and stalagmites of varied colours, often included in tours to this area.

Gran Vilaya → *Colour map 1, C4.*

The name Gran Vilaya was created by US explorer, Gene Savoy, one of the candidates for the original 'Indiana Jones', who discovered this extensive set of ruined complexes in 1985. There are about 30 sites spread over this vast area, 15 of which are considered significant. Among them are **Pueblo Alto**, **Pueblo Nuevo**, **Paxamarca** and **Machu Llacta**.

This area stretches west from the Río Utcubamba to the Río Marañón. Moist air pushing up from the Amazon Basin creates a unique biosphere of clouds and mist in which bromeliads and orchids thrive. Being near to the equator and over 3000 m above sea level, the daytime temperature is a constant 22°C. While the Marañón valley is a desert, the peaks are always misted from June to September and often drenched in rain the rest of the year. This creates a huge variety of mini-ecological zones, each with its own flora and fauna, depending on altitude and on which flank of the mountain they are on.

Gran Vilaya can be accessed from several points. From the north: **Cohechán**, 30 minutes' ride past Luya on the road to Cruzpata; **Inguilpata**, on a road that branches south off the road to Luya; and **Colcamar**, on a road that branches off the road to Leymebamba, just after it crosses to the west bank of the Utcubamba. The southern area is reached from the **Yumal Pass**, along the road that runs from Choctámal to Pizuquia.

The Inca roads in this region make for incredible trekking and many Chachapoyas operators offer tours here. Trails from the three northern access points and a road from Cohechán all lead to **Huaylla Belén**, a gigantic silted-in green valley with a spectacular panorama of the river meandering below. It is the only large flat spot in the zone. As it stands at about 2800 m, it can get frosts on clear nights. From here you cross the spine of the Andes on a 1.6-km Inca stairway, dropping into Gran Vilaya. You pass many ruins near Vista Hermosa (3½ to four hours from Belén). The 1600-1700 m climb to the Yumal Pass is 'a killer'. From Yumal a road and the trail thankfully descend to Choctámal where there is lodging (see Sleeping below). To trek across the area takes three to five days. It can be combined with a visit to Karajía and can also be done starting in the south at the Yumal Pass.

To the south of Yumal, along a trail that goes from Llaucán (1.5 km west of Choctámal) to Yomblón, is **Cerro Shubet** (3882 m), a striking flat-topped mountain with ruins and petroglyphs. The views from the top are excellent in good weather.

Gran Vilaya Region

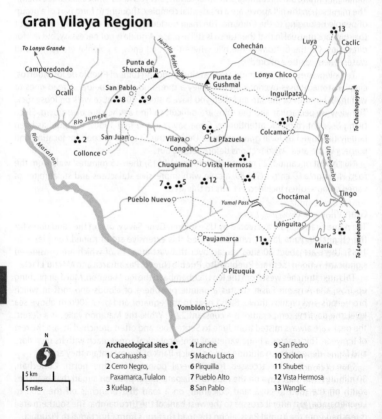

Archaeological sites ∴
1 Cacahuasha	4 Lanche	9 San Pedro
2 Cerro Negro, Paxamarca, Tulalon	5 Machu Llacta	10 Sholon
	6 Pirquilla	11 Shubet
3 Kuélap	7 Pueblo Alto	12 Vista Hermosa
	8 San Pablo	13 Wanglic

5 km
5 miles

Purunllacta and the route to Mendoza

Forty kilometres east from Chachapoyas, on the road to Mendoza, are the pre-Inca ruins of **Monte Peruvia** (known locally as **Purunllacta**). They consist of hundreds of white stone houses with staircases, temples and palaces. The ruins have been cleared by local farmers and some houses have been destroyed. A guide is useful as there are few locals from whom to ask directions. The ruins are about two hours walking from **Cheto**, which is south of the main road. There are no hotels in town but a house high up on the hill above the town with a balcony has cheap bed and board. The same family has a house on the plaza. There are two small shops and a small house with one room serves basic but good meals.

The road east from Chachapoyas continues through **Pipus** to **Molinopampa**, two hours' drive from Chachapoyas, it then passes the **Palmeras de Ocol** palm forest, to **Mendoza** (1500 m), capital and supply centre of the subtropical province of the same name (Rodríguez de Mendoza), which reportedly produces the best coffee in Peru. Organically grown coffee from the area is exported directly to Europe. There are several simple restaurants on Jr Rodríguez de Mendoza. There is a cave at **Omia** and thermal baths at **La Colpa de Tocuya**.

Mendoza is also the starting point for an ethnologically interesting area in the Guayabamba Valley where there is a high incidence of fair-skinned people. For a long while this gave rise to a wide variety of theories on the people's origin. These included the ideas that they originate from warring conquistador factions in the early 16th century, or that they are related to the cloud people, themselves descendants of the Vikings. Among the most important research to counter such romantic theories is the investigation into DNA samples. In Guayabamba these can be traced to one Spanish family who lived in the region for a long time and there is evidence that the people of Chirimoto were originally Italian and Spanish settlers in the 1820s. More wide-ranging, related research has looked at the DNA of the mummies found at Laguna de Cóndores and Scandinavian bog people and other European mummies.

There are roads and public transport to the small towns of Huambo, Santa Rosa, Totora, Limabamba, Chirimoto Viejo and Milpuc; and horse trails to other remote villages. Visitors going beyond Mendoza should be self sufficient.

North of Chachapoyas

The paved road north from Chachapoyas heads through the beautiful Utcubamba River canyon with steep mountains on either side. In places the road is cut into the canyon wall. **Pedro Ruiz** (altitude 1260 m) is a small but important junction at the confluence of the Río Ingenio and the Utcubamba. From here you can either head west to Chiclayo on the coast, east to Tarapoto, Yurimaguas and the jungle, or north to Ecuador via Bagua Grande and Jaén. There is a **Dircetur** tourist office at Marginal 176.

Gocta

There are many interesting options for walking in the surrounding hills, covered with patches of cloudforest and a good deal of undeveloped archaeology. The main attraction in the area is the magnificent **Gocta Waterfall** (see box, page 516). The best access is from Pedro Ruiz; many people travel on to Chachapoyas without realising that they have already passed by the waterfall. From Pedro Ruiz, take the Chachapoyas road for 16 km to **Cocahuayco** where there are two roads up to Gocta, along either bank of the Cocahuayco

Gocta Falls

In 2002 the German explorer Stefan Ziemendorff came across a waterfall in Amazonas department, near the Pedro Ruiz–Chachapoyas road, called Gocta. Its whereabouts was not revealed by locals who feared that a mermaid living in the waters below the fall would curse whoever disclosed its location. Ziemendorff has not been so timid, but there is no agreement on where the falls rank in the world's waterfall hierarchy. At 771 m (2530 ft: the upper waterfall is 231 m, the lower waterfall is 540 m), it could be the third highest, or the fifth, or the 14th, but Miles Buesst, formerly of South American Explorers in Lima, is certain of one thing: they are "utterly spectacular and well worth the visit: at one lookout there are eight separate waterfalls visible and The World Waterfall Database gives Gocta itself a 'scenic rating' of 96%, which I think is ungenerous!"

The most amazing overall view of Gocta is from a natural lookout point about 4.5 km from San Pablo. From about 5 km away, you can see both tiers completely as well as their forest surroundings. The village itself is some 300 m above the river, with views of several large waterfalls, canyons and the Río Utucubamba Valley, but the Gocta Waterfall is just around a bend. The approach to Gocta is relatively level, climbing gradually in 6 km to the bottom of the upper tier on a well maintained trail. About 4.5 km from the village is the turn-off to the right to the lookout. Most go first to the overlook, then head back up the 100 m to the trail to the base of the

upper tier. It takes about 1-1½ hours to walk to the lookout, then another 30 minutes to the upper tier. From there you have beautiful views from the edge of the 550-m drop and of the upper tier, the pools between the tiers and the surrounding woods. There are giant ferns that appear like small palm trees and the famous cock-of-the-rock.

Cocachimba is on the opposite side of the canyon from San Pablo, 150-200 m above the river. From the village you can see Gocta about 2-3 km away. It's an 8-km walk from there to the bottom of the lower tier. The walk goes down a well maintained trail, across two foot bridges and through some steep gullies. It takes about 1½-2½ hours, depending on your fitness. From the base there is an impressive view of the lower tier and a pool where one can swim (the water is cold and there are usually biting insects). From here it is possible to cross the river and climb the other side to the the top of the lower tier and the other viewpoints. An avid walker can possibly hike out of Cocachimba to the upper tier and back in one good day.

Jeffrey Powers of **Norton Rats** in Cuzco (who wrote most of the above description and who is planning to open a hotel near San Pablo) recommends starting the hike at San Pablo and finishing at Cocachimba. You can arrange transport to return to San Pablo at the end of the hike if staying there, or a ride to San Pablo to begin the hike if lodged in Cocachimba. The ride is about 30 minutes. This is a great way to get the full experience.

River. The first turn-off leads up to the village of **San Pablo de Valera** (1900 m, 6 km, 20 minutes by car) from which trails lead to the best overall view of the falls and to the base of the upper waterfall. The second turn-off, 100 m further on the main road, leads up to the village of **Cocachimba** (5.3 km, also 20 minutes), from which the base of the lower waterfall can be reached. Both routes are delightful and it is possible to connect from one trail to the other. Both communities are developing their tourist facilities fast and the district is implementing a project which includes a bridge across the river at the bottom of the falls. They offer similar services: entry fee is US$1.80, local guides cost US$7, horses can be hired for US$8.75 in San Pablo (ask if they can go all the way), and rubber boots and rain ponchos are available for rent (it is always wet by the falls). See Sleeping and Transport, below, for details of these services.

Besides the waterfall another area worth visiting from San Pablo is a plateau about 600-800 m above the village. There are rolling, grassy hills surrounded by natural rock formations and woods (with, reportedly, spectacled bears). Several large caves are found here, including **La Caverna de la Vieja Tomasa**, extending a couple of kilometres into the mountains. The area is largely unexplored.

Other beautiful waterfalls in the area include **Yumbilla**, 2½ to three hours' walk from the village of Cuispes (30 minutes' drive from Pedro Ruiz, US$1.50 by mototaxi), a multi-section waterfall with a total drop of 896 m (one section is about 250 m high; the water only flows seasonally) and the 150-m-high **Chinata** falls, two hours' walk from the village of San Carlos (one hour drive or two hours' walk from Pedro Ruiz).

Pomacochas Lake, 2150 m above sea level, is near the town of **Florida** along the road from Pedro Ruiz to Tarapoto. The blue-green water is surrounded by totora reeds. It's not possible to walk around the lake but boat trips across and around it can be arranged from the pier at US$1 per person, minimum five people. Take a combi from Pedro Ruiz to Florida or Balsapata (one hour, US$1.75), or take a taxis, US$15 with 1½-hour wait; there are good views of the lake from the road. There are a couple of hotels in the town and restaurants serve locally caught fish.

Near Florida is the **Río Chido** trail, a famous birdwatching site with some rare species, including the marvelous spatuletail hummingbird. Access is five minutes before the high point on the road to Florida, at San Ignacio. A highly recommended guide is Dilberto Faustino, who is very enthusiastic and knowledgeable. A second site to see the marvelous spatuletail is a 4-ha plot owned by Santos Montenegro. Take a mototaxi from Pomacochas to the *cruce* opposite the police control, US$0.50. Santos and his brother Wilmer guide birders to the sites where the birds are most likely to be feeding. The best months are May-July. A donation will help this private reserve to protect this unique bird. Pomacochas community has a reforestation project for trees favoured by hummingbirds on the road towards Pedro Ruiz. It is operated with the help of **ECOAN** (Asociación Ecosistemas Andinos, www.ecoanperu.org), which has various bird conservation projects in the Río Marañón and Alto Mayo corridor and others throughout Peru.

Chachapoyas Region listings

For Sleeping and Eating price codes and other relevant information, see pages 38-44.

Sleeping

Celendín *p504*

C-E Hostal Celendín, Unión 305, Plaza de Armas, T076-555041, hcgustavosd1@ hotmail.com. In a building with a central patio and wooden stairs. Some rooms have plaza view, hot water, TV, colourful bed linen, pleasant. It has 2 restaurants: **Rinconcito Shilico**, 2 de Mayo 816, for *parrilladas*, pizzas and seafood, and **Pollas a la brasa Gusys**.
E-F Loyer's, José Gálvez 410, T076-555210. The patio has a wooden balcony all round, cheaper without bath, nice place. All meals are charged extra.
F Hostal Imperial, Jr Dos de Mayo 568, 2 blocks from the plaza, T076-555492. Large rooms with bath, good mattresses, hot water, colour TV, a decent choice.
F Maxmar, Dos de Mayo 349, T076-555330. Cheaper without bath, hot shower extra, basic, clean, parking, good value, owners Francisco and Luis are very helpful. A kitchen and breakfast service are planned.
F Mi Posada, Pardo 388, next to Atahualpa bus, T074-979-758674. New in 2009, with breakfast, TV, soft beds, small cheerful rooms, family atmosphere.
F Raymi Wasi, Jr José Gálvez 420, T076-551133. With electric shower, cheaper without, TV, large rooms, has patio, quiet, parking, good value, restaurant and karaoke.
Orange, Jr Unión 333, T076-770590, www.celendinperu. com. The Dutch-Peruvian owners of the original *hostal* in the centre are builing a new place on the edge of town. See the website for developments. Meanwhile you can ask for advice on the area by emailing Susan van der Wielen in advance. There is 1 bedroom available in their home, but you must check first if it is free (price on request). This is also the HQ for **Proyecto Yannick**, a charity for children and the families of children with Down's Syndrome, www.proyectoyannick.org. If you would like to volunteer or help in other ways, see the website or contact Orange.

Chachapoyas and around
p505, map p506

B-C Casa Vieja, Chincha Alta 569, T041-477353, www.casaviejaperu.com. In a converted old house with lovely courtyard, very nicely decorated, all rooms different, family atmosphere, living room and *comedor* with open fire, includes breakfast, Wi-Fi, art gallery and library. Repeatedly recommended.
B-C Casona Monsante, Amazonas 746, T041-477702, www.lacasonamonsante.com. Converted colonial house with patio, comfortable rooms decorated with antiques, Wi-Fi in lobby, breakfast available.
B-C Villa París, 2 km from centre off road to Pedro Ruiz, T041-792332, www.hostalvilla paris.com. Comfortable rooms and cabins in a rural setting, Includes breakfast, good restaurant, small pool, nice grounds, parking.
C Puma Urco, Amazonas 833, T041-477871. Comfortable rooms, includes breakfast, Wi-Fi, **Café Café** next door, hotel and café receive good reports, run tours.
C-D Hostal Revash, Grau 517, Plaza de Armas, T041-477391, www.chachapoyaskuelap. com.pe. Traditional house with patio, steaming hot showers, Wi-Fi, breakfast available, friendly helpful owners, good local information, popular. Operate tours and sell local crafts.
D Gocta, Amazonas 721, T041-477698, carlaam6@hotmail.com. Brightly painted rooms with private bath, hot water, Wi-Fi, opened in 2009.
D Gran Vilaya, Ayacucho 755, T041-477664, www.hotelvilaya.com. Comfortable rooms, firm beds, includes breakfast, Wi-Fi, parking, English spoken. Knowledgeable owner, Gumercindo Zegarra.
D Las Orquídeas, Ayacucho 1231, T041-478271, www.hostallasorquideas.com.

Converted contemporary home, large rooms, includes breakfast, private bath, hot water, large garden, Wi-Fi, family run, friendly.
D-E Belén, Jr Ortiz Arrieta 540, Plaza de Armas, T041-477830, www.hostalbelen.com. With private bath, hot water, nicely furnished, pleasant sitting room overlooking the plaza, good value.
E El Dorado, Ayacucho 1062, T041-477047, ivvanovt@hotmail.com. With bathroom, electric shower, clean and helpful.
E Vista Hermosa, Puno 285-295, T041-477526. Nice ample rooms, some have balconies, private bath, electric shower, Wi-Fi, good value.
F Rumi Huasi, Ortiz Arrieta 365, T041-791100. With private bath, cheaper without, electric shower, small rooms, opened in 2009.

Levanto *p506*

D Levanto MS Lodge, behind the church, T041-478838, www.marvelousspatuletail.net. Joint venture between the community and **Chachapoyas Tours**. 2 circular buildings with tall, thatched roofs, **G** pp in small dorm (take your own sleeping bag), 2 basic, external bathrooms with hot shower, lounge with fireplace and kitchen, meals US$6-8. Volunteer programmes and tours, horses available for day trips. Advance booking required.

Kuélap *p508, map p508*

When walking up to Kuélap from Tingo, the last house to the right of the track (El Bebedero, just above a small spring) offers accommodation: bed, breakfast and evening meal for US$6; good food, friendly and helpful. A bit further, on the left, 100 m below the ruins, is the **Instituto Nacional de Cultura** (INC) hostel. It's a clean dormitory with room for about 12 people, in a lovely setting, US$1.75 per person, but may be fully booked by archaeologists, no running water (please conserve the rainwater in the buckets), simple meals may be available from the caretaker for US$1. There is free camping outside the hostel. If these options are booked, Gabriel Portocarrero, the caretaker at the ruins, and his friendly family run a very basic hostel just below the ruins, sleeping on a mat on the floor. Otherwise walk 2 hrs to María, below.

Tingo

A Estancia Chillo, Km 46 Carretera Chachapoyas-Leymebamba, 5 km south of Tingo on the east bank of the Utcubamba, T01-265 9158 (Lima), www.estancia chillo.com. On a 9-ha farm, includes dinner and breakfast, private bath, hot water, 24-hr electricity, transport service, tours, trekking, horse riding. Owner Oscar Arce knows the area well, he is a reliable Spanish-speaking guide. You can walk from Chillo to Kuélap, it is shorter than from Tingo and you can take an alternative trail back via Nogalcucho.
E-F Hospedaje Tingo, on the main highway, just north of the Río Tingo, T041-941 732251. Simple adequate rooms with bath, electric shower, restaurant.

F-G Hospedaje León, Jr Saenz Peña s/n, along the south bank of the Río Tingo, just upriver from the highway, T041-941-715685, hildegardlen@yahoo.es. Basic, shared bathroom, electric shower, guiding service, can arrange horses, friendly, run by Lucho León, who is knowledgeable.

Choctámal

C Choctámal MS Lodge, 3 km outside Choctámal towards Kuélap, T041-478838, www.marvelousspatuletail.com. Joint venture between the community and Chachapoyas Tours. Heated rooms, some have hot tub. Breakfast US$6, lunch and dinner US$8 each. In a lovely setting with great views, telescope for birdwatching (may see the endangered Marvelous Spatuletail hummingbird) or stargazing. Arrange tours, good day hikes. Advance booking required.
F Gran Shubet, at the entrance to town from Tingo. Very basic, shared bath, restaurant.

María

F Hospedajes There are 10 basic places to stay in town, some with private bath and hot water, meals are also available.

Leymebamba *p511*

The phone numbers listed correspond to the community phones closest to each hotel. These numbers will change when new private lines are installed (supposedly in 2010).
B-C La Casona, Jr Amazonas 223, T041-830106, www.casonadeleymebamba.com. Nicely refurbished old house, attractive common area with large balcony, includes breakfast, simple rooms with bath and hot water, hanging orchid garden, arrange tours and horses, very friendly. Recommended.
E Laguna de los Cóndores, Jr Amazonas 320, half a block from the plaza, T041-830104, www.loscondoreshostal.com. With private bath (cheaper without), electric shower, nice courtyard, friendly, also runs the shelter at Laguna de los Cóndores.

E La Petaca, Jr Amazonas 426, on the plaza, T041-830105. Good rooms with private bath and hot water, friendly owner.
F There are a couple of very basic *hospedajes* along 16 de Julio below the plaza.

Northwest of Chachapoyas *p512*
D Hostal Kuélap, Garcilaso de la Vega 452, Lamud, on the plaza. Clean, basic, friendly, cheaper without bath or hot water.
G Hostal Jucusbamba, in Luya. Basic accommodation.

East and north of Chachapoyas *p515*
Mendoza

E Prince Azul, Jr Amazonas 219, opposite the market, T041-504047. With bath, hot water, cheaper with cold water.
F Paraíso, Jr Huambo 314, opposite Restaurante Tívoli, T041-504025. With bath, hot water, cheaper with shared bath and cold shower.

North of Chachapoyas *p515*
Pedro Ruiz

E Casablanca, Av Marginal 122, the main highway road to the Chachapoyas turning, T041-830171. Private bathroom, hot water, comfortable and friendly. Also has a decent restaurant and opens early for breakfast.
E-F Amazonense, Av Marginal 146, near Policía Nacional on the main road, T01-998 811799. Simple rooms with bath, hot water, cheaper in older rooms with cold water, clean, small garden, friendly and helpful.

Gocta *p515*
San Pablo and Cocachimba both offer basic accommodation.

San Pablo de Valera

Luis Chuquimez and his wife Felipa offer lodging in their house a few metres from the main plaza, about US$2 for a bed. They have a telephone (satellite) and serve meals for US$1.50. There are a couple of similar places to eat or sleep available upon enquiry.

Cocachimba

Besides the hotel below, there are several less expensive locally run hostals. There are also a few humble restaurants where a meal costs about US$5-7.

A Gocta Andes Lodge, T042-522225, www.goctalodge.com (current name). Under same ownership as **Río Shilcayo** near Tarapoto. Beautifully located lodge overlooking the waterfall, luxuriously furnished bedrooms and en suite bathrooms, price includes breakfast. Packages available with other hotels in the group.

Pomacochas Lake

A-B Puerto Pumas, Carretera Fernando Belaúnde Terry Km 326, Florida, T01-242 5550, www.puertopalmeras.com.pe/pumas.htm. In the same group as **Puerto Palmeras** in Tarapoto, rooms with comfy beds, hot water and art gallery theme.
F-G Hostal Oro Verde and **Pensión Caja-marquino**, along the highway in Florida, basic.

🍴 Eating

Celendín *p504*

Few places open for breakfast unless you want to risk the main daily market (a new site for which is under construction).
🍴-🍴 La Reserve, José Gálvez 313. Good quality and value, extensive menu, from Italian to *chifa*.
🍴 Carbón y Leña, 2 de Mayo 410. For chicken, *parrillas* and pizzas.
🍴 Juguería Carolin, Bolognesi 384. One of the few places open early, from 0700-2200 daily, for juices, breakfasts and *caldos*.
🍴 Orange King, Ayacucho 491. Café, bar and disco, with good cocktails, snacks, music and lounge. Very friendly owner, Vilzeth Vásquez Bazán, has information on trekking in the area. See **Orange**, under Sleeping, above.

Chachapoyas and around

p505, map p506
🍴 El Tejado, Santo Domingo 424. Mon-Fri 1200-1600, 1900-2100, Sat-Sun midday only, but hours vary. Excellent upscale *comida criolla*, *tacu tacu* is the house specialty. Large portions, attentive service, nice atmosphere and setting around a garden. Also serves good value *menú ejecutivo* on weekdays. Recommended.
🍴 La Real Cecina, Jr Hermosura 676, Plazuela Burgos. Daily 0800-2300. Good for regional specialties; also lunch *menú* on weekdays.
🍴 La Tushpa, Jr Ortiz Arrieta 753. Mon-Sat 1300-2300. Good grilled meat and *platos criollos*, wine list, very clean kitchen, attentive service.
🍴-🍴 Romana, Ayacucho 1013. Daily 0700-2300. Choice of set meals and à la carte, attentive service.
🍴 El Edén, Grau y Ayacucho by the market. Sun-Thu 0700-2100, Fri 0700-1800. Good vegetarian, large helpings.
🍴 Mari Pizza, Ayacucho 832. Daily 1630-0100. Good pizza, home-made pasta and fresh fruit juices.
🍴 Matalaché, Ayacucho y Unión. Mon-Sat 0700-2100, Sun 0800-1600. Famous for their huge *milanesa* (breaded beef); also serves *menú* and à la carte.
🍴 Sabores del Perú, Jr 2 de Mayo 321. Daily 0700-2200. Breakfast, good value and quality *menú* at lunch, à la carte at night.

Cafés

Dulcería Santa Elena, Amazonas 800. Daily 0900-2230. Old-fashioned home-made desserts and sweets.
Fusiones, Chincha Alta 445. Mon-Sat 0730-1130, 1600-2100. Breakfast, fair-trade coffee, juices, snacks, Wi-Fi, book exchange, volunteer opportunities.
Heladería San Antonio, 2 de Mayo 521 and Amazonas 856. Good home-made ice cream, try the *lúcuma* and *guanábana* flavours.
Panadería Café San José, Ayacucho 816. Mon-Sat 0700-1300, 1500-2200. Bakery and café, good breakfasts, sweets and snacks.

Leymebamba *p511*

❦**Cely Pizza's**, Jr La Verdad 530, 2 blocks from Plaza de Armas. Daily 0700-1900. Good food, value and service, pizza and vegetarian dishes with advance notice, great for breakfast, clean and very friendly. Recommended.

❦**El Sabor Tropical**, 16 de Julio. Good chicken and chips, friendly.

Northwest of Chachapoyas *p512*

❦**María**, Lamud, down from **Hostal Kuélap**. Cheap, friendly and obliging, steak and chips is recommended, popular.

East and north of Chachapoyas *p515*

Some simple places in Mendoza and Pedro Ruiz: in the latter **Chuquichaka**, Marginal 154, is much the best place to eat, serving huge portions.

❀ Festivals and events

Celendín *p504*

16-29 Jul Celendín hosts its **Virgen del Carmen** festival. Bullfights with matadores from Spain and cock fighting are all part of the well-attended celebrations. All hotels put their prices up at this time.

Chachapoyas and around
p505, map p506

1st week of Jun Raymi Llacta and Semana Turística.

Mid Aug Fiestas Patronales in honour of Virgen Asunta.

▲ Activities and tours

Chachapoyas and around
p505, map p506

Most of the attractions can be visited on a tour. Prices vary according to season (higher Jul-Sep), distance to a site, number of passengers and whether meals are included. Full-day trips cost US$12.50-25 per person. Some operators have their own vehicles, but

also use taxis and combis, depending on the number of passengers. Several operators have daily departures to Kuélap and Gocta. Other popular destinations are Karajía, Quiocta, Leymebamba, and Revash. All-inclusive trekking tours cost about US$45 per person per day, Gran Vilaya and Laguna de los Cóndores are most popular.

Andes Tours, at Hostal Revash (see Sleeping above). Daily trips to Kuélap and Gocta, other tours to ruins and caves in the area and trekking trips to Gran Vilaya, Laguna de los Cóndores and less travelled destinations. The latter combine travel by car, on horseback and walking.

Chachapoyas Tours, Santo Domingo 432, T041- 478078 www.kuelapperu.com, in the USA contact **Northern Circuit of Peru**, T1-866-396 9582 or T1-407-325 0499. Reliable, with 20 years' experience, benefiting local communities, all-inclusive tours with accommodation at their lodges in Choctámal and Levanto, multilingual staff and guides, volunteer opportunities, good service. Recommended.

Kuelap Adventure, Pje Tupac Amaru 141, T041-478956, www.kuelapadventure.com. Multiple-day tours throughout northern Peru.

Martín Chumbi, is a local guide, contact through Restaurant Las Rocas, Jr Ayacucho 932, on the Plaza.

Nuevos Caminos, at Café Fusiones, T041-479170, www.nuevoscaminostravel.com. Alternative community tourism throughout northern Peru, volunteer opportunities.

Turismo Explorer, Jr Grau 509 and at Hotel Puma Urcu, T041-478162, www.turismo explorerperu.com. Daily tours to Kuélap, Gocta and other destinations, trekking tours including Laguna de los Cóndores and other archaeological sites outside Leymebamba, transport service.

Vilaya Tours, c/o Gran Hotel Vilaya, T041-477506, www.vilayatours.com. All-inclusive treks to off-the-beaten-path destinations throughout northern Peru. Run by Robert Dover, a very experienced and knowledgeable British guide, book ahead. Recommended.

Northwest of Chachapoyas *p512*
Angel Mestanza Bobadilla, Garcilaso de la Vega 458, Lamud, T041-780213/780223. He is a photographer and is recommended. Reasonable prices. One trip is to local caves (be prepared to get muddy; take a torch); also to waterfalls.

East and north of Chachapoyas *p515*
Augustus Grandez Loja, Mendoza, a local guide, can take travellers around the little-known environs of Mendoza. He can provide horses for longer treks. Ask for him in town.

⊖ Transport

Celendín *p504*
Bus
To **Cajamarca**, 107 km, 3½ hrs: with **Royal Palace's**, Jr Unión y José Gálvez, by Plaza de Armas, at 1400 daily; also **CABA** 2 a day, and **Rojas** 3 a day. Cars to Cajamarca leave when full from Ovalo Agusto Gil, Cáceres y Amazonas, 2½ hrs, US$6.75 per person. From the same place they go to **Chachapoyas**, 6 hrs, US$18 per person; also **Chachapoyas Express** combis to **Leymebamba**, Thu and Sun, 0800, US$7.15. Also here is **Móvil**, to Cajamarca daily 1500, US$3.50, to Chachapoyas, 0900, US$12.50, 9 hrs. **Virgen del Carmen**, Cáceres 117 by Ovalo A Gil, T076-792918, to Chachapoyas, daily except Tue and Sat at 1000, US$11, 6 hrs to Leymebamba, US$7.

Chachapoyas and around
p505, map p506
Air
There are no scheduled flights to Chachapoyas. The last attempt at a regular service, in 2010, was cancelled after a short while owing to lack of passengers.

Bus
To **Chiclayo**, 9 hrs, **Trujillo**, 12 hrs, and **Lima** (20-22 hrs), the best option is **Móvil Tours**, Libertad 464, T041-478545; to Lima daily at 1000, US$41; to Trujillo US$22, and Chiclayo US$16, both at 1930. **Trans Zelada**, Ortiz Arrieta 310, T041-478066, to Lima daily at 1500, US$40 (*cama*), US$32 (*semi cama*), to Trujillo US$21, to Chiclayo US$15. **Civa**, Salamanca y Ortiz Arrieta, T041-478048, to Lima at 1600, US$29, to Chiclayo at 1815, US$11. **Turismo Kuélap**, Salamanca 726, T041-478128, to Chiclayo Tue and Sat at 1900, other days at 2000, US$15. **GH Bus**, Jr Unión 330, T041-479200, to Lima at 1000, US$37.50, to Chiclayo at 1900, US$15. Will sell ticket on a connecting bus to **Tarapoto**, but involves a long wait in Pedro Ruiz. To **Celendín**, 8-9 hrs, and **Cajamarca**, 11-12 hrs: **Móvil Tours**, at 0600 daily, Celendín US$12.50, Cajamarca US$18; to Celendín with **Virgen del Carmen**, Salamanca 956, Mon at 1700, Thu and Sat at 0500, US$11. Cars to Celendín, **Raymi Express**, Salamanca 909, US$18, 8 hrs, best try early in the morning or arrange ahead. To **Pedro Ruiz** (1 hr), for connections to Chiclayo, Jaén, or Tarapoto, cars leave from Grau 310 y Salamanca, 0600-2100 (2100-2300 they depart from Grau in front of the market), US$4; combis every 2 hrs 0600-1800, from Ortiz Arrieta 370, US$2, also from Libertad y Ortiz Arrieta. To **Bagua Grande** for connections to Jaén, cars from Grau between Libertad and Salamanca 0600-2100 and Grau by the market 2100-0600, US$8, 2 hrs (in 2010 the road between Pedro Ruiz and Bagua Grande was under construction and daytime transit was restricted).

For **Kuélap**, US$7.15, 3½ hrs (will only go to Kuélap if they have enough passengers); **María** US$5.40, 3 hrs; **Lónguita** US$4.30, 2½ hrs; **Choctámal** US$3.60, 2 hrs; **Tingo** US$2.90, 1½ hrs: with **Roller's**, Grau corner Salamanca, combi or car, at 0300 (return from Kuelap around 1200); with **Sr José Cruz**, Grau 331, combi or car at 0530 (returns from María at 0800); with **Trans Shubet**, Pasaje Reyes off Grau, cars to Lónguita around 1400-1500. To **Tingo**, also with **Brisas del Utcubamba**, Grau 332, cars bound for Magdalena, 0500-1800 or transport going to Yerbabuena or

Leymebamba. Vehicles going to Chachapoyas pass Tingo from 0500. To **Choctámal**, also service going to Pizuquia (see below). To **Levanto**, cars from Av Cuarto Centenario y Sociego at the southeast end of town, daily 1200-1300, US$2.90; taxi return with a wait US$25. To **Jalca Grande**, from Jr Hermosura 325, 2 combis depart around 1400 and 1600 (return 0300-0400), US$4.30, 3 hrs. To **Yerbabuena**, from Grau below Libertad, combis at 0900 and 1200 (return 1200 and 1500) US$2.85, 2 hrs; cars around 0700-0800, US$3.60. For **Revash**, Comité Santo Tomás, Grau by Pasaje Reyes, to **Santo Tomás**, at 1000, 1300 and 1500 (return at 0300, 0400 and 0500), US$4.30, 3 hrs; get off at **Cruce de Revash** (Puente Santo Tomás), US$4.30, 2½ hrs; or with the same company to **San Bartolo** at 1400 (return 0600), US$4.30, 3 hrs. For **Cerro Olán**, Comité Santo Tomás, at 1200 and 1400 (return at 0300 and 0400) to **Montevideo**, US$3.60, and **San Pedro de Utac**, US$5.35. To **Leymebamba**, 83 km, 2½ hrs, reserve ahead, transport fills quickly: **Transportes Karlita**, Salamanca cuadra 9, combis at 1200 and 1600, US$3.60, and cars as they fill early in the morning US$7.15; with **Raymi Express**, Salamanca 909, cars as they fill, US$5.40; also combis from Grau below Libertad, at 1400 and 1600, US$3.60; **Móvil Tours**, Libertad 464, bus to Cajamarca at 0600, will sell tickets to Leymebamba if not full, US$3.60. To **Luya** and **Lamud**, from Libertad y Chincha Alta, cars 0400-1800, US$2.85, 1 hr to Lamud, same price to Luya. For **Gran Vilaya**: to **Cohechán**, cars from Luya, 0600-1700, US$1.80; to **Inguilpata**, cars from Jr Unión cuadra 3, near GH Bus, daily except Thu at 1300, US$2.90; to **Colcamar**, with Roller's, Grau y Salamanca, at 1100, US$2.85 and combis from Ortiz Arrieta 370 at 1500 and 1600 (both return at 0800), US$2.85, 1½ hrs. To **Huaylla Belén** (US$8.90) and **Congón** (US$10.70), car from Panadería Café San José, Ayacucho 816, at 0330; combis to San Juan de Rejo in the

Pizuquia area, US$6.45, 4 hrs, go by **Choctámal**, and the **Yumal Pass**, US$5.35, 3½ hrs, with Sr José Cruz, Grau 334, at 0330; **Roller's**, Grau y Salamanca, at 0330 and **Trans Shubet**, Pasaje Reyes y Grau, at 0400. To **Mendoza** (86 km), Trans Zelada, Ortiz Arrieta 310, bus at 1800, US$5.40, 4 hrs; cars 0500-1900, with Guayabamba, Ortiz Arrieta 372, US$9, 3½ hrs.Taxis may be hired from the plaza for any local destination.

Car
There are a petrol stations in Tingo and Leymebamba (not always open). Otherwise there is fuel in Chacha.

Leymebamba p511
To **Chachapoyas**, 2½ hrs, reserve ahead, transport fills quickly: **Transportes Karlita**, Jr Amazonas corner16 de Julio on the plaza, combis at 0400 and 0500, US$3.60, and cars as they fill early in the morning, US$7.15; with **Raymi Express**, Jr 16 de Julio at the plaza, cars as they fill, US$5.40; also combis from Jr Bolívar 347, at 0500 and 1400, US$3.60; **Móvil Tours**, Jr Amazonas 420, Cajamarca–Chachapoyas bus passes around 1500, US$3.60. To **Celendín**, 6-7 hrs, and **Cajamarca**, 9-10 hrs, book ahead: **Móvil Tours**, Jr Amazonas 420, T041-830097, passes Leymebamba about 0800, Celendín US$8.90, Cajamarca US$12.50; **Virgen del Carmen** buses will pick up passengers in Leymebamba if they have room, but you cannot book ahead; **Chachapoyas Express**, 16 de Julio below the plaza, combis to Celendín, Tue and Fri at 0600, US$7.15.

East and north of Chachapoyas p515
For **Purunllacta**: transport to **Cheto** from Salamanca y Jr Hermosura, Mon-Fri 0700-1400, cars US$2.90 and combis US$2.15.

From **Mendoza**, Trans Zelada buses, esq TRM con Braulio Redondo, run to **Chachapoyas**, 0900 daily, US$5.40, 4 hrs. Guayabamba cars from opposite Banco de la Nación, 0500-1900, US$9, 3½ hrs. To **Limabamba**, 3 daily between 1300 and 1500, 2 hrs, US$1.20.

To and from **Pedro Ruiz** there are many buses on the **Chiclayo**, **Tarapoto**, 8-9 hrs, and **Chachapoyas** routes. All pass through town. There is no way to reserve a seat and buses are often full. Bus companies are along Av Marginal on either side of the junction to Chachapoyas. **Móvil**, Av Cahuide 653/Av Marginal, T041-830085, is the choice company for buses to **Lima** and **Tarapoto**. To **Chachapoyas**, 54 km, 1 hr, cars 0600-2100, US$4 and combis US$2, both leave from the road to Chacha past the bridge. To **Bagua Grande**, cars US$4.30, 1 hr. To **Jaén**, Trans Fernández bus originating in Tarapoto passes Pedro Ruiz about 1400-1500 or take a car to Bagua Grande and another car from there. To **Nueva Cajamarca**, cars US$9, combis US$5.35, 3-3½ hrs. Cars to **Moyobamba**, US$10.70, 4 hrs.

Gocta *p515*
For Gocta: in Pedro Ruiz go to where the cars leave for Churuja (in the same direction). Either hire the whole car, US$9, or wait till the car fills to **San Pablo de Valera**, US$2.15, or to **Cocachimba**, US$1.80. A taxi to either Cocachimba or San Pablo US$25 with 5-6 hrs wait. To hire a car (with driver) from Chachapoyas will cost about US$20-30. You can hire one of the *autos* that run passengers between Chacha and Pedro Ruiz which line up by the central market. Chachapoyas operators offer tours to the falls US$12.50-21.

For either Cocachimba or San Pablo you go to the village of Cocahuayco (see page 515) where there are turn-offs to the respective villages. From Chachapoyas it is about 35 km, 1 hr, to Cocahuayco, from Pedro Ruiz it is 16 km, 30 mins.

❻ Directory

Celendín *p504*
Banks MultiRed ATM beside Banco de la Nación on 2 de Mayo may not accept all foreign cards; take cash. **Internet and telephone** Internet offices all round the centre. **Locutorio Roma**, 2 de Mayo on the plaza, also has phones. **Post** Jr Unión 415.

Chachapoyas and around
p505, map p506
Banks BCP, Ortiz Arrieta 576, Plaza de Armas. Visa and MasterCard ATM, changes US$ cash. **Banco de la Nación**, Ayacucho corner 2 de Mayo, Visa ATM. **Isamax** clothing store, Ayacucho 940, Plaza de Armas, Mon-Sat 0900-1300, 1500-1800, Sun 0900-1300, US$ cash only, fair rates. **Hostal Revash** changes US$ cash and sometimes euro. There is nowhere to change TCs. Exchange rates in Chachapoyas are lower than in other cities. **Internet** Many places around the plaza and elsewhere, US$0.35 per hr. **Laundry** Clean, Amazonas 817, US$1.40 per kg. **Post** Jr Ortiz Arrieta 632.

Leymebamba *p511*
Banks There are no banks, ATMs or *cambios* in Leymebamba, bring soles. At a pinch, try Hotel La Casona. **Internet** A couple of places around the plaza, US$0.35 per hr.

East and north of Chachapoyas *p515*
Banks Banco de la Nación, in Pedro Ruiz, Visa ATM and changes US$ cash. Better exchange rates in Chachapoyas.

To Ecuador and to the Amazon

The Carretera Marginal Fernando Belaúnde Terry toll road joins the northern coast with the jungle. From Pedro Ruiz (see page 515), it goes west for 65 km to Bagua Grande, at first through a lovely narrow gorge, the ridges covered with lush cloudforest, then along the broad and fertile lower Utcubamba Valley. It then crosses the Marañón at Corral Quemado. Further west at Chamaya a road branches north to Jaén and San Ignacio, then crosses the Peru-Ecuador border at La Balsa. This is a worthwhile scenic route for travelling from Chachapoyas or the jungle to Ecuador without going down to the coast. To the east of Pedro Ruiz the road climbs to the Abra Patricia Pass and descends through lovely cloudforest to Moyobamba, Tarapoto and Yurimaguas. ▸▸ *For listings, see pages 533-540.*

Chachapoyas - Vilcabamba (Ecuador)

Border essentials: Peru–Ecuador

Namballe–Zumba

The border is at La Balsa, with a simple comedor, a few small shops and money changers, but no lodgings. To leave Peru head directly to immigration; ask for the officer if he is not at his desk. When entering Peru, see immigration first, then get a stamp from the PNP and return to immigration. For Ecuadorean customs and immigration, also ask around if staff are not in their offices. Although small and relaxed, in 2010 this border provided all necessary services to cross with your own vehicle.

Transport From San Ignacio to Namballe and La Balsa, cars leave from Jr Porvenir (cuadra 2) y Jr Santa Rosa: to Namballe US$3.60, 1¾ hours; to La Balsa US$4.30, two hours. In Ecuador, rancheras run from La Balsa to Zumba at 1230, 1730 and 1930, US$1.75, 1¾ hours; Zumba to La Balsa 0800, 1430 and 1730. To get to Vilcabamba in one day, best leave Jaén by 0600 or San Ignacio by 0900. It is a long tiring journey and although the Jaén–Loja road is being improved in both countries, parts are subject to damage after rain. You may have to stay in Namballe or Zumba. Travelling to Peru, you should leave Vilcabamba by 0600 to reach San Ignacio the same day. There are Ecuadorean military controls before and after Zumba; keep your passport to hand.

To Ecuador → For listings, see pages 533-540.

The Baguas

The first town of note heading west from Pedro Ruiz is **Bagua Grande** (altitude: 450 m; phone code: 041). It is hot and dusty, sprawled along its main street, Avenida Chachapoyas, where most services are located (**E Hotel Bagua Grande** reported good; for a meal, try **El Chacho**, M Muro 357, open all day, clean and popular). The town is not safe however and suffers water shortages, Pedro Ruiz or Jaén are more pleasant places to spend the night. If changing buses in Bagua Grande note that there are several terminals, see Transport, page 537. In 2010 there was major reconstruction work on the road between Pedro Ruiz and Bagua Grande, with restricted travel times.

Some 24 km west of Bagua Grande, a side road heads north to Sarameriza, the first port on the Marañón (see below); off this road is **Bagua Chica**. Both Bagua Chica and Bagua Grande may be referred to as just 'Bagua', pay attention so you are not taken to the wrong one. The road north to Ecuador starts at **Chamaya**, 50 km west of Bagua Grande and 18 km south of Jaén; cars from Chamaya run to Jaén all day, US$1, 15 minutes.

Jaén and around → Colour map 1, B3. Phone code: 076. Population: 100,000. Altitude: 740 m.

Although it was founded in 1536, Jaén retains little of its colonial character. Rather, it is the modern and prosperous centre of a rich agricultural region producing rice, coffee, and cocoa (also, reputedly, opium poppies). It is a hot, noisy, busy but friendly place. The local **festival** of Señor de Huamantanga on 14 September is widely attended. **Municipal Tourist Office** ① Oficina de Cultura, Bolívar 1520 y Pardo Miguel, p 3, Mon-Fri 0800-1300, 1400-1645.

A colourful modern **cathedral** dominates the large plaza around which most services of interest to the visitor are clustered. A **museum** ① Instituto 4 de Junio, Hermógenes Mejía s/n, south of centre, mototaxi US$0.40, displays pre-Columbian artefacts from the Pakamuros culture.

To bathe in the **Marañón**, take a combi from the corner of Cajamarca and Eloy Ureta to Bellavista (40 minutes, US$0.50). From here it is a 45-minute walk beside rice paddies to the river, ask for directions. Swimming is possible but mind the strong current. Many locals go there on Sundays. A motorboat across the Marañón costs US$0.45 one way.

Jaén to the border → *Colour map 1, B3.*

A scenic road runs north from Jaén through rice fields. Just past Ambato-Tamborapa, 40 km north of Jaén, an unpaved road turns west towards La Coipa, Rumpite and **Tabaconas**. About 10 minutes along this road is good dry-forest birdwatching. Some 20 km further north, another short detour off the main road goes west towards Chirinos for more birdwatching in an area of rice paddies and mango trees. In 2010, the main road was paved as far north as Puerto Perico, 55 km from Jaén. Beyond, it runs alongside the Río Chinchipe to Puerto Ciruelos, where it leaves the river and climbs through forested hills to **San Ignacio** (phone code: 076, altitude: 1300 m), on route to the border with Ecuador. This is a friendly town with steep streets and a modern plaza. The **Fiesta de San Ignacio Loyola** is celebrated on 30 July. The area has good walking and plenty of birds amid the coffee plantations. You can visit waterfalls, lakes, petroglyphs at Faical, and ancient ruins in the surrounding green hills. A pleasant excursion is to Cerro Campana overlooking town. From San Ignacio a narrow, unpaved road runs 45 km north through more nice scenery to **Namballe**, 5 km from the border.

Just north of Namballe a dirt road goes west to the **Santuario Tabaconas-Namballe (SNTN)** ⓘ *ProSNTN, Av Santa Rosa 500, San Ignacio, T076-356490, prosntn@gmail.com; see www.sntabaconasnamballe.gob.pe,* a 29,500-ha reserve between 1200 m and 3800 m, protecting several Andean ecosystems, mainly páramo and cloud forest, with many endemic flora and fauna and a number of endangered and emblematic species, such as the spectacled bear and the mountain tapir. The southern section of the reserve is reached from Tabaconas (see above). Pieter Van de Sype of the Belgian Development Agency writes: "Although a visit is rough and time-consuming (at least three days from San Ignacio or Jaén) the scenery is spectacular and very different from most other treks in Perú. Furthermore, for the more adventurous trekker who is weary of encountering other tourists on their path, this is the ideal place: it is virtually unvisited. On an expedition we entered areas previously unexplored, which was pretty exciting, and although the policy of the park authorities is to keep the tourism within certain boundaries in the park, at this point many parts of the SNTN remain unexplored".

Easier to visit is the cloud forest of Chinchiquilla, where you can see the cock-of-the-rock (*gallito de las rocas*). It is near the charming little town of Nueve de Octubre, one hour from San Ignacio (if you leave before 0900 you can be back before dark). Together with the SNTN, it is the only area in the province which hasn't suffered substantial deforestation – they are too high for coffee cultivation.

To the coast

Heading west from Chamaya, the highway at first follows the canyon of the Río Chamaya, in which a dam and reservoir is being built near the town of Pucará. It then reaches the Abra de Porculla (at 2150 m, the lowest pass through the Peruvian Andes), before descending to join the old Pan-American Highway at Olmos (see page 451). From here you can go southwest to Chiclayo, or northwest to Piura. The road from Pedro Ruiz west to Olmos is paved, but prone to landslides in the rainy season.

The eastern branch of the road at Pedro Ruiz runs paved all the way to Yurimaguas. The area is prone to landslides in the wet season. In 2010 there was construction in a few sections causing delays. This is a very beautiful journey, first passing Laguna Pomacochas (see page 517), then leading to where the high Andes tumble into the Amazon Basin before your eyes. The descent from the heights of the **Abra Patricia Pass** to the Río Afluente at 1400 m is one of the best birdwatching areas in northern Peru. As you travel the road you may see groups of people with their binoculars tramping beside the highway, stopping at likely sites for rare species. Ideally several days should be taken to see as many birds as possible. ECOAN has a 'long-whiskered owlet biological station', **Estación Biológica Lechucita Bigotona (EBLB)** ① *Km 364.5, T041-816814, www.ecoanperu.org*, which provides lodging in bungalows at the **Abra Patricia Lodge** in our **A** range per person, meals extra. The lodge is in a fabulous mountain location with hummingbird feeders, good trails and a lovely central dining/seating area with library and free coffee and snacks all day long, very friendly, recommended. This private reserve is aimed at conserving the critically endangered long-whiskered owlet (*Xenoglaux loweryi*) and other rare species. There is abundabnt birdlife and a tower for canopy watching. You can go birdwatching by mototaxi with Roberto. Guiding costs US$50 per day although most of this money goes to ECOAN, not to the guide. ECOAN has information on many aspects of this area.

Further along, Nueva Cajamarca, Rioja, Moyobamba and Tarapoto are growing centres of population, with much forest clearance beside the Carretera Marginal de la Selva.

Nuevo Cajamarca → *Colour map 1, B4. Phone code: 042. Altitude: 940 m.*
After Florida, the road winds down then up through Buenos Aires to a cultivated zone around the villages of **La Esperanza**, **El Progreso** and **Oso Perdido**. A further forested descent leads to the town of **Nuevo Cajamarca**, 152 km east of Pedro Ruiz. There is a market and accommodation on the main road (**F Continental**, T042-556141, is the best) but this is not a safe town. Rioja, further east, has a better reputation.

Rioja → *Colour map 1, B5. Phone code: 042. Altitude: 900 m.*
Beyond Nueva Cajamarca, 22 km, is Rioja, a pleasant colonial town with a modern church. Straw hats and crafts are made here from the *bombonaje* straw, for example at **Artesanías Leito**, Jr Santo Toribio 1239. Colourful carnival celebrations are considered the best in the region. Rioja is the access point for the western section of the **Reserva Ecológica del Río Avisado-Tingana** (see below). Near town there are a number of caves (Diamante, Cascayunga) and river sources (Tioyacu, Negro), as *complejos* and *recreos turísticos*, which have accommodation, swimming pools and local foods.

Moyobamba → *Colour map 1, B5. Phone code 042. Population: 14,000. Altitude: 900 m.*
Moyobamba, a pleasant town in the attractive Río Mayo Valley, was founded in 1540 as the original capital of Maynas. It then became capital of Loreto before the establishment of the department of San Martín, of which it became capital in 1906. This area has to cope with lots of rain in the wet season and in some years the whole area is flooded. At the end of June the town celebrates its annual **tourist week festival** (San Juan); the **Fiesta de Santiago** is in late July and for three days around 1 November is the **Festival de la Orquídea**. The valley is renowned for its orchids. There are three places where you can see orchids around Moyobamba: **Jardín Botánico San Francisco** ① *Barrio Lluyllucucha, follow*

Jr Arequipa to the south, http://jardinbotanicomoyobamba.com, daily 0800-1700, US$0.35, a park at the west end of town; **Orquideario Waqanki** ⓘ *just before you get to the San Mateo thermal baths, www.waqanki.com, open 0700-1800, US$0.55,* where the orchids have been placed on the trees; and **Viveros AgrOriente** ⓘ *Jr Reyes Guerra 900, by Punta de Tahuishco, www.agroriente.com, daily 0800-1800, US$0.35,* a commercial orchid and tropical fruit nursery that also has a small zoo with regional animals and birds.

A pleasant promenade with nice views of the Río Mayo valley is **Punta de Tahuishco** (from the town centre follow Jirón Reyes Guerra seven blocks north). A steep path goes down from here to **Puerto Tahuishco**, the town's harbour on the Río Mayo. Boats can be hired for excursions on the river (US$1.80 per person) and a passenger boat serves communities upriver, going as far as Nueva Piura. **Morro de Calzada** ⓘ *take a Rioja-bound car or combi to the Calzada turnoff, US$0.55, 20 mins; mototaxis charge US$0.55 from the turnoff to the town of Calzada or US$2.50 to the start of the trail,* is an isolated outcrop in white sand forest, good for birdwatching. A nice path through forest leads to the top and a lookout. The walk from the town to the start of the trail takes 30 minutes, from there to the top about 1½ hours. There are Baños Termales at **San Mateo** ⓘ *5 km to the southeast, off the road to Jepelacio, open 0600-2200, US$0.55, US$0.70 after 1800,* which are hot and worth a visit.

For the **Paccha waterfalls** ⓘ *local guides in San Miguel will take you to the falls for a tip,* in a beautiful, unspoilt setting, take an *auto* or combi to Nuevo San Miguel past Jepelacio. Walk past town for 15 minutes; just before a bridge is a sign for the falls to the right. A trail follows the river upstream through lovely forest, the first falls are only ten minutes away. Getting to the other four falls requires crossing some log bridges. Salto del Alcalde, the highest, is 10 minutes from the first falls. At the house by the trailhead there is a small orchid nursery which can be visited.

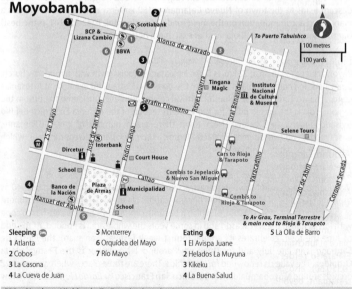

Moyobamba

Sleeping
1 Atlanta
2 Cobos
3 La Casona
4 La Cueva de Juan
5 Monterrey
6 Orquídea del Mayo
7 Río Mayo

Eating
1 El Avispa Juane
2 Helados La Muyuna
3 Kikeku
4 La Buena Salud
5 La Olla de Barro

The **Reserva Ecológica del Río Avisado-Tingana**, part of the Area de Conservación Aguajales Renacales del Alto Mayo, protects 3480 ha of seasonally flooded forest in the drainage of the Alto (upper) Mayo River. At 800 m, it is among the highest flooded forests in the world. It is rich in flora, including many epiphytes and several types of palms, and fauna including giant river otter, capuchin and squirrel monkeys, two-toed sloth and many birds. Community tourism projects operate in two areas of the reserve. The **Tingana** sector ① *T042-782679, www.tingana.org*, is reached via either Calzada or Yantaló to Boca del Río Huascayacu, 45 minutes by car, followed by one hour on a motor launch up the Río Mayo to Puerto Punga on the Avisado. The community offers lodging in the **D** range, meals and guided canoe tours. Further west, the **Lloros** sector ① *T042-782126, www.lloros.org*, is 26 km from Rioja, reached via Yuracyacu, along a side road that starts 7 km west of Rioja. The community offers guided canoe and walking tours and meals. They have a 12-m-high observation tower. Moyobamba operators offer tours to the reserve.

The **Oficina Municipal de Información** ① *Jr Pedro Canga 262, Plaza de Armas, T042-562191, Mon 0800-1300, 1430-1700, Tue-Fri 0800-1300, 1430-2000, Sat 0900-1300, 1600-2000, Sun 0900-1300*, is very helpful, and English is spoken. **Dircetur** ① *Jr San Martín 301, T042-562043, www.turismosanmartin.com, Mon-Fri 0730-1300, 1430-1700*, has some leaflets and a map. Information on excursions and hikes is available from the **Instituto Nacional de Cultura** ① *Jr Benavides 352*, which also has a small departmental **museum** ① *Mon-Fri 0800-1300, 1500-1800*. Also see www.moyobamba.net.

Tarapoto → *Colour map 1, C5. Phone code: 042. Altitude: 500 m.*

Tarapoto, 109 km southeast of Moyobamba, is a friendly city. Founded in 1782, it is today the largest commercial centre in the region. It is a busy place and competes with Iquitos for the record number of motorcycle taxis per square metre of road. They are not allowed in the plaza, although private motorcycles are. There are three parts to the town: Tarapoto itself, Morales to the west and La Banda de Shilcayo to the east. The **Museo Regional de la Universidad Nacional de San Martín** ① *Maynas, ½ a block from the plaza, behind the church, Mon-Fri 0800-2000, US$0.70*, contains a little of everything: paleontology, geology, ethnography, stuffed animals, and so on. In the second week of July is the town's rowdy **tourist week festival**, Santa Cruz de los Motilones, but between May and September, it seems like every weekend celebrates something. It doesn't take much for the Tarapoteños to party. Tourist information from **Oficina Municipal de Información** ① *Jr Ramírez Hurtado on Plaza, T042-526188, Mon-Sat 0830-1230, 1500-1900, Sun 0900-1300*, and Dircetur ① *Jr Angel Delgado Morey, cuadra 1, at Ministerio de Agricultura, T042-522567, tarapoto@mincetur.gob.pe, Mon-Fri 0730-1300, 1400-1700, helpful.*

Around Tarapoto

There are petroglyphs at **Demor** and **Pólish** east of the city, 4 km and 5 km respectively.

About 14 km from Tarapoto on the spectacular road to Yurimaguas are the 50-m **Ahuashiyacu Falls** ① *entry US$0.70 (toilets US$0.15), transport from La Banda de Shilcayo*, which can be visited by tour from Tarapoto (US$4.50 by mototaxi). A walkway leads up to a pool at the foot of one of the lower parts of the falls. You can swim here, but wait until after the sun has warmed the water; before 0900 it's freezing. This is a popular place at lunchtimes and weekends. The entire falls can be seen from the *recreo turístico* **El Paraíso Verde**, with a restaurant serving typical food, drinks, toilets, swimming pool (US$0.60), also popular. About 300 m beyond Ahuashiyacu is **El Mono y La Gata** restaurant, beyond which is **El Pozo**, a man-made pool for swimming and washing.

Carry on along the road to Yurimaguas for 22 km and you come to the **Baños Termales de San José** and **Cascada de Carpishoyacu**.

Lamas 22 km northwest of Tarapoto, off the road to Moyobamba, is a small town with a Quechua-speaking native community, descendants of the Chancas people. Set in the hills, Lamas is known as 'La ciudad de los tres pisos' (the city of three storeys). On the top level, by the antennas, is a lookout with good views, a hotel-restaurant and a recreo turístico. The main town occupies the middle level. Here, the small **Museo Los Chancas** ① Jr San Martín 1157, daily 0830-1300, 1430-1800, US$0.90, has interesting exhibits about the history of the region and cultural aspects of the native people; it also sells crafts. Uphill from the museum is **El Castillo de Lamas** ① Mon-Sat 0900-1230, 1400-1800, Sun 0930-1830, US$1.80, an art gallery and café set in a incongruous medieval castle. On the lower level is the neighbourhood of **Wayku**, where the native people live. Some of the women wear traditional dress; you may see them by their home making a clay pot or weaving, or at market (largest on Sunday) in the main town early in the morning. Lamas' Easter celebrations draw many Peruvian visitors, as do the **Fiestas Patronales** in honour of Santa Rosa de Lima, the last week in August. From Lamas you can visit several waterfalls including **Chapawanqui** ① US$0.70, taxi US$7, 15 mins, or take a car bound for Urcupata from Jr Lima corner 16 de Octubre, US$1 and get off at the turn-off.

Tarapoto

Sleeping 🛏		Eating 🍴	
1 El Mirador	6 Nilas	1 Café Plaza	6 La Patarashca Restaurant
2 July	7 Río Sol	2 Chifa Cantón	7 Real Grill
3 La Patarashca	8 San Antonio	3 El Maguaré	8 Tambo's Pizza
4 La Posada Inn	9 Tarapoto Inn	4 El Merendero	
5 Luna Azul		5 Helados La Muyuna	**Bars & clubs 🍸**
			9 Stonewasi

Tarapoto to Yurimaguas

From Tarapoto it is 129 km to Yurimaguas on the Río Huallaga (see page 597), along a spectacular paved road. From Tarapoto, the road climbs through lush country passing the Ahuashiyacu Falls (see above) to a tunnel. Stop at the police control for birdwatching, mototaxi US$5. From here the road descends through beautiful forest perched on rocky cliffs to **Pongo de Caynarachi** (several basic *comedores*), where the flats start. **Shapaja** is the port for Tarapoto, 14 km from town, served by *autos*. At Shapaja cargo boats can be caught to Yurimaguas. There's plenty of birdlife and river traffic to be seen. From Yurimaguas on the Río Huallaga, launches go to Iquitos.

Tarapoto to Tingo María

The Carretera Marginal Sur heads south from Tarapoto, crossing the Río Mayo a few kilometres west of its confluence with the Huallaga. A road on the north bank of the Mayo runs east to Shapaja and Chasuta. South of the river, **Laguna Azul** (or Laguna de Sauce) is a big lake 52 km south of Tarapoto, off the road to Juanjui, with a choice of accommodation; there are motor boats for hire and a couple of waterfalls nearby. You can go river rafting on the Río Mayo for US$10 per person. **Picota**, 59 km from Tarapoto on the Huallaga is promoting itself as a tourist destination with several waterfalls, thermal baths and a cave with oilbirds. There are several *alojamientos* and eateries. The road is paved from Tarapoto to Juanjuí. Juanjui–Tocache is unpaved (about seven hours by bus) and from Tocache to Tingo María is paved. The area around Tocache is less safe than other parts of this road, but hold-ups may occur anywhere.

⊚ To Ecuador and to the Amazon listings

For Sleeping and Eating price codes and other relevant information, see pages 38-44.

⊜ Sleeping

Jaén and around *p527*
C El Bosque, Mesones Muro 632, T/F076-431184, hoteleraelbosque@speedy.com.pe. On main road by bus terminals, just below roundabout for turn to San Ignacio. Includes breakfast, quiet rooms in back, gardens, a/c, frigobar, solar hot water, Wi-Fi, nice pool, good restaurant.
D Hostal Valle Verde, Mcal Castilla 203, Plaza de Armas, T076-432201. Very clean and modern, large comfortable rooms and beds, a/c (cheaper with fan), hot water, frigobar, Wi-Fi, parking, includes breakfast. Recommended.
D Prim's, Diego Palomino 1341, T076-431039. Includes breakfast, good service, comfortable, hot water, a/c (cheaper with fan), frigobar, Wi-Fi, friendly, small pool.

D-E César, Mesones Muro 168, T/F076-431491, hotelcesar-jaen@hotmail.com. Spacious comfortable rooms, fan, phone, TV, Wi-Fi in lobby, parking.
D-E Danubio, V Pinillos 429, T076-433110. Older place, nicely refurbished in 2009, many different rooms and prices, all with private bath, hot water, fan and Wi-Fi.
E Cancún, Diego Palomino 1413, T076-433511. Good rooms with bath, hot water, fan and Wi-Fi.
E Hostal Manantial, Alfonso Arana Vidal 450, T076-976 969003. 500 m from El Bosque, close to several bus lines. Very friendly and hospitable, clean, new and good value.
F-G Santa Elena, Sánchez Carrión 142, T076-803020. Cold water, cheaper with shared bath, basic rooms, some with fan.

Jaén to the border *p528*
San Ignacio
D-E Gran Hotel San Ignacio, Jr José Olaya 680 at the bottom of the hill, T076-356544, www.granhotelsanignacio.com.pe. Includes

breakfast, restaurant **Mi Tierra**, Wi-Fi, modern comfortable rooms, upmarket for San Ignacio.
E-F La Posada, Jr Porvenir 218, T076-356180. Simple rooms with private bath and hot water (cheaper with shared bath and cold water), restaurant, internet, small terrace upstairs.

Namballe
E Sol de la Frontera, 1 km north of Namballe, 4 km from La Balsa, soldelafrontera@ yahoo.es. British-run by Isabel Wood. Comfortable rooms, bathtubs, gas water heaters, continental breakfast (other meals not available), set in 2.5 ha of countryside. A good option if you have your own vehicle or bring some food.
F-G Hostal Maldonado, near the plaza, Namballe, T076-830011 (community phone). Private bath (cheaper with shared bath), cold water, basic.

Rioja p529
D Gran Bombonaje, Faustino Maldonado 515, T042-558013. Older hotel but well maintained, with bath, hot water, fan, frigobar, restaurant, offers tours.
D-E Borsalino Hostal, Jr Santo Toribio 958, near Plaza de Armas, T042-558050. Modern, with bath, hot water, frigobar, Wi-Fi.
E-F San Martín, Grau 540, T042-559490. Nice simple rooms with bath, cold water, sitting room, small patio, parking, good value.

Moyobamba p529, map p530
A-B Puerto Mirador, Jr Sucre, 1 km from the centre, T/F042-562050. Includes breakfast, lovely grounds but with monkeys in cages, nice views, good pool, Wi-Fi, good restaurant.
B-C Río Mayo, Jr Pedro Canga 415, T042-564193, www.riomayo.com. Includes breakfast, central location, modern comfortable rooms, frigobar, Wi-Fi, small indoor pool, parking, attentive service.
D La Casona, Alonso de Alvarado 682, T042-563858. Nicely refurbished old home, lovely courtyard with orchids, comfortable rooms, includes breakfast, private bath, electric shower. Recommended.

D Orquídea del Mayo, Jr San Martín 432, T042-561049, orquideadelmayohostal@ hotmail.com. Includes breakfast, bright modern comfortable rooms with bath, hot water, internet, opened in 2010.
E Atlanta, Alonso de Alvarado 865, T042-562063, atlantainn@hotmail.com. With bath, hot water (cheaper without), parking, TV, fan, some rooms have frigobar, clean and good but the front rooms are noisy.
E Monterrey, Jr Manuel del Aguila 584, on the plaza, T042-795899. Front rooms nice but noisy, back ones are cheaper, simpler and good value, all have private bath and cold water, friendly and helpful.
E-F La Cueva de Juan, Jr Alonso de Alvarado 870, T042-562488, lacueva870@hotmail.com. Rooms around a small courtyard, private bath, hot water, restaurant serves breakfast and lunch, central but reasonably quiet, good value, friendly.
F Cobos, Jr Pedro Canga 404, T042-562153. Private bath, cold water, simple but good, friendly.

Tarapoto p531, map p532
AL Puerto Palmeras, in La Banda de Shilcayo, T042-524100, www.puerto palmeras.com. Includes breakfast, good restaurant, nice rooms, helpful staff, pleasant grounds with horses and small zoo. Has a private reserve, **Lago Lindo**, off Juanjui road 2 hrs from town, with accommodation, lake and monkey island. Resorts in same group at Pomacochas and Yurimaguas.
A Río Shilcayo, Pasaje Las Flores 224, 1 km east of town in La Banda de Shilcayo, T042-522225, www.rioshilcayo.com. Includes buffet breakfast, excellent meals, pool (US$3.50 for non-guests), airport transfers. Packages available for 2-4 nights. Under the same ownership is the **Pumarinri Huallaga Lodge**, same phone, www.pumarinri.com, 30 km southeast of Tarapoto overlooking the Río Huallaga between Shapaja and Chasuta, with lovely rooms and good food, birdwatching, other activites and programmes.

B Nilas, Jr Moyobamba 173, T042-527331, www.hotelnilas.com. Includes breakfast, a/c, fridge, Wi-Fi, pool, jacuzzi, gym, airport transfers, conference facilities.

C Río Sol, Jiménez Pimentel 407, T042-523154, www.riosoltarapotohotel.com. Includes breakfast and airport transfers, small pool, restaurant and bar. Modern comfortable rooms with a/c, fridge, Wi-Fi.

C-D La Posada Inn, San Martín 146, T042-522234, laposada_inn@yahoo.es. Good central hotel, ageing but well maintained, comfortable rooms with a/c (cheaper with fan), private bath, hot water, fridge, Wi-Fi, nice atmosphere, small library of Spanish books on the region.

C-D Luna Azul, Jr Manco Capac 276, T042-525787, www.lunaazulhotel.com. Includes breakfast and airport transfers, with bath, hot water, a/c (cheaper with fan), Wi-Fi, frigobar, attentive service.

C-D Tarapoto Inn, Jr Jiménez Pimentel 115, T042-524213, www.hoteltarapoto.com. Multi-storey hotel, includes breakfast, a/c (cheaper with fan), private bath, hot water. Starting to show its age but still OK.

D El Mirador, Jr San Pablo de la Cruz 517, 5 blocks uphill from the plaza T042-522177, www.elmiradortarapoto.blogspot.com. With bath, electric shower (cheaper with cold water), fan, Wi-Fi, laundry facilities, very clean, breakfast available (US$3.50), hammocks on rooftop terrace with nice views, tours arranged. Family-run and very welcoming. Recommended.

D La Patarashca, Jr San Pablo de la Cruz 362, T042-528810, www.lapatarashca.com. Very nice hotel with ample rooms, includes breakfast, restaurant, private bath, electric shower, Wi-Fi, large garden with hammocks, tours arranged.

E July, Jr Alegría A de Morey 205, T042-522087. Adequate rooms with bath, electric shower, breakfast available.

E-F San Antonio, Jr Jiménez Pimentel 126, T042-525563. Small simple rooms with private bath, hot water and fan.

There are several *alojamientos* on Alegría Arias de Morey, cuadra 2, as well as cheap, basic accommodation by the bus terminals. Several other basic *hospedajes* in El Sauce.

Lamas *p532*
E Girasoles, Los Chancas s/n, on top of the hill, opposite the lookout, T042-543439, stegmaiert@yahoo.de. Nice wooden chalet, includes breakfast, with bath, hot water, nice views, pizzeria open Wed-Sun, German-Peruvian run, English also spoken, friendly and knowledgeable about the area.

F El Abuelo Felipe, Jr San Martín 1027, T042-543451. Nice simple place, with private bath, cold water, fan, friendly service.

Tarapoto to Tingo Maria *p533*
Laguna Azul, El Sauce
A El Sauce Resort, 3 blocks from the plaza, Tarapoto office: Jr Alegría A de Morey 140, T042-522588, www.elsauceresort.com. Full-service cottages by the lake, cheaper in rooms, includes breakfast, restaurant, pool, kayaks, transport from Tarapoto US$20 per person.

E-F Hosp El Moderno, Jr Leticia s/n, T042-830060. Simple, with bath, cold water.

🍴 Eating

Jaén and around *p527*
♙♙-♙ La Cabaña, Bolívar 1332 at Plaza de Armas. Daily 0700-2400. Daily specials at noon, à la carte in the evening, popular.

♙♙-♙ Lactobac, Bolívar 1378 at Plaza de Armas. Daily from 0730, but closed in the evening. Variety of à la carte dishes, snacks, desserts, good *pollo a la brasa*. Very popular and recommended.

♙ Claudy Chicken, Diego Palomino 1284. Sun-Fri 0700-2300. Selection of set meals at noon, Chinese and chicken in the evening.

Cafés

Café Los Amigos, Cajamarca 380. Serves good local coffee in a surprisingly trendy establishment.

Cenfrocafé, San Martín, 1 block from the Plaza. Excellently balanced, organic coffees, well-prepared and nicely served, *una perla escondida*. **Cenfrocafé**, www.cenfrocafe. com.pe, is a Jaén-based coffee farmers organization, regarded as the best of its kind in the region. A blend of Cenfrocafé coffee is served in **Arábica** café in Miraflores, Lima.

La Compana, Huamantanga y Castilla. Café and bakery which also sells delicious *chupetes*, try the coffee or algarrobina flavours.

Jaén to the border *p528*
San Ignacio

Many simple *comedores* on Jr Porvenir.
♥♥-♥ **El Tundal**, Av San Ignacio 140. Daily 0830-2300. Regional dishes and sea-food, à la carte only.
♥ **Cafetería Saja**, Jr Bolívar 263, ½ block from plaza. Daily 0700-2300. Capuccino, espresso, other coffees and snacks. Sells local coffee products.

Rioja *p529*

Helados La Muyuna, Jr San Martín 1034. Good natural jungle fruit ice cream.

Moyobamba *p529, map p530*

Many stands on Malecón San Juan between Punta Tahuishco and **Viveros AgrOriente** serve regional specialties on weekends.
♥♥-♥ **La Olla de Barro**, Pedro Canga 398. Mon-Sat 0900-2200, Sun to 1600. Typical food, expensive compared with other places in town but still good value. Also in Tarapoto.
♥♥-♥ **Kikeku**, Jr Pedro Canga 450, next to casino, open 24 hrs. Good *chifa*, also *comida criolla*, large portions, noisy.
♥ **El Avispa Juane**, Jr Alonso de Alvarado 1003. Closed Sun. Regional specialties and snacks.
♥ **La Buena Salud**, 25 de Mayo 227, by market. Sun-Fri 0800-1500. Vegetarian set meals, breakfast and fruit juices.

♥ **Helados La Muyuna**, Jr Pedro Canga 549. Good natural jungle fruit ice cream.

Tarapoto *p531, map p532*

Regional specialities include *cecina* (dried pork) and *chorizo*, both usually served with *tocacho* (fried green bananas), also *juanes*, *inchicapi* and *ensalada de chonta* as in Iquitos. Interesting juices are *cocona*, made with cloves and cinnamon, and *aguajina*, from the *aguaje* fruit (deep purple skin, orange inside, sold on street corners). Regional fruits include grapes and pineapples.
♥♥ **Real Grill**, Jr Moyobamba on the plaza. Daily 0830-2400. Regional and international food, also breakfast. One of the best in town and more expensive than elsewhere.
♥♥ **La Patarashca**, Jr Lamas 261. Daily 1200-2300. Tourist restaurant serving regional specialties à la carte.
♥♥-♥ **Chifa Cantón**, Jr Ramón Castilla 140. Mon-Fri 1200-1600, Sat-Sun 1200-2400. Chinese, very popular and clean.
♥♥-♥ **El Merendero**, Jr San Martín cuadra 1. Daily until 2300. *Comida criolla* à la carte.
♥♥-♥ **Tambo's Pizza**, Jr San Pablo de la Cruz 299. Mon-Sat 1830-0000, Sun 1830-2200. Pizza and pasta.
♥ **El Maguaré**, Jr Moyobamba corner Manco Cápac. Mon-Sat 1100-1530. Choice of set meals and à la carte, good food and service.

Cafés

Café Plaza, Jr Maynas corner Martínez, at the plaza. Mon-Sat 0730-1300, 1530-2200, Sun 0900-1300, 1730-2130. Breakfast, coffee, snacks, juices, Wi-Fi, popular.

Helados La Muyuna, Jr Ramón Castilla 271. Open 0800-2400 except closed Fri from 1700 until Sat at 1830. Good natural ice cream and drinks made with jungle fruits, fruit salads, also breakfast.

Italia Mozzarella, Jr Manco Capac 233. Shop selling good home-made yoghurt and a variety of cheeses.

Lamas *p532*
¶ **Rolly's**, San Martín 925, just off the plaza. Serves good food.

❶ Bars and clubs

Moyobamba *p529, map p530*
Kovachi, at Punta Tahuishco. Open Thu-Sun from 2100. Popular club, varied music.
Papillón, Carretera a Baños Termales. Also a popular club, sometimes has live music.

Tarapoto *p531, map p532*
For clubs, check out the neighbourhood of Morales, 2 popular ones are **Anaconda** and **Macumba**. Cover at weekends US$1.50. Several bars are clustered around Jr Lamas by San Pablo de la Cruz; **Stonewasi** is popular.

❍ Shopping

Tarapoto *p531, map p532*
Centro Artesanal, Moyobamba y San Pablo de La Cruz at corner of Plaza. Several stalls selling a variety of local crafts.

▲ Activities and tours

Moyobamba *p529, map p530*
Selene Tours, Jr Serafín Filomeno 150, T042-564471, www.selenetours.com. City and regional tours.
Tingana Magic, Jr Reyes Guerra 430, T042-563163, www.tinganaperu.com. Tours to regional attractions, birdwatching.

Tarapoto *p531, map p532*
Quiquiriqui Tours, Jiménez Pimente 309, T042-527863, www.quiquiriquitours.com. Regional tours, car and van rental with drive; also sell flight and bus tickets.

❍ Transport

The Baguas *p527*
Bus
Many buses pass through **Bagua Grande** en route from Chiclayo to Tarapoto and Chachapoyas and vice versa, by day or night. You can book for **Lima**, US$16-28, or **Chiclayo**, US$8.50, Transcade, Chachapoyas 1999, at 1000 and 2200, but for **Tarapoto**, US$10, or **Chachapoyas**, US$8, you must wait and see if there is space and they are often full. A better bet is to take a car or combi. Cars and combis to **Jaén** and **Bagua Chica** leave from Mcal Castilla y Angamos at the west end of town: to Jaén, cars US$3.20, 1 hr; combis US$1.80, 1¼ hrs. From R Palma 308 at the east end of town, cars leave to **Pedro Ruiz**, US$4.35, 1 hr, and **Chachapoyas**, US$7.85, 2½ hrs. Taking a mototaxi (US$0.55) between the 2 stops is a good alternative to walking in the heat.
    Marañón or **Cenepa** buses **Chiclayo**–Bagua Chica, 6 hrs, US$8, at 1030, 2100 and 2130.

Jaén and around *p527*
Bus
Terminals are strung along Mesones Muro, blocks 4-7, south of centre; many ticket offices, always enquire where the bus actually leaves from. Some companies also have offices in the centre: eg Civa, Mcal Ureta 1300 y V Pinillos (terminal at Bolívar 935). To **Chiclayo**: US$5.50-7, 6 hrs, many companies, eg **Móvil** (Mesones Muro cuadra 7, T076-433963), *bus cama* at 1330 and 2300, US$10; **Civa**, 1200 and 2230; **Linea**, 1200 and 2300; **Turismo Jaén**, 6 a day. Cars to Chiclayo from terminal at Mesones Muro cuadra 4, US$18, 5 hrs. To **Lima**: Móvil at 1600, 16 hrs, *bus cama* US$39, *semi-cama* US$32. **Civa**, 1700, US$32. Service to Lima also goes through **Trujillo**, US$7-9, **Emtrafesa**, US$11,

9 hrs. To **Piura** via Olmos: Sol Peruano, at 2230, US$14, 8 hrs. To **Tarapoto**: 490 km, US$11, 9-10 hrs; Jaén Express at 1000, 1700, Fernández, 3 a day; Sol Perú at 2030; daytime transit was restricted in 2010 because of construction. To **Moyobamba**: US$9, 7 hrs, same service as Tarapoto, likewise to **Pedro Ruiz**: US$7, 3½ hrs. To **Bagua Grande** (transfer here for Chachapoyas): cars from Mesones Muro cuadra 6, 0400-2000, US$3.20, 1 hr; combis from cuadra 9, US$1.80, 1¼ hrs. To **Bagua Chica**: combis US$1.50, 1¼ hrs. To **Chamaya**: cars from Mesones Muro cuadra 4, 0500-2000, US$1, 15 mins. To **San Ignacio** (for **Ecuador**), cars from Av Pacamuros, cuadra 19, 0400-1800, US$5.40, 2 hrs; combis from cuadra 17, US$3.60, 3 hrs.

Jaén to the border p528
Bus
From San Ignacio to **Chiclayo**, with Civa, Av San Ignacio 386 y Jr Porvenir, daily at 1830, US$9, 10-11 hrs; with **Trans Chiclayo**, Av San Ignacio 406, 1845 daily. To **Trujillo**, Ejetur, Av San Ignacio 425, 1800 daily, US$12.50, 13 hrs. To **Jaén**, from *óvalo* at south end of Av Mariano Melgar (many touts): cars US$5.40, 2 hrs; combis US$3.60, 3 hrs. For transport information to Ecuador, see Border essentials box, page 527.

Nuevo Cajamarca p529
Buses To/from Chiclayo and Tarapoto stop here (except express services such as Móvil Tours, T042-787886). Frequent service to **Rioja**, 20 mins, cars US$1.40, combis US$0.55. To **Pedro Ruiz**, 3 hrs, car US$9, combis US$5.35 To **Bagua Grande**, car US$12.50, 4 hrs; combis US$8.90, 5 hrs. To **Moyobamba**, 40 mins, cars US$1.80, combis US$1.10.

Rioja p529
Buses To/from Chiclayo and Tarapoto (except express services) stop here. To **Moyobamba**, 20 mins, car US$1.45, combi US$0.55. To **Nueva Cajamarca**, 20 mins, car US$1.40, combi US$0.55.

Moyobamba *p529, map p530*
Bus
Long distance The Terminal Terrestre is about 12 blocks from the centre on Av Grau, which leads out of town to the main highway (mototaxi to centre US$0.55). There is no service originating in Moyobamba; all buses are en route to/from Tarapoto. Several companies to **Tarapoto** (eg Tarapoto Tours, Paredes Estrella, Sol Peruano, Móvil Tours, T042-563720), US$3.60-5.35, 2 hrs. To **Yurimaguas**, US$9, 5-6 hrs, involves waiting in Tarapoto, it is better to go to Tarapoto and transfer there. Many buses heading west, en route from Tarapoto to **Pedro Ruiz**, US$9, 4 hrs, **Jaén**, US$9, 7 hrs, **Chiclayo**, US$14.30-23, 12 hrs, **Piura**, US$18, 14 hrs, **Trujillo**, US$21-29, *cama* US$36, 14-15 hrs and **Lima**, US$32-46, *cama* US$57, 23-25 hrs. They will not sell you a ticket the day before if you are going to an intermediate destination such as Pedro Ruiz, but they do take you if there's room when the bus arrives (Fernández will sell tickets to Pedro Ruiz for the full fare to Jaén, also try Ejetur).

Regional
Cars Empresa San Martín, Benavides 276, T042-562716 and ETRISA, Benavides 244, T042-562726, 0400-2100, both will pick you up from your hotel; to **Tarapoto**, US$7.15, 2 hrs, to **Rioja** US$1.45, 20 mins, to **Nueva Cajamarca**, US$1.80, 40 mins. There is no service direct to Pedro Ruiz or Yurimaguas unless you have enough people to fill a car. Taxi (4 passengers) to **Pedro Ruiz**, US$43, to **Chachapoyas** US$54.

Combis Turismo Selva, Jr Callao y Benavides, 0600-1800, leave when full; to **Tarapoto** US$3.60, 2½ hrs, **Rioja** US$0.55, 30 mins; to **Nueva Cajamarca** US$1.10, 1 hr. To **Jepelacio**, from General Benavides y Callao, 0600-1800, 30 mins, US$1.25; to **Nuevo San Miguel**, 1½ hrs, US$2.15.

Tarapoto *p531, map p532*
Air
Flights to **Lima**, with **LAN**, Ramírez Hurtado 183, on the plaza, T042-529318, 2 daily, US$180-225, and **Star Perú**, San Pablo de la Cruz 100, T042-528765, daily, US$97-117; to **Iquitos**, Tue, Thu and Sat, US$107-127. Book flights in advance, particularly in the rainy season. A taxi to the airport is US$3, mototaxi US$1.50. There's no bus service, but it's no problem to walk.

Bus
Long distance Buses leave from Av Salaverry, blocks 8-9, in Morales; mototaxi from the plaza, US$0.70, 15 mins. To **Moyobamba**, 116 km, US$3.60-5.35, 2 hrs. **Pedro Ruiz**, US$7.10 (companies going to Jaén or Chiclayo), 6 hrs; **Chiclayo**, 690 km, 15-16 hrs, US$12.50-23; **Trujillo**, US$21-29, 17-18 hrs; and **Lima**, US$32-46, *cama* US$57, 29-30 hrs. **Móvil Tours** is a reliable company on the above routes, at the top of the price range; to **Lima** at 0730, 1300 and 1530, to **Trujillo** at 1500, to **Chiclayo** at 1600. To **Jaén**, US$11, 10 hrs, **Fernández** at 0700, 1400, 1600, and **Jaén Express**, at 1200. For **Chachapoyas**, take a Jaén or Chiclayo-bound bus to Pedro Ruiz (you will probably have to pay full fare to Chiclayo) and a car from there. To **Piura** US$21.50, 18 hrs, with **Sol Peruano**, at 1200. To **Juanjui**, **Tocache**, **Tingo María** and **Pucallpa**, daily except Sun at 0800, **Transamazónica** and **Transmar** alternate days, Pucallpa, US$32, 22-24 hrs. (Note public safety problems on this route.)

Bus companies All on Av Salaverry unless noted otherwise: **Civa**, T042-522269. **Ejetur**, T042-526827. **Fernández**, Av Universitaria y Av Salaverry. **Jaén Express**, T042-531883. **Móvil Tours**, No 880, T042-528240, www.moviltours.com.pe. **Paredes Estrella**, T042-521202. **Sol Peruano**, No 804, T042-531861. **Tarapoto Tours**, No 935, T042-782204. **Transamazónica**, Av Universitaria 104 y Salaverry, T042-781636. **Transmar**, Av Universitaria y Av Salaverry, T042-232392.

Regional
To **Moyobamba**, cars with **Empresa San Martín**, Av Alfonso Ugarte 1456, T042-526327 and **ETRISA**, Jr Limatambo 504, T042-521944, both will pick you up from your hotel, US$7.15, 2 hrs; combis with **Turismo Selva**, Av Alfonso Ugarte, cuadra 11, US$3.60, 2½ hrs.

To **Yurimaguas**, good minibuses with Gilmer Tours, Av Alfonso Ugarte 1480, hourly 0500-1200, 1400-1800, US$5.35, 2½ hrs; cars with **Empresa San Martín**, address above, US$7.15, 2 hrs; combis with **Turismo Selva**, as above, US$3.60, 2½ hrs.

To **El Sauce/Laguna Azul**, from La Banda de Shilcayo, near the hospital, cars US$4.30, 1½ hrs; combis US$2.50, more frequent on weekends. To **Juanjui**, combis with Turismo Selva, address above, US$4.70, 3 hrs.

To **Lamas**, cars from Av Alfonso Ugarte cuadra 11, US$1.45, 30 mins.

❶ Directory

Jaén and around *p527*
Banks BBVA, Ramón Castilla y San Martín, at the plaza, ATM (Visa/MasterCard) and US$ cash. **BCP**, Jr Maynas y San Pablo de la Cruz, for ATM and cash. **BCP**, Bolívar y V Pinillos, at the plaza. ATM (Visa/MasterCard), US$ cash and TCs. Many *cambios* on V Pinillos 1 block north of plaza, US$ cash only. **John Lennon**, V Pinillos right on the plaza, fair rates, helpful. **Internet** Many places, US$0.40 per hr. **Post** Pardo Miguel y Bolívar.

Jaén to the border *p528*
San Ignacio
Banks Only US$ cash exchanged at Banco de la Nación, Av San Ignacio 150; and Comercial Unión, Av San Ignacio 454, Mon-Sat 0700-1300, 1430-1900, Sun morning only, fair rates. **MultiRed ATM**, on the plaza, takes Visa. **Internet** Several places, US$0.40 per hr.

Moyobamba *p529, map p530*
Banks BBVA, San Martín 494, ATM (Visa/ MasterCard), US$ cash and TCs. **BCP**, Alonso de

Alvarado 903 y San Martín. ATM (Visa/Master-Card). **Interbank**, San Martín y Callao, ATM (Visa/MasterCard), US$ cash and TCs, euro cash. **Lizana Cambio**, Alonso de Alvarado, cuadra 10. Cash US$ and euro, good rates. **Scotiabank**, Alonso de Alvarado y San Martín. ATM (Visa/MasterCard), US$ cash and TCs.

Tarapoto *p531, map p532*

Banks BBVA, Ramírez Hurtado, Plaza Mayor, with Visa/MasterCard ATM. **BCP**, Jr Maynas y San Pablo de la Cruz, for ATM and cash. **Interbank**, Grau 119, near the plaza. **La Inmaculada**, supermarket, Martínez de Compagñón, just off plaza, has Global Net ATM which accepts many cards. **Cambio Popi**, Jr Maynas 174, cash US$ and euro, good rates. **Scotiabank**, Ramírez Hurtado y Grau, corner of plaza. ATM for Plus/Visa and MasterCard/Maestro/Cirrus. **Internet** Several places in the centre, US$0.55 per hr.

Contents

Central Highlands

At a glance

⊖ **Getting around** Train as far as Huancavelica; by bus.

◉ **Time required** 1-2 weeks.

☀ **Weather** May-Sep is the dry season. Nov-Apr can be wet.

⊗ **When not to go** Travel can be difficult in the rainy season.

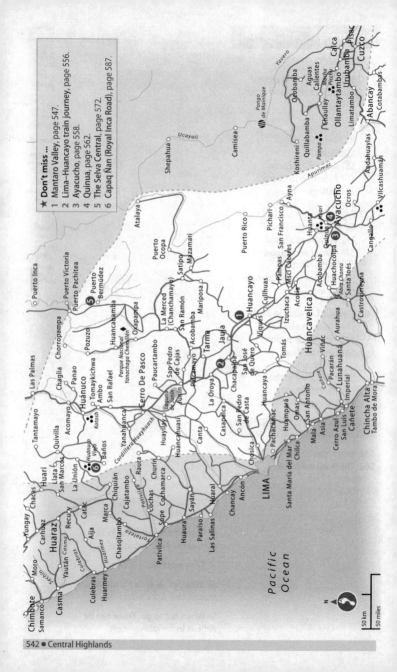

★ Don't miss ...
1 Mantaro Valley, page 547.
2 Lima–Huancayo train journey, page 556.
3 Ayacucho, page 558.
4 Quinua, page 562.
5 The Selva Central, page 572.
6 Capaq Ñan (Royal Inca Road), page 587.

Stretching from the southern end of the Cordillera Blanca right up to Cuzco department, this area of stunning mountain scenery and timeless Andean towns and villages is a must for those who appreciate traditional, good-quality textiles and ceramics. The main highlights include the cities of Huancayo, Ayacucho and the surrounding villages, which are the main production centres for handicrafts. The Central Railway from Lima to Huancayo has passenger services, so one of the most outstanding train rides in South America can be experienced once more. But Huancayo is still a little off the tourist compass. Meanwhile, Ayacucho hosts one of the largest and most impressive Holy Week celebrations in Latin America and at that time becomes a real focus of attention.

If you are seeking refuge from the Andean chill, the road through Tarma to the Selva Central is one of the most beautiful in Peru, leading to a relatively unexplored region of the country. More than just fabulous landscapes, this area also hides important pre-Inca sites, such as Kótosh (near Huánuco) and Huari (outside Ayacucho), two early examples of Andean urban civilizations. Stretches of the Royal Inca Road run from the temple fortress of Huánuco Viejo and up the Yanahuanca Valley, serving as reminders of this great imperial causeway. The Spaniards, too, have left their mark, with fine churches and mansions in Ayacucho.

Lima to Ayacucho

The Central Highway and the famous Central Railway take you up from the coast to the thin air of the metal-smelting zone of La Oroya. To get there you have to follow some of the highest routes in the continent. Beyond La Oroya are traditional towns and remains of pre-Hispanic cultures on the altiplano. Huancayo is the commercial centre of the region and the heart of a valley whose villages concentrate on making handicrafts and holding festivals. Head south towards Ayacucho on difficult roads, either via the departmental capital of Huancavelica, or through more remote but magnificent scenery. ▶▶ *For listings, see pages 549-557.*

Ins and outs

Getting there There are flights from Lima to Ayacucho and Huancayo. The Central Highway between Lima and Huancayo more or less parallels the course of the railway. At La Oroya (see page 545) it divides, with its southern branch following the valley of the Río Mantaro to Huancayo and on to Huancavelica or Ayacucho. Buses serve all the main towns. With the paving of roads from Lima to Huancayo and on to Huancavelica, Pisco to Ayacucho and Nazca to Abancay, there are now more options for getting to the sierra, but all other roads in this region are in poor condition, especially when wet.

Chosica, San Pedro de Casta and Marcahuasi → *Colour map 3, C4.*

Chosica (860 m), 40 km from Lima, is the real starting place for the mountains. It is warm and friendly and, known as 'la villa del sol', a great place to escape Lima's grey cloud. Beyond the town looms a precipitous range of hills almost overhanging the streets. There are some basic hostales in town and, outside, weekend resorts (see www.chosica.com). Around 40 km beyond Chosica, up the picturesque Santa Eulalia valley, is the village of **San Pedro de Casta** (3180 m), which has some interesting sights nearby. Above the village, at 3900-4100 m, is **Marcahuasi** ① *2½-3½ hrs' hike from San Pedro, depending on route, US$3.30 (US$1 for students)*, a table mountain (*meseta*) covering about 3 km by 3 km. There are three lakes here, a 40-m-high so-called 'Monumento a la Humanidad' and other mysterious lines, gigantic figures, sculptures, astrological signs and megaliths, which the late Daniel Ruzo describes in various publications, eg *La Cultura Masma* (Extrait de l'Ethnographie, Paris, 1956). Others speculate that the formations are the result of wind erosion and there are plenty of sites about its significance on the internet. The trail starts behind the village of San Pedro and bends to the left. About halfway you have to choose between the longer trail (the easier of the two) which goes to El Anfiteatro, and the shorter trail ending at el Monumento a la Humanidad, which is better for views of the valley below. Local guides can be hired, advisable in misty weather. Mules for carrying bags cost US$4.30 to hire from the tourist office; a horse costs US$5. Overnight camping is popular at the 'amphitheatre' at weekends, but this can be a noisy affair with loud parties. **Tourist information** ① *T01-297 2344, communal phone*, is available at the municipality on the plaza. Tours can be arranged with travel agencies in Lima.

La Oroya and around → *Colour map 3, C4.*

Beyond Chosica each successive valley looks greener and lusher, with a greater variety of trees and flowers. Between Río Blanco and **Chicla** (Km 127, 3733 m), Inca contour-terraces can be seen quite clearly. After climbing up from **Casapalca** (Km 139, 4154 m), there are glorious views of the highest peaks, and mines, at the foot of a deep gorge. The road climbs to the **Ticlio Pass**, before the descent to **Morococha** (Km 169, altitude 4600 m) and **La Oroya**. A large metal flag of Peru can be seen at the top of Mount Meiggs, not by any means the highest in the area, but through it runs **Galera Tunnel**, 1175 m long, in which the main line of the Central Railway reaches its greatest altitude, 4782 m. At the mouth of the tunnel (Km 132), on one side of a crater, is **Ticlio**, one of the highest passenger stations in the world at 4758 m. The railway is a magnificent feat of engineering, with 58 bridges, 69 tunnels and six zigzags, passing beautiful landscapes. It was the project of the great American railway engineer, Henry Meiggs (who died before it was finished) and built by the Pole, Ernesto Malinowski. It is definitely worth the ride on the new tourist service. ►► *See Transport, page 555.*

La Oroya (3755 m), the main smelting centre for the region's mining industry, can seem a dreary place with its slag heaps and appalling air pollution, but is nevertheless full of vitality. It stands at the fork of the Yauli and Mantaro rivers, 196 km from Lima by a road. Any traveller, but asthmatics in particular, beware, the pollution from the heavy industry causes severe irritation. ►► *For places to stay east and north of La Oroya, see pages 576 and 589.*

Jauja and around → *Colour map 3, C4. Altitude: 3330 m.*

Some 80 km southeast of La Oroya is Jauja, a friendly, unspoilt town in the middle of a good area for walking. It was Pizarro's provisional capital until the founding of Lima. It has a very colourful Wednesday and Sunday market. There's a **tourist office for Junín department** ① *Jr Grau 528, T064-362897, junin@mincetur.gob.pe (unlikely they will reply).* The **Museo Arqueológico Julio Espejo Núñez** ① *Jr Cusco 537, T064-361163, Mon and Wed 1500-1900, Sun 0900-1200, 1400-1700, donations welcome,* is a quaint but endearing little gem of a museum, with an eclectic mix of relics from various cultures and regions of Peru. It includes two mummies, one still wrapped in the original shroud. To enter, knock on door of La Casa del Caminante opposite, where the creator and curator of the museum lives. He also has a collection of fossils found in the area over the last 50 years. The **Cristo Pobre** church is claimed to have been modelled after Notre Dame and is something of a curiosity. On a hill above Jauja is a fine line of Inca storehouses and, on hills nearby, are the ruins of hundreds of circular stone buildings from the Huanca culture. There are also ruins near the **Laguna de Paca** ① *3.5 km away, colectivos leave regularly from Av Pizarro, 10 mins, US$0.30.* The western side of the lake is lined with restaurants that are good for lunch; try the delicious *ceviche de trucha* and, at weekends, *pachamanca*. It is possible to walk around the lake in about three hours. Many restaurants have launches offering half-hour boat trips at weekends, US$0.75 per person.

On the road to Huancayo 18 km to the south, is **Concepción** (altitude 3251 m), with a market on Sunday. From Concepción, a branch road leads for 6 km to the **Convent of Santa Rosa de Ocopa** ① *Wed-Mon 0900-1200 and 1500-1800, tours start on the hour and last 45 mins, US$1.10, colectivos run from the market in Concepción, 15 mins, US$0.25.* This Franciscan monastery, set in beautiful surroundings, was established in 1725 for training missionaries for the jungle. It contains a fine library with over 20,000 volumes and a biological museum with animals and insects from the jungle. The convent also contains a large collection of paintings.

Huancayo and around → *For listings, see pages 549-557. Colour map 3, C5. Altitude: 3271 m.*

The large, sprawling departmental capital of Huancayo is a functional kind of place. As the main commercial centre for inland Peru it has few tourist trappings. Huancayo's attractions are beyond the city boundaries. It lies in the beautiful Mantaro Valley, surrounded by villages that produce their own original crafts and celebrate festivals all year round, see page 553. The city has its own important festivals, however, when people flock from far and wide with an incredible range of food, crafts, dancing and music. At this height, nights are chilly and altitude can be a problem for those arriving straight from the coast.

Ins and outs

The nearest airport to Huancayo is outside Jauja (see above) and the city is served, if a bit haphazardly, by train to and from Lima and Huancavelica. Bus services are good and, as elsewhere in the Andes, serve the entire region. There is a small **tourist information booth** ⓘ *Real 481, in Plaza Huamanmarca, T064-238480/233251.* **Indecopi** ⓘ *Moquegua 730, El Tambo, T064-245180, abarrientos@indecopi.gob.pe.* See also www.hyoperu.com for information. **Touring y Automóvil Club del Perú** ⓘ *Jr Lima 355, T064-231204, huancayo@ touringperu.com.pe.* Beware of theft if arriving early in the morning. ▸▸ *See Transport, page 555.*

Sights

The Plaza de Armas is called **Plaza de la Constitución**. The main sights, though, as well as the Sunday market, are quite a way from the centre. The **Sunday market** gets going after 0900 every week and provides a little taste of Huancayo at festival time. The stalls on Jirón Huancavelica, 3 km long and four stalls wide, still sell typical clothes, fruit, vegetables, hardware, handicrafts and, especially, traditional medicines and goods for witchcraft. However, the market has been described as expensive and offering little choice; it is better to go to the villages for local handicrafts. There is also an impressive **daily market** behind the railway station and a **large handicrafts market** between Ancash and Real, block seven, offering a wide selection.

Museo Colegio Salesiano ⓘ *Pasaje Santa Rosa, north of the Río Shullcas, T064-247763, http://www.hyoperu.com/huancayo/museos/1, Mon-Fri 0800-1200, 1500-1800, Sun 1000-1200, US$1.75,* has over 5000 pieces, a fascinating Victorian-style cabinet of curiosities with everything ranging from two-headed beasts to an almost up-to-date collection of all the coins of the United States of America.

Parque de la Identidad Wanka ⓘ *Jr San Jorge, Barrio San Carlos, northeast of the city (35 mins' walk from plaza), free but contributions appreciated,* is a fascinating mixture of surrealistic construction, interwoven with indigenous plants and trees and the cultural history of the Mantaro Valley. It can get crowded at weekends. There are several restaurants serving traditional meals in the area.

Mantaro Valley

The main attraction in the area is the Mantaro Valley, which is rich in culture, music, local food, dances and handicrafts and plays host to numerous festivals. On the outskirts of town is **Torre-Torre** – impressive, eroded sandstone towers on the hillside. Take a bus to Cerrito de la Libertad and walk up. To the west of the Río Mantaro, 19 km from Huancayo, is **Viques**, which is known for the production of belts and blankets. **Huayucachi**, 7 km away, organizes festivals with dancing and impressive costumes in January and February and also makes embroidery.

The ruins of **Warivilca** ⓘ *15 km from Huancayo, daily 1000-1200 and 1500-1700, US$0.15; to get here take one of the micros for Chilca, which leave from C Real,* feature the remains of a pre-Inca temple of the Huanca culture. There is a museum in the plaza (open in the morning only), with deformed skulls, and modelled and painted pottery of successive Huanca and Inca occupations of the shrine.

The villages of **Cochas Chico** and **Cochas Grande**, 11 km from Huancayo on the east side of the Mantaro river, are both well worth visiting. Micros leave from the corner of Amazonas and Giráldez, US$0.25. This is where the famous *mate burilado*, or gourd carving, is done (see page 672). You can buy the gourds cheaply direct from the manufacturers, but ask around. You can also enjoy beautiful views of the Valle de Mantaro and Huancayo.

Hualahoyo, 11 km from Huancayo, has a little chapel with 21 colonial canvases, while **San Agustín de Cajas** (8 km) makes fine hats and **San Pedro** (10 km) makes wooden chairs. In the village of **Hualhuas**, 12 km from Huancayo, you can find fine alpaca weavings, which you can watch being made. The weavers take special orders; small items can be finished in a day. Negotiate a price.

The town of **San Jerónimo** is renowned for the making of silver filigree jewellery, on sale at the Wednesday market. Near the town are good places to eat *pachamanca* (meat and vegetables cooked on hot stones buried in the ground). A major fiesta is held in the town on the third Saturday in August, when one of the two plazas is converted into a temporary bullring. There are ruins two to three hours' walk above San Jerónimo, but seek advice before hiking to them.

Izcuchaca

On the railway line between Huancayo and Huancavelica, **Izcuchaca** is the site of a bridge over the Río Mantaro. On the edge of town is a fascinating pottery workshop whose machinery is driven by a water turbine. There is also a small shop. It's a nice hike to the chapel on a hill overlooking the valley (one to 1½ hours each way). Heading towards Ayacucho, there is a good road from Izcuchaca to the Quichuas hydroelectric scheme, but thereafter it is narrow with hair-raising bends and spectacular bridges. The scenery, however, is staggering.

Huancavelica and around → *For listings, see pages 549-557. Colour map 3, C5. Altitude: 3660 m.*

Huancavelica, capital of the next department south, is a friendly and attractive town, surrounded by huge, rocky mountains. Founded in the 16th century by the Spanish to exploit rich deposits of mercury and silver, Huancavelica has very few mines open now. It is predominantly an indigenous town, where people still wear traditional costume.

Ins and outs

Huancavelica is not on an air route, but the road between Huancayo and Huancavelica has been recently paved and is a delightful ride, if you can find a driver who will not scare the living daylights out of you. Mechanical problems aside, the Huancayo–Huancavelica train service should run daily, but is less comfortable than the buses now. Buses and colectivos serve the entire region. The **Dircetur office** ① *Victoria Garma 444, p 2, T067-452938, dircetur_hcv@hotmail.com, Mon-Fri 0800-1300, 1415-1730*, is very helpful. See also www.hellohuancavelica.com. Don't wander around the surrounding hills alone. Contact **Serenazgo** ① *Sebastián Barranca 265, T067-368637*, if you need to report a crime.

Sights

The **cathedral** on the Plaza de Armas has an altar considered to be one of the finest examples of colonial art in Peru. Also very impressive are the five other churches in town. The **church of San Francisco**, for example, has no less than 11 altars. Sadly, though, most of the churches are closed to visitors. Bisecting the town is the Río Huancavelica. South of the river is the main commercial centre. North of the river, on the hillside, are the **thermal baths** ① *0600-1500, US$0.15 for private rooms (water is not very hot), US$0.10 for the hot public pool*. There are also hot showers but take a lock for the doors. The **handicraft sellers** congregate in front of the Municipalidad on M Muñoz and the Biblioteca on the Plaza de Armas (V Toledo). The regional INC office ① *Plazuela de San Juan de Dios s/n, T067-453420, inc_huancavelica@yahoo.es*, is a good source of information on festivals, archaeological sites, history, and more. The institute also runs courses on music and dancing, and hosts lectures some evenings. There is an interesting but small **Museo Regional Daniel Hernández Morillo** ① *Plazuela de San Juan de Dios, Arica y Raimondi, Mon-Sat 1000-1300 and 1500-1900.*

Routes to Ayacucho → *Colour map 3, C5/6.*

If driving to Ayacucho and beyond, roads are amazingly rough. Don't go alone and count kilometres diligently to keep a record of where you are as road signs are poor. The direct route from Huancavelica to Ayacucho (247 km) goes via **Santa Inés** (4650 m) at Km 78. Out of Huancavelica, the road climbs steeply with switchbacks between herds of llamas and alpacas grazing on rocky perches. Around Pucapampa (Km 43) is one of the highest habitable *altiplanos* (4500 m), where the rare and highly prized ash-grey alpaca can be seen. Snow-covered mountains are seen as the road climbs to 4853 m at the **Abra Chonta Pass**, 23 km before Santa Inés. By taking the turn-off to Huachocolpa at Abra Chonta and continuing for 3 km you'll reach one of the highest drivable passes in the world, at 5059 m. Nearby are two lakes (Laguna Choclacocha), which can be visited in 2½ hours. Beyond Santa Inés at the **Abra de Apacheta** (4750 m), 98 km from Ayacucho, the rocks have oxidized into all the colours of the rainbow, with a violet river running through the fabulous scenery.   •

An alternative is to travel from Huancavelica to **Lircay**, a small village with accommodation. From here, catch a bus to **Julcamarca**, which has a colonial church, and a minibus from Julcamarca plaza to Ayacucho; beautiful scenery all the way.

There is another route to Ayacucho from Huancayo, little used by buses, which involves less climbing for cyclists. Cross the pass into the Mantaro Valley on the road to **Quichuas**. Then continue to **Anco** and **Mayocc**, where you'll find accommodation. From here the road crosses a bridge after 10 km and in another 20 km reaches **Huanta** (see page 563). A paved road runs from here to Ayacucho. ›› *See Transport, page 569.*

ⓞ Lima to Ayacucho listings

For Sleeping and Eating price codes and other relevant information, see pages 38-44.

⬤ Sleeping

Chosica, San Pedro de Casta and Marcahuasi *p544*

F Marcahuasi, just off the plaza in San Pedro de Casta. The best hotel in San Pedro (**G** per person without bath), clean, has a restaurant.

Locals in San Pedro will put you up, **G**; ask at tourist information at the municipality on the plaza, see above. Take all necessary camping equipment and water for Marcahuasi trek.

La Oroya *p544*

F Hostal Chavín, Tarma 281. Shared bathroom, cheap restaurant.
G Hostal Inti, Arequipa 117, T064-391098. Shared bathroom, warm water, clean but basic.

Jauja and around *p545*

D Hostal Manco Cápac, Jr Manco Cápac 575, T064-361620/T99-974 9119 (mob), www.hostal-mancocapac.com. Central, with variety of cosy rooms, doubles with private bath, or **E** per person in shared room, Wi-Fi, beautiful patio, pleasant, relaxing, good breakfast and coffee included, also lunch and dinner available. Owned by Bruno Bonierbale (ex-manager of **South American Explorers**), English, French and Spanish spoken. Recommended.

F Hostal María Nieves, Jr Gálvez 491, 1 block from the Plaza de Armas, T064-362543. Clean, safe, helpful, friendly, price includes large breakfast, hot water all day, parking. Good choice.

G Hostal Los Algarrobos, Huancayo 264, T064-362633. Shared bathroom, hot water in the morning, TV extra, a last resort, frequented by amorous couples.

Huancayo and around p546, map p546
The places listed below are all in Huancayo. Prices may rise in Holy Week.

A-B Presidente, C Real 1138, T064-231275, www.hoteles-del-centro.com. With bathroom, clean and classy, friendly, helpful, safe, with breakfast, restaurant attached. Recommended.

A-B Turismo, Ancash 729, T064-231072, ● www.hoteles-del-centro.com. In a restored colonial building, same owner as **Presidente** but more atmosphere. Rooms with bath and cable TV, some rooms are small but elegant, comfortable, quiet, Wi-Fi in strategic areas, money exchange. The restaurant (♈-♈) is a bit pricey but some of the dishes are well worth it, excellent service.

B El Marquez, Puno 294, T064-219202, www.elmarquezhuancayo.com. Rooms with bath and TV, continental breakfast included, extra heaters available, Wi-Fi, small business centre, good value and efficient, laundry, safe parking.

D Kiya, Giráldez 107, Plaza Constitución, T064-214955, www.hotelkiya.com. With bath, hot water, Wi-Fi, TV, clean and comfortable although in ageing modern block, helpful staff. Restaurant does not serve breakfast. Spectacular view of plaza.

D-E La Casa de la Abuela, Av Giráldez 691, T064-223303, www.incasdelperu.org/casa-de-la-abuela. **F** per person in dorms. Comfortable hostel in well-restored colonial building, plenty of services, discounts for Footprint readers and long-stay guests. Some

rooms with antique beds, good hot showers, breakfast included, meals available, games and TV rooms, free internet and Wi-Fi, laundry services, Spanish classes and tours arranged, English spoken, sociable staff. Good place to meet other backpackers. Free taxi pick-up from the bus station if requested in advance.

D-E Santa Felicita, Giráldez 145, Plaza Constitución, T064-235285, irmaleguia@ hotmail.com. With bathroom, hot water, more expensive with cable TV, good, breakfast extra.

E pp Casa Alojamiento de Aldo y Soledad Bonilla, Huánuco 332, no sign, half a block from Mcal Cáceres bus station, T064-232103. Renovated 2009. Rates quoted are full board, cheaper without, colonial house, owners speak English, laundry, secure, relaxing, nice courtyard, tours arranged, best to book ahead.

E Los Balcones, Puno 282, T064-214881. Very clean and comfortable rooms, free Wi-Fi, cable TV, hot water, helpful staff. Elevator makes it reasonably accessible for those with disabilities. View of the back of the cathedral. Highly recommended.

E Retama Inn, Ancash 1079, T064-219193, retamainn73@hotmail.com. All amenities but noisy location, hot water, comfortable beds, TV, helpful, café/bar, breakfast US$2.

F pp Peru Andino, Pasaje San Antonio 113-115, San Carlos, 1 block from Parque Tupac Amaru, just in the 1st block of Francisco Solano, left side of Defensoría del Pueblo, 10-15 mins' walk from the centre, T064-223956. Clean rooms with hot showers, private or shared bathroom, safe area, cosy atmosphere, run by Sra Juana and Sr Luis, they speak some English, friendly. Organize trekking and mountain bike tours, personal Spanish classes. Pick-up and transfer from Lima airport to bus station. Highly recommended.

G pp Hospedaje Familiar Tachi, Huamanmarca 125, T064-219980, saenz_nildy@hotmail.com. Central, but not the safest area, small, comfy, hot water, shared showers, family-run, nice atmosphere and views from terrace.

G Hostal Santo Domingo, Ica 655, T064-218890. Set around 2 pleasant patios, clean, basic, good value, pay in advance.

Mantaro Valley p547

In Izcuchaca ask in stores off the plaza. Many locals are enthusiastic about renting a room to a gringo traveller for a night. You may be offered a room in a run-down, adobe colonial mansion and make a friend for life.

E Hostal La Llamita, Jr Huancayo 445, Hualhuas. 30 rooms with bath, hot water, also dormitories (**G** per person with shared bath and cold water), friendly owner, swimming pool, laundry, restaurant and handicraft shop.

Huancavelica and around p548

A-B Presidente, Plaza de Armas, T067-452760, www.hoteles-del-centro.com. By far the poshest hotel in town, lovely colonial building, tourist or business rooms available. All rooms have cable TV, heating, shower, breakfast included, safe, parking, laundry, Wi-Fi, internet, smart restaurant serving *chifa* and *criollo* food (♥♥-♥), cafetería and room service.

D-E Ascención, Jr Manco Cápac 481 (Plaza de Armas), T067-451397/453103. A hidden treasure: no sign, go in the wooden door next to the Comisería and follow the 'hotel' sign. Rooms with cable TV and bath, cheaper without TV, cheaper still without bath, hot water, very clean, comfortable, wood floors.

E La Portada, Virrey Toledo 252, T067-453603. Very basic, but with secure metal doors, **G** without bath, hot water all day, small desks in rooms, extra heaters available at a small cost. Women may be put off by the public urinal in the shared shower area, but there is a better bathroom by the cafetería.

F Camacho, Jr Carabaya 481, T067-453298. Shared shower, hot water in morning only, good value, padlocks on doors. Old-fashioned and much religious iconography.

F San José, Jr Huancayo 299, at top of Barranca (past Santo Domingo), T067-452958. Padlocks on doors, with bath, solar heaters provide hot water during day only, cheaper without bath, clean but basic, comfortable beds, helpful.

F-G Tawantinsuyo, Carabaya 399 y Manchego Muñoz, T067-452968. Cheaper without washbasin, 24-hr hot water, wood floors and curtains.

There are several other cheap *hospedajes* in town.

Routes to Ayacucho p549

The following are all **G**. In **Santa Inés**, you can sleep at **Alojamiento Andino**, and there's a very friendly restaurant called **El Favorito**; several others. **Lircay** has an unnamed *hostal* at Sucre y La Unión, with bath and hot water. It's much better than **Hostal El Paraíso**, opposite, also with bath. **Hostal Villa Julcamarca**, near the plaza in **Julcamarca** has no tap water and is really basic. In **Quichas**, try **Hostal Recreo Sol y Sombra**, which is basic but helpful and charming, with a small courtyard. The **Hostal Gabi** in **Anco** is appalling but better than anything else.

🍽 Eating

Chosica, San Pedro de Casta and Marcahuasi p544

♥ **Don Alberto**, Av Lima Sur 280, Chosica, T064-3603557, http://donalbertorestaurante. com. Open Tue-Sun from 1200. An open-air restaurant serving lots of meat, chicken, trout and other *comida criolla* as well as pizza.

♥ **El Fondo Marino**, Jr Callao 137, Chosica, T064-3614340, http://elfondomarino.com. Open daily 1000-1900 with live music Sun and holidays. Marine decor, lots of seafood, *ceviche, tiradito*.

La Oroya and around p544

♥ **El Tambo**, 2 km outside La Oroya on road to Lima. Good trout and frogs, local dishes and cheese and *manjar*. Receives most of trade from coaches stopping on the way to/ from Lima. Recommended as the best in town.

Jauja and around p545

Centro Naturista, Huarancayo 138 (no sign). Serves fruit salad, yoghurt, granola, etc and sells medicinal drinks. Very basic interior.

D'Chechis, Jr Bolívar 1166, T064-368530. For lunch only, excellent food.

Ganso de Oro, R Palma 249, T064-362166. Restaurant in hotel of same name, which is not recommended. Varied prices, unpretentious. The *Ganso de Oro* cocktail, based on pisco, is cheap and lethal.

La Rotonda, Tarapacá 415, T064-368412. Tables in a pleasant courtyard or dining rooms, good lunch menu and pizzas in the evening.

Huancayo and around p546, map p546

Breakfast is served in Mercado Modelo from 0700. Better class, more expensive restaurants serve typical dishes for about US$4-5, plus tax, drinks can be expensive. Lots of cheap restaurants along Av Giráldez.

Detrás de la Catedral, Ancash 335, T064-212969. Pleasant atmosphere, good dishes, charcoal grill in the corner keeps the place warm on cold nights. Considered by many to be one of the best restaurants in town.

El Olímpico, Giráldez 199. For the past 50 years, locals have been calling El O 'the best restaurant in Huancayo', upscale, offers Andean and Creole dishes. The owner's model-car collection is displayed in glass cabinets throughout the restaurant.

La Cabaña, Av Giraldez 652. Pizzas, ice cream, *calentitos* and other dishes, excellent atmosphere, live music Thu-Sun (see **Incas del Perú** under Tour operators, below).

Pizzería Antojitos, Puno 599. Attractive, atmospheric pizzeria, live music some nights.

Chifa Xu, Giráldez 208. Good food at reasonable prices, always busy.

A La Leña, Paseo la Breña 144 (another branch on Ancash). Good salads, nice atmosphere, always popular, probably the best rotisserie chicken in town.

Chifa El Centro, Giráldez 238, T064-212575. Another branch in Av Leandra Torres 240.

Chinese food, good service, value and atmosphere (has a waterfall).

Donatelo's, Puno 287. Excellent pizza place with modern atmosphere, popular with families, fried chicken as well.

La Pérgola, Puno 444. Pleasant atmosphere, woody and warm, overlooking the plaza, 4-course *menú*.

Cafés

Café El Parque, Giráldez y Ancash, main plaza. Popular *juguería*, with sweets, cakes and coffee.

El Inka, Puno 530, T064-232550. Popular *fuente de soda* with milkshakes, real coffee, good desserts and Peruvian food.

El Paraíso, Arequipa 428. Average vegetarian food, juices, good service. There is another vegetarian restaurant opposite at No 429.

ImaginArte, Jr Ancash 260. Open from 1800. An interesting contemporary art gallery, often displaying work based on ethnic Peruvian culture. Good coffee and cakes.

Panadería Koky, Ancash y Puno, next to **Hotel Marquez**, T064-234707. Open 0700-2300. Good for breakfasts, sandwiches, pastries and cappuccino, also serves good main dishes (lunch 1230-1530), fancy, free Wi-Fi.

Mantaro Valley p547

Restaurant El Parque, on plaza, Izcuchaca. Opens 0700. Delicious food.

Huancavelica and around p548

There are lots of cheap, basic restaurants on C Muñoz and Jr Virrey Toledo. All serve typical food, mostly with a set menu for around US$1.50. There area also *chifas* on Toledo.

Mochica Sachún, Av Virrey Toledo 303. Great *menú*, sandwiches and full meals, friendly, popular.

Roma II, Manco Cápac 580, T067-452608. Open 1800-2300. Pizza smells delicious, friendly, delivery available.

Chifa El Mesón, Manchego Muñoz 153, T067-453570. Very popular, standard *chifa* fare, delivery available.

Joy, Virrey Toledo 230. Award-winning *criollo* and regional dishes, long-established. It's brightened by a Mondrian-like paint job, photos of masked dancers from local fiestas, and Beatles posters. Also **Joy Campestre**, Av De los Incas 870. Typical regional dishes in leisurely country environment.

🅞 Bars and clubs

Huancayo and around *p546, map p546*
All the *peñas* have folklore shows with dancing, normally Fri, Sat and Sun 1300-2200. Entrance is about US$2 per person. Try **Ollantaytambo**, Puno, block 2, or **Taki Wasi**, Huancavelica y 13 de Noviembre. Most clubs are open 2000-0200; some charge an entrance fee of US$3-4.
Galileo, Paseo La Breña 378. A high-class bar, live music some nights.
La Noche, Pasaje San Antonio 241. Nice disco.

Huancavelica and around *p548*
Huancavelica is the epicentre of entertainment for youth from the surrounding area. There are various *peñas* and karaokes on Virrey Toledo (although **Discotek Nighclub La Casona** at No 123 is depressing and unsafe). **Dancing Palace/Karaoke Ariana** (aka Skandalo), Jr Agustín Gamarra 177 and 179. These 2 establishments appear to be separate but in fact when you enter one, you end up in the other. Ariana is a karaoke bar with an older crowd. Dancing Palace is a spectacular *chichódromo* teeming with of hundreds of local teenagers hooking up and dancing to Peruvian pop music.
Discoteca las Casona, Manco Cápac 371. Salsa. Strange glow-in-the-dark zodiac paintings, black light, and smoke machine give this place a ghoulish atmosphere.

🅞 Festivals and events

Huancayo and around *p546, map p546*
1-6 Jan New Year celebrations.
19-31 Jan Festividad del Tayta Niño

20 Jan San Sebastián y San Fabián (recommended in Jauja).
16-17 Jul Virgen del Carmen.
8 Sep Festividad de la Virgen de Cocharcas.
30 Sep Festividad de San Jerónimo de Tunan.
4 Oct San Francisco de Asís.
18 Oct San Lucas.
28-30 Oct The culmination of month-long celebrations for **El Señor de los Milagros**.
1 Nov Día de Todos los Santos.
8 Dec Inmaculada Concepción.
25 Dec Navidad (Christmas).

Mantaro Valley *p547*
There are so many festivals in the Mantaro Valley that it is impossible to list them all. Practically every day of the year there is a celebration of some sort in one of the villages.
19-31 Jan Festividad del Tayta Niño, in Huayucachi.
Feb Carnival celebrations for the whole of the month, with highlights on 2 Feb, **Virgen de la Candelaria**, and later in the month **Concurso de Carnaval**.
Mar/Apr Semana Santa is impressive throughout the valley, especially the Good Friday processions.
1 May Fiesta de las Cruces also takes place throughout the valley.
15 Jun Virgen de las Mercedes.
24 Jun San Juan Bautista.
29 Jun San Pedro y San Pablo.
24-25 Jul Fiesta de Santiago.
4 Aug San Juan de Dios.
30 Aug Santa Rosa de Lima.
8 Sep La Virgen de Cocharcas is held in Concepción, Jauja and, more famously, in Sapallanga, 8 km south of Huancayo.
15 Sep Virgen de la Natividad.
23-24 Sep Virgen de las Mercedes.
29 Sep San Miguel Arcángel.
Sep The Semana Turística del Valle del Mantaro is held on different dates.

Huancavelica and around *p548*
The whole area is rich in culture with many festivals and dances.

4-8 Jan Fiesta de los Reyes Magos
y los Pastores.
Jan (moveable) **Fiesta del Niño Perdido**.
20 Jan-mid Mar Pukllaylay Carnavales.
Celebration of the 1st fruits from the ground.
Mar/Apr Semana Santa, Holy Week.
End May-beginning Jun Toro Pukilay.
May and Aug Fiesta de Santiago.
22-28 Dec Los Laygas or Galas
(scissors dance).

O Shopping

Huancayo and around *p546, map p546*
All handicrafts are made outside Huancayo
in the many villages of the Mantaro Valley
(see page 547). The villages are worth
a visit to see how the items are made.
Casa de Artesano, corner of Real and
Paseo La Breña, Plaza Constitución, has
a wide selection of good-quality crafts.
   There is also a **large market** between
Ancash and Real, block 7, offering a wide
selection of local handicrafts. Watch out
for pickpockets. Thieves hand out rolled-
up paper and pick your pocket when you
unravel them.

▲ Activities and tours

Huancayo and around *p546, map p546*
La Caminata is a popular hike from the city
to a glacier at 4850 m on **Huaytapallana** peak
(5572 m). It is organized at weekends by tour
operators: vehicles go to the **Virgen de las
Nieves**, with basic restaurant in 1-1½ hrs,
then a fairly good trail of 6-7 hrs goes around
lakes Carhuascocha and Cocha Grande to
the glacier tongue. Return the same day;
take warm clothing, About US$25 to hire
a vehicle, 6-8 passengers.

Guides
Marco Antonio Jurado Ames, T064-201260,
T064-964 227050 (mob), andinismo_peru@
yahoo.es. Organizes long-distance treks on
the 'hidden paths of Peru'. Many of these
include Huancayo, such as a 2-week trip
from Lima to Machu Picchu via Huancayo,
the Amazon lowlands and Vilcabamba.
Mountain trekking includes the Inka Trail
to Pariaccacca in the Central Andes and the
route from the Amazon to Machu Picchu via
Choquequirao. Also offers rock climbing and
mountaineering courses with the **Mountain
Guide School CEAM**, Huaraz.

Tour operators
American Travel & Service, Plaza
Constitución 122, of 2 (next to the cathedral),
T064-211181, T064-964 830220 (mob),
americtr@huncayotravel.com. Wide range
of classical and more adventurous tours in
the Mantaro Valley and in the central jungle.
Transport and equipment rental possible.
Most group- based day tours start at
US$8-10 per person.
Dargui Tours, Jr Ancash 367, Plaza
Constitución, T064-233705. Also have
office in Lima, Av Conquistadores 1020,
of 203, San Isidro, T01-422 7132,
www.darguitours.com. Standard tours.
Incas del Perú, Av Giráldez 652, T064-
223303, www.incasdelperu.org. Associated
with the **La Cabaña/Otra Lado** restaurants
and **La Casa de la Abuela**. Jungle, biking
and riding trips throughout the region,
as well as language and cultural courses
and volunteer programs. Very popular with
travellers in the region.
Peruvian Tours, Plaza Constitución 122,
p 2, of 1, T064-213069, T964-661044 (mob),
eaiperu@hotmail.com. Next to the cathedral
and **American Travel & Service**. Classic tours
of the Mantaro Valley, plus day trips up to
the Huaytapallana Nevados above Huancayo,
plus long, 16-hr excursions to Cerro de Pasco
and Tarma.

⊖ Transport

San Pedro de Casta and
Marcahuasi p544
Colectivo minibuses for **Chosica** leave from
Av Grau, Lima, when full, 0600-2100, US$0.75.
Most buses on the Lima–La Oroya route are
full so take a colectivo taxi from Chosica to
reach **La Oroya**, US$4, 3 hrs, very scenic,
passing the 2nd-highest railway in the
world. For **San Pedro de Casta**, buses
leave **Chosica** from Parque Echenique,
opposite the market, at 0900 and 1500,
4 hrs, US$2.50; return 0700 and 1400.

La Oroya and around p544
To **Lima** from La Oroya, 4½ hrs, US$5.50. To
Jauja (80 km), 1½ hrs, US$1. To **Tarma**, 1½ hrs,
US$1.50. To **Cerro de Pasco**, 131 km, 3 hrs,
US$2.20. To **Huánuco**, 236 km, 6 hrs, US$4.35.
Buses leave from Zeballos, adjacent to the train
station. Colectivos also run on all routes.

Jauja and around p545
Air
LC Busre flies daily from **Lima** to Francisco
Carle airport (just outside Jauja). Fares range
from US$70-130 one way, depending on
promotions, which include a transfer to
Huancayo (it is marketed as Lima–Huancayo).

Bus
Most companies have their offices on the
Plaza de Armas, but their buses leave from
Av Pizarro. To **Lima**, Cruz del Sur, Pizarro 220,
direct, 3 a day, 6 hrs, US$16 (US$25.40 bus
cama at holiday weekends). To **Huancayo**,
44 km, 1 hr, US$1.25; combis from 25 de Abril
y Ricardo Palma, 1¼ hrs, US$1. To **Cerro de
Pasco**, Turismo Central from 25 de Abril 144,
5 hrs, US$3.55.

Huancayo and around p546, map p546
Bus
Local To **Jauja**, 44 km, 1 hr. Colectivos
and combis leave every few mins from
Huamanmarca y Amazonas, and Plaza
Amazonas, US$1.50. Those via San Jerónimo

and Concepción have 'Izquierda' on the front.
Taxi to Jauja US$10, 45 mins. Most buses to
the **Mantaro Valley** leave from places around
the market area. Buses to **Hualhuas** and
Cajas leave from block 3 of Pachitea. Buses
to **Cochas** leave from Amazonas y Giráldez.

Long distance Most of the bus offices of
the better companies running to Lima are
2-3 blocks north of the main plaza, while those
of the cheaper companies are located to the
north of the Río Shullcas, a 10- to 15-min walk
from the centre. Bus companies to destinations
south of Huancayo, eg Huancavelica and
Ayacucho, are 4-5 blocks south of the
main plaza. A new bus terminal for all buses
is being planned, 3 km north of the centre.

To **Lima**, 6-7 hrs on a good paved road,
US$10-13. Travel by day for fantastic views
and for safety. If you must travel by night,
take warm clothing. Recommended are
Ormeño, Av Mcal Castilla 1379, El Tambo;
Cruz del Sur, Ayacucho 281, T064-235650;
Turismo Central, Jr Ayacucho 274,
T064-223128 (double-decker bus cama),
and **Transportes Rogger**, Lima 561, T064-
212687, cama and semi-cama at 1300 and
2330, comercial at 2230.

To **Huancavelica**, 147 km, 5 hrs, US$2.85.
Many buses leave daily, eg **Transportes Yuri**,
Ancash 1220, 3 a day. A private car from
Huancayo costs US$12-17 per person
depending on your negotiating skills. The
road is paved and the scenery spectacular.
The ride by car is much more comfortable
than the train.

To **Ayacucho**, 319 km, 9-10 hrs, US$10-12.
Molina, C Angaráes 334, T064-224501, 3 a
day, recommended; 1 a day with **Turismo
Central**, US$8. The road is paved for the first
70 km, then in poor condition and is very
difficult in the wet. Take warm clothing.

To **Cerro de Pasco**, 255 km, 5 hrs, US$4,
several departures. Alternatively, take a bus
to **La Oroya** (every 20 mins, from Av Real
about 10 blocks north of the main plaza)
and change (see above). The road to La
Oroya and on to Cerro is in good condition

and there are regular buses and colectivos. To **Huánuco**, 7 hrs, **Turismo Central** have a direct bus at 2115, US$6, good service.

To **Chanchamayo**, Angelitos/San Juan, Ferrocarril 161 and Plaza Amazonas, every 1½ hrs, and **Trans Los Canarios** hourly service via Jauja to **Tarma**, 3 hrs, US$3, some of which continue to **La Merced**, 5 hrs, US$4.70.

ETAS/Angoma, Loreto 744, T064-215424, travels to **Cañete** on the coast, 289 km, 10 hrs, US$4. Tickets are best bought the day before; the office is usually open until about 1930. It is a poor road though the stunning Cañete Valley, with beautiful mountain landscapes (best views on the right). The bus passes through **Llapay**, US$4.55 any time from 1130 in the dry season to 1500 in the wet season, **Yauyos** (2 hrs from Llapay), **Chavín** (3 hrs) and **Catahuasi** (3½ hrs) arriving in **Cañete** from 1930 onwards.

Train

There are 2 unconnected railway stations. The **Central station** (Av Ferrocarril 461, T064-217724/216662) serves **Lima**, via **La Oroya** (298 km). Service on this railway with trains at certain weekends is run by **Ferrocarril Central Andina**, T01-226 6363, www.fcca.com.pe. The fare is US$40 one way, US$62.65 return on the *tren clásico* (old British or Romanian rolling stock) or US$80/114 on the *tren turístico*. The train leaves Lima twice a month. Coaches on the tourist train have reclining seats, heating, restaurant, tourist information, toilets and nurse with first aid and oxygen. Information on forthcoming departures can be obtained from the websites or travel agents, see Activities and tours, page 554.

From the small station in Chilca suburb (15 mins by taxi, US$1), trains run 128.7 km to **Huancavelica**, on a narrow-gauge track (3 ft). There are usually 2 trains (but heavy rains in 2010 followed by line improvement works affected services): at 0630 daily, US$3, and 1300 daily, US$2.50. Tickets can only be

bought on the day of travel; get in the queue at 0600 at the latest. There are 38 tunnels and the line reaches 3676 m. This classic Andean train journey takes 7 hrs and has fine views, passing through typical mountain villages where vendors sell food and crafts. Expect random stops and, in some places, the train has to reverse and change tracks. You can hop off in Izcuchaca, buy bread, then jump back on the moving train.

Izcuchaca *p548*

Trains from Huancayo to **Huancavelica** pass at around 0900 and 1600. Trains from Huancavelica to **Huancayo**, pass at 0800 and 1400-1430. They tend to be very crowded. The direct bus from Huancayo to **Ayacucho** passes at 0800, alternatively take a truck – about 8 hrs to Ayacucho. There is a daily colectivo to Ayacucho at 1000-1100, 8 hrs.

Huancavelica and around *p548*
Bus

All bus companies are at the east end of town, around Parque M Castilla, on Muñoz, Iquitos, Tumbes and O'Donovan. To **Huancayo**, 147 km, 5 hrs, US$2.85, paved road. **Transportes Yuri** and **Transportes Ticllas**, O'Donovan 500. To go only as far as **Izcuchaca** costs US$1.45. To **Lima** there are 2 routes: 1 is via Huancayo, 445 km, 13 hrs minimum, US$5.70. **Libertadores** buses to Huancayo at 1830 go on to Lima, also Ticllas at 1700. The other route is via **Pisco**, 269 km, 12 hrs, US$7 and **Ica**, US$8, at 1730 daily, with **Oropesa**, O'Donovon 599. Buy your ticket 1 day in advance. The road is poor until it joins the Ayacucho–Pisco road. The views are spectacular, but most of the journey is done at night. Be prepared for sub-zero temperatures in the early morning as the bus passes snowfields, then for temperatures of 25-30°C as the bus descends to the coast.

The only direct transport from Huancavelica to **Ayacucho**, is 0430 Sat with **San Juan Bautista**, Plaza Túpac Amaru 107, T067-803062, US$5.70. On other days you have to catch a **San Juan Bautista** bus at 0430 to **Rumichaca** on the paved Pisco–Ayacucho road, just beyond Santa Inés, 4 hrs, then wait for a passing bus to Ayacucho, 1500, 3 hrs, US$2. From Rumichaca it's a spectacular but cold journey to Ayacucho on the paved road, which rarely drops below 4000 m for 150 km. The best alternative is to take a colectivo from Huancavelica to **Lircay**, and continue with the same company from Lircay Terminal Terrestre hourly from 0430 to **Julcamarca**, 2½ hrs, US$3. Minibuses run from Julcamarca plaza to Ayacucho, US$2, 2 hrs. The final option is to travel by bus or train from Huancavelica to **Izcucacha** and change for services to Ayacucho there.

Train

Just a little beyond the bus stations and about 500 m from the Plaza de Armas is the train station. Trains leave for **Huancayo** at 0630 and 1300, daily. Sit on the left for the best views.

❻ Directory

Jauja and around *p545*
Banks Dollar Exchange Huarancayo, on Jr Huarancayo, gives a better rate than BCP, Junín 790 (no TCs). If closed, cash dollars exchanged at clothes shop at Junín y Bolívar, just off the Plaza. **Internet** All along Junín blocks 9 to 12. **Post** Jr Bolívar. **Telephone** Ricardo Palma, opposite Hotel Ganso de Oro.

Huancayo and around *p546, map p546*
Banks BCP, Real 1039. Scotiabank, Real casi Ica. Interbank and Banco Continental are on block 6 of Real. There are several *casas de cambio* on Ancash. Street changers hang out on Giráldez, 100 block. The best place to change money is C Lima, parallel to Plaza Constitución. There are a number of kiosks that stamp your exchanged bills as a means of guaranteeing them. **Internet** Numerous places round Plaza Constitución on Giráldez, Paseo La Breña. Average price under US$0.75 per hr. **Language classes** Katia Cerna is a recommended teacher in Huancayo and Chanchamayo, T064-225332, katiacerna @hotmail.com. She can arrange homestays; her sister Karina works in adventure tourism in Huancayo and the jungle. Tailor-made classes include local trips taking in culture, food, celebrations and fiestas. **Incas del Perú** (see page 554) organize Spanish courses for beginners, US$140 per week, 3 hrs a day classroom tuition, including 5 nights' accommodation at **La Casa de La Abuela** and all meals, also more advanced courses, homestays, and other cultural classes. **Laundry** On Paseo La Breña around the corner from Casa de Artesano. **Medical services** Hospital: Daniel A Carrión, Av Daniel A Carrión 1552, T064-222157/232222. **Police** Av Ferrocarril 555, T064-211653. Tourist police: Av Ferrocarril 580, T064-219851. **Post** On Plaza Huamanmarca.

Huancavelica and around *p548*
Banks BCP, Virrey Toledo 381, west of Plaza. **Caja Municipal**, Virrey Toledo 283. MultiRed ATM on M Muñoz in front of the Municipalidad. **Internet** Despite what they say, internet places open around 0900 till 2100-2200. There are places on V Toledo and M Muñoz. **Librería Municipal**, Plaza de Armas, US$0.60 per hr. **Laundry** Lavandería, Jr Arica 246. **Post** On Ferrua Jos, at block 8 of M Muñoz. **Telephone** Carabaya y Virrey Toledo.

Ayacucho and its hinterland

→ *Colour map 5, A4. Altitude: 2748 m .*

The city of Ayacucho, the capital of its department, is famous for its hugely impressive Semana Santa celebrations, its splendid market and, not least, a plethora of churches – 33 of them no less – giving the city its alternative name La Ciudad de las Iglesias. A week can easily be spent enjoying Ayacucho and its hinterland. The climate is lovely, with warm, sunny days and pleasant balmy evenings. It is a hospitable, tranquil place, where the inhabitants are eager to promote tourism. It also boasts a large, active student population. ▸▸ *For listings, see pages 565-571.*

Ins and outs

Getting there and around The airport is to the east of the city along Avenida Castilla. A taxi to the centre costs US$2. Walk half a block down the street from the airport for a bus or colectivo to the Plaza Mayor. A new Terminal Terrestre opened in June 2008 in Urbanización Los Artesanos, at the end of Avenida Confraternidad, 10 minutes northwest of the centre. This is a large city but the interesting churches and colonial houses are all fairly close to the Plaza Mayor. Barrio Santa Ana is further away to the south and you will probably want to take a taxi to get to it (US$1; it's easy to walk back). Taxis are cheap and mototaxis are plentiful. ▸▸ *See Transport, page 569.*

Tourist information iperú ① *Portal Municipal 45, on the plaza, T066-318305, iperu ayacucho@promperu.gob.pe, Mon-Sat 0830-1930, Sun 0830-1430,* is very helpful. There is a desk at the airport to meet incoming flights and another desk in the Terminal Terrestre. Dircetur ① *Asamblea 481, T066-312548, Mon-Fri 0800-1300,* is also friendly and helpful.

Background

The city was founded on 9 January 1539 by the invading Spaniards, who named it San Juan de la Frontera. This was changed to San Juan de la Victoria after the Battle of Chupas, when the king's forces finally defeated the rival Almagrist power. Despite these Spanish titles, the city always kept its original name of Huamanga. It became an important base for the army of the Liberator Simón Bolívar in his triumphant sweep south from the Battle of Junín. It was here, on the Pampa de Quinua, on 9 December 1824, that the decisive Battle of Ayacucho was fought, bringing Spanish rule in Peru to an end. Huamanga was, therefore, the first city on the continent to celebrate its liberty. In the midst of the massive festivities, the Liberator decreed that the city be named Ayacucho, meaning 'City of Blood'. For much of the 1980s and early 1990s, this title seemed appropriate as the Shining Path terrorized the local populace, severely punishing anyone they suspected of siding with the military. Now, though, peace has returned to this beautiful colonial Andean city.

Sights

The construction of Ayacucho's many colonial religious buildings is said to have been financed by wealthy Spanish mine-owners and governors. Unfortunately many have fallen into disrepair and are closed to the public.

Ayacucho

To 2
To Pisco & Lima
To Museo Anfasep

Mercado Artesanal Shosake Nagase
Quinua
Manco Capac
Libertad
Garcilaso de la Vega
9 de Diciembre
Asamblea
Pasaje Cáceres
Los Andes
Miller
To Combis for Huari, Quinua & Huanta

Av Mariscal Cáceres
Colectivos to Julcamarca
To Combis for Huari, Quinua & Huanta

6
10
8
3
Santo Domingo
4
Bellido
9
Tres Máscaras
Sol
Cuzco
4

Casonas de los Marqueses de Mozobamba y del Pozo
Museo de Arte Popular Joaquín López Antay
Callao
Prefectura
Municipalidad
1
Casas de Cambio
5
Plaza Mayor
Cathedral
13
11
Lima
6
Arequipa
12

La Compañía de Jesús
Centro Turístico Cultural San Cristóbal
Casa Jaúregui
La Merced
San Martín
7
28 de Julio
Grau
Libertad

El Nazareno
9
Carlos F Vivanco
Arco del Triunfo
Av Ramón Castilla
Río Alameda
To 7, Airport & Cuzco
Londres
12

Santa Clara
Mercado de Abastos Carlos F Vivanco
San Francisco de Asís
Raymondi
Huancasolar

S J de Dios
5
Mercado 12 de Abril
C Chorro
Museo Andrés A Cáceres (Casona Vivanco)
8

N
100 metres
100 yards
Santa Teresa
San Cristóbal
To Barrio Santa Ana
To 2
2 de Mayo

Sleeping
1 Ayacucho Hotel Plaza
2 El Marqués de Valdelirios
3 El Mesón
4 Florida
5 Grau
6 Hosp El Centro
7 Hostal Tres Máscaras
8 Hostal San Blas
9 La Crillonesa
10 Marcos
11 San Francisco de Paula
12 Santa María
13 Santa Rosa
14 ViaVia Café Ayacucho

Eating
1 Brasa Roja
2 Cabo Blanco
3 Chifa Wa Lin
4 La Casona
5 La Miel
6 La Pradera
7 Las Flores
8 Mía Pizza
9 Nino
10 Pollería Dorado
11 Portal 1
12 Urpicha

Plaza Mayor and north

Ayacucho is built round the Plaza Mayor in the centre of which is a statue of Independence hero Antonio José de Sucre. Facing onto the plaza are the cathedral, Municipalidad, the Prefectura and the Supreme Court, housed in fine colonial buildings within the Plaza's arcades. The **cathedral** ① *1700-1900, Sun 0900-1700*, was built in 1612. The two towers are in green stone, while the portal is pink. It has three strong, solid naves of simple architecture, in contrast to the elegant decoration of the interior, particularly the superb gold-leaf altars. The cathedral is beautifully lit at night. Next to the cathedral is the **Universidad Nacional de San Cristóbal de Huamanga (UNSCH)**, in the Casona de Castilla y Zamora. It has a small courtyard in which grows a fig tree, after which the university café, **La Higuera**, is named.

On the north side of the Plaza Mayor, on the corner of Portal de la Unión and Asamblea, are the **Casonas de los Marqueses de Mozobamba y del Pozo**, also called Velarde-Alvarez. Recently restored as the Centro Cultural de la UNSCH, frequent artistic and cultural exhibitions are held here, worth a visit. The **Museo de Arte Popular Joaquín López Antay** ① *Portal de la Unión 28, in the BCP building, www.unsch.edu.pe/proyeccion/ museo.htm, Tue-Fri 1030-1700, Sat 1030-1230*, displays local craft work. Leading north from the Plaza is Jr Asamblea, full of eating places, internet cafés and commercial centres. The first two blocks are pedestrianized and called Boulevard del Jr Asamblea. On a parallel street, one of the city's most notable churches is **Santo Domingo** (1548) ① *9 de Diciembre, block 2, open for Mass daily 0700-0800*. Its fine façade has triple Roman arches and Byzantine towers.

North of the centre, **Museo de Memoria Anfasep (Asociación Nacional de Familiares de Secuestrados Detenidos y Desaparecidos del Perú)** ① *Prol Libertad 1229, T066-317170, www.youtube.com/watch?v=rzJ7aSkx4uM, 15 mins' walk from Mercado Artesanal Shosake Nagase, or mototaxi, entry free but give a donation*, provides an insight into the recent history of this region during the violence surrounding the Sendero Luminoso campaign and the government's attempts to counter it. In total, 69,280 people were killed.

South of Plaza Mayor

A stroll down Jr 28 de Julio towards the prominent **Arco del Triunfo** (1910), which commemorates victory over the Spaniards, passes **La Compañía de Jesús** (1605) ① *open only for Mass*. It has one of the most important façades of Viceregal architecture. It is of baroque style and guarded by two impressive 18th-century towers. Its altar is covered in gold leaf and large paintings of saints adorn the nave.

The first two blocks, Boulevard de 28 de Julio, are pedestrianized. Go through the arch to the church of **San Francisco de Asís** ① *28 de Julio, block 3, open daily for morning Mass and 1730-1830*. It dates from 1552 and has an elaborate gilt main altar and several others. It claims the largest bell in the city in its tower. Across 28 de Julio from San Francisco is the **Mercado de Abastos Carlos F Vivanco**, the packed central market. As well as all the household items, meat and other local produce, look for the cheese sellers, the breads and the section dedicated to fruit juices.

Santa Clara de Asís ① *Jr Grau, block 3, open for Mass*, is renowned for its beautifully delicate coffered ceiling and for the statue of Jesús de Nazareno, patron of Huamanga, which heads the procession on the Wednesday of Holy Week. Santa Clara is open for the sale of sweets and cakes made by the nuns (go to the door at Nazareno 184, it's usually open). On the fifth block of 28 de Julio is the late 16th-century **Casona Vivanco**, which houses the **Museo Andrés A Cáceres** ① *Jr 28 de Julio 508, T066-812360, Mon-Sat*

0900-1300, 1400-1800, US$1.25. The museum has a collection of baroque paintings and colonial furniture, some republican and contemporary art, and exhibits on Mariscal Cáceres' battles in the War of the Pacific.

Further south still, on a pretty plazuela, is **Santa Teresa** ① *28 de Julio, block 6, open daily for Mass usually 1600,* with its monastery dating from 1683. It has magnificent gold-leafed altars, heavily brocaded and carved in the churrigueresque style. The nuns here sell sweets and crystallized fruits and a *mermelada de ají,* made to a recipe given to them by God (apparently it is not *picante*). Opposite is tiny **San Cristóbal** ① *Jr 28 de Julio, block 6, rarely open,* with its single tower. This was the first church to be founded in the city (1540) and is one of the oldest in South America.

Back near the centre, the 16th-century church of **La Merced** ① *2 de Mayo, near San Martín, open for Mass,* is the second oldest in the city. The high choir is a good example of the simplicity of the churches of the early period of the Viceroyalty. In 1886 a flagstone was discovered with the sculpted image of a sleeping warrior, known popularly as the 'Chejo-Pacheco'. **Casa Jáuregui** ① *opposite La Merced on 2 de Mayo, Mon-Fri 0800-1700,* also called **Ruiz de Ochoa**, was built in the second half of the 18th century and became the Jáuregui family home, until Peruvian banks restored it in 1974-1997. Its outstanding feature is its doorway, which has a blue balcony supported by two fierce beasts with erect penises.

Barrio Santa Ana

For a fascinating insight into Inca and pre-Inca art and culture, a visit to **Barrio Santa Ana** is a must. Here, about 200 families have workshops making *artesanías*: textiles, *retablos*, ceramics and work in stone. Their work is distributed through the galleries in the Barrio. **Galería de Arte Latina** ① *Plazuela de Santa Ana 105, T066-528315,* is especially recommended. The owner, Alejandro Gallardo Llacctahuamán, and his son, Alexander, are very friendly and have lots of information on weaving techniques and the preservation of their culture. They plan to open a textile museum and Alexander is working with local communities. Also visit **Wari Art Gallery** ① *Jr Mcal Cáceres 302, Santa Ana, T066-312529,* run by Gregorio Sulca and his family, who will explain the Quechua legends, weaving and iconography. Next door is the Sulcas' **Instituto de Cultura Quechua**, which affords wonderful views of the city and surrounding hills from its roof. Both the Gallardos and the Sulcas are renowned internationally. A good grasp of Spanish is essential to appreciate the galleries fully. Note that the galleries in the barrio are closed on Sunday.

Around Ayacucho → *For listings, see pages 565-571.*

Vilcashuamán and Vischongo

The impressive Inca ruins of **Vilcashuamán** are four hours to the south of Ayacucho (120 km), beyond Cangallo. According to John Hemming, Vilcashuamán was an important provincial capital, the crossroads where the road from Cuzco to the Pacific met the empire's north–south highway. The tourist office on the Plaza in Ayacucho has a guidebook, in Spanish, which can be consulted. Near Vilcashuamán is the village of **Vischongo**, which has a market on Wednesday. About an hour's walk uphill from the village are the Inca baths of **Intihuatana**, which are worth seeing as much for their superb location on a beautiful lake as for the ruins themselves.

It is possible to see both ruins in a day, though it's more relaxing to spend the night in Vilcashuamán or camp at the lake near Vischongo. Tours to Vilcashuamán from Ayacucho

The Huari influence

The city of Huari had a population of 50,000 and reached its apogee in AD 900. Its influence spread throughout much of Peru: north to Cajamarca; along the north coast to Lambayeque; south along the coast to Moquegua; and south across the sierra to Cuzco. Before the Inca invasion, the Huari formed a *chanca* – a confederation of ethnic groups – and populated the Pampas river and an area west of the Apurímac. This political agreement between the peoples of Ayacucho, Andahuaylas, Junín and Huancavelica was seen by the Incas in Cuzco as a threat. The Incas fought back around 1440 with a bloody attack on the Huari on the Pampa de Ayacucho, and so began a period of Inca domination. The scene of this massacre is still known as *Rincón de los Muertos*.

include both Vischongo and Intihuatana. ▸▸ *See Activities and tours, page 569, and Transport, page 569.*

Huari

ⓘ *22 km from Ayacucho, daily 0800-1700, US$0.90.*

A good road going north from Ayacucho leads to Huari (frequently spelt Wari), dating from the 'Middle Horizon' (AD 600-1000), when the Huari culture spread across most of Peru. This was the first urban walled centre in the Andes and was used for political, administrative, ceremonial, residential and productive purposes. The huge irregular stone walls are up to 4 m high (although many are long and low) and rectangular houses and streets can be made out. There are large areas of flat stone, which may have been for religious purposes, and there are tomb complexes and subterranean canals and tunnels.

The most important activity here was artistic production. High-temperature ovens were used to mass produce ceramics of many different colours. The Huari also worked with gold, silver, metal and alloys such as bronze, which was used for weapons and decorative objects. The ruins now lie in an extensive tuna cactus forest (don't pick the fruit). There is a small museum at the site, but very little direction and the few explanations are only in Spanish. Tombs of the Huari nobles are being excavated along the road from Ayacucho to Quinua.

Quinua

This village, 37 km northeast of Ayacucho, has a charming cobbled main plaza and many of the buildings have been restored. There is a small market on Sunday. Nearby, on the Pampa de Quinua, a huge obelisk commemorates the battle of Ayacucho. The obelisk is 44 m high, representing 44 years of struggle for independence.

The village's handicrafts are recommended, especially ceramics, which range from model churches and nativity figures to humorous groups of musicians and gossiping women. The rich red local clay is modelled mainly by hand and decorated with local mineral earth colours. Traditionally, the model churches are set on the roofs of newly occupied houses to ward off evil spirits. Virtually every roof in the village has a church on it – including the church itself. **San Pedro Ceramics**, at the foot of the hill leading to the monument, and **Mamerto Sánchez**, Jr Sucre, are good places to find typical pieces but there are many others. By the *paradero* are several *recreos*, tourist restaurants serving typical food. The **Fiesta de la Virgen de Cocharcas** is held around 8 September.

Huanta Valley → *48 km northeast of Ayacucho. Colour map 5, A4.*
The town of **Huanta**, one hour from Ayacucho on the road to Huancayo, overlooks the valley and has a pleasant plaza with palms and other trees. It was in Huanta that the Pokras and Chancas warriors put up their last, brave fight against the Inca invasion. Huanta celebrates the **Fiesta de la Cruz** during the first week of May, with much music and dancing. Its Sunday market is large and interesting, while the permanent daily market covers quite an area. There are many places to eat around town.

The **Valley of Luricocha**, 5 km away, can be visited. It has a lovely, warm climate. The *recreos* (tourist restaurants) at Luricocha are famous for their *platos típicos*. Take a combi from Parque Hospital in Huanta (US$0.15).

The area is notable as the site of perhaps the oldest known culture in South America, 20,000 years old, evidence of which was found in the cave of **Pikimachay**. The cave is 24 km from Ayacucho, on the road to Huanta. It is a 30-minute walk from the road. The remains are now in Lima's museums.

Ayacucho to Cuzco → *For listings, see pages 565-571.*

Andahuaylas and around → *Colour map 5, A4.*
About 240 km from Ayacucho, in a fertile, temperate valley of lush meadows, cornfields and groves of eucalyptus, alder and willow, stands Andahuaylas (2980 m). The town offers few exotic crafts, but it has a good market on Sunday and the surrounding scenery is beautiful. The church of **San Pedro** ① *daily 1600-1670*, takes up the south side of the plaza, which has tulips and other trees, flowers and statues. On the north side is the Municipalidad, with a small **Museo Arqueológico**, which has a good collection of pre-Columbian objects, including mummies. **Dircetur** ① *Av Túpac Amaru 374, T083-421627, diturandahuaylas@hotmail.com.*

A good nearby excursion is to the **Laguna de Pacucha**, beautifully set among the hills. On the shore is the town of Pacucha and various places to eat. A road follows the north shore of the lake and a turn-off climbs to **Sóndor** ① *US$0.65 (beware overcharging by the guardian)*, an Inca archaeological site at 3300 m. Various buildings and small plazas lead up to a conical hill surrounded by concentric stone walls or terracing. At the summit is a large rock said to be an *intihuatana* (hitching post of the sun). There are wonderful views back to Pachuca and over the surrounding valleys. Each 18-19 June **Sóndor Raymi** is celebrated.

Abancay and around → *Colour map 5, A5.*
Nestled between mountains in the upper reaches of a glacial valley at 2378 m, this friendly town is first glimpsed after about two hours on the bus from Andahuaylas. The last few kilometres are on the paved highway from Nazca, a relief after the rough, tortuous descent from the high sierra. The town is a functional, commercial centre, growing in importance now that the paved Lima–Nazca–Cuzco road passes through. For information visit the **tourist office** ① *Lima 206, T083-321664, open 0800-1430*, or **Dircetur** ① *Av Arenas 121, p 1, T083-321664, apurimac@mincetur.gob.pe.*

Half-day tours are run to nearby sites such as the former haciendas of **Yaca** and **Illanya**. Near Yaca is a place where silk worms are bred. Also included is the colonial bridge at **Pachachaca** (which can be seen from any bus going to Andahuaylas), the **Mirador at Taraccasa**, for views over the city, and the thermal baths of **Santo Tomás**.

Santuario Nacional de Ampay ① *US$1.50*, north of town, encompasses lagoons, called Angasccocha (3200 m) and Uspaccocha (3820 m), a glacier on Ampay mountain at

5235 m and flora and fauna typical of these altitudes. By public transport, take a colectivo to Tamburco and ask the driver where to get off. It takes two days of trekking to get to the glacier, with overnight camping.

One hour out of Abancay, at a place called **Carbonera**, a road to the left goes to **Huanipaca** (40 minutes, US$15.15 in car, lodging available, and guides). It continues to Ccenhualla, from where Choquequirao is visible. You descend 1½ hours to **Hacienda San Ignacio** by the Río Apurímac, then climb 14 hours up to **Choquequirao** (much steeper than the Cachora route). Shortly after Carbonera is the turn to Cachora.►► *For Cachora and the route to Choquequirao, see West of Cuzco, page 220.*

Three kilometres from the main road to Cuzco, at 3000 m, is the **Saywite stone** ⓘ *Km 49 from Abancay, well-signed, allow 1-2 hrs to see the whole site. US$4, students US$2.* This large carved rock and its surroundings is a UNESCO World Heritage Site. The principal monolith is said to represent the three regions of jungle, sierra and coast, with the associated animals and Inca sacred sites of each. The holes around the perimeter suggest that it was covered in gold. It is said to have been defaced when a cast was made, breaking off many of the animals' heads; ask the guardian for a closer look. Six main areas spread away from the stone and its neighbouring group of buildings. Look out for a staircase beside an elegant watercourse of channels and pools; a group of buildings around a stone (split by lightning), called the **Casa de Piedra** (or Rumi Huasi), an *usnu* platform and another monolith, called the Intihuatana.

About 20 minutes from Saywite is **Curahuasi** (126 km from Cuzco), famous for its aromatic anise herb, which has several roadside restaurants and *hospedajes*. A good two-hour walk takes you up Cerro San Cristóbal to **Capitán Rumi**, a huge rock overlooking the Apurímac Canyon. The views are staggering, particularly if Salkantay and its snowy neighbours are free of cloud. Ask for directions, especially at the start.

Not far from the new road bridge over the Apurímac are the thermal baths of **Cconoc** ⓘ *US$1.80.* An unmade road twists down to the river's edge where several pools and spouts are fed by warm water coming out of the cliffs. They are fairly clean, but watch out for the biting midges.

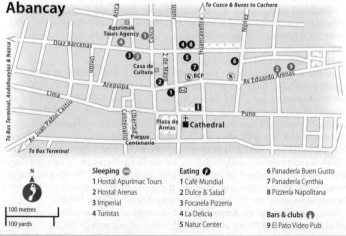

Abancay

Sleeping	Eating	
1 Hostal Apurímac Tours	1 Café Mundial	6 Panadería Buen Gusto
2 Hostal Arenas	2 Dulce & Salad	7 Panadería Cynthia
3 Imperial	3 Focarela Pizzería	8 Pizzería Napolitana
4 Turistas	4 La Delicia	
	5 Natur Center	Bars & clubs
		9 El Pato Video Pub

100 metres
100 yards

For Sleeping and Eating price codes and other relevant information, see pages 38-44.

⊜ **Sleeping**

Ayacucho *p558, map p559*

B Ayacucho Hotel Plaza, 9 de Diciembre 184, T066-312202, hplaza@derrama.org.pe. Beautiful colonial building but the rooms don't match up to the palatial splendour of the reception. It's comfortable, has TV, and some rooms overlook the plaza.

B-C Santa Rosa, Jr Lima 166, T066-314614, www.hotel-santarosa.com. Lovely colonial courtyard in the Casona Gutiérrez (1630); the Monja Alferez lived here for a while. It also served as the press HQ during the terrorist years. Rooms are very clean and warm, hot water all day, friendly, attentive staff, car parking, good restaurant (♥♥) with good-value menu, roof terrace. Breakfast and Wi-Fi included. Recommended.

C San Francisco de Paula, Jr Callao 290, T066-312353, www.hotelsanfranciscodepaula.com. Rather like an old museum with a nice patio, this is a friendly hotel and a popular choice. Breakfast is included, room service available, TV, Wi-Fi, comfortable rooms with private bathrooms and hot water, singles, large and small doubles and triples. Recommended. Will book El Encanto de Oro in Andahuaylas.

C Santa María, Arequipa 320, T066-314988, www.jianhoteles.com.pe/ayacucho. A modern hotel with suites and huge rooms, some on 2 floors (the stairs are a bit flimsy), price includes breakfast. Bedrooms are comfortable, with a proper bath, large TV and good fixtures and furnishings. There is a restaurant/bar, a garage in the basement and a great view from the roof.

C ViaVia Café Ayacucho, Portal Constitución 4, Plaza de Armas, T066-312834, www.viavia cafe.com. 10 rooms, from dorm to singles, solar hot water 24 hrs, TV room, Wi-Fi. The attached **ViaVia** restaurant and travellers' café overlooks the Plaza, offering international and

Peruvian food, a lunch *menú*, lounge and live music on Sat.

D Hostal El Marqués de Valdelirios, Alameda Bolognesi 720, T066-317040/ 318944. Go through the arch below Santa Teresa to the broad Alameda for this lovely colonial-style mansion, beautifully furnished, with blue flower pots, pickup from the airport US$3, reserve at least 24 hrs in advance. Breakfast, hot water, bar. Recommended.

D Marcos, 9 de Diciembre 143, T066-316867. A comfortable, modern hotel in a cul-de-sac ½ a block from the plaza. It's quiet, clean and rooms have bath, hot water and TV. The price includes breakfast in the cafeteria.

D-E La Crillonesa, El Nazareno 165, T066-312350. A big blue and white building just up from Santa Clara and the market, with colourful, locally made decorations and excellent services. The price, set specially for tourists, includes bath, hot water in the basins as well as the shower, kitchen and laundry facilities, discount for longer stay, great views from roof terrace. Café for drinks and snacks. English and Italian spoken, clean, friendly, lots of tourist information. Carlos will act as a local tour guide and knows everyone. Recommended.

E El Mesón, Jr Arequipa 273, T066-312938, hselmeson@hotmail.com. Colonial entrance to hotel extension with good views. Nice, clean, friendly, variety of room sizes, private bath, hot water.

E Florida, Jr Cusco 310, T066-312565. Small and pleasant: a leafy courtyard leads to a modern block with clean, quiet rooms with bath and TV, hot water, electric showers, Wi-Fi. Caged birds and plants on the patio.

E Hostal Tres Máscaras, Jr Tres Máscaras 194, T066-312921, www.hoteltresmascaras. galeon.com. New rooms with bath are better, but have less character, than the old ones, some of which have shared bathroom. This colonial building has a deep red patio with plants and caged parrots. Clean, basic rooms, hot water, Wi-Fi, breakfast extra, car park.

E-F Grau, Jr San Juan de Dios 192, T066-312695, hotelgrau192@hotmail.com.
On the 3rd floor , by the markets. With private or shared bath, hot water in all bathrooms, TV, clean, clothes washing facilities and laundry service, good value, safe, friendly, noisy, breakfast extra. Recommended.
F Hospedaje El Centro, Mcal Cáceres 1038, T066-313556. Rooms with or without bath and TV, large rooms, hot water, very clean, good value, but on a busy avenue.
F Hostal San Blas, Jr Chorro 167, T066-312712. Special tourist price represents good value, nice rooms with bath (cheaper without), hot water all day, clean, friendly, kitchen facilities and laundry service, cheap meals available, bicycles to lend, tourist information. Recommended.

Andahuaylas and around *p563*
D El Encanto de Oro, Av Pedro Casafranca 424, T083-723066, www.encantodeoro. 4t.com. A large modern hotel, 1 block from the market, 2 from the plaza, with spacious, comfortable rooms, well decorated and good facilities, breakfast included, TV, hot water 24 hrs, laundry service, restaurant with mirador, organizes trips on request. Advisable to reserve in advance.
E Sol de Oro, Jr Juan A Trelles 164, T083-721152, soldeorohotel@hotmail.com.
A tall blue building, with lift to upper floors, near the bus stations. Breakfast included, hot water, TV, clean, laundry service, garage and tourist information. **El Dorado Inn** restaurant alongside.
F El Encanto de Apurímac, Jr Juan Francisco Ramos 401, T083-723527. Close to Los Chankas and other bus stations, with bath, TV, hot water, clean, very friendly and helpful.
G Hostal Waliman, Av Andahuaylas 266, T083-422570. Cold water in the shared bathrooms, very basic but clean and helpful.
G Las Américas, Jr Ramos 410, T083-721646. Near the bus stations. A bit gloomy in the public areas, but rooms are fine if basic. Cheaper without bath, hot water, clean, friendly.

Abancay and around *p563, map p564*
C-D Turistas, Av Díaz Bárcenas 500, T083-321017, hotursa@terra.com.pe.
With bathroom, breakfast included. The original building is in colonial style, rooms (**D**) a bit gloomy, breakfast not included. Newer rooms on top floor (best) and in new block (**C**), including breakfast. Good restaurant (♔), enjoy a pisco sour over a game of billiards in the wood-panelled bar. Internet (US$0.60 per hr), parking space.
E Hostal Arenas, Av Arenas 192, T083-322107. A brand-new hotel is almost finished beside the old one, with well-appointed rooms, good beds, big showers, hot water, TV, restaurant, internet, parking, lift to top floor, which has good views. Hospitable.
E Imperial, Díaz Bárcenas 517, T083-321578, www.hotelimperial.pe. Rooms are around the central parking space in this hospitable, efficient and spotless hotel. Rooms have great beds, TV and hot water, Wi-Fi, laundry, café. Cheaper without private bath or breakfast. Helpful and good value.
F Hostal Apurímac Tours, Jr Cusco 421, T083-321446. New, rooms upstairs sleep 1-4, with tiny bathroom and hot water. Good value, helpful, laundry, TV, bar, café.

● Eating

Ayacucho *p558, map p559*
Those wishing to try *cuy* should do so here as it's cheaper than in Cuzco. Also try *mondongo*, a soup made from intestines, maize and mint. Many restaurants have this and *puca picante* (beef in a thick spicy sauce) on their Fri lunch menu. You can also find *mondongo* at the central market in the Sección Comidas in the main building, or at Pasajes 2 and 3 outside; ensure food is piping hot.

For a cheap, healthy breakfast try *maca*, a drink of maca (see introduction, page 583), apple and quinoa. It is sold opposite Santa Clara between 0600 and 0800. There are countless small, unnamed eating places around the centre. Few vegetarian options in town, so if required, buy food in the market and prepare it yourself in *hostales* with kitchen facilities.

On Av 26 de Enero, there are several *cevicherías*, such as La Choza del Norte, Sabor a Norte, El Piurano and Los Manglares de Tumbes, all ₹₹-₹. All much the same.

₹₹ **Las Flores**, Jr José Olaya 106, Plaza Conchopata, east of city. Open 0900-1900. Specializes in *cuy*, with *chicharrón*, *ccapchi* and beer, bougainvillea-filled patios, rustic. Similar restaurants on the plaza, boys guard cars, taxi US$1 from centre.

₹₹ **Urpicha**, Jr Londres 272, T066-813905. Recommended for typical food, which is its only cuisine. The dish called *urpicha* includes something of everything.

₹₹-₹ **La Casona**, Jr Bellido 463. Open 1200-2200. Dining under the arches and in dining room, regional specialities, try *puca picante*, *mondongo* and *cuy*, and a wide menu. Recommended for food, service and cleanliness.

₹₹-₹ **Nino**, Jr 9 de Diciembre 205, on small plaza opposite Santo Domingo church, T066-814537. Open daily, very nice dining rooms with pleasant decor, terrace and garden (look for the owls in the trees); chicken, pastas and pizzas, including takeaway, friendly.

₹ **Brasa Roja**, Jr Cuzco block 1. Relatively upmarket chicken place with food cooked *a la leña*, salads, very good.

₹ **Cabo Blanco**, Av Maravillas 198, T066-818740, close to Shosaku Nagase market (see Shopping, page 569). *Ceviches*, seafood and fish dishes, small place with friendly personal service.

₹ **Chifa Wa Lin**, Asamblea 257. Very popular Chinese, said to be the best in town.

₹ **La Pradera**, Lima 145 int 7. Open 0700-2200 daily. One of the few vegetarian places.

₹ **Mía Pizza**, Mcal Cáceres 1045, T066-313273. Open 1800-2400, for pizzas, pastas and karaoke (also has a bar to get you in the mood for singing).

₹ **Pollería Dorado**, Jr Asamblea 310. Excellent-value set menu and chicken dishes

in a long, cavernous dining room, mirrors and wood oven.

₹ **Salud y vida**, Jr Sol 380. Another vegetarian place, open every day.

Cafés
Centro Turístico Cultural San Cristóbal, 28 de Julio 178, has some expensive cafés (eg Lalo's, No 115, open 0900-2100, and New York, No 114) as well as other restaurants; all have tables set out in the pleasant courtyard.

La Miel, Portal Constitución 11-12, 2 locations. Good coffee, hot drinks, juices, shakes, cakes and snacks, also ice creams.

Portal 1, Portal Constitución 1. A good café on the corner of the plaza serving snacks, light meals and ice cream.

Huanta Valley *p563*
₹ **La Casona**, Gral Córdoba 162. A huge place on the plaza in Huanta serving traditional dishes, chicken and good-value *menú*.

Andahuaylas and around *p563*
₹ **El Dragón**, Jr Juan A Trellas 279. A recommended *chifa* serving huge portions, excellent value (same owner as Hotel El Encanto de Apurímac).

₹ **Il Gatto**, Jr G Cáceres 334. A warm pizzería, with wooden furniture, pizzas (generous toppings, thick crust) cooked in a wood-burning oven, very friendly.

₹ **Nuevo Horizonte**, Jr Constitución 426. Vegetarian and health food restaurant, clean, open for breakfast.

Abancay and around *p563, map p564*
₹ **Focarela Pizzería**, Díaz Bárcenas 521, T083-322036. Simple but pleasant decor, pizza from a wood-burning oven, fresh, generous toppings, popular (ask for 'vino de la casa').

₹ **Pizzería Napolitana**, Diaz Barcenas 208. With a wood-fired clay oven and wide choice of toppings.

Cafés

Café Mundial, Arequipa 301. Open early for breakfast and also for evening snacks.
Dulce & Salad, Arequipa y 2 de Mayo. 4 types of breakfast, daily salad specials, sandwiches, hot and cold drinks, cakes and a bar.
La Delicia, Díaz Bárcenas 210. A small vegetarian place serving breakfast, lunch buffet, juices, yoghurts and other products.
Natur Center, Díaz Bárcenas 211. An equally small vegetarian café with breakfast, lunch *menú*, juices and treatments.
Panadería Buen Gusto, Núñez 209. Good breads and cakes baked on the premises.
Panadería Cynthia, Huancavelica 311. With café serving enormous croissants.

☽ Bars and clubs

Ayacucho *p558, map p559*
By municipal decree in 2007, no discos are allowed within 2 blocks of the plaza, only *tabernas* with regional decoration and folkloric entertainment, open Mon-Fri til 2200, and 0200 at weekends. Among new places that have opened up are: **Bohemia Hard Rock**, Av Mcal Cáceres 944, bohemia peru@gmail.com, café-taberna and videos; **El Abuelo**, Asamblea 255, p 3, T066-403360, café, taberna and pizzería; **Karaoke El Buho** and **Karaoke Sol y Luna**, both at 9 de Diciembre 288, former has live music; **Magia Negra**, 9 de Diciembre 293.

Andahuaylas and around *p563*
El Garabato, on main plaza beside Municipalidad. Video and music club, with tree trunk tables, animal skins on the wall, woollen seat covers, expensive drinks, popular. There are many others around the plaza.

Abancay and around *p563, map p564*
Av Arenas has many *peñas turísticas*, bars and clubs. The best place for a beer is **El Pato Video Pub**, Arenas 176.

✺ Festivals and events

Ayacucho *p558, map p559*
This area is well known for its festivals throughout the year. Almost every day there is a celebration in one of the surrounding villages, even in Ayacucho itself. Check with the tourist office.
6 Jan Bajada de Reyes, when people pay to take gifts from an adorned Baby Jesus.
Feb/Mar Festival Internacional de la Tuna y Cochinilla (date varies, lasts for 15 days), for real 'dye' hards. **Carnival** has a respectable side and a riotous side, the *comparsas urbanas* and the *comparsas rurales*; ask Carlos at Hotel La Crillonesa about taking part.
Mar/Apr Ayacucho is famous for its **Semana Santa**, which begins on the **Fri before Holy Week**. There follows one of the world's finest Holy Week celebrations, with candle-lit nightly processions, floral 'paintings' on the streets, daily fairs (the biggest on Easter Sat), horse races and contests among peoples from all over central Peru. All accommodation is fully booked for months in advance of Holy Week. Many people offer beds in their homes during the week. Look out for notices on the windows of the bus company ticket offices.
25 Apr Anniversary of the founding of Huamanga province.
30 Aug One of the main festivals in **Barrio Santa Ana**, with processions and bull running in the plaza.
1-2 Nov Todos Los Santos follows Día de Los Muertos, the former celebrated with bread figures of people and horses, some as tall as 1 m; on the latter families visit the graves of their deceased relatives to eat, drink, sing and dance.

◯ Shopping

Ayacucho *p558, map p559*
Ayacucho is a good place to buy local crafts including filigree silver, which often uses *mudéjar* patterns. Also look out for little painted altars showing the nativity scene,

carvings in local alabaster, harps, or the pre-Inca tradition of carving dried gourds. The most famous goods are carpets and *retablos*. In both weaving and *retablos*, scenes of recent political strife have been added to more traditional motifs. Even the newspaper stands on the Plaza, along with the Coca Cola emblems, are painted like *retablos*.

Centro Turístico Cultural San Cristóbal, Jr 28 de Julio 178. Complex with a quiet courtyard, art galleries, shops and restaurants.
Familia Pizarro, Jr UNSCH 278, Barrio Belén, T066-313294. Textiles, masks for Carnaval and *piedra de huamanga* (local alabaster).
Mercado 12 de Abril, Chorro y San Juan de Dios. For fruit and vegetables.
Shosaku Nagase, Jr Quinua y Av Maravillas opposite Plazoleta de María Parado de Bellido, a large new Mercado Artesanal y Centro de Capacitación. Contact Faustino Contreras at Stand 89-A, **Apuarte**, apuarte2@hotmail.com, for a demonstration of ceramic-making. He also gives private classes at his house. Some of the same goods can be found in the **Mercado de Abastos Carlos F Vivanco** (see Sights).

▲ Activities and tours

Ayacucho *p558, map p559*
Tours to **Vilcashuamán** with travel agencies include Intihuatana, full day US$13, but they only run with 8 passengers. Alternatively stay overnight. Trips to **Huari, Quinua** village and the battlefield with travel agencies, US$7.55 per person, minimum 4 people.
Adán Castilla Rivera, T066-315789/T066-966-701746 (mob), castilla68@hotmail.com. An archaeologist who guides tours to local sites and the city, very knowledgeable.
Morochucos Reps, Jr Cuzco 355, T066-312542, www.morochucos.com. Tours locally and to other parts of Peru (has its own hostal in Nazca: **Guillén**, Av los Incas 117, T056-524272, nasca@morochucos.com), transport, hotel bookings, also flight and bus tickets.

Urpillay Tours, Portal Unión 33, T066-315074, urpillaytours@terra.com. All local tours and flight tickets.
Wari Tours, Portal Independencia 70, T066-311415. Local tours.
Willy Tours, Jr 9 de Diciembre 107, T066-314075. Personal guides, also handles flight and bus tickets.

Abancay and around *p563, map p564*
Apurimak Tours, at hotel **Turistas**, see Sleeping. Run local tours and 1- and 2-day trips to **Santuario Nacional de Ampay**: 1-day, 7 hrs, US$40 per person for 1-2 people (cheaper for more people). Also a 3-day trip to **Choquequirao** including transport, guide, horses, tents and food, just bring your sleeping bag, US$60 per person.
Carlos Valer, guide in Abancay – ask for him at hotel **Turistas** – knowledgeable and kind.

✈ Transport

Ayacucho *p558, map p559*
Air
To/from **Lima**, with LC Busre daily, depart Lima 0530, return 0700, US$114. To **Cuzco** and **Lima**, with StarPerú.
  Airline offices LC Busre, 9 de Diciembre 160, T066-316012. StarPerú, Portal Constitución 17, T066-316660. Most travel agents also sell tickets.

Bus
Local Combis to **Vilcashuamán** run from a new local terminal at Av Cuzco 350 (5 mins east of the centre, with municipal police station, plus Hostal Kankún and Restaurant Cartagena next door), daily 0400-1500 whenever full, 4 hrs, US$4.35. From Vilcashuamán to **Vischongo** costs US$0.75. The return journey from Vischongo to Ayacucho takes a little under 4 hrs, and costs US$2.75. Combis to **Huari**, 40 mins, US$0.75, and **Quinua**, a further 25 mins (US$0.50, US$1.10 from Ayacucho) leave from Paradero below the Ovalo de la Magdalena, at the

corner of Jr Ciro Alegría and Jr Salvador Cavero, when full from 0700 onwards. Ask the driver to go all the way to the Obelisco in Quinua for an extra US$0.50, then walk back to the town. Combis and cars to **Huanta** leave from the same place, US$1.90.

Long distance New Terminal Terrestre, built Jun 2008, in Urb Los Artesanos, at the end of Av Confraternidad, 10 mins northwest of the centre. Bus company offices are given below, but with full operation of the terminal, these may move. To **Lima**, 8 hrs on the good, paved Vía Los Libertadores, via **Ica** (5 hrs). For **Pisco**, 332 km, you have to take a Ica/Lima bus and get out at San Clemente, 10 mins from Pisco, and take a bus or combi (same fare to San Clemente as for Ica). Companies include **Antezana**, Manco Cápac 273, T066-311348, US$9 at 2030, US$10 at 2100, US$13.50 at 2200 (also to Ica only at 2145, US$12 with toilet), **Molina**, Jr 9 de Diciembre 458, T066-319989, US$10 at 0730, US$13.50 at 0800 and evening buses US$10-20, **Cruz del Sur**, Av Mcal Cáceres 1264, T066-312813, *imperial* at 1000, US$16.50, *crucero* at 2130, US$20-26.50, **Ayacucho Express**, Av Mcal Cáceres 1442, T066-328277, US$9 at 2100, US$13.50-16.50 at 2200, **Libertadores**, Tres Máscaras 493, T066-318967, US$10 at 0830 and evening buses, and **ReyBus**, Pasaje Cáceres 177, T066-319413. **Ormeño**, Jr Libertad 257, T066-312495, runs to Ica only, 2100, US$13.50.

To **Huancayo**, 319 km, 9-10 hrs, US$10 (0700 and 2000), US$12 (2100), with **Molina**, and US$8, 2030 with **Turismo Central**, Manco Cápac 499, T066-317873. The road is paved as far as **Huanta**, thereafter it is rough, especially in the wet season, but the views are breathtaking.

For **Huancavelica**, take a **Libertadores** 0730, **Molina** 0800 or **Cruz del Sur** 1000 bus as far as **Rumichaca**, US$2, where combis wait at 1030 for **Huancavelica**, 4 hrs. Otherwise take a Huancayo bus as far as **Izcuchaca**, then take another bus.

To **Andahuaylas**, 261 km, 10-11 hrs (more in the rainy season), the road is unpaved but in good condition when dry. Daytime buses stop for lunch at **Chumbes** (4½ hrs), which has a few eateries and some grim toilets. Departures are **Los Chankas**, Pasaje Cáceres 150, T066-312391, at 0630 (without toilet) and 1900 (with toilet), and **Celtur**, Pasaje Cáceres 174, T066-313194, 1830, all US$10.

Although you still have to change buses in Andahuaylas, **Los Chankas'** 1900 and **Celtur** services have a direct connection (no waiting) through to **Cuzco**. To get to **Abancay**, a further 138 km, 5 hrs, you must change buses and then go on to Cuzco, a further 195 km, 5 hrs. It takes 24 hrs to Cuzco. There are no direct buses. Road conditions are quite good, given the terrain crossed, but landslides a common occurrence in the wet season. The scenery, though, is stunning and makes up for it.

Huanta Valley *p563*

The *paradero* in Huanta is at R Castilla y Amazonas. **Expreso Huamanga**, Amazonas 404, and **Molina**, G Santillana at Parque Alameda, have night buses to **Lima**. Molina and **Turismo Central**, G Santillana 464, run daily to **Huancayo**.

Andahuaylas and around *p563*
Bus

Local Colectivo from Av Los Chankas y Av Andahuaylas, at the back of the market, to **Pacucha**, US$0.75, about 40 mins. To get to **Sóndor**, take a taxi from Andahuaylas, US$10, or catch the colectivo to Pacucha, then walk 8-10 km. Colectivos to **Argama** (also from behind Andahuaylas market), pass the entrance. With any form of public transport you will have to walk back to Pacucha, unless you're very lucky.

Long distance Daily buses to **Ayacucho**, minimum of 10 hrs, US$10, with **Los Chankas**, Av José María Arguedas y Jr Trelles, T083-722441, at 0600 and 1800 or 1840. Also

Celtur, 1 a day, US$10. To **Lima**, buses go via Ayacucho or Pampachiri and Puquio. On all night buses, take a blanket.

To **Abancay**, 5 hrs, Señor de Huanca, Av Martinelli 170, T083-721218, at 0600, 1300 and 2000 daily, US$3.40; Los Chankas at 0630, US$3.60. To **Cuzco**, San Jerónimo, Av José María Arguedas 425, T083-801767, via Abancay, 1800 or 1830, also 1900 Sun, US$15, and Los Chankas. Molina, Av José María Arguedas y Av Lázaro Castilla, over the bridge, also goes to Abancay and Cuzco at 1900.

Abancay and around *p563, map p564*
All interprovincial buses leave from the **Terminal Terrestre**, on Av Pachacútec, on the west side of town. It has a restaurant, internet and phones, a *cambio*, toilets and shops. Taxi to centre US$0.75, otherwise it's a steep 5 blocks up Av Juan Pablo Castro to Jr Lima. Several companies also have offices on or near the El Olivo roundabout at Av Díaz Bárcenas y Gamarra.

All buses on the **Lima–Nazca–Cuzco** route, via Chalhuanca and Puquio, pass through Abancay at about midnight. Abancay–Lima bus companies always reserve a few seats for **Puquio**, US$5.50, and **Nazca**, 464 km, US$7.50, if you wish to break the journey. The journey to **Cuzco** takes 4½ hrs and costs US$10. The scenery en route is dramatic, especially as it descends into the Apurímac valley and climbs out again. The road is paved and in good condition.

Buses to **Cachora** (for Choquequirao) depart from the terminal at Jr Prado Alto, between Huancavelica y Núñez (5 blocks uphill from Díaz Bárcenas; it's not the 1st Jr Prado you come to), daily 0500 and 1400, 2 hrs, US$1.50. Cars from the Curahuasi terminal on Av Arenas, charge US$10.

Bus company offices Bredde, Gamarra 423, T083-321643, 5 daily to **Cuzco**, including at 0600 and 1300. Cruz del Sur, Díaz Bárcenas 1151, T083-323028, serving the whole country. Los Chankas, Díaz Bárcenas 1011, El Olivo, T083-321485,

to Andahuaylas and Cuzco. Molina, Gamarra 422, T083-322646, 3 daily to Cuzco, also to **Andahuaylas** at 2330, US$4.25. San Jerónimo, to Cuzco at 2130 and Andahuaylas at 2130. Señor de Huanca, Av Arenas 198, T083-322377, to Andahuaylas at 0600, 1300, 2000, US$3.40. Several others to **Lima** and Cuzco.

🅞 **Directory**

Ayacucho *p558, map p559*
Banks BCP, Portal Unión 28, T066-314102. Visa ATM. **Continental BBVA**, Portal Unión 24, T066-327481. Interbank, opposite Hotel Ayacucho, Jr 9 de Diciembre 183, T066-312480, has ATM for Visa, MasterCard/Cirrus and Amex. 0915-1315, 1630-1830, Sat 0930-1230. Street changers can be found at Portal Constitución Nos 2, 3 and 5 on the plaza, they offer a good rate for cash, another on same side as BCP. **Internet** All over the centre. Around US$0.60 per hr. **Laundry** El Arco Iris, Jr Bellido 322. **Viclars**, Av Mcal Cáceres 876. **Medical services** Farmacia del Pino, 28 de Julio 123. Inka Farma, 28 de Julio 250. **Post** Asamblea 293. **Tourist police** Arequipa cuadra 1, T066-312055.

Andahuaylas and around *p563*
Banks BCP, Av Perú, 6th block east of the Plaza. MultiRed ATM on north side of Plaza. Cambio Machi, Jr R Castilla 371, closes 1800. Another *cambio* in Pizzería Napolitana. **Internet** Many places, all US$0.45 per hr.

Abancay and around *p563, map p564*
Banks BCP, Jr Arequipa 218, has ATM outside. There are several *cambios* on Jr Arequipa, opposite the Mercado Central, including Machi, No 202 (also at Díaz Bárcenas 105) and Oro Verde. **Internet** Plenty. Some have phone cabins. **Post** Junín y Arequipa. Mon-Sat 0800-2000, and Sun 0800-1500.

East of La Oroya and La Selva Central

From La Oroya, a paved road heads north towards Cerro de Pasco and Huánuco. After 25 km a turn-off branches east and drops 600 m before it reaches Tarma, which is 30 km off the Carretera Central. Beyond Tarma the road continues its steep descent. In the 80 km between Tarma and La Merced the road, passing by great overhanging cliffs, drops 2450 m and the vegetation changes dramatically from temperate to tropical. This is a really beautiful run, leading to Peru's central jungle area which, until recently, has received scant attention compared with the Iquitos and southeastern areas. All this is about to change. ➤➤ *For listings, see pages 576-582.*

Ins and outs

The main city of this region, Tarma, is easily reached by road from Lima in six hours, and from Huancayo in three hours. From Tarma, roads descend the eastern flanks of the Andes to the Selva Central. Tourist information is available in **Tarma** ① *Subgerencia de Turismo, 2 de Mayo 775 on the plaza, T064-321010, ext 107, turismo@munitarma.gob.pe, Mon-Fri 0800-1300, 1500-1800. See also www.tarma.info.* The office is very helpful and has good displays on the walls about the surrounding area.

Tarma and around → *For listings, see pages 576-582. Colour map 3, C4. Altitude: 3050 m.*

Tarma, 'the Pearl of the Andes', was founded in 1538 and is one of the oldest towns in Peru. Though this small, flat-roofed place, with plenty of trees, is now growing with garish

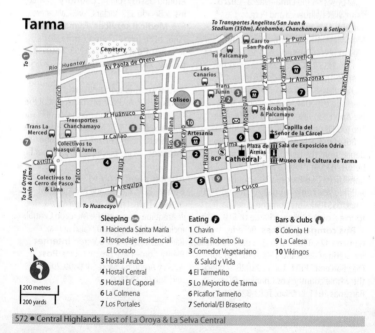

Tarma

Sleeping
1 Hacienda Santa María
2 Hospedaje Residencial El Dorado
3 Hostal Aruba
4 Hostal Central
5 Hostal El Caporal
6 La Colmena
7 Los Portales

Eating
1 Chavín
2 Chifa Roberto Siu
3 Comedor Vegetariano & Salud y Vida
4 El Tarmeñito
5 Lo Mejorcito de Tarma
6 Picaflor Tarmeño
7 Señorial/El Braserito

Bars & clubs
8 Colonia H
9 La Calesa
10 Vikingos

modern buildings, it still has a lot of charm. The Plaza de Armas and the large cathedral are very pleasant. Jr Lima is the main street, where many cafés, restaurants and other services are found. A former sanatorium town, Tarma still receives many Limeños attracted by the crisp mountain air and beautiful surroundings. The **Semana Santa** celebrations are spectacular, with a very colourful Easter Sunday morning procession in the main plaza. With its beautiful surrounding countryside, the town is also notable for its locally made fine **flower-carpets**. In 1999 it recorded the largest flower carpet in the world. ▸▸ *See Festivals and events, page 579.*

The **Sala de Exposición Odria** ① *at the Municipalidad Provincial, Jr Lima 199, Mon-Fri 0800-1300, 1500-1800, free,* celebrates the life of Tarma's most famous son, General Manuel Odria, who became president of Peru in the 1930s. The museum contains personal memorabilia. The **Museo de la Cultura de Tarma** ① *Jr Arequipa 190 (at the corner of Plaza de Armas), T064-321021 ext 114, open Tue-Sat 0930-1300, 1530-1800, Sun 1000-1300,* has archaeology, ethnography and regional customs exhibits. There is a large *artesanía* market at Lima 548 and a good, friendly market around Amazonas and Ucayali.

Around Tarma

About 8 km south of Tarma on the road to Huancayo, at **Tarmatambo**, is the start of a good section of Inca road that runs 3 km to Huasqui on the Tarma–La Oroya road. There are also ruins and caves and a spectacular view of terrace farming and of Tarma itself. It's 20 minutes by car from Tarma. Some 30 km from Tarma on the Huancayo road is **El Santuario Rupestre Pintish Machay**, near Huairicolca. Here is the largest site of cave paintings in Peru, some 600 pictures dating back 4000 to 10,000 years.

To the north, some 8 km from Tarma, the small hillside town of **Acobamba** has some attractive old buildings. There are festivities during May, see page 579. Some 2 km up beyond the town is the futuristic **Santuario de Muruhuay**, with a venerated picture painted on the rock behind the altar. Its design was inspired by Le Corbusier's work. It also has fine *tapices* made in San Pedro de Cajas, which depict the Crucifixion.

The **Grutas de Huagapo**, also known as 'La gruta que llora' (the cave that weeps), is 4 km from the town of **Palcamayo**, which is 15 km northwest of Acobamba. The caves can be entered for about 100 m, at which point it is up to 30 m high and 20 m wide. Guides with torches and ropes can be hired near the entrance to reach 300 m. Beyond that wet suits and simple caving gear are needed. Even without a guide you can penetrate the cave for some way with a torch. The cave is the deepest in South America and investigations, which have penetrated up to 2800 m, suggest that the system extends over 30 km underground. There is a small but impressive gorge, **Cañón de Ushtu**, 10 minutes' walk down river from the cave.

Northwest beyond Palcamayo, the road climbs steeply for 14 km to **San Pedro de Cajas**, a large village famed for its coloured sheep-wool weavings. The principal shops are on the central plaza and the road to Palcamayo. (This road joins up with the main road from La Oroya to Cerro de Pasco below Junín.) The town holds the **Festival de La Pukcha** (Hilado) on 28-30 June. There is accommodation and a couple of restaurants.

Three kilometres beyond San Pedro on the road to La Oroya is a **vicuña reserve** and cooperative, which is the best place to see vicuña at close range. The animals are accustomed to people and roam near the road. Every August they are sheared and the money from the sale of the fleece goes to the reserve.

The towns of San Ramón and La Merced, collectively known as Chanchamayo, are some 73 km east of Tarma. **San Ramón** is 11 km before La Merced on the banks of the Río Tarma. It is a busy, attractive town in the lower foothills of the Andes, where the temperature is noticeably higher than in Tarma. For information, visit **Dircetur** ① *Pardo 110, San Ramón, T064-331265*. The surrounding hills are covered in coffee plantations and there are many waterfalls in the area.

The main town and provincial capital, **La Merced**, lies in the fertile Chanchamayo Valley at 800 m, and is famous for its citrus and coffee production. For information, visit the **Subgerencia de Turismo** ① *Municipalidad Provincial de Chanchamayo, Av Zuchetti 125, Parque Integración, T064-531143, Mon-Fri 0730-1300, 1400-1615*, where there are pamphlets and limited information in Spanish only. La Merced was a colonial mission settlement first founded in 1635 as San Buenaventura de Quimiri in Campa-Asháninka territory. However, the first mule track from Tarma only went through in 1847 and the current city of La Merced was founded in 1869 near the original settlement. Italian and German settlers followed. Today the only remaining Asháninka community of Chanchamayo with 25 families is at Pampa Michi, 15 km from La Merced. Campa people can usually be found around the central plaza selling bows, arrows, necklaces and trinkets. La Merced has a central **market**, where you can usually find Campa articles, exotic herbs and jungle medicines such as *uña de gato* and *sangre de grado*. Other vendors can be found on street corners. The hill behind the town can be climbed up to **La Cruz** for a wonderful view of the entire Chanchamayo Valley, or you can hire a mototaxi for US$1. There is a restaurant and small recreation area here. At holiday times prices double as the area is full of Limeños seeking tropical warmth.

East of Chanchamayo

A 123-km paved road leads from Chanchamayo to **Satipo**. At Km 20, the confluence of the Chanchamayo and Paucartambo rivers forms the Río Perené. The road follows the river, winding through lush jungle and Asháninka villages, where indigenous artefacts are often for sale. At Km 70, palm-thatched huts signal the outskirts of **Pichanaki**.

A few years ago this village represented the remotest of Peruvian outposts, but its fertile lands and warm climate were ideal for coffee, bananas and citrus. Tens of thousands of Andean *campesinos* flocked to the region in search of jobs and land. A paved road reached the town in 1999 and it is now the commercial hub of the region. Its long sandy beaches on the Río Perené make an ideal retreat from the encircling jungle and a jumping-off point to visit the waterfalls, lakes and remote indigenous villages in the area. During the dry season (April-August), the town's plaza and streets are covered with drying coffee beans. Most of the good restaurants are at **Playa Pescadora** (El Puerto Pichanaki) and serve the local delicacy, *doncella* fish (**El Bambú** is recommended).

Beyond Pichanaki the paved road pulls away from the Río Perené and goes to the noisy, semi-modern jungle town of **Satipo**, the main centre of this region. One kilometre from town is **Isla de Fantasía** and **El Lagarto**, with restaurant, nightclub and swimming in the river.

A dirt road continues east to **Mazamari** and **Puerto Ocopa** (about four hours from Satipo) near the confluence of the Satipo and Perené rivers. Some 10 km along this road are the **Arcoiris waterfalls**. From here you can go by road (11 hours) or take a boat (1½ days) down the Río Tambo to its confluence with the Urubamba at **Atalaya**, where it forms the

Ucayali. It used to be a centre of the drugs trade, but now it is safe to visit with an army base on the outskirts. It has become a regional centre for commerce and travel, with several *hostales*, a market and a tourist office on the plaza that will help with day trips.

North of Chanchamayo → *For listings, see pages 576-582.*

Puerto Bermúdez → *Colour map 3, B5. Altitude: 260 m.*
About 25 km from La Merced along the road to Oxapampa, a road turns northeast to Villa Rica, centre of an important coffee-growing area. A very poor dirt road continues north to Puerto Bermúdez and beyond to join the Tingo María–Pucallpa road at Von Humboldt, 86 km from Pucallpa. **Puerto Bermúdez** is on the Río Pichis, an affluent of the Pachitea. This is a great base for exploring further into the Selva Central Peruana, with trips upriver to the Asháninka community. Puerto Bermúdez, at the geographic centre of Peru, is an authentic jungle town that has grown up along the now seldom-used airstrip. The town is an access point to two extensive natural reserves: **Bosque de Protección San Matías-San Carlos** and **Reserva Nativa Sira**, both with primary forest. The electricity supply is unreliable. Fifty kilometres north of Puerto Bermúdez, **Ciudad Constitución**, also known as Palcazú, is a dusty town straddling the Río Palcazú. East of town are a few dilapidated old buildings being reclaimed by the jungle. They are the remains of President Belaúnde Terry's grandiose plans for the future national capital – a Peruvian Brasília.

Oxapampa → *Colour map 3, B4. Altitude: 1794 m.*
Oxapampa is set on a fertile plain on the Río Huancabamba, a tributary of the Ucayali, 81 km from La Merced. A third of the inhabitants are descendants of a German-Austrian community of 70 families that settled in 1859 at **Pozuzo**, 80 km downstream, and spread later to Oxapampa. There is much livestock farming here, and coffee is planted on land cleared by the timber trade. On 5 August the town hosts a festival, the **Virgen de Las Nieves**. The tourist office ⓘ *Bolívar 466, 2nd floor, T063-462375, www.oxapampa online.com, Mon-Fri 0800-1230, 1400-1700*, sells maps and guidebooks.

North of Oxapampa
On the main road to Pozuzo, at the end of Oxapampa, go to Inrena for authorization to visit the **Yanachaga Chemillén National Park**, where there is good birdwatching very early in the morning and camping is possible for US$1.50. The staff are extremely helpful and will give you trekking information.

Some 25 km from Oxapampa is **Huancabamba**, from where it is 55 km to **Pozuzo**. The whole road between La Merced and Pozuzo is very rough, depending on the season, and crosses no less than 30 rivers. North of Pozuzo, 3 km, is **Prusia**, another Austro-Peruvian village, with two hotels that are very friendly. There is good hiking in the area. Downstream, 40 km from Pozuzo, is **Nuevo Pozuzo**; there is no transport between the two so it's a two-day walk. There is an interesting **museum** ⓘ *US$0.75*, opposite the church in the town centre. The town celebrates the **Semana Turística de Pozuzo** during the last week in July.

For Sleeping and Eating price codes and other relevant information, see pages 38-44.

◉ Sleeping

Tarma and around *p572, map p572*
Accommodation is hard to find at Easter but you can apply to the Municipalidad for rooms with local families. Also contact the tourist information office.

A Los Portales, Av Castilla 512, T064-321411, www.hoteleslosportales.com. On the edge of town, built 1954, traditional style, with bathroom, hot water, TV, heating, quiet, secluded, price includes breakfast, very good restaurant, but expensive.

A-B Hacienda Santa María, 2 km out of town at Sacsamarca 1249, T064-321232, www.haciendasantamaria.com. A beautiful (non-working) 17th-century hacienda, has less land than **La Florida** but beautiful gardens and antique furniture, great fireplace. Includes breakfast and light evening meal. Excellent guides will arrange local day trips for you. Recommended.

B Hacienda La Florida, 6 km from Tarma, T064-341041, www.haciendalaflorida.com. 18th-century working hacienda, 12 rooms, some furnished with antiques, with bath, hot water, price includes breakfast, other meal packages available, owned by German-Peruvian couple Inge and Pepe who arrange excursions. Great for kids as you can milk cows and ride tractors. Recommended. Also camping **G**.

C-D Hostal Campestre Auberge Normandie, beside the Santuario de Muruhuay, Acobamba, T064-341028, in Lima T01-365 9795, www.hotelnormandie.com.pe. Rooms sleep 2-4 people, hot water, phone, Wi-Fi, room service, TV in lounge, bar, restaurant, parking, fine views over the valley, tours offered.

D Hostal El Caporal, Lima 616, T064-323636, hostalelcaporal@yahoo.es. Includes breakfast, very clean, good location, nicely refurbished old house, comfortable rooms with large new bathrooms, hot water, cable TV. Recommended.

E Hostal Aruba, Jr Moquegua 452 near the market, T064-322057, www.tarma.info/aruba.html. Hot water, pleasant rooms with tiled floors, TV, private bathroom, good value.

E Hostal Central, Huánuco 614, T064-322625. Shared or private bathroom, hot water, friendly, laundry facilities, a bit run down but popular, has an observatory that opens Fri at 2000, US$1 for non guests.

F Hospedaje Residencial El Dorado, Huánuco 488, T064-321914, www.hospesdajeeldoradotarma.com. Colonial-style building, cheaper without bath, hot water, rooms set round a patio, 1st-floor rooms better, simple, clean, poor beds, safe, welcoming.

F La Colmena, Jauja 618, T064-321157. An old building with character, well-maintained considering its age, with or without bath, electric shower, clean, convenient for Huancayo buses.

Chanchamayo *p574*
There are many places to stay just outside San Ramón, off the main road to La Merced.

A-B Río Grande Inn, Av Victor Villachica Gambini s/n, Campamento Chino, Km 97, San Ramón, T064-332193, www.riogrande-bungalow.com. Price includes breakfast, bungalows, hot water, TV, fridge, fan, parking, internet access, laundry, swimming pool, very good service, overlooking river.

B-C El Refugio, Av del Ejército 490, San Ramón, T/F064-331082, www.hotelelrefugio.com.pe. 100 beds in double or triple rooms in bungalows set in a beautiful tropical garden, with pool, internet in rooms, friendly staff, restaurant used by tour parties, price includes breakfast, packages with tours available.

C-D Hostal Rey, Junín 103, La Merced, T064-531185. Same owner as **Reyna**, which is slightly more expensive, private bathroom, cable TV, internet access, laundry, brightly lit, luggage store, parking.

C-D Reyna, Palca 259, La Merced, T064-531780, www.hotelreyna.com. Clean rooms with private bath, cable TV, Wi-Fi, fridge on request, fan and, like its partner, brightly lit.
D El Rancho, Playa Hermosa, San Ramón, T064-331511, www.bungalowselrancho.i8.com. Bungalows set in large grounds with fruit trees, each with 2 double bedrooms and private bathrooms, breakfast included, camping US$5 per tent, local food in dining room.
E Conquistador, Progreso 298, San Ramón, T064-331771, conquistador@viabcp.com. Modern, with hot water, TV, parking.
E Elio's, Jr Palca 281, La Merced, T064-531229, hotelelios@hotmail.com. With bath, hot water, fan, tiled floors, friendly, a bit pricey for what it offers.
E El Parral, Uriate 355-361, San Ramón, T064-331128. Modern, with hot water, TV, clean, good restaurant serving local specialities, especially meat.
E Hospedaje Karol, Jr Tarma 373, on Plaza de Armas, La Merced, T064-335187, hospedajekarol@hotmail.com. With bath, electric shower, nice wooden floors, good location, very friendly.
E Hospedaje Virginia, Jr Arequipa 280, La Merced, T064-338022, vrginia@hotmail.com. Private bathroom, cold water, friendly but a bit pricey.
E Oscar's, Jr 2 de Mayo 201, La Merced, T064-531978, hostal_oscars@hotmail.com. Private bathroom, hot water, small modern rooms.
E Primavera, Arequipa 175, La Merced, T064-531433. Friendly, rooms with TV, fan, private bathroom, hot water. Recommended.
F-G Hospedaje Santa Rosa, 2 de Mayo 447, La Merced, T064-531012. With shared or private bath, clean, simple, good value.

East of Chanchamayo p574
D Hostal Majestic, on the plaza, Jr Fundadores 408, Satipo, T064-545762, www.majesticsatipo.com. With bathroom, hot water, cable TV, Wi-Fi, laundry, parking, noisy.

F Hostal Brando, Ene 120, Atalaya, T064-461128. New, tiled building, comfortable beds, TV, fan, cold water, helpful staff.
G Hostal Denis, Jr Raymondy 144, Atalaya, T064-461087. New building across from Plaza de Armas, quiet, TV, fan, with bathroom, cold water.

Puerto Bermúdez p575
F Hostal Pinto, Oxapampa s/n, T063-830048. Small rooms with bath, cold water, adequate.
F-G Hostal Tania, Av Ramón Castilla y Jr Oxapampa, T063-830021. Adequate screened rooms, cold water, pleasant grounds with hammocks, electric generator.
G pp Albergue Cultural Humboldt, by the river port (La Rampa), 4 mins' walk from the centre, T063-963 722363, www.alberguehumboldt.com. The knowledgeable owner, Basque writer Jesús López de Dicastillo, has created a haven for backpackers, with maps, book and video library and book exchange, music and coffee. Single, double, triple rooms, or tents and hammocks. Breakfast US$2, dinner US$3. 24-hr electricity. Highly recommended. Jesús arranges tours, from day trips to camping and trekking in the primary forest. He has a good relationship with many Asháninka communities that you can visit.

Ciudad Constitución
F Hospedaje Chura. Private bathroom, cold water, modern, small rooms, often no water.
F Madeleine, T063-830062. Private bathroom, cold water, fan, screened rooms, older place but clean and adequate. Many other basic places to stay.

Oxapampa p575
C Albergue Turístico Böttger, Jr Mcal Castilla 6th block, T063-462377, www.oxapampaonline.com/bottger. Very popular, in a quiet area, good service, breakfast included, serves good meals. They also have another lodge with 2 more rooms and self-catering country houses for 3 nights minimum.

D D'Palma Lodge, Prolongación Thomas Schaus, T063-462123, www.depalmalodge. com. Price includes breakfast. 6 rooms in main building and 5 log cabins with balcony set in a spacious area, hot water, friendly, tours, archery, local food, music and dance, children's playground. Permits camping at US$3 per tent.

E Posada Edelweiss, Carretera Central, Lote 58-Miraflores, T063-462567, www.oxapampaonline.com/edelweiss. Rooms sleep 1-4, private bath, hot water, games room, parking, laundry, childcare, tours. Buffet breakfast included, other meals available in rustic dining room, very friendly owner. Recommended.

F Don Calucho, San Martín 411, T063-462109, www.oxapampaonline.com/doncalucho . Rooms with private bath, quiet, pleasant, parking, a good option.

North of Oxapampa *p575*

B-E Hostal Tirol, Pozuzo, www.pozuzo.de. In 3 different buildings, also with bungalows. Breakfast US$4, lunch and dinner by request US$5-6. Clean, hot water in most rooms, some with shared bath, swimming pool. Tours. Recommended.

D Albergue Turístico Frau Maria Egg, Los Colonos, Pozuzo, T01-444 9927 (Lima), www.pozuzo.com. Includes typical local breakfast, garden, swimming pool, excursions, cheaper Nov-Apr. Recommended.

There are several other guesthouses in Pozuzo, such as **El Mango**, Pacificolgn 185, T063-287528, www.hellopasco.com/el_mango, with restaurant serving good German food (♥), Austro/Peruvian-owned.

❶ Eating

Tarma and around *p572, map p572*
Several eating places on Lima. Tarma's *manjar blanco* is famous, as is *pachamanca*, *mondongo* and *picante de cuyes*. In the central market try *cachanga* – fried bread with cinnamon. Good places to buy local produce

such as *manjar blanco* and honey are **El Tarmeñito**, Lima 149, or the **Señoritas Ferruso**, 2 de Mayo, cuadra 4, opposite the market, who make very good, home-made, natural *manjar blanco*.

♥ **Chavín**, Jr Lima 270 at Plaza de Armas. Open daily 0730-2230. Very good quality and variety in set meals (weekdays only), also à la carte. Recommended.

♥ **Chifa Roberto Siu**, Lima 569, upstairs, T064-414025. A good option for Chinese food, popular with locals.

♥ **Comedor Vegetariano**, Arequipa 695. Open 0700-2100, closed Fri after lunch and all day Sat. Vegetarian, small and cheap, sells great bread.

♥ **Don Pepe**, Jr Lima 799 y Jr Pasco. Open daily 0700-0100. *Pollo a la brasa*, bakery and sweets.

♥ **Lo Mejorcito de Tarma**, Arequipa 501, T064-321766. Open 0700-2300. Offers a good set *menú* with choices at US$1.50, local specialities, popular, has tourist information.

♥ **Picaflor Tarmeño**, Lima 306. A small place opposite the cathedral, good for snacks.

♥ **Salud y Vida**, Arequipa 677. Open 0730-2000, closed Fri after lunch and all day Sat. A small vegetarian place, good value.

♥ **Señorial/Pollería El Braserito**, Huánuco 138-140, T064-323334. **Señorial** open daily 0800-1530, **El Braserito**, 1800-2300. Good *menú* and à la carte options, extensive choice, excellent *sopa criolla*, popular with locals.

Chanchamayo *p574*

♥♥-♥ **Rincón Gaucho**, Jr Ancash cuadra 5, Parque Integración, La Merced, T064-337966. Best place for steak, anticuchos and other meat dishes, set meals, *menú turístico* and *menú económico*.

♥♥-♥ **Shambari-Campa**, Jr Tarma on the Plaza de Armas, La Merced. Open daily 0630-2400. It has an extensive menu, an excellent set *menú* at US$3, and hundreds of interesting old photos of the local area, some dating back to the start of the century, cover the walls. Highly recommended.

♥ **Café Prisci**, Progreso 256, San Ramón. Good for snacks, home-made lemon pie.
♥ **Chifa Felipe Siu**, Progreso 440, San Ramón. Also at Jr Arica 163, La Merced. Open daily 1200-1500 and 1830-2300. One of the most popular restaurants in town, along with Chifa Conquistador, see above.
♥ **Chipipizzas**, Junín 234, La Merced, T064-337966. Pizzas, burgers, pasta, sandwiches. Good service and clean.

Puerto Bermúdez *p575*
♥ **Las Palmeras**, Av Aviación, opposite the airstrip. Open daily 1200-1900. Very good à la carte fish and game, regional dishes, swimming pool open to the public 1000-1800, busy at weekends.

Ciudad Constitución
♥ **El Portal**, at north end of town, good set meals. Many others in town, keep an eye out for hygiene.

Oxapampa *p575*
♥ **La Casa de Baco**, Carretera Central, Miraflores Oxapampa. Typical food, good for meats.
♥ **Oasis**, Jr Bolognesi 120, T063-762206. This is a highly recommended restaurant.
♥ **Típico Oxapampino**, Plaza de Armas. Very popular, good food, friendly owner.

North of Oxapampa *p575*
♥ **Guten Appetit**, Av los Colonos, Pozuzo. A very popular restaurant in the town.
♥ **Típico Pozucino**, Av Los Colonos s/n, La Colonia-Pozuzo. Good, cheap food, try *albóndigas de carne* or potato salad.

🍷 Bars and clubs

Tarma and around *p572, map p572*
Colonia H, Jr Callao y Jr Pasco. Bar, good for *tragos exóticos*: regional drinks served hot.
La Calesa, Arequipa 433. An old, quiet pub-style bar.

La Esquina del Coco, Jr Arequipa y Jr Huancayo. The meeting place for Tarma's bohemian community.
Vikingos, Jr Huancayo y Jr Callao. The in place for dancing, varied music.

⊛ Festivals and events

Tarma and around *p572, map p572*
20-25 Feb Carnaval Tarmeño.
Mar/Apr Semana Santa and the Concurso de Alfombras de Flores (flower carpet competition).
May Festividad Señor de Muruhuay.
23-24 Jun Fiestas Patronales de San Juan.
27-28 Jun Circuito Turístico de Ciclismo de Montaña in Huasahuasi.
23-27 Jun Festival de la Papa in Huasahuasi.
24 Jun Tayta Inti ceremony is held in Tarmatambo.
23-29 Jul Semana Turística.
28-30 Sep Fiesta de la Siembra del Maíz, mainly in Acobamba, but also in Tarma.
Oct Señor de Los Milagros processions.

▲ Activities and tours

Tarma and around *p572, map p572*
For the local guides association, email taruma84@hotmail.com, or ask at the tourist office on the main plaza. Some tour operators have English-speaking guides. Regular and adventure (mountain biking, canyoning) tours are offered with a variety of day trips to local sites, leaving around 0930 and returning at 1800.
Centro Tour, Jr 2 de Mayo 658, T064-321104, turismocentrotours@hotmail.com.
Max Adventure, Jr 2 de Mayo 682, T064-323908, www.maxadventureperu.com, also has office in La Merced.
Perú Latino, Jr Lima 296, T064-321832, www.tarmatours.com.
Taruma Tours, Jr Paucartambo 439, T064-321635, taruma-tours@hotmail.com.

Chanchamayo *p574*

There are a number of informal tour operators on the main plaza in La Merced catering to Lima weekenders; they are often closed in low season. Check on safety record before taking part in any adventure sports.

Angel Tours, Jr Tarma 290, La Merced, T064-509534, www.angel-adventure.com. They offer tours to waterfalls, coffee-growing areas, native communities.

Impala Tours, Jr Tarma 290, La Merced, T064-532476, also Jr Progreso 290, San Ramón. Owner Gustavo de Madariaga is very helpful. They offer day trips to surrounding area.

Max Adventure, Jr Junín 224, La Merced, T064-532175, www.maxadventure.com.pe. They offer tours to waterfalls, coffee-growing areas, native communities, cycling and canyoning.

Puerto Bermúdez *p575*

Jesús at **Albergue Humboldt** offers an extensive selection of tours to natural and cultural attractions, these combine river travel and walking.

⊜ Transport

Tarma and around *p572, map p572*

In this area, locals use the terms *carros* and *stations* (from station wagon) rather than than *colectivos*.

Local To **Tarmatambo**: colectivos from Paucartambo y Arequipa US$0.95, combis from Av Pacheco (continuación Jr Jauja), cuadra 1, US$0.30. To **Pintish Machay**: cars from Av Pacheco, cuadra 1, US$12 for 4 passengers. To **Acobamba** and up to **Muruhuay**: Combis all along Jr Huánuco, US$0.30, 15 minutes to Acobamba, US$0.45 to sanctuary. Colectivos from Jr Huánuco y Moquegua or **Canary Tours** combis and colectivos from Jr Amazonas. To **Palcamayo** (Grutas de Huagapo): Colectivos from Bermúdez y Otero, US$1.10, 40 mins. Also for Palcamayo, continuing to **San Pedro de Cajas**: combis from Huancavelica y Paucartambo, US$1.10, colectivos from Av Francisco Paula de Otero y Jr Moquegua, cuadra 1, US$1.60.

Long distance Direct buses leave daily to **Lima**, 231 km, 6 hrs, US$4.70-6.50 normal, US$8 *semi-cama*, US$9.50-11 *cama*; **Transportes Chanchamayo**, Callao 1002, T064-321882, passes Tarma en route from La Merced daily about 0830 and 2300, except Fri and Sun at about 1330 and 2300. Also **Transportes Junín**, Amazonas 667, nicer buses, at 0845, 1015, 1130 (*semi-cama*), 1245 (*cama*) 2300 (*semi-cama*), 2330 (*cama*), 2345 (*cama*). **Trans Junín** in Lima: Av Nicolás Arriola 198, T01-224 9220, www.transpjunin. com. **Transportes La Merced**, Vienrich 420, 3 daily, at 1130, 1330 and 2300 (*cama*) and **Trans Los Canarios (Señor de Muruhuay)** at 0930 and 2200, (office at Jr Amazonas 694; office in Lima at Av Grau 491, T01-426 6599). The colectivos to Lima leave from Castilla y Vienrich, wait till full, US$12.50, 4 hrs. The road is paved for the entire route.

To **Jauja**, 2 hrs, US$2, and **Huancayo**, 3 hrs, US$3, with **Transportes/Angelitos San Juan** from the stadium 0800-1800, every 1½ hrs , en route from Chanchamayo; also **Trans Los Canarios**, 0500-1800 (13 daily, about 1 per hr). **Trans Junín** at 1200 and 2400. Colectivos (cars) depart when full from Callao y Jauja, 2 hrs, US$4 to **Jauja**, or 3 hrs, US$6, to **Huancayo**.

Buses to **La Oroya** leave regularly from opposite the petrol station on Av Castilla block 2, 1 hr, US$1.50, while colectivos leave from the petrol station itself, 45 mins, US$2.

To **Chanchamayo**, Transportes Angelitos/San Juan from the stadium 13 daily, 0600-2100, to La Merced US$1.60. Trans Junín, 0600, 0730, 0830, 0930, 1½ hrs, US$1.60 to **San Ramón**, and 2 hrs, US$2.50 to **La Merced**, 0930 bus continues to Satipo US$4.70, 5 hrs. Combis from the stadium to La Merced, US$1.60; colectivos from the stadium to La Merced US$3.80.

Chanchamayo p574

Air

There is a small airstrip in San Ramón where Aero Montaña, T064-339191/331074, rfmamsa@hotmail.com, has air taxis that can be chartered (*viaje especial*) to the jungle towns, including **Puerto Bermúdez**, 33 mins, with a maximum of 3 people. Flights cost US$250 per hr and you have to pay for the pilot's return to base. You can also just go to the air base, across the river, on the east of town.

Bus

Local There is a flow of combis and colectivos between San Ramón market and main plaza and Lima y Junín in La Merced, 15 mins, US$0.20 and US$0.30 respectively.

Long distance From San Ramón to Lima, Transportes La Merced, Paucartambo y Alvariño, 5 daily, 7 hrs, US$6. To **Huánuco**, Transportes León de Huánuco, Paucartambo 380, departs 2200, 6-7 hrs, US$7. To **Tarma**, Transportes Angelitos/San Juan, Progreso 105, hourly, 2 hrs, US$1.60.

From La Merced there is a large bus station on the east side of town, from which most buses, colectivos and combis arrive and depart. To **Satipo**, Transportes Lobato (not a reliable company according to the tourist office), 1130 and 2330, 2½ hrs, US$3; other buses passing through from Huancayo and Lima may also have room. Combis 0500-1800, US$3.20, 3 hrs; colectivos US$4.10. To **Oxapampa**, Empresa Santa Rosa, every ½ hr, 3 hrs, US$3; there are also regular colectivos, 2 hrs, US$5.50, combis 0400-1730, every 35 mins, US$3.20. To **Pozuzo**, Empresa Santa Rosa, 0430 and 0830, 6 hrs, US$4.50, combis at 0515 and 0830, US$4.10, 5½ hrs; the condition of the road improves after Oxapampa. To **Pichanaki**, colectivos 0500-2100, US$2.20, 1¼ hrs. To **Puerto Bermúdez**, Empresa Transdife and Villa Rica have 4WD pickups (US$14 in front or US$8 in the back, spending the extra is suggested because of

the extreme crowding) departing from 0400 and may pick up passengers from their hotels. You must buy your tickets in advance at the bus terminal. This is not a paved road and takes around 8-10 hrs or more in the dry season. Some vehicles continue to Ciudad Constitución. Note that there have been occasional armed holdups on this route. To **Lima**, US$8 regular, US$11 *cama* upper level, US$12.50 *cama* lower level, 7-8 hrs. Chanchamayo, Mon-Thu, Sat at 0630 and 2100, Fri and Sun at 1130 and 2100. Transmov, daily 2200 (in Lima 28 de Julio y Luna Pizarro, T01-494 4188). Junín, 7 daily. Angelitos/San Juan, 0730, 2100. To **Tarma**, Transportes Angelitos/San Juan, hourly, 2½ hrs, US$1.60, or colectivos, just over 1 hr, US$3.80. To **Huancayo** via Tarma, US$4.70, 4½ hrs. Transportes Angelitos/San Juan, hourly 0600-2000; Junín at 1030 and 2330; Transportes Lobato 1230 and 1830.

East of Chanchamayo p574

To reach **Atalaya**, catch a bus to **Satipo** (for transport to Satipo, see under Chanchamayo, above), 2 daily from Lima, 9 hrs, US$8.30; then take a colectivo to **Puerto Ocopa** (2½ hrs, US$5), and *lancha* to **Atalaya** (6 hrs downstream, 9 hrs upstream on Río Tambo, US$10). Buses to **Huancayo** and **Lima** depart from Satipo at night, a very cold journey, 12 hrs, US$9.50, with Apóstol San Pedro (more expensive but no better), Expreso Satipo and Lobato.

From Atalaya there are boats to **Pucallpa**, several a week, basic, hammock space, 36 hrs, US$16. They stop at all main towns, food is usually available, but take your own snacks, fruit and drinks. Hammocks can be bought in Sepahua or Atalaya. There are also flights from Atalaya to Pucallpa when demand is sufficient, usually several a week.

North of Chanchamayo p575

For transport to **Puerto Bermúdez**, see La Merced, under Chanchamayo, above. From Puerto Bermúdez, pickups and station wagons (colectivos) run to **Ciudad Constitución**,

0630-1730 when full, US$5 in front, US$3.20 in the back, 2½ hrs (4 hrs in wet season). From Ciudad Constitución to **Pucallpa**, Trans Pachitea-Palcazú 4WD pickups (office below **Hospedaje Chura**, T063-720245) at 0300 and 0430 if there are enough passengers, US$15 in front, US$11 in the back, 6 hrs in the dry, 8 hrs or more in the rainy season. From Ciudad Constitución to **La Merced** via Puerto Bermúdez and Villa Rica (where you can transfer for Oxapampa), 4WD pickups 0300-0400, US$17.50 in front, US$9.50 in the back, 12-13 hrs. Note that you can travel from Pucallpa to Puerto Bermúdez in 1 long day, but if travelling northbound from Puerto Bermúdez to Pucallpa you must spend the night in Ciudad Constitución and continue early the next morning.

Oxapampa p575
From Tarma to **Oxapampa**, Trans Los Canarios passes Tarma en route from Huancayo about 0945, US$4.70, 3½ hrs. Service from Lima (**Trans La Merced**, 11-12 hrs) to Oxapampa and **Pichanaki** usually goes full and does not take passengers in Tarma, better options from La Merced. **Empresa Santa Rosa**, Kennedy y Loaechle, T063-762582, to/from **La Merced**, US$2.50, 3 hrs. Combis to **Pozuzo**, 3-5 per day, US$3, 3-4 hrs. Oxapampa to **Cerro de Pasco** via Junín, Trans Junín, 0530 and 1300, US$3, 3 hrs. Colectivos to **Junín**, US$3.20, 1 hr, to Cerro de Pasco US$6.50, 2 hrs.

Directory

Tarma and around p572, map p572
Banks BCP, Lima 401. Changes TCs, cash, ATM. **Banco de la Nación**, Av Castillo 166, cash only; **Caja Municipal Huancayo**, Jr Lima 176, cash only, fair rates; **Mi Banco**, Jr Lima 543, cash only. Several cambios on Jr Moquegua near the Plaza de Armas, change US$ and euro, cash only, good rates. Also several ATMs. **Internet** Internet offices can be found all along Av Lima or Malecón José Gálvez just off Lima, US$0.30 per hr. **Telephone** Locutorios are everywhere, especially along Jr Lima.

Chanchamayo p574
Banks Banco de la Nación, Ancash y Lima. BCP, Junín y Tarma, changes cash and TCs. Several cambios around the Plaza de Armas, La Merced, change US$ and euro, cash only. **Internet** Internet cafés in La Merced. SoftService, Palca 279, and Selva net, Junín 210, are good. Next to El Parral on Uriate, San Ramón. **Post** Progreso 402, San Ramón; 2 de Mayo y Arica, La Merced.

North of Chanchamayo p575
Banks Banco de la Nación, Puerto Bermúdez, has no exchange services. Albergue Humboldt changes US dollars and euro cash. There are no exchange facilities in Ciudad Constitución. **Internet** Several places in Puerto Bermúdez, US$0.65 per hr. A couple of places in Ciudad Constitución, US$1.25 per hr. **Telephone** Public phones only, at Hostal Tania and Albergue Humboldt, Puerto Bermúdez, and Hotel Madeleine, Ciudad Constitución.

North of La Oroya and the Huallaga Valley

A paved road runs 130 km north from La Oroya to Cerro de Pasco. It runs up the Mantaro Valley through narrow canyons to the wet and mournful Junín pampa; at over 4250 m, it's one of the world's largest high-altitude plains. Blue peaks line the pampa in a distant wall. This windswept sheet of yellow grass is bitterly cold and the only signs of life are the young herders with their sheep and llamas. The road passes the eastern shores of the Lago de Junín, which is famous for its birdlife. From Junín to Cerro de Pasco the landscape is dominated by the cultivation of maca, through the Sierra Verde project; since it was declared that this tuber has strong nutritional value, demand has soared. Maca juice, cake, bread, liquor, etc, is sold from roadside stalls all around the lake. It is even claimed to have aphrodisiac properties.

The Central Highway from Cerro de Pasco continues northeast another 528 km to Pucallpa, the limit of navigation for large Amazon river boats. The western part of this road (Cerro de Pasco–Huánuco) is a good paved highway and the descent along the Río Huallaga is dramatic. The road drops 2436 m in the 100 km from Cerro de Pasco to Huánuco; most of it is in the first 32 km. From the bleak vistas of the high ranges the road plunges below the tree line into another world of tropical beauty. ➨ *For listings, see pages 589-592.*

Ins and outs
There are good roads all the way down to Huánuco, with bus services from the capital. There is also a road connection from the Callejón de Huaylas to Huánuco, so if you wish to stay in the sierra, you do not have to backtrack to the coast. For information, contact the **department of tourism** ① *T063-200550/51, junin@mitinci.gob.pe*, in Junín. **Dircetur Pasco** ① *Edif Estatal No 3, San Juan Pampa, Cerro de Pasco, T063-421029, dirceturpasco@ speedy.com*, in Cerro de Pasco, or **Dircetur** ① *Bolívar 381, T062-512980, huanuco@ mincetur.gob.pe*, in Huánuco. A useful website is www.webhuanuco.com.

Pampas de Junín ➔ *For listings, see pages 589-592.*

Junín ➔ *Colour map 3, B4. Altitude 4120 m.*
The town of Junín lies some distance south of Lago de Junín and has the desolate feel of a high puna town, bisected by the railway. Although small, it is typical of the lifestyle of the Peruvian Andes, with 16th-century architecture, strong local traditions and distinctive cuisine. It is a good starting point for seeing Andean wildlife and, as such, is becoming increasingly popular with birdwatchers and photographers.

The town has two plazas, one old, one new, called La Libertad. In the latter is a small underground museum with memorabilia from the battle. There is a large handicrafts centre at the southern entrance to the town. The Municipalidad is a few blocks from Plaza La Libertad. There are two **Inrena offices** ① *the Sede Administrativo at Jr San Martín 138, T064-344146, m-junin@inrena.gob.pe, and another at the west end of Jr Bolívar*, which administer three nearby protected areas: the Reserva Nacional de Junín (the lake and surroundings), the Santuario Nacional de Huayllay (Bosque de Piedras), and the Santuario Histórico de Chacamarca. Staff are very friendly.

Chacamarca
Three kilometres south of Junín, the **Chacamarca Historical Sanctuary** covers 2500 ha and includes the site of one of the most important battles of independence, at which

the Peruvians under Bolívar defeated the Spaniards in 1824. An obelisk marks the battlefield. Chacamarca is crowded during the annual commemoration of the battle on 6 August, but quiet the rest of the year. There's also an interesting underground museum and the remains of the pre-Inca citadel of Chacamarca. The wildlife of the high puna includes vicuña and foxes and there are springs at Yaropuquio. A taxi from the main street will cost you US$1.50-2.

Lago Junín National Reserve
ⓘ *US$5, ticket from Inrena in Junín. Altitude 4103 m.*

Peru's largest lake after Titicaca at 30 km by 14 km, Lago Junín (also known as Chinchaycocha) protects one of the best birdwatching sites in the central Andes, where all the highland waterbirds and raptors may be seen. It is a UNESCO Ramsar site and is said to be the highest lake of its size in the world. The surrounding fields abound with sierra-finches and ground-tyrants. Giant coot and even flamingos may be seen and, if you are really lucky, you can spot the diademed sandpiper and white-bellied cinclodes. Note that the *zambullidor de Junín*, Junin grebe, is in danger of extinction but can still be found here. In total, about 131 different species of bird can be found on the lake, 20% of which depend entirely on the lake's specific conditions for survival. Birdwatchers should sail around the lake; local fishermen are usually around to take visitors out.

There are several ways to get to the lake. The easiest is from the village of Huayre, 5 km south of **Carhuamayo** on the east side, from where it is a 20-minute walk down to the shore. Carhuamayo is the best place to stay near the lake, 50 minutes north of Junín. Nearby are Lago Shalipaico, the Minahuaraco fortress and Chuyroc caves. Another good viewing point is close to the village of **Ondores** on the west side of the lake; no paved roads here. There is an Inrena office in Ondores (one basic hostal, combi service throughout the day to/from Junín). Nearby are the interesting caves of Pachamachay with prehistoric paintings and El Mirador de Canoc lookout point. Beyond Ondores is San Pedro de Parl (one basic hostal, one combi a day to/from Junín, also some days to/from Cerro de Pasco). There is good birdwatching along the road. On the way you can stop to see some outstanding geological formations, ancient paintings on the rocks, the church of San Pedro and the Mirador de Comac Punta, with breathtaking views.

🌙 *The deep canyon of Goyllarisquisga (the 'place where a star fell'), 42 km north of Cerro de Pasco, is the highest coal mine in the world.*

Cerro de Pasco and around → *For listings, see pages 589-592. Colour map 3, B4.*
Altitude: 4330 m.

This long-established mining centre, 130 km from La Oroya by road, lies 8 km off the Carretera Central between Lago Patarcocha and the huge abyss of the mine above which its buildings and streets cling precariously. Not surprisingly for a place that claims to be the highest city in the world, nights are bitterly cold. Cerro de Pasco is famous as the site of a battle in the War of Independence. On 6 December 1820, local hero, Antonio Alvarez de Arenales, defeated Diego de O'Reilly's royalist troops at Cerro Uliachin (1 km from town). Although Cerro de Pasco is not an attractive place, the old corrugated iron buildings have a certain charm and it is very friendly.

Huayllay

Forty kilometres southwest of Cerro de Pasco is the **Santuario Nacional de Huayllay** (aka **Bosque de Piedras**) ① *visits are recommended Apr-Aug, US$1, payable only if the guides Ernesto and Christian are there*, which has unique weathered limestone formations in the shape of a tortoise, elephant, alpaca, etc. Four tourist circuits, at 4100 to 4600 m, pass spectacular rock formations, archeological remains, rock paintings, springs and beautiful high Andean landscapes. This is another great place for birdwatching. Camping is permitted within the sanctuary but be warned that nights become bitterly cold. The village of **Huallay**, is 20 minutes beyond the sanctuary entrance.

Also near Huallay are the ruins of an Inca community centre, **Bon Bón Marca**, which marks the course of a good section of Inca road, and the thermal springs of **Calera** ① *10 mins beyond the sanctuary entrance, daily 0700-2200, US$0.75*. The new individual baths, which can take up to four people, are the cleanest. Take a swimsuit; the baths are very hot and clean, ideal for a splash after a tiring day.

Yanahuanca Valley → *Colour map 3, B4.*

Some 65 km northwest of Cerro de Pasco, **Yanahuanca** (3200 m) is a quiet and very friendly town situated in the beautiful deep valley of the Río Chaupi Huaranga. It has well-stocked shops and adequate places to stay and eat (shopkeepers may change cash, best to take soles; internet in town US$0.30-0.50 per hour, phone services are unreliable). There are two sets of thermal baths at Villo and Tambochaca, facing each other on either side of the Río Chuapi Huaranga, connected by a footbridge. Those on the Tambochaca side are hotter, US$0.15 for the pool, US$0.65 for a private tub. The baths are a one-hour walk or 15 minutes by car from Yanahuanca plaza, US$0.50.

From the village you can reach one of the longest surviving stretches of Inca road by heading 2 km up the valley to where a lesser valley cuts northwards between the towering crags. The Inca road, its paving uneven and disturbed by countless horse and donkey convoys, leads up the smaller valley, its course sometimes shared by a stream, to the village of **Huarautambo**, about 4 km away, which is surrounded by many pre-Inca and Inca remains, as well as petroglyphs. (Cars from Yanhuanca plaza to Huarautambo, US$0.60, 30 minutes; it's a nice walk back down to Yanahuanca, one to two hours alongside cliffs and waterfalls.) The **Capaq Ñan** (Royal Inca road) is not only almost unbroken for more than 150 km from the Yanahuanca Valley, but it is also shown on the map issued by the **Instituto Geográfico Militar**. The clearest stretch ends at Huari in Ancash (see page 391). The Inca Road also climbs south of Yanahuanca to Chipipata and beyond, starting at an 'Inca-style' pedestrian bridge inaugurated in 2007, 30 minutes' walk from Yanahuanca.

Huánuco and the route to Huaraz → *For listings, see pages 589-592. Colour map 3, B4.*

Huánuco is an attractive Andean town on the Upper Huallaga at 1894 m. The city was founded in 1539, by Gómez de Alvarado, and is one of the oldest in Peru. It was originally known as 'Los Caballeros de León de Huánuco'. Its most famous son is Leoncio Prado, who refused to surrender to the Chileans at the Battle of Huamachuco in 1882 and is commemorated all over the city. There is a large main plaza fringed by enormous ficus trees, which are much more attractive than the modern cathedral. The natural history museum, **Museo de Ciencias** ① *Gen Prado 495, Mon-Fri 0900-1200, 1500-1800, Sat-Sun 1000-1200, US$0.50*, claims to have 10,000 exhibits of fauna from Peru's three regions, plus a good collection of shells and minerals. Many of the displays have multiple language signs. The town also holds an interesting market.

From Huánuco, a spectacular but very poor dirt road, impassable at times in the wet season, leads all the way to La Unión, capital of Dos de Mayo district (137 km). From Huánuco it climbs out of the Higueras Valley to **La Corona del Inca** (the 'Crown of the Inca'), also known as Lacsahuarina, meaning 'Two Princesses' in Quechua. This distinctive rock formation is at the pass before the descent into the upper canyon of the Río Marañón. The route then follows the Marañón to its confluence with the Río Vizcarra.

Kótosh

ⓘ *5 km from Huánuco on the road west to La Unión, admission US$0.75, including a guide (in Spanish). Taxi from Huánuco, US$5 including a 30-min wait.*

Investigations suggest that this archaeological site, at an altitude of 1912 m, was occupied for over 2000 years. Six distinct phases of occupation have been identified the oldest of which dates back some 4000 years. The Temple of Crossed Hands dates from 2000 BC; it was at one time regarded as the 'oldest temple in the Americas'. There are three main temple buildings, some of which have been partly reconstructed, though the original 'crossed hands' sculpture is now in the Archaeology Museum in Lima. The site has

Huánuco

To Tingo María & Pucallpa

Sleeping	6 Las Vegas	Eating
1 Caribe	7 Residencial Lima	1 Chifa Men Ji
2 El Roble		2 Govinda
3 Grand Hotel Huánuco		3 La Olla de Barro
4 Hostal Miraflores		4 Pizzería Don Sancho
5 Imperial		

200 metres
200 yards

an access bridge, is in good condition and has a small museum that gives clear explanations of Kótosh. A guide will take you around a marked circuit, which also passes through a small botanical garden of desert plants.

Tantamayo and around → *Colour map 3, B3. Altitude: 3600 m.*

Tantamayo 50 km beyond the turn off to La Unión is a farming village surrounded by pre-Columbian ruins from the Yarowillca culture. **Japallan** is perhaps the most scenically sited, guarding the entrance to the valley leading from the spectacular Marañón canyon. To get there, cross the river from Tantamayo and walk west to San Pedro de Pariarca; at the start of the village take the path to the right to Pariash (Upper Pariarca), and head for the ruins silhouetted on a ridge. The ruins of **Selinin** are just above Pariash. The most elaborate are **Piruru** – which was occupied continuously for 1700 years, from 3000 BC as a ceremonial, and later, a ceramics centre – and **Susupillu**. Both sites have high-rise stone dwellings. To reach Susupillu head northeast through the tiny village of La Florida. There are other ruins further afield.

All the above mentioned ruins are visible from Tantamayo and can be reached on foot in about three to four hours; guides are available to visit the sites. The walks to the ruins are arduous, so take warm clothing, a hat and suntan lotion, but the scenery is stunning. Pictures and information on the sites are available from Huánuco post office and on www.webhuanuco.com. In Tantamayo there are four basic hotels and one restaurant, Ortega, on the corner of the plaza. ▸▸ *See Huánuco transport, page 591.*

La Unión → *Colour map 3, B3. Altitude: 3204 m.*

La Unión is a regional supply town, with a large prison on the outskirts. The Plaza de Armas has a church with an interesting bell-tower but is not the centre of activity. Most shops are along two parallel streets: Jirón Dos de Mayo and Jirón Comercio. Although many people are friendly and helpful, tourists may nonetheless find themselves the object of much unwanted attention. The town straddles the Río Vizcarra. Electricity can be a problem and it gets very cold at night but there are good **hot baths** at Tauripampa, 5 km up the Vizcarra Valley, US$0.50 per person. The **Royal Inca Road** (Capac Ñan) runs north, just upriver from the baths on the north side of the valley, to Huari and south to Huánuco Pampa (Huánuco Viejo) and beyond. There is an INC office ① *Jr Comercio 1060*, which may have information about the road and associated archaeological sites.

You can hike to the **Cordillera Raura** from **Laguna Lauricocha**. To reach the lake from La Unión take a *camioneta* to **Baños**, then take another *camioneta* from there to **Antacolpa**. It's half a day's walk to the lake from here. In 1959, caves were discovered by the lake, containing 9500-year-old human remains and some paintings. This is where the Río Marañón rises, eventually becoming the Ucayali and then Amazon rivers, before spilling into the Atlantic Ocean, 5800 km away to the east.

Huánuco Viejo

① *2½ hrs' walk from La Unión, US$1.50; local farmer may be available to act as a guide (US$1).*
On the pampa above La Unión are the Inca ruins of Huánuco Viejo (or Huánuco Pampa), a great temple-fortress with residential quarters. To get there, take the very steep path starting behind the market and climb towards the cross, which is at the edge of a plateau (this takes one hour). Continue straight through the village on the wide path. Note that, though the locals are friendly, some of their dogs are not always well disposed to strangers. The views of the pampa, surrounded on all sides by mountains, are beautiful.

Seemingly at the foot of a mountain, in front and to your right, is the silvery metallic roof of a little chapel, behind which are the ruins, 4 km from the plateau's edge.

Huánuco Viejo was a major Inca settlement on the royal highway from Cuzco to Quito. The site has examples of very fine Inca stonework comparable with anything to be seen in Cuzco. This includes an *usnu*, measuring 30 m by 50 m and 4 m high, encased with superb stone blocks and with carved monkeys adorning the entrance and at one corner. An *usnu* was a ceremonial or judging platform, though its exact function is still uncertain. The *usnu* is surrounded by a huge central plaza, 547 m by 370 m, which, possibly, had to accommodate huge herds of animals. On the east side of the plaza are two *kallankas* (barracks), 84 m and 75 m long, nearly 10 m wide and two-storeys high, with thatched roofs. Running from the *kallankas* down to the royal Inca quarters and Inca bath are a series of six fine stone gateways adorned with beautifully carved pumas. Illa Tupac used the site as his stronghold from which he mounted resistance against the Spanish from 1536 until at least 1542. The site was then largely forgotten by the outside world and left untouched until the mid-20th century. It is the only major Inca settlement on the royal highway not to have been built over by a colonial or modern town.

Allow at least one hour to visit the main part of the site and at least two hours for the whole site, which covers over 2 sq km and contains the remains of over 3500 structures. You should take warm clothing and be prepared for some violent thunderstorms. A major festival, Fiesta del Sol, is held at the site on 27 July each year, but lodgings in the town are almost impossible to find at this time.

One of the finest stretches of the Royal Inca Road, or Capaq Ñan, runs northwest from the site to the Callejón de Conchucos. The Mountain Institute (www.mountain.org) has set up a six-day trek, known as the Inka Naani between Huánuco Viejo and the Pomachaca bridge, near San Marcos (see page 391; also see page 382 for the Mountain Institute's project at Vicos). The project, based on the work of Ricardo Espinosa (see page 695), involves conservation of the road and community tourism with villages along the route, which usually starts at Pomachaca. Apply to the Mountain Institute via the website for prices, departure dates, etc.

Huallanca (Huánuco) and on to Huaraz → *Colour map 3, B3.*
It is becoming easier to get to the Cordillera Blanca from Huánuco and La Unión. It's best to travel this route by day. El Rápido has two daily buses to Huaraz from La Unión via Chiquián (see page 592). Alternatively, take a colectivo to Huallanca and from there continue to Chiquián and Huaraz. The road from La Unión to Huallanca, follows the attractive and, in places, very narrow Vizcarra gorge for most of the journey. Beyond Huallanca a good road goes via Huansala all the way to Huaraz.

Often known as Huallanca (Huánuco) to distinguish it from the settlement of the same name in the Cañón del Pato, this is an attractive, unspoilt small town set between four hills in the Vizcarra valley. Large-scale mining projects in the area are bringing rapid change to the town and are polluting the Río Vizcarra.

For Sleeping and Eating price codes and other relevant information, see pages 38-44.

● Sleeping

Junín *p583*

F Leo, Jr San Martín 251, on Plaza La Libertad, T064-344199. The best of several small, basic *hostales* on the plaza, very clean, hot water, shared bathroom, pleasant.

G Hospedaje Paraíso, Av Chacamarca 164, half a block from Plaza de Armas, T064-344483. Small, simple and clean rooms, shared bath, tepid electric shower US$1 extra per person, good value.

Chacamarca *p583*

Gianmarco, Maravillas 454, and **Patricia**, Tarapacá 862, are the best of several basic *hostales* in Carhuamayo.

Cerro de Pasco and around *p584*

D Señorial, San Juan, 5 mins north of Cerro de Pasco by taxi, T063-422802, hotelsenorial @hotmail.com. The most comfortable hotel in Cerro, with hot water, TV, and a fine view back across the mine pit. There are some other good *hostales* in this district.

E Wong, Carrión 99, T063-421551. Hot water 24 hrs, TV, clean, comfortable, noisy, friendly, motorcycle parking.

F Hostal Arenales, Jr Arenales 162, near the bus station, T063-423088. Clean, modern, TV, friendly, hot water in the morning. Good.

F Welcome, Av La Plata 125, T063-721883, opposite the entrance to the bus station. Some rooms are without a window, hot water 24 hrs, clean, friendly.

Yanahuanca Valley *p585*

E-F Rocca's, Jr Soledad, T063-816501. Somewhat bare, modern rooms, electric shower (cheaper without), clean, views, good restaurant, family-run, friendly.

F Hostal Jamay Wasi, Jr 28 de Julio, T063-816549. Simple, clean and pleasant, rooms

with shower, most rented out long term, cheaper with shared bath and cold water.

Huánuco *p585, map p586*

A Grand Hotel Huánuco, Dámaso Beraún 775, T062-514222, www.grandhotelhuanuco. com. A hotel since the 1940s in a prime location on the Plaza de Armas. Includes breakfast, TV, free internet. Restaurant, pool, sauna, gym, parking. Recommended.

D Caribe, Huánuco 546, T062-513645. Large modern hotel with big rooms, bathroom, TV. **Hostal Mariño**, T062-513702 is next door.

D Imperial, Huánuco 581, T062-518737. Modern, breakfast included, with bath and hot water, TV, quiet and helpful. Recommended.

E Hostal Miraflores, Jr Hermilio Valdizan 564, T062-512848, www.granhostalmiraflores. com. Rooms with bath, hot water and cable TV, clean, quiet, safe, laundry.

F Las Vegas, 28 de Julio 940, on Plaza de Armas, T/F062-512315. Small rooms, hot water, TV. Restaurant next door. Good.

F Residencial Lima, 28 de Julio 922, on the Plaza de Armas. TV, hot water and private bathrooms, clean.

G El Roble, Constitución 629, T062-512515. Without bath, clean, good value.

La Unión *p587*

F Abilia Alvarado, Comercio 1196 y Grau. Hot water, large pleasant grounds, parking, restaurant has choice of good set meals and à la carte (best in town), disco at weekends. Rooms are old, musty and run down, poor beds. Helpful owners provide some information about visiting Huánuco Viejo.

F Hostal Picaflor, Jr Dos de Mayo 870 and 2nd location 2 blocks away at Jr Porvenir 517, T062-510222. Small, simple rooms, some with electric shower (connected only by advance arrangement, not reliable), laundry facilities, reasonably clean and adequate.

There are several other basic places to stay in town.

Huallanca (Huánuco) *p588*

E Hotel Milán, 28 de Julio 107. Modern, TV and hot water in all rooms, best in town. The restaurant is good and serves trout caught in lakes high above the town.

G Hostal Yesica, L Prado 507. Hot water, shared bathroom, the best of the basic ones.

🍴 Eating

Lago Junín National Reserve *p584*
There are numerous restaurants along the main road in Carhuamayo. The best is **Savoy**. You can also find locals selling *pachamanca*, fried frogs' legs and *maca* products.

¶ **Skorpion's**, Jr Bolívar 704 y Ayacucho, Plaza de Armas, Junín. Open daily. Friendly and attentive owner, good set meals, also fruit juices, sandwiches, sweets and hot drinks.

Cerro de Pasco and around *p584*
Local specialities are trout, fried frog, *ferro carril* (which is known elsewhere as *bistec a lo pobre*) and *maca*.

¶ **Los Angeles**, Jr Libertad, near the market. Excellent *menú*.

¶ **San Fernando** bakery in the plaza. Opens at 0700. First-rate hot chocolate, bread and pastries.

Huánuco *p585, map p586*
¶ **Chifa Men Ji**, 28 de Julio, block 8. Good prices, nice Chinese food, clean.

¶ **Govinda**, 2 de Mayo 1044. Reckoned to be the best vegetarian in town.

¶ **La Olla de Barro**, Gral Prado 852, close to main plaza. Serves typical food, good value.

¶ **Pizzería Don Sancho**, Prado 645. For the best pizzas in town.

La Unión *p587*
See **Abilia Alvarado**, in Sleeping, above. There are several other simple places to eat, keep an eye on hygiene.

Huallanca (Huánuco) *p588*

¶ **El Norteño**, Comercio 441. Apart from the Hotel Millán, this is the most popular place to eat.

⊗ Festivals and events

Junín *p583*
5-6 Aug Battle of Independence. Events in town and at Chacamarca, colourful and popular, hotels fill, prices rise, etc.

Cerro de Pasco and around *p584*
May Festival de La Chonguinada Cerreña is celebrated in the 1st week.
May/Jun Semana Turística de Huarica.
5 Aug Virgen de Las Nieves.
Last week in Nov Semana Turística de Pasco.

Huánuco *p585, map p586*
20-25 Jan Carnaval Huanuqueño.
21 Mar Festival de las Cataratas.
1 May Festival of El Señor de Chacos in San Rafael, in the province of Ambo.
3 May La Cruz de Mayo, in Huánuco.
16 Jul Fiesta de la Virgen del Carmen.
Jul Festival de la Perricholi (last week)
12-18 Aug Tourist Week in Huánuco.
15 Aug Founding of the city.
25-27 Sep Festival del Cóndor Pasa.
28-29 Oct Fiesta del Rey y del Señor de Burgos, the patron of Huánuco.
25 Dec Fiesta de los Negritos.

⊙ Transport

Junín *p583*
Buses, combis and cars all leave from Av Manuel Prado at the east end of town. To **Carhuamayo**, taxi colectivos charge US$1.50. To **Ondores**, US$0.90-1.50 for a 30-min ride, cars throughout the day. To **San Pedro de Pari**, US$1.50, 1 combi daily in early morning. To **Tarma**, cars leave throughout the day, US$2.50, 1½ hrs. To **Lima**, Empresa Junín,

4 daily, US$4.70-6.50, 5 hrs, Lima terminal at Nicolás Arriola 198, T01-224 9220. Also **Turismo Carhuamayo**, 3 daily, Lima terminal at Av Luna Pizarro 145, T01-330 7291. To **Huancayo**, several companies daily, US$2.80, 4 hrs. To **Cerro de Pasco**, several companies, frequent service throughout the day with buses passing through from Lima, US$1, 1½ hrs.

Lago Junín National Reserve p584
From Carhuamayo to **Cerro de Pasco**, 40 mins, colectivos charge US$1.50.

Cerro de Pasco and around p584
All services use the large, enclosed bus station. To **Lima**, several companies including Carhuamayo and Transportes Apóstol San Pedro, hourly 0800-1200, plus 4 departures 2030-2130, 8 hrs, US$4-5. If there are no convenient daytime buses, you could change buses in La Oroya. Buses to **Carhuamayo**, 1 hr, US$1; **Junín**, 1½ hrs, US$1; and **La Oroya**, 2½ hrs, US$2, leave when full, about every 20-30 mins. Colectivos (cars) also depart with a similar frequency to all places, eg, 1½ hrs, US$2.50, to La Oroya. To **Tarma**, Empresa Junín at 0600 and 1500, 3 hrs, US$2.50. Colectivos hourly, 1½ hrs, US$4. To **Huancayo**, various companies throughout the day, 5 hrs, US$4. To **Oyón**, Transportes Javier, 1230, 5 hrs, US$3.50; there is also a bus to the mine at **Raura**, 1100, 7 hrs, US$5. Minibuses to **Huayllay** leave throughout the day, about 1 hr, US$1; they return until 1800-1900. Taxis to the **Calera** thermal baths run throughout the day, US$1.50, 45 mins, or pick up a Huayllay combi, US$1.20, about 1 hr. To **Huánuco**, buses (US$2) and cars (US$4) leave when full, 2½ hrs and 1½ hrs.

Yanahuanca Valley p585
To/from **Cerro de Pasco**, cars leave when full throughout the day (from the Plaza de Armas in Yanahuanca), US$4.10, 2½ hrs. To **Huánuco**, Chavalito, Jr 28 de Julio, down the hill from the hospital, daily at 0400 and 1400, US$3.80, 4 hrs. From Huánuco daily at 0700

and 1200. To **Lima**, San Cristóbal de Huánuco, near Plaza de Armas, Wed, Fri, Sun at 1400, US$8, 13 hrs. From Lima (Huánuco 1538, La Victoria, T01-794 9337) Tue, Thu, Sat at 1930. Also **Hauynate**, Av Grau 707, Tue, Fri, Sun at 1500, from Lima Mon, Thu, Sat at 2030.

Huánuco p585, map p586
Air
Airport T062-513066. To **Lima**, LC Busre (2 de Mayo 1355, T062-518113), daily, 55 mins.

Bus
To **Lima**, US$11 *normal* to US$17 *cama*, 8 hrs, various companies: León de Huánuco, Malecón Alomía Robles 821, 3 a day; Bahía Continental, Valdizan 718, T062-519999, recommended; Transportes El Rey, 28 de Julio 1215. Most buses leave 2030-2200, most companies also have a bus at 0900-1000. Colectivo to Lima, US$23, 0400, 10 hrs; book the night before at Gen Prado 607, 1 block from the plaza. Recommended.

Bus to **Cerro de Pasco**, 3 hrs, US$2; colectivos less than 2 hrs, US$4. All leave when full from the roundabout, Ovalo Carhuayna, on the north side of the city, 3 km from the centre. To **Huancayo**, 7 hrs, US$6, with **Turismo Central**, Tarapacá 530, at 2130, or with **Trans Rey** at 2215, from depot on 28 de Julio, US$7, 7 hrs.

Colectivos run to **Tingo María**, from block 1 of Prado close to Puente Calicanto, 2½ hrs, US$5, also microbuses, US$2, either is recommended over the unsafe Etnasa bus, 3-4 hrs, US$2. For **Pucallpa**, take a colectivo to Tingo María, then a bus from there; see under Pucallpa, Transport, for direct buses. Travel by day and check the safety situation.

To **La Unión**, Turismo Unión, daily at 0730, 7 hrs, US$5, and **Turismo Marañón** daily at 0700. There are also El Niño colectivo services (Aguilar 530), departing when full, 5 hrs, US$7.15. To **Tantamayo**, Turismo Bella, San Martín 571, at 0630 and 0730, operate old buses on this rough route, but is recommended by locals, 8 hrs, US$6; also **Chasqui**, Mayro 572. To **Baños**,

Transportes **Legionario**, Independencia 656, run buses and truck-buses on alternate days, 0830; also **Transportes Romancero**, Tarapacá 500 block, 0900, 4 hrs, US$3.50.

La Unión *p587*

There is a small ramshackle bus and combi terminal on Jr Comercio at the west end of town, but some companies also have agencies in town.

To **Huánuco**, Turismo Unión, Jr Comercio 1224, daily at 0600, US$5, 7 hrs, and **Turismo Marañón**, Jr Comercio 1309, daily at 0700. There are **El Niño** colectivo services from Jr Comercio 12, T062-515952. To **Tantamayo**, several combis and buses daily, 5-6 hrs, US$4. However, it may be easier to take a combi to Tingo Chico at the Vizcarra/Marañón confluence, 1 hr, US$0.75, then wait for the bus services from Huánuco to Tantamayo. To **Huaraz**, El Rápido, 2 daily (1st at 0400), US$4.80, 4½ hrs. To **Huallanca** (**Huánuco**), combis leave from the market, about half hourly, when full and follow the attractive Vizcarra Valley, 1 hr, US$0.75; they return from the corner of Comercio y 28 de Julio in Huallanca. To **Lima**, Cavassa, daily at 0500 via Chiquián, 12 hrs, and at 1800 direct, 9 hrs, both US$8. From Lima daily at 0900 via Chiquián and 1800 direct (Lima terminal at Raymondi 129 y Paseo de la República). Also **Armonía**, daily at 1800, US$8, 9 hrs. From Lima daily at 1800 (Lima terminal at Leticia 520, off Av Abancay). Journey times will be reduced when the road to Huallanca is paved.

To **Huánuco Viejo**, combis bound for Baños leave from the bus terminal at about 0600 and 1300 daily (they fill early and get crowded), 1 hr to the archaeological site, US$0.65. To return to La Unión they pass **Huánuco Pampa** around 1100 and 1600, or walk down to town. Taxi to ruins, round-trip with wait, US$6.50-9.50, negotiable.

⊙ Directory

Junín *p583*

Banks Banco de la Nación, Jr San Martín y Suárez, 1 block from Plaza de Armas, Mon-Fri 0830-1700, Sat 0830-1300. Changes US$ cash only, fair rates, no TCs, no ATM, no cash advances. Botica Beatriz, Jr San Martín 578, near Av Manuel Prado where the buses stop, US$ cash only, poor rates. **Internet** A few places, US$0.50 per hr.

Cerro de Pasco and around *p584*

Banks BCP, Jr Bolognesi. Money changers on Jr Bolognesi between the market and the cathedral.

Huánuco *p585, map p586*

Banks BCP, at Dos de Mayo 1005. Casa de cambio at Gral Prado 635. **Internet** Several in the centre. **Post** 2 de Mayo on the plaza, Mon-Sat 0800-2000, Sun 0800-1400. **Telephone** Telefónica del Perú, 28 de Julio 1170.

La Unión *p587*

Banks Banco de la Nación, Jr Dos de Mayo 798 y Jr Unión, fair rates for US$ cash only, Mon-Fri 0900-1730, Sat 0900-1300. No TCs, ATM or cash advances. **Internet** Several places US$0.65 per hr. Mundo Satelital, Jr Unión 260, is good and fast.

Contents

Amazon Basin

At a glance

⊖ **Getting around** Small plane and by boat.

◉ **Time required** 1 week in the northern jungle; 1 week in the southern jungle.

☀ **Weather** Apr-Oct is the dry season. Nov-Mar/Apr is the rainy season and can be oppressively hot. Expect some rain at any time of year.

✖ **When not to go** As well as the heat and rain, there are more mosquitoes in the wet season.

ECUADOR

COLOMBIA

Pantoja

Copal Urco

Curaray

Marsella

San Jacinto
Andoas

Tigre

Intuto

Mazán
Indiana

Amazonas

Pebas

Trompeteros

2 Iquitos **3**

Caballococha

San Pablo

Leticia
Santa Rosa

Nauta

Morona

Pastaza

Marañón

BRAZIL

Borja

San Ramón

Lagunas

1 Reserva Nacional
Pacaya-Samiria

Ucayali

Balsapuertos

Yurimaguas

Moyobamba

Lamas

Tarapoto

Huallabamba

★ **Don't miss ...**

1 Pacaya-Samiria Reserve, page 597.
2 Iquitos, page 600.
3 Stay in a jungle lodge, pages 609 and 629.
4 Manu Biosphere Reserve, page 620.
5 Tambopata National Reserve, page 627.

Tocache Nuevo

L Yarinacocha

Pucallpa

Aucayacu

Tournavista

La Morada

Aguaytía

Pampas de Sacramento

Huaraz

Tingo María

Acomayo

Huánuco

Cerro
De Pasco

Huancabamba

Atalaya

Iñapari
Iberia

San
Ramón

Junín

Mazamari

Manu
Biosphere
Reserve

4 Madre Dios

Boca
Colorado

Puerto
Maldonado

La Oroya

Tarma

Boca Manu

Itahuania

3

Jauja

Shintuya

Laberinto

LIMA

Huancayo

Atalaya

Bahuaja-Sonene
National Park

5 Tambopata
National Reserve

Huancavelica

Ayna

Calca

Ica

Ayacucho

Cuzco

Nazca

The Amazon Basin covers a staggering 4,000,000 sq km, roughly equivalent to three-quarters the size of the United States. But despite the fact that 60% of Peru is covered by this green carpet of jungle, less than 6% of its population lives here, meaning that much of Peru's rainforest is still intact. The area is home to 10,000,000 living species, including 2000 species of fish and 300 mammals. It also has over 10% of the world's 8600 bird species and, together with the adjacent Andean foothills, 4000 butterfly species. This incredible biological diversity brings with it an acute ecological fragility. The Amazon rainforest is reckoned to produce 20% of the Earth's oxygen and any fundamental change could have disastrous implications for our future on this planet.

The two major tourist areas are the northern and southern jungles. In the north the focus is the River Amazon itself, with Iquitos at the heart of life on the river. To get into the wilds, head for Peru's largest national reserve, Pacaya-Samiria. In the south the Manu Biosphere Reserve and Tambopata National Reserve are also far removed from the modern world. In fact most of Manu is off limits to tourists. Many lodges in the area are close to the river port of Puerto Maldonado.

Wildlife viewing in these two areas is quite different. Northern Peru is dominated by flood plains and vast rivers, with much of the land regularly submerged. In remote spots, there are chances of seeing manatees, giant otters and pink and grey Amazonian dolphins. Terrestrial mammals seem to be thinly distributed through the jungle. The Southern Amazon has several faster-running rivers and rapids that prevent dolphins and manatees reaching the upper sections. A huge variety of forest types and diverse habitats have led to more bird species here than anywhere else on the planet. Moreover, in protected areas such as Manu and Tambopata, some larger mammals, like tapir, giant anteaters, otters and primates, are fairly easy to spot due to lack of hunting pressure.

Northern Jungle

From the heights of the Andes down to the Amazonian lowlands a road runs to Pucallpa, the second city of this region of Peru. It passes through the Huallaga Valley, not the safest part of the country owing to the narcotics trade, but if you stick to the main route you should be OK. From Pucallpa and Yurimaguas, further north, you can venture into the jungle if you want to continue beyond; the only way is to spend several days in a boat, getting to know the rivers and their traffic.

Standing on the banks of the Amazon itself, the city of Iquitos still retains something of a frontier feel. It became famous during the rubber boom of the late 19th century and is now attracts tourists to this part of the country to experience the authentic Amazon river. For jungle visits there are many lodges to choose from and two fine protected areas, Pacaya-Samiria and Allpahuayo-Mishana.

▶▶ For listings, see pages 606-619.

Tingo María to Iquitos → For listings, see pages 606-619.

The overland route from the central Andes to Pucallpa runs from Huánuco east to Tingo María on a paved road, and gives the first views of the vast green carpet of jungle. Beyond Huánuco the road begins a sharp climb to the heights of Carpish (3023 m). A descent over 58 km brings it to the Huallaga river again; the road continues along the river to Tingo María. The road is paved from Huánuco to Tingo María, including a tunnel through the Carpish hills. Landslides along this section are frequent and construction work causes delays. Although this route is reported to be relatively free from terrorism and violence related to drug cultivation and trafficking, robberies do occur and it is advisable to travel only by day. Seek local advice.

Tingo María → Colour map 3, A4. Phone code: 062. Altitude: 655 m.

Tingo María is on the Middle Huallaga, in the Ceja de Montaña, or edge (literally, eyebrow) of the mountains. The Cordillera Azul, the front range of the Andes, covered with jungle-like vegetation to its top, separates it from the jungle lowlands to the east. The mountain that can be seen from all over the town is called La Bella Durmiente – The Sleeping Beauty. The meeting here of sierra (highlands) and selva (jungle) makes the landscape extremely striking. Bananas, sugar cane, cocoa, rubber, tea and coffee are grown. The main crop of the area, though, is coca, grown on the chacras (smallholdings) in the countryside, and sold legitimately (and otherwise) in Tingo María. These crops thrive in the tropical climate, with an annual rainfall of 2642 mm. In the height of the rainy season the town can be isolated for days. The altitude, however, prevents the climate from being oppressive: the maximum temperature is 34°C, minimum 18°C, with a relative humidity of 77.5%. A small university outside the town, beyond the Hotel Madera Verde, has a little **museum/zoo** ① free but a small tip would help to keep things in order; it also maintains botanical gardens in the town. There is also a **Dircetur tourist office** ① Av Ericson 158, T062-562310, perucatapress@gmail.com.

On a rough road, 6.5 km from Tingo, is a fascinating cave, the **Cueva de las Lechuzas** ① US$0.90. Take a mototaxi from town, US$1.75, and cross the Río Monzón by the new bridge. Take a torch, and do not wear open shoes. There are many oilbirds in the cave and parakeets near the entrance. The cave is in the 18,000-ha **Parque Nacional de Tingo María** ① US$2.50, the second national park created in Peru. A mototaxi to the entrance costs US$0.75. There are other caves and waterfalls in the area.

North to Yurimaguas

The Río Huallaga winds northwards for 930 km from its source to the confluence with the Marañón. The Upper Huallaga is a torrent, dropping 15.8 m per km between its source and Tingo María, but by the time it becomes the Lower Huallaga it moves slowly through a flat landscape. The main port of the Lower Huallaga, **Yurimaguas**, is below the last rapids and only 150 m above the Atlantic Ocean, yet distant from that ocean by over a month's voyage. Between the Upper and Lower lies the Middle Huallaga: the third of the river that is downstream from Tingo María and upstream from Yurimaguas.

At **Tulumayo**, soon after leaving Tingo María, a road runs north down the Huallaga past **La Morada** to **Aucayacu**, which has a couple of poor hotels, and **Tocache**, which also has a couple of hotels, plus an airport. The road has been pushed north from Tocache to join another built south from Tarapoto and has now been joined at Tarapoto to the Olmos–Bagua–Yurimaguas Transandean Highway to the coast at Chiclayo. The road is paved to Tocache, 169 km. The stretch from Tocache to Juanjuí is unpaved, 178 km, seven hours by public transport. Thereafter it is paved to Tarapoto. Colectivos run between towns on the Tingo María–Tarapoto road. Occasional hold-ups occur.

Yurimaguas → *Colour map 1, B5. Phone code: 065. Population: 25,700. Altitude: 160 m.*

Yurimaguas is a very friendly, relaxed jungle town. It is the road head on the lower Río Huallaga, an ideal starting point for river travel in the Peruvian Amazon. The town has a fine church of the Passionist Fathers, based on the Cathedral of Burgos in Spain. A colourful market is held from 0600-0800, full of fruit and animals. In addition to the **tourist information office** ① *in the Consejo Regional building on the main plaza, T065-352676, Mon-Fri 0800-1600,* there is a small **Museo Arqueológico** (same hours). There are some interesting excursions in the area too, including the gorge of **Shanusi** and the lakes of **Mushuyacu** and **Sanango**.

Lagunas → *Colour map 1, B6.*

The river journey to Iquitos can be broken at Lagunas, 12 hours from Yurimaguas; all *lanchas* stop here. This is a good access point for the Pacaya-Samiria Reserve.

Reserva Nacional Pacaya-Samiria → *Colour map 2, C2.*

① *Reserve office in Iquitos, C Moore 1430, T065-226944, Mon-Fri 0800-1300, 1500-1800, has information and an up-to-date list of tour operators authorized to enter the reserve. You must go here to obtain proof of payment for the entry fee (US$20 per day); payment itself must be made at Banco de la Nación. To make the most of the park, stay for a minimum of 5 days.*

Pacaya-Samiria Reserve, at 2,080,000 ha, is the country's largest such protected area. It is bounded by the rivers Marañón and Ucuyali – and a tributary of it, the Canal de Puinahua – narrowing to their confluence near the town of **Nauta** (two hours by road from Iquitos). The reserve's waterways, lakes and swamps provide habitat for mammals such as the manatee, tapir, river dolphins and giant river otters, as well as black cayman, boas and the *charapa* (yellow-headed river turtle), 193 species of fish and some 330 bird species. Many of the animals found here are in danger of extinction. Trips are mostly on the river, sleeping in hammocks, and include fishing. Iquitos operators enter through Nauta to Yarina where there is a shelter, also through Requena. Other entry points are the villages of **Maipuco**, 18-20 hours from Yurimaguas, **Leoncio Prado**, on the Marañón, opposite the outflow of the Río Samiria (*hospedajes* 5 **Hermanitos** and Ruiz), and **Bretaña** on the Canal de Puinahua.

Androgynous Amazonians

The Amazon is the longest river in the world. It rises high up in the Andes as the Marañón, then joins the Ucayali and winds its way east to disgorge itself finally into the Atlantic, over 6000 km from its source. At its mouth, the Amazon river is a massive 300 km wide. This mighty waterway was named by the Spaniard Francisco de Orellana during his epic voyage in 1542, following an encounter with a hostile, long-haired indigenous group whom he took to be the fearsome women warriors of Greek legend.

The main part of the reserve is off-limits to tourists, but some 'ecotourism zones' have been set up where, with the correct permits (see above), river trips can be undertaken and some controlled camping is possible. As no building is allowed, nor use of motors, trips are limited. Do not join a tour that involves living off the land or any other activity that will endanger the wildlife in the reserve. Take bottled water, or purifier, and mosquito repellent and make sure that any boat has enough fuel to get you to the reserve.

Tingo María to Pucallpa → *Colour map 3, A4/5.*

From Tingo María to the end of the road at Pucallpa is 255 km, with a climb over the watershed – the Cordillera Azul – between the Huallaga and Ucayali rivers. The road is paved all the way and goes through Aguaytía. It can be affected by mud and landslides in the rainy season. Apart from its insecurity, another reason not to travel this road at night is that you will miss the tremendous views as you go from the high jungle to the Amazon Basin. Sit on the right side of the bus to appreciate the landscape and the hairpin bends and sheer drops. When the road was being surveyed it was thought that the lowest pass over the Cordillera Azul was more that 3650 m high, but an old document stating that a Father Abad had found a pass through these mountains in 1757 was rediscovered, and the road now goes through the pass of Father Abad, a gigantic gap 4 km long and 2000 m deep. At the top of the pass is a Peruvian customs house; the jungle land to the east is a free zone. Concrete stairs and metal handrails have been built for viewing the waterfalls. Coming down from the pass the roadbed runs along the floor of a magnificent canyon, the **Boquerón Abad**. It is a beautiful trip through luxuriant jungle, with ferns and sheer walls of bare rock punctuated by occasional waterfalls plunging into the roaring torrent below. East of the foot of the pass the road goes over the flat pampa, with few bends, to the village of **Aguaytía**. Here you'll find a narcotics police outpost, petrol, accommodation and two restaurants. Nearby is the 20-m-high **Velo de la Novia** waterfall, in a beautiful setting. From Aguaytía the road continues for 160 km to Pucallpa – five hours by bus. There is a fuel station three hours before Pucallpa.

Pucallpa → *Colour map 3, A5. Phone code: 061. Population: 600,000. Altitude 150m.*

The capital of the department of Ucayali is a busy jungle city on the Río Ucayali, navigable by vessels of 3000 tons from Iquitos, 533 nautical miles away. It is the transfer point for most cargo to and from Iquitos and a transport hub for visitors. At the Plaza de Armas, where locals stroll in the evening, are a modern cathedral and municipality. Artists perform on weekend evenings at the Malecón Grau, a pleasant riverfront promenade with a clock tower (El Reloj Público). Mototaxis make the city very noisy. The climate is tropical. The dry season is from June to October when it's hot and dusty. The rainy seasons are October to November and February to March and the dirt roads leading to port areas of town can be muddy through to May.

There is narcotics activity in the area. The city centre is relatively safe until about 2200, but avoid deserted areas and don't travel at night. The tourist office is **Dircetur** ⓘ *Jr 2 de Mayo 111, T061-578400, ucayali@mincetur.gob.pe, Mon-Fri 0730-1300, 1330-1515.* Information is also available at **Gobierno Regional de Ucayali (GOREU)** ⓘ *Raymondi 220, T061-575018, www.regionucayali.gob.pe.*

The Parque Natural de Pucallpa has gardens, recreation areas, a zoo, and houses the **Museo Regional** ⓘ *Carretera Federico Basadre Km 4.2, www.parquenaturalpucallpa.com, entry US$1.10, Mon-Fri 0800-1630, Sat-Sun 0900-1730.* The museum has some good examples of Shipibo ceramics, as well as some delightful pickled snakes and other reptiles. You will probably want to take a taxi or mototaxi to visit it. **Usko Ayar Amazonian School of Painting** ⓘ *Jr LM Sánchez Cerro 465-467, Pucallpa, see www.pablo amaringo.com,* is in the house of artist Pablo Amaringo (1943-2009), a former *vegetalista*

Pucallpa

Sleeping
1 Antonio's
2 Barbtur
3 Hostal Arequipa
4 Hostal Komby
5 Hostal Sun
6 Mercedes
7 Sol del Oriente

Eating
1 C'est si Bon
2 Chifa Xin Xin
3 El Viajero
4 La Favorita
5 Tropitop Heladería

(healer). The school provides art classes for local people and is financially dependent upon selling their work. The internationally renowned school welcomes overseas visitors for short or long stays to study painting and learn Spanish and/or teach English with Peruvian students. The painting is oriented around the Amazonian cultures, including the healing and hallucinogenic effects of *ayahuasca*.

The economy of the area is based around sawmills, plywood factories, an oil refinery, fishing and boat building; timber is trucked out to the highlands and the coast. Large discoveries of oil and gas are being explored. **Maple Gas oilfield** has a 75-km pipeline to the Pucallpa refinery.

Lago Yarinacocha

The main attraction of the area is Lago Yarinacocha, to the northeast of Pucallpa, a U-shaped oxbow lake linked to the Río Ucayali by a canal at the northern tip of its west arm. River dolphins can be seen here. Puerto Callao, also known as Yarinacocha or Yarina, is the main town, located at the southern tip of the U, it is reached by road from Pucallpa. There are a number of restaurants and bars here and it is a popular place for weekend outings among locals. From Yarina, a road continues along the western arm to San José, San Francisco and Santa Clara. Other villages are reached on foot or by boat. The area is populated by the Shipibo people, who make traditional ceramic and textile crafts. The area between the eastern arm of the lake and the Río Ucayali has been designated as a reserve. Here, towards the northwestern shore of the east arm is the beautifully located **Jardín Botánico Chullachaqui**, reached by boat from Puerto Callao to Pueblo Nueva Luz de Fátima. It's a 45-minute trip, then an hour's walk to the garden; entry is free. For information about traditional medicine contact **Moroti Shobo**, at the Plaza de Armas in Puerto Callao.

Pucallpa to Iquitos

The Río Ucayali meanders a great deal, making travel time longer than expected for the distance as the crow flies. Distance here is measured in bends, eg the next town is three curves away. In the dry season there are many sandbanks; larger boats may travel only by day and tie up along the shore at night, making the trip much longer. The exposed banks are covered in bright green rice fields (*arroz de verano*), which attract many birds including Jabiru storks (*tuyuyo*). Some of the more important towns along the way are **Contamana** with a floating dock, a large town with a frontier feel (**F Hospedaje Venus**, T065-551460, with TV, cheaper with shared bath; several others in town), **Orellana** (**F Hospedaje Alejandro**, T065-830014, with bath, fan; and a couple of other places), **Bretaña** on the Canal de Puinahua (see Pacaya-Samiria, above), and **Requena**, a couple of hours south of the confluence with the Amazon, from where speedboats (*rápidos*) go to Iquitos.

Iquitos → *For listings, see pages 606-619. Colour map 2, B4. Phone code: 065. Population: 600,000.*

Capital of the Department of Loreto and chief town of Peru's jungle region, Iquitos is some 800 km downstream from Pucallpa and 3646 km from the mouth of the Amazon. It is a tropical city, an urban oasis, completely isolated except by air and river. It is active, generally friendly and has gained a reputation for some of its restaurants' gastronomy. The atmosphere is quite different from the rest of Peru. It remains the best place for access to the Peruvian Amazon proper. With its jungle lodges and natural areas such as Pacaya-Samiria, this is the only part of the Peruvian jungle where Victoria Regia lilies and pink dolphins can be seen. In the city it may seem that Iquitos is attempting a new world

Iquitos

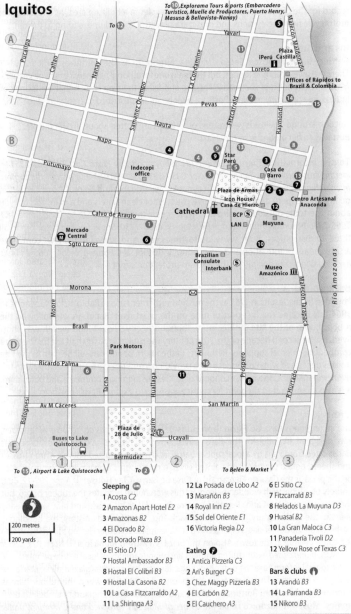

To 12, Explorama Tours & ports (Embarcadero Turístico, Muelle de Productores, Puerto Henry, Masusa & Bellavista-Nanay)

To 10, Airport & Lake Quistococha

To 2

To Belén & Market

200 metres
200 yards

Sleeping
1 Acosta *C2*
2 Amazon Apart Hotel *E2*
3 Amazonas *B2*
4 El Dorado *B2*
5 El Dorado Plaza *B3*
6 El Sitio *D1*
7 Hostal Ambassador *B3*
8 Hostal El Colibrí *B3*
9 Hostal La Casona *B2*
10 La Casa Fitzcarraldo *A2*
11 La Shiringa *A3*

12 La Posada de Lobo *A2*
13 Marañón *B3*
14 Royal Inn *E2*
15 Sol del Oriente *E1*
16 Victoria Regia *D2*

Eating
1 Antica Pizzería *C3*
2 Ari's Burger *C3*
3 Chez Maggy Pizzería *B3*
4 El Carbón *B2*
5 El Cauchero *A3*

6 El Sitio *C2*
7 Fitzcarrald *B3*
8 Helados La Muyuna *D3*
9 Huasaí *B2*
10 La Gran Maloca *C3*
11 Panadería Tivoli *D2*
12 Yellow Rose of Texas *C3*

Bars & clubs
13 Arandú *B3*
14 La Parranda *B3*
15 Nikoro *B3*

record for the highest concentration of motorcycles in a built-up area. As a result of the motorcycle noise, televisions and music are played at top volume, adding to the din.

Ins and outs

Getting there Francisco Secada Vigneta **airport** is in the southwest, T065-260147. There are several ports in Iquitos, but the main one for all long-haul service in large vessels is Masusa, 2 km north of the centre. The rise and fall of the river is such that the islands off Iquitos are constantly moving. **Ports** for river boats are described in Transport, page 616.

Getting around Iquitos is well spread out. Hotels are dotted about all over the place. The best way to get around is by mototaxi.

Tourist information iperú ① *Loreto 201 y Raymondi, by Plaza Castilla, T065-236144, iperuiquitos@promperu.gob.pe, Mon-Sat 0830-1930, Sun 0830-1400; also at the airport, open at flight times*. Staff at both offices are knowledgeable and helpful. If arriving by air, go first to the **iperú** desk. They will give you a list of clean hotels and a map, and tell you about the touts outside the airport, etc. **Dircetur tourist office** ① *La Condamine 183, T065-234609, loreto@mincetur.gob.pe, Mon-Fri 0730-1430*. Some English is spoken in all three tourist offices. Both www.iquitostimes.com and www.iquitosnews.com have articles, maps, information and advertising. **Indecopi** ① *C Putumayo 464, T065-243490, jreategui@indecopi.gob.pe*, for the tourism protection service.

Background

Founded by the Jesuits in 1757 as the mission settlement of San Pablo de los Napeanos, in 1864 this became the first port of note on the great river. Rapid growth followed the rubber boom of the late 19th century, though the city's new-found wealth was short lived. By the second decade of the 20th century the rubber industry had left for the more competitive oriental suppliers. Remnants of the boom period can still be seen in the fine houses decorated with Portuguese tiles, providing a reminder of former beauty along the river embankment. The main economic activities are logging, commerce and petroleum. It is also the main starting point for tourists wishing to explore Peru's northern jungle.

Sights

The incongruous **Casa de Fierro (Iron House)** ① *Plaza de Armas at Próspero y Putumayo*, was designed by Eiffel for the Paris exhibition of 1889. It is said that the house was transported from Paris by a local rubber baron, and it is constructed entirely of iron trusses and sheets, bolted together and painted silver. It now houses a pharmacy downstairs. Also on the plaza, is the **Casa de Fitzcarrald** or **Casa de Barro (Clay House)** ① *Napo 200-12*. Built entirely of adobe, with wooden balconies, this warehouse predates the rubber boom, but the famous *cauchero*, Carlos Fermín Fitzcarrald, used it as his house and office in the early years of the 20th century. This is now a bank and, apart from its history, the building is nothing special; descendants of Fitzcarrald still live upstairs. Werner Herzog's film *Fitzcarraldo* is a cause célèbre in the town. Also on the plaza is a **Museo Municipal** ① *Napo 224, under renovation and closed*, with stuffed animals and woodcarvings of local native peoples.

Of special interest are the older buildings, faced with *azulejos* (glazed tiles). Many are along the Malecón. They date from the boom of 1890-1912, when the rubber barons imported the tiles from Portugal and Italy and ironwork from England to embellish their homes. **Museo Amazónico** ① *on the corner of Malecón Tarapacá and C Morona, under*

Rubber barons

The conquest and colonization of the vast Amazon Basin was consolidated by the end of the 19th century with the invention of the process of vulcanizing rubber. Many and varied uses were found for this new product and demand was such that the jungle began to be populated by numerous European and North American immigrants who came to invest their money in rubber.

The rubber tree grew wild in the Amazon but the indigenous peoples were the only ones who knew the forests and could find this coveted tree. The exporting companies set up business in the rapidly expanding cities along the Amazon, such as Iquitos. They sent their 'slave hunters' out into the surrounding jungle to find the native labour needed to collect the valuable rubber resin. These people were completely enslaved, their living conditions were intolerable and they perished in their thousands, leading to the extinction of many indigenous groups.

One notable figure from the rubber boom was Fitzcarrald, son of an immigrant Englishman who lived on the Peruvian coast. He was accused of spying during the 1879 war between Peru and Chile and fled to the Amazon where he lived for many years among the indigenous people.

Thanks to Fitzcarrald, the isthmus between the basin of the Ucayali river and that of the Madre de Dios was discovered. Before this, no natural form of communication was known between the two rivers. The first steamships to go up the Madre de Dios were carried by thousands of native workers across the 8-km stretch of land that separated the two basins. Fitzcarrald, one of the region's richest men, died at the age of 36 when the ship on which he was travelling sank.

The rubber barons lived in the new Amazonian cities. Every imaginable luxury was imported for their use: latest Parisian fashions for the women; finest foreign liqueurs for the men; even the best musical shows were brought over from the Old World. But this period of economic boom came to an end in 1912 when rubber grown in the French and British colonies in Asia and Africa began to compete on the world market.

renovation in 2010, is housed in the Prefetura palace. It has a lovely carved wooden ceiling. Amazon art is on display and there are sculptures by Lima artist Letterstein. The *malecón*, referred to as El Boulevard, although refurbished is no longer residential and has lost some of its charm. It offers good views around sunset. Along the malecón, at the bottom of Calle Napo is the **Centro Artesanal Anaconda**, a craft market on stilts, selling paintings and other regional crafts.

Belén, the picturesque waterfront district, is lively, but not safe at night. Most of its huts were built on rafts to cope with the river's 10-m change of level during the year: it begins to rise in January and is highest from May to July. Now, the cabins are built on wooden or concrete stilts (floating houses can still be seen below the north end of Malecón Maldonado). The main plaza has a bandstand designed by Alexandre Gustave Eiffel. In the high-water season canoes can be hired on the waterfront (US$3 an hour) to visit Belén. The market at the end of the Malecón is worth visiting, though you should get there before 0900 to see it in full swing. On Pasaje Paquito, one of its side streets, vendors sell local medicinal herbs and potions and bars sell local sugarcane rum. It is not recommended to walk between the Plaza de Armas and Belén because, along the way, much of the riverbed (which is silting up) has been taken over by squatters.

Around Iquitos

There is a pleasant beach, with white sand and palms, at **Tipishca**, reached in 20 minutes by speedboat from Puerto de Santa Clara near the airport; it gets quite busy at weekends. A quieter beach is **Santa Rita**, reached from Puerto de Pampa Chica, on a turnoff, off the road to the airport. Beaches appear when the river is low, July-September.

Allpahuayo-Mishana Reserve ① *Instituto de Investigaciones de la Amazonía Peruana (IIAP), Av Quiñones on the way to the airport, T065-265515*, is some 25 km south of Iquitos by road or two to three hours by boat from Bellavista. This reserve protects the largest concentration of white-sand jungle (*varillales*) in Peru. Part of the Napo ecoregion, biodiversity here is among the highest in the Amazon Basin, with many birds (500 species have been recorded) and several endangered species including the very rare Iquitos Gnatcatcher (*Polioptila clementsi*), two primates and some endemic species. It also has a **Jardín de Plantas Medicinales** ① *at Km 24, T065-267733, 0800-1400, US$3.35* with over 2400 species. With a smaller number of plants, but various departments dedicated to the scientific study of medicinal plants is **Jardín Botánico del Instituto de Medicina Tradicional** ① *IMET, Pasaje San Lorenzo 205, Guayabamaba, at Km 2 of Av Abelardo Quiñones, T065-265629, villacresvallejo@yahoo.com, 0700-1500*.

Some 4 km south of the city, **Lake Quistococha** is beautifully situated in lush jungle, with a fish hatchery at the lakeside. On the lake, **Parque Zoológico de Quistococha** ① *0900-1700, US$1*, gives an insight into the local wildlife, though conditions are squalid. At the entrance are interesting pictures and texts of local legends. The ticket office will supply a map of the lake and environs. There's a good two-hour walk through the surrounding jungle on a clearly marked trail, bars and restaurants on the lakeside and a small beach. Boats are for hire on the lake and swimming is safe but take insect repellent against the sandflies.

On the road to Quistococha is the turn-off to the village of **Santo Tomás**. Take a left turn just before the airport, and then another left 300 m further on. Then it's about 4 km to the village. You can swim at the lake, canoes are available daily and water skis sometimes. Basic restaurants are open on Sunday (not recommended). The village hosts a fiesta on 22-25 September. Mototaxi from Iquitos US$3.20.

Pilpintuwasi Butterfly Farm ① *near the village of Padre Cocha, T063-232665, www.amazon animalorphanage.org, Tue-Sun 0900-1600, US$5, students US$3*. As well as butterflies, it also has a small well-kept zoo and animal rescue centre, Austrian-Peruvian run.

Iquitos to the Brazilian/Colombian border → *For listings, see pages 606-619.*
Colour map 2, B5/6.

The village of **Pebas**, on the north bank, is three hours from Iquitos. **Pijuayal**, a part of Pebas, is a military area. One of the greatest of Peru's abstract painters, Francisco Grippa, lives in Pebas. His house overlooks the river and you can stay there if you are interested in his work and art in general. Anyone in town will tell you where he lives. If you want to see his paintings, but don't want to stop in Pebas, there are several on display in the Hotel El Dorado in Iquitos.

San Pablo, a further three hours downstream, is a refuelling stop, where children swim next to the jetty. You can buy crackers and drinks during the five-minute halt; the boat will wait for you. After another hour you reach **Chimbote**, where there is a police and customs point. Your passport will be stamped and your bags checked. Food can be bought, but it's not that hygienic.

Border essentials: Peru–Brazil/Colombia

Santa Rosa–Tabatinga–Leticia

Open 24 hours a day. When leaving Peru, check procedures in Iquitos first at immigration (see page 619) or with the Capitanía at the port. Travelling by *rápido*, you get your exit stamp at the police station in Santa Rosa in front of the jetty. After clearing customs and getting your exit stamp, the *rápido* will take you to Tabatinga across the river (five minutes).

If you go to Brazil or Colombia from Santa Rosa, you will need a Peruvian exit stamp, which means that you will need an entry and exit stamp from either Colombia or Brazil if you want to re-enter Peru. There is an immigration office in the port of Tabatinga. Your best bet is to take a taxi and ask the driver to take you to the Polícia Federal, whose office is on the main road, some 2 km from the port. The process is straightforward; Brazilian immigration is friendly and there is always somebody who speaks English. If you intend to stay in the border region, choose Brazilian immigration formalities over Colombian, which take longer, with more questions asked. All immigration services are free of charge. Once you have a Brazilian or Colombian entry stamp, you can move freely between Leticia and Tabatinga as there is no border between the two. Nobody will check your passport if you just walk or drive (if you take a boat, for which there is no need, between Tabatinga and Leticia, the Colombians may give you a hard time). US citizens need a Brazilian visa; if you don't have one, enter via Colombia. If you go to any other destination in Brazil, you will have to get a Brazilian entry stamp. The same goes for Colombia. Peruvian immigration will give you a 30-day entry stamp in Santa Rosa.

Note For sleeping options and transport details to the border, see pages 610 and 617.

Caballococha, 45 minutes from Chimbote, is the kind of town you always imagined when reading the books of García Márquez: lost in the jungle and in time, hot, humid and nostalgic. It's built on a small arm of the river, surrounded by lush green tropical vegetation.

Between Caballococha and Santa Rosa, the journey is beautiful, taking about two hours. To your left are the rolling green hills of Colombia's Amacayacu National Park. The Iquitos–Tabatinga *rápidos* usually take the narrow, southern arm of the river, which does not give views of Colombia, so ask before you buy your ticket which route it will take. Otherwise you must take a Leticia–Caballococha boat.

Santa Rosa is the small Peruvian military base across the river from **Leticia** (Colombia) and **Tabatinga** (Brazil), in the region known as the 'tri-border'. It is the only place with a good beach, so it gets busy at weekends. It only has one very basic *hostal* next to the jetty and the large, pleasant café on the waterfront only sells *refrescos*, no water or coffee. There are no money changers.

Iquitos to the Ecuadorean border → *For listings, see pages 606-619.*

About 70 km downriver from Iquitos is the confluence of the Amazon and the Río Napo, which provides the only river access to Ecuador with border formalities. The Napo area is home to mestizos as well as Kichwa, Huitoto and Arabela Indians. Towns along the route offer a chance to experience life on the river. The first port of call, 12 hours on a fast *lancha* from Iquitos, is **Mazán**, on the lower Napo, a pleasant riverside town with basic services. It is connected to the Amazon by two paved tracks through the forest: when the water level is low the one to **Indiana** is used (US$1, 15 minutes by mototaxi), when the water is high, the path to El Varadero (US$0.65, 10 minutes). These overland shortcuts can save some 150 km of navigation between Iquitos and Mazán. One day further upstream is **Santa Clotilde**, another pleasant town with well-stocked shops and basic services. A trail goes upstream parallel to the river to the village of San José, a pleasant one-hour walk. There are *rápidos* between Mazán and Santa Clotilde, which again cut the travel time on the slower *lanchas*. A further 28 hours upstream is the Kichwa town of **Angoteros** and 17 hours ahead the pretty border town and military garrison of **Cabo Pantoja**, set on hilly ground at the confluence of the Napo and Aguarico rivers. You can hire a motorized canoe (US$100 per day) to visit nearby lakes where dolphins may be seen, or follow a track from town to see jungle. Peruvian immigration is on top of the hill, near the military base, if the officer is not in, ask around town. In addition to immigration, you may have to register with the navy on either side of the border so have your passport at hand. For full details of river traffic, see Transport, page 618.

Nuevo Rocafuerte (Ecuador), another friendly town, is further upriver along the Napo. You must hire a speedboat as there is no public service. Canoes go from Nuevo Rocafuerte to Coca four times per week. Nuevo Rocafuerte has simple hotels, eateries, a phone office and shops and is a good place from which to reach the east end of Parque Nacional Yasuní. Ecuadorean immigration is next to the navy dock; if the officer is not in, enquire in town.

◉ Northern Jungle listings

For Sleeping and Eating price codes and other relevant information, see pages 38-44.

● Sleeping

Tingo María *p596*
Hotels are often fully booked.
AL-B Madera Verde, Av Universitaria s/n, a way out of Tingo María on the road to Huánuco, near the university, T/F062-561800. Built in the 1930s. Several chalets set in beautiful surroundings, with and without bathroom, restaurant, swimming pool.
C Albergue Ecológico Villa Jennifer, Km 3.4 Carretera a Castillo Grande, 10 mins from Tingo María, T062-962-603509, www.villa jennifer.net. This Danish/Peruvian-owned hotel offers breakfast in the price, 2-4 night packages, from US$50-90 per person, and tours to local sites, birdwatching, mini-zoo, pool, restaurant, laundry service. Phone ahead to arrange bus station pickup. Surrounded by local flora, with lots of birdlife.
C Nueva York, Av Alameda Perú 553, T062-562406, joferjus@hotmail.com.

With bath and TV, cheaper without, hot water, restaurant, laundry, good value.
D Hostal Marco Antonio, Jr Monzón 364, T062-562201. Quiet, restaurant of the same name next door.
F Hostal Central, Av Tito Jaime Fernández 440, T062-562027. Central, as the name suggests, OK.
F Hostal Cusco, Raimondi 671, T062-562046. Basic, but very cheap.

Yurimaguas *p597*
A-B Puerto Pericos, Jr San Miguel 720, Malecón Paranapura, T065-352009, www.puertopalmeras.com.pe. Same group as **Puerto Palmeras** in Tarapoto, includes breakfast, with hot water, restaurant and gardens. Remodelled in 2008.
C Luis Antonio, Av Jaúregui 407, T065-352061, antonio@vibcp.com. With fan and bath, **E** without a/c, cold water, balconies overlooking small pool, clean, friendly and helpful. Recommended.
D Hostal Residencial El Naranjo, Arica 318, T065-352860, hotel_elnaranjo@hotmail.com.

Best in town, with bath, a/c (**E** with fan), hot water, comfy, small pool, good restaurant.
D Leo's Palace, Sargento Lores 106, Plaza de Armas, T065-351404. Good, **F** without a/c, friendly, reasonably priced, restaurant.
D Posada Cumpanama, Progreso 403, T062-352905, http://posadacumpanama. blogspot.com. Cheaper without a/c, with breakfast, tastefully decorated, pool, very pleasant.
E Hostal El Caballito, Av Jáuregui 403, T065-352864. With bath, cold water, fan, clean and pleasant, good value.
There are several other hotels near the intersection of Jáuregui and Tacna.

Lagunas p597

F Hostal Isabel, C Miraflores, 1 block from plaza. Shared bath, cold water, basic, meals available.
F Hostal La Sombra, Jr Vásquez 1121. Shared bathroom, basic, friendly, good food.

Reserva Nacional Pacaya-Samiria p597

Amazon Ecolodge, in the park near Bretaña, office in Pucallpa at Fitzcarrald 384, T061-799214, www.amazon-ecolodge.com. One of a chain of small lodges in the area, rustic construction, shared showers, dining rooms, guides, excursions. US$390-576 for 2-4 night packages; see website for other prices.
Pacaya Samiria Amazon Lodge, Lima office: Av José Pardo 601, of 602, Miraflores, T01-446 2739, www.pacayasamiria.com.pe. In Iquitos at Urbanización Las Palmeras A-9, T065-225769. Beautifully designed, luxurious lodge on a hill overlooking the Marañón, just inside the boundaries of the Reserve, one of the best locations for wildlife viewing. All buildings in indigenous style, with balconies and en suite bathrooms, restaurant, bar. Boat trips, community visits and specialist birdwatching trips are included in the price. Camping trips (with official permits) can be arranged deeper inside the reserve. A 6-day trip including 2 days at a jungle camp costs US$1600 per person, but US$705 per person if 4 people book together.

Pucallpa p598, map p599

A Sol del Oriente, Av San Martín 552, T061-575154, www.soldelorientehoteles. com. Price includes airport transfer, breakfast and welcome cocktail. With bathroom, a/c, internet, pool, parking and good restaurant. The hotel also has a mini-zoo. In the same group are **Albergue Turístico La Maloka Ecolodge** at Yarinacocha and **Complejo Ecoturístico La Caoba**.
B Divina Montaña, Carretera Federico Basadre Km 11.3, outside Pucallpa on the road to Tingo María, T061-600060, http://divinamontana.com. Bungalows, restaurant, swimming pool, sports facilities.
B-C Mercedes, Raimondi 610, T061-575120, ghotelmercedes@hotmail.com. Older hotel with some refurbished rooms, breakfast included, fridge, a/c. Good but noisy, with bar and restaurant attached, swimming pool.
C-E Antonio's, Jr Progreso 545, T061-573721. A variety of rooms and prices, cheaper in older rooms or with fan instead of a/c, cable TV, garden, pool, jacuzzi, parking. Has airport pickup.
C-E Hostal Arequipa, Jr Progreso 573, T061-571348, www.hostal-arequipa.com. With bathroom, fan or a/c, rooms with a/c include breakfast and fridge, good, comfortable rooms with safe, cable TV, clean, restaurant, friendly staff.
E-F Barbtür, Raimondi 670, T061-572532. With or without bathroom, friendly, central, good beds, cold water, noisy.
E-F Hostal Komby, Ucayali 360, T061-571562, www.hostalkomby.com.pe. Fan, cold water, private bath, noisy over street, back rooms quiet. Comfortable, excellent value.
E-F La Suite de Petita's Inn, Jr Fitzcarraldo 171, 3 blocks from Plaza de Armas, T061-572831. Includes simple breakfast, bath, cold water, fan, fridge, internet, parking, good value.
F Hostal Sun, Ucayali 380, next to Komby, T061-574260. With bathroom, cheaper without, simple to basic, not so clean, front rooms noisy, just adequate.

Lago Yarinacocha *p600*

AL Jana Shobo Amazonian Lodge, T061-596943, www.janashobo.tk. A small lodge set in 10 ha of forest on the lakeshore, living room, reading room and kitchen. Price is for 3 days/2 nights and includes meals and airport transfer, other packages and tours available.

A pp **Pandisho Amazon Ecolodge**, north of the village of 11 de Agosto, towards the northern tip of the eastern shore of the west arm, T061-591517, www.amazon-ecolodge.com (in Pucallpa Fitzcarrald 384, T061-799214). Full board, good resort with cabins by the lakeshore, also offers packages of varying length and rainforest expeditions.

E-F Los Delfines, opposite **Electroucayali** in Puerto Callao. Rooms with bathroom, fan, fridge, some with TV, clean.

Iquitos *p600, map p601*

Around Independence Day (27 and 28 Jul) and Easter, Iquitos gets crowded. Prices rise at this time. At all times, hotels are more expensive than in the rest of the country, but discounts can be negotiated in the low season (Jan-Apr). Taxi drivers and touts at the airport and ports are paid commission by some hotels; insist on being taken where you want to go. To avoid noise, ask for a room away from the street.

LL El Dorado Plaza, Napo 258 on main plaza, T065-222555, www.eldoradoplazahotel.com. 5 stars, very good accommodation and restaurant, bar, internet, prices include service charge, welcome drink, transfer to/from airport extra. The hotel offers special 3-day/2-night packages in conjunction with some of the Amazon lodges. Recommended.

AL Victoria Regia, Ricardo Palma 252, T065-231983, www.victoriaregiahotel.com. Price includes breakfast and airport transfer, a/c, fridge, cable TV, Wi-Fi in rooms for US$6.50, free map of city, safety deposit boxes in rooms, good restaurant and pool. Good service. Recommended.

AL-A El Dorado, Napo 362, T065-232574, www.hoteldoradoiquitos.com. Same owners as El Dorado Plaza, pool (open to restaurant

users), a/c, cable TV, bar and restaurant, prices include breakfast, service and airport transfer. Popular with business people.

AL-B La Casa Fitzcarraldo, Av La Marina 2153, T065-601138, http://sites.google.com/site/lacasafitzcarraldo/home. Prices vary according to room, suite or bungalow. Includes breakfast and airport transfer, with private bath, Wi-Fi, satellite TV, minibar, 1st-class restaurant, treehouse, pool in lovely gardens. The house was the home of Walter Saxer, the executive-producer of Werner Herzog's famous film, lots of movie and celebrity memorabilia. Recommended.

A Sol del Oriente, Av Quiñónez Km 2.5 on the way to the airport, T065-260317, www.soldelorientehoteles.com. Includes breakfast, airport transfers, a/c, cable TV, pool, internet in hall, nice gardens, decoration is a bit kitsch.

B Acosta, Calvo de Araujo y Huallaga, T065-231761, www.hotelacosta.com. Price includes breakfast, a/c, cable TV, safety deposit boxes, airport transfer available, noisy.

B Amazon Apart Hotel, Aguirre 1151, T065-266262, www.amazonaparthotel.com. 1- and 2-bedroom furnished apartments, a/c, hot water, Wi-Fi, pool, airport transfers.

B Marañón, Nauta 285, T065-242673, www.hotelmaranon.com. Includes breakfast and airport transfers, small pool, a/c, hot water, comfortable. Recommended as good value, but double-check bookings.

C Amazonas, Napo 303, on Plaza de Armas, T065-232149. Good location but faded and noisy, breakfast and TV included, a/c, phone, fridge bar.

C Hostal Ambassador, Pevas 260, T065-233110, www.paseosamazonicos.com/hotel_ambassador.htm. Includes breakfast, a/c, transport to and from airport, cafeteria, see also **Sinchicuy Lodge** below.

C La Posada de Lobo, Pantoja 417 y Yavari, T065-236140. A/c, hot water, TV, fridge, swimming pool, jacuzzi, gym, laundry, price includes breakfast and internet, relaxed atmosphere, pleasant and good value.

D Hostal El Colibrí, Nauta 172, T065-241737, hostalelcolibri@hotmail.com. 1 block from plaza and 50 m from river, nicely refurbished house, TV, a/c, cheaper with fan, hot water, secure, good value, helpful. Recommended.

D Hostal La Casona, Fitzcarrald 147-A, T065-234394, www.lacasonadeiquitos.com. Ample rooms with bathroom, cold water, ceiling fan, kitchen facilities, small patio, Wi-Fi and internet, pool, popular with travellers. Recommended.

D Royal Inn, Aguirre 793, T065-224244. Includes breakfast, Wi-Fi and airport transfer, a/c, frigobar, hot water, bidet, modern and comfortable.

E El Sitio, Ricardo Palma 541, T065-234932. With private or shared bathroom, very clean, fan, cable TV, cafeteria, good value. Recommended.

E La Shiringa, Fitzcarrald 465, T065-243293. Private bathroom, fan, a reasonable option although this part of Fitzcarrald has lots of traffic noise.

Jungle lodges

See Activities and tours, page 613, for general hints on booking tours. Note especially the advice on checking credentials.

Amazon Yarapa River Lodge, Av La Marina 124, T065-993 1172, www.yarapariver lodge.com. On Río Yarapa, tributary of the Amazon, in a pristine location, this award-winning lodge has a field laboratory in conjunction with Cornell University. It uses ecofriendly resources and local materials, and works with nearby villages. Flexible and responsible. Prices from US$600 per person for 4-day/3-night stay with transport, excursions and meals.

Blue Morpho Tours, Av Guardia Civil 515, T065-263454, www.bluemorphotours.com. A rustic camp on Carretera Nauta, Km 52.5. Centre for shamanic studies and workshops, 9-day shamanic trips US$2190, all inclusive except for bar and snacks.

Cumaceba Lodge and Expeditions, Putumayo 184 in the Iron House, T/F065-232229, www.cumaceba.com. Overnight visits to Cumaceba Lodge, 35 km from Iquitos, and tours of 1-4 nights to the Botanical Lodge on the Amazon, 80 km from Iquitos, birdwatching tours, *ayahuasca* ceremonies. A good option for those with limited time in Iquitos.

Explorama Tours, by the riverside docks on Av La Marina 340, T065-252530, www.explorama.com. Highly recommended, with over 40 years in existence, they are certainly the biggest and most established. Their sites are: **Ceiba Tops**, 40 km (1½ hrs) from Iquitos, a comfortable resort, 75 a/c rooms with electricity, hot showers, pool with hydromassage and beautiful gardens. The food is good and, as in all Explorama's properties, is served communally. There are attractive walks and other excursions, a recommended jungle experience for those who want their creature comforts, US$270 per person for 1 night/2 days, US$115 for each additional night (1-2 people).

Explorama Lodge, at Yanamono, 80 km (2½ hrs) from Iquitos. Palm-thatched accommodation with separate bathroom and shower facilities connected by covered walkways, cold water, no electricity, good food and service. US$365 for 3 days/2 nights and US$100 for each additional day (1-2 people).

Explornapo Lodge, at Llachapa on the Sucusai creek (a tributary of the Napo). In the same style as **Explorama Lodge**, but further away from Iquitos, 160 km (4 hrs), and is set in 105,000 ha of primary rainforest, so is better for seeing wildlife, US$950 for 5 days/4 nights. Nearby is the impressive canopy walkway 35 m above the forest floor and 500 m long, "a magnificent experience and not to be missed". It is associated with the **Amazon Center for Tropical Studies** (ACTS), a scientific station, only 10 mins from the canopy walkway.

Explor Tambos, 2 hrs from **Explornapo**. Offers more primitive accommodation, 8 shelters for 16 campers, bathing in the river, offers the best chance to see fauna. Close to Explornapo is the ReNuPeRu medicinal plant garden, run by a *curandero*. Members of South American Explorers are offered 15% discount.

Heliconia Lodge, Ricardo Palma 242, T065-231959, www.amazonriverexpeditions.com.

On the Río Amazonas, 1¼ hrs from Iquitos, the lodge has hot water, electricity for 5 hrs a day, good guiding and staff; rustic yet comfortable, 3 days/2 nights US$282. Under same management as Zungarococha Bungalows 15 kms from Iquitos on a lake off the Río Nanay, and in the same group as Hotels **Victoria Regia** and **Acosta**, see above. They organize trips to Allpahuayo-Mishana, Pacaya-Samiria and the ACTS canopy walkway.

Muyuna Amazon Lodge, Putumayo 163, ground floor, T065-242858, T065-993 4424 (mob), www.muyuna.com. 140 km upstream from Iquitos, on the Río Yanayacu, before San Juan village, in an area less spoilt than some parts of the forest downstream. Packages from 1-5 nights available, 2 nights/3 days US$340 per person for 2-10 people. Everything is included in the price. Trusted guides (including female guides), accommodation in 1st-class bungalows, good food and service, family-friendly. Well organized and professional, flexible, radio contact, will collect passengers from airport if requested in advance. They offer birdwatching and full-day camping trips deep in the forest. Because of its isolated location the lodge guarantees that you will see animals, even rarities such as the piuri (wattled curaçao, *Crax globulosa*). Highly recommended.

Paseos Amazónicos Ambassador, Pevas 246, T/F065-231618, www.paseos amazonicos.com, operate the **Amazonas Sinchicuy Lodge**. The lodge is 1½ hrs by boat northeast of Iquitos on the Sinchicuy river, near the village of Santa María de Ojeal, 25 mins by boat from the Amazon river. It consists of several wooden buildings with thatched roofs on stilts, cabins with bathroom, no electricity but paraffin lamps are provided, good food, activities, disabled facilities, includes visits to local villages, US$221 per person 3 days/2 nights. Recommended. They also have **Tambo Yanayacu** and **Tambo**

Amazónico lodges, organize visits to Pacaya-Samiria and local tours.

Tahuayo Lodge, Amazonia Expeditions, 10305 Riverburn Dr, Tampa, FL 33647, toll-free T+1 800-262 9669, www.perujungle.com. Near the Reserva Comunal de Tamshiyacu-Tahuayo on the Río Tahuayo, 145 km upriver from Iquitos, clean, comfortable cabins with cold shower, buffet meals, good food, laundry service, wide range of excursions, excellent staff. An 8-day/7-night programme costs US$1555, all inclusive, extra days US$100. The lodge is associated with the **Rainforest Conservation Fund** (www.rainforest conservation.org), which works in Tamshiyacu-Tahuayo, one of the world's richest areas for primate species and for amphibians (there is a poison dart frog management programme), birds, other animals and plants.

Iquitos to the Brazilian/Colombian border *p604*

There are several basic *hostales* in Caballococha, including **Plaza**, Progreso 105, T065-291423.

Iquitos to the Ecuadorean border *p605*

E Casa Blanca, Malecón y Nicolas Torres, T+593-6-238 2184, **Nuevo Rocafuerte** (Ecuador). Cold water, fan, nice simple place, welcoming, refurbished in 2009.

There are a couple of other basic places to stay in Nuevo Rocafuerte.

F Hospedaje Bella Durmiente, Santa Clotilde. With bath, pleasant, clean, some rooms with fan, best in town.

F Hospedaje Gorety, across from the health centre, no sign, T065-254660 (leave message for Edwin Capinoa), Mazán. Private bath, basic rooms but it is the cleanest and best in town.

F Hospedaje Municipal Napuruna, Pantoja. With bath, simple but adequate.

F-G Hostal El Cielo, Santa Clotilde, next to Bella Durmiente. With shared bath, a bit run down but adequate.

Eating

Local specialities Try palm-heart salad (*chonta*), or a *la loretana* dish; also try *inchicapi* (chicken, corn and peanut soup), *cecina* (fried dried pork), *tacacho* (fried green banana and pork, mashed into balls and eaten for breakfast or tea), *patarashca* (barbecued fish wrapped in bijao leaves), and *juanes* (chicken, rice, olive and egg, seasoned and wrapped in bijao leaves). Many jungle species such as deer, wild boar, paiche (now seriously overfished), turtle (eg *zarapatera*, a spicy soup made with turtle meat served in its shell), and alligator still figure prominently in restaurants. Please be responsible. Try the local drink *chuchuhuasi*, made from the bark of a tree, which is supposed to have aphrodisiac properties but tastes like fortified cough tincture, and *jugo de cocona*, the alcoholic *cola de mono* and *siete raíces* (aguardiente mixed with the bark of 7 trees and wild honey). *Camu-camu* is an interesting but acquired taste, said to have one of the highest vitamin-C concentrations in the world.

Tingo María *p596*
¶ **El Antojito 2**, Jr Chiclayo 458. Good local food.
¶ **Girasol**, Av Raimondi 253, T062-562065. Chicken, burgers, cakes, juices.

Yurimaguas *p597*
¶¶ **Pizzería**, Jáuregui at Plaza de Armas. Pizza, snacks and drinks.
¶ **Prosperidad**, Jáuregui y Próspero. *Pollo a la brasa* and fruit juices.
¶ **Helados La Muyuna**, Jr Simón Bolívar 116. Good natural jungle fruit ice cream.
There are several other simple *comedores*. On the 2nd block of Jáuregui is a small juice bar serving cold drinks and home-made jungle fruit ice cream.

Pucallpa *p598, map p599*
¶¶-¶ **C'est si Bon**, Jr Independencia 560 y Pasaje Zegarra, Plaza de Armas. Daily 0800-

2400. Chicken, drinks, sweets, ice cream.
¶¶-¶ **Chifa Xin Xin**, Jr Tarapacá 515 and Av Raimondi 603. Daily 1200-1600 and 1830-2300. Authentic Chinese cooking, set meals and à la carte, Tarapacá location is considered better.
¶¶-¶ **El Viajero**, Jr Libertad 374. Sun-Fri 0800-1630. Choice of very good set meals, also à la carte, very popular. Recommended.
¶¶-¶ **La Favorita**, Jr Adolfo Morey e Inmaculada. Daily 0800-1600. Regional and home cooking, good set meals Mon-Sat and parrilladas on Sun, popular.
¶ **Tropitop Heladería**, Jr Sucre y Tarapacá 401 (Plaza de Armas). Good, cheap, typical breakfasts.

Lago Yarinacocha *p600*
¶¶-¶ **La Anaconda**, floating restaurant serves regional and international dishes, set meals and à la carte, shows at weekends.
¶¶-¶ **La Maloka**, in Puerto Callao. Restaurant and hotel, regional specialities, set meals and à la carte.

Iquitos *p600, map p601*
¶¶¶ **Al Frío y al Fuego**, on the water, go to Embarcadero Turístico and their boat will pick you up, T065-224862. Mon 1830-2300, Tue-Sat 1130-1600 and 1830-2300, Sun 1130-1600. Good upscale floating restaurant with regional dishes, seafood specialties.
¶¶¶ **Fitzcarrald**, Malecón Maldonado 103 y Napo. Smart, pizza, also pastas and salads.
¶¶¶ **La Gran Maloca**, Sargento Lores 170, opposite **Banco Continental**. A/c, high class, good food.
¶¶ **Ari's Burger**, Plaza de Armas, Próspero 127. Fast food, good breakfasts, popular with tourists, but not the most hygienic place.
¶¶ **El Cauchero**, at the end of Raymondi on Plaza Castilla. New restaurant run by a French-trained local chef, serving fusion cuisine: "Iquitos and the rest of the world".
¶¶ **Yellow Rose of Texas**, Putumayo 180. Varied food, Texan atmosphere. Open 24 hrs so you can wait here if arriving late at night, good breakfasts,

rather dirty, lots of information, also has a bar, Sky TV and Texan saddle seats.

¶¶-¶ Antica Pizzería, Napo 159. Sun-Thu 0700-2400, Fri-Sat 0700-0100. Great pizza and Italian dishes, pleasant ambiance especially on the upper level, also serves breakfast.

¶¶-¶ Chez Maggy Pizzería, Raymondi 177. Daily 1800-0100. Wood-oven pizza and home-made pasta.

¶ Darshan, Dos de Mayo 469, T065-243657. Open 0700-1400, 1900-2200. Vegetarian.

¶ El Carbón, La Condamine y Napo, evenings only. Grilled meats, salads, regional side-dishes such as *tacacho* and *patacones*.

¶ El Sitio, Sargento Lores cuarda 4, evenings only. A simple place for kebabs (*anticuchos*) for all tastes including vegetarian, popular.

¶ Huasaí, Fitzcarrald 131 half a block from the plaza. Daily 0715-1600. Varied and innovative menu, daily *menú* US$3.30 (more on Sun), popular and recommended.

¶ La 5ta de Abtao, Abtao 527. Open daily 1000-1700. Small simple restaurant serving good food.

Cheap local breakfasts can be found at kiosks outside the market on Sargento Lores, block 5.

Cafés

Café de María, Pevas 2nd block. Sandwiches, pies and the best cappuccino in Iquitos.

Helados La Muyuna, Jr Próspero 621. Good natural jungle fruit ice cream.

Panadería Tívoli, Ricardo Palma, block 3. A variety of good bread and sweets.

Iquitos to the Brazilian/Colombian border *p604*

¶ Restaurant El Sabroso, next to the port, in Caballococha. This is the best place to eat, good sandwiches for about US$1. There are several cheap *comedores* around the main plaza, which is also next to the port.

🎔 Bars and clubs

Pucallpa *p598, map p599*

Los Pericos, Av las Alamedas opposite Universidad Alas Peruanas. Popular dancing spot with several halls and varied music, mixed crowd.

Iquitos *p600, map p601*

El Pardo, Mariscal Cáceres y Alzamora. Large, popular dance centre, live Latin music with thousands dancing at weekends.

La Parranda, Pevas, cuadra 1. Drinks, live music, dancing, Latin music, 80s rock.

Nikoro, Pevas at the shore. Floating bar, pleasant atmosphere.

Noa Noa, Pevas y Fitzcarrald. Open Tue-Sat. Disco, popular with locals and tourists, varied music, An Iquitos classic, can get crowded, young clientele.

Snack Bar Arandú, Malecón Maldonado. Good views of the Itaya river.

✳ Festivals and events

Pucallpa *p598, map p599*
24 Jun Fiesta de San Juan.
5-20 Oct Pucallpa's Aniversario Político and the Ucayali regional fair.

Iquitos *p600, map p601*
5 Jan Anniversary of Founding of Iquitos.
Feb/Mar During Carnival you can see the local dance La Pandilla.
24 Jun Festival of San Juan, patron saint of Loreto. Tourist week, with regional music, held in the Mercado Artesanal de San Juan, is celebrated around the same time.
28-30 Aug Santa Rosa de Lima is celebrated in Rumococha.
22-25 Sep Santo Tomás is celebrated in the village of the same name.
8 Dec La Purísima, celebrated in Punchana, near the docks.

O Shopping

Pucallpa *p598, map p599*
Many Shipibo women carry and sell their products around Pucallpa and Yarinacocha.
Agustín Rivas, at Jr Tarapacá 861, above a small restaurant whose entrance is at No 863 (ask for it), Pucallpa. For local woodcarvings visit the workshop of this sculptor. His work is made from huge tree roots and when Sr Rivas is in town he is happy to chat over a cup of tea. His family runs the gallery when he is in Iquitos or Germany.
Artesanías La Anaconda, Pasaje Cohen, Plaza de Armas. Good selection, indigenous crafts.
SBS, Jr Zavala 467, Urb Callería Ucayali. Bookshop.

Iquitos *p600, map p601*
Good hammocks in the markets in Iquitos cost about US$8. For bookshops try **SBS**, Nauta 248.
   The following are good for arts and crafts:
Amazon Arts and Crafts, Napo block 100;
Centro Artesanal Anaconda, Malecón Tarapacá at the bottom of Napo; **Mercado Artesanal de San Juan**, Av Quiñónez 4 km from the centre in the San Juan district, on the road to the airport (take a colectivo). Cheapest in town with more choice than elsewhere; **The Point**, Napo 423.
Comisesa, Arica 471, rubber boots, torches (flashlights), rain ponchos and other gear.
Mad Mick's Trading Post, Putumayo 163, top floor. Hires out rubber boots for those going to the jungle.

▲ Activities and tours

Yurimaguas *p597*
There are some small tour operators in town, offering trips into the jungle: eg **Manguares Expeditions**, Sargento Lores 126, near Plaza de Armas. Also **Nilo Hidalgo**, Maynas 710, T065-502442. US$50-80 per person per day for guide, transport and food, but excluding park entry fees and lodging.

Reserva Nacional Pacaya-Samiria *p597*
For Pacaya-Samiria Reserve, there are 5 registered operators in Lagunas. Local guides from Lagunas or other access points offer tours to the reserve for about US$40 per day including food and equipment. Trips to Pacaya-Samiria can also be arranged in Iquitos. Expeditions must be booked in advance.
Asiendes (Asociación Indígena en Defensa de la Ecología Samiria), asiendesperu@hotmail.com, Tavara 1258, T965-861748, asiendesperu@hotmail.com. Sr Manuel Ahuanari is a local association which runs trips into Pacaya-Samiria, promoting the jungle and benefiting the community, from 4 to 7 days, US$50 per day, all inclusive except boat passage from Iquitos and price of entry to the park. You stay at rangers' stations or can camp. With all tours make sure you know exactly what is involved on the trip, such as where you will stay, whether the food you will eat will be hunted on the trip, etc.

Pucallpa *p598, map p599*
Jungle tours from Pucallpa are not very well organized. You can negotiate a price for a group with the boatmen on the waterfront. Only use accredited guides.

Iquitos *p600, map p601*
See Sleeping above for jungle lodges and the trips that they offer. Agencies arrange 1-day or longer trips to places of interest with guides speaking some English. Package tours booked in Lima or abroad are much more expensive than those booked in Iquitos and personal approaches to lodge operators will often yield better prices than booking through an agency or the internet. Take your time before making a decision and don't be bullied by the hustlers at the airport (they get paid a hefty commission). If concerned, check with iperú if there have been any complaints about the guide and/or agency you are thinking of employing. In our experience, you have to ask about the specific one, they will not hand out a list of people/agencies, but they will tell you if you pin-point one of them.

Do not go with a company that does not have legal authorization; there are many unscrupulous people about. Find out all the details of the trip and food arrangements before paying (a minimum of US$45 per day). Speed boats for river trips can be hired by the hour or day at the **Embarcadero Turístico**, at the intersection of Av de la Marina and Samánez Ocampo in Punchana. Prices vary greatly, usually US$10-20 per hr for a *peque-peque*, U$80 per hr for a speedboat, and are negotiable. In fact, all prices are negotiable, except **Muyuna**, **Heliconia** and **Explorama**, who do not take commission.

Take a long-sleeved shirt, waterproof coat and shoes or light boots on jungle trips and a good torch, binoculars, as well as *espirales* to ward off mosquitoes at night – they can be bought from pharmacies in Iquitos. **Premier** is the most effective local repellent. Check with your tour operator if the places that you will be visiting are free of malaria. Also check in advance if you are required to have a yellow fever vaccination. The dry season is Jul-Sep (Sep is the best month to see flowers and butterflies).

Before taking *ayahuasca* in a ceremony with a shaman, read the note on page 59.
Amazon River Expeditions, Ricardo Palma 259, T01-421 9195/ 442 4515, www.amazonrex.com.

Amazon Tours and Cruises, 336 Requena St, T065-222440, www.amazoncruisesonline.com. An American-owned company offering a variety of cruises, many for nature watching. Also peacock bass fishing, trips to villages (including Pevas), jungle cabin at Llachama and more.
Aqua Expeditions, Huallaga 215, T065-601053, www.aquaexpeditions.com. Runs luxury 3-, 4- and 7-night cruises upstream from Iquitos to Nauta, Pacaya-Samiria and beyond. Each suite on the vessel is a/c.
Blue Morpho, Centre for Shamanic Studies and Workshops, Av Guardia Civil 515, T065-263454, www.bluemorphotours.com. A rustic camp on Carretera Nauta, Km 52.5. Centre for shamanic studies and workshops, 9-day shamanic trips US$2190, all inclusive except for bar and snacks.
Dawn on the Amazon, Malecón Maldonado 185 y Nauta, T065-223730, www.dawnonthe amazon.com. Offer a variety of day tours around Iquitos on the 14-passenger vessel *Dawn on the Amazon* (US$65 per person) and the luxurious 20-passenger *Dawn on the Amazon III* (US$120 per person). Also offer custom-made cruises for several days. Ask here about the 9-hole **Amazon Golf Course**, off the road to Quistacocha and Nauta, www.amazongolfcourse.com (pay and play, US$25 for 18 holes including clubs and balls), and **Iquitos Times**, www.iquitostimes.com.

Jungle Expeditions (Junglex), Av Quiñónez 1980, T065-262340, www.junglex.com. A good local operator.
Tambo Visits, Alfonso Ugarte 565, T065-226686, grupotambo@terra.com.pe. Offer day trips in and around Iquitos.

⊙ Transport

Tingo María *p596*

Buses to **Huánuco**, 119 km, 3-4 hrs, US$2 with **Etnasa** (but this company is not recommended because of theft and drug-trafficking). Better to take one of the several micros daily, US$2 per seat, or colectivos, US$5, 2 hrs. Direct buses continue to **Lima**, 12 hrs, with **Trans Rey** (in Lima Av Bauzate 228 y Meza, T01-423 0664, leaves Lima 1800), US$22 bus cama, **León de Huánuco**, **Bahía Continental** (recommended, T01-424 1539), US$15 regular, and **Interbus Chocano**, Enrique Pimentel 182, T062-406509. To **Pucallpa**, 255 km, 7-8 hrs, US$8.50 by bus, eg **Etposa**. **Turismo Ucayali** colectivos, Raimondi y Callao, and **Selva Express**, Av Tito Jaime 218, T062-562380, 7 hrs, US$15. There are other colectivos and taxis. Transport may be cancelled in the rainy season.

North to Yurimaguas *p597*

Colectivos run from Tingo María to **Tocache** US$13, 4½ hrs; or bus US$9.50, 6 hrs. **Tarapoto**–Tocache, US$7.50 by colectivo. Colectivos and taxis run from Tocache to **Yurimaguas**. A daily *camioneta* runs from Tarapoto to Yurimaguas, US$7-9, 6-8 hrs. The **Juanjui**–Tocache road has 4 bridges and a ferry just before Juanjui (US$9.20 per vehicle). Juanjui–Tarapoto by colectivo US$12.50.

For the river journey, start early if you do not wish to spend a night at the river village of **Sión**. There are no facilities, but the nights are not cold. The river runs through marvellous jungle with high cliffs. Boats sometimes run aground in the river near Sión. Take food and bottled water. Balsa wood rafts also ply this stretch of river.

Yurimaguas *p597*

The road to Tarapoto is paved. **Paredes Estrella**, office on 5th block of Mariscal Cáceres, 0430 daily to **Lima** (30 hrs, US$32) via **Tarapoto** (US$4), **Moyobamba** (US$9, 5-6 hrs), **Pedro Ruiz** (for Chachapoyas), **Chiclayo** (20 hrs) and **Trujillo**. Also Ejetur, 0400 to **Lima**, 30 hrs, US$36. Faster than the bus to Tarapoto are: **Gilmer Tours**, C Victor Sifuentes 580, hourly mini-buses 0500-1200, 1400-1800, US$5.35, 2½ hrs; cars (eg **San Martín**) US$7.15; and combis (Turismo Selva) US$3.60.

By *lancha* to **Iquitos** takes 3 days and 2 nights. Fares usually include meals, US$22 2nd-class hammock, US$38 1st class hammock, US$38-48 for 1 bunk in a cabin. **Eduardo**, Elena Pardo 114, T065-352552, is the best company. Buying a hammock costs US$5.75-8.50 in Yurimaguas, on Jáuregui (make sure to buy string to tie it up with). Arriving bus passengers are surrounded by touts trying to sell boat tickets to Iquitos. See page 33 for general tips on river travel.

Pucallpa *p598, map p599*

The airport is to the northwest of the town. Bus from the airport to town, US$0.25; motos US$1; airport taxi US$6, outside taxi US$3. One daily flight to/from **Lima** (1 hr) and **Iquitos**, with Star Perú (7 de Junio 865, T061-590585), and **LAN** (Jr Tarapacá 805 y San Martín, T061-579840).

There are regular bus services to **Lima**, 812 km, 18-20 hrs (longer in the rainy season, Nov-Mar). **Transmar**, Av Raimondi 770, T061-579778 (in Lima Av Nicolás de Piérola 197, T01-265 0190). Regular at 1030 and 1800, US$17.50; *bus cama* with a/c at 1300, US$28, without a/c at 1330, US$25. **Trans Junín**, Av Raimondi 897, T061-573963, at 1800, US$14; **Interbus Chocano**, Av Raimondi 742, T061-577659 (in Lima Av Luna Pizarro 240, T01-330 4286, in Huánuco Jr Crespo 690 y Castillo, T062-511944); **Rey Tours**, Av Raimondi 677 y 7 de Junio (Lima address above), at 1500, US$12.50. Take blankets as the crossing of the Cordillera at night is bitterly cold. To **Tingo María**, 255 km, 7-8 hrs, US$8.50, Regular (not *bus cama*) buses bound for Lima stop in Tingo María, also **Etposa**, 7 de Junio 843, at 1700. Colectivos leave early in the morning, depending on passenger demand, US$15, 7 hrs: **Selva Express**, Jr 7 de Junio 841, T061-579098; **Turismo Ucayali**, Jr 7 de Junio 799 y San Martín, T061-593002. To **Huánuco**, US$9.50, 11 hrs, regular buses bound for Lima stop here, also **Etposa** (see above). Transmar at 0930 continues to **Huancayo** US$12.50, 15 hrs. To **Ciudad Constitución**, Trans Pachitea-Palcazú, Av Raimondi 730, T061-572421, 4WD pickups at 0630, additional departures if there is demand, US$14.50 in front, US$11 in the back, 6 hrs in the dry, 8 hrs in the rainy season. On occasion they also continue to **Puerto Bermúdez**, otherwise transfer for Puerto Bermúdez which you can reach from Pucallpa in 1 long day.

Different ports are used depending on the level of the river, they are all just mud banks without any facilities. 2 blocks downriver from the Malecón Grau, at the bottom of Jr Inmaculada, is Puerto Inmaculada, used with mid to low water. Several blocks further downriver, at Jr Arica y Manco Cápac is Puerto Henry, a private port used year-round only by **Henry**'s vessels bound for Iquitos. When the water level is very high, Puerto Manantay, 4 km south of town is used. By river to **Iquitos**, down the Ucayali and Amazon, 3-4 days downriver, longer if the water level is low and larger boats must travel only by day, hammock US$35, berth US$43-65 per person. **Henry** is a large company with departures Mon, Wed, Fri and Sat; their newer boats, *Henry 6* and *7*, have some cabins with private bath; another good boat is *Pedro Martín 2* sailing from Puerto Inmaculada. To **Atalaya** up the Ucayali, cargo barges, 3-4 days upriver, 2-3 days downriver, US$19 in hammock (no berths available). Sometimes there are also canoes that are faster but more crowded. See page 33 for general tips on river travel.

Lago Yarinacocha *p600*
Yarinacocha is 20 mins by colectivo or bus from Pucallpa, or 15 mins by taxi. Buses and cars to Yarinacocha (Puerto Callao) go along Jr Ucayali. Colectivos from Puerto Callao to San Francisco and Santa Clara US$0.65 per person. There are also boats, these do not always have enough passengers, you may have to hire the entire boat, about US$6.50 per hr.

Iquitos *p600, map p601*
Air
Francisco Secada Vigneta airport, T065-260147. Check times in advance as itineraries change. A taxi to the airport costs US$4.80 per car. A motocarro (motorcycle with 2 seats) is US$2. To take a city bus from the airport, walk out to the main road; most bus lines run through the centre of town, US$0.55. **LAN** (3-4 direct), **Peruvian Airlines** (2 a day) and **Star Perú** (direct or via Tarapoto) have daily flights to **Lima**.

Airline offices LAN, Próspero y Putumayo, T065-224177, Mon-Fri 0900-1900, Sat 0900-1700, Sun and holidays 0900-1200. **Peruvian Airlines**, Próspero 215, T231074. **Star Perú**, Napo 260, T065-234173, Mon-Sat 0830-1900, Sun 0900-1300.

Bus
To get to **Lake Quistococha**, combis leave every hr until 1500 from Plaza 28 de Julio, Iquitos. The last one back leaves at 1700. Alternatively take a mototaxi there and back with a 1-hr wait, which costs US$6. Another option is to hire a motorbike and spend the day there. The road can be difficult after rain. To **Nauta**, colectivos (station wagons), from Atahualpa y Grau, opposite Mercado Sachachorro, US$3.50, 1½ hrs.

Boat
Av La Marina leads from the centre north to Punchana, the ports district. Closest to town is **Muelle de Productores**, by the Mercado de Productores, from where speedboats and older, slower boats leave for local destinations. Next to it, at the intersection

of Samánez Ocampo, is the **Embarcadero Turístico**, also known as **El Huequito**, used by tour operators and by speedboats going to the Brazilian/Colombian border. Further along, is **Puerto Henry**, used by *Henry* vessels going to Pucallpa and the *Eduardo* line bound for Yurimaguas. About 2 km from the centre is **Puerto Masusa**, the main port for long-haul service in large vessels, a dangerous area at night. At the end of Av de la Marina is **Puerto Bellavista-Nanay** used by small boats providing local service. Other ports serving local destinations are near the airport. If arriving in Iquitos on a regular, slow boat, take extreme care when disembarking. Things get very chaotic at this time and theft and pickpocketing is rife.

For information about boats, go to the corresponding ports of departure for each destination, except for speed boats to the Brazil/Colombian border, which have their offices clustered on Raymondi cuadra 3. See page 33 for general tips on river travel.

Local To **Indiana** from Muelle de Productores: run-down *yates* at 1000 and 1400, returning at 0600 and 1300, US$1.60, 3 hrs; *deslizadores* have departures through the day depending on demand, last one returns to Iquitos about 1700, US$3.80, 45 mins. If the water level is high, transport goes to the nearby **El Varadero** port instead of Indiana. Mototaxis take passengers from either of these ports to **Mazán** on the Río Napo.

To **Pilpintuwasi Butterfly Farm** take a colectivo boat from Bellavista to Padre Cocha, 20 mins (US$0.30, leave when full), walk from there. If the river is high, boats can reach Pilpintuhuasi directly (no need to walk), a speedboat charges US$25 return including waiting time (pay at the end).

Long distance All boats leave from the docks described above. All sailings around 1800-2000, the first night's meal is not included. To **Pucallpa**, 4-5 days upriver along the Amazon and Ucayali although it can be longer if the water level is low and larger boats must travel only by day, hammock US$35, berth US$43-65 per person. *Henry*

(T065-263948) has 4 departures per week from Port Henry (see under Pucallpa for recommended vessels); likewise *Pedro Martín 2* from Puerto Masusa. To **Yurimaguas**, 3-4 days up river along the Amazon, Marañón and Huallaga, 2nd-class hammock space US$22, 1st-class hammock space US$38, berth US$38-48 per person. **Eduardo** company (T065-960404) with 8 boats is recommended, they sail from Puerto Henry Mon-Sat; *Eduardo IV* and *Eduardo V* are good.

Iquitos to the Brazilian/Colombian border *p604*
Boat
Lanchas to **Islandia**, 2-3 days downriver on the Amazon, hammock space US$16-17.50, berth US$25-30, leave from Masusa. With increased availability of *rápidos* on this route, there are fewer *lanchas* and these seem more run down. Passengers disembark in Peru for immigration formalities (no exchange facilities), then take another boat to **Marco** (US$2.50), the port for **Tabatinga**, Brazil. Most boats for **Manaus** depart from Marco. *Rápidos* for **Santa Rosa** and **Tabatinga** leave from the Embarcadero Turístico, Tue-Sun 0600 (board 0500-0530), be at the port 0445 for customs check, 8-10 hrs journey, US$60. There are no boats direct to Manaus. Boats go to Santa Rosa for immigration formalities then take passengers across to Tabatinga. A few boats may continue to **Leticia** (Colombia). Purchase tickets in advance from company offices, most are clustered on Raymondi, block 3 and a couple on Arica, they open Mon-Sat 0800-1900, some close for lunch, a few also open Sun 0800-1200. Not all *rápidos* are the same, some have faster inboard engines while others have outboard motors of different sizes, some are new and in better shape than others; ask around and if possible have a look at the boat before purchasing your ticket. Each company has 3 weekly departures in each direction, those departing Iquitos Sun, Wed, Fri return from Tabatinga Tue, Thu, Sat, those departing Tue, Thu, Sat return from Tabatinga Sun, Wed, Fri.

iperú has a list of companies registered with them, but there are other good ones: **Brastur**, Arica 746, T065-223232, **Trans Turismo Amazonas**, Raymondi 348, T065-231486, or **Golfinho**, Raymondi 378, T065-225118, www.transportegolfinho.com; **Golfinho II** is a jet boat, about 3 hrs quicker than *rápidos*, US$70 including 2 meals, Wed and Sun 0600. **Thor**, Arica 381, T065-243671, Sun, Wed, Fri. All include a small breakfast of a sandwich and coffee, a passable lunch and mineral water (ask for it). All carry life jackets and most have bathrooms. Luggage limit is 15 kg. Most travel agencies sell tickets. Hotels have details of sailings; ask around which boats are reliable. From Tabatinga departures for **Iquitos** Tue-Sun 0500-0600, the trip takes slightly longer upriver. Small boats between **Tabatinga** and **Santa Rosa**, or **Leticia** and Santa Rosa are readily available and charge US$2 per passenger.

Slow boats between **Iquitos** and **Santa Rosa** stop in **Caballococha**. *Rápidos* between **Iquitos** and **Tabatinga** only make a brief stop, so to see the sun, take a *rápido* boat from **Leticia** (Colombia), 2-3 hrs depending on the number of stops, then catch a **Grupo 42** flight out or a *rápido* the next day. If you plan to stop off along the way at small villages on the river in Peru (see Iquitos to the Brazilian/Colombian border, page 604), you can usually get a passing boat to make an unscheduled stop by flagging it down with a white sheet. This method doesn't work on the Brazilian part of the river, where boats don't make unscheduled stops. The only way to board a Brazilian boat between stops is to hire a canoe to take you out to meet it in mid-river then flag it down.

Iquitos to the Ecuadorean border *p605*
Boat
To **Pantoja** (for Ecuador), 5-7 days up river on the Napo, there are 2 boats: the better boat is *Cabo Pantoja*, contact through the Municipio de Torres Causana, Iquitos T065-226575, or try to inquire at one of the following private phones in Pantoja: T811616, T830055.

Hammock space US$35, US$3 per day extra for a berth. The other, shabbier boat is *Jeisawell*, Iquitos T065-613049. To shorten the voyage, or visit towns along the way, you can go to **Indiana** from Muelle de Productores (see above), then take a mototaxi to **Mazán** on the Río Napo. From Mazán, there are *rápidos* to **Santa Clotilde** Mon, Tue, Thu, Fri and Sat around 0900-1100 (Santa Clotilde to Mazán Tue, Wed, Fri, Sat and Sun), US$24 includes a snack, 4-5 hrs, information from **Forestal Export HM**, T065-251315, or **Familia Ruiz**, T065-251410 (Iquitos). From Mazán to Pantoja the *lancha* costs US$22-25, from Santa Clotilde to Pantoja US$16-19. There is no public transport from Pantoja to **Nuevo Rocafuerte** (Ecuador), you must hire a private boat, US$50-60 per boat; try to share the ride. From Nuevo Rocafuerte to **Coca**, large motorized canoes sail Sun, Tue, Wed and Fri at 0500, US$15-20, 12-14 hrs; from Coca to Nuevo Rocafuerte Mon, Tue, Thu and Fri between 0700-0800, 10 hrs. Be at the dock early.

See page 33 for general tips on river travel.

Motorcycle hire
Park Motors, Tacna 643, T/F065-231688. The tourist office has details of other companies. Expect to pay US$2.20 per hr, US$19 for 24 hrs; remember that traffic in town is chaotic.

❶ Directory

Tingo María *p596*
Internet Several places on Raimondi and in the streets near Plaza de Armas; fast, cheap.

Yurimaguas *p597*
Banks Interbank or travel agents charge poor rates. **Negocios Zerimar**, Júrequi half a block from plaza, changes US$ cash, Mon-Sat 0700-2100, Sun 0700-1500. **Internet** Café on Plaza de Armas, US$1.70 per hr.

Pucallpa *p598, map p599*
Banks There are lots of street changers (watch them carefully). BCP, Raimondi y Tarapacá. Mon-Thu 0900-1830, Fri 0900-1930,

Sat 0900-1300. Cash advances can be made on Visa. **Interbank**, Av Raimondi y Ucayali, Mon-Fri 0900-1800, Sat 0915-1230, cash and TCs at fair rates, ATM. **Scotiabank**, Av Raimondi 192 y Tacna, Mon-Fri 0900-1330, 1600-1830, Sat 0915-1230, cash and TCs, ATM. **Cambios**, several at Av Raimondi corner Ucayali. **Internet** Many around town. **Police** Policía Nacional, Jr Independencia 3rd block, T061-575211. **Post** Tarapacá y San Martín.

Iquitos *p600, map p601*
Banks BCP, Plaza de Armas. Visa ATM around the corner on Próspero. **BBV Continental**, Sgto Lores 171. **Banco de la Nación**, Condamine 478. Good rates. **Interbank**, Próspero y Sgto Lores, cash and TCs at fair rates, ATM. *Casa de cambio* at **Tienda Wing Kong**, Próspero 312, Mon-Sat 0800-1300, 1500-2000, Sun 0900-1200. Western Union, Napo 359, T065-235182. Don't change money on the streets. **Consulates** Brazil, Sargento Lores 363, T065-235153, www.abe.mre.gov.br. Mon-Fri 0800-1400, visas issued in 2 days. **Colombia**, Calvo de Araujo 431, T065-231461, Mon-Fri 0900-1230, 1500-1700. Germany, Max Axel Georg Druschke, Pevas 133-B, T065-233466, mdruschke@terra.com.pe. **Note** There is no Ecuadorean consulate. If you need a visa, you must get it in Lima or in your home country. **Immigration** Mcal Cáceres 18th block, T065-235371, Mon-Fri 0800-1615. **Internet** There are places everywhere,

US$0.50- 0.65 per hr. **Laundry** At Ricardo Palma, blocks 4 and 5, and at Putumayo, block 1. **Medical services** Clínica Ana Stahl, Av la Marina 285, T065-252535. **Police** Tourist police: Sargento Lores 834, T065-231851. In emergency T065-241000 or 241001. Better to take complaints to iperú than to tourist police or Indecopi. **Post** On the corner of C Arica with Morona, near Plaza de Armas, daily 0700-1700. **Telephone** *Locutorios* everywhere.

Iquitos to the Brazilian/Colombian border *p604*
Banks There is no exchange office in Santa Rosa, but you can pay in reais. You can use Colombian pesos in Brazil and reais in Colombia. Peruvian soles are not accepted in Colombia, but sometimes you can pay with soles in Brazil. There are no exchange facilities in Tabatinga port, but there are several *casas de cambio* in Leticia, the best place to change money, even for reais into soles. US dollars are accepted everywhere. **Internet** The only place with internet is Leticia. Slow connection.

Iquitos to the Ecuadorean border *p605*
Banks Shopkeepers in Pantoja exchange US$ cash at poor rates, but may not give you US$ for soles. **Telephone** Public phones: Mazán, T065-811613, T065-812225, T065-254660; Santa Clotilde, T065-811014, T065-830040; Pantoja T065-811616, T065-830055, T065-812229.

Southern Jungle

Both the Manu Biosphere Reserve and Tambopata National Reserve offer amazing wildlife spotting, large parts being remote and pristine, with such highlights as macaw clay licks and birdwatching on undisturbed lakes. The southern selva is found mostly within the Department of Madre de Dios, created in 1902, and contains the Manu National Biosphere Reserve (2.05 million ha), the Tambopata National Reserve (254,358 ha) and the Bahuaja-Sonene National Park (1.1 million ha).
▶▶ *For listings, see pages 629-640.*

Background

The forest of this lowland region (altitude: 260 m) is technically called subtropical moist forest, which means that it receives less rainfall than tropical forest and is dominated by the flood plains of its meandering rivers. One of the most striking features is the former river channels that have become isolated as oxbow lakes (*cochas*). These are home to black caiman and giant otter and a host of other species. Other rare species living in the forest are jaguar, puma, ocelot and tapir. There are also capybara, 13 species of primate and many hundreds of bird species, including macaws, guans, currasows and the giant harpy eagle. If you include the cloudforests and highlands of the Manu Biosphere Reserve, the bird species count almost totals 1000.

The relative proximity to Cuzco of Manu in particular has made it one of the prime nature-watching destinations in South America. Despite its reputation, Manu is heavily protected, with visitor numbers limited and a large percentage of the park inaccessible to tourists. Nevertheless, there is no need to worry that this level of management is going to diminish your pleasure. There is more than enough in the way of birds, animals and plants to satisfy the most ardent wildlife enthusiast. Tambopata does have a town in the vicinity, Puerto Maldonado, and the area is under threat from exploitation and settlement. The suspension of oil exploration in 2000 led to a change of status for a large tract of this area, giving immediate protection to another of Peru's zones of record-breaking diversity.

Since 2003 the new emerging threat to the forests of Madre de Dios is the planned construction of the Interoceánica, a road linking the Atlantic and Pacific Oceans via Puerto Maldonado and Brazil. The paving of this road system, creating a high-speed link between the two countries, will certainly bring more uncontrolled colonization in the area, placing the forests of the Tambopata region under further pressure. The uncontrolled colonization of the Bahuaja-Sonene's southern border, in the Tambopata headwaters area is another cause for concern. On top of that is illegal logging and the issue of new oil exploration contracts for most of Madre de Dios outside of the conservation concessions. This, in spite of the fact that they overlap heavily with the indigenous territories concession, including the lands of indigenous peoples living in voluntary isolation.

Manu Biosphere Reserve → *For listings, see pages 629-640. Colour map 4, C4.*

No other rainforest can compare with Manu for the diversity of its life forms. It is one of the world's great wilderness experiences, with the best birdwatching as well as offering the best chance of seeing giant otters, jaguars, ocelots and several of the 13 species of primate that abound in this pristine tropical wilderness. The more remote areas of the reserve are home to uncontacted indigenous tribes and many other indigenous groups with very little knowledge of the outside world. Covering an area of 2,041,137 ha, Manu Biosphere Reserve is also one of the largest conservation units on Earth, encompassing the complete drainage of the Manu river, with an altitudinal range of 200-4100 m above sea level.

Ins and outs

Getting there and around The multiple-use zone of Manu Biosphere Reserve is accessible to anyone and several lodges exist in the area (see Lodges in Manu below). The

Manu Biosphere Reserve

Sleeping
1 Amazonia Lodge
2 Boca Manu &
  Yine Lodges
3 Casa Machiguenga
4 Cock of the Rock
  Lodge
5 Erika Lodge
6 Manu Cloud
  Forest Lodge
7 Manu Lodge
8 Manu Wildlife Center
9 Pantiacolla Lodge
10 Posada San Pedro
   Cloud Forest Lodge
11 Proyecto Selva Inca
12 Yanayaco Lodge

Cultural Zone

reserved zone is accessible by permit only and entry is strictly controlled (see below). The frontier town of Puerto Maldonado is the starting point for expeditions to the Tambopata National Reserve and is only a 30-minute flight from Cuzco. ►► *See Activities and tours, page 635, and Transport page 638.*

Best time to visit The climate is warm and humid, with a rainy season from November to March and a dry season from April to October. A cool air mass descending from the Andes, called a *friaje*, is characteristic of the dry season, when temperatures drop to 15-16°C during the day, and 13°C at night. Always bring a sweater at this time. The best time to visit is during the dry season when there are fewer mosquitoes and the rivers are low, exposing the beaches. This is also a good time to see birds nesting and to view the animals at close range, as they stay close to the rivers. A pair of binoculars is essential and insect repellent is a must.

Information Manu National Park Office ① *Av Micaela Bastidas 310, Cuzco, T084-240898, pqnmanu@terra.com.pe, 0800-1400.* They issue a permit for the former Reserved Zone, costing S/.150 per person (about US$54). This is included in package tour prices. For information on conservation issues: **Asociación Peruana para la Conservación de la Naturaleza (Apeco)** ① *Parque José Acosta 187, p 2, Magdalena del Mar, Lima 17, T01-264 0094, www.apeco.org.pe;* and **Pronaturaleza** ① *Alfredo León 211, Miraflores, Lima 18, T01-447 9032 and Jr Cajamarca, cuadra 1 s/n, Puerto Maldonado, T082-571585, www.pronaturaleza.org.* **Perú Verde** ① *Ricaldo Palma J-1, Santa Mónica, Cuzco, T084-226392, www.peruverde.org,* is a local NGO that can help with information and has free video shows about Manu National Park and Tambopata National Reserve. Staff are friendly and helpful and also have information on programmes and research in the jungle area of Río Madre de Dios.

The park areas

The biosphere reserve is divided into the **Manu National Park** (1,692,137 ha), where only government-sponsored biologists and anthropologists may visit with permits from the Ministry of Agriculture in Lima, the **Manu Reserved Zone** (257,000 ha) (within the Manu National Park), set aside for applied scientific research and ecotourism, and the **Cultural Zone** (92,000 ha), containing acculturated native groups and colonists, where the locals still employ their traditional way of life. To enter these tourism and recreational areas visitors may only go under the auspices of an authorized operator with an authorized guide. Permits are limited and reservations should be made well in advance, though it is possible to book a place on a trip at the last minute in Cuzco. In the former Reserved Zone there are two lodges, the rustic **Casa Machiguenga** run by the Machiguenga communities of Tayakome and Yomibato with the help of a German NGO, and the upmarket **Manu Lodge**. In the Cocha Salvador area, several companies have tented safari camp infrastructures, some with shower and dining facilities, but all visitors sleep in tents. Some companies have installed walk-in tents with cots and bedding.

The Cultural Zone is accessible to anyone and several lodges exist in the area. It is possible to visit these lodges under your own steam. Among the ethnic groups in the Cultural Zone (a system of buffer areas surrounding the core Manu area) are the Harakmbut, Machiguenga and Yine in the Amarakaeri Reserved Zone, on the east bank of the Alto Madre de Dios. They have set up their own ecotourism activities, which are entirely managed by indigenous people. Associated with Manu are other areas protected by conservation groups or local people, for example the Blanquillo reserved zone, a conservation concession in the adjacent Los Amigos river system and some cloudforest parcels along the road. The **Nuhua-Kugapakori Reserved Zone** (443,887 ha), set aside for these two nomadic groups, is the area between the headwaters of the Río Manu and headwaters of the Río Urubamba, to the north of the Alto Madre de Dios.

To Manu and Puerto Maldonado from Cuzco → For listings, see pages 629-640.
Colour map 5, A5/6.

The arduous trip over the Andes from Cuzco to Pilcopata takes about 16-18 hours by bus or truck (20-40 hours in the wet season). On this route, the scenery is magnificent.

Leaving Cuzco
From Cuzco you climb up to the Huancarani pass before **Paucartambo** (3½ hours), before dropping down to this picturesque mountain village in the Mapacho Valley at the border between the departments of Cuzco and Madre de Dios. For more information about Paucartambo, see page 213. The road then ascends to the Ajcanacu pass (cold at night), after which it goes down to the cloudforest and then the rainforest. On the way you pass **Manu Cloudforest Lodge, Cock of the Rock Lodge** and the **San Pedro Biological Station** (owned by Tapir Tours, visited in their Manu programmes). After 12 hours you reach **Pilcopata** at 650 m.

Atalaya
After Pilcopata, the route is hair-raising and breathtaking. Even in the dry season this part of the road is appalling and trucks often get stuck en route to Atalaya, the first village on the Alto Madre de Dios river and about an hour away from Pilcopata. Atalaya consists of a few houses, and basic accommodation can be found here. Meals are available at the very friendly family home of Rosa and Klaus, where you can also camp. Boats here will take you across the river to **Amazonia Lodge**, see page 629. The village is also the jumping-off point for river trips further into the Manu. The route continues to **Salvación**, where a Manu Park office is situated. There are basic hostels and restaurants.

Shintuya and Itahuania → Colour map 5, A6.
The road now bypasses Shintuya, a commercial and social centre, as wood from the jungle is transported from here to Cuzco. There are a few basic restaurants and you can camp (beware of thieves). The priest will let you stay in the dormitory rooms at the mission. Supplies are expensive. There are two Shintuyas: one is the port and mission and the other is the indigenous village. The next town is **Itahuania**, the starting point for river transport, but it won't be long before the port moves down river as the road is pushed through to Nuevo Edén, 11 km away, and on to Diamante. The road is one day planned to reach Boca Colorado. **Note** It is not possible to arrange trips to the Reserved Zone of the National Park from Itahuania, owing to park regulations; all arrangements must be made in Cuzco.

Boca Manu
Boca Manu is the connecting point between the rivers Alto Madre de Dios, Manu and Madre de Dios. It has a few houses, an airstrip and some food supplies. It is also the entrance to the Manu Reserve and to go further you must be part of an organized group. The park ranger station is located in **Limonal**, 20 minutes by boat from Boca Manu. You need to show your permit here; camping is allowed if you have a permit. There are no

regular flights from Cuzco to Boca Manu. These are arranged the day before, if there are enough passengers. Check at Cuzco airport or with the tour operators in Cuzco.

To the Reserved Zone
Upstream on the Río Manu you pass the **Manu Lodge** (see page 629) on the Cocha Juárez, three to four hours by boat. You can continue to Cocha Otorongo, 2½ hours, and Cocha Salvador, 30 minutes, the biggest lake with plenty of wildlife where the **Casa Machiguenga Lodge** is located and several companies have safari camp concessions. From here it is two hours to **Pakitza**, the entrance to the National Park Reserved Zone. This is only for biologists and others with a special permit.

Boca Colorado
From Itahuania infrequent cargo boats sail (when fully laden, about six to eight a week) to the gold-mining centre of Boca Colorado on the Río Madre de Dios, via Boca Manu, passing several ecotourism lodges including **Pantiacolla Lodge** and **Manu Wildlife Centre**, see page 629. The trip takes around nine hours, and costs US$15. Basic accommodation can be found here but is not recommended for lone women travellers. From Boca Colorado a road now runs to Puerto Maldonado, 4½ hours by colectivo and a ferry crossing (see Transport, page 638). Some lodges in the Manu area now use this route: flight to Puerto Maldonado, a vehicle to Boca Colorado and then a boat upstream to the lodge.

Between Boca Manu and Colorado is **Blanquillo**, a private reserve (10,000 ha). Bring a good tent with you and all food if you want to camp, or alternatively accommodation is available at the **Tambo Blanquillo** (full board or accommodation only). Wildlife is abundant, especially macaws and parrots at the macaw lick near Manu Wildlife Centre. There are occasional boats to Blanquillo from Shintuya, six to eight hours.

Puerto Maldonado → *For listings, see pages 629-640. Colour map 6, A3. Phone code: 082. Population: 45,000. Altitude: 250 m.*

Puerto Maldonado is an important starting point for visiting the southeastern jungles of the Tambopata Reserve, or for departing to Brazil or Bolivia. Most visitors do not see much of the place because they are whisked through town on their way to a lodge on the Río Madre de Dios or the Río Tambopata. The city dwellers haven't been too pleased about this, preferring tourists to spend some time in town, which is a major timber, gold mining, Brazil nut and tourism centre. Its expansion is bound to continue as a bridge, part of the Interoceánica highway, is being built across the Río Madre de Dios. Even before its completion (late 2010 or 2011, forecasts vary – at the time of writing two of the supports were in place) the town is becoming an increasingly active commercial centre for trade and business travellers from Lima and Brazil. Facilities to accommodate them are popping up in the form of more modern hotels with air-conditioning and cable TV, in contrast to the more traditional tourist jungle lodges. It's a safe place, with *chicha* music blaring out from most street corners. There are tourist offices at the airport and at **Dircetur** ① *Urb Fonavi, take a mototaxi to the Posta Médica, which is next door.*

Ins and outs
The road from Cuzco to Puerto Maldonado is being upgraded as part of the Interoceánica highway. There are regular bus services. As paving proceeds, journey times will lessen and the road's susceptibility to bad weather will decrease. In its

pre-upgrading state it was expertly described in Matthew Parris' book *Inka-Cola*. (See www.southamericanpictures.com/collections/inter oceanic-highway/interoceanic-highway.htm for a photo essay). The road passes through Ocongate and Marcapata before reaching **Quincemil**, 240 km from Urcos, a centre for alluvial gold-mining. Petrol is scarce here because most vehicles continue on 70 km to **Mazuko**, where it's cheaper. The changing scenery is magnificent. Take warm clothing for travelling through the sierra. For an alternative route, see page 623.

Sights

Puerto Maldonado overlooks the confluence of the rivers Tambopata and Madre de Dios. From the park at the end of Jirón Arequipa, across from the Capitanía, you get a good view of the two rivers, the ferries across the Madre de Dios (soon to be replaced by the new

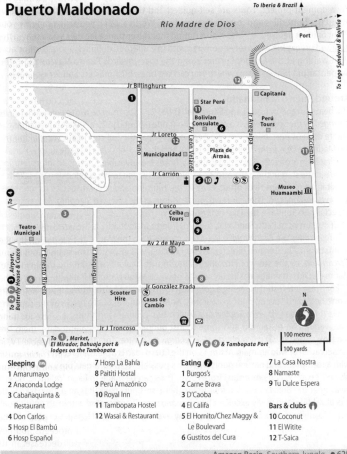

Puerto Maldonado

To Iberia & Brazil

Río Madre de Dios

Port

To Lago Sandoval & Bolivia

Jr Billinghurst

Star Perú
Capitanía

Bolivian
Consulate
Perú
Tours

Jr Loreto

Municipalidad

Plaza de Armas

Jr Carrión

Museo
Huamaambi

Jr Cusco

Ceiba
Tours

Teatro
Municipal

Av 2 de Mayo

Lan

Jr González Prada

Scooter
Hire

Casas de
Cambio

Jr J Troncoso

To 1, Market,
El Mirador, Bahuaja port &
lodges on the Tambopata

To 5

To 4 9 & Tambopata Port

100 metres
100 yards

N

Jr Puno
Av León Velarde
Jr Arequipa
Jr 26 de Diciembre
Jr Ernesto Rivero
Jr Miaquegua

To 4
To Airport,
Butterfly House & Cuzco

Sleeping
1 Amarumayo
2 Anaconda Lodge
3 Cabañaquinta & Restaurant
4 Don Carlos
5 Hosp El Bambú
6 Hosp Español
7 Hosp La Bahía
8 Paititi Hostal
9 Perú Amazónico
10 Royal Inn
11 Tambopata Hostel
12 Wasai & Restaurant

Eating
1 Burgos's
2 Carne Brava
3 D'Caoba
4 El Califa
5 El Hornito/Chez Maggy & Le Boulevard
6 Gustitos del Cura
7 La Casa Nostra
8 Namaste
9 Tu Dulce Espera

Bars & clubs
10 Coconut
11 El Witite
12 T-Saica

bridge) and the stacks of lumber at the dockside. The Brazil-nut harvest is from December to February and the crop tends to be good on alternate years. Nuts are sold on the street, plain or coated in sugar or chocolate. **El Mirador** ⓘ *at the junction of Av Fitzcarrald and Av Madre de Dios, Mon-Fri 0700-1200, 1500-2100 (officially, not always obeyed), US$0.60*, is a 47-m-high tower with 250 steps and three platforms giving fine views over the city and surrounding rainforest. There is also a toilet at the top – no curtains – from which there is an equally fine view over the city! **Museo Huamaambi** ⓘ *26 de Diciembre 360, US$1*, contains photos and artefacts pertaining to the Harakmbut culture of central Madre de Dios and is now also home to **Fenamad** ⓘ *26 de Diciembre 276*, a local organization for the protection of the lands and cultures of people from jungle communities. **Inkaterra** is currently managing the **Mariposario (Butterfly House)** ⓘ *adjoining the airport entrance (a 5-min walk from the terminal building), open 0800-1330, US$5*, which breeds butterflies as part of a sustainable development project. Tours are self-guided and there are plaques with information about the butterflies and tortoises you will see. Worth a visit if you arrive early for your flight or if it is delayed. It's also worth noting that the entrance fee gets you a seat in the cool and breezy Inkaterra reception area with free internet; definitely more comfortable than waiting at the airport. Further along the road towards Puerto Maldonado is the **Serpentarium (Snake Farm)** where you can see boas, bushmasters and fer-de-lances.

Around Puerto Maldonado

The beautiful and tranquil **Lago Sandoval** ⓘ *US$9.50, you must go with a guide; this can be arranged by the boat driver*, is a one-hour boat ride (about US$25 a day, plus fuel, from the Madre de Dios port, minimum two people, don't pay the full cost in advance) along the Río Madre de Dios from Puerto Maldonado, and then a 5-km walk into the jungle. Parts of the first 3 km are a raised wooden walkway; boots are advisable. There is an interpretation centre at the start of the trail and a 35-m-high observation tower overlooking the lake. It is possible to see giant river otters early in the morning and several species of monkeys, macaws and hoatzin. There are two jungle lodges at the lake, see Sleeping. At weekends, especially on Sundays, the lake gets quite busy.

Upstream from Lago Sandoval, towards Puerto Maldonado, is the wreck of a steamer that resembles the *Fitzcarrald*. It lies a few metres from the Madre de Dios in the bed of a small stream. The German director, Werner Herzog, was inspired to make his famous film, *Fitzcarraldo*, by the story of Fitzcarrald's attempt to haul a boat from the Ucuyali to the Madre de Dios drainage basins (in what is now the Manu National Park).

For those interested in seeing a gold-rush town, a trip to **Laberinto** is suggested. There is one hotel and several poor restaurants. At Km 1.5 on the Cuzco road you will find the **Kapievi Ecoaldea** ⓘ *www.kapievi.org*, which has cultural workshops, a children's play area, vegetarian restaurant and some tourist bungalows. Further along at Km 11 is the **Amazon Shelter** ⓘ *www.amazonshelter.org*, a centre for the rehabilitation and conservation of wild animals. At Km 13 on the Cuzco road is a pleasant recreational centre with a restaurant and natural pools where it's possible to swim. It gets busy at weekends. It's US$2 each way by mototaxi from town. Trips can be made to **Lago Valencia**, 60 km away near the Bolivian border; four hours there, six hours back. It is an oxbow lake with lots of wildlife, and many excellent beaches and islands are located within an hour's boat ride. Mosquitoes are voracious. You can stay overnight with local families or at a refuge.

Tambopata National Reserve (TNR) → *For listings, see pages 629-640. Colour map 6, A3.*

From Puerto Maldonado you can visit the Tambopata National Reserve by travelling up the Tambopata river or down the Madre de Dios. The area was first declared a reserve in 1990 and is a very reasonable alternative for those who do not have the time or money to visit Manu. It is a close rival in terms of seeing wildlife and boasts some superb oxbow lakes. There are a number of lodges here which are excellent for lowland rainforest birding. **Explorers' Inn** is perhaps the most famous, but the **Posada Amazonas/Tambopata Research Centre** and **Tambopata EcoLodge** are also good. In an effort to ensure that more tourism income stays in the area, a few local families have established their own small-scale *casas de hospedaje*, which offer more basic facilities and make use of the nearby forest.

Ins and outs
If not visiting the Reserve on a lodge package, you need to visit the **INRENA office** ⓘ *Av 28 de Julio 482, T082-573278, Mon-Fri 0830-1300, 1430-1800, Sat 0900-1200.* ›› *For Transport, see page 640.*

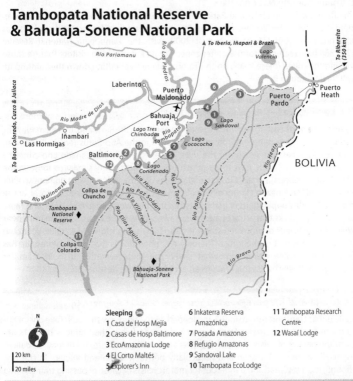

Tambopata National Reserve & Bahuaja-Sonene National Park

N
20 km
20 miles

Sleeping
1 Casa de Hosp Mejía
2 Casas de Hosp Baltimore
3 EcoAmazonia Lodge
4 El Corto Maltés
5 Explorer's Inn
6 Inkaterra Reserva Amazónica
7 Posada Amazonas
8 Refugio Amazonas
9 Sandoval Lake
10 Tambopata EcoLodge
11 Tambopata Research Centre
12 Wasaí Lodge

Border essentials: Peru–Brazil

Iñapari-Assis Brasil

A suspension bridge from Iñapari to Assis Brasil now links the two countries. Peruvian immigration is in Iñapari. Exit stamps can be obtained between 0800 and 1830. Walk across the bridge over the Río Acre to Assis Brasil, where there is no Policía Federal office. Travel on to Brasiléia to obtain your Brazil entry stamp at Policía Federal in the Rodoviária (bus station). You must have a yellow fever certificate to enter Brazil.

There is a road from Assis Brasil to Brasiléia in Brazil (120 km, buses run in the dry season, 2½ hours, US\$3.60; 4WD vehicles in the wet season), from where a new bridge has been opened to Cobija in Bolivia. There are no exchange facilities en route and poor exchange rates for Brazilian currency at Iñapari. Crossing between Peru and Bolivia on this route is not easy.

Note Check in advance that you do not need a consular visa for Brazil; they are not issued at the border. For transport to the border, see page 640.

Bahuaja-Sonene National Park

The **Bahuaja-Sonene National Park** runs from the Río Heath, which forms the Bolivian border, across to the Río Tambopata, 50-80 km upstream from Puerto Maldonado. It was expanded to 1,091,416 ha in August 2000, with the Tambopata National Reserve (254,358 ha) created to form a buffer zone. The park is closed to visitors though those visiting the *collpa* (macaw lick) on the Tambopata or river rafting down the Tambopata will travel through it.

Río Las Piedras → *For listings, see pages 629-640.*

Lying to the northeast of, and running roughly parallel to the Río Manu, this drainage runs some 700 km from remote rainforest headwaters in the Alto Purús region. The lower, more easily accessible section of the river, closer to Puerto Maldonado and currently outside state protection, runs through rich tropical forests, very similar to those in the Manu and Tambopata areas. Close to 600 species of birds, at least eight primate species and some of the Amazon's larger mammals, jaguar, puma, tapir and giant anteater, are all present. Healthy populations of giant otters exist in the rivers and oxbow lakes, and there are several clay licks that attract parrots, macaws and, in some cases, larger mammals as well. Due to its lack of protected status it's also fairly straightforward to tailor your own itinerary in this part of the forest. The only real downside is that hunting pressure has resulted in wildlife being somewhat shyer and more secretive than in Manu or Tambopata. Nevertheless this remains an excellent wildlife destination.

To Iberia and Iñapari → *For listings, see pages 629-640. Colour map 4, C6.*

Daily public transport runs to Iberia and Iñapari on the border with Brazil. Take one of the frequent ferries that crosses from Puerto Maldonado (while the bridge is being built). Until the paving of this section of the Interoceánica is complete, there may be delays, especially in the wet season and particularly between Iberia and Iñapari. In the dry, though, it is a fast road and dangerous for motorcyclists because of passing traffic. Along the road there remains no primary forest, only secondary growth and small *chacras* (farms). There are also picturesque *caseríos* (settlements) that serve as collecting and processing centres for the Brazil nut industry. Approximately 70% of the inhabitants in the Madre de Dios are involved in the collection of the prized nut.

Iberia, at Km 168, has accommodation. Just outside the town the local rubber tappers' association has set up a reserve with an information centre. **Iñapari**, at the end of the road and the border with Brazil (see box, opposite), Km 235, has two accommodation options, but **Assis Brasil** across the border is more attractive.

◉ Southern Jungle listings

For Sleeping and Eating price codes and other relevant information, see pages 38-44.

◉ Sleeping

Manu Biosphere Reserve *p620, map p621*
The following lodges offer various packages:
Amazonia Lodge, on the Río Alto Madre de Dios just across the river from Atalaya, T084-816131, www.amazonialodge.com; in Cuzco at Matará 334, piso 3, T/F084-231370. An old tea hacienda run by the Yabar-Calderón family, famous for its bird diversity and fine hospitality, a great place to relax, meals included, US$70 per person per night, birding or natural history tours available, contact in advance to arrange a pickup.

Casa Machiguenga, contact **Manu Expeditions** or the **Apeco NGO**, T084-225595. Near Cocha Salvador, upriver from Manu Lodge, Machiguenga-style cabins run by the local community of Tayakome with NGO help.

Cock of the Rock Lodge, www.tropical naturetravel.com. On the road from Paucartambo to Atalaya at San Pedro, at 1600 m, next to a Cock of the Rock lek, 10 private cabins with en suite bath, US$595 per person for 3 days/2 nights, including tours, guide and meals.

Erika Lodge, contact **Manu Ecological Adventures**, Plateros 356, Cuzco T084-261640, www.manuadventures.com (see Activities and tours, page 636). On the Alto Madre de Dios, 25 mins from Atalaya. Like Amazonia Lodge, this is good place for birds.

It offers basic facilities and is cheaper than the other, more luxurious lodges.
Manu Cloud Forest Lodge, owned by Manu Nature Tours (see Activities and tours, page 636). Located at Unión at 1800 m on the road from Paucartambo to Atalaya, 6 rooms with 16-20 beds.

Manu Lodge, run by **Manu Nature Tours** (see Activities and tours, page 636) and only bookable as part of a full-package deal with transport. Situated on the Manu river, 3 hrs upriver from Boca Manu towards Cocha Salvador. It's a fine location overlooking Cocha Juárez, an oxbow lake, which often plays host to a family of giant otters. The lodge has an extensive trail system, and stands of mauritia palms near the lake provide nesting sites for colonies of blue and yellow macaws.

Manu Wildlife Center, book through **Manu Expeditions**, which runs it in conjunction with the conservation group Peru Verde, www.manuwildlifecenter.com. 2 hrs down the Río Madre de Dios from Boca Manu, near the Blanquillo macaw lick. 22 double cabins, all with private bathroom and hot water. It also has a tapir lick and canopy tower for birdwatching.

Pantiacolla Lodge, www.pantiacolla.com. 14 rooms in bungalows, book through Pantiacolla Tours. 30 mins downriver from Shintuya. Owned by the Moscoso family. This lodge is located at the foot of the Pantiacolla Mountains, which boasts vast biological diversity, particularly with birds. There is a good trail system. Lots of tours

available and all-inclusive packages with transport and guides. Also managed by Pantiacolla is the **Yine Lodge**, see below.
Yanayaco Lodge, Procuradores 46, Cuzco, T084-248122, www.yanayacolodge.com. About 1 hr by boat above Diamante village on the southern bank of the Madre de Dios, close to a small parrot *collpa* (mineral lick); claims to offer frequent sightings of large mammals. Using local river transport to arrive at the lodge rates are very reasonable, prices depend on length of stay. The lodge also offers several different itineraries in Manu.

To Manu and Puerto Maldonado from Cuzco *p623*
Posada San Pedro Cloud Forest Lodge, San Pedro, on the road from Paucartambo to Atalaya, before Pilcopata. 14 rooms. Included as an overnight stop in many tour operators' Manu programmes.
Proyecto Selva Inca, Av Sumar Pacha s/n, Pilcopata, T084-231625 or T084-984 756207 (mob), in Cuzco Urb Marcavalle C-25, Wanchac, www.selvainka.com. Run by Evelyne Vega Oblitas, this is a safe, friendly and inexpensive option in Pilcopata, staying at the **Albergue Turístico La Casa del Kshipaktona**. Due to its village position this is more a social project than an opportunity to see rare wildlife, but we've received several positive reports regarding their sustainable development programmes and work with local communities. Contact in advance to see what options are available.
Turismo Indígena Wanamei, Av 26 de Diciembre 276, Puerto Maldonado, T082-572539, and Av El Sol 814 p 2, of 212, Cuzco, T084-234608, T084-984 754708 (mob), www.ecoturismowanamei.com. 8 indigenous communities from the Amarakaeri Communal Reserve introduce visitors to their ancestral lands, located between Manu and Tambopata. Their 9-day trip, starting in Cuzco, costs US$2640 for 2 people. Accommodation includes lodges, communities and camping. The trips aim to offer not only excellent wildlife viewing opportunities but also an insight into

the daily life of indigenous peoples in the early 21st century. To gain the most from this unusual experience you need to speak Spanish (or Harakmbut!) and to have some experience of hiking over difficult terrain. Tents can be hired in Cuzco. Porters can be hired at US$10 per day.
D Boca Manu Lodge, book through **Emperadores Tours**, Procuradores 190, Cuzco, T084-239987, empetcusco@hotmail. com. Run by long-standing Manu resident Juan de Dios Carpio. Juan owns a general store in Boca, so if you're stranded in Boca Manu and you're looking for a reasonably priced place to stay this could be an option – just ask at the store.
G Hospedaje Manu, Boca Colorado, on street beside football field. Cell-like rooms, open windows and ceilings but comfy mattresses and mosquito netting.
G Hostal, Boca Manu, run by the community. Basic accommodation.
G The Mission, Shintuya. The priest will let you stay in the dormitory rooms. There are a few basic restaurants and you can camp (beware of thieves). Supplies are expensive.
G Sra Rubella, Pilcopata. This unnamed place is very basic, but friendly.

Lodges
Yine Lodge, next to the airstrip, Boca Manu. A smart cooperative project run by **Pantiacolla Tours**. Actually, the native Yine community of Diamante operates its own tours into the community and surroundings.

Puerto Maldonado *p624, map p625*
B Anaconda Lodge, 600 m from airport, T082-982 611039 (mob), www.anaconda junglelodge.com. **E** with shared bath, Swiss/Thai-owned bungalows, hot showers, swimming pool, Thai restaurant, tours arranged, has space for camping, very pleasant, family atmosphere.
B Don Carlos, Av León Velarde 1271, T082-571029, www.hotelesdoncarlos.com. Nice view over the Río Tambopata, a/c, restaurant, TV, phone, pool, good.

B Wasaí Maldonado, Billinghurst, opposite the Capitanía, T082-572290, www.wasai.com. Price includes breakfast, a/c, TV, shower. In a beautiful location overlooking the Madre de Dios, with forest surrounding cabin-style rooms that are built on a slope down to the river. The hotel may be affected because of its proximity to the new bridge. A/c, TV, shower, small pool with waterfall, good restaurant (local fish a speciality). Recommended. They can organize local tours and have a lodge on the Tambopata River.

C Cabañaquinta, Jirón Cuzco 535, T082-571045, www.hotelcabanaquinta.com.pe. With buffet breakfast, bathroom, a/c, small pool, sauna, good restaurant, friendly, lovely garden, very comfortable, price includes airport transfer if needed. Recommended.

C Paititi Hostal, G Prada 290 y Av León Velarde, T082-574667, paititihostal@ hotmail.com. All mod-cons, executive and standard rooms, TV, a/c, breakfast included, Wi-Fi. Reserve in advance. Recommended.

C Perú Amazónico, Jr Ica 269, T082-571799, peruamazonico@hotmail.com. Brand new, modern and comfortable, cable TV, frigobar, a/c, Wi-Fi. No outdoor space, but popular with business travellers and those who need a break from the jungle.

E Amarumayo, Libertad 433, T082-573860, residenciamarumayo@hotmail.com. Price includes breakfast. Comfortable, with pool and garden, good restaurant, 10 mins from the centre. Recommended.

E Hospedaje La Bahía, 2 de Mayo 710, T082-572127. Cheaper without bath or TV, large rooms, clean. Best of cheaper options.

E Hospedaje Español, González Prada 670, T082-572381. Comfortable, set back from the road in a quiet part of town. Garden setting, clean, friendly.

E Royal Inn, Av 2 de Mayo 333, T082-573464, mitsukate4@hotmail.com. Modern and huge, clean, rooms at back are less noisy, rooms have ceiling fans and TV, secure parking.

F Hospedaje El Bambú, Jr Puno 837, T082-793880. New, basic and small but well-kept rooms with fan, family atmosphere, breakfast

and juices not included in price but served in dining room. A good budget option.

F pp Tambopata Hostel, Av 26 de Diciembre 234, www.tambopatahostel.com. The only real backpacker hostel in town, dorm beds. Nice atmosphere, they also organize local tours.

F Hotel Toni, in Quincemil, on the road from Cuzco to Puerto Maldonado. Friendly, clean, cold shower, good meals.

Tambopata National Reserve (TNR)
p627, map p627

Most of the lodges in the Tambopata area use the term 'ecotourism', or something similar, in their publicity material, but it is applied pretty loosely. **Posada Amazonas'** collaboration with the local community is unique in the area, but fortunately no lodge offers trips where guests hunt for their meals. Wi-Fi and mobile phone access now seems to be standard in the larger, upmarket lodges along the Tambopata. To escape this you would leave to stay somewhere smaller, such as a community-run lodge like **Baltimore**. Prices are given only for standard 3-day/ 2-night packages that include all transport links, accommodation on a full-board basis and guiding. Lodges on the Tambopata are reached by vehicle to Bahuaja port, 15 km upriver from Puerto Maldonado, by the community of Infierno, then by boat. Some of the lodges mentioned above also offer guiding and research placements to biology and environmental science graduates. For more details send an SAE to **TReeS: UK**, c/o J Forrest, PO Box 33153, London NW3 4DR, www.tambopata.org. Long-term visitors should be aware that leishmaniasis exists in this area.

Río Madre de Dios

Casa de Hospedaje Mejía, book via **Ceiba Tours**, Av L Velarde 420 in Puerto Maldonado (see Activities and tours, page 638), T082-573567/571428, turismomejia@hotmail.com. A small, family-run, rustic lodge close to Lago Sandoval, with 10 double rooms, none en suite. Canoes available to explore the lake. An English-speaking guide can be arranged. 3 days/2 nights costs US$190.

Eco Amazonia Lodge, book through their office in Lima: Enrique Palacios 292, Miraflores, Lima, T01-242 2708; in Cuzco: Garcilazo 210, of 206, T084-236159, www.ecoamazonia.com.pe. On the Madre de Dios, 1 hr downriver from Puerto Maldonado (ofice Jr Lambayeque 774, T082-573491). 45 basic bungalows and dormitories, good for birdwatching with viewing platforms and tree canopy access, has a pool and Monkey Island, with animals taken from the forest, US$210-230 for 3 days/2 nights including tours.

El Corto Maltés, in Puerto Maldonado, T082-573831, www.cortomaltes-amazonia.com. On the south side of the Madre de Dios river, one of the closest to Puerto Maldonado, halfway to Sandoval, the focus of most visits. Bungalows are very well spaced out and all have a river view. Hot water, huge dining room, well run, pool planned. Ayahuasca sessions can be arranged. US$240 for 3 days/2 nights.

Estancia Bello Horizonte, 20 km northwest of Puerto Maldonado, office in Puerto Maldonado, Jr José María Grain 105, T/F082-572748, www.estanciabellohorizonte. com. In a nice stretch of forest overlooking the Madre de Dios, a small lodge with bungalows for 20 people, with private bath, hammock and pool, transport and breakfast included, or book a package, 3 days/2 nights US$240 with all meals and tours with guide. The lodge belongs to APRONIA and profits fund a home for children with learning difficulties. Suitable for those wanting to avoid a river trip.

Inkaterra Reserva Amazónica Lodge, Rio Madre de Dios Km 15, Margen Izquierda, T082-573534, 45 mins by boat. To book: Inkaterra, Andalucía 174, Lima 18, T01-610 0400, Plazoleta Nazarenas 167 p 2, Cuzco T084-245314, and Cuzco 436, Puerto Maldonado, www.inkaterra.com. A hotel in the jungle with rooms and suites in 35 tastefully decorated, thatched-roof cabañas with solar electricity and hot water, good food in huge dining room supported by a big tree. Jungle tours available with multilingual guides in its own 10,000-ha reserve and to Lago Sandoval, plus a 350-m canopy walkway with a canopy treehouse, two 30-m canopy viewing towers and a Monkey Island (Isla Rolín), for the recovery of primates, which are readapted to their natural environment. 3 day/2 night packages from US$1080 all-inclusive; several packages and room-only otions available. Has the largest number of ant species recorded in a single location: 362. Also offers guided visits to the Hacienda Concepción research centre.

Sandoval Lake Lodge, to book, InkaNatura, Manuel Bañón 461, San Isidro, Lima, T01-440 2022, www.inkanatura.com/sandovallake lodge.asp. Also have offices in Cuzco, C Ricardo Palma J1, Santa Mónica, T084-255255, and Puerto Maldonado, Jr San Martín 755, T082-571037. 1 km beyond Mejía on Lago Sandoval, usually accessed by canoe across the lake after a 3-km walk or rickshaw ride along the trail, this lodge, on a *cocha*, is part-owned by local Brazil-nut collectors. It can accommodate 50 people in 25 rooms, bar and dining area, electricity, hot water. There is a system of trails nearby, guides are available in several languages. Price for 3 days/2 nights is US$278-298 per person based on 2 sharing.

Río Tambopata

Casas de Hospedaje Baltimore, several families in the community of Baltimore on the banks of the Río Tambopata, 60 km upriver. In Puerto Maldonado, Junín cuadra 1, Mz 2-Lote 10F, T082-572380, info@baltimore peru.org.pe. They offer the opportunity to experience the forest close-up, and an insight into daily life in the forest at a more economical price. US$165 double, 4 days/ 3 nights. The 1st night is spent camping, the next 2 staying in a family home. Guiding in Spanish; English-speaking guide can be arranged for US$25. Researchers and volunteers also welcomed by arrangement.

Explorer's Inn, www.explorersinn.com, or book through **Peruvian Safaris**, Alcanfores 459, Miraflores, Lima, T01-447 8888, www.peruviansafaris.com. The office in Puerto Maldonado is at Fonavi H15, T/F082-572078. 7 thatched bungalows, candle lit at night, solar electricity only in the central building with dining room. The lodge is in the TNR, in the part where most research work has been done, 58 km from Puerto Maldonado. It's a 2½-hr ride up the Río Tambopata (1½ hrs return, in the early morning, so take warm clothes and rain gear), one of the best places in Peru for seeing jungle birds (more than 580 species have been recorded here), butterflies (more than 1230 species), also giant river otters, but you probably need more than a 2-day tour to benefit fully from the location. Offers tours through the adjoining community of La Torre to meet local people and find out about their farms (*chacras*) and handicrafts.

Posada Amazonas Lodge, on the Tambopata river, 1½ hrs by vehicle and boat upriver from Puerto Maldonado. Book through **Rainforest Expeditions**, San Francisco de Paula Ugariza 813, Of 201, San Antonio-Miraflores, Lima, T01-241 4880, reservations at T01-997 903650, www.peru nature.com. A collaboration between the tour agency and the local native community of Infierno. Attractive rooms with cold showers, visits to Lake Tres Chimbadas, with good birdwatching including the Tambopata Collpa. Offers trips to a nearby indigenous primary health care project where a native

healer gives guided tours of the medicinal plant garden. Service and guiding is very good. Recommended. The **Tambopata Research Centre**, the company's more intimate, but comfortable lodge, is about 6 hrs further upriver. Rooms are smaller than Posada Amazonas, shared showers, cold water. The lodge is next to the famous Tambopata macaw clay lick. 2 hrs from Posada Amazonas, Rainforest Expeditions also has the **Refugio Amazonas**, close to Lago Condenados. It is the usual stopover for those visiting the collpa. 3 bungalows accommodate 70 people in en-suite rooms, large, kerosene lit, open bedrooms with mosquito nets, well- designed and run, atmospheric. Prices for a 5 day/4 night package at the Posada or Refugio range from US$908-2127. There are many more packages at the different lodges and lots of add-ons.

Tambopata EcoLodge, on the Río Tambopata, make reservations at Nueva Baja 432, Cuzco, T084-245695, operations office at Jr Gonzales Prada 269, Puerto Maldonado, T082-571726, www.tambopatalodge.com. The lodge has rooms and suites with solar-heated water, accommodates 59. Good guides, excellent food. Trips go to Lake Condenados, some to Lake Sachavacayoc, and to the Collpa de Chuncho, guiding mainly in English and Spanish, package from US$307 per person for 3 days/2 nights. Naturalists programme provided.

Wasaí Lodge and Expeditions, on the Río Tambopata, 120 km (4½ hrs) upriver from Puerto Maldonado, T082-572290,

3 hrs return, same owners as Hotel Wasaí in town, www.wasai.com. Small lodge with 7 bungalows for 40 people, 20 km of trails around the lodge, guides in English and Spanish. 3 days/2 nights costs US$337; 5 days/4 nights costs US$596. See also Activities and tours, page 638.

Río Las Piedras p628
Amazon Rainforest Conservation Centre, Las Piedras Amazon Tours, Jr Los Cedros B-17, Los Castaños, Puerto Maldonado, T082-573655, www.laspiedrasamazontour.com. Roughly 8 hrs up Río Las Piedras, in a magnificent location overlooking Lago Soledad, a beautiful oxbow lake, which has a family of giant otters. Surrounding the lodge is a 7000-ha private reserve. 8 comfortable bungalows, with bath, hot water, small balcony. Activities include a viewing platform 35 m up an ironwood tree, a hide overlooking a macaw lick, and walks on the extensive trail network. Most trips break the river journey half way at Tipishca Camp, overlooking an oxbow lake with a family of otters. A 5-day/4- night package costs US$1055 (6-, 7- and 8-day tours available, cheaper for larger groups).
Las Piedras Biodiversity Station is, in effect, a *casa de hospedaje*, T/F082-573922, www.rainforestresearch.netfirms.com. A small lodge in a 4000-ha concession of 'primary' rainforest 90 km up Río Las Piedras. Visitors camp en route to the lodge. With only 20 beds in 10 rooms the lodge offers a more personalized experience of the rainforest. Central dining room, shared bath, no electricity, library, guiding in English/Spanish. Owing to the remoteness of the lodge the minimum package is for 4 days/3 nights, US$470 per person based on a group of 2-3 people, falling to US$239 per person for groups of 10-14 people. Birdwatching trips cost more. They also offer volunteer placements.

To Iberia and Iñapari p628
F Hostal Aquino, Iberia, Km 168. The better of the 2 hotels here. Basic, cold shower.
G Hostal Milagros, Iñapari, at the end of the road, Km 235. Of the 2 basic hotels here, this is the better. With restaurant.

In Assis Brasil, across the border, there are 3 hotels (**E-F**), 2 restaurants and shops.

⬤ Eating

Puerto Maldonado p624, map p625
The best restaurant in town is at the **Hotel Wasaí**, the best lunchtime menu is at the **Cabañaquinta** (see above).
⑪-⑪ Burgos's, Billinghurst 480 y Puno. An atmospheric restaurant with a lovely terrace overlooking the Madre de Dios, serves traditional dishes and has a good set lunch menu, creole buffet Tue-Sun. Good variety and good reputation among locals.
⑪-⑪ Carne Brava, on the Plaza de Armas. One of the smart places for a steak and chips. Similar, also on the Plaza, is **Vaka Loca**.
⑪-⑪ El Califa, Piura 266. Often has bushmeat, mashed banana and palm hearts.
⑪-⑪ El Hornito/Chez Maggy, on the plaza. Cosy atmosphere, busy at weekends, good pizzas, pasta dishes are not such good value.
⑪ D'Caoba, Madre de Dios 439. Serves the most delicious *pollos a la brasa* in town.
⑪ La Casa Nostra, Av León Velarde 515. The best place for snacks, cakes and coffee. Sells huge fruit juices, *tamales*, *papas rellenas* and enormous fancy cakes.
⑪ Namaste, Av León Velarde 469. Moroccan and Indian food, sandwiches, breakfasts and set lunches, in chilled out surroundings.

Cafés
Gustitos del Cura, Loreto 258, Plaza de Armas. An ice cream parlour run by a project for homeless teenagers, offering an amazing range of delicious and unusual tropical juices. The "last delicatessen before the jungle".
Tu Dulce Espera, Av L Velarde 475. Good for evening juices and snacks.

🌙 Bars and clubs

Puerto Maldonado *p624, map p625*
Coconut, east side of the plaza. Disco.
El Witite, Av León Velarde 153. A popular,
good disco, latin music, open Fri and Sat.
Le Boulevard, behind **El Hornito**.
Live music, popular.
T-Saica, Loreto 335. An atmospheric bar
with live music at weekends.
Vikingo and **Juzal**, 26 de Diciembre y 2 de
Mayo. Two popular bars/open-air discos.

⛰ Activities and tours

Manu Biosphere Reserve *p620, map p621*
The tour operators listed below are situated in
Cuzco, the gateway to the reserve. Beware of
pirate operators on the streets of Cuzco who
offer trips to the Reserved Zone of Manu and
end up halfway through the trip changing the
route 'due to emergencies', which in reality
means they have no permits to operate in the
area. The following companies organize trips
into the Multiple Use and Reserved Zones.
Contact them for more details.
Amazon Trails Peru, Tandapata 660, San Blas,
Cuzco, T/F084-437499, T984-714148 (mob),
www.amazontrailsperu.com. Small agency
owned and operated by ornithologist Abraham
Huamán, who has many years' experience
guiding in the region, and Ulrike (Ulla) Maennig.
Mainly offers interesting itineraries into Manu

National Park and to Manu Blanquillo, a private
reserve adjoining the national park. Well-
organized tours include visits to macaw and
tapir licks. Guaranteed deperature dates with
minimum 2 people. Recommended. Also
operate trekking tours in the Cuzco area and
run the **Amazon Hostel** next door to the office,
T084-236770, www.amazonhostelcusco.com.
Bonanza Tours, Suecia 343, T084507871,
www.bonanzatoursperu.com. 3- to 8-day tours
to Manu with local guides, jungle walks, rafting,
kayaking and camp-based excursions. Tours
go down the Madre de Dios as far as the
Blanquillo clay lick, not to the Reserve area.
Expediciones Vilca, Plateros 359, T/F 084-
244751, www.manuvilcaperu.com. Manu
jungle tours of 4-8 days. Will supply sleeping
bags at no extra cost. Minimum 5 people,
maximum 10 per guide. This is the only
economical tour that camps at the Otorongo
camp, which is supposedly quieter than
Salvador where many agencies camp.
There are discounts for students and **SAE**
members. Very efficient, good service.
InkaNatura Travel, Manuel Bañón 461, San
Isidro, Lima, T01-440 2022, www.inkanatura.
com. Also in Cuzco and Chiclayo. A non-profit
organization with proceeds directed back into
projects on sustainable tourism and conservation. Arranges trips to the Manu Reserved Zone,
Manu Wildlife Centre, The Biotrip, 6 days/
5 nights, which takes you through the Andes
to lowland jungle, and **Sandoval Lake Lodge**
in Tambopata. They sell a book called *Peru's*

Amazonian Eden – Manu, US$80, proceeds go to the projects. The same title can be found in other bookshops at a much inflated price.

Manu Ecological Adventures, Plateros 356, T084-261640, www.manuadventures.com. Manu jungle tours, either economical tour in and out overland, or in by land and out by plane, giving you longer in the jungle. Options include a mountain biking descent through the cloudforest and 3 hrs of whitewater rafting on the way to **Erika Lodge** on the upper Río Madre de Dios. Good for guides, food and value. They operate with a minimum of 4 people and a maximum of 10 people per guide.

Manu Expeditions, Clorinda Matto de Turner 330, Urb Magisterial, Cuzco, T084-225990, www.manuexpeditions.com. Mon-Fri 0900-1300, 1530-1900; Sat 0900-1300. English spoken. Run by ornithologist and British Consul Barry Walker of the **Cross Keys Pub**. 3 trips available to the reserve and Manu Wildlife Centre. 2 of the trips on 1st Sun of every month visit a lodge run by Machiguenga people and cost an extra US$150.

Manu Nature Tours, Av Pardo 1046, T084-252721, www.manuperu.com. Owned by Boris Gómez Luna, English spoken. This company aims more for the luxury end of the market. Owns **Manu Lodge** (see page 629) and part-owns **Manu Cloudforest Lodge**. Tours are based around these sites, thus entailing less travel between different areas. Manu Lodge has an extensive trail system and also offers canopy climbing for an additional US$45 per person.

Manu Cloud Forest Lodge

Cock-of-the Rock Dance Company
Performances: Twice daily, year-round

manu nature tours
Manu National Park tour operators since 1985

Manu Lodge, Manu National Park

You would not be yawning if you saw this kitty!
Picture by: R. Quirmbach. German tourist

Avenida Pardo 1046. Cusco-Perú. T (+5184) 252721 or (+5184) 252521
F+ 5184 234793 info@manunaturetours.com   www.manuperu.com

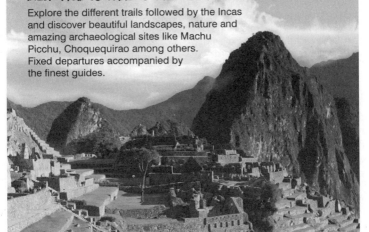

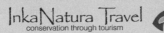

Oropéndola, Av Circunvalación s/n, Urb Guadalupe Mz A Lote 3, Cuzco, T084-241428, www.oropendolaperu.org. Guide Walter Mancilla Huamán is a flora and fauna expert. 5-, 7- and 9-day tours from US$800 per person plus park entrance of US$50. Tours finance the non-profit Oropéndola Project, which manages a 500-ha reserve and operates Oropéndola Lodge and Manu Camping Lodge.
Pantiacolla Tours, Saphy 554, Cuzco, T084-238323, www.pantiacolla.com. Manu jungle tours: 5- and 7-day trips include return flights, the 9-day trip is an overland return. Prices do not include park entrance fee. Guaranteed departure dates regardless of number, maximum 10 people per guide. The trips involve a combination of camping, platform camping and lodges. All clients are given a booklet entitled *Talking About Manu*, written by the Dutch owner, Marianne van Vlaardingen, who is a biologist. She is extremely friendly and helpful. Marianne and her Peruvian husband Gustavo Moscoso have recently opened an ecotourism lodge in conjunction with the Yine native community of Diamante. Yine guides are used and community members are being trained in the various aspects of running the project.

Puerto Maldonado *p624, map p625*
All guides should have a carnet issued by the Ministry of Tourism (DIRCETUR), which verifies them as suitable for trips to other places and confirms their identity. Check that the carnet has not expired. Reputable guides are **Hernán Llave Cortez**, **Romel Nacimiento** and the **Mejía** brothers, all of whom can be contacted on arrival at the airport, if available. Also recommended: **Carlos Borja Gama**, a local guide offering specialist birdwatching and photography trips as well as traditional jungle tours; contact him through **Wasai** (see below) or see www.carlosexpeditions.com.
Víctor Yohamona, T082-968 6279 (mob), victorguideperu@hotmail.com. Speaks English, French and German. Boat hire can be arranged through the Capitanía del Puerto (Río Madre de Dios), T082-573003.

Ceiba Tours, Av L Velarde 420, T082-573567, turismomejia@hotmail.com. Organize local trips, including to their lodge at Lago Sandoval.
Perú Tours, Loreto 176, T082-573244, peru toursytravel@hotmail.com. Organize local trips.

Tambopata National Reserve (TNR)
p627, map p627
Peruvian Safaris, Alcanfores 459, Miraflores, Lima 18, T01-447 8888, www.peruviansafaris. com. For reservations for the Explorer's Inn.
Tambo Tours, 4405 Spring Cypress Rd Suite 210, Spring, Texas, 77388, USA, T1-888-2-GO-PERU (246-7378), T001-281 528 9448, www.2GOPERU.com. See page 164.
Wasaí Lodge and Expeditions, contact Las Higueras 257, Residencial Monterrico, La Molina, Lima 12, T01-436 8792, or Plaza Grau 1, Puerto Maldonado, T/F 082-572290, www.wasai.com. Offering a variety of traditional and innovative tours including river trips, wildlife observation, birdwatching, canoeing, volunteer work, etc. Also offering budget tours for backpackers, see their website for details. For lodge, see page 633.

⊖ Transport

Manu Biosphere Reserve *p620, map p621*
Air
There is an airstrip at **Boca Manu**, but no regular flights from Cuzco. These are arranged the day before, usually by Manu tour operators, if there are enough passengers.

Road
From the Coliseo Cerrado in Cuzco 3 bus companies run to **Pilcopata** Mon, Wed, Fri, returning same night, US$10. They are fully booked even in low season. The best are **Gallito de las Rocas**; also Unancha from Calle Huáscar near the main plaza. Trucks to Pilcopata run on same days, returning Tue, Thu, Sat, 10 hrs in wet season, less in the dry. Only basic supplies are available after leaving Cuzco, so take all your camping and food essentials, including insect repellent.

Transport can be disrupted in the wet season because the road is in poor condition although improvements are being made. *Camioneta* service runs between Pilcopata and **Salvación** to connect with the buses, Mon, Wed, Fri. The same *camionetas* run **Itahuania–Shintuya–Salvación** regularly, when there are sufficient passengers, probably once a day, and 2 trucks a day. On Sun, there is no traffic whatsoever. To **Boca Manu** you can hire a boat in Atalaya, be it a *peque-peque*, or a motorboat it will cost you several hundred dollars. It's cheaper to wait or hope for a boat going empty up to Boca Manu to pick up passengers, when the fare will be US$15 per passenger. Itahuania-Boca Manu in a shared boat with other passengers is US$7.50. A private chartered boat will also be over US$100. From Itahuania, cargo boats leave for **Boca Colorado** via Boca Manu, but only when the boat is fully laden; about 6-8 a week, 9 hrs, US$20. From Boca Colorado colectivos leave from near football field for Puerto Carlos, 1 hr, US$5, ferry across river 10 mins, US$1.65, then colectivos run to **Puerto Maldonado**, 3 hrs, US$10, rough road, lots of stops (in Puerto Maldonado Turismo Boca Colorado, Tacna 342, T082-573435, leave when full). Tour operators usually use their own vehicles for the overland trip from Cuzco to Manu.

Puerto Maldonado *p624, map p625*
Air
To **Lima**, daily with **Lan** and **Star Perú**, via Cuzco. Combis to the airport run along Av 2 de Mayo, 10-15 mins, US$0.75. A mototaxi from town to the airport is US$3.

Airline offices Lan, Av León Velarde y 2 de Mayo, T082-573677. **Star Perú**, Av León Velarde 151, T082-982 7074.

Bus
There are daily buses from the Terminal Terrestre in **Cuzco** with **Transportes Iguazú**, **Mendivil** and **Móvil Tours**. All are on Av Tambopata, blocks 3 and 5 in Puerto

Maldonado. Fare is US$15, depart 1400 from Puerto Maldonado; **Móvil** (at No 529, T082-795785) 1830, 1930, US$16, also have daily service to **Rio Branco** (Brazil), 1200, US$35. Another option is to go from Cuzco to **Urcos**, 1 hr, US$2.25, then look for the Transportes Juan Carlos bus in Urcos' main plaza. This is a Volvo truck modified with seats and windows. To Puerto Maldonado it charges US$13; it leaves about 1500 daily. There are also daily buses from **Mazuko** to Puerto Maldonado with **Transportes Bolpebra** and **Transportes Señor de la Cumbre**, US$3. To **Laberinto**, combis take 50 mins, US$1.50, uncomfortable (return in afternoon daily). To **Juliaca**, Transportes Tambopata and Transportes Aguilas/Tahuamanu, Fizcarrald 609, daily services via San Gabán, at 1700 and 1900 respectively, 18 hrs, US$17. These routes form part of the Interoceánica highway and are being upgraded and paved. More and more public transport companies are using tourist minibus-style vehicles on the Cuzco-Puerto Maldonado route; ask around for a colectivo, they usually leave from close to the bus station. Journey times are decreasing: in Oct 2010 it took 9 hrs in a private vehicle. Public transport takes longer and there may be delays in the wet season but once the highway is complete, expect speedy journeys.

Motorcycles/taxis
Scooters and mopeds can be hired from San Francisco, and others, on the corner of Puno and G Prada for US$1.15 per hr or US$10 per day. No deposit is required but your passport and driving licence need to be shown. Mototaxis around town charge US$0.60; riding pillion on a bike is US$0.30.

Boat
For **Boca Manu** and **Itahuania** take a *colectivo* to **Boca Colorado** and then take a cargo boat (no fixed schedule). From Itahuania there is transport to **Pilcopata** and **Cuzco** (see above under Manu Biosphere Reserve).

Tambopata National Reserve (TNR)
p627, map p627

Boat

A river taxi makes 2 journeys a week, Mon and Thu upriver, Tue and Fri down, up to 10 hrs, US$5 to travel as far as **Wasaí Lodge**. It leaves Puerto Maldonado between 0600 and 0900.

To Iberia and Iñapari *p628*

To the border with **Brazil**, daily buses leave from Jr Ica y Jr Piura for **Iberia** and **Iñapari**. Recommended companies are **Turismo Imperial** and **Real Dorado**. Car colectivos also run from where the road starts across the river, 4 hrs, US$10. See also **Móvil Tours**, above.

🅞 Directory

Puerto Maldonado *p624, map p625*
Banks 0900-1300, 1700-1900. **BCP**, cash advances with Visa, ATM, no commission on TCs. **Banco de la Nación**, cash on MasterCard, quite good rates for TCs. Both on the south side of the plaza. Best rates for cash are at the casas de cambio/gold shops on Puno 6th block. **Consulates** Bolivia, on the north side of the plaza.
Immigration Peruvian immigration, Ica 727, p 2, T082-571069, get your exit stamp here. **Internet** All over town.
Laundry On block 4 of Av León Velarde, next to **Ceiba Tours** office. **Post** Serpost, Av León Velarde 6th block, 0800-2000 (0800-1500 Sun). **Telephone** Telefónica, west side of plaza, adjoining the Municipalidad. Phone office on the plaza, next to **El Hornito**.

Contents

Footprint features

Background

History

Pre-Columbian history

Despite Peru's formidable geographical difficulties and frequent natural disasters, archaeologists have uncovered a pre-Columbian history of highly advanced societies that prevailed against these awesome odds. The coastal desert from Lambayeque department south to Paracas has revealed an 'American Egypt', although this has meant a bias towards the coastal region and a reliance on the contents of tombs for information. Knowledge of these tombs often only comes to light following their looting by gangs of huaqueros (grave robbers), incited by demand from the international antiquities market.

The Incas told the Spaniards that before they established their Tawantinsuyo Empire, the land was overrun by primitives constantly at war with one another. There were, in fact, many other civilized cultures dating back to before 2000 BC. The most accomplished of these were the Chavín and Sechín (circa 900-200 BC), the Paracas-Nazca (circa 200 BC-AD 500), the Huari-Tiahuanaco (circa 750 BC-AD 1000), and the Moche-Chimú (200 BC-AD 1400).

Early settlement

It is generally accepted that the earliest settlers in Peru were related to people who had crossed the Bering Straits from Asia and drifted through the Americas from about 20,000 BC. However, theories of early migrations from across the Pacific and Atlantic have been rife since Thor Heyerdahl's raft expeditions in 1947 and 1969-1970, see also under Túcume, page 448.

The earliest evidence of human presence has been found at three sites: Pikimachay near Ayacucho, Pachamachay in Junín and the Guitarrero Cave in the Callejón de Huaylas. All have a radiocarbon date prior to 9000 BC. It had been thought that village settlement in Peru, on the central coast at Pampa, dated from 2500 BC. The theory was that, between these two dates, people lived nomadically in small groups, mainly hunting and gathering but also cultivating some plants seasonally. Domestication of llamas, alpacas and guinea pigs also began at this time, particularly important for the highland people around the Titicaca basin. Caral, however, has overturned many of the accepted tenets of Peruvian archaeology for this period. Caral is a city, 20 km from the coast in the Supe Valley whose date is about 2600 BC. It is a monumental construction and appears to be easily the oldest city in South America, flourishing for some 500 years. The evidence points to complex urban society beginning much earlier than previously thought and the city seems to have had a primarily religious, rather than warlike purpose. If these deductions are correct, they also upset some long-held beliefs about city-building worldwide being principally bellicose rather than peaceful.

The abundant wealth of marine life produced by the Humboldt Current, especially along the north coast, boosted population growth and settlement in this area. Around 2000 BC climatic change dried up the lomas ('fog meadows'), and drove sea shoals to deeper water. People turned to farming and began to spread inland along river valleys.

Origins of Andean civilization

From the second millennium BC to around the first century BC is known as the Formative Period (also called Preceramic Period VI and Initial Period) when the first signs of the high culture of Andean society appeared. During this period sophisticated irrigation and canal systems were developed, farming productivity increased and communities had more time to devote to building and producing ceramics and textiles. The development of pottery also led to trade and cultural links with other communities. Distribution of land and water to the farmers was probably organized by a corporate authority, and this may have led to the later '*Mit'a*' labour system developed by the Incas.

Above all, this period is characterized by the construction of centres of urban concentration (Caral notwithstanding) that promoted labour specialization and the development of cultural expression. The earliest buildings built were *huacas*, adobe platform mounds, centres of cult or sacred power. Huaca Florida was the largest example of this period, near the Río Rimac, later replaced by Huaca Garagay as a major centre for the area. Similar centres spread along the north coast, such as El Aspero and Piedra Parada.

During this period, however, much more advanced architecture was being built at Kótosh, in the central Andes near Huánuco. Japanese archaeological excavations there in the 1960s revealed a temple with ornamental niches and friezes. Some of the earliest pottery was also found here, showing signs of influence from southern Ecuador and the tropical lowlands, adding weight to theories of Andean culture originating in the Amazon. Radiocarbon dates of some Kótosh remains are as early as 1850 BC.

Chavín and Sechín

For the next 1000 years or so up to circa 900 BC, communities grew and spread inland from the north coast and south along the northern highlands. Farmers still lived in simple adobe or rough stone houses but built increasingly large and complex ceremonial centres, such as at Las Haldas in the Casma Valley (dated at 1700 BC). As farming became more productive and pottery more advanced, commerce grew and states began to develop throughout central and north-central Peru, with the associated signs of social structure and hierarchies.

Around 900 BC a new era was marked by the rise of two important centres; **Chavín de Huantar** in the central Andes and **Sechín Alto**, inland from Casma on the north coast (some date the latter from 1600 BC).

Chavín takes its name from the site of Chavín de Huantar in the northern highlands. This was the first of several 'horizon styles' that were of the greatest importance in Peru and had very widespread influence. The other later ones, the Huari-Tiahuanaco and the Inca, were pan-Peruvian, affecting all parts of the country. The chief importance of Chavín de Huantar was not so much in its highly advanced architecture as in the influence of its cult coupled with the artistic style of its ceramics and other artefacts. The founders of Chavín may have originated in the tropical lowlands as some of its carved monoliths show representations of monkeys and felines.

Objects with Chavín traits have been found all along the coast from Piura to the Lurin valley south of Lima, and its cult ideology spread to temples around the same area. Richard L Burger of Yale University has argued that the extent of Chavín influence has been exaggerated. Many sites on the coast already had their own cult practices and the Chavín idols may have been simply added alongside. There is evidence of an El Niño flood that devastated the north coast around 500 BC. Local cults fell from grace as social order was disrupted and the Chavín cult was snatched up as a timely new alternative.

Chavín cult

The Chavín cult was paralleled by the great advances made at this time in textile production and in some of the earliest examples of metallurgy (whose origins have been attributed to some gold, silver and copper ornaments found in graves in Chongoyape, near Chiclayo, which show Chavín-style features). But earlier evidence has been discovered in the Andahuaylas region, dating from 1800 to 900 BC. The religious symbolism of gold and other precious metals and stones is thought to have been an inspiration behind some of the beautiful artefacts found in the central Andean area. The emergence of social hierarchies also created a demand for luxury goods as status symbols.

The cultural brilliance of Chavín de Huántar was complemented by its contemporary, **Sechín**. This huge granite-faced complex near Casma, 370 km north of Lima, was described by JC Tello as the biggest structure of its kind in the Andes. According to Michael Moseley of Harvard University, Chavín and Sechín may have combined forces, with Sechín as the military power that spread the cultural word of Chavín, but their influence did not reach far to the south where the Paracas and Tiahuanaco cultures held sway.

Upper Formative Period

The Chavín hegemony, which is also known as the Middle Formative Period (or Early Horizon), broke up around 300 BC. The 'unity' of this period was broken and the initial phase of the regional diversification of Andean cultures began. The process of domestication of plants and animals culminated in the Upper Formative Period. Agricultural technology progressed leading to an economic security that permitted a considerable growth in the centres of population. Among the many diverse stylistic/cultural groups of this period are: the Vicus on the north coast; Salinar in the Chicama valley; Paracas Necrópolis on the south coast; and Huarás in the Ancash highlands.

Paracas Necrópolis was the early phase of the Nazca culture and is renowned for the superb technical quality and stylistic variety in its weaving and pottery. The mantos (large, decorated cloth) rank amongst the world's best, and many of the finest examples can be seen in the museums of Lima. The extreme dryness of the desert here has preserved the textiles and ceramics in the mummies' tombs which have been excavated.

Paracas Necrópolis is, in fact, a cemetery located on the slopes of Cerro Colorado, in the Department of Ica, from which 429 funerary bundles were excavated (see page 306). Each bundle is a mummy wrapped in many fine and rough textiles. Paracas Necrópolis corresponds to the last of the 10 phases into which Paracas ceramics have been divided. The previous ones, known as Paracas Cavernas, relate to the Middle Formative Period and were influenced by the Chavín cult.

Nazca culture

The Regional Development Period up to about AD 500, was a time of great social and cultural development. Sizable towns of 5000-10,000 inhabitants grew on the south coast, populated by artisans, merchants, government administrators and religious officials.

One of the most famous cultures of this period, or indeed of pre-Columbian history was the Nazca. The Nazca Lines are a feature of the region. Straight lines, abstract designs and outlines of animals are scratched in the desert surface forming a lighter contrast that can be seen clearly from the air. There are many theories of how and why the lines were made but no explanation has yet been able definitively to establish their place in Peruvian history (see Nazca Lines, page 321). There are similarities between the style of some of the line patterns and that of the pottery and textiles of the same period. It is clear from the scale of the lines and quality of the work that they were important to the Nazca culture.

In contrast to the quantity and quality of the Nazca artefacts found, relatively few major buildings belonging to this period have been uncovered in the southern desert.

Dos Palmas is a complex of rooms and courtyards in the Pisco Valley, while Cahuachi in the Nazca Valley is a large area including adobe platforms, pyramids and a 'wooden Stonehenge' cluster of preserved tree trunks. Most recently excavated are the architectural complex of Los Molinos, with large buildings, patios and passages, and the necropolis of La Muña, both near Palpa. As most of the archaeological evidence of the Nazca culture came from their desert cemeteries, little is known about the lives and social organization of the people. Alpaca hair found in Nazca textiles, however, indicates that there must have been strong trade links with highland people.

Moche culture

Nazca's contemporaries on the north coast were the militaristic Moche who, from about AD 100-800 built up an empire whose traces stretch from Piura in the north to Casma, beyond Chimbote, in the south. The Moche built their capital in the middle of the desert, outside present day Trujillo. It features the pyramid temples of the Huaca del Sol and Huaca de la Luna (see page 423). The Moche roads and system of way stations are thought to have been an early inspiration for the Inca network. The Moche increased the coastal population with intensive irrigation projects. Skillful engineering works were carried out, such as the La Cumbre canal, still in use today, and the Ascope aqueduct.

The Moche's greatest achievement, however, was its artistic genius. Exquisite ornaments in gold, silver and precious stones were made by its craftsmen. Moche pottery progressed through five stylistic periods, most notable for the stunningly lifelike portrait vases. A wide variety of ceremonial and everyday scenes were created in naturalistic ceramics, telling us more about Moche life than is known about other earlier cultures, and perhaps used by them as 'visual aids' to compensate for the lack of a written language (see also page 424).

A spectacular discovery of a Moche royal tomb at **Sipán** was made in February 1987 by Walter Alva, director of the Brüning Archaeological Museum, Lambayeque. Reports of the excavation in the National Geographic magazine (October 1988 and June 1990), talked of the richest unlooted tomb in the New World (see page 446). The find included semi-precious stones brought from Chile and Argentina, and seashells from Ecuador (the Moche were also great navigators).

The cause of the collapse of the Moche Empire around AD 600-700 is unknown, but it may have been started by a 30-year drought at the end of the sixth century, followed by one of the periodic El Niño flash floods (identified by meteorologists from ice thickness in the Andes) and finished by the encroaching forces of the Huari Empire. The decline of the Moche signalled a general tipping of the balance of power in Peru from the north coast to the southern sierra.

Huari-Tiahuanaco

The ascendant Huari-Tiahuanaco movement, from circa AD 600-1000, combined the religious cult of the Tiahuanaco site in the Titicaca basin, with the military dynamism of the Huari, based in the central highlands. The two cultures developed independently but, as had occurred with the Chavín-Sechín association, they are generally thought to have merged compatibly.

Up until their own demise around AD 1440, the Huari-Tiahuanaco had spread their empire and influence from Cajamarca and Lambayeque in the north and across much of southern Peru, northern Bolivia and Argentina. The Huari introduced a new concept in urban life, the great walled urban centre, the best example of which is their capital city,

22 km north of Ayacucho (see page 562). They also made considerable gains in art and technology, building roads, terraces and irrigation canals across the country.

The Huari-Tiahuanaco ran their empire with efficient labour and administrative systems that were later adopted and refined by the Incas. Labour tribute for state projects had been practised by the Moche and was further developed now. But the empire could not contain regional kingdoms who began to fight for land and power. As control broke down, rivalry and coalitions emerged, and the system collapsed.

Chimú culture

After the decline of the Huari Empire, the unity that had been imposed on the Andes was broken. A new stage of autonomous regional or local political organizations began. Among the cultures corresponding to this period were the Kuélap, centred in the Chachapoyas region (see page 503), and the Chimú.

The Chimú culture had two centres. To the north was Lambayeque, near Chiclayo, while to the south, in the Moche valley near present-day Trujillo, was the adobe walled city of Chan Chán. At 20 sq km, this was the largest pre-Hispanic Peruvian city (see page 425).

Chimú has been classified as a despotic state that based its power on wars of conquest. Rigid social stratification existed and power rested in the hands of the great Lord Siquic and the Lord Alaec. These lords were followed in social scale by a group of urban couriers who enjoyed a certain degree of economic power. At the bottom were the peasants and slaves. In AD 1450, the Chimú kingdom was conquered by the Inca Túpac Yupanqui, the son and heir of the Inca ruler Pachacuti Inca Yupanqui.

Inca Dynasty

The origins of the Inca Dynasty are shrouded in mythology. The best known story reported by the Spanish chroniclers talks about Manco Cápac and his sister rising out of Lake Titicaca, created by the Sun as divine founders of a chosen race. This was in approximately AD 1200. Over the next 300 years the small tribe grew to supremacy as leaders of the largest empire ever known in the Americas, the four territories of Tawantinsuyo, united by Cuzco as the umbilicus of the universe. The four quarters of Tawantinsuyo, all radiating out from Cuzco, were: Chinchaysuyo, north and north-west; Cuntisuyo, south and west; Collasuyo, south and east; Antisuyo, east.

At its peak, just before the Spanish Conquest, the Inca Empire stretched from the Río Maule in central Chile, north to the present Ecuador-Colombia border, containing most of Ecuador, Peru, western Bolivia, northern Chile and northwest Argentina. The area was roughly equivalent to France, Belgium, Holland, Luxembourg, Italy and Switzerland combined (980,000 sq km).

The first Inca ruler, Manco Cápac, moved to the fertile Cuzco region, and established Cuzco as his capital. Successive generations of rulers were fully occupied with local conquests of rivals, such as the Colla and Lupaca to the south, and the Chanca to the northwest. At the end of Inca Viracocha's reign the hated Chanca were finally defeated, largely thanks to the heroism of one of his sons, Pachacútec Inca Yupanqui, who was subsequently crowned as the new ruler.

From the start of Pachacútec's own reign in AD 1438, imperial expansion grew in earnest. With the help of his son and heir, Topa Inca, territory was conquered from the Titicaca basin south into Chile, and all the north and central coast down to the Lurin Valley. The Incas also subjugated the Chimú, their highly sophisticated rivals on the coast (see above). Typical of the Inca method of government, some of the Chimú skills were assimilated into their own political and administrative system, and some Chimú nobles were even given positions in Cuzco.

Perhaps the pivotal event in Inca history came in AD 1527 with the death of the ruler, Huayna Capac. Civil war broke out in the confusion over his rightful successor. One of his legitimate sons, Huáscar, ruled the southern part of the empire from Cuzco. Atahualpa, Huáscar's half-brother, governed Quito, the capital of Chinchaysuyo. In AD 1532, soon after Atahualpa had won the civil war, Francisco Pizarro arrived in Tumbes with 167 conquistadores, a third of them on horseback. Atahualpa's army was marching south, probably for the first time, when he clashed with Pizarro at Cajamarca.

Francisco Pizarro's only chance against the formidable imperial army he encountered at Cajamarca was a bold stroke. He drew Atahualpa into an ambush, slaughtered his guards, promised him liberty if a certain room were filled with treasure, and finally killed him on the pretext that another Inca army was on its way to free him. Pushing on to Cuzco, he was at first hailed as the executioner of a traitor: Atahualpa had ordered the death of Huáscar in AD 1533, while himself a captive of Pizarro, and his victorious generals were bringing the defeated Huáscar to see his half-brother. Panic followed when the conquistadores set about sacking the city, and they fought off with difficulty an attempt by Manco Inca to recapture Cuzco in AD 1536.

Inca society

The Incas were a small aristocracy numbering only a few thousand, centred in the highland city of Cuzco, at 3400 m. They rose gradually as a small regional dynasty, similar to others in the Andes of that period, starting around AD 1200. Then in the mid-1400s, they began to expand explosively under Pachacútec, a sort of Andean Alexander the Great, and later his son, Topa. Under 100 years later, they fell before the rapacious warriors of Spain. The Incas were not the first dynasty in Andean history to dominate their neighbours, but they did it more thoroughly and went further than anyone before them.

Empire building

Enough remains today of their astounding highways, cities and agricultural terracing for people to marvel and wonder how they accomplished so much in so short a time. They seem to have been amazingly energetic, industrious and efficient – and the reports of their Spanish conquerors confirm this hypothesis.

They must also have had the willing cooperation of most of their subject peoples, most of the time. In fact, the Incas were master diplomats and alliance-builders first, and military conquerors only second, if the first method of expansion failed. The Inca skill at generating wealth by means of highly efficient agriculture and distribution brought them enormous prestige and enabled them to 'out-gift' neighbouring chiefs in huge royal feasts involving ritual outpourings of generosity, often in the form of vast gifts of textiles, exotic products from distant regions, and perhaps wives to add blood ties to the alliance. The 'out-gifted' chief was required by the Andean laws of reciprocity to provide something in return, and this would usually be his loyalty, as well as a levy of manpower from his own chiefdom.

Thus, with each new alliance the Incas wielded greater labour forces and their mighty public works programmes surged ahead. These were administered through an institution known as *mit'a*, a form of taxation through labour. The state provided the materials, such as wool and cotton for making textiles, and the communities provided skills and labour.

Mit'a contingents worked royal mines, royal plantations for producing coca leaves, royal quarries and so on. The system strove to be equitable, and workers in such hardship posts as high altitude mines and lowland coca plantations were given correspondingly shorter terms of service.

Organization

Huge administrative centres were built in different parts of the empire, where people and supplies were gathered. Articles such as textiles and pottery were produced there in large workshops. Work in these places was carried out in a festive manner, with plentiful food, drink and music. Here was Andean reciprocity at work: the subject supplied his labour, and the ruler was expected to provide generously while he did so.

Aside from *mit'a* contributions there were also royal lands claimed by the Inca as his portion in every conquered province, and worked for his benefit by the local population. Thus, the contribution of each citizen to the state was quite large, but apparently, the imperial economy was productive enough to sustain this.

Another institution was the practice of moving populations around: inserting loyal groups into restive areas, and removing recalcitrant populations to loyal areas. These movements of *mitmakuna*, as they were called, were also used to introduce skilled farmers and engineers into areas where productivity needed to be raised.

Communications

The huge empire was held together by an extensive and highly efficient highway system. There were an estimated 30,000 km of major highway, most of it neatly paved and drained, stringing together the major Inca sites. Two parallel highways ran north to south, along the coastal desert strip and the mountains, and dozens of east-west roads crossing from the coast to the Amazon fringes. These roadways took the most direct routes, with wide stone stairways zig-zagging up the steepest mountain slopes and rope suspension bridges crossing the many narrow gorges of the Andes. The north-south roads formed a great axis that eventually came to be known as **Capaq Ñan** – 'Royal', or 'Principal Road', in Quechua – which exceeded in grandeur not only the other roads, but also their utilitarian concept. They became the Incas' symbol of power over men and over the sacred forces of nature. So marvellous were these roads that the Spaniards who saw them at the height of their glory said that there was nothing comparable in all Christendom.

Every 12 km or so there was a *tambo*, or way station, where goods could be stored and travellers lodged. The *tambos* were also control points, where the Inca state's accountants tallied movements of goods and people. Even more numerous than *tambos*, were the huts of the *chasquis*, or relay runners, who continually sped royal and military messages along these highways.

The Inca state kept records and transmitted information in various ways. Accounting and statistical records were kept on skeins of knotted strings known as *quipus*. Numbers employed the decimal system (although Italian engineer Nicolino De Pasquale claimed in 2006 the number system was based on 40), and colours indicated the categories being recorded. An entire class of people, known as *quipucamayocs*, existed whose job was to create and interpret these. Neither the Incas nor their Andean predecessors had a system of writing as we understand it, but there may have been a system of encoding language into *quipus*. Archaeologists are studying this problem today. History and other forms of knowledge were transmitted via songs and poetry. Music and dancing, full of encoded information that could be read by the educated elite, were part of every major ceremony and public event information was also carried in textiles, which had for millennia been the most vital expression of Andean culture.

Textiles

Clothing carried insignia of status, ethnic origin, age and so on. Special garments were made and worn for various rites of passage. It has been calculated that, after agriculture, no activity was more important to Inca civilization than weaving. Vast stores of textiles were maintained to sustain the Inca system of ritual giving. Armies and *mit'a* workers were partly paid in textiles. The finest materials were reserved for the nobility, and the Inca emperor himself displayed his status by changing into new clothes every day and having the previous day's burned.

Most weaving was done by women, and the Incas kept large numbers of 'chosen women' in female-only houses all over the empire, partly for the purpose of supplying textiles to the elite and for the many deities, to whom they were frequently given as burned offerings. These women had other duties, such as making *chicha* – the Inca corn beer that was consumed and sacrificed in vast quantities on ceremonial occasions. They also became wives and concubines to the Inca elite and loyal nobilities. And some may have served as priestesses of the moon, in parallel to the male priesthood of the sun.

Religious worship

The Incas have always been portrayed as sun-worshippers, but it now seems that they were mountain-worshippers too. Recent research has shown that Machu Picchu was at least partly dedicated to the worship of the surrounding mountains, and Inca sacrificial victims have been excavated on frozen Andean peaks at 6700 m. In fact, until technical climbing was invented, the Incas held the world altitude record for humans.

Human sacrifice was not common, but every other kind was, and ritual attended every event in the Inca calendar. The main temple of Cuzco was dedicated to the numerous deities: the Sun, the Moon, Venus, the Pleiades, the Rainbow, Thunder and Lightning, and the countless religious icons of subject peoples which had been brought to Cuzco, partly in homage, partly as hostage. Here, worship was continuous and the fabulous opulence included gold cladding on the walls, and a famous garden filled with life-size objects of gold and silver. Despite this pantheism, the Incas acknowledged an overall Creator God, whom they called Viracocha. A special temple was dedicated to him, at Raqchi, about 100 km southeast of Cuzco. Part of it still stands today.

Military forces

The conquering Spaniards noted with admiration the Inca storehouse system, still well-stocked when they found it, despite several years of civil war among the Incas. Besides textiles, military equipment, and ritual objects, they found huge quantities of food. Like most Inca endeavours, the food stores served a multiple purpose: to supply feasts, to provide during lean times, to feed travelling work parties, and to supply armies on the march.

Inca armies were able to travel light and move fast because of this system. Every major Inca settlement also incorporated great halls where large numbers of people could be accommodated, or feasts and gatherings held, and large squares or esplanades for public assemblies.

Inca technology is usually deemed inferior to that of contemporary Europe. Their military technology certainly was. They had not invented iron-smelting, and basically fought with clubs, palmwood spears, slings, wooden shields, cotton armour and straw-stuffed helmets. They did not even make much use of the bow and arrow, a weapon they were well aware of. Military tactics, too, were primitive. The disciplined formations of the Inca armies quickly dissolved into melees of unbridled individualism once battle was joined. This, presumably, was because warfare constituted a theatre of manly prowess, but was not the main priority of Inca life. Its form was ritualistic. Battles were suspended by both sides for religious observance. Negotiation, combined with displays of superior Inca strength, usually achieved victory, and total annihilation of the enemy was not on the agenda.

Architecture
Other technologies, however, were superior in every way to their 16th century counterparts: textiles; settlement planning; and agriculture in particular with its sophisticated irrigation and soil conservation systems, ecological sensitivity, specialized crop strains and high productivity under the harshest conditions. The Incas fell short of their Andean predecessors in the better-known arts of ancient America – ceramics, textiles and metalwork – but it could be argued that their supreme efforts were made in architecture, stoneworking, landscaping, roadbuilding, and the harmonious combination of these elements.

These are the outstanding survivals of Inca civilization, which still remain to fascinate the visitor: the huge, exotically close-fit blocks of stone, cut in graceful, almost sensual curves; the astoundingly craggy and inaccessible sites encircled by great sweeps of Andean scenery; the rhythmic layers of farm terracing that provided land and food to this still-enigmatic people. The finest examples of Inca architecture can be seen in the city of Cuzco and throughout the Sacred Valley. As more evidence of Inca society is uncovered each year, our knowledge of these remarkable people can only improve: in 2002 alone two new cities in the Vilcabamba region were revealed, as well as the huge cemetery at Purucucho (see Lima, page 97) and a mummy at Machu Picchu.

Ruling elite
The ruling elite lived privileged lives in their capital at Cuzco. They reserved for themselves and privileged insiders certain luxuries, such as the chewing of coca, the wearing of fine vicuña wool, and the practice of polygamy. But they were an austere people, too. Everyone had work to do, and the nobility were constantly posted to state business throughout the empire. Young nobles were expected to learn martial skills, as well as read the quipus, speak both Quechua and the southern language of Aymara, and know the epic poems.

The Inca elite belonged to royal clans known as panacas, which each had the unusual feature of being united around veneration of the mummy of their founding ancestor – a previous Inca emperor, unless they happened to belong to the panaca founded by the Inca emperor who was alive at the time. Each new emperor built his own palace in Cuzco and amassed his own wealth rather than inheriting it from his forebears, which perhaps helps to account for the urge to unlimited expansion.

This urge ultimately led the Incas to overreach themselves. Techniques of diplomacy and incorporation no longer worked as they journeyed farther from the homeland and met ever-increasing resistance from people less familiar with their ways. During the reign of Wayna Cápac, the last emperor before the Spanish invasion, the Incas had to establish a northern capital at Quito in order to cope with permanent war on their northern frontier. Following Wayna Cápac's death came a devastating civil war between Cuzco and Quito, and immediately thereafter came the Spanish invasion. Tawantisuyo, the empire of the four quarters, collapsed with dizzying suddenness.

Conquest and after

Peruvian history after the arrival of the Spaniards was not just a matter of conquistadores versus Incas. The vast majority of the huge empire remained unaware of the conquest for many years. The Chimú and the Chachapoyas cultures were powerful enemies of the Incas. The Chimú developed a highly sophisticated culture and a powerful empire stretching for 560 km along the coast from Tumbes south to present-day Lima. Their history was well-recorded by the Spanish chroniclers and continued through the conquest possibly up to about 1600. The Kuélap/ Chachapoyas people were not so much an empire as a loose-knit "confederation of ethnic groups with no recognized capital" (Morgan Davis *Chachapoyas: The Cloud People*, Ontario, 1988). But the culture did develop into an advanced society with great skill in roads and monument building. Their fortress at Kuélap was known as the most impregnable in Tawantinsuyo. It remained intact against Inca attack and Manco Inca even tried, unsuccessfully, to gain refuge here against the Spaniards.

In 1535, wishing to secure his communications with Spain, Pizarro founded Lima, near the ocean, as his capital. The same year Diego de Almagro set out to conquer Chile. Unsuccessful, he returned to Peru, quarrelled with Pizarro, and in 1538 fought a pitched battle with Pizarro's men at the Salt Pits, near Cuzco. He was defeated and put to death. Pizarro, who had not been at the battle, was assassinated in his palace in Lima by Almagro's son three years later.

For the next 27 years each succeeding representative of the Kingdom of Spain sought to subdue the Inca successor state of Vilcabamba, north of Cuzco, and to unify the fierce Spanish factions. Francisco de Toledo (appointed 1568) solved both problems during his 14 years in office: Vilcabamba was crushed in 1572 and the last reigning Inca, Túpac Amaru, put to death.

For the next 200 years the Viceroys closely followed Toledo's system, if not his methods. The Major Government – the Viceroy, the Audiencia (High Court), and *corregidores* (administrators) – ruled through the Minor Government (indigenous chiefs put in charge of large groups of natives), a rough approximation to the original Inca system.

Towards independence

There was an indigenous rising in 1780, under the leadership of an Inca noble who called himself Túpac Amaru II. He and many of his lieutenants were captured and put to death under torture at Cuzco. Another indigenous leader in revolt suffered the same fate in 1814, but this last flare-up had the sympathy of many of the locally born Spanish, who resented their status, inferior to the Spaniards born in Spain, the refusal to give them any but the lowest offices, the high taxation imposed by the home government, and the severe restrictions upon trade with any country but Spain.

Help came to them from the outside world. José de San Martín's Argentine troops, convoyed from Chile under the protection of Lord Cochrane's squadron, landed in southern Peru on 7 September 1820. San Martín proclaimed Peruvian independence at Lima on 28 July 1821, though most of the country was still in the hands of the Viceroy, José de La Serna. Bolívar, who had already freed Venezuela and Colombia, sent Antonio José de Sucre to Ecuador where, on 24 May 1822, he gained a victory over La Serna at Pichincha.

San Martín, after a meeting with Bolívar at Guayaquil, left for Argentina and a self-imposed exile in France, while Bolívar and Sucre completed the conquest of Peru by defeating La Serna at the battle of Junín (6 August 1824) and the decisive battle of Ayacucho (9 December 1824). For over a year there was a last stand in the Real Felipe fortress at Callao by the Spanish troops under General Rodil before they capitulated on 22 January 1826. Bolívar was invited to stay in Peru, but left for Colombia in 1826.

Post-independence Peru

Following independence Peru attempted a confederation with Bolivia in the 1830s but this proved temporary. Then, in 1879 came the disastrous War of the Pacific, in which Peru and Bolivia were defeated by Chile and Peru lost its southern territory.

Economic change

Peru's economic development since independence has been based upon the export of minerals and foodstuffs to Europe and the United States. Guano, a traditional fertilizer in Peru and derived from the manure of seabirds, was first shipped to Europe in 1841. In the three decades that followed it became an important fertilizer in Europe and by the early 1860s over 80% of the Peruvian government's revenues were derived from its export. Much of this income, though, went to pay off interest on the spiralling national debt. By the 1870s the richer deposits were exhausted and cheaper alternatives to guano were being discovered. One of these was nitrates, discovered in the Atacama desert, but Peru's defeat by Chile in the War of the Pacific ensured that she would lose her share of this wealth.

After the decline of guano, Peru developed several new exports. In the 1890s the demand in Europe and USA for Amazonian rubber for tyres and for use in electrical components led to a brief boom in both the Brazilian and Peruvian Amazon. The Peruvian industry was based around the port of Iquitos. This boom was short-lived as cheaper rubber was soon being produced from plantations in the East Indies. Peru's colonial mineral exports, gold and silver, were replaced by copper, although ownership was mainly under control of foreign companies, particularly the US-based Cerro de Pasco Copper Corporation and Northern Peru Mining. Oil became another important product, amounting to 30% of Peruvian exports by 1930. Further exports came from sugar and cotton, which were produced on coastal plantations, see also page 660.

Social change

Independence from Spanish rule meant that power passed into the hands of the Creole elite with no immediate alternation of the colonial social system. The *contribución de indíginas* (the colonial tribute collected from the native peoples) was not abolished until 1854, the same year as the ending of slavery.

Until the 1970s land relations in the sierra changed very little, as the older landholding families continued to exert their traditional influence over 'their' peones. The traditional elite, the so-called '44 families', were still very powerful, though increasingly divided between the coastal aristocracy with their interests in plantation agriculture and trade, and the serrano elite, more conservative and inward looking.

The pattern of export growth did, however, have major social effects on the coast. The expansion of plantation agriculture and mining led to the growth of a new labour force; this was supplied partially by Chinese indentured labourers, about 100,000 of whom

War of the Pacific

One of the major international wars in Latin America since independence, this conflict has its roots in a border dispute between Chile and Bolivia. The frontier between the two in the Atacama desert was ill-defined.

There had already been one conflict, in 1836-1839, when Chile defeated Peru and Bolivia, putting an end to a confederation of the two states. The discovery of nitrates in the Atacama only complicated relations, for in the Bolivian Atacama province of Antofagasta nitrates were exploited by Anglo-Chilean companies.

In 1878 the Bolivian government, short of revenue, attempted to tax the Chilean-owned Antofagasta Railroad and Nitrate Company. When the company refused to pay, the Bolivians seized the company's assets. The Chilean government claimed that the Bolivian action broke an 1874 agreement between the two states. When Peru announced that it would honour a secret alliance with Bolivia by supporting her, the Chilean president, Aníbal Pinto, declared war on both states.

Control of the sea was vital, and this was where Chile concentrated her efforts. Following a successful naval campaign, the Chileans invaded the southern province of Tarapacá and then landed troops north of Tacna, seizing the town in May 1880 before capturing Arica, further south. In January 1881 the Chilean armies seized control of Lima.

Despite these defeats and the loss of their capital, Peru did not sue for peace, although Bolivia had already signed a ceasefire, giving up her coastal province. Under the 1883 peace settlement Peru gave up Tarapacá to Chile. Although the provinces of Tacna and Arica were to be occupied by Chile for 10 years, it was not until 1929 that an agreement was reached under which Tacna was returned to Peru, while Chile kept Arica. Apart from souring relations between Chile and her two northern neighbours to this day, the war gave Chile a monopoly over the world's supply of nitrates and enabled her to dominate the southern Pacific coast.

arrived between 1855 and 1875, partly by the migration of indigenous people from the sierra and partly by the descendants of black slaves.

Political developments

19th century

For much of the period since independence Peruvian political life has been dominated by the traditional elites. Political parties have been slow to develop and the roots of much of the political conflict and instability which have marked the country's history lie in personal ambitions and in regional and other rivalries within the elite.

The early years after independence were particularly chaotic as rival caudillos (political bosses) who had fought in the independence wars vied with each other for power. The increased wealth brought about by the guano boom led to greater stability, though political corruption became a serious problem under the presidency of José Rufino Echenique (1851-1854) who paid out large sums of the guano revenues as compensation to upper class families for their (alleged) losses in the Wars of Independence. Defeat by Chile in the War of the Pacific discredited civilian politicians even further and led to a period of military rule in the 1880s.

Early 20th century

Even though the voting system was changed in 1898, this did little to change the dominance of the elite. Voting was not secret so landowners herded their workers to the polls and watched to make sure they voted correctly. Yet voters were also lured by promises as well as threats. One of the more unusual presidents was Guillermo Billinghurst (1912-1914) who campaigned on the promise of a larger loaf of bread for five cents, thus gaining the nickname of 'Big Bread Billinghurst'. As president he proposed a publicly funded housing programme, supported the introduction of an eight hour day and was eventually overthrown by the military who, along with the elite, were alarmed at his growing popularity among the urban population.

The 1920s This decade was dominated by Augusto Leguía. After winning the 1919 elections Leguía claimed that Congress was plotting to prevent him from becoming president and induced the military to help him close Congress. Backed by the armed forces, Leguía introduced a new constitution which gave him greater powers and enabled him to be re-elected in 1924 and 1929. Claiming his goal was to prevent the rise of communism, he proposed to build a partnership between business and labour. A large programme of public works, particularly involving building roads, bridges and railways, was begun, the work being carried out by poor rural men who were forced into unpaid building work. The Leguía regime dealt harshly with critics: opposition newspapers were closed and opposition leaders arrested and deported. His overthrow in 1930 ended what Peruvians call the *Oncenio* or 11-year period.

The 1920s also saw the emergence of a political thinker who would have great influence in the future, not only in Peru but elsewhere in Latin America. José Carlos Mariátegui, a socialist writer and journalist, argued that the solution to Peru's problems lay in the reintegration of the indigenous people through land reform and the breaking up of the great landed estates. See also page 677.

The formation of APRA Another influential thinker of this period was Víctor Raúl Haya de la Torre, a student exiled by Leguía in 1924. He returned after the latter's fall to create the Alianza Popular Revolucionaria Americana (APRA), a political party which called for state control of the economy, nationalization of key industries and protection of the middle classes, which, Haya de la Torre argued, were threatened by foreign economic interests.

In 1932 APRA seized control of Trujillo; when the army arrived to deal with the rising, the rebels murdered about 50 hostages, including 10 army officers. In reprisal the army murdered about 1000 local residents suspected of sympathizing with APRA. APRA eventually became the largest and easily the best-organized political party in Peru, but the distrust of the military and the upper class for Haya de la Torre ensured that he never became president.

A turning point in Peruvian history occurred in 1948 with the seizure of power by General Manuel Odría, backed by the coastal elite. Odría outlawed APRA and went on to win the 1950 election in which he was the only candidate. He pursued policies of encouraging export earnings and also tried to build up working class support by public works projects in Lima. Faced with a decline in export earnings and the fall in world market prices after 1953, plus increasing unemployment, Odría was forced to stand down in 1956.

In 1962 Haya de la Torre was at last permitted to run for the presidency. But although he won the largest percentage of votes he was prevented from taking office by the armed forces who seized power and organized fresh elections for 1963. In these the military obtained the desired result: Haya de la Torre came second to Fernando Belaúnde Terry.

Belaúnde attempted to introduce reforms, particularly in the landholding structure of the sierra; when these reforms were weakened by landowner opposition in Congress, peasant groups began invading landholdings in protest.

At the same time, under the influence of the Cuban revolution, terrorist groups began operating in the sierra. Military action to deal with this led to the deaths of an estimated 8000 people. Meanwhile Belaúnde's attempts to solve a long-running dispute with the International Petroleum Company (a subsidiary of Standard Oil) resulted in him being attacked for selling out to the unpopular oil company and contributed to the armed forces' decision to seize power in 1968.

The 1968 coup

This was a major landmark in Peruvian history. Led by General Juan Velasco Alvarado, the Junta had no intention of handing power back to the civilians. A manifesto issued on the day of the coup attacked the 'unjust social and economic order' and argued for its replacement by a new economic system 'neither capitalist nor communist'. Partly as a result of their experiences in dealing with the insurgency, the coup leaders concluded that agrarian reform was a priority.

Wide-ranging land reform was launched in 1969, during which large estates were taken over and reorganized into cooperatives. By the mid-1970s, 75% of productive land was under cooperative management. The government also tried to improve the lives of shanty-town dwellers around Lima, as well as attempting to increase the influence of workers in industrial companies. At the same time efforts were made to reduce the influence of foreign companies. Soon after the coup, IPC was nationalized, to be followed by other transnationals including ITT, Chase Manhattan Bank and the two mining giants Cerro de Pasco and Marcona Mining. After a dispute with the US government, compensation was agreed.

Understandably, opposition to the Velasco government came from the business and landholding elite. The government's crack-down on expressions of dissent, the seizure of newspapers and taking over of TV and radio stations all offended sections of the urban middle class. Trade unions and peasant movements found that, although they agreed with many of the regime's policies, it refused to listen and expected their passive and unqualified support. As world sugar and copper prices dropped, inflation rose and strikes increased. Velasco's problems were further increased by opposition within the armed forces and by his own ill-health. In August 1975 he was replaced by General Francisco Morales Bermúdez, a more conservative officer, who dismantled some of Velasco's policies and led the way to a restoration of civilian rule.

Belaúnde returned to power in 1980 by winning the first elections after military rule. His government was badly affected by the 1982 debt crisis and the 1981-1983 world recession, and inflation reached over 100% a year in 1983-1984. His term was also marked by the growth of the Maoist movement **Sendero Luminoso** (Shining Path) and the smaller, Marxist **Movimiento Revolucionario Túpac Amaru** (MRTA) – see box page, 658.

Initially conceived in the University of Ayacucho, Shining Path gained most support for its goal of overthrowing the whole system of Lima-based government from highland indigenous and migrants to urban shanty towns. The activities of Sendero Luminoso and the MRTA were effectively curtailed after the arrest of both their leaders in 1992. Víctor Polay of MRTA was arrested in June and Abimael Guzmán of Sendero Luminoso was captured in September. Although Sendero did not capitulate, many of its members in

1994-1995 took advantage of the Law of Repentance, which guaranteed lighter sentences in return for surrender, and freedom in exchange for valuable information. Meanwhile, MRTA was thought to have ceased operations (see below).

In 1985 APRA, in opposition for over 50 years, finally came to power. With Haya de la Torre dead, the APRA candidate Alan García Pérez won the elections and was allowed to take office by the armed forces. García attempted to implement an ambitious economic programme intended to solve many of Peru's deep-seated economic and social problems. He cut taxes, reduced interest rates, froze prices and devalued the currency. However, the economic boom that this produced in 1986-1987 stored up problems as increased incomes were spent on imports. Moreover, the government's refusal to pay more than 10% of its foreign debt meant that it was unable to borrow. In 1988 inflation hit 3000% and unemployment soared. By the time his term of office ended in 1990 Peru was bankrupt and García and APRA were discredited.

Modern Peru

Peru under Fujimori

In presidential elections held over two rounds in 1990, **Alberto Fujimori** of the Cambio 90 movement defeated the novelist **Mario Vargas Llosa** (see box, page 680), who belonged to the Fredemo (Democratic Front) coalition. Fujimori, without an established political network behind him, failed to win a majority in either the senate or the lower house. Lack of congressional support was one of the reasons behind the dissolution of congress and the suspension of the constitution on 5 April 1992. The president declared that he needed a freer hand to introduce market reforms and combat terrorism and drug trafficking, at the same time as rooting out corruption.

In elections to a new, 80-member Democratic Constituent Congress (CCD) in November 1992, Fujimori's Cambio 90/Nueva Mayoría coalition won a majority of seats. Though three major political parties – APRA, Acción Popular and the Movimiento de Libertad – boycotted the elections, they satisfied many aid donor's requirements for the resumption of financial assistance.

A new constitution drawn up by the CCD was approved by a narrow majority of the electorate in October 1993. Among the new articles were the immediate re-election of the president (previously prohibited for one presidential term), the establishment of a single-chamber congress, the designation of Peru as a market economy and the favouring of foreign investment. As expected, Fujimori stood for re-election on 9 April 1995 and the opposition chose as an independent to stand against him former UN General Secretary, Javier Pérez de Cuéllar. Fujimori was re-elected by a resounding margin, winning about 65% of the votes cast. The coalition that supported him also won a majority in Congress.

The government's success in most economic areas did not appear to accelerate the distribution of foreign funds for social projects. Rising unemployment and the austerity imposed by economic policy continued to cause hardship for many, despite the government's stated aim of alleviating poverty.

Dramatic events on 17 December 1996 thrust several of these issues into sharper focus: 14 Túpac Amaru terrorists infiltrated a reception at the Japanese Embassy in Lima, taking 490 hostages. Among the rebel's demands were the release of their imprisoned colleagues, better treatment for prisoners and new measures to raise living standards. Most of the hostages were released and negotiations were pursued during a stalemate that lasted until 22 April 1997. The president took sole responsibility for the successful, but risky assault that freed all the hostages (one died of heart failure) and killed all the terrorists. By not yielding to Túpac Amaru, Fujimori regained much popularity.

But this masked the fact that no steps had been taken to ease social problems. It also deflected attention from Fujimori's plans to stand for a third term following his unpopular manipulation of the law to persuade Congress that the new constitution did not apply to his first period in office. His chances of winning looked remote as demands grew for a more open, democratic approach, though opposition to his standing for a third term of office remained fragmented. Ultimately, his chances hinged on the economy, which looked to be improving until the worst El Niño of the 20th century hit Peru in late 1997, causing chaos, many deaths and devastating damage.

Fujimori's unpopularity was further driven home by Shell-Mobil's withdrawal from the multi-million dollar Camisea natural gas project, which was supposed to pull Peru out of its energy deficit. In July 1998, a 1.4 million-name petition was presented to the National Electoral Authority, requesting a referendum on whether Fujimori should be allowed to stand for a third term. In spite of the amendment to the constitution following Fujimori's auto golpe in 1993, allowing presidents to run for only two successive terms, the president had, in 1996, pushed through congress a law of 'authentic interpretation' of the constitution, allowing him to run for election once more on the grounds that the new constitution did not apply to his first term. All the same, until the last month of campaigning for the 2000 presidential elections, Fujimori had a clear lead over his rivals, who insisted that he should not stand. Moreover, local and international observers voiced increasing concern over the state domination of the media. Meanwhile, the popularity of a fourth candidate, Alejandro Toledo, a former World Bank official of humble origins, surged to such an extent that he and Fujimori were neck and neck in the first poll. Toledo, a pro-marketeer given to left-wing rhetoric, and his supporters claimed that Fujimori's slim majority was the result of fraud, a view echoed in the pressure put on the president, by the US government among others, to allow a second ballot. The run-off election, on 28 May 2000, was also contentious since foreign observers, including the Organization of American States, said the electoral system was unprepared and flawed, proposing a postponement. The authorities refused to delay. Toledo boycotted the election and Fujimori was returned unopposed, but with scant approval. Having won, he proposed "to strengthen democracy".

This pledge proved to be utterly worthless following the airing of a secretly shot video on 14 September 2000 of Fujimori's close aide and head of the National Intelligence Service (SIN), Vladimiro Montesinos, allegedly handing US$15,000 to a congressman, Alberto Kouri, to persuade him to switch allegiances to Fujimori's coalition. Fujimori's demise was swift. His initial reaction was to close down SIN and announce new elections, eventually set for 8 April 2001, at which he would not stand. Montesinos was declared a wanted man and he fled to Panama, where he was denied asylum. He returned to Peru in October and Fujimori personally led the search parties to find his former ally. Peruvians watched in amazement as this game of cat-and-mouse was played out on their TV screens. While Montesinos himself successfully evaded capture, investigators began to uncover the extent of his empire, which held hundreds of senior figures in its web. His activities encompassed extortion, money-laundering, bribery, intimidation, alleged arms and drugs dealing and possible links with the CIA and death squads. Swiss bank accounts in his name were found to contain about US$70 million, while other millions were

Revolutionary movements – until the final victory

Officially speaking, the Peruvian civil war ended in 1992. On 12 September of that year, leader of the Shining Path, Abimael Guzmán, stood after his arrest in front of the television cameras, reduced from "National Enemy Number One" to "Prisoner Number 1509". Nobody knows how many people died in the carnage that lasted for more than a decade, the most conservative estimates speak of 35,000.

The Maoist Shining Path was officially fighting for the resurrection of the Inca state and against Western imperialism and white supremacy in this racially and economically divided society. However, its methods were brutal and counter-productive. They included intimidation and the killing of several progressive leaders and hundreds of members of other revolutionary movements (including the contemporaneous Movimiento Revolucionario Túpac Amaru – MRTA). The plan was to reduce Peru's economy to ashes by destroying its infrastructure, military and police posts, power plants, tourism and other 'strategic targets'.

Both the army and the Shining Path were responsible for the eradication of countless towns and villages in the jungle and Andes, mass executions and torture of civilians. Sandwiched between these opposing forces, villagers in the mountains were forced to migrate to the coast, settling in enormous shantytowns, doubling the population of Lima in little more than a decade. Both sides forcibly recruited children from poor neighbour-hoods and controlled the traffic in drugs (they took it in turns to 'tax' the same airstrips used by Colombian drug cartels).

During his term of office ex-president Fujimori did remove terrorism from Peru, however questionable the methods now appear. Evidence has recently come to light that many war crimes initially blamed on the Shining Path were in fact committed by the armed forces, even though it suited the terrorists to claim responsibility at the time. And investigations into the web of intrigue surrounding Fujimori's henchman, Vladimiro Montesinos, indicate some form of 'working relationship' with Sendero Luminoso. The Fujimori-Montesinos propaganda machine managed to discredit the entire Peruvian Left by comparing it to the Shining Path. Consequently, when the war ended, there was almost no legitimate opposition in the country from this end of the political spectrum.

Both Professor Guzmán (who graduated from the Philosophy Department of the University of Arequipa and was a respected expert on the German philosopher Kant) and Víctor Polay (leader of the Marxist MRTA) are now locked away in underwater cells in the navy bunker on the island of San Lorenzo (Callao). They were condemned to life imprisonment by military tribunal. Nevertheless, many Peruvian and foreign analysts believe that both Shining Path and MRTA are recruiting again, albeit with softer methods, gaining support in the jungle, the Andes and in Lima. Unless the gap between the rich and poor can be narrowed, this period of relative peace in Peru may be at risk.

discovered in accounts in the Cayman Islands and elsewhere. In early 2001 he was eventually captured in Venezuela and returned to Peru where he was tried on, and convicted of, a multitude of charges. Fujimori, on the other hand, fled to Japan from where, on 20 November 2000, he sent Congress an email announcing his resignation. Congress rejected this, firing him instead on charges of being "morally unfit" to govern.

An interim president, Valentín Paniagua, was sworn in, with ex-UN Secretary General Javier Pérez de Cuéllar as Prime Minister, and the government set about uncovering the depth of corruption associated with Montesinos and Fujimori. In 2004, prosecutors sought to charge exiled Fujimori with authorizing death squads at Barrios Altos (1991) and La Cantuta (1992) in which 25 people died. This followed the Truth and Reconciliation Committee's report (2003) into the civil war of the 1980s and 1990s, which stated that over 69,000 Peruvians had been killed. With attempts to extradite Fujimori from Japan coming to nothing, prosecution could not proceed. Meanwhile Fujimori declared that he would be exonerated and stand again for the presidency in 2006. To this end he flew to Chile in November 2005 with a view to entering Peru, but the Chilean authorities jailed him for seven months and then held him on parole until an extradition request was finally approved in September 2007. In December that year the first of several trials began, Fujimori being charged with, but strenuously denying, the Barrios Altos and La Cantuta murders, kidnapping and corruption. He was found guilty of human rights abuses in 2009 and sentenced to 25 years in prison. As further convictions followed, he vowed to appeal and support for him was likely to continue as his daughter, Keiko, planned to stand for the presidency in 2011.

Post-Fujimori In the run-up to the 2001 elections, the front-runner was Alejandro Toledo, but with far from a clear majority. Ex-President Alan García emerged as Toledo's main opponent, forcing a second ballot on 3 June. This was won by Toledo with 52% of the vote. He pledged to heal the wounds that had opened in Peru since his first electoral battle with the disgraced Fujimori, but his presidency was marked by slow progress on both the political and economic fronts. With the poverty levels still high, few jobs created and a variety of scandals, Toledo's popularity plummeted. A series of major confrontations and damaging strikes forced the president to declare a state of emergency in May 2003 to restore order. Nor could Toledo escape charges of corruption being laid at his own door; accusations that he and his sister orchestrated voter fraud in 2000 were upheld by a congressional commission in May 2005.

The April 2006 elections were contested by Alan García, the conservative Lourdes Flores and Ollanta Humala, a former military officer and unsuccessful coup leader who claimed support from Venezuela's Hugo Chávez and Evo Morales of Bolivia. García and Humala won through to the second round, which García won, in part because many were suspicious, even critical of the 'Chávez factor' and the latter's interference in Peruvian affairs. Many were equally suspicious of García's ability to overcome his past record as president, but prior to taking office he pledged to rein in public spending and not squander the benefits of a growing economy. Humala's Unión por el Perú-Partido Nacionalista Peruano (UPP-PNP) won 45 seats in Congress, compared with 36 for APRA, forcing García to forge allies with right-leaning parties in order to sustain a majority for his policies. His first cabinet included APRA members and independents, as well as an unprecedented number of women (six), to help tackle social problems.

Much depended upon García's ability to succeed where no previous government seems to have made significant progress, namely alleviating poverty. Congress' approval of a trade pact with the United States in 2006 became the focus of protests as many claimed that food exports were taking precedence over the domestic market, where prices for food began to rise sharply. US-Peru Trade Promotion Agreement (PTPA) came into force in 2009 and Peru has also entered into, or is negotiating similar agreements with a number of other countries, including Canada, China and the EU. Between 2005 and 2008 the economy grew strongly, but suffered in line with world recession and low commodity prices in 2009. García's free-market policies were judged to have failed to address the inequality of income distribution and major demonstrations were held through 2007 and 2008. Even worse events occurred in mid-2009 when indigenous protestors from near Bagua Grande (Amazonas) clashed with police over oil-drilling rights on their land. Many feared that Peru's mineral exploration policies would put areas of the Peuvian Amazon under threat of deforestation and the fact that this protest led to over 50 deaths and claims of human rights abuse highlighted the extreme sensitivity of the issue.

Constitution and government

Peru has a single chamber 120-seat congress. Men and women over 18 are eligible to vote, and registration and voting is compulsory until the age of 70. Those who do not vote are fined. The president, to whom is entrusted the executive power, is elected for five years. Peru is split into 25 regions (divided into 150 provinces, subdivided into 1321 districts), plus the province of Lima.

Economy

Structure of production
Agriculture and **forestry** account for about 8% of GDP and employ about a third of the labour force. The coastal region is the most productive area of the country and has traditionally been the dominant economic region. Occupying 11% of the total land area, most of the export crops are grown here: cotton, rice, sugar, artichokes, asparagus and fruit where the coastal desert is irrigated. Most food production is in the sierra, where revitalization of agriculture, with the aim of returning to the self-sufficiency of Inca times, has been a long-term goal. There have been improvements in living standards, but two-thirds of the inhabitants of the sierra still live in poverty and prices for many crops remain very low. Peru has the potential to be the world's leading exporter of fishmeal, as in 2001-2002, but the industry is susceptible to the Niño current forcing the main catch, anchovy, out of Peruvian waters. When this happens, as for instance in 1983 and 1997-1998, fishing suffers a dramatic decline.

International statistics indicate that Peru accounts for about 45% of world **coca** production, being the largest grower of coca leaf, if not having the largest area under cultivation (it is second to Colombia). Following efforts to curb the cultivation of coca for the production of cocaine, United Nations officials recorded a 5% drop in coca production in 2003, but subsequently the area under coca cultivation according to those same officials has risen year-on-year to 59,900 ha in 2009 (up 6.8% on 2008). Major efforts are being made to introduce alternative crops such as oil palm, organic coffee and tea and fruits, but production of the leaf thrives in the tropical valleys and policies to eradicate coca in Colombia appear to have encouraged growers in Peru.

Manufacturing, mining and **fishing/fish processing** contribute 32% of GDP. Food processing, fishmeal, oil refining, metals and transport equipment are important sectors. Mining has traditionally been important in Peru since pre-Conquest times. The sector contracted sharply in the 1980s because of poor world prices, strikes and terrorist activity in mining areas, but a new Mining Law in 1992 encouraged domestic and foreign investment and the sector has since boomed. Copper and iron deposits are found on the south coast, but the sierra is the principal mining area for all minerals, including silver,

A way of life

Coca leaves have long been used by the people of the Andes as a tonic. As casual as a coffee-break and as sacred as Communion, coca chewing is an ancient ritual.

The coca leaves are chewed with a piece of *cal*, or lime, which activates with the saliva. Some cocaine is absorbed into the bloodstream through the mouth, providing a slight numbing of cheek and tongue and more is absorbed in the stomach and intestinal tract. The desired effect is to numb the senses, which helps stave off hunger pangs and exhaustion, and to help people live at high altitude with no ill-effects.

As well as being a prerequisite for manual workers, such as miners, coca is also taken in a social context. The native population used to deny this because, in the eyes of their Spanish bosses and clergy, an increase in labour productivity was the only permissible reason for tolerating consumption of 'the devil's leaf'. The only places where coca is not chewed is in church and in the marital bed. The masticated leaves are spat out at the bedside.

Coca is also used in various rites, such as in offerings to Pachamama, or Mother Earth, to feed her when she gets hungry. Various items such as flowers and sweets, along with the coca leaves, are put together in bundles called *pagos* and burned on the mountains at midnight. In Andean markets different *pagos* are sold for different purposes: to put into the foundation of a new house; for help in matters of health, business or love; or for magic, white or black. The leaves are also used for fortune-telling.

gold, lead and zinc. The largest gold mine in Latin America, Yanacocha, is in Cajamarca, contributing the majority of Peru's annual production of 130 tonnes. Another major project is the Antamina in Ancash, the world's leading combined copper and zinc mine.

Oil production comes from the northeast jungle, although some is produced on and off the northwest coast. No major new reserves of oil have been found since 1976 and proven reserves are put at 448 million barrels. Peru is a net importer of oil. However, the Camisea gas and condensates field in the southeast jungle is huge and overall proven reserves are 334 billion cu ft of natural gas. The Camisea project and its associated pipeline and processing facilities on the coast is also hugely controversial, primarily for environmental and humanitarian reasons.

Since the early 1990s, when the threat of terrorism had receded, numbers of foreign **tourists** to Peru have grown steadily, with the sector contributing about 4% to GDP. Traditionally tourism has been the third largest sector of GDP, but it dropped back to fourth place in 2009, behind mining, agriculture and fishing, largely as a result of the negative impact of world recession. The total number of visitors in 2009 was 1.75 million (compared with 1.82 million in 2008), with receipts of some US$2 billion (Observatorio Turístico del Perú, www.observatorioturisticodelperu.com). Most visitors come from the USA, followed by Canada, Chile, Mexico, the UK, Spain and France.

Society

The most remarkable thing about Peru is its people. For most Peruvians life is a daily struggle to survive in the face of seemingly insurmountable problems. Most people do get by, through a combination of ingenuity, determination and sheer hard work. Many work full time and study at night school. Those without work (and employment opportunities are few and far between) invent their own jobs.

Peru may not be the poorest country in South America and a thriving economy since 2002 has helped to reduce levels of poverty, but recent estimates put the number of poor at about 45% of the population, while almost a fifth of people live in extreme poverty. Over a third of homes have no electricity or running water and a third of children suffer from chronic malnutrition.

Health

There have been major improvements in health care in recent years, but almost a third of the population has no access to public health services. The infant mortality rate is 21 deaths under age one per 1000 births (2005-2010, INEI – Instituto Nacional de Estadística e Informática); the figure rises steeply in some rural areas where one in 10 infants dies within a year of birth. Life expectancy is 73 years.

As only a small percentage of the population contributes to social security schemes, medical consultations are not necessarily free. People also have to pay for prescribed medicines, which are very expensive, and so rarely finish a course of treatment. As with other areas, there is a huge gulf between those who can afford to pay for health care and those who cannot. Lack of health education and limited primary health care also means that many women die in childbirth. Abortion is illegal in Peru, but those with cash can always find a private doctor. Those without the means to pay for a doctor run the risk of death or infection from botched abortions.

Education

Education is free and compulsory for both sexes between six and 14. Adult literacy in 2007 stood at 93%. There are public and private secondary schools and private elementary schools. There are 32 state and private universities, and two Catholic universities. But resources are extremely limited and teachers earn a pittance. Poorer schoolchildren don't have money to buy pencils and notebooks and textbooks are few and far between in state schools. Furthermore, many children have to work instead of attending school; a quarter of those who start primary school don't finish. This is also due to the fact that classes are taught in Spanish and those whose native tongue is Quechua, Aymara or one of the Amazonian languages find it difficult and give up.

Migration

The structure of Peruvian society, especially in the coastal cities, has been radically altered by internal migration. This movement began most significantly in the 1950s and 1960s as people from all parts of Peru sought urban jobs in place of work on the land. It was a time of great upheaval as the old system of labour on large estates was threatened by the peasant majority's growing awareness of the imbalances between the wealthy cities and impoverished sierra. The process culminated in the agrarian reforms of the government of General Juan Velasco (1968-1975). Province-to-city migration was given renewed impetus during the war between the state and Sendero Luminoso in the 1980s. Many communities that were depopulated in that decade are now beginning to come alive again.

Culture

People

Peruvian society today is a melting pot of Native Andeans, Afro-Peruvians, Spanish, immigrant Chinese, Japanese, Italians, Germans and, to a lesser extent, indigenous Amazon tribes. The total population in 2007 was 28.2 million (INEI census statistics), with an annual average growth rate of 1.6%. The INEI estimates the total at 29.5 million in 2010. The urban population represents 73% of the total.

Criollos and mestizos

The first immigrants were the Spaniards who followed Pizarro's expeditionary force. Their effect, demographically, politically and culturally, has been enormous. They intermarried with the indigenous population and the children of mixed parentage were called mestizos. The Peruvian-born children of Spanish parents were known as criollos, though this word is now used to describe people who live on the coast, regardless of their ancestory, and coastal culture in general.

Afro-Peruvians

Peru's black community is based on the coast, mainly in Chincha, south of Lima, and also in some working-class districts of the capital. Their forefathers were originally imported into Peru in the 16th century as slaves to work on the sugar and cotton plantations on the coast. The black community represents between 2-5% of the total population.

Asian immigrants

There are two main Asian communities in Peru, the Japanese and Chinese. Large numbers of poor Chinese labourers were brought to Peru in the mid-19th century to work in virtual slavery on the guano reserves on the Pacific coast and to build the railroads in the central Andes. The culinary influence of the Chinese can be seen in the many *chifas* found throughout the country.

The Japanese community, now numbering some 100,000, established itself in the first half of the 20th century. The normally reclusive community gained prominence when Alberto Fujimori, one of its members, became the first president of Japanese descent outside Japan anywhere in the world. During Fujimori's presidency, many other Japanese Peruvians took prominent positions in business, central and local government. The nickname 'chino' is applied to anyone of Oriental origin.

Europeans

Like most of Latin America, Peru received many emigrés from Europe seeking land and opportunities in the late 19th century. The country's wealth and political power remains concentrated in the hands of this small and exclusive class of whites, which also consists of the descendants of the first Spanish families. There still exists a deep divide between people of European descent and the old colonial snobbery persists.

Peru's indigenous people

Peru has a substantial indigenous population, only smaller as a percentage of the total than Bolivia and Guatemala of the Latin American republics. The literacy rate of the indigenous population is the lowest of any comparable group in South America and their diet is 50% below acceptable levels. The highland communities bore the brunt of the conflict between Sendero Luminoso and the security forces, which caused thousands of deaths and mass migration from the countryside to provincial cities or to Lima. Many indigenous groups are also under threat from colonization, development and lost road-building projects. Long after the end of Spanish rule, discrimination, dispossession and exploitation are still a fact of life for many native Peruvians.

Quechua

Predominantly an agricultural society, growing potatoes and corn as their basic diet, they are largely outside the money economy. Today, there remain two enduring legacies of Inca rule; their magnificent architecture and their language, Quechua, which, although predating the Incas themselves, has become synonymous with the descendants of their subjects. Quechua is one of the key channels of continuity with the captivating pre-European past and indigenous identity of the Andes. Sadly, that continuity still takes the form of a distinctly underprivileged status in relation to the dominant Spanish and it is only the remoteness of many Quechua speakers which has preserved the language in rural areas. This isolation has also helped preserve many of their ancient traditions and beliefs. Most speakers today are bilingual in Spanish and Quechua is still losing ground fast. It remains primarily a spoken, in-group language, strongly bound up with the distinct indigenous identity, but unlike the Aymara (see below), the seven million or so Quechua-speakers have generally been much less successful in asserting themselves. There is no real sense of unity between the disparate groups of speakers scattered through Ecuador, Peru and Bolivia. Some recent developments in these three countries have at last been more positive. The language is now increasingly written and is being fitfully introduced in primary education, though the impact of Spanish, and polemics about standardization, continue to have a very disruptive effect. At least some Quechua-speaking communities are gradually recovering a long-deserved semblance of pride in their native tongue and culture, such as the successful Otavalo traders in Ecuador, or the Jalq'a and Tarabuco peoples around Sucre in Bolivia thanks to their beautiful weaving traditions. See also Festivals, on page 674.

Aymara

High up in the Andes, in the southern part of Peru, lies a wide, barren and hostile plateau, the *altiplano*. Prior to Inca rule Tiahuanaco on Lake Titicaca was a highly organized centre for one the greatest cultures South America has ever witnessed: the Aymara people. Today, the shores of this lake and the plains that surround it remain the homeland of the Aymara. The majority live in Bolivia, the rest are scattered on the southwestern side of Peru and northern Chile. The climate is so harsh on the *altiplano* that, though they are extremely hard working, their lives are very poor. They speak their own unwritten language, Aymara. More so than the scattered group of different peoples that speak Quechua, the Altiplano Aymara people form a compact group with a clear sense of their own distinct identity and in many respects have been able to preserve more of their indigenous traditions and belief system.

The Afro-Peruvian experience since 1532

The first person of African descent to arrive in the Americas came in 1492 with Christopher Columbus. He was a mulatto from Spain, and a free man. During the next three centuries an estimated 15 million Africans arrived in the Americas as slaves. Francisco Pizarro brought the first black slaves to Peru. They were present at the capture of Atahualpa in Cajamarca in 1532 and saved the Spanish during Manco Inca's siege of Cuzco in 1536, when they put out the fire engulfing the great hall of Sunturwasi, where the *conquistadores* had taken refuge.

When Hernando de Soto returned to Spain in 1534 bearing Atahualpa's gold and silver ransom, he asked the crown for permission to take 100 slaves back to Peru. By 1550, their number had risen to 3000 – half of whom lived in Lima – and by 1640 to 30,000. In total, between 1532 and 1816, an estimated 100,000 African slaves were transported to Peru.

They were sent to replace an indigenous labour force ravaged by the destruction of its sociopolitical infra-structure and by European diseases. Some worked in the cities as servants, artisans or porters, others in the mines of Huancavelica or Potosí and the majority toiled on the coast in sugar cane plantations, cotton fields and vineyards.

Indigenous and African workers transformed Peru into the richest of all the Spanish colonies in the 16th and 17th centuries. Many fortunes, including that amassed by the Jesuits, were made using slave labour. The ownership of black slaves was a status symbol and even some Afro-Peruvians who had achieved their own freedom subsequently acquired slaves.

The location of Afro-Peruvian communities today reflects the colonial distribution of black labour. They are concentrated in the coastal areas once dominated by the great haciendas: Chincha, Cañete and Ica, the northern departments of Lambayeque and Piura, and the cities, especially Lima. Here, the vibrant culture created by slaves from diverse African heritages lives on in local art, music, dance, religion, food and folklore (see pages 44 and 672).

The wars of independence spread the libertarian ideal of emancipation. Promised their freedom, hundreds of Afro-Peruvians joined the republican armies, only to find their situation little changed in 1821 under the fledgling government. In 1854, Generals Ramón Castilla and José Rufino Echenique engaged in civil war and were in need of troops. To attract black recruits Echenique offered freedom to those who would join him and, in reply, Castilla announced the abolition of slavery, paying off landowners with awards raised from guano exports.

The 25,000 black slaves freed in 1854 were received by society with contempt and remained oppressed by labour laws. Racism continues to live on today. Colour is still identified with inferiority in everyday attitudes and in the poverty and marginalization of black communities and their lack of representation in government.

Some one hundred and 50 years after abolition, those who shared the hardships of the *conquistadores* have still not shared in either their glory or their wealth.

The Aymaras are a deeply religious people whose culture is permeated with the idea of the sacred. They believe that God, the Supreme Being, gives them security in their daily lives and this God of Life manifests him/herself through the deities, such as those of the mountains, the water, wind, sun, moon and *wa'qas* (sacred places). As a sign of gratitude, the Aymara give *wax'ta* (offerings), *wilancha* (llama sacrifices) and *ch'alla* (sprinkling alcohol on the ground) to the *achachilas* (the protecting spirits of the family and community), the Pachamama (Mother Earth), Kuntur Mamani and Uywiri (protecting spirits of the home).

The remote mountains of the bleak *altiplano* are of particular importance for the Aymara. The most sacred places are these high mountains, far from human problems. It is here that the people have built their altars to offer worship, to communicate with their God and ask forgiveness. The community is also held important in the lives of the Aymara. The achachila is the great-great grandfather of the family as well as the protector of the community, and as such is God's representative on earth.

The offerings to the sacred mountains take place for the most part in August and are community celebrations. Many different rituals are celebrated: there are those within the family; in the mountains; for the planting and the harvest; rites to ask for rain or to ask for protection against hailstorms and frosts; and ceremonies for Mother Earth.

All such rituals are led by Aymara Yatiris, who are male or female priests. The Yatiri is a wise person – someone who knows – and the community's spiritual and moral guide. Through a method of divination that involves the reading of coca leaves, they guide individuals in their personal decision-making.

Amazonian peoples

Before the arrival of the Europeans, an estimated six million people inhabited the Amazon Basin, comprising more than 2000 tribes or ethnic-linguistic groups who managed to adapt to their surroundings through the domestication of a great variety of animals and plants, and to benefit from the numerous nutritional, curative, narcotic and hallucinogenic properties of thousands of wild plants.

It's not easy to determine the precise origin of these aboriginal people. What is known, however, is that since the beginning of colonial times this population slowly but constantly decreased, mainly because of the effect of western diseases such as influenza and measles. This demographic decline reached dramatic levels during the rubber boom of the late 19th and early 20th centuries, due to forced labour and slavery.

Today, at the basin level, the population is calculated at no more than two million inhabitants making up 400 ethnic groups, of which approximately 200,000-250,000 live in the Peruvian jungle. Within the basin it is possible to distinguish at least three large conglomerates of aboriginal societies: the inhabitants of the varzea, or seasonally flooded lands alongside the large rivers (such as the Omagua, Cocama and Shipibo people); the people in the interfluvial zones or firm lands (such as the Amahuaca, Cashibo and Yaminahua) and those living in the Andean foothills (such as the Amuesha, Asháninka and Machiguenga).

The Amazonian natives began to be decimated in the 16th century, and so were the first endangered species of the jungle. These communities still face threats to their traditional lifestyles, notably from timber companies, gold miners and multinational oil and gas companies. There appears to be little effective control of deforestation and the intrusion of colonists who have taken over native lands to establish small farms. And though oil companies have reached compensation agreements with local communities, previous oil exploration has contaminated many jungle rivers, as well as exposing natives to risk from diseases against which they have no immunity.

Andean mysticism

Since the 1990s Andean shamanism and mysticism have attracted increasing attention, though they have always played an important part in the lives of indigenous people.

In highland cities, especially, it is common to engage a ritual specialist, called an altomisayoq, to perform a *pago*, or offering, when laying the foundations of a house or starting a business. Ritual objects for use in these ceremonies are sold at specialized stands in local markets. Another type of ritualist, a *curandero*, is summoned when someone is ill.

Some of these healers are experts in the use of dozens of medicinal plants, while others invoke spirit powers to expel illness. Sometimes eggs or guinea pigs are passed over the patient's body, and then cracked, or killed, in order to read the innards and diagnose the illness. Inevitably this field has its share of charlatans, but there are also *curanderos* who have many attested cures to their credit.

One thing shamans from all the Andean regions have in common is the use of a *mesa* – a layout of ceremonial power objects – which is thought to attract spirit power and channel it to the shaman. Another feature running through all strains of Andean mysticism, despite the usual presence of Christian elements, is a living connection, via innumerable practices and associations, to Peru's pre-Columbian past.

Ritualists who seek to communicate with 'the other side' in their ceremonies often use psychoactive plants. These vary according to the region. On the coast, curanderos often take an infusion of the San Pedro cactus, a form of mescaline. The highland shamans invariably chew coca leaf, a much milder psychoactive, but with broader uses. Coca is burned with every offering, and many ritualists cast the leaves to read the fortunes of their clients. These shamans usually invoke the power of the mountain deities in their ceremonies. In the rainforest regions shamans use the powerful psychedelic vine, *ayahuasca* (vine of the dead – so called because it is believed to transport the user to the spirit world), as they have for millennia.

Religion

The Inca religion (described on page 649) was displaced by Roman Catholicism from the 16th century onwards, the conversion of the inhabitants of the 'New World' to Christianity being one of the stated aims of the Spanish *conquistadores*. Today, statistics vary between 81% and 89% of the population declaring itself Catholic.

One of the first exponents of Liberation Theology, under which the Conference of Latin American Bishops in 1968 committed themselves to the 'option for the poor', was Gustavo Gutiérrez, from Huánuco. This doctrine caused much consternation to orthodox Catholics, particularly those members of the Latin American church who had traditionally aligned themselves with the oligarchy. Gutiérrez, however, traced the church's duty to the voiceless and the marginalized back to Fray Bartolomé de las Casas (see *The Peru Reader*, page 695).

The Catholic Church faced a further challenge to its authority when President Fujimori won the battle over family planning and the need to slow down the rate of population growth. Its greatest threat, however, comes from the proliferation of evangelical Protestant groups throughout the country. Some 6% of the population now declare themselves Protestant and one million or more people belong to some 27 different non-Catholic denominations.

Although the vast majority of the population ostensibly belongs to the Roman Catholic religion, in reality religious life for many Peruvians is a mix of Catholic beliefs imported from Europe and indigenous traditions based on animism, the worship of deities from the natural world such as mountains, animals and plants. Some of these ancient indigenous traditions and beliefs are described throughout this section.

Arts and crafts

Peru has a rich variety of handicrafts. Its geographic division into four distinct regions – coast, mountains, valleys and Amazon Basin – coupled with cultural differences, has resulted in numerous variations in technique and design. Each province, even each community, has developed its own style of weaving or carving.

The Incas inherited 3000 years of skills and traditions: gold, metal and precious stonework from the Chimú; feather textiles from the Nazca; and the elaborate textiles of the Paracas. All of these played important roles in political, social and religious ceremonies. Though much of this artistic heritage was destroyed by the Spanish conquest, the traditions adapted and evolved in numerous ways, absorbing new methods, concepts and materials from Europe while maintaining ancient techniques and symbols.

Textiles and costumes

Woven cloth was the most highly prized possession and sought after trading commodity in the Andes in pre-Columbian times. It is, therefore, not surprising that ancient weaving traditions have survived. In the ninth century BC camelid fibre was introduced into weaving on the south coast. This allowed the development of the textiles of the Paracas culture that consist of intricate patterns of animalistic, supernatural and human forms embroidered onto dark backgrounds. The culture of the Chancay valleys cultivated cotton for white and beige dyed patterned cloth in preference to the camelid fibres used by the Paracas and Nazca cultures. The Incas inherited this rich weaving tradition. They forced the Aymaras to work in *mit'as* or textile workshops. The ruins of some enormous *mit'as* can be seen at the temple of Raqchi, south of Cuzco (see page 216). Inca textiles are of high quality and very different from coastal textiles, being warp-faced, closely woven and without embroidery. The largest quantities of the finest textiles were made specifically to be burned as ritual offerings – a tradition which still survives. The Spanish, too, exploited this wealth and skill by using the mitas and exporting the cloth to Europe.

Prior to Inca rule Aymara men wore a tunic (*llahua*) and a mantle (*llacata*) and carried a bag for coca leaves (*huallquepo*). The women wore a wrapped dress (*urku*) and mantle (*iscayo*) and a belt (*huaka*); their coca bag was called an *istalla*. The *urku* was fastened at shoulder level with a pair of metal *tupu*, the traditional Andean dress-pins. Inca men had tunics (*unkus*) and a bag for coca leaves called a *ch'uspa*. The women wore a blouse (*huguna*), skirts (*aksu*) and belts (*chumpis*), and carried foodstuffs in large, rectangular cloths called *llicllas*, which were fastened at the chest with a single pin or a smaller clasp called a *ttipqui*. Women of the Sacred Valley now wear a layered, gathered skirt called a *pollera* and a *montera*, a large, round, red Spanish type of hat. Textiles continue to play an important part in society. They are still used specifically for ritual ceremonies and some even held to possess magical powers. One of the most enduring of these traditions is found among the Aymara people of Taquile island on Lake Titicaca.

A belt for every occasion

The belt plays a particularly important role in the lives of the indigenous peoples. The Incas developed a range of belts, or *chumpis*, of ritual and spiritual significance which are still used today.

Chumpis are believed to have protective and purifying qualities. In the Cuzco area, some communities place *chumpis* on sacred mountain tops, or *apus*, in order to communicate with the gods. Traditionally women give birth lying on a *chumpi* and the baby is wrapped in a softer version, known as a *walt'ana*, which ensures he or she will grow up properly. From adolescence, women wear a *chumpi* under their skirt to encourage a lover or deter an unwanted suitor. It is even common practice for the bridegroom to lasso his bride with one. The age-old tradition of burying the dead with the family *chumpi* is still occasionally observed.

Textile materials and techniques

The Andean people used mainly alpaca or llama wool. The former can be spun into fine, shining yarn when woven and has a lustre similar to that of silk, though sheep's wool came to be widely used following the Spanish conquest. A commonly used technique is the drop spindle. A stick is weighted with a wooden wheel and the raw material is fed through one hand. A sudden twist and drop in the spindle spins the yarn. This very sensitive art can be seen practised by women while herding animals in the fields.

Spinning wheels were introduced by Europeans and are now prevalent owing to increased demand. In Ayacucho and San Pedro de Cajas, centres of the cottage textile industry, the wheel is the most common form of spinning. Pre-Columbian looms were often portable and those in use today are generally similar. A woman will herd her animals while making a piece of costume, perhaps on a backstrap loom, or waist loom, so-called because the weaver controls the tension on one side with her waist with the other side tied to an upright or tree. The pre-Columbian looms are usually used for personal costume while the treadle loom is used by men for more commercial pieces.

The skills of dyeing were still practised virtually unchanged even after the arrival of the Spanish. Nowadays, the word *makhnu* refers to any natural dye, but originally was the name for cochineal, an insect that lives on the leaves of the nopal cactus. These dyes were used widely by pre-Columbian weavers. Today, the biggest centre of production in South America is the valleys around Ayacucho. Vegetable dyes are also used, made from the leaves, fruit and seeds of shrubs and flowers and from lichen, tree bark and roots.

Symbolism

Symbolism plays an important role in weaving. Traditionally every piece of textile from a particular community had identical symbols and colours that were a source of identity as well as carrying specific symbols and telling a story. One example is on the island of Taquile where the Inti (sun) and Chaska (Venus) symbols are employed as well as motifs such as fish and birds, unique to the island.

Animal figures dominated the motifs of the Chavín culture and were commonly used in Paracas textiles. Specimens of cotton and wool embroidery found in Paracas graves often show a puma as a central motif. Today, this and other pre-Columbian motifs are found on many rugs and wall-hangings from the Ayacucho region. Other symbols include Spanish figures such as horses and scenes depicting the execution of Túpac Amaru.

Pottery

The most spectacular archaeological finds in South America have been made in Peru. The Nazca culture (100 BC-AD 900) excelled in polychrome painting of vessels with motifs of supernatural beings, often with strong feline characteristics, as well as birds, fish and animals. Many of the Nazca ceramic motifs are similar to those found in Paracas textiles.

Moche or Mochica vessels combined modelling and painting to depict details of Moche daily life. Human forms are modelled on stirrup spout vessels with such precision that they suggest personal portraits. The Moche also excelled in intricate linear painting often using brown on a cream base.

Inca ceramic decoration consists mainly of small-scale geometric and usually symmetrical designs. One distinctive form of vessel that continues to be made and used is the arybola. This pot is designed to carry liquid, especially *chicha*, and is secured with a rope on the bearer's back. It is believed that arybolas were used mainly by the governing Inca elite and became important status symbols. Today, Inca-style is very popular in Cuzco and Pisac.

With the Spanish invasion many indigenous communities lost their artistic traditions, others remained relatively untouched, while others still combined Hispanic and indigenous traditions and techniques. The Spanish brought three innovations: the potter's wheel, which gave greater speed and uniformity; knowledge of the enclosed kiln; and the technique of lead glazes. The enclosed kiln made temperature regulation easier and allowed higher temperatures to be maintained, producing stronger pieces. Today, many communities continue to apply pre-Hispanic techniques, while others use more modern processes.

Jewellery and metalwork

Some of the earliest goldwork originates from the Chavín culture – eg the Tumi knife found in Lambayeque. These first appeared in the Moche culture, when they were associated with human sacrifice. Five centuries later, the Incas used Tumis for surgical operations such as trepanning skulls. Today, they are a common motif.

The Incas associated gold with the Sun. However, very few examples remain as the Spanish melted down their amassed gold and silver objects. They then went on to send millions of indigenous people to their deaths in gold and silver mines.

During the colonial period gold and silver pieces were made to decorate the altars of churches and houses of the elite. Metalworkers came from Spain and Italy to develop the industry. The Spanish preferred silver and strongly influenced the evolution of silverwork during the colonial period. A style known as Andean baroque developed around Cuzco embracing both indigenous and European elements. Silver bowls in this style – *cochas* – are still used in Andean ceremonies.

False filigree This was practised by some pre-Hispanic cultures. The effect of filigree was obtained with the use of droplets or beads of gold. True filigree work developed in the colonial period. Today, there are a number of centres. Originally popular in Ayacucho, the tradition continues in the small community of San Jerónimo de Tunan, near Huancayo. Here, silversmiths produce intricate filigree earrings, spoons and jewellery boxes. Catacaos near Piura also has a long tradition of filigree work in silver and gold.

Seeds, flowers and feathers These continue to be used as jewellery by many Amazonian peoples. Pre-Hispanic cultures also favoured particular natural materials; eg the sea shell spondylus was highly revered by the Chavín and Moche. It was found only along part of the

From pagan ritual to folk art

Retablos – or St Mark's boxes, as they were originally known – were introduced to Latin America by the Spanish in the 16th century. These simple, portable altars containing religious images were intended to aid in the task of converting the native population to Catholicism. Early examples often contained images of St James, patron saint of the Spanish army.

The *retablos* were made from a variety of materials and two distinct styles evolved to suit different needs. Those of clay, leather and plaster were destined for the native rural population, while those for use by the colonial hierarchy were made of gold and silver, or the famous alabaster of Ayacucho, known as Huamanga stone.

Traditional *retablos* had two floors inside a box. On the top floor were the patron saints of animals: St Mark, patron saint of bulls; St Agnes, patron saint of goats; and St Anthony, patron saint of mules, among others. On the lower floor was a scene of a cattle thief being reprimanded by a landowner.

From the 17th century onwards, the native rural population used the *retablo* in ceremonies accompanying cattle branding. During August, a ritual believed to have its roots in pagan fertility festivals took place in which the *retablo* was placed on a table and surrounded by offerings of food and coca leaves. People danced round and sang in front of the box, asking for protection for their animals and celebrating their well-being.

In the 1940s the first *retablo* reached Lima, by which time the art of making them had virtually disappeared. However, with the new-found outside interest a revival began. The traditional elements began to be varied and the magical or ritualistic value was lost as they became a manifestation of folk art. The artist Joaquín López and his family created the early examples, but today they are made in many workshops.

The figures are made from a mixture of plaster and mashed potato, modelled or made in moulds, sealed with glue, then painted and positioned inside the brightly painted box. Some miniature versions are made in chiclet boxes or egg shells, while, at the other end of the scale, some have five floors and take months to complete.

Extracted from *Arts and Crafts of South America*, by Lucy Davies and Mo Fini, Tumi.

Ecuadorean coast and must have been acquired through trade. The western fashion for natural or ethnic jewellery has encouraged production, using brightly coloured feathers, fish bones, seeds or animal teeth.

Woodcarving

Wood is one of the most commonly used materials. Carved ceremonial objects include drums, carved sticks with healing properties, masks and the Incas' *keros* – wooden vessels for drinking *chicha*. Keros come in all shapes and sizes and were traditionally decorated with scenes of war, local dances, or harvesting coca leaves. The Chancay, who lived along the coast between 100 BC and AD 1200, used *keros* carved with sea birds and fish. Today, they are used in some Andean ceremonies, especially during Fiesta de la Cruz, the Andean May festival.

Glass mirrors were introduced by the Spanish, although the Chimú and Lambayeque cultures used obsidian and silver plates, and Inca *chasquis* (messengers) used reflective stones to communicate between hilltop forts. Transporting mirrors was costly so they were produced in Lima and Quito. Cuzco and Cajamarca then became centres of production. In Cuzco the frames were carved, covered in gold leaf and decorated with tiny pieces of cut mirror. Cajamarca artisans, meanwhile, incorporated painted glass into the frames.

Gourd-carving

Gourd-carving, or *mate burilado*, as it is known, is one of Peru's most popular and traditional handicrafts. It is thought even to predate pottery – engraved gourds found on the coast have been dated to some 4500 years ago. During the Inca empire gourd-carving became a valued art form and workshops were set up and supported by the state. Gourds were used in rituals and ceremonies and to make poporos – containers for the lime used while chewing coca leaves. Today, gourd-carving is centred around the small communities of Cochas Grande and Chico, near Huancayo.

The information on arts and crafts in this guidebook has been adapted from *Arts and Crafts of South America*, by Lucy Davies and Mo Fini, published by Tumi, 1994. Tumi, the Latin American Craft Centre, specializes in Andean and Mexican products and produces cultural and educational videos for schools: at Unit 2, Ashmead Business Centre, Ashmead Road, Keynsham, Bristol BS31 1SX, T0117-986 9216. Tumi Music (www.tumi.com) specializes in different rhythms of Latin America.

Music and dance

The music of Peru can be described as the very heartbeat of the country. Peruvians see music as something in which to participate, and not as a spectacle. Just about everyone, it seems, can play a musical instrument or sing. Just as music is the heartbeat of the country, so dance conveys the rich and ancient heritage that typifies much of the national spirit. Peruvians are tireless dancers and dancing is the most popular form of entertainment. Unsuspecting travellers should note that once they make that first wavering step there will be no respite until they collapse from exhaustion.

Each region has its own distinctive music and dance that reflects its particular lifestyle, its mood and its physical surroundings. The music of the sierra, for example, is played in a minor key and tends to be sad and mournful, while the music of the lowlands is more up-tempo and generally happier. Peruvian music divides at a very basic level into that of the highlands (Andina) and that of the coast (Criolla). For a celebration of many Peruvian dance styles, see the film *Soy Andina* and its accompanying website www.soyandina.com. Made by Mitch Teplitsky in 2007 it documents two women, both living in the USA, rediscovering their roots in Peru through its music and traditions.

Highlands

When people talk of Peruvian music they are almost certainly referring to the music of the Quechua- and Aymara-speaking people of the highlands that provides the most distinctive Peruvian sound. The highlands themselves can be very roughly subdivided into some half dozen major musical regions, of which perhaps the most characteristic are Ancash and the north, the Mantaro Valley, Cuzco, Puno and the Altiplano, Ayacucho and Parinacochas.

Musical instruments Before the arrival of the Spanish in Latin America, the only instruments were wind and percussion. Although it is a popular misconception that Andean music is based on the panpipes, guitar and charango, anyone who travels through the Andes will realize that these instruments only represent a small aspect of Andean music. The highland instrumentation varies from region to region, although the harp and violin are ubiquitous. In the Mantaro area the harp is backed by brass and wind instruments, notably the clarinet. In Cuzco it is the charango and quena and on the *altiplano* the sicu panpipes.

The *quena* is a flute, usually made of reed, characterized by not having a mouthpiece to blow through. As with all Andean instruments, there is a family of quenas varying in length from around 15-50 cm. The sicu is the Aymara name for the *zampoña*, or panpipes. It is the most important pre-Hispanic Andean instrument, formed by several reed tubes of different sizes held together by knotted string. Virtually the only instrument of European origin is the Charango. When stringed instruments were first introduced by the Spanish, the indigenous people liked them but wanted something that was their own and so the charango was born. Originally, they were made of clay, condor skeletons and armadillo or tortoise shells.

Highland dances The highlands are immensely rich in terms of music and dance, with over 200 dances recorded. Every village has its fiestas and every fiesta has its communal and religious dances.

Comparsas are organized groups of dancers who perform for spectators dances following a set pattern of movements to a particular musical accompaniment, wearing a specific costume. They have a long tradition, having mostly originated from certain contexts and circumstances and some of them still parody the ex-Spanish colonial masters.

One of the most notable is the comical Auqui Auqui (*auqui* is Aymara for old man). The dance satirizes the solemnity and pomposity of Spanish gentlemen from the colonial period. Because of their dignified dress and manners they could appear old, and a humped back is added to the dancers to emphasize age. These little old men have long pointed noses, flowing beards and carry crooked walking sticks. They dance stooped, regularly pausing to complain and rub aching backs, at times even stumbling and falling. Another dance parody is the Contradanza, performed in the highlands of La Libertad.

Many dances for couples and/or groups are danced spontaneously at fiestas throughout Peru. These include indigenous dances which have originated in a specific region and ballroom dances that reflect the Spanish influence. One of the most popular of the indigenous dances is the **Huayno**, which originated on the *altiplano* but is now danced throughout the country. It involves numerous couples, who whirl around or advance down the street arm-in-arm, in a Pandilla. During fiestas, and especially after a few drinks, this can develop into a kind of uncontrolled frenzy.

Two of the most spectacular dances to be seen are the **Baile de las Tijeras** (scissor dance) from the Ayacucho/Huancavelica area, for men only, and the pounding, stamping **Huaylas** for both sexes. Huaylas competitions are held annually in Lima and should not be missed. Also very popular among indigenous and/or mestizo people are the Marinera, Carnaval, Pasacalle, Chuscada (from Ancash), Huaylas, Santiago and Chonguinada (all from the Mantaro) and Huayllacha (from Parinacochas).

Urban and other styles Owing to the overwhelming migration of peasants into the barrios of Lima, most types of Andean music and dance can be seen in the capital, notably on Sundays at the so-called 'Coliseos', which exist for that purpose. This flood of migration to the cities has also meant that the distinct styles of regional and ethnic groups have become blurred. One example is **Chicha music**, which comes from the *pueblos jóvenes*, and was once the favourite dance music of Peru's urban working class. Chicha is a hybrid of Huayno music and the Colombian Cumbia rhythm – a meeting of the highlands and the tropical coast.

Tecno-cumbia originated in the jungle region with groups such as Rossy War, from Puerto Maldonado, and Euforia, from Iquitos. It is a vibrant dance music which has gained much greater popularity across Peruvian society than *chicha* music ever managed. There are now also many exponents on the coast such as Agua Marina and Armonía 10. Many of the songs comment on political issues and Fujimori used to join Rossy War on stage. Tecno-cumbia has evolved into a more sophisticated form with wider appeal across Peruvian society. Listen to Grupo 5, from Chiclayo, for instance.

Coast

Música Criolla The music from the coast, could not be more different from that of the sierra. Here the roots are Spanish and African. The immensely popular **Valsesito** is a syncopated waltz that would certainly be looked at askance in Vienna and the **Polca** has also undergone an attractive sea change. Reigning over all is the **Marinera**, Peru's national dance, a splendidly rhythmic and graceful courting encounter and a close cousin of Chile's and Bolivia's Cueca and the Argentine Zamba, all of them descended from the Zamacueca. The Marinera has its 'Limeña' and 'Norteña' versions and a more syncopated relative, the Tondero, found in the northern coastal regions, is said to have been influenced by slaves brought from Madagascar. All these dances are accompanied by guitars and frequently the cajón, a resonant wooden box on which the player sits, pounding it with his hands. Some of the great names of 'Música Criolla' are the singer/composers Chabuca Granda and Alicia Maguiña, the female singer Jesús Vásquez and the groups Los Morochucos and Hermanos Zañartu.

Afro-Peruvian Also on the coast is the music of the small but influential black community, the 'Música Negroide' or 'Afro-Peruano', which had virtually died out when it was resuscitated in the 1950s, but has since gone from strength to strength, thanks to Nicomedes and Victoria Santa Cruz who have been largely responsible for popularizing this black music and making it an essential ingredient in contemporary Peruvian popular music. It has all the qualities to be found in black music from the Caribbean – a powerful, charismatic beat, rhythmic and lively dancing, and strong percussion provided by the cajón and the quijada de burro, a donkey's jaw with the teeth loosened. Its greatest star is the Afro-Peruvian diva Susana Baca. Her incredible, passionate voice inspired Talking Head's David Byrne to explore this genre further and release a compilation album in 1995, thus bringing Afro-Peruvian music to the attention of the world. Other notable exponents are the excellent Perú Negro, one of the best music and dance groups in Latin America, and the singer Eva Ayllón. In the footsteps of the dynamic Gotan Project (Argentine musicians who have taken a radical approach to the interpretation of the tango), Novalima, a group of internationally based Peruvian musicians, have produced new arrangements of many classic Afro-Peruvian tracks (see www.novalima.net). Some of the classic dances in the black repertoire are the Festejo, Son del Diablo, Toro Mata, Landó and Alcatraz. In the last named one of the partners dances behind the other with a candle, trying to set light to a piece of paper tucked into the rear of the other partner's waist.

Festivals

Fiestas (festivals) are a fundamental part of life for most Peruvians, taking place the length and breadth of the country and with such frequency that it would be hard to miss one, even during the briefest of stays. This is fortunate, because arriving in any town or village during these frenetic celebrations is a great Peruvian experience.

Day of the Dead

One of the most important dates in the indigenous people's calendar is the 2 November, the 'Day of the Dead'. This tradition has been practised since time immemorial. In the Incaic calendar, November was the eighth month and meant Ayamarca, or land of the dead. This celebration, or 'All Saints' as it is also known, is just one example of religious adaptation in which the ancient beliefs of ethnic cultures are mixed with the rites of the Catholic Church.

According to Aymara belief, the spirit (*athun ajayu*) visits its relatives at this time of the year and is fed in order to continue its journey before its reincarnation. The relatives of the dead prepare for the arrival of the spirit days in advance. Among the many items necessary for these meticulous preparations are little bread dolls, each one of which has a particular significance. A ladder is needed for the spirit to descend from the other world to the terrestrial one. There are other figures that represent the grandparents, great grandparents and loved ones of the person who has 'passed into a better life'. Horse-shaped breads are prepared that will serve as a means of transport for the soul in order to avoid fatigue.

Inside the home, the relatives construct a tomb supported by boxes over which is laid a black cloth. Here they put the bread, along with sweets, flowers, onions and sugar cane. This latter item is an indispensable part of the table as it symbolizes the invigorating element that prevents the spirit from becoming tired on its journey towards the Earth. The union of the flowers with the onion is called *tojoro* and is a vital part of the preparations. It ensures that the dead one does not become disoriented and arrives in the correct house.

The tomb is also adorned with the dead relative's favourite food and drink, not forgetting the all-important glass of beer as, according to popular tradition, this is the first nourishment taken by the souls when they arrive at their houses. Once the spirit has arrived and feasted with its living relatives, the entire ceremony is then transported to the graveside in the local cemetery, where it is carried out again, beside the many other mourning families.

This meeting of the living and their dead relatives is re-enacted the following year, though less ostentatiously, and again for the final time in the third year, the year of the farewell. It does not continue after this; just as well as the costs can be crippling for the family concerned.

While Peru's festivals can't rival those of Brazil for fame or colour, the quantity of alcohol consumed and the partying run them pretty close. What this means is that, at some point, you will fall over, through inebriation or exhaustion, or both. After several days of this, you will awake with a hangover the size of the Amazon rainforest and probably have no recollection of what you did with your backpack.

Peruvian festivals also involve widespread balloons-filled-with-water fights, bags of flour and any other missile guaranteed to cause a mess. In the Amazon region various petroleum by-products are favoured ingredients, which can be bad news for smokers. Some travellers complain that they are being picked on, but to someone from the *altiplano*, a 6-ft tall, blond-haired gringo makes an easier target. So, don't wear your best clothes, arm yourself with plenty of water bombs, get into the spirit and have some fun!

With over 3000 fiestas, there are too many to mention them all. The main national ones are described on page 44, and details of local fiestas are given under the listings for each town. You can also check the websites of PromPerú and South American Explorers, see Tourist information, page 66.

Meaning of fiestas

It is only when they don their extravagant costumes and masks and drink, eat and dance to excess that the indigenous Peruvians show their true character. The rest of the time they hide behind a metaphorical mask of stony indifference as a form of protection against the alien reality in which they are forced to live. When they consume alcohol and coca and start dancing, the pride in their origins resurfaces. This allows them to forget the reality of poverty, unemployment and oppression and reaffirms their will to live as well as their unity with the world around them.

The object of the fiesta is a practical one, such as the success of the coming harvest or the fertility of animals. Thus the constant eating, drinking and dancing serves the purpose of giving thanks for the sun and rain that makes things grow and for the fertility of the soil and livestock, gifts from Pachamama, or Mother Earth, the most sacred of all gods. So, when you see the Aymara spill a little *chicha* (maize beer) every time they refill, it's not because they're sloppy but because they're offering a *ch'alla* (sacrifice) to Pachamama.

The participants in the dances that are the central part of the fiesta are dressed in garish, outlandish costumes and elaborate masks, each one depicting a character from popular myth. Some of these originate in the colonial period, others survive from the Inca Empire or even further back. Often the costumes caricature the Spanish. In this way, the indigenous people mock those who erased their heritage.

Literature

Quechua

The fact that the Incas had no written texts in the conventional European sense and that the Spaniards were keen to suppress their conquest's culture means that there is little evidence today of what poetry and theatre was performed in pre-conquest times. It is known that the Incas had two types of poet, the *amautas*, historians, poets and teachers who composed works that celebrated the ruling class' gods, heroes and events, and *haravecs*, who expressed popular sentiments. There is strong evidence also that drama was important in Inca society.

Written Quechua even today is far less common than works in the oral tradition. Although Spanish culture has had some influence on Quechua, the native stories, lyrics and fables retain their own identity. Not until the 19th century did Peruvian writers begin seriously to incorporate indigenous ideas into their art, but their audience was limited. Nevertheless, the influence of Quechua on Peruvian literature in Spanish continues to grow.

Colonial period

In 16th-century Lima, headquarters of the Viceroyalty of Peru, the Spanish officials concentrated their efforts on the religious education of the new territories and literary output was limited to mainly histories and letters.

Chroniclers such as Pedro Cieza de León (*Crónica del Perú*, published from 1553) and Agustín de Zárate (*Historia del descubrimiento y conquista del Perú*, 1555) were written from the point of view that Spanish domination was right. Their most renowned successors, though, took a different stance. Inca Garcilaso de la Vega was a mestizo, whose *Comentarios reales que tratan del origen de los Incas* (1609) were at pains to justify the achievements, religion and culture of the Inca Empire. He also commented on Spanish society in the colony. A later work, *Historia General del Perú* (1617) went further in condemning Viceroy Toledo's suppression of Inca culture. Through his work, written in Spain, many aspects of Inca society, plus poems and prayers have survived.

Writing at about the same time as Inca Garcilaso was Felipe Guaman Poma de Ayala, whose *El primer nueva corónica y buen gobierno* (1613-1615) is possibly one of the most reproduced of Latin American texts (eg on T-shirts, CDs, posters and carrier bags). Guaman Poma was a minor provincial Inca chief from Ayacucho province whose writings and illustrations, addressed to King Felipe III of Spain, offer a view of a stable pre-conquest Andean society (not uniquely Inca), in contrast with the unsympathetic colonial society that usurped it.

In the years up to Independence, the growth of an intellectual elite in Lima spawned more poetry than anything else. As criollo discontent grew, satire increased both in poetry and in the sketches that accompanied dramas imported from Spain. The poet Mariano Melgar (1791-1815) wrote in a variety of styles, including the yaraví, the love-song derived from the pre-Columbian *harawi* (from *haravek*). Melgar died in an uprising against the Spanish but played an important part in the Peruvian struggle from freedom from the colonial imagination.

After Independence
After Independence, Peruvian writers imitated Spanish *costumbrismo*, sketches of characters and lifestyles from the new Republic. The first author to transcend this fashion was Ricardo Palma (1833-1919), whose inspiration, the *tradición*, fused *costumbrismo* and Peru's rich oral traditions. Palma's hugely popular *Tradiciones peruanas* is a collection of pieces which celebrate the people, history and customs of Peru through sayings, small incidents in mainly colonial history and gentle irony.

Much soul searching was to follow Peru's defeat in the War of the Pacific. Manuel González Prada (1844-1918), for instance, wrote essays fiercely critical of the state of the nation: *Páginas libres* (1894), *Horas de lucha* (1908). José Carlos Mariátegui, the foremost Peruvian political thinker of the early 20th century, said that González Prada represented the first lucid instant of Peruvian consciousness. He also wrote poetry, some Romantic, some, like his *Baladas peruanas*, an evocation of indigenous and colonial history, very pro-Indian, very anti-White.

20th-century prose
Mariátegui himself (1895-1930), after a visit to Europe, considered the question of Peruvian identity. His opinion was that it could only be seen in a global context and that the answer lay in Marxism. With this perspective he wrote about politics, economics, literature and the indigenous question (see *Siete ensayos de interpretación de la realidad peruana*, 1928).

Other writers had continued this theme. For instance Clorinda Matto de Turner (1854-1909) intended to express in *Aves sin nido* (1889) her "tender love for the indigenous people" and hoped to improve their lot. Regardless of the debate over whether the novel achieves these aims, she was the forerunner by several years of the 'indigenist' genre in Peru and the most popular of those who took up González Prada's cause.

Other prose writers continued in this vein at the beginning of the 20th century, but it was Ciro Alegría (1909-1967) who gave major, fictional impetus to the racial question. Like Mariátegui, Alegría was politically committed, but to the APRA party, rather than

Marxism. Of his first three novels, *La serpiente de oro* (1935), *Los perros hambrientos* (1938) and *El mundo es ancho y ajeno* (1941), the last named is his most famous.

Contemporary with Alegría was José María Arguedas (1911-1969), whose novels, stories and politics were also deeply rooted in the ethnic question. Arguedas, though not Indian, had a largely Quechua upbringing and tried to reconcile this with the hispanic world in which he worked. This inner conflict was one of the main causes of his suicide. His books include *Agua* (short stories, 1935), *Yawar fiesta* (1941), *Los ríos profundos* (1958) and *Todas las sangres* (1964). They portray different aspects of the confrontation of indigenous society with the changing outside world that impinges on it.

In the 1950s and 1960s, there was a move away from the predominantly rural and indigenist to an urban setting. At the forefront were, among others, Mario Vargas Llosa, Julio Ramón Ribeyro, Enrique Congrains Martín, Oswaldo Reynoso, Luis Loayza, Sebastián Salazar Bondy and Carlos E Zavaleta. Taking their cue from a phrase used by both poet César Mora and Salazar Bondy (in an essay of 1964), "Lima, la horrible", they explored all aspects of the city, including the influx of people from the sierra. These writers incorporated new narrative techniques in the urban novel, which presented a world where popular culture and speech were rich sources of literary material, despite the difficulty in transcribing them.

Many writers, such as Vargas Llosa (see box, page 680), broadened their horizons beyond the capital. His novels after *La ciudad y los perros* encompassed many different parts of the country. An additional factor was that several writers spent many years abroad, Vargas Llosa himself, for instance, and Ribeyro (1929-1994). The latter's short stories, though mostly set in Lima, embrace universal themes of delusion and frustration. The title story of *Los gallinazos sin pluma* (1955), a tale of squalor and greed amid the city's rubbish tips, has become a classic, even though it does not contain the irony, pathos and humour of many of his other stories or novels.

Other writers of this period include Manuel Scorza (1928-1983), who wrote a series of five novels under the general title of *La guerra silenciosa* (including *Redoble por Rancas*, *El jinete insomne*, *La tumba del relámpago*) which follow the tradition of the indigenist struggle, and also emphasize the need to defend indigenous society with growing militancy if necessary.

Alfredo Bryce Echenique (born 1939) has enjoyed much popularity following the success of *Un mundo para Julius* (1970), a brilliant satire on the upper and middle classes of Lima. His other novels include *Tantas veces Pedro* (1977), *La última mudanza de Felipe Carrillo* (1988), *No me esperen en abril* (1995), *Dos señoras conversan* (1990), *La amigdalitis de Tarzan* (2000) and *El huerto de mi amada*, which won the Premio Planeta (Barcelona) in 2002. Other contemporary writers of note are: Rodolfo Hinostroza (born 1941), novelist, playwright and poet, whose books include *Cuentos de Contranatura* (1972) and *Extremo occidente* (2002); Mario Bellatín (born 1960 in Mexico but educated in Peru), among whose works are the excellent short novels *Salón de belleza* (1994) and *Damas chinas* (1995); Jaime Bayly (born 1965), who is also a journalist and TV presenter. His novels include *Fue ayer y no me acuerdo*, *Los últimos días de la prensa*, *No se lo digas a nadie*, *La noche es virgen* and *Y de repente, un ángel*.

Recent trends for novelists include confronting the violence and the after-effects of the Sendero Lumnioso/MRTA and Fujimori/Montesinos period, with powerful, neorealist novels and stories. Among the best examples are Alonso Cueto (born 1954), *Grandes miradas* (2003), *La hora azul* (2005); and Santiago Roncagliolo (born 1975), see *Abril rojo* (2006). His newest book is *Tan cerca de la vida*, published in 2010. Another new voice is Daniel Alarcón, born in Lima in 1977 but brought up in Birmingham, Alabama, whose first collection of stories, *War by Candlelight* (*Guerra en la penumbra* – 2005) is set almost entirely in Lima but is written in English. His first novel, *Lost City Radio* (2007) tells the story of a radio presenter, whose most popular show unites people separated by civil war, and her relationship with a young boy who comes in person to deliver such a message. Another strand is writing about the reality of immigrant communities in Lima, such as Augusto Higa Oshiro's novel, *Final del porvenir* (1992), and Siu Kam Wen's stories in *El tramo final* (2009).

20th-century poetry

At the end of the 19th century, the term Modernism was introduced in Latin America by the Nicaraguan Rubén Darío, not to define a precise school of poetry, but to indicate a break with both Romanticism and Realism. In Peru one major exponent was José Santos Chocano (1875-1934), who labelled his poetry 'mundonovismo' (New Worldism), claiming for himself the role of Poet of South America. He won international fame (see, for example, *Alma América*, 1906), but his star soon waned.

A much less assuming character was José María Eguren (1874-1942) who, feeling alienated from the society around him, sought spiritual reality in the natural world (*Simbólicas*, 1911; *La canción de las figuras*, 1916; *Poesías*, 1929). It has been said that with Eguren the flourishing of Peruvian 20th century poetry began.

Without doubt, the most important poet in Peru, if not Latin America, in the first half of the 20th century, was César Vallejo. Born in 1892 in Santiago de Chuco (Libertad), Vallejo left Peru in 1923 after being framed and briefly jailed in Trujillo for a political crime. In 1928 he was a founder of the Peruvian Socialist Party, then he joined the Communist Party in 1931 in Madrid. From 1936 to his death in Paris in 1938 he opposed the fascist takeover in Spain. His first volume was *Los heraldos negros* in which the dominating theme of all his work, a sense of confusion and inadequacy in the face of the unpredictability of life, first surfaces. *Trilce* (1922), his second work, is unlike anything before it in the Spanish language. The poems contain (among other things) made-up words, distortions of syntax, their own internal logic and rhythm, graphic devices and innovative uses of sounds, clichés and alliterations. *Poemas humanos* and *España, aparta de mí este cáliz* (written as a result of Vallejo's experiences in the Spanish Civil War) were both published posthumously, in 1939.

In the 1960s writers began to reflect the broadening horizons of that increasingly liberal decade, politically and socially, which followed the Cuban Revolution. One poet who embraced the revolutionary fervour was Javier Heraud (born Miraflores 1942). His early volumes, *El río* (1960) and *El viaje* (1961) are apparently simple in conception and expression, but display a transition from embarking on the adventure of life (the river) to autumnal imagery of solitude. In 1961 he went to the USSR, Asia, Paris and Madrid, then in 1962 to Cuba to study cinema. He returned to Peru in 1963 and joined the Ejército de Liberación Nacional. On 15 May 1963 he was shot by government forces near Puerto Maldonado. Heraud's friend César Calvo, now living in Cuba, is a poet and essayist.

Other major poets born in the early 20th century are Emilio Adolfo Westphalen (1911) and Jorge Eduardo Eielson (see his book *Celebración*). Others who began to publish in the 1960s were Luis Hernández (1941-1977), Antonio Cisneros (born 1942) and Marco Martos (born 1942).

In the 1970s, during the social changes propelled by the Velasco regime (1968-1975), new voices arose, many from outside Lima, eg the Hora Zero group (1970-1973 – Enrique Verástegui, Jorge Pimentel, Juan Ramírez Ruiz), whose energetic poetry employed slang

Mario Vargas Llosa

The best known of Peru's writers, Mario Vargas Llosa, was born in 1936 in Arequipa and educated in Cochabamba (Bolivia), from where his family moved to Piura. After graduating from the Universidad de San Marcos, he won a scholarship to Paris in 1958 and, from 1959 to 1974, lived first in Paris then in London in voluntary exile. In 2010, while teaching at Princeton University in the US, he was awarded the Nobel Prize for Literature, "for his cartography of structures of power and his trenchant images of the individual's resistance, revolt and defeat". At the time of winning, he said "This Nobel goes to Latin American literature. It is a recognition of everything that surrounds me." Much has been written about his personal life, and his political opinions have been well documented, but, as befits an author of the highest international standing and one of the leading figures in the so-called 'Boom' of Latin American writers in the 1960s, it is for his novels that Vargas Llosa the writer is best known.

The first three – La ciudad y los perros (1963), La casa verde (1966) and Conversación en la Catedral (1969) – with their techniques of flashback, multiple narrators and different interwoven stories, are an adventure for the reader. Meanwhile, the humorous books, like Pantaleón y las visitadoras and La tía Julia y el escribidor cannot be called lightweight. La guerra del fin del mundo marked a change to a more direct style and an intensification of Vargas Llosa's exploration of the role of fiction as a human necessity, extending also to political ideologies. La fiesta del chivo (2000) is another fictionalized account of historical events, this time the assassination of President Trujillo of the Dominican Republic in 1961 and the intrigue and fear surrounding his period in office. It is a gripping story, widely regarded as one of his best. More recently he has written Travesuras de la niña mala (2006 – The Bad Girl), which the author called his first 'love story', and, due out at the time of going to press in 2010, El sueño del celta, about the Irishman, Roger Casement.

Vargas Llosa has always maintained that in Peruvian society the writer is a privileged person who should be able to mix politics and literature as a normal part of life. This drive for authenticity led to his excursion into national politics. He stood as a presidential candidate in 1990, losing to Alberto Fujimori. He has since taken up Spanish citizenship (2007) with homes in Lima, Paris, Madrid and London.

and obscenities and other means to challenge preconceptions. Other poets of the 1970s and after include José Watanabe (1946-2007), a film-maker as well as poet, with Album de familia (1971), Historia natural (1994) and the anthology Elogio del Refrenamiento (2004). Renato Cisneros (born 1976) is a poet (Ritual de los prójimos, 1998; Maquina fantasma, 2002), novelist (Nunca confíes en mí, 2010) and blogger (Busco novia, see www.renatocisneros.net).

Women poets and novelists In addition to Clorinda Matto de Turner (see above), modern writers worth checking out are: Blanca Varela (1926-2009), who was married to sculptor Fernando de Szyszlo (see below), published volumes of poetry from 1959 (Ese puerto existe) to her anthology Como Dios en la nada (covering 1949-1998). Her work was championed by the Mexican Octavio Paz, among others. Carmen Ollé (born 1947) introduced a style of writing that is regarded as feminist and confessional. Her best known poetry collection is *Noches de adrenalina* (1981), while her prose includes *Las dos caras del deseo* (1994) and *Una muchacha bajo su paraguas* (2002). Giovanna Pollarolo is a poet, short story writer and screenwriter (born 1952) whose collections include *Huerto de olivos*, 1982, *Entre mujeres solas*, 1996, *La ceremonia de adios*, 1997 and *Atado de nervios*, 1999. Rocio Silva Santiesteban (born 1967) has published short stories as well as the poetry collections *Asuntos circunstanciales* (1984), *Este oficio no me gusta* (1987) and *Mariposa negra* (1996). Laura Riesco's (1940-2008) novel *Ximena de dos caminos* (1994) is an episodic tale of a young girl growing up in the Sierra, experiencing the clash between the oral culture of the local people who look after her, the mining company her father works for, city people who visit and the life of the coast where she goes on holiday. Younger poets of note are: Ericka Ghersi (born 1972), *Zenobia y el anciano* (1994), *Contra la ausencia* (2002), Rosella di Paolo (born 1960), *Piel alzada* (1993), *Tablillas de San Lázaro* (2001) among other collections, and Marita Troiano, whose works include *Mortal in puribus* (1996) and *Secreto a veces* (2003). Novelists include Alina Gadea (born 1966), with *Otra vida para Doris Kaplan* (2009), and Giselle Klatic (born 1976), *Alguien que me quiera* (2010).

Fine art and sculpture

The Catholic church was the main patron of the arts during the colonial period. The churches and monasteries that sprang up in the newly conquered territories created a demand for paintings and sculptures, met initially by imports from Europe of both works of art and of skilled craftsmen, and later by home-grown products.

Colonial period

An essential requirement for the inauguration of any new church was an image for the altar and many churches in Lima preserve fine examples of sculptures imported from Seville during the 16th and 17th centuries. Not surprisingly, among the earliest of these are figures of the crucified Christ, such as those in the cathedral and the church of La Merced by Juan Martínez Montañés, one of the foremost Spanish sculptors of the day, and that in San Pedro, by his pupil Juan de Mesa of 1625. Statues of the Virgin and Child were also imported to Lima from an early date, and examples from the mid-16th century survive in the cathedral and in Santo Domingo by Roque de Balduque, also from Seville although Flemish by birth.

Sculptures were expensive and difficult to import, and as part of their policy of relative frugality the Franciscan monks tended to favour paintings. In Lima, the museum of San Francisco now houses an excellent collection of paintings imported from Europe, including a powerful series of saints by Zubarán, as well as other works from his studio, a series of paintings of the life of Christ from Ruben's workshop and works from the circles of Ribera and Murillo, see page 80.

The Jesuits commissioned the Sevillian artist Juan de Valdés Leal to paint a series of the life of St Ignatius Loyola (1660s) which still hangs in San Pedro. The cathedral museum has a curious series from the Bassano workshop of Venice representing the labours of the monks and dating from the early 17th century. Another interesting artistic import from Europe that can still be seen in San Pedro (see Lima Churches) are the gloriously colourful painted tile decorations (*azulejos*) on the walls of Dominican monastery, produced to order by Sevillian workshops in 1586 and 1604.

Viringo

If you go to a Peruvian museum at a coastal archaeological site, you may see an elegant dog, with a long, thin nose and arched neck near the entrance. It might be a bit shy, and, if the weather is cold, it may be wearing a little woollen jacket. This is because the dog has no hair.

The Peruvian hairless, or viringo, is a rare breed today, but in Inca times was a companion animal whose main job was to warm his master's bed. The Chavín, Moche and Chimú cultures represented it on their ceramics, but its origins are unknown. The most likely theory is that it accompanied the first migrants to the Amercian continent from Asia. In its most common, hairless form, it has no fleas and no smell.

Breeders note that it needs protecting against the sun and the cold, but there is also a coated variety (called 'powder puff' in the dog world).

In recognition of the importance of this dog in its history, the Peruvian government decreed in Law number 27537 that every site museum on the coast must have at least one viringo on the premises.

In 2006 archaeologists announced the discovery of over 40 mummified dogs at tombs of the Chiribaya people in the Ilo valley, dating from AD 900-1350. They weren't viringos, but a distinct breed, christened 'Chiribaya shepherds' as it is supposed that they herded llamas.

Painters and sculptors soon made their way to Peru in search of lucrative commissions including several Italians who arrived during the later 16th century. The Jesuit Bernardo Bitti (1548-1610), for example, trained in Rome before working in Lima, Cuzco, Juli and Arequipa, where examples of his elegantly Mannerist paintings are preserved in the Jesuit church of the Compañia, see Arequipa page 264.

Another Italian, Mateo Pérez de Alesio worked in the Sistine Chapel in Rome before settling in Peru. In Lima the Sevillian sculptor Pedro de Noguera (1592-1655) won the contract for the choirstalls of the cathedral in 1623 and, together with other Spanish craftsmen, produced a set of cedar stalls decorated with vigorous figures of saints and Biblical characters, an outstanding work unmatched elsewhere in the Viceroyalty.

Native artists

European imports, however, could not keep up with demand and local workshops of Creole, mestizo and indigenous craftsmen flourished from the latter part of the 16th century. As the Viceregal capital and the point of arrival into Peru, the art of Lima was always strongly influenced by European, especially Spanish models, but the old Inca capital of Cuzco became the centre of a regional school of painting that developed its own characteristics.

A series of paintings of the 1660s, now hanging in the Museo de Arte Religioso, see Cuzco page 134, commemorate the colourful Corpus Christi procession of statues of the local patron saints through the streets of Cuzco. These paintings document the appearance of the city and local populace, including Spanish and Inca nobility, priests and laity, rich and poor, Spaniard, Indian, African and mestizo. Many of the statues represented in this series are still venerated in the local parish churches. They are periodically painted and dressed in new robes, but underneath are the original sculptures, executed by native craftsmen. Some are of carved wood while others use the pre-conquest technique of maguey cactus covered in sized cloth.

A remarkable example of an indigenous Andean who acquired European skills was Felipe Guaman Poma de Ayala whose 1000-page letter to the King of Spain celebrating the Andean past and condemning the colonial present contained a visual history of colonial and precolonial life in the Andes, see also page 677.

One of the most successful native painters was Diego Quispe Tito (1611-1681) who claimed descent from the Inca nobility and whose large canvases, often based on Flemish engravings, demonstrate the wide range of European sources that were available to Andean artists in the 17th century. But the Cuzco School is best known for the anonymous devotional works where the painted contours of the figures are overlaid with flat patterns in gold, creating highly decorative images with an underlying tension between the two- and three-dimensional aspects of the work. The taste for richly decorated surfaces can also be seen in the 17th- and 18th-century frescoed interiors of many Andean churches, as in Chinchero, Andahuaylillas and Huaro, and in the ornate carving on altarpieces and pulpits throughout Peru.

Andean content creeps into colonial religious art in a number of ways, most simply by the inclusion of elements of indigenous flora and fauna, or, as in the case of the Corpus Christi paintings, by the use of a setting, with recognizable buildings and individuals.

Changes to traditional Christian iconography include the representation of one of the Magi as an Inca, as in the painting of the Adoration of the Magi in San Pedro in Juli. Another example is that to commemorate his miraculous intervention in the conquest of Cuzco in 1534, Santiago is often depicted triumphing over indigenous people instead of the more familiar Moors. Among the most remarkable 'inventions' of colonial art are the fantastically over-dressed archangels carrying muskets which were so popular in the 18th century. There is no direct European source for these archangels, but in the Andes they seem to have served as a painted guard of honour to the image of Christ or the Virgin on the high altar.

Independence and after

Political independence from Spain in 1824 had little immediate impact on the arts of Peru except to create a demand for portraits of the new national and continental heroes such as Simón Bolívar and San Martín, many of the best of them produced by the mulatto artist José Gil de Castro (died Lima 1841). Later in the century another mulatto, Pancho Fierro (1810-1879) mocked the rigidity and pretentiousness of Lima society in lively satirical watercolours, while Francisco Laso (1823-1860), an active campaigner for political reform, made the Andean people into respectable subjects for oil paintings.

It was not until the latter part of the 19th century that events from colonial history became popular. The Museo de Arte in Lima (see Lima page 79) has examples of grandiose paintings by Ignacio Merino (1817-1876) glorifying Columbus, as well as the gigantic romanticized 'Funeral of Atahualpa' by Luis Montero (1826-1869). A curious late flowering of this celebration of colonial history is the chapel commemorating Francisco Pizarro in Lima cathedral which was redecorated in 1928 with garish mosaic pictures of the conqueror's exploits.

Impressionism arrived late and had a limited impact in Peru. Teofilo Castillo (1857-1922), instead of using the technique to capture contemporary reality, created frothy visions of an idealized colonial past. Typical of his work is the large 'Funeral Procession of Santa Rosa' of 1918, with everything bathed in clouds of incense and rose petals, which hangs in the Museo de Arte, in Lima. Daniel Hernández (1856-1932), founder of Peru's first Art School, used a similar style for his portraits of Lima notables past and present.

20th century to today

During the first half of the 20th century, Peruvian art was dominated by figurative styles and local subject matter. Political theories of the 1920s recognized the importance of Andean indigenous culture to Peruvian identity and created a climate which encouraged a figurative indigenista school of painting, derived in part from the socialist realism of the Mexican muralists. The movement flourished after the founding of the Escuela de Bellas Artes in 1920. José Sabogal (1888-1956) is the best known exponent of the group which also included Mario Urteaga (1875-1957), Jorge Vinatea Reinoso (1900-1931), Enrique Camino Brent (1909-1960), Camilo Blas (1903-1984) and Alejandro González (1900-1984). Their work can be seen in the Museo de Arte and the Museo Banco Central de Reserva in Lima.

The Mexican muralist tradition persisted into the 1960s with Manuel Ugarte Eléspuru (1911) and Teodoro Núñez Ureta (1914), both of whom undertook large-scale commissions in public buildings in Lima. Examples of public sculpture in the indigenist mode can be seen in plazas and parks throughout Peru, but it was in photography that indigenism found its most powerful expression. From the beginning of the century photographic studios flourished even in smaller towns. Martín Chambi (1891-1973) is the best known of the early 20th-century Peruvian photographers but there were many others, including Miguel Chani (1860-1951) who maintained the grandly named Fotografía Universal studios in Cuzco, Puno and Arequipa.

From the middle of the century artists have experimented with a variety of predominantly abstract styles and the best known contemporary Peruvian painter, Fernando de Szyszlo (1925) has created a visual language of his own, borrowing from Abstract Expressionism on the one hand and from pre-Columbian iconography on the other. His strong images, which suggest rather than represent mythical beings and cosmic forces, have influenced a whole generation of younger Peruvian artists. Look for his monument, Intihuatana 2000, near the sea in Miraflores.

Other leading figures whose work can be seen in public and commercial galleries in Lima include Venancio Shinki, Tilsa Tsuchiya, José Tola, Ricardo Weisse, Ramiro Llona and Leoncio Villanueva. Carlos Revilla, whose wife is his muse and principal subject of his painting, is clearly influenced by Hieronymus Bosch, while Bill Caro is an important exponent of hyperrealism. Víctor Delfín, a painter and sculptor (with beautiful work in iron) can be visited at his house in Barranco (Domeyko 366). His piece, The Kiss (El beso), is in the Parque del Amor in Lima. Pedro Azabache (from Trujillo) is a disciple of José Sabogal; his work is much broader in scope than the indigenism of his mentor. There are many other new artists whose work could be mentioned (Luz Letts, Eduardo Tokeshi, Carlos Enrique Polanco, Bruno Zepilli, Christian Bendayan – try to contact him in Iquitos, Flavia Gandolfo, Claudia Coca) and there are plenty of galleries in Lima with representative exhibitions. A new foundation is working towards opening a museum of contemporary art in Barranco, Lima, which is long overdue in a country where art is constantly changing. One striking modern piece outside Lima is the mosaic mural at the Ciudad Universitaria UNT in Trujillo, which, at almost 1 km long, is the longest mosaic mural in the world.

Land and environment

Geography

Peru is the third largest South American country, the size of France, Spain and the United Kingdom combined, and presents formidable difficulties to human habitation. Virtually all of the 2250 km of its Pacific coast is desert. From the narrow coastal shelf the Andes rise steeply to a high plateau dominated by massive ranges of snow-capped peaks and gouged with deep canyons. The heavily forested and deeply ravined Andean slopes are more gradual to the east. Further east, towards Brazil and Colombia, begin the vast jungles of the Amazon Basin.

Geology

The geological structure of Peru is dominated by the Nazca Plate beneath the Pacific Ocean, which stretches from Colombia in the north southwards to mid Chile. Along the coastline, this Plate meets and dives below the mass of the South American Plate that has been moving westwards for much of the Earth's geological history. Prior to the middle of the Tertiary Period, say 40 million years ago, marine sediments suggest that the Amazon Basin drained west to the Pacific, but from that time to the present, tectonic forces have created the Andes range the length of the continent, forming the highest peaks outside the Himalayas. The process continues today as shown by the earthquakes and active volcanoes and, in spite of erosion, the mountains still grow higher.

Coast

The coastal region, a narrow ribbon of desert 2250 km long, takes up 11% of the country and holds 44% of the population. It is the economic heart of Peru, consuming most of the imports and supplying half of the exports. When irrigated, the river valleys are extremely fertile, creating oases that grow cotton throughout the country, sugar-cane, rice and asparagus in the north, and grapes, fruit and olives in the south. At the same time, the coastal current teems with fish, and Peru has on occasion had the largest catch in the world.

Not far beyond the border with Ecuador in the north, there are mangrove swamps and tropical rainforest, but southwards this quickly changes to drier and eventually desert conditions. South of Piura is the desert of Sechura, followed by the dry barren land or shifting sands to Chimbote. However, several rivers draining the high mountains to the east more or less reach the sea and water the highly productive 'oases' of Piura, Trujillo, Cajamarca and Chimbote.

South of Chimbote, the Andes reach the sea, and apart from a thin strip of coastland north of Lima, the coastal mountains continue to the Chilean border at Arica. This area receives less rain than the Sahara, but because of the high Andes inland, over 50 Peruvian rivers reach the sea, or would do naturally for at least part of the year. As in the north, there are oases in the south, but mostly inland at the foot of the mountains where the river flow is greatest and high sunshine levels ensure good crop production.

The climate of this region depends almost entirely on the ocean currents along the Pacific coast. Two bodies of water drift northwards, the one closest to the shore, known as the Humboldt Current, is the colder, following the deep sea trench along the edge of the Pacific Plate. The basic wind systems here are the South-East Trades crossing the continent from the Atlantic, but the strong tropical sun over the land draws air into Peru from the Pacific. Being cool, this air does no more than condense into mist (known as the *garúa*) over the coastal mountains. This is sufficient to provide moisture for some unusual flora but virtually never produces rain, hence the desert conditions. The mixing of the two cold ocean currents, and the cloud cover that protects the water from the strongest sunlight, creates the unique conditions favourable to fish, notably sardines and anchovy, giving Peru an enormous economic resource. In turn, the fish support vast numbers of seabirds whose deposits of guano have been another very successful export for the country. This is the normal situation; every few years, however, it is disrupted by the phenomenon known as 'El Niño', see page 688.

Highlands

The highlands, or la sierra, extend inland from the coastal strip some 250 km in the north, increasing to 400 km in the south. The average altitude is about 3000 m and 50% of Peruvians live there. Essentially it is a plateau dissected by dramatic canyons and dominated by some of the most spectacular mountain ranges in the world.

Mountains

The tallest peaks are in the Cordillera Blanca (Huascarán; 6768 m) and the neighbouring Cordillera Huayhuash (Yerupajá; 6634 m). Huascarán is often quoted as the second highest point in South America after Aconcagua, but this is not so; there are some five other peaks on or near the Argentina-Chile border over 6770 m. The snowline here, at nine degrees south, is between 4500 m and 5000 m, much lower than further south. For example, at 16 degrees south, permanent snow starts at 6000 m on Coropuna (6425 m). Peru has more tropical glaciers than any other country in South America, but in recent years scientists have recorded rapid shrinkage of snow and glaciers from Peruvian peaks. This loss is blamed on global warming.

The reasons for this anomaly can be traced again to the Humboldt current. The Cordillera Blanca is less than 100 km from the coast, and the cool air drawn in depresses temperatures at high altitudes. Precipitation comes also from the east and falls as snow. Constant high winds and temperatures well below freezing at night create an unusual microclimate and with it spectacular mountain scenery, making it a mecca for snow and ice mountaineers. Dangers are heightened by the quite frequent earthquakes causing avalanches and landslides which have brought heavy loss of life to the valleys of the region. In 1970, 20,000 people lost their lives when Yungay, immediately west of Huascarán, was overwhelmed.

Canyons

Equally dramatic are the deep canyons taking water from the high mountains to the Pacific. The Colca Canyon, about 100 km north of Arequipa, has been measured at 3200 m from the lower rim to the river, more than twice as deep as the Grand Canyon. At one point it is overlooked by the 5227 m Señal Yajirhua peak, a stupendous 4150 m above the water level. Deeper even than Colca is the Cotahuasi Canyon, also in Arequipa Department, whose deepest point is 3354 m. Other canyons have been found in this remote area yet to be measured and documented.

In spite of these ups and downs, which cause great communications difficulties, the presence of water and a more temperate climate on the plateau has attracted people throughout the ages. Present day important population centres in the Highlands include Cajamarca in the north, Huancayo in central Peru and Cuzco in the south, all at around

3000 m. Above this, at around 4000 m, is the 'high steppe' or puna, with constant winds and wide day/night temperature fluctuations. Nevertheless, fruit and potatoes (which originally came from the puna of Peru and Bolivia) are grown at this altitude and the meagre grasslands are home to the ubiquitous llama.

Volcanoes

Although hot springs and evidence of ancient volcanic activity can be seen almost anywhere in Peru, the southern part of the sierra is the only area where there are active volcanoes. These represent the northernmost of a line of volcanoes which stretch 1500 km south along the Chile-Bolivia border to Argentina. Sabancaya (5977 m), just south of the Colca canyon, is currently active, often with a dark plume downwind from the summit. Beyond the Colca canyon is the Valle de los Volcanes, with 80 cinder cones rising 50-250 m above a desolate floor of lava and ash. There are other dormant or recently active volcanoes near the western side of Lake Titicaca – for example Ubinas – but the most notable is El Misti (5822 m), which overlooks Arequipa. It is perfectly shaped, indicating its status as active in the recent geologic past. Some experts believe it is one of the most potentially dangerous volcanoes in South America. Certainly a major eruption would be a catastrophe for the nearby city.

Lake Titicaca

The southeastern border with Bolivia passes through Titicaca, with about half of the lake in each country. It is the largest lake in South America (ignoring Lake Maracaibo in Venezuela, which is linked to the sea) and at 3812 m, the highest navigable body of water in the world. It covers about 8300 sq km, running 190 km northwest to southeast, and is 80 km across. It lies in a 60,000 sq km basin between the coastal and eastern Andes that spread out southwards to their widest point at latitude 18 degrees south.

The average depth is over 100 m, with the deepest point recorded at 281 m. Twenty-five rivers, most from Peru, flow into the lake and a small outlet leaves the lake at Desaguadero on the Bolivia-Peru border. This takes no more than 5% of the inflow, the rest is lost through evaporation and hence the waters of the lake are slightly brackish, producing the totora reeds used to make the mats and balsa boats for which the lake dwellers are famed.

The lake is the remnant of a vast area of water formed in the Ice Age known as Lake Ballivián. This extended at least 600 km to the south into Bolivia and included what is now Lake Poopó and the Salar de Uyuni. Now the lake level fluctuates seasonally, normally rising from December to March and receding for the rest of the year but extremes of 5 m between high and low levels have been recorded. This can cause problems and high levels in the late 1980s disrupted transport links near the shoreline. The night temperature can fall as low as -25°C but high daytime temperatures ensure that the surface average is about 14°C.

Eastern Andes and Amazon Basin

Almost half of Peru is on the eastern side of the Andes and about 90% of the country's drainage is into the Amazon system. It is an area of heavy rainfall with cloudforest above 3500 m and tropical rainforest lower down. There is little savanna, or natural grasslands, characteristic of other parts of the Amazon Basin.

There is some dispute on the Amazon's source. Officially, the mighty river begins as the Marañón, whose longest tributary rises just east of the Cordillera Huayhuash. However,

When the wind blows

Anyone who tuned into a weather forecast during late 1997 now knows about the climatic effect called El Niño, which means 'Christ child'. El Niño was so named by Peruvian fishermen who noticed the warming of the waters of the eastern Pacific around Christmas time.

Every three to seven years, for some as yet unexplained reason, the trade winds that usually blow west from South America subside. So the warm waters of the Pacific – a giant pool the size of Canada – drift eastwards towards South America. The result is worldwide weather chaos.

In 1997 El Niño made its third visit of the decade. The eastern Pacific heated faster than at any time in recorded history to become the most devastating climatic event of the century, surpassing even the 1982-1983 El Niño, which killed thousands and caused almost US$14 billion in damage.

The 1997 El Niño caused drought in Australia, New Zealand, Thailand, Malaysia and Papua New Guinea, forest fires in Indonesia, famine in North Korea, hurricanes along the US Pacific coast and the failure of the fish harvest in Peru. El Niño also sparked epidemics of cholera, encephalitis and bubonic plague.

The 1997-1998 event, the worst for 50 years, was the last in a rapid succession in the 1990s. Since then there have been weak-to-moderate events in 2002-2003, 2006-2007 and 2009-2010, but nothing of the strength of 1997-1998. Scientists still appear to know little about El Niño, but monitoring and research continue around the globe.

the longest journey for the proverbial raindrop, some 6400 km, probably starts in southern Peru, where the headwaters of the Apurímac (Ucayali) flow from the snows on the northern side of the Nevado Mismi, near Cailloma.

With much more rainfall on the eastern side of the Andes, rivers are turbulent and erosion dramatic. Although vertical drops are not as great – there is a whole continent to cross to the Atlantic – valleys are deep, ridges narrow and jagged and there is forest below 3000 m. At 1500 m the Amazon jungle begins and water is the only means of surface transport available, apart from three roads which reach Borja (on the Marañón), Yurimaguas (on the Huallaga) and Pucallpa (on the Ucayali), all at about 300 m above the Atlantic which is still 4000 km or so downstream. The vastness of the Amazon lowlands becomes apparent and it is here that Peru bulges 650 km northeast past Iquitos to the point where it meets Colombia and Brazil at Leticia. Oil and gas have recently been found in the Amazon, and new finds are made every year, which means that new pipelines and roads will eventually link more places to the Pacific coast.

Climate

Coast

On the coast summertime is from December to April, when temperatures range from 25° to 35°C and it is hot and dry. Wintertime is May to November, when the temperature drops a bit and it is cloudy.

The coastal climate is determined by the cold sea-water adjoining deserts. Prevailing inshore winds pick up so little moisture over the cold Humboldt current, which flows from Antarctica, that only from May to November does it condense. The resultant blanket of sea-mist (called *garúa*) extends from the south to about 200 km north of Lima. It is thickest to the south as far as Chincha and to the north as far as Huarmey, beyond which it thins and the sun can be expected to break through.

Sierra
From April-October is the dry season. It is hot and dry during the day, around 20°-25°C, and cold and dry at night, often below freezing. From November to April is the wet season, when it is dry and clear most mornings, with some rainfall in the afternoon. There is a small temperature drop (18°C) and not much difference at night (15°C).

Selva
April to October is the dry season, with temperatures up to 35°C. In the jungle areas of the south, a cold front can pass through at night. November to April is the wet season. It is humid and hot, with heavy rainfall at any time.

Flora and fauna

Peru is a country of great biological diversity. The fauna and flora are to a large extent determined by the influence of the Andes, the longest uninterrupted mountain chain in the world, and the mighty Amazon river, which has the largest volume of any river in the world. Of Earth's 32 known climate zones Peru has 28, and of the 117 recognized microclimates Peru has 84. Throughout the country there are 61 protected natural areas.

Natural history
This diversity arises not only from the wide range of habitats available, but also from the history of the continent. South America has essentially been an island for some 70 million years joined only by a narrow isthmus to Central and North America. Land passage played a significant role in the gradual colonization of South America by species from the north. When the land-link closed these colonists evolved to a wide variety of forms free from the competitive pressures that prevailed elsewhere. When the land-bridge was re-established some four million years ago a new invasion of species took place from North America, adding to the diversity but also leading to numerous extinctions. Comparative stability has ensued since then and has guaranteed the survival of many primitive groups like the opossums.

Coast
The coastal region of Peru is extremely arid, partly as a result of the cold Humboldt current (see Climate above). The paucity of animal life in the area between the coast and the mountains is obviously due to this lack of rain, though in some areas intermittent lomas, which are areas of sparse scrubby vegetation caused by moisture in the sea mist. The plants which survive provide ideal living conditions for insects which attract insectivorous birds and humming birds to feed on their nectar. Cactuses are abundant in northern Peru and provide a wooded landscape of trees and shrubs including the huarango (*Prosopis juliflora*). Also common in the north is the algorrobo tree – 250,000 ha were planted in 1997 to take advantage of the El Niño rains. Algorrobo forests (*algorrobales*), scrub thicket (*matorrales*) and coastal wetlands each provide habitat for some 30 species of birds. Mammals include foxes, three species of deer and six species of dogs from pre-Columbian times.

Andes

From the desert rise the steep Andean slopes. In the deeply incised valleys Andean fox and deer may occasionally be spotted. Herds of llamas and alpacas graze the steep hillsides. Mountain caracara and Andean lapwing are frequently observed soaring, and there is always the possibility of spotting flocks of mitred parrots or even the biggest species of hummingbird in the world (*Patagonia gigas*).

The Andean zone has many lakes and rivers and countless swamps. Exclusive to this area short-winged grebe and the torrent duck which feeds in the fast flowing rivers, and giant and horned coots. Chilean flamingo frequent the shallow soda lakes. The puna, a habitat characterized by tussock grass and pockets of stunted alpine flowers, gives way to relict elfin forest and tangled bamboo thicket in this inhospitable windswept and frost-prone region. Occasionally the dissected remains of a Puya plant can be found; the result of the nocturnal foraging of the rare spectacled bear. There are quite a number of endemic species of rodent including the viscacha, and it is the last stronghold of the chinchilla. Here pumas roam preying on the herbivores which frequent these mountain – pudu, a tiny Andean deer or guemal and the mountain tapir.

Tropical Andes

The elfin forest gradually grades into mist enshrouded cloudforest at about 3500 m. In the tropical zones of the Andes, the humidity in the cloudforests stimulates the growth of a vast variety of plants particularly mosses and lichens. The cloudforests are found in a narrow strip that runs along the eastern slopes of the spine of the Andes. It is these dense, often impenetrable, forests clothing the steep slopes that are important in protecting the headwaters of all the streams and rivers that cascade from the Andes to form the mighty Amazon as it begins its long journey to the sea. This is a verdant world of dripping epiphytic mosses, lichens, ferns and orchids that grow in profusion despite the plummeting overnight temperatures. The high humidity resulting from the 2 m of rain that can fall in a year is responsible for the maintenance of the forest and it accumulates in puddles and leaks from the ground in a constant trickle that combines to form myriad icy, crystal-clear streams that cascade over precipitous waterfalls. In secluded areas, orange Andean cock-of-the-rock give their spectacular display to females in the early morning mists. Woolly monkeys are also occasionally sighted as they descend the wooded slopes. Mixed flocks of colourful tanagers are commonly encountered as are the golden-headed quetzal and Amazon umbrella bird.

Amazon Basin

At about 1500 m there is a gradual transition to the vast lowland forests of the Amazon Basin, which are warmer and more equable than the cloudforests clothing the mountains above. The daily temperature varies little during the year with a high of 23-32°C falling slightly to 20-26°C overnight. This lowland region receives some 2 m of rainfall per year most of it falling from November to April. The rest of the year is sufficiently dry, at least in the lowland areas to inhibit the growth of epiphytes and orchids that are so characteristic of the highland areas. For a week or two in the rainy season the rivers flood the forest. The zone immediately surrounding this seasonally flooded forest is referred to as terre firme forest.

The vast river basin of the Amazon is home to an immense variety of species. The environment has largely dictated their lifestyle. Life in or around rivers, lakes, swamps and forests depend on the ability to swim and climb – amphibious and tree-dwelling animals

The debonair dolphin

Two species of dolphin live in the Amazon, the pink *Inia geoffrensis* and the grey *Sotalia fluvialis*. The pink dolphin is mainly solitary, but small groups are often found. Instead of a dorsal fin, it has a hump on its back and it also has a long bottle nose but because of its surfacing habits, you are unlikely to see its nose. The grey dolphin swims in groups and is a more 'conventional' shape, with a dorsal fin and shorter snout. When surfacing it often jumps right out of the water. For centuries the dolphins have lived peacefully with man on the river and, as a result, many myths have grown up around them. Sadly, destruction of habitat and pollution have threatened this harmonious coexistence.

The best-known legend concerns the night-time exploits of the pink dolphin. Indigenous people of the Amazon call it the *bufeo* and believe that it lives in an underwater city in Lake Caballococha, near the Peru-Colombia border. By night, the *bufeo* transforms himself into a suave gentleman in a white linen suit and, in this guise, he preys on local women. Even today, unwanted pregnancies are sometimes blamed on this magical animal. For some communities the dolphin is a semi-divine being, for others an untrustworthy witchdoctor. Its teeth, says Alex Shoumatoff in *The Rivers Amazon*, are claimed to cure children's diarrhoea, its ear to grant a long-lasting erection and its "grated left eye is an aphrodisiac powder".

In scientific circles, the pink river dolphins were, until recently, a forgotten species, considered extinct. All that remained was the skeleton of one in Paris, brought back from South America as a gift to Napoleon, and a few vague scientific papers dating from the 19th century in the Natural History Museum in London. The *bufeo* was rediscovered by a British expedition in 1956, then forgotten again until 1987, when Jacques Cousteau astounded TV viewers around the world with the first-ever pictures of pink dolphins frolicking in Amazon.

Now many Amazon lodges take travellers on dolphin-spotting expeditions. With some patience you can see one, or both types of dolphin in the flesh. The more curious pink ones circle quite close to the boat, while the grey will be further away, plunging into the river in unison – a fantastic sight. Back on land, however, female travellers should beware a charming, smartly dressed gentleman who doesn't raise his hat (it covers his blowhole).

---

are common. Once, the entire Amazon Basin was a great inland sea and the river still contains mammals more typical of the coast, eg manatees and dolphins.

Here in the relatively constant climatic conditions animal and plant life has evolved to an amazing diversity over the millennia. It has been estimated that 3.9 sq km of forest can harbour some 1200 vascular plants, 600 species of tree, and 120 woody plants. Here, in these relatively flat lands, a soaring canopy some 50 m overhead is the power-house of the forest. It is a habitat choked with strangling vines and philodendrons among which mixed troupes of squirrel monkeys and brown capuchins forage. In the high canopy small groups of spider monkeys perform their lazy aerial acrobatics, whilst lower down, cling to epiphyte-clad trunks and branches, groups of saddle-backed and emperor tamarins forage for blossom, fruit and the occasional insect prey.

Symbol of the Andes needs a helping paw

Possessor of many names, the Andean or spectacled bear, or ukuku, or oso de Anteojos has always loomed large in South American mythology. For the Incas the bear was seen as a connection between the human and spiritual or natural worlds and a force to restore order in times of chaos. At the Qoyllur Rit'i festival don't be surprised if a man dressed as a bear comes and gives you a good whipping if you misbehave on the way up to the glacier's frosty edge. In other Andean cultures the ukuku is considered an almost comic character, the Lord of Misrule, and further north the U'wa indigenous people of the Sierra Nevada del Cocuy, Colombia, think of Manoba (their name for the bear) as the ancestor of men, a creature with semi-human qualities.

The real Andean or spectacled bear, endemic to the region and the last of an ancient group of 'short-faced bears' that included the biggest bear that ever lived, is at least as intriguing in real life. The bears have been little studied and only now, in the early 21st century are these complex and resourceful creatures beginning to be understood. Spectacled Bears are so named because of the facial patterns formed by white fur around the eyes and sometimes extending down to their chests. Individuals can be identified by the unique markings. The bear's eyesight is not that good (so maybe a pair of glasses would be appreciated), but their sense of smell more than compensates for this with individuals able to smell a meal from several kilometres away. Love of fruits and bromeliads growing high in the forest canopy, as well as insects, honey, birds and eggs – anything that comes within a paw's distance – has made this South American omnivore a world champion climber. A larger male is able to pull his hefty, 175-kg frame up even vertical trunks, an impressive example of strength and agility. So confident are bears in this arboreal realm that they often construct tree 'nests' for a snooze.

Bears seem to prefer cool, mist-laden cloudforests and moist boggy *páramo* where bromeliads and puya plants are

The most accessible part of the jungle is on or near the many meandering rivers. At each bend of the river the forest is undermined by the currents during the seasonal floods at the rate of some 10-20 m per year leaving a sheer mud and clay bank, whilst on the opposite bend new land is laid down as broad beaches of fine sand and silt.

A succession of vegetation can be seen. The fast growing willow-like Tessaria first stabilizes the ground enabling the tall stands of caña brava Gynerium to become established. Within these dense almost impenetrable stands the seeds of rainforest trees germinate and over a few years thrust their way towards the light. The fastest growing is a species of Cercropia that forms a canopy 15-18 m over the *caña* but even this is relatively short-lived. The gap in the canopy is quickly filled by other species. Two types of mahogany outgrow the other trees forming a closed canopy at 40 m with a lush understory of shade tolerant Heliconia and ginger. Eventually even the long-lived trees die off to be replaced by others providing a forest of great diversity.

easily found, but they occur in habitats ranging from lowland dry forests to the edges of the Amazon and up to the snowline at nearly 5000 m. These wide-ranging habits, combined with shrinking wild areas because of agricultural expansion, are leading to greater human/bear conflict. Perhaps due to lack of natural food, the normally shy bears are increasingly raiding farmers' fields, and some claim bears actively hunt cattle. This is a matter of some debate among scientists, some of whom believe bears only scavenge from puma kills or animals dying from natural causes, a controversy that may continue for years to come.

Nobody knows how many of these highly elusive creatures remain. Estimates range from 2000 to 15000, but with bears being killed by angry farmers, hunted for claws, bile and gale bladders used in Oriental medicine, captured for 'dancing bear acts' in circuses or as pets, plus their homes being ruined as forests disappear, the bears need as many friends as they can find. Fortunately many dedicated study and conservation projects have begun through the Central and Northern Andes, from Venezuela to Bolivia. Volunteer projects provide fascinating opportunities for bear trackers (how often do you see that on a CV?) to community teachers to more general project work preserving the bears' habitat. All can make a difference to the bears' long-term survival. Spectacled Bears are a symbol of the Andes, its people, history and an indicator of clean and healthy mountain environments.

The Wildlife Conservation Society, www.wcs.org, runs a Northern Andes Conservation Progamme and a specifc Andean bear project in several South American Countries. In Peru, the Chaparrí Private Reserve near Santa Catalina de Chongoyape (see page 448) has a project that protects and rehabilitates captured bears for release into the wild. Tourists can stay at the community-run ecolodge (www.chaparrilodge.com), which feeds entrance fees and profits back in the reserve and provides local employment. Long-distance supporters can 'adopt a bear': www.wildlifeprotection.info.

Jungle wildlife

The meandering course of the river provides many excellent opportunities to see herds of russet-brown capybara – a sheep-sized rodent – peccaries and brocket deer. Of considerable ecological interest are the presence of oxbow lakes, or *cochas*, since these provide an abundance of wildlife that can easily be seen around the lake margins. The best way to see the wildlife, however, is to get above the canopy. Ridges provide elevated view points. From here, it is possible to look across the lowland flood plain to the foothills of the Andes, some 200 km away. Flocks of parrots and macaws can be seen flying between fruiting trees and troupes of squirrel monkeys and brown capuchins come very close.

The lowland rainforest of Peru is particularly famous for its primates and giant otters. Giant otters were once widespread in Amazonia but came close to extinction in the 1960s owing to persecution by the fur trade. The giant otter population in Peru has since recovered and is now estimated to be at least several hundred. Jaguar and other predators are also much in evidence. Although rarely seen their paw marks are commonly found along the forest trails. Rare bird species are also much in evidence, including fasciated tiger-heron and primitive hoatzins.

The (very) early morning is the best time to see peccaries, brocket deer and tapir at mineral licks (collpa). Macaw and parrot licks are found along the banks of the river. Here at dawn a dazzling display arrives and clambers around in the branches overhanging the clay-lick. At its peak there may be 600 birds of up to six species (including red and green macaws, and blue-headed parrots) clamouring to begin their descent to the riverbank where they jostle for access to the mineral rich clay. A necessary addition to their diet that may also neutralize the toxins present in the leaf and seed diet. Rare game birds such as razor billed curassows and piping guans may also be seen.

A list of over 600 species has been compiled. Noteworthy are the black-faced cotinga, crested eagle, and the Harpy eagle, the world's most impressive raptor, easily capable of taking an adult monkey. Mixed species flocks are commonly observed containing from 25 to 100-plus birds of perhaps 30 species including blue dacnis, blue-tailed emerald, bananaquit, thick-billed euphoria and the paradise tanager. Each species occupies a slightly different niche, and since there are few individuals of each species in the flock, competition is avoided. Mixed flocks foraging in the canopy are often led by a white-winged shrike, whereas flocks in the understorey are often led by the bluish-slate antshrike.

Books

Culture and history

Bingham, Hiram *Lost City of the Incas*, (new illustrated edition, with introduction by Hugh Thomson, Weidenfeld & Nicolson, London, 2002).

Bowen, Sally *The Fujimori File. Peru and its President 1990-2000* (2000). A very readable account of the last decade of the 20th century; it ends at the election of that year so the final momentous events of Fujimori's term happened after publication. Bowen has also written, with **Jane Holligan**, *The Imperfect Spy: the Many Lives of Vladimiro Montesinos* (2003), Peisa.

Hemming, John *The Conquest of the Incas* (1970). The one, invaluable book on the period of the conquest.

MacQuarrie, Kim *The Last Days of the Incas*, a thrilling account of the events that led to the Incas' final resistance and of the explorers who have tries to uncover the secrets of their civilization (2007) Piatkus.

Morrison, Tony *Qosqo. The Navel of the World* (1997) Condor Books. Cuzco's past and present with an extensive section of photographs of the city and its surroundings. *Pathways to the Gods: The Mystery of the Andes Lines* (1978), Michael Russell, obtainable in Lima; and *The Mystery of the Nasca Lines* (1987), nonesuch Expeditions, with an intro by Marie Reiche.

Mosely, Michael E *The Incas and their Ancestors: The Archaeology of Peru* (2001) Thames and Hudson.

Muscutt, Keith *Warriors of the Clouds: A Lost Civilization in the Upper Amazon of Peru* (1998) New Mexico Press. Excellent coffee table book and Chachapoyas memoir; also refer to its website (www.chachapoyas.com).

Starn, Orin, **Carlos Iván Degregori**, and **Robin Kirk**, *The Peru Reader* (2nd edition, 2005), Duke Univeristy Press. A good collection on history, culture and politics.

Urton, Gary, *The Social Life of Numbers* (1997), University of Texas Press, on the significance and philosophy of numbers in Andean society. Related to Urton's other studies on khipus and Inca mythology.

Capaq Ñan, the Royal Inca Road

Espinosa, Ricardo, *La Gran Ruta Inca, The Great Inca Route* (2002), Petróleos del Perú. A photographic and textual record of Espinosa's walk the length of the Camino Real de los Incas, in Spanish and English. He has also walked the length of Peru's coast, described in *El Perú a toda Costa* (1997) Editur. The same company has published *Zarzar, Omar, Por los Caminos del Perú en Bicicleta*.

Muller, Karin *Along the Inca Road. A Woman's Journey into an Ancient Empire* (2000), National Geographic.

Portway, Christopher *Journey Along the Andes* (1993) Impact Books. An account of the Andean Inca road.

Non-Peruvian Fiction

Matthiessen, Peter *At Play in the Fields of the Lord* (1965).

Shakespeare, Nicholas *The Vision of Elena Silves* (1989).

Thubron, Colin *To the Last City* (2002) Chatto & Windus.

Vltchek, Andre *Point of No Return* (2005) Mainstay Press.

Wilder, Thornton *The Bridge of San Luis Rey* (1941) Penguin.

Travel

Murphy, Dervla *Eight Feet in the Andes* (1983).

Parris, Matthew *Inca-Kola* (1990).

Shah, Tahir *Trail of Feathers* (2001).

Simpson, Joe *Touching the Void* (1997) Vintage. A nail-biting account of Simpson's accident in the Cordillera Huayhuash.

Thomson, Hugh *The White Rock* (Phoenix, 2002), describes Thomson's own travels in the Inca heartland, as well as the journeys of earlier explorers. *Cochineal Red: Travels through Ancient Peru* (Weidenfeld & Nicolson, 2006), explores pre-Inca civilizations.

Trekking and climbing
Biggar, John *The Andes. A Guide for Climbers* (1999) Andes Publishing.

Box, Ben *Footprint Cuzco and the Inca Heartland* (Footprint).

Gómez, Antonio, and Tomé, Juan José *La Cordillera Blanca de Los Andes* (1998) Desnivel, Spanish only, climbing guide with some trekking and general information, available locally. Also *Escaladas en los Andes. Guía de la Cordillera Blanca* (1999) Desnivel (Spanish only), a climbing guide.

Ricker, John F *Yuraq Janka, Cordilleras Blanca and Rosko* (1977), The Alpine Club of Canada, The American Alpine Club.

Sharman, David *Climbs of the Cordillera Blanca of Peru* (1995) Whizzo. A climbing guide, available locally, from South American Explorers, as well as from Cordee in the UK and Alpenbooks in the USA.

Simpson, Joe *Touching the Void* (1997) Vintage. A nail-biting account of Simpson's accident in the Cordillera Huayhuasah.

Wildlife
Clements, James F and Shany, Noam *A Field Guide to the Birds of Peru* (2001) Ibis.

Schulenberg, Thomas S, Stotz, Douglas F, et al *Birds of Peru* (2007), Helm. A comprehensive field guide.

TReeS (see under Jungle tours from Puerto Maldonado: Tambopata, for address) publish *Tambopata – A Bird Checklist, Tambopata – Mammal, Amphibian & Reptile Checklist* and *Reporte Tambopata*; they also produce tapes and CDs of *Jungle Sounds* and *Birds of Southeast Peru* and distribute other books and merchandise.

Valqui, Thomas, *Where to Watch Birds in Peru* (2004), www.granperu.com/bird watchingbook/. Describes 151 sites, how to get there and what to expect once there.

Walker, Barry, and Jon Fjeldsa *Birds of Machu Picchu*.

Contents

Footnotes

Index → *Entries in bold refer to maps*

Advertisers' index

Credits

Footprint credits

Project editor: Nicola Gibbs
Layout and production: Emma Bryers
Cover and colour section: Pepi Bluck
Maps: Kevin Feeney and Robert Kunstaetter
Proofreader: Ria Gane
Managing Director: Andy Riddle
Commercial Director: Patrick Dawson
Publisher: Alan Murphy
Publishing Managers: Felicity Laughton, Nicola Gibbs
Digital Editors: Jo Williams, Jen Haddington
Marketing and PR: Liz Harper
Sales: Diane McEntee
Advertising: Renu Sibal, Elizabeth Taylor
Finance and administration: Elizabeth Taylor

Photography credits

Front cover: Christian Kapteyn/photolibrary.com
Back cover: Hervé Hughes/hemis.fr
Page 1: Eitan Simanor/Robert Harding
Pages 2-3: Hervé Hughes/hemis.fr
Page 6: Beren Patterson/Alamy; Kuelap shot xx??; Pawel Wysocki/hemis.fr; Toño Labra/age fotostock
Page 7: Ran Mor/Dreamstime.com; Stefano Torrione/hemis.fr
Page 8: Hervé Hughes/hemis.fr
Page 9: Theodore Scott; Kevin Schafer/age fotostock; Yoshio Thomii Photo Studio/photolibrary.com; Kristian Peetz/Alamy
Pages 10-11: Jean-Daniel Sudres/hemis.fr
Page 12: Eye Ubiquitous/photolibrary.com; Stefano Torrione/hemis.fr
Page 13: Craig Lovell/age fotostock; Christan Kapteyn
Page 14: Pete Oxford/naturepi.com; Eric Baccega/naturepi.com; Thomas Marent/Minden Pictures/FLPA; Eric Baccega/naturepi.com
Page 15: Tui De Roy/Minden Pictures/FLPA
Page 16: Tui De Roy/Minden Pictures/FLPA

Footprint feedback

We try as hard as we can to make each guide as up to date as possible but, of course, things always change. If you want to tell us about your experiences – good, bad or ugly– send in your comments at www.footprintbooks.com.

Publishing information

Footprint Peru
8th edition
© Footprint Handbooks Ltd
February 2011

ISBN: 978 1 90726327 9
CIP DATA: A catalogue record for this book is available from the British Library

® Footprint Handbooks and the Footprint mark are a registered trademark of Footprint Handbooks Ltd

Published by Footprint
6 Riverside Court
Lower Bristol Road
Bath BA2 3DZ, UK
T +44 (0)1225 469141
F +44 (0)1225 469461
discover@footprintbooks.com
www.footprintbooks.com

Printed in India by Nutech Print Services, Delhi. Pulp from sustainable forests.
Distributed in the USA by Globe Pequot, Press, Guildford, Connecticut.

Ben Box

One of the first assignments Ben Box took as a freelance writer in 1980 was sub-editing work on the *South American Handbook*. From this humble beginning came editorship of the *Handbook* itself in 1989. Involvement in many of Footprint's other Latin American titles has meant that he has been able to travel in the region for 30 years. Whilst not daring to express a preference for any country in South America, he finds Peru totally captivating and is eager for others to share the joys of exploring its grandeur and intricacies. Having a doctorate in Spanish and Portuguese studies from London University, Ben maintains a strong interest in Latin American literature. In the British summer he plays cricket for his local village side and year round he and his wife Sarah attempt to achieve some level of self-sufficiency in fruit and veg in a rather unruly country garden in Suffolk (UK).

Acknowledgements

As ever the preparation of this edition would not have been possible without the support of a huge number of people. Above all, Ben Box is extremely grateful to Sarah Cameron, Robert and Daisy Kunstaetter and Nicola Gibbs of Footprint for their invaluable help in seeing the book through to completion. At Footprint Ben would also like to thank Alan Murphy, Liz Harper, Andy Riddle, Kevin Feeney and Emma Bryers.

Sarah Cameron edited the following chapters: Arequipa, Lake Titicaca, the Cordilleras Blanca and Huayhuash and the Central Highlands, while Heather MacBrayne did research for Lima, Cuzco, Lake Titicaca, Arequipa, the South Coast and the Southern Jungle. She would like to thank for their assistance and hospitality Lucio Avila and family (Tambo Real Titikaka), Jesús Alemán Palomino (Hotel Sillustani), Lilian G Cotrado Chevarria (Nayra Travel) and Javier Lucio (Transturin) in Puno, Eduardo Indacochea and family (La Casa de Margott) in Arequipa and the Kuntur Wasi Family in Cabanaconde, Mozes Martens (Villa Jazmin) in Ica, Carla de Cabrera and family (Hostal Tambo Colorado) in Pisco, Duncan Griffin (The Lighthouse) in Lima, Abigail Gómez Canessa (Wasai Lodge and Expeditions) in Puerto Maldonado, Carlos Mendoza (Terrazas del Inca) and Laura "Lala" Rodríguez in Aguas Calientes. Aaron Zarate updated the Cordilleras Blanca and Huayhuash chapter, while Alberto Cafferata of Pony Expeditions, Caraz, also sent new information on the Cordillera Blanca.

Robert and Daisy Kunstaetter updated most of the Northern Highlands chapter and their thanks are given in the South American Handbook. They also edited all the maps..

The author is also most grateful to Walter Eberhart of Trujillo for updating Trujillo, Huanchaco and Cajamarca.

Other much appreciated contributions to the text were received from Analía Sarfati of Muyuna, Iquitos, John and Julia Forrest (London), Paul Cripps (Cuzco), Michael White (Trujillo), Meriel Larkin (London and Puno), Mariella Bernasconi, Alberto Miori and Zoe Gillett (Cuzco), Víctor Melgar Morales (Lima) and Ulla Holmquist (Museo Larco, Lima).

We are also grateful to all those travellers who have written to the South American Handbook and Footprint's website, www.footprinttravelguides.com, in particular Olga van Bruggen; Penny Hale (Spain); Joachim Holtz (Germany); Samir Kumar Sharma (Cuzco); Jonathan Ley; Lukas; Beat Reber (Switzerland); Nicole Saure (Switzerland); Carol Sevitt (Canada); and Pieter Van de Sype (Belgium).

Ben Box and Sarah Cameron visited Peru late 2009. For their help and hospitality they would like to thank the following: in Lima, Ana Cecilia Vidal (Hoteles Libertador); Claudia Miranda and Fiorella Llanos Pretell (Sonesta); Rodrigo Custodio (InkaNatura), also Daniel and Patricia Vargas (Chiclayo), Siduith Ferrer and Rick Vecchio of Fertur; Mónica Moreno (La Posada del Parque); Judy Kamiche; Raúl Meza; Miles Buesst; Carolina Morillas (Cóndor Travel); Alessandro Fassio, Josué Maguiña and Nataly Rodríguez of Il Tucano Perú, and Rafael Tapia (PromPerú). In Cajamarca, Pim Heister. In Trujillo, Walter and Friedy Eberhart; and Clara Bravo. In Celendín, Susan van der Wielen and Vilzeth Vásquez Bazán. Also Cecilia Kamiche (Mórrope); Andrea Martin of Rancho Santana (Pacora); Rosana Correa (Los Horcones, Túcume); Piedad y Aldo of San Roque, Lambayeque; in Chiclayo the hotels Las Musas, La Casa de la Luna and Gran Chiclayo; Luis Ocas and Ever Reyes. In Santiago deViñac: Enrique Umbert of Mountain Lodges of Peru and Elisabeth Leitner-Rauchdobler

In September 2010 Ben Box was back in Peru and he would like to thank the following: the staff of El Albergue, Ollantaytambo; Nick Asheshov in Urubamba, and Violeta Mariscal Gamboa of Posada Tres Marías. For all their hospitality in Cuzco Ben is most grateful to Paul Cripps and Carol Thomas, Dougie Stewart, Jeffrey Powers, Mary Finn of South American Explorers, Mariella Bernasconi, Roberto Díaz and Melissa Gold Pérez at Chicha and the staff at Limo. Ben was most pleased to visit two LATA Foundation projects based in Cuzco: Threads of Peru at Rumira Sondormayo, with Ariana Svenson, Urbano, Norman and Daniel Soncco Gayoso; and ChildHope at Barrio Alto San Martín with Gricelda Salazar and Mery, with thanks also to Ligia Alencastre and Rosario Salazar of Amhauta and Emily Mulville of ChildHope. From 22-24 September the Footprint Team attended the TravelMart LatinAmerica, with thanks to the staff of William H Coleman, Inc, especially Manuel Cuevas, and the Sheraton Hotel. Last but not least Ben would like to thank most warmly the following in Lima: Andrés Alvarez Calderón and Yvonne Casabonne of Museo Larco; Matt Barker and guide Miguel of Peru for Less; Cynthia Cáceres, Blanca Romero and driver Jimmy of Lima Mentor; Alvaro del Carpio of Casa Andina; Siduith Ferrer and Rick Vecchio; Cecilia Kamiche; Kathrine Lindholm of South American Explorers; and Víctor Melgar Morales of La Catedral del Pisco and Hostal Víctor.